Lecture Notes in Computer Science 2438
Edited by G. Goos, J. Hartmanis, and J. van Leeuwen

Springer-Verlag
Berlin Heidelberg GmbH

Manfred Glesner Peter Zipf
Michel Renovell (Eds.)

Field-Programmable Logic and Applications

Reconfigurable Computing Is Going Mainstream

12th International Conference, FPL 2002
Montpellier, France, September 2-4, 2002
Proceedings

Springer

Series Editors

Gerhard Goos, Karlsruhe University, Germany
Juris Hartmanis, Cornell University, NY, USA
Jan van Leeuwen, Utrecht University, The Netherlands

Volume Editors

Manfred Glesner
Peter Zipf
Technische Universität Darmstadt
Institut für Datentechnik, FG Mikroelektronische Systeme
Karlstraße 15, 64283 Darmstadt, Germany
E-mail: {glesner,zipf}@mes.tu-darmstadt.de

Michel Renovell
LIRMM, Microelectronics Department
161 rue Ada, 34392 Montpellier Cedex, France
E-mail: renovell@lirmm.fr

Cataloging-in-Publication Data applied for

Die Deutsche Bibliothek - CIP-Einheitsaufnahme

Field programmable logic and applications : reconfigurable computing is going mainstream ; 12th international conference ; proceedings / FPL 2002, Montpellier, France, September 2 - 4, 2002. Manfred Glesner ... (ed.).

(Lecture notes in computer science ; Vol. 2438)
ISBN 978-3-540-44108-3 ISBN 978-3-540-46117-3 (eBook)
DOI 10.1007/978-3-540-46117-3

CR Subject Classification (1998): B.6-7, C.2, J.6

ISSN 0302-9743
ISBN 978-3-540-44108-3

http://www.springer.de

Originally published by Springer-Verlag Berlin Heidelberg New York in 2002

Typesetting: Camera-ready by author, data conversion by Boller Mediendesign
Printed on acid-free paper SPIN: 10870229 06/3142 5 4 3 2 1 0

Preface

This book is the proceedings volume of the 12th International Conference on Field-Programmable Logic and Applications (FPL) held on September 2–4, 2002. The conference was hosted by the Laboratoire d'Informatique, de Robotique et de Microélectronique de Montpellier (LIRMM), France. The FPL conference covered areas like reconfigurable logic and reconfigurable computing, as well as their application in various areas like DSP, communication and cryptography. Its subtitle "Reconfigurable Computing Is Going Mainstream" emphasizes the extensive role reconfigurable logic has started to play.

The annual FPL series is the oldest international conference in the world covering configware and all its aspects (also see: http://www.fpl.org). It was founded in 1991 at Oxford University (UK) and is two years older than its two most important competitors, which usually take place in Monterey and Napa. FPL has been held in Oxford (three times), Vienna, Prague, Darmstadt, London, Tallinn, Glasgow, Villach, and Belfast. It brings together experts, users, and newcomers from industry and academia in an informal, social, and productive atmosphere that encourages stimulating and profitable interaction between the participants.

Covered topics. The scope of this conference has been substantially extended over the past years and today also covers evolvable and adaptable systems, coarse-grain reconfigurable (sub)systems, their synthesis methods and applications, and their indispensable role in System-on-a-Chip (SoC) development, as well as reconfigurable computing (RC) as an emerging new paradigm, threatening to shake the general foundations of computer science: computing in space vs. computing in time. The application of field-programmable logic in different areas has gained increasing importance also, and the number of according submissions has grown.

Still growing importance. The size of FPL conferences has grown rapidly from 1991 to 2001. The figure below shows the numbers of submitted and accepted papers, starting in 1996. The 214 papers submitted in 2002 represent

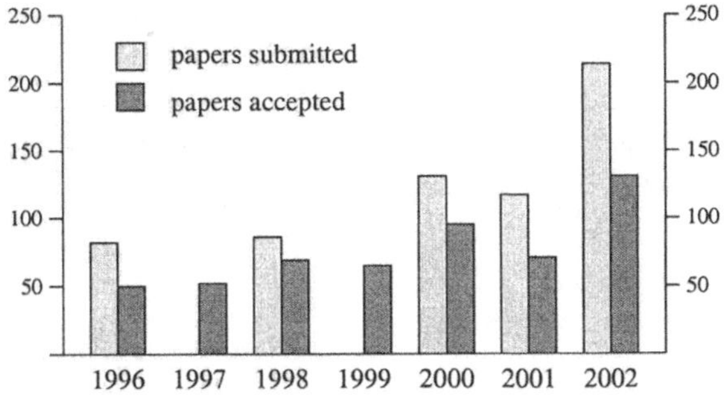

Numbers of submitted and accepted papers by year

an 83% increase compared to the year 2001. The program was assembled from 104 selected regular papers and 27 posters, resulting in a very interesting and attractive book. Another four papers are invited, including three keynotes. Because of the huge number of accepted contributions, this year for the first time the FPL program consisted of three parallel sessions. The selected contributions were submitted by researchers from 26 different countries:

USA:	30	Canada:	5	Ireland:	2	Lebanon:	1
UK:	15	Poland:	5	Portugal:	2	Mexico:	1
Germany:	12	Hong Kong:	4	Slovakia:	2	New Zealand:	1
Japan:	11	The Netherlands:	4	Australia:	1	Switzerland:	1
Spain:	9	Belgium:	3	Brazil:	1	Singapore:	1
France:	6	Czech Republic:	3	Greece:	1		
Italy:	6	Finland:	3	Iran:	1		

We gratefully acknowledge the reviewing work done by the PC members and many additional reviewers who contributed with their expertise to successfully compile the program.

Trends at FPL 2002. The main focus, set by the number of papers, was on the use of field-programmable logic for applications, mainly in the area of DSP (3 sessions), but also in various other areas (7 sessions, including two about arithmetic and two about cryptography). The use of field-programmable logic for communication applications (2 sessions) has been a sustaining field of interest. Reconfiguration and reconfigurable computing remain major points of interest, and are covered by 7 sessions ranging from custom computing engines to reconfigurable processors and issues of dynamic reconfiguration. Finally, low-power issues are receiving growing attention which is reflected in a new session dedicated to that topic.

Acknowledgements. We would like to thank the authors for submitting their first versions and for preparing the final versions of the accepted papers, as well as the members of our Program Committee and all other reviewers listed on the following pages. We also thank Reiner Hartenstein for making the event public on the web. We especially thank Thilo Pionteck and Ralf Ludewig from Darmstadt University of Technology for their help in managing the reviewing process and for their assistance while the proceedings volume was being assembled. We thank as well Alberto Garcia Ortiz, Octavian Mitrea, Juan Jesus Ocampo Hidalgo, Gilles Sassatelli, and Clemens Schlachta for supporting them. We gratefully acknowledge the excellent cooperation with Alfred Hofmann from Springer-Verlag, now FPL's official publisher for the 10th year.

June 2002

Manfred Glesner,
Peter Zipf,
Michel Renovell

Organization Committee

Program Chair:	Manfred Glesner Darmstadt University of Technology, Germany
General Chair:	Michel Renovell LIRMM, University of Montpellier II, France
Publicity Chair:	Reiner Hartenstein University of Kaiserslautern, Germany
Local Chair:	Lionel Torres LIRMM, University of Montpellier II, France
Proceedings:	Peter Zipf Darmstadt University of Technology, Germany
Sponsors:	Pascal Nouet LIRMM, University of Montpellier II, France
Exhibition:	Michel Robert LIRMM, University of Montpellier II, France
Social:	Daniel Auvergne, Nadine Azémard LIRMM, University of Montpellier II, France
Finance:	Marie-Lise Flottes, Denis Deschacht LIRMM, University of Montpellier II, France

Program Committee

Nazeeh Aranki	Jet Propulsion Laboratory/NASA, USA
Peter Athanas	Virginia Tech, USA
Neil Bergman	Queensland University of Technology, Australia
Dinesh Bhatia	University of Texas, USA
Eduardo Boemo	University of Madrid, Spain
Gordon Brebner	University of Edinburgh, UK
Stephen Brown	University of Toronto, Canada
Klaus Buchenrieder	Infineon Technologies AG, Germany
Stephen Casselman	Virtual Computer Corp., USA
Charles Chiang	Synopsys, Inc., USA
André DeHon	California Institute of Technology, USA
Carl Ebeling	University of Washington, USA
Hossam ElGindy	University of New South Wales, Australia
Manfred Glesner	Darmstadt University of Technology, Germany
John Gray	Independent Consultant, UK
Herbert Grünbacher	Carinthia Tech. Institute, Austria
Steven Guccione	QuickSilver Technology, USA
Reiner Hartenstein	University of Kaiserslautern, Germany
Scott Hauck	University of Washington, USA
Brad Hutchings	Brigham Young University, USA

Tom Kean	Algotronix Consulting, UK
Andres Keevallik	Tallinn Technical University, Estonia
Andreas Koch	University of Braunschweig, Germany
Dominique Lavenier	IRISIA and CNRS Univ. of Montpellier II, France
Philip Leong	Chinese University of Hong Kong, China
Jason Lohn	NASA Ames Research Center, USA
Wayne Luk	Imperial College London, UK
Patrick Lysaght	Xilinx, Inc., USA
Bill Mangione-Smith	University of California at Los Angeles, USA
Reinhard Männer	University of Mannheim, Germany
Oskar Mencer	Bell Labs, USA
Georges Milne	University of Western Australia
Toshiaki Miyazaki	NTT Network Innovation Labs, Japan
Fernando Moraes	PUCRS, Brazil
Sebastien Pillement	ENSSAT, France
Viktor Prasanna	University of Southern California, USA
Michel Renovell	LIRMM, University of Montpellier II, France
Jonathan Rose	University of Toronto, Canada
Zoran Salcic	University of Auckland, New Zealand
John Schewel	Virtual Computer Corp., USA
Hartmut Schmeck	University of Karlsruhe, Germany
Rainer Spallek	Dresden University of Technology, Germany
Adrian Stoica	Jet Propulsion Laboratory/NASA, USA
Jürgen Teich	University of Paderborn, Germany
Lothar Thiele	ETH Zürich, Switzerland
Lionel Torres	LIRMM, Univ. of Montpellier II, France
Stephen Trimberger	Xilinx, Inc., USA
Ranga Vemuri	University of Cincinnati, USA
Roger Woods	Queen's University of Belfast, UK

Additional Reviewers

Shailendra Aulakh	University of Texas, USA
Shankar Balachandran	University of Texas, USA
Marcus Bednara	University of Paderborn, Germany
Rajarshee P. Bharadwaj	University of Texas, USA
Elalaheh Bozorgzadeh	University of California at Los Angeles, USA
G.A. Bundell	University of Western Australia, Australia
Ney Calazans	PUCRS, Brazil
Gaston Cambon	LIRMM, Univ. of Montpellier II, France
Daniel Chillet	LASTI, University of Rennes, France
Seonil Choi	University of Southern California, USA
George Constantinides	Imperial College London, UK
Tim Courtney	Queen's University Belfast, UK

Didier Demigny	ETIS/ENSEA, France
Arran Derbyshire	Imperial College London, UK
Dirk Fischer	University of Paderborn, Germany
Thomas Geocaris	Synopsys, Inc., USA
Soheil Ghiasi	University of California at Los Angeles, USA
Herbert Grünbacher	Carinthia Tech. Institute, Austria
Manish Handa	University of Cincinnati, USA
Frank Hannig	University of Paderborn, Germany
Christian Haubelt	University of Paderborn, Germany
Fabiano Hessel	PUCRS, Brazil
Thomas Hollstein	Darmstadt University of Technology, Germany
Lorentz Huelsbergen	Bell Labs, USA
Minoru Inamori	NTT Network Innovation Labs, Japan
Ju-Wook Jang	University of Southern California, USA
Rajeev Jayaraman	Xilinx, Inc., USA
Adam Kaplan	University of California, LA, USA
Ryan Kastner	University of California, LA, USA
Jamil Kawa	Synopsys, Inc., USA
Jawad Khan	University of Cincinnati, USA
Ryusuke Konishi	NTT Network Innovation Labs, Japan
Gareth Lee	University of Western Australia, Australia
Norris Leong	Chinese University of Hong Kong, China
Stan Y. Liao	Synopsys, Inc., USA
Gaye Lightbody	Amphion Semiconductor, UK
Ralf Ludewig	Darmstadt University of Technology, Germany
Reinhard Männer	University of Mannheim, Germany
Chi-Yu Mao	Synopsys, Inc., USA
César Marcon	PUCRS, Brazil
Maire McLoone	Queen's University Belfast, UK
Seda Ogrenci Memik	University of California, LA, USA
Peter Moceyunas	Synopsys, Inc., USA
Sumit Mohanty	University of Southern California, USA
Rolf Fredi Molz	Universidade de Santa Cruz du Sul, Brazil
John Morris	University of Western Australia, Australia
Madhubanti Mukherjee	University of Cincinnati, USA
Takahiro Murooka	NTT Network Innovation Labs, Japan
Kouichi Nagami	NTT Network Innovation Labs, Japan
Ulrich Nageldinger	Infineon Technologies AG, Germany
Yoshiki Nakane	NTT Network Innovation Labs, Japan
Abdulfattah Obeid	Darmstadt University of Technology, Germany
Alberto Garcia Ortiz	Darmstadt University of Technology, Germany
Thilo Pionteck	Darmstadt University of Technology, Germany
Michel Robert	LIRMM, University of Montpellier II, France
Majid Sarrafzadeh	University of California at Los Angeles, USA
Gilles Sassatelli	Darmstadt University of Technology, Germany

Clemens Schlachta	Darmstadt University of Technology, Germany
Ron Scrofano	University of Southern California, USA
Alexander Sedlmeier	Infineon Technologies AG, Germany
Olivier Sentieys	IRISA, University of Rennes, France
Seung Kim	University of California, USA
Tunemichi Shiozawa	NTT Network Innovation Labs, Japan
Shiva Navab	University of California, USA
Reetinder Pal Sidhu	University of Southern California, USA
Subramanyan D. Siva	University of Cincinnati, USA
Frank Slomka	University of Paderborn, Germany
Vijay Sundaresan	University of Cincinnati, USA
Russ Tessier	University of Massachusetts Amherst, USA
Sudhir K. Vaka	University of Texas, USA
Vicky Vrolijk	University of Western Australia, Australia
Wendong Hu	University of California, USA
Ralph Weper	University of Paderborn, Germany
Lyndon While	University of Western Australia, Australia
Cliff Young	Bell Labs, USA
Yumin Zhang	Synopsys, Inc., USA
Peter Zipf	Darmstadt University of Technology, Germany

Michal Servit Award Committee

Gordon Brebner	University of Edinburgh, UK
Manfred Glesner	Darmstadt University of Technology, Germany
Reiner Hartenstein	University of Kaiserslautern, Germany
Wayne Luk	Imperial College London, UK
Paul Master	QuickSilver Technology, USA (sponsor)
Michel Renovell	LIRMM, University of Montpellier II, France
Roger Woods	Queen's University of Belfast, UK

Steering Committee

Manfred Glesner	Darmstadt University of Technology, Germany
John Gray	Independent Consultant, UK
Herbert Grünbacher	Carinthia Tech Institute, Austria
Reiner Hartenstein	University of Kaiserslautern, Germany
Andres Keevallik	Tallinn Technical University, Estonia
Wayne Luk	Imperial College London, UK
Patrick Lysaght	Xilinx, Inc., USA
Michel Renovell	LIRMM, University of Montpellier II, France
Roger Woods	Queen's University of Belfast, UK

Table of Contents

DSP Applications 1

Reconfigurable Fabrics

Dynamic Reconfiguration 1

DSP Applications 2

Routing & Placement

Dynamic Reconfiguration 2

Power Estimation

Synthesis Issues

Keynote Address

Communication Applications 1

New Technologies

Reconfigurable Architectures

Communication Applications 2

Multimedia Applications

FPGA-based Arithmetic 1

Reconfigurable Processors

Image Processing

Crypto Applications 1

Keynote Address

Multitasking

Special Architectures

Crypto Applications 2

Compilation Techniques

DSP Applications 3

Complex Applications

Architecture Implementation

Design Flow

Miscellaneous

Short Papers

A Cryptanalytic Time-Memory Tradeoff: First FPGA Implementation

Jean-Jacques Quisquater, Francois-Xavier Standaert, Gael Rouvroy, Jean-Pierre David, and Jean-Didier Legat

UCL Crypto Group
Laboratoire de Microelectronique
Universite Catholique de Louvain
Place du Levant, 3, B-1348 Louvain-La-Neuve, Belgium
{quisquater,standaert,rouvroy,david,legat}@dice.ucl.ac.be

Abstract. A cryptanalytic time-memory tradeoff allows the cryptanalysis of any N key symmetric cryptosystem in $O(N^{\frac{2}{3}})$ operations with $O(N^{\frac{2}{3}})$ storage, if a precomputation of $O(N)$ operations has been done in advance. This procedure is well known but did not lead to any realistic implementations. In this paper, the experimental results for the cryptanalysis of DES[1] that are presented are based on a time-memory tradeoff using distinguished points, a method which is referenced to Rivest [2]. For this task, a fast hardware implementation of DES was designed using FPGA technology. The target is a 40-bit DES which is obtained from DES by fixing 16 key bits to arbitrary values. The precomputation task is performed with a purpose-built FPGA design, whereas the search algorithm corresponding to the online attack is reported to be feasible on any PC within about 10 seconds, with a success rate of 72%. The cost of an expansion to 56-bit DES is evaluated.

1 Introduction

Generally speaking, a block cipher allows to encrypt a n-bit text using a k-bit key to produce a n-bit ciphertext. Let $q = \lceil \frac{k}{n} \rceil$. If q plaintext/ciphertext pairs are known, with a high probability, the key can be determined by exhaustive key search, but it requires a too long processing time. Another possibility is a chosen plaintext attack using a precomputation table where an attacker precomputes the encryptions of q chosen plaintexts under all possible keys and stores the corresponding ciphertext/key pairs, but it requires a too large memory. The aim of a time-memory tradeoff is to mount an attack which has a lower online processing complexity than exhaustive key search and lower memory complexity than a precomputation table.
In this paper, we present a cryptanalytic time-memory tradeoff in the context of a chosen plaintext attack on DES. In this way, we designed fast hardware implementations of DES using FPGA technology. Basically, the programmable

[1] DES : Data Encryption Standard

M. Glesner, P. Zipf, and M. Renovell (Eds.): FPL 2002, LNCS 2438, pp. 780–789, 2002.

hardware device was used as a dedicated computer in order to perform some precomputation tasks (like cryptographic encryption and chaining) at very high frequencies. We designed a machine that can break a 40-bit DES block cipher in about 10 seconds, using one PC[2], with a high success rate (72%). An exhaustive search of the key on the same PC would have taken about 50 days. We also evaluate the hardware cost of an expansion to a 56-bit DES block cipher. Finally, this paper underlines the efficiency of FPGA's in cryptanalytic applications in terms of brute computational power.

2 Definitions

Let E : $\{0,1\}^n \times \{0,1\}^k \rightarrow \{0,1\}^n$ be a block cipher with block length n and key length k. The encryption of one block is written as:

$$C = E_K(P) \tag{1}$$

Where $C \in \{0,1\}^n$, $K \in \{0,1\}^k$ and $P \in \{0,1\}^n$ denote the ciphertext, the secret key and the plaintext.
We define two functions. The first one just mixes its arguments and rejects z bits to reach the key size $k = n - z$. $g : \{0,1\}^n \rightarrow \{0,1\}^k$.

$$g(C) = g(C_1, C_2, ..., C_n) = (C_{perm(1)}, C_{perm(2)}, ..., C_{perm(n-z)}) \tag{2}$$

Where $C \in \{0,1\}^n$ is the ciphertext and *perm* denotes a simple permutation. We call g a mask function. There are many possibilities to define g, namely $(n-z)!$
We also define a function $f : \{0,1\}^k \rightarrow \{0,1\}^k$

$$f(K) = g(E_K(P)) \tag{3}$$

Finally, for a random start point $SP \in \{0,1\}^k$, we define a chain K_0, K_1, K_2, ..., K_t of length t as

$$K_0 = SP \tag{4}$$

$$K_i = f(K_{i-1}) = f^i(K_0) \tag{5}$$

Definition of a DP-property: Let $\{0,1\}^k$ be the key space and $d \in$ {1,2,3,...,k-1}. Then $DP - d$ is a DP-property of order d if there is an easily checked property which holds for 2^{k-d} different elements of $\{0,1\}^k$. In our application, having d bits locked to a fixed value, say 0, is a DP-property of order d.

Definition of a distinguished point: Let $K \in \{0,1\}^k$ and $d \in$ {1,2,3,...,k-1}. Then K is a distinguished point (DP) of order d if the DP-property defined beforehand holds for K. Note that using this definition of distinguished point, we do not need to store the fixed bits and reduce the memory requirements of the tradeoff.

[2] 256Mbytes RAM/350MHz

3 Algorithms

The algorithm proposed requires the choice of a DP-property of order d and a maximum chain length t. We precompute r tables by choosing r different mask functions. For each mask function m different start points (DP) will be randomly chosen. For each start point a chain will be computed until a DP is encountered or until the chain has length $t+1$. Only start points that iterate to a DP in less than t iterations will be stored with the corresponding chain length, the others will be discarded. Moreover, if the same DP is an end point for different chains, then only the chain of maximal length will be stored.

Precomputation algorithm: Generate r tables with (SP,EP,l)-triples, sorted on EP.

1. Choose a DP-property of order d.
2. Choose r different mask functions g_i, $i = 1, 2, ..., r$. It defines r different f functions: $f_i = g_i(E_K(P))$, $i = 1, 2, ..., r$.
3. Choose the maximum chain length t.
4. For $i = 1$ to r
   (a) Choose m random start points $SP_1^{(i)}, SP_2^{(i)}, ..., SP_m^{(i)}$.
   (b) For $j = 1$ to m, $l = 1$ to t
      i. Compute $f_i^l(SP_j^{(i)})$.
      ii. If $f_i^l(SP_j^{(i)})$ is a DP then store the triple $(SP_j^{(i)}, EP_j^{(i)} = f_i^l(SP_j^{(i)}), l)$ and take next j.
      iii. If $l > t$ "forget" $SP_j^{(i)}$ and take next j.
   (c) Sort triples on end points. If several end points are identical, only store the triple with the largest l.
   (d) Store the maximum l for each table: l^i_{max}.

For the search algorithm, a table only has to be accessed when a DP is encountered during an iteration. Moreover, if the encountered DP is not in the table, then one will not find the target key by iterating further. Hence the current search can skip the rest of this table.

Search algorithm: Given $C = E_K(P)$ find K.

1. For $i = 1$ to r
   (a) Look up l^i_{max}.
   (b) $Y = g_i(C)$.
   (c) For $j = 1$ to l^i_{max}
      i. If Y is a DP then
         A. If Y in table i, then
            – Take the corresponding $SP^{(i)}$ and length l in the table.
            – If $j < l$
               • Compute predecessor $\tilde{K} = f_i^{l-1-j}(SP_l^{(j)})$.
               • If $C = E_{\tilde{K}}(P)$ then $K = \tilde{K}$: STOP.
               • If $C \neq E_{\tilde{K}}(P)$, take next i.
         B. Else take next i.
      ii. Set $Y = f(Y)$.

4 Hardware Description

All our experiments were carried out on a Virtex1000BG560-4 FPGA board, developed by DICE[3]. The board is composed of a control FPGA (FLEX 10K) and a VIRTEX1000 FPGA associated with several processors (ARM and PIC) and fast access memories. We used a PCI[4] to communicate between the PC and the FPGA.

5 Implementation: A Hardware/Software Co-design

The implementation choices were enforced by both precomputation and search algorithms. Obviously, the search algorithm corresponds to an online attack that we want to be efficient on any PC and therefore is being dealt with in the software part. On the other hand, we performed the precomputation task with an optimal usage of the FPGA considering its limited size. It led us to carry out some parts of the precomputation by software like the sort on EP. We also wanted our hardware circuit to be parametric in order to change the tradeoff parameters by software. Therefore, some tasks are hardware implemented with a software control. The next list summarizes the hardware vs software design decisions.

Task	HW	SW	SW controlled
SP generation	X	-	-
DES chaining	X	-	-
Mask functions	X	-	X
Rejection of long chains	X	-	X
Rejection of short chains	X	-	X
DP detection	X	-	-
Length computation	X	-	-
Triples storage	-	X	-
Sort on EP	-	X	-
Merger rejection	-	X	-
Online attack	-	X	-

In a cryptanalytic point of view, the main advantage of FPGA's is to parallelize algorithms in order to reach very high encryption rates. Practically, we implemented DES in the following way:
DES is a block cipher with 64-bit block size and 56-bit keys. The algorithm proceeds in three steps:

1. The given plaintext P_0 is divided into two parts of 32 bits according to an initial permutation $IP : IP(P_0) = L_0R_0$.
2. 16 iterations of a round function are computed and sixteen keys K_1, K_2, ..., K_{16}, each bit strings of length 48 are derived from the initial key K.

[3] Microelectronics laboratory, Universite Catholique de Louvain, Belgium
[4] Parallel Computer Interface

3. The inverse permutation IPP is applied to the bit string $L_{16}R_{16}$, obtaining the ciphertext C_0.

A fast implementation can be obtained by inserting registers between each round of the algorithm as suggested by Figure 1.

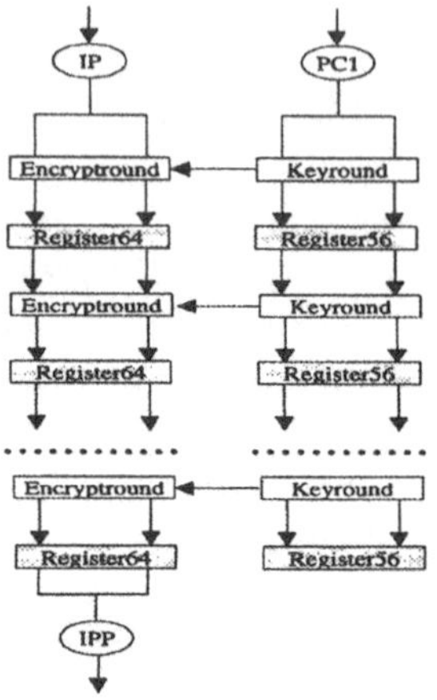

Fig. 1. Fast DES implementation

The following table summarizes the practical results of our implementation:

	Number of LUT	Work Frequency
Pipeline DES	4736	66 MHz

Finally, the start point of our hardware design (Figure2) is a pipeline DES which runs at 66M encryptions/second. As a plaintext is encrypted in 16 clock edges, we deal simultaneously with 16 start points: $K1, K2, ..., K16$. Initially, they do not need to be different because each start point has its own mask function. The design of Figure 2 computes triples for 16=2^4 different mask functions. We parallelized 4 units on the FPGA which corresponds to 64=2^6 different mask functions.
The triples computed by the FPGA are communicated to the PC via a FIFO memory.

6 Cryptanalysis of a 40-bit DES Block Cipher: Experimental Results

The Data Encryption Standard encrypts a 64-bit plaintext using a 56-bit secret key. We define a 40-bit DES by fixing 16 key-bits to arbitrary values and propose a chosen plaintext attack to recover the 40 bits of the secret key.

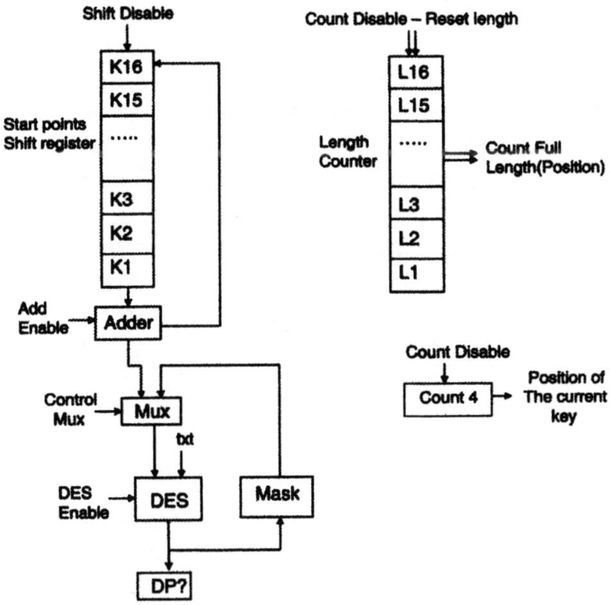

Fig. 2. Precomputation design

6.1 Precomputation Task

The objective of the precomputation task is to reach the condition:

$$r \times Nbr.Triples.Stored \times Average.chain.length \geq 2^{40} \tag{6}$$

We define three quantities to evaluate the precomputation task:

1. Let $E =$ (Number of triples stored after sort and mergers rejection)/(Number of triples computed) be the effectiveness of the precomputation task.
2. Let $ALBS$ be the average chain length before sort and mergers rejection.
3. Let $ALAS$ be the average chain length after sort and mergers rejection.

The tradeoff parameters should be chosen such as to avoid the following situations:

- A saturation phenomenon. After the computation of an amount of triples, mergers of chains become critical and the effectiveness of the computation decreases.
- A variation of the average length of chains: $ALBS \gg ALAS$.

Consequently, we performed a heuristic evaluation of the parameters and defined a set of adequate values.

1. DP-property: $d = 11$.
2. Length of chains: $2^9 < l < 2^{13}$.

We succeeded in storing $2^{19.5}$ triples with an average length of $2^{10.97}$ for every mask function and therefore decided to fulfil condition (6) by taking 2^{10} different mask functions. In terms of precomputation time, we ran the FPGA with 16 different configurations because we could only fit 2^6 mask functions on one FPGA. It took us about one week. In terms of memory requirements, we stored all triples on 16 CDROM's[5] corresponding to 16 sets of 2^6 mask functions. Finally, we give the precomputation results.

Number of triples stored	$2^{19.5}$
Average length of chains	$2^{10.97}$
Number of mask functions	2^{10}
Memory requirements	16 CDROM's
Key space cover of one CDROM	$2^{36.47}$

6.2 Online Attack

In order to evaluate the practical success rate of our attack and the amount of overlaps between mask functions, we define the following quantities:
Let the theoretical key space cover be defined in terms of memory usage as:

$$TKSC = Number.of.CDROM's \times 2^{36.47} \tag{7}$$

It corresponds to the cover that we would have observed without any overlap between the chains computed with different mask functions.
If i is the number of CDROM's used for the online attack, let the practical key space cover be defined in function of the experimental success rate of the attack:

$$PKSC(i) = \frac{Number.of.keys.found(i)}{Number.of.keys.tried(i)} \times 2^{40} \tag{8}$$

Differences between $TKSC$ and $PKSC$ are due to the overlap problem and we define an overlap factor such as:

$$TKSC = PKSC \times Overlap.factor \tag{9}$$

Finally, we define the experimental success rate of the attack as:

$$SR(i) = \frac{Number.of.keys.found(i)}{Number.of.keys.tried(i)} \tag{10}$$

We summarize the online attack results:

Nbr of CDROM's	Nbr of keys tried	Nbr of keys found	SR
1	3000	260	8.6%
2	3000	510	17%
4	3000	941	31.4%
8	3000	1490	49.7%
16	3000	2160	72%

[5] 650Mbytes

Nbr of CDROM's	TKSC	PKSC	Overlap factor
1	$2^{36.47}$	$2^{36.47}$	1
2	$2^{37.47}$	$2^{37.44}$	1.02
4	$2^{38.47}$	$2^{38.33}$	1.1
8	$2^{39.47}$	$2^{38.99}$	1.39
16	$2^{40.47}$	$2^{39.53}$	1.92

The online attack was performed on a single PC[6] and we recovered one key in about 10 seconds with a success rate of 72%. An exhaustive key search on the same PC would have taken about 50 days. Remark that the overlap factor denotes a saturation problem when multiplying the number of mask functions.

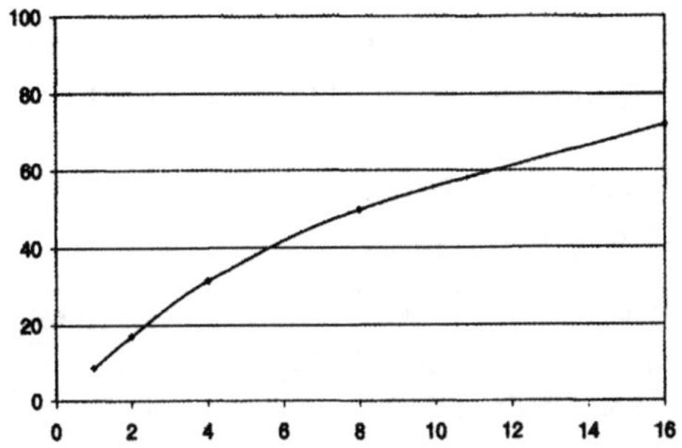

Fig. 3. Success rate (%) in terms of memory usage (CDROM's).

7 Expansion to a 56-bit DES Block Cipher

In order to evaluate the possibility of a cryptanalytic tradeoff on a complete DES block cipher (with a 56-bit key), we modified our hardware design and performed a sample of the precomputation task with the following parameters:

1. *DP*-property: $d = 18$.
2. Chain lengths: all.
3. Storage until saturation.
4. Number of mask functions: $r = 16$.

Figure 4 illustrates the saturation phenomenon encountered in the precomputation task which restricts the number of triples stored to 2^{22}. It corresponds to 5 days of computation. As the average chain length after sort was $\simeq 2^{18}$, we concluded that 2^{16} mask functions are necessary to fulfil the condition:

$$r \times Nbr.Triples.Stored \times Average.length.of.chains \simeq 2^{56} \quad (11)$$

[6] 18Gbytes memory/256Mbytes RAM/350MHz

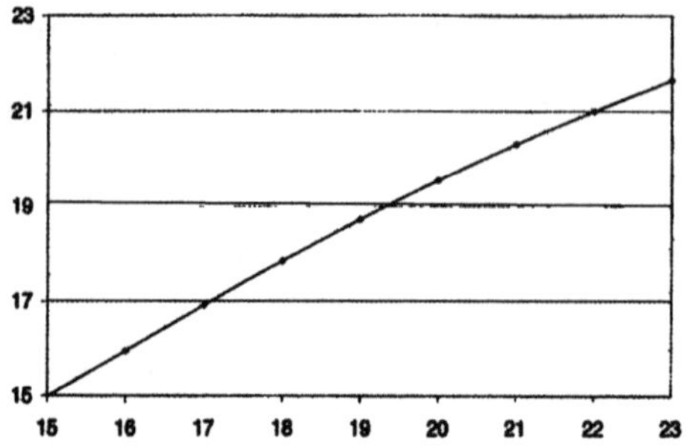

Fig. 4. X = Triples computed in log_2 scale - Y = Triples stored in log_2 scale.

However, a key space cover of 2^{46} only needs 2^6 mask functions and therefore 5 $\times$ 5 = 25 days of computation. It should allow us to reach a success rate close to $\frac{1}{2^{10}} \simeq 0.1\%$.
Finally, the next list indicates the possibilities to increase the precomputation power by using larger and faster FPGA's.

Family	Device	System gates	Internal clock
VIRTEX 2.5V FPGA	XCV1000	1M	200 MHz
VIRTEX-E 1.8V FPGA	XCV3200E	4M	300 MHz
VIRTEX-2 1.5V FPGA	XC2V8000	8M	400 MHz

For example, a VIRTEX-2 FPGA with 8M gates would certainly allow to gain a factor 16 in the precomputation time. Consequently, a parallelization of several VIRTEX-2 FPGA's would allow us to reach significant success rates (1% to 10%).
Concerning the online attack, the processing complexity roughly depends on the product: $ALAS \times r$. Then we can compare different attacks:

1. DES-40 with cover $= 2^{40}$: Complexity $\simeq 2^{10.5} \times 2^{10} = 2^{20.5}$.
2. DES-56 with cover $= 2^{46}$: Complexity $\simeq 2^{18} \times 2^{6} = 2^{24}$.
3. DES-56 with cover $= 2^{56}$: Complexity $\simeq 2^{18} \times 2^{16} = 2^{34}$.

We conclude that an attack against DES-56 with 0.1% success rate is only 16 times slower than the attack developed in this paper against DES-40. Therefore, a software implementation of the attack is thinkable. However, high success rate attacks against DES-56 involve long processing times and should probably use a hardware coprocessor (for example a FPGA) for the distinguished points computation during the attack.

8 Conclusion

We performed a first implementation of a time-memory tradeoff using distinguished points and presented experimental results that confirm its effectiveness

in the context of block ciphers cryptanalysis. The resulting chosen plaintext attack significantly improves all existing complete cryptanalytic attacks attempted against DES or other block ciphers in terms of speed. Note that the attack is general and could be applied to any block cipher without changing algorithms. In case of a 40-bit DES and compared to exhaustive key search, we recover a key in 10 seconds instead of 50 days with a success rate of 72%.
Moreover, we evaluated the cost of a possible expansion to 56-bits DES. With our current equipment[7], a success rate of 0.1% is achievable. With recent FPGA's, we could gain a factor from 8 to 16 or more if the parallelization of several devices is considered. Anyway, the time-memory tradeoff attack can be dangerous even when the size of the key space is too large to be exhaustively searched (say 2^{80}). Consider an application where immediate inversion of a single cipher can be disastrous (e.g. an online bank transfer), then, constructing tables that would cover "only" 2^{60} points would allow online inversion with probability 2^{-20}, which is not negligible.
Finally, this work confirms the effectiveness of FPGA's in cryptanalytic applications. Due to hardware constraints, some parts of the precomputation had to be software-implemented to make it less memory-consuming, but the resulting design is deployed on reasonably expensive hardware and allows a first implementation of a cryptanalytic time-memory tradeoff against a practical cipher. Future devices combined with high speed processors should reduce hardware constraints and permit the implementation of a variety of cryptanalytic attacks on FPGA's. In terms of cost and effectiveness, this could replace distributed computations in the coming years.

References

1. M.Hellman, *A Cryptanalytic Time-Memory Tradeoff*, IEEE transactions on Information Theory, Vol 26, 1980, pp.401-406.
2. D.Denning, *Cryptography and Data Security*, p.100, Addison-Wesley, 1982, Out of Print.
3. National Bureau of Standards. *Data Encryption Standard*, U.S.Department of Commerce, Washington DC, USA, January 1977.
4. J.Borst, B.Preneel and J.Vandewalle, *On the Time-Memory Tradeoff Between exhaustive key search and table precomputation*, Proc. of the 19th Symposium in Information Theory in the Benelux, WIC, 1998,
5. K.Kusuda and T.Matsumoto, *Optimization of Time-Memory Tradeoff Cryptanalysis and its Applications to DES, FEAL-32 and Skipjack*, IEICE Transactions on Fundamentals of Electronics, Communications and Computer Science, EP79-A, 1996, pp.35-48.
6. J.J.Quisquater, F.X.Standaert,G.Rouvroy,J.P.David,J.D.Legat, *A Cryptanalytic Time-Memory Tradeoff: First FPGA Implementation*, UCL Technical Report CG-2002/2, http://www.dice.ucl.ac.be/crypto/techreports.html
7. A.J.Menezes, P.C.van Oorschot and S.A.Vanstone, *Handbook of applied cryptography*, CRC Press, 1997.
8. Xilinx: *Virtex 2.5V Field Programmable Gate Arrays Data Sheet*, http://www.xilinx.com.

[7] We used only one VIRTEX1000BG560-4

Creating a World of Smart Re-configurable Devices

Extended Abstract

Rudy Lauwereins

IMEC & K.U.Leuven, Kapeldreef 75, B-3001 Leuven, Belgium
Rudy.Lauwereins@imec.be
http://www.imec.be

Abstract. We often hear the world is evolving towards ambient intelligence. Is this another buzzword like artificial intelligence with which it shares the abbreviation AI? What are the properties of ambient intelligence? What will be needed from a technological point of view? Electronic devices in an ambient intelligent environment should combine power efficiency with run-time flexibility. These are conflicting requirements. Re-configurable devices could be an answer, but what should be their properties?

1 A View into an Ambient Intelligence Future

Let's have a look at electronic devices as I expect them to be available in 2010. In sports, athletes, for example runners, will have sensors all over their body, measuring blood composition, electro-cardiogram, electro-encephalogram, breathing condition, motion, stress and position of the joints, etc. These smart sensors will contain the actual solid-state sensing device, analog conditioning circuitry, digital signal processing and RF interface. Using a wireless Body Area Network (BAN), they continuously transmit their measured data to a Wearable Digital Assistant (WDA). The WDA does further processing and transmits all information via a wireless interface to a base-station along the running track, where it can be analyzed by the coach and medical team. This allows the athlete to come as close as possible to his physical limits, in all safety.

Similar setups can be employed for improving medical diagnosis and health care, gaming, entertainment, communication, etc. They all show us that ambient intelligence is centered around four major properties:

- Embedded, ubiquitous, distributed *wearable computing*;
- Ubiquitous *wireless communication*;
- Pro-active *non-keyboard user interfaces*, putting the electronics in the background and people in the foreground;
- *Distributed transducer* systems with sensors and actuators for physical and chemical properties.

2 Properties of the Required Platforms

A Global System for Ambient Intelligence (GSIA, instead of GSM) will consist of one Wearable Digital Assistant per person and in the order of hundred smart sensors and actuators per person-aura.

M. Glesner, P. Zipf, and M. Renovell (Eds.): FPL 2002, LNCS 2438, pp. 790-794, 2002.

The WDA will execute all multimedia and game processing, determine global position (GPS), analyze biometric input, monitor health and control its environment. It will be able to see, hear and feel, as well as speak, show and stimulate. Using a radio interface with multiple antennas, it can communicate in a multi-mode manner with several wireless networks: long distance (kilometers) via GSM/GPRS/UMTS, medium distance (tens of meters) to wireless local area network (WLAN) base-stations and other WDAs with which it forms ad-hoc networks, short distance (one meter) to the smart sensors in its aura. Computing performance is estimated to be 10 to 100 billion operations per second at a power consumption below two Watt, i.e. a power efficiency of 10 to 50 MOPS/mW. The latter is necessary since they are battery operated and should last on a single battery charge for at least one day. Applications can be upgraded and new services downloaded to the WDA. Hence, they should be flexible.

The smart sensors and actuators combine the actual sensing or actuating device, the signal conditioning and digital processing and the wireless interface in one package, which often should be bio-compatible. They do not have to be flexible as they are expected to perform one function throughout its entire life. Most of them need to transmit or receive only a few hundred bits per second, in short bursts, and have very moderate compute requirements. However, their power consumption is limited to a hundred microwatt, since they do not possess a battery and should generate the necessary energy from their environment (e.g. motion, temperature, light, ...). The required power efficiency is estimated at 100 MOPS/mW.

Power efficiency and flexibility are conflicting requirements (Figure 1). What can be seen is that power efficiency of traditional microprocessors today is two to three orders of magnitude less than for hardwired logic. On the contrary, microprocessors offer the highest degree of flexibility. The power efficiency needed for ambient intelligence can only be met today by hardwired logic; however, this does not provide the required flexibility. It can be seen on the graph that in a few years, when we are at the 65nm feature size, a mixture of hardwired logic, some re-configurable logic and a few processors for the less demanding tasks will make ambient intelligence feasible.

3 Case Study of a Smart Re-configurable Device

As a case study, we want to show what can be achieved today in building a smart re-configurable device. Assume you have 4 separate appliances: an MP3 audio player, an MPEG-2 video player, a PDA and a mobile phone. Each of these devices contains a few Instruction Set Processors (ISP) and several hardwired accelerators (marked as 'ASIC' in Figure 2).

What the consumer really wants to have is a single device that can run all listed applications at wish, even multiple at the same time. In that case, we add a re-configurable hardware section to the platform. Let us assume for example that the consumer wants to see a full motion full screen video on his/her appliance (Figure 3).

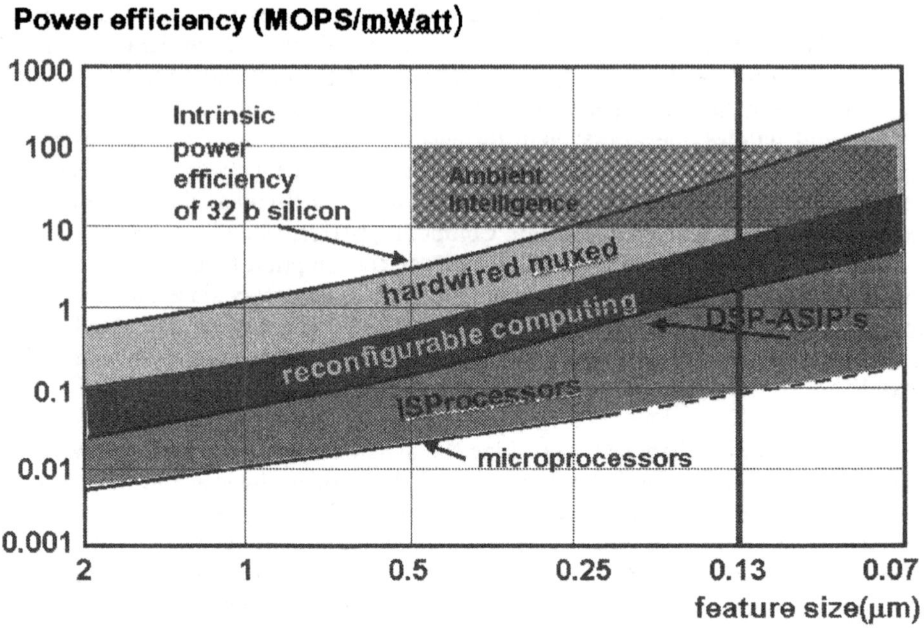

Fig. 1. Power efficiency versus feature size (Source: T.Claasen et al. (ISSCC99).

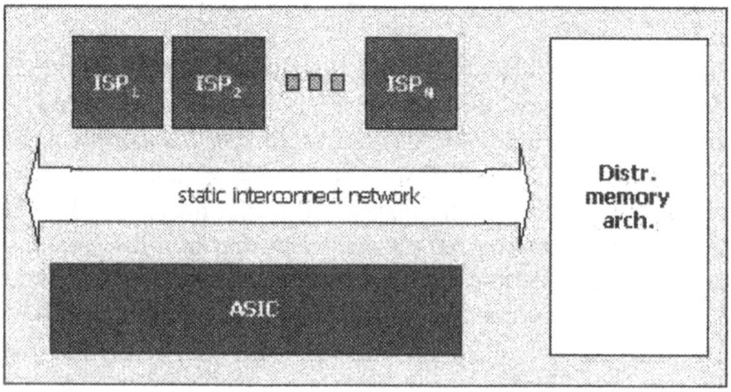

Fig. 2. Typical hardware structure of a traditional System-on-a-Chip (SoC) for a battery operated consumer electronics appliance.

Fig. 3. Multiple application appliance, running an MPEG-2 video decoder full screen.

For power reasons, we do not run the video decoder in software on an ISP, but we map it onto the re-configurable hardware (Figure 4).

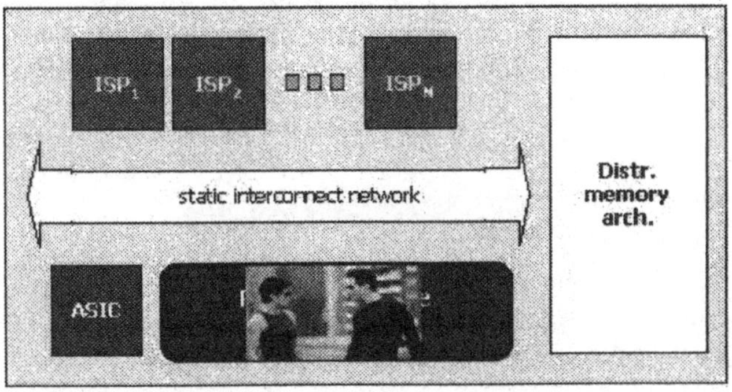

Fig. 4. For power reasons, the full motion full screen video decoder is mapped onto the re-configurable hardware.

When the consumer gets bored by the scene and wants to switch to a downloaded 3D game, while still seeing the movie as a picture-in-picture (Figure 5), the Real-Time Operating System (RTOS) moves the video decoder from hardware to software to free the re-configurable hardware resource for the computationally demanding 3D game; the reduced size video decoder fits on an ISP (Figure 6).

Fig. 5. The appliance now runs two concurrent applications: a full screen 3D game as well as a video decoder as picture-in-picture.

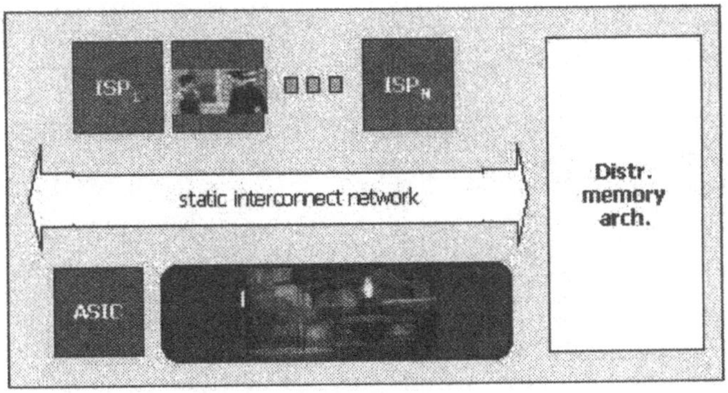

Fig. 6. The video decoder has been moved to software, to make the re-configurable hardware available for the demanding 3D game application.

To demonstrate the feasibility of this hardware-to-software migration under operating system support, without interrupting the running application and hence by automatically migrating the 18-bit wide words of the application status in the hardware to an equivalent 32-bit wide status in the software, we implemented this scenario on a Compaq iPaq, enhanced with a board containing a Xilinx Virtex II-6000 (Figure 7).

Fig. 7. Prototype platform demonstrating the migration of applications between hardware and software under operating system control.

4 Conclusion

Ambient intelligent appliances need a large compute power at very low energy. This can only be achieved by combining hardware accelerators, re-configurable logic and instruction set processors. Real-time operating system support must be provided to enable multi-threading in hardware as well as in software and to enable easy migrating of applications between hardware and software without interrupting the application.

Interconnection Networks Enable Fine-Grain Dynamic Multi-tasking on FPGAs

Théodore Marescaux, Andrei Bartic, Dideriek Verkest*, Serge Vernalde, and Rudy Lauwereins**

IMEC vzw.,
Kapeldreef 75, 3001 Leuven, Belgium
marescau@imec.be

Abstract. Multimedia support appears on embedded platforms, such as WAP for mobile phones. However, true multimedia applications require both the computation power that only dedicated hardware can provide and the flexibility of software implementations. To this end, we are investigating reconfigurable architectures, composed of an instruction-set processor running software processes and coupled to an FPGA on which hardware tasks are spawned by dynamic partial reconfiguration. This paper focuses on two main aspects. It explains how separating communication from computation enables hardware multi-tasking and it describes our implementation of a fixed communication-layer that decouples the computation elements, allowing them to be dynamically reconfigured. This communication layer is an interconnection network, implemented on a Virtex FPGA, allowing fast synchronous communication between hardware tasks implemented on the same matrix. The network is a 2D torus and uses wormhole routing. It achieves transfer rates up to 77.6 MB/s between two adjacent routers, when clocked at 40 MHz. Interconnection networks on FPGAs allow fine-grain dynamic partial reconfiguration and make hardware multi-tasking a reality.

1 Introduction

Nowadays, numerous multimedia applications are emerging on portable devices such as personal digital assistants (PDA) or mobile phones. Typical applications such as MPEG players or 3D games are usually computationally intensive, preventing them from being implemented on general-purpose embedded processors. To achieve the minimal Quality of Service (QoS) required for these applications, traditional designs of multimedia platforms contain dedicated hardware accelerators, which lack flexibility, or application specific instruction-set processors (ASIP), which are limited to their specific application domains.

Based on our experience in reconfigurable systems [1], we believe that the combination of instruction-set processors (ISP) with reconfigurable hardware is

* also professor at Vrije Universiteit Brussel
** also professor at Katholieke Universiteit Leuven

M. Glesner, P. Zipf, and M. Renovell (Eds.): FPL 2002, LNCS 2438, pp. 795–805, 2002.

the best trade-off for such a platform. The platform has to support true hardware/software (HW/SW) multitasking, i.e. tasks are executed either on the ISP or on the reconfigurable hardware, a Field Programmable Gate Array (FPGA) in our case. A hard real-time operating system (RT-OS) manages the applications by distributing the different tasks on the available resources. Our platform is composed of a Compaq iPaq^{TM} PDA, running RT-Linux [3] on its StrongArm processor SA-1110 (206MHz) and controlling a Xilinx Virtex^{TM} XCV800 running hardware tasks.

The applications running on our platform [2] are composed of several software threads and of several hardware tasks. These HW and SW components must therefore be able to inter-communicate, i.e. a specific HW communication layer, compatible with SW communication, has to be designed.

Hardware resources are shared by dividing the FPGA into logical tiles of coarse granularity, such as a JPEG decoder. However, the reconfiguration grain is fine, i.e. an AES encryption module could replace the JPEG decoder. Tasks can be dynamically instantiated in the tile matrix by partial reconfiguration. Our communication-layer is a packet-switched Inter-Connection Network (ICN) and is fixed in place to allow Dynamic Partial Reconfiguration (DPR).

This paper presents the use of on-FPGA interconnection networks to enable fine-grain dynamic partial-reconfiguration. To this end, Sect. 2 develops how separating communication from computation allows hardware multitasking on FPGAs. Sect. 3 presents a simple packet-switched network that is used to create a fixed communication layer. Sect. 4 details the implementation of our interconnection network on the Virtex family. Specific issues about Virtex column-based DPR are treated in Sect. 5. Sect. 6 discusses the performances of our reconfigurable System on Chip (SoC) platform. Finally, Sect. 7 concludes.

2 Separating Communication from Computation Enables Fine-Grain Dynamic Partial-Reconfiguration

In order to do multitasking, the FPGA must be partitioned into an array of identical tiles, each tile running a hardware task, equivalent to a software thread. Whereas the granularity of the tiles is coarse, a JPEG decoder for example, the reconfiguration grain is fine: the same tile can be configured to run an image filter as well as a data encryption module. This approach differs from previous works [4] where the FPGA is divided into simple computation elements, difficult to manage by an OS and requiring specific component libraries.

The ability to dynamically reconfigure tasks depends on the control over the boundaries between them. Indeed, with the traditional design-flow, if we reconfigure an AES encryption module in place of a Laplace edge detector, their interfaces do not match and we have to perform a Place and Route (P&R) on the whole FPGA. However, by adding constraints to the positioning of the interface, the P&R phase is only required at design-time because it yields hardware components with an identical input/output topology (Sect. 5).

Hardware tasks are thus encapsulated into a fixed layer providing them with a unified way of communicating. This communication layer raises the abstraction level of the hardware blocks, allowing easy Intellectual Property (IP) block integration.

Various fixed communication layers such as buses and on-chip interconnection networks can be used to this end. However, we prefer a packet-switched network to a bus for three reasons. A simple bus is a major bottleneck because its routing resources are shared by all connected blocks, whereas in a network routing resources are distributed. A network is therefore easily scalable, whereas the complexity of a bus arbiter increases with the number of blocks controlled. Finally, networks are more power efficient than buses, because idle parts can be powered off, whereas buses must always drive long lines.

3 Choosing a Packet-Switched Network for SoC Reconfigurable Platforms

3.1 SoC Reconfigurable Platforms Require Specific Interconnection Networks

One can think of an interconnection network as being an array of routers interconnecting an array of processors (Fig. 1(a)). In general each processor has direct access to a local memory, without using the ICN. Interconnection net-

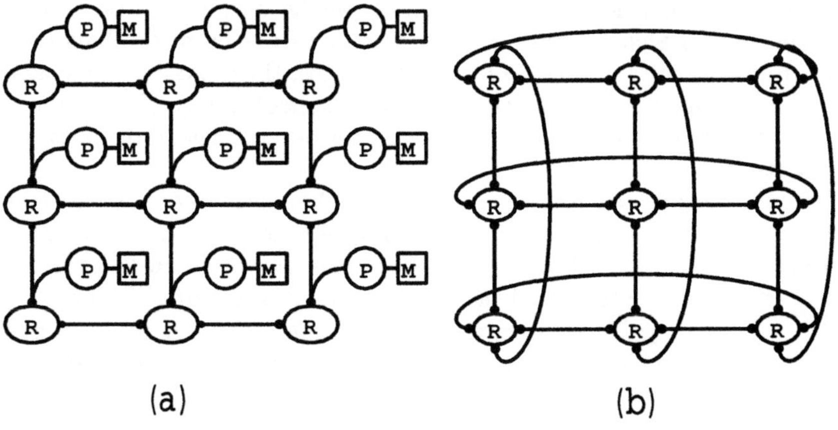

Fig. 1. In an ICN (a), each processor (P) is connected to a router (R). Each processor has access to local memory (M). In a 2D torus (b), each row and column of routers is connected in a ring, reducing router complexity with respect to a 2D mesh.

works have been successfully used in the world of multi-processor computing, such as the J-Machine [6], with various forms of architectures (k-ary n-cubes, hyper-cubes, butterflies, crossbars) and routing policies (virtual cut-through, wormhole, mad-postman switching) [9]. However, they are multi-chip circuits, whereas for reconfigurable SoC we have to implement the whole network and all the processors on the same FPGA ! The choice for our ICN is therefore dictated by the need for low hardware overhead. A network, and therefore its complexity, are described by two parameters: topology and routing algorithm [9].

3.2 The Interconnection Network Has a 2D Torus Topology to Limit Hardware Overhead

An FPGA is a 2-dimensional chip, so we naturally considered 2D network topologies. In a mesh-topology such as the one in Fig. 1(a) a router has to be able to route in all directions: North, South, East and West. It is possible to reduce the router complexity by using a similar topology, called a torus network (Fig. 1(b)). Such a network folds the mesh along the horizontal and vertical directions and therefore only requires routing along two directions, i.e. East and South. However, this complexity reduction comes at the expense of a 15% increase (for a $4 * 4$ folded torus) [7] in power consumption with respect to a mesh network.

3.3 The Network Uses Wormhole Packet-Switching

The routing algorithm we use on our 2D torus is called Wormhole Routing [8]. It is a blocking, hop-based, deterministic routing algorithm. It uses relative addresses and thus does not require a global knowledge of the network. In wormhole switching, message packets are pipelined through the network. This technique relieves routers from buffering complete messages, thus making them small and fast [9]. A message is broken into flits (flow control units). Flits come in two types: header flits, containing routing information and data flits containing the message itself.

The two header flits give the number of channels that must be traversed respectively in the X and Y directions. Packets are routed first along the X direction, then along the Y direction before reaching their target. The value in the X header flit is decremented each time a router is traversed. When it reaches zero, the X heading flit is discarded and routing starts on the Y dimension. When Y equals zero, the message enters the destination hardware block.

3.4 Two Virtual Channels Are Used to Avoid Deadlocking

Our network uses two time-multiplexed Virtual Channels (VC) to avoid deadlocks. Deadlocks in an interconnection network occur when no message can advance toward its destination because all queues are full with messages not destined to neighboring routers (Fig. 2(a)) [8]. Fig. 2(b) shows the virtual channel usage on a 1D torus. Router 0 only sends messages on VC_0, whereas the other routers may initiate messages only on VC_1. This virtual channel management policy avoids deadlocks by breaking the torus into a spiral [9].

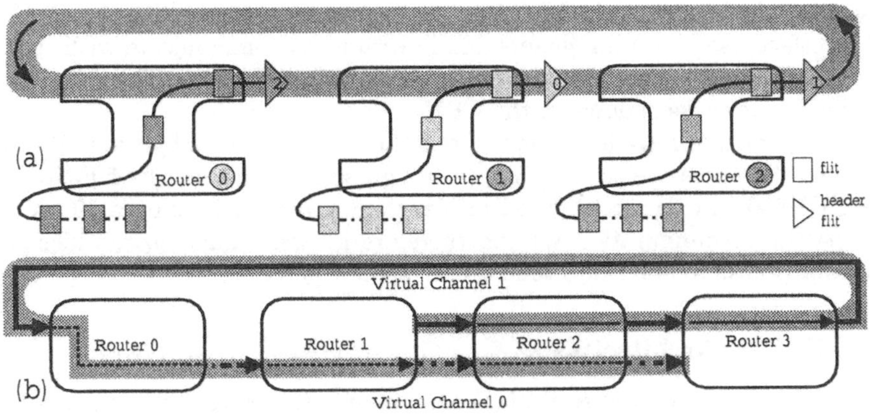

Fig. 2. When message queues are full with messages destined to non-neighboring routers (a) no message can be sent, the network is deadlocked. Using two virtual channels avoids dead-locking by breaking the 1D torus into a spiral(b).

4 Architecture of Our Interconnection Network

This section details our implementation of a packet-switched ICN on a Virtex XCV800. However, the figures can be easily extrapolated to the Virtex II XC2V6000, which is the target of our final demonstrator. Reconfigurable designs should target the Virtex II, because it features 6 columns of block-RAMs (BRAMs), allowing implementation of up to 6 routers, whereas the Virtex I has only 2 (Sect. 5).

4.1 Implementation Overview

The data-path width is chosen to maximize the network's throughput. However, it can not be too wide, because on the Virtex I family the BRAM element is 16-bit wide. Moreover, reconfigurable modules have to use the scarce number of long-lines connecting tri-state buffers (Sect. 5) to connect routers together and to get access to resources such as BRAMs or multipliers. We have chosen to prioritize the availability to these resources. Therefore, on our network, messages are segmented into 16-bit flits. The Maximum Transfer Unit (MTU) is fixed to 128 data flits per message, enabling a Virtex I to buffer two messages in a BRAM. The ICN is fully pipelined and achieves, between two routers, a peak rate of 38.8 MBytes/s per virtual channel (Sect. 6), when clocked at 40 MHz.

Hardware tasks can be slow compared to the network's bitrates. Therefore to avoid blocking, the hardware tasks are decoupled from the network using interfaces. These interfaces use dual-port BRAMs to buffer messages and work as a network abstraction layer for the hardware task.

In our demonstrator, the ICN is connected to the memory bus of the StrongArm SA1110 on a Compaq iPaq 3760. A specialized interface (IO interface) resides at the border of the FPGA to enable communication with the CPU. The IO interface uses control registers and interrupts to communicate with the CPU and its message buffers are memory mapped to the SA1110. The scheduling of the hardware tasks is done on the CPU.

Moreover, the reconfiguration of the Virtex is also done by the CPU, which accesses the Virtex select-map port through some glue-logic. At 50MHz a Virtex XCV800 can be reconfigured in less than $11ms$ ($39.5ms$ on a XC2V6000). For partial reconfiguration we can therefore go well under $5ms$, which allows hardware tasks to start in a time a user cannot perceive.

4.2 Router Architecture

On a 2D torus, rows are equivalent to columns, therefore the torus can be decomposed into rows of 1D toruses connected to columns of 1D toruses. We can chain two simple 1D routers to obtain a 2D router and produce a more modular network.

A 1D-router has two input/output channels. A message entering a router can either be forwarded along the current direction or sent orthogonally, either on a column if the Y header-flit is non-zero, or into a hardware task. Each channel is composed of a 16-bit data path and of 3-bit control signals. Two control-bits are used to signal the presence of a message and its destination and the third is a back-pressure signal (nack) used to block a message entering a busy router or interface.

The routers handle two time-multiplexed VCs to avoid deadlocking (Sect. 3.4) [9]. These VCs are interleaved, with one clock cycle each.

For efficiency, the router is fully pipelined. Because the data channels are interleaved the control signals are also interleaved and precede data by one clock cycle. The nack signal, used for blocking, is back-propagated along the message path. It takes two ticks for a flit to get out of a router, therefore at each clock cycle data is transmitted on, alternating VCs.

A 1D-router (Fig. 3), is composed of one input controller per channel, one arbiter and an output-controller. The input controllers issue output requests to a round-robin arbiter and decrement header-flits when routing. Each output channel has a 2-flit deep buffer to be able to resume blocked messages. The output controller is composed of a 2-input crossbar-switch and of the nack logic.

4.3 Architecture of the Interface between Task and Router

An interface decouples the hardware task from the network using DP-RAMs as message buffers. The hardware task can then use independent data-width and clock rates, allowing easy IP integration. The interfaces are designed to cope with the sustained bit-rates required by the ICN and perform multiple-message buffering to reduce network congestion.

Moreover the interface, called a "net-cell", provides the hardware task (or IP-block) with high-level communication by means of routing tables. Hardware

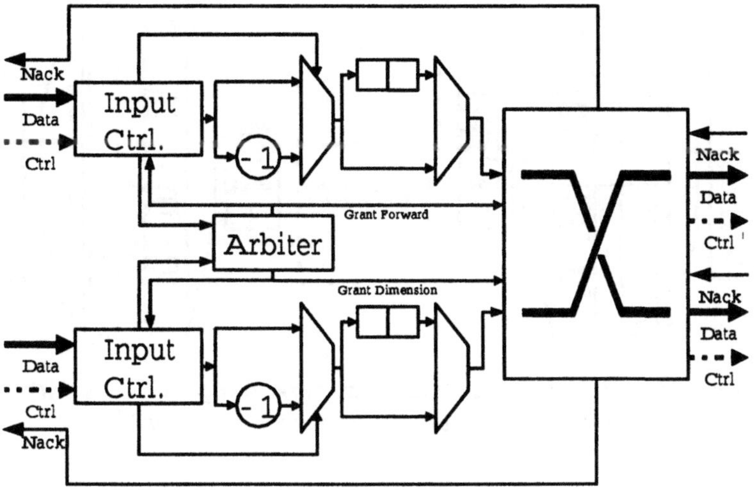

Fig. 3. 1D-Router has 1 input controller per channel, 2-flit deep buffers are included in the output controller/switch.

tasks within an application communicate through a tuple composed of a logical address and a port number, similar to the IP address and UDP port number for the UDP protocol. Routing tables transform a destination logical address into the number of X and Y hops on the network. The routing tables are updated by the RT-OS to match the position of the IP-block in the network. Therefore, a task does not need to know where it is situated in the network and whether the tasks it communicates with are running in hardware or software. The RT-OS adapts the routing tables after an IP-block reconfiguration. Therefore, there is no need for complex run-time circuit re-routing as required in previous works [5] and circuit integrity is guaranteed. Routing tables can also be modified at any time without having to reset or stop the hardware task. This is very useful if some other task from the same application is switched in or out of the network as a function of the available resources and the QoS policy.

Our implementation of a net-cell buffers two input and two output messages on a Virtex I and eight on the Virtex II. Each message buffer is complemented by a control register bank giving the length and origin/destination of the message. This high-level protocol information such as port number or net-cell origin is piggy-backed in the Y-header flit and does not require extra bandwidth.

As Fig. 4 shows, our net-cell is composed of a process reading the local router and steering the storage of messages in a circular linked-list of message buffers and control registers. The hardware task is encapsulated in a block that always presents the same fixed interface giving access to a message-in presentation layer and a message-out presentation layer. Moreover this fixed block also gives ports to extra local resources such as BRAMS or even multipliers on a Virtex II. The presentation layers abstract the internals of the net-cell from the IP-block.

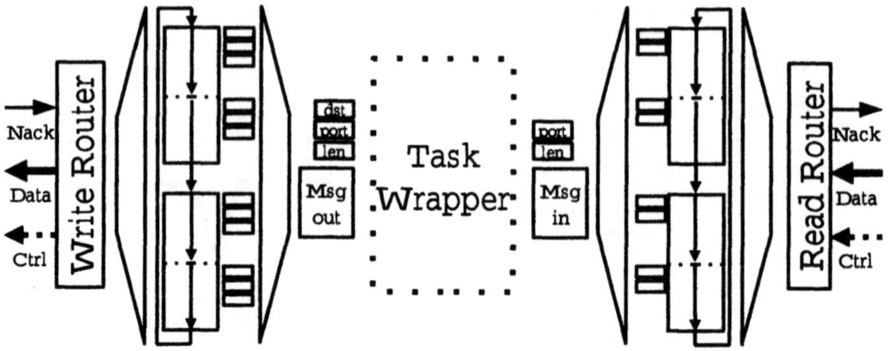

Fig. 4. Net-cell encapsulates the hardware task and provides it with high-level communication primitives (destination, port, message length).

4.4 Architecture of the Interface between CPU and FPGA

Our reconfigurable platform is composed of an ISP (SA-1110) coupled to an FPGA through its memory bus. A special interface, similar to a net-cell (c.f. Sect. 4.3), has been designed to allow fast and efficient communication between them by means of memory-mapped registers and interrupts.

The Virtex I implementation can buffer 8 input and 8 output messages in its BRAMs. These are mapped in the memory space of the SA-1110 to allow fast access. Indeed, on an iPaq 3760 the SA-1110 has a maximum access speed of up to 103 MHz on its memory bus.

5 Dynamic Partial Reconfiguration on Xilinx Virtex FPGAs

The full design is composed of fixed router modules and replaceable IP modules. The IP modules can be loaded dynamically, according to the user actions. When a new IP module is to be loaded into the FPGA it will be placed into a free predefined area, or will replace a module that is no longer needed. In order to be able to dynamically reconfigure the design, partial bitstreams of the IP modules must be available.

We have generated the partial bitstreams for the IP modules following the Partial Reconfiguration (PR) methodology developed by Xilinx [10] (ISE tool suite v4.2 and higher). According to the Xilinx methodology, the design has to be partitioned in fixed and reconfigurable modules. Naturally, routers are fixed and hardware tasks are the reconfigurable modules.

In principle, during the partial reconfiguration process all the modules can continue working, except for the reconfigured module. However this is not possible in our design, because the network has to maintain communication between modules. According to the PR methodology, the reconfigurable modules must span the whole chip from top to bottom [10]. Therefore the 2D torus must be folded into a 1D structure and consequently the communication between routers has to traverse the reconfigurable modules (Fig. 5). The communication with the

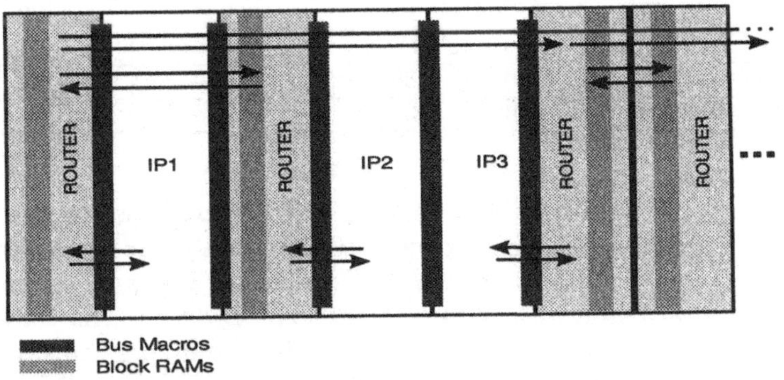

Fig. 5. Placement of routers and IP modules a Virtex II 6000.

reconfigurable modules can only take place through a "Bus Macro" (BM). The BM ensures the reproducibility of the design routing and is implemented using tri-state buffers. The tri-state buffers force the routing to always pass through the same places. At the same time they decouple the modules from each other during reconfiguration, avoiding possible harmful transitory situations. In this way, a 4 bit per row communication channel is possible between adjacent modules. This limitation comes from the current Virtex architecture and its limited routing resources.

The Virtex II 6000 has 96 rows, limiting the total number of bits passing through the interface to 384. Moreover, the BMs only support unidirectional signals, strongly limiting the minimum size of an FPGA that can be used to implement our network.

The current Xilinx tool suite requires the modules to have widths in multiples of 4 columns. A Virtex II 6000 has 88 columns which sets the upper limit of the possible modules to 22. However, the main limitation in the number of modules comes from the fact that all resources, such as BRAMs, present inside the area reserved for a module can only be used by that module. Because the routers use BRAMs, the maximum number of routers is given by the number of BRAM columns available on the FPGA: 2 for a Virtex I and 6 for a Virtex II 6000.

6 Results

The use of an ICN brings in some hardware overhead (Tab. 1). The synthesis has been performed with Synopsys Design Compiler on a Virtex $XCV800$. For the $2*2$ torus network we implemented, the hardware overhead on a Virtex $XCV800$ amounts to 35%, but drops to 9.5% on a bigger Virtex $XC2V6000$. The ICN is fully pipelined and it takes 2 clock cycles to transmit one 16-bit flit on a given

Table 1. Hardware overhead induced by an ICN.

Element	$XCV800$ (slices)	$XCV800$ (%)	$XC2V6000$ (%)
1D-Router	223	2.4	0.7
Net-Cell	259	2.8	0.8
FPGA-CPU Interface	716	7.6	2.1
$1*4$ 1D-Torus (estimated)	2385	25.4	7.1
$2*2$ 2D-Torus (estimated)	3227	34.8	9.5

VC. There are 128 data flits in a message and two extra header flits plus two more for the message tail. The bandwidth between two adjacent routers, per VC is therefore: $(16-bit*20MHz*128/132)/8 = 38.8MBytes/s$. On a $2*2$ torus network, the total bandwidth is therefore $310.4MBytes/s$. The throughput of the network is however limited by the deterministic routing scheme. If each task is simultaneously sending a message, the throughput drops to 20%. A technique to overcome this problem is to clock the network faster than the hardware tasks.

7 Conclusions

This paper presents the three steps that enable us to use interconnection networks to perform fine-grain dynamic multi-tasking on FPGAs. In the first place, one must separate communication from computation by using a fixed communication layer. To this end, interconnection networks are to be preferred over bus architectures because they are more scalable and consume less power. Our interconnection network is a fully-pipelined 2D-torus that uses wormhole routing to minimize hardware overhead and achieves $77.6MBytes/s$ at $40MHz$. Finally, dynamic partial reconfiguration is possible on Virtex FPGAs by folding the 2D-network into a 1D-structure fitting the Virtex column-based architecture.

Interconnection networks enable fine-grain dynamic multi-tasking on FPGAs for a low hardware overhead. Hardware tasks can be dynamically instantiated in the network by partial reconfiguration, opening the way to a new class of hybrid applications dynamically mixing hardware and software components.

References

1. D. Desmet, P. Avasare, P. Coene, S. Decneut, F. Hendrickx, T. Marescaux, J.-Y. Mignolet, R. Pasko, P. Schaumont, D. Verkest: Design of Cam-E-Leon: A Run-time Reconfigurable Web Camera, in Embedded Processor Design Challenges, LNCS Springer 2002.
2. J-Y. Mignolet, S. Vernalde, D. Verkest and R. Lauwereins: Enabling hardware-software multitasking on a reconfigurable computing platform for networked portable multimedia appliances, ERSA 2002.
3. P. Coene, V. Nollet: RT-Linux Strong-Arm port (`http://www.imec.be/rtlinux`).
4. G. Brebner. A virtual hardware operating system for the Xilinx XC6200, Proc. 6th International Workshop on Field Programmable Logic and Applications, Springer LNCS 1142, 1996, pp 327-336.

5. J. Burns et al.: A dynamic reconfiguration run-time system, Proc. 5th Annual IEEE Symposyum on FPGAs for Custom Computing Machines, IEEE, 1997, pp 66-75.
6. W.J. Dally et al.: The J-Machine: A Retrospective, Retrospective in 25 Years of the International Symposia on Computer Architecture - Selected Papers. pp 54-58.
7. W.J. Dally and B. Towles: Route Packets, Not Wires: On-Chip Interconnection Networks, Proceedings of the 38th Design Automation Conference, June 2001.
8. W.J. Dally and C.L. Seitz: The torus routing chip, Distributed Computing, 1:187 196, 1986.
9. J. Duato, S. Yalamanchili, L. Ni: Interconnection networks, an engineering approach, September 1997. ISBN 0-8186-7800-3.
10. Xilinx Inc., An Implementation Flow for Active Partial Reconfiguration Using 4.2i, XAPP290 (v0.5) February 2002.

Multitasking Hardware on the SLAAC1-V Reconfigurable Computing System*

Wesley J. Landaker, Michael J. Wirthlin, and Brad L. Hutchings

Department of Electrical and Computer Engineering
Brigham Young University, Provo, Utah 84602
{wjl,wirthlin,hutch}@ee.byu.edu

Abstract. Configurable computing systems traditionally operate as single user systems. The availability of configurable systems can be improved by supporting multiple users simultaneously. This paper presents a configurable system using the SLAAC1-V that supports multitasking configurable hardware. The techniques used to support hardware context-switching are described and the run-time performance of the system is evaluated.

1 Introduction

Configurable computing machines (CCMs) are systems increasingly being used to provide orders of magnitude improvement in performance over software for many application-specific computing challenges. These systems achieve notable levels of performance by executing an application-specific digital circuit on programmable logic resources.

Conventional configurable machines are single-user systems – only one user or process can actively operate the CCM board at a given time. Configurable applications are typically controlled by a program executing on the CCM host. This host program controls CCM configuration, operation flow, I/O transfer and often performs additional post-processing. As long as these host programs are active, they retain exclusive ownership of the resource. Unfortunately, this approach can lead to poor utilization of the expensive configurable resource – a host program that does not actively use the CCM will prevent other users or programs from utilizing the resource.

A more efficient way of utilizing the expensive CCM resource is to allow multiple users access to the resource at the same time. With an appropriate form of resource management, user requests for the CCM resources can be arbitrated to provide seemingly exclusive ownership of the configurable hardware. This resource sharing is very similar to multitasking on modern operating systems

* This effort is sponsored by the Defense Advanced Research Projects Agency (DARPA) under contract number DABT63-96-C-0047. The U.S. Government is authorized to reproduce and distribute reprints for Governmental purposes notwithstanding any copyright annotation thereon.

M. Glesner, P. Zipf, and M. Renovell (Eds.): FPL 2002, LNCS 2438, pp. 806–815, 2002.

– multiple software processes execute "simultaneously" on the CPU by time-sharing their execution.

There are a number of situations in which multitasking configurable hardware will lead to improved resource utilization. First, multitasking can be used during verification when the board is used relatively infrequently, but is locked for long periods of time. Second, multitasking can be used while a non-interactive configurable computing application is blocked waiting for host I/O or asynchronous data. Much like a preemptive multitasking software environment, a multitasking architecture switches configurable applications in and out of hardware to *maximize utilization* of the hardware resources.

Multitasking and context-switching configurable resources is not a new idea. Several projects have proposed or designed FPGAs that provide multiple hardware contexts on a single programmable device[1, 2, 3]. These multi-context FPGAs are designed to rapidly switch between hardware contexts to increase the virtual hardware available to the designer. Other work, such as [4], describes multitasking architectures using reconfigurable processors. While the techniques presented in these papers are related to our effort, we take a different approach. This work does not attempt to context-switch in a single cycle or to introduce new hardware architectures. Instead, this work will perform context-switching relatively infrequently (i.e. measured in seconds) using readily-available commercial FPGAs. While multitasking reconfigurable computing systems have been proposed, very few have demonstrated these techniques in actual systems. This work presents an actual demonstration and evaluation of hardware multitasking using *commercially available* FPGAs. This paper demonstrates that context-switching today's FPGAs is not only possible, but is practical in a number of operating situations.

2 Context-Switching for Configurable Systems

The steps involved in context-switching are relatively straightforward and have been used for many years in multitasking operating systems. Modern CPUs have been designed to facilitate these steps and improve the time required for context-switching. Context-switching for configurable hardware, however, requires techniques and capabilities not intrinsic to most configurable systems. This section will discuss the four steps required for context-switching and relate it to configurable systems.

2.1 Stopping Hardware

The first step of a hardware context-switch is stopping the hardware. All of the FPGAs must be stopped *simultaneously* to insure that the entire system has been halted in a known and restorable state. The most straightforward method of simultaneously stopping synchronous hardware is to stop the global clock. When the global synchronous clock has been stopped, the configurable hardware will no longer modify its state registers or memory.

2.2 Capturing Hardware State

Like software multitasking, a hardware multitasking system must capture and store the state of the hardware process. Unlike software multitasking, hardware systems contain a large amount of state that is difficult to access. The state associated with a configurable application includes the design configuration, every flip-flop and memory element within its FPGAs, and the contents of any external memories attached to the programmable logic. This large amount of state requires a large memory space for state storage and a relatively long time for accessing the state.

Although the large amount of state posses technical challenges for a hardware multitasking system, the biggest hurdle is accessing the internal state of the programmable logic. Most FPGA vendors do not provide access to the internal flip-flops and memories of the FPGA device. Reconfigurable systems that use such devices must add additional circuitry to provide external access to the internal state. One such approach involves the automatic insertion of scan chains to access circuit state[5]. Xilinx FPGAs provide a state-capture capability called Readback[6]. This feature allows a designer to read (but not modify) the state of internal flip-flops and memories through the device configuration port.

2.3 Restoring Hardware State

Restoring the hardware state of a programmable logic circuit is the most difficult task of a hardware context-switch. Currently, few vendors provide the capability of setting the state of internal registers and memories. Again, scan chain can be used here, but while this approach provides state capture and restoration, it consumes large amounts of programmable logic resources and may affect the overall timing of a user design.

An alternative approach for setting the state of internal registers is to *modify* the original design to reflect the saved state of the hardware process. This modified design is then configured onto the resource to restore both the hardware configuration and hardware state onto the configurable resources.

State restoration of flip-flops is implemented by changing the reset/preset behavior of each flip-flop in the design. Most FPGA vendors provide flip-flop libraries that support both preset and reset options. The state of internal registers can be modified by individually setting the preset or reset mode of each flip-flop. For example, flip-flops with an initial "1" state are replaced by flip-flops in preset mode and flip-flops in the "0" state are replaced by flip-flops in reset mode. Once the design has been modified, a global reset is performed on the device and each register is restored to the appropriate state value.

Figure 1 demonstrates this technique with a four-bit register. When the circuit is first loaded, the global reset line is strobed and the four bit register is initialized to `0000`. After executing for a number of cycles, the circuit is stopped and the register is found to hold the value `0110`. This value is saved as part of the state of the design, and the circuit configuration is modified to reflect the state `0110`. The two middle flip-flops are each changed from a flip-flop in the reset mode to a flip-flop in the preset mode. Thus, when the design is restored and reset, the register will contain the value of its last known state.

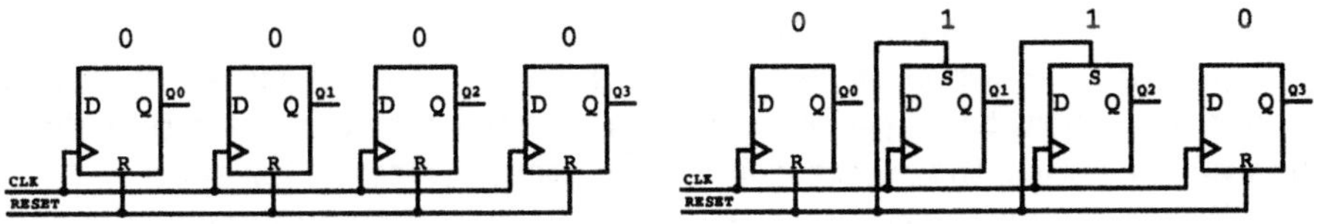

(a) Before (b) After

Fig. 1. Restoring State to a Register.

Modifying a design and performing technology mapping during a context-switch would require an unreasonable amount of time. To avoid technology mapping, these simple design modifications can be made by modifying the design *bitstream*. Low-level tools such as JBits[7] can be used to rapidly make such bitstream modifications. Such bitstream modification tools can be used to modify the preset/reset characteristics of each flip-flop to represent the appropriate state value upon configuration. Modifying the bitstream with custom tools to restore FPGA state is the method used in the context-switching architecture described in this paper.

2.4 Restarting Hardware

The final step in a hardware context-switch is restarting the hardware. The hardware is restarted simply by enabling the global synchronous clock. If the state is properly restored before the clock is cycled, the hardware process will restart and operate as though the circuit had never been removed from the hardware resources.

3 Multitasking Architecture

A multitasking configurable computing system was created to demonstrate the feasibility of multitasking hardware and evaluate its run-time performance. The primary function of this multitasking system is to correctly perform the hardware context-switch as described above. This section will describe the multitasking architecture and the approach used for a hardware context-switch.

This hardware multitasking system was created using the SLAAC1-V CCM developed at USC-ISI[8]. This particular CCM is particularly useful for multitasking; it provides control of the clock and device Readback. Although the SLAAC1-V contains three Xilinx Virtex FPGAs and ten megabytes of external memory, the current system only utilizes a single FPGA and does not save external memory as part of a context-switch. Future work on this system will include context-switching the other two FPGAs and handling external memory.

Our multitasking architecture includes the following components (see Figure 2): a SLAAC1-V CCM, a hardware server process executing on the host, and an arbitrary number of hardware client applications. Hardware clients communicate with the server using a network socket-based client-server protocol. The hardware server is a process executing on the host computer that directly communicates with the configurable computing system. This process "owns" the CCM and manages access to its resources based on external client requests. Hardware clients are processes that communicate with the hardware server to use the shared CCM resource. Client processes may execute locally on the host computer, or remotely on any device networked to the hardware server using standard network sockets.

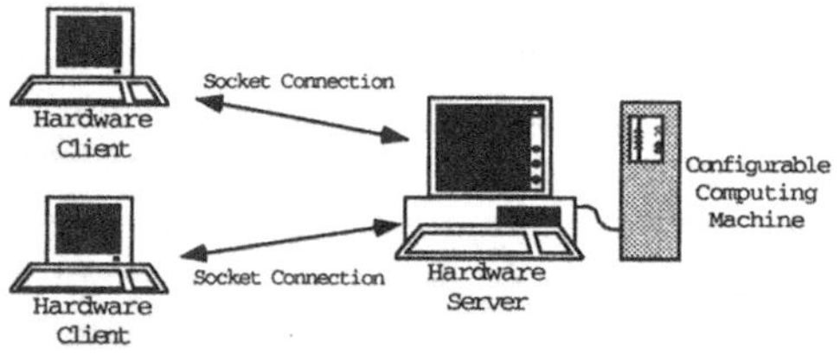

Fig. 2. Multitasking Architecture Overview.

3.1 Hardware Server

The hardware server is a software process executing on the host workstation that owns and manages the shared configurable resource. Much like the kernel in a modern operating system, the hardware server determines which process executes on the CCM hardware and manages the state of suspended processes. The server performs hardware context-switching by executing the four steps of a context-switch described earlier. To arbitrate the shared configurable resource between multiple hardware processes, the hardware server always maintains exclusive ownership of the CCM. Client applications must access the board through the hardware server. Once the CCM has been initialized, the hardware server is ready to schedule hardware client processes on the hardware resource. As clients connect, they will request for configurations to be loaded, for execution to begin, and for results to be returned. The hardware server schedules these operations efficiently to maximize device utilization and to reduce context-switching overhead.

With exclusive ownership of the hardware resource and a mechanism for communicating with hardware clients, the server performs all operations on behalf of a client process. The server knows how to save and restore all the state needed to make context-switching of client processes possible. In addition, the hardware server can perform I/O with the board as requested by clients. By owning the hardware resource, the hardware server can arbitrate the sharing of the resources while simulating exclusive access to the resource for each client.

3.2 Client/Server Protocol

This hardware multitasking architecture uses standard network sockets to communicate between the hardware server and client hardware processes. The communication protocol used is simple but extensible. It mirrors (and simplifies) the interface to the CCM that a client would typically see when using the SLAAC1-V board directly.

The use of network sockets allows users to access the hardware resource from a machine that does not contain the CCM. Since network sockets are universal on networked systems, hardware clients do not have to use the language or operating system in which the hardware device driver code is written.

The socket-based client-server protocol provides a basic set of commands to configure and use the hardware resources. These commands are similar to the software API calls that are traditionally provided with a CCM device driver. These commands include conventional operations such as configuration, clock control, as well as special operations for checkpointing and state restoration. Additional commands can be easily added to our extensible protocol when they are implemented on the server.

Open/Close When an Open or Close command is sent to the hardware server, the CCM device is not actually opened or closed – it has already been opened and locked by the server. Instead, the Open command establishes a hardware session with the server. The Close command ends the hardware session by removing all data structures associated with the client process.

Configure The Configure command does not immediately configure the hardware resource. When the server receives the Configure command, it simply caches the configuration bitstream sent with the command and marks the bitstream as active. Later, when the client process is scheduled to execute on the hardware resource (via a Run or Cycle command), the bitstream is actually configured onto the hardware.

Cycle/Run/Stop The Cycle command is used to initiate execution of a bitstream on the hardware resource. When the Cycle command is executed, the hardware server will first perform a context-switch if the current client is not already active. When the command has completed execution, the server will save the state of the hardware before proceeding to the next scheduled operation. If the current process is still active when another process is scheduled, it will be context-switched away with its state saved until it is scheduled again. The Run command initiates continuous execution. This is done by internally issuing Cycle commands for finite numbers of clock cycles until the Stop command is received. Thus even in Run mode, multitasking takes place.

Save/Restore Since the hardware server always has the state of each client process, the server may provide the client with a snapshot of its state using the Save command. Unlike Readback, the Save command only provides the state of each state element and not the configuration data associated with the Readback command. The Restore command is used to restore an arbitrary snapshot of a client's state onto the hardware resource.

Readback The client may obtain the results of a hardware Readback (full state plus *configuration* information) by issuing the Readback command. As described earlier, Readback is used in conjunction with context-switching by the server; this command simply allows this raw information to be exposed to the client application in an undistilled form.

Other operations not shown above are general I/O transfers between the CCM and the client application. The multitasking architecture is completely transparent to these operations, as long as the state they involve (i.e. memories) is context-switched with the FPGA state.

3.3 Hardware Clients

A hardware client is a software process that executes on any machine with network access to the hardware server. The client connects to the hardware server and sends various commands (as described above) to the server to control the configurable computing machine. Unlike traditional CCM application software, hardware clients do not directly access the CCM hardware; all requests for hardware resources go through the hardware server. Despite the hidden network layer, the client makes calls to the board in the same way that it would if the client were exclusively accessing the board. Multitasking and context-switching is completely transparent to the client. In addition, the use of context-switching allows the additional feature of hardware checkpointing and restoration through the Save and Restore commands, which the client may, but is not required, to use.

Because the client talks over the network to the server in a simple protocol, clients may run on any operating system and be written in any programming language that provides the use of sockets. Hardware clients written in C++, Java, and Ruby have been developed and tested with the hardware server. In fact, interfacing with the SLAAC1-V through the server proves much easier than writing code directly for the board. Because of this, various general clients and user-interfaces can easily be developed as well as application-specific drivers.

3.4 Run-Time Example

To illustrate the operation of this multitasking architecture, consider two users using the board simultaneously: User A has designed a brute force decrypting application to run on the available CCM. Her application may need to run for days. User B has been working on an ATR application targeted at the same CCM, and is now in the verification stage. Using an interactive environment, he needs to step the hardware and verify that that the circuit is functioning correctly. He doesn't need to execute more than a few cycles at a time on the board and will likely wait minutes between each cycle as the results are analyzed.

While the actual execution on the board may be limited to a few seconds, his entire hardware verification sessions may involve several hours over multiple days.

Without any kind of hardware multitasking system, user A would tie up the board indefinitely and prohibit the use of the board by user B. Further, if user B is using the board interactively to verify an application the resource, user A cannot use the board to run her application. The only solution in this case seems to be to purchase extra CCM hardware, despite the fact that the given hardware may already be under-utilized. However, with a multitasking configurable hardware system, users A and B may use the programmable logic resources in harmony.

User A starts her decryption application running through the hardware server, and as the only application on the CCM, it will simply run with no interruption. User B then arrives and begins an interactive hardware debugging session. He opens a connection to the server and issues the Open and Configure commands. Because he has not yet issued a command that requires his design to be actually configured into the CCM, user A is not interrupted. Next, user B issues a Cycle command to cycle his design 10000 cycles and a Readback command to get results. The hardware server schedules this command next, deciding to preempt the long-running decryption application. User A's design is saved and suspended, then user B's design is configured onto the programmable device. The cycle command is issued, followed by the Readback command. Results are returned to user B, and user B takes a few minutes to review the results before cycling again.

Finally, the hardware server schedules user A's hardware application, since there are no other pending commands. The design is reconfigured onto the device with the state that was saved previously, and it is put back into run mode, pending more commands from other users.

In this example, users A and B were all able to share a single CCM resource. Although there was overhead from context-switching, user B was able to get results interactively without locking the board for the duration. User A's decryption results may be slightly delayed from the context-switching overhead, but without multitasking hardware in place, she may have never even been able to *start* her application!

4 Multitasking Performance

The multitasking architecture described was implemented using the SLAAC1-V configurable computing board. The system was executed and tested for correctness and to measure run-time performance. The host computer used was a Pentium III 500MHz machine with 512MB of RAM, running Linux. Two simple applications used for testing include a 168-bit LFSR, and an IEEE Floating Point adder. Several instances of each of these hardware client programs were run from several different similar computers and connected to the hardware server through a standard 10BaseT Ethernet network. Measurements were taken to show the relative performance and bottlenecks of various components of hardware context-switching.

As seen in Table 1, the average context-switch time seen in our current implementation (only one FPGA, no memories) is a little over one second. The two most time consuming operations performed on the SLAAC1-V board is configuration and Readback. This result is due to the large size of the configuration and Readback bitstreams (about 766 Kbytes), and the slower configuration clock that must be used by both operations when communicating with the FPGAs. Also, the board communicates over a standard PCI bus, which only operates at 33MHz. Part of the timing taken for raw Readback and reconfiguration includes the overhead of state extracting, bitstream manipulation, and transferring to or from the CCM.

Stage	Exec. Time	% of Total
Raw Readback	407ms	33%
State Extraction	465ms	38%
Reconfiguration	365ms	29%
Total	1237ms	100%

Table 1. Average Execution Time for Stages of a Hardware Context-Switch

After a Readback has been performed, the entire raw data stream must be examined, state information extracted, and the original bitstream modified so that it can be later reconfigured into the correct state. This process, tabulated as "State Extraction," is performed completely in software. Because of the large amount of processing required for state extraction, state extraction execution time would be reduced by simply using a faster host computer.

Clearly, hardware context-switches are fairly expensive in comparison to software context-switches. There is additional network overhead when clients are run remotely versus on the host computer, making remote operation useful mostly interactive sessions. However, because CCM hardware often is run in short bursts with lots of idle time in between (especially in verification stages, but also in many applications), using hardware context-switching can still increase board utilization with acceptable overhead.

5 Conclusions and Future Work

The multitasking hardware architecture presented by this work demonstrates that configurable hardware can be shared using traditional context-switching techniques. By exploiting the ability to capture the hardware state and providing techniques for restoring the hardware state, this system can dynamically move hardware processes in and out of the configurable resource. Such context-switching can be used to maximize utilization and efficiency of configurable computing resources.

Context-switching programmable logic resources is an essential component of a multitasking configurable system. However, it is necessary to capture and restore the state of other components within a configurable system to *fully* support multitasking. The state of external memories, I/O interfaces, and other non-programmable logic state must also be captured and restored as part of the configurable system context-switch. Future efforts will investigate techniques for capturing and restoring all system state and supporting multitasking of a complete configurable system. As additional hardware multitasking techniques are identified and the performance of hardware multitasking improves, expensive configurable computing resources will be more effectively used and available to more users and developers.

References

[1] Steve Trimberger, Dean Carberry, Anders Johnson, and Jennifer Wong. A time-multiplexed FPGA. In J. Arnold and K. L. Pocek, editors, *Proceedings of IEEE Workshop on FPGAs for Custom Computing Machines*, pages 22–28, Napa, CA, April 1997.

[2] S. M. Scalera and J. R. Vazquez. The design and implementation of a context-switching FPGA. In J. M. Arnold and K. L. Pocek, editors, *Proceedings of IEEE Workshop on FPGAs for Custom Computing Machines*, pages 78–85, Napa, CA, April 1998.

[3] T. Fujii, K. Furuta, M. Motomura, M. Nomura, M. Mizuno, K. Anjo, K. Wakabayashi, Y. Hirota, Y. Nakazawa, H. Ito, and M. Yamashina. Dynamically reconfigurable logic engine with a multi-context/multi-mode unified-cell architecture. In *Proceedings of the 1999 46th IEEE International Solid-State Circuits Conference (ISSCC'99)*, pages 364–365, 1999.

[4] A. Chien and J. H. Byun. Safe and protected execution for the morph/amrm reconfigurable processor. In K. L. Pocek and J. M. Arnold, editors, *Proceedings of the IEEE Workshop on FPGAs for Custom Computing Machines*, page n/a, Napa, CA, April 1999. IEEE Computer Society, IEEE.

[5] Timothy Wheeler, Paul Graham, Brent Nelson, and Brad Hutchings. Using design-level scan to improve FPGA design observability and controllability for functional verification. In *Field-Programmable Logic and Applications. Proceedings of the 11th International Workshop, FPL 2001*, Lecture Notes in Computer Science, pages 483–492. Springer-Verlag, August 2001.

[6] Xilinx Corporation. *Virtex Series Configuration Architecture User Guide*, September 27, 2000. XAPP151 (v1.5).

[7] Philip James-Roxby and Steven A. Guccione. Automated extraction of run-time parameterisable cores from programmable device configurations. In Kenneth L. Pocek and Jeffrey M. Arnold, editors, *Proceedings of the IEEE Symposium on FPGAs for Custom Computing Machines (FCCM '00)*, pages 153–161. IEEE Computer Society, IEEE Computer Society Press, April 2000.

[8] P. Chodowiec, K. Gaj, P. Bellows, and B. Schott. Experimental testing of the Gigabit IPSec-compliant implementations of rijndael and triple DES using SLAAC1-V FPGA accelerator board". In *Proceedings of 2001 Information Security Conference*, pages 220–234, October 2001.

The Case for Fine-Grained Re-configurable Architectures: An Analysis of Conceived Performance

Tuomas Valtonen[1,2], Jouni Isoaho[1,2], Hannu Tenhunen[3]

[1] Turku Center for Computer Science (TUCS), Lemminkäisenk. 14A, 20520 Turku, Finland
[2] Lab. of Electronics and Communication Syst., Dept. of IT, University of Turku, Finland
tuomas.valtonen@utu.fi
[3] Lab. of Electr. and Comp. Syst., Dept. of Microelectr. and IT, R. Instit. of Tech., Sweden

Abstract. In the coming years, the semiconductor industry will face new design challenges due to growing complexity, evolving and diversifying demand and decreasing time-to-market. Re-configurable IC architectures (RAs) add flexibility and decrease silicon-level complexity, but are inefficient in terms of traditional cost functions. Due to increased system-level integration on ICs, the focus will move to system or even end-user conceived performance issues from traditional module-level performance criteria, such as area, power, clock speed, and design efficiency. Other characteristics – dependability, scalability, product-level inter-generation compatibility and effective lifetime – should also be considered. Obviously, traditional cost functions are insufficient to express the full range of design considerations. In this article we outline a methodology for evaluating performance from the user's perspective, analyze various IC architectures using qualitative performance metrics, and present a novel IC architecture, specifically designed to exhibit high qualitative performance.

1 Introduction

As we move into the era of million-gate RAs, a number of considerations in IC design may need to be revised. In [1], four key challenges for future RAs are stated: (a) the proportionally increasing routing delay, (b) long compilation and re-configuration times due to scale and complexity, (c) the task of partitioning of functionality into fixed and configurable structures for optimal performance, and (d) eliminating the impact of fabrication defects, e.g. through redundancy. The need for a methodological change in the research and development of RAs is further emphasized in [2]. Here general-purpose fine-grained RAs (FGRAs) are considered too slow and area-inefficient to fulfill future demand for constantly increasing computing power. Coarse-grained RAs (CGRAs), using a combination of hardwired blocks and a programmable switching network, are anticipated as a reasonable compromise between high performance and programmability. A number of ongoing research projects [3] have proposed new RAs composed of cells with a grade of built-in functionality. The shared objective of such coarse-grained approaches is to provide better performance than conventional FPGAs, whilst imposing some constraints on flexibility.

It is apparent that all four issues (a–d) need to be addressed by the designers of future ICs. However, we should first define and prioritize the desired characteristics: do we need more speed and capacity, higher area and power efficiency, or perhaps better reliability, lower cost, greater flexibility or longer effective product lifetimes? In this

M. Glesner, P. Zipf, and M. Renovell (Eds.): FPL 2002, LNCS 2438, pp. 816-825, 2002.

article, we strive to broaden our conception of performance from traditional cost functions towards qualitative performance and features that are directly beneficial to the user. In chapter 2, we discuss traditional metrics in the light of human need, and present a number of qualitative metrics. In chapter 3, we illustrate the impact of using qualitative performance metrics for guiding design decisions: by prioritizing flexibility, dependability and cost, we arrive at a novel IC architecture that would easily be ignored using traditional cost functions. Finally, chapter 4 contains a broad qualitative analysis of performance in existing and potential future IC architectures. This article focuses on technology-related aspects of performance metrics; a further discussion on the commercial significance of performance metrics can be found in [4].

2 A New Methodology for the Evaluation of Performance

In order to achieve the optimal outcome from a number of options, we require a reliable and appropriate method for evaluating different scenarios; i.e., for converting real-world complexity into humanly tangible measures. In the IC design process, the vast complexity of options is squeezed into simple cost functions, measuring mainly quantitative properties. In this chapter, we shall raise the question upon the sufficiency and optimality of quantitative performance metrics. We shall also outline a novel user-oriented methodology for evaluating the performance of IC architectures.

2.1 Traditional Cost Functions

Today's commonly used cost metrics, such as speed, area and energy efficiency, give a basic idea of the trade-offs between different IC architectures. Hard-wired ICs, such as ASICs and SoCs, provide high speed and area-efficiency, but are expensive to design. CGRAs provide less raw performance, but also require less engineering work. FGRAs and the AET architecture (see Section 3.2) are slow and area-inefficient, but entail low design effort, due to the cellular structure. Designing a microprocessor is work-intensive and expensive, but the creation of applications as software is straightforward. Hence, the optimal architectural approach can be reached by partitioning the specified functionality into hardwired and configurable portions: if speed is the dominant requirement, then all or most of the functionality should be hardwired (ASIC, SoC); if speed and some re-configurability are required, critical portions should hardwired (CGRA); or if configurability is more essential than speed, then little or none of the functionality should be hardwired (FGRA, μP, AET). Traditional performance metrics for various IC architecture classes[1] are illustrated in table 1.

[1] We have classified the range of IC technologies into six main categories: ASIC, SoC, CGRA, FPGA, μP and AET. The "ASIC" category represents hardwired ICs, where functionality is fixed spatially and runtime re-configuration is not possible. The "SoC" category differs from the former mainly by its design methodology. System-on-Chip ICs are typically designed modularly, so that various Intellectual Property (IP) blocks can be replicated and reused; the connectivity of IP blocks is albeit fixed in the design phase. Here we assume that a SoC is not re-configurable; although, hybrid systems can be constructed with both hardwired IP blocks and e.g. re-configurable μP cores [5]. ICs in the "CGRA" category consist similarly of IP blocks (and possible μP cores), but are connected with a re-configurable switching network. The "FGRA" category represents classical fine-grained RAs, such as FPGAs and CPLDs, assuming homogeneousity, although this is not always the case [6]. The "μP" category refers to conventional hardwired μPs controlled by software; this is generally the case, although some μPs today are partially configurable [7][8]. Finally, the "AET" category is the class of the architectures described in section 3.2.

Table 1. Traditional cost functions for various IC architectures.

	ASIC	SoC	CGRA	FGRA	μP	AET
1. Chip fabrication						
– Granularity	One unit	Coarse	Coarse	Fine	One unit	Fine
– Manufacturing cost[2]	Very high	High	Medium	Low	Low	Very low
– Chip design effort	High	Medium	Medium	Low	Very high	Very low
2. Application design						
– Re-configurability	N/A	N/A	Spatial	Spatial	Temporal	Spatial
– Design effort	Very high	High	Medium	Medium	Low	Medium
3. Raw performance						
– Clock frequency	Very high	High	Low	Very low	High	Very low
– Area efficiency	Very high	High	Low	Very low	Medium	Very low
– Power consumption for fixed function	Very low	Low	Medium	High	High	Low

2.2 Conceived Performance Vs. Raw Performance

Advances in *raw performance* of ICs, such as clock frequency, processing power and storage capacity of ICs, are well known and frequently referred to when envisioning future technology generations with even higher raw performance. However, while raw performance may currently be the primary objective of IC designers, it is but one of several attributes of a real-world ICT product. These include, among others, the (a) effective product lifetime, (b) flexibility, (c) expandability, (d) inter-generation compatibility, (e) dependability, (f) cost, and (g) energy efficiency. In general, features that the user considers beneficial increase the externally visible or *conceived performance* of the product – and vice versa, undesirable features decrease such performance.

The prevailing view in today's ICT industry is that the demand for more raw performance will persist, and even increase in future [9]. Primary drivers for seeking higher raw performance are (a) the increasing amount of multimedia content distributed and (b) growing number of users in the Internet, mobile networks and – in future – ubiquitous communication networks. However, a recent study [10] suggests that raw performance is only one factor required for the creation of diverse future Internet and mobile applications envisioned by major governmental instances. New potential application areas range from healthcare, social, educational and environmental applications to financial, industrial and security purposes. Key design issues for future ICT technology include methods for adaptable interaction with users from diverse cultural backgrounds, management of mobile communication, techniques for providing secure and reliable information services, context-based models for flexible information storage and distribution, and high-speed server equipment and networks, both fixed and mobile, allowing for remote access to digital libraries.

2.3 The Impact of Performance Metrics on IC Design

Traditional performance metrics do not necessarily directly correlate with the real-world value of IC architectures and ICT products. Hence, in order to create products that accurately match user needs, we should evaluate alternative IC architectures from the user's perspective. Using a broader set of performance metrics allows for exploration in a variety of design concepts and IC architectures, including those typically abandoned due to insufficient raw performance. One such architecture, the Autonomous Error-Tolerant cellular fabric, is briefly described in the following chapter.

[2] Estimates based on the expected production volumes.

3 Case: The Autonomous Error-Tolerant Cellular Fabric

In this chapter, we present a case study of an architecture designed with primary emphasis on conceived performance, the Autonomous Error-Tolerant (AET) cellular fabric. We first discuss the principles and design focus, and then briefly illustrate the technical implementation of the architecture.

3.1 Overview and Target Characteristics

In [12] a number of fundamental principles for flexible and robust IC architectures were discussed. Firstly, the concept of physical autonomy, the ability for an entity to maintain its electrical characteristics regardless of the outside system (provided power is available), was introduced. Partitioning the overall system into physically autonomous cells was offered as a robust approach to creating defect-tolerant ICs. Secondly, if the cellular fabric was completely homogeneous and the fixed data operations in each cell were fine-grained, it would be possible to construct a highly flexible re-programmable cellular fabric by straightforward replication and interconnection of cells. Thirdly, homogeneousity and physical autonomy together would allow for ultra large-scale, even wafer-scale, integration, because individual fabrication defects could no longer jeopardize the integrity of the IC. Hence, (a) physical autonomy, (b) homogeneousity and (c) fine-granularity of operations in cells were defined as the target characteristics for the cellular fabric.

3.2 AET Cell Architecture and Inter-cellular Connectivity

The basic architecture for the AET cell was introduced in [12]. The hexagonal cell comprised 18 input lines that could each be switched to any set of 18 output lines. In addition, any two inputs could be channeled through a data operation (AND, OR, XOR), and each input line and output could also be negated. Finally, any input could synchronize any set of output lines.

The interconnection of AET cells was described in [13]. Firstly, each cell was connected to its six neighboring cells with short wires. In addition, each cell was also connected to six third-next cells over wires parallel to cell edges, and to six other third-next cells via wires perpendicular to cell edges; hence, a total of 18 inter-cellular I/O line pairs connected each cell to its neighbors.

An AET cell can be configured by another cell using standard communications lines. Commands contain 17 bits of data, which are sent sequentially over to an unused input of the destination cell. In addition, synchronization signals are sent via a third-party cell between the source and destination cells. Commands include settings for input lines, output lines, data operations and general maintenance commands. A cell can store its configuration in short-term memory, or permanently in re-writable EEPROM cells. Programming issues are described in further detail in [14].

In order to guarantee physical autonomy, each AET cell comprises an independent power management subsystem. Power management has two primary functions: (1) monitoring power consumption in each of six neighboring cells and (2) disconnecting the cell from the power supply (V_{DD}) upon request by any neighboring cell. In practice, the power consumption of a cell is determined by the difference in voltage between V_{DD} and the average voltage inside the cell (V_{AVG}). If V_{AVG} persists significantly lower than V_{DD}, the cell is assumed to be short-circuited and should be disconnected. Likewise, if V_{DD} is exactly V_{AVG}, the cell is assumed to be idle and is temporarily shut down. Cells are powered down by sending a signal to one of six power-switching transistors that physically separate the V_{DD} from the cell's internal power distribution network. The power management sub-system is explained further in [15].

Finally, AET cells can be dynamically interconnected to form cell clusters with reconfigurable functionality. An *AET being* is a special case of a cell cluster that: (a) is protected against accidental or malicious re-configuration, (b) is able to relocate itself, (c) is able to rotate itself, and (d) is able to stretch or reshape itself.

4 A Qualitative Analysis of Conceived Performance

The paradigm shift from raw performance to conceived performance will require a new model for the evaluation of IC architectures. Hence, we must broaden our performance measurements from pure quantitative to *qualitative*; conceived performance, after all, is merely an indicator of how well the user's expectations are met. From the user's perspective, conceived performance adds value; raw performance itself does not. Before specifying the requirements for an ICT product, we should first prioritize attributes of conceived performance to match user needs as accurately as possible. In the remainder of this chapter, we conduct a qualitative analysis of today's ICT products by asking a series of questions, which are answered simply as (a) yes, (b) no, or (c) not applicable.

4.1 Flexibility, Scalability, and Inter-generation Compatibility

An analysis on flexibility, scalability and compatibility (table 2) reveals a number of fundamental differences between the architectural approaches. Firstly, CGRAs are mainly limited to functionality that can be anticipated today. By hard-wiring specific functionality into cells, we accept the fact that ICT products based on CGRAs must be updated or replaced at regular intervals. Furthermore, because the structure of cells varies over time, compatibility between different IC generations may cause problems. FGRAs are in this sense more versatile, because the structure of each autonomous cell is kept simple, thus allowing for re-configuration as new demands emerge.

FPGA cells are logically autonomous, i.e. the architecture contains external control, synchronization and communication mechanisms. In order to create a large homogeneous mass of FPGA cells, specific interfaces and control mechanisms between ICs and FPGA boards are required. The same applies to the microprocessor: although internally very flexible, externally it is embedded in a fixed-wired circuit board, allowing thus for very limited configuration or expansion. In a homogeneous and physically autonomous FGRA that completely lacks external subsystems for control, synchronization and communication, expansion is merely as task of extending inter-cellular links physically from one IC to another (e.g. by using a scarce mesh of optical diodes between wafer-scale ICs), and arbitrary configuration is possible by reorganizing both inter-cellular and intra-cellular connections.

Another advantage of creating the network from a homogeneous mass of cells is that processing capacity, when required, can be flexibly increased where it is most economical or necessary. For instance, computation-intense applications would be physically located in network servers containing large masses of cells. Mobile or ubiquitous terminals, containing limited cellular capacity, would access all services via the network. However, if the network is slow, or the user wishes to perform more computation off-line, terminals could be upgraded simply by adding cellular capacity.

Table 2. Flexibility, scalability and inter-generation compatibility of various IC architectures.

	ASIC	SoC	CGRA	FGRA	µP	AET
1. Can IC behavior be changed after fabrication						
– to tasks known or envisioned in the design phase?	NO	NO	YES	YES	YES	YES
– to tasks unforeseen in the design phase?	NO	NO	NO	YES	YES	YES
2. As functionality of the system changes						
– will terminals require IC replacements?	YES	YES	YES	NO	NO	NO
– will network servers require IC replacements?	YES	YES	YES	NO	NO	NO
– will terminals require expansion ICs?	N/A	N/A	N/A	N/A	N/A	NO
– will network servers require expansion ICs?	N/A	N/A	N/A	N/A	N/A	NO
3. As raw performance requirements grow						
– will terminals require IC replacements?	YES	YES	YES	YES	NO	NO
– will network servers require IC replacements?	YES	YES	YES	YES	YES	NO
– will terminals require expansion ICs?	N/A	N/A	N/A	N/A	N/A	NO
– will network servers require expansion ICs?	N/A	N/A	N/A	N/A	N/A	YES
4. As the system grows, is interfacing required						
– between ICs of the same technology generation?	YES	YES	YES	YES	YES	NO
– between ICs of the different technology generations?	YES	YES	YES	YES	YES	NO

4.2 Dependability

An analysis on dependability (table 3) highlights the benefits of physical autonomy. As discussed in chapter 3, physical autonomy entails that each cell can operate independently of other cells or any external top-level mechanisms. Hence, a fabric of physically autonomous cells has no shared components or wiring for communication, synchronization or configuration: all wiring is point-to-point between two cells. If defect cells can be shut down by neighboring cells and defect wires are excluded from use, arbitrary fabrication defects only disable individual cells (unless they span more than one cell) – while the integrity of the IC in whole persists uncompromised.

Table 3. Dependability of various IC architectures.

	ASIC	SoC	CGRA	FGRA	µP	AET
1. Does the IC include						
– global wiring and/or shared components for communication?	YES	YES	YES	YES	YES	NO
– global wiring and/or shared components for synchronization?	YES	YES	YES	YES	YES	NO
– global wiring and/or shared components for configuration?	N/A	N/A	YES	YES	YES	NO
– global power distribution wiring?	YES	YES	YES	YES	YES	NO
– potential single points of overall failure?	YES	YES	YES	YES	YES	NO
2. After the fabrication stage						
– can all physical defects be detected?	NO	NO	NO	NO	NO	N/A
– can all physical defects be remedied?	NO	NO	NO	NO	NO	N/A
3. During operation, can we detect and remedy						
– short-circuits due to defects?	NO	NO	NO	NO	NO	YES
– inconsistent behavior due to defects?	NO	NO	NO	NO	NO	YES[3]
– logical errors due to defects?	NO	NO	NO	NO	NO	YES[4]
4. As the density of arbitrary physical defects grows						
– will the IC operate predictably?	NO	NO	NO	NO	NO	YES
– will the functionality of the IC persist?	NO	NO	NO	NO	NO	YES[4]

As the defect density grows, the processing capacity of the fabric degrades in a predictable manner. To a certain extent of degradation, algorithmic structures (e.g. AET

[3] Applicable when a special AET being for cell verification is available.

[4] Applicable when AET beings are designed robustly (until the number of operational cells is insufficient).

beings in the AET fabric) of the IC should maintain normal operation, assuming that these are capable of moving, reshaping and rotating within the remaining cells.

4.3 Design and Fabrication Cost

Major design challenges for the IC design process include (1) design for sharing and reuse, (2) increased system and silicon complexities, (3) systematic improvement of design process and productivity [7]. In conventional ASICs, SoCs and CGRAs, all or portions of the IC functionality is hardwired according to assumptions of future applications. Although this approach improves raw performance, it diminishes potential reuse, and thus entails continuous re-design work as requirements evolve. Accommodation of increased demand for raw performance, e.g. by establishing greater parallelism, may also involve additional logic-level design work, unless the architecture is freely scalable. Electrical anomalies at silicon-level are another future challenge for IC design; if these cannot be completely eliminated, the system must comprise mechanisms for coping with such unsolicited phenomena.

Table 4. Design and fabrication cost for various IC architectures.

	ASIC	SoC	CGRA	FGRA	µP	AET
1. When the designing the IC architecture						
– should potential applications be first identified?	YES	YES	YES	NO	NO	NO
– is it designed primarily for specific applications classes?	YES	YES	YES	NO	NO	NO
– are other potential application classes ruled out?	YES	YES	YES	NO	NO	NO
2. Is the functionality of the IC implemented as						
– individually designed functional blocks?	YES	NO	NO	NO	YES	NO
– various classes of replicated functional blocks?	NO	YES	YES	NO	NO	NO
– a single class of replicated cells?	NO	NO	NO	YES	NO	YES
3. Is the wiring of the IC implemented as						
– individually placed wires between blocks?	YES	YES	YES	YES	YES	NO
– shared communication bus wiring?	YES	YES	YES	YES	YES	NO
– a constant self-repetitive wiring pattern?	NO	NO	NO	NO	NO	YES
4. Does the IC also require design of a sub-system						
– for communication between blocks?	YES	YES	YES	YES	YES	NO
– for synchronization between blocks?	YES	YES	YES	YES	YES	NO
– for the configuration of blocks?	N/A	N/A	YES	YES	N/A	NO
5. As the number of blocks grows arbitrarily, must we						
– re-design the communication sub-system?	YES	YES	YES	YES	YES	NO
– re-design the synchronization sub-system?	YES	YES	YES	YES	YES	NO
– re-design the configuration sub-system?	N/A	N/A	YES	YES	N/A	NO
6. Is further logic-level design work required when						
– functionality requirements change significantly?	YES	YES	YES	NO	YES	NO
– raw performance requirements increase significantly?	YES	YES	YES	YES	YES	NO
– new technology generations emerge?	YES	YES	YES	YES	YES	NO
7. Is further layout-level design work required when						
– functionality requirements change significantly?	YES	YES	YES	NO	YES	NO
– raw performance requirements increase significantly?	YES	YES	YES	YES	YES	NO
– new technology generations emerge?	YES	YES	YES	YES	YES	YES
8. Is it worthwhile for IC manufacturers to						
– design the entire IC as a full-custom implementation?	NO	NO	NO	NO	NO	YES
– fabricate large (e.g. 20") wafer-scale ICs?	NO	NO	NO	NO	NO	YES
– mass-produce very large amounts of identical ICs?	NO	NO	NO	NO	NO	YES

System-level complexity also increases the amount of design work required per IC. This can be alleviated via architectural modularity and reusable components, such and Intellectual Property (IP) blocks. Besides isolated functional blocks, various top-level sub-systems are essential in conventional IC architectures: e.g. for communication, synchronization and configuration. Naturally, these require additional design work, and ultimately limit the scalability of the IC [7].

Maintaining cost-efficiency in IC manufacturing will become an intricate challenge, because of (a) short product life cycles, (b) production yield constraints and (c) heterogeneous functionality requirements. As IC life cycles grow shorter, time-to-market becomes increasingly critical, adding further pressure for acceleration of the design process. Moreover, the rising probability of fabrication defects in increasingly large and transistor-packed ICs shall have a negative impact on production yield, unless effective redundancy techniques or error-tolerant components are used. Finally, when ICs are designed and optimized for specific applications and life cycles are short, batch sizes remain relatively small in comparison to an alternative scenario where identical and flexible ICs could be mass-produced cost-effectively to fulfill a long-term global demand. Furthermore, if the ICs contained only identical and simple cells, very little design work would be required. Ideally if such ICs were immune to fabrication defects, i.e. built from physically autonomous cells, production yields would persist high even for large wafer-scale ICs.

4.4 Computation Power, Latency, and Power Consumption

Traditional metrics of raw performance, such as speed, chip area and power consumption, are the strongest arguments for the proponents of hardwired or semi-hardwired IC architectures. However, in terms of conceived performance, it is difficult to identify a practical case that *simultaneously* requires high speed and capacity together with small area and low power consumption. In a global fixed-wired core network of high-capacity servers, processing and storage capacity can be cost-efficiently increased at central server sites. Mobile and ubiquitous terminals, accessed via wireless networks, on the contrary need only contain the minimum of processing capacity required for interfacing between the user and network. Typically, computation-intensive services should reside within the high-capacity core network, and the terminal should serve as a local interface. For (potentially) trillions of miniature terminals to be deployed in future ubiquitous networks, reliability and flexibility shall be more significant attributes than raw performance.

Again, when considering conceived performance, we look at the system from the user's perspective. The user cannot observe raw performance of individual components within a system; the user can only determine whether or not the system fulfills his or her expectations. Hence, in a fast-speed network, it is irrelevant whether a task is accomplished in a local mobile terminal or in the network, as long as the task *can* be accomplished in the *expected* time. Here the first parameter is capacity: does the system have enough capacity to perform the task at all? The second parameter is initial response-time: how fast can the system reply? The third parameter is delivery time: how fast can the result be computed and delivered back to the user?

A traditional stand-alone ICT terminal has its limitations: some tasks can be completed, others cannot. Shifting computation fully or partially to powerful network servers allows for more demanding tasks; however, modern ICT technology cannot be scaled to deal with arbitrary-scale tasks (due to limitations of networking protocols etc.) Also, response times in data networks are typically not guaranteed even when the network speed is adequately high, due to various randomized mechanisms for network traffic control [11]. Computation time depends on network server capacity and link speed. If faster computation is required, server capacity can be increased to a certain extent, but not arbitrarily. These constraints apply to all conventional ICs (ASIC, SoC, FPGA, µP) and future CGRAs. The freely scalable AET cellular fabric, on the contrary, can theoretically be scaled to cope with tasks of any scale, or to compute tasks extremely fast using massively parallel datapaths. When communication algorithms (i.e., AET link beings) are designed correctly and link speeds are sufficient, the response time to user requests can also be guaranteed.

Finally, power consumption in conventional synchronous ICs can be divided into five main categories: (a) data operations in functional blocks, (b) the clock distribution network, (c) data transport between functional blocks, (d) transistor power leakage and (e) dynamic switching of data between functional blocks. In hardwired synchronous ASICs and SoCs, the first four categories are relevant, whereas in conventional synchronous re-configurable ICs, all categories of power consumption are present. The AET cellular fabric consumes power in the first, third and last categories.

Table 5. Computation power, latency and power consumption in various IC architectures.

	ASIC	SoC	CGRA	FGRA	µP	AET
1. Is the expansion of computing power restricted						
– in a stand-alone system?	YES	YES	YES	YES	YES	YES
– without specific physical constraints (space, weight, power)?	YES	YES	YES	YES	YES	NO
– in today's ICT networks?	YES	YES	YES	YES	YES	N/A
– in a network of identical cellular masses?	N/A	N/A	N/A	N/A	N/A	NO
2. In a network with adequate speed, is a reasonable response-time (e.g. 150 ms for humans) guaranteed using						
– today's networking protocols and devices?	NO	NO	NO	NO	NO	N/A
– an interconnected network of AET cellular fabrics?	N/A	N/A	N/A	N/A	N/A	YES
3. Is power consumption of the IC caused by						
– data processing in functional blocks?	YES	YES	YES	YES	YES	YES
– clock distribution network?	YES	YES	YES	YES	YES	NO
– data transport between functional blocks?	YES	YES	YES	YES	YES	YES
– transistor power leakage?	YES	YES	YES	YES	YES	NO
– dynamic switching between functional blocks?	NO	NO	YES	YES	NO	YES

5 Conclusions and Future Work

In this article, we discussed the concept of performance. We showed that when focusing only on traditional cost functions, other forms of performance are easily neglected. We showed that raw performance given by traditional cost functions can significantly differ from conceived performance indicators. Especially flexibility, scalability, inter-generation compatibility and dependability are significant in conceived performance metrics; in classical metrics, these play but a minor role. The examination of computation power, latency and energy efficiency revealed that a network-oriented approach could be more viable than aiming for higher raw performance in all ICs and ICT products. We also presented a case study of a novel RA, designed with primary focus on conceived performance and conducted an analysis on IC architectures using conceived performance metrics. The next step will be to extend the evaluation model from qualitative to quantitative: creating new cost functions for comparison of alternative architectural strategies, taking a range of qualitative design attributes into account. In time, we expect that conceived performance will gain the status of raw performance today, and will shape the IC market accordingly.

Acknowledgements

We wish to thank Nokia Foundation for financial assistance to this research.

References

[1] J. Rose et al: "Architectural and Physical Design Challenges for One-Million Gate FPGAs and Beyond", ACM Symp. on FPGAs (FPGA'97), Feb. 1997, pp. 129–132 (invit.)

[2] R.W. Hartenstein: "The Microprocessor is no more General Purpose: why Future Reconfigurable Platforms will win", Int'l Conf. on Innovative Systems in Silicon (ISIS'97), Austin, TX, USA, October 8–10, 1997 (invited).

[3] R.W. Hartenstein: "A Decade of Reconfigurable Computing: a Visionary Retrospective", embedded tutorial at Int'l Conf. on Design Automation and Testing in Europe – and Exhibit (DATE'01), Munich, Germany, 2001.[5]

[4] T. Valtonen et al: "Conceived Performance of Re-Configurable IC Architectures", accepted to the 8th Biennial Conf. On Electronics and Microsystem Technology (BEC 2002), Tallinn, Estonia, Oct. 6–9. (URL: http://users.utu.fi/tuoval/research/BEC02.pdf)

[5] A. Hemani et al: "Network on Chip: An architecture for billion transistor era", in the Proc. 18th IEEE NorChip Conf., Turku, Finland, Nov. 2000, pp. 166–173.

[6] S. Brown et al: "FPGA and CPLD Architectures: A Tutorial", in IEEE Design and Test of Computers, Vol. 12, No. 2, pp. 42–57, Summer 1996.

[7] Semiconductor Industry Association: "International Technology Roadmap for Semiconductors, 2001 Edition – Design", 2001.

[8] Intel Corporation: "Mobile Intel® Pentium® 4 Processor-M and Intel 845MP Chipset Performance Brief", Doc. no. 250725-001, March 2002.

[9] Semiconductor Industry Association: "International Technology Roadmap for Semiconductors, 2001 Edition – Test and Test Equipment", 2001.

[10] T. Valtonen: "Governmental Visions for Future Info-Communication – A Survey of the European Union, the United States and Japan", Turku Center for C.S., Tech. Rep. 425, Turku, Finland, May 2001. (URL: http://users.utu.fi/tuoval/research/TUCSTR425.pdf)

[11] T. Valtonen: "Quality of Service in the 3rd Generation Transmission Network and the Internet", M.Sc. Thesis 837, Helsinki Univ. of Tech., Helsinki, Finland, May 2000. (URL: http://users.utu.fi/tuoval/research/MScThesis.pdf)

[12] T. Valtonen et al: "An Autonomous Error-Tolerant Cell for Scalable Network-on-Chip Architectures", Proc. 19th IEEE NorChip Conf., Kista, Sweden, Nov. 12–13, 2001. (URL: http://users.utu.fi/tuoval/research/NorChip01.pdf)

[13] T. Valtonen et al: "Interconnection of Autonomous Error-Tolerant Cells", Proc. IEEE Int'l Symp. on Circuits and Systems, Scottsdale, AZ, USA, May 26–29, 2002. (URL: http://users.utu.fi/tuoval/research/ISCAS02.pdf)

[14] T. Valtonen et al: "Cell Configuration in the Autonomous Error-Tolerant Cellular Fabric", submitted to 20th IEEE NorChip Conf., Copenhagen, Denmark, Nov. 11–12, 2002. (URL: http://users.utu.fi/tuoval/research/NorChip02.pdf)

[15] T. Nurmi et al: "Power Management of the Autonomous Error-Tolerant Cell", accepted to the 15th Annual IEEE Int'l ASIC/SoC Conf., Rochester, NY, USA, Sept. 25–28, 2002. (URL: http://users.utu.fi/tuoval/research/ASICSoC02.pdf)

[5] A broad overview of global RA research, with forward references to numerous RA projects.

An FPGA Implementation of a Multi-comparand Multi-search Associative Processor

Zbigniew Kokosiński and Wojciech Sikora

Cracow University of Technology, Faculty of Electrical & Computer Eng.
ul. Warszawska 24, 31-155 Kraków, Poland;
zk@pk.edu.pl

Abstract. The multi-comparand associative search paradigm is shown to be efficient in processing complex search problems from many application areas including computational geometry, graph theory, and list/matrix computations. In this paper the first FPGA implementation of a small multi-comparand multi-search associative processor is reported. The architecture of the processor and its functions are described in detail. The processor works in a combined bit-serial/bit-parallel mode. Its main component is a multi-comparand associative memory with up to 16 programmable prescription functions (logic searches). Parameters of implemented FPGA devices are presented and discussed.

1 Introduction

Searching is one of the key concepts in computer science and engineering [12]. Searching problems arise in different application areas. As a result of increasing searching tasks at hand time requirements are becoming more critical. Therefore, new techniques that can speed up search operations are required. One solution is provided by massively parallel computing.

Among many parallel models associative machines, that belong to broader SIMD category of parallel processors, are particularly well suited for performing fast parallel search operations. In content-addressing mode associative memories use build-in multiple comparison capability [2,3,20,22]. Recent advances in associative processing include : classification and forwarding network search engines [27,28], massively parallel associative processor IXM2 [6], experimental optical associative architecture [16], new applications in databases, computational geometry and artificial intelligence [11], new selection and extreme search algorithms for fully parallel memories resulting from average-case analysis [17], multiassociative/hybrid search [4], etc.

Most associative machines work in bit-serial word-parallel mode, with a single comparand and multiple data. Results of multiple comparisons are stored in a tag memory and are resolved by a specialized circuitry (logical tag resolver). However, many alternative paradigms were also developed. Other commonly used working modes include fully parallel (bit-parallel word-parallel), word-serial,

M. Glesner, P. Zipf, and M. Renovell (Eds.): FPL 2002, LNCS 2438, pp. 826–835, 2002.

block-oriented, etc. Various machines implement different sets of basic logical matching functions. There exist architectures without tag memory, and solutions with separated tag and word mask circuitry. Logical tag resolvers often vary in their function and structure. All this leads to a variety that fits many particular processing requirements.

One common drawback of mainstream associative models is usage of a single comparand only. Although there exist particular applications, where simultaneous many-to-many comparisons are feasible without any need to use an external comparand vector [8,9], a common practice is to process many-to-many comparisons sequentially, by performing a sequence of one-to-many compare operations. Eventually, parallelization is achieved through processing of many copies of input data simultaneously. Design of a processor with multiple-comparand processing capability would make the multi-comparand associative search much faster. The problem was stated for the first time in [1], where a versatile search memory with many-to-many comparison was proposed. Recently, associative algorithms with multi-comparand search operations were developed for six representative problems from various complexity classes, i.e. SET INCLUSION, GEOMETRIC RANGE SEARCH, MATRIX INCLUSION, NEIGHBOURHOOD, MULTIPLE SEARCH and MULTI-LIST RANKING [14].

At first the idea of multi-comparand search was rejected due to a fundamental missunderstanding (see [3], pp. 198-202). High cost of the required hardware seemed to be the second obstacle in developing new associative architectures.

Current progress of IC technology resulted in successful ASIC designs of conventional single-comparand associative processors with extended search operations and memory cells designed on the transistor level [5,7,18,21]. Single-comparand memories became embedded features of Spartan-II and Virtex programmable FPGA devices from Xilinx. New FPGA-based asociative memory designs "XAPP 20x" were presented in the recent years [23,24,25,26]. However, to our best knowledge, no attempt was reported to build a multi-comparand associative processor using ASIC/FPGA technology.

In this paper low cost experimental FPGA design of a simple hierarchical associative processor is reported, that implements the idea of multi-comparand search [14,19]. A multiple-comparand associative memory with 2D tag memory is a key module of the processor. The memory implements up to 16 different logic search functions. In order to extract global features of processed data, associative search capability is introduced into the 2D tag memory too. Thus, the associative search is organized hierarchically, on the two levels.

The design was performed with Xilinx Foundation Series Software (Student Edition v.2.1). We used low cost XS40 demo board from XESS with single Xilinx XC4005XL FPGA device. The obtained results are very promissing having in mind steady effort to take advantage of associative processing implemented in FPGA technology [23,24,25,26].

In the next section the processor architecture is described. Section 3 is devoted to associative memory design on logic level. In section 4 implementation data of a small FPGA prototypes are collected. Section 5 suggests possible directions of a further research.

2 The Multi-comparand Processor Architecture

The multi-comparand associative memory may be described as follows. Basic data processing is organized in bit-serial word-parallel mode, but the conventional single-comparand register is replaced by a comparand array, and the tag memory is extended to the size of the Carthesian product of data and comparand sets. Processing is performed neither in the data array, nor in the comparand array, but exclusively in the 2D tag memory. In each consecutive step of processing each tag memory cell is updated according to : its previous state, the corresponding data/comparand values, and so called prescription function that defines type of the search (24 logical and 10 arithmetical searches are valid [1]). Type of the search determines also the initial state of the tag memory. The possibility to define a prescription function for each tag cell separately is a source of the memory's versatility but it requires an extra logic and $\lceil log_2 q \rceil$ control bits for each cell, where q is the number of different prescription functions. Obviously, presumptively homogenous cell functions could be handled in a less hardware consuming way, reducing the number of control bits. Applying current technology, the processor's tag memory can be implemented as a reconfigurable logic, with configuring data loaded from a PRAM, providing substantial hardware savings and essential improvement of time parameters. Comparison results collected in the 2D tag memory have to be further processed in order to extract global search results. Otherwise, partial intermediate data collected in the tag memory are difficult to interpret. This implies a need of providing the 2D tag memory with basic associative processing capabilities (exact match/mismatch). As a result, a simple multi-comparand multi-search associative processor architecture is obtained, which is depicted in Fig.1. The processor consists of the following components [14]:

DATA ARRAY (DA) - n × p binary data matrix;
COMPARAND ARRAY (CA) - m × p binary comparand matrix;
DM - n × 1 data and tag (TM and T2) mask vector;
CM - m × 1 comparand mask vector;
SM1 - 1 × p mask vector for multi-comparand search;
(DM, CM and SM1 select proper submatrices of DA and CA for multi-comparand search)
BPC - bit position counter; (generates consequtive bit slices selected by SM1 for bit-serial processing; bit slice l is generated by bit BPC[l]=1; for all j ≠ l: BPC[j]=0)
TAG MEMORY (TM) - n × m binary tag matrix; (memory for processing and storing current comparison results; each cell TM[i, j] process and stores results of comparison of subsequent pairs of bits {DA[i, l], CA[j, l]}, where l is the coordinate of processed bit slice, according

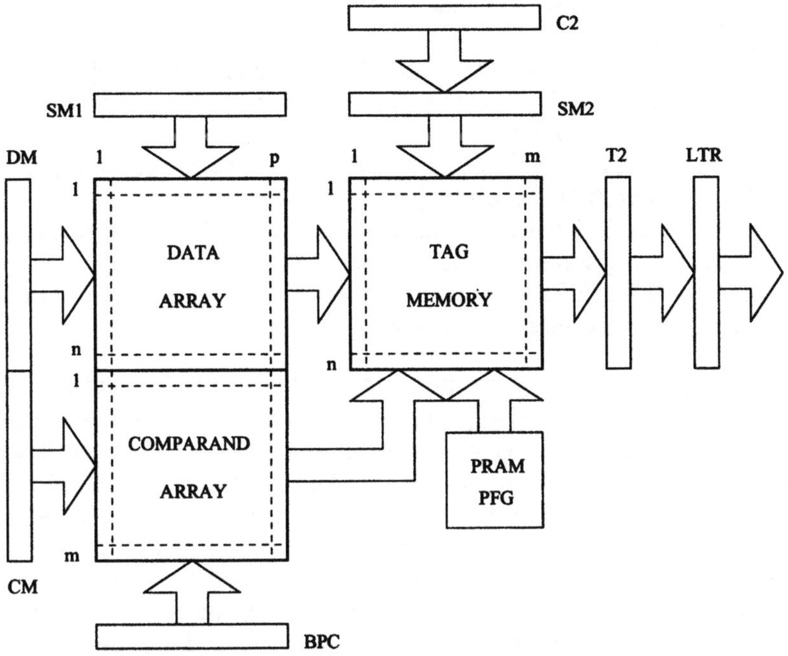

Fig. 1. A multi-comparand multi-search associative processor.

to a presription function loaded into TM from PRAM PFG; TM has built-in capability of fully parallel (bit-parallel word-parallel) associative processing its content with single comparand C2 and search mask SM2 - results of single comparand EQUALITY search in TM are stored in T2; TM can also perform SELECT FIRST function [3] in each column)

PRAM PFG - PRAM prescription function generator; (for our needs the number of prescription functions is 6, 12 or 16 but in general this set can be freely modelled for a given application)

C2 - 1 × m binary comparand vector;

SM2 - 1 × m TM mask vector;

T2 - n × 1 binary tag vector for TM;

LTR - logical tag resolver; (in particular, it computes binary variables w and u : w = 1 iff at least one unmasked bit of T2 is equal 1, while u = 1 iff all unmasked bits of T2 are equal 1; variable w, often denoted as SOME/NONE, is commonly used in tag resolvers [3,11]; variable u, which can be denoted as ALL/NOT ALL is used in [11]).

The above processor architecture is described in a basic configuration. Depending on particular application it is necessary to add a number of the optional architecture components:

COUNTER OF RESPONDERS - counter of the number of responders for T2 [3];
SELECT FIRST - circuit for each column of TM and T2 [3];
(p,k)-COMBINATION GENERATOR - hardware mask generator for SM1 (and, eventually, similar one for SM2 [13];
(p,k)-PERMUTATION GENERATOR - hardware comparand generator placed between DA and CA [13];
CONTROLLERS for sequencing processor operations in TM (required for processing some specific problems only).
MEMORY REGISTERS - storage of temporary results of computations, like tag vectors, mask vectors, etc.

The machine model is powerfull and flexible enough to satisfy numerous requirements in fast associative processing. The model is a parametrized generalization of many other simpler models proposed earlier and can substitute them functionally, i.e. process all algorithms derived for those models. For instance, models of single-comparand processors are equivalent to our model with the parameter m=1. In many cases, where multi-comparand searching is crucial, the model provides a significant improvement of algorithms' performance.

The proposed architecture satisfies the following design assumptions which can be used for evaluation of combinatorial algorithms developed in our model:

1. single bit-serial search operation lasts a unit time;
2. all bit-serial word-parallel search operations last a time proportional to the number of bit slices, i.e. O(p) or less;
3. TM prescription functions can be loaded from PRAM PFG in O(1) time;
4. single mask programming is performed in O(1) time;
5. single comparand permutation is performed in O(1) time;
6. LTR, SELECT FIRST circuits and COUNTER of the number of respondes consume a time that depends on the construction of these components and available technology. In general that time is a logarithmic function of n.

3 The Design

The processor architecture consists of data and comparand registers, associative memory TM, output register T2, specialized output circuits and a control unit. The architecture is easy scalable since its basic components have very regular structure. Below we will describe in detail the most important unit, i.e. associative memory TM.

Tag memory TM is built of identical cells designed for 16 different logic searches. We started from implementing 6 basic logic operations and gradually increased their number to all 16 possible searches. Two variants of TM cell were considered: one with latches and the second with D flip-flops as storage elements. Each cell has the 9 inputs – CM (mask), S0-S3 (search selector), DA (data bit), CA (comparand bit), WRITEEN (write enable), CLEAR (clear), two state variables – P, Q (memory state) and output O (search result).

The following notation is used: p - word size; i - bit position ($0 \leq i \leq p-1$); Q_i - state of memory element Q in ith cycle ($Q_0=0$), O_i - result of ith comparison (if S3=0 then $O_i=\neg Q_i$, otherwise $O_i=Q_i$).

Description of a Tag Memory cell with full logic capabilities (16 logic searches) is presented in Table 1.

Table 1. Description of Tag Memory cell with 16 logic searches

Variable	CM	S0	S1	S2	S3	DA_i	CA_i	Q_{i+1}	O_{i+1}
Masking	0	X	X	X	X	X	X	X	0
DA∩CA="0"	1	0	0	0	0	0	∅	Q_i	$\neg Q_i$
	1	0	0	0	0	1	0	Q_i	$\neg Q_i$
	1	0	0	0	0	1	1	0	1
DA∩CA≠"0"	1	0	0	0	1	0	∅	Q_i	Q_i
	1	0	0	0	1	1	0	Q_i	Q_i
	1	0	0	0	1	1	1	1	0
DA≤CA	1	0	0	1	0	0	0	Q_i	$\neg Q_i$
	1	0	0	1	0	0	1	0	1
	1	0	0	1	0	1	0	1	0
	1	0	0	1	0	1	1	Q_i	$\neg Q_i$
DA>CA	1	0	0	1	1	0	0	Q_i	Q_i
	1	0	0	1	1	0	1	0	0
	1	0	0	1	1	1	0	1	1
	1	0	0	1	1	1	1	Q_i	Q_i
DA≥CA	1	0	1	0	0	0	0	Q_i	$\neg Q_i$
	1	0	1	0	0	0	1	1	0
	1	0	1	0	0	1	0	0	1
	1	0	1	0	0	1	1	Q_i	$\neg Q_i$
DA<CA	1	0	1	0	1	0	0	Q_i	Q_i
	1	0	1	0	1	0	1	1	1
	1	0	1	0	1	1	0	0	0
	1	0	1	0	1	1	1	Q_i	Q_i
DA=CA	1	0	1	1	0	0	0	Q_i	$\neg Q_i$
	1	0	1	1	0	0	1	0	1
	1	0	1	1	0	1	0	0	1
	1	0	1	1	0	1	1	Q_i	$\neg Q_i$
DA≠CA	1	0	1	1	1	0	0	Q_i	Q_i
	1	0	1	1	1	0	1	1	0
	1	0	1	1	1	1	0	1	0
	1	0	1	1	1	1	1	Q_i	Q_i
DA= ¬CA	1	1	0	0	0	0	0	0	1
	1	1	0	0	0	0	1	Q_i	$\neg Q_i$
	1	1	0	0	0	1	0	Q_i	$\neg Q_i$
	1	1	0	0	0	1	1	0	1

Table 1. (continued)

Variable	CM	S0	S1	S2	S3	DA_i	CA_i	Q_{i+1}	O_{i+1}
DA≠ ¬CA	1	1	0	0	1	0	0	1	0
	1	1	0	0	1	0	1	Q_i	Q_i
	1	1	0	0	1	1	0	Q_i	Q_i
	1	1	0	0	1	1	1	1	0
DA∩CA=DA	1	1	0	1	0	0	∅	Q_i	$\neg Q_i$
	1	1	0	1	0	1	0	0	1
	1	1	0	1	0	1	1	Q_i	$\neg Q_i$
DA∩CA≠DA	1	1	0	1	1	0	∅	Q_i	Q_i
	1	1	0	1	1	1	0	1	0
	1	1	0	1	1	1	1	Q_i	Q_i
DA∩CA=CA	1	1	1	0	0	0	∅	Q_i	$\neg Q_i$
	1	1	1	0	0	1	0	Q_i	$\neg Q_i$
	1	1	1	0	0	1	1	0	1
DA∩CA≠CA	1	1	1	0	1	0	∅	Q_i	Q_i
	1	1	1	0	1	1	0	Q_i	Q_i
	1	1	1	0	1	1	1	1	0
DA∪CA="0"	1	1	1	1	0	0	0	0	1
	1	1	1	1	0	0	1	Q_i	$\neg Q_i$
	1	1	1	1	0	1	∅	Q_i	$\neg Q_i$
DA∪CA≠"0"	1	1	1	1	1	0	0	1	0
	1	1	1	1	1	0	1	Q_i	Q_i
	1	1	1	1	1	1	∅	Q_i	Q_i

4 The FPGA Prototype

For prototyping Xilinx Foundation Series Software (Student Edition v.2.1) and a demo board with a single Xilinx XC4005XL FPGA device, which is one of the smallest of XC4000 series, were used. The XC4005XL device - with density 9k gates - contains 196 CLBs and 112 IOBs.

Prototyping work was twofold. The first aim was to build a small multi-comparand processor with basic functionality. Only six logic searches were implemented, i.e. $\{=, \neq, <, >, \leq$ and $\geq\}$. The maximum size of the prototype obtained was 6×6×4. In that case 36 simultaneous comparisons were performed with the clock rate 68 ns per bit. Parameters of exemplary processor projects are shown in Table 2.

Table 2. Associative processor parameters (XC4005XL FPGA).

processor size	max. clock frequency	min. clock rate	CLBs utilization (max. 196 available)	
	MHz	ns	cells	%
3×3×3	24,9	40,1	63	25
5×5×5	18,7	53,2	157	80
6×6×4	14,7	68,0	194	99

Table 3. Associative memory parameters (XC4005XL FPGA).

memory type			max. clock frequency	min. clock rate	CLBs utilization (max. 196 available)	
TM size	embedded searches	memory element	MHz	ns	cells	%
5×5	6	latch	68,3	14,6	80	40
5×5	6	D-FF	66,5	15,0	74	37
5×5	12	latch	63,4	15,7	75	38
5×5	12	D-FF	58,2	17,1	64	34
5×5	16	latch	54,3	18,4	156	80
5×5	16	D-FF	51,0	19,6	147	75

Asymptotic circuit complexity is $O(n^2)$ (it is dominated by TM size), while the clock rate decreases slower then linearly with n. Therefore the second purpose was to build and test only TM array which consumes most of the circuit CLBs. TM was build in three versions: with 6, 12 and 16 build–in logic operations. The maximum size of the prototype obtained was 5×5 and about 75% of device resources were used. Higher functionality is traded for circuit speed but the resulting TM array is surprisingly quite fast. Designs with latches instead of D flip-flops are a bit faster and smaller in terms of circuit size. Parameters of exemplary TM array projects are shown in Table 3.

If XC4085 FPGA was used (which has the highest density in XC4000 series) with 4 times more IOBs and 16 times more CLBs the estimated TM array size could be 10 x 10 due to I/O limitations, with 600 out of 3136 CLBs used (utilization about 30%).

All designs were carefully tested [19]. Small instances of SET INCLUSION, GEOMETRIC RANGE SEARCH, MULTIPLE SEARCH and MATRIX INCLUSION problems were processed in our multi-comparand multi-search processor with associative algorithms described in [14]. The analysis of waveforms confirmed correctness of the designed devices.

5 Concluding Remarks

In this paper an FPGA implementation of multi-comparand multi-search associative processor was proposed which enables highly parallel search operations. The processor is versatile and flexible enough to meet a wide range of requirements, and solve combinatorial problems belonging to various complexity classes including polynomial, P-complete, isomorphic-complete and NP-complete problems.

It is not recommended to implement Tag Memory array as a separate FPGA device. In high density FPGAs the main bottleneck is limited number of IOBs. Hence, one processor should be implemented in single FPGA. There is a need to evaluate sizes of necessary data array DA and comparand array CA and resolve their read/write operations taking into account existing limitations. Basically, all necessary additional components should be included within one chip. Sometimes however, implementation of some procesor components as separate devices may be reasonable.

In cases when one processor is not sufficient for given problem size, a number of processors may be applied using known multiassociative/hybrid techniques described in [4]. Partitioning particular problem data and deriving global solutions from distributed partial results still remains an important research problem.

Some particular topics may be objects of further investigation. For instance, establishing the relationships between desired associative memory cell structure and embedded macrocell functions may contribute to better utilization of FPGA hardware. Various techniques of speeding up search operations may still be discovered (see [17]). Finally, a closer inspection of various classes of combinatorial problems should significantly extend the application domain as well as result in many new algorithms developed on the basis of multi-comparand search operations.

References

1. Digby D.W.: A search memory for many-to-many comparisons. IEEE Transactions on Computers **C-22** (1973) 768-772
2. Fernstrom C., Kruzela I., Svensson B.: LUCAS associative array processor. Design, programming and application studies, LNCS **216** (1986)
3. Foster C.C.: Content addresable parallel processors. Van Nostrand Reinhold (1976)
4. Herbordt M.C., Weems C.C.: Associative, multiassociative and hybrid procesing. [in:] Krikelis A. Weems C.C. (eds): Associative processing and processors. IEEE Computer Society Press (1997) 26-49
5. Herrmann F.P. *et al.*: A dynamic three-state memory cell for high-density associative processors. IEEE Journal of Solid-State Circuits **26** (1991) 537-541
6. Higuchi T. *et al.*: The IXM2 parallel associative processor for AI. Computer **27** (1994) 53-63
7. Jalaleddine S.M.S., Johnson L.G.: Associative IC memories with relational search and nearest-match capabilities. IEEE Journal of Solid-State Circuits **27** (1992) 892-900
8. Kapralski A., Kokosiński Z., Mól W.: An electronic circuit for the maximum selection in a RAM. Patent No. 146021, Polish Patent Office (1989)
9. Kapralski A.: The maximum and minimum selector SELRAM and its application for developing fast sorting machines. IEEE Transactions on Computers **38** (1989) 1572-1576
10. Kapralski A.: Supercomputing for solving a class of NP–complete and isomorphic complete problems. Computer Systems Science & Eng. **7** (1992) 218-228.
11. Kapralski, A.: Sequential and parallel processing in depth search machines. World Scientific (1994)
12. Knuth D.E.: The art of computer programming. Sorting and searching, Addison-Wesley (1973)
13. Kokosiński Z.: Mask and pattern generation for associative supercomputing. Proc. 12th Int. Conf. on Applied Informatics AI'94, Annecy, France (1994) 324-326

14. Kokosiński Z.: An associative processor for multi-comparand parallel searching and its selected applications. Proc. Int. Conf. on Parallel and Distributed Processing Techniques and Applications PDPTA'97, Las Vegas, USA (1997) 1434-1442
15. Krikelis A. Weems C.C. (eds): Associative processing and processors. IEEE Computer Society Press (1997)
16. Louri A., Hatch J.A.: An optical associative parallel processor for high-speed database processing. Computer **27** (1994) 65-72.
17. Parhami B.: Extreme-value search and general selection algorithms for fully parallel associative memories. The Computer Journal **39** (1996) 241-250
18. Schultz K.J., Gulak P.G.: Fully parallel integrated CAM/RAM using preclassification to enable large capacities. IEEE Journal of Solid-State Circuits **31** (1996) 689–699
19. Sikora W.: Synthesis of a programmable associative memory operating on two data sets. MS thesis, Politechnika Krakowska, Kraków, Poland (2000)
20. Stüttgen H.: A hierarchical associative processing system. LNCS 195 (1986)
21. Yamagata T. *et al.*: A 288-kb fully parallel content addressable memory using a stacked-capacitor cell structure. IEEE Journal of Solid-State Circuits **27** (1992) 1927-1933
22. Yau S.S., Fung H.S.: Associative processor architecture - a survey. Computing Surveys **9** (1977) 3-27
23. An overview od multiple CAM designs in Virtex Devices. Application Note XAPP 201, http://www.xilinx.com (1999)
24. Content addresable memory (CAM) in ATM applications. Application Note XAPP 202, http://www.xilinx.com (2001)
25. Design flexible, fast CAMs with Virtex family FPGAs. Application Note XAPP 203, http://www.xilinx.com (1999)
26. Using block RAM for high performance read/write CAMs. Application Note XAPP 204, http://www.xilinx.com (2000)
27. NetLogic Microsystems. Product Data, http://www.netlogicmicro.com (2002)
28. SiberCore Technologies. Product Data, http://www.sibercore.com (2002)

AES Implementation on FPGA: Time - Flexibility Tradeoff

Anna Labbé, Annie Pérez

Laboratoire L2MP-ICF (UMR CNRS 6137), IMT
Technopôle de Château Gombert
13451 Marseille Cedex 20, France
labbe@up.univ-mrs.fr
perez@up.univ-mrs.fr

Abstract. This paper presents some FPGA-based implementations of the private key Advanced Encryption Standard (AES) cryptography algorithm. The technological fixed target is one V1000BG560 Xilinx Virtex FPGA. A basic architecture is presented first for a 256-bit Cipher Key and a 256-bit Block configuration. Partially pipelined structures were also implemented and perform a throughput rate proportional to the pipeline degree. These improved architectures can ensure high speed encryption by processing several Blocks of the plaintext concurrently. In return they need more logic resources. The resources being limited to the Virtex device ones, the highest speed implementations will loose flexibility as for the choice of the number of bits coding the Cipher Key or the Blocks. Different implementation results illustrating this time – flexibility tradeoff are presented and commented.

1 Introduction

Nowadays electronic transactions become extremely important. Most of the applications in this field need security since they concern payments and/or confidential data. For proof a lot of actual projects concern secure multi-application platforms. A powerful tool to solve the security problem is the encryption of the concerned data. Indeed cryptography algorithms are able to ensure data authenticity, integrity and confidentiality [1;2].

These algorithms can be implemented in software or in hardware. Since the technology enables to realize fast electronic transactions, the encryption/decryption process must be fast too. For superior performances as well as for physical security many applications require to realize cryptography algorithms in hardware.

This paper concerns the implementation on Field Programmable Gate Arrays (FPGA) of the recent private-key Advanced Encryption Standard (AES) algorithm [3] successor of the classical standard Data Encryption Standard (DES) [4]. AES implementation needs storage RAMs, look-up table ROMs, shift registers and simple Boolean functions, so the fine grain structure of FPGA is quite suitable. Moreover inherent parallelism and flexibility of the algorithm can be exploited in FPGA [5-9].

M. Glesner, P. Zipf, and M. Renovell (Eds.): FPL 2002, LNCS 2438, pp. 836-844, 2002.

AES algorithm involves several rounds that can be performed in parallel. This same parallelism can be introduced in the hardware structure though pipelining techniques and will lead to a throughput increase. In return these efficient architectures will need more resources; if the target FPGA resources are not sufficient, the system will loose flexibility as for the choice of the number of bits coding the Cipher Key or the Blocks. Different implementations results illustrating this time-flexibility tradeoff are given and commented.

This paper is organized as follows. Section 2 briefly presents the AES algorithm as well as different working modes (ECB, CBC) [10]. Section 3 gives our architectural choices responding to the imposed constraints. The implementation results and associated performances are given in Section 4. Finally section 5 gives some conclusion.

2 AES Algorithm

AES is a private key block cipher. The length of the Block and of the Cipher Key can be independently chosen equal to 128, 192 or 256 bits. In order to illustrate the different steps of this algorithm, let us take a 256-bit Block and a 256-bit Cipher Key. More complete and mathematical AES descriptions can be found in reference [3]. The Block and the Cipher Key are considered as a byte array of four rows and eight columns.

2.1 Encryption Algorithm

AES encryption algorithm iterates Round transformation of the data. Intermediate result during the Round transformation is called the State (4x8 byte array). Each round operates on the State through the RoundKey. This sub-section will summarize the Round transformation process and give the RoundKey generation method.

Round transformation :
The round transformation (**Fig.1**) is iterated fourteen times (in fact, the number of rounds depends on the Block and Cipher Key length). Each round involves four steps. The entry of the first three steps is the State while the last step entries are the State and the RoundKey, as shown below:

```
Round (State, RoundKey)
    {
    ByteSub(State);
    ShiftRow(State);
    MixColumn(State);
    AddRoundKey(State, RoundKey);
    }
```

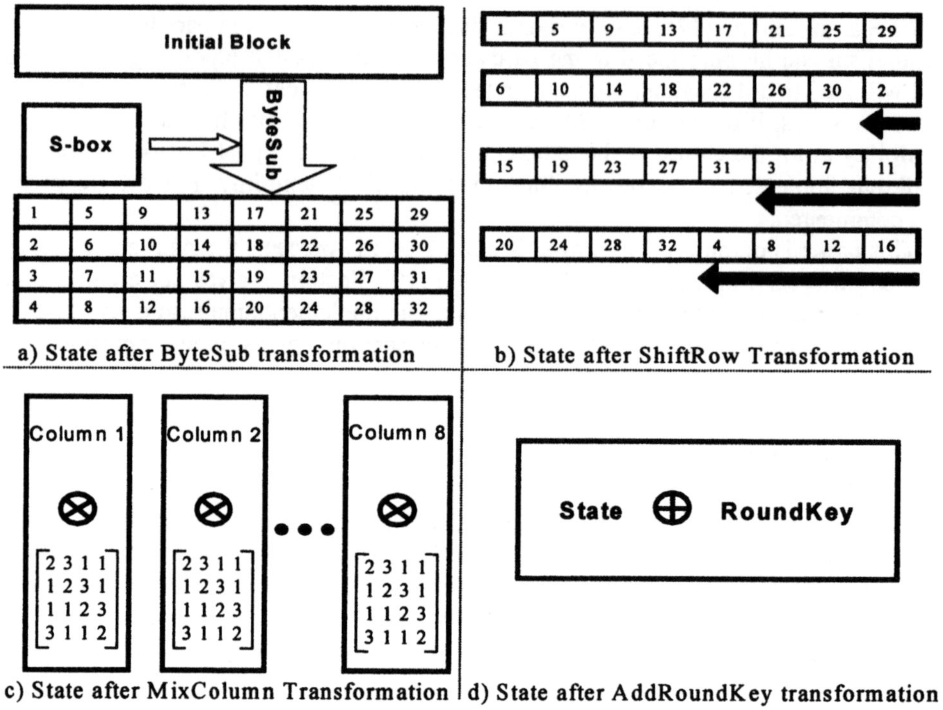

Fig. 1. Round transformation

ByteSub is a non linear byte substitution. Each byte of the State is replaced by another byte which can be calculated or found in the substitution table S-box. **Fig.1a** illustrates this transformation and the resulting State.

ShiftRow transformation acts on the rows of the State. As shown in **Fig.1b**, Row 1 remains unchanged while Row 2 is rotated to the left by one bit, Row 3 by three bytes and Row 4 by four bytes. Other rotation offsets must be taken for other Block sizes.

MixColumn transformation operates on the columns of the State and over the Galois Field GF(2^8). Each column of the State is multiplied by the matrix indicated in **Fig.1c** to give the updated State column.

Finally in the AddRoundKey transformation (**Fig.1d**) the State and the RoundKey are bitwise XORed (i.e. added over GF(2^8)) to give the final State of the round.

Each round involves these four steps, except the last round which avoids the MixColumn operation. Moreover the first round must be preceded by an initial AddRoundKey step.

RoundKey generation :

As we previously saw each round transformation needs a RoundKey. The RoundKeys are generated from the Cipher Key through the following two steps :

```
RoundKey generation (Cipher Key)
    {
    KeyExpansion;
    RoundKey Selection;
    }
```

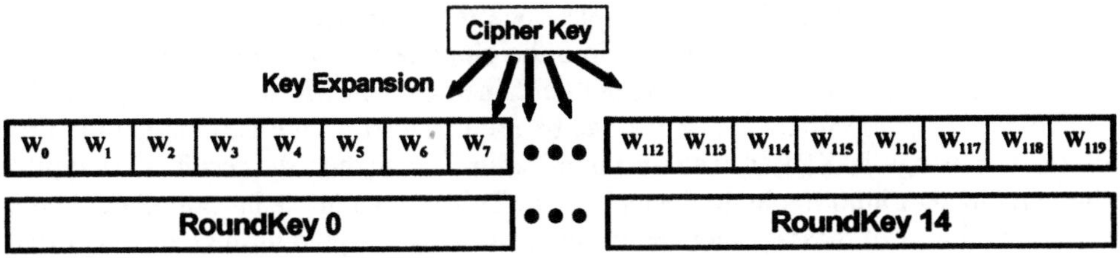

Fig. 2. RoundKey generation

The Cipher Key must be expanded to the so called Expanded Key coded on N bits. N is equal to the Block length multiplied by the number of rounds plus 1, i.e. N = 3840 for the case of 256-bit Blocks illustrated here. The Expanded Key is a linear array of 4-byte words W (**Fig.2**). The first eight word group (W_0 to W_7) is no more than the Cipher Key itself; each following word W_i is obtained by XORing the previous word (W_{i-1}) with the word situated eight positions earlier (W_{i-8}), except when the index i is a multiple of 8 or 4.

In these last cases (W_{i-1}) must be transformed before the XOR. Indeed if the index i is a multiple of 4, the SubByte step (table lookup application to all four bytes of the word) must be applied. If the index i is a multiple of 8 the transformation is a little bit more complex : a Rot Byte transformation (rotation of the bytes in the word) is applied followed by the SubByte step and the result is finally XORed with a round constant.

Then the Round Keys are selected among the words of the Expanded Key : each successive Round Key results of the concatenation of eight contiguous words as shown in **Fig.2**.

2.2 Decryption Algorithm

The decryption process is roughly the same as the encryption one. The same kind of operations are involved. Indeed the decryption steps are analog to the encryption ones and are called : Inverse ByteSub, Inverse ShiftRow, Inverse MixColumn. Moreover the transformation Inverse MixColumn must be applied to the Key. Since the coefficients of the matrix which multiplies each column during the Inverse MixColumn step are grater than those of the MixColumn transformation (see **Fig.1c**), the decryption process is more time consuming than the encryption one.

2.3 Cipher Modes

Several ways of using AES are recommended [7;10]. The so called cipher modes are mainly of two kinds : the Electronic CodeBook mode (ECB) and the Cipher Block Chaining mode (CBC). In both cases the same sequence drives the encryption as well as the decryption process. Let us focus on encryption.

ECB encryption mode is rather simple since the plaintext block is directly transformed through the encrypt algorithm into the ciphertext. However if the same message is sent twice with the same key, both obtained ciphers will be identical. In order to avoid this situation the CBC mode can be used instead. In the CBC mode the first block of message is XORed with an initialization vector then the result is encrypted through the algorithm to obtain the ciphertext. This first cipher is in turn XORed with the second block of message and the resulting word is encrypted through the algorithm and so on.

Concerning hardware implementation, the chaining in the CBC mode implies a feedback and thus a Block encryption can start only if the previous Block is encrypted. This disables parallelism. The ECB mode involves no feedback and allows the introduction of pipeline processing. This capability will be explored in the work presented here.

3 Implementation Architecture

3.1 Design Constraints, Choices, and Tools

For our FPGA AES implementations the following choices and constraints have been taken into account :

- The selected operating mode is the ECB cipher mode because it allows the implementation of a pipelined architecture;
- The fixed FPGA target is the Virtex Xilinx V1000BG560-4 [11]; this circuit has a high capacity, high speed performance and provides embedded RAMs useful for AES implementation;
- The RoundKey generation and Round transformation modules are implemented together.

The architecture was described in VHDL using the design tool NCVHDL of Cadence. The Known Answer Test vectors (KAT) proposed by the National Institute of Standard and Technology (NIST) [10] where applied to debug and verify the VHDL source code. This code was then added as an entry into the Xilinx Foundation tool (version 3.1i) for implementing the design into the target FPGA. The global architecture of the resulting design will be presented. Then the RoundKey generation module will be detailed, followed by the description of several versions of the Round transformation module.

3.2 Basic Iterative Architecture

The block diagram corresponding to the AES implementation is shown in **Fig.3**. The right part concerns the RoundKey generation module and the left part the Round transformation module. The control signals are generated by a state machine.

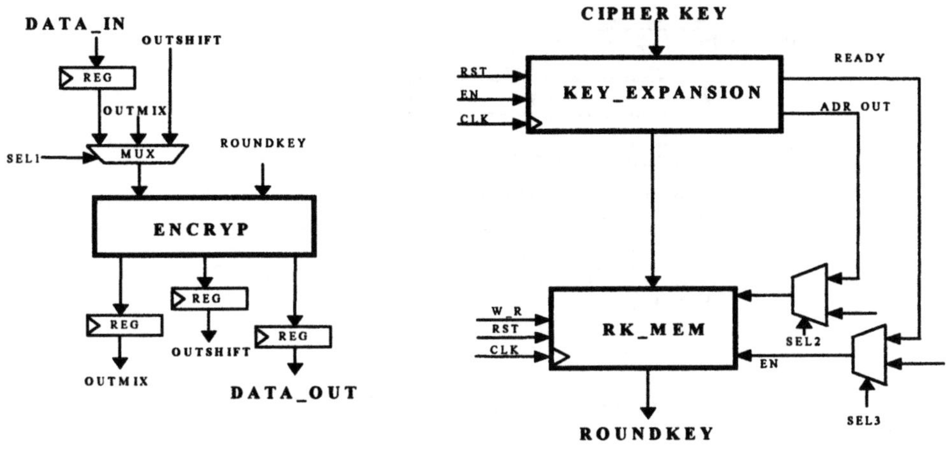

Fig. 3. AES encryption

RoundKey generation module :
This module contains two components : the KEY_EXPANSION and the memory RK_MEM where the generated RoundKeys are stored. The entry of KEY_EXPANSION is the 256-bits Cipher Key and the output is the RoundKey. This component contains logic gates, the lookup table used in the SubByte step and the ROM memory which contains the round constants.

Since the chosen FPGA provides embedded RAMs, we used them to implement RK_MEM by invoking the Single Port Block Memory core in the CORE Generator of the Foundation implementation tool. The CORE Generator was also employed to implement the memories of the KEY_EXPANSION component.

Round transformation module :
The left part of **Fig.3** presents the basic architecture of the Round transformation module; this basic solution minimizes the hardware requirements since only one ENCRYP block is implemented. ENCRYP contains the combinational logic dedicated to process the steps AddRoundKey, ByteSub, ShiftRow, MixColumn (in this order). ENCRYP will be reused at each round computing say at each clock cycle.

3.3 Multiple-ENCRYP Blocks Architecture

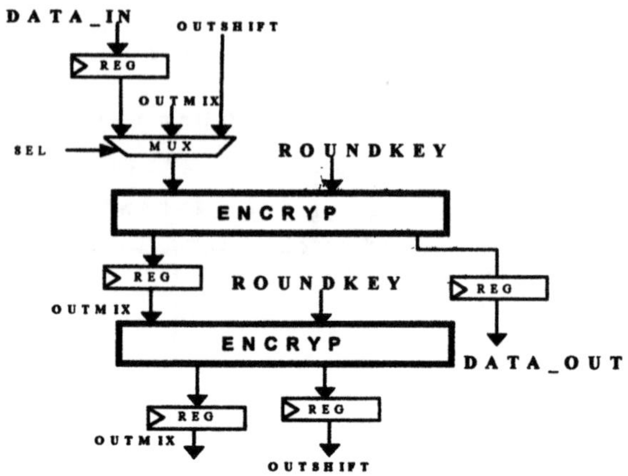

Fig. 4. Partially pipelined structure (PP_2)

In order to increase the throughput an alternative architecture for the Round transformation is a pipelined architecture [5-7]. **Fig.5** gives by instance the architecture of a partially pipelined of degree 2 (PP_2) where the ENCRYP block and associated registers are duplicated. This kind of solution allows to increase the number of data Blocks that can be concurrently encrypted. However it requires more hardware resources as compared to the basic iterative implementation.

4 Results

We implemented into the Virtex V1000BG560-4 FPGA designs corresponding to all the possible AES Block lengths (128, 192, 256 bits), for the basic architecture as well as for different pipeline degrees (PP_2, PP_5). The results concerning the quantity of logic resources, the maximum clock frequency and the throughput are reported in **Table 1**.

The throughput is defined as follows :

Throughput = Block_size . (Number_of_blocks_processed_simultaneously / Latency)

Where the latency is the encryption latency, i.e. the time necessary to encrypt a single Block of plaintext :

Latency = (Cycles_per_encrypted_block / Clock_frequency)

Table 1. Implementation results

Blocks # of bits	Archi-tecture	Slices # (%)	LUTs # (%)	RAMs # (%)	f_{max} (MHz)	Throughput (Mbits/s)
128	basic	2,151 (17)	3,841 (16)	4 (12)	30.81	394.32
128	PP_2	3,543 (29)	6,410 (26)	4 (12)	31.08	795.75
128	PP_5	8,767 (71)	16,957 (69)	4 (14)	29.86	1911.04
192	basic	2,960 (24)	5,327 (22)	6 (19)	31.01	496.10
192	PP_2	5,048 (41)	9,179 (37)	6 (19)	27.70	886.46
256	basic	3,892 (32)	6,946 (28)	8 (25)	27.13	496.04
256	PP_2	6,676 (54)	12,083 (49)	8 (25)	27.76	1007.91

So the implementations of 256 or 192-bit Block architectures show that a maximum pipeline degree of 2 is reached and that in this case the 256-bits structure presents better throughput results. For obtaining even higher throughput rates, the pipeline degree must be increased. Taking into account that the target FPGA is fixed, more pipeline stages can be implemented only for the 128-bits Blocks architecture. Thus saving encryption time must be paid by less Block length flexibility.

5 Conclusion

Overcoming the reduced flexibility associated with ASIC solutions, this paper proposes AES architectures optimized for FPGA. Moreover a FPGA solution provides reduced time and complexity for designing. We implemented a no feedback cipher mode of the AES algorithm on one fixed target FPGA (Virtex V1000BG560). The architecture includes the Key schedule and the Encryption module. The Foundation CORE Generator tool was very efficient to generate the different memories modules while optimizing the logic resources.

Inherent parallelism and flexibility of the algorithm have been exploited. Partial pipelined structures were designed and performed high throughput rates. However the time – flexibility tradeoff imposes lower Block length for higher pipeline degree architectures. Exploiting the dynamically reconfigurability of the target devices could probably avoid this tradeoff.

References

1. Dhem,J.F., Veithen, D., Quisquater,,JJ.: SCALPS : Smart Card for Limited Payment Systems. IEEE Micro, Juin 1996, pp. 42-50
2. Naccache,D. ,M'Raïhi,D.: Cryptographic Smart Cards. IEEE Micro, Juin 96, pp. 14- 24.
3. Daemen, J., Rijmen, V., AES Proposal : Rijndael http://www.esat.kuleuven.ac.be/~rijmen/rijndael/, September 1999
4. Biham,E., Shamir,A.: Differential cryptanalysis of DES-like cryptosystems. Journal of Cryptology, Vol.4, n°1, 1991,pp.3-72

5. Elbirt, A.J., Yip, W., Chetwynd, B., Paar,C. : An FPGA Implementation and Performance Evaluation of the AES Block Cipher Candidate Algorithm Finalist, Proc. AES3 Candidate Conference, New York, USA, April 13-14, 2000 http://csrc.nist.gov/encryption/aes/round2/conf3/aes3conf.htm
6. Chodowiec,P., Khuon, P., Gaj,K.,: Fast implementation of secret-key block ciphers using mixed inner- and outer-round pipelining. Proc. ACM/SIGDA International Symposium on Field Programmable Gate Arrays, FPGA'01, Monterey, CA, Febrary 11-13, 2001
7. Gaj,K., Chodowiec,P. : Fast implementation and fair comparison of the final candidates for Advanced Encryption Standard using Field Programmable Gate Arrays. Proc. RSA Security Conference – Cryptographer's Track San Francisco, CA, April 8-12, 2001
8. Dandalis, A., Prasanna, V.K., Rolim, J.D. : A Comparative Study of Performance of AES Final Candidates Using FPGAs, CHES 2000, Lectures Notes in Computer Science vol 1965, pp125-140, 2000
9. Mroczkowski P.: Implementation of the Block Cipher Rijndael Using Altera FPGA; Public Comments on AES Candidate Algorithms - Round 2. http://csrc.nist.gov/encryption/aes/round2/pubcmnts.htm
10. Description of Known Answer Tests and Monte Carlo Tests for Advanced Encryption Standard (AES) Candidate Algorithm Submissions; derived from Draft NIST Special Publication 800-17: Modes od Operation Validation System: Requirements and Procedures,May 1996.
11. Xilinx products http://www.xilinx.com/

An FPGA Implementation of the Linear Cryptanalysis

Francois Koeune, Gael Rouvroy, Francois-Xavier Standaert,
Jean-Jacques Quisquater, Jean-Pierre David, and Jean-Didier Legat

UCL Crypto Group
Place du Levant, 3, B-1348 Louvain-La-Neuve, Belgium
{koeune,rouvroy,standaert,quisquater,david,legat}@dice.ucl.ac.be

Abstract. This paper deals with cryptographic concepts. It presents a hardware FPGA implementation of linear cryptanalysis of DES[1]. Linear cryptanalysis is the best attack known able to break DES faster than exhaustive search. Matsui's original attack [4, 5] could not be applied as such, and we had to implement a modified attack [1] to face hardware constraints. The resulting attack is less efficient than Matsui's attack, but fits in our hardware and breaks a DES key in 12-15 hours on one single FPGA, therefore becoming the first practical implementation to our knowledge. As a comparison, the fastest implementation known so far used the idle time of 18 Intel Pentium III MMX, and broke a DES key in 4.32 days.

Our fast implementation made it possible for us to perform practical tests, allowing a comparison with theoretical estimations.

Keywords: Cryptography, linear cryptanalysis, FPGA, DES.

1 Introduction

Linear cryptanalysis [1, 4, 5] is a cryptanalytic technique that takes advantage of possible input-output correlations over a cipher. Evaluating this relationship for an sufficient number of plaintext/ciphertext pairs (typically 2^{43}, for a full DES), it is possible to recover some bits of the key faster than an exhaustive search.

Although linear cryptanalysis is the best attack known against DES nowadays, this attack still has a "theoretical" flavour, in the sense that very few experimental applications have actually been performed: a single experimentation for a full DES cipher has been performed in [5], and, until recently, remained the only practical test to our knowledge.

However, recent technological advances have made the required computing power reachable, as is witnessed by a set of 21 experiments [2, 3], using the idle time of 18 Intel Pentium III MMX, capable of performing an attack in 4.32 days.

[1] DES : Data Encryption Standard, the old U.S. cipher standard

M. Glesner, P. Zipf, and M. Renovell (Eds.): FPL 2002, LNCS 2438, pp. 845–852, 2002.

This paper proposes an FPGA implementation completing the attack in 12-15 hours, using hardware roughly worth $3500. We believe that our implementation is the fastest implementation known. Due to tight memory constraint, Matsui's original attack could not be implemented as such. Therefore we implement a variant of it ([1]), which turns out to be less efficient on a theoretical point of view, but gave birth to a very fast implementation. In fact, this attack can be considered as more efficient than Matsui's, in the sense that it requires less plaintext-ciphertext (2^{42} vs. 2^{43}) pairs, but recovers only 7 (resp. 14, by using the dual equation) key bits rather than 13 (resp. 26).

The paper is organized as follows: section 2 describes our FPGA's main characteristics; section 3 reminds the basic principles of linear cryptanalysis; section 4 presents the modified attack and its expected theoritical efficiency; section 5 discusses the attack completion (i.e. recovering the full key); finally, section 6 summarizes the results we obtained on a set of 27 practical tests.

2 Hardware Ressources

All our experiments were carried out on a Virtex1000BG560-4 FPGA board developed by DICE [2]. The board is composed of a control FPGA (FLEX 10K) and a VIRTEX1000 FPGA[3] associated with several processors (ARM and PIC) and fast access memories. The board has multiple compatible PC interfaces (PCI, RS232,USB). To carry out our simulations we used a PCI communication.

3 Linear Cryptanalysis

This section is a brief reminder of Matsui's linear cryptanalysis [4, 5]. This attack is based on the existence of some unbalanced linear relationship between input and output of a reduced-round version of the target encryption scheme. In the case of DES, Matsui used the relationship

$$\begin{aligned}P_L[15] \oplus P_H[7,18,24,29] \oplus C_L[7,18,24] = K_1[22] \oplus K_3[22] \oplus K_4[44]\\ \oplus K_5[22] \oplus K_7[22] \oplus K_8[44] \oplus K_9[22] \oplus K_{11}[22] \oplus K_{12}[44] \oplus K_{13}[22]. \quad (1)\end{aligned}$$

Basically, this relationship means that the exclusive-or of some well-chosen bits of the plaintext (namely, the 7th, 18th, 24th, 29th bits of its high-order part) and some well-chosen bits of the ciphertext is equal to the exclusive-or of some well-chosen bits of the key with probability different from $\frac{1}{2}$.

We can easily calculate its dual, obtained by reversing the expression

$$\begin{aligned}P_L[7,18,24] \oplus C_L[15] \oplus C_H[7,18,24,29] = K_2[22] \oplus K_3[44] \oplus K_4[22]\\ \oplus K_6[22] \oplus K_7[44] \oplus K_8[22] \oplus K_{10}[22] \oplus K_{11}[44] \oplus K_{12}[22] \oplus K_{14}[22], \quad (2)\end{aligned}$$

[2] UCL Microelectronics laboratory (see `http://www.dice.ucl.ac.be`).
[3] This FPGA counts about 6144 CLB's.

where $X[7,18,24] := X[7] \oplus X[18] \oplus X[24]$. Those characteristics are the best linear approximations of 14-round DES cipher. They are satisfied with probability $p = \frac{1}{2} - 1.19 \times 2^{-21}$.

Expression[4] (1) is then extended to the full 16 rounds by adding two non-linear round functions respectively in the first and 16-round:

$$\begin{aligned} P_L[7,18,24,29] \oplus P_H[15] \oplus F_1(P_L,K_1)[15] \oplus C_H[7,18,24] \oplus \\ F_{16}(C_L,K_{16})[7,18,24] = K_2[22] \oplus K_4[22] \oplus K_5[44] \oplus K_6[22] \oplus \\ K_8[22] \oplus K_9[44] \oplus K_{10}[22] \oplus K_{12}[22] \oplus K_{13}[44] \oplus K_{14}[22], \end{aligned} \quad (3)$$

where $F_1(P_L, K_1)$ denotes the first round function. This relationship keeps exactly the same probability as eq. (1). In fact only 6 bits of K_1 (resp. K_{16}) influence the value of $F_1(P_L, K_1)[15]$ (resp. $F_{16}(C_L, K_{16})[7,18,24]$).

If we compute this equation for all 4096 possibilities of the key K_1 and K_{16} a large number of plaintexts, knowing that only one of these 4096 keys is correct, we will find one significative probability corresponding to the 12 correct key bits. The following algorithm summarizes this idea:

Algorithm

1. For each candidate K^i (i=1,2,...4096) of (K_1,K_{16}), let T_i be the number of plaintexts such that the left side of the eq. (3) is equal to zero.
2. Let T_{max} be the maximal value, T_{min} the minimal value of all T_i's and N the number of plaintexts/ciphertexts.
   If $|T_{max} - \frac{N}{2}| > |T_{min} - \frac{N}{2}|$, then adopt the key candidate corresponding to T_{max}.
   If $|T_{max} - \frac{N}{2}| < |T_{min} - \frac{N}{2}|$, then adopt the key candidate corresponding to T_{min}.

An extra bit can be found thanks to relation (3). Indeed, as K_1 and K_{16} were found thanks to the precedent algorithm, we can derive the value of $K_2[22] \oplus K_4[22] \oplus K_5[44] \oplus K_6[22] \oplus K_8[22] \oplus K_9[44] \oplus K_{10}[22] \oplus K_{12}[22] \oplus K_{13}[44] \oplus K_{14}[22]$. It is therefore possible to recover 12+1 bits of the key. The same treatment can be applied to the dual equation (3), thus yielding a total of 26 bits. The remaining 30 unknown key bits have to be searched exhaustively.

4 A Chosen-Plaintext Linear Cryptanalysis

As described in [5], Matsui's Linear Cryptanalysis allows to find these 26 key bits with 2^{43} known-plaintext. Nevertheless, for a hardware implementation, the main problem of this attack is the 2×2^{12} counters (43-bits wide) needed to perform the key guess. Knowing that we have about 24000 LUT's on our FPGA, the implementation of 2^{12} parallelized counters is much too expensive to be realistic (more than 350000 LUT's).

[4] We will leave the second relationship aside in this discussion, since it is the first one's dual.

So, we have to reduce the number of needed counters. Looking back at equation (3)[5], we see that these counters are induced by the terms $F_1(P_L, K_1)[15]$ and $F_{16}(C_L, K_{16})[7, 18, 24]$, each of which depends on 6 key bits. If we could force one of these terms (say, F_1) to a constant value, we would get rid of 2^6 counters.

Due to the non-linear character of F_1 (remember that F_1 – or at least the parts of its output we are interested in – basically corresponds to the S-box S_5), the only way to force $F_1(P_L, K_1)[15]$ to a constant value seems to be to fix its input. As the key bits are obviously constant, all we have to do is to fix 6 bits of P_L to a constant value. As a consequence, this attack becomes a chosen-plaintext attack. It is an attack proposed in [1].

Let us have a look at the success rate of this algorithm. In [4], the following lemmas are proposed:

Lemma 1. *Let N be the number of given random plaintexts and p be the probability that equation 3 holds, and assume $|p - \frac{1}{2}|$ is sufficiently small. Then, the success rate of the algorithm depends on $l_1, l_2, \ldots, l_d$ (as defined in Lemma 2), and $\sqrt{N}|p - \frac{1}{2}|$ only.*

Generally speaking, it is not easy to calculate numerically the accurate probability above. However, under a condition it can be possible as follows.

Lemma 2. *With the same hypotheses as Lemma 1, let $q^{(i)}$ be the probability that the following equation holds for a subkey $K_n^{(i)}$ and a random variable X:*

$$F_n(X, K_n)[l_1, l_2, \ldots, l_d] = F_n(X, K_n^{(i)})[l_1, l_2, \ldots, l_d] \tag{4}$$

Then if $q^{(i)}$'s are independent, the success rate of the algorithm is

$$\int_{x=-2\sqrt{N}|p-\frac{1}{2}|}^{\infty} \Big(\prod_{K_n^{(i)} \neq K_n} \int_{-x-4\sqrt{N}(p-\frac{1}{2})q^{(i)}}^{x+4\sqrt{N}(p-\frac{1}{2})(1-q^{(i)})} \frac{1}{\sqrt{2\Pi}} e^{\frac{-y^2}{2}} dy \Big) \frac{1}{\sqrt{2\Pi}} e^{\frac{-x^2}{2}} dx \tag{5}$$

where the product is taken over all subkey candidates except K_n.

In the case we are considering, we have $d = 3$ and $l_1 = 7, l_2 = 18, l_3 = 24$. Then a numerical calculation of expression (5) is as follows.

N	$\lvert p - \frac{1}{2}\rvert^{-2}$	$2\lvert p - \frac{1}{2}\rvert^{-2}$	$4\lvert p - \frac{1}{2}\rvert^{-2}$	$8\lvert p - \frac{1}{2}\rvert^{-2}$	$16\lvert p - \frac{1}{2}\rvert^{-2}$
Success rate	20.1%	37.8%	64.1%	88.8%	98.8%

Table 1. Success rate

[5] The dual equation can be treated similarly.

In addition we can write this table with $p = \frac{1}{2} - 1.19 \times 2^{-21}$:

N	2^{37}	2^{38}	2^{39}	2^{40}	2^{41}	2^{42}	2^{43}	2^{44}	2^{45}	2^{46}
Success rate	2.1%	3.0%	4.6%	8.0%	14.6%	27.8%	50.2%	77.8%	95.7%	99.8%

Table 2. Success rate with $p = \frac{1}{2} - 1.19 \times 2^{-21}$

It is of course difficult to compare this to Matsui's results, since the latter recovers 13 bits[6] rather than 6+1. As a comparison basis, we nevertheless used equation (5) to show the theoretical success probability of Matsui's 14-round attack[7], which is as follows:

N	$\lvert p-\frac{1}{2}\rvert^{-2}$	$2\lvert p-\frac{1}{2}\rvert^{-2}$	$4\lvert p-\frac{1}{2}\rvert^{-2}$	$8\lvert p-\frac{1}{2}\rvert^{-2}$	$16\lvert p-\frac{1}{2}\rvert^{-2}$
Success rate	4.8%	17.7%	51.3%	87.0%	98.8%

Table 3. Success rate in Matsui's case

N	2^{37}	2^{38}	2^{39}	2^{40}	2^{41}	2^{42}	2^{43}	2^{44}	2^{45}	2^{46}
Success rate	0.1%	0.1%	0.3%	0.8%	2.5%	9.3%	31.9%	71.8%	95.3%	99.8%

Table 4. Success rate in Matsui's case with $p = \frac{1}{2} - 1.19 \times 2^{-21}$

Therefore we can see that this method needs less plaintext/ciphertext pairs than Matsui's one, but retrieves less key bits. The next section discusses the implication this has on a complete attack.

5 Completing the Attack

Once these 6+1 bits of information have been obtained, the question becomes of course: "how can they be exploited to obtain the complete key".

Since the 6 bits yielded by the previous attack belong to the 12 involved in the classical form of the linear cryptanalysis, we can now set up a classical attack[8], with these 6 bits fixed to the values we found in preceding phase. This would give the 6 other bits and only require 2^6 counters to maintain, which is clearly achievable by the FPGA. Applying the same treatment to the dual equation (eq. (3)) would provide us with a total of 26 key bits.

[6] The 13 other bits recovered by Matsui's attack are obtained by using the dual characteristic; as will be shown in next section, the same can be done in our case.

[7] Due to the large (4095) number of factors involved, the equation could not be computed exactly; therefore we used an approximation.

[8] A known plaintext attack.

Let us consider the success rate of this method. The characteristic we use in the second phase has probability $\frac{1}{2} - 1.19 \times 2^{-21}$. Using equation (5), we obtain the following values[9]:

N	2^{37}	2^{38}	2^{39}	2^{40}	2^{41}	2^{42}	2^{43}	2^{44}	2^{45}	2^{46}
Success rate	2.1%	3.1%	5.0%	8.9%	17.6%	35.4%	63.9%	90.1%	99.3%	100%

Table 5. Success rate to complete the attack with $p = \frac{1}{2} - 1.19 \times 2^{-21}$

We obtain the success probability of the global attack by multiplying the probabilities of the first and second phase (tables 2 and 5), as summarized in table 6. This is to be compared with Matsui's success rate, given by table 4.

N	2^{37}	2^{38}	2^{39}	2^{40}	2^{41}	2^{42}	2^{43}	2^{44}	2^{45}	2^{46}
Success rate	0.0%	0.1%	0.2%	0.7%	2.6%	9.8%	32.1%	70.1%	95.0%	99.8%

Table 6. Success rate of global attack

It turns out that these two tables are very close one to the other. One could thus be tempted to conclude that this two-phase attack is as efficient as Matsui's. Unfortunately, it is not possible to reuse for second phase the plaintext/ciphertext pairs used in first phase. As these pairs were explicitly constructed to make the first round constant, they cannot teach us any information about the corresponding key bits.

Consequently, this attack finally requires twice the amount of plaintext/ciphertext pairs required by Matsui for comparable efficiency. Its only advantage (besides the fact that 6 bits of information are already available at mid-course) is that it fits in our FPGA, and can actually be carried out in roughly 12 hours (as a comparison, the only actual implementation of linear cryptanalysis that we know [2, 3] performs an attack in 4.32 days. An exhaustive search of the remaining 30 bits would take about 3 seconds.

Remark: The above estimations only take into account the probability for the right key to be the *first* one in our guess list. In fact, a more efficient method is used in [5]: the candidates are sorted according to their ranking in the linear estimation, and are successively used as basis for exhaustive search. Similarly, we could of course simultaneously treat the 2^t more likely candidates yielded by first phase, combining them with all possible values for the 6 remaining bits. In view of the place left by our implementation on the Xilinx FPGA, it appears we could set $t = 3$. Corresponding success probabilities are difficult to derive theoretically (Matsui's estimations were obtained by extrapolating the results obtained against an 8-round DES). The next section summarizes the results we obtained by actually running the attack.

[9] These value are not the same as table 5, since the considered S-box (and thus $d, l_1, \ldots l_i$) is different.

6 Experimental Results

In this section, we give a description of the results we got running the first phase of the attack (recover 6 key bits) on one single Xilinx FPGA. We carried out the experiments at a work frequency = 66.6 MHz (=2^{26}) and we parallelized 6 attack blocks. Therefore we are able to compute 6×2^{26} equations per second. So, 2^{43} evaluations take about 6 hours.

We carried out tests with 27 different keys. Table 7 summarizes the experimental success rate to rank first the right subkey candidate for various amounts N of chosen-plaintext/ciphertext pairs:

N	2^{36}	2^{37}	2^{38}	2^{39}	2^{40}	2^{41}	2^{42}	2^{43}
Success rate	0%	0%	0%	4%	4%	19%	37%	70%

Table 7. Experimental success rate in the first phase

These experimental results probably suggest that Matsui's theoretical analysis is slightly pessimistic (see table 2). Our hardware design could help to accurate existing mathematical model.

7 Conclusion

This paper presented the first known FPGA implementation of linear cryptanalysis. Due to FPGA constraints, we choose an adapted attack that makes it less memory-consuming. The resulting attack is less efficient (by a factor 2) than the original one, but can actually be deployed on reasonably expensive hardware and is capable of breaking a full DES key in 12-15 hours, including final exhaustive search. In addition, it is worth noting that with the new Xilinx FPGA[10], we would be able to carry out the same attack in about 1 hour, without changing the HDL code. Therefore, in some applications, FPGA's can be used as powerful cryptographic calculation tools.

References

[1] L.R. Knudsen and J.E. Mathiassen A Chosen-Plaintext Linear Attack on DES. In Bruce Schneier, editor, *Proc. of FSE'00*, LNCS, pages 262–272. Springer, 2000.

[2] P. Junod. Linear cryptanalysis of DES. Master's thesis, Swiss Institute of Technology, Zurich, 2000.

[3] P. Junod. On the complexity of Matsui's attack. In *Proc. of SAC'01*, LNCS, pages 216–230. Springer, 2001.

[4] M. Matsui. Linear cryptanalysis method for DES cipher. In Tor Helleseth, editor, *Advances in Cryptology - EuroCrypt '93*, pages 386–397, Berlin, 1993. Springer-Verlag. Lecture Notes in Computer Science Volume 765.

[10] Xilinx VIRTEX-II XC2V8000.

[5] M. Matsui. The first experimental cryptanalysis of the Data Encryption Standard. In Yvo Desmedt, editor, *Advances in Cryptology - Crypto '94*, pages 1–11, Berlin, 1994. Springer-Verlag. Lecture Notes in Computer Science Volume 839.
[6] J.M. Rabaey. *Digital Integrated Circuits.* Prentice Hall, 1996.
[7] Xilinx. Virtex 2.5V field programmable gate arrays data sheet. available from `http://www.xilinx.com`.

Compiling Application-Specific Hardware

Mihai Budiu and Seth Copen Goldstein

Carnegie Mellon University
{mihaib,seth}@cs.cmu.edu

Abstract. In this paper we describe ASH, an architectural framework for implementing Application-Specific Hardware. ASH is based on automatic hardware synthesis from high-level languages. The generated circuits use only localized computation structures; in consequence, we expect these circuits to be fast, to use little power and to scale well with program complexity.

We present in detail CASH, a scalable compiler framework for ASH, which generates hardware from programs written in C. Our compiler exploits instruction level parallelism by using aggressive speculation and dynamic scheduling. Based on this compilation scheme, we evaluate the computational resources necessary for implementing complex integer-based programs, and we suggest architectural features that would support the ASH framework.

1 Introduction

For five decades the relentless pace of technology, expressed as Moore's law, has supplied computer architects with ample materials in their quest for high performance. The abundance of resources has translated into increased complexity. This complexity has already become unmanageable in several respects:

- Verification and testing costs escalate dramatically.
- Manufacturing costs grow dramatically with each new hardware generation.
- Defect density control gets more expensive as the feature size shrinks; in the near future we will be unable to manufacture large defect-free integrated circuits.
- The clock frequency has increased to a point where only a small fraction of the chip is reachable in a single cycle.
- The number of exceptions generated by the CAD tools requiring manual interventions grows quickly with design complexity.
- The dissipated power density (watts/mm^2) of state-of-the-art microprocessors reaches values that make air-cooling infeasible.
- Today's processors use extremely complicated hardware structures to enable the exploitation of the instruction-level parallelism (ILP) in large windows; however, the sustained performance is rather low.

Under the assumption that hardware density continues to improve at an exponential pace for the next decade, we propose in Section 2 an alternative approach to implement general-purpose computation, which consists of synthesizing — at compile time — application-specific hardware, on a reconfigurable-hardware substrate. We argue that such hardware can solve or alleviate all of the above problems. We call this model

M. Glesner, P. Zipf, and M. Renovell (Eds.): FPL 2002, LNCS 2438, pp. 853–863, 2002.

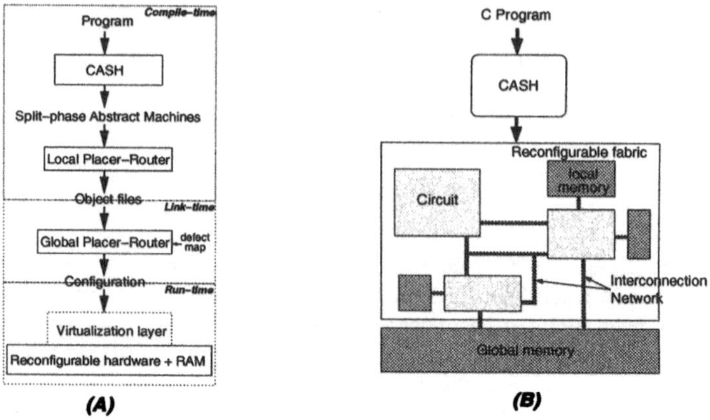

Fig. 1. *(A) The ASH tool-flow (B) Translation of programs into hardware.*

ASH, for Application-Specific Hardware. We propose a method for directly synthesizing custom, application-specific dataflow machines in hardware. ASH implementations have low overhead, as they are precisely tailored to the program parallelism. ASH circuits can be used stand-alone to implement the whole application, or in tandem with a general-purpose processor. The main component of the ASH framework is **CASH**, a Compiler for ASH, presented in Section 3. CASH spans the realms of traditional compilation and hardware synthesis.

In Section 4 we evaluate the hardware resources needed to implement realistic programs within the ASH model of computation. Section 5 describes some implications of the ASH architecture on computer system design.

2 Application-Specific Hardware

In this section we give an overview of the ASH model of computation. The core of ASH is a reconfigurable fabric; compilation subsumes the role of traditional software compilation and hardware synthesis, translating high-level language programs into hardware configurations.

The left of Figure 1 summarizes our framework. Programs written in general-purpose high-level languages are the input to the CASH compiler.

From each procedure in the program, CASH constructs three different types of objects: computation structures, interconnection links and local memories (see Figure 1, right). In this paper we address only the construction of the hardware circuits.

Each procedure is independently optimized, synthesized, placed, and routed. The pre-placed and routed circuits for each procedure are then connected together in a global place and route phase. The resulting "executable" is a configuration for a reconfigurable hardware platform.

The procedures communicate asynchronously with each other. Each contains computation and possibly a small local memory. All the internal signals of the procedure have predictable latency, including the access to local memory. Procedures can however invoke remote operations, which have unpredictable latencies.

Whenever a procedure needs to execute an operation that has unpredictable latency it uses the interconnection network: remote memory accesses, and control-flow transfers are conceptually transformed into messages which can be routed dynamically on a network.

During program execution a procedure can be in one of three states: (1) Inactive: if is not being executed, does not have live state, and need not consume power; (2) Active: if is actively switching, being at the "top" of the stack; (3) Passive: if stores live values, but is blocked waiting for the completion of a callee (occasionally there may be some concurrent execution between a caller and a callee).

An example. Here we illustrate, using an example, the atomic operations and how they are assembled together to implement a simple C program. The program is an iterative implementation of the Fibonacci function, displayed in the left side of Figure 2; its ASH implementation is given in the right side.

CASH partitions each C procedure into a collection of *hyperblocks*, transforms each hyperblock into straight-line code using *speculation* and next translates each hyperblock into a dataflow circuit. The compilation process is discussed further in Section 3. Once a hyperblock starts execution, every one of its operations is executed exactly once.

In order to understand how ASH circuits operate, one should think of the data as produced by a source operator and consumed by a destination operator. Once the data is consumed, it is no longer available. In general, an operator is *strict*, i.e. cannot compute unless all its input data items are present. An operation may fanout the data value it produces to multiple consumers.

Dataflow circuits can be easily used to express straight-line code. In order to allow the implementation of control-flow constructs (branches, procedure calls), ASH augments the set of dataflow operations with two special constructs: *merge* and *eta* nodes[1]. These nodes are used between hyperblocks. Merge and eta nodes are sufficient for synthesizing circuits corresponding to arbitrary flow of control, including that of irreducible graphs. Merge is denoted by a triangle pointing upwards, while eta (η) is a triangle pointing downwards.

The *eta* operation has one data input, one *predicate* input and one data output. If the predicate is *true*, the input data is copied to the output, otherwise the input data is just consumed and no output is generated. Thus, an eta node is a gateway, which lets data flow to a different part of the circuit depending on the predicate. For instance, the eta nodes in hyperblock 1 will steer data to either hyperblock 2 or 3, depending on the test `k != 0`. Note that the etas going to hyperblock 2 are controlled by this predicate, while the eta going to hyperblock 3 is controlled by its complement.

Merge is the only non-strict operator. It has n inputs and one output; it copies one available data input to the output. A merge node accepts information from multiple sources, but only one of the sources should be active at some point. There are merge nodes in hyperblocks 2 and 3. The merge nodes in hyperblock 2 accept data either from hyperblock 1 or from the back-edges in hyperblock 2 itself. The back-edges denote the flow of data along the *while* loop. The merge node in hyperblock 3 can accept control either from hyperblock 1 or from hyperblock 2. The constant "1" feeding the "return"

[1] This terminology is historical, borrowed from the dataflow machine literature [18].

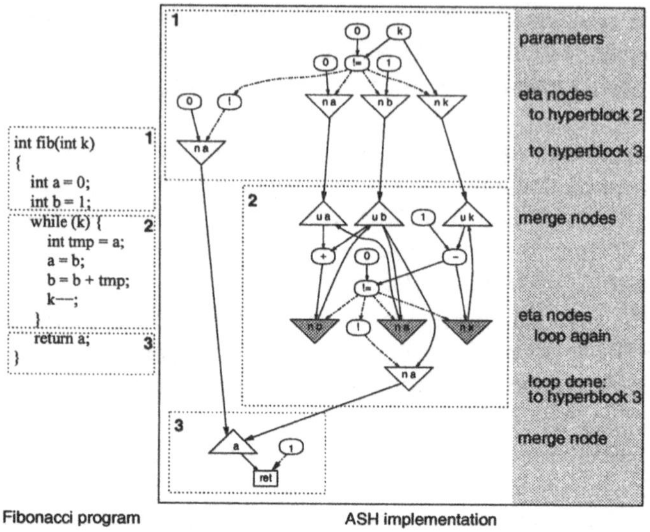

Fig. 2. *C program for Fibonacci and its ASH implementation. The program is decomposed by CASH into 3 hyperblocks, depicted by dotted lines. Hyperblocks are described in Section 3.*

instruction is a predicate, showing that the return is (from a control-flow point of view) unconditionally executed, i.e., it fires as soon as its input data is available.

A formal definition of the semantics of all the basic ASH constructs can be found in [4]. This type of operational semantics, where data is explicitly produced and consumed, is also used in some types of asynchronous circuit descriptions and in dataflow machine architectures.

3 CASH

In this section we describe CASH, our current implementation of the ASH Compiler. Our compiler infrastructure is built around the SUIF 1.3 research compiler [20]. Currently, we do not use any of the parallelizing components of SUIF. Due to space restrictions this presentation is very abstract; for more details please refer to [4].

Hyperblocks. The main abstraction we use at the program level is the hyperblock. A hyperblock is part of a program control-flow graph (CFG) with a single entry point but possibly multiple exits. Hyperblocks have been introduced in the context of predicated execution [12] to uncover instruction-level parallelism (ILP) by removing the control dependences through the predication of the instructions within the hyperblock.

Using hyperblocks as a unit of compilation for reconfigurable hardware was earlier proposed by Callahan and Wawrzynek [6]. Their proposal was heavily influenced by resource constraints and selected only high-profile loop body fragments to map to hardware. Our method of hyperblock selection is unconstrained by resource limitations. We cover each procedure with disjoint hyperblocks, using a linear-time algorithm.

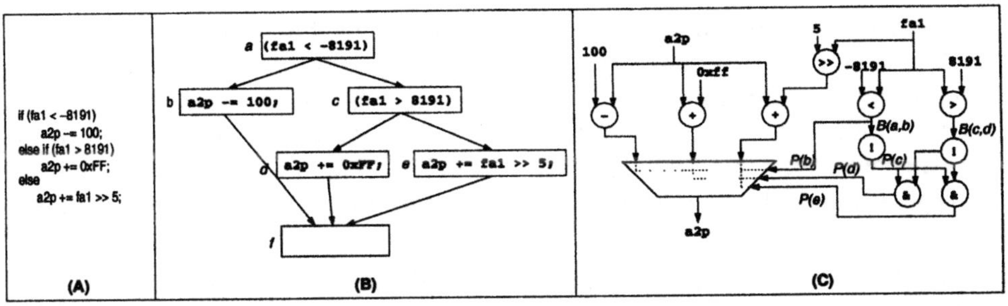

Fig. 3. *(A) Code fragment (B) Control-flow graph (C) Speculative implementation.*

Work in predicated architectures developed a set of heuristics for hyperblock selection [12] (considering hyperblock fragmentation, code duplication, loop peeling and other optimizations). Currently we are using a simple heuristic, building hyperblocks of maximal size.

Some hyperblocks will be loop bodies; we follow the same approach as Callahan and consider the back-edges as part of the hyperblock. If a loop has multiple back-edges, all of them are considered part of the same hyperblock. We next synthesize each hyperblock separately; later merge and eta nodes are used to connect hyperblocks to each other.

Hyperblock synthesis. Through the use of predication, each hyperblock is transformed into straight-line code. Next the code is brought into static-single assignment form (SSA) [9] through variable renaming. The computation of the combinatorial portion of each hyperblock (i.e. excluding the back-edges) is next implemented speculatively in the style of predicated static-single assignment [8] and predicated speculative execution [1], as described in [6].

To illustrate the implementation, we use the example in Figure 3, a code snippet from the `g721` Mediabench [10] program.

Path Predicates. Each basic block in a hyperblock has an associated *path predicate*, as described in [8]; the path predicate associated to block B is true if and only if block B is executed during the current loop iteration. The predicates corresponding to blocks are recursively defined: $P(entry) = True$ and $P(s) = \vee_{p \in Pred(s)}(P(p) \wedge B(p,s))$, where $B(p,s)$ is true if block p branches to s. This is read as: "Block s is executed if and only if one of its predecessors p is executed and p jumps to s."

We next use *instruction promotion* [12] which removes predicates from some instructions or replaces them with weaker predicates, enabling their speculative execution. If the hyperblock code is in static-single assignment form, any instruction with no side-effects can be safely and completely promoted to be executed unconditionally.

Since predicate computations do not need to be guarded, they can be implemented like any regular computation. The predicates are then used for three tasks: (1) to guard the execution of instructions with side-effects (memory writes, memory reads that can trigger exceptions, function calls and returns), (2) to control looping, and (3) on exit from the current hyperblock to indicate which successor hyperblock is executed.

Each edge in the CFG contributes one term to the predicate computation, so the implementation of all predicates is linear in the hyperblock size.

The speculative program implementation just described is essentially a gated static single assignment representation (GSA) [14] of the predicated program. The ϕ operators used by the SSA form become in our representation multiplexors, selecting among the many definitions of a value that reach a join point in the CFG. The multiplexor selectors are path predicates. Unlike other proposed SSA representations for predicated code [8], we explicitly build the circuitry to compute the ϕ functions, which become multiplexors in hardware (see Figure 3C).

Multiplexor placement and optimization. As already noted, the placement of multiplexors corresponds to the placement of ϕ functions in SSA form. However, multiplexor placement is simpler than ϕ placement, because all the back edges in a hyperblock go to the entry point and the rest of the hyperblock is a directed acyclic graph.

We next run a multiplexor simplification pass, which repeatedly applies one of the following rules: (1) constant selector predicates values can be removed; (2) multiple identical data inputs of a mux are merged into a single input and the predicate is set to the logical "or" of the corresponding predicates (3) a mux with a single data input is removed and the input is connected directly to the output (4) two chained mux are transformed into a single mux (whose predicates are the logical "and" of the two muxes).

Merge and eta insertion. The circuits generated for the hyperblocks are "stitched" together using merge and eta operations as follows: (1) for each live variable at the entry of a hyperblock we create a merge node; (2) for each live variable at an exit of a hyperblock (i.e., on a hyperblock exit edge) we create an eta node; the eta is controlled by the edge predicate. The eta's output is connected to the input of the corresponding merge node of the successor hyperblock.

Scheduling and synchronization. Crucial for performance is the efficient scheduling of the dataflow operations. Here we depart from Callahan's proposal, by implementing dynamic scheduling using a completely distributed synchronization scheme. The difference between these two methods is analogous to the difference between VLIW and superscalar processors. Static scheduling requires little hardware support (in the form of a very simple sequencer, which is implemented as a circular shift register in Garp), while dynamic scheduling requires a more complicated handshaking protocol.

The producer of data must signal that data is valid, while the consumer(s) must signal that they have extracted the data, i.e., that the channel can be reused. This protocol is essentially the Two-Phase Bundled Data convention used in asynchronous hardware implementations. ASH is perfectly suitable for an asynchronous implementation.

We expect that mixed implementations that combine static and dynamic scheduling are feasible: portions of the computation between unpredictable latency operations can use simple sequencers that are started by a "data valid" signal. "Data valid" signals are also used to preserve the original program order between instructions which have side effects. Notice that these signals ensure that operations are issued in the original program order; they do not specify the order in which they will complete.

Lenient evaluation. One problem of predicated-execution architectures is that execution time on speculated control-flow paths may be unbalanced [2]. For instance, assume that subtraction takes much longer than addition; then the leftmost path in Figure 3C is the critical path. We propose to solve this problem by using *lenient, fully decoded multiplexors*.

Fully-decoded multiplexors have as many selector bits as there are inputs. Each selector bit selects one of the inputs, as shown by the dotted lines in Figure 3C. These multiplexors do not need complicated decoding logic. A lenient multiplexor can generate its output as soon as one selector predicate is *true* and the corresponding selected data item is valid. We use lenient evaluation both for boolean operations and multiplexors.

4 Resources Required for ASH Implementations

In this section we present a preliminary evaluation of the required resources for the complete implementation of programs in hardware. We analyze a set of programs from the Mediabench [10] and SpecInt95 [17] benchmark suites.

Resources. Table 1 displays the resources required for the complete implementation of these programs in hardware. We do not include in these numbers the standard library or the operating system kernel. All the values are static counts. The lines of code were counted with the sloccount program [19], which skips whitespace and comments. We have used a conservative approximation of the program call-graph to eliminate some of the procedures which are never called.

For some of the operations it is fairly easy to estimate the required hardware resources; we listed these under the heading "bits", and the values indicate the approximate number of bit-operations required to implement them. For remote operations (memory access, call/return), the implementation size can vary substantially, depending for instance on the nature of the interconnection network. For these we report just operation counts.

Comments: The raw computation resources required (the total of the "bits" columns) is below 2.2 million for all benchmarks except `mesa`, which is below 5 million (without any floating-point resources). Even by today's standards, these are reasonably small and many of them can be implemented completely in hardware now—the rest will soon fit within a single chip.

This data doesn't include the savings that can be achieved by implementing computations of custom sizes. Research has shown [5] that simple static methods can eliminate 20% of the bit computations in these benchmarks.

Notice that the resources taken by the predicate computations are minor compared to the actual computation; this suggests that coarse-grained reconfigurable fabrics are more suitable for ASH systems than today's fine-grained FPGAs.

5 Benefits of the ASH Model

The ASH model has better scalability properties than traditional CPU architectures. For instance:

- The verification and testing of a homogeneous reconfigurable fabric is much simpler than general purpose microprocessors. ASH translates the applications directly into

			Units				Bit-operations			
Program	LOC	Circuits	tokens	memory	call/ret	fp	predicates	mux	flow	arithmetic
adpcm_e	183	6	12	10	8	0	53	1,408	1,749	4,450
adpcm_d	183	6	7	9	8	0	36	832	1,653	2,114
g721_e	924	39	115	148	86	0	421	2,816	8,673	25,488
g721_d	922	46	113	153	108	0	493	3,200	8,464	30,741
gsm_e	4156	247	761	1,080	463	0	1,951	15,104	52,707	291,065
gsm_d	4155	243	751	1,069	459	0	1,966	14,976	51,865	290,552
epic_e	1632	254	323	379	231	53	1,389	8,928	252,613	124,164
epic_d	1538	127	310	474	112	6	139	864	175,386	69,670
mpeg2_e	5123	553	2,490	2,482	876	197	6,714	37,152	205,309	430,367
mpeg2_d	6854	457	1,297	1,714	837	11	3,820	18,816	102,395	254,513
jpeg_e	15623	1,705	3,605	7,429	1,676	153	11,624	42,016	702,402	701,323
jpeg_d	15039	1,651	3,386	6,993	1,605	153	11,099	38,848	695,943	713,640
pegwit_e	5013	320	1,008	1,711	604	0	2,412	8,832	69,231	194,744
pegwit_d	5013	320	1,008	1,711	604	0	2,412	8,832	69,231	194,744
mesa	47063	3,299	10,491	19,742	4,104	4,900	125,938	175,008	2,024,765	2,032,393
129.compress	1431	84	216	241	82	3	214	1,760	19,007	24,794
124.m88ksim	12910	750	4,225	4,951	2,080	47	25,650	50,208	178,035	373,232
099.go	25665	2,229	11,324	9,516	2,966	0	35,889	139,360	961,999	817,972
130.li	4888	653	2,000	2,251	1,672	13	4,480	30,560	87,436	101,028
132.ijpeg	17563	1,658	3,609	7,632	1,854	157	10,182	29,216	649,388	741,338
134.perl	23365	1,960	26,835	14,143	4,924	47	140,598	191,040	1,045,737	858,553
147.vortex	49224	1,165	17,389	20,054	7,665	4	53,324	147,744	693,659	966,205

Table 1. *Static resource consumption for each benchmark. Some resources are expressed in units, while other are expressed in bit-operations.* **LOC:** *lines of source code,* **hypers:** *number of hyperblocks generated;* **tokens:** *token-merging operators;* **memory:** *loads and stores;* **call/ret:** *calls and returns;* **fp:** *floating-point operations;* **predicates:** *boolean operations computing predicates;* **mux:** *multiplexors;* **flow:** *control-flow operators;* **arithmetic:** *integer arithmetic. We do not include the cost of handshaking control circuitry.*

hardware, so there is no interpretation layer (i.e., the CPU) which can contain bugs. By using the translation validation [15], (used by a certifying compiler to emit a formal proof that the executable is equivalent with the input program) we completely eliminate one complex layer needing verification and testing.

- Only one hyperblock is actively switching at any time, requiring little power.
- ASH implementations use only local signals, which scale well with clock frequency. All inter-procedural communication can be made using a switched, pipelined interconnection network, so there is no need for global electrical signals.
- Dynamic methods of extracting ILP from programs (as implemented in today's out-of-order processors) are hindered by limited issue windows. Our compiler analyzes large program fragments and can uncover substantially more parallelism than processor issue windows.

The main disadvantage of the ASH paradigm is the requirement for substantial hardware resources. However, this can be alleviated through use of virtualization, or by hardware-software partitioning between a CPU and an ASH fabric. According to data presented in Section 4, the evolution of component density according to Moore's law will soon provide sufficient resources for all but the most complex programs.

6 Related Work

This work has two different lineages: research on intermediate program representation and compilation for reconfigurable hardware architectures.

Many researchers have addressed the problem of compiling high-level languages for reconfigurable architectures: e.g., [16, 6, 3, 13, 11]. Our compilation scheme is most closely related to the scheme proposed by Callahan in the Garp compiler [6, 7]. While we exploit many of the ideas in his proposal, we differ in the following respects:

- Our approach reflects our different assumptions about the amount of available computational resources. In his proposal each hyperblock becomes a separate configuration. In our implementation we translate entire procedures into hardware: each procedure is decomposed into a collection of disjoint hyperblocks, and inter-hyperblock communication is synthesized. We also handle procedure calls and returns in hardware, albeit with some restrictions (currently we do not handle recursion).
- In Callahan's work, the synthesized hyperblock implementation is statically scheduled, using a fixed sequencer. We propose the use of a dynamically scheduled execution, which, despite requiring potentially more hardware resources to implement, has the capability to gracefully absorb unpredictable latency operations. Our dynamic scheduling scheme naturally generalizes his software-pipelining scheme.

The output of our compiler is a series of circuits. These bear a striking resemblance to some forms of intermediate representations of the program in other optimizing compilers. Our circuits are most closely related to predicated static-single assignment [8]. Our circuits are also closely related to dataflow machines [18], but are meant to be implemented directly in hardware and not interpreted on dataflow machines using token-passing.

7 Conclusions

In this paper we have presented a proposal for a new model of computation, called Application-Specific Hardware (ASH), which implements programs completely in hardware, on top of a reconfigurable hardware platform. Our preliminary evaluations suggest that soon there will be enough hardware resources to accommodate complete realistic programs, and that the sustained performance of this model will be comparable to processor-based computations.

We have discussed the compilation technology which can scalably translate large programs written in high-level languages into hardware implementations. Our compilation strategy transforms hyperblocks into circuits which execute many operations speculatively, and thus expose a substantial amount of instruction-level parallelism. The execution of the hardware is dynamically scheduled by using only local synchronization structures, tolerating unpredictable latency events.

We have also outlined those features of the ASH model of computation that promise to make this model *scalable*. ASH implementations can easily and naturally take advantage of the exponentially increasing amount of hardware resources, avoiding many of the problems that the increased complexity brings to standard CMOS-based microprocessor design and manufacturing.

8 Acknowledgements

This research is funded in part by the National Science Foundation under Grant No. CCR-9876248 and by Darpa under contract #2156-CMU-ONR-0659. We are grateful to Tim Callahan for his comments on a preliminary version of this paper.

References

[1] David I. August, Daniel A. Connors, Scott A. Mahlke, John W. Sias, Kevin M. Crozier, Ben-Chung Cheng, Patrick R. Eaton, Qudus B. Olaniran, and Wen mei W. Hwu. Integrated predicated and speculative execution in the IMPACT EPIC architecture. In *Proceedings of the 25th Annual International Symposium on Computer Architecture*, pages 227–237, June 1998.

[2] David I. August, Wen mei W. Hwu, and Scott A. Mahlke. A framework for balancing control flow and predication. In *Proceedings of the 30th International Symposium on Microarchitecture*, December 1997.

[3] Jonathan Babb, Martin Rinard, Csaba Andras Moritz, Walter Lee, Matthew Frank Rajeev Barua, and Saman Amarasinghe. Parallelizing applications into silicon. In *Proceedings of the Seventh Annual IEEE Symposium on Field-Programmable Custom Computing Machines*, 1999.

[4] Mihai Budiu and Seth Copen Goldstein. Pegasus: An efficient intermediate representation. Technical Report CMU-CS-02-107, Carnegie Mellon University, May 2002.

[5] Mihai Budiu, Majd Sakr, Kip Walker, and Seth Copen Goldstein. BitValue inference: Detecting and exploiting narrow bitwidth computations. In *Proceedings of the 2000 Europar Conference*, volume 1900 of *Lecture Notes in Computer Science*. Springer Verlag, 2000.

[6] Timothy J. Callahan and John Wawrzynek. Instruction level parallelism for reconfigurable computing. In Hartenstein and Keevallik, editors, *FPL'98, Field-Programmable Logic and Applications, 8th International Workshop, Tallinin, Estonia*, volume 1482 of *Lecture Notes in Computer Science*. Springer-Verlag, September 1998.

[7] Timothy J. Callahan and John Wawrzynek. Adapting software pipelining for reconfigurable computing. In *Proceedings International Conference on Compilers, Architecture, and Synthesis for Embedded Systems (CASES) 2000*, 2000.

[8] Lori Carter, Beth Simon, Brad Calder, Larry Carter, and Jeanne Ferrante. Path analysis and renaming for predicated instruction scheduling. *International Journal of Parallel Programming, special issue*, 28(6), 2000.

[9] R. Cytron, J. Ferrante, B. Rosen, M. Wegman, and K. Zadeck. Efficiently computing static single assignment form and the control dependence graph. *ACM Transactions on Programming Languages and Systems*, 13(4):451–490, 1991.

[10] Chunho Lee, Miodrag Potkonjak, and William H. Mangione-Smith. MediaBench: a tool for evaluating and synthesizing multimedia and communications systems. In *Micro-30, 30th annual ACM/IEEE international symposium on Microarchitecture*, pages 330–335, 1997.

[11] Yanbing Li, Tim Callahan, Ervan Darnell, Randolph Harr, Uday Kurkure, and Jon Stockwood. Hardware-software co-design of embedded reconfigurable architectures. In *DAC 2000*, 2000.

[12] Scott A. Mahlke, David C. Lin, William Y. Chen, Richard E. Hank, and Roger A. Bringmann. Effective compiler support for predicated execution using the hyperblock. In *Proceedings of the 25th International Symposium on Microarchitecture*, pages 45–54, Dec 1992.

[13] Ken Mai, Tim Paaske, Nuwan Jayasena, Ron Ho, William J. Dally, and Mark Horowitz. Smart memories: A modular reconfigurable architecture. In *Proceeding of the International Conference on Computer Architecture 2000*, June 2000.

[14] Karl J. Ottenstein, Robert A. Ballance, and Arthur B. Maccabe. The program dependence web: a representation supporting control-, data-, and demand-driven interpretation of imperative languages. In *Proceedings of the Conference on Programming Language Design and Implementation PLDI 1990*, pages 257–271, 1990.

[15] Amir Pnueli, Michael Siegel, and Eli Singerman. Translation validation. In Springer Verlag, editor, *Proceedings of TACAS'98*, volume 1384 of *LNCS*, pages 151–166, 1998.

[16] Rahul Razdan. *PRISC: Programmable reduced instruction set computers*. PhD thesis, Harvard University, May 1994.

[17] Standard Performance Evaluation Corp. *SPEC CPU95 Benchmark Suite*, 1995.

[18] Arthur H. Veen. Dataflow machine architecture. *ACM Computing Surveys*, 18 (4):365–396, 1986.

[19] David A. Wheeler. More than a gigabuck: Estimating GNU/Linux's size. http://www.dwheeler.com/sloc, November 2001.

[20] Robert P. Wilson, Robert S. French, Christopher S. Wilson, Saman P. Amarasinghe, Jennifer M. Anderson, Steve W. K. Tjiang, Shih-Wei Liao, Chau-Wen Tseng, Mary W. Hall, Monica S. Lam, and John L. Hennessy. SUIF: An infrastructure for research on parallelizing and optimizing compilers. In *ACM SIGPLAN Notices*, volume 29, pages 31–37, December 1994.

XPP-VC: A C Compiler with Temporal Partitioning for the PACT-XPP Architecture

João M.P. Cardoso and Markus Weinhardt

PACT Informationstechnologie AG, Muthmannstrasse 1, 80939 Munich, Germany
jmpc@acm.org, mw@pactcorp.com

Abstract. *The eXtreme Processing Platform (XPP) is a unique reconfigurable computing (RC) architecture supported by a complete set of design tools. This paper presents the XPP Vectorizing C Compiler XPP-VC, the first high-level compiler for this architecture. It uses new mapping techniques, combined with efficient vectorization. A temporal partitioning phase guarantees the compilation of programs with unlimited complexity, provided that only the supported C subset is used. A new loop partitioning scheme permits to map large loops of any kind. It is not constrained by loop dependences or nesting levels. To our knowledge, the compilation performance is unmatched by any other compiler for RC. Preliminary evaluations show compilation times of only a few seconds from C code to configuration binaries and performance speedups over standard microprocessor implementations. The overall technology represents a significant step toward RC architectures which are faster and simpler to program.*

1 Introduction

Many applications are characterized by data-intensive processing and both low power consumption and high performance requirements. It is more and more evident that these requirements cannot be fully accomplished with today's microprocessor technology. Accelerating specific tasks using ASICs relieves some of the processing burden and adds some required features, but limits flexibility and requires high non-recurring engineering (NRE) costs and long design cycles. FPGAs eliminate the NRE costs and add flexibility, but still require hardware design expertise. Because of their fine-grain structure, FPGAs are not a particularly suitable target platform for compiling high level algorithmic descriptions.

New coarse-grained RC architectures are being introduced to tackle these problems [1]. One of the new promising architectures is the XPP [2][3]. It features a coarse-grain, data-driven, runtime reconfigurable ALU array. The XPP was designed to support pipelining, both instruction- and task-level parallelism, and dataflow and stream-based computations. The C compiler described in this paper was developed to drastically reduce the time to program an XPP device, and to hide architecture details from the user. A novel temporal partitioning technique allows to map programs without size limits.

M. Glesner, P. Zipf, and M. Renovell (Eds.): FPL 2002, LNCS 2438, pp. 864–874, 2002.

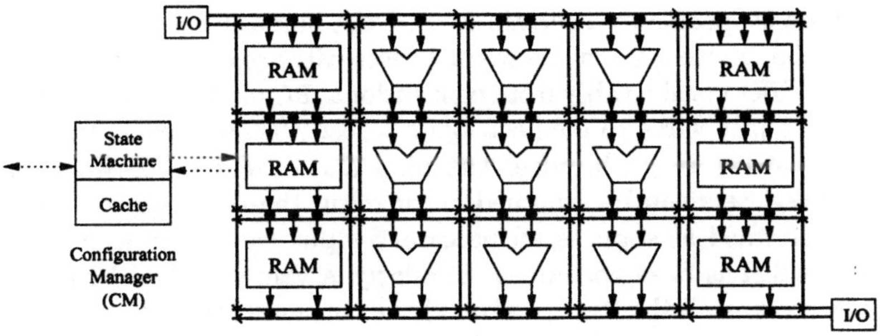

Fig. 1. Simplified structure of an XPP array.

This paper is organized as follows. The next section briefly describes the features of the XPP technology relevant for XPP-VC. Section 3 outlines compilation to the XPP and section 4 describes the temporal partitioning steps. Section 5 shows some experimental results, section 6 points out the main differences between this and previous work, and finally section 7 concludes the paper and enumerates ongoing and future work.

2 XPP Technology

The XPP technology consists of an RC architecture [3] delivered as a device or an IP core, and a complete development tool suite consisting of a place and router, a simulator, and a visualizer [2]. The tools use the proprietary *Native Mapping Language* (NML), a structural language with reconfiguration primitives [2].

The architecture is based on a 2-D array of coarse-grained, adaptive processing elements (PEs), internal memories, and interconnection resources. XPP has some similarities with other coarse-grained RC architectures which were especially designed for stream-based applications (*e.g.*, KressArray [1], RaPiD [4]). XPP's main distinguishing features are its sophisticated configuration mechanisms and the dataflow protocols implemented in the interconnection resources.

Array Structure: Fig. 1 shows the structure of a simple XPP. It contains a 3×3 square of PEs in the center and one column of independent internal memories on each side. There are two I/O units which can either be configured as ports for streaming data or as interfaces for external RAM. The PEs perform common arithmetic and logical operations, comparisons, and special operations such as counters. In each configuration, each PE performs one dedicated operation. Each thick line in the figure represents several segmented busses which can be configured to connect the output of a PE with other PE's inputs. The array is attached to a *Configuration Manager* (CM) responsible for the runtime management of configurations, for downloading configuration data from external memory into the configurable resources of the array. Besides a finite state machine, the CM has cache memory for configuration data.

Data and Event Synchronization: The interconnection resources of an XPP consist of two independent sets of busses: data and event busses. The number of busses is specific to a certain XPP. Data busses have a uniform bit width specific to the device type, while event busses carry one-bit control information. The busses differ considerably from conventional RC architectures (*e.g.*, FPGAs). They are not just wires to connect logic: a ready/acknowledge protocol implemented in hardware synchronizes the data and events processed by the PEs. Pipelining registers can be switched on or off in the bus segments. A PE operation is performed as soon as all necessary input values are available and the previous result has been consumed. Similarly, a value produced by a PE is forwarded as soon as all the PE's receivers have consumed the previous value. Thus it is possible to map a dataflow graph directly to the array, and to pipeline input data streams through it. Note that an XPP is a synchronous design operating at a fixed clock frequency.

Events transmit state information which can be used to control a PE's execution or memory accesses. The PEs can perform selective operations such as MERGE, DEMUX, and MUX. MERGE uses an event to select one of two operands. MUX has a similar functionality, but discards the data on the input not selected. Finally, DEMUX forwards its input data to the selected output. DEMUX can also be used to selectively discard data. Thus conditional computations are feasible. Some PE operations generate events depending on results or exceptions. A counter, *e.g.*, generates a special event only after it has terminated. Events can even trigger a self-reconfiguration of the device as explained below.

Configuration: In the XPP every configurable object (*e.g.*, PE, memory) locally stores its current configuration state, *i.e.*, if it is part of a configuration or not (states "configured" or "free"). If a configuration is requested, its configuration data is first copied to the internal cache. Then the CM downloads the configuration onto the array, synchronizing with the configurable objects. Once an object is configured, it changes its state to "configured". This prevents the CM from reconfiguring an object which is still used by another configuration.

Objects are released (*i.e.*, changed to state "free") by events on a special input. These events are automatically broadcast along all connected PEs such that the entire configuration is removed. Events on release inputs can be explicitly generated by the CM or created in the array itself by a PE. Hence, running applications can request a self-reconfiguration of the device, making possible to execute an application consisting of several configurations without any external control. When a computation is finished, the PE detecting the end (*e.g.*, a counter) can generate the event to be broadcast or can send an event to the CM requesting the next configuration.

The configuration time can be reduced by prefetching mechanisms: during the loading of a configuration onto the array other configurations can be loaded to the CM cache. Thus it need not be loaded from external memory when configurable objects become available. The same is true if a configuration has been used before and its configuration data is still in the CM cache.

Because of its coarse-grained nature, an XPP can be configured rapidly. Since only the configuration of those array objects actually used is necessary, the configuration time depends on the application.

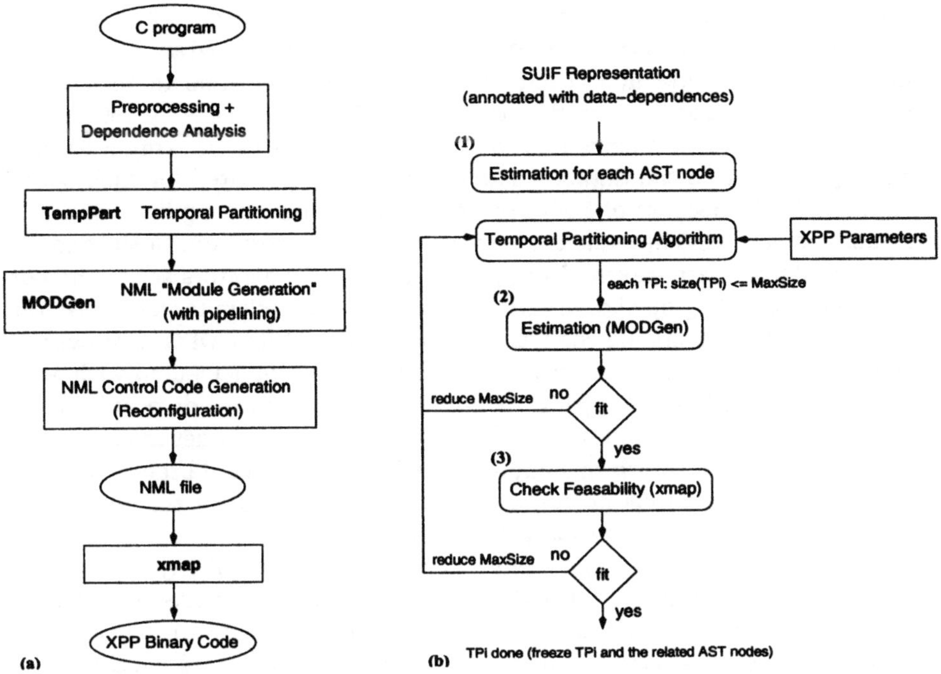

Fig. 2. (a) XPP-VC compilation flow. (b) Temporal partitioning process realized by `TempPart`.

3 Compiling C Code with XPP-VC

The XPP Vectorizing C Compiler XPP-VC is based on the SUIF compiler framework [5]. XPP-VC translates C programs to NML files. The currently supported C subset excludes `struct` and floating-point data types, pointers, irregular control flow, and recursive and system calls. A compiler options file specifies the parameters of the target XPP and the external memories connected to it. To access XPP I/O ports specific C functions are provided.

Fig. 2(a) shows the compilation flow. First, some architecture-independent preprocessing passes based on well-known compilation techniques [6] are executed. During this phase, user-annotated FOR loops are automatically unrolled. Then the compiler performs a data-dependence analysis and tries to vectorize inner FOR loops. In XPP-VC, vectorization means that loop iterations are overlapped and executed in a pipelined, parallel fashion. This technique is based on the *Pipeline Vectorization* method [7]. Next, `TempPart` splits the C program into several temporal partitions if required (see section 4). Then, `MODGen` generates one NML module for each partition and NML reconfiguration code is added. Each NML module is placed and routed automatically by `xmap`, which uses an enhanced force-directed placer with short runtimes. Finally, the configuration data for each partition and the binary code to program the CM, which represents the flow of configurations, are generated.

We now describe how C code is transformed to NML code. First, program data is allocated to memory resources. `MODGen` maps each program array to internal or external RAM and scalar variables needing registers to registers in the array. Next, a control/dataflow graph (CDFG), which directly reflects the NML structure needed, is generated. Straight-line code without array references is directly mapped to the dataflow model. One PE is allocated for each operator in the CDFG. Because of the data-driven mechanism, no explicit control or scheduling is needed. The same is true for conditional execution. Both branches of an IF statement are executed in parallel and MUX operators select the correct output depending on the condition, as in many compilers targeting FPGAs, [8]. Fig. 3(a) shows a simple conditional statement and its CDFG. However, IF statements containing array references or loops are not implemented with MUX operators. Instead, DEMUX operators are used. They forward data only to the branch selected by the IF condition. The outputs of both branches are connected to the subsequent PEs. With this implementation, only selected branches receive data and execute and thus no conflict occurs. Fig. 3(b) shows the conditional statement of Fig. 3(a) implemented this way.

Accesses to the same memory have to be controlled explicitly to maintain the correct execution order. MERGE operators forward addresses and data in the correct order to the RAM, and DEMUX operators forward values read to the correct subsequent operator. Finite state machines for generating the correct sequence of events (to control these operators) are synthesized by the compiler. I/O port accesses are handled in a similar way. Fig. 3(c) shows the implementation of the statements `x = arr[a]; y = arr[b];`. In this example, the events controlling the MERGE and DEMUX operators are simply generated by an event register with a feedback cycle. The register is preloaded with "0" and is configured to invert its output value.

All scalar variables updated in the loop body are treated as follows. In all but the last iteration, a DEMUX operator routes the outputs of the loop body back to the body inputs. Only the results of the last iteration are routed to the loop output. The events controlling the DEMUX are generated by the loop counter of FOR loops or by the comparator evaluating the exit condition of WHILE loops. Note that the internal operators' outputs cannot just be connected to subsequent operators since they produce a result in each loop iteration. The required last value would be hidden by a stream of intermediate values. As opposed to registers in FPGAs, the handshaking protocol requires that values in XPP registers are consumed or explicitly discarded before new values are accepted. Fig. 3(d) shows the (slightly simplified) CDFG for the following C code:

```
a = x;
for (i = 1; i <= 10; i++) a = a + i;
```

Note that the counter generates ten data values (1..10), but eleven events. After ten loop iterations a "1" event routes the final value of a to the output.

If the loop body contains array or I/O accesses, a loop iteration may only start after the previous iteration has terminated since the original access order must be maintained. The compiler generates events enforcing this. For generating more efficient XPP configurations, `MODGen` generates pipelined operator networks for

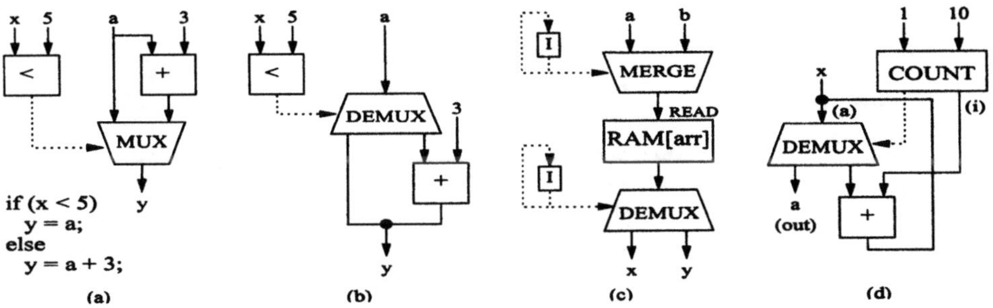

Fig. 3. C compilation examples. Data busses are represented as solid arrows, and event busses as dotted arrows. Black dots denote combined data busses: (b) and (d). I represents an event register with an inverted output (c).

inner loops which have been annotated for vectorization by the preprocessing phase. In other words, subsequent loop iterations are started before previous iterations have finished. Data flows continuously through the operator pipelines. By applying pipeline balancing techniques, maximum throughput is achieved.

To reduce the number of memory accesses, the compiler automatically removes some redundant array reads. Inside loops, loads of subsequent array elements are transformed to a single load and a shift register scheme.

4 Temporal Partitioning

A program too large to fit in the target XPP is handled by performing temporal partitioning, *i.e.*, by splitting it into several sequential parts such that each one is mappable. The problem can be formulated as follows. Given a C program and a specific XPP device, determine the set of feasible temporal partitions which results in the fastest overall program execution.

Fig. 2(b) shows the main steps for the temporal partitioning process. A first level of estimations ((1) in Fig. 2(b)) computes the XPP resources needed for each SUIF abstract syntax tree (AST) node in the code. Then, the temporal partitioning algorithm is performed. The algorithm starts with a partition for each AST node in the highest level of the SUIF representation and then iteratively merges adjacent partitions. During the merging the algorithm checks if the resulting partitions are feasible, *i.e.*, lead to segments of code entirely mappable in the available XPP resources. The iterative process runs until a single partition is achieved, or no more merges are feasible. To decide on a certain merge the compiler considers that a partition must define, on the control flow graph of the program, a region of code with a single entry and possibly multiple exists.

Only if an AST, in the hierarchical level being traversed by the algorithm, does not fit into the available XPP resources, the algorithm is applied recursively to the inner nodes of the AST[1]. Large loops are partitioned by a new method,

[1] Note that loops are consequently executed in a single configuration whenever possible. This has the advantage of using an active configuration as long as possible.

```
int i;
...
for(i=0;i<N;i++) {
   stmt 1;
--->
   stmt 2;
}
stmt3;
...
```

(a)

```
      int i;
      int comm[1];
      ...
      i=0;                      ] conf.1
      comm[0] = i;
..............................
lab1: i = comm[0];
      if(i>=N) goto lab2;       ] conf.2
      stmt 1;
..............................
      i = comm[0];
      stmt 2;                   ] conf.3
      comm[0] = ++i;
      goto lab1;
..............................
lab2: stmt3;                    ] conf.4
      ...
```

(b)

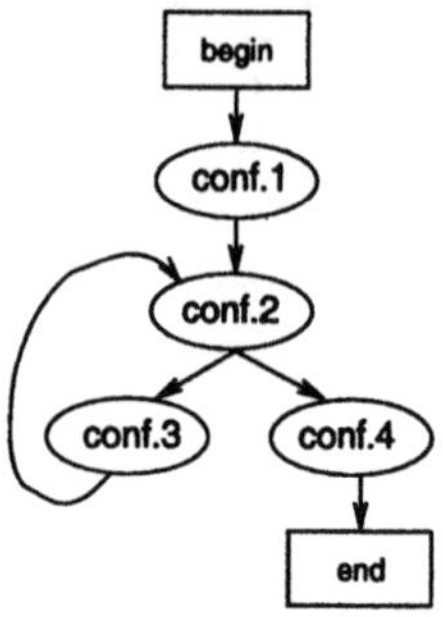

(c)

Fig. 4. Applying *loop dissevering*: (a) original code: the arrow identifies the place where the loop must be partitioned; (b) transformed code with configuration boundaries and buffer statements for the variable `i`; (c) graph representing the flow of configurations.

called *loop dissevering*[2]. The scheme transforms the loop into straight line code with a conditional jump to loop-exit or to the next iteration (see Fig. 4) and uses the capability of a reconfiguration controller to orchestrate the flow of configurations needed (see Fig. 4(c)). In the case of the XPP, the controller is directly realized by the CM. In other architectures it can be supported by a host CPU. *Loop dissevering* can be applied to any type of loop and is not constrained by any type of dependences or nested structures (*e.g.*, nested loops).

Estimations derived from a high level representation are fast but not accurate. Since we need to ensure that each partition generated fits onto the available XPP resources, our methodology also uses two other levels (see (2) and (3) in Fig. 2(b)). In level (2) each processed partition is checked with estimations performed on the CDFG generated by `MODGen`. If the size exceeds the available resources, the algorithm revokes the last merges, and proceeds by tightening the size constraint (diminishing the maximum number of available resources). Level (3) tests if each configuration successfully checked in level (2) can be really mapped to the XPP. This check uses the placer and router (`xmap`). If it does not fit, the algorithm once more revokes the last merges and proceeds by tightening the size constraint.

Currently, arrays assigned to internal memories are used as inter-partition storage for scalar variables[3], as illustrated by the communication of the variable `i` in Fig. 4(b) via the array `comm`. The arrays (those initially used in the program plus the added ones to communicate data) are assigned to the XPP's internal memories based on their lifetimes, as determined by the flow of configurations exposed. This permits, in some cases, to use fewer internal memories since they can be time shared among different configurations.

[2] In some cases loop partitioning can be dealt with by applying *loop distribution* [6]. However, we do not currently apply *loop distribution* automatically.

[3] The internal XPP RAMs keep, by default, their data during reconfiguration.

5 Experimental Results

We have done a preliminary evaluation of the XPP-VC compiler with a set of benchmarks. Table 1 shows their main properties. They have 18-228 lines of C code (loC), 2-16 loops, and 2-6 array variables. Table 2 shows the results obtained with XPP-VC. The second column shows the CPU time (using a PC with a Pentium III at 933MHz) to compile each example with XPP-VC (from the C program to the binaries). In the experiments we use an XPP array of 16×16 PEs. Columns #Part, #PEs, and #Max represent the number of partitions, number of PEs used (in the cases with more than one partition, we show the number of PEs of the largest configuration and the sum of PEs for all configurations), and the maximum number of PEs concurrently executed (as an indication of ILP degree), respectively. Columns 5 and 6 show the overall computation time of the configurations on the array and the total execution time (taking into account setup, fetching, configuring, data communication and computation), respectively, both in number of clock cycles. The last column shows the speedup obtained with XPP at 150MHz implementations (using the total execution time) over the examples compiled with `gcc` and running on a PIII at 933MHz.

The compiler has achieved speedups from 2.8 to 98. Since, as far as the clock frequency is concerned, the PIII's is 6.2 times faster than the considered XPP, the results are very promising. Note that no benchmark was specially rewritten to exploit the XPP architecture more efficiently (*e.g.*, partitioning of arrays among the internal memories) and thus some results could be further improved. Also note that there are other advantages to use the XPP instead of a microprocessor (*e.g.*, power consumption reduction).

Each benchmark was compiled in less than 6 seconds, including placement and routing. This shows that it is possible, when targeting the XPP platform, to have compilation runtimes comparable to the ones achieved by software compilation, and to still accomplish efficient implementations.

In order to show the capabilities of *loop dissevering*, Table 3 presents the results obtained with `dct`, `bpic`, and `life`. The technique was applied in order to allow mapping to a smaller array. With *loop dissevering*, the implementations needed 34-56% fewer PEs. Additionally, `dct` and `life` have not exhibited significant differences in the execution time. However, `bpic` needed over twice the number of clock cycles. This performance reduction is related to the configuration overhead, when the computation time on configurations called several times is short. Such configuration overhead could almost be neglected on architectures with several on-chip configuration planes.

6 Related Work

We now compare briefly our high-level compilation and temporal partitioning approach with closely related work.

Compilation: High-level compilation for reconfigurable logic has been the focus of many researchers since the first attempts [8]. Most of this work targets

Table 1. Properties of the benchmarks used.

Benchmark	Source	#loC	#loops / #arrays	primary data size	description
dct	in-house	90	8/4	512×512	8×8 block 2-D DCT (based on matrix multiplications) traversing an image
fir	in-house	18	2/3	10,000	1D FIR filter with 32 taps
bpic	COSYMA	151	8/5	512×512	binary pattern image coding algorithm
edge_det	UTDSP	188	16/6	512×512	edge detector with smooth (3×3) and using vertical and horizontal 2-D convolutions
life	Rawbench	118	10/2	8×8	Conway's Game of Life (4 iterations)
fdct	TI C62x^{tm} DSP	228	3/3	512×512	8×8 block 2-D FDCT with rounding (pointer-free version)
median	MIT Bitwise	96	4/6	10,000	median filter (5×9)

Table 2. Results obtained with XPP-VC.

Benchmark	loop unrolling (#loops)	Compilation time (sec)	#Part	#PEs	#Max	computation (#ccs)	total (#ccs)	Speedup
dct	yes (2)	2.2	1	240	26	11,239,424	11,252,333	2.9
fir	yes (1)	0.9	1	132	67	11,942	16,853	40.0
bpic	yes (3)	3.4	1	237	12	945,984	1,047,733	2.8
edge_det	yes (2)	5.6	5	54/225	12	3,536,384	3,541,818	9.3
fdct	no	1.8	2	150/299	14	1,231,872	1,240,078	12.7
median	yes (3)	1.3	2	201/231	44	22,906	28,090	98.0

Table 3. Results using *loop dissevering.*

	w/o loop dissevering			w/ loop dissevering			Ratio	
Benchmark	#Part	#PEs	total (#ccs)	#Part	#PEs	total (#ccs)	PEs	ccs
dct (16 8×8 blocks)	1	123	148,215	5	54/132	152,182	0.44	1.02
bpic (16×16 image)	1	148	13,752	5	97/189	32,737	0.66	2.38
life	4	185/317	124,286	8	102/325	113,698	0.55	0.92

fine-grain devices (*e.g.*, FPGAs) which require logic synthesis and/or module generators. In addition, fine-grain architectures also need very time consuming backend phases (mapping and place and route) and iterative refinements over the entire compilation flow. Even when pre-placed and pre-routed components are used, the compilation time is still in the order of minutes or hours. Since XPP is a coarse-grained architecture, which directly supports arithmetic and other operations occurring in high-level languages, complex synthesis and mapping phases are not needed. XPP-VC uses the *pipeline vectorization* method presented in [7], while other compilers such as Garp-C [9] and Napa-C [10] are based on software pipelining techniques. The control structure generation, based on the event handling mechanisms of the XPP, is completely new. Those structures are also directly mapped to XPP resources handling events.

Temporal Partitioning: Temporal partitioning at the behavioral level has already been successfully conducted on FPGAs [11]. The temporal partitioning algorithm used in the XPP-VC compiler is based on some ideas presented in [12]. *Loop dissevering*, a new method for partitioning loops, is proposed in this paper. Previous approaches, which target FPGAs, consider a type of *loop distribution* for loops not fitting in the available resources [11]. Thus, large loops which could not be distributed could not be compiled. Our method is always applicable and can handle programs with unlimited complexity, provided only the supported C subset is used.

7 Conclusions and Future Work

We have described the new Vectorizing C Compiler XPP-VC which maps programs in a C subset to PACT's XPP architecture. Assisted with a fast place and route tool, it provides a complete "push-button" path from algorithms to XPP configuration binaries with short compilation times. Speedup factors of upto 98 for a 150MHz XPP core over a 933MHz PIII have been achieved, using this compiler. It integrates both temporal partitioning and a new loop partitioning mechanism, which allows to map large programs containing hundreds of lines of code. Since the XPP includes a configuration manager, programs are compiled to a single, self-contained XPP binary file that can be executed without assistance of an external host processor, even when several configurations are used. Our evaluation showed that XPP reconfiguration is fast enough to make runtime reconfiguration worthwhile if medium-size data sets are processed between reconfigurations. Work on the XPP architecture to accelerate reconfiguration even more is being carried out.

Ongoing work on the XPP-VC focuses on optimizing the compilation, on removing the current restrictions for pipelining loops, and on supporting other loop transformations. We are also researching a temporal partitioning algorithm which will consider the overlapping of fetch, configure, and compute stages as well as configuration prefetching techniques to minimize the overall execution time.

References

1. R. Hartenstein, "A Decade of Reconfigurable Computing: a Visionary Retrospective," In *Proc. Design, Automation and Test in Europe*, 2001, pp. 642-649.
2. PACT Informationstechnologie GmbH, Germany, "The XPP White Paper," Release 2.0, June 2001. http://www.pactcorp.com
3. V. Baumgarte, et al., "PACT XPP - A Self-reconfigurable Data Processing Architecture," In *Journal of Supercomputing*, Kluwer Academic Publishers, (to appear).
4. D. C. Cronquist, P. Franklin, C. Fisher, M. Figueroa, C. Ebeling, "Architecture Design of Reconfigurable Pipelined Datapaths," In *20th Anniversary Conference on Advanced Research in VLSI*, Atlanta, GA, USA, March 1999, pp. 23-40.
5. SUIF Compiler system, http://suif.stanford.edu
6. Muchnick, S. S., *Advanced Compiler Design and Implementation*, Morgan Kaufmann Publishers, Inc., San Francisco, CA, USA, 1997.

7. M. Weinhardt and W. Luk, "Pipeline Vectorization," In *IEEE Transactions on Computer-Aided Design of Integrated Circuits and Systems*, Feb. 2001, pp. 234-248.
8. Ian Page and Wayne Luk, "Compiling occam into FPGAs," In *FPGAs*, Will Moore and Wayne Luk, editors, Abingdon EEI&CS Books, 1991, pp. 271-283.
9. T. J. Callahan, J. R. Hauser, and J. Wawrzynek, "The Garp architecture and C compiler," In *IEEE Computer*, 33(4), April 2000, pp. 62-69.
10. Maya B. Gokhale, Janice M. Stone, "NAPA C: Compiling for a Hybrid RISC/FPGA Architecture," in *Proc. IEEE 6th Symposium on Field-Programmable Custom Computing Machines*, Napa Valley, CA, USA, April 1998, pp. 126-135.
11. Meenakshi Kaul, Ranga Vemuri, Sriram Govindarajan, Iyad E. Ouaiss, "An Automated Temporal Partitioning and Loop Fission approach for FPGA based reconfigurable synthesis of DSP applications," in *Proc. IEEE/ACM Design Automation Conference*, New Orleans, LA, USA, June 21-25, 1999, pp. 616-622.
12. João M. P. Cardoso, "A Novel Algorithm Combining Temporal Partitioning and Sharing of Functional Units," In *Proc. IEEE 9th Symposium on Field-Programmable Custom Computing Machines*, Rohnert Park, CA, USA, April 30 - May 2, 2001.

Sea Cucumber: A Synthesizing Compiler for FPGAs

Justin L. Tripp, Preston A. Jackson, and Brad L. Hutchings

Brigham Young University, Provo, Utah

Abstract. Sea Cucumber (SC) is a synthesizing compiler for FPGAs that accepts Java class files as input (generated from Java source files) and that generates circuits that exploit the coarse- and fine-grained parallelism available in the input class files. Programmers determine the level of coarse-grained parallelism available by organizing their circuit as a set of inter-communicating, concurrent threads (using standard Java threads) that are implemented by SC as concurrent hardware. SC automatically extracts fine-grained parallelism from the body of each thread by processing the byte codes contained in the input class files and employs conventional compiler optimizations such as data-flow and control-flow graph analysis, dead-code elimination, constant folding, operation simplification, predicated static single assignment, if-conversion, hyperblock formation, etc. The resulting EDIF files can be processed using Xilinx place and route software to produce bitstreams that can be downloaded into FPGAs for execution.

1 Introduction

The principal challenge facing developers of synthesizing compilers for FPGAs that are based on sequential programming languages is the discovery and extraction of sufficient parallelism. FPGA systems typically operate at a clock rate less than 1/10 that of a processor fabricated in the same process. In order to overcome this clock rate penalty, an FPGA circuit must exploit more than *an order of magnitude* more available parallelism than a conventional software compiler. Extracting parallelism from sequential descriptions is already a very difficult problem. Requiring that the compiler automatically extract even more parallelism will only make the problem that much more difficult.

SC takes a pragmatic approach to the problem of extracting parallelism. SC requires that programmers expose coarse-grained parallelism by organizing their application as standard Java threads that intercommunicate using provided library functions. SC then analyzes the body of each thread and uses a variety of compiler and circuit optimization techniques to extract fine-grained parallelism. Experience has shown that programmers can do a reasonable job of manually organizing software as relatively coarse units that operate in parallel[1]. In addition, there is a great body of work that deals with automated discovery and exploitation of fine-grained parallelism in the compiler literature[2]. It is believed that by combining these two approaches (programmer-exposure of coarse-grained

M. Glesner, P. Zipf, and M. Renovell (Eds.): FPL 2002, LNCS 2438, pp. 875–885, 2002.

parallelism and automated discovery of fine-grained parallelism), SC can produce FPGA circuitry that exploits much more available parallelism.

SC is a work in progress and this paper gives a brief overview of its current status, including an overview of the programming model, presentation of analysis techniques for extracting fine-grained parallelism, and suggestions for future work.

2 Related Work

Compiling from Java byte codes is not new. Past efforts, including GALADRIEL and NENYA[3] and a previous BYU effort[4], compile using byte-codes as their input. Collectively, these efforts indicate the advantages of using byte codes. The advantages include, among others, the lack of writing and maintaining a parser, access to standard compiler and debugging tools, and access to a wide range of available byte-code analysis and modification tools.

SC significantly differs from these projects in various ways. First, unlike GALADRIEL, SC directly generates EDIF files as output. GALADRIEL generates VHDL as output and thus requires the use of an additional synthesis tool to generate EDIF files. It should be noted that because SC performs only limited circuit optimizations, the ultimate quality of circuits could be lower with SC than with a mature synthesis tool. We feel that this discrepancy is assuaged by the ease of working with SC as a single integrated tool. Working with two separate synthesis tools forces the user to be conversant in both to debug problems. Second, unlike the earlier work at BYU, SC programs can be verified by compiling the Java files with the standard Java compiler and executing the class-files in the standard Java Virtual Machine. This feature eliminates the need for circuit simulation to verify behavior as used in the earlier BYU effort.

Snider et al. [5] were the first to articulate the general idea of using a general-purpose language to describe programmer-exposed coarse parallelism and automatic discovery of fine-grained parallelism to an FPGA audience. SC has adopted this coarse/fine approach along with the use of predicated static single assignment (PSSA)[6] and other compiler optimizations described by Snider et al. However, their coarse-level parallel programming model uses a custom approach based on C++ and inheritance whereas SC adopts the standard Java thread model and augments it with a communication model based on Communicating Sequential Processes (CSP)[7]. In addition, SC uses hyperblocks and if-conversion optimizations that are not discussed by Snider et al. and provides ways to control the bit-width of variables in Java.

The Garp project[8] applies some of the techniques and data structures found in VLIW compiler research to FPGA synthesis. In particular, Garp isolates a critical path in a code segment and synthesizes it to a reconfigurable co-processor. SC uses many of the same techniques and data structures but differs from Garp in the extent to which they are used. SC extends the critical-path synthesis performed in Garp to entire system synthesis with multiple paths and multiple parallel threads.

3 Programming Model

The general programming model used by SC is based on Java. Users write circuit descriptions in Java, exposing coarse-level parallelism as concurrent threads that communicate via protocols that are based on CSP. The hardware and software implementations of the communicating functions are provided by SC. Bit-precision of variables is specified by the programmer using a BitWidth package that is also provided as a part of SC. SC also performs bit-precision analysis following the specification to eliminate unnecessary precision of intermediate signals. Finally, programmers verify the behavior of their application by compiling their Java source and executing and debugging it using standard Java Virtual Machines (JVM) and debuggers—no simulation is necessary. Once satisfied with the behavior, the programmer invokes the SC compiler on the relevant class file to generate an EDIF netlist and further invokes Xilinx place and route software to create a bitstream from the synthesized EDIF netlist. SC supports standard Java class-files; however, there are some restrictions. Use of the `new` operator, object references, static native Java calls (e.g. `System.out.println()`), string manipulation, and exception handling are restricted in the current version of SC.

Java was chosen to be the source programming language for SC because it is popular, portable, widely available, and a generally more productive programming environment when compared to C or C++. SC designs can be compiled, debugged, and simulated with standard tools that are freely available on the internet. Also, unlike C/C++, threads are a part of the language specification making it easier to exploit a programmer base that already understands the Java threading model.

As discussed above, Java threads are used by the programmer to express coarse-level parallelism. Typically, in software, threads give the illusion of concurrency for programming expediency, or limited concurrency if multiple processors are available. However, when compiled by SC, each thread is implemented using dedicated hardware thereby guaranteeing full concurrency. In order to facilitate thread hardware synthesis, it was necessary to create an inter-thread communication scheme that eliminates shared memory access, by limiting all communication to a specified channel. This scheme is based on CSP.

CSP was chosen for inter-thread communcation because it provides a programmable, well-behaved model for communication. Handel-C[9], and SystemC[10] are other tools that provide CSP as a communication model. Hoare's CSP[7] provides a theoretical basis for consistent and provable behavior. The provided CSP channels simplify communication and free the programmer to concentrate on the design and behavior of threads.

As described in [11], channels connect two threads and manage the communication of data between them. A channel is unbuffered, one-way, and self-synchronizing. Communication in both directions between two threads requires two channels. Both sending and receiving threads must be ready before code execution will continue in either thread. Since the threads synchronize around the channel communication, it is the responsibility of the programmer to avoid deadlock.

BitWidth is a library of variable precision functions for exactly specifying and simulating the width in bits of integer and floating-point values and operations in Java. BitWidth provides function calls which indicate the sizes of variables in the Java source code. The functions calls become markers in the classfile after the Java source is compiled. After compilation, BitWidth processes the classfile and produces a new classfile in which the operations on the variables have been replaced with bit-corrected versions. The BitWidth produced version can be executed to test the behavior of the code with the correct variable bit-width. The bit-width markers are used during synthesis to determine the size of registers and wires.[1]

4 Sea Cucumber Compilation and Synthesis Process

SC synthesizes from Java class files into EDIF. Figure 1 outlines the different steps involved in SC. The basic steps are as follows: pre-processing, byte-code analysis, extracting fine-grain parallelism, compiler optimizations, and net-list generation.

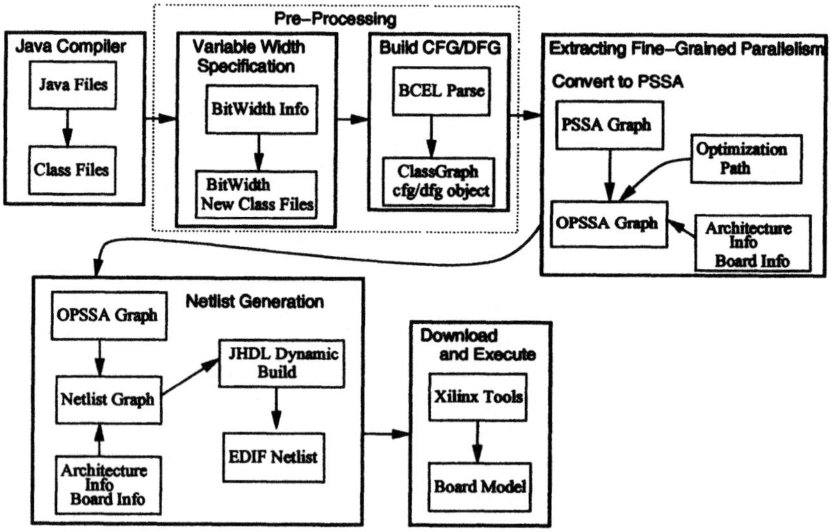

Fig. 1. Overview of Sea Cucumber

4.1 Preprocessing

Preprocessing involves two steps: bit-width analysis to obtain the bitwidth behavior as described in section 3, and class-file stitching which determines the relationship of different class files.

[1] Due to a re-write of the interface layer to the byte code parser, SeaCucumber does not currently use BitWith information. BitWidth can be used for bit-correct simulation, but a static data structure is used to communicate the sizes of variables.

In this stage of SC, bit-width analysis locates the bit-width markers in the byte code and records them for use in netlisting and optimization. The bit-width markers are found by parsing the byte-code, locating the function call signatures, and parsing the inputs to the function calls. If the byte code has not been updated with the BitWidth package, then the natural Java variable size is used. (e.g. a `byte` is eight bits, an `int` is thirty-two bits, etc.)

The class-file stitcher reads the input class file and parses the byte code of the `main()` method in order to determine the structure of the SC design. The constructors of the different channels and threads are located and the inputs to the constructors are determined. This information is passed back to SC, so that all of the threads can have their byte-code parsed and the channels can be connected properly.

```
if (a < b) {
  c = d + e;
} else {
  if (a < 0) {
    c = d - e;
  } else {
    c = c * 2;
  }
}
```

(a) Code

```
if (a_1 < b_1) {
  c_2 = d_1 + e_1;
} else {
  if (a_1 < 0) {
    c_3 = d_1 - e_1;
  } else {
    c_4 = c_1 * 2;
  }
}
c_6 =  φ(c_2, c_3, c_4)
```

(b) SSA

Fig. 2. Example Code and SSA Converstion

4.2 Byte-Code Analysis

SC dissassembles the Java class files in order to perform control-flow and data-flow analysis using the same static analysis and emulation of Java byte code as is done in [4]. The result is a control-flow graph (CFG) which contains vertices called basic blocks. A basic block is a sequence of straight-line code that has a single entry point at the beginning and a single exit point at the end[2]. Each basic block contains a data-flow graph, which is a directed-acyclic graph representing the operations and data dependencies of that basic block. The CFG and DFGs are further modified to expose greater parallelism.

As part of the DFG generation, all references to variables are uniquely numbered using Static Single Assignment (SSA). In SSA, each variable can only be assigned once. Each new assignment to a variable creates a unique variable name. As can be seen in figure 2(b), the first assignment to variable c is called c_2, the second assignment c_3, and so on. Operations in this format can be scheduled as soon as their real data dependencies have been met.

Once the DFGs and CFGs are formed, the DFGs are traversed in order to form ordered lists of operations. The traversal is accomplished by recursively visiting every vertex in the DFG, determining its type and creating a corresponding operation in the list. DFGs for channel communication recieve special handling, since the hardware has already been laid out by hand. An example of an operation graph is in figure 3(b).

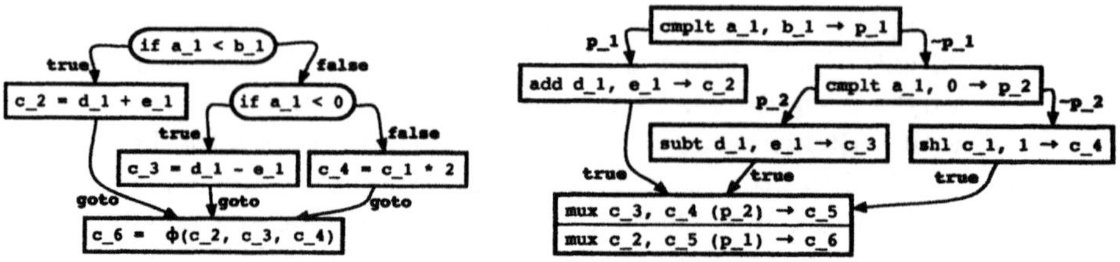

(a) CFG (b) Operation lists

Fig. 3. Creation of the DFG and CFG

4.3 Extracting Fine-Grained Parallelism

SC uses the hyperblock to maximize fine-grained parallelism. A hyperblock, described in [12], is an extended basic-block of instructions which has one input path but may have any number of output paths. To form hyperblocks, SC uses instruction predicates[6] and if-conversion[13]. An instruction predicate is a field which indicates whether or not an instruction should be executed. If-conversion is the process of forming these predicates from if-statements and edges in the CFG. It allows instructions which fall into parallel if- and else-blocks to be executed in parallel. After execution, the results of both paths are multiplexed together and the correct result is selected using the instruction predicate.

The goal of hyperblock formation is to combine as many instructions together as possible. Having a large number of instructions in each hyperblock enables greater fine-grained parallelism and optimization. In practice, however, the amount of exploitable parallelism is ultimately limited by the amount of available hardware. For example, in VLIW processors, the number of functional units determines how many operations can proceed in parallel. The size of the hyperblock must be limited using heuristic algorithms based on execution profiles. In contrast, SC assumes that infinite hardware resources are available and forms hyperblocks of maximum size, thus ensuring a greater degree of parallelism.

In order to form hyperblocks, all of the operations[2] in the graph must be predicated. Before if-conversion, each vertex in the CFG contains a list of unpredicated operations extracted from the DFG. These vertices are connected by edges which represent branches in the control-flow. Each edge is labeled with the boolean expression which indicates when the branch is taken. For example, in figure 3(b) the labels on the edges are derived from the results of the compare operations, p_1 indicates that the branch taken when the first instruction evaluates to `true`. Likewise, ~p_1 indicates the branch taken when the first operation is `false`. SC forms predicates for the operations using these edge expressions

[2] In SC, we use the term *operation* instead of *instruction* because each operation is explicitly built in hardware.

during if-conversion. When if-conversion is complete, the information stored on each forward edge in the CFG is also stored in each operation's predicate.

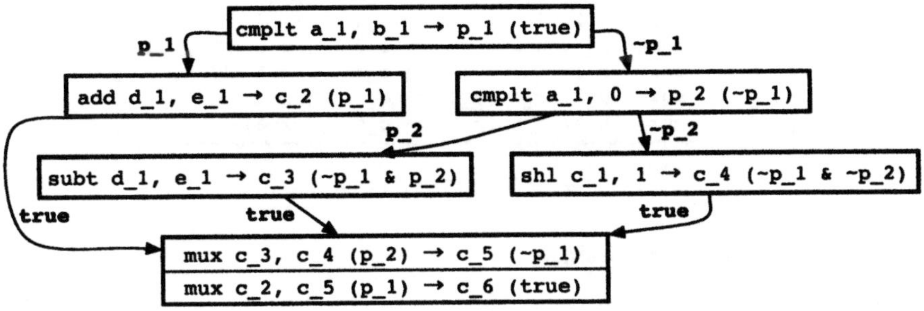

Fig. 4. Predicated Operations

If-conversion was originally written to exploit parallelism for vector processors. In SC, it is used to form operation predicates. During if-conversion, each edge in the graph is tagged as a forward or backward edge. A forward edge represents a branch to a later section of code and a backward edge represents a branch to an earlier section of code. The edge labels are used to form predicates in all of the operations which follow it in the graph. The edge label is added to each operation predicate across multiple basic-blocks until a backward edge is found. In figure 4 the `shl` instruction has a predicate of `(~p_1 & ~p_2)`. This predicate means that this instruction follows the ~p_1 and ~p_2 branches in the graph. Terminating at backward edges prevents the endless application of predicates around a loop in the CFG. An example of added predicates can be seen in figure 4. Each operation contains the value indicating when its result is valid.

Once the edge expressions of each forward edge are retained in the operation predicates, SC forms hyperblocks by removing the forward edges. There are two ways to merge basic-blocks into hyperblocks. First, if a basic-block has two children, representing two alternative execution paths, they can be merged together into a single hyper-block. This type of merging is called a parallel-merge. Second, when two blocks fall in a single execution path, they can be merged using serial-merging. When the merging is complete the forward edges have been removed and the basic-blocks are replaced with hyperblocks. The difference can be seen between figure 4 and figure 5. In figure 5 all of the forward branches have been removed and the instructions all reside in a single hyperblock.

After merging basic blocks, each new merged block will contain multiple operator lists that must also be merged. This merging step is complicated by input and output considerations. Consider outputs – when merging two lists in parallel, the outputs of both lists must be unique. If not, then a `mux` operator must be added to select the correct value from the two outputs. When merging two lists serially, similar problems arise. For example, if the second list reads a variable from the first list, the first output becomes a local variable to the new merged list. Also, inputs common to both lists must read from the same variable and outputs must be unique.

cycle	operation		predicate
0	cmplt a_1, b_1	→ p_1	(true)
0	add d_1, e_1	→ c_2	(p_1)
0	cmplt a_1, 0	→ p_2	(~p_1)
0	subt d_1, e_1	→ c_3	(~p_1 AND p_2)
0	shl c_1, 1	→ c_4	(~p_1 AND ~p_2)
1	mux c_3, c_4 (p_2)	→ c_5	(~p_1)
2	mux c_2, c_5 (p_1)	→ c_6	(true)

Fig. 5. Hyperblock

4.4 Compiler Optimizations

Sea Cucumber uses compiler optimizations to simplify the code before it is synthesized. As in [5] optimizations are performed at different levels of abstraction. In the compiler, optimizations occur at the operation level, the hyper-block level and the at the graph level.

Optimizations at the operation level examine only a single operation. Operation simplification and constant folding can be performed at this level. Typically the Java compiler will take care of constant math operations, but these operations can be created as side-effects of the SC programming style or other optimizations. Operation simplification converts an operation to one that is simpler to implement for the given platform. Examples of such optimizations are additive and multiplicative identities, multiplying or dividing by 2^i, and multiply or shifting by zero.

Hyper-block optimizations consider an entire hyper-block and examples of these optimizations are the dead-code removal, and scheduling. Dead-code occurs for several different reasons: side-effects of optimization, hyper-block formation, channel communication and array formation. Through the optimization process, dead-code is located and the predicate of those operations will be set to `false`. These invalid operations are removed from the hyperblock, but this must be done iteratively in order to remove all operations that contributed to the removed operation. The removal of this dead-code can result in an empty hyperblock. The empty hyperblock is removed from the graph and the control flow is updated appropriately.

Scheduling is one of the last optimizations to be performed. Scheduling is required for circuit generation and state-machine creation. Currently, SC schedules operations by dependence. As soon as the inputs to an operation are made available, the operation will be scheduled. The scheduler calculates the cycle in which a given operation must be executed (see figure 5). With this information a state-machine for the given thread can be created. The state machine controls flow of execution in the hyperblock and is used to determine which and when outputs of operations will be written to registers.

4.5 Net-List Generation and Bit-Stream Synthesis

Net-list generation is the process by which the SC intermediate form, a CFG with PSSA operations, is converted into a generic circuit object. PSSA operations in a hyper-block lend themselves to direct synthesis into the netlist. State machines are generated by examining the operations and creating the circuitry necessary. CSP channels are implemented with custom-built circuits. SC produces an EDIF netlist which can be used as the input to bitstream synthesis tools.

State machines are used in SC to determine the flow of execution between hyperblocks, and control when variable registers are updated. In a thread, only one hyperblock is active. The active hyperblock is responsible for calculating which succeeding hyperblock should be activated next. The state machine generator examines the exit edges of a hyperblock and correlates the conditions of exit from the predicates found in that hyperblock. For example, if all future operations are predicated `A` and the exit edge is predicated `~A`, then the state machine generator will know that in the cycle where `A` is calculated, the future hyperblock at the end of the `~A` edge can be sent a start signal. If the exit edge points to the same hyperblock from which it came (a loop), the hyperblock will return to its initial state.

After the state machine has been generated, SC generates data-path elements using the hyperblock's operation list. Each operation contains an operator, a list of operands, and a predicate. All operators are directly synthesized using module generators or logical operations. The operation's operands represent wires in the netlist. Because these operand names are generated in PSSA form, each wire has a unique name. This transformation can be seen in figure 6.

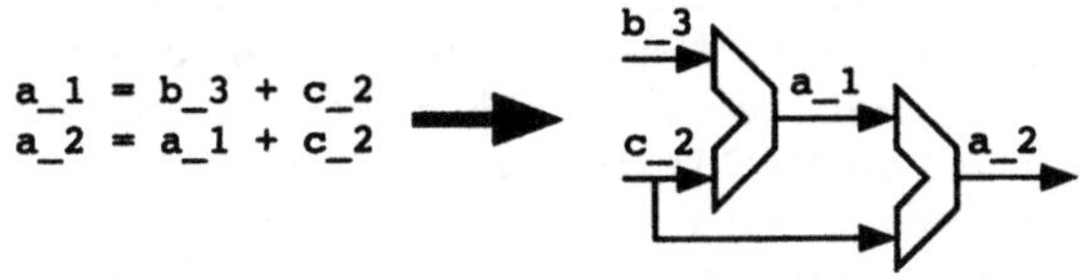

Fig. 6. Synthesis of hyperblock operations

The operation predicates are synthesized using boolean logic gates. The output of these gates is used in two cases. First, when a result of a computation must be saved for use in other hyperblocks, the output acts as the enable line to the storage register. Second, the output is used by the state machine to control the next-state transitions and early-exits of the hyperblock.

The CSP channels synthesize to hardware in a straightforward fashion. On each side of the channel a write and read operation blocks until its complementary operation is ready. This behavior is implemented easily using simple waiting state machines on both sides of the channel. The channel circuitry is simply an interface to which both threads can connect to transfer data. When both operations are ready and the data has been transfered, the state machines release control of the thread and execution proceeds.

In the SC project, we do not tackle the problem of generating a configuration file for the FPGA, rather we break the tool chain and the user must run the platform specific configuration-file generation tools. SC produces an EDIF netlist which can be processed using manufacturer-provided place and route software to produce bitstreams that can be downloaded into FPGAs for execution. Once this side step in the tool chain has been completed the design is ready to run in hardware.

5 Closing Remarks

Sea Cucumber brings a novel programming model to FPGA synthesis. Using standard Java threads to expose coarse-grained parallelism and VLIW techniques to increase fine-grained parallelism, SC provides a paradigm to exploit large amounts of parallelism. Different from some other tools, programming and simulating a design happens in the same environment.

SC is a work in progress. It currently produces simulatable JHDL designs and can netlist EDIF. We are working on the seamless support for a Virtex II board so that designs can be downloaded to hardware. Future work will explore the impact of programming and synthesizing other communication models and determining which optimizations bring the greatest levels of parallelism.

References

[1] M. P. I. Forum, "MPI: A message-passing interface standard," Tech. Rep. UT-CS-94-230, 1994.

[2] S. S. Munchnick, *Advanced Compiler Design and implementation.* San Fransisco, California, USA: Morgan Kaufmann Publishers, Inc., third ed., 1997.

[3] J. M. P. Cardoso and H. C. Neto, "Macro-based hardware compilation of java bytecodes into a dynamic reconf igurable computing system," in *Proceedings of the IEEE Workshop on FPGAs for Custom Computing M achines* (K. L. Pocek and J. M. Arnold, eds.), (Napa, CA), p. n/a, IEEE, 1999.

[4] M. J. Wirthlin, B. L. Hutchings, and C. Worth, "Synthesizing rtl hardware from java byte codes," in *Field Programmable Logic and Applications: 11th International Conference proceedings / FPL 2001*, pp. 1–10, Springer-Verlag, 2001.

[5] G. Snider, B. Shackleford, and R. J. Carter, "Attacking the semantic gap between application programming languages and configurable hardware," in *FPGA 2001*, (Monterey, CA), pp. 115–124, ACM, ACM, February 2001.

[6] L. Carter, B. Simon, B. Calder, L. Carter, and J. Ferrante, "Predicated static single assignment," in *IEEE PACT*, pp. 245–255, 1999.

[7] C. A. R. Hoare, *Communicating Sequential Processes.* London, UK: Prentice-Hall, 1985.

[8] T. Callahan and J. Wawrzynek, "Adapting software pipelining for reconfigurable computing," in *Proceedings of the International Conference on Compilers, Architecture, and Synthesis for Embedded Systems (CASES)*, (San Jose, CA), ACM, 2000.

[9] Celoxica, *Handel-C Language Reference Manual.* Celoxica Limited, 2001.

[10] S. Swan, D. Vermeersch, D. Dumlugöl, P. Hardee, T. Hasegawa, A. Rose, M. Coppolla, M. Janssen, T. Grötker, A. Ghosh, and K. Kranen, *Functional Specification for SystemC 2.0.* Open SystemC Initiative, 2.0-p ed., October 2001.

[11] G. Hilderink, J. Broenink, W. Vervoort, and A. Bakkers, "Communicating Java Threads," in *Parallel Programming and Java, Proceedings of WoTUG 20* (A. Bakkers, ed.), vol. 50, (University of Twente, Netherlands), pp. 48–76, IOS Press, Netherlands, 1997.

[12] S. A. Mahlke, D. C. Lin, W. Y. Chen, R. E. Hank, and R. A. Bringmann, "Effective compiler support for predicated execution using the hyperblock," in *25th Annual International Symposium on Microarchitecture*, 1992.
[13] J. R. Allen, K. Kennedy, C. Porterfield, and J. D. Warren, "Conversion of control dependence to data dependence," in *Symposium on Principles of Programming Languages*, pp. 177–189, 1983.

Practical Considerations in the Synthesis of High Performance Digital Filters for Implementation on FPGAs

J.E. Carletta and M.D. Rayman*
Department of Electrical and Computer Engineering
The University of Akron, Akron, OH USA
{carlett@uakron.edu, mdrayman@ieee.org}

Abstract. The quality of a hardware implementation of a digital filter should be measured in terms of both hardware measures such as hardware cost, throughput and latency, and quality of performance measures such as the degree to which the implemented filter's frequency response matches a stated ideal. Here, practical considerations for the implementation of high performance digital filters on field programmable gate arrays are outlined, and the effect of design and implementation decisions on both hardware and quality of performance measures are considered. A synthesis system for high performance digital filters is described. Results show that the synthesized filters are slightly smaller than and have twice the throughput of comparable filters synthesized with Altera's *FIR Compiler Megacore Function.*

1.0 Introduction

A finite impulse response (FIR) filter computes $y[n] = \sum_{k=0}^{n-1} h[k]x[n-k]$. High performance FIR filters are key to many applications, including satellite communications, image compression, and signal denoising. This work describes an architecture for automatically synthesized multiplierless FIR filters. It describes practical considerations related to filter coefficient quantization and intermediate signal bit width that must be made when implementing the architecture on a field programmable gate array (FPGA).

Two traditional forms for FIR filters, *transposed* and *direct*, are shown in Figure 1. While the two architectures are functionally equivalent, the direct form has an advantage from a hardware performance perspective, in that its adders, shown as a cascade in the figure, can be reorganized into a tree structure. We use a variation on the direct form, shown in Figure 2, that uses two well-known techniques to improve performance. The first is to replace the filter coefficients $h[k]$ in the weighted sum with val-

*. J.E. Carletta was supported in part by a Summer Faculty Fellowship at the National Aeronautics and Space Administration (NASA) Glenn Research Center. M.D. Rayman was supported by an Ohio Aerospace Institute Space Grant Consortium Graduate Fellowship.

M. Glesner, P. Zipf, and M. Renovell (Eds.): FPL 2002, LNCS 2438, pp. 886-896, 2002.

ues that can be represented as sums or differences of powers of two, called *SPT coefficients*. For example, we may have that 0.46875 = 0.5 - 0.03125. This allows multiplications to be replaced with faster shifts and additions. We often constrain the filter

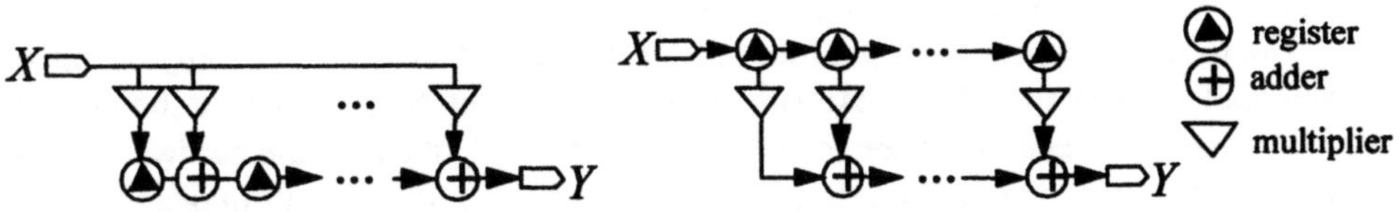

Figure 1. Finite impulse response filter forms

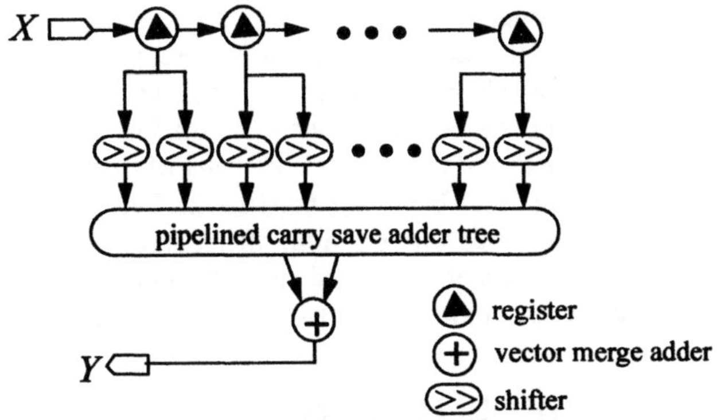

Figure 2. High performance version of direct form

coefficients to those values that can be written as a sum or difference of limited number of power-of-two terms to limit the number of additions required, and hence exercise indirect control over the size of the hardware. We will elaborate on the trade-off in Section 2.0.

The second technique is the use of *carry save addition* for large pipelined adder trees. Carry save addition propagates two separate partial results, rather than one complete sum. Thus, each carry save adder (CSA) takes three data words in, and produces two words at the output (denoted a *sum* word and a *carry* word). By splitting the sum and carry information into two separate words to be dealt with independently, the carry save adder has the highly desirable property that its delay is simply the delay of a full adder, independent of the bit width of the signals being added. Carry save addition is ideal for FPGA applications using Xilinx or Altera parts because the pipelined CSA element maps extremely well to the logic cells on the chip. In the pipelined tree, the largest combinational delay is that of the CSA element, only one full adder or one logic cell deep. In designing the tree, there is a trade-off between the bit-widths of internal (intermediate) signals (and therefore hardware cost) and the quality of the resulting filter's frequency response; this is detailed in Section 3.0.

The only part of the system that has a combinational delay longer than that of a single full adder is the vector merge addition that must be done at the base of the carry save adder tree. This adder sums the two outputs of the tree to produce the final result. Because the vector merge adder is only a small part of the system, it is relatively easy to parallelize it so that it does not become the performance bottleneck. For this work, a bank of ripple carry adders, working in round robin fashion, was used. The details of the adder bank are presented in Section 4.0.

The resulting architecture produces a new output at each clock, and enjoys a high throughput due to its small critical path. The latency of the architecture, or the number of clock cycles of delay between the point at which an input enters the hardware to the point at which the first result using that input appears at the output, depends on the depth of the pipelined carry save adder tree. This depth grows logarithmically with the total number of sums of powers of two in all of the filter coefficients. For high order filters, with many coefficients, the combinational logic paths are the same as for low order filters; this means that high order filters are also capable of achieving high throughput. (As filters get larger, they are more difficult to route, so throughput will go down somewhat as routing delay along critical paths increases.) The main penalties to pay for higher order filters are simply longer latency, and a larger hardware cost.

The main novelty of this design lies in the combination of SPT coefficients and carry save addition with the use of the round-robin bank of ripple carry adders to prevent the vector merge adder from being the bottleneck. Other researchers have proposed FIR filter synthesis methods with full multipliers, based on multiply-accumulate units [3][9]; our uses SPT coefficients to avoid multiplication entirely. Others, like [4], use SPT coefficients, but with a more traditional vector merge addition technique.

2.0 Quantization of SPT Coefficients

The architecture used in this work achieves its high throughput by replacing multiplications with shifts and adds. To do so, the filter coefficients must first be approximated as sums and differences of powers-of-two. One design decision involves the number of non-zero powers-of-two (here, called *SPT terms*) to be used in approximating the coefficients. Each SPT term will require an input to the carry save adder tree. The more SPT terms that are used, the lower the error in the approximation, and so the higher the quality of the frequency response of the filter, but the greater the size and latency of the resulting hardware. The number of SPT terms does not directly affect the throughput of the filter.

A number of researchers have developed optimization methods for choosing the SPT terms, given an ideal set of (real) filter coefficients and a criteria for the quality of the result; see [6] and [2], for example. The optimization method used should be chosen based on the performance metrics most important to the target application, whether that be overall adherence to an ideal frequency response as measured by absolute maximum difference in magnitude of frequency response, or matching frequency response in a particular frequency band (such as maximizing flatness in the pass band, or minimizing peak ripple in the stop band). Because the coefficient optimization technique is not the main focus of this work, we illustrate concepts using a simple iterative greedy approach, starting with zero terms, and at each iteration allocating an additional SPT term to the approximated coefficient that is farthest from its ideal value. Any other optimization technique is compatible with the architecture and could be easily substituted; our goal is simply to illustrate the trade-off between hardware cost and quality of frequency response. We use as an example the low pass analysis filter for the biorthogonal 4.4 wavelet [8]. The filter has eight bits of input, and is symmetric, with nine coefficients as shown in Table 1. The table also shows an approximation for the coefficients that uses a total of eighteen SPT terms, along with the number of terms for each coefficient.

Table 1. Filter coefficients for the example filter

coefficient	ideal value	*T*=18 approx.	#SPT terms
h[0], h[8]	0.026748757411	0.027343750	2
h[1], h[7]	-0.016864118443	-0.015625000	1
h[2], h[6]	-0.078223266529	-0.078125000	2
h[3], h[5]	0.266864118443	0.265625000	2
h[4]	0.602949018236	0.601562500	4

Our experimental setup starts with a set of ideal, real filter coefficients. A Matlab script finds the SPT approximations for the filter coefficients, given the desired total number of SPT terms, *T*. Given the SPT coefficients from Matlab, filter synthesis software, written in C, generates a synthesizable VHDL description of the filter. The Altera Max+plusII version 10.1 software package is used for logic synthesis, placement and routing on an EPF10K20TC144-3 Altera FPGA, a member of the Flex10K family. The filter designs are verified by comparing the output of a Max+plusII simulation of the implemented filter with the expected output from Matlab. The Max+plusII software is used to analyze critical path delays, and to determine hardware size, measured here in terms of number of Altera logic cells. For this experiment, we carefully synthesize the filter with enough precision on intermediate signals so that no bits of information are ever lost; this allows us to separate the effects of coefficient quantization from other implementation issues.

Figure 3 illustrates the change in the frequency response characteristics of the filter as a function of *T*, the number of SPT terms used in implementation. It shows the magnitude of the frequency response on a linear scale. Because care is taken to keep the filter symmetric throughout the coefficient approximation process, all filters exhibit identical linear phase. As can be seen, frequency response of the implementations grows closer to ideal as *T* increases. For *T*=18, which uses an average of two SPT terms for each filter coefficient, frequency response can not be distinguished from the ideal case on the figure.

Table 2 shows relative hardware and performance metrics for the three systems. From the results, we see that *T*, the number of SPT terms, is a good predictor of the resulting hardware area; the number of logic cells is very close to a linear function of *T*. We also note that the achieved throughput varies only slightly from filter to filter. This is because all the filters, regardless of size, have the same combinational logic along the critical paths; any difference comes from differences in routing delay. Note

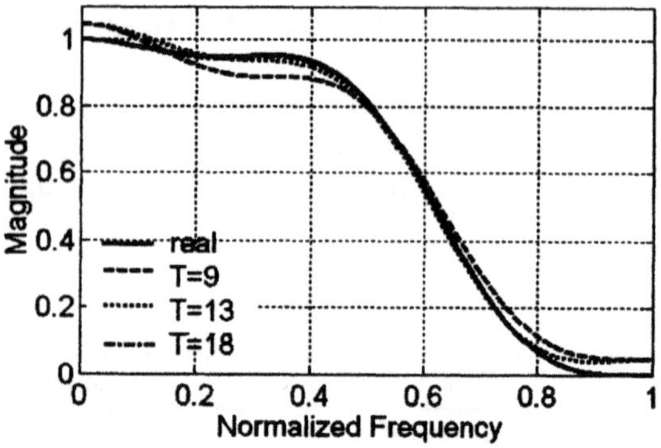

Figure 3. Frequency response for 9-tap filter implementations with various values of *T*, the number of SPT terms used

that the maximum absolute deviation from ideal frequency response is the maximum absolute difference between the ideal and implemented filters in magnitude of frequency response for 512 points spread evenly around the unit circle, and is one measure commonly used to quantify how well a hardware filter implements an ideal filter.

Table 2. Hardware and quality metrics for the three implementations of the example nine-tap filter with varying values for the number of SPT terms *T*

	T=18	T=13	T=9
area (in logic cells)	729	585	462
latency (in clock cycles)	12	12	11
throughput (in Mresults/sec)	119.04	113.63	116.27
max. abs. deviation from ideal frequency response	0.00628	0.04688	0.06443
maximum zero displacement	0.03189	0.61647	0.65244

3.0 Precision of Intermediate Values

When we are designing a digital filter for implementation on a FPGA, we have full control over the bit widths of each signal in the system. This degree of freedom gives us an additional degree of control over the trade-off that exists between the amount of hardware required and the quality of the frequency response of the filter.

In the previous section, the fixed point formats of all intermediate signals were specified so as to achieve the same precision that we would get if we used floating point hardware; this was accomplished by specifying a format for each intermediate computation large enough to handle the full range of values possible at that point, with no overflow or round-off. For the nine-tap (T=18) wavelet filter, this meant that the signals grew from a width of eight bits at the input to a total of twenty-one bits at the output. In what follows, we refer to this as a "full precision" system. The least significant of the full twenty-one bits play only a small role in the eight-bit result, and we may leave some of them out to save hardware. Of course, doing so will affect frequency response of the filter, as truncation occurs in intermediate signal values.

For our filter synthesis system, the goal was to allow exploration of the design trade-off between signal bit width and frequency response by providing a mechanism for handling intermediate signals of varying bit width in a practical way. We did so by writing our adder descriptions in VHDL so that they are capable of adding together data inputs of *arbitrary* fixed point format. Within the adder, the inputs are sign-extended and zero-padded as necessary prior to addition. Here, a fixed point format of (n, f) means that the data input has a total of n bits, with the least significant bit in the 2^f's place. Once the adders are defined in this way, it is easy to constrain the fixed point formats of intermediate signals while synthesizing the filter.

We devised an experiment to illustrate the effect of the precision of intermediate signals on the quality of the implemented filter. We start with the T=18 set of sums-of-power-of-two (SPT) filter coefficients that were used in the last section. This filter, implemented in floating point math, is taken as our "ideal" case; we compare to the T=18 filter, rather than to the original wavelet filter with real coefficients, so that we can separate out just the effects due to precision of intermediate signals, without effects due to coefficient quantization. We then use our filter synthesis software to generate several synthesizable VHDL descriptions of the filter. Each differs in the maximum number of integer and fraction bits allowed in representing intermediate signals. Here, we specify enough integer bits to avoid overflow, so that only errors due to truncation of intermediate signals at the least significant end affect the result. As before, we synthesize for an EPF10K20TC144-3 Altera FPGA. We obtain frequency response data for the implemented filters by generating an input stream of high frequency content (using the 'chirp' function in Matlab to sweep frequency linearly), passing that stream through the filter in a Max+plusII simulation, and porting the resulting output stream back to Matlab for frequency analysis and direct comparison to the ideal, full precision case.

Figure 4 and Table 3 summarize the results of the experiment. Figure 4 shows the magnitude on a linear scale and phase in degrees of the frequency responses of the implemented filters. The figure shows that magnitude and phase both deteriorate as we use fewer bits to represent intermediate signals. Table 3 shows the area, latency, and throughput of the hardware. Latency, which depends only on the number of SPT terms used for the coefficients, does not change here. Throughput, which is affected primarily by differences in routing delay, is also not much changed. Table 3 also shows the maximum absolute difference in magnitude of frequency response between the filter and an ideal T=18 filter implemented with floating point math, and the biggest absolute error in the output for the chirp input stream, which should be put into context by noting that the ideal output for that input stream lies in the range [-127, +136]. Figure 5 plots filter implementation quality, in terms of how well a filter implementation's frequency response magnitude matches an ideal value, versus filter implementation area, in terms of number of logic cells. The resulting plot is the classical shape for area/performance trade-off curves. Which point on the curve is the best depends, of course, on the application.

We note that the exact results of an experiment of this sort will vary with the organization of the carry save adder tree. It is possible to organize the additions so as to minimize the total number of full adders [7]. To do so, rearrange the inputs of a level of the tree so that each carry save adder adds data inputs that are as similar in format as possible. This reduces the need for zero padding and sign extension, and the overall bit width of each carry save adder. However, the hardware saved comes at the expense of additional routing delay, as the signals going from one level of the tree to the next are permuted. Because routing delay is a significant portion of overall delay in an FPGA-based implementation, we did not attempt to use this technique here.

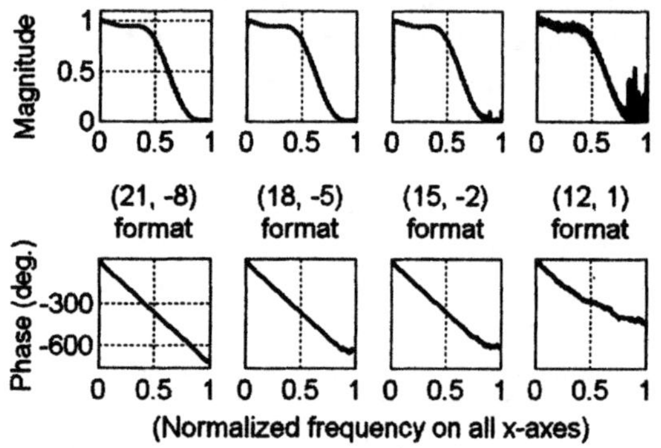

Figure 4. Frequency response for implementations of the example nine-tap (T=18) filter with varying maximum formats

Table 3. Hardware and quality metrics for implementations of the example nine-tap (T=18) filter with varying maximum formats

max. format	(21, -8)	(18, -5)	(15,-2)	(12,1)
area (in logic cells)	729	650	517	366
latency (in clock cycles)	12	12	12	12
throughput (in Mresults/sec)	119.04	112.35	125.00	125.00
max. abs. dev. from ideal (full precision) freq. response	0	0.0137	0.1092	0.5333
max. output error	0	0.1328	1.9453	18.051

4.0 Implementation Issues

In actually implementing a designed digital filter on a field programmable gate array, care must be taken to achieve the highest possible throughput. In particular, the following can become performance bottlenecks.if they are not carefully considered: the vector merge adder producing the final result; the control signal generation; and the

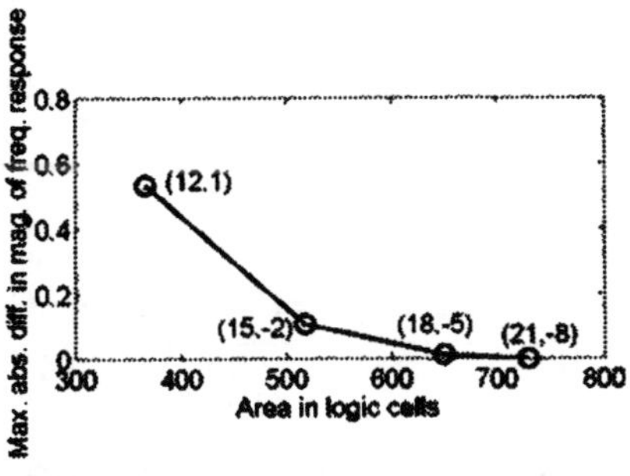

Figure 5. The area/performance trade-off for intermediate signal bit width

placement of the controller. We address these three considerations in the next three subsections, showing how to successfully implement the design.

4.1 The Vector Merge Adder

The vector merge adder at the base of the carry save adder tree is a traditional adder responsible for calculating the final filter output, and is the only part of the system that has combinational delay longer than that of a single full adder. A key point is that while the natural choice in a VLSI system would be implement the vector merge adder with a sophisticated addition technique such as carry look-ahead addition and square root carry select addition [5] to improve delay, it makes no sense to use anything other than simple ripple carry addition in an FPGA implementation. The reason is that FPGAs have special purpose routing for carry chains. This routing goes directly from one logic cell to its neighbor, without the high capacitive loading inherent in the more general purpose routing. Non-ripple carry adders are unable to fully exploit the carry chains and so suffer from significantly more routing delay. As a result, the more sophisticated addition techniques actually have a longer critical path when implemented on an FPGA. Figure 6 shows worst case combinational delay as a function of bit width for a ripple carry and carry look ahead adder (with four-bit carry look ahead sections, rippled together) implemented on an Altera EPF10K30C356-3 device and synthesized using MAX+PlusII ver. 9.6 software. Clearly, the ripple carry adder is the better choice.

To keep the vector merge adder from being the bottleneck for the entire system in terms of critical path delay, we implement it as a bank of ripple carry adders operating in parallel, round-robin style. If there are b adders in the bank, each ripple carry adder gets a new result to add every bth clock, and has b clock periods in which to complete a computation. At every clock, a b-to-1 multiplexer at the output of the bank switches to pass the most recently completed addition result through to the filter output. When the multiplexer is larger than two-to-one, it is pipelined to avoid becoming the critical path. We make the number of adders in the bank large enough so that the bank is no longer the performance bottleneck for the system. For our wavelet filter example, we

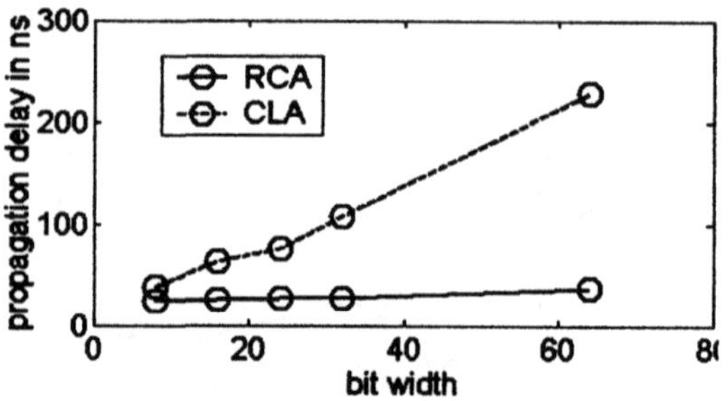

Figure 6. Delay of FPGA implementations of ripple carry (RCA) and carry look ahead (CLA) adders

found that the ripple carry adder needed for the vector merge adder had a delay of 15.2 ns, whereas the worst carry save adder in the rest of the system had a delay of 8.4 ns. As a result, two bank adders were used.

Even with a bank of adders operating in parallel, and a fully pipelined output multiplexer, careful synthesis must be done in order to keep the adder bank from forming the critical path of the system. Some pertinent issues are described next.

4.2 Use of One-Hot Distributed Control

The only significant control required for the filter is for the parallelized bank of adders that form the vector merge adder. A *b*-phase enable signal is required; enable*b* is used as a load signal for the input and output registers around the *b*th adder. On an Altera FPGA, the most straightforward way to implement the load signal for the register is to take advantage of the enable pins available in the D flip-flops within the logic cells. The enable*b* signal is also used as a select signal for a multiplexer used to switch the filter output to connect to each of the bank adder outputs in turn.

To generate the *b*-phase enable signal, we use a *b*-bit circular shift register, seeded upon reset to hold a single "1". While other schemes are possible, one-hot control helps us preserve the fast clock period of the architecture. Because the enable signals travel farther through the routing than the inherently local data signals, they already have significantly long routing delays. Any kind of logic cell delay on the enable signal paths would push the delay of those paths high enough to form critical paths for the system. Implementing the one-hot control successfully, using only flip-flops for the circular shift with no intervening logic, required disabling one of Max+plusII's default logic synthesis options (specifically, "not gate pushback") for the controller logic.

Functionally, a single *b*-bit circular shift register is sufficient to generate the one-hot enable signals for the entire adder bank. However, we found that in practice that routing a single set of enable signals throughout the adder bank resulted in unacceptably high routing delay. The solution for this problem is to *distribute* the control throughout the adder bank. Each register in the adder bank (and each part of the pipelined output multiplexer) has its own *b*-bit, one-hot controller. Because each copy of the controller can be placed directly next to the unit that it is controlling, the routing delay along the enable signal paths is significantly less.

5.0 Results

We compare our synthesized filters to ones generated by Altera's commercially available *FIR Compiler Megacore Function* [1]. For the comparison, we implemented filters with full precision results. In the *FIR Compiler*, we chose to use a parallel architecture with full pipelining; that combination, the fastest available, gives a filter that produces one result per clock, and so corresponds most closely to ours. We did two versions of the *FIR Compiler*-generated filter. One used the original real-valued coefficients for the nine-tap wavelet filter, converted to fixed point values with sixteen bits of precision; the other used the (T=18) sums-of-powers-of-two (SPT) coefficients used in our implementation. Because the FIR Compiler can not take advantage of SPT coefficients in producing the filter hardware, the two versions of the *FIR Compiler*-generated filter are not significantly different in terms of area or throughput.

Table 4 shows the results of the comparison. Our synthesis and architecture results in about twice the throughput of the commercially-generated filters. For our choice of using eighteen SPT terms in the coefficients, our filter is also about ten percent smaller; however, the area comparison is not a completely fair one, because the area of our filter depends on the degree to which the user wants the filter's frequency response to match some ideal. However, it is fair to say that our architecture allows a higher degree of control over the area/quality of frequency response trade-off, because approximating the coefficients more roughly makes for a direct savings in the number of logic cells, as the number of inputs to the carry save adder tree falls. With a non-SPT coefficient design, control over the trade-off is more indirect, and involves only how many bits of precision are used in the array multipliers that do the coefficient multiplication.

Table 4. Comparison to FIR filters synthesized by commercial tool

	Altera (original coeffs)	*Altera* (T=18)	*ours* (T=18)
area (in logic cells)	819	817	729
latency (in clock cycles)	11	11	12
throughput (in Mresults/sec)	60.24	61.34	119.04

6.0 Conclusions

Issues involving the design of high performance digital filters for implementation on FPGAs are discussed, and a synthesis tool is presented. The work shows that a carefully implemented filter using sums-of-powers-of-two coefficients to replace multiplication with shifts and adds can operate at about twice the speed of traditional filter architectures that employ multipliers. The architecture and synthesis scheme also allow a more direct trade-off between area and filter quality than traditional architectures.

References

1. Altera Corporation, *FIR Compiler Megacore Function User Guide*, www.altera.com, 1999.
2. Cho, N.-I. and S.U. Lee, "Optimal Design of Finite Precision FIR Filters Using Linear Programming with Reduced Constraints," *IEEE Trans. on Signal Processing*, Vol. 46, No. 1, Jan. 1998, pp. 195-199.
3. Chou, C.-J., S. Mohanakrishnan, and J.B. Evans, "FPGA Implementation of Digital Filters," *Proc. 4th Int'l. Conf. on Signal Processing Applications and Technology*, 1993.
4. Evans, J.B., "Efficient FIR Filter Architectures Suitable for FPGA Implementation," *IEEE Trans. Circuits & Systems*, July 1994.
5. Flynn, M.J. and S.F. Oberman, *Advanced Computer Arithmetic Design*, John Wiley & Sons, 2001.
6. Lim, C.-L., Yang, R., Li, D., and J. Song, "Signed Power-of-Two Term Allocation Scheme for the Design of Digital Filters," *IEEE Trans. on Circuits and Systems - II: Analog and Dig. Sig. Proc.*, Vol. 46, No.5, May 1999, pp. 577 - 584.
7. Mehendale, M., Sherlekar, S.D., and G. Venkatesh, "Synthesis of Multiplier-less FIR Filters with Minimum Number of Additions," *IEEE/ACM Intl. Conf. on Computer-Aided Design*, 1995, pp. 668-671.
8. Strang, G. and T. Nguyen, *Wavelets and Filter Banks*, Wellesley-Cambridge Press, 1997.
9. Woods, R., S. Ludwig, J. Heron, D. Trainor, and S. Gehring, "FPGA Synthesis on the XC6200 using IRIS and Trianus/Hades", *Proc. of the 5th IEEE Symposium on FPGA-based Custom Computing Machines*, 1997, pp. 155-164.

Low Power High Speed Algebraic Integer Frequency Sampling Filters Using FPLDs

U. Meyer-Baese[1], J. Ramírez[1,2], and A. García[2]

[1] Department of Electrical and Computer Engineering, Florida State University, 2525 Pottsdamer St., Tallahassee, Florida 32310-6046.
Uwe.Meyer-Baese@ieee.org

[2] Dept. of Electronics and Computer Technology, University of Granada, 18071 Granada, Spain
{jramirez, agarcia}@ditec.ugr.es

Abstract. Algebraic integers have been proven beneficial to DFT, DCT, and non-recursive FIR filter designs since algebraic integers can be dense in $\mathbb{C}$, resulting in short-word-width, low power, and high-speed designs. This paper uses another property of algebraic integers; namely, algebraic integers can produce exact pole zero cancellation pairs that are used in recursive complex FIR, frequency sampling filter designs. Design synthesis results for Xilinx and Altera FPLDs are provided.

1 Introduction

Driven by increased level of integration and higher device speed, power dissipation has become a crucial design constraint. A power-aware design improves battery life, reduces packaging and cooling costs and results in a higher reliability. Power in CMOS devices usually is modeled by switching power, short-circuit, and DC leakage power dissipation. Short-circuit and leakage can become dominant in deep sub-micron devices or if the ramp time is long. High speed design typically are dominated by switching power and are a function of capacitance, voltage, clock rate, active gate count, and switching activity. Historically, semiconductor improvement in capacitance and supply voltage scaling has been the most adopted approach to power optimization. On system level the primary optimization of high speed DSP and communication designs is a reduction in gate count preserving a high throughput. This impact on a DSP filter design using algebraic integers is studied in this paper.

2 Algebraic Integer Processing

An element of $\mathbb{C}$ is an algebraic integer if it is a zero of a monic polynomial in $F[x]$ where F is one of the fields $\mathbb{Z}$, $\mathbb{Z}_M$, or $\mathbb{Z}_p$. M is taken to be composite, and p is assumed to be prime. If R is a commutative ring with unity, and $p(x)$ is an irreducible polynomial in $R[x]$, then the quotient ring $R[x]/\langle p(x)\rangle$ is a field.

M. Glesner, P. Zipf, and M. Renovell (Eds.): FPL 2002, LNCS 2438, pp. 897–904, 2002.

Therefore, in such a field for non-zero N, N^{-1} exists. For frequency sampling filters (FSFs), if $p(x)$ is monic, then the ring properties of $\mathbb{Z}_M/\langle p(x)\rangle$ are sufficient to support the developed purpose in the paper. Specially, $p(x)$ will be selected so that algebraic integers can be used to describe the complex plane. In this context, it should be noted that if $p(x) = x^N - 1$, then $\mathbb{Z}_M[x]/\langle x^N - 1\rangle \cong \mathbb{Z}_M[W_N]$, where $W_N = e^{j2\pi/N}$. The quotient ring $\mathbb{Z}_M[x]/\langle x^N - 1\rangle$ is cyclic and has order N. Addition of polynomials $A(x), B(x) \in \mathbb{Z}_M[x]/\langle x^N - 1\rangle$ is given by $A(x) + B(x) = \sum_{k=0}^{N-1}(a_k + b_k)\, x^k$ and multiplication is given by

$$A(x) \cdot B(x) = \sum_{k=0}^{N-1}\left(\sum_{l=0}^{N-1} a_l b_{\langle k-l\rangle_N}\right) x^k \tag{1}$$

where $\langle\cdot\rangle_m$ is a modular reduction of $\cdot$ modulo m. Addition of polynomials in the field $\mathbb{Z}_M[x]/\langle x^N - 1\rangle$ is the usual component-wise addition operation. However, the multiplication of polynomials given above is recognized as cyclic convolution. An interesting property of the multiplication given above is that if $B(x) = x^l$, the product is simply a cyclic rotation of the coefficients of $A(x)$.

2.1 Implementation Issues of Algebraic Integer Filters

Not all N components $e_k = W_N^k$ are necessary; most of them are linear combinations of the others. A potential decrease in system complexity has been suggested. Cozzens, Finkelstein, and Games [1, 2] have used algebraic numbers defined over the cyclotomic polynomial $C_N(x)$, (i.e., the quotient ring $\mathbb{Z}_M/\langle C_N(x)\rangle$) to lower the number of vectors from N to $\phi(N)$, where $\phi(N)$ is the Euler totient function. Only those components e_k must be kept that are totative to N, that is, $\gcd(N, k) = 1$. Instead of $x^N - 1$, it is sufficient to use the *cyclotomic polynomial* [3]

$$p(x) = C_N(x) = \prod_{\substack{\gcd(N,k)=1\\ 0<k<N}} x - W_N^k. \tag{2}$$

In frequency sampling filter designs, the aim is to generate as many points N as possible on the unit circle for a fixed $\phi(N)$. A lower bound for $\phi(N)$ is provided by Landau [4]. That the Landau bound is not accurate for small values of N can be seen from Figure 1.

A polynomial defined modulo a cyclotomic polynomial $A(x) \in \mathbb{Z}_M/\langle C_N(x)\rangle$ can now be expressed as $A(x) = a_0 + a_1\cdot x + a_2\cdot x^2 + \ldots + a_{\phi(N)-1}\cdot x_N^{\phi(N)-1}$ with $a_k \in \mathbb{Z}_M$. Addition of two polynomials, $A(x)$ and $B(x)$, in this ring is component-wise and is given by $A(x) + B(x) = \sum_{k=0}^{\phi(N)-1}(u_k + v_k)\, x^k$. The multiplication is a convolution sum of the coefficients modulo the cyclotomic polynomials $C_N(x)$. That is,

$$A(x) \cdot B(x) = (a_0 b_0) + (a_0 b_1 + a_1 b_0)\, x\ + \ldots. \tag{3}$$

The *conversion* from complex numbers to algebraic integers (with $N > 4$) has been investigated [2, 5]. A direct approach (with less accuracy and complexity) for conversion of *real* integers to algebraic integers uses only the first

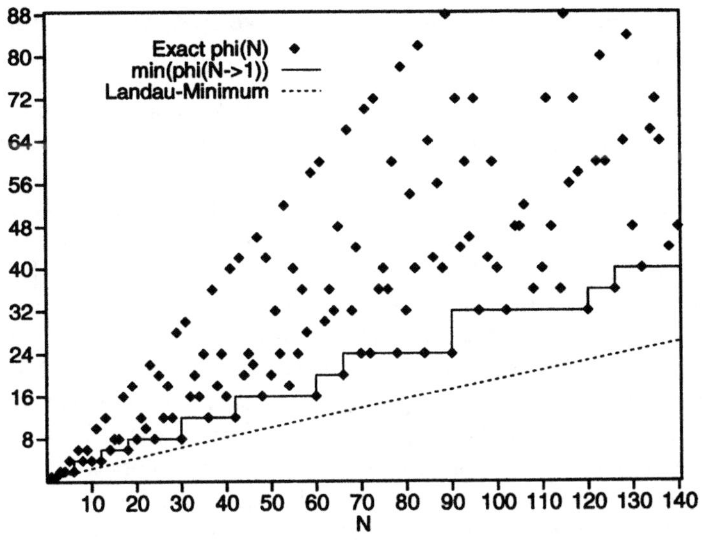

Fig. 1. Order of $C_N(x)$, which is $\phi(N)$ (symbol ♦). Computation of lower bound (solid line) starting with a high N value (1000) and computation of $\phi(N)$ down to $N = 1$. Lower bound approximation by Landau (dashed line).

component, forcing all other components to zero (i.e., $A = (a_0, 0, 0, \ldots)$). Similarly, the *imaginary* part can be assigned to the component $W_N^{N/4}$ if 4 divides N. The conversion from algebraic integers to complex numbers can be efficiently implemented using the CORDIC algorithm [6].

3 Frequency Sampling Filters

A classical FSF consists of a comb filter cascaded with a bank of frequency selective resonators [7, 8]. The resonators independently produce a collection of poles that annihilate the zeros produced by the comb pre-filter. Gain adjustments are applied to the output of the resonators so as to approximately profile the magnitude frequency response of a desired filter. An FSF can also be created by cascading all-pole filter sections with all-zero filter (comb) sections as suggested in Figure 2(a). The delay of the comb section, namely $1 \pm z^{-D}$, is chosen so that its zeros cancel the poles of the all-pole pre-filter. It can be observed that wherever there is a complex pole, there also exists an annihilating complex zero. The filter has pole/zero symmetry on the unit circle which results in linear phase and constant group delay properties. FSFs of this type are known to provide very efficient multi-rate interpolation and decimation solutions and may serve as high decimation rate filters for RF-to-baseband conversion of radio signals [9]. If the filter of Figure 2(a) is realized with a non-recursive FIR, then D (complex) multiplications and $D - 1$ additions are used. In contrast, the recursive design uses only one algebraic multiplication and one subtraction!

3.1 Improvement of Frequency Selective Properties Using Algebraic Integers

To motivate the contribution of the paper, consider again the filter shown in Figure 2(a). It can be argued that first-order filter sections produce poles at angles 0° and 180°. Second-order pole sections with integer coefficients can produce poles at angles 60°, 90°, and 120°, according to the relationship $2\cos(2\pi K/D)$=1, 0, and −1. For sections of higher order, only multi-passband filters can be implemented with integer coefficients as shown by Meyer-Baese et al. [10]. The design algorithm works for filter banks with few channels. This FSF design paradigm produces poor results for filter banks containing fifteen to twenty channels, such as those used in high quality speech processing. The reason is that higher order pole sections generate multiple passbands and the complexity for the mandatory anti-aliasing filter can be greater than that of the FSF section. To meet this challenge, algebraic integers will be introduced to construct *single* passband FSF building blocks. Because algebraic integers can be used to represent N, exact numbers located on the unit circle, cyclotomic polynomials can provide a framework for pole assignment of a single frequency filter having poles on the unit circle.

3.2 Example Designs for Algebraic Integer Processing

Figure2(a) presents a single stage, single passband FSF with algebraic integer processing, having a *single* pole angle of 360°/12 = 30°. Figures 2(b) and 2(c) show two realization options, Figure 2(b) without cyclotomic polynomial reduction (i.e., $p(x) = x^{12} - 1$), and Figure 2(c) uses algebraic integers over the cyclotomic polynomial $C_{12}(x) = x^4 - x^2 + 1$. For the realization found in Figure 2(b), twelve components are used, resulting in twelve comb filter sections. The realization with the cyclotomic polynomial requires one more subtraction for the pole realization, but only four comb filter sections. The complexity reduction through the use of cyclotomic polynomials is obvious.

Neglecting the quantization error from sine and cosine functions, the architectures generate identical impulse responses and eigenfrequency test results. The filter behaves identically to a non-recursive FIR realization. To compare this realization with that previously found by the authors [10], it should be emphasized that the algebraic integer realization has a higher complexity (four times as many comb filter sections), but has a single complex pole and is, therefore, a *single* passband filter. Consequently, this system does *not* need an additional anti-aliasing filter.

4 Multirate Implementation

For interpolation or decimation applications, it is possible to take advantage of flow graph manipulations. Let S be the number of comb sections. A reduction of comb delays by a factor of R can be achieved for Figure 3(a), if $R|D$, by

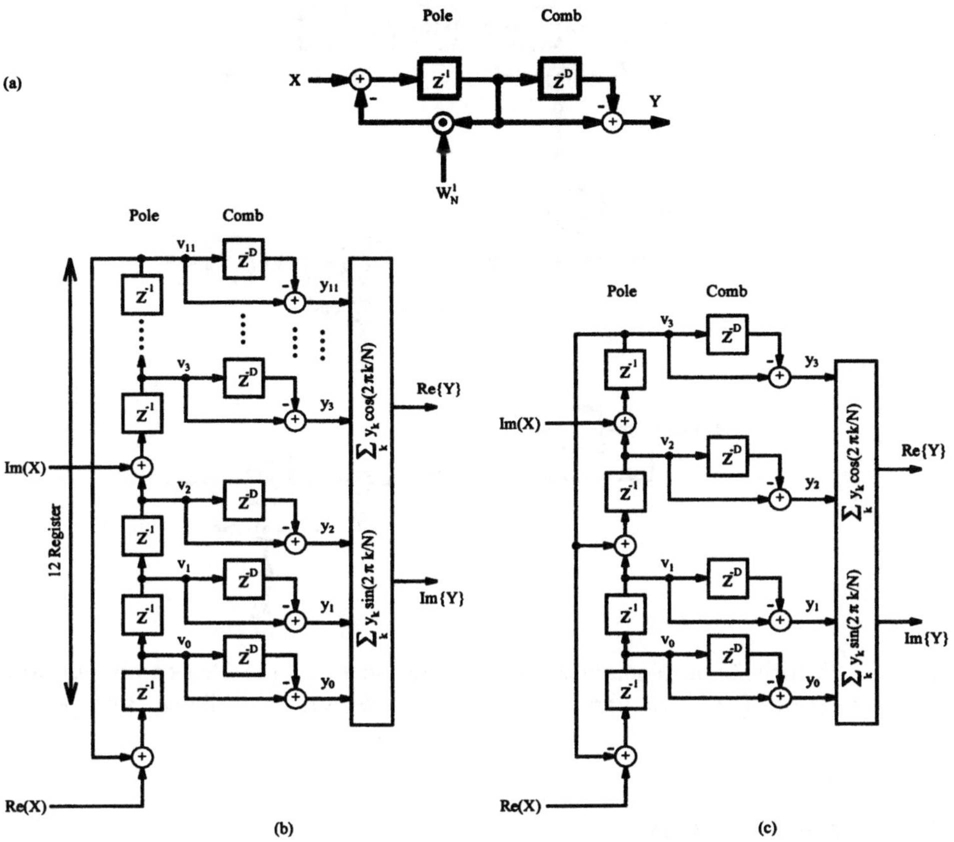

Fig. 2. One stage FSF for $N = 12$ and pole at W_{12}^{1}. (a) One pole FSF filter (shadowing symbolizes the processing in parallel channels for algebraic integers). (b) Without cyclotomic polynomial reduction. (c) Using the cyclotomic polynomial $C_{12}(x)$.

exchanging the down-sampler and the comb sections. For the solution in Figure 3(b), only 2 channels are needed in the algebraic comb sections for the real and imaginary part if $4|N$. Counting only the used register, the effort for the comb section becomes

$$\begin{matrix}\#\text{Reg. in}\\ \text{Fig.3(a)}\end{matrix} = \frac{SD\phi(N)}{R} \gtrless SD2 = \begin{matrix}\#\text{Reg. in}\\ \text{Fig.3(b)}\end{matrix}, \qquad (4)$$

i.e., for $\frac{\phi(N)}{R} < 2$ solution from Figure 3(a) will be advantageous.

For an interpolator design (see Figure 3(c)), the exchange of $\uparrow R$ upsampler and comb sections saves a factor R in delay elements, if $R|D$.

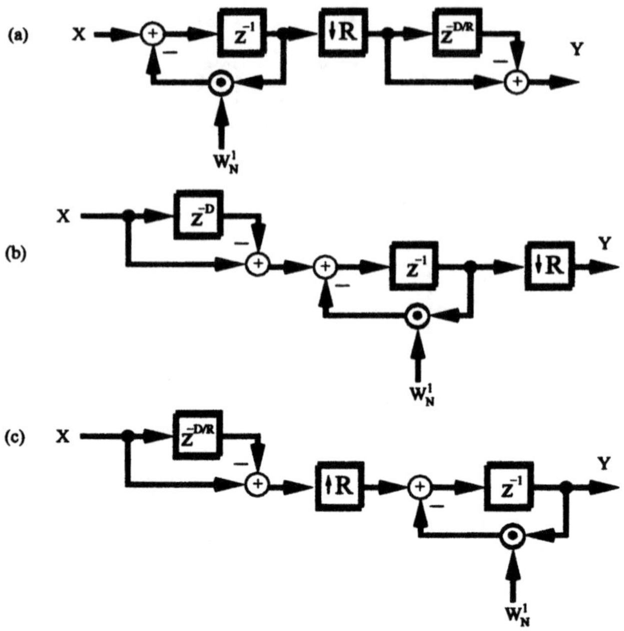

Fig. 3. Multirate implementation of algebraic FSF. (a) Pre comb sampling rate reduction. (b) Two channel comb section design. (c) Efficient interpolator configuration.

5 Design Example

To judge better the presented design paradigm, chip area measurements for Altera and Xilinx FPLDs are provided in the following. Similar to the one stage design shown in Figure 2(c), a multirate bandpass filter with a pole angle at 30° and $\phi(12) = 4$ algebraic integer components has been designed and will be compared with a conventional complex nonrecursive FIR filter in transposed form. The filter length was $L = 36$ and the sampling rate reduction $R = 9$. This results in a comb delay of $D = 4$ and from Equation (4) follows that the multirate configuration shown in Figure 3(a) is preferred. The filters were implemented with 8 bit input/output and internal 16 bit precision to avoid dynamic overflow.

Circuits have been synthesized from their VHDL description and optimized for speed and size with synthesis tools from Altera and Synopsys.

5.1 Altera Synthesis Results

A EPF10K30RC208-3 FPLD device from Altera was selected which has the fast carry arithmetic support typical for the 10K and 20K families and sufficient numbers of logic cells (LCs) such that the device can host the largest design. The designs have been synthesized using Altera's Max+plus II Version 10.0 tools.

Table 1. Altera FPLD synthesis results for multirate FSF with pole at 30° and $L = R \cdot D = 9 \cdot 4 = 36$.

	non-	Algebraic integer	
	recursive	no conversion	with conversion
LCs	1045	409	606
F / MHz	24.63	41.32	35.97

Table 1 shows the FPLD synthesis results for the nonrecursive design and the recursive "algebraic integer" design. One Altera LC consists of two 3 input LUTs and a flip-flops. We notice that the algebraic solution is superior both in terms of chip size (gate count) as well as of registered performance. The effort for the algebraic to complex conversion is measured with 32% for this design and was implemented directly with CSD coefficients.

5.2 Xilinx Synthesis Results

A XC4020XL-09PQ240 FPGA device from Xilinx was selected which has the fast carry arithmetic support typical for the XC4K family and sufficient numbers of configurable logic blocks (CLBs) such that the device can host the largest design. The designs have been compiled using Xilinx Foundation package F2.1i which includes synthesis tool from Synopsys.

Table 2 shows the Xilinx synthesis results for the nonrecursive design and the recursive "algebraic integer" design. One Xilinx CLB consists of two 4 input LUTs, one 3 input LUT, 2 flip-flops, and the Xilinx Foundation Series tool combines these circuits into a single metric called an equivalent "gate count." We notice that the algebraic solution is superior both in terms of chip size (gate count) as well as of registered performance.

Table 2. Xilinx FPGA synthesis results for multirate FSF with pole at 30° and $L = R \cdot D = 9 \cdot 4 = 36$.

	non-	Algebraic integer	
	recursive	no conversion	with conversion
4 input LUTs	1231	106	261
3 input LUTs	3	148	148
Flip-flops	1068	346	399
Gates	22565	3767	5848
F / MHz	14.31	33.58	26.35

The effort for the algebraic to complex conversion is measured with 35% for this design and was implemented directly with CSD coefficients. The effort in percentage will decrease if the filter has more than one stage and can also be reduced with an iterative CORDIC processor design [6], but the iterative algorithm will have a greater latency.

Acknowledgements

The authors would like to thank Altera and Xilinx for their support under the University Programs.

6 Conclusion

The Hogenauer [9] idea of a cascade integrator comb filter was extended to complex bandpass filtering. Using a digital signal processing scheme with algebraic integers provides single passband frequency sampling filter building blocks. These filters are of low complexity and are multiplier free, so that a wide selection of passband frequencies may be implemented without the high cost of anti-aliasing filters as previously proposed [10]. Synthesis results for a typical design example have been compiled and show an improvement in size of 73% for Altera FPLDs and an equivalent "gate count" factor of 3.8 for Xilinx FPGAs compared with the conventional non-recursive design, preserving or improving registered performance.

References

[1] Cozzens, J., Finkelstein, L.: Computing the Discrete Fourier Transform Using Residue Number Systems in a Ring of Algebraic Integers. *IEEE Transactions on Information Theory*, (1985) 580–8

[2] Games, R.: Complex Approximations Using Algebraic Integers. *IEEE Transactions on Information Theory*, (1985) 565–579,

[3] T. Nagell, *Introduction to Number Theory*, Chelsea, 1964.

[4] E. Landau, *Handbuch der Lehre von der Verteilung der Primzahlen*, Vol. 1, Chelsea publishing company, 1953.

[5] Marcellin, M., Fischer, T.: Encoding Algorithms for Complex Approximations in $Z[e^{2\pi i/8}]$. *IEEE Transactions on Information Theory*, April (1989) 1133–6.

[6] Meyer-Baese, U., Meyer-Baese, A., W. Hilberg, W.: **CO**ordinate **R**otation **DI**gital **C**omputer (CORDIC) Synthesis for FPGA. in *Lecture Notes in Computer Science*, Vol. 849. Springer-Verlag, Berlin Heidelberg New York (1994) 397–408.

[7] Meyer-Baese, U.: *Digital Signal Processing with Field Programmable Gate Arrays*, Springer Verlag, Berlin Heidelberg New York (2001)

[8] Meyer-Baese, U., Taylor, F.: Optimal Algebraic Integer Implementation With Application to Complex Frequency Sampling Filters. Transactions on C&S II **48** (2001) 2061–2064

[9] Hogenauer, E. B.: An Economical Class of Digital Filters for Decimation and Interpolation. *IEEE Transactions on Acoustics, Speech and Signal Processing*, Vol. 29. (1981) 155–162

[10] Meyer-Baese, U., Mellott, J., Taylor, F.: Design of RNS Frequency Sampling Filter Banks. in *IEEE International Conference on Acoustics, Speech, and Signal Processing*, Vol. 3. (1997) 2061–2064

High Performance Quadrature Digital Mixers for FPGAs*

Francisco Cardells-Tormo[1] and Javier Valls-Coquillat[2]

[1] R&D Dept., Hewlett-Packard InkJet Commercial Division (ICD)
08190 Sant Cugat del Valles, Barcelona, Spain
fcardell@bpo.hp.com

[2] Department of Electronic Engineering, Polytechnic University of Valencia (UPV),
Camino de Vera s/n, 46022 Valencia, Spain
jvalls@eln.upv.es

Abstract. This paper deals with the optimized implementation of high performance quadrature mixers for transmission. This work examines the most relevant architectures that may be used on FPGAs such as memory compression techniques and the CORDIC algorithm. Each technique is optimized for Virtex FPGAs in terms of area and throughput using relationally placed macros. In order to exploit the high-speed capabilities of these devices we have evaluated several VLSI architectural transforms and arithmetic techniques and we have identified which ones are still successful on FPGAs. We have applied the results of this study to the design of mixers attaining clock rates close to 280 MHz.

1 Introduction

The current trend in software radios is to perform digital signal processing closer and closer to the antenna (digital front-end) [1, 2, 3] thus requiring sampling rates as high as several hundred megasamples per second (MSPS). Reconfigurability is compulsory because of this radio technology being multi-system and multi-standard. At this point FPGAs become the only reconfigurable device that can achieve the required performance.

One of the most critical components in a software radio system are high performance quadrature digital mixers which are required to translate channel frequency from baseband to the intermediate frequency (IF) for transmission. As an example a QPSK modulator for the Digital Video Broadcasting (DVB) standard [4] requires at least a symbol rate of 20.3 MBauds. This means that if the IF frequency is 70 MHz the mixer must run at a clock rate higher than 160.3 MHz. Indeed, the higher the clock rate is the more negligible the effect the frequency response of the D/A converter becomes.

* This work was supported by the Spanish "Ministerio de Ciencia y Tecnologia" under grant number "TIC2001-2688-C03-02" and in part by the "Universitat Politecnica de Valencia" (UPV) under the Research Funding Program. Francisco Cardells-Tormo acknowledges the support of Hewlett-Packard ICD in the preparation of his Ph.D. thesis.

M. Glesner, P. Zipf, and M. Renovell (Eds.): FPL 2002, LNCS 2438, pp. 905–914, 2002.

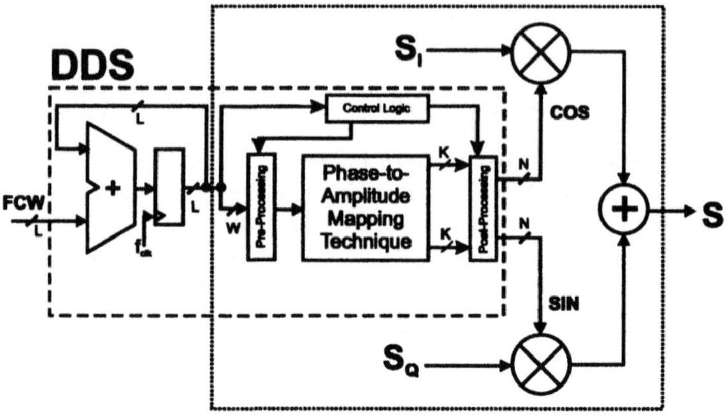

Fig. 1. Building Blocks of a Quadrature Digital Mixer

Conventional quadrature digital mixers (figure 1) consist of two real multipliers and a quadrature direct digital synthesizer (DDS). The carrier frequency is given by the frequency control word (FCW). DDS consist of an accumulator, which generates the phase word, and a phase-to-amplitude converter [5]. If instead of generating a whole period we benefit from quarter-wave symmetry, the DDS must be provided with a pre-processing stage, and a post-processing stage (dashed box in figure 1) in order to mirror and flip the amplitude signal. Several phase-to-amplitude mapping techniques exist in the literature, they are all summarized in [6]. We will focus on memory compression techniques [7, 8]. An alternative method to perform the digital mixing uses the CORDIC algorithm [9, 10]. The CORDIC-based mixer generates the quadrature waveforms and computes the complex-number multiplication at the same time, thus avoiding the extra multipliers used in the conventional case [11]. It therefore replaces the blocks enclosed in the dotted box in figure 1. Finally if the sampling frequency is chosen exactly four times higher than the carrier frequency, a very simple architecture emerges.

In order to get the most out of FPGAs, designs must be conceived having in mind the target technology. As we will later see, designing for FPGA implies forgetting about well established VLSI design practices and learning new rules. Throughout this paper we will have the opportunity to study high performance digital modulators and see the impact of all these new design rules in efficient designs. The FPGA technology we are aiming at is the Xilinx Virtex/E family [12]. The cores presented in this paper have been developed by instantiation of relationally placed macros (RPMs) in our code and we have specified their relative position in the FPGA. This design methodology improves the cores in two ways. On the one hand our cores have a performance which is independent of the degree of area utilization or of their relative position inside the FPGA. On the other hand logic circuitry has already been mapped and placed by us in the FPGA, thus avoiding all the problems associated to automatic placement processes and thus making designs completely independent of the synthesis tool or the HDL coding style. We have used Synplify as synthesis tool and vendor-supplied software for FPGA placement and routing.

The goal of this paper is twofold. On the one hand, we will apply the existing knowledge of FPGA-based DDS for the design of high performance mixers. On the other hand, we will evaluate the impact that VLSI architectural transforms and arithmetic have on speed and area, in order to push the clock rate as high as possible. We will apply our designs to a particular case study: the mixer should send data to a 14-bit D/A converter. Throughout this paper we will design mixers for a transmission system with a carrier frequency of 70 MHz and a bandwidth of 25 MHz per arm. Finally we will compare the different techniques and architectures based on the attained performance.

2 CORDIC-Based Mixers

2.1 Efficient Architectures for FPGAs

The mixer consists of a CORDIC processor and an accumulator. Both building blocks can be implemented with simple arithmetic operators such as hardwired shifters, adders and subtracters, all of them can be pipelined without difficulties. The main advantage is that no multipliers or memories are needed at all. In figure 2, we represent the overall architecture for transmission. There are subtle features in the design of CORDIC processors. In fact there are several CORDIC architectures which could be used to cover the $[-\pi, \pi)$ range [6, 13, 14, 15]. They have been systematically evaluated in [16] for FPGAs in terms of spectral purity, precision, area and speed and it is concluded that the optimum architecture is that based on [15].

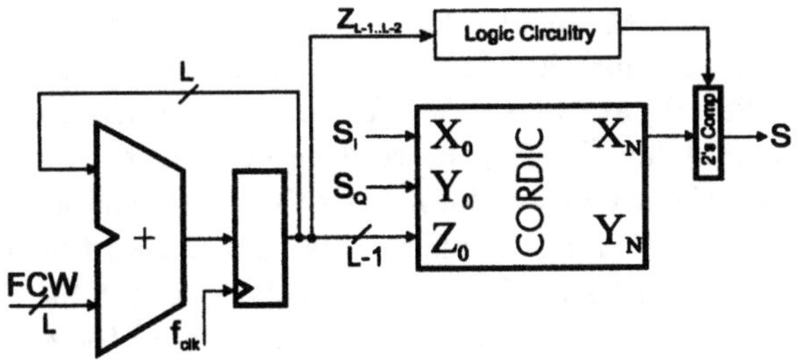

Fig. 2. Mixer based on the CORDIC Algorithm for Transmission

We have designed a generic intellectual property (IP) core for Virtex devices using a bit-parallel, pipelined and unfolded CORDIC-based implementation [17], using the scheme developed in [15] but using RPMs. Besides, we have incorporated design principles for FPGA-based arithmetic processors [18]: replication of the logic associated to driving signals with a very high fan-out. For instance, in order to reduce the high fan-out of the control signal coming from the most significant bit of the Z signal, the Z datapath adder/subtracters have to be redesigned with a two-bit sign extension. At the same time we have reduced the Z datapath wordlength as iterations progress to save area. From our point of view it presents the ideal features to become a general purpose core: it can be easily resized and the same circuit can be used for signal reception, complex mixing or frequency synthesis but for changes in the input signals.

Looking back at our case study, the CORDIC processor must have 15 stages. The inner wordlength for the X and Y datapath becomes 20-bit long and the Z datapath requires a 19-bit wordlength. The implementation results for a XCV400-4 are: maximum frequency 113 MHz, and area 440 slices. The clock frequency is clearly too low for our design specifications. Using a more modern device such as the Virtex-E, the maximum clock speed can be pushed to 200 MHz for the highest speed grade (8).

2.2 Improvements Based on Arithmetic and Architectural Transforms

But for certain applications we might not be happy with this result. There are several advantages in working with the a sampling rate as high as possible. For instance, the higher the sampling frequency is, the less important the impact the frequency response of the D/A converter has on the signal spectrum becomes. On the other hand the maximum clock speed at which a Virtex-E device could work is claimed to be 400 MHz. Yet, we cannot always rely on the release of faster devices. We must focus on improving our design so as to achieve such a high clock rate and benefit from the full potential of our device.

Looking back at our design we realize that the most critical combinational path includes the following: a clock to output delay (Tcko), plus a fan-out delay due to the add-sub signals (net), plus a delay due to the carry chain, and last we must take into account the set-up to clock delay (Tick). Nevertheless, the shortest combinational path in an FPGA is defined by the sum of the following: the clock to output delay (Tcko), the routing delay with a unity fan-out (net), the LUT delay and the set-up to clock delay (Tick). We should apply our efforts towards minimizing the overall value of this sum. According to Xilinx and for our speed grade we could already say that Tcko will not be higher than 0.8 ns and that Tick will not exceed 0.7 ns, which leaves room for another 1 ns coming from routing. We should orient our efforts towards simplifying our logic paths. In this section we will examine the impact that VLSI transformations have on speed and critical path reduction.

Bit-Level Pipelining Having all these ideas in mind, our first thought was to divide the long carry chains of the X and Y datapaths by two, i.e pipeline our adder-subtracters. The throughput could be doubled at the expense of also doubling speed and latency. But Virtex carry chains are already optimized in a way that there is only a slight difference in speed between a 10 and an 20-bit adder/subtracter. In actual fact, the most important delay comes from the dedicated XOR gate that is located at the end of the carry-chain. We had to make a bit-level partition of the operators as we realized that this is the only way to somewhat increase the speed in a noticeable way. By doing this, the carry signal does not have to go through neither the dedicated carry chain nor the dedicated XOR gate thus reducing the combinational delay up to 1ns. But bit-level pipelining has some drawbacks: latency grows dramatically up to 300 clock cycles (20 times 15) and the datapath area is increased by five, although it can be kept that low thanks to a LUT based shift register (SRL16). This macro is only present in Virtex FPGAs, if we had worked with another reconfigurable device we would not have even thought about this technique.

Carry-Save Arithmetic A design based on the use of carry-save adders instead of ripple-carry adders also gets rid of the carry chain. It has the advantage that latency is only doubled, i.e. 30 clock cycles, but area is equivalent to the bit-level pipelined design. After the X and Y carry-save datapath we need a Vector Merging Adder, which this time is a bit-level pipelined adder. Our design is very close to a register-net-LUT-register scheme so it should bring about outstanding clock rates. This scheme is therefore better than the precedent.

We have presented two alternatives for replacing the adder-subtractors in the X, Y datapath of our former design by more efficient arithmetic units. Nevertheless the angle controlpath speed must be increased accordingly. We could first use a bit-level pipelined adder-subtractor with all the disadvantages already mentioned. But this solution is too area hungry for control signals must be registered in order for every full adder to receive the right order, and a reasonable layout becomes impossible. On the other hand carry-save datapaths could be controlled by a carry-save angle control path but at the expense of not knowing the sign in a straightforward way. Redundant versions of the CORDIC algorithm, although outstanding for VLSI, were ruled out for FPGAs in [18]. Instead, control signals should be obtained thanks to some techniques developed in the literature [13, 19] which predict the micro-rotations from the input angle. Let us focus on the latter techniques. We have examined both techniques for our target device. Using [19] micro-rotations can be known in advance and both X and Y datapaths can be directly driven. Our critical path is the minimum path we described above but according to the timing analyzer the maximum clock rate falls to 240 MHz. Arithmetic units are quite large, and there is a huge amount of data lines crossing from one datapath to the other so as to make net delays increase up to 2.5 ns.

When we tried to translate the VLSI design described in [13] to our device, we merged the first 7 stages in a Virtex BRAM but speed fell again to 196 MHz as critical net delays raised to 3.5ns. Neither technique was successful in FPGAs even though they would have clearly been for VLSI. In [12] we found data which casted some light into our work: Virtex devices have typical net delays, for fan-out equal to one, ranging from 1ns to 3.5 ns, which means that the maximum

Architecture	Fmax [MHz]	Latency (rel.)	Area (rel.)
Parallel Processing	280	2x	2x
Bit-level Pipelining RCAs	240	18x	6x
Carry-Save Arithmetic[19]	240	2x	5x
Carry-Save Arithmetic[13]	196	1x	3x
CORDIC Mixer	200	1x	1x

Table 1. Comparison of High-Speed CORDIC-based Mixers. Target Device XCV1000E-8.

sustainable clock rate that can be guaranteed is 196 MHz in a Virtex-E-8 device. Any design going beyond this value should be considered as acceptable. On the other hand, these delays become more critical with long interconnection nets and with crossing paths. So our designs should be kept as compact as possible.

Parallel Processing With all the above ideas in mind we took another route. In this design we re-used our former CORDIC core which had already been optimized. We have parallelized two CORDIC blocks each running at half the maximum clock rate as in figure 3. The input values are registered and shared between the two processing units and the output values are interleaved by a multiplexer creating the output sequence. We have already shown that each processor is able to work at a clock rate well in excess of 200 MHz. In theory this system should run at 400 MHz, but the place and route tool does not predict more than 280 MHz in the high frequency side. This occurs due to the net delays from the output registers to the multiplexer. The inescapable conclusion is that it is impossible to have a sustainable speed of 400 MHz all wide and long the FPGA. In our design, the external oscillator frequency becomes 140 MHz and it is doubled by one of the internal DLLs to 280 MHz. The area is of course doubled, even though frequency is not. Looking at table 1 we see that no other VLSI technique has provided similar results.

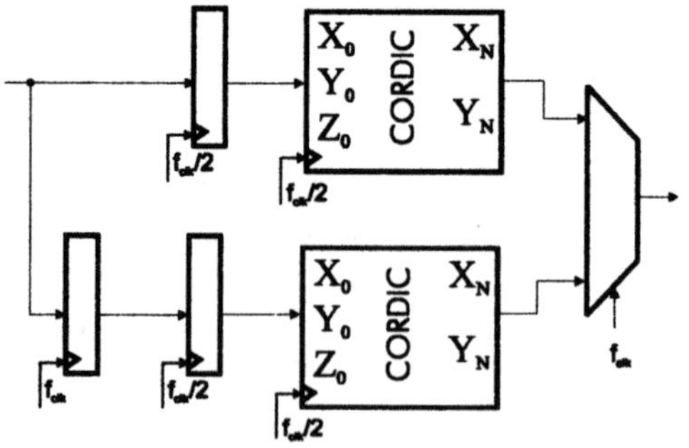

Fig. 3. Mixer based on CORDIC Parallelization

3 Memory-Based Mixers

3.1 Efficient Architectures for FPGAs

We will study the implementation of a mixer following the scheme shown in figure 1 with a DDS based on ROM partitioning techniques. In these section we will independently study the multipliers and the frequency synthesizer. Let us focus on the DDS block. ROM partitioning techniques approximate a goal function by adding the contents of a coarse and a fine ROM instead of addressing a single ROM. Trigonometric approximations, such as [20] and the so-called Nicholas architecture [21], have been presented as a way to reduce the overall storage requirements for DDS. In [16] we gave some design guidelines which differ from those for VLSI designs: instead of using the most complex algorithm, we should use an algorithm which fits into one of the BRAM configurations, even if this implies using the simplest compression algorithm.

Multiplier Style	Frequency [MHz]	Latency [Clock cycles]
Pipelined Tree (ours)	124.7 (8.017ns)	4 (32.07 ns)
Pipelined Array (ours)	130.0 (7.692ns)	14 (107.69 ns)
Pipelined Tree [22]	123.4 (8.106ns)	4 (32.42 ns)

Table 2. Comparison of Two's Complement Multiplier Implementations on FPGA using RPMs. Wordlength 14-bit. Device XCV300-4-PQ240

As it has already been described, the mixing operation consists in multiplying the input signal by a sinusoidal signal. We will then deal with the implementation of multipliers. There are several alternatives in VLSI but for FPGA implementations the choice is reduced to two. They are in particular Ripple carry (RC) array multipliers and RC tree multipliers, being the former of the Baugh-Wooley type and the latter requiring sign extension [23, 24, 25]. We should now check if any of all of these multipliers could be run at least at the same speed of the synthesizer. We have studied both schemes, the results are summarized for both fully pipelined and combinational cores in table 2.

Apart from latency, differences between the alternatives presented in table 2 are quite small. In the end the architecture of our choice is the fully pipelined tree multiplier because of its low latency. Each multiplier of this architecture represents an additional cost, in terms of area, of 125 Slices.

For our case study the mixer requires a total area of 358 Slices plus 2 BRAMs. In terms of speed we attain a clock rate of 121 MHz for an XCV400-4 device, which is clearly insufficient. The same design in an XCV400E-8 device runs at 163 MHz. The bottleneck in a DDS based on memory compression techniques is not the multiplier as it might occur in VLSI designs. The critical path consists of the clock to output value in the BRAM (Tbcko), plus the net delay (net) plus the setup-to-clock delay (Tdick). Net delays continue to be the bottleneck for high-speed designs.

3.2 Improvements Based on Architectural Transforms

The maximum clock rate that we obtained in the previous section is too close to the Nyquist frequency, so we must find a way to increase it. As we have already proved in the previous section, we should focus only on parallel processing techniques in order to improve the throughput. When applying this technique to memory-based mixers, we also attain 280 MHz for a Virtex-E device with a speed grade 8 because the bottleneck is again in the high frequency clock domain.

4 Simplified Mixers

For certain conditions the mixer can be simplified in an extraordinary way. For instance, if we go beyond the Nyquist frequency and we make the sampling frequency four times the carrier frequency, the mixer circuit reduces to that in figure 4. Let us now focus on the implementation for our target device. The first solution (A) is to directly map each of the logic elements into the FPGA architecture. We define a block which is the multiplexer and another which is the two's complementor. A first result for a XCV50E-8 is: area 15 Slices and speed 277 MHz. Area can be halved by merging the multiplexer and the two's complementor into a single row of Slices (B). This can be done just by realizing that there are four input signals and that the carry chain is used after this logic. Area is reduced to 7 slices and speed results in 271 MHz.

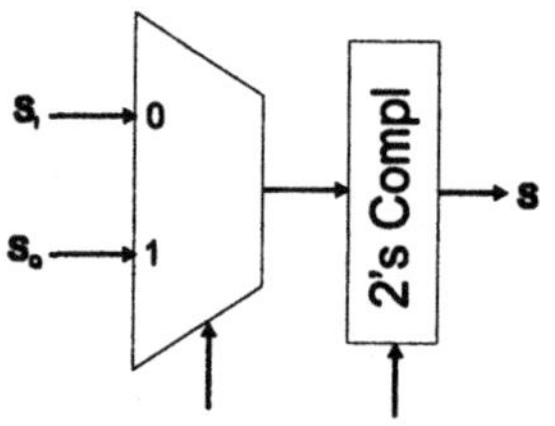

Fig. 4. Simplified Mixer

The Virtex carry chain is fast enough to achieve our goals, but we could still try to avoid it and increase the overall speed of the circuit. We could improve our design and either use an FPGA with a lower speed grade or run at a higher clock rate. We are going to evaluate the impact on area. We reproduce the same work that we carried out before, i.e we pipeline at a bit level the two's complementor. Again thanks to the SLR16 block area is as low as 49 Slices, and speed for a XCV50E-6 we obtain 290 MHz and for a XCV50E-8 340 MHz. By multiplying area in slice by the cost of a single slice for each speed grade we could know which solution is the most interesting in terms of economy. No further architectural transforms are necessary for we already obtain the maximum possible speed, and they will increase area requirements. In order to make direct comparisons, we have summarized in table 3 the main implementation results.

Modulator	Area Slices/BRAMs	Frequency MHz	Applicable Architectural Transform
CORDIC	440/0	200	Parallel processing
Memory Compression	358/2	163	Parallel processing
Simplified ($f_{CLK} = 4 \cdot f_c$)	7/0	271	Bit-level pipelining

Table 3. Modulators in FPGA. Device XCV400E-8

5 Conclusions

We have reviewed all the existing architectures of quadrature mixers for FPGAs. We have focused on the two most successful ones which are based on CORDIC and on memory partitioning techniques. For each technique we could find many architectures in the literature. We have implemented all of them in our target device, the Virtex family, and we have made out the most efficient for this technology. When comparing pipelined modulation cores we see the clear superiority of CORDIC: this core can realize multiple functions, it can be easily stretched to match more demanding applications and it runs at frequencies high enough for communication applications: 200 MHz for an XCV300E-8 device.

Nevertheless, we found necessary to increase the clock rates to a value around 280 MHz. We have incorporated to our design VLSI techniques such as architectural transforms and carry-save arithmetic to realize that most VLSI techniques are not very succesful in FPGAs. The only techniques which leaded to a significant improvement in speed are parallelization and replication of logic blocks. For instance, it was possible to attain 280 MHz for a XCV300E-8 by the means of parallel processing both with memory-based mixers and CORDIC-based mixers.

Finally we have optimized and implemented a simplified mixer. We have realized that if we are able to comply with the carrier frequency/clock rate ratio this architecture presents the best performance in terms of area and throughput.

References

[1] Cummings, M., Haruyama, S.: FPGA in the software radio. IEEE Communications Magazine (1999) 108–112

[2] Hentschel, T., Henker, M., Fettweis, G.: The digital fron-end of software radio terminals. IEEE Personal Communications (1999) 40–46

[3] Dick, C., Harris, F.: Configurable logic for digital communications: Some signal processing perspectives. IEEE Communications Magazine (1999)

[4] E.T.S.I.: Digital Video Broadcasting (DVB). framing structure, channel coding and modulation for 11/12 Ghz satellite services. European Standard EN 300 421 (1997)

[5] Tierney, J., Rader, C.M., Gold, B.: A digital frequency synthesizer. IEEE Transactions on Audio and Electroacoustics **19** (1971) 48–57

[6] Vankka, J.: Methods of mapping from phase to sine amplitude in direct digital synthesis. IEEE Transactions on Ultrasonics, Ferroelectrics, and Frequency Control **44** (1997) 526–534

[7] H. T. Nicholas, I., Samueli, H.: A 150-MHz direct digital frequency synthesizer in 1.25-um CMOS with -90-dBc spurious performance. IEEE Journal of Solid-State Circuits **26** (1991) 1959–1969
[8] Tan, L.K., Samueli, H.: A 200 MHz quadrature digital synthesizer/mixer in 0.8um CMOS. IEEE Journal of Solid-State Circuits **30** (1995) 193–200
[9] Volder, J.E.: The CORDIC trigonometric computing technique. IRE Transactions on Electronics and Computers (1959) 330–334
[10] Walther, J.S.: A unified algorithm for elementary functions. (1971) 379–385
[11] Loehning, M., Hentschel, T., Fettweis, G.: Digital down conversion in software radio terminals. In: 10th European Signal Processing Conference (EUSIPCO).Tampere, Finland. Volume 3. (2000)
[12] Xilinx: The programmable logic data book (2001)
[13] Madisetti, A., Kwentus, A.Y., Willson, Jr., A.N.: A 100-MHz, 16-b, direct digital frequency synthesizer with a 100-dBc spurious-free dynamic range. IEEE Journal of Solid-State Circuits **34** (1999) 1034–1043
[14] Gielis, G.C., van de Plassche, R., van Valburg, J.: A 540-MHz 10-b polar-to-cartesian converter. IEEE Journal of Solid-State Circuits **26** (1991) 1645–1650
[15] Cardells-Tormo, F., Valls-Coquillat, J.: Optimisation of direct digital frequency synthesizer based on CORDIC. IEE Electronics Letters **37** (2001) 1278–1280
[16] Cardells-Tormo, F., Valls-Coquillat, J.: Optimized FPGA-implementation of quadrature DDS. In: IEEE International Symposium on Circuits and Systems. (2002)
[17] Andraka, R.: A survey of CORDIC algorithms for FPGA based computers. In: ACM/SIGDA International Symposium on Field Programmable Gate Arrays. Monterey, CA. (1998) 191–200
[18] Valls, J., Kuhlmann, M., Parhi, K.K.: Evaluation of CORDIC Algorithms for FPGA design. To be published in the Journal of VLSI Signal Processing (2002)
[19] Kuhlmann, M., Parhi, K.K.: A high-speed CORDIC algorithm and architecture for DSP applications. In: IEEE Workshop on Signal Processing Systems (SiPS99). (1999) 732–741
[20] Sunderland, D.A., Strauch, R.A., Wharfield, S.S., Peterson, H.T., Cole, C.R.: CMOS/SOS frequency synthesizer LSI circuit for spread spectrum communications. IEEE Journal of Solid-State Circuits **sc-19** (1984) 497–506
[21] Nicholas, H.T., Samueli, H., Kim, B.: The optimization of direct digital frequency synthesizer performance in the presence of finite word length effects. In: Proceedings 42nd Annual Frequency Control Symposium 1988. (1988) 357–363
[22] Xilinx: Core generator system. (http://www.xilinx.com/products/logicore/-coregen/index.htm)
[23] Chapman, K.: Fast integer multipliers using FPGAs. XCELL Review The Quarterly Journal for Xilinx Programmable Logic Users (1994) 28–31
[24] Wiatr, K., Jamro, E.: Implementation of multipliers in FPGA structures. In: Proceedings of the 2001 International Symposium on Quality Elctronic Design. (2001) 415–420
[25] Tagzout, S., Sahli, L.: Compact parallel multipliers using the sign-generate method in FPGA. In: Proceedings of the 21st International Conference on Microelectronics. Volume 2. (1997) 815–818

HAGAR: Efficient Multi-context Graph Processors

Oskar Mencer[1], Zhining Huang[2], Lorenz Huelsbergen[1]

[1] Bell Labs, Murray Hill
NJ 07974, USA.
{mencer,lorenz}@research.bell-labs.com

[2] Department of Electrical Engineering
Princeton, NJ 08544, USA.
znhuang@ee.princeton.edu

Abstract. Graph algorithms, such as vertex reachability, transitive closure, and shortest path, are fundamental in many computing applications. We address the question of how to utilize the bit-level parallelism available in hardware, and specifically in FPGAs, to implement such graph algorithms for speedup relative to their software counterparts.

This paper generalizes the idea of a data-structure residing in reconfigurable hardware that, along with support logic and software in a microprocessor, accelerates a core algorithm. We give two examples of this idea. First, we draw parallels to content addressable memories. Second, we show how to extend the idea of mapping the adjacency matrix representation of a graph to a HArdware Graph ARray (HAGAR). We describe HAGAR implementations for graph reachability and shortest path. Reachability is a building block that can further be used to implement transitive closure, connected components, and other high-level graph algorithms. To handle large graphs where such an approach can excel relative to software, we develop a methodology, using FPGA internal small RAM blocks, to store and switch between multiple contexts of a regular architecture. The proposed circuits are implemented within the PAM-Blox module generation environment using Compaq's PamDC, and run on an FPGA accelerator card.

1. Introduction

Graph algorithms are fundamental to many applications in computing: routing layouts in networks and VLSI CAD, computer graphics, and scientific programs, are just a few examples. Software implementations of graph algorithms usually involve "walking" the graph by following chains of pointers, or by repeatedly indexing into a 2D array containing the graph's adjacency matrix. The limiting factor for the performance of such implementations is memory latency, which is recognized by the computer architecture community to be a major bottleneck that will become ever more severe as processor speeds increase faster than memory performance [WALL95]. The non-local and irregular memory accesses implied by pointer chasing further diminish the effectiveness of the caches introduced to mitigate this processor/memory speed imbalance.

M. Glesner, P. Zipf, and M. Renovell (Eds.): FPL 2002, LNCS 2438, pp. 915-924, 2002.

Custom (or reconfigurable) computing suggests using an FPGA in conjunction with a general-purpose processor to accelerate performance limited applications. Most work in this area (e.g. [SONIC00]) focuses on algorithm's computational parts that, for example, require more arithmetic power than is available from a microprocessor. Such applications are often called *compute-bound.* A complementary set of applications, limited by memory performance, consists of *memory-bound* applications. It is primarily this latter set of applications that our data-structure+algorithm approach addresses.

We propose building circuits that incorporate a data structure—potentially quite complex—and support logic for algorithms specific to this data structure. Some simple data structures and algorithms such as LIFO/FIFO for example, are already common hardware building blocks. We believe that hardware structures for tasks typically relegated to software are feasible and that FPGAs coupled with microprocessors are an ideal vehicle for their realization. The algorithm itself may be distributed among the reconfigurable and microprocessor pieces or may reside almost completely in one or the other.

Typically, a single access to the circuit on the FPGA initiates an operation on the data structure within the FPGA. Implemented operations depend on the particular data structure under consideration. For graphs (which we consider in this paper), the operations insert or delete graph vertices or edges. We present accompanying graph algorithms for shortest unit[1] path and reachability. Using reachability, higher level algorithms such as transitive closure and connected components can also be implemented [HUELS00].

Before venturing into our implementation of graph algorithms, let us take a look at a well known hardware implementation of a non-trivial algorithm and data structure: the Content Addressable Memory (CAM)[FLYNN61]. The CAM extends the idea of SRAM memory to an associative memory. A CAM implicitly implements a search through all elements; i.e. a search in a CAM takes one clock cycle, only slightly longer than an access to conventional SRAM memory, and at a cost of four additional transistors within each memory cell. CAMs are used for applications such as processor caches[HP90], internet routers [PEI91], and simple compression algorithms[KOM93].

We take an idea that is conceptually similar to CAMs and apply it to graphs. Let us define as usual a directed graph $G(V,E)$ as a set of N vertices (or nodes) $V=\{v0,v1,v2,...,vN\text{-}1\}$, and a set of directed edges (or arcs) E between the vertices. We construct an adjacency matrix that fully describes a particular instance of such a graph. Matrix element $a(i,j)=1$ *iff* there is an edge from vertex v_i to v_j; otherwise $a(i,j)=0$. The matrix has $N=|V|$ rows and columns and thus the matrix has a size of $O(N^2)$.

This paper describes how efficient multi-context circuits can compute with graphs represented in their adjacency matrix form—each cell of the resulting two-dimensional hardware array corresponds to one entry in the adjacency matrix. This idea, called Dynamic Graph Processors (DGP), is first developed in Huelsbergen [HUELS00]. Here we give three extensions to this prior work: (1) a streamlined implementation via tri-state logic that can increase density and therefore graph size,

[1] All edges have uniform weight of one.

(2) a scheme for scaling the hardware arrays to larger graphs by splitting them into multiple contexts, and (3) an embedding of the graph accelerator circuits in a module generation environment.

An early approach to implementing graphs on FPGAs is part of the RAW project [RAW96]. In contrast to our solution, RAW's graphs are stored in the FPGA by creating a circuit that directly resembles the graph—edges are routes connected to logic representing vertices. As a consequence, changing nodes and edges requires completely rerouting and reconfiguring the entire FPGA circuit, which is extremely costly in time. In our approach, a circuit represents a graph of a particular size, while edges are state bits that can be changed quickly at runtime. Another prior effort eliminates graph specific circuits by synthesizing a technology dependent design "based on the specific domain [algorithm,target]" [DAND99]. Unlike this prior work, our approach admits graph modifications at runtime and performs them in a single write (clock cycle) to the FPGA.

2. Representing Graphs in Reconfigurable Hardware

The approach shown here adapts ideas from [HUELS00] (and originally implemented on the Xilinx XC6200) to the Xilinx XC4000 and Virtex families of FPGAs. In particular, we extend the earlier work to use internal tri-state buffers. This more compactly implements the desired functionality—a compact implementation can hold larger graphs and operate more quickly. Figure 1 shows the general idea of the hardware graph accelerator using tri-state buffers. The tri-state buffer is a controlled switch. The flip-flop connected to its control input stores an entry of the adjacency matrix and decides whether or not the row signal is forwarded to the column—i.e., if the row node has an edge to the column node.

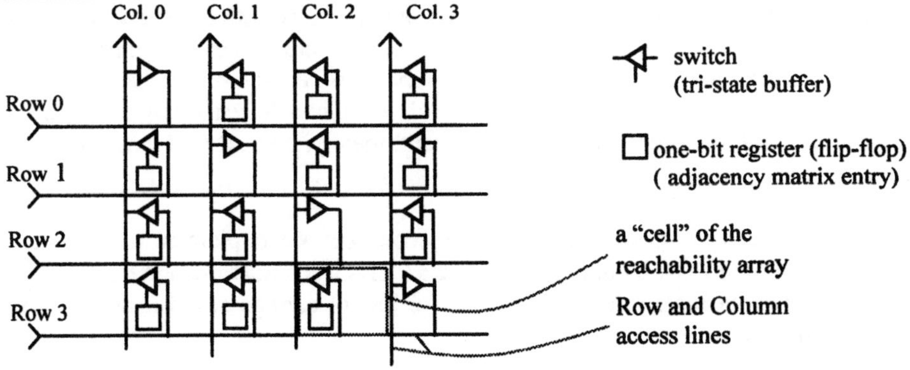

Fig. 1. Buses and tri-state switches implement the graph adjacency matrix in hardware.

It is apparent from the figure that an FPGA of a fixed size can only hold graphs up to a fixed number of nodes. Although the FPGA size places an upper bound on the number of graph nodes, the number and location of the graph's edges is unbounded in this approach. Inserting an edge into the graph consists of writing a '1' to the register at position (source, destination) in the array. Notice that the cells along the diagonal differ from the other cells in the array. This difference in cell structure implements the propagation of a vertex's value onto its out edges and is crucial to how the array evaluates a graph algorithm such as reachability, described next.

3. Reachability for Small Graphs

As a starting point, we take the simple design illustrated in Figure 1 above and implement a graph with a small number of nodes so that the entire adjacency matrix fits into one FPGA configuration. Section 4 shows how to create multi-context versions with identical functionality but for larger graphs.

Reachability is a graph primitive from which many graph algorithms, such as transitive closure and connected components, may be constructed. It takes as input a source and a destination node and decides if there is a path from the source to the destination; in other words, if the destination node is reachable from the source node.

How do we use the structure proposed in the previous section to compute reachability? After the graph adjacency matrix is loaded into the registers in the cells, it suffices to drive a value of '1' onto the source node's row and to observe the row of the destination node. In fact, all rows corresponding to nodes that are reachable from the source node will be driven high ('1') within the time it takes the signal to propagate through the graph circuit. Thus, the performance of computing reachability is converted to the propagation delay of a combinational circuit.

4. Multi-context Arrays for Large Graphs

Since the size of the adjacency matrix grows quadratically with the maximum number of graph vertices, the size of the FPGA limits the absolute size of the graph. HAGARs address this problem by partitioning the graph into several pieces called contexts. During evaluation of the algorithm, HAGARs switch between these contexts in an orchestrated fashion to obtain the desired result. Ideally, context switches should be as fast as possible.

Instead of using FPGA configurations as contexts, we implement a multi-context circuit within the FPGA by using the FPGA's CLBs as context memories, albeit small ones. A four-input lookup table (LUT) has 16 bits of storage and can therefore store up to 16 contexts.

4.1 Multi-context Reachability

Consider a HAGAR for N vertices $V=\{v0,v1,v2,...,vN-1\}$. M rows per context gives $C=N/M$ contexts (or partitions). Context 0 consists of the first M rows of the HAGAR, context 1 holds the second set of M rows, etc. Suppose the partitioned blocks have M rows and N columns. We store C contexts in FPGA lookup tables configured as distributed RAMs and switch between them to compute reachability.

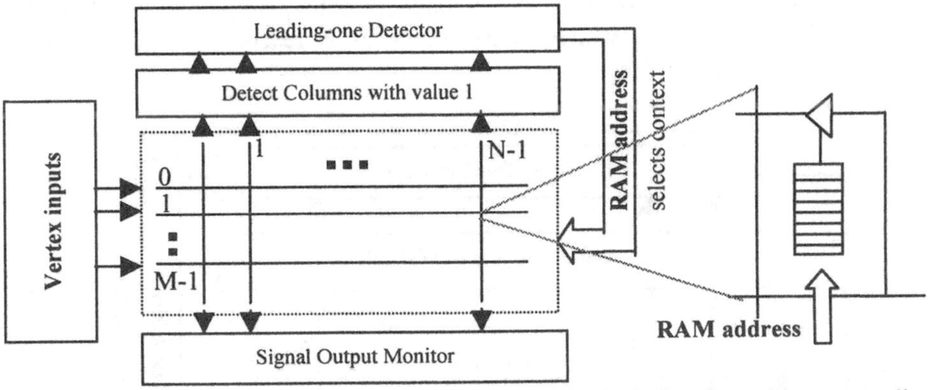

Fig. 2. Diagram of a multi-context HAGAR for reachability, including the multi-context cell architecture.

During a context switch, column values stay unchanged. At every column, a register at the top of the array retains the column value. Once a column receives a signal and becomes high, the column bus remains high during the entire evaluation, which in general consists of multiple context switches.

The algorithm works as follows: Assume we want to compute the reachability of vertex *v0*, and thus we switch to context 0, and drive a '1' on row 0. The '1' signal on row 0 now propagates to the connected columns. Suppose column *M*+2 and 2*M*+4 become '1'. At the next clock cycle, the current context will be swapped for another. Candidates for swapping-in are those who have received a '1' signal but have not yet been checked. Vertex *v0* has signal '1' but has been checked. Vertices *v*(*M*+2) and *v*(2*M*+4) now become candidates. We simply pick up the first candidate (leading-one detector on top of the array), and switch to context 01. When there are no more unchecked candidates, the computation is done. By monitoring column outputs, the set of vertices reachable from *v0* consists of the vertices with column values of '1'.

Figure 2 shows the general organization of the HAGAR circuit. Changing the distributed RAM addresses effects a context switch.

4.2 Multi-context Shortest Path

A HAGAR implementation of shortest path algorithm is slightly more complex than reachability. The shortest path algorithm also takes two input nodes, a source and a destination. From the set of paths from source to destination, a shortest such path is the result of the algorithm; otherwise, the algorithm indicates that no path exists from source to destination.

In this section we explain how to find the shortest path between two vertices using a hardware array. To find the shortest path, we use a special partition of the adjacency matrix, with contexts being single rows ($M=1$) of the original square HAGAR circuit. Contexts still contain N columns where N is the number of vertices in the graph. There are therefore $C=N$ contexts stored in the distributed RAMs, named context 0 to context (*N*-1). We start with the source vertex, say vertex *v0* and context 0. The computation ends when we reach the destination vertex, say vertex *v7*. If column 7 changes from '0' to '1', which means vertex *v7* is reached, the shortest path is available in the register file.

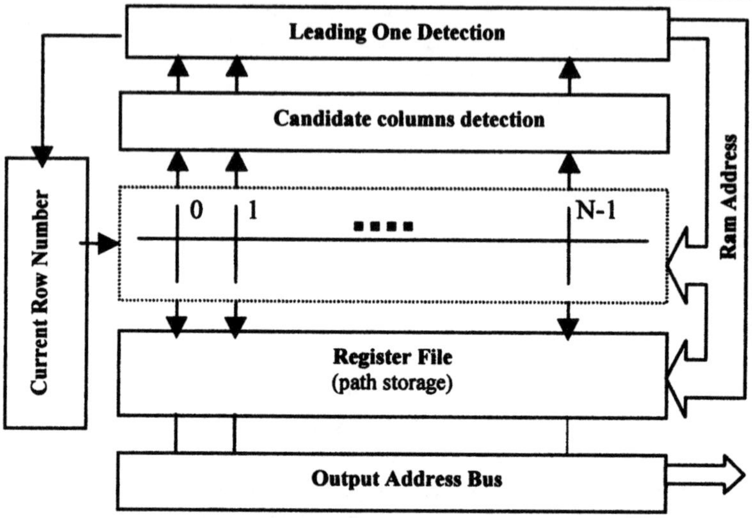

Fig. 3. HAGAR circuit for a multi-context implementation of shortest path.

The general organization of the HAGAR circuit for finding the shortest path is shown in Figure 3. The register file holds vertices in the traversed path. For each column *i* (where *i* is between *0* and *N-1*) the register file keeps the log(*N*) bits that identify the vertex that immediately precedes column *i* on the shortest paths. For example, if column 8 goes from '0' to '1' during a cycle, this means that vertex *v8* is reached. If the current context is 11, vertex *v8* is reached via vertex *v11*.

We keep a distance counter in the circuit to count how many steps we are away from the source vertex. At each step *k* there is a set of vertices that needs to be checked. This set of vertices contains the vertices that can be reached from the source vertex in a minimum of *k* steps. After all vertices have been checked, the distance counter is increased by one.

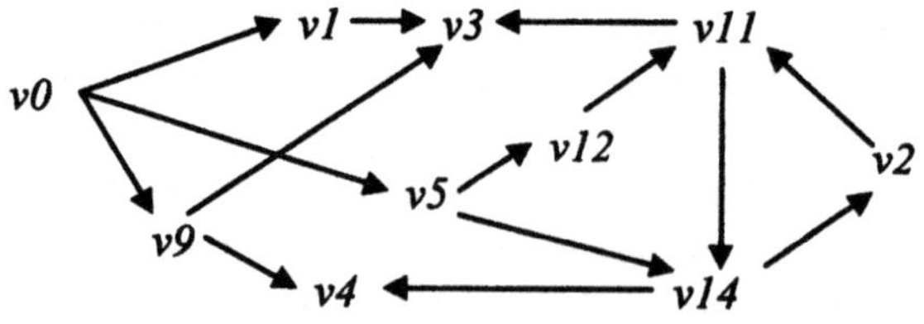

Fig. 4. Graph for shortest path example (*v0* → *v5* → *v12* → *v11*).

Consider for example the graph of Figure 4 where the vertex *v0* is taken as the source and has edges to *v1*, *v5*, and *v9*. The vertex set {*v1*,*v5*,*v9*} is therefore checked during step (distance) one. From *v1* we can reach *v3*; from *v5* we can reach *v12* and *v14*; from *v9* we can reach *v3* and *v4*. Vertices *v3*, *v4*, *v12*, and *v14* now form the set that needs to be checked in step two. This process continues until the destination vertex *v11* is reached, or no progress is made. The registers in each column record the context number as the column goes from '0' to '1'. Context numbers correspond to vertex numbers. In our example, the registers at columns 1, 5, and 9 record zero while the register at column 3 records a one. When the destination vertex is reached, we retrieve the shortest path from the register file as follows. The recorded values form a linked list. In our example with destination vertex *v11*, we first read out the value 12 from the register at column 11. At column 12 we read the value 5. At column 5 we read the value 0 (the source), and thus have a shortest path: *v0* → *v5*→*v12*→*v11*.

In case of a cycle in the graph, or multiple paths to the same node, the algorithm records the first time the node is reached. Any subsequent visit to the same node is ignored since it can not indicate a path shorter than the one through which the node was initially visited.

5. Implementation and Results

We implemented our HAGARs using the PAM-Blox II module generation environment[PBLOX02], built on top of the register transfer level (RTL) FPGA design library for C++, Compaq PamDC[PAM92]. The circuits were implemented on a Xilinx Virtex 300E FPGA (speedgrade –6) using Xilinx place-and-route tools (with effort level 4). The results below include the HAGAR and associated I/O circuitry for a PCI-based FPGA accelerator card.

Figure 5 shows the increase of cycle time for multi-context reachability. The performance of the HAGARs for reachability and shortest path—i.e. the worst case time to compute the reachability for a particular input is $O(|V|)$ while the worst case for shortest path is $O(|E|)$. The speedups are not obtained by improving the underlying complexity of the algorithm, but by reducing the time of their central computational primitive by a large factor [HUELS00].

We expect average performance to increase with increasing context size, especially with regard to shortest path computations. Average execution time depends strongly on the shape and size of the graph. Due to the larger contexts of reachability, average execution time for reachability should be much shorter than average execution time for shortest path. While the cycle time does not vary much with the number of contexts, the largest number of nodes (88 nodes on an XCV300E) can only be handled by *8* contexts, suggesting a tradeoff between context overhead and HAGAR size. We observe that the cycle time for shortest path is less sensitive to an increase in the number of nodes due to the single row context, and the bus-based architecture, as shown in Figure 6.

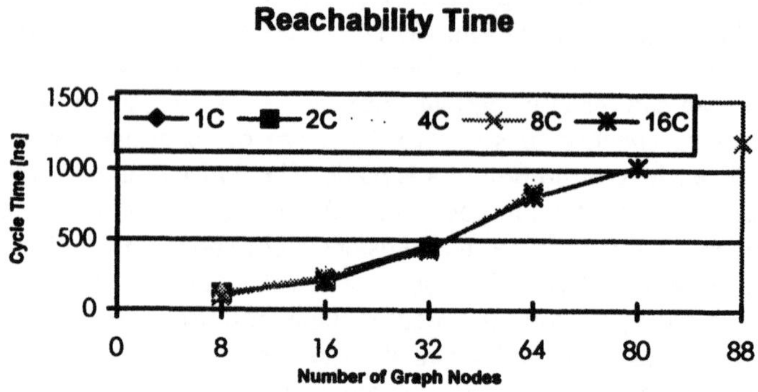

Fig. 5. Maximal delay or minimal clock cycle time, in [ns] for the multi-context reachability circuit, as a function of the number of graph nodes. Results show 1-16 contexts (1C-16C).

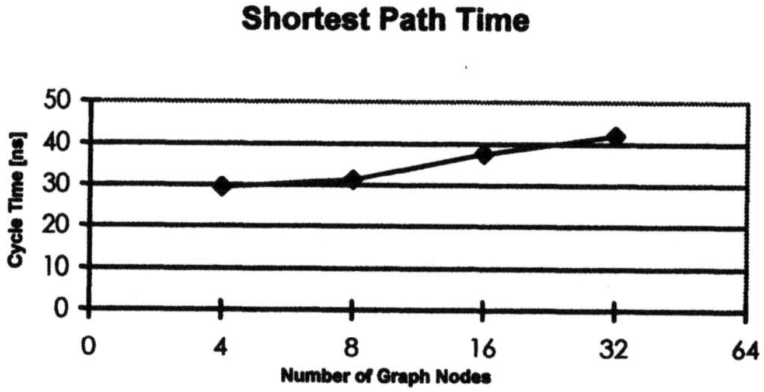

Fig. 6. Maximal delay, or minimal clock cycle time, in [ns] for the multi-context shortest path circuit, as a function of the number of graph nodes.

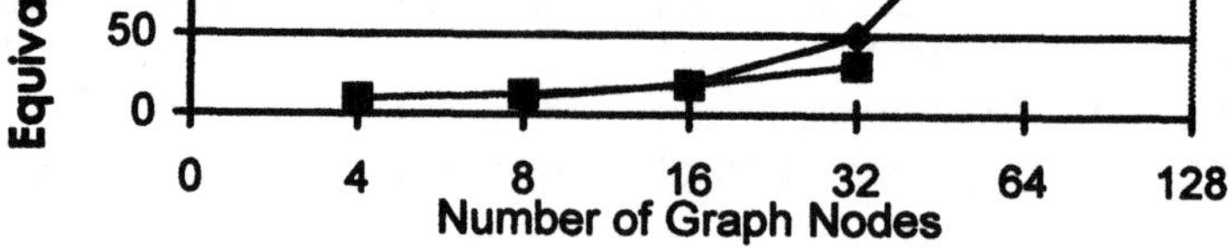

Fig. 7. Area in equivalent gates for the shortest path circuits, and reachability circuits with 4-context circuits.

Figure 7 shows the results for the area requirements of the proposed circuits for reachability and shortest path. The results for shortest path are limited to 32 nodes because the current implementation uses only a single small (32 bit) RAM for contexts. Larger graphs could be implemented by using multiple RAMs.

6. Conclusions and Future Work

This paper describes multi-context FPGA solutions for graph reachability and shortest path algorithms. It is possible to extend these ideas to other graph algorithms including transitive closure and connected components as described by [HUELS00], as well as to graph coloring, minimum spanning trees, etc. Implementation details of such additional algorithms are future work.

An additional improvement over the proposed method could be obtained by using multiple small RAMs, or larger block RAMs, for keeping contexts and/or storing temporary results. Such block RAMs are available in most current FPGAs. Furthermore, a finer balance between the usage of tri-state buffers and lookup tables could further improve the efficiency of the resulting circuits. However, even without these improvements we expect our HAGAR generators to scale to hundreds of nodes on the largest currently available FPGAs and to achieve speedups of orders of magnitude over general purpose microprocessor implementations.

Our work has the potential to help with one of the main problems in computer architecture: the growing gap between processor speed and time to access memory. Instead of software data structures constructed from pointers residing in a microprocessor's memory, complex data-structure+algorithm combinations can, as we have shown, be implemented very efficiently as HAGAR FPGA circuits. Thus, HAGARs have the potential to mitigate the memory bottleneck of certain algorithms and applications by representing the central data structure as a reconfigurable circuit.

Acknowledgements

Thanks to Rae McLellan, Rob Pike, Miron Abramovici, and Wayne Luk for helpful discussions and comments on this work.

References

[WALL95] W.A. Wulf, S.A. McKee, "Hitting the Memory Wall: Implications of the Obvious," Computer Architecture News, 23(1):20-24, March 1995.

[SONIC00] S.D. Haynes, J. Stone, P.Y.K. Cheung, W. Luk, "Video Image Processing with the Sonic Architecture," IEEE Computer, April 2000.

[FLYNN61] M. Flynn, "Operations in an Associative Memory," PhD Thesis, EE Dept., Purdue Univ., June 1961.

[HP90] J. Hennessy, D. Patterson, "Computer Architecture: A Quantitative Approach," Morgan Kaufmann, 1990.

[PEI91] T.B. Pei, C. Zukowski, "Routing Tables: Tries and CAMs," Proc. Infocom 1991.

[KOM93] E. Komoto, T. Homma, T. Nakamura, "A High-Speed and Compact-Size JPEG Huffman Decoder using CAM," Symposium on VLSI Circuits, Kyoto, Digest of Technical Papers ch. 61 v pp. 37-X3, 1993.

[HUELS00] L. Huelsbergen, "A Representation for Dynamic Graphs in Reconfigurable Hardware and its Application to Fundamental Graph Algorithms," Proc. ACM Int. Symposium on Field Programmable Gate Arrays (FPGA 2000), Monterey, Feb. 2000

[RAW96] J. Babb, M. Frank, A. Agarwal, "Solving graph problems with dynamic computation structures," High-Speed Computing, Digital Signal Processing, and Filtering Using Reconfigurable Logic, Proc. SPIE 2914, 1996.

[DAND99] A. Dandalis, A. Mei, V.K. Prasanna, "Domain Specific Mapping for Solving Graph Problems on Reconfigurable Devices," 6th IEEE Reconfigurable Architectures Workshop (RAW), April 1999.

[PBLOX02] O. Mencer, "PAM-Blox II: Design and Evaluation of C++ Module Generation for Computing with FPGAs," IEEE Symposium on Field Programmable Custom Computing Machines, FCCM, Napa Valley, CA, 2002.

[PAM92] P. Bertin, D. Roncin, J. Vuillemin, "Programmable Active Memories: A Performance Assessment," ACM FPGA Conference, Monterey, Feb. 1992.

Scalable Implementation of the Discrete Element Method on a Reconfigurable Computing Platform

Benjamin Carrión Schäfer[1], S.F.Quigley[1], A.H.C. Chan[2]

[1]Dept. of Electronic, Electrical and Computer Engineering, University of Birmingham
Edgbaston, Birmingham B15 2TT, United Kingdom
schaferb@ieee.org, s.f.quigley@bham.ac.uk
[2]Dept. of Civil Engineering, University of Birmingham
Edgbaston, Birmingham B15 2TT, United Kingdom
a.h.chan@bham.ac.uk

Abstract. The Discrete Element Method (DEM) is a numerical method for the simulation of the behaviour of media consisting of discrete particles, and is important for the optimisation of production processes in the food processing and pharmaceutical industries. The DEM is computationally very expensive, but can benefit from the properties of reconfigurable computing. This paper presents the design of an optimised dedicated hardware architecture for the DEM implemented on a Reconfigurable Computing platform based on a Field Programmable Gate Array. A single FPGA version shows a 30-fold speed-up compared to an optimised software version running on a fast PC. The design of a multi-FPGA board solution is also presented; this provides approximately 30 times more speed up for each FPGA used.

1 Introduction

The Discrete Element Method (DEM) is an algorithm that is widely used by civil and chemical engineers. It is particularly important for the optimisation of manufacturing processes for the food and pharmaceutical industries. However, its application is limited by its extremely heavy computational demands. DEM simulations take hours to days to run on fast workstations. Conventional parallel computers suffer from load balancing and communication overhead problems when solving the DEM, which means that they give a relatively disappointing speed up.

This paper presents results for the implementation of a 2-D DEM simulator on a Pentium PC augmented by reconfigurable computing boards containing FPGA and RAM. This paper advances over our previous reported results [1] in that it considers the scaling of the design up to realistic problem sizes, and across multiple FPGA boards. The speed-up compared to an optimized software version is a factor of 30 per FPGA board, and this speed-up increases slightly less than linearly with the number of boards, because of the synchronization of both boards after every completed cycle.

M. Glesner, P. Zipf, and M. Renovell (Eds.): FPL 2002, LNCS 2438, pp. 925-934, 2002.

2 Implementation of the Discrete Element Method

The DEM models the behaviour of assemblies of granular materials. Granular materials can be defined as large conglomerations of discrete macroscopic particles. Like liquids, they can flow and assume the shape of the container, and like a solid, they can support weight; however they can not normally support a tensile stress.

A flow chart for the method is shown in Fig. 1. The method is based on the assumption that particles only exert forces on one another when they are in contact. A simulation starts by assuming some initial configuration of particle positions, and then computing which of the particles are touching. The simulation then proceeds by stepping in time, applying the sequence of operations of fig. 1 at each step. The force between two particles can be calculated from the strength of the contact between them [2]. The resultant force on a particle is the vector sum of the forces exerted by each of its neighbours. Once the resultant force on each particle has been computed, it is simple to compute a velocity and position increment for each particle. Finally, the list of which particles are in contact must be re-computed.

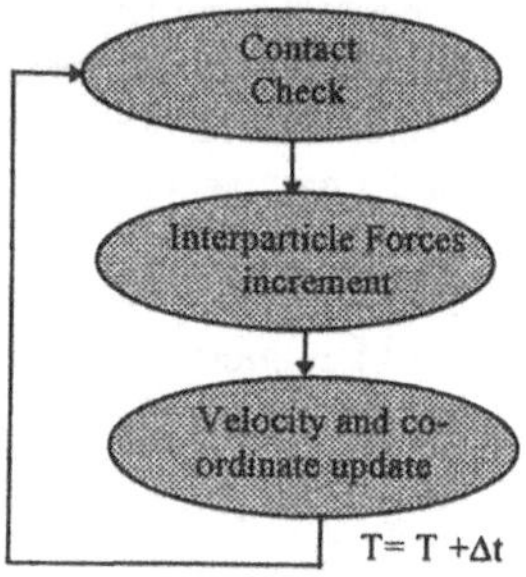

Fig. 1 DEM Flow chart

Every particle's force interaction, acceleration and movement is calculated individually at each time step. The assumptions underlying the method are only correct if no disturbance can travel beyond the immediate neighbours of a particle within one time step. This generally means that the time step must be limited to a very small value, thus making the DEM extremely computationally expensive.

2.1 Contact Check

For each particle, a "contact list" is formed, which contains references to each of the particles with which it comes into close proximity. This is achieved by checking if their bounding boxes overlap, a simple operation requiring just two subtractions and two comparisons.

For our investigation, we have assumed that all particles are of the same radius R. For this circumstance, simple geometry shows that for a 2-D simulation, the maximum number of contacts that each ball can have is 6. This means that contact information can be represented by a simple data structure, in which each particle has six memory slots allocated to hold the identities of the particles in contact. If there are N particles within a region of the DEM, then the number of contact checks that must be performed is N^2.

2.2 Inter-particle Forces Increment

For each pair of particles whose bounding boxes overlap (fig. 2), the degree of indentation between the two is calculated as

$$\Delta n = R_1 + R_2 - \sqrt{(x_1 - x_2)^2 + (y_1 - y_2)^2} \quad (1)$$

where x_i y_i are the co-ordinates of each particle's centre and R_1 and R_2 are the respective radii.

For this study, a simple force-displacement law is adopted; therefore the resulting force between two balls is proportional to the indentation between the balls (where k_i is the stiffness (normal and shear), M is the moment, and R is the radius of the particles). The resultant force on a particle is the vector sum of the forces caused by each contact with its neighbours.

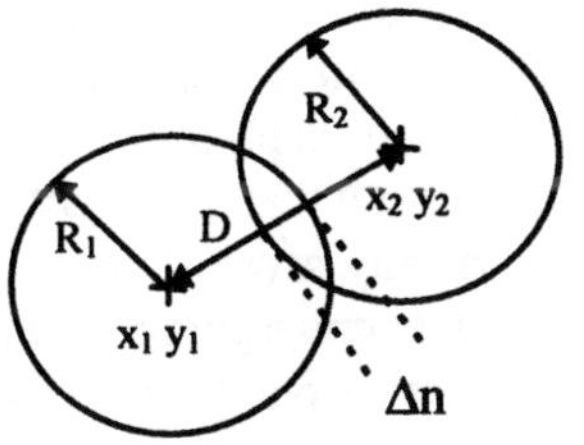

Fig. 2 Balls in contact

$$F_{xi} = k_n \Delta n_{xi} \tag{2a}$$

$$F_{yi} = k_s \Delta n_{yi} \tag{2b}$$

$$M = F_s R \tag{2c}$$

2.3 Position Update

Once the resultant force on each particle has been calculated, these forces are used to find new accelerations using Newton's second law. These accelerations are integrated to obtain the velocities in the x and y direction and the angular velocity

$$v_x = v_{x0} + \frac{F_x}{m} \Delta t \tag{5a}$$

$$v_y = v_{y0} + \frac{F_y}{m} \Delta t \tag{5b}$$

$$\theta' = \theta' + \frac{M}{I} \Delta t \tag{5c}$$

As is usual for time integration schemes, the time step has to be small enough that no disturbance can travel beyond one contact in one time step. The new coordinates can be found adding the original coordinates with the incremental displacement obtained by integrating the obtained velocities:

$$x = x_0 + v_x \Delta t \tag{6a}$$

$$y = y_0 + v_y \Delta t \tag{6b}$$

$$\theta = \theta + \theta' \Delta t \tag{6c}$$

2.4 Hardware Implementation

The hardware architecture used to process the domain is shown in fig. 3. It is implemented in a single Xilinx Virtex 2000E-8 FPGA mounted on a Celoxica RC-1000 PCI card containing 4 banks of 2 Mbyte of RAM.

The architecture divides the internal block RAM of the FPGA into six dual port RAMs. At any given time, six of the columnar cells of fig. 4 will be stored within the FPGA and undergoing processing. Each word of data within the block RAM corresponds to one particle, and is 256 bits wide. Each 256 bit word contains 16-bit representations for the particle's position and angle co-ordinates x, y, θ, the velocities v_x , v_y θ', the forces and moment F_x F_y, M, a type flag for the particles, and the identity of up to 6 neighbouring particles that have been identified during the contact check.

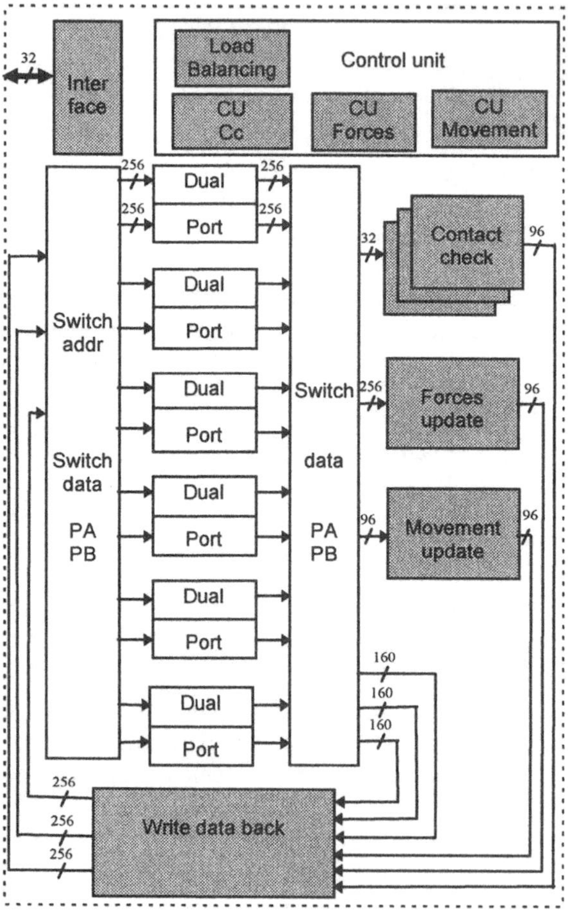

Fig. 3 The Hardware Architecture

The contact check unit, the force update unit, and the co-ordinate update unit are each implemented as a pipeline that consumes one 256-bit input and produces one 256-bit output per clock cycle. The control units generate the necessary control signals to synchronise data between the blocks, and to steer the data output by the RAMs through the switch array to the inputs of the appropriate computation unit. The control units also generate the addresses to read and write data back to the internal and external memory.

The hardware requirements for each of the main functional units are shown in table 1. Constant coefficient multipliers (KCMs) require much less hardware resource than multipliers that have both inputs free to vary. The contact checking unit is very simple, requiring little hardware resource, and capable of operation at high clock speeds. The force update unit requires a large amount of hardware. It also operates at a comparatively low clock speed of 7.5 MHz. The movement update unit has an intermediate level of hardware complexity.

Each of the three stages (contact checking, resultant force calculation and position updating) can be built as a hardware pipeline that produces one result per clock cycle

Table 1 Hardware requirements for the building blocks

Contact checking	Force update	Movement update
2 additions	18 adders	7 adders
2 subtractions	10 multipliers	15 KCM
	8 KCM	
	1 divider	
	1 LUT	

It can be seen that for realistic sizes of N, contact checking is by far the most time consuming stage. However, its hardware requirements are quite modest, so many contact check units can be instantiated in parallel.

Table 2 Clock cycles needed to stream data through each unit of fig. 3

Unit	clk cycles needed
Co-ordinates update	N
Forces	6N
Contact checking	$^1/_2N^2$

3 Domain Decomposition

As shown in table 2 the contact check unit is the most time consuming part as it grows with the square of the number of particles in the domain. For N particles the execution time will grow as $O(N^2)$. This is true whether the DEM is implemented in hardware or software. This can be alleviated by dividing the domain up into smaller cells [3]. Each particle is tagged as belonging to a particular cell, and it will only be checked for contacts with particles within the same cell, and the neighbouring ones if this particle is close to the cell boarder. If there are C particles per cell, the execution time is then proportional to $^N/_C\ O(C^2)$. This technique is used in most software implementations of the DEM.

The computationally challenging nature of the DEM has led to considerable interest in mapping the DEM onto multiprocessor parallel computers. This is normally done by decomposing the domain into cells, and then mapping a cell onto each processor within the parallel computer.

In an “ideal” parallel problem, the speed up would be proportional with the number of processors used to perform the calculations. However, for the DEM is this not normally the case. Particles transitioning from one cell to another create communication and synchronisation overheads [3], slowing the whole system down considerably. Also, if some cells become more populated than others, there will be inefficiencies due to load imbalance between the processors.

These factors limits the degree of speed up achieved by running the DEM on parallel computers. For example a parallel implementation on a 64 node Alta Technologies T805 achieved a rather modes 8-fold speed up compared to a serial implementation [4]. Another implementation on a Swiss T0-Dual machine achieved a speed up of 2 for a 8 node system[5].

It is the difficulty in achieving a good level of speed up with a parallel computer that motivated our investigation into the acceleration of DEM by reconfigurable computing.

4 Domain Decomposition on the FPGA Implementation

The domain decomposition used for our implementation is shown in fig. 4. The domain is split into vertical columnar cells. Each particle belongs to a particular cell, and for most particles contact checking and force updating need only be performed against the other particles within the same cell. For the small number of particles that are close to a boundary between two cells, more complicated arrangements are necessary.

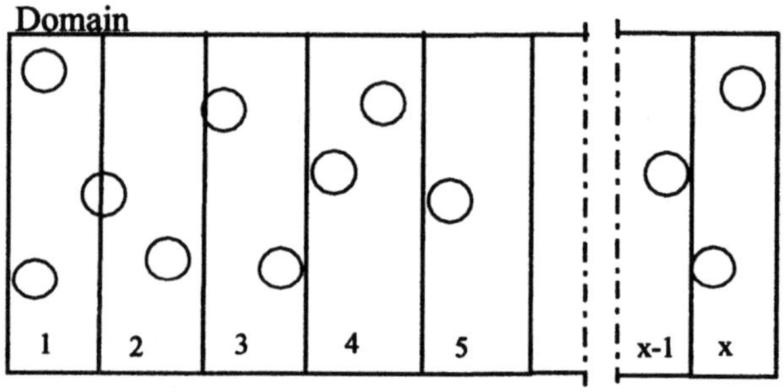

Fig. 4 Decomposition of the domain

As an example of the scheduling, consider the situation where the six dual port block RAMs of fig. 3 respectively contain the particle data for columns 1,2,3,4,5 and 6 of the domain of fig. 4 The particle x,y co-ordinate data for column 5 is streamed through the contact check unit and the particle contact list data is written back into the block RAM. At the same time, the data for column 2 is streamed through the force update unit, and the data for column 1 is streamed through the co-ordinate update unit. The results are written back into the appropriate region of the FPGA's block RAM. The data for column 1 is then written into an external RAM, and new data for column 7 is read from external RAM.

The block RAMs now respectively contain the data for columns 7,2,3,4,5 and 6. Computation now recommences, with contact checking being performed on column 6, force updating on column 3 and co-ordinate updating on column 2.

4.1 Load Balancing

With contact checking, force updating and co-ordinate updating being performed in parallel, load balancing problems appear, since the overall system speed will be limited by the speed of the slowest of the three units. As shown in tables 1 and 2, the co-ordinate check is the most time consuming, but requires very simple hardware and can operate at high clock speed.

In order to improve the load balance, many contact check units are instantiated, and they operate in parallel. The number of contact checks used is a parameter of the design, which can be easily changed. The contact check control unit can generate all the required control signals to steer the data between the different check units. Also, the contact check units run at four times the clock speed (30 MHz) of the force update unit and co-ordinate update unit (7.5 MHz).

It can also be seen from table 2 that the co-ordinate update unit will finish much earlier than the forces update unit. The spare time available at the end of the co-ordinate update is used to write the data from the block of RAM corresponding to co-ordinate update (which has now finished being processed for this timestep) into external RAM, and to read in a new set of data from external RAM corresponding to the next column of the domain that is to be processed.

In this way, writing to and reading from external RAM can be fully overlapped with computation, and the number of particles that can be processed at full speed is limited only by the size of the external RAM. This means that problems containing tens of millions of particles can be processed easily.

In order for the system to run at highest efficiency, there should be enough contact check units operating in parallel so that contact checking takes the same length of time as force updating. This length of time should also be equal to the total time taken for co-ordinate update and communication with the external RAM.

4.2 Handling Cell Boundaries

Several complications arise as a result of interactions at boundaries between the columns of particles.

Firstly, a particle close the boundary may be in contact not only with particles from its own column, but also from an adjacent column. This situation is handled by an auxiliary memory located within the control unit that handles inter-cell boundaries. So for example during the contact check of column 5, each particle of column 5 is checked to determine whether it is within 2R of the boundary with column 6. If it is, then after the particle has completed contact check, its data is written back as normal into the block RAM for column 5; its address is *also* copied into the auxiliary memory within the control unit. Once the contact check of column 5 has finished contact check of the particles stored in the control unit's auxiliary memory are checked for contacts in column 6. Once the correct contact list has been generated for a particle, all subsequent computation will proceed correctly, even if a contact straddles a boundary.

Secondly, a particle close to a boundary may transition from one column to another during co-ordinate update. For such a particle, after the results of the co-ordinate update are written back to the RAM, the particle has the correct co-ordinates, but is stored in the wrong block of RAM. This is automatically detected and corrected by the contact check unit in its following sweep through the data at the next time step. One of the responsibilities of the contact check control unit is to detect when a particle is in the wrong column, and to write it back to the correct column.

A third complication is that as simulation progresses, particles will move between columns, and some columns may become heavily populated, whilst others are sparsely populated. It is then necessary to move the cell boundaries, thus expanding some cells and contracting others. This is needed in order to provide good load balancing, and also to prevent overflow of the block RAMs.

Movement of cell boundaries is fairly simple. The control unit monitors how many particles are held in each block RAM. When the number falls below a minimum threshold or rises above a maximum, the boundary is moved by a distance R so as to expand or contract the cell. When the boundary moves, a number of cells will find that their data is stored in the wrong column of RAM, but this will be automatically detected and corrected by the mechanisms described earlier for handling particles close to boundaries.

Using the procedures described here, the transition of particles from one cell to another is handled without causing any loss of performance. Also, the cell size is adaptively optimised so that good load balancing is always achieved.

5 Multiple FPGA Design

The domain decomposition used also facilitates the spreading of the simulation across multiple FPGA boards with minimal communications overhead, which means that near linear speed-up can be achieved. Figure 5 shows the appearance of a system containing N RC1000 boards. Each board contains an FPGA, whose block RAM is organised as 6 dual port RAMs each of which is used to contain the data for a sub-domain. This data is swopped in and out four banks of static RAM present on each RC1000 board.

The boards communicate with one another across the PCI bus. As long as the amount of data being transferred across the PCI bus between the boards remains small, linear speed up can be expected as more FPGA boards are added.

Initially the domain is split across the boards so as to equalise the workloads between each board. After the first time step is completed, each board needs to exchange its right most column (including the data structures that catch particles transitioning across sub-domain boundaries) with its right hand neighbour, and its leftmost column with its left hand neighbour. If this transfer can be completely

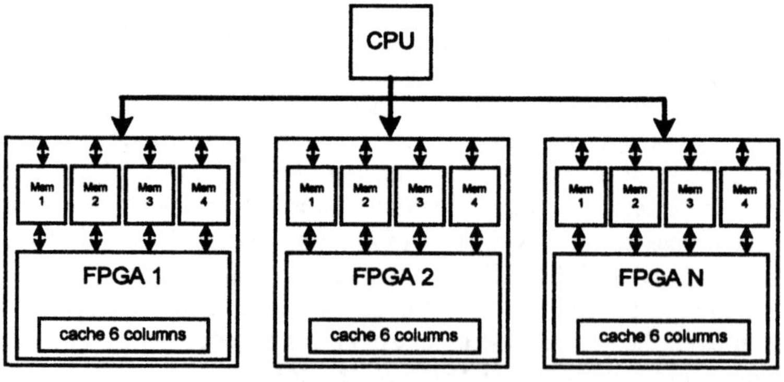

Fig. 5 Multi-FPGA system

overlapped with computation, then none of the computational pipelines on the FPGAs need ever stall, and speed up should be linear (i.e. use of N boards should provide N times more speed-up than a single board).

The data for each particle consists of 10 bytes (2 bytes each for n_x, n_y, v_x, v_y, θ'), and the number of particles in a column is limited to 256 (in order to avoid overflow of the block RAM, the method will adaptively reduce the size of any domain that has a number of particles approaching this limit). So for N boards, the maximum amount of data transferred across the PCI bus for each time step of the DEM method is $10 \times 256 \times 4 \times N$ bytes, = 10 N kByte.

Within each board, the FPGA uses one RAM bank at a time. Transfer of edge data to an adjacent board can be initiated when a bank of memory is released by the FPGA, and must be completed before the FPGA attempts to re-acquire that bank (which occurs after it has finished processing the contents of the other three RAM banks on the board). This amounts to a time of 3 × (time taken to process one sub-domain) × (number of sub-domains per RAM). The slowest operation in processing a sub-domain containing M particles is the contact checking, which takes M^2/(no. of contact check units × 30 MHz). Each RAM contains 2 Mbyte/(256 × 10) sub-domains. For typical sub-domain occupancy, this means that the length of time available for transfers between adjacent boards is in the range 100 - 400 ms.

This can be used to estimate a worst case transfer rate required across the PCI bus of 100 N kByte/s for N boards. The boards are capable of sustaining DMA transfers across the PCI bus at about 12 Mbyte/s, which means that saturation of the bus will not occur for values of N below about a hundred. This means that if ideal load balancing is achieved then speed-up can be expected to be linear.

6 Results

For DEM simulations, a software program reads the initial data (e.g. domain size and constants) and generates the particles randomly in the domain. The actual DEM simulation can be handled either in software or hardware. For hardware simulation, the parameters required by the FPGA are generated by the software; these parameters and the particle data are then downloaded into the RC1000 board. The results are uploaded from the board into the memory of the computer once the end of the simulation has finished. Software routines then handle graphical feedback of results to the user.

A domain with 25,000, 50,000, 75,000, 100,000, 125,000 and 150,000particles was generated and simulated for 1,000 time steps. The performance of the software version was measured and compared with the results obtained for the Hardware version using a single FPGA board. The software version ran on a 1 GHz Pentium III processor with 1.3 Gbyte of RAM. The results are shown in table 3.

Table 3. Comparisons of speed-up obtained by hardware DEM for a single FPGA

No. of particles	50,000	75,000	100,000	125,000	150,000
Speed $up_{measured}$ (1 board)	35.3	31.0	29.8	30.2	29.5
Speed $up_{measured}$ (2 board)	54.0	55.2	54.7	53.7	54.9

The hardware simulation was able to provide an accurate solution for problems of a realistic size across a thousand time steps in spite of its use of 16 bit arithmetic. The speed-up achieved was in the range 30-35, with some slight variation due to variations in the efficiency of the domain decomposition for different particle densities.

The hardware simulation for a system with two boards gave a result slightly worst than the expected linear speed up of a factor of 60. This is due to the synchronization of the FPGAs as after every cycle the fastest FPGA needs to wait for the slowest one, as it is impossible to have a completely balanced system.

7 Conclusions

The DEM is an algorithm that is increasing in importance, but its deployment is inhibited by its very heavy computational demands. Models of many hundreds of thousands of particles may take several hours to several days on single processor machines. Conventional parallel computing solutions tend to give disappointing speed-up due to load imbalance and communications overheads.

A dedicated chip architecture implemented on a reconfigurable computing board has shown a speed up of to 30 times compared to a fast PC. Further speed up and accuracy can be achieved using newer FPGAs, with higher logic densities and clock speeds, and boards with faster memory. Such methods could easily raise the speed up to a factor of over 100.

The design of a multi-board system has been implemented, and as more boards are added, almost linear speed up is achieved. Only the synchronization of the FPGAs after every time step keeps the speed up slightly worse than linear. The overall performance depends on how well the system loading is balanced: the most heavily loaded FPGA limits the speed up of the entire system.

References

1 B. Carrión Schäfer, S.F. Quigley, A.H.C. Chan. *Analysis and Implementation of the Discrete Element Method using a Dedicated Highly Parallel Architecture in Reconfigurable Computing,* 2002 IEEE Symposium on Field-Programmable Custom Computing Machines (FCCM 2002)

2 P.A. Cundall O.D.L. Strack, *A discrete numerical model for granular assemblies.* Geotechnique 29, pp. 1-8, 1979

3 Mario Antonioletti. *The DEM application demonstrator* pp.7. Available at http://www.epcc.ed.ac.uk/epcc-tec/JTAP/DEM.html

4 Andrew I. Hustrulid. *Parallel implementation of the discrete element method.* Available at http://egweb.mines.edu/dem/

5 ML Sawley & PW Clearly. CSIRO Mathematical & Information Sciences, Clayton, Australia. *A Parallel discrete element method for industrial granular flow simulations,* EPLF Supercomputing review -SCR No 11, Nov. 99

On Computing Transitive-Closure Equivalence Sets Using a Hybrid GA-DP Approach

Kai-Pui Lam and Sui-Tung Mak

Department of Systems Engineering and Engineering Management
The Chinese University of Hong Kong, Shatin, Hong Kong

Abstract. The computation of transitive-closure equivalence sets has recently emerged as an important step for building static and dynamic models for biological DNA sequencing. We present a hybrid method of integrating genetic algorithm (GA) with dynamic programming (DP), and offer an efficient FPGA (field programmable gate array) implementation platform for the required computation. The dynamic programming calculation of transitive closure makes use of the Floyd-Warshall algorithm that forms the basic fitness evaluation in genetic algorithm, for selecting candidate chromosome strings generated by applying basic genetic operators. The complete high-level design is developed using Xilinx's System Generator tool, which provides an efficient generation of VHDL code for verification on targeted FPGA hardware such as the Virtex-800. Successful testing results for finding 5-node equivalence sets for a 30-node genetic network are reported.

1 Introduction

The rapid advance in technology such as DNA microarrays makes available voluminous experimental data [1,2] for the analysis and development of models for large scale genetic network comprising thousands of genes. Information extraction and reduction to meaningful patterns from the data has become an urgent but rather computationally demanding task. In [1] the idea of partitioning genes into equivalence sets was proposed, with reference to a Boolean matrix R obtained from the gene expression patterns resulting from disruption or forced expression. The equivalence sets allows effective grouping of "closed-loop" genes (where the relationships of gene $'a'$ affects gene $'b'$ and gene $'b'$ affects gene $'a'$ coexist in the set), and can be derived from transitive closure computation. Subsequently dynamic models are estimated from the identified equivalence sets for capturing network behavior.

While the transitive closure for an N-node genetic network can be readily obtained by sequential dynamic programming techniques such as Floyd-Warshall or Bellman-Ford [10,4], the procedure is computationally intensive for practical network size where N is large. Subsequent search to obtain all possible M-node (with M much less than N) equivalence sets is further needed. In this paper we propose a hybrid genetic-algorithm, dynamic-programming (GA-DP) approach,

M. Glesner, P. Zipf, and M. Renovell (Eds.): FPL 2002, LNCS 2438, pp. 935–944, 2002.

which provides an alternative solution and is more efficient in requiring the transitive closure computation of only M-node network.

The essential idea of this hybrid approach is to embed the dynamic programming calculation for an M-node network within a GA search procedure. An exhaustive brute-force search for all the possible M-node equivalence sets for an N-node genetic network is not viable, simply because of combinatorial problems. However, GA has long been known to be a highly efficient global search procedure than brute-force, provided that a meaningful fitness evaluation for candidate solutions (or so-called chromosome strings in a population) is known. For our specific application on equivalence sets, this fitness evaluation is straight forward by simply summing the entries of the Boolean matrix resulted from transitive closure computation for an M-node network.

The common GA operators such as selection, crossover, and mutation are used in the following study of finding 5-node equivalence sets on a sample 30-node genetic network. Hence, $N = 30, M = 5$. The population size N_p chosen in the GA is 10. In each of the N_p chromosomes, we have 5 genes to represent the 5 nodes for the corresponding equivalence set. Using binary encoding, a 6-bit string is adequate for representing a single gene of a 30-node network (e.g. 000101 represents node 5). Hence a chromosome string consisting of 5 genes is a 30-bit string (e.g., 000001 000010 000011 000100 000101 is the chromosome encoding for a set of 5 nodes 1, 2, 3, 4, 5).

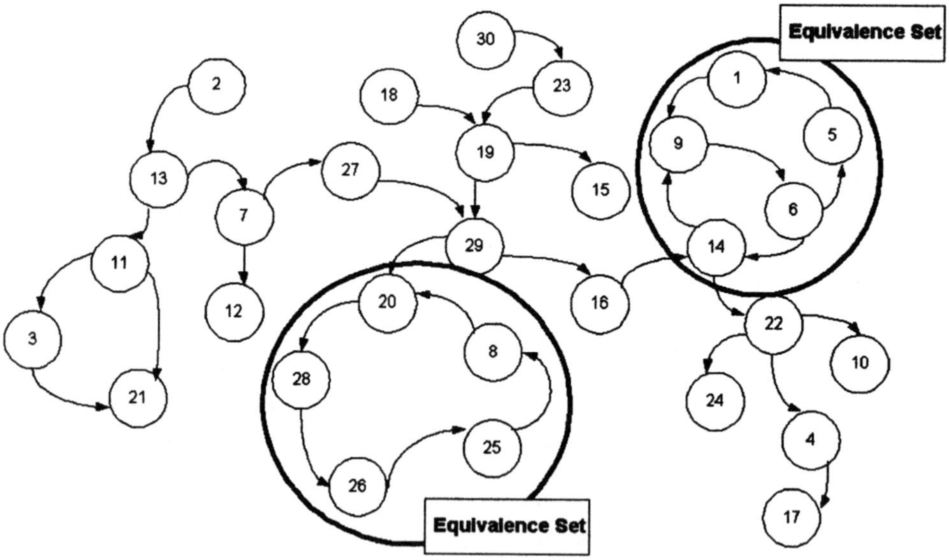

Fig. 1. A 30-node genetic network with two equivalence sets

The sample 30-node genetic network with unidirectional arcs is shown in Fig. 1. The nodes are representing the genes and the arcs are representing the affection between genes in this figure. If there is a set of genes $\{i, j, k\}$ in which gene $'i'$ can be affected by gene $'j'$ and $'k'$, gene $'j'$ can be affected by gene $'i'$ and $'k'$ and gene $'k'$ can be affected by gene $'i'$ and $'j'$, we say that they form a 3-node equivalence set. There are 2 quoted equivalence sets: $\{1, 5, 6, 9, 14\}$ and $\{8, 20, 25, 26, 28\}$ in Fig. 1.

We have implemented the hybrid GA-DP approach using field-programmable gate array (FPGA), a real-time custom computing platform that has seen growing usage for GA [7,8,9]. With the use of a recently available high-level digital signal processing (DSP) tool, Xilinx's System Generator [11], the tedious tasks of design, simulation, and testing were undertaken with much ease. In Section 2 we give an overview of our GA-DP architecture as implemented under the Simulink environment, with further details of individual GA and DP blocks given in Section 3. Sections 4 and 5 summarize our simulation and testing results of the GA-DP approach.

2 GA-DP Architecture

2.1 Design Flow

Our logic-level design makes extensive use of Xilinx's System Generator (SG) that works under MATLAB's Simulink environment. Simulink provides a schematic design environment and blocks of logic gates, which could be connected by wires directly. SG then generates the VHDL code automatically from the schematic design. Subsequently, Syplicity Pro is used to convert the VHDL files to EDIF format. Using Xilinx's Design Manager and Hardware Debugger, the EDIF file is converted to a bit stream file which can then be readily downloaded to a XESS devlopment board [6] containing the FPGA (XCV800 HQ240).

On the system level, MATLAB is also used as software simulation tool. This allows cross verification of the system outputs with that generated from lower-level simulation results obtained from SG.

2.2 System Overview

Figure 2 shows a GA-DP system overview. It mainly consists of 2 computational parts: the GA and the Floyd-Warshall algorithm. Traditional GA operators are implemented as different functional blocks, including selection, one-point crossover, mutation, and fitness evaluation. The Floyd-Warshall algorithm is embedded as part of the fitness value evaluation of the GA. In the system, there are 3 different memory allocations used for different purposes. The Temp RAM is 10×30-bit for storing 10 sets of transition chromosomes in the GA operation. A ROM is used to store the Boolean network matrix. The matrix is mapped into a one-dimension vector storing in the ROM. The Elite RAM is used to store the always-best chromosome, which has the highest score of fitness value among the chromosomes. The system controller is used to control the operations of the functional blocks. Since only one block is operating at a time, the other non-working blocks are switched off by the system controller.

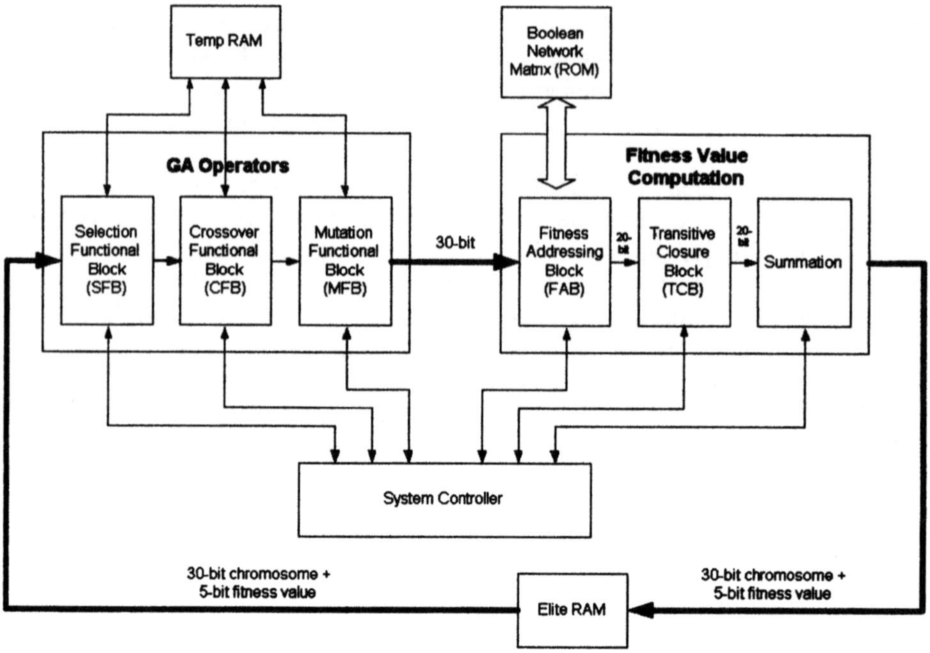

Fig. 2. GA-DP System overview

All functional blocks are controlled asynchronously, where the blocks are triggered by an up bit signal from the system controller. When the system starts to run, ten sets of randomly initialized chromosomes are stored in the Temp RAM. The FAB will read in the chromosomes from the RAM one at a time. In the FAB, the chromosome will be sliced into 5 genes (each has 6 bits) and output a 20-bit string representing the interconnection between the genes. The string is stored in the RAM right after the FAB, and the procedure is repeated for the remaining chromosomes.

After the FAB finishes the task for all the 10 sets of chromosomes, a complete signal will be sent to the system controller and the system controller will trigger the transitive closure computing. The Transitive Closure Block (TCB) reads one set of 20-bit data, which is representing the interconnection of genes, and performs transitive closure calculation using the Floyd-Warshall algorithm. Before the results are saved in the RAM, a summation functional block will convert the 20-bit string into a fitness value. The TCB reads in another set of chromosomes. and repeats the fitness value computing and stores all fitness values for each of the remaining sets. A complete signal will then be sent to the Selection Functional Block (SFB).

In the SFB, 2 sets of chromosomes will be randomly selected from the RAM. Their corresponding fitness values are retrieved and compared using a comparator. The one with higher fitness value will be chosen by a multiplexer as the output that will be saved in the RAM. The SFB continues with the processing until 10 sets of child chromosomes are saved. A completion signal then triggers the Crossover Block.

In crossover, the 10 sets of chromosomes will be divided into 2 groups. Group one contains chromosome one to five, and group two contains chromosome six to ten. Each time one chromosome is chosen from each group. By slicing each of them into 5 genes and specifying a crossover rate, they will exchange the genes. After the exchange process, they would be concatenated into 2 new child chromosomes. These 2 new chromosomes will then be stored in the RAM with the same address as their parents. After applying crossover five times, a complete signal will trigger the Mutation Block.

The Mutation Block reads in a chromosome from the RAM, and slices the chromosome into 5 genes. Each gene will have a chance to mutate based on a specified mutation rate. The genes will then be concatenated as a child chromosome and saved right after the Mutation Block. After completing mutation for the 10 sets of chromosomes, a complete signal alerts the Constraint Satisfaction Block. This block checks whether there are duplicate genes in each chromosome, and will generate a new gene whenever there are repeating genes.

The best-score chromosomes are stored in the Elite RAM together with their corresponding fitness values. The output of the Elite RAM drives an LED decoder connected to seven-segment display LEDs, so that results can be interpreted and verified.

3 Design of GA-DP Blocks

In our hardware implementation, the calculation for the fitness value for a chromosome is complex and involves 3 functional blocks (FAB, TCB, and summation) before its fitness value is stored into the RAM.

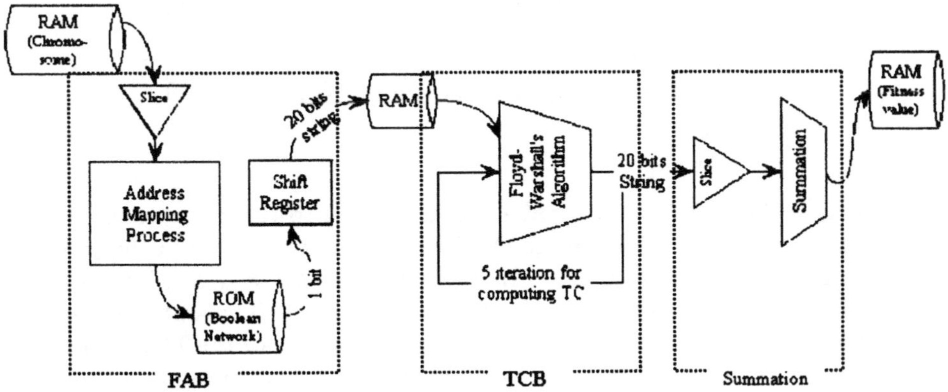

Fig. 3. Fitness Value Computation Logic Flow

3.1 Fitness Address Block (FAB)

The FAB reads in a chromosome from the RAM and slices it into 5 genes. Each gene is represented by 6 bits for our 30-node network. A computation unit for address index calculation of $f(p,q)$ can be formulated as:

$$f(p,q) = \begin{cases} q + p \times 29 & \text{if } p < q \\ q + p \times 29 + 1 & \text{otherwise} \end{cases} \quad \text{if } p \neq q \text{ and if } p,q = 0,1,\ldots,28,29 \quad (1)$$

In Eqn. 1 p, q stand for the gene number, and $f(p,q)$ is the address of the ROM which stores the Boolean value on whether gene $'p'$ can affect gene $'q'$ or not. There are 20 sets of result, because each gene can connect to 4 other genes. Therefore 20 bits are used to represent the interconnection of genes. The output from the ROM is either 1 or 0 ($R(p,q) = 1$ means that gene $'p'$ is affecting gene $'q'$. if $R(p,q) = 0$, then there is no effect from gene $'p'$ to gene $'q'$). The 20 sets of R from the ROM will then pass through a 20-bit register which will be concatenated to a string as the block output.

3.2 Transitive Closure Block (TCB)

The 20-bit string output from the FAB is used as the input to the TCB. The TCB carries out the Floyd-Warshall algorithm under the control of iteration loops. In implementing the Floyd-Warshall algorithm, the 20-bit string is reconstructed as a 5 by 5 square matrix with zero diagonal elements. All the combination of rows is under the OR operation and the required one is selected by the multiplexer. The matrix with excluded diagonal elements will be finally mapped to a 20-bit string as output.

3.3 Summation Block

The summation block receives the 20-bit string from the TCB. The 20 bits will be sliced into individual bits, which are added up to give the fitness value.

$$K_i = \sum_{\substack{p,q=0 \\ q \neq q}}^{p,q=29} F(f(p,q)) \text{ where } p,q = 0,1,\ldots,28,29 \quad (2)$$

The K_i is the output fitness value corresponding to the chromosome i. The fitness value will be stored in the RAM. Reading a chromosome in the previous RAM of FAB has a latency of 1. In the FAB, the 20 sets of $F(f(p,q))$ are computed in parallel. The latency for the multiplier is 1. The shift register and concatenation need 20 clock cycles to generate the output for the TCB. Therefore the FAB requires 22 clock cycles for computing one set of chromosomes. In the TCB we use a synchronous design that requires 183 clock cycles. The total computation time for computing one set of chromosomes sums up to 205 clock cycles.

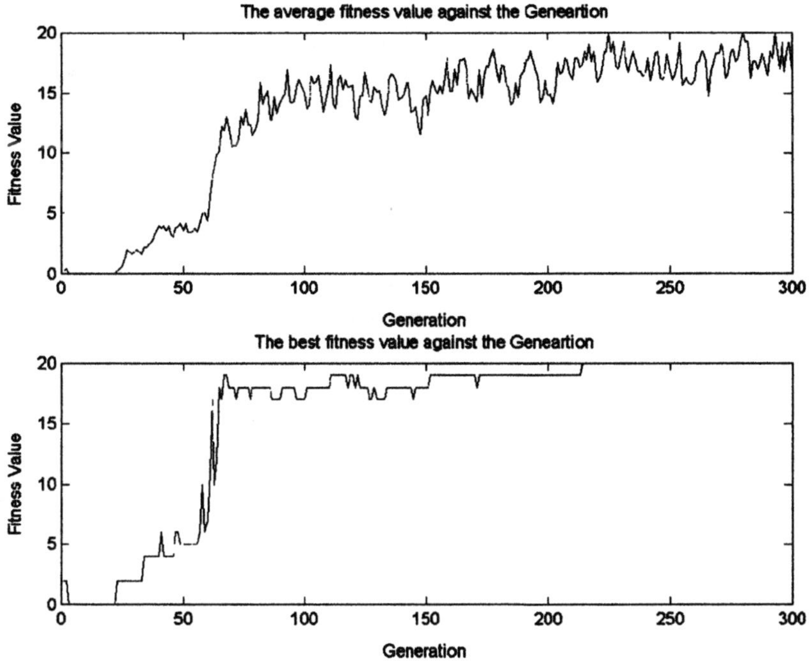

Fig. 4. GA-DP searching performance using MATLAB program

4 Simulation Results

A MATLAB program is prepared which implements the same algorithm as the GA-DP hardware for verification and performance comparison. Both the MATLAB software program and the hardware are searching the 5-node equivalence sets. The termination criterion for the GA iteration is 300 generation. The fitness value of GA in each generation is captured. The global optimal (5-node equivalence set is found) is reached once the fitness value equals 20. But for searching an equivalence set with size N, the global optimal is found once the fitness value equals $N \times (N-1)$.

The results of software and hardware simulation for performance comparison are shown in Figs. 4 and 5. In the graph, the y-axis is the fitness value and x-axis is the number of generation performed.

When comparing Figs. 4 and 5, the hardware has similar performance with that from the MATLAB simulation. The fitness values of both software and hardware system converge to the global optimal: The MATLAB program converges after around 220 generations while the hardware system converges after 70. Their difference in converging time is mainly due to the stochastic nature of GA. The random number generations for mutation and for crossover are constructed differently. The best fitness value of the hardware system has sharp

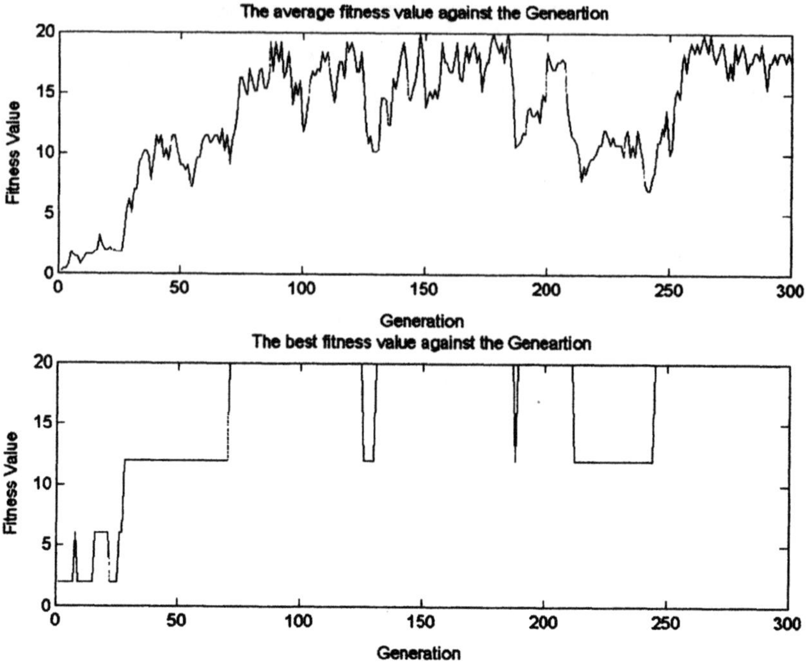

Fig. 5. GA-DP searching performance for FPGA

decreases at the 120th, 180th and 210th generation, but recovers back to the global optimal several iterations after. Apparently, this sharp-fall, sharp-rise effect is the consequence of mutation in the best chromosome.

4.1 Timing Analysis

Table 1. Upper bound of computing time for the GA-DP module

	Matlab Software Program Simulation(A)	FPGA 50Mhz Simulation(B)	FPGA speed up (A/B)
GA 300 Generation	PIII450MHz 41.69 seconds (CPU time)	XVC800 with clock 50MHz 0.01361 second	3063.1888
GA1000 Generation	142.7250 seconds (CPU time)	0.04538 seconds (CPU time)	3145.1080

In Table 1, the computation time of the MATLAB software program and the FPGA is compared. The speed up rate is around 3000 for the GA-DP system on FPGA hardware over software implementation. The GA-DP system requires 2269 clock cycles for one GA generation, and hence the total computation time for 300 generations equals $2269 \times 300 \div 50MHz = 0.01361s$. The speed up is mainly due to clock rate increase, and the required computation time also depends on the size of the equivalence set. The computation time can be formulated as $I \times (5N + N^3)$, where N is the size of the equivalence set (number of genes in an equivalence set), and I is the number of GA generation. The Floyd-Warshall algorithm has a computational complexity of N^3, while the other GA functional blocks have $O(N)$ complexity. Hence, the GA-DP system's computation complexity is $O(N^3)$. In our experimental study, the GA will converge after around 300 generations. Obviously, for a larger network a greater number of iterations are required to find the optimal.

Resource allocation The system consumes 64% of the FPGA resources called slices in the Virtex-800 devices.

5 Implementation

We have successfully implemented the GA-DP system on one FPGA processor. For the FPGA implementation, we verified the successful operation of the GA-DP system by reading the RAM data which capture the always-best score chromosome using a much slower clock. Data integrity check was performed by comparing the LED display in the XESS board. After using a 22.5 MHz clock running the FPGA for a while, we reduced the clock rate close to 0.92 Hz. The LED displayed the relevant values for the best chromosome. For instance, 14→5→9→6→1→ 31→20→14→5→9→6→1→31→20...

The value 31 was the starting indicator. Fitness value and chromosomes were sequentially displayed. We could see that {14, 5, 9, 6, 1} was found and was exactly one of the equivalence sets shown in Fig. 1.

6 Conclusion

The search of equivalence sets in large scale genetic network is an important step in gene expression data analysis. Our proposed GA-DP system has shown to give an efficient solution to the rather demanding computational problem. It also provides a realization of GA and Floyd-Warshall's algorithm using the FPGA platform. In our test case of a 30-node network, the equivalence set solution was found within 0.01361 second at a 50MHz clock rate, which is 3063 times faster than using a PIII 450 MHz computer. Correct results have been validated with both MATLAB simulation and FPGA implementation.

7 Acknowledgement

This research project was support by Hong Kong Research Grant Council (RGC) Earmarked Grant 4132/97E

References

1. Y.Maki, et al.: Development of a system for the inference of large scale genetic network. Proc. Pacific Symposium on Biocomputing (2000)
2. T. Akutsu, et al: Identification of gene regularity networks by strategic gene disruptions and gene over expressions. Proc. 9th ACM-SIAM Symp. Discrete Algorithm, 695(1998)
3. W. M. Fung, H.S. Ng, K.P. Lam: Digital FPGA implementation for Bellman-Ford computation, Proc. SPIE (ITCOM 2001), 4525-10, (2001)
4. K.P. Lam, C. W. Tong: Closed semiring connectionist network for the Bellman-Ford computation. IEE Proc. Comput. Dig. Tech., Vol. 143(3), (1996)
5. Xilinx Data Book 2000 - Programmable Logic Product, [Online], Available HTTP: http://www.xilinx.com/partinfo/databook.htm
6. XESS XSV Board Product Description, [online], Available HTTP: http://www.xess.com/prob014_4.php3
7. B. Shackleford, et al.: An FPGA-based genetic algorithm machine. Eigth ACM Int. Symp. on FPGA, Feb 10-11, (2000)
8. P. Graham, B. Nelson: Genetic algorithms in software and in hardware - a performance analysis of workstation and custom computing machine implementations. Proc. Fourth Annual IEEE Symp. on FPGAs for Custom Computing Machines, 216-225, (1996)
9. J. Koza et al.: Evolving computer programs using rapidly reconfigurable field programmable gate arrays and genetic programming. Proc. of the ACM Sixth Int. Symp. on FPGA, 209-219, (1997)
10. T.H. Cormen et al.: Introduction to algorithms. MIT Press, (1990)
11. Xilinx System Generator for Simulink: Xilinx blockset reference guide and basic tutorial. Xilinx, (2000)

REFLIX: A Processor Core for Reactive Embedded Applications

Zoran Salcic[1,2], Partha Roop[1], Morteza Biglari-Abhari[1], Abbas Bigdeli[1]

[1] Department of Electrical and Electronic Engineering, The University of Auckland, Private Bag 92019, Auckland, New Zealand,
[2] on leave at The University of Technology Vienna, Institute of Communications, Gusshausstr. 25/389, 1040 Vienna, Austria
z.salcic@auckland.ac.nz

Abstract: Efficient and reliable interaction with the environment (reactivity) is a key feature for many embedded system applications. Current implementation technologies that include standard microprocessors and microcontrollers, or fully customized systems, are not ideally suited to such reactive tasks. We propose novel microprocessor architecture that has native support for reactivity, with the flexibility to be customized at much higher level than usual microprocessor-based solutions. The proposed microprocessor architecture is an extension of our existing FLIX processor open core. The new processor core, called REFLIX (Reactive FLIX), guarantees at most one instruction cycle delay for priority resolution and preemption and supports design style for reactive applications used in Esterel programming language.

1 Introduction

Embedded systems most often have a dedicated microprocessor or a microcontroller that executes a non-terminating control program, which controls the environment that constitutes of a set of sensors and actuators, which are used for interaction with the environment. The control program repeatedly determines the status of the environment (by checking the status of the sensors and actuators) and then reacts based on the current status (hence embedded systems are often called *reactive systems)* [1], [2]. Determination of the environment status can be made either by polling (which checks for the presence of certain signals routinely) or by using interrupt mechanism (which is like an alert mechanism when certain signals occur in the environment). Polling is also known as *busy waiting* since CPU cycles are wasted while checking for the presence of signals in environment. Interrupts avoid busy waiting but have context switching overhead since the occurrence of an interrupt requires the execution of specific code (called interrupt service routine) leading to a change in the standard control flow of the program. Hence, the context of program execution needs to be saved prior to branching for interrupt handling and has to be restored after interrupt handling is completed. Such context-switching overhead can be considerable in an embedded system where environment interaction is a key. Moreover, as the interrupt handling is executed concurrently with the main control task, there is a danger of inconsistent

M. Glesner, P. Zipf, and M. Renovell (Eds.): FPL 2002, LNCS 2438, pp. 945-954, 2002.

system behavior due to mishandling of common resources (data). Also, different events often have different level of importance and priority-based interrupt schemes have to be used.

This paper describes a novel processor core, called REFLIX, which is aimed at reactive embedded applications. REFLIX provides a primitive set of features and instructions suited to such task in addition to a set of standard set of instructions found in common microprocessors. The proposed approach provides mechanism to avoid busy waiting associated with polling, when required, and context switching associated with interrupts completely. The environment interaction model of a reactive programming language Esterel [3] for embedded systems inspires this mechanism. The major contributions of this paper are the following:

a) We propose a microprocessor architecture that supports reactivity through a set of native instructions, which are lacking in previous architectures. All instructions, including those that look like conventional instructions for polling, perform in the same time equal to 4 machine cycles contributing to both efficiency and predictability of program execution.
b) REFLIX supports preemption and priority resolution based on external events using a new native instruction called abort, which can be nested to achieve priorities of external events. Our proof of concept prototype can resolve 4 levels of external event priorities during preemption, which is guaranteed to happen in a single instruction cycle. This is an extremely important feature for implementation of real-time tasks.

Section 2 gives background and framework for REFLIX design. In section 3, we introduce the REFLIX architecture and instruction set with emphasis on features that support reactivity. In section 4, we describe in more details the REFLIX data path and control unit together with some implementation aspects. Section 5 presents some concluding remarks related to the current implementation and our future work.

2 Related Work

One of the trends in implementation of embedded systems is to rely on processors for specific applications that better match requirements of those applications than general-purpose instruction processors [4]. There are several approaches suggested or used for customisation of those processors. Some of them rely on using existing architectures, such as those from ARM or MIPS [5, 6, 7]. Standard fixed processor cores are connected to programmable logic to implement additional instructions and functions. Some of the solutions are using parameterized processor cores that are customized at the time of their compilation/synthesis for FPGAs, such as Altera NiOS processor [5], or in run-time during system operation [8, 9]. Another processor cores [10,11] provide generic mechanisms for new instruction implementation that execute in functional units external to the processor core and are readily supported by software. A further step towards generalization has been proposed in [12], where a number of processor "templates" is used to provide a framework for different customization strategies. All above processors have general-purpose processor RISC-type architecture with more or less usual instruction sets that belong to RISC-type processors. None of those processors addresses aspects of reactive applications by supporting generic mechanisms for reactivity and preemption beyond usual interrupt structures and mechanisms found in conventional processors.

3 REFLIX Framework

REFLIX operation is inspired by Esterel, which is a synchronous reactive programming language that provides a neat set of constructs for modeling, verification and synthesis of reactive systems. The environment of any Esterel program consists of a set of sensors and signals, which can be modeled abstractly using constructs available in the language. The activation clock of the Esterel program is a predefined event called the *tick* event. During every tick the Esterel kernel samples its environment and performs a set of *instantaneous* reactions based on the values present in its environment during the present tick. The main constructs for interacting with the environment are *await* (which is a delay construct), *emit* (which performs signal emissions to the environment), *sustain* (which sustains a signal forever), *abort* (which is preemption construct), and *trap* (which is similar to software interrupts). In addition to such constructs for control flow Esterel supports data handling through host language such as C or Java.

REFLIX is a processor core designed to capture main ideas of Esterel interaction model with the environment. For that purpose REFLIX provides a set of native instructions suitable for reactive. These include native facilities for *delay*, *signal emission*, *priorities*, *preemption* and *task execution* facility using functional units. REFLIX essentially represents another customization of our existing FLIX processor [10,11] open core. By adopting Esterel model for reactivity and by supporting it on machine instruction level, we achieve two major goals: a) the same processor core can be used to implement different reactive algorithms for different applications by changing only programs and not processor hardware and b) preserve performance predictability by guaranteeing execution times for all primitive instructions. In this way we provide a generic platform for implementation of a large class of embedded applications, which would otherwise be implemented either by separately synthesized hardware (usually finite state machine - FSM) or by complicated software means that can be implemented on standard microprocessors but with many difficulties.

4 REFLIX Core Architecture and Features

The current version of REFLIX has adopted the original FLIX core for its base with removal of the interrupt structure and asynchronous event handling altogether. REFLIX preserves FLIX word length (16 bits) and instruction execution principles (4 machine cycles make one instruction cycle). Main departures and extensions to the original core that directly aim reactive applications are:

- Variable numbers of input sensor and output sensor lines. Support for up to16 sensor input lines, Sin[15..0], and 16 signal output lines, Sout[15..0].
- Notion of real-time in terms of numbers of instruction cycles. One instruction cycle corresponds to one tick of the Esterel reaction clock and equals to four machine cycles.
- Introduction of internal timers that generate user programmable TimeOut signals. Number of internal timers is customizable and represented by a design parameter. TimeOut signals can be used for interaction with the environment or can be fed back to the REFLIX core itself and used for synchronization purposes.
- Introduction of *abort* mechanism for preemption based on external events. Any piece of code can be wrapped up within *abort* statement (abort body) and immediately abandoned in case that an external event on specified sensor input or timing event occurs.

4.1 Reactive Instructions

There are five basic instructions in the reactive category and they are presented in Table 1. Most of REFLIX instructions are only one word long, but some of the reactive instructions require two words for immediate operands or address information.

Table 1 REFLIX instructions supporting reactive processing

Instruction syntax	**Length and format** (No of bits in parenthesis)	**Function/Description**
SAWAIT signal	W1: Opcode(8) Signal(4)	Wait until signal is present.
TAWAIT delay	W1: Opcode(8) W2: Time(16)	Immediate delay— wait until specified time elapses (wait at least one system tick - time is expressed in the number of instruction cycles)
EMIT signal	W1: Opcode(8) Signal(4)	Specified signal is set high for one instruction cycle
SUSTAIN signal	W1: Opcode(8) Signal(4)	Specified signal is raised forever
ABORT <Timer/Signal> continuation-address	W1:Opcode(10) Timer(2)/Signal(4) W2: Address(16)	Preemption instruction. Abort has a body up to the instruction whose address is indicated by the continuation address. Signal can be either external one or from an internal timer

In order to illustrate the use of new reactive instructions, let's look to a simple example of a program that controls a seat-belt alarm controller. After every time a car's ignition is turned on, check if the driver's seat belt is fastened within some C1 time. If seat belt is not fastened within this time, generate an alarm until alarm-input is turned off. The following is a simple REFLIX program to implement this behavior:

```
start:
  SAWAIT IGNITION-ON;                   wait until IGNITION-ON
     START Timer1, C1;                  initialize Timer1 with C1
     ABORT Timer1 addr1;                abort activated on Timer1 timeout
       AWAIT BELT-ON;                   wait until BELT-ON
addr1: ABORT ALARM-INPUT-OFF addr2; abort activated on
                                        ; ALARM-INPUT-OFF
         SUSTAIN ALARM;                 activate ALARM
addr2:   JMP start;                     back to beginning
```

4.2 Preemption Support

Native ABORT instruction is introduced to support preemption with priorities. In the current REFLIX prototype ABORT instruction can work with up to 16 different external input signals and up to four internal timers generated signals. ABORT instructions can be nested to support up to four levels of priorities.

An ABORT instruction is active from the instant it is executed until its entire body is executed or until an event on the signal occurs that preempts all unexecuted instructions within the body. Format of the instruction is as follows:

OPCODE (10)	Timer(2)/Signal(4)
Continuation-address (16)	

Two different operation codes are used for abort operations, one for an abort on an external signal and the other for an abort on a timer. The ABORT instruction is executed in two stages with the support of a dedicated hardware unit called the abort-handling block:

- **Abort activation**. It is executed immediately after the fetching and decoding ABORT instruction, when REFLIX starts monitoring change (activation) of the designated signal. The continuation address, from where the program will continue execution if preemption happens, is stored into the REFLIX abort handling block.
- **Abort termination**. Once the designated signal is activated, the abort is taken and an unconditional jump to the continuation address is executed, or, if the continuation address is reached and the designated signal has not been activated, the abort is automatically terminated.

The abort handling block (AHB) also supports nesting and prioritizing of abort statements. Current proof of concept implementation supports nesting to up to 4 levels of aborts. The AHB contains active abort signal register (AASR) block with 4 registers with the length that equals the number of input sensing signals, which can abort current program execution. Registers are used to store the code of the signal line that starts to be monitored for signal activation. Each signal line has an unique code generated using a one-hot encoding scheme (only one bit can have value 1). Addresses of AASR registers, 0 to 3, at the same time represent, in ascending order, priorities of signals that are monitored. The first executed ABORT instruction always stores the monitored signal code into AASR(0), next nested ABORT instruction stores its monitored signal code into AASR(1), and so on. Summary information on all currently monitored signals that can abort program sequence is stored in joint abort signal register (JASR). Its value is obtained by bit-wise OR-ing values of all AASRs:

$$JASR_i = AASR_i(0) + \ldots + AASR_i(3) \text{ for } i=0, 1, \ldots, 15$$

As JASR can't preserve information on priorities of monitored signals, each AASR is associated with a single bit flag called abort flag (AF), and individual AF bits will be set if corresponding AASR register (with the same address) is non-empty (with AF(0) being 1 for highest priority monitored signal). Summary joint abort flag (JAF) contains information on presence of monitored signals, or

$$JAF = AF(0) + AF(1) + AF(2) + AF(3)$$

The REFLIX control unit determines an action path during instruction execution based on the value of the JAF bit as it is shown in section 4. Another register block contains four active abort address registers (AAARs), which are used to store continuation addresses of currently active abort instructions. Highest priority ABORT instruction (outermost one) continuation address is in AAAR(0), next lower priority continuation address is in AAAR(1) and so on.

Signal input register (SIR) is used to capture (latch) activation of signals on individual input sensing lines. This information is used, together with the information on currently monitored signals, to identify existence of pending (non-processed) abort events. For that purpose, another flag, called pending abort event flag (PAEF) is introduced and used by REFLIX control unit to provide proper and immediate reaction when events on monitored signal lines occur. It's value is derived as

$$PAEF = (SIR_0\ JASR_0) + \ldots + (SIR_{15}\ JASR_{15})$$

Abort termination stage happens when monitored event occurs, or when abort instruction reaches its continuation address without occurrence of event. Termination of an ABORT instruction causes also termination of all other ABORT instruction nested within its body that are of the lower priority.

Two pointers called abort read pointer (ARP) and abort write pointer (AWP) are used to up-date addresses of registers within the AHB from which information will be read or written to and they are not user visible. They are used only by the control unit and can be considered as its part.

Other parts of programming model include signal output register (SOR) with individually controllable/writtable bits, and pool of timers that appear as memory mapped registers with some programmable features. The level of their programmability is application dependant and can be customized by the selection of configuration (VHDL generics) parameters. Their meanings are more or less obvious and they are described further in the following section where we discuss the REFLIX data path.

5 REFLIX Design and Implementation

REFLIX data path with emphasized differences to original FLIX data path is shown in Figure 1. The data path is organized around two internal buses, called ABUS and DBUS, which are used for transfers of address and data information between internal registers, respectively, and enable to carry two register transfers, between two pairs of registers, at the same time (machine cycle). Abort handling block is shown with the shaded background in Figure 1.

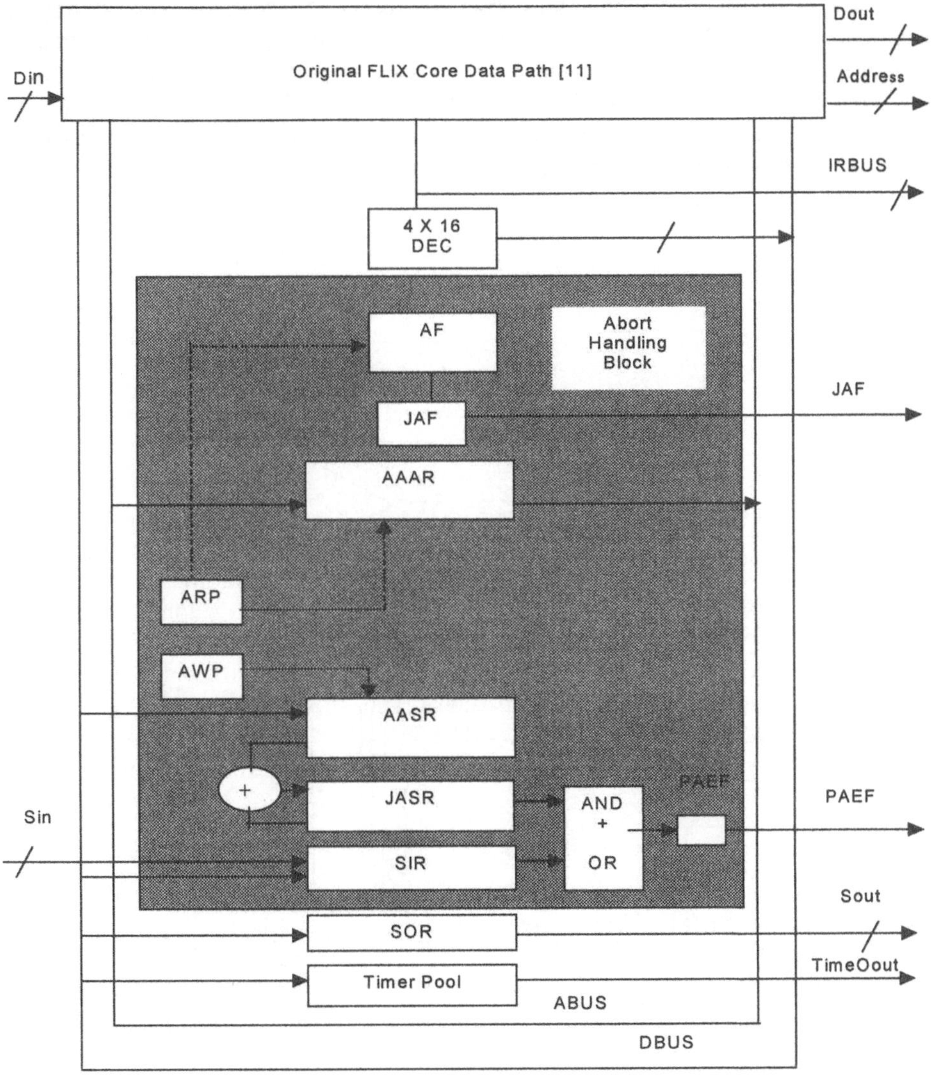

Figure 1 REFLIX data path

One of the major issues in the overall REFLIX design was to fit it within the basic and very simple FLIX framework and to preserve some of the original core features, which have been found useful when using them in a number of customization projects. The instruction cycle is one of those features, which permits each of the instructions to be completely executed in four machine cycles. This leads to the easy maintenance of time, both REFLIX global time and individual timing relationships, especially those which use locally generated relative times and timing based events. Both the global clock and locally generated non-overlapping four clock phases are available to external logic to drive external circuits (including FUs).

A conceptual REFLIX instruction execution cycle, which also depicts control unit operation, is shown in Figure 2. All events on monitored signals recorded during one instruction cycle will be given attention in the next instruction cycle (tick of time). In case of the absence of pending events, the control unit performs two actions:

- Next instruction is fetched from memory and executed. Although there is no special difference between instructions, the ABORT instruction is emphasized in diagram of Figure 2, as it carries operations on the registers of the AHB.

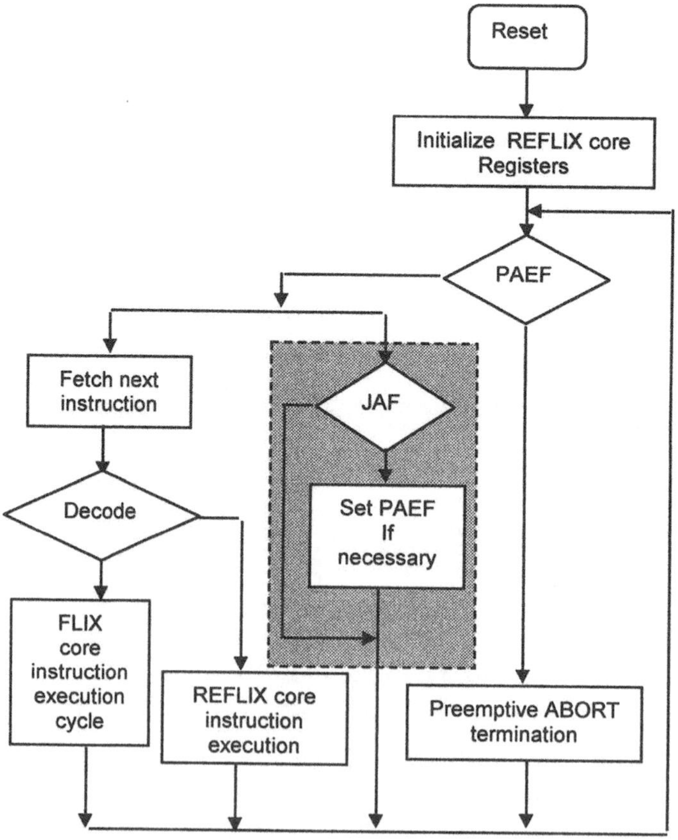

Figure 2 REFLIX control unit global operation

- Non-preemptive termination of ABORT instruction, if any, is performed in parallel with instruction fetching and execution.

For REFLIX implementation and prototyping we have used field-programmable logic devices (FPLDs). There two major reasons for this: (a) FPLDs provide an ideal prototyping environment with very fast turn-around time between two versions of the design, and (b) with the appearance of huge FPLDs with millions usable equivalent gates, it becomes feasible to build whole systems on programmable chips (SoPC).

On the other hand FPLDs are accompanied with advanced design tools and HDLs that enable design of parameterized designs that can be relatively easily customized for specific applications. This aspect of REFLIX design has not been emphasized in the paper. The first implementation is used as a proof of concept and incorporates parameterization of only some of resources, such as number of timers, number of sensing input signals, number of output signals and number of priority levels of external events (depth of nesting).

6 Conclusions

The REFLIX approach represents a novel way for supporting reactive systems at the processor hardware level. Inspired by Esterel language, the first REFLIX implementation supports dealing with input and output signals in Esterel-like model of computation, without true concurrency. However, by supporting constructs for synchronization and preemption on random and timing signals, REFLIX enables writing programs, which can be easily verified. REFLIX programs are predictable in their temporal performance and provide guaranteed reaction times on external events without unnecessary overheads and context-switching found in conventional microprocessors. Processor supports notion of time, which can easily be derived based on fact that each instruction performs in time equal to 4 machine cycles. In concrete FPLD implementations minimum clock cycle can go to up to 25ns, which defines temporal features of the solution.

REFLIX architecture is based on a concept of flexible instruction execution unit, which is well suited to embedded systems by keeping the core simple and small (essential for embedded systems) and providing facilities for interaction with a set of functional units to achieve more complex tasks (which is also very similar in spirit to the Esterel tasking model).

The REFLIX core is generic in many respects, by providing parameterized configuration that can be easily customized and instantiated for specific application. As such it is suited for SoPC applications. It fits in a fraction of typical high-capacity FPLD, thus leaving plenty of space for modifications, additions and customisation.

The major limitation of the current implementation is that it does not support fully Esterel model of computation, which is one of our goals, particularly true concurrency and valued signals. Despite of that, we have found a number of applications that can be described much more clearly and concisely than with the assembly languages of the conventional processors, which don't have similar support for reactivity, and also verified using formal methods.

References

[1] Harel D. Statecharts: A Visual Formalism for Complex Systems, Sci. Comput. Prog., 8; 1987, pp. 231-274

[2] Pnueli A. Application of temporal logic to the specification and verification of reactive systems: a survey of current trends, Lecture notes in computer science, 224; pp. 510-584. Springer Verlag, 1986

[3] Berry G. and Gonthier G. The ESTEREL synchronous programming language, Sc. Comput. Prog., 19; 1992, pp. 87-152

[4] Fisher J.A. Customized instruction sets for embedded processors. In Proc. 36th Design Automation Conference, pp. 253–257,1999.

[5] Altera Corporation. Excalibur Embedded Processor Solutions, http://www.altera.com

[6] Triscend. The Configurable System on a Chip, http://www.triscend.com

[7]] Xilinx Corporation. IBM and Xilinx team to create new generation of integrated circuits, http://www.xilinx.com/prs rls/ibmpartner.htm

[8] Wirthlin M and Hutchings B. A dynamic instruction set computer. In Proc. IEEE Symp. on Field Programmable Custom Computing Machines, pp. 99–107. IEEE Computer Society Press, 1995.

[9] Donlin A. Self modifying circuitry - a platform for tractable virtual circuitry. In Field Programmable Logic and Applications, LNCS 1482, pp. 199–208. Springer, 1998

[10] Salcic Z. and Maunder B. "CCSimP - an Instruction-level Custom-Configurable Processor for FPLDs" , in *Field-Programmable Logic FPL '96, Lecture notes in Computer Science 1142* (R.Hartenstein, M.Gloessner and M.Servit editors), Springer, 1996, pp. 280-289

[11] Salcic Z. and Mistry T. FLIX Environment for Generation of Custom-Configurable Machines in FPLDs for Embedded Applications, *Elsevier Journal on Microprocessors and Microsystems*, vol.23(8-9), December 1999, pp. 513-526

[12] S.P. Peng, W. Luk and P.K.Y Cheung. Flexible instruction set processors. Proceedings *CASES'00,* November 17-19, 2000, San Jose, California

Factors Influencing the Performance of a CPU-RFU Hybrid Architecture

Girish Venkataramani, Suraj Sudhir, Mihai Budiu, and Seth Copen Goldstein

Carnegie Mellon University
Pittsburgh PA 15213
{girish,ssudhir,mihaib,seth}@cs.cmu.edu

Abstract. Closely coupling a reconfigurable fabric with a conventional processor has been shown to successfully improve the system performance. However, today's superscalar processors are both complex and adept at extracting Instruction Level Parallelism (ILP), which introduces many complex issues to the design of a hybrid CPU-RFU system. This paper examines the design of a superscalar processor augmented with a closely-coupled reconfigurable fabric. It identifies architectural and compiler issues that affect the performance of the overall system. Previous efforts at combining a processor core with a reconfigurable fabric are examined in the light of these issues. We also present simulation results that emphasize the impact of these factors.

1 Introduction

The continued scaling of the minimum feature size of CMOS technology provides the chip real estate necessary to place a sizable reconfigurable fabric on the same die as a processor. Reconfigurable computing devices have been shown to achieve substantial performance improvements over conventional processors on some computational kernels [4]. These benefits arise from hardware customization, which avoids the mismatch between the basic requirements of the algorithms and the architectures of the processors. Previous research has shown that closely coupling conventional processor cores with such reconfigurable fabrics is the preferred method of deploying these devices, since these devices can be ill-suited in executing entire applications due to space limitations, and inefficiency in implementing some operations (e.g. floating-point arithmetic).

Modern superscalar architectures present powerful techniques to exploit Instruction Level Parallelism (ILP) from a dynamic instruction stream. These processors allow multiple instruction issue and out-of-order execution. Augmenting these processors with a reconfigurable fabric may offer many opportunities to significantly boost performance, since several instructions, from the CPU and Reconfigurable Functional Unit (RFU), can be executed concurrently.

We focus on automatically mapping general-purpose applications to a hybrid architecture, and identify critical factors that can affect this system's performance. These factors fall into two broad categories – the CPU-RFU interface design, and compiler support. The former is heavily influenced by the CPU architecture. For example, the ability to concurrently execute CPU instructions and RFU configurations can better exploit

M. Glesner, P. Zipf, and M. Renovell (Eds.): FPL 2002, LNCS 2438, pp. 955–965, 2002.

the features of superscalar architectures. However, if they are both allowed to access a shared address space, then memory consistency becomes an issue. Compiler support determines what kind of code regions (instruction sequences, loops, whole functions) will form *RFUops*. An RFUop is an operation that executes on the fabric.

This paper identifies and describes a number of factors that represent potential bottlenecks to performance. Resolving these problems gives direction to the design of the hybrid system. In Section 2, we present the architectural issues that are relevant in hybrid machine design. In Section 3, we examine the necessary compiler support required to boost performance. In Section 4, we describe our tool-chain. Our experimental framework is presented in Section 5, where we also analyze our results. In Section 6, we discuss previous hybrid designs in the light of the issues presented in this paper.

2 The Hybrid Architecture

Many choices face the designer of a hybrid processor. For every feature under consideration, the costs and benefits must be weighed. The costs may come in the form of additional hardware support, runtime overheads, and complexity. The primary benefit of adding a new capability to the reconfigurable fabric is enlarging the selection space of possible RFUops that can be placed on the fabric, leading to increased performance.

2.1 ISA Additions

An RFUop may be represented as a series of instructions that trigger the RFUop's execution, allow access to data, and write back results. This can either be done with a single instruction or with multiple instructions. We have chosen to use multiple instructions, since it gives us more flexibility to experiment with the design. We define `inputrfu` to be an instruction that will transfer the RFUop's input data from the CPU's register file to the fabric. The `startrfu` instruction triggers the execution of the RFUop. This instruction must specify the RFUop's identification number to select the RFUop. The `outputrfu` instruction transfers the results of the RFUop back to the register file.

The number of registers that can be specified with a single `inputrfu` (or `outputrfu`) instruction is limited by the instruction encoding width. Multiple `inputrfu` (or `outputrfu`) instructions are used if necessary.

2.2 Effect on the Superscalar Pipeline

Superscalar architectures are characterized by a multiple instruction issue, out-of-order core, with the ability to execute speculatively. In our hybrid architecture, the RFUop instructions go through the pipeline just like the rest of the instructions. When an RFUop is executing, the `outputrfu` instruction does not commit until the RFUop completes. Since, instructions are always committed in order, no instructions beyond the `outputrfu` instructions can commit. This causes a structural hazard, since the reorder buffer will soon fill up.

The effect of this hazard can be ameliorated by re-ordering instructions such that the `outputrfu` instruction appears as late in the instruction stream as possible (e.g.

just before the first instruction that is data dependent on the RFUop). Similarly, the `inputrfu` and `startrfu` instructions can be moved up the instruction stream, in order to start RFUop execution as soon as possible. The instructions appearing between the `startrfu` and `outputrfu` instructions can execute and commit, thereby reducing the pipeline congestion.

2.3 Memory Interface

The most suitable type of memory access interface depends intimately on the kind of applications that are targeted. Some previous research has focused exclusively on accelerating streaming multimedia and image processing applications on the reconfigurable fabric. In such cases, it is often useful to have Direct Memory Access (DMA), since access patterns are regular and predictable [10, 5].

Our research focuses on general-purpose C programs. In such applications, it is difficult to gather RFUops of reasonable sizes without including load/stores. Since both the CPU and the RFU can access a share address space, the memory interface needs to synchronize all accesses to ensure consistency.

In superscalar processors, memory accesses are dispatched from a structure such as a load-store queue (LSQ). The LSQ checks for dependencies between its entries, thereby ensuring memory consistency. When the CPU executes concurrently with an RFUop, there is a possibility that memory accesses from the RFUop arrive at the LSQ after a memory reference instruction that follows the RFUop in the program order. In this situation, memory inconsistency could arise if both the memory references access the same memory blocks. We can imagine three different scenarios:

- No Memory Accesses by RFUop: In the trivial case, the memory instructions following the RFUop can be issued freely.
- CPU and RFU access disjoint memory addresses: These accesses can also be permitted.
- CPU and RFU access common memory addresses: To maintain memory consistency, there has to be a mechanism to serialize such accesses.

While ensuring memory consistency, it is important to limit the negative impact on performance that this can potentially cause. Thus we define a protocol which allows memory access from the first two classes to execute in parallel with the RFUop while those in the third class are not issued until the RFUop completes. The accesses from the first and second cases can be scheduled between the `startrfu` and `outputrfu` instructions, while the memory accesses in the third case must appear after the `outputrfu` instruction. However, implementing this policy effectively is difficult since completely disambiguating memory accesses is hard even with the best pointer analyses [7].

An orthogonal issue is the sequence of accesses that originate from the fabric alone. Due to the placement of the RFUop on the fabric, it may be the case that memory references don't arrive at the LSQ in program order, although they are issued in order. A memory reference from later in the program may be placed closer to the fabric's external interfaces, and thus may arrive at the LSQ before an earlier reference.

2.4 Concurrent Active Configurations

With superscalar processors, it is possible to issue multiple `startrfu` instructions concurrently. However, support for multiple active configurations introduces other complexities - contentions for fabric resources, like external I/O pins, and space availability. When the RFUops contain memory references, memory consistency is an issue. If all the references in two RFUops cannot be disambiguated, then they may have to be serialized.

Not allowing concurrent execution of RFUops, on the other hand, could severely restrict the pipeline. Starting with the second RFUop all instructions will stagnate in the fetch queue, waiting for the first RFUop to complete. Compiler directed instruction re-ordering can help in this case if instructions that are not dependent on the second RFUop are scheduled before it.

3 Compiler Support

In this paper we are interested in automatic compilation of high-level languages to hybrid systems. The compiler support is thus essential for the successful utilization of an RFU. In addition to standard optimizations, the key component of such a compiler is to partition the code between the RFU and the CPU and to generate the configurations for the RFU, as well as the interface code between the two. We are addressing here just the automatic application partitioning.

The primary objective of code partitioning is to identify code fragments that can be accelerated by execution on the fabric. A number of architectural constraints may restrict the types of the RFUops that are eventually extracted. Some operations may be too costly to implement in reconfigurable hardware (e.g., floating point computations), or may require complex non-computational processing (e.g., procedure calls, exceptions, system calls).

The potential search space for RFUop selection is huge. Hence, we need to develop a systematic approach to finding the code segments that are most likely to form RFUops. The selected segments should have sufficient parallelism, and should be sufficiently large to amortize the overhead cost of the RFUop invocation. From a structural point of view, the following types of code fragments can be selected for implementation as an RFUop:

- Short sequences of dependent instructions which do not fully utilize the processor datapath. These can be collapsed into *custom instructions*, which are implemented very efficiently on the RFU.
- Basic blocks: are attractive since they are relatively easy to analyze. However, the average size of basic blocks is small, resulting in small RFUops which often cannot amortize the RFU invocation overhead.
- Loops: are a natural candidate for classical parallelizing compilers. Similarly, they are attractive as RFUops, as loops can concentrate a large percentage of the program running time, and can benefit from pipelining.
- Hyperblocks: are contiguous groups of basic blocks, having a single control-flow entry point, but possibly multiple exits. Hyperblocks offer the potential for increased

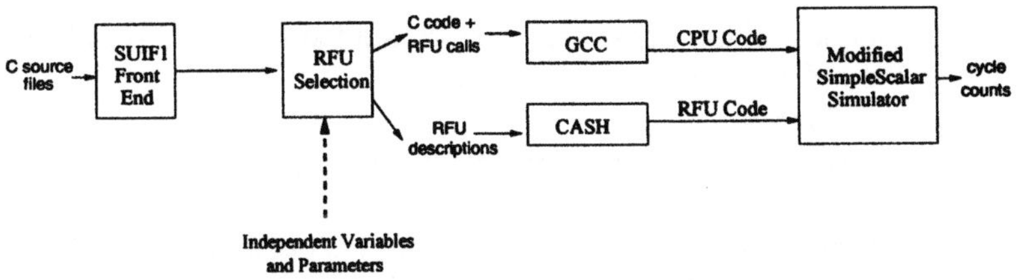

Fig. 1. The Compiler-Simulator tool chain of the system.

ILP through the use of predicated execution, which removes control dependences by speculating execution along many control-flow paths.

- Single Entry—Single Exit (SESE) Regions: hyperblocks implemented as RFUops raise the additional complication of returning not only data from the RFU, but also control-flow information on RFUop execution termination, which requires a more complicated hardware-software interface. SESE regions do not suffer from this problem. Moreover, natural loops often form SESE regions.
- Whole functions: are particular cases of SESE regions. Prior research has not considered this partitioning strategy, as RFUops were mostly constrained by the available hardware resources. The exponential increase of hardware resources however will make this factor less important, and will thus make whole function selection an attractive solution. The main advantage of this approach is simplicity: there are few alternatives to consider, no new interfaces have to be introduced into the program, functions represent "autonomous" regions of computation, with relatively few inputs and outputs, and program ILP profiles roughly correspond to function divisions.
- Larger application fragments. The best reported speed-ups for hybrid systems involve hand-partitioned applications, where the portions with high parallelism are implemented on the RFU, and the rest of the computation is handled by the CPU. However, automatic parallelism extraction from large application fragments is still an elusive goal of compiler research.

4 Tool Chain

In this section we describe the tool chain we have used to conduct our experiments (Figure 1). It has two parts: Compilation, and CPU-RFU simulation. There are two major phases in compilation - RFUop selection and configuration code generation for the RFU.

The RFUop selection pass is influenced by a number of independent parameters and constraints. These parameters may be classified under two broad categories—architectural and policy-driven. The architectural constraints define the boundaries of the RFU and the CPU-RFU interface. Currently, we support the parameterization of the following architectural constraints—whether memory operations are permissible from the fabric, and the maximum number of permissible RFUop inputs and outputs. The policy-driven parameters aid in refining the potential RFUop search space within the given architectural constraints. These variables define the structural profile of the selected RFUops. We define the following policies:

- Select only natural loops
- Select only short sequences of dependent instruction sequences; i.e., custom instructions
- Restrict the minimum size of RFUops (in terms of the number of instructions)

Further, we assume that there are two hard architectural constraints that are not parameterizable—RFUops must have only one control exit, and RFUops must be self-contained, i.e., RFUops cannot invoke other RFUops or other functions meant to execute on the CPU.

We can view these constraint categories as filters that help in selecting the best RFUops. In addition to these two filters, it is essential to have another filter that diagnoses the goodness of the RFUops selected by the first two filters. This filter will use heuristics like RFUop latency, area and average-ILP estimates to determine RFUop goodness. Without this, the selection process blindly generates too many RFUops. This increases total execution time for two reasons. First, it increases the RFUop invocation overhead. Second, and most importantly, it reduces the effectiveness of traditional compiler optimizations by creating regions of the program which are opaque to the compiler; effectively disallowing certain instruction sequences from being considered by the optimizer. In our present compiler, this filter uses a simple heuristic that computes a quick estimate of the Cycles-per-instruction (CPI) of the RFU. If this CPI is greater than a threshold, then the RFU is rejected.

The compiler translates the selected RFUops to hardware implementations by aggressively speculating and exposing various parallelism forms, such as bit-, instruction-, pipeline- and loop-level parallelism [2]. Currently, it generates a C program that represents a custom timing and functional simulator of the RFUop; a Verilog back-end is in progress.

The compiler is implemented within the SUIF1 compiler infrastructure [13]. The SUIF-based compiler partitions the code and generates a lower level C program that is then compiled with gcc and simulated for measurements. Our experience with this tool flow indicates that the interaction between the base SUIF passes and gcc tends to introduce extraneous instructions in the application, creating a substantial amount of noise in our measurements. For instance, SUIF introduces a number of temporaries in the source code, which causes gcc to create register spills. For the decoder version of the `epic` benchmark from Mediabench [8], compiling with SUIF and then gcc causes the the execution time to increase by 10% compared to when it is compiled just with gcc. Further, the number of memory references increases by about 30%.

We use a modified version of the SimpleScalar simulation infrastructure [1] to measure the performance of the various benchmarks on our architectural model. Our simulation framework has two components—RFUop Simulation and CPU simulation. For the former, we use the automatically generated RFU simulator, as described above. A modified version of the SimpleScalar out-of-order simulator is used to perform cycle-accurate CPU simulation [12]. The ISA is augmented to include `inputrfu`, `startrfu` and `outputrfu` instructions. When a `startrfu` instruction is encountered, a separate RFUop simulation thread is invoked.

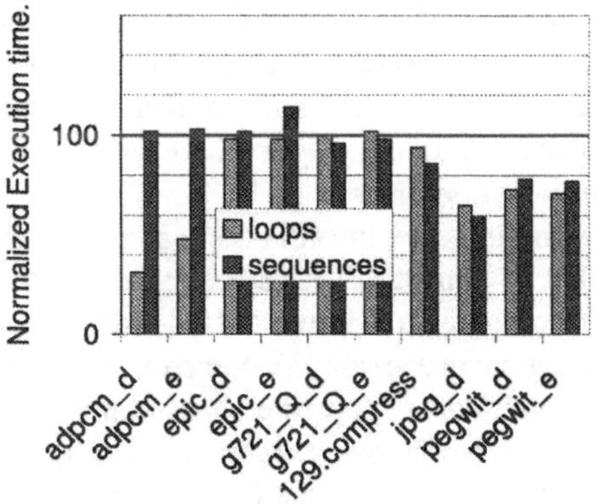

Fig. 2. *Performance comparison between a (single-issue, in-order) MIPS core with the same core augmented with an RFU*

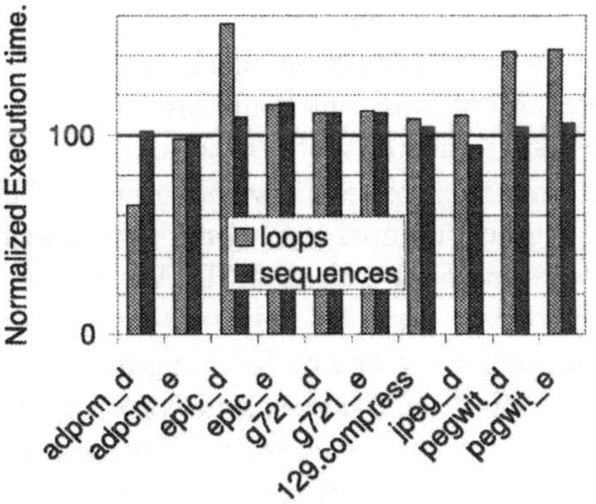

Fig. 3. *Performance comparison between a (4-issue, out-of-order) superscalar core with the same core augmented with an RFU*

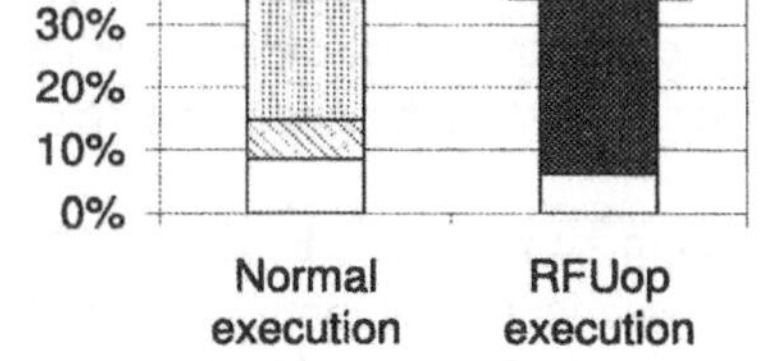

Fig. 4. *Relative breakdown of total execution time by Fetch Queue sizes. The fetch queue is almost always full during RFUop execution, implying that the pipeline mostly stalls during RFUop execution*

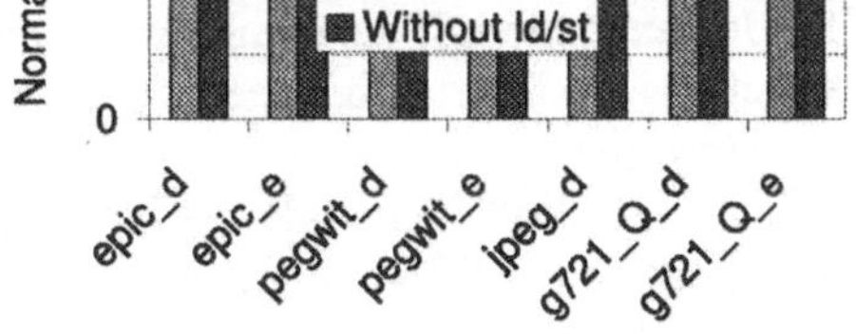

Fig. 5. *Effect of RFUops containing memory references.*

5 Experimental Results

We set up our experiments to compare the performance of our hybrid system with a CPU core. We compiled benchmarks from the Mediabench [8] and SPEC95 [11] benchmark suites. Most programs in the Mediabench suite have an encoder and a decoder version; these are indicated with _e and _d suffixes respectively. In the graphs where we compare performance, we have always normalized the execution times.

Figure 2 compares a hybrid system with a single-issue, in-order core, and the same core augmented with an RFU. We can see that in almost all cases the hybrid system outperforms the CPU-only version. Figure 3 compares a 4-issue, out-of-order superscalar processor, and an RFU augmented to the same processor. We compare two kinds of RFUop selection policies in these figures—when only loops are chosen, and when custom instructions are selected. In spite of the fact that the same compilation and mapping techniques were used in the two hybrid systems, we see that the performance of the superscalar+RFU system does not always match the performance of the superscalar processor. This implies that the techniques employed in the in-order hybrid architecture do not scale to the superscalar hybrid architecture. We attribute the slowdown to four principal factors:

- Parallelism: Currently, we do not reschedule any independent instructions between the `inputrfu`/`startrfu` and `outputrfu` instructions. Hence, the re-order buffer becomes a structural hazard when an RFUop is executing. Moreover, our current model does not support concurrent execution of multiple RFUops. This can severely affect the CPU pipeline. Figure 4 shows the relative breakdown of total execution time (of the adpcm_d benchmark) by fetch queue sizes. Notice that the fetch queue is almost always full during RFUop execution, which implies that the CPU is unable to issue any instructions as the pipeline stalls. Figure 6 shows the effect of stalling the CPU when an RFUop executes. In one case, the CPU is not allowed to issue any instructions after a `startrfu` is dispatched. The second is the default case when instructions are issued, but not committed until the `outputrfu` commits. Even with the restricted model in the latter case, there is up to 18% performance speedup. This shows that there is a lot of opportunity to issue more instructions in the CPU during RFUop execution. If the compiler can reorder instructions such that independent instructions are inserted between `startrfu` and `outputrfu`, the performance can only improve.
- RFUop selection: The code partitioning pass needs to be refined. The policy filter may need to be different. Selecting just instruction sequences or loops restricts us to a smaller domain of candidate RFUops. Moreover, our heuristic for diagnosing RFUops is simplistic. This tends to generate RFUops that produce more overhead than benefits. In Figure 7, we describe the effect of restricting the minimum RFUop size. When the minimum size of all RFUops is 15 static instructions, the performance is much better than when the minimum RFUop size is 5. Using a simple policy decision, we see that we can reduce some of the unnecessary overhead.
- Speculation: If an RFUop contains an entire loop, the compiler synthesizes a circuit that supports extensive pipelining and speculation. However, we do not speculate across loop iterations. This can cause a cascaded effect on performance if the critical path of the loop body contains memory references (with potentially large laten-

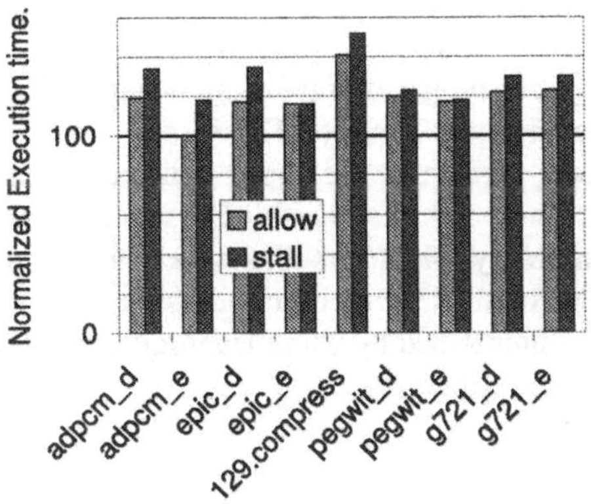

Fig. 6. *Effect of stalling CPU during RFUop execution*

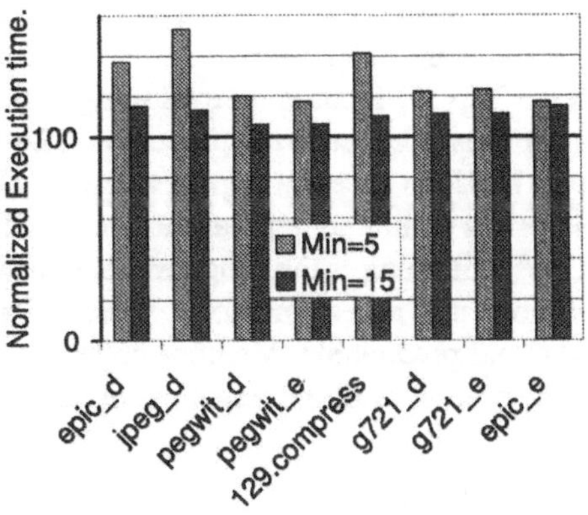

Fig. 7. *Effect of restricting the minimum RFUop size (in terms of number of instructions)*

cies). On the superscalar processor, speculation is supported across all conditional branches. Figure 5 shows that the performance of the system is better when RFUops don't contain memory references.

- Our tool flow introduces a substantial amount of noise. Hence, in some cases, the results are not indicative of a realistic evaluation.

6 Related Work

We can classify previous research based on the host CPU: those that augment a in-order core, and those that use a superscalar processor.

PRISC [9] is the first to explore the feasibility of a RFU on the datapath of a MIPS processor. All custom instructions must fit within a two-input/one-output signature, read and write the register file, and take a single processor cycle to execute.

GARP [3] augments an RFU co-processor to a MIPS core. The compiler attempts to accelerate loops by pipelining them using techniques similar to those used in VLIW compilers. The RFUops are chosen from hyperblocks that have loops embedded within them. The RFU can access the processor's caches and main memory directly.

The T1000 architecture [14] is an extension of the PRISC, although the CPU is a superscalar processor. The focus of this work is on developing a selective algorithm that is used to extract RFUops. Each RFUop is always assumed to execute in a single cycle, no matter how big it is, and the RFUops are not allowed to contain memory instructions. Also, the architecture has multiple RFUs on its datapath. Hence, concurrent RFUop execution comes naturally.

Chimaera [6] uses a superscalar processor in its model. It relies on fine-grained optimizations to obtain speedups. Hence, the compiler tries to extract sub-word parallelism from ALU instructions and map such sequences to RFUops. Memory instructions are not included in the RFUops.

OneChip [5] focuses on exploiting ILP in streaming multimedia applications. The host CPU is a superscalar processor. The architecture supports DMA, and assumes that all RFUops access a regular memory block, perform certain operations, and write back results to another regular memory block. Their compiler doesn't extract candidate RFUops, but requires the programmer to use a library, which contains calls to load configurations and access memory. These calls make all RFU memory accesses explicit, regular and predictable. Memory coherence is maintained by using techniques similar to those used in multiprocessors to maintain cache coherence.

7 Conclusions

While the idea of integrating a reconfigurable functional unit (RFU) into a general-purpose RISC processor has been studied extensively in the past, there have been few studies that have examined the new issues that arise when augmenting a high-performance superscalar architecture with a reconfigurable fabric. In fact, previous spectacular results often overlook progress that has been made in traditional architectures. Many previous studies either hand-code applications, ignore the extra ILP that can be extracted by out-of-order processors, or ignore negative interactions between an RFU and the main pipeline of the CPU.

Our work focuses on how to positively integrate an RFU into a superscalar pipeline. We target general-purpose applications and require automatic compilation of programs to the target hybrid architecture. The critical component of such a system is the compiler that can automatically map applications written in high-level languages to such architectures. The compiler must be cognizant of the factors that could influence performance. It is imperative that the compiler employs good heuristics in the code partitioning phase, so that performance is maximized and overhead is minimized. When using a shared memory space, memory consistency is a factor. While consistency must be maintained, the compiler must attempt to minimize the negative impact this can have on performance. In superscalar architectures, it is important to exploit all system resources and to minimize pipeline stalls. It is clear that much work needs to be done before an RFU can successfully boost total performance on an entire application.

Acknowledgments

This research is funded by the National Science Foundation (NSF) under Grant No. CCR-9876248.

References

[1] Todd Austin, Eric Larson, and Dan Ernst. SimpleScalar: An infrastructure for computer system modeling. *Computer*, 35(2):59–67, February 2002.

[2] Mihai Budiu and Seth Copen Goldstein. Pegasus: An efficient intermediate representation. Technical Report CMU-CS-02-107, Carnegie Mellon University, May 2002.

[3] Timothy J. Callahan and John Wawrzynek. Instruction Level Parallelism for Reconfigurable Computing. In Hartenstein and Keevallik, editors, *FPL'98, Field-Programmable Logic and Applications, 8th International Workshop, Tallinin, Estonia*, volume 1482 of *Lecture Notes in Computer Science*. Springer-Verlag, September 1998.

[4] André DeHon. The density advantage of configurable computing. *Computer*, 33(4):41–49, April 2000.

[5] Jorge E. Carrillo E. and Paul Chow. The effect of reconfigurable units in superscalar processors. In ACM/SIGDA, editor, *Ninth ACM International Symposium on Field-Programmable Gate Arrays (FPGA'01)*, pages 141–150, February 2001.

[6] S. Hauck, T. W. Fry, M. M. Hosler, and J. P. Kao. The Chimaera reconfigurable functional unit. In *IEEE Symposium on FPGAs for Custom Computing Machines (FCCM '97)*, pages 87–96, April 1997.

[7] Michael Hind and Anthony Pioli. Evaluating the effectiveness of pointer alias analyses. *Science of Computer Programming*, 39(1):31–55, January 2001.

[8] Chunho Lee, Miodrag Potkonjak, and William H. Mangione-Smith. Mediabench: a tool for evaluating and synthesizing multimedia and communications systems. In *Micro-30, 30th annual ACM/IEEE international symposium on Microarchitecture*, pages 330–335, 1997.

[9] R. Razdan and M. D. Smith. A high-performance microarchitecture withv hardware-programmable functional units. In *Proceedings of the 27th Annual International Symposium on Microarchitecture*, pages 172–80. IEEE/ACM, November 1994.

[10] Hartej Singh, Guangming Lu, Eliseu M. C. Filho, Rafael Maestre, Ming-Hau Lee, Fadi J. Kurdahi, and Nader Bagherzadeh. MorphoSys: case study of a reconfigurable computing system targeting multimedia applications. In *Proceedings of the 37th Conference on Design Automation (DAC-00)*, pages 573–578, NY, June 5–9 2000. ACM/IEEE.

[11] Standard Performance Evaluation Corp. *SPEC CPU95 Benchmark Suite*, 1995.

[12] Suraj Sudhir. Simulating processors with reconfigurable function units. Master's thesis, Carnegie Mellon University, Electrical and Computer Engineering Department, Carnegie Mellon University, Pa 15213, May 2002.

[13] R. Wilson, R. French, C. Wilson, S. Amarasinghe, J. Anderson, S. Tjiang, S.-W. Liao, C.-W. Tseng, M. Hall, M. Lam, and J. Hennessy. SUIF: An infrastructure for research on parallelizing and optimizing compilers. In *ACM SIGPLAN Notices*, volume 29, pages 31–37, December 1994.

[14] Xianfeng Zhou and Margaret Martonosi. Augmenting modern superscalar architectures with configurable extended instructions. In José Romlin et al., editor, *Proceedings of 15th International Parallel and Distributed Processing Symposium*, pages 941–950. Springer-Verlag, Berlin, May 2000.

Implementing Converters in FPLD

A. Sanz , J.I. García-Nicolás, I. Urriza

Department of Electronics and Communications Engineering
Centro Politécnico Superior, University of Zaragoza, Spain
C/ María de Luna 1, Zaragoza 50015-E
{asmolina, jign, urriza}@posta.unizar.es

Abstract. This paper describes a new technology to implement AD and DA converters using digital FPLD and few external components. To explain this technology we present two example designs; a new broadband modem mixed-signal front end (MxFE) and a narrow band modem both for Power Line Communications (PLC). The key point of this technology is the use of digital output as voltage or current source and passive RLC network to implement continuous time multi-bit sigma-delta converter architecture. The DAC uses mismatch-shaping and multi-bit modulator. The ADC is high-order single-bit continuous time modulator. The quantizer used to implement the ADC is a low cost ultrafast single supply comparator and few external components.

1 Introduction

The Power Line medium provide a low cost and easy to install network to connect the appliances in a home. Nowadays a key problem of the SoC solution for PLC is the integration of analog and digital side of design in a low cost digital technology. Right now there is a problem to integrate in the same chip the analog and digital side of a HF-PLC broadband modem, from 1.6MHz to 30Mhz, using advanced digital technologies. A HF-PLC broadband modem is an large digital design including base band DSP, equalization, and MAC tasks [1,2]. The use in the integration in a SoC of a non optimum advanced digital technology increases the final cost of the system.
This work presents the first design results of a new broadband MxFE for a PLC modem that can be integrated in a SoC solution using an advanced digital technology and only few low cost external components. This system can be tested in a new board including a Virtex2000E, ZBT RAM, static RAM, FLASTH and the external components of converters
This work also presents the results of a new narrowband modem for PLC. The modem for the power line medium uses a multi-bit sigma-delta converter [3] in the ADC and DAC. The DAC transmitting stage uses a sigma-delta architecture with a fifth order modulator, a quantizer of fifteen non regular levels and mismatch-shaping. The narrow band network is complementary with broadband home network oriented to Internet applications. This system was tested in a new board including a Xilinx XC4085E FPGA, static RAM, EPROM and the external components of converters. The system clock is an 11.0592 MHz oscillator

M. Glesner, P. Zipf, and M. Renovell (Eds.): FPL 2002, LNCS 2438, pp. 966-975, 2002.

2 MxE Block Description

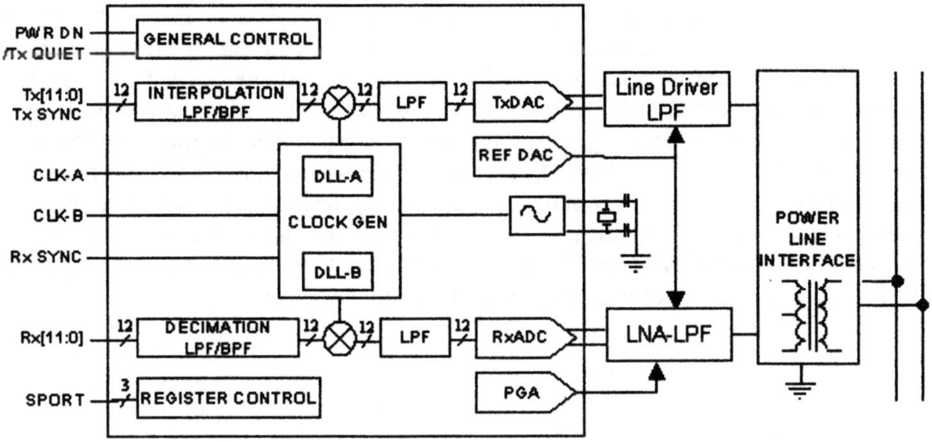

Fig.1. broadband modem MxFE for Power Line Communications

The Fig.1 shows the general architecture of the presented MxFE. The general architecture of the presented MxFE is similar to the architecture of AD9876 [5] the lastest Broadband Modem Mixed-Signal Front End of Analog Devices. Both devices are oriented to Powerline Networking, Home Phone Networking, xDSL, Broadband Wireless and Home RF. We will present, in the actual work, similar results that the AD9876 [4] but the presented device is an VHDL IP block that can be integrated in the digital side of a final SoC solution for a broadband PLC modem using any advanced digital technology. This IP block is optimized to minimize the size and cost of necessary external components. This external components are no more costly than those used in a typical 10 bits, 100 MSPS MxFE. The whole system can use the same DC power supply (3.3V or 2.5V) in both, the digital and analog sides. The system clock is 200Mhz, this signal is obtained from a 50 Mhz external single crystal or a clock input oscillator. All the IP block is a synchronous digital system.

The presented MxFE receives from the base band processor the signal to transmit in the base band frequency with 12 bits and a configurable sample rate from 12.5 MSPS to 100MSPS. The device contains in the transmit path an Interpolation Filter, a mixer low pas filter and a DAC, and in the receive path a LPF, an ADC, a mixer, a decimator and low-pass or band-pass filter. The mixers and filters in the transmit path and receive path can adapt the base band frequency of the signal to any channel in the range from 1.6Mhz to 30Mhz. The registers control sets the frequency of local oscillators DLL-A and DLL-B and the value of the REF DAC. A serial port can be used to configure this registers. The local oscillators DLL-A and DLL-B use DDS and a 200Mhz global clock to provide the signal to mixers.

The REF DAC provides the reference voltage to bias the analog external components.

3 Transmit Path

In the transmit path, the interpolation filter uses a selectable digital interpolation low-pass or band-pass filter to further oversample transmit data to the 200MSPS. The mixer and low-pass filter adapt the base band frequency of the signal to any channel in the range of 1.6Mhz to 30Mhz. Finally the TxDAC and line driver LPF provide the analog transmit signal. The TxDAC and line driver LPF conform a multi-bit sigma-delta converter architecture [5]. The TxDAC uses mismatch-shaping multi-bit output to improve the signal line driver LPF [6]. The line driver LPF is an active amplifier that performs the current to voltage conversion, the impedance adaptation, the power amplification and a continuous time third order low-pass filtering. The TxDAC outputs are standard LVDS or LVPECL digital outputs that are used by the line driver LPF as current sources of a 200MSPS sigma-delta converter.

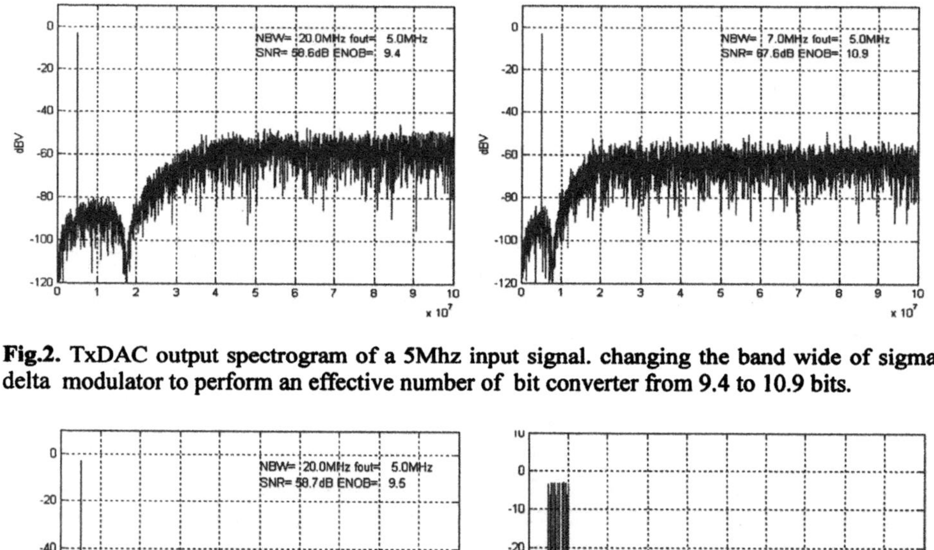

Fig.2. TxDAC output spectrogram of a 5Mhz input signal. changing the band wide of sigma-delta modulator to perform an effective number of bit converter from 9.4 to 10.9 bits.

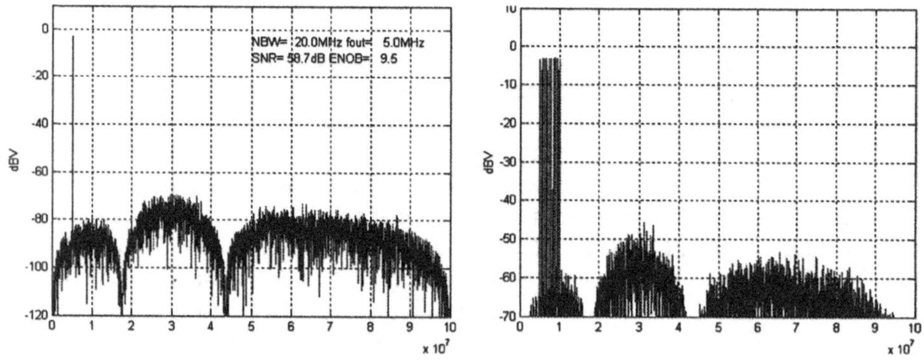

Fig.3. Line driver LPF output spectrogram of a 5Mhz and multi tone input signal.

The left figure 3 shows the simulation result of line driver LPF output that perform the current to voltage conversion, the impedance adaptation, the power amplification and a continuous time third order low-pass filtering of previous TxDAC output of a 5Mhz pure signal. The right figure 3 shows the simulation result of line driver LPF output of 10 channel signal from 5Mhz to 10Mhz. To test the TxDAC system we use a dual tone (Fig .4) and a multi tone (Fig.5) input signal

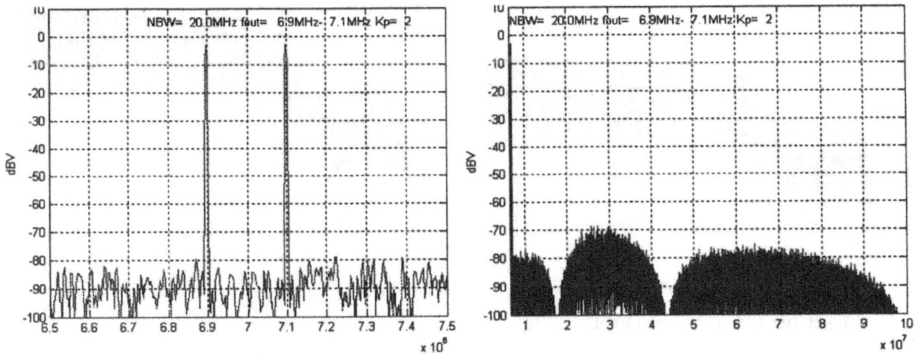

Fig.4. Dual tone spectral plot of line driver LPF output in the frequency band and in the complete band. The output signal is harmonic free in band and out band. The SNR is around 90dB (ENOB=14) and higher that 80dB in the band of 0 to 20MHz

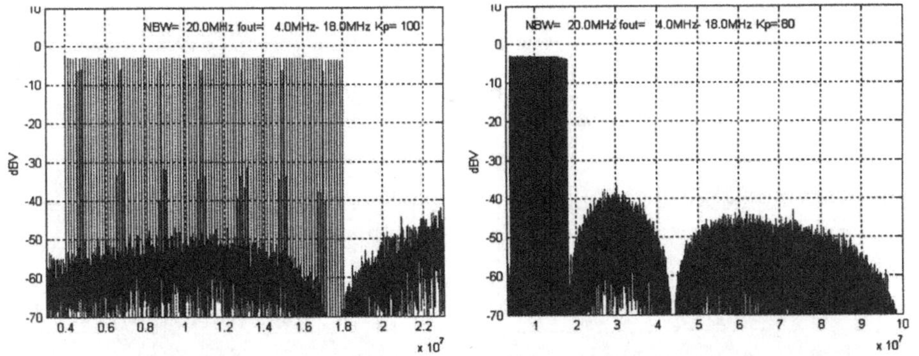

Fig.5. Multi tone spectral plot of line driver LPF output in the frequency band and in the complete band. The input signal include 80 channels from 4MHz to 18MHz. The output signal is harmonic free in band and out band. The SNR is around 56dB (ENOB=9) and higher that 50dB in the band of 0 to 20MHz. To improve the linearity of DAC we will uses noise-shaping principle to the errors caused by element mis-match [6-8]

4 Receive Path

In the receive path, the LNA-LPF and the RxDAC conform a high order multi-bit sigma-delta converter architecture. The DAC of RxDAC modulator uses mismatch-shaping multi-bit output to improve the dynamic range. The PGA control the LNA-LPF to provide a control of global gain of the conversion. The LPF filters the converter out of band noise. The mixer and LPF/BPF adapt to the base band frequency the signal from any channel in the range of 1.6Mhz to 30Mhz. Finally the decimation provide to the base band processor the signal in the base band frequency whit 12 bits and 12.5MSPS to 100MSPS.

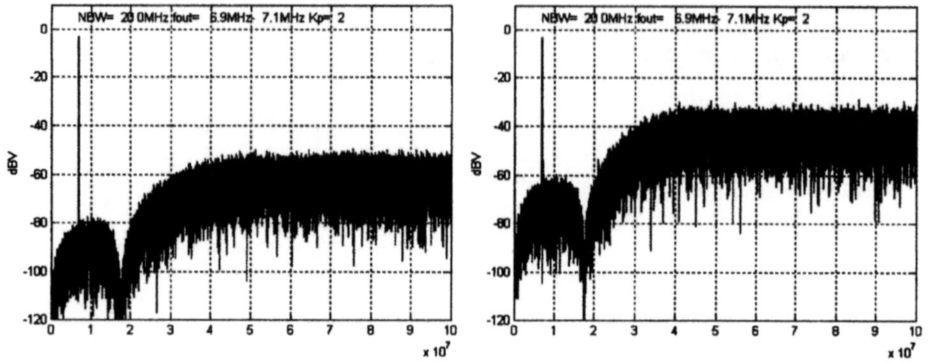

Fig.6. Dual tone spectral plot changing the number of level (31 in the left and 4 in the right) in the quantizer for the dual tone input signal

To define the architecture of the RxDAC modulator we are evaluated some design alternatives. The first question is to evaluate the impact of the number of level of the quantizer in the general performances of the system. According to the lineal model the reduction in the number of quantization level increases 18dB the noise level in the frequency band is;

$$Log_2\left(\frac{31}{4}\right) * 6.02 = 17.78\ dB \tag{1}$$

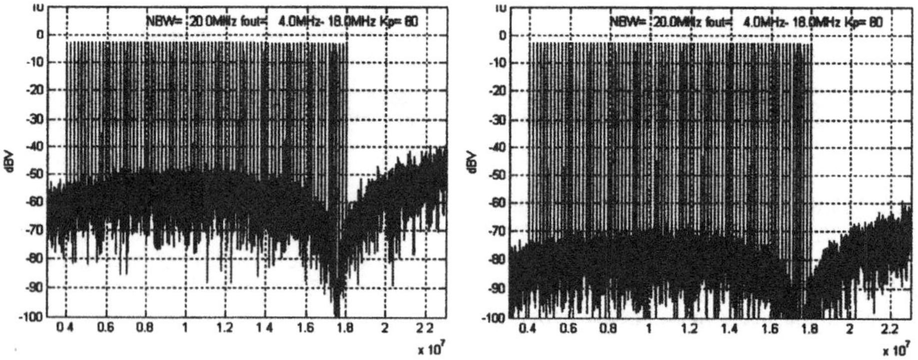

Fig.7. Multi tone spectral plot, 80 channels from 4MHz to 18MHz, changing the number of level in the quantizer

To improve this performance we can uses multibit quantizer. The figures 7 show, in the left, the result of a third order modulator using a 4.95bit (31 level) low cost quantizer and in the right figure a third order modulator using a 8bit (256 level) low cost quantizer. Then the uses of a 8bit low cost quantizer provide a ENOB=12.

The dynamic range of a ΔΣ modulator employing pure differentiation noise transfer functions depends on the oversampling ratio R, the order of the noise shaping filter L, and the internal quantizer resolution N, according to [9]

$$DR = \frac{3}{2}\left(\frac{2L+1}{\pi^{2L}}\right)\left(2^{N}-1\right)^{2} R^{2L+1} \qquad (2)$$

We are considering some design alternatives to archive a good compromises of target performances and complexity. The next table show the resulted DR and the equivalent numbers of bit ENOB

Table 1. The order of the noise shaping filter L, and the internal quantizer resolution N versus the resulting DR and the equivalent numbers of bit ENOB

L	N	SNR	ENOB
3	1	43.5992	6.9500
6	1	70.6441	11.4425
3	2	53.1416	8.5352
3	3	60.5012	9.7577

A good alternative can been a cascaded multibit $\Delta\Sigma$ modulator. The modulator consist of a second-order stage with a cascade of two stages with 1-bit quantization the first and N-bit the second one [10]. The input to the second stage is the difference between the output and the input of the first-stage quantizer. That is, the input to the second stage is the quantization error of the first stage. In this architecture the cascade modulator does not display any harmonic distortion, a consequence of the second-order shaping and the fact that the input to the second stage is the quantization error of the first stage, which is substantially decorrelated from the input to the modulator.

5 Architecture of Narrowband Modem for PLC

The architecture of this modem is oriented to attain low complexity and low power. The modem included in EHSoC [11] a System on Chip (SoC) implementation of a complete node for the European Home Systems specifications (EHS) [12]. It uses multi-bit sigma-delta converters in both the Analog to Digital Converter (ADC) and the Digital to Analog Converter (DAC). The DAC uses multi-bit mismatch shaping.

We have used a non-traditional demodulation method to decrease the hardware complexity and the power consumption. Usually the FSK demodulation in a modem is implemented using a superheterodyne schema [13] composed by: a narrow band amplifier, a mixer block to change to an IF, a second narrow band filter and a demodulator. With this architecture, a modem for power line communication according to EHS needs more that 1Mflop for the reception and demodulation sections. The method that we have used is the measure of period time. The filtered output of the ADC is connected to a zero crossing block. The logic unit counts the numbers of clock cycles between N zero crossings. If the count is in the range [fmin,fp] then a logic '1' has been received (RxD=1, /CD=0). If the count is in the range [fp,fmax] then a logic '0' has been received (RxD=0, /CD=0). If the count is out of range [fmin,fmax] there is no reception (RxD=X, /CD=1). This architecture needs less than 300Kflop for the reception and demodulation sections.

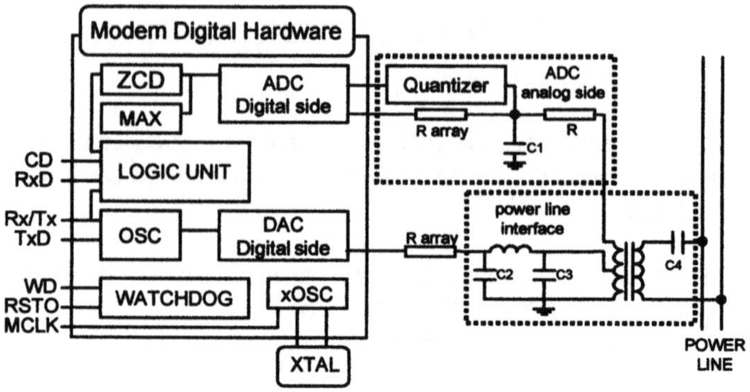

Fig. 8. Modem architecture

In the transmission stage, a class D output amplifier is embedded in the DAC to decrease the power consumption. This digital design is powered by a single 3.3V supply and requires a small number of external passive components to be fully implemented. All these aspects and the low internal complexity of this architecture will make viable a final very small system.

6 Analog Converters in the Narrowband Modem for PLC

The analog converters are the design key points of this modem. The different types of topologies and the different types of loads connected to the power line, make necessary a large dynamic range in reception [14-15].

The traditional approach to this problem is to use an Automatic Gain Control (AGC). The use of an analog AGC imposes restrictions in the technology that can be used to implement the modem. The FPGA and the Gate Array technologies don't include analog devices. This is the reason that we have used a new approach.

The modem for the power line medium uses a multi-bit sigma-delta converter in the ADC and DAC. The DAC transmitting stage uses a sigma-delta architecture with a fifth order modulator, a quantizer of fifteen non regular levels and mismatch-shaping. As Fig.8 shows, this DAC uses the digital CMOS output to control a resistors array in D class configuration. The resistors array and the input impedance of power line interface configure a non-uniform quantizer.

The Fig.9 left shows the output of DAC, with load impedance of 10Ω, without mismatch shaping to control the external resistors array. The noise floor is lower bounded by the fifth order modulator. The Fig.9 right shows the output of DAC, with load impedance of 10Ω, with mismatch-shaping to control the external resistors array. The noise floor is lower bounded by the mismatch-shaping noise. The result is a DAC with Equivalent Number of Bits (ENOB)=7.7, BandWidth (BW)=1MHz and 11 Mega Samples per Second (MSPS).

When the power line interface is connected to the DAC the noise floor is further reduced, and the result is a DAC with ENOB=8.9, BW=1MHz & 11MSPS.

To provide the necessary large dynamic range in reception the ADC uses a multi-bit sigma-delta converter with a continuous time modulator and few external analog components (Fig.8). The ADC modulator uses a DAC with a fifteen non-uniform levels quantizer and mismatch shaping. In the transmission stage, we use the digital CMOS output to control an array or seven resistors in a D class configuration to decrease the power consumption.

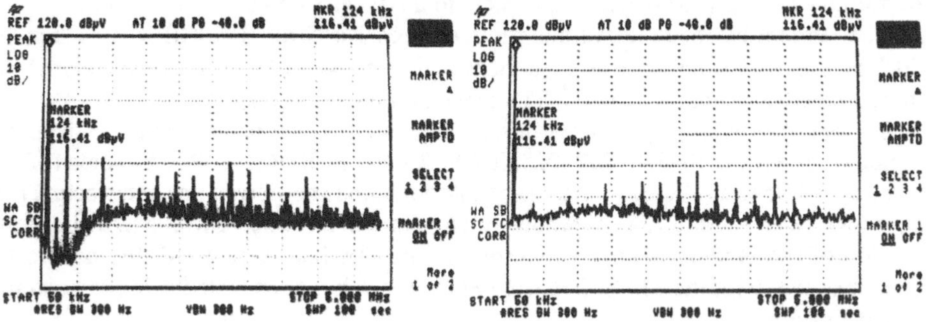

Fig. 9. The left hand side figure shows the Output DAC spectrum without mismatch-shaping, the right hand side figure shows the Output DAC spectrum with mismatch-shaping

EHS, for power line medium, sets a maximum output level of 116dBµV (631mVrms). The traditional solution uses a B class amplifier powered by a 10V supply and a line adapter with a voltage transformation rate of 5. The power efficiency is 70%. The use of D class output amplifier increases the power efficiency to 90%. Moreover using a D-class output amplifier, the whole system is powered by a 3.3V DC supply.

The power line interface provides the electrical isolation, filtering, and impedance and level signal adaptation to the power line. We have used an inductive coupling in this design but it is also possible to use a capacitive coupling. The capacitive coupling will reduce the size of the system, but it does not provide electrical isolation.

The output level of modem agrees with the EN50065-1/A1 norm. The power line medium is characterized by a large, and variable, range of impedance. To assure the communication it is crucial to maintain the signal emission level in a wide range of load impedance.

The emission level is related to the serial capacitor impedance used in the power line interface. It is possible to increase the signal emission level using a bigger output capacitor.

Table 2. emission level versus load impedance using a 470nF output capacitor

Load (Ω)	Emission (dBµV)
80	112
10	109
1	103
0,5	92
0,1	83

7 Results and Conclusion

This paper presents a new technology to implement AD and DA converters using digital FPLD and few external components. To explain this technology we was present two example designs; a new broadband modem mixed-signal front end (MxFE) and a narrow band modem both for Power Line Communications (PLC). The performances of this MxFE are equivalent to a typical 10 bits, 100 MSPS MxFE.

The modem has been tested and the measured Bit Error Rate (BER) is better that 10^{-5} in the condition of use in a home. For a 44dBµV (154µVrms) signal the measured BER is better than 10^{-4}. The dynamic range is 72db.

To test the whole system we have designed a specific test board, this board includes a Xilinx FPGA (XC4085XLA), RAM, EPROM, a PLCC socket for a standard 80C51, an ADC, a serial port interface and the power line interface. These board has been used to test the whole system (microcontroller, MAC and a simplified version of the modem) mapped into the FPGA. The final version of the modem has been mapped, with the MAC, into the FPGA and it has been tested using the external microcontroller.

The size of the EHSoC is 3192 CLB in a XC4000 FPGA, (1050 for the 8051, 486 for the MAC and 1656 for the modem).

Mapped in the XC4085XLA the minimum clock cycle is 75 ns (13 MHz), and the system uses an 11.0592 MHz oscillator. The critical path is in the arithmetic unit of the microcontroller. Using faster devices (i.e. Xilinx VirtexE), the clock cycle will be reduced to 25 ns.

References

1. Antonio Hidalgo, Antonio Luque, "INSONET In-Home and SoHo Networking trough the mains Network" ISPL2001 Proceedings of the 5th international Symposium on Power-Line Communications and its Applications, Pag.:59-65 Malmö, Sweden, April 2001
2. Steve Gardner, "The HomePlug Standard for PowerLine Home Networking" ISPL2001 Proceedings of the 5th international Symposium on Power-Line Communications and its Applications, Pag.:66-72 Malmö, Sweden, April 2001
3. S. R. Norsworthy, R. Schreier, G. C. Temes. D. Liu, E. Flint, B.Guacher and Y. Kwark: Delta-Sigma Data Converters. Theory, Design, and Simulation. IEEE Press, New York (1996)
4. Analog Devices, "AD9876; Broadband Modem Mixed-Signal Front End" Analog Devices, Inc., 2001
5. S. R. Norsworthy, R. Schreier, G. C. Temes. D. Liu, E. Flint, B.Guacher and Y. Kwark. Delta-Sigma Data Converters. Theory, Design, and Simulation. IEEE Press. IEEE Circuits & Systems Society, sponsor ISBN 0-7803-1045-4 NY 1996
6. R.W. Adams and T. W. Kwan, "Data-directed scrambler for multi-bit noise-shaping D/A converters" U.S. Patent 504142, Aprli 4, 1995
7. R.T. Baird and T.S. Fiez, "Improved $\Delta\Sigma$ DAC linearity using data weighted averaging" Proc. 1995 IEE Int. Symp. Circuits Sys., vol 1, pp. 13-16, May 1995.
8. R.Schreier and B. Zhang, "Noise-shaped multibit D/A converter employing unit elements" Electron. Lett., vol 1, no. 20, pp. 1712-1713, Sept. 1995.
9. B.Brandt, "Oversampled Analog-to-Digital Conversion" Ph.D. Dissertation, Stanford Univesity, Aug. 1991

10.L. Longo and M.Copeland "A 13 bit ISDN-band oversampled ADC using two-stage third order noise shaping" Proc. IEEE 1988 Custom Integrated Circuit Conf., pp 2120-1244, nov 1988
11.A. Sanz, J.I. García Nicolás, I. Urriza, A. Valdovinos."A complete node for the Power Line medium of European Home Systems specifications" ISPL2001 Proceedings of the 5th international Symposium on Power-Line Communications and its Applications, Pag.:66-72 Malmö, Sweden, April 2001
12.EHSA: European Home Systems Specification Release 1.3. EHSA Zavenem, Belgium (1997)
13.Leon W. Couch II: Digital and Analog Communication Systems. Prentice Hall Inc. (1997)
14.J. B. B'Neal: The Residential Power Line Circuit as a Communication Medium. IEEE Transactions on Consumer Electronic, vol 45 n.4, IEEE Press, New York (1999) 1087-1097
15.D. Liu, E. Flint, B.Guacher and Y. Kwark: Wide Band AC Power Line Characterization. IEEE Transactions on Consumer Electronic, vol 45 n.4, IEEE Press, New York (1999) 1087-1097

A Quantitative Understanding of the Performance of Reconfigurable Coprocessors

Domingo Benitez

University of Las Palmas G.C., Campus de Tafira, Edificio de Informatica,
35017 Las Palmas, Spain
dbenitez@dis.ulpgc.es

Abstract. The goal of this work is to explore the architectural behavior of FPGA-based coprocessors that are part of general-purpose computer systems. Our analysis shows maximum performance improvements of up to two orders of magnitude in comparison with current high-performance processors. However, the performance benefits exhibited by reconfigurable coprocessors may be deeply influenced by some design parameters. We have studied the impact of hardware capacity, reconfiguration time, memory organization, and system bus bandwidth on the performance achieved by FPGA-based coprocessors. Our results suggest that an unappropriated bandwidth both for the reconfigurable data-path and host bus can degrade enormously the performance improvement. Since the variation of bus bandwidths encountered in contemporary computer systems is substantial, we found that reconfigurable coprocessors are more efficient when placed as close to the processor as possible without being part of its data-path.

1. Introduction

One of the open research problems of computing with FPGAs is understanding the limitation of FPGAs when competing with microprocessors [8]. In this paper we describe a performance evaluation of computation-intensive and data-parallel applications on FPGA-based coprocessors that are part of general-purpose computers. An important motivation is the architectural characterization of reconfigurable systems that interact with current high-performance processors. We compare the performance of a successful Pentium III processor with various FPGA-based coprocessors.

Further motivating our study is the large role memory hierarchy plays in limiting performance. From our experiments, we can explain why the reconfigurable coprocessor performance is highly dependent on an efficient memory organization and the associated bandwidth of data transmission. We observe that our benchmarks demand not only sufficient CLB count and memory size, but also a large number of memory banks and a high-bandwidth host bus. If these architectural elements were not well dimensioned, they would limit seriously the achievable performance. Based on our quantitative approach, we explain why some current reconfigurable coprocessors do not provide the achievable performance improvement. We present these results with the goal of aiding future reconfigurable system design.

2. Experimental Methodology

This paper studies the reconfigurable system model shown in Figure 1. Its architecture is composed of a current general-purpose processor and a coprocessor based on

M. Glesner, P. Zipf, and M. Renovell (Eds.): FPL 2002, LNCS 2438, pp. 976-986, 2002.

FPGAs and memory blocks. The reconfigurable coprocessor has a remote interface since the general-purpose processor and the reconfigurable hardware are connected through the „System Bus". The instruction-set processor and the reconfigurable data-path may support data processing in parallel or concurrently. Customizing the hardware configuration of the coprocessor, higher performance can be provided.

The Local Memory (M) is analogous to a data cache. It is made up from several banks and all of them can be accessed in parallel by the reconfigurable data-path. The general-purpose microprocessor can access to the memory banks through the „Local Bus". As we will see, a dedicated local memory organized in banks is key for reconfigurable architectures to achieve high performance. However, this architectural element is not found in some reconfigurable systems. Another component is the „Interface Controller (IC)". We suppose that its integrated DMA controller can handle data transfers with variable bandwidths. We don't consider any implementation technology for the design of the coprocessor. All of its components may be put on a chip, board, or integrated with the microprocessor on the same chip. Our architectural study tries to understand the impact of several factors of the system design such as memory organization and bus bandwidth on the coprocessor performance.

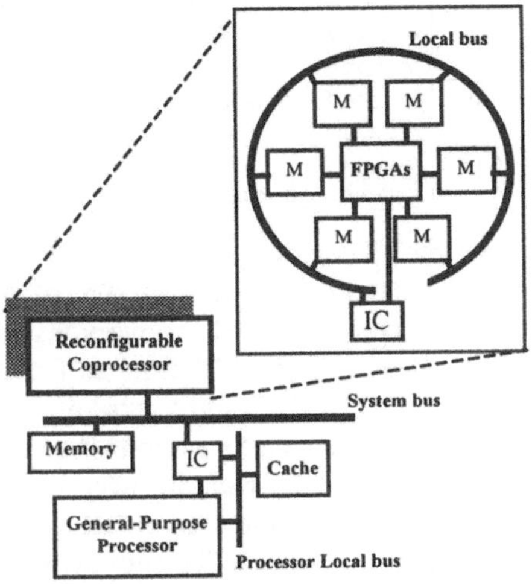

Fig. 1. Block diagram of the FPGA-based general-purpose syst

We use an experimental platform that is composed of:

- A C compiler for FPGAs called Handel-C ver. 2.1 [7]. We also use its simulator which allows verify the functionality of programs without using real hardware and obtain the number of cycles that the FPGA spends in processing a piece of code.
- The Xilinx Foundation design suite ver. 3.1. It is used for generating FPGA bitstreams from the netlist obtained by Handel-C. These tools allow the maximum clock rate of the synchronous hardware to be estimated.
- The Intel VTune Performance Analyzer ver. 4.5. It allows the code generated by the compiler MS C++ 6.0 on a Pentium III processor to be simulated.
- A PCI coprocessor board called RC1000-PP with a one million-gate FPGA [2].

For our study, we employ the real benchmarks and data sets that are described in Table 1. These applications were chosen from the media-processing domain where configurable computing may provide greater speedup than other architectural solutions. They are representative kernels for image-processing applications. Note that we do not include applications as JPEG or MPEG encoder/decoder, which are used in studies of general-purpose processors ([13], [14], [18]). We found that our benchmarks exhibit workload characteristics that are different from those of applications that really consist of kernels. Our conjecture, which is shared by other authors, is that reconfigurable coprocessors can speed up application programs by exploiting parallelism at kernel level [11].

Table 1. Summary of the image-processing benchmarks used in this study

FDCT	Integer implementation of the Forward Discrete Cosine Transform [5] adopted by JPEG, MPEG and MediaBench [10]. Data set: images of 256x256 pixels, 1024 blocks of 8x8 16-bit data.
EDGE	Edge detector performed by subtracting the pixel values for adjacent horizontal and vertical pixels, taking the absolute values and thresholding the result [12]. Data: images of 256x256 16-bit pixels.
ME	Motion Estimation stage of MPEG-2 implemented by the Full Search Block Matching method [9]. Data set: 1 search block of 24x24 8-bit pixels, and matching blocks of 16x16 8-bit pixels.
ATR	Automatic Target Recognition application that automatically detects, classify, recognize and identifies chromatic patterns [1]. Data set: color images of 256x256 24-bit pixels.

Using VTune, we profiled the C++ versions of the benchmarks to identify key procedures that spend more than 99% of cycle count on a Pentium III. Then, we obtained the cycle count and CPI for every instruction type in every performance category. The variation of average CPIs ranges from 0.63 (ME) to 1.01 (ATR). It means that the conventional ILP features exploit different levels of parallelism that the image-processing benchmarks exhibit. On average and in percentage terms, 61,2% of all the instructions require memory access, and the respective cycle count is 68,4%. These results differ from those reported in others studies where it is shown an average 22% of memory instructions for multimedia workload [14].

On the other hand, 43,4% of all the instructions use the ALU functional unit, and only a 6,6% of all the instructions are branches. The reduced percentage of branch instructions is associated with a relative large percentage of stall cycles due to missprediction (9,15%). Overall, reducing basically both the number of instructions and the stall time originated by data dependencies and memory latencies, FPGA coprocessors allow the performance of the computer system to be improved. As we will show, when the FPGA is used to implement the image-processing workload, those applications that exhibit lower CPI require higher hardware cost to achieve the same performance improvement.

We manually coded the four benchmarks using exclusively the programming language Handel-C. Each benchmark was coded in five different ways corresponding to five hardware microarchitectures. Then, the compiled code was simulated using the Handel-C simulator in order to collect the cycle count required by the FPGA. Every Handel-C program was tested to verify the same output results exhibited by the C++ version. Finally, we automatically synthesized the netlist files generated by the Handel-C compiler with the Xilinx development suite. So, the maximum operating frequency for each microarchitecture was estimated. Some of the implementations were also tested on the real FPGA-based board RC1000-PP.

We use the speed-up of the reconfigurable coprocessor over the Pentium III processor as the primary metric to evaluate its performance benefits. The speed-up is evaluated by dividing the cycle count required by both architectures and scaling the clock speeds. We assume that a representative Pentium III processor fabricated with 0,18 μm technology operates at 1 GHz. We obtained the maximum clock rate for the FPGA from the place and route tools taking a Xilinx Virtex(-4) device fabricated with 0,22 micron technology. The results shown in this paper would be even more optimistic for the reconfigurable coprocessor if the transistor density were the same. When the FPGA reconfiguration time or the system bus bandwidth are considered, the cycle count for the FPGA is increased proportionally. We also studied the influence of other parameters such as the number of configurable blocks, the bandwidths between local memory and the FPGAs, and the number of memory banks for further insights into the reconfigurable system behavior.

3. Improving System Performance

In this section we study some architectural properties of FPGA-based coprocessors that provide performance improvement. Further, we discuss factors limiting their benefits.

3.1 Alternative Architectures for FPGA-based Coprocessors

Several microarchitectures were used to develop different implementations of each benchmark. These microarchitectures are targeted at FPGA-based coprocessors and each of them executes completely all benchmarks. They apply a combination of well-known hardware techniques that improve performance: muticycle, pipelining, and replication of data-paths. We report results for five variations of the coprocessor microarchitecture called „uA1, uA2, ..., uA5". The combinations of hardware techniques used for each microarchitecture are shown in Table 2. Note that each of them can be multicycle or pipelined, and this architectural feature is used for one or several identical replications of the processing hardware called „hw path". Each hardware path exploits the data level parallelism inherent to the respective benchmark.

Table 2. Characteristics of the microarchitectures and their clock rates in MHz

Name	FDCT		EDGE		ME		ATR	
uA1	Multicycle, 1 hw path	48	Multicycle, 1 hw path	113	One cycle, 1 hw path	50	Multicycle, 1 hw path	52
uA2	Pipelined, 1 hw path	55	Pipelined, 1 hw path	113	One cycle, 2 hw paths	47	Pipelined, 1 hw path	77
uA3	Pipelined, 2 hw paths	49	Pipelined, 2 hw paths	98	One cycle, 8 hw paths	43	Pipelined, 2 hw paths	69
uA4	Pipelined, 8 hw paths	42	Pipelined, 8 hw paths	92	One cycle, 32 hw paths	40	Pipelined, 8 hw paths	62
uA5	Pipelined, 32 hw paths	40	Pipelined, 32 hw paths	81	One cycle, 256 hw paths	35	Pipelined, 32 hw paths	50

Each microarchitecture followed the software development flow described in the previous section. The maximum clock frequencies obtained in the logic synthesis of each microarchitecture are shown in Table 2. Note that the microarchitectures allow process images at rates that vary in the range from 40 MHz to 113 MHz. The variation of rates is in accordance with two factors. On one hand, the complexity of computation demanded by the benchmarks imposes the number of CLBs involved in the propagation of signals between registers, which are synchronized by the same clock signal. This complexity is the highest for FDCT and ME and the lowest for EDGE. Thus, FDCT and ME exhibit the lowest clock rates. On the other hand, the higher demand for CLBs exhibited by the microarchitectures that support more hardware paths makes the propagation delay within the FPGA larger. We observed that the hardware compiler and synthesizer might influence these results. However, all microarchitectures were compiled and synthesized with the same options.

3.2 Impact of FPGA-based Architectures

For each benchmark, Figure 2a presents speed-up measurements for the five variations of the coprocessor architecture described above. The way in which these results were collected was described in Section 2.

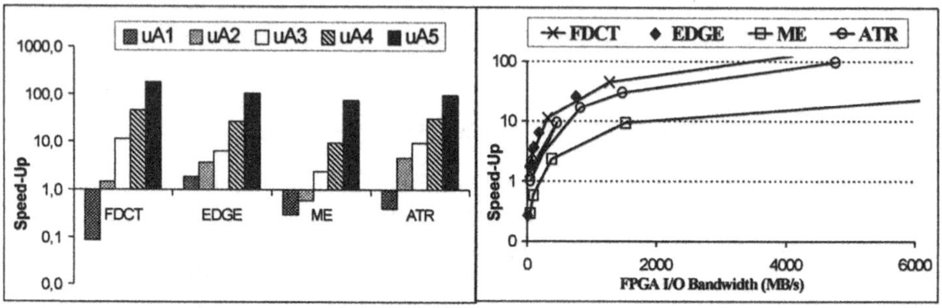

(a) (b)

Fig. 2. (a) Performance improvement of the reconfigurable coprocessor over a Pentium III. (b) Impact of the bandwidth between local memory and the FPGA (I/O Bandwidth) on the speed-up

The reconfigurable coprocessor may provide significant performance improvement for all benchmarks, with maximum values that reach factors of 180X (see Figure 2a). On average, we observe that an FPGA coprocessor can improve the performance of the Pentium III by a factor of 114X. These results can be even better if more parallelism is applied. Figure 2b presents some additional data. Each line represents the bandwidth between the FPGA and local memory that is required by the architectures uA*x* for one of the benchmarks. Note that the bandwidth becomes higher as the speed-up increases.

One justification of these results is the existence of pipelined hardware paths. All the benchmarks are essentially composed of loops that provide regularity to the computation. The operations of each loop can be divided into blocks that have no data dependence and then pipelined. For example, the pipelined microarchitectures uA2 can load new data and store results on every clock cycle, thus demanding higher bandwidth than the multicycle implementations named uA1.

Three of the benchmarks (FDCT, EDGE and ATR) experiment performance benefits from pipelining. We found that computation can be deeply pipelined in EDGE and ATR, and moderately in FDCT. For ME, the main computation can be reduced to one operation, so pipelining has no effect on the number of data accessed each clock cycle.

A second justification for these higher FPGA I/O bandwidth requirements is due to that more parallelism may be applied since multiple hardware paths can be synthesized. They operate in parallel on independent or shared data sets. Therefore, I/O throughput is higher because the image-processing workload allows synthesize FPGA data-paths that are massively multithread and fully pipelined.

Note that some reconfigurable microarchitectures may exhibit lower performance when compared to the general-purpose processor (uA1 for FDCT, ME and ATR; and uA2 for ME). A low I/O bandwidth does not allow FPGA to provide better performance than current processors. This low FPGA I/O bandwidth may be originated by hardware microarchitectures that do not exploit enough parallelism though FPGAs make use of specialized operators and reduce the overhead of branch instructions. In these cases, the ILP parallelism of current processors provides more benefits than FPGAs.

We observe a correlation between the level of performance experimented by three of the benchmarks (FDCT, ME, ATR) and the respective distributions of retired instructions and cycle counts for the Pentium III processor. Considering a level of performance improvement, those benchmarks with higher percentage of instructions and cycle count in the category of memory access demand higher FPGA I/O bandwidth.

Other studies on general-purpose processors have shown that the image-processing kernels exhibit high memory stall times unaffected by larger caches. In these cases, using software prefetching it is possible to achieve high performance improvements on superscalar general-purpose processors. But after applying software prefetching, the benchmarks revert to being compute bound [13]. Thus, general-purpose processors exploit a limited parallelism on image-processing kernels. FPGA-based systems can improve the performance of computer systems by exploiting more parallelism than processors. Our results show that reconfigurable coprocessors with higher FPGA I/O bandwidth achieve better performance. The limit is associated with the number of iterations in each benchmark. Normally, it is the same as the number of pixels or data blocks. On average, an increment of FPGA I/O bandwidth improves the speed-up by the same factor, if hardware resources are not limited. Therefore, using FPGA technology, all image-processing kernels revert to being I/O bound.

3.3 Hardware Cost

Figure 3 presents the results obtained for the area when the microarchitectures uA*x* (*x*=1,...,5) are implemented on a Virtex FPGA. These amounts are given in Xilinx CLB slices. Each CLB is equivalent to approximately 90 gates. Our experiments show that for each image-processing benchmark, the CLB increase has benefits associated with improved performance due to more parallelism. However, the CLB increase does not correspond to an equivalent performance improvement.

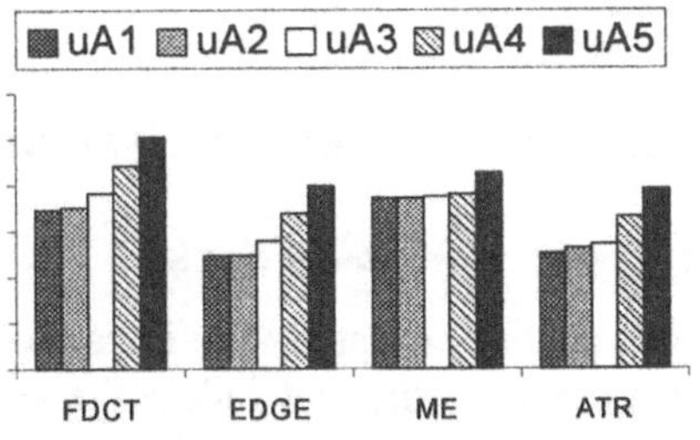

Fig. 3. CLB counts that are required to synthesize the microarchitectures uA*x* (*x*=1, ..., 5) on a Virtex FPGA

An average increase of 2,5X in CLBs (range of 1,6X to 2,9X) provides an average factor of 5,1X performance improvement (range of 3X to 8,1X). Combining these results with those shown previously, we observe that the benefits from FPGAs are more efficiently achieved when more I/O bandwidth is supported.

3.4 Reconfiguration Time

If the configuration for the FPGA is shared by the execution of one application on multiple images, the negative impact of the reconfiguration time is reduced. Supposing that each of our benchmarks makes data processing on successive frames at a rate of 25 images/s (25 Hz), Figure 4 shows the real speed-up of the reconfigurable coprocessor for the microarchitectures that ideally achieve higher performance than Pentium III. These measurements are given as percentages of the maximum performance improvements. We suppose that the reconfiguration process is static and is made before image processing starts. Additionally, we suppose a loading time of 11,6 μs. per CLB. This is a realistic value taken from Virtex FPGAs. Obviously, those microarchitectures with higher CLB count need more processing time using the same configuration to exhibit performance improvement. Examining the variation of processing times needed to get a real speed-up of 1 across the microarchitectures and benchmarks, we observe that it is correlated to the maximum speed-up in the same way as the CLB count does. During few seconds, uA5 exhibits lower performance benefits compared to the remaining microarchitectures. However, uA5 could exhibit the maximum performance improvement if the processing time is larger than a threshold proportional to the CLB count.

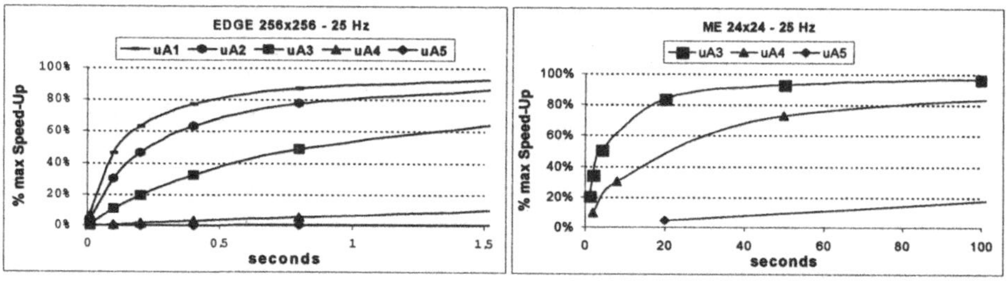

Fig. 4. Impact of the reconfiguration time. The data show the percentage of maximum speed-up obtained by the FPGA coprocessor when a time interval of continuous processing has elapsed

4. Analysis of Memory System Performance

4.1 Impact of Memory Banks

In this section, we study the impact of memory banks on the performance of FPGA-based coprocessors that follow the architectural model shown in Figure 1. Each microarchitecture u*Ax* (*x*=1,..,5) requires a different number of local memory modules. For each benchmark, Figure 5 presents the bank count for the microarchitectures that provide performance improvement. Overall, our results show that higher levels of speed-up require larger bank count. Examining the performance improvement across the benchmarks, we observe that it is mainly due to data level parallelism. The reduction of processing time is due to the increased number of parallel data-paths that operate on reduced data sets, which are stored in local memory banks.

Except for ME, the total size of local memory was kept fixed (FDCT & EDGE: 128 KB, ATR: 192 KB). In these cases, the total memory size depends on the image size. Larger images would require larger memory to get the same performance improvement. Similar to our results but in the domain of general-purpose architectures, Ranganathan et al. found that the size of data cache needed to exploit the reuse in superscalar processors depends on the image size [13]. However, we found that if the bank count is kept fixed, the memory size has no impact on the benefits achieved by FPGA coprocessors for three kernels.

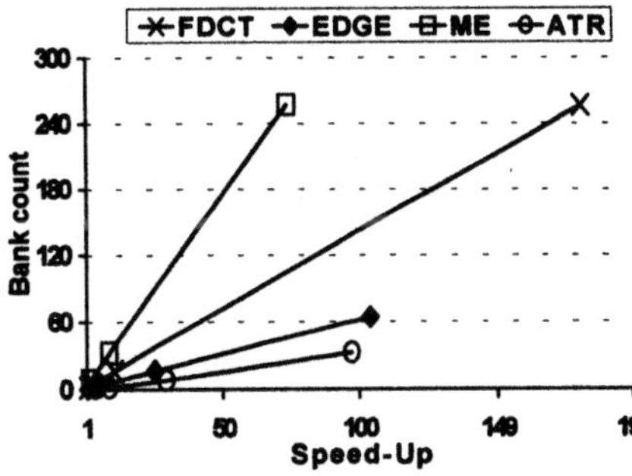

Fig. 5. Impact of the bank count of memory

The ME application achieves performance improvement by replicating the reference block. In this case, the limit to the performance benefits is associated with the number of possible displacements within a search block. Each matching block is stored in an independent memory bank and assigned to an independent data-path in the FPGA. So, the size of local memory for ME ranges from 1,25 KB to 65 KB. Therefore, for this application, performance improvement is achieved by increasing both the total memory size and the bank count. However, ME exhibits less benefits than other benchmarks when the bank count is fixed. On the other hand, Figure 5 shows that all image-processing kernels demand a different bank count for a fixed level of performance. We observe that this fact is related to the variation of CPI for memory instructions that have been executed by Pentium III. ME exhibits the lowest CPI for memory instructions and demands the highest bank count. For ATR, we found the opposite. Therefore, the addition of memory banks to reconfigurable coprocessors improves the performance by reducing the memory stall time exhibited by general-purpose processors. This improvement is linear with the bank count as shown in Figure 5. It is only limited by the number of supported data-paths and the maximum data-level parallelism that the application allows.

4.2 Impact of System Bus Bandwidth

Real coprocessors require an initial stage in which data are transmitted from the host memory to the coprocessor memory. So, the limited bandwidth of the system bus may cause the performance improvements degrade. Figure 6 shows the performance impact of the system bus bandwidth for those microarchitectures that ideally provide performance improvement. Now, the latency of data transmission is added to the cycle count required by the FPGA. For ME, the copying of the reference block is also considered.

For our kernels, a minimum 400 MB/s bus bandwidth is needed to get performance improvement. With 1 GB/s, all applications see a speed-up reduction that is higher than 50%. A 10 GB/s system bus allows the speed-up to reach the 70% of the maximum speed-up. EDGE and FDCT require a minimum bandwidth to exhibit performance improvement that is higher than those required by the remaining kernels. EDGE

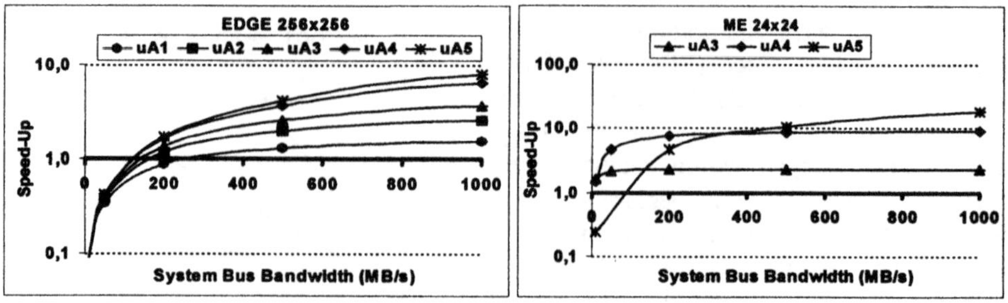

Fig. 6. Speed-up of the coprocessor over a Pentium III taking account the system bus bandwidth

and FDCT operate on images and their results are also images. Thus, the higher impact of system bus bandwidth is due to the transmission of complete images in both directions. On the other hand, ATR and ME operate on images but the results correspond to smaller data structures. Then, these applications spend less time in data transmission. Additionally, we observe that the microarchitectures that implement ME exhibit a variation of speed-up that is distinct from those exhibited by the remaining benchmarks. For ME, the microarchitecture that supports larger parallelism is associated with larger data structures since the number of copies of matching blocks is higher. Then, those microarchitectures that ideally provide higher performance require higher bus bandwidth to get the same real improvement. On the remaining kernels, the greater parallelism and bank count inherent to a microarchitecture are associated with the reduction of size of every memory bank while keeping the total memory size fixed. In these cases, the microarchitecture that ideally performs better requires less system bus bandwidth to achieve a determined level of real speed-up. Overall, these results are dependent on the image dimensions. For larger images, the bandwidth requires to be incremented proportionally in order to exhibit the same performance improvement. For example, taking the worst case (uA2 for FDCT) and 1024x1024 16-bit images, an speed-up equal to 1 requires a host bandwidth of 6,2 GB/s.

5. Related Work

Most of reconfigurable systems have demonstrated their innovative characteristics on multimedia applications. Some studies have shown that computing systems integrating a high-performance processor with a reconfigurable functional unit exhibit a maximum factor of 2X performance improvement over superscalar processors ([4], [18]). On the other hand, reconfigurable systems can provide even higher performance for multimedia applications ([3], [6], [11], [15], [17]). However, the performance analysis in these papers is usually limited to a mention of the benefits. There is little quantitative understanding of the causes of the performance benefits, bottlenecks, or impact of alternative architectures. Some researchers have claimed that there have been very few attempts to quantify the trade-offs in reconfigurable systems [16]. So, this paper provides a quantitative analysis of systems that perform the same tasks using a conventional computing model relative to another where a reconfigurable coprocessor with remote interface has been added.

Quantitative studies of multimedia applications on general-purpose processors have been given a growing attention. Ranganathan et al. reported that using SIMD-style media instruction set architecture extensions and software prefetching, all their image-processing benchmarks are compute-bound [13]. This effect limits the performance improvement, which can be enhanced by using remote reconfigurable coprocessors. Slingerland and Smith studied the caching behavior of multimedia applications. They observed that multimedia applications exhibit relatively low instruction miss ratios and comparable data miss ratios when contrasted with other workloads. The reuse exhibited by image-processing applications (more than 98%) is highly exploited by the cache memory in current processors [14]. As it was described previously, the computation model that follows some FPGA-based systems can provide higher performance improvement if the memory organization supports numerous banks of memory that are accessed in parallel. For our workload, this memory organization exploits more data locality than caches.

6. Summary

6.1 FPGA-based Coprocessor Design

In this paper, we have provided a quantitative analysis of three important design parameters for FPGA-based coprocessors in order to support image-processing applications.
Hardware capacity. A moderate FPGA capacity of 10E+5 CLBs was found to provide two orders of magnitude of performance improvement over a Pentium III-1GHz processor for most of applications.
Memory bank count. We found performance improvement when the bank count for the coprocessor memory is increased. About 200 memory banks of 256 bytes can provide the maximum speed-up for the hardware capacity mentioned above.
System bus bandwidth. We found that the maximum speed-up depends on the amount of data processed by the coprocessor. Taking images with 256 x 256 pixels, those benchmarks that can exhibit a performance improvement by up to two orders of magnitude would require a bus bandwidth as high as 30 GB/s.

6.2 Conclusions

Based on our quantitative approach, we explain why some reconfigurable coprocessors that are currently available do not provide the achievable two orders of magnitude performance improvement for the applications studied here. This conclusion was verified using the PCI bus plug-in board RC1000-PP. It has one Virtex XCV1000 FPGA with four local memory banks [2]. The FPGA device can provide a hardware complexity equivalent to 12288 CLBs. The bandwidth supported by PCI slots in a computer is typically 132 MB/s. So, the maximum achievable speed-up is 7,8X for ME, and 2X for ATR (see Figure 6). For the remaining benchmarks, the limited bandwidth does not allow achieve any performance improvement, which was verified. The four banks of memory and the one million of gates would achieve a factor of 2,8X (FDCT) to 9,4X (ATR) performance improvement. ME requires a minimum of eight memory banks to see a factor of 2,3X performance improvement over Pentium III-1 GHz (see Figure 5). These results illustrate that the four memory banks supported by

RC1000-PP are not sufficient to get a minimal speed-up. Therefore, an unappropriated bandwidth both for the reconfigurable data-paths and host bus can degrade enormously the performance improvement that is achievable by current FPGAs. In conclusion, we found that FPGA coprocessors are more efficient when placed as close to the processor as possible without being part of its data-path.

Acknowledgments

This work was supported by the Ministry of Education and Science of Spain under contract TIC98-0322-C03-02, Xilinx and Celoxica. We thank Daniel Herrera and the referees for helpful feedback is preparing this paper.

References

1. Benitez, D.: Modular Architecture for Custom-Built Systems Oriented to Real-Time Computer Vision: Application to Color Recognition. Journal of System Architecture 42, 8 (1997) 709-723
2. celoxica.com
3. Callahan, T. et al: The Garp Architecture and C Compiler. IEEE Computer 33, 4 (2000) 62-69
4. Chou, Y., et al: PipeRench Implementation of the Instruction Path Coprocessor. Proceedings of the 33rd International Symposium on Microarchitecture (2000)
5. Conte, T.M., et al: Challenges to Combining General-Purpose and Multimedia Processors. IEEE Computer 30, 12 (1997) 33-37
6. Goldstein, S., et al: PipeRench: A Reconfigurable Architecture and Compiler. IEEE Comp. 33, 4 (2000) 70-77
7. Embedded Solutions Ltd. (now Celoxica): Handel-C Language Reference Manual (1998)
8. Hartenstein, R.: Reconfigurable Computing: a New Business Model - and its Impact on SoC Design. Proceedings of the Euromicro Symposium on Digital Systems Design (2001)
9. Komarek, T., Pirsch, P.: Array Architectures for Block Matching Algorithms. IEEE Transactions on Circuits and Systems 36 (1989) 1301-1308
10. Lee, C., et al: MediaBench: A Tool for Evaluating and Synthesizing Multimedia and Communications Systems. Proceedings of the 30th Intl. Symposium on Microarchitecture (1997) 330-335
11. Miyamori, T., Olukotun, K.: A Quantitative Analysis of Reconfigurable Coprocessors for Multimedia Applications. Proc. of the IEEE Symp. on FPGAs for Custom Computing Machines (1998) 2-11
12. Pratt, W.: Digital Image Processing. 2nd edn.. John Wiley & Sons (1991)
13. Ranganathan, P. et al: Performance of Image and Video Processing with General-Purpose Processors and Media ISA Extensions. Proceedings of the 26th Int. Symp. on Computer Architecture (1999) 124-135
14. Slingerland, N.T., Smith, A.J.: Cache Performance for Multimedia Applications. Proceedings of the 15th ACM International Conference on Supercomputing (2001) 204-217
15. Singh, H., et al: MorphoSys: An Integrated Reconfigurable System for Data-Parallel and Computation-Intensive Applications. IEEE Transactions on Computers 49, 5 (2000) 465-481
16. Villasenor, J., Hutchings, B.: The Flexibility of Configurable Computing. IEEE Signal Processing Magazine 15, 5 (1998) 67-84
17. Vassiliadis, S., et al: The MOLEN pu-coded processor. Lecture Notes in Computer Science Vol. 2147, Springer (2001) 275-285
18. Ye, Z., et al: Chimaera: A high-performance architecture with tightly-coupled reconfigurable functional unit. Proceedings of the 27th International Symposium on Computer Architecture (2000) 225-235

Integration of Reconfigurable Hardware into System-Level Design

Klaus Buchenrieder, Ulrich Nageldinger, Andreas Pyttel, Alexander Sedlmeier
Infineon Technologies AG, Corporate Logic
D-81730 Munich, Germany
{Klaus.Buchenrieder|Ulrich.Nageldinger|Andreas.Pyttel|Alexander.Sedlmeier}@infineon.com

Abstract: In this paper, we present a design methodology for high-performance systems based on heterogeneous models. These models contain functions, that are implemented with reconfigurable hardware components. During the stepwise refinement-based design process, a hardware/software system prototype is developed. In the process, we start with a conceptual, implementation independent design at the system-level. Hereby, we employ the commercial Cadence® Cierto VCC (Virtual Component Codesign) tool, which allows to model the system with an architectural-, behavioral-, timing-, and performance view. Standard C or C++ serve as modeling language and description of the software-only system and the refinement process. During refinement, selected blocks are evaluated and transformed in stepwise fashion to hardware using Handel-C for subsequent mapping to Xilinx® Virtex 1000E FPGAs attached to a standard PC. The hardware implementations on reconfigurable logic are seamlessly integrated into the VCC environment by stub modules, which perform the hardware/software interfacing and communication via shared memory DMA transfers.
This paper presents the methodology and illustrates it using an example of a Viterbi encoder/decoder.

1 Introduction

For system-level design, three basic Codesign approaches exist: Early Partitioning - Late Integration based Codesign (cosynthesis) [3], Refinement-based Codesign [3] and Platform-based Codesign [4]. Furthermore, some non-commercial approaches [6] [7] [8] or the OCAPI system [5] [9] developed at the IMEC institute are also well known.

For commercial development of embedded systems, platform-based codesign has proven to be most effective, in that platforms are viewed as the catalyst for systematic reuse, rapid development, and integration of derivative products, and can drive dramatic reductions in time-to-market. The effective use of platform-based design throughout the supply and design chains of industrial systems design enables better interaction of suppliers of architectures, components and software, and system customers.

Platform-based design fosters the concurrent development of reliable hardware and software technology that presents a reliable and quantifiable translation from a modeled behavior to an implementation architecture with constraints and asserts imposed. Typical are aggregations of intellectual property modules (IP) that serve as the basis for multiple derivative system-on-chip products (SOC) that carry functional components. Thus, platform-based development depends on the existence of: (1) defined and

M. Glesner, P. Zipf, and M. Renovell (Eds.): FPL 2002, LNCS 2438, pp. 987-996, 2002.

verified, market-specific IP, (2) a clear division of system behavior in function, architecture and constraints, (3) performance estimation and functional verification/validation methods, (4) an integration-oriented design flow, and (5) tool, application and system support.

We have chosen the Cadence® Cierto VCC (Virtual Component Codesign) environment for hardware/software partitioning and design space exploration at the system-level. VCC employs a strict separation of behavior, architecture and timing information. In VCC, module definitions and functional specifications are described in C or C++. For one behavioral block, several functional descriptions (*views*) can be stored, representing e.g. different levels of functional refinement. For the simulation, any one of the views may be selected. The simulator and performance estimator employs an event-driven paradigm, appropriate for data- and control-flow intensive applications.

In the first step of our design method, we use VCC for system-level exploration and software-based system-simulation. In the subsequent partitioning step, we replace blocks of the VCC model by hardware modules, which are implemented using the Handel-C [1] design flow. Handel-C is a hardware oriented derivative of the C programming language designed for compiling programs into hardware images of FPGAs.

In our approach, we design the system platform-based with VCC, transform C/C++ modules into hardware using Handel-C and implement a true hardware/software prototype, that adheres to all constraints imposed, using Xilinx FPGA integrated into a PC. The example shown in this contribution, consists of blocks implementing a transmission channel containing a Viterbi encoder and decoder with all modules described with VCC.

Due to the high level of abstraction, some drawbacks are inevitable:

- Inaccurate delay times:
  Delay times that express the reply instance are imprecise, because clocking and CPU cycles are not accurately modeled at the system-level. For this reason, delays are based on the information provided by the user.
- Number representations:
  As C(++) is being used at the system level, the algorithm is specified with floating point or 32 bit integer precision respectively. However, the actual hardware rather relies on fixed-point representation and often on reduced integer bit widths for cost reasons. The impact of this reduced precision on the results can hardly be modeled at the system level in our example (although VCC allows reduced integer bit-widths for communication between blocks).
- Bit-level operation overhead:
  Some blocks employ extensive bit-level operations, which include a large computational overhead when being implemented in a high-level language.
- Simulation time due to computational complexity:
  Since we use the event-based simulation paradigm, processing a large number of data is time consuming.

In the approach brought forward in this contribution, we employ an integrated hardware/software approach to overcome the drawbacks mentioned before. All functions requiring floating-point arithmetic and computationally intensive functions are run in software on the PC. Other functions processing large volumes of data, such as the Viterbi en- and decoder, are implemented with FPGA logic. All dedicated, non processor hardware is described in Handel-C.

The Handel-C environment has been chosen for a number of reasons:

- The C-based description facilitates the mapping of VCC behaviors to Handel-C.
- Handel-C allows to describe parallel executing functions.
- Handel-C also provides communication channels as a powerful mechanisms for synchronized, data-driven communication (between parallel sections of code).
- The communication between PC and FPGA board (RC1000 / PCI bus) is supported by Handel-C macros facilitating access to various interfaces.

After the integration of the hardware parts, the complete system resembles a hardware-software prototype, that can be efficiently controlled using the VCC graphical user interface. The existing VCC simulation environment is significantly enhanced, as the Handel-C compiler also generates delay estimations as required by the VCC performance simulator.

In [10], we have shown a similar methodology using the OCAPI system from the IMEC institute. OCAPI is targeted for digital ASIC design and is also based on C++ to capture the system behavior with data flow semantics. However, VCC provides a higher level of abstraction and a more general simulation paradigm, which is better suited for controlflow-oriented applications.

2 System-Level Design with Cadence® VCC

The Cadence® Cierto VCC (Virtual Component Codesign) tool is projected for system-level design space exploration and hardware/software partitioning in the concept engineering phase of a complex hardware/software system. It allows both functional and performance simulation and fast redesign using a graphical user interface.

VCC employs a strict separation of behavior and architecture. The behavior of the system can be described in functional blocks using C or C++ (further supported options for behavioral capturing are beyond the scope of this paper.) The functional blocks (behavioral virtual components) feature an event-driven simulation approach, i.e. the functionality of a block is activated, as soon as a data token arrives at any inputport. This technique is adequate for both data-flow and control-flow intensive applications. Once the behavior is captured completely, a *functional simulation* can be performed to verify the correct behavior of the system.

The system behavior described above features zero delay times for all functional blocks. To add timing information, the behavior must be mapped onto an appropriate architecture, which is also built using several architectural modules. In the context of such a mapping, delays can be added to behavioral descriptions. The total timing is then determined by the specified delays and the additional timing caused by the interaction of the behaviors running on the architectural components. With the timing given, a *performance simulation* of the system can be done. As behaviors can be mapped to different architectural blocks, a design space exploration can be performed, finding the optimal partitioning of the functional modules onto the architectural elements.

3 Implementation Methodology

Initially, we follow the VCC design approach with modelling and simulating the entire system using functional blocks with a behavior specified in C. This simulation also determines some low-level aspects of the subsequent prototyping, e.g. the necessary bitwidth for the Viterbi error values.

After this, three steps lead to a prototype implementation for a combination of an FPGA (dedicated logic) and a processing element (represented by the VCC environment running on a Pentium III PC). In the first step towards implementation, a VCC description is partitioned into executable C and Handel-C. Hereby, blocks featuring floating-point calculations and OS-routines are retained as C models, thus representing the software part, while data intensive computations are targeted for the FPGA. In the second step, interfaces are generated for communication via shared memory and synchronization of hardware and software components. Finally, descriptions of VCC targeted for hardware implementation are translated to Handel-C.

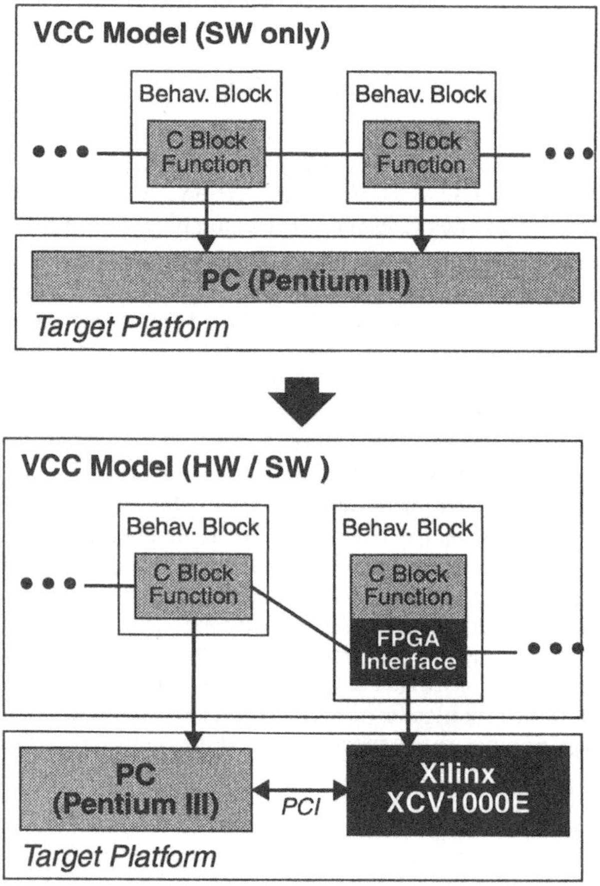

Fig. 1. Integration of HW modules into VCC

3.1 Partitioning a VCC System Description into Hardware and Software Modules

The system modeled in VCC contains functions, which perform computationally sophisticated floating-point operations as required for calculations such as of white noise. These functions cannot be easily mapped onto an FPGA structure and hence are implemented in software. Other functionality like the Viterbi encoder and decoder, which process a high amount of data with bit-level operations, are efficiently realized using FPGAs for higher execution speed. The hardware implementation of these modules allows to exploit parallelism inherent in the Viterbi realization. The partitioning process is driven by the complexity and computational cost of individual modules.

The VCC model itself represents a software-only model, so the behavior blocks aimed for PC execution are simply left untouched. To those blocks being selected for hardware implementation, an additional *view* is added, i.e. an alternative behavioral implementation for this block. This new view does not implement the block's functionality, but realizes interfacing functions for FPGA communication and control. Figure 1 provides an overview of the mapping process.

3.2 Interface Generation

For the communication and synchronization of hardware and software, two basic interfaces are supported. The shared memory interface and the synchronized point-to-point interface. Large data transfers are conducted via shared memory. This memory is accessed through an optimized PCI-DMA transfer mechanism from the software side. Block transfer is predominant for reconfigurable hardware. A semaphore like mechanism, supported by a C library, synchronizes the access to the shared memory. The point-to-point interface serves as control port for communication from the software to the hardware domain, and conversely as status-port. The implementation is software mastered, so that the configuration of the FPGA and the calculation of computationally expensive functions can be directly obtained from the initial VCC model. Library modules exist for both the shared memory and the point-to-point communication interfaces.

3.3 Mapping VCC Models to Handel-C

Handel-C [1] [2] enables compiling high-level algorithms directly into gate-level hardware. It is an extended subset of C syntactically in compliance with conventional ANSI C. It contains parallel constructs to exploit inherent parallelism, variable bit-width for variables and data-structures. In addition, a channel construct expresses synchronized communications between parallel branches of code.

The timing semantics of the language is straight forward, in that assignments require exactly one clock-cycle and expressions or control logic consume no cycles to evaluate. One or more cycles are necessary for communications over channels, since those are implemented with a blocking scheme, that waits until sender and receiver become ready. The Handel-C compiler generates EDIF or VHDL files for Xilinx and Altera FPGAs.

The functional blocks of VCC, and the event-triggered behaviors generally translate to parallel functions and channels in Handel-C. However, the mapping from VCC specifications to Handel-C functions requires the designer to take certain low-level decisions, which are not dealt with in VCC, e.g. the bitwidth of the variables. Furthermore, the channel semantics of Handel-C, which are similar to the Rendezvous synchronization of ADA, do not exactly correspond to the event-based synchronization of VCC. Handel-C semantics, however, have shown to be powerful enough to allow porting from VCC without major problems. Transfers of complete data blocks, which are supported in VCC, are not so efficiently done over Handel-C channels. In this case, the use of shared memories in Handel-C is the recommended method, especially as they are also available in VCC. The decision for shared memory in VCC, however, has to be taken in an early design phase.

4 System Design Environment

The system design environment encompasses the execution environment and the HW/SW system prototyper platform. The system prototyper platform, embedded in the execution environment, consists of a RC1000-PP board [2] plugged into the PCI slot of a Pentium III PC, running at 600 MHz. The RC1000-PP board hosts a Xilinx Virtex XCV1000E FPGA and four banks of memory with 2 MBytes each. This allows, to prototype, i.e., telecommunication subsystems, with embedded memories or provide sets of local test-stimuli. All four memory banks are accessible by the FPGA and any device on the PCI bus.

Communication between the reprogrammable Xilinx FPGA and any device connected to the PCI bus is conducted via the PLX PCI9080 PCI controller located on the RC1000-PP board. Different methods of data transfer from the host PC or the environment to the FPGA are available:
(1) Large amounts of data or test vectors are transferred between FPGA and PCI through the memory banks Mem0 to Mem3.
(2) Streams of bytes are most conveniently communicated through the unidirectional 8-bit control- and status-ports (figure 2).

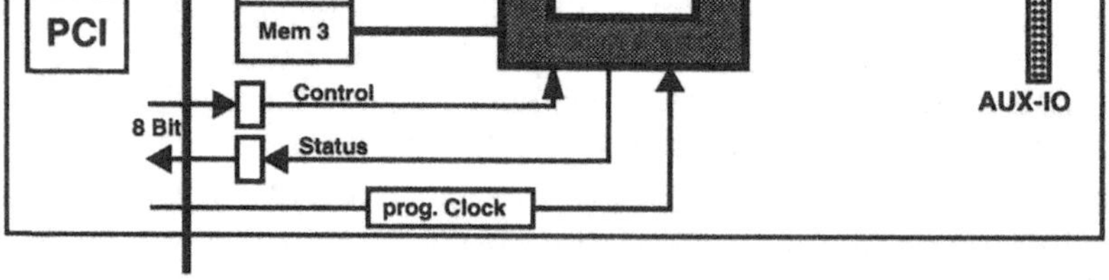

Fig. 2. Schematic view of the RC1000-PP Board

The RC1000-PP board is supported with a macro library that simplifies the process of initializing and talking to the hardware. This library comprises driver functions for initialization and selection of a board, handling of FPGA configuration files and data transfer between PC and the RC1000-PP board. These library functions can be

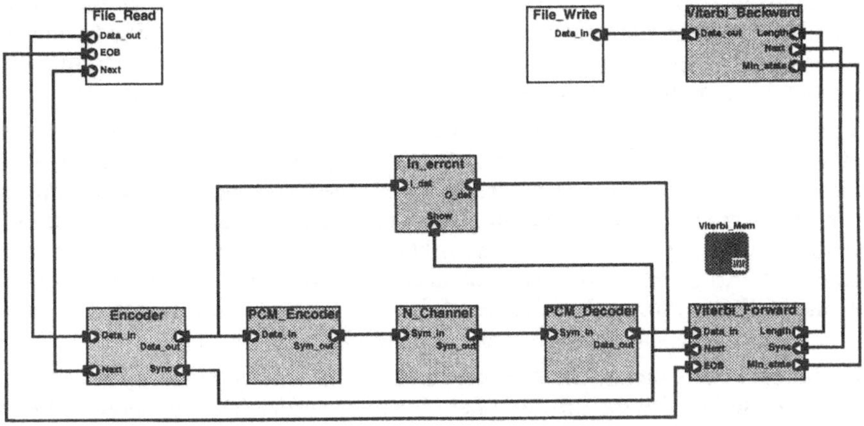

Fig. 3. VCC Block Diagram of the Viterbi Example

included in a C or C++ program, that runs on the host PC and performs data transfer via the PCI bus.

5 Viterbi Channel Example

Our example application implements a Viterbi encoder/decoder transmitting data over a noisy channel. The VCC block-diagram system is depicted in figure 3. The contents of a binary file is encoded by a convolutional encoder, transmitted over a channel, which inflicts noise, and decoded by a Viterbi decoder [11] [12]. After the decoding, which is done in a forward and a backward pass, the result is written to another file. An analyzer module compares the input and output data and measures the amount of erroneous bits. Additionally, the channel outputs the number of bits altered by the added noise. Both values allow a rating of the Viterbi decoder. By changing system parameters like block size or noise amplitude, several system variants can be examinated.

The system is realized in both hardware and software running on the host PC. The modules for reading and writing the binary files and the noise generator, which performs floating-point operations, are implemented in C or C++ and executed by the host. Other functional blocks, that process a large amount of data using partially bit-level functions, are transformed into Handel-C and mapped onto a Xilinx Virtex 1000E FPGA. Data exchange between hardware and software modules is established via shared memory. Additionally, a memory is used to exchange data efficiently between the forward and the backward phase of the Viterbi decoder. This is necessary, because the backward phase reads the data from memory in the reverse sequence as it was written by the forward phase.

For examination, 112201 bytes of input data is copied to the RC1000 memory using DMA. As the Viterbi-algorithm is block-oriented, the file is written to the memory and processed in blocks of parameterizable size. Input block data are encoded by a convolutional encoder, generating a 3-bit value out of each input bit. A further decoding step transforms this value into one of the eight symbol values (-7, -5, -3, -1, +1, +3,

+5, +7) by means of a lookup-table. The convolutional encoding module has been efficiently realized in hardware using a shift register and XOR gates. Subsequently, the channel block adds noise values to the data symbols using a 16 bit fixed-point representation (7 bit integer, 9 bit fractional part). The noise values are read from memory, where they have been stored by the noise generator implemented in software.

The Viterbi Decoder consists of two parts: the forward and the backward phase. The forward phase is the more complex one and begins with decoding the input symbols into 3-bit values using thresholds. As we use the hamming distance for error measure in our example, sixteen hamming units calculate the hamming distances of the input value to the possible values. In a further step, error values are added up with the accumulated errors and the lowest value is selected for each of the eight accumulated error values. One bit for each node, specifying the selected value, is stored in memory. All operations of the sub phases execute in parallel.

In the backward phase, the original bitstream is reconstructed by traversing the memory data written by the forward phase in reverse order. This function is efficiently done by a shift register and a multiplexer. The reconstructed bitstream is stored bytewise in another memory block of the RC1000 board. Additionally, the data that were changed by the noise are stored in this block. The contents of this memory is transferred to the host by DMA and written to a file. At last, the original data and the processed data are analyzed and the number of erroneous bits determined.

6 Results

The combination of VCC and Handel-C into a single high-level design environment allows to the model and analyze complex systems and provides a flexible link to implementation.

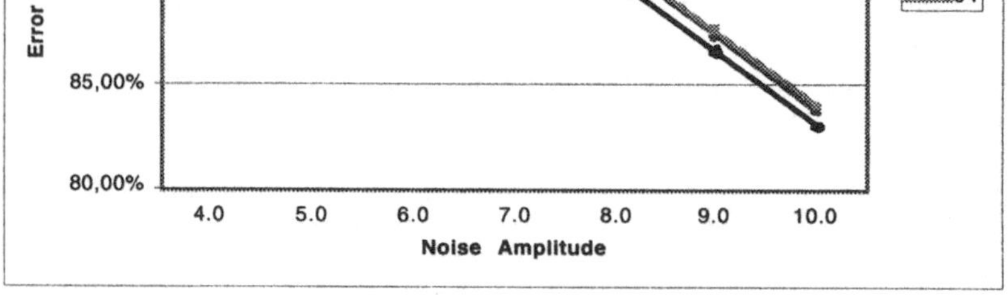

Fig. 4. Error Correction for different Block sizes

For our experiments, we chose a Viterbi implementation with adjustable block size and noise amplitude. For comparison, we implemented a software-only prototype and a HW/SW solution. Different parameter settings were employed in 28 runs of each case. The FPGA implementation used up 475 slices of a Xilinx Virtex XCV1000E at a clock speed of 20 MHz.

The HW/SW system completed all runs in about five minutes, while the SW-only implementation needed 90 minutes on a 600 MHz Pentium III PC. This shows a significant speed-up of the HW/SW solution. The simulation time decreases with increasing block-size due to less communication overhead.

The influence of increasing noise on the error correction is shown in figure 4 for three different block sizes. The figure shows the expected decrease of corrected errors with increasing noise amplitude and better error correction with increasing block-size. Note, that the dependency of the error rate on the block size is not linear.

The fixed-point arithmetic for noise-mixing in the HW/SW system reveals imprecision of the channel modelling, resulting in a slightly better performance of the Viterbi algorithm. The expected impact of the fixed-point arithmetic on the results, however, is smaller than expected and occurs mainly at low noise amplitudes and error rates (figure 5).

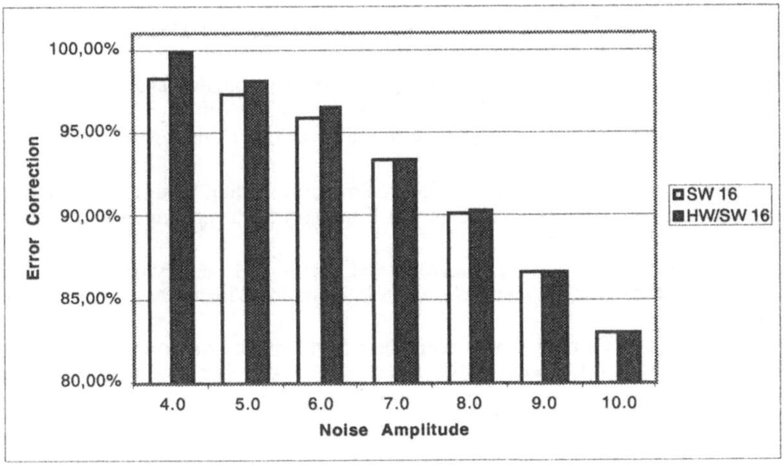

Fig. 5. Comparison of HW/SW and SW results

7 Conclusions

In this paper, we illustrated a methodology to get from a system-level software-only model down to a hardware/software prototype. It combines standard C or C++ with Handel-C and covers specification, system synthesis and FPGA realization. To demonstrate our approach, we designed and evaluated a Viterbi encoder and decoder with a noise-inflicted channel.

In the presented method, we followed a strict top-down Hardware/Software Codesign paradigm. Starting from the VCC model, which is based on functional modules, we partitioned the set of modules into software- and hardware-modules.

The blocks selected for hardware implementation were enriched by an additional view providing an interface to the FPGA hardware. Thus, hardware functionality could be smoothly integrated into the existing model. The behavioral descriptions of the hardware modules were translated to Handel-C, subsequently compiled and mapped onto Xilinx Virtex 1000E FPGAs, while the software parts were executed in the VCC environment on the host PC.

8 References

1. M. Bowen: Handel-C Language Reference Manual, Embedded Solutions Ltd., 1999
2. R. Kress, A. Pyttel, A. Sedlmeier: FPGA based Prototyping for Product Definition, FPL 2000, Villach , Austria.
3. K. Buchenrieder: Hardware / Software Codesign, 2nd edition, IT Press Bruchsal, 2001, ISBN: 3-929814-26-9
4. http://www.cadence.com/datasheets/vcc_environment.html
5. S. Vernalde, P. Schaumont, I. Bolsens: An Object Oriented Programming Approach for Hardware Design", IEEE Computer, Society Workshop on VLSI'99, Orlando, April 1999
6. G. DeMicheli, M. Sami: Hardware/Software Co-Design, Kluwer Academic Publishers, 1995, ISBN: 0-7923-3882-0
7. D.D. Gajski, F. Vahid, S. Narayan, J. Gong: Specification and Design of Embedded Systems, Prentice Hall, 1994, ISBN: 0-13-150731-1
8. W. Wolf: Object-oriented co-synthesis of distributed embedded systems, ACM Transactions on Design Automation of Electronic Systems, 1(3), 1996
9. C++ based hardware design of complex digital systems, Course Notes, IMEC Belgium, 2000.
10. K. Buchenrieder, A. Pyttel, A. Sedlmeier: A Powerful System Design Methodology Combining OCAPI and Handel-C for Concept Engineering; to appear in Proc. of DATE02, March 4-8, 2002, Paris, France.
11. Viterbi, A.J., Error Bounds for Convolutional Codes and an Asymptotically Op-timum Decoding Algorithm, IEEE Transactions on Information Theory, April 1967; IT - 13 (2) : pp. 260 - 269.
12. Viterbi, A.J., Convolutional Codes and Their Performance in Communication Systems, IEEE Transactions on Communications Technology, October 1971; COM - 19 (5) : pp. 751 - 772.

A Retargetable Macro Generation Method for the Evaluation of Repetitive Configurable Architectures

Frank Wolz and Reiner Kolla

Universität Würzburg, Lehrstuhl für Technische Informatik
{wolz,kolla}@informatik.uni-wuerzburg.de

Abstract. In this paper, we present a new retargetable macro generation strategy for LUT-based sequential circuits. It is a first part of a new design system for performing studies on arbitrary configurable architectures with repetitive structures. Besides retargetability, the main characteristics of our method are the interlocking of circuit partitioner and macro generator, further a fitting strategy, that performs routing before placement.

1 Introduction

Previous Work. Studies on configurable architectures have been performed relatively early [8] and there is still some research, that takes care of area and delay effects after placement and routing while scaling the structures [1]. Furthermore, there have been investigations about special features, like segmentation and buffering in routing structures [3], cluster-based logic blocks [5] or reduction of crossbar density [4], for example. However, all these studies employed the well-known island-style architecture for their analyses. Additionally, there has been developed also a CAD tool [2], that works good on this architecture type and that supports architectural research for similar commercial devices.

Our Approach. The scope of our research is to study area and delay behaviour on arbitrary field-programmable architectures with repetitive structures. Therefore, we developed a new, more general architecture model, that provides even multidimensionality, and searched for more universal placement and routing methods. As detailed routing is a hard problem for its own, especially general methods, that can take into account only less of an architecture's overall structural properties, must compete with complexity, if all specified features of an architecture should be exploited to optimize results. Because of this complexity aspect, we decided to perform a place and route concept with macros. That means, a circuit to implement is decomposed into subcircuits. By placing and routing these subcircuits, macros are formed in respect of a given target architecture, and finally, the macros are floorplanned and routed. Our basic idea was, to create a timing-driven placement and routing method, that invests higher complexity to get good results at macro level, and by controlling the macro size, we hope to balance complexity and quality of the results, despite compared architectures are very different in capabilities.

Outline. Section 2 introduces shortly our architecture model. Section 3 gives a more precise overview on our macro generation method, while implementation details are presented in section 4. Finally, section 5 shows some results on five architectures.

M. Glesner, P. Zipf, and M. Renovell (Eds.): FPL 2002, LNCS 2438, pp. 997–1006, 2002.

2 Architecture Model

Our architecture model is based on finite periodic graphs. Although this class of regular graphs has only been paid relatively less attention, it is well suitable for FPGA architectural research.

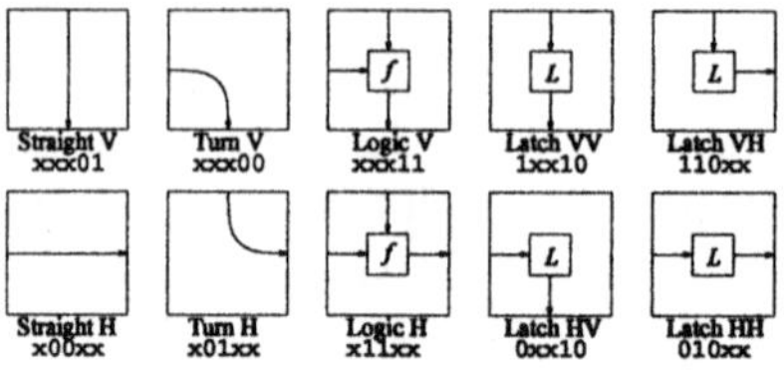

Fig. 1. Configurable Cell Example

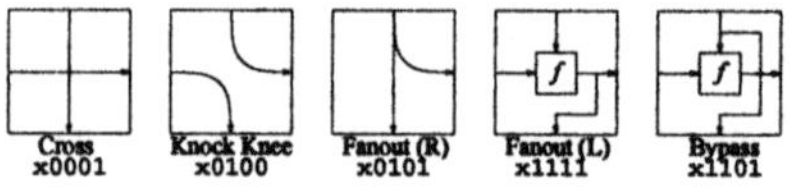

Fig. 2. Task Combination

A main advantage results from the compact description of an architecture: by creating a so-called static graph, that represents an architecture segment, we get a regular architecture instance of variable size by simply unrolling the static graph. Furthermore, the model also provides multidimensional architectures, that have not been studied before on FPGA realm. A first important fact on our architecture model is, that all configurability of an architecture is captured in nodes of the periodic graph. In consequence, nodes are representing configurable cells, that can perform logic and/or routing tasks, while the edges of the periodic graph are representing fixed links between configurable cells. An architecture can consist of one or more configurable cell types. Figure 1 illustrates the task list of an example cell. All tasks are encoded by bitstrings over $\{0, 1, x\}$, where the compatibility of a set of tasks is expressed by boolean containment. For example, the tasks *Straight V* and *Turn H* can be combined to realize a fanout routing, because their bitstrings xxx01 and x01xx can be combined to x0101. Some more possible task combinations are shown in figure 2. Figure 3 shows a static graph description of a simple sea-of-gates-style architecture with double-mesh routing structure. While using the cell type from figure 1 would lead to a fully homogeneous architecture, the capability of each logic cell (LC) could also be specified different. Note, that this is not a toroidal architecture, but a description for unrolling an architecture graph, whose peripheral edges (nil edges) do not have either a source or a target node.

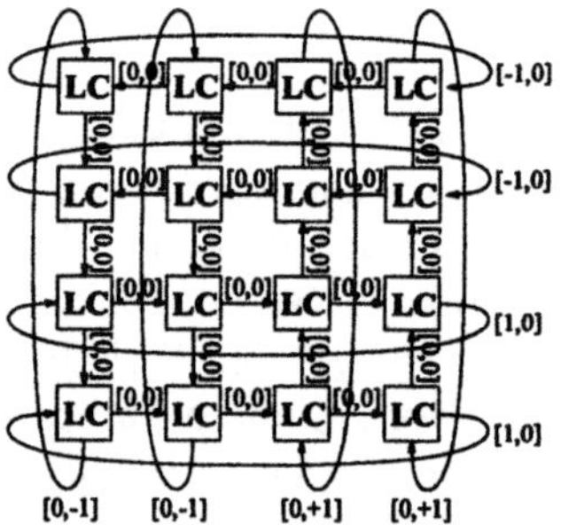

Fig. 3. Double-Mesh Architecture

3 General Approach

Our macro generator is mainly composed of two parts: we interlocked the partitioning method from [11] with an iterative placement and routing algorithm. The partitioning method performs a simultaneous construction of subcircuit clusters with timing-driven cost functions and suggests a list of best block candidates, that should be added to existing macro instances. If placing and routing of such a candidate block at its destination macro instance was not successful, the block is rejected and its destination macro will be locked for it. In this case, same procedure is performed for the second block in candidate list and so on. However, if a candidate block could be placed and routed at its destination macro instance, the partitioner recalculates the cost measures and suggests a next set of block candidates. While most known methods are first placing a block and then are trying to find short routings, our macro generation method first routes and then places the block. This is done by a simultaneous shortest path search of all nets adjacent to the block candidate. A placement, i.e. an assignment to a logic or latch resource is valid, if the resource is able to realize the candidate block's function and all required nets are available at its pins. Nets from or to neighbour blocks, that are not realized in the current macro instance, are routed from periphery of the architecture segment to avoid congestions by later routings. However, if the appropriate neighbour node is selected for placement at this macro instance, such nets are ripped up. Of course, simultaneous routing entails the occurence of conflicting routes, i.e. a routing resource is used by more than one route. This problem is addressed by a penalty factor in our routing cost function, which is increased at further iterations. This concept seems to be similar to the pathfinder method [6]. However, in contrary to the pathfinder algorithm, our route-then-place method determines the location of the target net terminals during search. Furthermore, re-routing due to conflicting routes can be limited to a maximum number of iterations. After this limit is exceeded, the destination resource found is locked and another re-iteration can be started. While the number of re-iterations after locking a resource is naturally limited to the set of free resources on the architecture segment, it is also possible to reduce the maximum number of repeats. After all blocks are fitted into macros, the architecture segment of each macro is shrinked to a minimum cube. Macros are shrinked by a maximum shorting of all routes to periphery and by cutting unused architecture segments around placed logic and routings. This is done, to get small instances for a subsequent floorplanning process.

4 Macro Generation

Overview. An important objective while developing our macro generation method was its ability to compete especially with strongly restricted routing and logic resources. Hence, the basic idea of our incremental method for placing and routing block candidates was to determine a feasible realization by finding routes for all required nets, first. We called the algorithm realizing this concept the *simultaneous path search method* (SPS). The core of our routing algorithm consists of majorly independent shortest-path methods, where the role of nodes and edges is switched: routing is performed from edge to edge of the periodic graph, while free routing tasks in the nodes are determining adjacency.

Classification of Nets. During our incremental macro generation method, there might be several unrealized neighbour blocks of a block candidate. To avoid blockings by later routings, our method reserves a route to the periphery of the macro space for each adjacent net. At first, this strategy oftenly preserves facilities for placing such a neigbour block later. However, at least, this always guarantees external availability of all nets. For realization of this strategy, we introduce the following classification of nets in respect of a partition P. *Internal Nets* are nets with no terminals outside of P. *IntExt Nets* are nets with more than one terminal in P and at least one terminal outside of P. *External Nets* are nets with exactly one terminal in P and at least one terminal outside of P. In respect of nets, we generally regard multi-point nets, that are to realize by configurable trees (CTree), which consist of one or more configurable routes, connecting a source terminal with one or more destination terminals. We call a configurable route a *temporary route*, if its appropriate net has a source terminal in P and a target terminal outside of P or vice versa. During macro generation we now keep the following invariants about routes: 1. The CTree of an IntExt Net or an Ext Net contains exactly one route to periphery. 2. The route of an Ext Net is a temporary route. 3. The route of an IntExt Net from or to the periphery is a temporary route. 4. All subroutes of a temporary route are also temporary routes.

Generating Searches. Let B be the block candidate to place and route in a destination macro space M. Let *pred*(B) be the set of predecessor blocks and *succ*(B) be the set of successor blocks of B. Let $\mathcal{N}$ be the set of nets adjacent to B. For each net $N \in \mathcal{N}$, we first deconfigure its temporary route, if one exists, from the preplaced part of macro M. Then, for all blocks $B' \in$ *pred*(B), we generate forward searches. If *succ*$(B) \neq \emptyset$, we also generate one backward search. For each instantiated search, the search front is initialized as follows:

Forward Searches: If a net $N \in \mathcal{N}$ is already realized in M, we walk along the appropriate CTree and initialize the search front with all configurable fanout possibilities. If N is not yet routed in M, and the predecessor block B_N of B via N is not realized, too, then we have to search for a temporary route from the periphery of M. In this case, we initialize the search front with all incoming nil edges of M, that are unused, yet. However, if B_N is realized in M, then the search front simply contains the outgoing edge of B_N's realization.

Backward Search: For all blocks $C \in$ *succ*(B), that are already realized in M, we initialize the search front with all unused ingoing edges of C's realization. However, if no $C \in$ *succ*(B) is realized in M, we have to search for a temporary route from the periphery of M back to B's output and initialize the search front with all outgoing nil edges of M, that are unused, yet.

Generating these searches, we ensure the simultaneous routing of all nets required by the candidate block. However, while Ext Nets and fanoutless Int Nets nets are always routed completely, for general Int Nets and IntExt Nets some additional fanout route requirements can occur. We will address this below. The principle of simultaneous path search is rather simple: the search fronts of all instantiated searches are extended in round-robin manner, until all fronts get empty. The front extension routine itself is nearly the same, as in a common shortest path algorithm, with the only exception that the role of nodes and edges are interchanged in contrary to the classical sense. Regard a forward search S, for example. We have to check the target node of each edge in the front of S for free routing tasks. If the successor edge e of a free routing task has not been reached cheaper by S, then update the costs of e in respect of search S and insert it to the search front of S. The backward search is managed in a similar way.

Note, that searches run completely independent from each other. Nevertheless, there are not less possibilities for creating an efficient implementation of such a search method, from using a priority queue or other specialized data structures, up to parallelization approaches.

Deciding Placeability. One main question, however, is, how SPS determines the best realization of a block candidate B on the macro space. This is done by solving matching problems between the set of required nets and the set of inputs of a cell: Let c be a configurable cell. If a net N has been previously routed to c or if the search of net N reaches a pin of c, then N is registered for c as an *available net*. If the nets of all searches are available at c, then for each configurable task t, which is able to realize B, check, if there is an injective mapping λ from the set of required nets to the set of t's inputs. This is equal to a maximum matching problem on a bipartite graph, that can be solved efficiently by network flow methods. We call a solution (t, λ) of this problem a *net matching* for the configurable cell c.

Realizing Routes. After finishing SPS, assuming that a net matching for the candidate block B was found, each search reconstructs its shortest route by tracing back over the "best" routing tasks. Note, that this step is the earliest stage, where we are able to determine efficiently, if there are in fact conflicting routes. The reconstruction of routes, including the test for disjointness is performed sequentially search by search. For each route to reconstruct, we have to check all previously reconstructed routes for already used resources. A placement and routing is only valid, if a net matching was found and all routes were non-conflicting. Then, the block candidate and its routes are configured on the macro instance M – with the provisio, that, as mentioned above, the remaining fanout routes can be found. Such remaining fanout routes for a net N are occuring in exactly three cases: 1. A net N has been routed to a block B by a forward search, but there is at least one other block already realized in M, that needs signal N for input. 2. A net N has been routed by backward search from one successor block to the output of a block B, but there is at least one other successor block already realized in M. 3. A net N has been routed by backward search, but the net has also successor blocks not realized in M. In this case, a temporary route has to be found. We compute these routes sequentially by a simple path expansion method. If valid routes can be constructed, we configure them on M and return. Else, if path expansion failed, we deconfigure routes and realization of B to start another SPS after locking the realization task of B and all other tasks of that cell using the same output pin.

Cost Function. The main objectives of our macro generation method are block realizability and routing delay minimization. While the first objective is addressed by the concept of temporary routes, the cost functions of the partitioner and the route-then-place method are targetting the second objective. The partitioner works only on the circuit's structure and calculates a slack-based *relative delay criticality* measure (RDC), assuming that realizations of all nets would cause equal delays. Two significant properties of RDC for a net N are: $0 < \mathrm{RDC}(N) \leq 1$ and $\mathrm{RDC}(N) = 1 \iff$ a critical path runs over net N. The cost function of our route-then-place method primarily takes into account this structural RDC measure, but also concrete delay values as they are specified by the given architecture description. Consider a front extension step of the SPS method for routing a net N: let t be a configurable routing task from edge u to edge v. Then, the new routing delay to edge v is $d_v = d_u + c_{u,N} + (\delta_t \cdot \rho) + \gamma_u$: The distance to edge v consists of the distance to edge u, the cost $c_{u,N}$ for routing net N on edge u and the delay δ_t of the routing task t, scaled by a factor ρ. Additionally, we introduced a random part γ_u. More exactly, we have: $c_{u,N} = p_u \cdot (2 - \text{RDC}(N))$ By this addend, we are scaling the structural criticality RDC of the net N, delivered by the partitioner, by a penalty factor p_u. For conventional iterations, it is $p_u = 1$. However, if edge u was a conflicting edge in previous iterations, we set $p_u = r_u \cdot n_i$ where r_u is the number of routes requested edge u and n_i is a factor increased by the numbers of re-iterations. The factor ρ has its purpose in reduction of routing costs for temporary routes. This is because temporary routes are ripped up later anyway, either if the appropriate neighbour block is selected for placement at the current macro instance, or even before the final routing procedure after floorplanning all macros. The neutral value of factor ρ is one. By selecting lower values, we observed more compact placements on benchmark circuits. Finally, the addend γ_u was introduced to cause slight differences in the routing cost measure of edge v for all searches. The default value of γ_u is zero. However, if v has been a conflicting edge in previous iterations, we add a random part of the basic routing costs $c_{u,N}$ for edge u. Hence, γ_u acts as an arbiter for competing routes.

5 Experimental Results

In this section, we present the first results with our new macro generation method on several architectures. Our experiments were focussed on two areas. First, we observed our plain place-then-route method fitting complete benchmark circuits into minimally dilated architectures. Second, we examined the decomposition of some bigger circuits into placed and routed macros, also for different architectures. We constructed several architectures based on two-input look-up tables and latches, but with different routing structures. Therefore, the benchmark circuits were mapped into two-input functions using SIS [9]. Our test architectures are introduced in section 5.1. With great regret, we had to remove all figures and tables of our experimental results from this article because of rigid space restrictions. They can be requested from the authors instead.

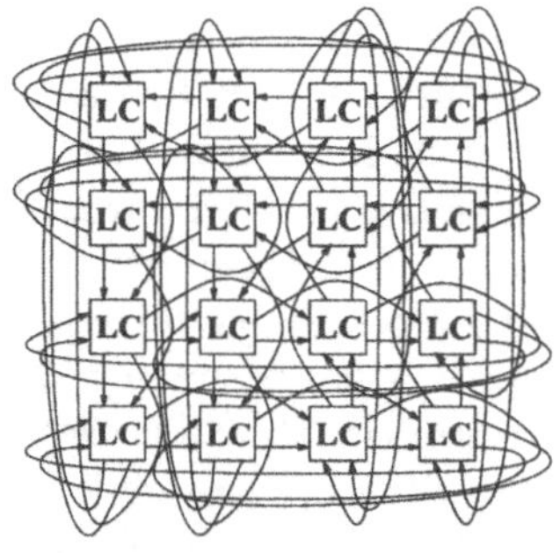

Fig. 4. 2D-Double-Mesh with Double Lines *(DMDouble)*

5.1 Test Architectures

DMSingle. The first architecture we examined, is the two-dimensional sea-of-gates architecture, already introduced in figure 3, provided with the configurable cell from figure 1. The simple double-mesh structure only allows direct-neighbour routings.

DMDouble. Figure 4 shows the description of a similar architecture, but its routing capabilities have been extended to double span routings.

ISSingle. The island-style architecture depicted in figure 5 consists of a logic cell (LC), surrounded by connector box cells (CB), that are linked by a switch box cell (SB). The logic cell contains one two-input look-up-table and one latch. The CB cells provide a connection of LC's inputs and outputs to single-span wires between CB and SB cells and it provides also wire track jumps. The SB cells can realize horizontal and vertical signal turns.

ISDouble. The *ISDouble* architecture in figure 6 is similar to the *ISSingle* architecture, but CB cells provide two double span routing tracks (marked by dashed lines), that bypass the neighbour SB cell.

IS3D. Finally, the *IS3D* architecture in figure 7 is a three-dimensional variant of the *ISSingle* architecture. The original architecture segment of *ISSingle* has been duplicated and flipped, routing capabilities have been extended for three-dimensional routings (shown by dashed lines).

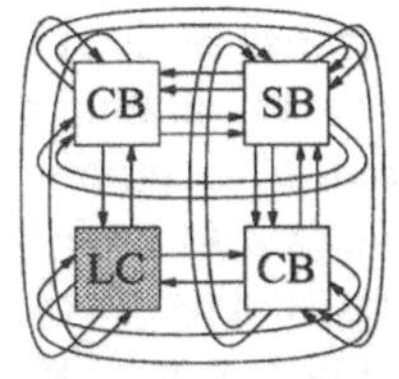

Fig. 5. 2D-Island-Style Architecture *(ISSingle)*

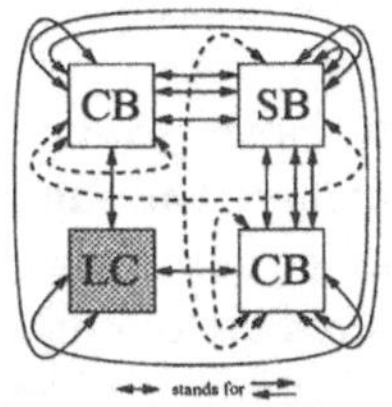

Fig. 6. 2D-Island-Style with Double Lines *(ISDouble)*

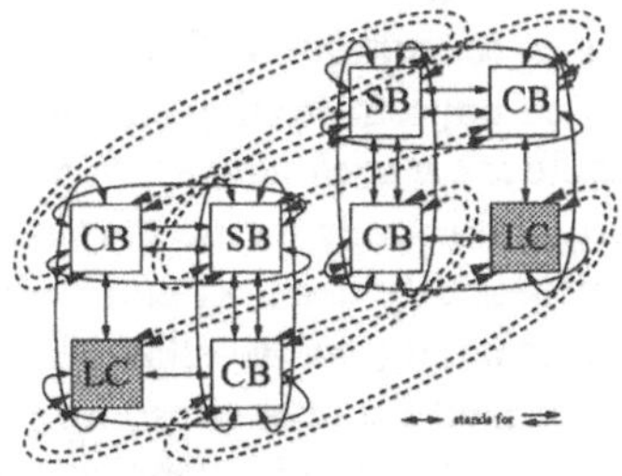

Fig. 7. 3D-Island-Style Architecture *(IS3D)*

5.2 Area and Delay Calculation

Area Consumption. All configurable cells of our architectures are specified on the basis of concrete realizations using look-up-tables, latches and multiplexers. These realizations have been evaluated by the area model suggested in [7], with the difference of normalizing all values to NAND2 gate equivalents (instead of inverters).

Delay Calculation. As edges of our architecture graph are representing fixed wires between nodes (i.e. configurable cells), they do not provide any delay. On the other hand, our specification of a configurable cell allows different delay values for all tasks. However, for these experimental purposes, we set all delay values to one, in order to calculate the maximum number of routing switches and look-up-tables along any combinational path.

5.3 Route-Then-Place Results

From the MCNC'93 benchmark set, we selected 12 small circuits with up to 92 functional blocks after mapping procedure. Each circuit was placed and routed completely on each architecture: starting with a single architecture segment, we enlarged the dilation until the circuit fitted. In order to use our incremental route-then-place method without interaction of the partitioner, we needed a valid placement order of all the circuit's blocks, because preplaced subcircuit and added block must be connected. To obtain a valid placement order, we used the following simple heuristic: We started with a block of maximum number of adjacent ExtNets and IntExtNets, that means, which is connected to the circuit's primary inputs or outputs as strong as possible. The remaining blocks were ordered by performing a breadth-first-search on the circuit. The maximum number of re-iterations has been set to 10 for conflicting routes and to half the volume of the architecture graph for task locking. The scale factor ρ for temporary routes has been set to 0.5.

Area Usage and Area Consumption. After a circuit has been completely fitted, the architecture's dilation was shrinked to the minimum bounding box of the entire placement and routing. For purpose of area comparisons, we calculated three measures: the area consumption of the minimum bounding box, the actual area consumption of the circuit's implementation and furthermore, area (and delay) values for a fictitious circuit-specific *ideal architecture*. *Bounding Box Area:* The sum of the area consumption of all configurable cells inside the bounding box. Note, that not all cells in a bounding box are necessarily used. *Actual Area Consumption:* The sum of the area consumption of the used configurable cells (inside the bounding box). *Ideal Area Consumption:* We first summarized the area consumption of the circuit's look-up-tables and latches. Then, in respect of the circuit's nets, we supposed, that with an ideal architecture, every fanout branch of a net would be routable by simply one 2:1-MUX to its appropriate destination. For each of our five architectures and also for the ideal architecture, we averaged the values over the circuits. Then, we calculated the proportion between the actual area consumption and the bounding box area consumption as the *bounding box usage*. By setting the actual area consumption into proportion to the ideal area consumption, we determined an *area overhead* measure.

Comments of the results about bounding box usage: Architectures of worst usage are *DMDouble* and *IS3D*, followed by *DMSingle*. While this behaviour was expected for *IS3D* architecture due to a larger 3D bounding box, a reason for the *DMDouble* architecture's worse result is, that the routing flexibility is still too low and the circuit's layout stretches widely over the double lines. Significantly better usage results were produced from the 2D island-style architectures, because they provide more flexibility. However, on contrary to double mesh architectures, the single and double subtypes show a reversed behaviour, that results probably from a more advantageous proportion between single and double span routing resources.

Comments of the results for area overhead in respect of ideal circuit-specific architectures: Despite the *DMSingle* architecture components are of lowest costs, this architecture obviously sacrifies too much look-up-table and latch resources due to a lack of routing resources. A simple insertion of double lines reduces area overhead drastically, as the result for *DMDouble* shows. However, in respect of island-style architectures, it is to observe, that investing double span resources could also lead to a larger overhead. Architecture *IS3D* segments are more expensive than *ISDouble* segments and, hence, produced larger overhead results.

Critical Path. As expected, there is a significant speed-up for architectures with additional double lines in respect of architectures with only nearest-neighbour connections. But also the *IS3D* architecture shows a positive behaviour due to connectivity into third dimension architecture layers.

5.4 Macro Generation Results

Finally, the complete macro generation method was tested with 12 larger circuits. The macro space dilation was fixed to a quadratic shape with a total amount of 144 look-up-tables for 2D architectures and 128 look-up-tables for the 3D architecture. The maximum number of placer's re-iterations has been set to 10 for conflicting routes and to 5 for task locking. The scale factor ρ for temporary routes has been set to 0.1. As expected, the decomposition process produced more partitions for more routing-restricted architectures.

Area Usage and Area Consumption. Except for *ISDouble* and *IS3D* architectures, these results are roughly equal to those of our placement experiments. The average usage of the bounding box for *ISDouble* architecture is now much lower. This is because the selected macro space dilation (144 look-up-tables) was relatively large, such that the partitioner's demands dominated the capacity restrictions. The better results for *IS3D* architecture confirm this phenomenon, as we selected a slightly smaller macro space of 128 look-up-tables. Note again, that the dilation of each macro has been shrinked segment by segment after finishing the macro generation process to a minimum dilation, such that placements of functional blocks, fanout realizations of nets and their subsequent routes were preserved. Surely, a high bounding box usage, if it results from a compact layout, is desirable for minimizing delay, but on the other hand, a low bounding box usage can possibly be good for a subsequent macro floorplanning step, as there could be preserved a higher macro overlap degree and more chances for through routings. Now, for all circuits, we summarized the actual area consumption (gate equivalents) of all macros and averaged the sums over all circuits. As architecture segments of the *DMSingle* and *DMDouble* architectures are relatively cheap, these architectures produced best results in area consumption. An interesting observation is, that the 3D architecture *IS3D* shows slightly better area results, than the 2D *ISDouble* architecture, although the first's segment costs are much larger. However, whether a 3D embedding is eventually more area efficient (in respect of actual area consumption) than a 2D with double lines, has to be examined more precisely and we will keep track of this observation in further investigations.

Critical Path. For each generated macro and its appropriate subcircuit, we calculated the length of the critical path and determined again a critical path overhead factor. While relatively worse values for single line architectures were expected, an apparently surprising fact is, that the 3D architecture, although it has only nearest-neighbour links, shows similar results like the *ISDouble* architecture. Even though the five examined architectures are relatively simple, there are still many open questions, we could not address at this place. For example, the examination of a 3D mesh architecture, a reduction of the number of look-up-tables and latches at the mesh architectures, multi span lines or only a 3D island-style architecture with double lines or even tests with completely new and different architectures of coarser granularity (larger look-up-tables).

6 Conclusion and Future Works

We presented a new retargetable macro generation method, that has been developed to be a part of a universal sequential circuit layout tool for the evaluation of configurable architectures with repetitive structures. The macro generation method consisted of an interlocked process between a circuit partitioner and an incremental placer and router. The route-then-place method, based on a simultaneous path search, was also newly designed for this purpose and we could not find any other similar approaches in previous publications. Furthermore, we are using an architecture model, that is based on finite periodic graphs, which support a compact specification of repetitive architectures and an efficient resizing of architecture spaces. Currently, we are profiling an interlocked routability- and timing-driven floorplanning and final routing system, comprising the floorplanning method from [10]. Our further investigations direct to a refinement of our retargetable layout system, the study of different architectures, especially the effect of multidimensionality in architecture design and a possible interdependency with multi span wires.

References

1. E. Ahmed, J. Rose: *The Effect of LUT and Cluster Size on Deep-Submicron FPGA Performance and Density*, Proceedings of the 8th International ACM/SIGDA Symposium on Field-Programmable Gate Arrays, pp. 3-12, 2000
2. V. Betz, J. Rose: *VPR: A New Packing, Placement and Routing Tool for FPGA Research*, Proceedings of the 7th International Conference on Field-Programmable Logic and Applications, pp.213-222, 1997
3. V. Betz, J. Rose: *FPGA Routing Architecture: Segmentation and Buffering to Optimize Speed and Density*, Proceedings of the 7th International ACM/SIGDA Symposium on Field-Programmable Gate Arrays, pp. 59-68, 1999
4. G. Lemieux, D. Lewis: *Using Sparse Crossbars within Clusters*, Proceedings of the 9th International ACM/SIGDA Symposium on Field-Programmable Gate Arrays, pp. 59-68, 2001
5. A. Marquardt, V. Betz, J. Rose: *Using Cluster-Based Logic Blocks and Timing-Driven Packing to Improve FPGA Speed and Density*, Proceedings of the 7th International ACM/SIGDA Symposium on Field-Programmable Gate Arrays, pp. 37-46, 1999
6. L. McMurchie and Carl Ebeling: *PathFinder: A Negotiation-Based Performance-Driven Router for FPGAs*, Proceedings of the 3rd International ACM/SIGDA Symposium on Field-Programmable Gate Arrays, pp. 111-117, 1995
7. S. Müller and W. J. Paul: *The Complexity of Simple Computer Architectures*, Springer, 1995
8. J. Rose, S. D. Brown: *Flexibility of Interconnection Structures for FPGAs*, IEEE Journal of Solid-State Circuits, 26(3):277-282, March 1991
9. Ellen M. Sentovich et al.: *SIS: A System for Sequential Circuit Synthesis*, http://www-cad.eecs.berkeley.edu, 1992
10. F. Wolz and R. Kolla: *A New Floorplanning Method for FPGA Architectural Research*, Proceedings of the 10th International Conference for Field-Programmable Logic and Applications, pp. 432-442, 2000
11. F. Wolz and R. Kolla: *Bubble Partitioning for LUT-based Sequential Circuits*, Proceedings of the 11th International Conference for Field-Programmable Logic and Applications, pp. 336-345, 2001

The Integration of SystemC and Hardware-Assisted Verification

Ramaswamy Ramaswamy and Russell Tessier

Department of Electrical and Computer Engineering
University of Massachusetts, Amherst, MA 01003
{rramaswa,tessier}@ecs.umass.edu

Abstract. In this research a refined interface between high-level design languages and hardware verification platforms is developed. Our interface methodology is demonstrated through the integration of a communication system design, written in C and SystemC, with a multi-FPGA logic emulator from Ikos Systems. We show that as designs are refined from a high-level to a gate-level representation, our methodology improves verification performance while maintaining verification fidelity across a range of abstraction levels.

1 Introduction

C-based system level design environments, such as SystemC [6], have recently been introduced to allow for modeling of entire systems in high-level language. C-based hardware modeling, enabled with the use of C++ based class libraries, allows for concurrent verification of both system hardware and software and the definition of interfaces between them. Although software can efficiently be tested using processor-based tools, the latter stages of hardware development frequently involve the use of verification hardware, such as parallel simulators or logic emulators. Traditionally, the interface between software test environments and hardware verification has, at best, been inefficient. Although it is currently possible to integrate software written in high-level languages, such as C/C++, with hardware descriptions written in HDLs, such as Verilog and VHDL, the overhead of passing data between the two verification domains can be a bottleneck, limiting verification performance [5]. The need to integrate system-level software (SystemC) with verification hardware motivates a new, modular integration approach.

In this paper, a design methodology is described which allows for the integration of parallel logic verification equipment with C/C++ system design languages. Our approach [4] *isolates* individual SoC component models from standard SystemC inter-component interfaces. Both component logic and interfaces are structured to allow for straightforward update as individual portions of the design are refined. This methodology allows for the optimization of the verification hardware interface to SystemC and similar system-design languages. Specifically, hardware verification approaches involving transaction-based processing [3] and data buffering can be accommodated to provide a transition from

M. Glesner, P. Zipf, and M. Renovell (Eds.): FPL 2002, LNCS 2438, pp. 1007–1016, 2002.

software to hardware domains. Communication support between components is provided at the functional, bus-cycle accurate, and cycle-accurate levels.

Our approach is demonstrated by the integration of SystemC with a VirtuaLogic emulation system [2] from Ikos Systems. To illustrate the system's capabilities for SoC designs, a modular communication system design is verified using SystemC with the FPGA-based emulator. Initially, the entire design is modeled in software using SystemC. After logic component and on-chip communication refinement, a portion of the design is migrated to the emulator. We show that it is possible to achieve increased verification accuracy with the use of our integration methodology over a range of modeling abstraction levels (from behavioral to gate-level). Additionally, we show that the interface approach is superior to previous process-based tool interfaces, such as PLI, used by logic simulators.

2 Background

Traditionally, it has been difficult to verify entire systems at a cycle-accurate level using a high-level language. Often, a complete design re-write has been necessary to translate behavioral portions of a hardware design into a format that can be synthesized to hardware. *SystemC* [6] provides high-level support for cycle-accurate hardware through the use of a set of C++ class libraries and a simulation kernel that supports clock-based hardware modeling. The result of this specification is the standardization of all design information, the capability to quickly re-specify and evaluate design changes, and the ability to increase overall verification speed compared to coupled high-level language/HDL simulator approaches. The SystemC class library provides special support for process concurrency and clocked hardware evaluation [6].

Current approaches for integrating logic simulators with C-based designs are too slow and inefficient for parallel verification. For simulators, data is passed between language domains by means of remote procedure calls or inter-process communication approaches such as sockets [5]. Emulation generally requires special operations regarding support for multi-cycle data transactions [3] and data buffering to support fast data rates. Further complicating the integration of SystemC and verification hardware is the design evolution of most SoC components. Most designs require the development of both logic functionality (IP cores) *and* inter-core interfaces. Not only does this require validation and refinement of the logic at behavioral, RTL, and logic levels, but it also requires the gradual refinement of the protocols necessary to connect these modules. The capability to verify communication using abstract ports (functional), untimed bus protocols (bus-cycle accurate), and clock-based protocols (cycle-accurate) is an important aspect of SystemC [1] [6]. The component isolation offered by these representations allows SystemC to model hardware accurately at various stages of the design cycle. Additionally, component isolation allows for a framework in software for emulator interfacing.

SC_MODULE - Basic object definer for SystemC objects.
SC_CTOR - Constructor used for initializing signals and declaring process types.
SC_METHOD - Instantiates a function which executes in zero functional time.
SC_SLAVE - Indicates slave process will start when value received on input port.
sensitive() - When the value of the enclosed signal changes, the process executes.
wait() - Suspends execution of a process until sensitivity signal changes.
sc_in, sc_out - Specifies input and output ports.
sc_outmaster - Output port of a master process.
sc_inslave - Input port of a slave process.

Fig. 1. SystemC Terminology

3 Integration Approach

Our design methodology can be demonstrated through a series of code examples. System design languages, such as SystemC, contain a range of constructs, shown in Figure 1, which can be used to define functionality and component interfacing. In Figure 2, a set of *untimed functional* (UTF) modules are shown. The UTF level of functional abstraction provides for the highest-level specification of a system. The example system consists of modules **master**, **slave** and **main** that communicate over *functional* channels in a sequential fashion. Data operation and execution order are modeled accurately, but time is not. All processes execute in zero time. In SystemC, the internal, *untimed* functional model of each module can be refined to either a *timed* functional or *cycle-accurate* model without modifying the module port structure or surrounding modules which interface with the module.

Communication between the two child modules in Figure 2, **master** and **slave**, takes place via the SystemC master-slave library [6]. Systems that contain DSPs, custom ASIC cores and processor cores communicating over a set of buses can be modeled with library structures as an interconnection of sequentially communicating blocks. When **master** writes a value to its output port through the *extract()* process, the *accumulate()* process in **slave** is invoked. Master output port (*sc_outmaster*) and slave input port (*sc_inslave*) are linked by an abstract channel, defined by the SystemC keyword *sc_link_mp*. A write to an output port starts the second slave function through *sc_link_mp*. The slave process executes inline with the master process and returns control to the master process after execution. This approach is amenable to communication synthesis. The top-level module (**main** in Figure 2) indicates connectivity of communication.

SystemC provides two levels of inter-component communication, *functional* and *bus-cycle accurate* (BCA). Migration from functional to BCA communication takes place in conjunction with migration of logic functionality from untimed functional to gate-level representation. The bus-cycle accurate definition specifies inter-component interaction at the cycle-accurate level. Communication

```
// master module
SC_MODULE(master) {
sc_outmaster<int> d;
sc_in<int> xin;

 // functionality
 void extract() {
   int a;
   a = xin;
   d = a & 1;
   }
}

// module constructor
SC_CTOR(master) {
   SC_METHOD(extract);
   sensitive(xin);
}
}
```

```
// slave module
SC_MODULE(slave) {
sc_inslave<int> in1;
int sum;

 void accumulate() {
     sum = sum + in1;
 }

 SC_CTOR(slave) {
     SC_SLAVE(accumulate, in1);
     sum = 0;
 }
};
```

```
// main module
int main(int argc, char* argv[])
{
     sc_signal<int> IN;
     sc_link_mp<int> link;
     slave.in1(link);
     master.xin(IN);
     master.d(link);
}
```

Fig. 2. UTF Master-Slave Module

between SoC components is made cycle-accurate with respect to bus handshake protocols while component functionality is unchanged. Abstract ports such as *sc_outmaster* and *sc_inslave* are adapted to form bus ports; hierarchical entities that group together specific terminals for data, address and control signaling. Three bus protocols are supported: no-handshake, enable-handshake and full-handshake. User-defined protocols can also be established.

Figure 3 shows how functional communication through abstract channels at the UTF level can be refined to a full-handshake bus protocol. Refinement is accomplished through the use of protocol conversion modules, ***abs2full*** and ***full2abs***. In the full-handshake protocol, the ports have three terminals - ***data***, ***req***, and ***ack***. Each data transfer cycle proceeds as a sequence. The ***abs2full*** module at the data sender asserts ***req*** and places the data to be transfered on ***data***. When the ***full2abs*** module receives the data, it asserts ***ack***. When ***abs2full*** receives the ***ack*** signal, the next data item can be transferred. The use of such protocol conversion modules separates component functionality from inter-component communication. This provides a pluggable environment where different modules implementing functionality and communication can be swapped easily.

The Transaction Interface Portal (TIP) [2] from Ikos Systems is a verification environment that enables a C model running on a host workstation to communicate with an RTL model implemented on the emulator. This capability provides a verification methodology called *co-modeling*. A common application of co-modeling is verification of a design under test (DUT) which is implemented on the emulator. A testbench or supporting system model is implemented as a C application running on the host workstation. Driver software coordinates data transfer with the DUT running on the emulator. The Transaction Application Programming Interface (TAPI), a series of C drivers, is used to control

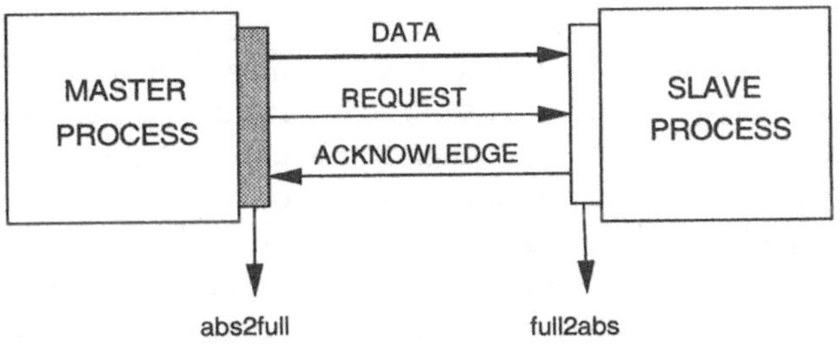

Fig. 3. Protocol conversion modules integrated with master-slave modules

```
// master module
SC_MODULE(master) {
sc_outmaster<int> d;
sc_in<int> xin;

  // functionality
  void extract() {
    int a;
    a = xin;
    d = temp & 1;
    }
 }

// module constructor
SC_CTOR(master) {
   SC_METHOD(extract);
   sensitive(xin);
 }
}
```

```
// slave module
SC_MODULE(slave) {
sc_inslave<int> in1;
int sum;

  void accumulate() {
     tapi_enable(); // open emulator
     tapi_wr_construct; // build write object
     tapi_write(in1);
     tapi_rd_construct; // build read object
     tapi_read(sum); // get result
  }

  SC_CTOR(slave) {
     SC_SLAVE(accumulate, in1);
  }
};
```

Fig. 4. Modified SystemC Slave

the operation of the emulator. A workstation-based PCI card provides physical communication between the workstation and the emulator.

The TIP architecture can be used in one of two ways - *data streaming* or *reactive co-modeling*. In data streaming, data transfers are independent of each other and allow for constant interaction between the user application and DUT. In reactive co-modeling, the data transfer sent by the user application depends on the previous transfer. The user application waits for the DUT to process the current transfer before a new one is sent, potentially leading to an application idle period.

SystemC modules can be modified to allow for emulator calls. In the example shown in Figure 4, a series of TAPI driver calls allow for a software-hardware interface for the UTF **slave** function shown in Figure 2. The inter-component communication infrastructure remains the same as for software-only verification. The isolation of inter-component communication supported by SystemC provides an ideal interface for parallel verification hardware. By taking advantage of this isolation, a number of optimizations for emulation can be supported.

Logic emulator interfaces often require special synchronization techniques to allow for efficient data transfer. Event-based and cycle-based synchronization are examples of fine grained synchronization in which the verification platforms synchronize at every event and clock cycle, respectively. Due to this tight coupling, the entire system proceeds at the rate of the slowest domain, limiting performance. An alternative approach is to synchronize data transactions only when necessary via *transactions* [3]. A transaction is a multi-cycle communication sequence between two verification domains. Transactions contain both data and synchronization information. A single transaction results in multiple verification cycles of work being performed by a verification platform (logic emulator). The transaction can be as simple as a memory read or as complex as the transfer of an entire structured packet through a channel.

4 Experimental Methodology

To evaluate our approach of integrating SystemC and hardware-assisted verification, the functionality of two testbench designs were verified using combinations of SystemC, logic simulation, and a logic emulator. All software tests were performed on an unloaded 360 MHz Sun Ultra 60 workstation with 512 MB of RAM. The workstation interfaces to an Ikos VirtuaLogic VLE-2M logic emulator containing 128 Xilinx 4036EX FPGAs via an SPCI card. The emulator clock speed was set to 30MHz for all designs. Data transfer between the workstation and the emulator was performed through the use of data streams and data transactions.

Two cores, a Reed Solomon encoder/decoder core (51,825 gates and 1,233,397 vectors) and a palindrome detector circuit (13,577 gates and 200,000 vectors) were used to validate the functionality of the SystemC-emulator interface.

Each of these cores was verified in three formats:

1. The cores were first modeled in functional SystemC code and compiled using **gcc** and SystemC library version 1.2 [6].
2. A gate-level model of each core, created from synthesized RTL models of the cores, was simulated using the Cadence Affirma NC-VHDL tool set.
3. A gate-level model of each core was mapped to the emulator using the Ikos VirtuaLogic compiler [2].

To fully test the interaction of the cores in a heterogeneous verification environment, two test scenarios were created. For the commercial *Reed Solomon* coder, a testbench written in SystemC code was created from the vectors obtained from the commercial core vendor. The testbench code was modeled separately at untimed, timed, and cycle-accurate levels, as described in Section 3. The three versions of the testbench were interfaced with three different implementation versions of the cores (SystemC, simulated gate-level, emulated gate-level) via functional and bus-cycle accurate methods of communication. This provided the capability to measure transfer rates between software and hardware verification tools under differing accuracy levels. The vectors used with the Reed Solomon coder are representative of the effort needed to decode an eight bit 200 x 200 Portable Greymap (PGM) image. To further test the Reed Solomon coder in an *integrated* system environment, an entire communication system, including the Reed Solomon core as a critical component, was modeled in software. This

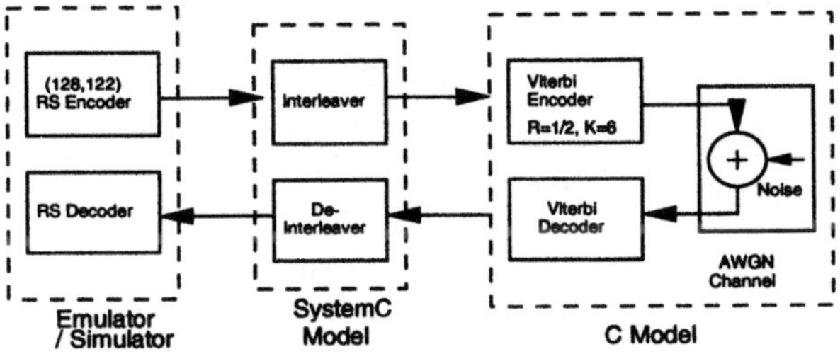

Fig. 5. Modeled communication system

system, shown in Figure 5, consists of the Reed Solomon coder, interleaver/de-interleaver functions [7] and a Viterbi coder.

The variety of components associated with the system makes it ideal for testing SystemC integration. Interleaving and de-interleaving was performed using SystemC models. The Viterbi portion of the system was implemented as a C model. The interleaver, de-interleaver and Viterbi portions of the system were run on the host workstation as thread processes which communicate with each other via abstract master-slave ports. In separate experiments, the Reed Solomon encoder/decoder was modeled using SystemC at the functional level and on the Affirma simulator and VirtuaLogic emulator at the gate level. Communication with the Reed Solomon coder is through PLI based socket calls for simulation and via transaction-based processing for emulation. A similar testbench-based environment was also created for the *palindrome* circuit. Several implementations of the testbench in varying accuracy levels were created and interfaced to the modeled core using functional and bus-cycle timing.

5 Experimental Results

To validate our approach of isolating emulation resources with modular communication constructs, three sets of experiments were performed with the experimental methodology described in Section 4. In the first experiment, a direct comparison of execution time of verification environments which include only SystemC with those that include simulation and emulation is provided. Table 1 shows the times taken to verify the three test configurations. For *Reed-Solomon* and *palindrome*, the test cores were interfaced to testbenches written in untimed functional SystemC, as described in Section 3. For *RS System*, the Reed Solomon core was interfaced to a software version of the communication system described in Section 4. Results in the Table 1 include:

- In the *SystemC* configuration (row 2), the entire design along with the testbench is implemented in SystemC as untimed models.
- In the *SystemC+Sim.* configuration (row 3), the untimed testbench used in the previous configuration is coupled with an RTL description of the DUT running on a simulator. Both testbench and simulator run on the workstation

	Reed Solomon	Palin-drome	RS System
SystemC	0.09s	0.4s	0.34s
SystemC+Sim.	2190s	312s	93s
SystemC+Emul.	175s	16s	43s

Table 1. Verification times

Palindrome Detector				
Data Transfer Abstraction Level	Time (sec)		Transfer Rate (kbps)	
	Simulation	Emulation	Simulation	Emulation
Untimed Functional	285	16	44.91	800.00
Timed Functional	291	19	43.98	673.68
Bus Cycle Accurate	301	24	42.52	533.33
Cycle Accurate	328	29	39.02	441.38
Reed Solomon Coder				
Data Transfer Abstraction Level	Time (sec)		Transfer Rate (kbps)	
	Simulation	Emulation	Simulation	Emulation
Untimed Functional	2260	175	52.39	676.61
Timed Functional	2447	204	48.38	580.42
Bus Cycle Accurate	2524	266	46.91	445.14
Cycle Accurate	2649	290	44.69	408.30

Table 2. Verification times with data transfer modeled at various levels of abstraction

as distinct processes. Communication between the processes is done via PLI-based socket interfaces.
- In the *SystemC+Emul.* configuration (row 4), the untimed testbench, running on the workstation, is coupled with the benchmark core implemented on the emulator.

It can be seen that the same modeling fidelity can be preserved by transitioning from a SystemC model to an implementation on the emulator. Although gate-level emulation takes longer compared to behavioral SystemC verification, accuracy for the cores is enhanced.

In a second experiment, verification times for SystemC testbenches interfaced to cores at various data transfer abstraction levels were determined. In the experiment, testbenches were interfaced to gate-level cores modeled on the emulator and simulated with the NC-VHDL simulator. For each configuration, master-slave interfaces were described in SystemC at various levels of abstraction. Overall run time for the *palindrome* and *Reed Solomon* benchmarks are shown in Table 2 and were measured using *gprof* and the profiling option in the Affirma simulator. Simulation-based verification is significantly slower than emulation-based verification due to the overhead of PLI calls and the sequen-

Test Bench	Number of vectors	Workstation (sec) Verify	Workstation (sec) Compare	Emul. (usec)
T1	61714	0.499	1.4	795
T2	68066	0.538	1.6	612
T3	128270	1.022	2.65	621
T4	170594	1.34	3.45	706
T5	179804	1.41	3.65	791
T6	275262	2.15	5.55	-

Table 3. Times taken for emulation with the testbench on the host workstation and the emulator

tial nature of execution. Transfer rates indicate achieved data rates between the SystemC testbench and NC-VHDL (simulation) and the emulator (emulation). Columns 4 and 5 show the transfer rate across the interfaces for different levels of abstraction. The transfer rates become slower at lower levels of inter-component communication abstraction. Moving from untimed functional to cycle-accurate modeling offers increased modeling accuracy at the cost of longer verification time. The variation in transfer rate is more noticeable for emulation.

A significant portion of verification time is spent in transferring fixed test vectors between software and hardware verification domains. In a final experiment, testbench vectors, which were previously implemented in SystemC on the host workstation, were migrated to memory resources located on the logic emulator. The testbench located on the emulator was partitioned into two separate memories. One portion contained the input test vectors and the other portion contained the expected output vectors. The test commences when the workstation sends a signal to emulator indicating that vector sequencing should start. Subsequently, individual test vectors are applied sequentually to the emulated design and results are collected and compared to expected vector outputs. After the final vector, a pass/fail result is returned to the workstation. A pass result is sent if all output vectors match expected results.

The above method was implemented with the Reed Solomon coder for varying testbench sizes. Table 3 compares results of storing test vectors on the workstation versus migrating the vectors to the emulator. The numbers in the third column represent the time taken to send and receive the entire set of test vectors to the emulator by a testbench on the host workstation. The fourth column represents the time taken to compare output result vectors with expected output vectors. This comparison was performed by a C program on the host workstation. The last column represents the verification time when the testbench is entirely implemented on the emulator. This also includes the time taken to compare output result vectors with expected output vectors. It can be seen that the verification performance when the testbench is migrated onto the emulator is 5000 times faster on average, than when the testbench is located on the host workstation and transmitted to the emulator. All run times were measured with *time()* function calls in the user application.

The number of test vectors that can be stored on the emulator depends on the amount of free memory available on the emulator. The largest testbench, T6, did not fit on the emulator due to a lack of memory in the system.

6 Conclusions

In this paper we have outlined a new design methodology for integrating system-design languages, such as SystemC, with parallel verification hardware. By isolating the interface to a specific module, optimizations such as data buffering, testbench migration, and transaction-based data transfer can be supported for logic emulation. To overcome data transfer bottlenecks, it was possible to seamlessly migrate benchmark data across the workstation/emulator interface to the emulator. These approaches led to an improvement in verification time while maintaining support of existing inter-component interfaces in software and associated benchmarks

7 Acknowledgments

This work was supported by Ikos Systems, Texas Instruments, and National Science Foundation Grant CCR-0081405.

References

[1] K. Bartleson. *A New Stardard for System-Level Design.* Synopsys, Inc., 2000. http://www.systemc.org/.
[2] Ikos Systems, Inc. *VirtuaLogic VLE-5 Emulation System Manual*, Jan. 2001. http://www.ikos.com/products/vsli/index.html.
[3] M. Kudlugi, S. Hassoun, C. Selvidge, and D. Pryor. A Transaction-Based Unified Simulation/Emulation Architecture for Functional Verification. In *ACM/IEEE Design Automation Conference (DAC)*, June 2001.
[4] R. Ramaswamy. The Integration of SystemC with a VirtuaLogic Emulation System. Master's thesis, University of Massachusetts, Department of Electrical and Compter Systems Engineering, September 2001. http://www.ecs.umass.edu/ece/tessier/systemc-thesis.pdf.
[5] L. Semeria and A. Ghosh. Methodology for Hardware/Software Co-verification in C/C++. In *Asia and South Pacific Design Automation Conference*, Jan. 2000.
[6] SystemC. *SystemC 1.2Beta User Guide*, 2000. http://www.systemc.org.
[7] S. Wicker. *Error Control Systems for Digital Communication and Storage.* Prentice Hall, Edgewood Cliffs, N.J., 1994.

Using Design Hierarchy to Improve Quality of Results in FPGAs

Alireza S. Kaviani

Xilinx Inc, 2100 Logic Drive, San Jose, CA95124, USA
alireza.kaviani@xilinx.com

Abstract. This paper presents and analyzes a methodology for improving the quality of results in Field Programmable Gate Arrays (FPGAs) by taking advantage of the design hierarchy. We use a representative case study, which is a real design, to demonstrate how taking advantage of the hierarchy may lead to higher area-efficiency and better speed-performance. According to our results, an area saving of 18% along with a speedup of 15% is achievable; these area and speed improvements may result in a cost saving of a factor of two for volume production. Our analysis also shows that the above savings will not have a negative impact on routability and power consumption.

1 Introduction

Field Programmable Devices (FPDs) consist of a set of logic blocks and a flexible routing structure to connect them together. Using automated CAD tools, a designer is able to program the logic blocks and their corresponding interconnect to implement any desired application within a reasonable amount of time. Accommodating such flexibility for FPDs requires a larger number of transistors compared to their alternative Application Specific Integrated Circuits (ASICs) such as standard cells. Recent advances in silicon process technology have led to aggressive scaling of transistors, making it possible to integrate a large number of them on the same chip. Therefore, SRAM-based FPGAs at the leading edge of FPDs have been able to take advantage of process technology advancements to grow faster than other ASIC solutions.

FPGA users enjoy a fast time to market and possibility of design changes even when they are close to shipping their products. Rapid growth of FPGAs has made them a viable solution for many more applications. FPDs are the only reasonable solution in some cases with a low to medium shipment volume. Nonetheless, the speed and area gap between FPGAs and standard cells remains significant, and any improvement in area-efficiency and speed of FPGAs will expand their application domain. In addition, the designers whose target market is high volume often decide to prototype their designs in FPGAs. In many cases, state-of-the-art FPGAs allow these customers to implement their designs in FPGAs with the real performance specification (as opposed to ASIC emulation at lower speeds). Such customers would rather stay with FPGAs as long as it is cost-effective.

This paper explains how to take advantage of the embedded hierarchy in a typical design to direct the automated flow for the purpose of performance and area improvements. We also show how these improvements may translate into 50% cost reduction. This paper's suggested methodology can be used in two forms: 1) future

M. Glesner, P. Zipf, and M. Renovell (Eds.): FPL 2002, LNCS 2438, pp. 1017-1026, 2002.

FPGA tools may embed some or all of the paper's recommendations into their automatic flow to improve the quality of results. 2) The designers may decide to spend one to two additional months to impose the suggested flow manually, for the purpose of timing closure or cost saving. The next section outlines the necessary background for this paper. Section 3 explains the methodology using a representative case example, followed by Section 4 that summarizes the results and discusses the benefits of the proposed method. In Section 4 we also analyze the results to achieve a better understanding of the reasons for improvements and to assure that our method does not have any adverse power or routability effects.

2 Background

In this section, we first review some related work, and then introduce the standard flow of implementing designs in Xilinx FPGAs. We also explain and justify our choice of target device and design. FPGA vendors provide and sometimes even recommend a so-called push-button flow, which produces the final bitstream from the original circuit. The push-button flow is often easy to use, but hides various steps of the CAD flow.

2.1 Related Work

Recently, there has been a revived interest in manual designer intervention with the standard tool flow to push the limits of silicon capability. Brian Dipert's key message in his 1997 article for improving the speed of FPGA designs [1] is to not rely on the FPGA tools. In a panel in FPGA 2000 symposium, Ray Andraka presents an extreme example to support that the desginers may boost the speed by up to 30% by taking advantage of floorplanning [2]. We agree with the potential benefits, but these efforts often require a complete knowledge of the design, and can not be used directly to improve the standard tool flow. In FPGA 2002 symposium, a university tool, called EVE, is introduced that provides an interactive environment for manual designer intervention [3]. While this tool is an interesting first step to help us understand the potential for improvements in the FPGA CAD tools, it is only applicable to very small designs. This is due to the time consuming greedy algorithms in the tool that consider all possible alternatives to the one chosen by the push-button flow.
In contrast with the above works we consider a large real design with realistic timing constraints. Also, the main information that we use is the design hierarchy, which is readily available to the tools and may be leveraged for potential future improvements. In addition, our methodology can be applied without a complete knowledge of the design and at a step close to the end of the design cycle.

2.2 Standard Xilinx Design Flow

Xilinx flow starts with the original circuit in either schematic or a Hardware Description Language (HDL). The ideas in this paper mostly apply to large applications, where the input circuit is represented in some HDL format. The first step in the flow is synthesis, which creates a structural EDIF netlist. The ideas in this paper can be applied regardless of the choice of synthesis tool. After the EDIF netlist is generated Xilinx internal tool processes the design in several steps.

The top-end of Xilinx tool, called *ngdbuild*, reads the EDIF netlist and User Constraint File (UCF) and creates a single file in Xilinx native format. We will explain UCF further later on, because it plays an important role in our methodology. Then another part of Xilinx tools, called *map*, reads the design in internal format and technology maps the design into LUTs and other basic elements specific to Xilinx devices. Map also creates a constraint file, called Physical Constraint File (PCF), which will be used by the next part of the tool. Perhaps the most sophisticated part of Xilinx tools is placement and routing, which happens in one single command but in separate steps. This part, called *Par*, uses the PCF to follow the physical or timing directives imposed by either the designer or synthesis tool. Finally, the resulting bitstream can be generated and configured into the FPGA. After the design is routed the timing can be verified using Xilinx timing analyzer, which is called *trce*.

2.3 Target Device and Design

Our ideal target platform is Virtex™-II, which is recently introduced to the market. However, our goal was to analyze a real working design. At the time, a large Virtex-II design with realistic timing constraints was not available and internal chip delays were not established for the timing analyzer. Consequently, we chose Xilinx Virtex™-E, which has been available to market for some time, as our target device. We base our conclusions on the improvements gained on Virtex-E devices, but we also consider Virtex-II architecture for our analysis as explained in Section 5. Moving along with this paper, we mention some architecture differences of Virtex-E and Virtex-II regarding our proposed methodology.

All Virtex devices consist of Configurable Logic Blocks (CLBs), which are connected using a rich set of routing resources. Each Virtex-II CLB contains four slices (two in Virtex-E), where each slice consists of two 4-input LUTs, two FFs, and a variety of dedicated circuitry to accommodate more efficient implementation of some specific logic. A good measure of area utilization of a design in Virtex devices is the slice count. Accurate slice count of a design is only available after the Map step of the Xilinx tools. Although the LUT count of a design is often available after synthesis and can be used as an estimate of area, it is somewhat optimistic. This is because aggressive packing of LUTs into slices (or CLBs) may result in unroutability issues; we consider slice count reported after Map as our area measure.

Approximately, 70% of Xilinx applications are in the communication area. Our real design example in Virtex-E is from a vendor in the communication area, providing fixed broadband wireless access. The design has two clock domains and contains a number of general-purpose modules including CPU, PCI, peripheral, SRAM interface and several proprietary modules. Virtex-E FPGAs meet the timing requirements of the application, but they were initially too expensive for their target OEM. Therefore the company plans to eventually move to standard cell ASIC for the purpose of cost reduction. Although the price of FPGAs may fall to an acceptable level quickly, some

designers would like to avoid any methodology that complicates their transition to ASIC. Our methodology in the next section complies with this desire.
In addition to CLB fabric, typical applications also require blocks such as memory or I/O pins. If a design does not fit in a device due to lack of resources other than CLB fabric, the proposed methodology in this paper will not apply and other measures should be taken. However, in the case of our example, which represents the majority of the designs, CLB fabric dictates the device size, and thus any reduction in slice count would be desirable.

3 Methodology

Our methodology involves advance planning to ensure proper design partitioning followed by incremental compilation of each partition. Since our method involves manual intervention in the flow, an intelligent partitioning will speedup the overall process. After partitioning we compile each portion of the design separately to meet the timing requirements in the minimum area. Then we add partitions incrementally to build the whole design.

3.1 Partitioning

First, we start by creating a top-level module that contains IOBs and global resources such as tri-state buffers and clock management instantiations. The amount of logic in the top module is optional, but we would like to keep it as small as possible to avoid long waiting period for each step. This is because the top-level module will be compiled with each partition. Next, we should synthesize the top level to create an EDIF netlist containing the top-level logic and a number of black boxes representing each partition. In addition, we create a separate EDIF netlist for each partition. The majority of customer designs use a single EDIF netlist to represent the whole circuit. While multiple netlists are not a requirement for our methodology, it will significantly ease up the process especially for those partitions that are expected to be timing critical.

The netlist creation step varies depending on the synthesis vendor. Using Synplicity, we added a simple directive after the module declaration so that the synthesis tool considers the corresponding module as black_box [4]. Generating a separate EDIF netlist for each partition simply involves synthesizing the top module of that partition and disabling IO insertion. Keep in mind that the choice of partition is independent of the choice of hierarchy, which is already decided by the designer. Any parts outside the partitions will remain in the top module. The choice of partitioning at this level may be revisited after observing partial results, but the implication would be repeating part of the process.

3.2 Incremental Compilation

For each partition we create a corresponding UCF that contains its related timing requirements from the original UCF. Then, we go through the standard Xilinx flow with the following differences:

a) The option "–u" should be used for "ngdbuild" and "Map" commands to prevent the removal of unused logic. This is because we are only compiling a portion of the design.
b) The option "-c 1" and "-r" should be used for "Map" command to use as few slices as possible, and disable register ordering. These options are not recommended unless accompanied by appropriate area constraints, as in our methodology. Otherwise, using these options may lead to unroutability and timing penalty.
c) The appropriate area region constraint should be added to the UCF corresponding to each partition. For example, partition *P1* in module *M3* of the design *TOP* can be constrained as follows:
INST *TOP/M3/P1* AREA_GROUP = *FPAG_P1*;
AREA_GROUP *FPAG_P1* COMPRESSION = 1;
AREA_GROUP *FPAG_P1* RANGE = SLICE_Xx_1Yy_1:SLICE_Xx_2Yy_2;

The italic portions of the area constraints depend on the design and designer's choice and the rest are keywords. The range keyword determines the size, shape, and position of each partition or module and will be discussed further in the next subsection. The format of the coordinates is slightly different for Virtex-E architecture, but the concept is the same. Also, separate area ranges for the memory blocks and tri-state buffers are required. More information on the syntax and detailed explanation of each keyword is available from [4]. Note that we can define more than one area region for each partition. After the area regions for all partitions and modules are determined, we add them to the original UCF. Then we compile the whole design with all the partitions to obtain a single routed circuit. In this final step we do not require "-u" option explained in part (a). As a result, the final area regions are slightly larger than their absolute lower bounds. Depending on the designer's requirements, they can be adjusted to reduce the area further, or left as is so that Par can use the extra room to achieve a better timing. The incremental approach helps us to identify the potential timing violations as early as possible in our flow.

3.3 Area Characteristics

Perhaps, the most difficult part of this methodology is determining the best location and dimension for each area region. The goal is selecting the combination of location and dimensions that minimizes the area and maximizes the speed without adverse effect on routability. Although these choices strongly depend on the design and the designer's needs, there are some general tips that are helpful. The minimum size of an area region is available from the mapper report. Xilinx tools currently support only rectangular areas, and we need to specify two dimensions to determine the shape. We refer to these dimensions as width and height (or x and y), respectively. The maximum size of the carry-chain in each hierarchy is the lower bound on the height (y) of its corresponding area region. The size of the largest carry-chain can be obtained using Xilinx *Floorplanner*. If the carry-chain is longer than the height of the area region, Par will exit with a placement failure message.

Since Xilinx routing structure is *segmented* [5, 6], the best internal timing for each area region or hierarchy is achieved when the region is square. Figure 1 demonstrates this fact by showing the best frequency that can be achieved when applying various area constraints to the same module. Each data point on the graph corresponds to a constraint (x, y), representing the width and height of its area region. The size of area region is approximately the same for all the data points in the figure to assure that the tools have the same degree of freedom to place various components of the module.

Figure 1 shows that the internal speed of the modules in a hierarchy improves as much as 36% when its area is square, but this is not always true for the timing between various area regions. The number of available routing resources between the current hierarchy and other portions of the design increases proportional to the periphery of the area region, which is (x+y). If the number of available connections between modules increases, better routability and timing can be achieved. Therefore, the ratio of the number of inputs/outputs for each hierarchy to its size (x.y) is a good measure for the shape of the area region. The higher the ratio the more rectangular the area should be.

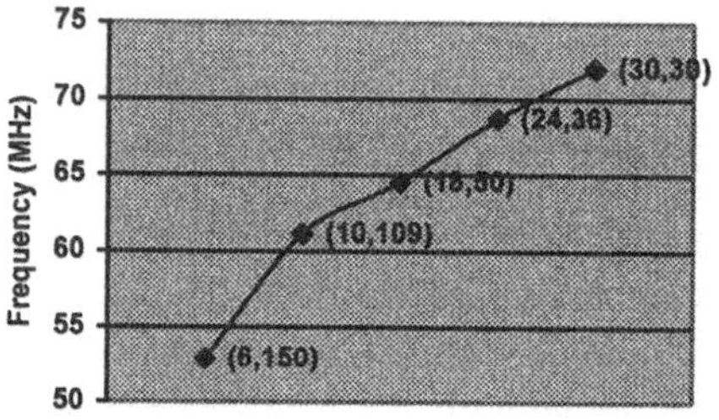

Fig. 1. Area region dimensions

4 Results

The best method to evaluate the advantage of using hierarchy would be to apply the proposed techniques to a large number of benchmark circuits and observe the results. However, such method would not be practical due to the difficulty of manual intervention and unavailability of realistic timing constraints for a large number of designs. Instead, we have chosen a representative example and we will reach our conclusions by accurately analyzing the results before and after applying our techniques.

4.1 Area and Speed

Our design targets XCV2000E-7 from Virtex-E family with 99% area utilization. We created two UCFs based on the original timing requirements: The first constraint file, which is referred to as standard, uses standard Xilinx flow without the area regions. The second UCF has also area constraints based on the hierarchy and uses our suggested flow, as described in Section 3. We refer to the second UCF and the results associated with it as hierarchical. Figure 2 shows the normalized speed and area results for both flows. We used version 4.1i of Xilinx tools to provide these results. We also repeated our experiments with the older 3.1i version, and achieved similar results. According to our results, the slice count (or area) of the design using standard flow is 18% higher than that of hierarchical design flow. In addition, the highest speed for the fast clock domain is 15% lower than that of hierarchical flow. At the same time the placement and routing tool finishes slightly faster when using the hierarchical flow, showing that routability is not affected negatively. Keep in mind that the original design has not been modified, and the benefits are due to changes in the UCF and methodology.

Our methodology can be considered any time in the design cycle even close to product release. However, FPGA designs close to product release are likely to have IOB constraints, because PCB design often goes in parallel with FPGA design. Our design example was no exception, but the results in Figure 2 show the improvements without the IOB constraints. We also tried our flow with IOB constraints added to both standard and hierarchical UCFs. The area improvement remained the same but the speed improvements declined by roughly 1%. Also, the engineering time to find the appropriate area regions to meet the timing requirements increased. Most of the timing violations were due to IOB placement, which was fixed independent of the design methodology. Therefore, it makes sense to consider using our methodology right before IO pins on the FPGA design are fixed. The design with the new methodology was successfully tested in the field to assure functional correctness.

4.2 Cost Reduction

Although gaining higher speed and area-efficiency is extremely important, today's FPGAs are often fast enough for a large variety of the designs. In that case there is no need for performance improvements, but our methodology can still be used to reduce the cost. There are three speed grades for XCV2000-E device: "-6", "-7", and "-8". The slowest and also least expensive device is "–6" grade, which is roughly 25% slower than the "–8" device. Figure 3 shows the approximate cost of two devices of our interest in Virtex-E family with two different speed grades. The prices are online

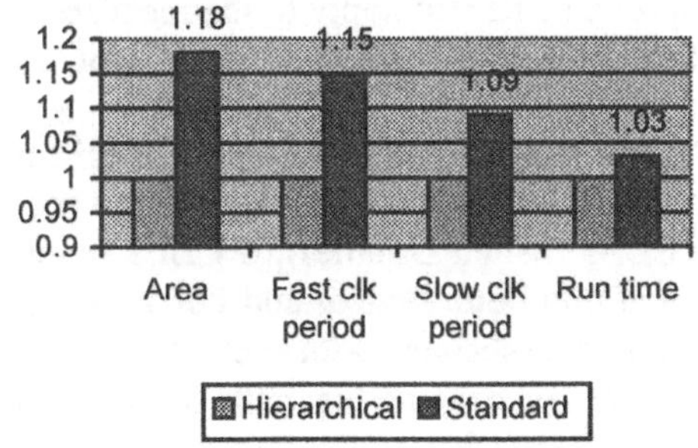

Fig. 2. Quality of results

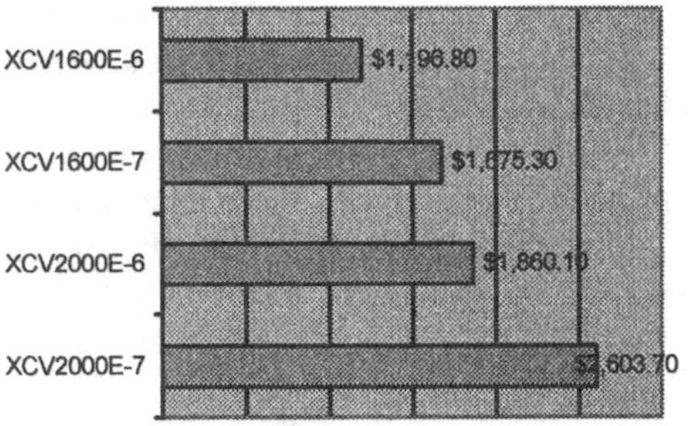

Fig. 3. Cost reduction

quotes from independent distributors of Xilinx chips for quantities of 100 devices in summer 2001. The packaging option is bg560 for all the cases in Figure 3. Our design met the timing requirements in "-7" grade using the standard flow. The same design meets the same timing requirements in XCV2000E-6 device using our hierarchical flow. Therefore, using the hierarchical design flow will translate to roughly 40% cost saving on each device. In addition, the area saving may lead to a significant cost reduction in some cases. For example, XCV2000E and XCV1600E devices contain 19200 and 15552 slices, respectively.

Most of the designers tend to leave some additional space in their FPGA device to allow for easy modifications. Any 2000E design with 81% or lower utilization may fit in 1600E device. Therefore, an approximate 18% area reduction, which is achievable using the hierarchical flow, may cause a 2000E design to fit in 1600E device with the same packaging and number of IOBs. This, along with the speed improvements leads to a cost saving more than a factor of 2, according to Figure 3. In our example case, we needed 4% more area reduction to fit the design in 1600E device. This could be achieved by implementing some of the logic in free memory blocks; roughly 40% of the memory blocks are not used in our example case. However, implementing logic in memory blocks might complicate the ASIC migration process, as it was the case in our example. It is clear that the expense of roughly two man-months of engineering efforts should be considered against the cost reduction.

4.3 Analysis of Results

Our area saving comes from the fact that we guide Xilinx tools to pack LUTs into CLBs aggressively without adversely affecting routability. It is possible to use the options in our flow without the area guidelines based on the design hierarchy. In that case Map still produces low slice count, but Par fails to route the design within an acceptable time. In other words, using hierarchy as a guideline for packing is essential for successful routing. While area savings due to our methodology are somewhat intuitive, the reason for speed improvements is not clear. Also, we would like to analyze the effects of our methodology on power dissipation. The best way to do this is to compare the utilization of routing resources. So far we have evaluated our methodology based on Virtex-E family for the sake of accuracy. In this subsection we consider Virtex-II for two reasons: 1) to make sure improvements still apply to the most recent FPGAs, and 2) to protect the proprietary information of the original circuit, which is designed for Virtex-E.

Virtex-II uses a *segmented* routing structure to minimize the number of transistors and wires that a signal needs to traverse to reach its destination. The segmented routing architecture includes wires that travel 2 CLBs (called Doubles), 6 CLBs (called Hexes), and the length of the chip (called Longs), in both vertical and horizontal dimensions. There are also pass transistors and buffers associated with each set of wires. For example, when we refer to a Hex switch we are considering both wire and its supporting transistors. There are also two types of switches to connect the wire segments to the inputs and outputs of each CLB; we refer to these types as Input Multiplexer (IMUX) and Output Multiplexer (OMUX). Figure 4 compares interconnect resource utilization for both hierarchical and standard flows. According to Figure 4, the number of IMUX, Double, Hex, and Long switches that are utilized in the standard flow are 3%, 21%, 27%, and 32% higher than that of hierarchical flow, respectively. The only slight increase in resource utilization due to the hierarchical flow is in OMUX (roughly 1%). The slight increase in OMUX is expected since they are often used for direct connections between CLBs.

Lower routing resource utilization in the hierarchical flow insures that we have not complicated routability. Furthermore, fewer interconnect resources are likely to lead to lower power dissipation, if the design is to run in the same frequency. To confirm this we estimated the dynamic power dissipation for both flows, assuming the switching activity of 10% for all resources [7]. According to our estimation, the dynamic power dissipation in the design using standard flow is 11% higher than that of hierarchical flow. This agrees with our utilization and speed results. Note that capacitance associated with a Long switch is higher than that of a Hex switch, which in turn is higher than that of a Double switch. Lower capacitances imply higher speed and lower power consumption.

We also examined the local routing congestion by counting the number of CLBs with a specific utilization. Figure 5 shows that there is no local congestion due to hierarchical flow. The horzontal axis in the figure corresponds to the utilization for each resource, and the vertical axis represents the numbers CLBs with the specific utilization. The CLB occurences at or around 100% utilization are not increased for the hierarchical flow, implying that encountering routability issues is unlikely.

It is rare to obtain performance improvements in three area, speed, and power domains at the same time. We believe our good results are due to the fact that we are taking advantage of human design factor. Designers tend to minimize number of I/Os in their modules to ease their task. Taking advantage of embedded hierarchy in the design is equivalent to using already existing human intelligence, which has optimized the number of connections between various hierarchies.

5 Concluding Remarks

Despite rapid growth in FPGA usage, there is still a wide performance gap between FPGAs and the standard ASIC. Improving quality of results will reduce this gap, and allows for wider use of FPGAs. Also, when the high-end FPGA devices are initially introduced to market they are expensive but by the time they are to be shipped in volume the price falls. In some cases this price reduction does not happen fast enough and the FPGA customers turn to ASIC alternatives.

We showed that by taking advantage of embedded hierarchy in a design we could increase the area-efficiency and speed-performance by 18% and 15%, respectively. At the same time power dissipation is likely to go down by 11%. Depending on the design cycle, and the volume of the products, these savings translate into a cost reduction by more than a factor of two. Potential future work includes applying our methodology to other designs and comparing the results. Also, it is desirable to automate part or all of our methodology to minimize the manual intervention.

Acknowledgements

I would like to thank Tony Quang, Khuong Ngo, and Amir Ameri who helped me with the original design constraints. Without their help this work would have been much more difficult. The opinions expressed by the author are his alone and do not represent the opinions of Xilinx and are not an indication of any future policy on FPGA software held by Xilinx.

Fig. 4. Interconnect resource utilization

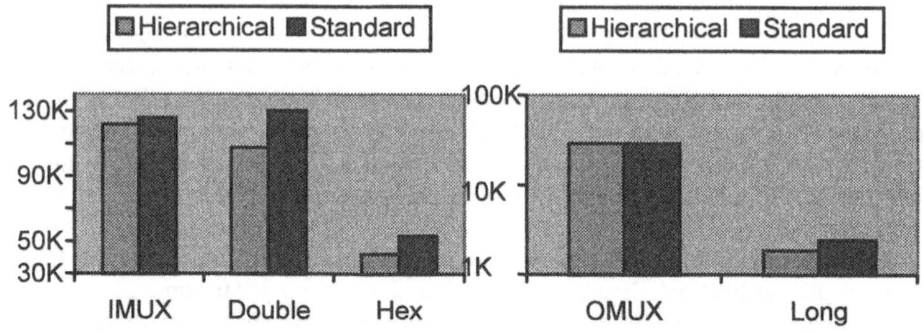

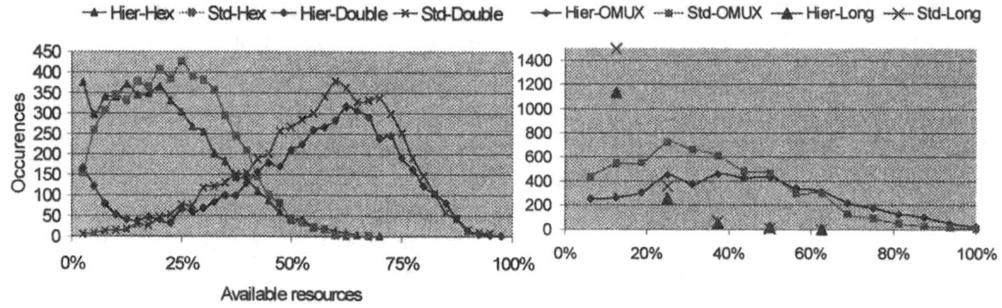

Fig. 5. Interconnect local congestion

References

1. Brian Dipert, "Shattering the programmable-logic speed barrier," EDN Magazine, May 1997, http://archives.e-insite.net/archives/ednmag/reg/1997/052297/11cs.htm.
2. Craig Matsumoto, "FPGA synthesis tools lose battle with John Henry (panel on FPGA2000)," EE Times, Feb 2000, http://www.eetimes.com/story/OEG20000211S0011.
3. W. Chow, J. Rose, "EVE: A CAD Tool for Manual Placement and Pipelining Assistance of FPGA Circuits," International Symposium on FPGAs, Feb. 2002, pp. 85-94.
4. Xilinx Inc. " www.support.xilinx.com "
5. Xilinx Inc. "The Programmable Logic Data book," *2000.*
6. Xilinx Inc. "Virtex-II Platform FPGA Handbook," Dec. *2000.*
7. L. Shang, A. Kaviani, K. Bathala, "Dynamic Power Consumption in Virtex-II FPGA Family," International Symposium on FPGAs, Feb. 2002, pp. 157-164.

Architecture Design of a Reconfigurable Multiplier for Flexible Coarse-Grain Implementations*

G. Koutroumpezis[1], K. Tatas[1], D. Soudris[1], S. Blionas[2], K. Masselos[2], and A. Thanailakis[1]

[1]Dept. of Electrical and Computer Engineering, Democritus University of Thrace, Greece
{gkoytroy,ktatas,dsoudris,thanail}@ee.duth.gr
[2]INTRACOM S.A., Hellenic Telecom and Electronics Industry, Peania 19002, Greece
{sbli, kmas}@intracom.gr

Abstract. A run-time reconfiguable array of multipliers architecture is introduced. The novel multiplier can be easily reconfigured to trade bitwidth for array size, thus maximizing the utilization of available hardware, multiply signed or unsigned data, and uses part of its structure when needed. The proposed reconfigurable circuit consists of an array of m×m multipliers, a few arrays of adders each adding three numbers, and switches. Also small blocks for the implementation of the reconfiguration capabilities, mentioned above, consist of adders, multiplexers, inverters, coders and registers. The circuit reconfiguration can be done dynamically through using only a few control bits. The architecture design of the reconfigurable multiplier, with hardware equivalent to one 64×64 bit high precision multiplier, which can be dynamically reconfigured to produce an array of the products in different forms is described in detailed manner.

1. Introduction

The accelerating need for higher performance, due to complex and real-time applications, for instance a large number of new wireless communication standards and multimedia algorithms, combined with tight time-to-market constraints, has made reconfigurable architectures the best platform for solving such problems. Reconfigurable computing has flourished recently due to many efforts from both academia and industry Garp [1], MATRIX [2], REMARC [3], MorphoSys [4], Pleiades [5], PipeRench [6], KressArray [7]. These implementations are characterised as coarse-grain reconfigurable architectures and tackle mainly DSP/multimedia issues. Therefore, the design of efficient coarse-grain reconfigurable modules is critical for realizing modern applications. For that purpose, reconfigurable modules have been designed either for the above platforms or for non- specific platforms [8].

In this paper the detailed architecture design of a coarse-grain reconfigurable multiplier is introduced. It resolves the design conflict between versatility, area, and computation speed, and makes it possible to build a feasible and highly flexible processor with multiple multipliers for data intensive applications. Furthermore, the proposed multiplier exhibits two kinds of reconfigurability: i) the wordlength of the multiplier's operands and ii) their arithmetic representation. Also, the addition and the

* This work was partially supported by the project AMDREL IST-2001-34379 funded by EC.
M. Glesner, P. Zipf, and M. Renovell (Eds.): FPL 2002, LNCS 2438, pp. 1027-1036, 2002.

structure of the partial products, as well as the operation of the interface units and arithmetic conversion circuits allow the lower power consumption of the whole system.

The proposed reconfigurable multiplier will be used in a prototype platform to measure the performance of an OFDM wireless communication system in two different scenarios using high and low number of bits in the multipliers of the FIRs in the I/Q block of the system.

In the following paragraphs, we will describe the real life problem from wireless communications, which makes the use of a reconfigurable multiplier necessary. Then, we will describe the detailed architecture design of the multiplier itself.

2. IQ Block Description

Modern wireless communications systems use digital modulation techniques like QPSK and QAM that require a conversion of the received signals to Inphase and Quadrature components (I/Q). The same stands for the transmitter part and a conversion from I/Q to the output signal has to be performed. This may take place either at the analog part of the system or at the digital. Digital I/Q is considered of higher precision and performance. A digital I/Q unit (receiver and transmitter), consists of FIR filters and their implementation may use a variable number of bits and is a trade-off between complexity and performance. For high SNR figures, low number of bits would be sufficient, in case of bad quality transmission channel, high number of bits would ensure high Bit Error Rates performance by sacrificing area and power consumption.

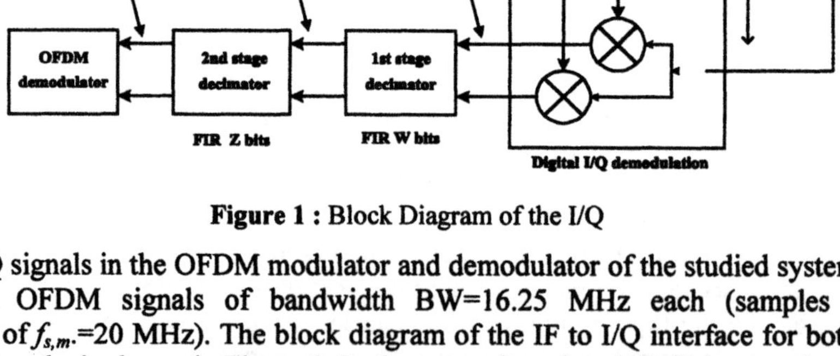

Figure 1 : Block Diagram of the I/Q

The I/Q signals in the OFDM modulator and demodulator of the studied system are base-band OFDM signals of bandwidth BW=16.25 MHz each (samples with frequency of $f_{s,m}$.=20 MHz). The block diagram of the IF to I/Q interface for both the Tx and Rx paths is shown in Figure 1. In the transmitter four FIR filters together with the respective upsampling unit, form four interpolators (two for the I branch and two for the Q branch). In the receiver four FIR filters together with the respective downsampling unit, form four decimators (two for the I branch, and two for the Q branch). The FIRs have symmetric coefficients. The interpolating filters need 16 and

14 multiplications, and the decimating needs 20 and 8, both at $f_{s,m}$. Hence the interface requires a total of 136 multiplications, or 10.88 multiplications per ns.

The baseband OFDM modem handles 16-bit signals. The data converters are 10-bit. The arithmetic of the internal operations in the FIRs of the I/Q block, could be different for each FIR in the decimators and interpolators. Various options may be considered for the number of bits of the operands. Depending on the SNR conditions of the communication channel, high bitwidth would be used for low SNR and lower for better channels.

The capability offered by the configurable bitwidth multipliers proposed here in this paper is of significant importance to the performance of an OFDM communication system by compromising (whenever possible), with the power consumption.

3. Reconfigurable Multiplier Architecture

The proposed reconfigurable multiplier shown in Fig. 2 consists of: i) the Interface Unit (IU), ii) the Arithmetic Selection Unit (ASU), iii) the Multiplication Function Unit (MFU), and iv) the Reconfiguration Register (RR). Furthermore, the first two units include two logic modules, which manipulate the incoming data stream, i.e. the multiplier and multiplicand operands as well as the outcoming stream, i.e. the final result. In particular, the IU performs the data transfers from/to bus. Generally, the bus bitwidth and the input/output data wordlength are different and thus, a control logic circuit within IU is designed to tackle with issue. The Arithmetic Selection Unit performs conversion between different arithmetic representations (i.e. 2's complement and unsigned numbers). The third unit, MFU, performs multiplication for various wordlengths of input data. It uses as elementary module a 4×4 array multiplier [9], assuming unsigned digit operations. Finally, the RR consists of nine bits and sends to IT, ASU, and MFU the appropriate bit stream to perform the reconfiguration. The detailed description of the above hardware will be given in the following paragraphs.

3.1 Multiplication Part

3.1.1 Construction of Array of Multipliers

The whole approach is based on the following algebraic equation:

$$\sum_{0\le i,j\le 7} X_i Y_j 2^{i+j} = \sum_{0\le m,n\le 1} \sum_{\substack{4m\le i\le 3+4m \\ 4n\le j\le 3+4n}} X_i Y_j 2^{i+j} \quad (1)$$

Here X and Y are two 8-bit numbers, and $X=X_7...Xi...X_0$ and $Y=Y_7...Yj...Y_0$

We build partial 4×4 product matrices, which will be used to compose an 8×8 partial product matrix as shown in Figure 3. The weighted bits of the four products of the four multipliers are added by two adders to result in the final product of the 8×8 multiplier.

The approach described above for decomposition of an 8×8 partial product matrix into four 4×4 ones can be applied recursively for larger size inputs of such computations. For example, to construct such a larger processor with (s, m)=(16, 4), four pieces of Block-1, one 3-n 16-b adder, and a few additional switches (controlled by bit C2) are sufficient. It is easy to verify that this structure can produce the product of two numbers of 16 bits by setting both C1 and C2 to state 1; or the array of 4 16-bit products by setting C1 to state 1, C2 to state 0; or the array of 16 8-bit products by setting C1 to state 1, C2 to state 0.

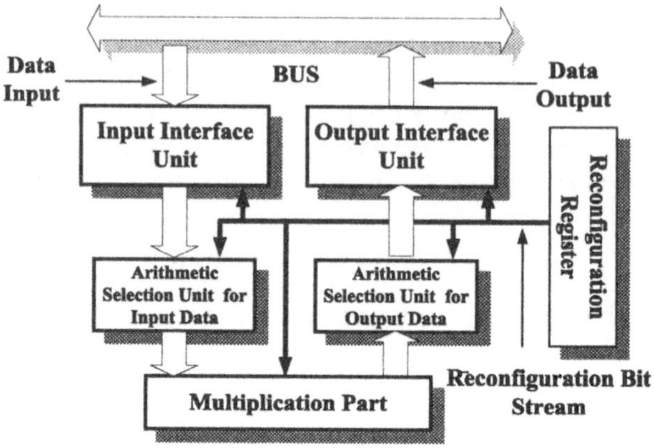

Figure 2. The block diagram of the proposed reconfigurable multiplier

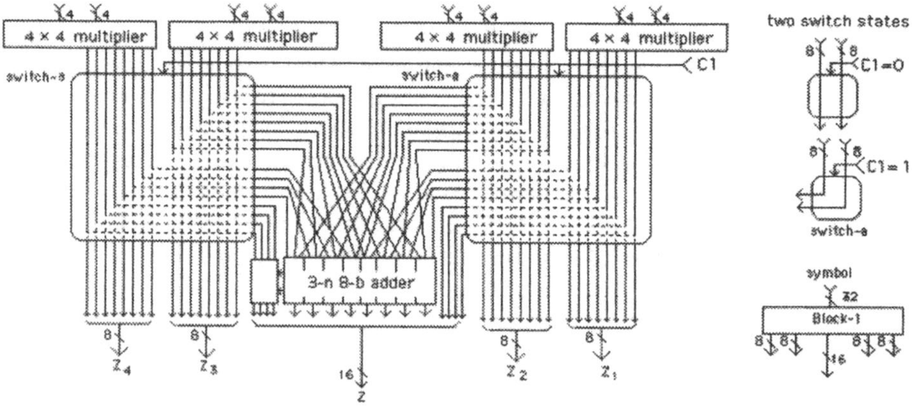

Figure 3. The reconfigurable array of multipliers of (s, m)=(8, 4), with 4 4×4 multipliers.

We can proceed in two levels of further extensions of the process. The processor of Fig. 4 can produce an array of 256 products of 8-bit items in 1 pipeline cycle; an array of 64 products of 16-bit items in 2 pipeline cycles, an array of 16 products of 32 bits in 3 pipeline cycles, an array of 64-bit products of 4 bits in 4 pipeline cycles, and a 128-bit product in 5 pipeline cycles. Processors with m≥8 can be constructed similarly.

3.1.2 The Input Networks

To duplicate and distribute the input data stream to the array of multipliers we need the following two additional simple sub-networks, as shown in Fig. 5, (for the array of multipliers with (s, m)=(16, 4)):

1. The input duplication network with the reconfiguration switches as shown in Figure 5(a) and (b). It duplicates data received from ports in one of the three levels according to the reconfiguration options. It consists of a fixed wire net and an array of reconfigurable switches with three switch states shown in Fig. 5(b).
2. The duplicated input data distribution network as shown in Figure 5(c). It is a fixed wire net which permutes data to the base 4×4 multipliers. By attaching these two sub-networks, we have the complete input network.

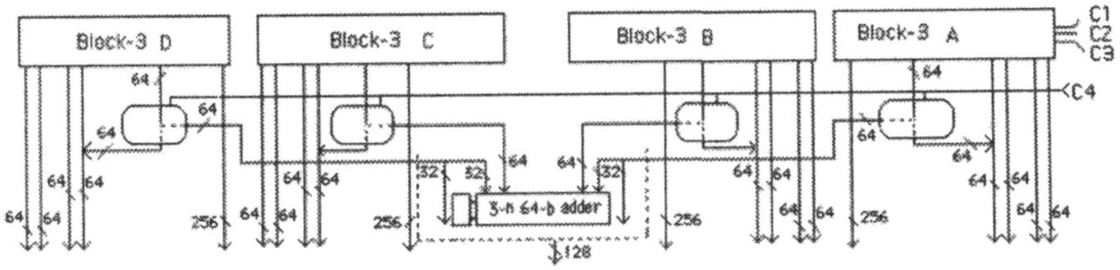

Figure 4. Reconfigurable array of multipliers of s=64, m=4, using 256 4×4 multipliers

Once the inputs are duplicated and distributed to the array of base multipliers, the corresponding levels of reconfigurable modules as described in the previous sections will be able to perform the pre-selected computation in pipeline to yield the desired results. In Figure 5(c) the 4 and 8-bit items have number indicators just for enumeration. If we want to multiply two 4-bit numbers we will put them in the right switches. There is an easy algorithm to find which the appropriate switches are. For this example we will put X1, Y1 to switches 17, 1 (X1, Y1 [17,1]) respectively. The switches are numbered from the right to the left (Fig. 7). For the rest we have:

Table 1.

Pairs X,Y	X1,Y1	X2,Y2	X3,Y3	X4,Y4	X5,Y5	X6,Y6
Switches	17,1	18,5	21,2	22,6	19,9	20,13
Pairs X,Y	X7,Y7	X8,Y8	X,Y 9	X,Y 10	X,Y 11	X,Y 12
Switches	23,10	24,14	25,3	26,7	29,4	30,8
Pairs X,Y	X,Y 13	X,Y 14	X,Y 15	X,Y 16		
Switches	27,11	28,15	31,12	32,16		

In the same manner, the network for a reconfigurable array of multipliers of s=64, m=4 can be constructed, with a total of 512 5-state switches connected to 256 4×4 multipliers.

3.2 Interface Unit

3.2.1. Main Part

In this approach we assume a 32-bit bus. A way is proposed to distribute an input array pair with $h=(s/b)^2$ b-bit items in parallel. Correct synchronized switches and trade transfer cycles (the time needed for a single (32-bit) word to be transferred from the bus) for register width.

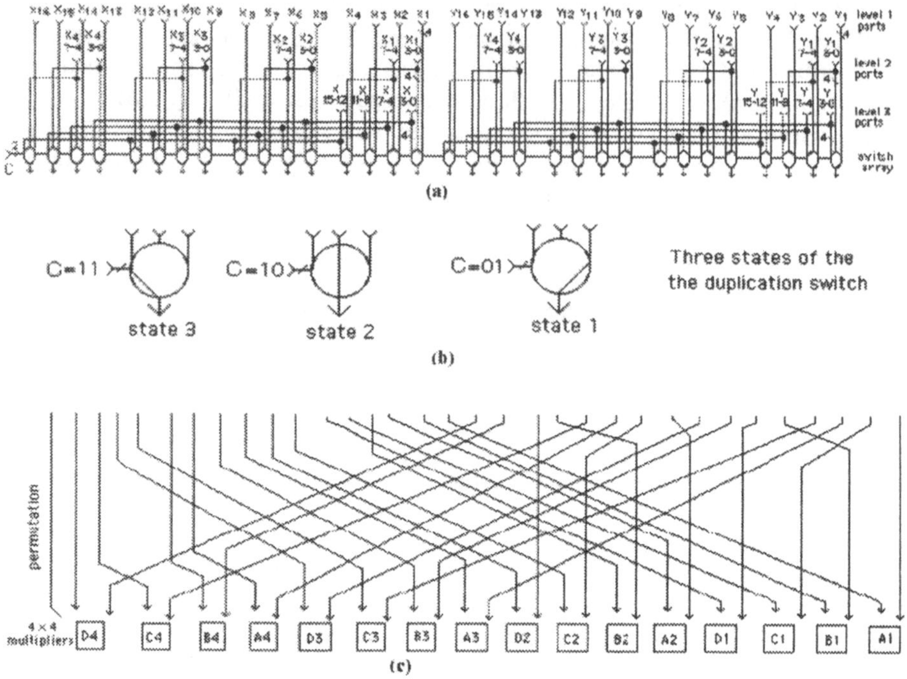

Figure 5. The input duplication sub-networks for array of multipliers of (s, m)=(16, 4). (a) The input duplication network with reconfiguration switches. (b) The reconfiguration switch states for input options: state 1 (2, 3), receiving data from level-1 (level-2, level-3) ports. (c) The input distribution network (fixed).

The basic unit which will realize the above is that of Fig. 6. In this figure the demultiplexer distributes its 32-bit input to two multiplexers. These multiplexers provide the 32-bit registers with new data only when the demultiplexer is referring to them and new data are provided to the demultiplexer from the outer circuit (this accomplished with the smux_a and clk_2 signals). Otherwise the registers are reloaded with their data. When both these registers are loaded with new data, the 64-bit register is triggered and loaded with these. Thus, the two sequential numbers transferred from the bus through the multiplexer are forming a single 64-bit number. The signals clk_* will be explained later. The rst signal resets the register.

Fig. 8 illustrates the whole circuit. In particular, Demultiplexer 2 distributes the data among the two blocks 64, which contain the above-mentioned logic. Its control signal sd_latch_4 (we will see the use of mux_a later) has a four times greater period than the data transfer period. In this way it provides each block with two sequential data words. A period of this signal is the time needed to load the two block_64 with data. Therefore the clk_3 signal of Fig. 6 is the same one, signal clk_2 has half the period of the previous one (sd_latch_2) because it controls the demultiplexer and clk_1 has the transfer data period.

Each of the signals sd_latch_2, sd_latch_4, sd_latch_8 has half the period of its next. They are outputs from a circuit of sequential D-latches where each one has as clock input the output of the previous latch.

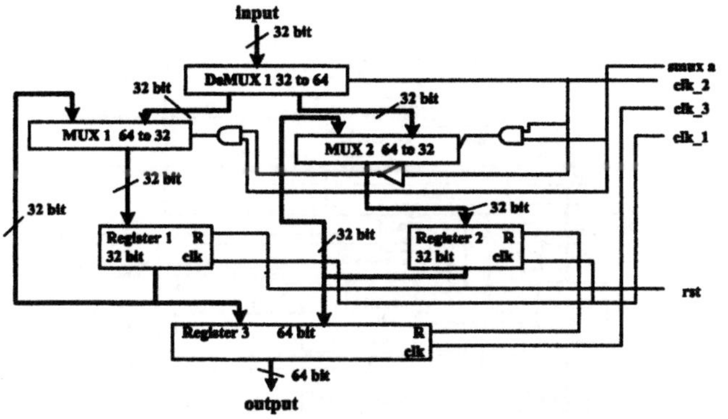

Figure 6. The logic structure of Block 64

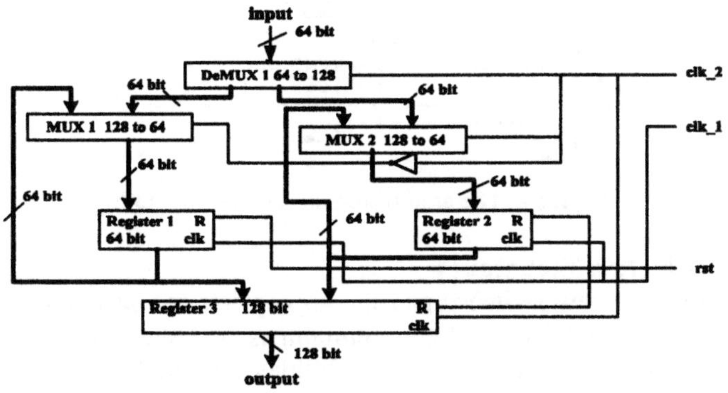

Figure 7. The logic structure of Block 32

The outputs of each block 64 are distributed to two demultiplexers. The Recon 1 (similar to C4 of Fig. 4) is their control signal. If it is '1', their input is driven to the multiplier and if it is '0' is driven to the next stage of the network. The next stage is similar but simpler than the first. As we see its units are twice the size of the ones in block 64. Block 32 is shown in Fig. 6. The Recon 2 (similar to C3 of Fig. 4) is the signal that determines if we will take the 4 pairs of 32-bit numbers or continues, in the same way as before, to the next level.

Let us return now to the structure of the multiplier described in the first part. Between each pipeline stage, the product of the multiplication, before it is fed to the next stage, is stored in a register. This register is triggered by the same signals (sd_latch_2, sd_latch_4, sd_latch_8) we used to control the multiplexers and demultiplexers, in order to accomplish the data synchronization. A simple multiplexer is providing these signals to the register. The multiplexer is controlled by the C1, C2, C3, and C4 bits.

The inverse procedure is followed after the data are processed, so that they can be driven back to the bus. This procedure is contained in the output interface unit. The new block that corresponds to block 64 is blockA 64, illustrated in Fig. 9.

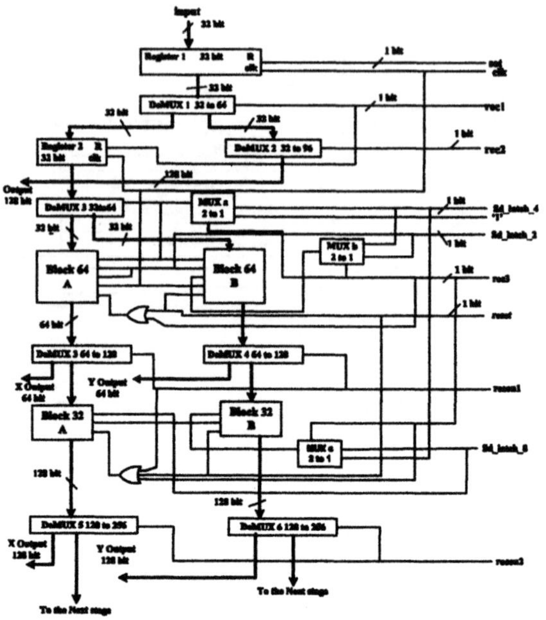

Figure 8. The architecture of the Interface unit

3.2.2 Power Reduction Techniques

With an addition of a few switches and the appropriate reconfiguration bits needed, we can use part of the structure (our minimum is half the structure in this case), wasting of course part of the processors capabilities gaining though, in the area of the adaptability to the problem and power reduction.

Two techniques are demonstrated: (i) In Figure 8, Mux_a controls Demux 3. If Rec 3 assumes the value of '1', the Demux 3 will pass its input always to block 64 B. Therefore half the circuit will not be in use, leading to no switching activity for its signals, meaning power reduction. The mux b,c units are providing the new control signals (with half the period from before), for the register and the multiplexers. When we refer to half the circuit we mean half of the structure of the multiplier. Of course we can't have the same number of parallel processed products. (ii): In Fig. 8 we can locate the demultiplexer 1. If Rec 1 is '1' the data from the bus pass to demultiplexer 2. This unit is controlled through the two bits of signal Rec 2 and passes its data directly to the multiplication part considering them 4 pairs of 4-bit numbers (Rec2="00"), or 2 pairs of 8-bit numbers (Rec 2="01") and a pair of 16-bit numbers (Rec 2="10"). In both examples a great part of the multiplier has inactive inputs leading to great power reduction if needed.

3.3. Arithmetic Selection Unit

The conversion of a binary number to its equivalent 2's complement (i.e. by inverting it and add '1') and of a signed to an unsigned number, gives the opportunity to use different arithmetic data representation on the same processor. This is possible just by using the appropriate circuit for converting the data into a plain unsigned binary number before it enters the multiplier and a circuit of reverse function after the MFU operation.

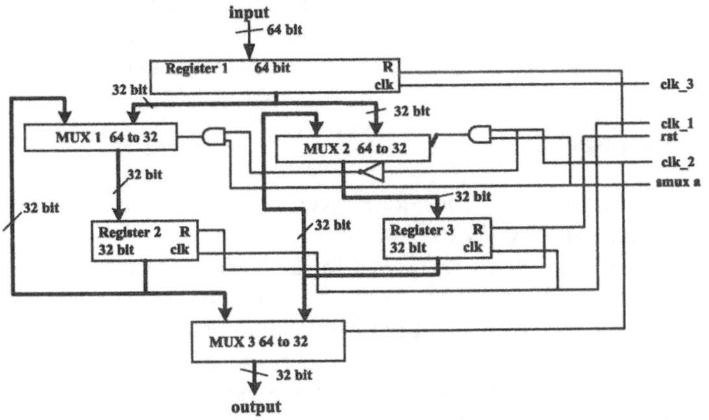

Figure 9. The logic structure Block A 64

The proposed circuits are shown in Fig. 10 for processing two 64-bit numbers. In the case of unsigned numbers, we keep both recon5, recon6 to '0', while for signed numbers, we set recon5 to '1'and keep recon6 at '0'. In this way the 127th bit and 63rd bit, which keep the sign of each number are changed to '0'. Thus, the two numbers are processed like two unsigned ones. Their signs are examined through an XOR gate and if they are different (i.e. zero is for positive and one for negative), the result is '1'(negative number) otherwise (both positive, both '0' or both negative '1') the result is '0' (positive number. The output of the XOR is put to the 127th bit of the result, which keeps the sign of the number.

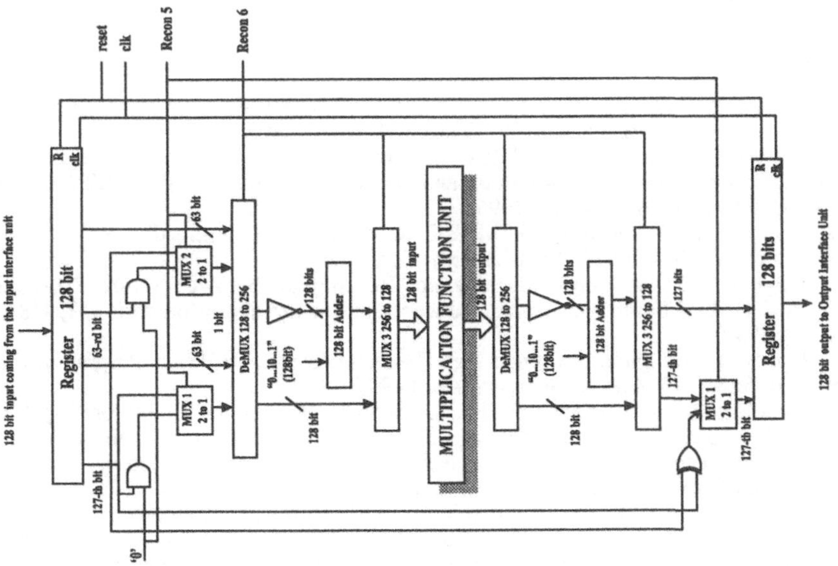

Figure 10. Interface units

Assuming of 2's complement numbers, we put recon5 to '1'and keep recon6 to '1'. Recon5 should be equal to '1' because in 2's complement arithmetic the numbers is signed. Because recon6='1' the numbers will be inverted and added with 0...1 (=64 bit) each, modified in this way to unsigned plain binary numbers. The inverse procedure modifies them back to the original form after the multiplication.

4. Measurements

The implementation costs of the alternatives presented above when the I/Q block implemented on a XILINX VirtexE2000-6 FPGA for the 16 bits arithmetic was 33% utilization of the device, while 50% was for the case of 24 bits. Power consumption has similar figures. By moving from the 24 bitwidth to the 16 bits, power consumption decreases by 33%. An implementation on a XILINX XC4000XV FPGA (device, 40150XVPG559) led to a comparison against a dedicated hardware multiplier. For an ordinary 16×16 multiplier we measured a maximum frequency of 51 MHz for a single 32 bit product in one clock cycle and for the presented multiplier a maximum frequency of 41.5 MHz for 16 32 bit products in 3 pipeline cycles.

5. Conclusions

A reconfigurable array of multipliers design has been presented. The processor can be run-time (or dynamically) reconfigured to trade bitwidth for matrix size. Specifically, for constructing an array of multipliers of size s=maximum input item bitwidth=2^{k+2} (k=0,1,2,...), a total of $(s/m)^2 = 4^k$ m×m multipliers is needed and it can process an input array pair with $h=(s/b)^2$ b-bit items in parallel in each pipeline step. The superiority of the design is achieved by reusing modules. This fact gives the opportunity to use part of the structure when for example power reduction is needed.

References

1. J. Hauser and J. Wawrzynek: Garp: A MIPS Processor with a Reconfigurable Coprocessor;Proc. IEEE FCCM '97, Napa, CA, USA, April 16-18, 1997.
2. E. Mirsky, A. De Hon: MATRIX: A Reconfigurable Computing Architecture with Configurable Instruction Distribution and Deployable Resources; Proc. IEEE FCCM '96, NAPA, CA, USA, April 17-19, 1996.
3. T. Miyamori and K. Olokotun: REMARC: Reconfiguirable Multimedia Array Coprocessor; Proc. ACM/SIGDA FPGA '98, Monterey, Feb. 1998
4. H. Singh, et al.: MorphoSys: An Integrated Re-Configurable Architecture; Proceedings of the NATO RTO Symp. On System Concepts and Integration, Monterey, CA, USA, April 20-22, 1998.
5. J. Rabaey: Reconfigurable Computing: The Solution to Low Power Programmable DSP; Proc. ICASSP '97 Munich, Germany, April 1997.
6. S. C. Goldstein, H. Schmit, M. Budiu, S. Cadambi, M. Moe, and R.Taylor "PipeRench: A Reconfigurable Architecture and Compiler" in IEEE Computer, Vol.33, No. 4, April 2000.
7. Reiner Hartenstein, "A Decade of Reconfigurable Computing: a Visionary Retrospective", Embedded Turorial, Asia-Pacific DAC, 2001.
8. Rong Lin ,A Run-Time Reconfigurable Array of Multipliers Architecture, in Proc. of 8th Reconfigurable Architectures Workshop (RAW 2001, in conjuction with International Parallel & Distributed Processing Symposium 2001, San Fransisco, April 2001.
9. Behrooz Parhami, "Computer Arithmetic: Algorithms and Hardware Designs," Oxford University Press, 2000.

A General Hardware Design Model for Multicontext FPGAs

Naoto Kaneko and Hideharu Amano

Keio University, 3-14-1 Hiyoshi Yokohama, 222-8522, Japan
{kaneko, amano}@am.ics.keio.ac.jp

Abstract. We propose a general multicontext hardware design model to promote the use of multicontext FPGAs in wide range of applications. There are two major problems to be overcome in multicontext FPGAs programming. One is the complexity of programming an application in multicontext. The design model provides the context scheduling mechanisms to free the programmers from the low-level context management. The other is the difficulty in scheduling non-algorithmic applications. Our distributed demand-driven dynamic scheduler facilitates their implementation. We have applied the design model to a network interface controller Martini. The result supports the effectiveness of our design model.

1 Introduction

Multicontext FPGA programming is an intricate task. In addition to implementing an application, programmers must also manage it into multiple hardware contexts. This includes (1) partitioning the design into contexts, (2) scheduling the contexts in run order, and (3) adapting the context for switching. These low-level toils perhaps make a multicontext FPGA an uneasy solution, in a way comparable to a computer without an operating system. The standard method to separate them from the application programming need to be developed; otherwise, multicontext FPGAs will never be accepted by the real world. Under such motivation, we propose a general hardware design model for multicontext FPGAs.

There are two popular approaches to time-multiplex a design into an FPGA. One is a data-flow graph based method [1] [2], and the other is micro-cycle sequencing [3]. The former usually aims to replace software systems by executing algorithms in hardware speed. By contrast, our design model aims to accommodate an existing hardware design to a multicontext device. The latter time-slices a clock to multiple contexts at the net-list level. Whereas our design model partitions a hardware design at a task module level.

It is often infeasible to context-schedule a hardware design statically because of its unpredictable patterns of task demand. This is especially when the design is interactive, multi-data-path, and/or exception raising. We loosely classify this class of application non-algorithmic: if C language does not suit to describe the

M. Glesner, P. Zipf, and M. Renovell (Eds.): FPL 2002, LNCS 2438, pp. 1037–1047, 2002.

application, it is probably non-algorithmic. In order to cope with the problem, our design model adopts a distributed demand-driven dynamic context scheduler.

The discussion in this paper revolves around the context scheduler. The next section introduces the conceptual outlook of the multicontext hardware design model. Section three goes through the procedural details of the context scheduling. Section four visits the issues on context partitioning. Then, section five exhibits an application of the design model to a practical network interface controller. Finally, the last section concludes the paper casting a few future works.

2 Multicontext Hardware Design Model

2.1 Target Device

Our design model targets a multicontext FPGA with partial reconfigurability. Its concept has been there for a while already, but the real chips are implemented only recently.

A multicontext FPGA is an FPGA which houses several sets of configuration data on-chip. Each set of the configuration data is also called a hardware context. Only one context is selected at a time to be active—that is, programmed on the logic surface. By switching the active context sequentially at run time, a large design is integrated into a smaller logic resource.

The partial reconfigurability divides the logic plane into independently context-switchable sections. This flexibility is indispensable for implementing non-algorithmic applications efficiently. It is indeed a popular capability for a multicontext FPGA as found in NEC's DRL [4].

2.2 Organization

Figure 1 depicts the conceptual organization of the design model.

A *module* is the atomic element of the structure. Each module contains a fragment of the function; the complete set of the modules possesses an equivalence to the single context implementation. Requests for the dynamic scheduling are issued at the module level.

Every module belongs either to the *fixed region* or *shared region*. This assignment is a critical issue for it is concerned with an area-to-performance trade-off. Modules allocated to the fixed region reside constantly on the logic plane. Heavily accessed modules, like FIFO queue, are the good candidates to be in the fixed region. Whereas modules allocated to the shared region are the subject of context switching; thus, they exist on the logic plane only as they are needed.

The shared region is divided into *context groups*, then, further into *contexts*. Every module in the shared region is a member of one of the contexts; there may be more than one module in a context. A context group corresponds to a section of the logic plane that is switched together in the partial reconfiguration. Each context group is tied with a set of contexts, and only one context out of the set

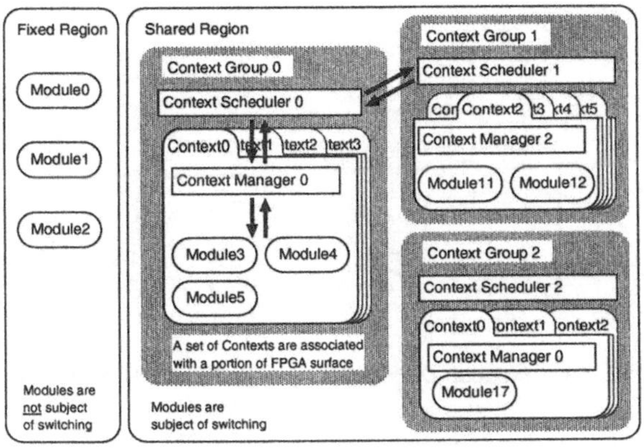

Fig. 1. Design model organization

is active at a time. The selection of which context to activate is determined by the context scheduling, and it takes place locally at each context group.

The context scheduling is carried out in cooperation of a *context scheduler* and its subordinating *context managers*. A context scheduler is attached to each context group. Likewise, context managers are attached to the respective contexts in the context group. As a part of a context, they are also subject of switching. Consequently, only the context manager of the active context can actually communicate with its context scheduler. The next section provides the procedural details of the request based scheduling.

3 Demand-Driven Dynamic Context Scheduling

3.1 Hierarchical Request Passing

A context scheduler commands the context switching based on the request information provided by its context managers. The request comes from the natural demand of the modules to advance the process. To compile the request information, a context manager keeps track of the run status of their modules.

1. Modules requested to run in this context
2. Modules still running
3. Modules requested to run in the next context

Upon the context activation, the list of modules requested to run is passed down to the context manager by the context scheduler. While the request is issued at the module level, not necessary every module in the active context joins the process. The context stays active as long as there are modules still running. The modules request another module as the process demands it. If the requested module were in the same context, it is added to the modules requested to run in this context. Else if the requested modules reside in another context, it is added to the modules requested to run in the next context.

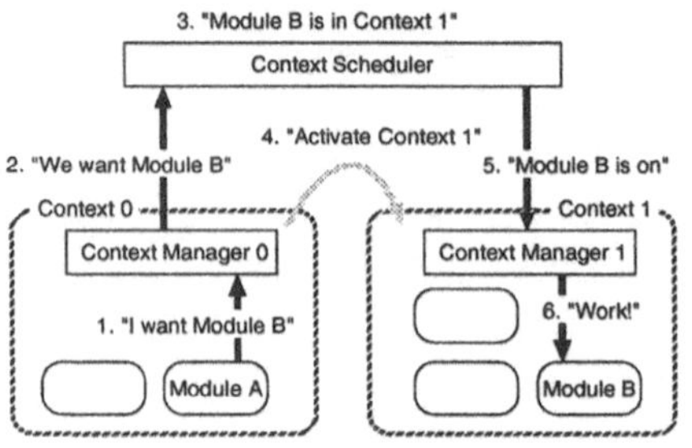

Fig. 2. Hierarchical request passing

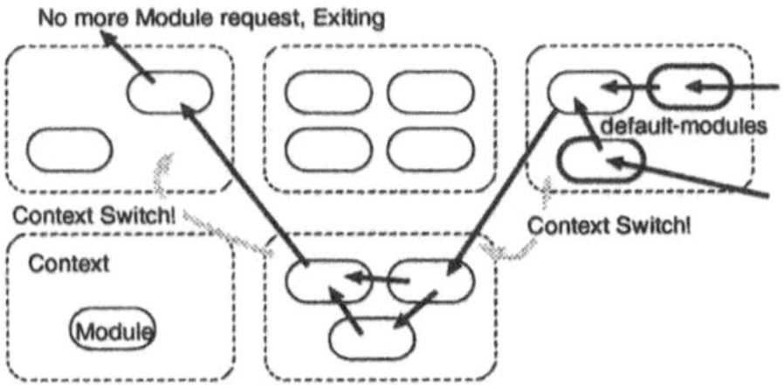

Fig. 3. Request flow

When eventually there is no more module running, the context manager declares the context is ready to go inactive. At this point, it passes up the accumulated result of the modules requested to run in the next context. The context scheduler looks up to what context the requested modules belong to, then switches the active context. The list of requested modules is again passed down to the new context. The cycles of these request management add up to the on-demand dynamic scheduling.

As illustrated in Fig.2, the request messages are passed up and down the stack of layers. Each layer communicates only with its adjacent layers, meanwhile their boundaries clearly separate the job of interest. The design model defines (1) the interface between the layers and (2) the state machines of the context scheduler and context manager. The actual implementation method is not specified because it must be dealt with according to the target application and device.

The hierarchical model benefits the FPGA programmers in two ways. First, it makes the multicontext FPGA programming much more comprehensible. Handling everything in one chunk is not only burdensome but also bug inducing. Second, it lets the programmers concentrate on their true objective, the application. Besides designing and partitioning the application, they need only to feed the interface to the upper layer with necessary information. The rest is taken care of by the schedulers, which are implemented elsewhere by whoever with knowledge of the target device.

3.2 Process Execution Model

We perceive the executing process as a flow of the requests. Figure 3 gives an intuitive diagram to this concept. The solid arrows indicate the direction of the module requests. Starting at the *default-modules*, a process travels through modules. Each participating module contributes a piece of function and passes the task on to the next module. When the request crosses the context border the context switching takes place. This routine continues until there's no more module to request. The wake of the requests is called the "flow."

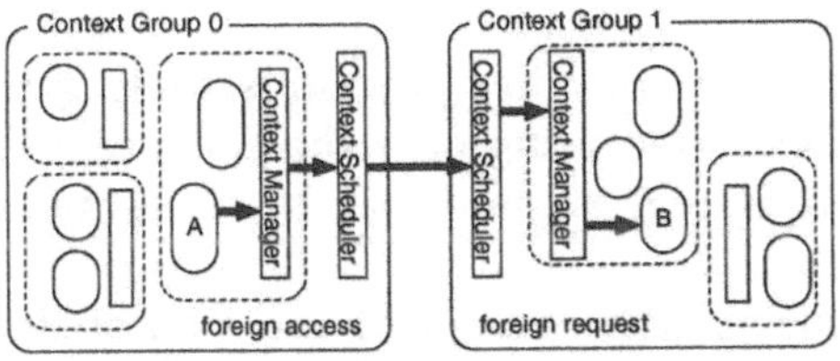

Fig. 4. Inter-context-group communication

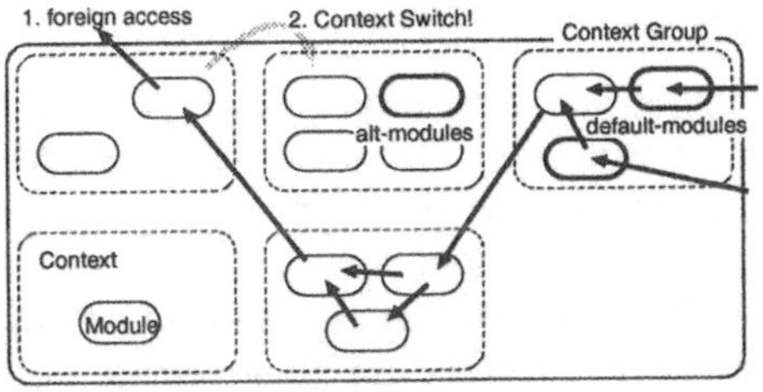

Fig. 5. Foreign access issued

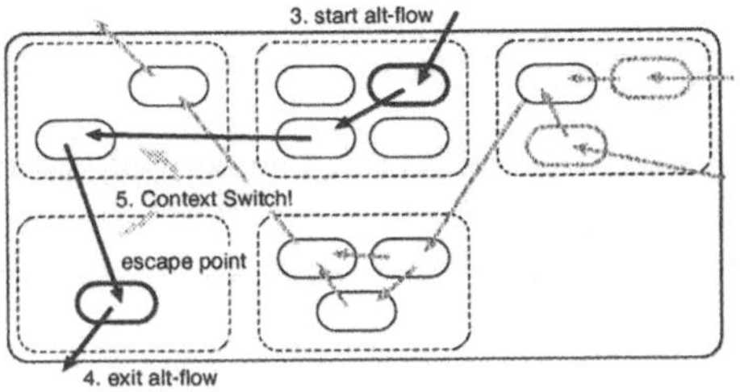

Fig. 6. Alt-flow executed

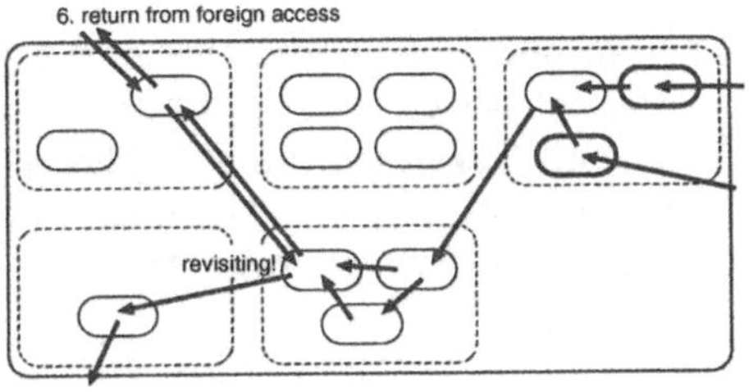

Fig. 7. Main-flow recovered

3.3 Inter-Context-Group Communication

Modules are allowed to access not only the modules inside its own context group but also those outside, *foreign-modules*. Figure 4 depicts the idea, using the example of module A sending a request for module B. The context managers and context schedulers sit in the middle of the transaction to make various adjustments. We call this exchange of the requests for foreign-modules inter-context-group communication. For convenience, let us name the request received from foreign-modules *foreign request* and the request issued for foreign-modules *foreign access.*

A context scheduler pends foreign requests as long as the currently running process has the next modules to request. When the request flow finally terminates, the next process is initiated from the modules of the foreign request, instead of the usual default-modules. The rest of the process is treated similarly as the request flow started locally in the context group.

The context that has issued a foreign access has to wait until the process returns. While waiting, the context is either *blocked* or *suspended.* If blocked, the entire context group is frozen at the location. Otherwise if suspended, the context runs another process for the time it is waiting. Although the suspension potentially brings a substantial performance improvement, a few but essential restrictions apply to its realization. A brief discussion on the restrictions follows.

3.4 Suspension

Suspension lets a secondary process run while the first process is waiting for foreign access. The secondary process is executed using only the parts that do not interfere with the primary process. It is only single depth, but it demands no extra resource either.

To consider the mechanism of suspension, the concept of the request flow must be brought up to attention. During suspension, there are two flows of requests in a context group: *main-flow* and *alt-flow*. The main-flow is the request flow of the primary process, and it is stopped at the foreign access. The alt-flow is the request flow of the secondary process. It starts from *alt-modules* and terminates at an *escape point*. A typical plot of suspension is like following.

1. A suspendable module issues a foreign access. Suspension kicks in, and the context is switched for alt-modules (Fig.5).
2. The alt-flow is executed and leaves from an escape point. The context group comes back to where the main-flow was left off (Fig.6).
3. The main-flow recovers from the foreign access and pursues its process (Fig.7).

Whether modules are suspendable depends on if a valid alt-flow can be formed. To form an alt-flow, the modules, which wish to suspend, must arrange alt-modules in advance at the design time. If no satisfactory alt-modules were found, it means those modules are not able to suspend and therefore have to be blocked. The "satisfactory alt-modules" are able to form the alt-flow which satisfies the next requirements.

- Does not collide with the main-flow
- Reaches an escape point definitely

Like in the example of Fig.6, the main-flow and alt-flow are not supposed to cross each other on a module. Any change to the process of the main-flow by the alt-flow may cause incoherency to the primary process. It is always possible that the main-flow revisits its previous modules, expecting their states to be unchanged (e.g. in Fig.7). This imposes the alt-flow some or large constraints on its contents of the process.

An escape point is where the alt-flow can safely withdraw from a process. A state that the main-flow is ready to terminate is one instance to be included in the escape points. There may be several escape points in a context group, and it does not matter which one is included. The bottom line is that the alt-flow will reach any one of them for certain. Otherwise, the main-flow is kept from re-entering the process.

4 Context Partitioning

The safeness of the design is probably the biggest concern in multicontext design. It may create a deadlock in scheduling, produce wrong results, or even

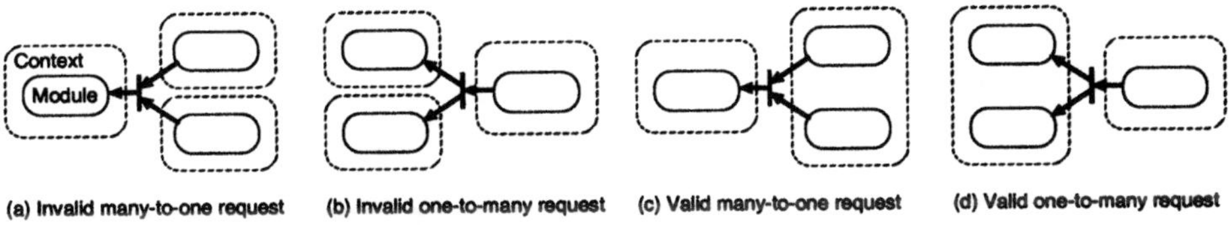

Fig. 8. Context partitioning rules

be unmappable to the device in the first place. Our design model avoids such hazards by applying the following rules at the partitioning time. We assume the original single context design is safe.

1. The number of contexts in a context group is no more than the device supports
2. The area after partitioning is no larger than the device capacity
3. No request forks out to separate contexts in the same context group
4. No request joins from separate contexts in the same context group
5. No foreign access cycles back to the original context group

The first two rules should be immediately recognized as obvious restrictions, as they simply forbid violating the physical limits of the target device. For the second rule, the area after partitioning is given with the formula below.

$$Partitioned\ Area = Fixed\ Region + \sum^{\forall}(Largest\ Context + Context\ Scheduler) \quad (1)$$

The second term represents the size of the shared region, the sum of all context groups. As seen, the size of a context group is determined by its largest context, however small all other contexts are. In addition to the logical size, the device overhead may have to be taken into account as well. For instance, DRL achieves eight contexts with 35% of the area overhead [4].

The next two rules prevent the conduct beyond scheduler's capability, i.e. the lack of concurrent context handling (see Fig.8). The forking and joining demands the simultaneous presence of modules in different contexts. Nonetheless our scheduler singles one context out to be activated. As the result, the modules in the ignored party are not able to receive proper input. This inhibits the proper update of their outputs and/or states, leading to wrong results and possibly deadlock. The rules avoid such hazard by securing that all requested modules are activated to receive correct input.

The last rule avoids the cyclic dependency among context groups. Once a request flow goes out of a context group, it cannot re-enter the context group. The context group cannot accept the foreign request because it is halt by the foreign access issued by the request flow itself. This is unless the context group suspends so that the request flow can continue its process. Cautions need be taken to design such suspension, however.

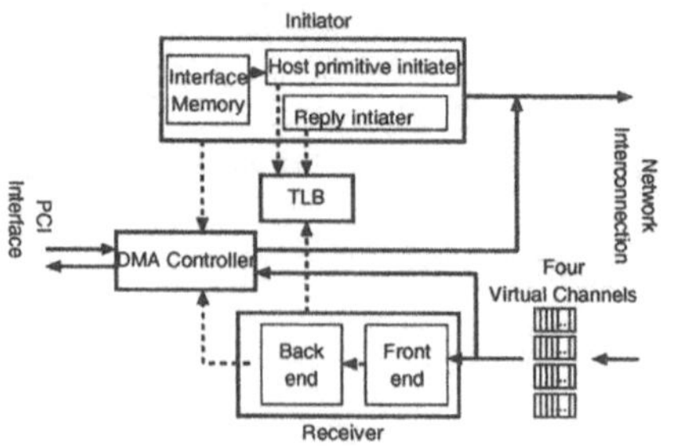

Fig. 9. Block diagram of the hardwired core

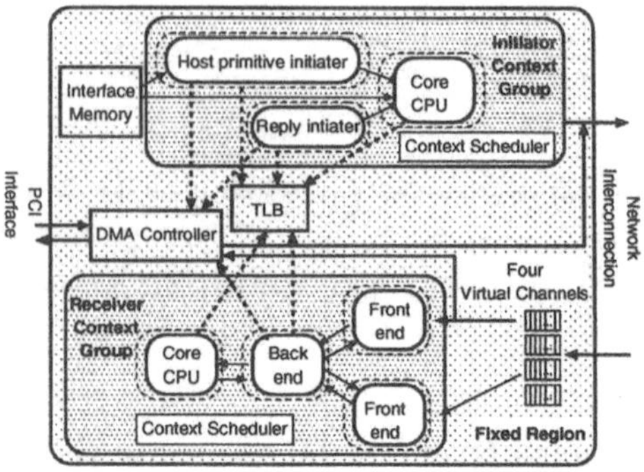

Fig. 10. Multicontext hardwired core

5 Design Example and Evaluation

As an example of the multicontext design, we applied the design model to a network interface controller, called Martini.

5.1 A Network Interface Controller Martini

Martini is a high-end network interface controller designed for heterogeneous PC clusters [5]. Martini communicates using two primitive commands, "push" and "pull." Push sends a cluster of memory data on the local host, and pull requests that on the remote host. They are fully implemented in a hardwired core—a core CPU software kicks in only when exceptions need be handled—called a primitive handler. As shown in Fig.9, the hardwired core consists of an initiator and a receiver. The initiator generates packets, while the receiver handles incoming packets.

A primitive process is started when the local host writes the command into a specific address of the interface memory modules. The host primitive initiator refers the Table Look-aside Buffer (TLB), compiles a packet header, and requests DMA. The header is transferred to the interconnection interface unit, and the packet body follows as soon as it is ready. On the remote end, the receiver front-end analyzes the packet header, and the back-end issues a DMA request if necessary.

The receiver front-end watches the incoming packets to its four concurrent virtual channels. This is actually the problematic part of the Martini design because it complicates the logic and burdens a long verification time. The original implementation sequentially checks the channels and processes if a packet were arrived. Later on, our scheduling mechanism presents another solution to this problem.

5.2 Martini Design on the Multicontext FPGA

We've focused on the primitive handler as a target of the multicontext design. Figure 10 sketches out the implementation and the request flow among the modules. The interface memory module and the TLB are assigned to the fixed region since these modules are frequently accessed. The rest of the modules are assigned to the shared region, thus they are subject of context switching. The shared region modules form two context groups: an initiator context group and a receiver context group.

The initiator context group consists of a host primitive initiator module, reply initiator module, and core CPU module. Each module is assigned to a context of its own. The host primitive initiator is activated by the request from the local host. The reply initiator is activated by the request from the receiver. The core CPU is activated when TLB miss-hits.

The receiver context group consists of two front-end modules, a back-end module, and a core CPU module. Again, each module is assigned to a context of its own. The front-ends are activated upon the arrival of a packet to the virtual channels. To what virtual channel the packet arrives determines which one of two front-end is activated. The back-end is activated by the front-end when it is ready for DMA, and if necessary, the back-end activates back the front-end. The core CPU is activated when TLB miss-hits.

For the context scheduler and context manager, we've used the generic implementation. They provide the state machine and interface that is defined by the design model, as mentioned in section three. With minor adjustments of parameters, they are readily fit in the design.

5.3 Simulation

The multicontext Martini is described in Verilog-HDL and simulated with a logic level simulator. While no Verilog-HDL simulator supports multicontext FPGA, we emulate the device by inserting the clocks only to the active contexts. We assume the multicontext FPGA switches from one context to another in one clock, as it is so with DRL.

The design is synthesized using Synopsys FPGA Compiler II. For the purpose of comparison, we assume the same CPLD (Altera APEX20KE) for both the original and multicontext design. The original Martini actually uses Hitachi 0.14μm CMOS ASIC.

5.4 Evaluation

The simulation result confirms the functional validity of the multicontext design. Martini correctly executes push and pull primitives even after the redesign to multicontext.

The simulation also supports the scheduling efficiency. The primitives are executed in multicontext with a matter of only a few clocks increased. A pull of 512byte costs 66 clocks in the original and 68 clocks in the multicontext Martini.

Table 1. Required logic blocks for the initiator

Original initiator			**5535**
Multicontext initiator			**2315**
	Contexts		*2282*
		Host primitive initiator	2282
		Reply initiator	1740
		16 bit core CPU	1500
	Context scheduler		*33*

Table 2. Required logic blocks for the receiver

Original receiver			**4949**
Multicontext receiver			**1692**
	Contexts		*1659*
		Front-end × 2	1077
		Back-end	1659
		16 bit core CPU	1500
	Context scheduler		*33*

Likewise, a push costs 177 clocks and 184 clocks respectively. The critical path of both the initiator (14MHz) and receiver (11MHz) remain the same even after the redesign. Therefore, it is safe to assess the scheduling overhead is negligibly small to the performance of Martini.

The synthesis results demonstrates the successful extraction of the area efficiency (Tbl.1 and Tbl.2). The initiator context group requires 2315 logic blocks (2282 + 33, refer equation (1)). Even accepting 35% of the device overhead, the area is almost half the original design. Similarly for the receiver context group, the required logic block is reduced from 4949 to 1692, which is less than half the original. Notice also, the size of the context scheduler is so small that it realizes the multicontext design with very little area overhead.

The area efficiency is not the only benefit of the multicontext hardware design. In situations it may even present solutions to the hardware design issues. As mentioned earlier in this section, Martini is confronted with the problems of the virtual channels control. Logically, it supports 32 channels but the control complexity restrains the realistic number to four. The multicontext Martini overcomes this problem by having the context scheduler toggle the front-end for the channel that demands attention. As a result, the front-end module is much simplified, and its size has dropped from 1638 to 1077 logic blocks. Moreover, additional channels come without any area penalty as long as there are still free contexts in the device.

6 Conclusion

Multicontext FPGAs are promising device, but they are hard to program. To address this problem, we propose a general multicontext hardware design model. Our design model improves their programmability by separating the low-level tasks from the application. Furthermore, its distributed demand-driven dynamic context scheduler accommodates not only algorithmic but also non-algorithmic applications. As an example, a network interface controller Martini has been applied to the model. The result confirms the effectiveness of our design model.

There are still more work left for us to be done. First, we need to examine the design model with the further variety of the target. Applications in telecommunication is one area we are interested in. Then, we need to implement the design on real multicontext FPGAs. We have already designed a four-DRLs testbed, and it is now under debugging. We are hoping to see their results chart up the practical methodology of the device utilization.

References

1. X.-P. Ling and H. Amano, "WASMII: A Data Driven Computer on a Virtual Hardware," *Proceedings of IEEE Workshop on FPGAs for Custom Computing Machines*, pp. 33-42, 1993.
2. E. Caspi et al, "Stream Computations Organized for Reconfigurable Execution (SCORE)," *Proceedings of the International Workshop on Field-Programmable Logic and Applications*, pp. 605-614, 2000.
3. S. Trimberger "Scheduling Designs into a Time-Multiplexed FPGA," *Proceedings of the IEEE Workshop on FPGA's for Custom Computing Machines*, pp. 153-160, 1998.
4. M. Yamashina et al, "Reconfigurable Computing: Its concept and practical embodiment using newly developed DRL LSI," *Proceedings of ASP-DAC*, pp. 329-332, 2000.
5. K. Watanabe et al, "Preliminary Evaluation of Martini: a Novel Network Interface Controller Chip for Cluster-based Parallel Processing," *Proceedings of International Symposium on Applied Informatics*, pp.390-396, 2002.

Dynamically Reconfigurable Hardware – A New Perspective for Neural Network Implementations

Mario Porrmann, Ulf Witkowski, Heiko Kalte, and Ulrich Rückert

Heinz Nixdorf Institute, System and Circuit Technology,
University of Paderborn, Germany,
porrmann@hni.upb.de, http://wwwhni.upb.de/sct

Abstract. In this paper we discuss the usability of dynamic hardware reconfiguration for the simulation of neural networks. A dynamically reconfigurable hardware accelerator for self-organizing feature maps is presented. The system is based on the universal rapid prototyping system RAPTOR2000 that has been developed by the authors. The modular prototyping system is based on XILINX FPGAs and is capable of emulating hardware implementations with a complexity of more than 24 million system gates. RAPTOR2000 is linked to its host – a standard personal computer or workstation – via the PCI bus. For the simulation of self-organizing maps a module has been designed for the RAPTOR2000 system, that embodies an FPGA of the Xilinx Virtex (-E) series and optionally up to 128 MBytes of SDRAM. A speed-up of about 50 is achieved with five FPGA modules on the RAPTOR2000 system compared to a software implementation on a state of the art personal computer for typical applications of self-organizing maps.

1 Introduction

System-on-chip designs with a complexity of more than a million logic gates and several hundred kBytes of internal SRAM memory can be mapped on state-of-the-art Field Programmable Gate Arrays (FPGAs). Clock rates approach several hundred MHz boosting the chip-computational power above 10^4 MOPS (million operations per second) at a power consumption of a few Watts. In this paper we want to show that FPGA-based architectures are well suited for the implementation of hardware accelerators for neural networks.

In recent years various hardware implementations for different neural network architectures have been presented [1,2,3]. The main benefit of special purpose hardware is the speedup compared to software implementations. However, many of the proposed architectures are dedicated to single neural network algorithms or groups of similar algorithms. The aim of our project is to deliver a system that is capable of accelerating a wide range of different neural algorithms. Additionally, in most applications, different methods of information processing are combined. For example, artificial neural networks are combined with fuzzy logic or with techniques for knowledge-based information processing. In contrast to

M. Glesner, P. Zipf, and M. Renovell (Eds.): FPL 2002, LNCS 2438, pp. 1048–1057, 2002.

implementing different components for data pre- and postprocessing and for neural networks we use a dynamically (i.e. during runtime) configurable hardware accelerator to implement all of the algorithms that are required for a special application. The system can be reconfigured for the different tasks in one application (e.g. different configurations for pre- and postprocessing may be selected). Because of the reconfigurability the hardware can be mapped optimally to the requirements of the application, thus allowing an easy expansion by new algorithms to improve flexibility and performance.

In this paper we will focus on self-organizing maps (SOMs) [4], that are successfully used for a wide range of technical applications, in particular, dealing with noisy or incomplete data. Examples of use are controlling tasks, data analysis and pattern matching. In cooperation with an industrial partner we are using SOMs for the analysis of IC (Integrated Circuits) fabrication processes. The large amount of data, that is captured during fabrication, has to be analyzed in order to optimize the process and to avoid a decrease of yield [5,6]. Software simulations of medium sized maps on state of the art workstations require calculation times from hours up to several days for these large data sets. The simulation of large maps (i.e. more than one million neurons with vector dimensions in the order of thousands) seems promising but is not feasible with state of the art PCs or workstations. From the various possibilities to speed up neural computations we have chosen the design of a hardware accelerator for neural networks. Our goal is to integrate the system into state of the art workstations if very high performance is required and to enable access to the accelerator via the internet if the accelerator is only sporadically used.

2 Using Reconfigurable Hardware for Neural Networks

Dynamic reconfiguration (or runtime reconfiguration) offers an opportunity for problem specific implementations on a dedicated hardware environment. Different levels of dynamic reconfiguration can be distinguished. For example in [7] three categories are presented: algorithmic reconfiguration, architectural reconfiguration and functional reconfiguration.

The goal in algorithmic reconfiguration is to reconfigure the system with a different computational algorithm that implements the same functionality, but with different performance, accuracy, power, or resource requirements [7]. In the field of neural network hardware, algorithmic reconfiguration can be used e.g. to implement algorithms with variable precision. For self-organizing feature maps a low precision of e.g. 8 bit is sufficient for a rough ordering of the map in the beginning of the learning process. For fine tuning of the map, the precision of the hardware is increased (e.g. to 16 bit). Using a lower precision allows us to set up an optimized architecture that can be faster, smaller or more energy efficient than a high precision architecture.

In architectural reconfiguration the hardware topology and computation topology is modified by reallocating resources to computations. The need for this type of reconfiguration arises e.g. if resources become unavailable or if additional resources become available. Designing massively parallel architectures for neural networks with a large number of processing elements, an interesting approach for architectural reconfiguration is to check the functionality of the processing elements during start up. Processing elements that are not working correctly can be disabled. This makes it possible, especially when working with application specific integrated circuits (ASICs), to enhance the yield, because problems in single processing elements can be tolerated in this way.

Functional reconfiguration is used to execute different algorithms on the same resources. Thus limited hardware resources can be used to implement a wide range of different algorithms. In neural network simulation we are often interested in providing as much computing power as possible to the simulation of the algorithm. But pre- and postprocessing of the input and output data often also requires quite a lot of calculations. In this case dynamic reconfiguration offers us the opportunity to implement special preprocessing algorithms in the beginning, switch to the neural network simulation and in the end reconfigure the system for postprocessing. Thus we do not require the system resources that would be necessary to calculate all algorithms in parallel. An example for functional reconfiguration in this sense is the use of self-organizing maps as a preprocessing stage for radial basis function networks, as proposed e.g. by [8].

Our implementation allows us to add additional functionality for data postprocessing like U-matrix calculation. The integration of postprocessing algorithms on the one hand speeds up computation time, on the other hand it often drastically reduces communication time because the amount of data, that has to be transferred from the hardware accelerator to the host computer is reduced by these algorithms. In the case of data visualization we are able to offer a speed up compared to a postprocessing algorithm on the host computer, that enables us to display U-matrices online, during learning with nearly no loss in performance.

3 The Dynamically Reconfigurable Hardware Accelerator RAPTOR2000

The hardware accelerator for self-orgainizing feature maps, that is presented in this paper is based on the modular rapid prototyping system RAPTOR2000. The system consists of a motherboard and up to six application specific modules (ASMs). Basically, the motherboard provides the communication infra"-structure between the ASMs and links the RAPTOR2000 system via the PCI bus to a host computer. Additionally, management functions like bus arbitration, memory management and error detection services are integrated in two Complex Programmable Logic Devices (CPLD). The various communication schemes that can be used between different ASMs and between the ASMs and the host computer are depicted in the block diagram in figure 1. Every ASM slot is connected to the Local Bus for internal communication with other devices or ASMs and for external communication with the host processor or with other PCI bus devices. An additional Broadcast Bus can be used for simultaneous communication between the ASMs. Additionally, a dual port SRAM can be accessed by all ASMs via the Broadcast Bus (e.g. utilized as a buffer for fast direct memory accesses to the main memory of the host system). Direct communication between adjacent ASMs is realized by 128 signals that can be variably used, depending on the actual implementation.

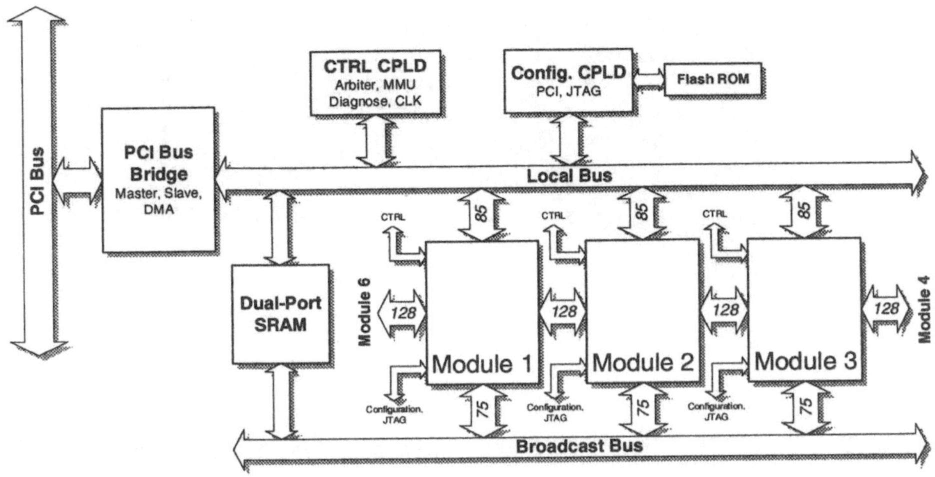

Fig. 1. Architecture of the RAPTOR2000 system

A crucial aspect concerning FPGA designs is the configuration of the devices. Each ASM that carries an FPGA has to be configured by an application specific data stream that determines the function of the device. In order to utilize dynamic reconfiguration (i.e. during runtime) it is necessary to minimize this reconfiguration time, therefor the configuration algorithms have been implemented in hardware. Reconfiguration of an ASM can be started by the host computer, another PCI bus device or by another ASM. Thus, it is possible that an FPGA autonomously reconfigures itself by configuration data that is located anywhere in the system. Due to the hardware implementation of the reconfiguration algorithm, a Xilinx Virtex 1000 FPGA can be completely reconfigured within less than 20 ms. The configuration algorithm implemented into the hardware also supports the partial reconfiguration of the system [9].

For the simulation of self-organizing feature maps the module DB-VS has been designed for the RAPTOR2000 system. This ASM embodies an FPGA of the Xilinx Virtex (-E) series and optionally up to 128 MBytes of SDRAM. The ASM can be equipped with various chips, that emulate circuits with a complexity of 400,000 to 4 million system gates. The SDRAM controller is integrated into the FPGA logic. A photo of the RAPTOR2000 system with two DB-VS modules is shown in figure 2. In the context of this paper we focus on the implementation of self-organizing feature maps on RAPTOR2000. Because of the flexibility of the system many other neural and conventional algorithms may be mapped to

Fig. 2. Photo of the RAPTOR2000 system with two ASMs of type DB-VS

the system. As another example for neural networks we have analyzed the implementation of neural associative memories on the RAPTOR2000 system [10]. Another case study focuses on the implementation of octree based 3D graphics [11]. To accelerate an octree based CAD tool, the most time consuming algorithms have been implemented in several hardware configurations. Depending on the algorithm, that is actually required by the user, the appropriate hardware configuration is downloaded to the RAPTOR2000 system during runtime.

4 Implementing Self-Organizing Maps on RAPTOR2000

Self-organizing maps as proposed by Kohonen [4] use an unsupervised learning algorithm to form a nonlinear mapping from a given high dimensional input space to a lower dimensional (in most cases two-dimensional) map of neurons. Our goal is to find an efficient implementation on state of the art FPGAs that, on the one hand delivers the required high performance and, on the other hand, fits into the limited resources of current FPGAs. Because of their internal structure FPGAs seem to be very well suited for the implementation of neural networks. Previous work of the authors concerning highly optimized ASIC implementations of self-organizing maps has emphasized, that avoiding memory bottlenecks by using on-chip memory is a must in order to achieve optimal performance [12]. We use XILINX Virtex FPGAs for our implementations, because these devices come with large internal SRAM blocks that can be used for internal weight storage.

In order to limit the hardware requirements for the implementation, the original SOM-algorithm has been simplified. In particular the Manhattan distance is used for calculating the distance between the input vector and the model vectors to avoid multiplications as required for the euclidean distance (which is typically used in SOM implementations). The internal precision is set to 16 bit and the accuracy of the input vector components and of the model vectors is set to eight bit. Restricting the values of the neighborhood function to negative powers of two gives us the opportunity to replace the multiplications that are required for adaptation by shift operations. Of cause these simplifications do not come for free (e.g. the convergence time may increase in some cases), but it has been shown that the simplified algorithm is well suited for a lot of applications [13]. Furthermore the actual generation of Xilinx FPGAs (Virtes II) comes with integrated multipliers and our implementations on these chips will thus be able to use euclidean distance instead of manhattan distance with no loss in performance.

Data pre- and postprocessing is a crucial and often ignored aspect in neurocomputer design. The use of reconfigurable hardware enables us to implement optimally fitting hardware implementations - not only for neural networks but also for pre- and postprocessing. As an example, we have integrated the main visualization techniques for self-organizing maps, that had to be performed in software so far, into hardware. The visualization of component maps and pattern position maps is supported as well as all kind of distance matrices like the U-Matrix. Implementing these algorithms in hardware dramatically reduces communication and thus enables a more efficient utilization of the hardware accelerator [14].

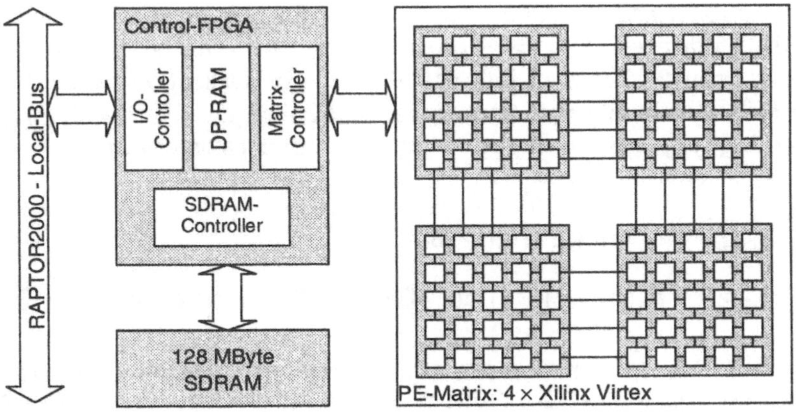

Fig. 3. Architecture of a hardware accelerator for self-organizing maps on the basis of the RAPTOR2000-system

Our SOM-implementation consists of processing elements that are working in SIMD-manner and that are controlled by an external controller. Nearly all calculations are performed in parallel on all processing elements. A bidirectional bus is used for data transfers to dedicated elements and for broadcasting data to groups of processor elements (or to all processor elements). Single elements and groups of elements are addressed by row and column lines that are connected to the two-dimensional matrix. The externally generated instructions are transferred to the processor elements via an additional control bus. Two more signals are used for status messages from and to the controller. The architecture is able to simulate virtual maps, i.e. it is possible to simulate maps that are larger than the array of processor elements that is implemented. Apart from the typical two dimensional grid of neurons, any other kind of network topology can be implemented (e.g. one dimensional or toroidal maps). Because the values for the adaptation factors are provided by an external controller, any adaptation function and neighborhood function may be realized with the proposed hardware (without any changes in the FPGA configuration).

In order to implement the proposed architecture on the RAPTOR2000 rapid prototyping system, five DB-VS modules are applied. Four ASMs are used to implement a matrix of processing elements while the fifth is used to implement the matrix controller, an I/O controller for the connection to the local bus of the RAPTOR2000 system and a dual port SRAM that is used to buffer input- and output-data. An integrated SDRAM interface controls the external 128 MBytes of SDRAM. The dual port SRAM is used to store single input vectors, commands from the host computer and the results (e.g. best match positions or postprocessed visualizations of the map). The large SDRAM is used to store one or more input data sets. During learning of a self-organizing map, the whole input data set has to be presented to the map for several times. Thus it is recommendable to transfer the whole data set in one fast block transfer via the PCI bus to the hardware accelerator in order to minimize the load of the PCI bus.

The design has been described in VHDL and synthesized using the Synopsys FPGA compiler and the Xilinx Alliance tools for place and route. Using Virtex XCV812E-6 devices, $N_{PE} = 70$ processing elements can be implemented, each equipped with 2 kBytes of internal SRAM. The utilization of the FPGAs is about 68%. The numbers of clock cycles that are required for recall (c_{recall}) and for learning (c_{adapt}) of an input vector with a dimension of l are:

$$c_{recall,v} = n_v \cdot (l + 2 \cdot \lceil \mathrm{ld}(l \cdot 255) \rceil + 4) \tag{1}$$

$$c_{adapt,v} = n_v \cdot (2 \cdot l + 2 \cdot \lceil \mathrm{ld}(l \cdot 255) \rceil + 12); \qquad \text{with} \quad n_v \leq \left\lfloor \frac{l_{max}}{l} \right\rfloor$$

The variable n_v is the number of neurons, that is emulated by one processing element. Using Virtex XCV812E-6 devices, a clock frequency of 65 MHz has been achieved for the FPGAs. The maximum performance is achieved, if every processing element represents one neuron ($n_v = 1$). In this case about $P_{C,r} = 17500$ MCPS (Million Connections per Second) can be achieved with

Table 1. Number of processing elements, maximum vector dimension and performance of the proposed implementation of self-organizing feature maps on various FPGAs of the Xilinx Virtex series

Device	N_{PE}	l_{max}	f_{FPGA} [MHz]	$P_{C,r}$ [MCPS]	$P_{C,l}$ [MCUPS]	Utilization of Slices
XCV1000-6	64	256	50	2835	326	48%
XCV812E-6	70	2048	65	4465	495	68%
XCV2000E-6	160	512	65	9735	1098	77%
XCV3200E-6	208	512	65	12655	1427	59%
XC2V6000-6	288	1024	105	29084	3244	78%
XC2V10000-6	384	1024	105	38914	4340	58%

the proposed architecture (consisting of five DB-VS modules) during recall and $P_{C,l} = 2000$ MCUPS during learning. Simulating larger maps by emulating more than one neuron with each processing element, the performance decreases. Using a benchmark data set with a vector dimension of $l = 9$, maps with up to 250×250 Neurons can be simulated with a performance of $P_{C,r} = 4400$ MCPS and $P_{C,l} = 665$ MCUPS, respectively. For the calculation of the performance $P_{C,l}$ during learning, only those neurons are taken into account, that are updated during learning. In [15] it has been shown, that the number of neurons that are updated during learning is approximately 22% for typical learning parameters. With an optimized software implementation on a state of the art personal computer (AMD Athlon, 1 GHz) only a performance of 85 MCPS and 22 MCUPS can be achieved for this problem.

Apart from the described Xilinx XCV812E devices, other FPGAs with BG560 package may be used on DB-VS. Xilinx Virtex devices may be used as well as Virtex E devices. The design has been synthesized to different Xilinx devices leading to a maximum performance of more than 50 GCPS and 5,7 GCUPS on Xilinx XCV3200E-6 devices. Currently we are developing a new ASM that incorporates an FPGA of the new Xilinx Virtex II series.

Table 1 shows the number of processing elements and the maximum vector dimension that can be achieved with some typical devices of the Xilinx Virtex family (using only one Xilinx device). An important design aspect was the optimal utilization of the embedded SRAM blocks in order to be able to simulate maps as large as possible. Because of different ratios of logic blocks to SRAM blocks the maximum vector dimension l_{max} changes between the different devices. In all examined cases the resulting utilization of logic blocks was small enough to enable synthesis to the clock frequency that is given in table 1 (An increase in device utilization normally leads to a decrease in the achievable clock frequency). The implementation on Xilinx Virtex-II FPGAs is not yet realized (the presented data is based on synthesis results) and does not take into account the special features of these FPGAs (like integrated multipliers). The final performance, that will be achieved with these devices will thus be even larger than the values presented here.

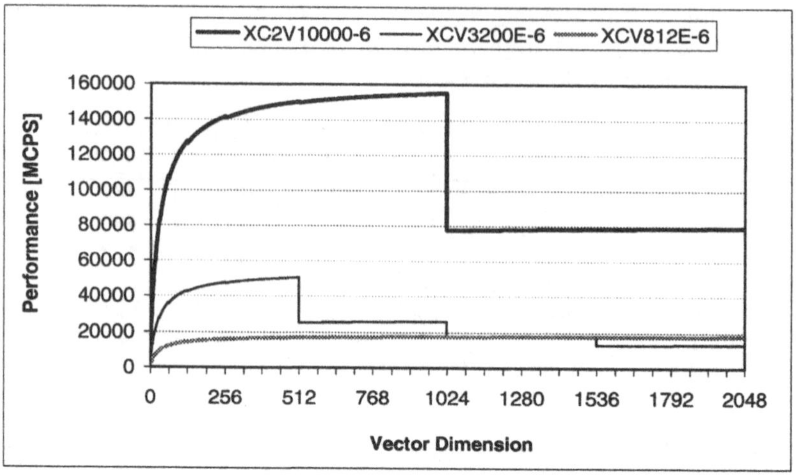

Fig. 4. Performance that can be achieved with the proposed system, composed of five DB-VS modules, for different Xilinx devices

The performance data that is given in table 1 is based on the assumption that the size of the simulated neural network is identical to the number of neurons and the vector dimension is maximal. Figure 4 shows the performance that can be achieved with the proposed system, composed of five DB-VS modules, during recall for different Xilinx Virtex devices. For the performance estimation it has been assumed, that for a given vector dimension the size of the simulated map is set to the maximum possible size. Performance increases until the maximum vector dimension for the particular FPGA, that is given in table 1, is reached. Larger vector dimensions are implemented by reconfiguring the FPGA for large vector dimensions with less processing elements and thus with smaller performance.

5 Conclusion

A dynamically reconfigurable hardware accelerator for the simulation of self-organizing feature maps has been presented. Equipped with five FPGA modules, the system achieves a maximum performance of more than 50 GCPS (Giga Connections per Second) during recall and more than 5 GCUPS (Giga Connection Updates per Second) during learning. Even higher performance numbers can be achieved by using new FPGA architectures like the Xilinx Virtex-II series. Apart from the high performance the system is capable of doing pre- and postprocessing tasks – either by use of the implemented visualization features or by dynamically reconfiguring the devices during runtime. The latter is supported by the RAPTOR2000 rapid prototyping system by means of the ability to reconfigure the FPGAs very fast via the PCI bus.

6 Acknowledgement

This work has been partly supported by the Deutsche Forschungsgemeinschaft (German Research Council) DFG Graduate Center "Parallele Rechnernetzwerke in der Produktionstechnik".

References

1. Glesner, M., Pochmüller, W.: "Neurocomputers: An Overview of Neural Networks in VLSI", Chapman Hall, 1994.
2. Rückert, U.: "ULSI Implementations for Artificial Neural Networks", 9th Euromicro Workshop on Parallel and Distr. Processing 2001, Feb. 7-9, 2001, Mantova, Italien, pp. 436–442.
3. Ienne, P.: "Digital Connectionist Hardware: Current Problems and Future Challenges", Biological and Artificial Computation: From Neuroscience to Technology, Vol. 1240 of Lecture Notes in Computer Science, pp. 688–713, 1997, Springer, Berlin.
4. Kohonen, T.: Self-Organizing Maps. Springer-Verlag, Berlin, (1995).
5. Goser, K., Marks, K.-M., Rückert, U., "Selbstorganisierende Parameterkarten zur Prozeßüberwachung und -voraussage", Informatik-Fachberichte Nr. 227, 1989, pp. 225–237, Springer, München.
6. Rüping, S., Müller, J.: "Analysis of IC Fabrication Processing using Self-Organizing Maps", Proc. of ICANN'99, Edinburgh, 7.-10. Sept. 1999, pp. 631–636.
7. Neema, S., Bapty, T., Scott, J.: "Adaptive Computing and Runtime Reconfiguration", 2nd Military and Aerospace Applications of Programmable Devices and Technologies Conference, MAPLD99, Laurel, Maryland, USA, September 1999.
8. Tinós, R., Terra, M. H.: "Fault detection and isolation in robotic manipulators and the radial basis function network trained by Kohonen's SOM". In Proc. of the 5th Brazilian Symposium on Neural Networks (SBRN98), Belo Horizonte, Brazil, pp. 85–90, 1998.
9. Porrmann, M., Kalte, H., Witkowski, U., Niemann, J.-C., Rückert, U.: "A Dynamically Reconfigurable Hardware Accelerator for Self-Organizing Feature Maps", Proc. of SCI 2001 Orlando, Florida USA, 22.-25. Juli, 2001, pp. 242–247.
10. Porrmann, M., Witkowski, U., Kalte, H., Rückert, U.: "Implementation of Artificial Neural Networks on a Reconfigurable Hardware Accelerator", 10th Euromicro Workshop on Parallel, Distributed and Network-based Processing (PDP 2002), 9.-11. Januar 2002, Gran Canaria Island, Spain.
11. Kalte, H., Porrmann, M., Rückert, U.: "Using a Dynamically Reconfigurable System to Accelerate Octree Based 3D Graphics", PDPTA'2000, June 26-29, 2000 Monte Carlo Resort, Las Vegas, Nevada, USA, pp. 2819–2824.
12. Porrmann, M., Rüping, S., Rückert, U.: "The Impact of Communication on Hardware Accelerators for Neural Networks", Proc. of SCI 2001 Orlando, Floriada USA, 22.-25. Juli 2001, pp. 248–253.
13. Rüping, S., Porrmann, M., Rückert, U., "SOM Accelerator System", Neurocomputing 21, pp. 31–50, 1998.
14. Porrmann, M., Rüping, S., Rückert, U., "SOM Hardware with Acceleration Module for Graphical Representation of the Learning Process", Proc. of the 7th Int. Conference on Microelectronics for Neural, Fuzzy and Bio-Inspired Systems, pp. 380–386, Granada, Spain, 1999.
15. Porrmann, M.: "Leistungsbewertung eingebetteter Neurocomputersysteme", Phd thesis, University of Paderborn, System and Circuit Technology, 2001.

A Compilation Framework for a Dynamically Reconfigurable Architecture

Raphael David[1], Daniel Chillet[1], Sebastien Pillement[1], and Olivier Sentieys[1,2]

[1] LASTI - University of Rennes I, 6, rue de kerampont, F-22300 Lannion, France
name@enssat

[2] INRIA / IRISA, Campus de Beaulieu, F-35042 Rennes cedex, France
sentieys@irisa.fr

Abstract. In addition to high performance requirements, future generation mobile telecommunications brings new constraints to the semiconductor design world. In order to associate the flexibility to the high-performances and the low-energy consumption needed by this application domain we have developed a functional level dynamically reconfigurable architecture, DART. Even if this architecture supports the processing complexity of the UMTS while allowing the portability of the devices and their evolutions, another challenge is to develop efficient high-level design tools. In this paper, we discuss about a methodology allowing the definition of such development tool based on the joint used of compilation and behavioral synthesis schemes.

1 Introduction

Moreover the high performance requirements inherent to multimedia processings or to access technics such as the W-CDMA (Wide-band Code Division Multiple Access), a data processing sequence of third generation brings new constraints to the semiconductor design world. In fact, the success of the Universal Mobile Telecommunication System (UMTS) will be linked to a greater flexibility of the standard than that of the current generation mobile networks such as the Global System for Mobile Communication (GSM) or the north American Interim-Standard(IS)-95.

Hence, UMTS must be able to support various standards and algorithms, for each kind of processing, and their evolutions as well as the integration of new services which still have to be imagined. For example, a speech signal can be coded according to the GSM norm with an Enhanced Full Rate (EFR) coder but also with a more powerful and adaptative AMR (Adaptative Multi Rate) coder, which is recommended for third generation telecommunications. Moreover, from an architectural point of view, a multimedia terminal will successively have to ensure the execution of very different applications in terms of calculation and data access patterns, and which handles various data types. For example, a Viterbi coder working at the bit-level could follow an MPEG coder working on 8-bit data. These processing modifications are then much more problematics

M. Glesner, P. Zipf, and M. Renovell (Eds.): FPL 2002, LNCS 2438, pp. 1058–1067, 2002.

since it will be necessary, in order to be efficient, to dynamically adapt the architecture to these changes.

Traditionally, signal applications are implemented in hardware or in software. Hardware implementations are based on the use of dedicated piece of silicon which are optimized for one application (ASIC) or eventually one set of applications (ASIP). These solutions allow to support the processings in a very efficient way and the designer may optimize its design in area, time, power or even a combination of these three parameters. On the other hand, software implementations are not limited to few applications since they use a programmable processor which may support every kinds of processing. This flexibility is however obtained at the price of a large amount of energy and performance waste since, to be generic, a programmable processor has to integrate a lot of resources that will, most of the time, not be used during the execution.

Between these two kinds of implementations, a third way has been proposed by FPGAs. This kind of architecture allows to optimize the circuit for one type of application but, if the processing has to be changed, the circuit can be reconfigured, in some milliseconds, to be fitted to these new computation patterns. This solution allows new trade-off between performance, energy consumption and flexibility. However, even if it can be attractive for numerous applications, its flexibility (limited by the time of the reconfiguration) and its performances (limited by the extra-cost introduced for the genericity of the architecture) prohibits its use for high complexity tasks or for those that successively have to execute different calculation patterns. Hence, the concept of reconfigurable architectures has evolved in order to allow some far more quick reconfigurations while offering a very high-level of performance and consuming very few energy [1],[2].

Within the scope of the next generation mobile telecommunication systems, we have developed the DART architecture that is reconfigurable at the functional level. It deals with previously mentioned constraints by associating high-performance, flexibility and low-energy consumption [3]. This architecture will be quickly described in the next section in order to exhibit its programming model. Since the calculation power of DART will be exploited only if efficient high-level design tools can be developed, we defined a simple programming model during the design of DART. The development flow, based on the joint use of compilation and behavioral synthesis schemes, will be presented in the section 3. This paper will finally be concluded by discussing about the work in progress and the work to come.

2 The DART Architecture

Since DART is to be embedded in portable multimedia devices, it has to deal with very different applications in terms of granularity, calculation patterns or timing constraints. Hence, this architecture has been broken up into clusters that may work independently the one with the others. This allows the partitioning of the application into distinct tasks (image processing, speech coding, W-CDMA) which may be computed concurrently on different clusters. In order to ensure the cluster independence, each one of them have its own controller and its own storage resources. Thanks to this hierarchical organization, some time and energy efficient interconnect networks can have been designed inside the clusters and between them.

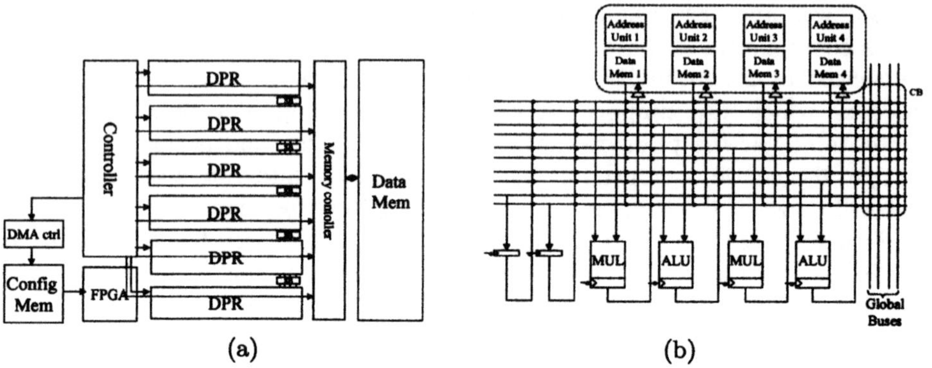

Fig. 1. Cluster (a) and DPR (b) architecture of DART

In the highest abstraction level of DART, a task controller have to distribute the tasks (and hence the configurations) to the clusters according to urgency and resource availability constraints. These reconfigurations are translated, at the cluster level (figure 1(a)), into modifications of the cluster controller program et by cluster internal data memory loading. The cluster controller program is constituted of configuration sequences, dynamically distributed towards two kind of targets: Reconfigurable DataPath (DPR) and FPGA. In fact, in order to have some calculation resources able to be in adequacy with every kind of processings we have integrated this two calculation primitives. The FPGA will be used for the bit-level manipulations which can be found in low-level processings such as the channel coding while the DPRs will be used for the arithmetic processings. Each DPR integrates one FPGA and 6 DPRs, as illustrated in figure 1(a). These DPRs are interconnected thanks to a segmented mesh network which allows some flexibility in their interconnection. According to the parallelism degree of the application to be implemented, the DPRs can be interconnected to compute it in a highly parallel fashion, or be disconnected to work independently on different threads.

Each DPRs (figure 1(b)) integrates 2 multipliers and 2 ALUs, interconnected according to a totally flexible interconnect network. These units are dynamically reconfigurable and are working on data stored in 4 local memories on top of which 4 local controllers are in charge of providing the addresses of the data handled inside the DPR. Moreover these 4 memories, 2 registers are also available in each DPR. These registers are particularly useful for data flow oriented applications where the different functional units are working on the same data flow but on samples delayed from one iteration to the following. In that case, these registers will be used to build a delay chain to share the data in the time and hence, to minimize the number of data memory accesses.

One of the main feature of DART is to support two DPR reconfiguration modes which ensues from the familiar 80-20 rule. This rule asserts that 80% of execution time is consumed by about 20% of a program code, that 20% usually being nested loops. In fact, during this 20% of regular program code a same calculation pattern is used during long periods of time. On the other hand, for the 80% of remaining irregular code, the calculation pattern is changing very often, eventually at each cycle. From these two types of processing, have resulted two types of reconfiguration.

2.1 Hardware Reconfiguration

These configurations are used for a long time and are adapted to the regular processings such as loop kernels. Since their modifications are very occasional, they can require a large amount of data without disturbing the execution of the entire processing. Hence, in that case, a total flexibility of the DPR will be ensured thanks to 4 52-bit instructions.

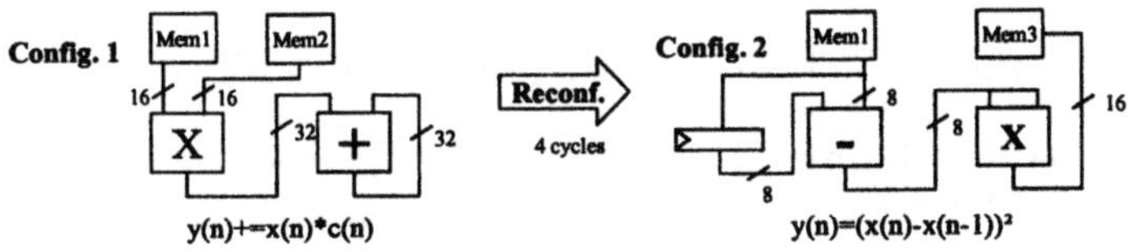

Fig. 2. Hardware reconfiguration

This kind of configuration can for example be illustrated by the figure 2. In this figure, the datapath is optimized at first in order to compute a filtering based on Multiply-ACcumulate operations. Once this configuration has been specified, the computation model is of dataflow type and no other instruction memory readings are done during the filtering. At the end of the computation, after a reconfiguration step which needs 4 cycles, a new datapath is specified in order to be in adequacy with the calculation of the square of the difference between x(n) and x(n -1). Once again, no control is necessary to conclude this computation.

2.2 Software Reconfiguration

For irregular processings that need to change the configuration of the DPRs at each cycle without particular order and in a non repetitive way, a software reconfiguration is used. In order to be able to reconfigure the DPR in one cycle with an instruction of reasonable size, their flexibility has been limited. It has been decided to adopt a calculation pattern of *Read-Modify-Write* type, such as that of conventional DSP. In that case, for each operator useful for the execution, the data are red, computed, then the result is stored in the memory associated with this operator at each cycle.

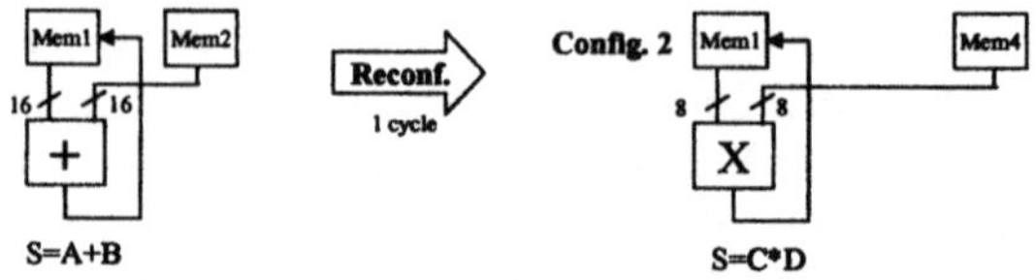

Fig. 3. Software reconfiguration

This software reconfiguration thus concerns only the functionality of the operators, the size of the data and their origin. Thanks to these flexibility limitations, the DPR may be reconfigured at each cycle with only one 52-bit instruction. This is illustrated on figure 3 which represents the reconfiguration needed to replace an addition on data stored in the memories 1 and 2 by a multiplication on data stored in memories 1 and 4.

2.3 Performance and Energy Efficiency of DART

A DART cluster have been synthesized with the *Synopsys* design tool framework with a 1.95V ST Microelectronic 0.18μm technology. Thanks to the DART simulator (see §3.5), the overall energy consumption of the architecture is evaluated from the activity of the different architectural modules (functional units, memories, glue-logic, ...) and their average energy consumption per access, estimated by *Design Power* with 10.000 test vectors randomly generated.

The synthesis leads to an operating frequency of 130 MHz. Running at 130MHz, DART is able to provide up to 1.56MMACS/cluster while consuming 0.34W which can be translated in a worst case energy efficiency of 9.2MIPS/mW. In fact, since an instruction includes an address generation, a memory access and up to 2 operations per multiplier (1 shift and 1 multiply(+saturate)) or 3 operations per ALU (2 shift + 1 ALU operation), this figure is equal to 32MOPS/mW @10.9GOPS. Practically, previous implementations from the application domain (DCT, autocorrelation, complex despreading [4]) show that DART provide between 11.6 and 16.7 MIPS for each mW consumed.

3 Development Flow

To exploit the computation power of DART, the conception of an efficient development flow is the key to enhance the status of the architecture. Hence, we develop a compilation framework based on the joint use of a front-end allowing the transformation and the optimisation of a C code, a retargetable compiler and a behavioral synthesis tool, as described in the figure 4. As in most development methodologies for reconfigurable hardware, the key of the problem has been to distinguish the different kinds of processing. In fact, this approach had already been used with success in the PICO (Program-In Chip-Out) project developed at HP labs in order to distinguish regular codes, implemented in systolic array, and irregular ones, executed in a VLIW processor [5]. Other related works such as the Pleiades project [6] or GARP [7] are also distinguishing regular processings and irregular ones to implement massively parallel processings on circuits respectively reconfigurable at the functional and at the gate level.

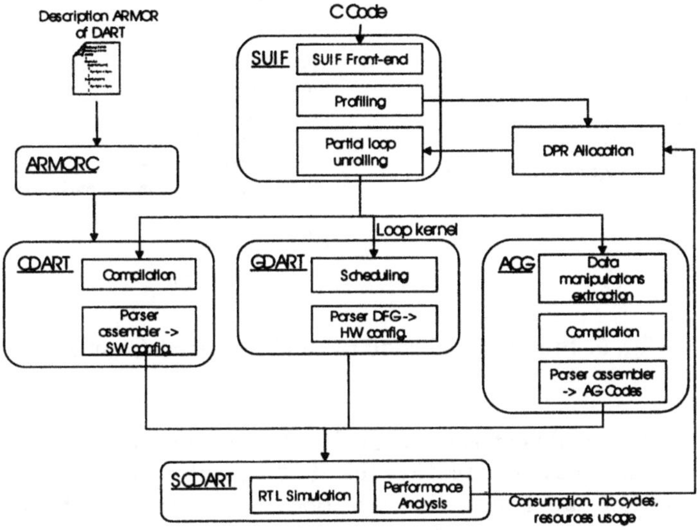

Fig. 4. DART Development flow

The development flow depicted in the figure 4 allows the user to describe its applications in C. These high-level descriptions are first translated into Control and Data Flow Graph (CDFG) from which some automatic transformations (loop unrolling, loop kernel extractions, ...) are done in order to optimize the execution times. After these transformations, the distinction between regular codes, irregular ones and data manipulations permits to translate, thanks to the compilation and the architectural synthesis, a high level description of the application into binary executable codes for DART.

3.1 The Suif Front-End

The Front-end of this development flow is based on the Suif [8] framework developed at Stanford. The main goal of this module is to generate a CDFG from which other modules can operate. Moreover, this module has to extract the loop kernels inside the C code. In fact, these loop kernels will be mapped as Hardware reconfigurations whereas the rest of the code will be implemented as Software reconfigurations and address generation instructions. For example, the C code of the figure 5(a) have to be translated into the modified C code of the figure 5(b) in order to bring to the fore the three kinds of processings of the task:

1. The irregular codes (x(n)=A.B; h(0)=B+D;) must be translated in Software reconfigurations by cDART (see §3.2);
2. The data manipulations (Mem1=x(i); Mem2=h(N-i-1); y(n)=Mem3;) must be translated in address generation instructions by ACG (see §3.4);
3. The loop kernels (Mem3=Mem3+Mem1*Mem2;) must be translated in Hardware reconfigurations by gDART (see §3.3).

```
x(0)=A*B;
h(0)=C+D;
For (i=0; i<N; i++)
        y(n)+=x(i)*h(N-i-1);
```

(a)

```
x(0)=A*B;
h(0)=C+D;
For (i=0;i<N;i++){
        Mem1=x(i);
        Mem2=h(N-i-1);
        Mem3=Mem3+Mem1*Mem2;
}
y(n)=Mem3
```

(b)

Fig. 5. Suif entry C code (a) and Modified C code (b)

Moreover these code extractions, Suif is also in charge of unrolling the nested loops. In fact, the only information that is transmitted to gDART is the loop kernel description and hence, this tool does not have any information about the parallelism degree of the application. Thus, to exploit the parallelism of an application, it must be extracted before the Hardware code generation. This is notably done by unrolling the loop. This unrolling depends on a module in charge of specifying the number of DPRs allocated to the application in the cluster. According to this information, Suif is thus able to establish the number of calculation units available in the cluster and so the unrolling order that can be realized. For example, on the previous pseudo FIR filter code, if 4 DPRs are allocated to the application, the loop will be unrolled by a factor of 8, in order to extract 8 multiplications and 8 additions.

3.2 Software Code Generation

In order to generate the Software reconfiguration instructions, we have integrated a compiler, cDART, into our development flow. This tool have been generated thanks to CALIFE [9] which is a retargetable compiler framework, developed inside the COSI project of the IRISA/INRIA, aiming at providing a compilation tool for a processor described in the ARMOR language.

In order to generate cDART, we first have to model DART in the ARMOR language. The main purpose of this step is to provide the informations needed by the flexible code generator. These informations come up from the inherent needs of the three main compiling activities which are the code selection, the allocation and the scheduling, and from the architectural mechanisms used by DART. It has to be noticed that the software reconfigurations implies some limitations about the DPRs flexibility and hence, the architecture subset concerned by this reconfiguration is very simple and orthogonal since it is constituted by 4 independent functional units working on 4 memories in a very flexible manner, i.e. there is no limitations about the use of the instruction parallelism.

The next step to generate cDART have been to translate the DART ARMOR description into a grammar able to analyze expression trees in the source code, thanks to the ARMORC tool. Finally, to built the compiler, the CALIFE framework allows us to choose the different compilation passes (e.g. code selection, resource allocation, scheduling, ...) that have to be implemented in cDART. In CALIFE, while the global compiler structure is defined by the user, module adaptations are automatically performed by the framework. Thus, thanks to this tool we have been able to generate a compiler optimized for DART, since each compiler structure efficiency can easily be checked and new compilation passes can quickly be added or subtracted from the global compiler structure.

3.3 Hardware Code Generation

If the software reconfiguration instructions can be generated thanks to classical compilation schemes, the hardware reconfiguration instructions have to be generated according to more specific synthesis tasks. In fact, as it has been said before, a hardware reconfiguration can be specified by a set of instructions that exhibit the DPRs structure. Hence, the tool developed, gDART, has to generate a DataPath in adequacy with the processings to be implemented during a loop. The entry point of this tool is thus a Data Flow Graph (DFG) representing the computation pattern that must be synthesized. The parallelism exhibition has been done during the Suif transformations and the only task that must be done by gDART is to find the datapath structure allowing the DFG implementation.

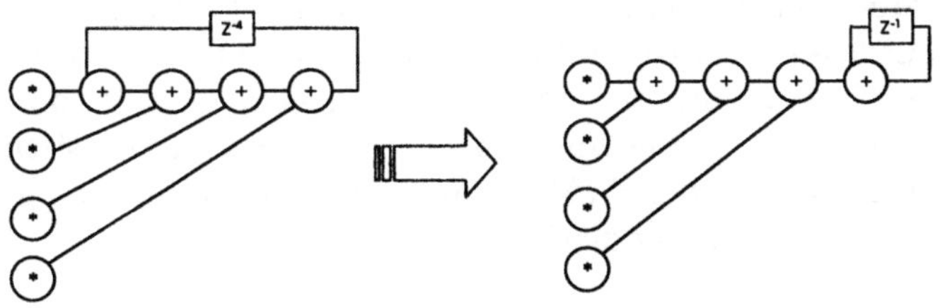

Fig. 6. Critical loop reduction

However, even if the DPR architecture is very flexible, it has some limitations. The main constraint to schedule the DFG is that it is impossible to share intermediate results between several cycles. Thus, the critical loops must be computed in one cycle. This problem can be illustrated by the FIR filter DFG represented on the figure 6 and mainly concerns the accumulations. In this particular case, the solution is to transform the DFG in order to reduce the critical loop timing to an only one cycle by swapping the additions. This solution can be generalized by swapping the operations of a critical loop according to the associativity and distributivity rules associated to the operators.

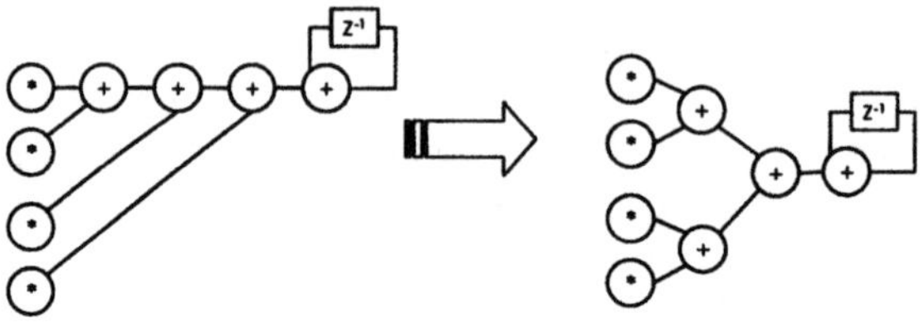

Fig. 7. DFG optimization

Moreover, the figure 7 shows a quite high latency of execution pipeline and if the iteration number of innermost loop is small, this feature is quite prejudicial. Hence, another scheduling algorithm has been developed in order to exploit the implementation parallelism and to obtain the DFG represented on figure 7. Thanks to this new algorithm, execution pipeline can now be filled in only 4 cycles while 5 cycles was previously needed. If unrolling factor is extended to 8, latency will be decreased more drastically from 10 cycles to 5 cycles.

3.4 Address Code Generation

if gDART and cDART allow the definition of the datapath, they do not take into consideration the data supplying. Hence, a third tool, ACG (Address Code Generator), has been developed in order to obtain the address generation instructions which will be executed on the address generators of each DPRs [3]. Since the address generators architecture is similar to a small RISC (a small controller manage a datapath built around a register file and an ALU), the generation of these instructions can be done by classical compilation steps thanks to CALIFE. The entry of the compiler is this time a subset of the initial entry code (Mem1=x(i), Mem2=h(N-i-1) and y(n)=Mem3 on the figure 5) which corresponds to the data manipulations.

3.5 Simulation

The different configurations of DART can be validated thanks to a bit-true and cycle-true simulator (SCDART), developed in SystemC. This simulator also generates some informations about the performance and the energy efficiency of the implementation realized. In order to have a good relative accuracy, the DART modeling have been done at the Register Transfer Level and each operator has been characterized by an average energy consumption per access. These energy consumption figures are coming from logical synthesis realized with *Synopsys* and from gate level consumption estimations realized via *Design Power* with randomly generated test vectors.

4 Conclusion

In this paper we have presented a dynamically reconfigurable architecture, which aim at supporting the next generation telecommunication constraints, and its associated development methodology. We have first verified that this architecture is in adequacy with our application domain then we have focused on the development tools. Since this architecture exhibits a quite simple execution model we have been able to partition the methodology into reasonable complexity tasks that are issued from compilation and behavioral synthesis tools. Hence, by discussing about 5 modules, from which some are still in development (ACG, cDART), we have described the overall methodology. The next step in our study is thus to complete the specification of this development tools, to validate it, and to study the system architecture of DART that will support a Real-Time Operating System.

References

[1] Rabaey, J.: Reconfigurable Processing : The Solution To Low-Power Programmable DSP. In: IEEE International Conference on Accoustics, Speech and Signal Processing (ICASSP). (1997)

[2] Hartenstein, R.: A Decade of Reconfigurable Computing : A Visionary retrospective. In: Design Automation and Test in Europe (DATE). (2001)

[3] David, R., Chillet, D., Pillement, S., Sentieys, O.: DART : A Dynamically Reconfigurable Architecture dealing with Next Generation Telecommunications Constraints. In: RAW. (2002)

[4] David, R., Chillet, D., Pillement, S., Sentieys, O.: Mapping Future Generation Mobile Telecommunication Applications on a Dynamically Reconfigurable Architecture. In: ICASSP. (2002)

[5] Schreiber, R., Aditya, S., al.: PICO-NPA : High-Level Synthsis of NonProgrammable Hardware Accelerators. Technical Report HPL-2001-249, Hewlett-Packard Labortories (2001)

[6] Wan, M.: Design Methodology for Low Power Heterogeneous Digital Signal Processors. PhD thesis, Berkeley Wireless Design Center (2001)

[7] Hauser, J.: Augmenting a microprocessor with reconfigurable hardware. PhD thesis, University of California, Berkeley (2000)

[8] Wilson, R., al.: SUIF : An Infrastructure for Research on Parallelizing and Optimizing Compilers. Technical report, Computer Systems Laboratory, Stanford University (1994)

[9] Charot, F., Messe, V.: A Flexible Code Generation Framework for the Design of Application Specific Programmable Processors. In: International Symposium on Hardware/Software Co-design (CODES). (1999)

Data Dependent Circuit for Subgraph Isomorphism Problem

Shuichi Ichikawa and Shoji Yamamoto

Department of Knowledge-based Information Engineering
Toyohashi University of Technology
1-1 Tempaku, Toyohashi, Aichi 441-8580, JAPAN
ichikawa@tutkie.tut.ac.jp
http://meta.tutkie.tut.ac.jp/~ichikawa/index-e.html

Abstract. The subgraph isomorphism problem has various important applications, although it is generally NP-complete and difficult to solve. This paper examines the feasibility of a data dependent circuit for the subgraph isomorphism problem, which is particularly suitable for FPGA implementation. For graphs of 32 vertices, the average logic scale of data dependent circuits is only 5% of the corresponding data independent circuit. The circuit is estimated to be 460 times faster than the software for 32 vertices. Even if the circuit generation time is included, a data dependent circuit is expected to be two times faster than software when there are 32 vertices. For larger graphs, the performance gain would be far larger.

1 Subgraph Isomorphism Problem

The subgraph isomorphism problem is a simple decision problem. Given two graphs G_α and G_β, it is determined whether G_α is isomorphic to any subgraph of G_β. For example, see Figure 1. In this figure, G_β has a subgraph that is isomorphic to G_α, while G_γ does not.

The subgraph isomorphism problem has many applications, including scene analysis in computer vision and search operation in chemical structural formula database. However, the subgraph isomorphism problem is generally NP-complete [1] and computationally difficult to solve.

To solve the subgraph isomorphism problem practically, several algorithms have been proposed. Ullmann [2] proposed a depth first search algorithm with a

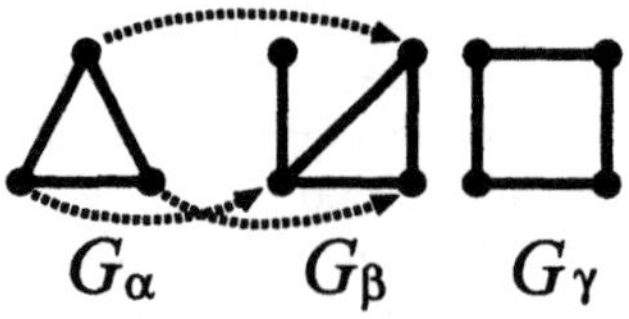

Fig. 1. Subgraph Isomorphism

M. Glesner, P. Zipf, and M. Renovell (Eds.): FPL 2002, LNCS 2438, pp. 1068–1071, 2002.

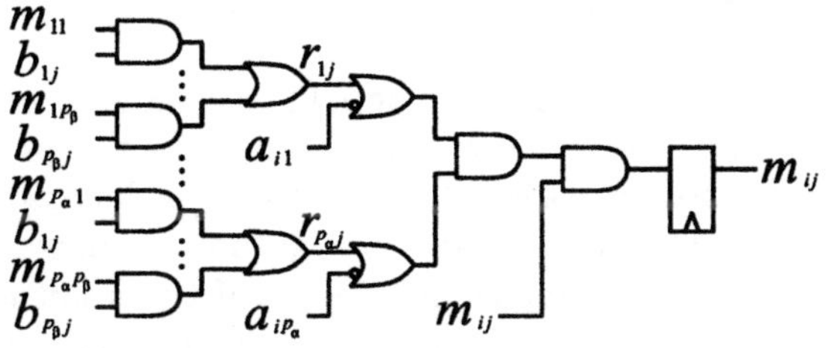

Fig. 2. Element Circuit for Refinement Procedure

smart pruning procedure (*refinement procedure*), which is now the most popular and frequently used algorithm for this problem.

2 Custom Circuit for Subgraph Isomorphism Problem

Ullmann pointed out that his refinement procedure can be implemented with asynchronous hardware [2]. Let p_α and p_β be the number of vertices of graph G_α and G_β, respectively. The adjacency matrices of graph G_α and G_β are represented as $A = [a_{ij}]\,(1 \leq i, j \leq p_\alpha)$ and $B = [b_{ij}]\,(1 \leq i, j \leq p_\beta)$. The temporary matrix $M = [m_{ij}]\,(1 \leq i \leq p_\alpha, 1 \leq j \leq p_\beta)$ is also used in the refinement procedure. Figure 2 illustrates the element circuit to calculate m_{ij}, which was proposed by Ullmann [2]. The whole circuit includes a $p_\alpha \times p_\beta$ array of this element circuit, which requires $O(p_\alpha {p_\beta}^2)$ logic gates. Experimental evaluations revealed, however, the fact that the Ullmann circuit requires too many logic gates for FPGA [3].

In this paper, we examine the data dependent implementation of the Ullmann circuit, which drastically reduces the number of logic gates. Generally, the circuit can be reduced if any input of the logic circuit is set to a constant. This reduction can be recursively applied. Therefore, a data dependent circuit can be smaller than a data *independent* circuit for the same function. Smaller circuits usually work at a higher frequency, and thus can be faster. A data dependent circuit would be more cost-effective, because it is smaller (thus cheaper) and faster than a data independent circuit.

Data dependent circuits are well suited for FPGA implementation due to their nature. On the other hand, the evident problem is that a circuit must be designed (or generated) for each input instance. Hence, the time for logic synthesis, mapping, placement and routing is also important, along with the execution time itself.

For computationally difficult problems such as subgraph isomorphism, the execution time for larger problems grows very quickly. As we show later, the circuit generation time could be inferior and negligible compared to the execution time. This is one of the reasons the authors considered a data dependent approach for computationally difficult problems.

3 Design Approaches

First of all, the original Ullmann circuit should be evaluated as a basis for further evaluation. The VHDL source code was taken from the previous project [3], which is detailed in another paper [4]. This design is denoted "INDEP" in this paper, because it is independent from input graph instances.

Next, we examine a data dependent design. If the input graph G_α is fixed, each a_{ij} in Figure 2 becomes constant. That is, we can replace a_{ij} with the corresponding constants in VHDL source code. At the same time, we can remove the flipflops to store the adjacency matrix A. Once a_{ij} is replaced by a constant, unnecessary logic gates are automatically reduced by logic synthesis software. It is all the same when fixing the adjacency matrix B. We will obtain a maximum reduction when both A and B are fixed.

Though it is easy and natural to leave logic reduction for the logic synthesis system, it takes much memory and execution time. As we mainly need simple and problem-specific optimization, we can manage a substantial part of the reduction in the source code generation phase. This preprocessing drastically reduces the total circuit generation time. Let us denote this design process, in which both input graphs are fixed, by "BOTH2".

4 Evaluation

Each of the results shown in this section is the average value of 50 pairs of G_α and G_β, which are randomly generated trees. Trees were chosen for inputs because they are the sparsest connected graphs. To reduce simulation parameters, $p_\alpha = p_\beta$ is also assumed in simulations. It would be better to investigate dense graphs, disconnected graphs, and the graphs of $p_\alpha < p_\beta$, but these are left for future studies.

Logic synthesis was performed by Synopsys FPGA Compiler II on a Duron 800 MHz PC. Mapping to Lucent OR2C FPGA was done with ORCA Foundry 9.4a on a Pentium II 450 MHz PC. In this study, we did not try the placement and routing. Software implementation of Ullmann's algorithm was evaluated on a Pentium III 600 MHz PC for comparison.

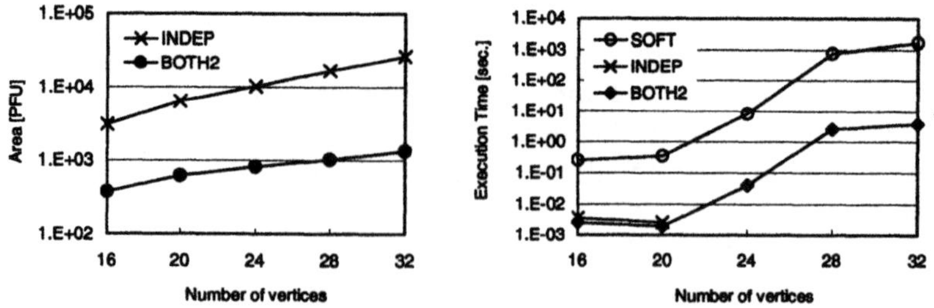

Fig. 3. Logic Scale (Left) and Execution Time (Right)

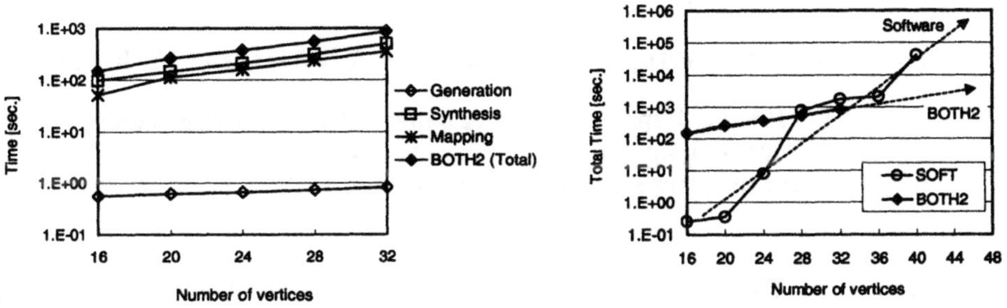

Fig. 4. Circuit Generation Time (Left) and Total Processing Time (Right)

Figure 3 (left) summarizes the logic scale, which is taken from the synthesis report. The logic scale is measured by the number of PFU (programmable function unit) of OR2C FPGA. The logic scale of BOTH2 is only 12%–5% that of INDEP for 16–32 vertices. Greater reduction is expected for larger graphs. Figure 3 (right) shows the expected execution time, which was estimated by the cycle count derived from the simulator and the operational frequency derived from the mapping report. SOFT denotes the software execution time, and BOTH2 denotes the estimated execution time of BOTH2 hardware. The acceleration ratio is 99–460 for 16–32 vertices. The ratio becomes larger in larger graphs.

Figure 4 (left) shows the details of circuit generation time in BOTH2. Circuit generation time grows gradually, and the execution time is negligible compared to generation time. Figure 4 (right) compares the total time (generation + execution) of a data dependent circuit to the software execution time. The data dependent circuit is faster for 28-vertice or larger graphs. The performance advantage would be greater for larger graphs.

Acknowledgment

This work was partially supported by a Grant-in-Aid for Scientific Research from the Japan Society for the Promotion of Science (JSPS) and a grant from the Telecommunications Advancement Foundation (TAF).

References

[1] Garey, M.R., Johnson, D.S.: Computers and Intractability. Freeman (1979)
[2] Ullmann, J.R.: An algorithm for subgraph isomorphism. J. ACM **23** (1976) 31–42
[3] Ichikawa, S., Saito, H., Udorn, L., Konishi, K.: Evaluation of accelerator designs for subgraph isomorphism problem. In: Proc. 10th Int'l Conf. Field-Programmable Logic and Applications (FPL2000). LNCS1896, Springer (2000) 729–738
[4] Saito, H.: A study on hardware implementation of Ullmann's algorithm. Master's thesis, Dept. Knowledge-based Information Engineering, Toyohashi University of Technology (2000) (in Japanese).

Exploration of Design Space in ECDSA

Jan Schmidt, Martin Novotný, Martin Jäger, Miloš Bečvář, and Michal Jáchim

CTU FEE Prague, Department of Computer Science and Engineering
Karlovo nám. 13, 121 35 Praha 2, Czech Republic
[schmidt|novotnym|xjager|becvarm|xjachim]@fel.cvut.cz

Abstract. The paper compares FPGA implementation of scaled polynomial basis and normal basis arithmetic units in the context of cryptographic coprocessor performing operations on elliptic curve points with coordinates in $GF(2^m)$. The hardware uses GCD division in polynomial basis and Itoh-Teechai-Tsujii inversion in normal basis. Where an optimal normal basis exists, the normal basis arithmetic performs better. The digit width of 6 is shown to give the best area/performance ratio for optimal normal basis arithmetic.

1 Introduction

Elliptic Curve Digital Signature Algorithm (ECDSA) with point coordinates in $GF(2^m)$ proved attractive for hardware implementations. Moreover, much shorter keys suffice for the same cryptographic strength as provided by the classic RSA.

Although ECDSA has been standardized [7], [1], there is still considerable degree of freedom in options such as key length, concrete elliptic curve used, or the field basis (poolynomial or normal), collectively called domain parameters. Even for a fixed set of domain parameters, multiple algorithms exist for operations required by ECDSA, offering different trade-offs between cost and performance.

This paper deals with one such trade-off. In normal bases, multiplication is more efficient than in polynomial bases. On the other hand, division in polynomial bases can be performed by the extended Euclidean algorithm [2], which takes less cycles than the Itoh-Tsujii algorithm [11], applicable to any basis. We are interested in the interaction of these choices in a realistic context, that is, in an elliptic curve processor implemented in an FPGA.

After a brief review of previous work and algorithms, we present the design of elliptic processor and the arithmetic units to describe the context of the study. Quantitative results of implementations for multiple key width follow together with their discussion and implementation.

2 Previous Work

For an overview of software implementations, please refer to [4]. The implementations using normal basis ([3], [10]) and polynomial basis ([9] and [8]) seem to

M. Glesner, P. Zipf, and M. Renovell (Eds.): FPL 2002, LNCS 2438, pp. 1072–1075, 2002.

be equally frequent. Closest to our work is the implementation of Orlando and Paar [8], which combines Itoh-Tsujii inversion with polynomial basis multiplication, and therefore would form an useful third apex to the two approaches studied here. Unfortunately, projective coordinates have been used as opposed to affine coordinates in that study.

3 Design of the Processor

The tested elliptic curve coprocessor implements scalar multiplication (by the add-and-double algorithm), addition and doubling of points on an elliptic curve over $GF(2^m)$. The points are represented by their affine coordinates. Field operations are performed in an arithmetic unit, which comes in two variants: one for normal basis and the other for polynomial basis representation. The processor works with fixed key length and basis. Configurations for different lengths are obtained from custom generators.

The polynomial basis unit consists of a squarer and a combined multiplication/division subunit. Division is done by the extended Euclidean algorithm [2] in a four-register structure. Three of the four registers also serve for a LSB-first mutiplier.

Multiplication in normal bases is computed using pipelined Massey-Omura multiplier [6] with digit width fixed by configuration. Inversion is done by the algorithm of Itoh, Teechai and Tsujii [11]. The multiplier is built around three sfift registers, with small number of data paths added to pass intermediate results during inversion, and three $\log m$-bit counters in the local controller.

The Itoh-Tsujii inversion algorithm calls for approximately $\log m$ exponentiations, by different exponents. As the actual exponents offer no opportunity for combining, the shifter would be in fact a multiplexer. implemented by $m(\log m - 1)$ two-input elements. A bit-serial Massey-Omura multiplier has $3m - 1$ two-input elements [5]. The time saved by the shifter is $O(m)$, but multiplication time is $O(m \log m)$. For m of interest in ECDSA, the shifter would be almost as large as the multiplier and the acceleration is not considered worth the additional area, which has been confirmed by implementation results. Therefore, the shifting ability of one of the three registers is also used for iterative squaring.

4 Implementation and Results

Xilinx Virtex XCV400E-8-PQ240 has been chosen for the implementation. Synthesis has been performed by Mentor Graphics Leonardo Spectrum 2001 and physical design by Xilinx ISE 4.1. The implementation results are presented in Table 1. Polynomial basis version (PB) with GCD inversion is compared to optimal normal basis version (ONB) with Itoh-Tsujii inversion (IT). The clock frequency has been obtained from static timing analysis of placed and routed designs. The area presented has been also measured on placed and routed design. The area $19.2m + 225$ and $11.4m + 0.54mD + 192$ for polynomial basis and optimal normal basis, respectively. Bit-serial ONB implementation has 63 %

Table 1. Performance and area of the processor

Basis	Inversion algorithm	m	D	Clock [MHz]	$P+Q$ [μs]	$2*P$ [μs]	$k*P$ [μs]	Total #slices	Arith. #slices
PB	GCD	162	1	74	6.6	4.4	1800	3343	1801
PB	GCD	180	1	81	8.2	4.5	2041	3660	1968
PB	GCD	210	1	88	8.8	6.1	2530	4267	2299
ONB	IT	162	1	113	17.9	16.3	5543	2128	586
ONB	IT	180	1	118	22.1	20.45	7662	2324	632
ONB	IT	210	1	103	27.3	25.10	11002	2701	733
ONB	IT	162	6	120	4.5	4.15	1404	2559	1017
ONB	IT	180	6	119	5.5	5.2	1934	2832	1140
ONB	IT	210	6	107	6.6	6.2	2691	3261	1293

area complexity of the polynomial one, while time complexity is 370 %. Digit-serial ONB implementation for digit size $D = 6$ has the same (94 %) speed as polynomial one, but it is smaller (77 %).

When scaling up the ONB multiplier, only the multiplication logic in the arithmetic unit actually scales. Although the design is quite minimal, the presence of parts that do not scale results in sub-linear growth of the whole arithmetic unit with D.

During that scale-up, the length of the critical path rose more slowly than expected. This can be attributed to timing-driven operation of both the synthesis and the physical design software.

Both these phenomena combined to give optimum area/performance trade-off at $D = 6$, where, incidentally, the area is close to that of the polynomial arithmetic.

It is apparent that the gain in cycle count obtained from GCD inversion can be compensated by scaling the polynomial multiplier. The Itoh-Tsujii inversion is expressed in terms of addition and multiplication. Therefore, it scales whenever the multiplier does.

5 Conclusions

The elliptic curve coprocessor has been implemented in FPGA. The processor has interchangeable arithmetic units, which enabled us to compare closely polynomial basis arithmetic and normal basis arithmetic. In all cases, inversion algorithm considered optimal for the particular arithmetic has been used.

For m where an optimal normal basis exist, the normal basis gives better results. To match the bit-serial polynomial basis multiplier in area, the digit width of $D = 6$ has to be used. This is also optimal for the multiplier itself with respect to the area/performance ratio.

Besides the comparison, the viability of GCD inversion in hardware has also been confirmed.

The quantitative study is currently being extended to multiplication in suboptimal normal bases and digit-serial polynomial basis multiplication.

6 Acknowledgement

This work was partially supported by GAČR 102/99/1017 and the ASICentrum company.

References

1. *ANSI X9.62-1999 Public Key Cryptography For The Financial Services Industry: The Elliptic Curve Digital Signature Algorithm (ECDSA).* 1999
2. B. Brunner, A. Curiger, M. Hofstetter: *On Computing Multiplicative Inverses in* $GF(2^m)$. IEEE Transactions on Computers, vol. 42, pp. 1010-1015, 1993.
3. L.Gao, S.Shrivastava, G.Sobelman: *Elliptic curve scalar multiplier design using FPGAs.* In: C.Koc and C.Paar, editors, Workshop on Cryptographic Hardware and Embedded Systems (CHES'99), volume LNCS 1717. Springer-Verlag, August 1999
4. J.Lopez, R.Dahab: *Fast Multiplication on Elliptic Curves over* $GF(2^M)$ *without Precomputation.* In C.Koc and C.Paar, editors: Workshop on Cryptographic Hardware and Embedded Systems (CHES'99), vol. LNCS 1717, Springer-Verlag, August 1999
5. R. Mullin, I. Onyszchuk, S. Vanstone, R. Wilson: *Optimal Normal Bases in* $GF(p^n)$. Discrete Applied Mathematics, vol. 22, pp. 149–161, 1989.
6. Omura, J., Massey, J.: Computational Method and Apparatus for Finite Field Arithmetic. U.S. patent number 4,587,627, 1986
7. IEEE P1363 *Standard for Public-key Cryptography (Draft Version 8).* IEEE, October 1998
8. G.Orlando, Ch.Paar: *A High Performance Reconfigurable Elliptic Curve Processor for* $GF(2^M)$. Workshop on Cryptographic Hardware and Embedded Systems (CHES'00), volume LNCS 1965. Springer-Verlag, August 2000
9. M.Rosner: *Elliptic curve cryptosystems on reconfigurable hardware.* Master's thesis, ECE Dept., Worchester Polytechnic Institute, Worchester, USA, May 1998
10. S.Sutiknp, R.Effendi, and A.Surya: *Design and implementation of arithmetic processor* $GF(2^{155})$ *for elliptic curve cryptosystems..* In: The 1998 IEEE Asia-Pacific Conference on Circuits and Systems, pp 647-650, November 1998
11. T. Itoh, O. Teechai, S. Tsujii: *A Fast Algorithm for Computing Multiplicative Inverses in* $GF(2^t)$ *using normal bases.* J. Society for electronic Communications (Japan) 44 (1986), 31-36.

2D and 3D Computer Graphics Algorithms under MORPHOSYS

Issam Damaj, Suhaib Majzoub, and Hassan Diab

Department of Electrical and Computer Engineering
Faculty of Engineering and Architecture
American University of Beirut
P.O. Box 110236
Beirut, Lebanon
issamwd@ieee.org; s_majzoub@hotmail.com; diab@aub.edu.lb

Abstract. This paper presents new mappings of 2D and 3D geometrical transformation on the MorphoSys (M1) reconfigurable computing (RC) prototype [2]. This improves the system performance as a graphics accelerator [1-5]. Three algorithms are mapped including two for calculating 2D transformations, and one for 3D transformations. The results presented indicate an improved performance. The speedup achieved is explained as well as the advantages in the mapping of the application. The transformations on an 8x8 RC array were run, and numerical examples were simulated to validate our results, using the MorphoSys mULATE program, which simulates MorphoSys operations. Comparisons with other systems are presented, namely, with Intel processing systems and Celoxica RC-1000 FPGA.

1 Introduction

Reconfigurable computing (RC) is becoming more popular and increasing research efforts are being invested in it. It employs reconfigurable hardware and programmable processors. The application is mapped such that the workload is divided between the general-purpose processor and the reconfigurable device. The use of RC opens the way for an increased speed over general-purpose processors and a wider functionality than application specific integrated circuits (ASICs). It is a good solution for applications requiring a wide range of functionality and speed at the same time [1].

2 MorphoSys Design

One of the emerging RC systems includes the MorphoSys designed and implemented at the University of California, Irvine. It is composed of: 1) an array of reconfigurable cells called the RC array, 2) its configuration data memory called context memory, 3) a control processor (TinyRISC), 4) a data buffer called the frame buffer, and 5) a DMA controller [2].

M. Glesner, P. Zipf, and M. Renovell (Eds.): FPL 2002, LNCS 2438, pp. 1076-1079, 2002.

A program runs on MorphoSys in the following manner: General-purpose operations are handled by the TinyRISC processor, while operations that have a certain degree of parallelism, regularity, or intensive computations are mapped to the reconfigurable array (RC-Array).

3 Geometrical Transformations

3.1 First 2D Algorithm Mapping

The main usage of the MorphoSys is, as any parallel processor, to perform fast computations of algorithms that need a certain computational power requirements. Computer graphics algorithms represent one of these families. A basic part in computer graphics operations is geometrical transformations, which require fast computations of matrix operations, namely, matrix multiplication which is the core part of any geometrical transformation. The emphasis in this paper is the mapping of matrix multiplication on the MorphoSys for the use with computer graphics 2D transformations, using the supported internal configuration of the RCs.

This Algorithm could be mapped onto the M1 RC-Array as follows: The contents of the matrix A are passed row by row through the context words. The contents of matrix B are broadcasted row by row to the columns of the RC-Array. The multiplication stage (row x column) is done by using the CMUL ALU operation where the output of the reconfigurable cell is: Out (t) = A x B. Then, the results output from the ALU of each RC need to be accumulated in a row-wise manner so we can get the first row of the output matrix C from the last column of the RC-Array. This is done by using the ALU-operation CMULOADD where Out (t + 1) = Out (t) + Out [From Left Cell]. Indeed, the contents of column 7 of the RC-Array are stored back to the frame memory and then to the main memory. The same steps are repeated with the same context word but with different constant field containing the data from matrix A until obtaining the resultant matrix C.

3.2 Second 2D Algorithm Mapping

Using the same above algorithm, in this section, we introduce a new mapping, taking the advantages of the MorphoSys reconfigurable array topologies. The new mapping uses the upper left quadrant along with the bottom right quadrant. Where, the matrices are considered to be of size 4x4.

3.3 3D Geometrical Transformations

The basic purpose of composing transformations is to gain efficiency by applying a single composed transformation to a point, rather than applying a series of transformations, one after the other. Our proposed mapping assumes column broadcast mode where all the cells in the same column perform the same function. The desired functions of the interconnection are: Out(t+1) = A×C, Out(t+1) = A×C + Out(t), and Out(t+1) = A×C – Out(t).

4 Performance Analysis

The performance is based on the execution speed of the algorithms. The MorphoSys system is considered to be operational at a frequency of 100 MHz. Comparisons among the suggested systems are given in Table 1 recalling some previous findings from [4-5], showing the speedup factor of the M1 over the other suggested systems. The speedup factor is calculated as the ratio in number of cycles between the M1 and the other suggested systems. Comparisons with the RC-1000 Celoxica FPGA are shown in Table 2.

Table 1. Comparisons with other systems.

Algorithm	System	N# of Cycles	Speedup
Vector-Vector Operations (Translation) "64-Elements". [5]	M1	96	
	80486	769	8.01
Vector-Scaling Operations (Scaling) "64-Elements". [6]	M1	55	
	80486	578	10.5
Combined Translations "64-Elements". [7]	M1	150	
	80486	898	5.99
Combined Translation and Scaling "64-Elements". [7]	M1	96	
	80486	3395	62.62
Combined Scaling "64-Elements". [8]	M1	66	
	Pentium	2053	31.1
	80486	6147	93
General Composite Algorithm Using Matrix Algorithm "64-Elements". Algorithm 1.	M1	256	
	Pentium	10151	39.65
	80486	27038	105.61
General Composite Algorithm Using Matrix Algorithm "16 Elements". Algorithm 2.	M1	70	
	Pentium	1328	18.97
	80486	3354	47.91
General Composite Algorithm Using Matrix Algorithm "64-Elements". Algorithm 3.	M1	45	
	Pentium	2551	56.67
	80486	6773	150.5

Table 2. Comparisons with RC-1000 FPGA.

Algorithm	**System**	**N# of Cycles**	**Speedup of the RC-1000 over the M1 RC-System.**
General Composite Algorithm Using Matrix Algorithm "64-Elements". Algorithm 1.	M1	256	
	RC-1000	15	17
General Composite Algorithm Using Matrix Algorithm "16 Elements". Algorithm 2.	M1	70	
	RC-1000	12	5.8
General Composite Algorithm Using Matrix Algorithm "64-Elements". Algorithm 3.	M1	45	
	RC-1000	12	3.7

5 Conclusion

New mapping techniques for some linear algebraic functions are recalled [5 – 8]. New mappings for 2D and 3D geometrical transformations are introduced and justified dealing with transformations operations and their performance analysis under MorphoSys. The speed of this mapping is calculated. Results compared with other processing systems. The superiority of the presence of a reconfigurable coprocessor is apparent from the calculated speedups. Effort could be invested in trying to map other algorithms that make use of the mapped ones for more advanced algorithms for computer graphics.

References

1. Abdennour E., Diab, H., Kurdahi, F.: FIR Filter Mapping and Performance Analysis on MorphoSys. *Proceedings of the Seventh IEEE International Conference on Electronics, Circuits and Systems.* Kaslik, Lebanon. (17-20 December 2000) 99-102.
2. Maestre R., Kurdahi, F., Bagherzadeh, N., Singh, H., Hermida, R., Fernandez, N.: Kernel Scheduling in Reconfigurable Computing. *Proceedings of Design and Test in Europe* (DATE'99). Munich, Germany, March 1999.
3. Bagherzadeh N., Kurdahi, F., Singh, H., Lu, G., Lee, M., Filho, E.: MorphoSys: A Reconfigurable Architecture for Multimedia Applications. *Proceedings of the XI Brazilian Symposium on Integrated Circuit Design.* Rio De Janeiro, October 1998.
4. Damaj I., Diab, H.: Performance Analysis of Extended Vector-Scalar Operations Using Reconfigurable Computing. *Proceedings of the ACS/IEEE International Conference on Computer Systems and Applications.* Beirut, Lebanon. (25-29 June 2001) 227-232.
5. Damaj I., Diab, H.: Graphics Acceleration Using Reconfigurable Computing. *Proceedings of the 13th International Conference on Microelectronics* Rabat, Morocco (29-31 October 2001).

A HIPERLAN/2 – IEEE 802.11a Reconfigurable System-on-Chip

S. Blionas, K. Masselos, C. Dre, C. Drosos, F. Ieromnimon, T. Pagonis, A. Pneymatikakis, A. Tatsaki, T. Trimis, A. Vontzalidis, and D. Metafas

INTRACOM SA, Development Programmes Department
19,5km Markopoulou Ave., P.O. Box 68, GR-19002 Peania, Attika, Greece
sbli@intracom.gr

Abstract. In this paper the design of a partly reconfigurable System-on-Chip (SoC) for wireless LANs is described. The reconfigurable System-on-Chip will realize both HIPERLAN/2 and IEEE 802.11a wireless LAN systems. The initial version of the system will include Mobile Terminal functionality. Future firmware versions will upgrade system's functionality to allow its operation as Access Point. Functionality for operation in outdoor environments in wireless point-to-point links will be also targeted by future firmware upgrades. A system's prototype is currently under development on the ARM integrator platform.

1. Introduction

From the quantity of the worldwide shipments and the estimated Network Interface Card (NIC) prices [5] it becomes clear that a System on a Chip (SoC) solution is a cost-efficient solution for the realization of the baseband processing for the OFDM reception in HIPERLAN/2 and IEEE 802.11a (compared to a realization based on discrete components). An Access Point implementation using the same SoC as used for a NIC would allow a significant reduction in Access Point prices.

The realization and verification of a HIPERLAN/2-IEEE 802.11a NIC/AP SoC system is a very complex task and would require a long time-to-market. A partly reconfigurable SoC implementation platform would allow incremental realization of the target functionality and faster time to market. A first version of the SoC may realize only the NIC functionality. Following firmware versions may upgrade the SoC to operate as an AP and even in outdoor environments for wireless Point-to-Point links. The presence of embedded reconfigurable hardware in the target SoC will also allow modification of baseband algorithms after fabrication and hardware sharing between tasks that are not active simultaneously to further reduce the system cost.

The rest of the paper is organized as follows: In section 2 the functionality that will be realized on the target System-on-Chip is described in detail. Architectural issues are described in section 3. First results from the realizations of different parts of the target functionality either in hardware or in software are presented in section 4. Finally conclusions are presented in section 5.

M. Glesner, P. Zipf, and M. Renovell (Eds.): FPL 2002, LNCS 2438, pp. 1080-1083, 2002.

2. Target Functionality and Implementation Issues

The main differences between HIPERLAN/2 and IEEE 802.11a are in the Data Link Control (DLC)/Medium Access Control (MAC) layer. The HIPERLAN/2 [1] protocol stack includes one or more convergence layers (X-Specific CL) on top of the data link control (DLC) layer. The medium access is based on a TDD/TDMA approach. The control is centralized to an "Access Point" (AP). The HIPERLAN/2 MAC frame duration is fixed to 2 ms. The IEEE 802.11 [3] MAC protocol includes two functions: a Distributed Coordination Function (DCF) implementing a Carrier Sense Multiple Access/Collision Avoidance (CSMA/CA) protocol and a Point Coordination Function (PCF) implementing a polling access method. The transmission time for a PSDU frame in IEEE 802.11a is not fixed. The higher levels of the protocol stacks (DLC) are assigned to instruction set processors given their small complexity. The demanding parts of the MAC sublayers and the MAC/Physical interfaces of both standards (which are completely different) require acceleration and may share the same reconfigurable hardware resources to reduce the area cost of the target system.

The physical layers of both HIPERLAN/2 and IEEE 802.11a systems are based on coded OFDM modulation scheme [2] and are almost identical [4]. Timing constraints impose custom hardware realization of physical layer. The differences of HIPERLAN/2 and IEEE 802.11a at the physical layer will be implemented as additional operation modes for the given blocks. Opportunities for exploiting reconfigurable hardware at the physical layer concern: a) complex tasks with more than one algorithmic instances b) tasks with complexities depending on the mode of operation and c) tasks with non-overlapping lifetimes.

Access Points (AP) and Mobile Terminals (MT) in HIPERLAN/2 have only few differences in physical layer. In IEEE 802.11a CF-pollable MTs have the same physical layer and MAC functions as APs (Point Coordinator–PC). The interfaces of APs and MTs to the external system entities are different. In the target system a PCI or Ethernet MAC controller will be implemented in the reconfigurable part of the SoC for MTs and APs respectively. DLC requirements of APs and MTs in both HIPERLAN/2 and IEEE 802.11a are different.

As far as outdoor operation (point-to-point) is concerned, the same comments made above are valid for the interface and the DLC. As far as the physical layer is concerned parameters that may improve the distance of the link include: higher number of subcarriers, additional decoding unit and higher bit precision at the equalization block. The related blocks (FFT/IFFT, additional decoder, equalizer) should be assigned to reconfigurable hardware.

3. Architecture

The architecture of the target reconfigurable SoC is shown in figure 1. Two ARM processors are included. One serves as protocol processor, while the other as networking processor. Customized hardware blocks (mainly for the modem), reconfigurable hardware blocks, internal memory, a DMA engine for fast data-transfers (featuring a configurable number of request channels) plus a number of peripheral components for I/O and auxiliary tasks are also included. All these blocks are organized as master and slave peripherals of a central AMBA (AHB) bus.

Two alternative architectures/implementations have been studied for the target reconfigurable SoC. In both cases an ARM RISC core (ARM7 TDMI or ARM9 depending on the protocol stack complexity) is used. In one case the MAC/PHY interface is realized on reconfigurable hardware (to support both standards) while in the other it is realized on a customized microcontroller.

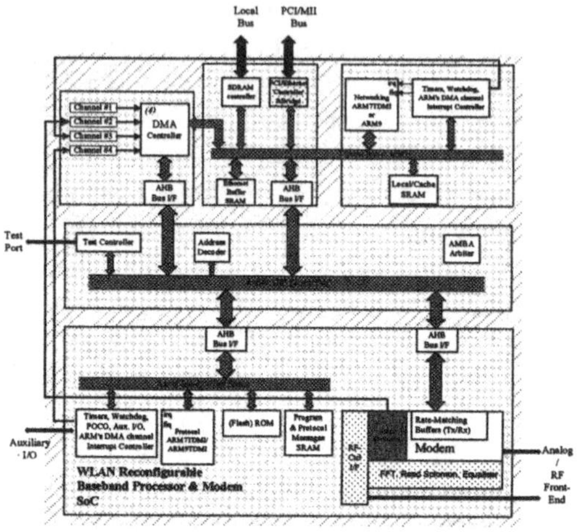

Fig. 1. Reconfigurable SoC architecture

4. First Implementation Results

Target system's prototyping is in progress on the ARM integrator platform. For the tasks assigned to instruction set processors C code is developed running on ARM7. Execution times for basic tasks of HIPERLAN/2 DLC and MAC layers are presented in tables 1, 2. Operation frequency of 50 MHz (cycle 20 ns) is assumed. The modem has been mapped to two core modules (Xilinx xcve2000-6 FPGAs) of the ARM integrator platform. In the first one the frequency and data domain blocks of the receiver are mapped. The second FPGA includes the transmitter, the time domain blocks of the receiver, the interface to MAC and a slave interface to an AMBA bus. The total utilizations of the FPGAs are 79% and 81%. The utilization per resource type for the logic modules is presented in tables 3, 4.

Task	Execution time
AP-Scheduler	71 μs
AP/MT-TxCL	340 μs
AP/MT-TxBuilder (full frame)	250 μs
AP/MT-TxBuilderCopy (580 bytes – word transfer)	110 μs
AP/MT-RxDecoder	200 μs
AP/MT-RxCL	400 μs

Table 1. Execution times for basic tasks of HIPERLAN/2 DLC layer

MT-BCH/FCH Decoder Modem Ctrl	
Subtask	**Execution time**
Initialisation Phase (Reset & Config @ slot commands)	1.50 μs
Synchronisation Phase (BCH_SRCH, Rx_FCH with rpt = 1, Rx_ACH)	3.80 μs
BCH decoding and BCH CRC checking	12.40 μs
Decoding of a single IE (UL)	6.14 μs
Decoding of 3 IEs (2 ULs, 1 DL) including CRC checking & Puncturing	41 μs

Table 2: Execution times for basic subtasks of the MT-BCH/FCH Decoder Modem Ctrl HIPERLAN/2 MAC layer process

Resource	Used	Available	Utilization
IOs	87	512	16.99%
Function Generators	14319	38400	37.29%
CLB Slices	7160	19200	37.29%
Dffs or Latches	3271	40812	8.01%

Table 3: Utilization per resource type for the first FPGA

Resource	Used	Available	Utilization
IOs	276	512	53.91%
Function Generators	12617	38400	32.86%
CLB Slices	6309	19200	32.86%
Dffs or Latches	5943	40812	14.56%

Table 4: Utilization per resource type for the second FPGA

5. Conclusions

The development of a reconfigurable System-on-Chip for wireless LANs has been described. The system will realize the HIPERLAN/2 and IEEE 802.11a wireless LAN systems and functionality both for Mobile Terminals and Access Points. Functionality for operation in outdoor environments for wireless point-to-point links is also targeted. The selected heterogeneous System-on-Chip implementation platform is expected to lead to an optimal trade-off between implementation efficiency and flexibility. Currently the system is under prototyping on the ARM integrator platform.

References

[1] ETSI, "Broadband Radio Access Networks (BRAN); HIPERLAN type 2; Physical (PHY) layer", V 1.2.1 (2000-11).

[2] R. van Nee, R. Prasad, "OFDM for Mobile Multimedia Communications", Boston: Artech House, Dec. 1999.

[3] IEEE Std 802.11a/D7.0-1999, Part11: Wireless LAN Medium Access Control (MAC) and Physical Layer (PHY) specifications: High Speed Physical Layer in the 5 GHz Band.

[4] Andreas Hettich and Matthias Schrother, "IEEE 802.11 or ETSI BRAN HIPERLAN/2: Who will win the race for a high speed wireless LAN standard ?", Wireless Conference, 1999.

[5] Cahners-In-Stat, "Life, Liberty and WLANs: Wireless Networking Brings Freedom to the Enterprise", Nov 2000.

SoftTOTEM: An FPGA Implementation of the TOTEM Parallel Processor

Stephanie McBader[1], Luca Clementel[1], Alvise Sartori[1], Andrea Boni[2], Peter Lee[3]

[1] NeuriCam S.p.A, Via S M Maddalena 12, 38100 Trento (TN), Italy
[mcbader , clementel , sartori]@neuricam.com
[2] University of Trento, Via Mesiano, 77, I-38050 Povo (TN), Italy
andrea.boni@ing.unitn.it
[3] University of Kent at Canterbury, Canterbury, Kent, CT2 7NT, UK
P.Lee@ukc.ac.uk

Abstract. TOTEM is digital VLSI parallel processor ideally suitable for vector-matrix multiplication. As such, it provides the core computational engine for digital signal processing and artificial neural network algorithms. It has been implemented in the past as a full-custom IP core, achieving high data throughput at clock frequencies of up to 30 MHz. This paper presents the 'soft' implementation of the TOTEM neural chip, and compares its cost and performance to previous 'hard' implementations.

1. Introduction

The TOTEM neural processor [1,2] is a DSP core which integrates 32 parallel processing units to achieve high performance in object recognition and classification. One TOTEM chip flexibly implements multi-layer perceptrons with up to tens of layers, over 8000 connections and a width of up to 32 neurons. The versatile memory-like interface makes TOTEM very easy to integrate with microcontrollers to build recognition systems [3], filters or signal compressors [4], and fuzzy controllers based on neural networks [5]. It can also be used to implement complex computations required in DSP operations [6].

Previous implementations of TOTEM have been realised in full-custom VLSI design. This, of course, resulted in highly powerful chips of optimum layouts at minimal power consumption. However, rapid advances in process technologies require that the full-custom layout is manually modified to match newer, smaller transistor dimensions. In fact, any modification or enhancement on the TOTEM architecture resulted in several man-months of effort and a new silicon run.

The alternative, 'fast-track' approach to this problem necessitates the existence of a 'soft' core, designed at a high level of abstraction. This paper presents the merits of such approach, and reports the obtained performance and incurred costs from porting the TOTEM architecture into its VHDL equivalent, SoftTOTEM, and implementing it on a Xilinx FPGA.

M. Glesner, P. Zipf, and M. Renovell (Eds.): FPL 2002, LNCS 2438, pp. 1084-1087, 2002.

2. Architecture Overview

The TOTEM SIMD architecture is based on a pipelined digital data stream, feeding 32 fixed-point fully-parallel multiply-and-accumulate processors (MACs), as shown in figure 1. The architecture is optimised for the execution of the MAC operation:

```
Acc(n+1) = Acc(n) + DataIn*Weight(n)
```

Where 16-bit `DataIn` is received from a common broadcast bus, in 2's complements format. Weights or filter parameters are stored locally to each neuron. Weight blocks are organised as 256x10-bits and are closely coupled to the MAC units. The 34-bit output of the accumulator is loaded into an output register before passing through a 34-bit input/16-bit output barrel shifter for scaling of results to the 16-bit interface.

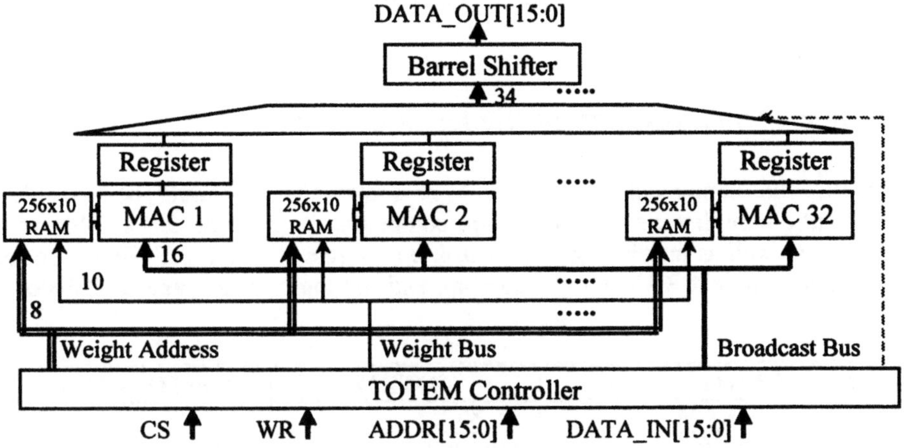

Fig. 1. TOTEM Architecture

3. SoftTOTEM Implementation

SoftTOTEM was implemented on a Xilinx XCV2000-E FPGA using VHDL for porting the full-custom design of TOTEM. Weight memories were instantiated as Xilinx-specific RAM Blocks, while the multiplier component of the MAC unit was implemented first as a Xilinx core, and then as a soft IP core using the Pezaris algorithm for multiplication. The prototyping platform used to test SoftTOTEM communicates with the host PC using a standard parallel port working in EPP mode.

SoftTOTEM was evaluated using the same approach that was used to test TOTEM chips. A test program generates random test vectors, and as it sends instructions to the hardware, it passes a copy to a TOTEM emulator, which computes the expected output in software. Once the test vectors have all been consumed, the output of the all neurons is read and compared to those of the emulated neural array.

Instruction	Description
`Setbarrel`	Set Barrel Shifter Window
`Outneuron`	Select Output Neuron
`Writewmem`	Write to Weight Memory
`Startaddr`	Set Memory Start Address
`Lregister`	Load Result Register
`Clearaccu`	Clear Accumulator
`Increment`	Increment Memory Address
`Calculate`	Compute MAC Operation
`Calcincrm`	Calculate then Increment Memory Address

Table 1. The TOTEM Instruction Set

4. Soft Vs. Hard Implementations: Comparison

Synthesis and implementation results have shown that it should be possible to implement a complete SoftTOTEM chip, comprising 32 neurons, 256x10-bit weight memories as well as interfacing and control, on a single Virtex 600-E FPGA, because it contains sufficient RAM blocks on-chip, and the logic would take up 95% of the device.

Characteristics	TOTEM	SoftTOTEM
Neurons/RAM	32, 80 K	32, 80 K
Processing Power	960 MOPS	3880 MOPS
Max. Clock Frequency	30 MHz (TOTEM limitation)	40 MHz (EPP limitation)
Area	747,166 transistors 186,792 gates? (Exc. Control)	718,076 gates 6,570 Slices (Inc. Control)
Power Consumption	1W @ 5V	2.455 W @ 1.8 V
Man-Months: Complete Design	6-12 Months	3 Months
Man-Months: Modification	4~6 months	< 1 week
Implementation	Min. 3 months (silicon run)	A few hours
Price/Chip	$42.4 (Exc. NRE [7])	$378 XCV600-E (Feb. 2002)

Table 2. TOTEM vs. SoftTOTEM

As shown in Table 2, SoftTOTEM outperforms its full-custom equivalent, at the cost of area and higher power consumption. This cost, however, is not a threatening one – products that are based on the TOTEM chip normally require an FPGA on-board to provide control for the neural array, as well as communication with the external system [8].

5. Conclusion & Further Work

The SoftTOTEM design and implementation illustrates a typical example of the merit of using field programmable logic as opposed to full-custom VLSI design. Fast development times and reduced efforts are not the only advantages of the 'soft' approach to implementing neural processing chips. It has been demonstrated that the soft implementation outperforms its full-custom rival, as it benefits directly from improvements in FPGA technology. Moreover, the use of VHDL permits design re-use and illustrates the merits of design portability.

Future work would concentrate on the advantages of integrating a host RISC processor into the FPGA, so as to complete a stand-alone system based on the neural approach to problem solving in a variety of applications. This level of integration has become even simpler than ever with the introduction of hard processing cores and multipliers into FPGA architectures [9].

References

1. R. Battiti, P. Lee, A. Sartori, G. Tecchiolli, "TOTEM: a Digital Processor for Neural Networks and Reactive Tabu Search", *Proc. of the 4th Int. Conf. on Microelectronics for Neural Networks and Fuzzy Systems*, pp. 17-25, Turin, Italy, September 26-28, 1994
2. NeuriCam S.p.A, "NC3003 Datasheet: TOTEM Digital Processor for Neural Networks", Rel. 12/99, www.neuricam.com
3. NeuriCam S.p.A, "Number Plate Recognition System", www.neuricam.com
4. R. Battiti, A. Sartori, G. Tecchiolli, P. Tonella, A. Zorat, "Neural Compression: an Integrated Application to EEG Signals", *Int. Workshop on Application of Neural Networks to Telecommunications*, Stockholm, Sweden, May 1995.
5. A. Zorat, A. Satori, G. Tecchiolli, L. Koczy, "A Flexible VLSI Processor for Fast Neural Network and Fuzzy Control Implementation", *Conf. of Soft Computing*, Iizuka, Japan October 1996.
6. NeuriCam S.p.A, "Using the NC3001 for DSP Applications: computing the DFT of a 256x256 image", Application Note AN005, www.neuricam.com
7. Xilinx, "Spartan ASIC Alternatives", www.xilinx.com
8. NeuriCam S.p.A, "Parallel Signal Processing Boards: TOTEM PCI Technical Reference Manual", Rel. 12/99, www.neuricam.com
9. Peter Alfke, "Evolution, Revolution and Convolution. Recent Progress in Field-Programmable Logic", FPL2001.

Real-Time Medical Diagnosis on a Multiple FPGA-based System

Takashi Yokota[1], Masamichi Nagafuchi[1], Yoshito Mekada[2], Tsutomu Yoshinaga[3], Kanemitsu Ootsu[1], and Takanobu Baba[1]

[1] Dept. Information Science, Utsunomiya University,
7–1–1 Yoto, Utsunomiya, Japan.
yokota@is.utsunomiya-u.ac.jp
http://aquila.is.utsunomiya-u.ac.jp/
[2] Graduate School of Engineering, Nagoya University, Nagoya-shi, Japan.
[3] Graduate School of Information systems, The University of Electro-Communications, Chofu-shi, Tokyo, Japan.

Abstract. The concentration index is a novel characteristic measurement that indicates the degree of concentration of lines to a certain point. Its typical application is medical diagnosis; for example, gastric cancer has a distinctive nature that folds concentrate to the lesion. Its large computational complexity requires much computing time. This paper presents a multiple FPGA-based computing architecture which accelerates the concentration index calculation and enables real-time diagnosis of gastric cancer. Evaluation results reveal that gate- and pin- counts are within those of todays' FPGA devices, and that the diagnosis process should be accelerated about 100 times faster than ordinal workstations..

1 Concentration Index for Medical Diagnosis

An interesting phenomenon, that gastric folds concentrate to a cancer lesion, is widely observed at about 80 percents of patients. By using this characteristic, an automatic diagnosis is proposed. It uses the concentration index filter.

The concentration index (C-index, [1]) is a characteristic measurement which indicates the degree of concentration of lines to a certain point in an image. The C-index at a point P is calculated as follows. A neighboring area of P is defined as $R = \{Q \mid r_{min} < r \leq r_{max},\ r = \overline{PQ}\}$. R has a doughnut-like shape whose minimum and maximum radiuses are r_{min} and r_{max}, respectively. Line segments are divided into small sections, called line elements (LEs). At any point Q in the neighboring area R, if Q has an LE on it, a direction component of the LE is described as $dx|\cos\alpha|$, where dx and α are the length and angle of the line element, respectively (Fig. 1). The C-index at the point P (we denote $C(\mathrm{P})$) is defined as follows.

$$C(\mathrm{P}) \quad = \quad \sum_{\mathrm{R}} \frac{dx|\cos\alpha|}{r} \ \Big/ \ \sum_{\mathrm{R}} \frac{dx}{r} \tag{1}$$

where r is the distance from P to the LE and $\sum_{\mathrm{R}}$ means the summation in the neighboring space R.

M. Glesner, P. Zipf, and M. Renovell (Eds.): FPL 2002, LNCS 2438, pp. 1088–1091, 2002.

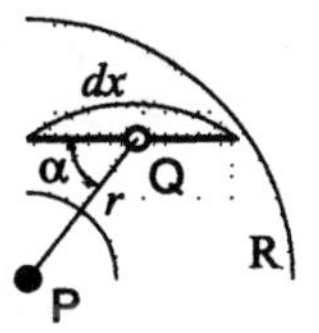

Fig. 1. Calculation of a Concentration Index

2 Applying FPGAs to C-index Operations

As shown in Equation (1) and Figure 1, the C-index operation requires huge computation, although, its computational structure is simple and suitable to FPGA implementation. We propose an FPGA-based C-index operation engine with the following two features[2,3]: (a) it offers sufficiently high performance and flexibility, and (b) it should be scalable enough to utilize the parallelism.

Reducing Complexity. Without loss of exactness, LEs are limited to eight patterns. This conducts considerable reduction of computational complexity: we can prepare two pre-calculated tables for $(dx|\cos\alpha|/r)$ and dx/r. Each table is accessed by the LE index and relative position (dx and dy).

Changing Order of Operations. A naive algorithm, derived from Equation (1), first picks up a point P and then its neighboring point Q. This algorithm essentially includes `if` statements in the kernel loop, and prevents extracting parallel operations. We solve this problem by changing the order of the operation; we first pick up Q and then P in its neighboring area. The modified algorithm is equivalent to the original one. Fig. 2 illustrates the simplified code of the kernel loop. In this figure, the neighboring area is approximated as a circumscribed square whose side is `WindowSize` × 2.

Determining Optimal Precision. The C-index operation is sensitive to the data precision and requires floating-point operations. Needless to say, wider bit-width leads to larger circuit and slower speed. Thus we have to determine optimal data width. Since required accuracy is 10^{-4}, number of mantissa bits is at least 14 ($= \lceil \log_2 10^4 \rceil$). The number of exponent bits depends on the size and shape of neighboring area R (Fig. 1). With proper approximation, we estimated 7-bit exponent for typical application. Thus, we use 24-bit data representation (16-bit mantissa, 7-bit exponent, and 1 sign bit).

Extracting Parallelism. The modified algorithm, shown in Fig. 2, allows us to extract sufficient parallelism. Actual limitation of parallelism is caused by pin-count bottleneck. Since the system handles a lot of floating-point data, and

```
for( j=WindowSize; j<Ysize-WindowSize; j++ ){
  for( i=WindowSize; i<Xsize-WindowSize; i++){
    n = line_data[i][j];
    if( n>=0 && n<8 ){
      for( k=j-WindowSize,q=0; k<=j+WindowSize; k++,q++){
        for( l=i-WindowSize,p=0; l<=i+WindowSize; l++,p++){
          sum_ev[l][k] += tbl_ev[n][p][q];
          sum_fr[l][k] += tbl_fr[n][p][q];
}}}}}
```

Fig. 2. Simplified Code of the Modified Algorithm

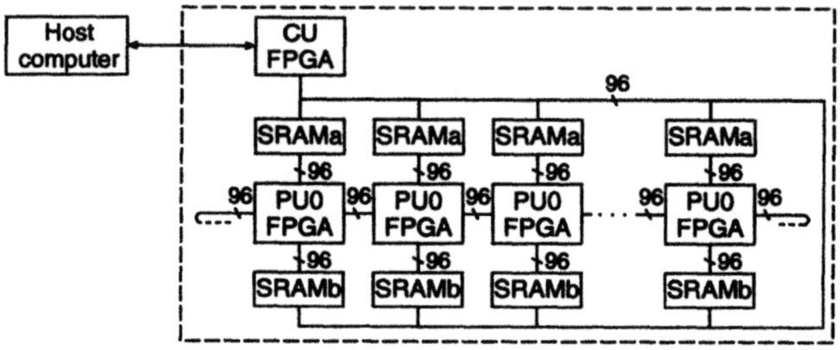

Fig. 3. System Configuration

no FPGA device today can contain all data, external memory devices are required. Thus the number of simultaneous data access to the memory bounds the parallelism. Our current design uses two sets of SRAMs, each connected by 96-bit bus (four 24-bit data).

Scalability. We can use multiple FPGAs by splitting the input image. This shows that the system has good scalability. For simplicity, we limit splitting method only in horizontal direction, thus FPGAs are connected in an array style (Fig. 3). Using multiple FPGAs increases parallelism, although, the neighboring area R requires additional boundary processing.

3 Evaluation

The proposed system is designed by Verilog-HDL. We use a Verilog simulator for verifying functional correctness and for estimating the number of steps to complete the C-index calculation. Furthermore, logic compilation tools are used to evaluate the circuit scale (i.e., gate count) and the maximum clock frequency.

Performance Estimation. We use an actual X-ray image which is 1600-by-1700 dots grayscale. Neighboring area R is a doughnut-like shape whose inner and outer diameters are 101 and 201, respectively.

A one-FPGA system requires about 4.8 billion clocks to complete the whole calculation. When using multiple FPGAs, a constant 8 million steps of boundary processing is required. A 15 FPGA system runs about 12 times faster than single FPGA system. This shows good scalability.

Logic Compilation. We use LeonardoSpectrum (Exemplar) for Altera APEX-20K devices and DesignCompiler (Synopsys) for Xilinx Virtex-E devices. The number of signal pins is 401. An APEX-20K device requires 7761 LCs with the maximum clock frequency of 22.1 MHz. A Virtex-E device needs 5833 CLBs (23332 LUTs) and its maximum clock frequency is 19.68 MHz.

Using the practically maximum configuration of 15 FPGAs, whole C-index operations complete in a few seconds. Current workstation, using a 750 MHz UltraSPARC-III processor, requires about four minutes for the same operations. Thus, the system achieves about 100 times speed-up.

4 Concluding Remarks

In this paper, we discussed about hardware acceleration of the C-index operations by applying FPGAs. The resulting architecture involves inherent parallelism and good scalability. Our prototype design, targeting current FPGA technology, will complete the C-index calculation in a few seconds. This indicates 100 times faster processing than current workstations.

Acknowledgment This research was supported in part by the Grant-in-Aid for Scientific Research (B)14380135 and (C)14580362, and Grant-in-Aid for Young Scientist (B)14780186 of Japan Society for Promotion of Science (JSPS).

References

1. Mekada, Y., Hasegawa, J., Toriwaki, J., Nawano, S., Miyagawa, K.: Automated extraction of cancer lesions from double contrast x-ray images of stomach, K.Doi et al.(Eds.) Computer-Aided Diagnosis in Medical Imaging, Elsevier Science B.V. (1999) 407–412.
2. Nagafuchi, M., Yoshinaga, T., Yokota, T., Ootsu, K., Baba, T.: Speed-up of the Medical Image Processing using the Parallel FPGA System, Tech. Report of IEICE, CPSY2001–44, (2001). (in Japanese).
3. Yokota, T., Nagafuchi, M., Mekada, Y., Yoshinaga, T., Ootsu, K., Baba, T.: A Scalable FPGA-based Custom Computing Machine for a Medical Image Processing, Proc. FCCM02 (2002).

Threshold Element-Based Symmetric Function Generators and Their Functional Extension

Kazuo Aoyama and Hiroshi Sawada

NTT Communication Science Laboratories, NTT Corporation
2-4, Hikaridai, Seika-cho, Soraku-gun, Kyoto 619-0237, Japan
{issei,sawada}@cslab.kecl.ntt.co.jp

Abstract. This paper presents threshold element-based symmetric function generators (SFG) and techniques for their functional extension. Any symmetric function of k input variables is realized by SFGs with $(k+1)$ configuration bits. When less than k input variables are applied to the SFGs, certain logic functions beyond symmetric functions can be achieved by configurations of interconnection resources. Logic functions achieved by the extended SFGs are compared with those by SRAM-based look-up tables. It is demonstrated that the SFGs have flexibility in achievable function classes and utilize configuration bits economically.

1 Introduction

Logic functions are symmetric if and only if the functions maintain the same value for any permutation of input variables. Such symmetric functions are an important function class in logic functions. Owing to the symmetry, the number of symmetric functions is much less than that of logic functions. For k input variables, there are $2^{(k+1)}$ symmetric functions and $2^{(2^k)}$ logic functions. Only $(k+1)$ configuration bits are required for symmetric function generators. Symmetric function generators are economical in terms of configuration bits.

Symmetric functions can be realized by simple networks with threshold elements. Threshold elements output a logical 1 or 0 depending on a result obtained by comparing a weighted sum of input variables ($\sum_{i=1}^{k} W_i \cdot X_i$) with a threshold ($Th$). Symmetry of input variables is easily achieved by using the same value to the weights, namely $W_i = W$. Threshold elements can be implemented in floating-gate devices with a simple structure [1]. The device outputs a logical 0 when a weighted sum ($\sum_{i=1}^{k} W \cdot X_i$) exceeds its threshold Th, and a logical 1 otherwise. A reconfigurable logic circuit realizing any symmetric function has been presented on the basis of these technologies [2].

This paper describes techniques for the functional extension of threshold element-based symmetric function generators and their properties. Symmetric function generators (SFG) used in this paper are a certain type of reconfigurable logic circuit, which comprises floating-gate devices capable of handling more input variables [3]. In Section 2, a structure and an operation of SFGs are described. Section 3 presents techniques for their functional extension that enable

M. Glesner, P. Zipf, and M. Renovell (Eds.): FPL 2002, LNCS 2438, pp. 1092–1096, 2002.

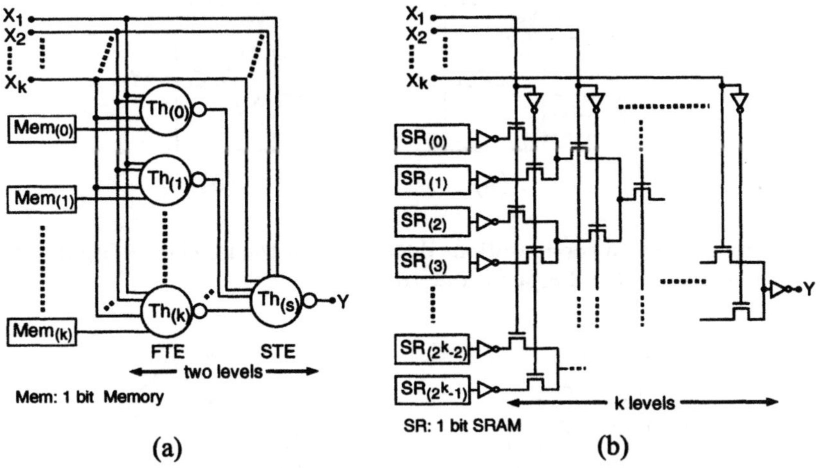

Fig. 1. Structures of two function generators with k input variables. (a) Threshold element-based symmetric function generator. (b) SRAM-based look-up table.

SFGs to generate logic functions beyond symmetric functions. And achievable logic functions in SFGs with functional extension are compared with those in SRAM-based look-up tables (LUT).

2 Symmetric Function Generators

A threshold element-based symmetric function generator with k input variables is illustrated in Fig. 1 (a). This is a two-level feed-forward circuit, and has $(k+1)$ first-level threshold elements (FTE) and one second-level threshold element (STE). A memory circuit for storing configuration data is added to each FTE. In contrast, an SRAM-based LUT with k input variables, shown in Fig. 1 (b), has 2^k SRAM cells and a decoder constructed with a k-level pass-transistor circuit [4]. The SFG has the advantages of two-level logic independent of k and the number of memory circuits.

Threshold elements are characterized by weights and a threshold. All input variables are input to FTEs and STE, and their weights are set at 1. A threshold of a *j-th* FTE (FTE[j]) in Fig. 1 (a) is $(j+0.5)$ and $(j-0.5)$ depending on a logical 1 and 0 stored in a *j-th* memory ($\text{Mem}_{(j)}$), respectively. A threshold $Th_{(s)}$ of STE is $(k+0.5)$. Let us define a weighted sum $(\sum_{i=1}^{k} X_i)$ as an *input status*. When an input status is Z $(0 \leq Z \leq k)$, the STE outputs a logical value stored in $\text{Mem}_{(Z)}$. Any totally symmetric function is generated on the basis of this multiplexer function using an input status.

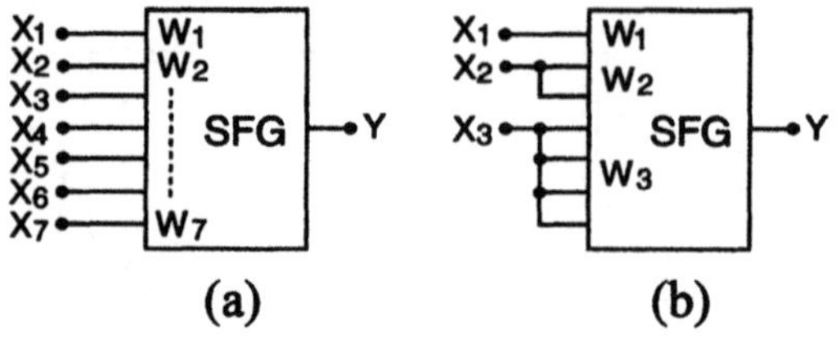

Fig. 2. Interconnection configurations depending on the number of input variables. (a) 7 input variables. (b) 3 input variables.

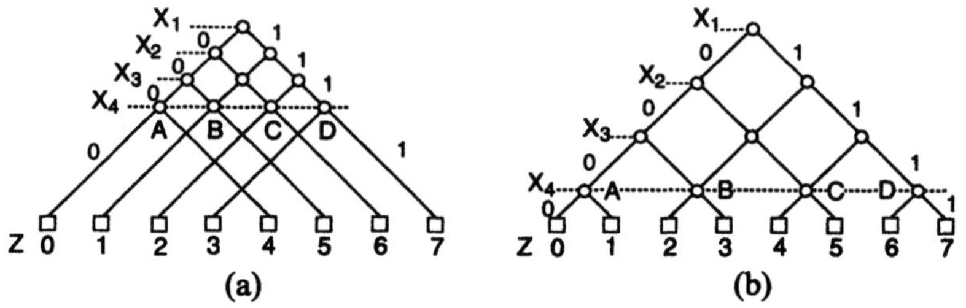

Fig. 3. Graphical representations clarifying the equality of two different transformations for the 7-input SFGs with 4 input variables. (a) $(W_1, W_2, W_3, W_4) = (1, 1, 1, 4)$. (b) $(W_1, W_2, W_3, W_4) = (2, 2, 2, 1)$.

3 Functional Extension of SFGs

SFGs can achieve logic functions beyond totally symmetric functions by connecting lines for some input variables in interconnection resources (IR). Such configurations in IRs generate various weight vectors. A weight vector given to a threshold element determines a function class. Two configurations in IRs of a 7-input SFG are shown in Fig. 2. Any totally symmetric function of 7 input variables and any logic function of 3 input variables are realized in Fig. 2 (a) and (b), respectively. When 4 to 6 input variables are given to the 7-input SFG, certain partially symmetric functions are achieved.

Achievable partially symmetric functions are discussed in detail. Let us assume that 4 input variables are input to the 7-input SFG. The integer 7 is partitioned to 4 positive integers such as $7 = (1+1+1+4) = (1+1+2+3) = (1+2+2+2)$. Each term of these sums represents a weight. Only input variables multiplied by an equal weight are symmetry. A weight vector including an equal weight transforms some input vectors to a certain input status. Those input vectors are called *degenerating input vectors.* Different weight vectors that generate the same set of degenerating input vectors can achieve the same partially symmetric functions, such as $(W_1, W_2, W_3, W_4) = (1, 1, 1, 4)$ and $(W_1, W_2, W_3, W_4) = (2, 2, 2, 1)$.

A graphical representation is introduced in order to identify achievable partially symmetric functions. Graphs in Fig. 3 (a) and (b) show the transformations

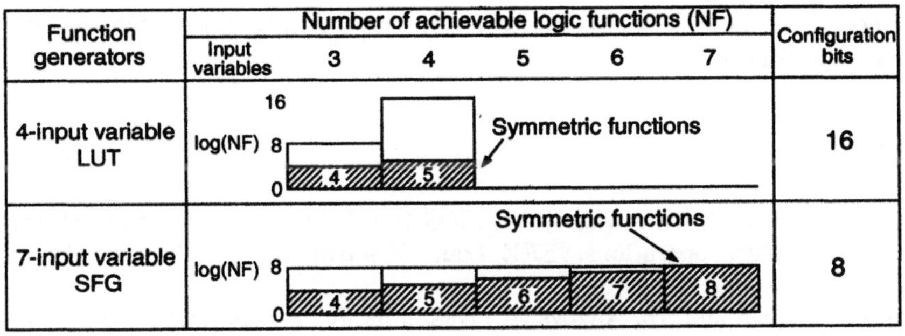

Fig. 4. Number of achievable logic functions and symmetric functions for the 4-input LUTs and the 7-input SFGs, depending on the number of available input variables.

with the above-mentioned two weight vectors. These graphs are different from binary decision diagrams (BDD) in that a length of their branches is weighted with a weight. Let us express a symmetric function with one logical 1 in X_1, X_2, and X_3 by $S^1_{\{1,2,3\}}$. Then, the nodes A, B, C and D in Fig. 3 (a) and (b) can be expressed by $S^0_{\{1,2,3\}}, S^1_{\{1,2,3\}}, S^2_{\{1,2,3\}}$, and $S^3_{\{1,2,3\}}$, respectively. Terminal nodes of both graphs are represented by $S^i_{\{1,2,3\}} \cdot X_4$, $(i = 0, 1, 2, 4)$, although the values of Z corresponding to $S^i_{\{1,2,3\}} \cdot X_4$ are different. These graphs are equivalent in terms of the transformation of input vectors to input statuses.

Let us define a *function group* by functions generated by a certain transformation of input vectors to input statuses. The SFGs realize a logic function by two steps. In the first step, a certain function group is determined by the number of input variables and an interconnection configuration. In the second step, a logic function is selected from the function group by assigning binary values to each terminal node represented by $Z = 0, 1, 2, \cdots, 7$ as shown in Fig. 3.

Achievable logic functions in the 7-input SFGs are compared to those in 4-input LUTs as shown in Fig. 4. The LUTs can realize any logic function of 4 input variables using 16 configuration bits. More than 4 input variables, however, cannot be handled. In contrast, the SFGs can achieve 2^8 logic functions of less than 8 input variables using *half* the configuration bits of the LUTs. The SFGs realize any logic function for 3 input variables like the LUTs, and can generate all symmetric functions of 4 to 7 input variables at least. Configuration bits of the SFGs are utilized economically.

4 Conclusions

Symmetric function generators can achieve various function classes: any logic function, partially symmetric functions and any totally symmetric function, depending on the number of input variables. Configurations in interconnection resources are utilized to generate the function classes. Relationships between the configurations and achieved logic functions were described. Achievable logic functions with the 7-input SFG and the 4-input LUT were compared. It was confirmed that the SFG utilizes effectively the 8 configuration bits to generate various logic functions.

References

1. Shibata, T., Ohmi, T.: A functional MOS transistor featuring gate-level weighted sum and threshold operations. IEEE Trans. Electron Devices Vol. 39 (1992) 1444–1455
2. Aoyama, K., Sawada, H., Nagoya, A., Nakajima, K.: A threshold logic-based reconfigurable logic element with a new programming technology. FPL2000, Lecture Notes in Computer Science 1896, Springer-Verlag (2000) 665–674
3. Aoyama, K.: A reconfigurable logic circuit based on threshold elements with a controlled floating gate. IEEE Intl. Symp. Circuits and Systems (2002) V-381–V-384
4. Chow, P., Seo, S. O., Rose, J., Chung, K., Páez-Monzón, G., Rahardja, I.: The design of a SRAM-based field-programmable gate array–part II: Circuit design and layout. IEEE Trans. VLSI Systems Vol. 7 (1999) 321–330

Hardware Implementation of a Multiuser Detection Scheme Based on Recurrent Neural Networks

Wolfgang Schlecker[1], Achim Engelhart[2], Werner G. Teich[2], and Hans-Jörg Pfleiderer[1]

[1] Microelectronics Department, University of Ulm, Germany
[2] Department of Information Technology, University of Ulm, Germany

Abstract. In this paper we describe the hardware (HW) implementation of a discrete–time channel matrix computation and a multiuser detection (MUD) scheme. We propose a MUD scheme based on recurrent neural networks (RNN) for the TDD mode of UMTS Terrestrial Radio Access. This algorithm achieves a performance which is close to the optimum MUD, while keeping the computational complexity low. To reach the high real–time data throughput we implemented the algorithm with parallel multipliers on a field programmable gate array (FPGA).

1 Introduction

In the 3rd generation mobile communication standard Universal Mobile Telecommunication System (UMTS) Code Division Multiple Access (CDMA) is an important part. To achieve full capacity of the system, multiuser detection (MUD) must be applied. The disadvantage of MUD is its large complexity, compared to the singleuser detection (SUD). MUD based on RNN (MU–RNN) have a moderate complexity and show a performance close to the optimum MUD. Another advantage of MU–RNN is its regular structure which allows a hardware implementation with a high data throughput. The most important question is how we can do the more than $5 \cdot 10^9$ multiplications per second in order to achieve the realtime data throughput.

The HW implementation is based on the TD–CDMA (time division CDMA) system as given by the time division duplex (TDD) mode of the UMTS terrestrial radio access (UTRA) interface.

2 Nonlinear MUD Based on RNN

In the following we use a discrete–time channel matrix model for the TDD mode of UTRA ([6]) to describe the function of the MUD based od RNN. The transmission of a packet of $N_B = 61$ information symbols and K subchannels with spreading sequence of length K can be calculated by a matrix–vector convolution: $\underline{\tilde{x}}[k] = \underline{R}[k] * \underline{x}[k] + \underline{\tilde{n}}[k]$. A detailed description can be found in [1].

M. Glesner, P. Zipf, and M. Renovell (Eds.): FPL 2002, LNCS 2438, pp. 1097–1100, 2002.

Due to the burst structure of the transmission we can define transmission and receive packet vectors, which contain all data symbols of all subchannels of one data symbol field:
$\underline{x} = (\underline{x}[1]^T, \underline{x}[2]^T, \ldots, \underline{x}[N_B]^T)^T, \underline{\tilde{x}} = (\underline{\tilde{x}}[1]^T, \underline{\tilde{x}}[2]^T, \ldots, \underline{\tilde{x}}[N_B]^T)^T$. The matrix–vector convolution can be written as a matrix–vector multiplication $\underline{\tilde{x}} = \underline{R} \cdot x + \underline{\tilde{n}}$. $\underline{R}$ is the packet channel matrix with the dimension $(K \cdot N_B) \times (K \cdot N_B)$. It has a regular block–Toeplitz structure and only elements near the diagonal are not equal to zero. $\underline{\tilde{n}}$ is the colored noise vector of dimension $K \cdot N_B$.

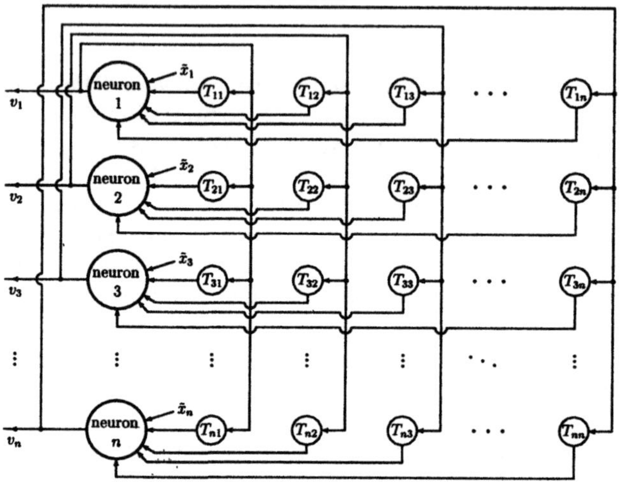

Fig. 1. Discrete–time recurrent neural network

For the detection of the received signal we consider a nonlinear MUD based on RNN as described for example in [1,3,4,5]. The performance of these detectors comes close to the performance of an optimal MUD. Fig. 1 shows the structure of a recurrent neural network. A MUD based on this scheme can be seen as iterative interference cancellation. In Fig. 1, n is equal to $K \cdot N_B$. In each neuron the inputs are summed and weighted by a nonlinear activation function. The outputs of the neurons are multiplied with T_{ij} and fed back to the inputs of all neurons. For the coefficients $T_{ij} (j \neq i)$ the negative values of the packet channel matrix $\underline{R}$ are used. The coefficients T_{ii} on the main diagonal of $\underline{T}$ are zero. The value $v_i[\kappa + 1]$ of the neuron i in iteration $\kappa + 1$ can be calculated as follows:

$$v_i[\kappa+1] = \sigma\left(\sum_{j=1}^{i-1} T_{ij} v_j[\kappa+1] + \sum_{j=i+1}^{n} T_{ij} v_j[\kappa] + \tilde{x}_i\right) . \tag{1}$$

3 Hardware Implementation

The most important aspect for the HW implementation is the wordlength of the received symbols and the channel matrix. Simulations showed that 11 binary digits after the decimal point lead only to a small degradation of the BER. Further investigations have shown that for the received symbols $\tilde{x}_i$ only six binary digits after the decimal point are sufficient [5].

The HW realization of the RNN algorithm is based on Equation (1) and on the specific structure of the packet channel matrix $\underline{R}$ (in our case only 80 elements in one line are not equal to zero, see [2,5]). We observe that we need 80 complex multiplications and additions to compute the value of one neuron in one iteration. For a symmetric uplink/downlink (UL/DL) allocation of the time bursts $5 \cdot 10^9$ real valued multiplications and additions have to be done in one second.

One multiplication needs about 15 ns. Therefore we have to do a lot of multiplications in parallel. The problem of parallel multiplications is the required parallel data access. We organized the memory of the $\underline{T}$ matrix and the values of the neurons in such a way that we can access eight complex values at once. That means we can do eight complex, i. e. 32 real–valued multiplications, in parallel. An access of more values at once is not possible without wasting too much memory. Fig. 2 shows a part of the architecture which computes Equation (1).

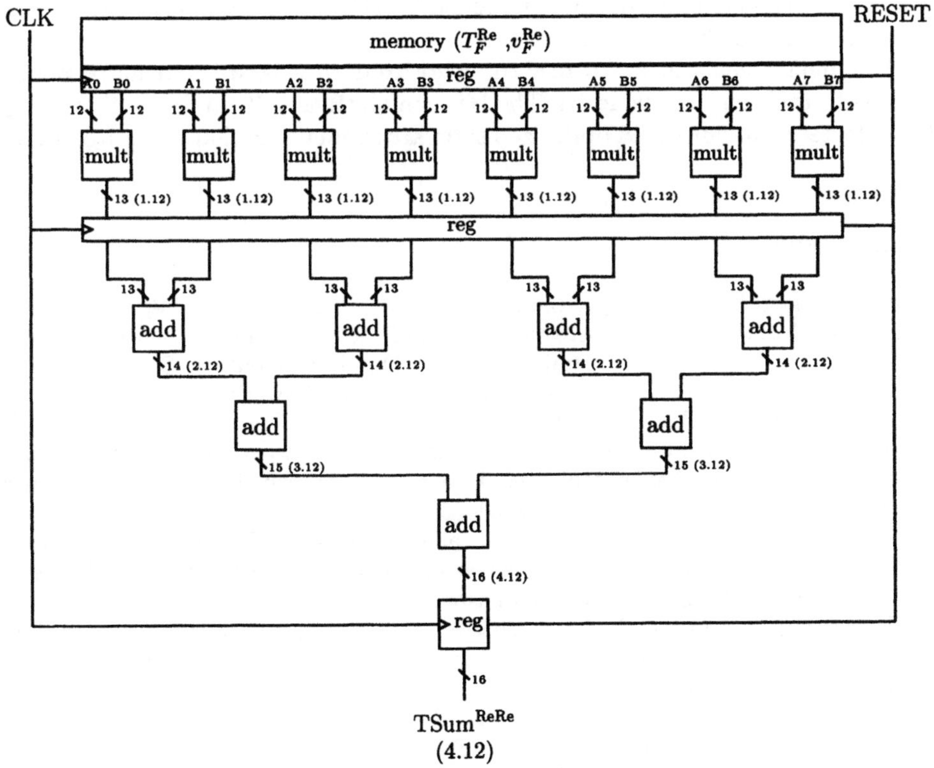

Fig. 2. One of four architectures with eight parallel multipliers. (x.y) means x binary digits before and y binary digits after the decimal point

This part is built four times, so 32 multiplications can be done in one clock cycle. We also use pipelining to reach the high data throughput. We implemented the whole algorithm in a VirtexE FPGA from XILINX and reached a maximum frequency of 70 MHz. So we can do the MUD for one datafield in 2.65 ms. But it should be done in 0.625 ms. So we need five architectures, each with 32 parallel multipliers and adders to do the MUD for a symmetric UL/DL allocation. Our implemented algorithm needs 24 BRAMs and about 3600 SLICEs. So we can include five parallel algorithms in one XCV2000E (160 BRAMs, 19200 SLICEs).

4 Summary

In this paper we presented a HW implementation based on FPGAs. A piece-wise linear approximation of the activation function and 12 binary digits of the channel matched filter outputs and the discrete–time channel matrix elements turned out to be sufficient. We mapped the algorithm to a VirtexE FPGA of XILINX. We used 32 parallel multipliers and adders to calculate the value of one neuron. The VHDL code and the post synthesis VHDL code could be verified by simulation. Parts of the algorithm have also been tested in HW. We estimate that a real–time detection of a symmetric UL/DL allocation can be done with one XCV2000E FPGA.

Our next steps will be to test the algorithm on a board and make further tests with different wordlengths. The HW simulations will run more than 10000 times faster than our speed optimized software simulations that are programmed in C.

References

1. A. Engelhart, W. G. Teich, J. Lindner, G. Jeney, S. Imre, and L. Pap: A Survey of Multiuser/Multisubchannel Detection Schemes Based on Recurrent Neural Networks. To appear in Wireless Communications and Mobile Computing, Special Issue on Advances in 3G Wireless Networks, Wiley Publishers, New York.
2. W. Schlecker, A. Engelhart, W. G. Teich, and H.–J. Pfleiderer: FPGA Implementation of a Multiuser Detection Scheme Based on Recurrent Neural Networks. Proc. COST262 Workshop Multiuser Detection in Spread Spectrum Communications, Schloss Reisensburg/Germany, 53–60, 2001.
3. C. Sgraja, A. Engelhart, W. G. Teich, and J. Lindner: Equalization with recurrent neural networks for complex–valued modulation schemes. Proc. 3. Workshop Kommunikationstechnik, Schloss Reisensburg/Germany, 7–12, 1999
4. W. G. Teich and M. Seidl: Code Division Multiple Access Communications: Multiuser Detection based on a Recurrent Neural Network Structure. Proc. ISSSTA '96, Mainz, Germany, 3:979–984.
5. W. G. Teich, W. Schlecker, A. Engelhart, R. Gessler, and H.–J. Pfleiderer: Towards an Efficient Hardware Implementation of Recurrent Neural Network Based Multiuser Detection. Proc. ISSSTA 2000, New Jersey, USA, 6:662–665, 2000.
6. ETSI/SMG2: The ETSI UMTS Terrestrial Radio Access (UTRA) ITU–R RTT Candidate Submission. May/June 1998

Building Custom FIR Filters Using System Generator

James Hwang and Jonathan Ballagh

Xilinx Inc. 2100 Logic Drive, San Jose, CA 95124 (USA)
{Jim.Hwang, Jonathan.Ballagh}@xilinx.com

Abstract. System Generator is a high level design tool well suited to creating custom DSP data paths in FPGAs. While providing a high level abstraction of an FPGA circuit, it can be used to build designs comparable to hand crafted implementations in terms of area and performance. In this paper we use a MAC-based FIR filter design example to demonstrate the interplay between mathematical abstraction and hardware-centric considerations enabled by System Generator. We demonstrate how an algorithm can be efficiently mapped onto FPGA resources and present the hardware results of several System Generator FIR filter implementations.

1 Introduction

There has been considerable recent progress in software tool development to support DSP applications in FPGAs. System Generator is a high-level design tool for Xilinx FPGAs that extends the capabilities of Simulink® to include bit and cycle accurate modeling of FPGA circuits, and generation of an FPGA circuit from a Simulink model [3,4]. System Generator provides robust Simulink libraries for arithmetic and logic functions, memories, and DSP functions. By supporting high level modeling and automatic code generation, System Generator creates new opportunities to explore the interplay between mathematical abstraction and hardware-centric considerations.

In this paper we discuss several implementations of FIR filters. We use System Generator to map an algorithm onto FPGA resources, including shift register logic, dedicated multipliers, memory structures, and the logic fabric of Virtex™ and Virtex-II™ FPGAs. We then compare area-performance tradeoffs for different filter structures.

2 Hardware Modeling in System Generator

Virtex family FPGAs provide dedicated circuitry for building fast, compact adders, multipliers, and flexible memory architectures in the logic fabric [1]. System Generator provides abstractions for these resources; the use of a silicon feature is either inferred or available through configuration parameters on the block interfaces.

The Addressable Shift Register (ASR) block abstracts the SRL16 memory configuration [5], with the capability of running delay and address inputs at different rates. System Generator Multiplier blocks provide options for combinational and pipelined structures built in the FPGA fabric, and where available, embedded multipliers. The memory blocks can target either distributed or block RAM, the latter in either a single ported or dual ported configuration.

M. Glesner, P. Zipf, and M. Renovell (Eds.): FPL 2002, LNCS 2438, pp. 1101–1104, 2002.

3 Building MAC-based FIR Filters

A versatile FIR filter architecture that maps well onto FPGA resources employs multiply-accumulate (MAC) engines. In general, N MAC operations are required to compute an output sample for an N-tap filter. A System Generator model of a single-MAC FIR filter is shown in Figure 1. This architecture is very compact, and is a reasonable choice for low throughput applications or when N is small.

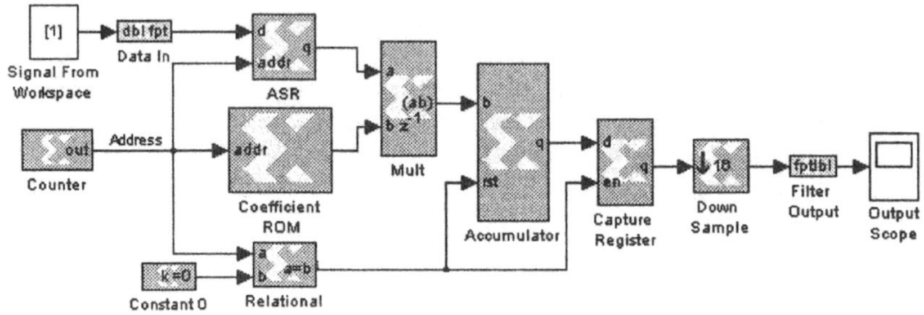

Fig. 1. Single-MAC FIR Filter

3.1 Configuring the Data Path

The tapped delay line is implemented using an ASR, which provides both a compact design and simple addressing requirements. The delay line runs at the data rate, but the rest of the filter, including the address port of the ASR, runs at N-times this rate. The impulse response of the filter is stored in a single port ROM having user-specifiable output precision (total and fractional bits), arithmetic type (signed or unsigned), and implementation option (distributed or block RAM).

The multiply-accumulate (MAC) engine is comprised of a multiplier and accumulator block. The multiplier computes the product of a filter tap and a sample from the data buffer, and the accumulator computes a running sum of these products. The multiplier can be implemented either in the logic fabric or using embedded multipliers. The accumulator is configured to reinitialize upon reset to its current input value to avoid a one-clock cycle stall at the end of each sum-of-products computation. A register captures the output of the MAC engine before it is reset. The capture register output is down sampled so the filter output rate matches its input rate.

The filter coefficient ROM is initialized from a MATLAB array bound to the model from the MATLAB workspace. Memory, counter, and down-sampler block parameters are specified in terms of this array. Multiplier and accumulator widths are defined as MATLAB functions of ROM wordsize, coefficient values, and filter input precision. Consequently, the model requires no modification to accommodate a change in the impulse response. The implications of this ability in System Generator to exploit the MATLAB interpreter during model customization should not be underestimated.

3.2 Filter Control Logic

A single counter, configured to count from 0 to $N-1$ repeatedly, generates addresses for both the coefficient ROM and input data ASR block. The counter's output sample period defines the rates of the downstream data and coefficient buffers using Simulink's sample time propagation rules. Since the filter requires addresses to change at N times the input data rate d_{rate}, the sample period is $\frac{1}{d_{rate} \cdot N}$.

For every new input sample, the accumulator block is reset to its current input, and the capture register latches the MAC engine output. This occurs when the address is zero; a relational block detects the condition.

3.3 Multiple-MAC Architectures

A single-MAC architecture has the drawback that throughput is inversely proportional to the number of filter taps. Throughput can be increased dramatically by exploiting parallelism. In theory the computation can be fully parallelized, *e.g.*, using a direct-form implementation [6], but System Generator and the FPGA allow a preferable solution that matches resource usage and availability to throughput.

The tapped delay line of the single-MAC architecture can be partitioned into cascaded sections, each serviced by a separate MAC engine. The outputs of these MAC engines are combined in an adder tree to compute the filter output. With this approach it is possible to increase the throughput over a single-MAC filter while keeping the resource consumption as small as possible. The entire data path can be fully pipelined in System Generator.

As an example, suppose a MAC engine can operate at 150 MHz, and a 144-tap filter is required to run at a data rate of 3.125 MHz. Then the MAC can service 150/3.125, or 48 filter taps, which implies a cascade section length of 48, and 144/48, or three such sections for the filter.

4 Results

All results were obtained using the Xilinx ISE Series 4.2i software and XST synthesis tool to target an XC2V250-6 part. All models use dedicated multipliers, block memory for coefficient storage, and 12-bit precision for filter input and coefficients.

Table 1. Performance of 16-tap MAC FIR filters with pipelined and non-pipelined dedicated multipliers.

Pipelined Multiplier	fs (MHz)	Frequency (MHz)	Slices	% Utilization
No	5.95	95.21	51	3
Yes	13.10	209.63	77	5

The results in Table 1 demonstrate the effectiveness of using the pipeline stages of the dedicated multipliers. If the lower throughput is tolerable, the filter can be implemented in only 51 slices.

Table 2 illustrates the tradeoff between filter size and throughput by providing the performance results of three 64-tap FIR filters with a varying number of MAC engines. It can be seen that in this experiment, the operating clock frequency is not particularly sensitive to the number of MAC-engines employed.

Table 2. Performance of fully pipelined non-symmetric 64-tap FIR filters with one, two, and four MAC engines.

MAC Engines	fs (MHz)	Frequency (MHz)	Slices	% Utilization
1	3.04	194.74	110	7
2	5.69	182.18	187	12
4	12.12	193.98	313	20

5 Conclusions

Modern FPGAs are capable of implementing high performance DSP functions, but the relative unfamiliarity of many DSP engineers with hardware design has slowed their wider adoption. Tools like System Generator provide means for both high level modeling of DSP algorithms, and implementing custom high performance DSP data paths in FPGAs. Through the use of simple examples, we have demonstrated several general techniques for building efficient MAC-based FIR filters from a system level development environment.

References

1. Xilinx, Inc., *Virtex-II Platform FPGA Handbook*, 2001.
2. The Mathworks Inc., "Matlab, Getting Started with Matlab," Natick, Massachusetts, 1999.
3. The Mathworks Inc., "Simulink, Dynamic System Simulation for Matlab, Using Simulink," Natick, Massachusetts, 1999.
4. J. Hwang, B. Milne, N. Shirazi, and J. Stroomer, "System Level Tools for DSP in FPGAs," *FPL 2001*, Lecture Notes in Computer Science, pp 534-543, 2001.
5. K. Chapman, "Saving Costs with the SRL16E," *Xilinx techXclusive*, 2000.
6. S. Mitra, "Digital Signal Processing: A Computer Based Approach 2nd Edition," McGraw-Hill, 2001.

SoC Based Low Cost Design of Digital Audio Broadcasting Transport Network Applications

Klaus Feske, Georg Heinrich, Berndt Fritzsche, Mark Langer
FhG IIS Erlangen - Branch Lab Design Automation Dresden,
Zeunerstr. 38, 01069 Dresden, Germany
e-mail: {feske | georg | fritzsche | langer}@eas.iis.fhg.de

Abstract. In order to enhance efficiency in designing Digital Audio Broadcasting (DAB) transport network applications we combine Protocol Compiler-based high level design methods with the Atmel System Designer SoC development suite. We define DAB requirements and outline design as well as validation of a Ensemble Transport Interface Monitoring Unit (EMU). Experimental results and conclusions concerning the efficiency of design and validation are given.

1 Introduction and Related Work

This paper reports our experiences in designing low cost System-on-a-Chip (SoC) based applications. For this purpose we combine domain specific high level modeling principles with the Atmel System-on-Chip technology.

The requirements of the controller design for telecommunication applications like Digital Audio Broadcasting (DAB) are the starting point of our work. Therefore, we studied high level approaches like the Protocol Compiler [1], useful for high level modeling, compiling and debugging of structured data processing controllers. Various application reports [2,3] indicate an improved design productivity exploiting the capabilities of this high-level synthesis approach.

The paper is structured as follows. Section 2 defines the DAB design requirements. In Section 3 first we explain modeling principles using the Protocol Compiler and our extended SoC design flow. Afterwards we describe dedicated design processes by a case study named ETI Monitoring Unit (EMU) and present synthesis results achieved for the FPSLIC SoC. Section 4 discusses two approaches to validate the designs. Finally we draw some conclusions and discuss opportunities for further activities.

2 Project Requirements

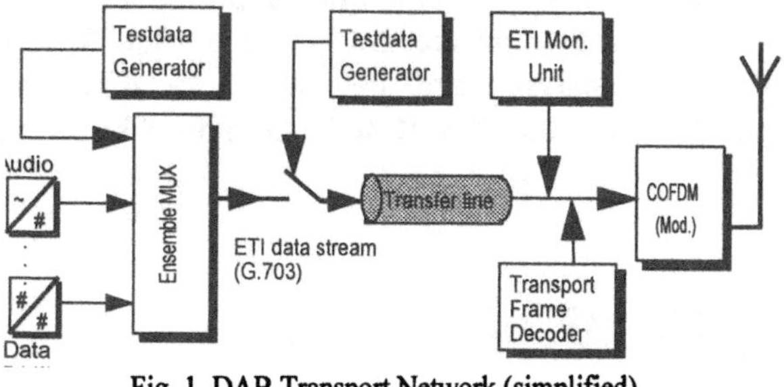

Fig. 1. DAB Transport Network (simplified) and additional test and monitoring facilities

The digital radio system DAB [4] is a broadband system which transmits multiple programs in a common frame. The digitized audio and data services as well as the control information are put together by the Ensemble Multiplexer to the Ensemble Transport Interface ETI [4]. In form of an ETI

M. Glesner, P. Zipf, and M. Renovell (Eds.): FPL 2002, LNCS 2438, pp. 1105-1109, 2002.

data stream they are distributed to the transmitters. Our Department has developed several DAB processing equipments, consequently, a suitable DAB test data generator represents an effective facility to support the test of complex DAB transport networks (Fig. 1). For monitoring purposes a further facility called *ETI Monitoring Unit* is placed into the DAB environment.

3 Extended Design Flow Using Protocol Compiler

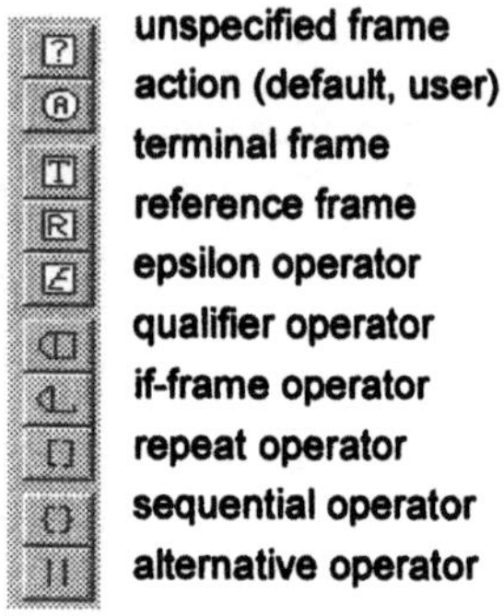

Fig. 2. Frame operators

In our current DAB project we extended our design environment by the ATMEL FPSLIC rapid prototyping platform and the dedicated HW-SW-Design Flow. The system development comprises two main aspects: HW design and SW design as described in [6]. As a new element of this flow, the Protocol Compiler is set on the top. In the field of telecommunication applications it supports the design of controller circuits for processing data protocols. Regarding the protocol level, a high-level specification is composed using a graphical entry (Fig. 2). Being similar to the Backus-Naur-Form the graphical symbolic format closely matches the requirements of high-level protocol specifications.

3.1 Modeling ETI Monitoring Unit EMU

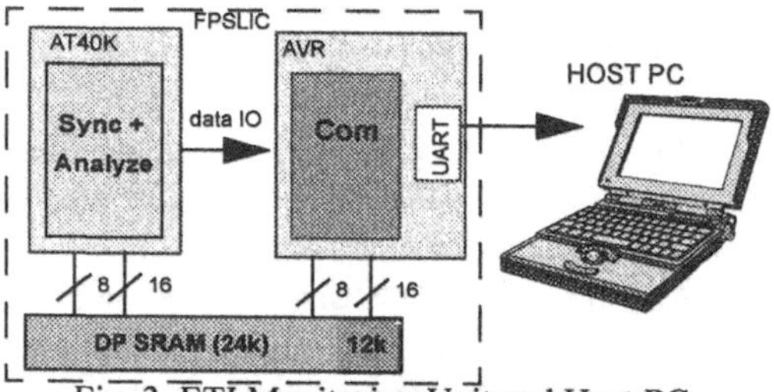

Fig. 3. ETI Monitoring Unit and Host PC

The *ETI Monitoring Unit* (*EMU*) is the counterpart to our *Test Data Generator* (*TDG*) [3,6]. As a low cost and mobile solution it utilizes the ATMEL FPSLIC features and enables analyzing basic DAB data stream properties like frame synchronization and several protocol components. The main parts of this SoC consist of a 8 bit AVR RISC CPU, a 36 kB internal dual-port SRAM, an AT40K FPGA and various periphery. The AVR connects the AT40K to an UART via the AVR internal bus and via a reserved SRAM range. Figure 3 shows the block diagram. Statical protocol data are transferred via the internal bus while dynamic data are transferred via the SRAM range. While the AT40K accomplishes the analysis of the data stream the AVR processes the extracted data and transports it out of the FPSLIC to be monitored by a host PC.

3.1.1 Frame Synchronization

In order to analyze ETI data correctly our EMU synchronizes the incoming ETI data. Since each ETI frame starts with one of two alternating synchronization words (FSYNC0 and FSYNC1) there are four synchronization levels according to

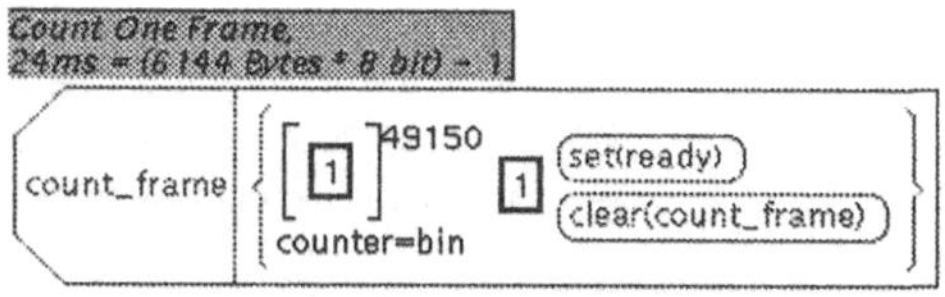

Fig. 4. Observing the frame length

the ETI Standard [4]. If three consecutive turns from FSYNC1 to FSYNC0 are recognized the synchronization is completed. To model this synchronization steps using the high-level HW description language of the Protocol Compiler our EMU consists of concurrent processes.The graphical modelled process in Figure 4 observes the correct frame size of 24ms. Four further processes are responsible to determine the synchronization level. Figure 5 shows the simplified state machine generated by the Protocol Compiler (a), and in detail the process (b) of the synchronization level 0. If the input

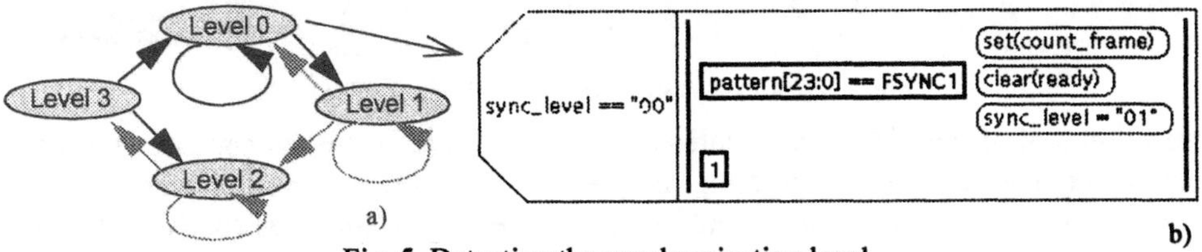

Fig. 5. Detecting the synchronization level

stream includes synchronization word FSYNC1 the EMU enters synchronization level 1 (*sync_level = "01"*). Furthermore the observation of the frame length is initialized by *set(count_frame)*.

3.1.2 Frame Analysis

The analyzing unit of the EMU filters particular protocol components from the DAB stream. Using the high-level descriptions of the Protocol Compiler the same modeling principles and operators are used as in [3]. The two related models of the Frame Characterization are visualized in Fig. 6. Comparing both models the consistency is visible: the main protocol elements are reference frames with coupled actions. During assembling (a) data stream elements are collected (tx_byte) and conversed (PS_Conversion) from parallel to a serial output. The analysis inside the EMU (b) is composed of several serial-parallel conversions and a storing process into variables or the SRAM. This comparison illustrates how easy it is to apply graphical composition of control logic for data transmission as well as protocol recognition tasks.

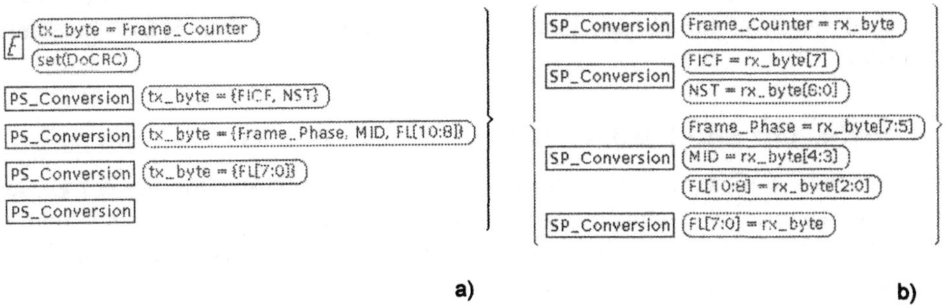

Fig. 6. Frame Characterization a) Assembling (TDG [3]) b) Analysis (EMU)

3.2 Synthesis Results

Both the TDG and the EMU were synthesized targeting the Atmel FPSLIC architecture. TDG synthesis results can be found in [6]. The synthesis results for the synchronization unit of the EMU are visualized in Fig. 7 - we compare the number of utilized cells and the maximum operating frequency. The different results were reached exploiting the code generating capabilities of the Protocol Compiler confronted with a manual edited VHDL model. To summarize the obtained results we found that a manual VHDL model is often a good solution. But a graphical model including the matching encoding style can more easily reach comparable results.

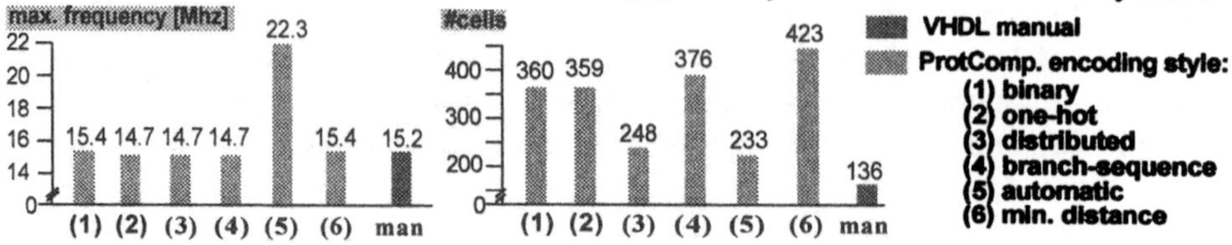

Fig. 7. Synthesis results for SYNC-Unit of EMU

4 Simulation and Prototyping

The testbench for verifying the hardware descriptions in VHDL utilizes both the TDG and the EMU (Fig. 8). The correct data stream generation can be examined using a waveform viewer or utilizing the analyzing capabilities of the EMU. So a useful VHDL testbench can be created and the verification of the generated data stream is simplified (1). To test the synchronizing and analyzing capabilities of the EMU stimuli data are required. So we composed an adapted testbench: The ETI data stream, generated by the TDG, was used as stimuli for the EMU, which can be understood as graphical composed stimuli data (2). After the iterative functional validation is done we check the correctness of the TDG and EMU prototypes in a DAB environment utilizing the Transport Frame Decoder FD1000 [5] for a meaningful testing.

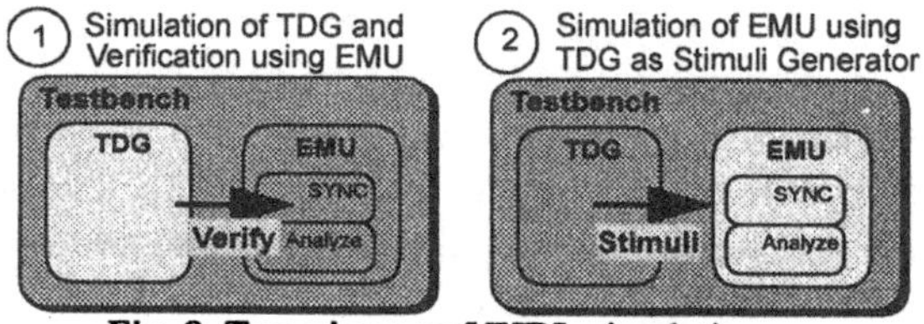

Fig. 8. Two views on VHDL simulation

5 Conclusions and Future Work

We extended a SoC design environment by a graphical high level design entry. This enables an application-oriented modeling style for structured data processing controllers at the specification level. Additionally this approach enhances design efficiency and leads to quick design explorations. The aim of our case studies was to evaluate our SoC-based design flow and to study the features of the achieved low cost solutions based on the FPSLIC. Our future work aims at applying this approach to other design projects in the field of telecommunications and networking.

Acknowledgment

The authors thank Mr. Cox, Atmel, and Sven Mulka, G. Döring, FhG IIS, for fruitful discussions. This work has been partially supported by the DFG Project SFB 358.

References

[1] SYNOPSYS: "V2000.05 Protocol Compiler User's Guide", Synopsys Inc., 2000.

[2] Holtmann, U.; Blinzer, P.: „Design of a SPDIF Receiver using Protocol Compiler", DAC'98, June 1998, San Francisco, CA, USA.

[3] Scholz, M.; Döring, G.; Feske, K.: „Design of a Digital Audio Broadcasting (DAB) Test Data Generator using the Synopsys Protocol Compiler", SNUG'99, Munich, 1999.

[4] ETS 300 799, Digital Audio Broadcasting (DAB); Distribution interfaces; Ensemble Transport Interface.

[5] Betriebshandbuch Transport Frame Decoder FD1000, Rohde & Schwarz, München.

[6] Feske, K.; Mulka, S; Schneider, J.; Heinrich, G.: „SoC Integration of Digital Audio Applications Using Protocol Compiler and Atmel FPSLIC", 14th ASIC/SOC Conference, Washington, 2001.

Dynamic Constant Coefficient Convolvers Implemented in FPGAs

Ernest Jamro, Kazimierz Wiatr

AGH Technical University, Institute of Electronics
Mickiewicza 30, 30-059 Kraków, POLAND
jamro/wiatr@agh.edu.pl

Abstract. This paper describes different techniques for implementing in FPGAs convolution operation for which coefficients are relatively constant. Multiplication is a very basic operation required for convolution, therefore a thorough study of different multipliers (Constant Coefficient Multiplier vs. Dynamic Constant Coefficient Multiplier vs. Variable Coefficient Multiplier), their hardware efficiency and dynamic change of the coefficient are described.

1 Introduction

An N-tap convolution (FIR filter) can be expressed by an arithmetic sum of products:

$$y(i) = \sum_{k=0}^{N-1} h(k) \cdot x(i-k) \qquad (1)$$

where: $y(i)$, $x(i)$ and $h(i)$ represent response, input at the time i and the convolution coefficients, respectively.

Multiplication is the most complex operation in the convolver, and several techniques have been adopted to perform it more efficiently. First at all, coefficient values are usually constant, therefore the values of the coefficient can be built-in the circuit, this solution is further denoted as a Constant Coefficient Multiplier (KCMs). The KCM occupies 17÷23% on average or 29÷41% on maximum [1], area of a fully functional, Variable Coefficient Multiplier (VCM). Consequently, the KCM should be implemented whenever the coefficient values are constant. Alternatively, when coefficients are changed infrequently, a part of the FPGA can be reconfigured in order to change the coefficient. A FPGA can be reconfigured in time of a few milliseconds, nevertheless a new multiplier circuit must be redesign and re-implemented, which is much more time consuming than the FPGA reconfiguration. Therefore, this approach can be practically adopted provided that only a finite number of coefficient values are allowed. In this case every coefficient value has a separate pre-implemented entry which can be quickly download into the FPGA.

FPGAs implement logic cells as a Look Up Table (LUT) memory, therefore the inherent way of performing multiplication seems the LUT based Multiplication (LM) [2, 3] where the value of the coefficient is coded into the contents of the LUT memory. The coefficient change can be obtained by a proper sequence of writes into the LUT memory [1, 4]. This multiplication technique allows for quick change of the

M. Glesner, P. Zipf, and M. Renovell (Eds.): FPL 2002, LNCS 2438, pp. 1110-1113, 2002.

coefficient and is further denoted as Dynamic Constant Coefficient Multiplier (DKCM).

2 Dynamic Constant Coefficient Multiplier (DKCM)

The DKCM [1] (or self-configurable binary multiplier [4]) is the LUT based multiplier for which ROMs are replaced by RAMs. The idea behind the dynamic change of the coefficient is to properly change the contents of the memories. This, however, requires an additional RAM Programming Unit (RPU) which feeds RAM memory with proper address and data sequence while changing coefficient value. An example of the DKCM is shown in Figure 1. It should be noted that this example is equivalent to the KCM.

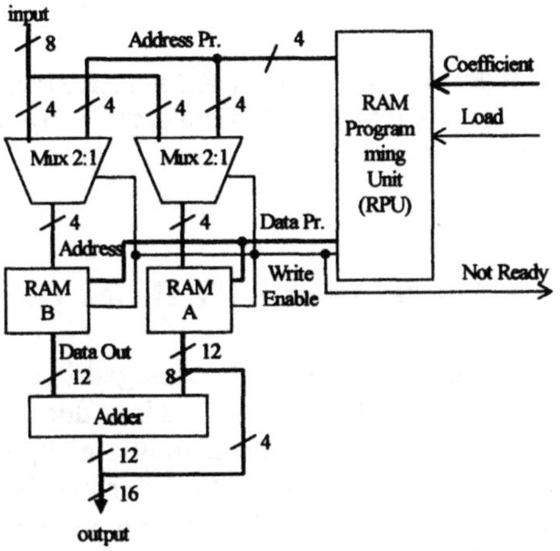

Fig. 1. An example of the DKCM for input data and coefficient width equal 8

The KCM can be implemented using either the LM or MM and the MM is getting more and more attractive as the coefficient width increases. Furthermore, even the LM can employ advance optimisation techniques which are suitable only for the KCM [1]. The KCM architecture varies significantly for different coefficients, which causes a great difference in area occupied. Therefore, to compare the DKCM with the corresponding KCMs, two different statistical costs of the KCM can be used: average and maximum area occupied by KCM for a given coefficient range (usually $1 \div 2^K - 1$).

The comparison of the KCM and DKCM is given in Figure 2. For small values of K, area occupied by the DKCM is much greater than for the KCMs due to the strong influence of the RPU; on Figure 2 the cost of the RPU is illustrated as the difference between DKCM-T (multiplexing in tri-state buffers) and maximum cost of the KCM-LM. As K increases, the relative cost of the RPU decreases, and additional cost of the DKCM over the KCM is related rather to the comparison strategy (the average or maximum cost of the KCM).

Recently, Xilinx Co. has introduced dedicated 18 bit × 18 bit fully functional multipliers to Virtex II family. Therefore it might seem that the VCM should be employed all the time. Nevertheless the number of dedicated multipliers is limited to 4 for XC2V40 and to 192 for XC2V10000 [6], so in a great number of designs the number of dedicated multipliers is still insufficient, and therefore the standard DKCM or KCM should be still considered.

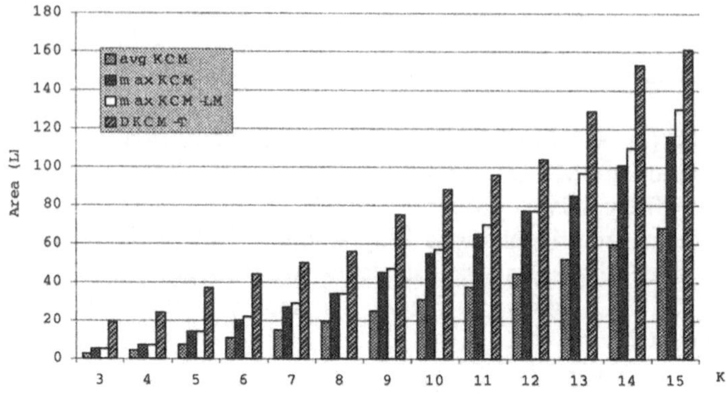

Fig. 2. Area for Xilinx XC4000, occupied by: the DKCM-T, maximum area of the KCM-LM and KCM (the best architecture of the MM or LM) and average area for the KCM. The input range $0 \div 2^K-1$ and the coefficient range $1 \div 2^K-1$

3 Dynamic Constant Coefficients LUT Based Convolver (DKLC)

For the DKLC, the value of coefficients can be changed in similar way, as it is in the case for the DKCM; rearranging the order of adders does not influence the LUTs programming schedule. For the DKCM, address multiplexing is located at the input of each RAM. Similarly for the DKLC, the multiplexer can be placed at the input of each multiplier (RAM). Let us denote this option as DKLC-M. An alternative solution, denoted as DKLC-C, is to place the multiplexer at the convolver input, so the address sequence for programming LUTs will propagate through the convolution delay elements to the input of the LUTs. The drawback of this method is a more sophisticated control logic. Besides, the number of programming cycles increases because of additional propagation time through the filter delay elements.

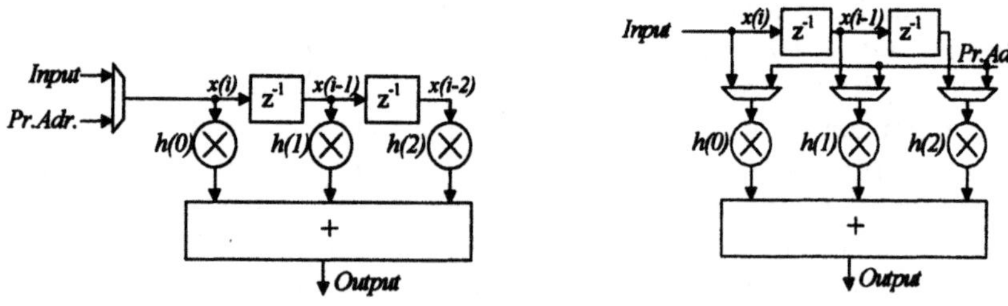

Fig. 3. Different strategies for dynamic change of coefficients

It should be noted that the LUTs can be programmed either in sequence: a single multiplier is programmed at the time, or in parallel, when all multipliers are programmed simultaneously. The serial option has longer programming time but a single RAM Programming Unit (RPU) is required. The parallel option has short programming time but each multiplier requires its own RPU and therefore this option occupies more hardware. The choice between the serial and parallel option should be taken after considering the average time between coefficients changes in similar way as it was described in Section 2.

4 Conclusions

Convolution is a fundamental operation for digital signal processing [10], therefore its efficient implementation in FPGAs is getting more and more important, as FPGAs are recognised as the best solution for high speed data driven algorithms. The significant part of this paper describes implementation of different multipliers in FPGA. A multiplication is a very basic operation for the convolution and, what is more important, can be smoothly described by the average or maximum area for the given coefficient and input ranges. The statistic area of the multiplier can be further analysed in order to find the best solution for the given parameters of the convolver.

Design automation is one of the most significant design factor, often more important that occupied area. Consequently, an Automated Tool for generating Convolvers in FPGAs (AuToCon) has been designed by the authors of this paper [3, 9]. The AuToCon can therefore automatically generate an optimised and synthesizable VHDL description of the convolver, only input parameters such as: the input width, convolution kernel size, coefficient values, pipelining parameter need to be entered.

References

[1] Wiatr K., Jamro E. *Implementation of Multipliers in FPGA Structures,* Proc. of the IEEE Int. Symposium on Quality Electronic Design, San Jose, March 2001, pp. 415-420.

[2] Omondi A.R *Computer Arithmetic Systems. Algorithms Architecture and Implementations,* Prentice Hall 1994.

[3] Wiatr K., Jamro E. *Constant Coefficient Multiplication in FPGA Structures,* Proc. of the IEEE Int. Conf. Euromicro, Maastricht, 2000, Vol. I, pp. 252-259.

[4] Wojko M., ElGindy H., *Configuration Sequencing with Self Configurable Multipliers,* Proc. 10th Sym. on Parallel and Distributed Processing, San Juan, April 1999, pp. 643-651.

[5] Do T.T., Reuter C., Pirsch P. *Alternative approaches implementing high-performance FIR filters on lookup table-based FPGAs: A comparison.* SPIE Conference on Configurable Computing and Applications, Boston, pp. 248-254, 2-3 Nov. 1998.

[6] Xilinx Inc. *The Programmable Logic Data Book,* San Jose, 2000.

[7] Sanchez E., Sipper M., Haenni J., Beuchat J., Perez-Uribe A. *Static and Dynamic Configurable Systems,* IEEE Trans. on Computers, col. 48, no. 6, pp. 556-563, June 1999

[8] Wirthlin M. J., Hutchings B.L., *Improving Functional Density Using Run-Time Circuit Reconfiguration,* IEEE Trans. on VLSI Systems, vol. 6, no. 2, June 1998.

[9] Jamro E., Wiatr K., *Genetic Programming in FPGA Implementation of Addition as a Part of the Convolution,* Proc. of the IEEE Int. Conf. Digital System Design, Warszawa, 2001, pp. 466-473, IEEE Computer Society Press.

[10] Jamro E., Wiatr K. *Implementation of convolution operation on general purpose processors* Proceedings of the Euromicro Conf. Warszawa, 2001, pp. 410-417, IEEE Computer Society Press.

VIZARD II: An FPGA-based Interactive Volume Rendering System

Urs Kanus[1], Gregor Wetekam[1], Johannes Hirche[1], and Michael Meißner[2]

[1] WSI/GRIS, Universität Tübingen, 72076 Tübingen, Germany,
[urs,gwetekam,jhirche]@gris.uni-tuebingen.de,
http://www.gris.uni-tuebingen.de
[2] Viatronix,
Stony Brook, NY, USA

Abstract. In this paper we present a volume rendering system that implements a Direct Volume Rendering algorithm on a Xilinx FPGA being capable of visualizing 3D-datasets with highest image quality at interactive frame rate. The volume renderer utilizes a cache optimized memory scheme for maximum memory bandwidth and a fully pipelined architecture of the computational expensive rendering calculations. The used ray-casting algorithm was adapted in critical parts to fit the specific need of an efficient hardware usage, with respect to available resources and computational power, without limiting rendering features.
Using a FPGA approach offers full flexibility to the implementation of the algorithm making it easy to adapt and extend new features to the rendering pipeline without the need of time consuming redesigns, especially important in a scientific environment.

1 Introduction

Direct Volume rendering is a key technology in the visualization of volumetric datasets. It is widely used in fields that use three dimensional sampled data, e.g. medical applications and scientific simulations.
The volume rendering process creates a 2D-image out of a 3D-dataset, [2] which highlights information based on a set of parameters, adjustable by the user.
Due to the three dimensional nature of the source data the rendering process requires large memory resources and and is computational expensive.
A variety of solutions have been proposed to this problem using software renderers, standard graphics cards or dedicated hardware [3], [4]. All existing solutions are either limited in the available rendering features, do not provide sufficient image quality or lack interactivity.
To overcome this limitation, we implemented a FPGA based volume rendering accelerator on a custom PCI-board with off-the-shelf components that offers highest image quality at interactive speed and is not limited to a specific set of rendering features due to its reconfigurability.

M. Glesner, P. Zipf, and M. Renovell (Eds.): FPL 2002, LNCS 2438, pp. 1114–1117, 2002.

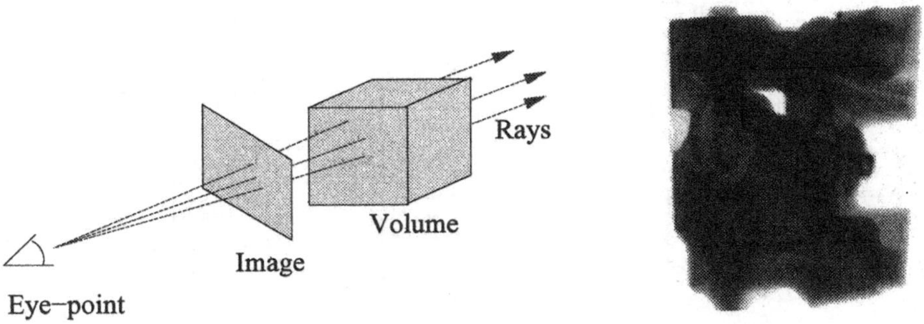

Fig. 1. Illustration of casting rays from the eye-point through the volume and a Volume rendered image of an engine block with a semi-transparent hull and opaque inner parts.

2 Algorithms

For each pixel of the final image a ray is cast from the eye-point through the volume, as illustrated by Figure 1 a). A volume consists of voxels (the 3D equivalent to pixels) that are located on a 3D grid. After determining the first intersection of the ray and the volume, sample values are calculated at equidistant points along the ray until the ray exits the volume. Because not all sample positions are directly at a voxel position, samples are tri-linearly interpolated from the eight surrounding voxels (see Figure 1 b)).

In the classificaton stage the sample values are interpreted as color , opacity and lighting properties to provide a meaningful interpretation of the volume data.

To enhance the three dimensional perception of the volume data a local illumination model is applied to the sample. For this shading operation a gradient is required at sample position. This gradient is tri-linearly interpolated from eight surrounding precomputed gradients, that are stored with the voxels as an attribute. The colored sample is finally accumulated in the compositing stage with the color and opacity values of previous samples along the same ray. A final pixel value C is reached after all samples of one ray have been accumulated: The final color value for each pixel on the view plane is therefore a composition of filtered samples of the original volume data.

To speed up the ray-casting algorithm, rays can be terminated before they exit the volume if the opacity reaches a certain threshold. This early ray termination avoids the computation of samples that do not contribute to the final pixel value, effectivly reducing the overall number of samples needed to render an image.

3 Implementation

VIZARDII is the first complete ray-casting implementation on an FPGA. Previous attempts on FPGA based volume rendering [3], [1] implemented only parts

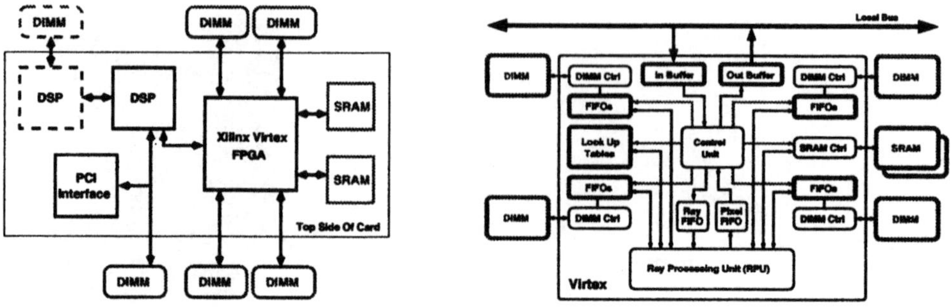

Fig. 2. Left: Architecture of the PCI board. Right: Architecture of the ray-casting engine.

of the rendering pipeline in hardware, due to limited device capacity and the high algorithmic complexity of the volume rendering algorithm. In the meantime, FPGA devices have grown considerably in size and performance and high level design tools have matured significantly, allowing more complex designs to be implemented. Before describing the ray-casting implementation on the Virtex FPGA, we give a brief description of the VIZARDII board.

VIZARDII Board The PCI-board is a custom Printed Circuit Board design, equipped with a PCI bridge (a PLX9054), a Digital Signal Processor (Analog Devices SHARC-21160), a Xilinx Virtex 2000E FPGA, two SRAMs and five SODIMM memory modules (256MByte each) as shown in Figure 2. Four SODIMM-modules are used as volume memory, connected to the Virtex FPGA. Each SODIMM can be independently addressed. The fifth SODIMM serves as local program- and data-memory for the DSP. Two SRAMs (1 Mbit) are used to store large lookup-tables, which would not fit into on-chip RAM. The DSP is responsible for the communication to the host system and performs the ray setup, while the FPGA contains the full ray-casting engine.

Ray-Casting Implementation The ray-casting engine (Figure 2) consists of a central control unit, which handles communication with the DSP, render modi, dataset- and look-up-table-download, and global control for the rendering pipeline. Four SDRAM and one SRAM memory controller interface to external memory. Addresses to and data from SDRAM memory is fifoed to allow continuous pipeline operation, even if one SDRAM is in a precharge or refresh cycle. All computations are performed in the ray processing unit (RPU), which receives ray-, voxel-, and look-up-table-data and delivers RGBα-Pixels.

4 Results

The VIZARDII rendering engine is implemented in more than more than 30k lines of VHDL-code. After synthesis and place&route, the rendering engine uses three quarters of the CLB Slices of a Virtex 2000E FPGA and 80 BlockRams. This compares to 2.3 Million nand-gate equivalents including on-chip memory. Currently, the FPGA can be clocked at 65 MHz but with proper floor-planning and a few optimization in timing critical design regions, 100 MHz is within reach.

Performance: The current implementation of the rendering pipeline computes a maximum of 65 million tri-linearly interpolated and Phong-shaded samples per second (one sample per clock cycle). This allows for interactive rendering of large (512^3) datasets at high quality, but due to the view and classification dependency, the frame-rate is not constant.

Design Flexibility: Volume rendering is not a "one algorithm fits all" application, therefore flexibility in the choice of the algorithm was a strong reason to choose a FPGA. Given a set of different algorithms, each in it's own configuration bit-stream, the host application can choose at run-time, which algorithm to use, by reconfiguring the FPGA. So far, we have not investigated partial reconfiguration of the FPGA, due to the lack of proper design tools. However, recent improvements of these tools may make it worthwhile to do so.

Image Quality: Our rendering engine supports different rendering modes, such as standard ray-casting, Pre-Integrated Rendering and Maximum Intensity Projection and produces images at arbitrary oversampling rates in x, y, and z-dimension further increasing the image quality.

Conclusions This paper presented the algorithm, the architecture and the implementation of a volume rendering PCI-board. It is the first fully FPGA based implementaion of a ray-casting pipeline, providing high quality images at interactive framerates. For an in-depth description of VizardII see http://www.gris.uni-tuebingen.de/.

References

[1] Michael Dao, Todd A. Cook, Deborah Silver, and Paul S. D Urbano. Acceleration of template-based ray casting for volume visualization using FPGAs. *Proceedings of the IEEE Symposium on FPGA's for Custom Computing Machines (FCCM '95)*, pages 116–124, 1995.

[2] R. A. Drebin, L. Carpenter, and P. Hanrahan. Volume Rendering. *Computer Graphics*, 22(4):65–74, August 1988.

[3] G. Knittel. A PCI-based volume rendering accelerator. In *Proc. of Eurographics/SIGGRAPH Workshop on Graphics Hardware*, pages 73–82, Maastricht, The Netherlands, August 1995.

[4] H. Pfister, J. Hardenbergh, J. Knittel, H. Lauer, and L. Seiler. The VolumePro Real-Time Ray-Casting System. In *Computer Graphics*, Proc. of ACM SIGGRAPH, pages 251–260, August 1999.

RHiNET/NI: A Reconfigurable Network Interface for Cluster Computing

Naoyuki Izu, Tomonori Yokoyama, Junichiro Tsuchiya, Konosuke Watanabe, and Hideharu Amano

Dept. of ICS, Keio University, 3-14-1 Hiyoshi Yokohama 223-8522 Japan
pdarch@am.ics.keio.ac.jp

Abstract. A reconfigurable network interface called RHiNET/NI is developed for parallel processing with PCs distributed within one or more floors of a building. Two configurations: the HS (High Speed) configuration only with a high speed primitive and the DSM (Distributed Shared Memory) configuration which supports sophisticated primitives can be selected by the network requirements.

1 RHiNET

RHiNET(RWCP high performance network)[1] is a new class of networks which has the advantages of both system area networks (SANs) used in common PC clusters and local area network (LANs). It consists of network switches and network interfaces each of which provides electric/optical interface converters.

RHiNET/NI(Fig. 1), a network interface of RHiNET consists of PCI interface, an optical interconnection interface, memory modules for data buffer (SDRAM) and tables (SRAM), and a CPLD (Altera's FLEX10K 250ABC600-1) for the reconfigurable primitive handler(Fig.2).

Fig. 1. RHiNET/NI

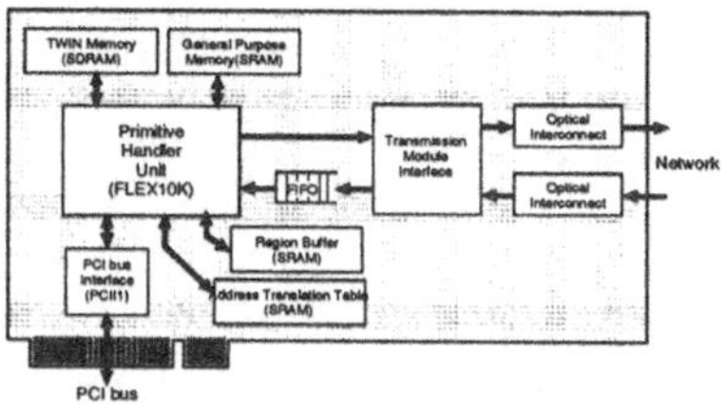

Fig. 2. Block diagram

In most network interfaces, a simple processor with dedicated DMA hardware is used for primitive processing like LANai in Myrinet[5]. However, we adopted a reconfigurable primitive controller for high speed zero copy communication as well as flexible operations.

Configuration data sets of the primitive controller are stored in the host memory, and can be replaced through the PCI bus in order to satisfy network requirements. Now, *High Speed (HS) configuration* which is advantageous when

M. Glesner, P. Zipf, and M. Renovell (Eds.): FPL 2002, LNCS 2438, pp. 1118–1121, 2002.

the parallel program is executed only with simple message passing libraries, and *Distributed Shared Memory (DSM) configuration* for building a distributed shared memory are available.

2 Two Configurations

2.1 HS Configuration

"push" is a zero-processor-copy remote DMA primitive from the host memory to the remote memory. In zero-processor-copy remote DMA communication, the network interface directly copies data from/to the user processes' memory space. Memory copy between user space and kernel space, which is usually performed on both sides of the communication, is not needed.

As shown in Fig. 3a), in a primitive handler for the HS configuration, a receive unit with the receive controller and the send unit with the send controller are implemented as individual modules, and work in the pipelined manner. So, this configuration attain high clock frequency. Page tables are provided in SRAM units outside the CPLD, and shared with the sender and receiver.

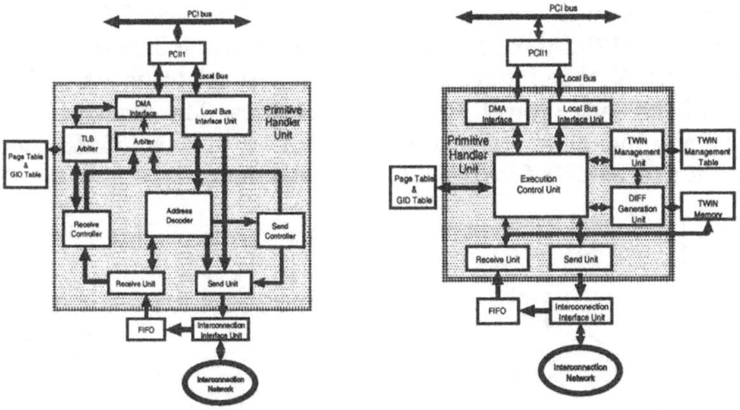

a)HS Configuration b) DSM Configuration

Fig. 3. HS and DSM configuration

The data flow control is achieved using the double buffer which in both local bus interface unit and sender / receiver. Note that the primitive handler executes every above operation with the reconfigurable hard wired logic.

2.2 DSM Configuration

Following primitives are provided in the DSM configuration.

- *push* and *pull* for remote zero-copy DMA transfer.
- *lock/unlock* for exclusive operations.

- primitives for multiple-writer protocol[2]: *pull_with_twin:* copies the receiving data to the memory in the network interface during the data is transferring to the main memory of the host with the DMA. *push_diff:* compares the sending data from the initiater memory with the data in the the network interface memory, and the difference is only transferred.
- other primitives: *barrier:* is a synchronization primitive which broadcasts a packet when all registered nodes execute the primitives. *push_bitmap:* transfers the data from the initiater memory to the remote memory according to the bit map stored in the network interface memory. Only the data corresponding bit in the bit map is "1" is written to the remote memory. This primitive is useful for array data transfer with a specific stride.

Unlike the HS configuration, the centralized execution control unit manages all communication as shown in Fig. 3b). Instead of the pipelined execution in the HS configuration, it controls complicated data flow sequentially. Sophisticated primitives pull_with_twin and push_diff are managed with dedicated controller units.

3 Evaluation Results

The performance is evaluated with a real system. Two host PCs (Intel Pentium III 800MHz with 512Mbyte main memory and 33MHz PCI) are connected with the RHiNET-2/SW. The interconnect frequency is set to be 100MHz, thus the bandwidth of the each optical link becomes 1Gbps. The clock of RHiNET/NI is set to be the maximum of each configurations: that is, 25MHz for the HS configuration and 20MHz for the DSM configuration.

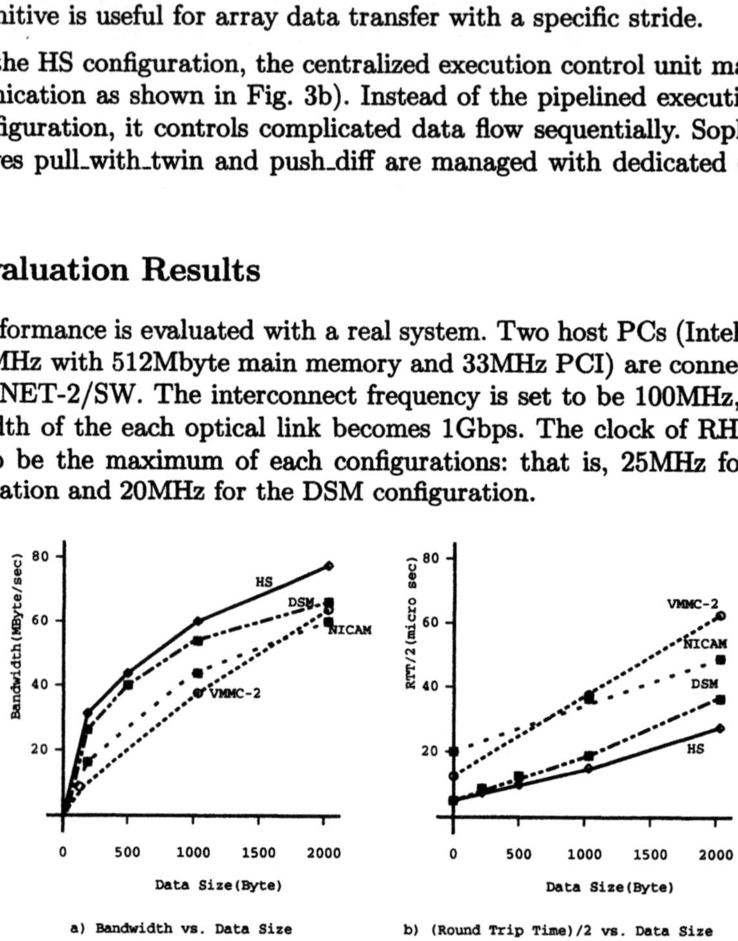

Fig. 4. Performance of RHiNET/NI

3.1 Bandwidth and Latency

Fig. 4 shows the bandwidth and latency of the HS configuration and DSM configuration. The latency is measured by the half of the round trip time of data ping-pong program using "push" primitive. For comparison, the evaluation results of traditional PC clusters: VMMC-2[3] and NICAM[4] are added in the graph. Both systems use Myrinet's LANai7[5] as their network interfaces.

As shown in Fig. 4, the HS configuration achieves better performance compared with traditional systems. Especially, the latency (round trip time) is much reduced. The performance of the DSM configuration is lower than that of the HS configuration because of its complicated functions, but it is not worse than traditional systems. This results demonstrates that the reconfigurable approach can achieve better performance compared with network interface with dedicated hardware and processor core.

3.2 The Performance of Sophisticated Primitives

Table 1 shows the execution time of pull_with_twin operation. The same operation can be done with a simple pull primitive and data copy in the host memory. "Software" in the table shows required time for such software execution. Using the reconfigurable logic, pull_with_twin achieves more than twice performance compared with the software execution. Table 1 also shows the execution time of push_diff operation. In this case, the same operation can be done with the bit map generation by the software and push_bitmap primitive. The figures in the table shows that the similar performance improvement is observed in this case.

Table 1. The execution time of DSM primitives (micro sec)

	pull_with_twin			push_diff		
Data size (byte)	512	1024	2048	512	1024	2048
RHiNET/NI	21	29	44	25	39	69
Software	35	55	97	38	63	119

Through this empirical evaluation, it appears that the HS configuration much improves the latency of data transfer, while the DSM configuration achieves more than twice performance for executing sophisticated operations as that of software implementation.

References

1. T.Kudoh, et.al, "RHiNET: A network for high performance parallel processing using locally distributed computers," Proc. of 1999 International Workshop on Innovative Architectures pp.69-73
2. C.Amza et al. "TreadMarks: Shared Memory Computing on Networks of Workstations," Computer, Vol.29, No.2, pp18-28, Feb. 1996.
3. S.Dubnicki, et.al, "VMMC-2: Efficient Support for Reliable, Connection-Oriented Communication," Hot Interconnects V, August 1997.
4. Y.Tanaka, et.al, "COMPaS: A Pentium Pro PC based SMP Cluster and its Experience," IPPS Workshop on Personal Computer Based Network of Workstations, LNCS 1388, pp.486-497, 1998.
5. http://www.myri.com/

General Purpose Prototyping Platform for Data-Processor Research and Development

Filip Miletić, Rene van Leuken, and Alexander de Graaf

DIMES, Delft University of Technology
Mekelweg 4 H16 CAS, 2628 CD, Delft, The Netherlands
rene@dimes.tudelft.nl

Abstract. This paper describes a general purpose prototyping platform, which allows for fast prototyping of data processors. It is based on publicly available components and design tools. Additions to the original models are described and hardware and software issues are explained. The prototyping platform is in use by educational and research groups.

1 Introduction

The availability of large FPGA's has enabled fast prototyping of large digital systems. The goal of the prototyping environment is to test and debug the developed model in real hardware. The model under development should be placed in a 'black box' environment, where only the model and the software necessary to control the model are visible: the prototyping platform. The basic components of such a prototyping platform are: CPU, memory, I/O devices, a co-processor interface, and a communication bus. The LEON is a synthesizable VHDL description of a SPARC compatible processor. The model and development tools built around GNU C are available for download at [1].

2 The LEON Co-processor Interface

Design goal was making a comfortable testing environment for data processors. Ideally, one would be able to plug in a design as co-processor without delving into abundant detail of the enviroment. LEON allows for one serial and one parallel co-processor unit be present. The serial unit must be a FPU, while the parallel unit can be either a FPU or a general purpose co-processor. The co-processor unit consists of two modules: the interface and the execution unit. The interface is an instruction decoder, which also contains the co-processor register file. In SPARC, the co-processor registers are denoted as *%c0*,*%c1* and so on. They are used for data transfer from memory and as source and destination operands for the co-processor instructions. LEON can be configured to provide a generic interface to a special-purpose co-processor. One co-processor instruction can be started each cycle as long as there are no data dependencies. When finished, the result is written back to the co-processor register files.

M. Glesner, P. Zipf, and M. Renovell (Eds.): FPL 2002, LNCS 2438, pp. 1122–1125, 2002.

Co-processor Access. To illustrate the use of the co-processor, consider the listing 1.1. First the *cp_enabled* flag of the program status register must be set. This is done in software by *cp_en*, shown in line 16 of listing 1.1. The *nop* instructions following line 20 are required as the pipeline might defer actual setting of the flag.

Listing 1.1. Using co-processor from within GNU C

```
   #define cpop1(opc,rs1,rs2,rd) \
2    ".word␣(0x81B00000␣+␣\
     (("␣rs1␣"  & 0x1F) << 14) + "\
4    "(("rd "␣&␣0x1F)␣<<␣25)␣+␣\
     ("rs2" & 0x1F) +"␣\
6    "(("opc "␣&␣0x1FF)␣<<␣5)␣)"
   #define cpop2(opc,rs1,rs2,rd) \
8    ".word␣(0x81B80000␣+␣\
     (("␣rs1␣" & 0x1F) << 14) +"␣\
10   "(("rd"␣&␣0x1F)␣<<␣25)␣+␣\
     ("rs2" & 0x1F) +"␣\
12   "(("opc"␣&␣0x1FF)␣<<␣5)␣)"
   #define rC0 "0"
14 #define rC2 "2"
   #define rC4 "4"
16 void cp_en() {  */
     asm(     "mov␣%%psr,␣%%g1"
18     "set␣0x2000,␣%%g2"
       "wr␣%%g1,␣%%g2,␣%%psr"
20     "nop"
       "nop"
22     "nop"  : : : "g1", "g2");
   }
24 void loadc0(long a) {
     asm("ld␣␣%0,␣%%c0" : : "m" (a) );
26 }
   void storec0( long *a) {
28   asm("st␣%%c0,␣%0" : "=m" (*a) );
   }
30 void cpop1() {
     asm(cpop1("0x49", rC0, rC2, rC4));
32 }
```

The co-processor communicates with the rest of the system using load and store instructions to move data to and from co-processor registers. GNU Assembler can recognize transfers involving co-processor registers and will generate appropriate instructions. The *asm* clause in lines 25 and 28 of listing 1.1 follows the GNU C conventions. The *m* flag will force GNU Assembler to generate loads and stores from memory in case parameter *a* gets passed in a register. Two generic instructions are provided for co-processor operation control, *cpop1* and *cpop2*. *cpop1* must not modify flags, while *cpop2* is allowed to do so. Both have a 9 bit opcode field, allowing up to 512 different instructions. The co-processor operation instruction is specified in line 31. Each generic instruction has four arguments [3], the encoding of which is given in figure 1. This instruction is not supported by GNU Assembler, so in listing 1.1 we give co-processor defines which embed *cpop1* and *cpop2* using the *word* directive. The first argument is the opcode, a number that distincts between the different operations requested from the co-processor to perform. We use a value of 49_{16}, chosen at random, but requiring that the instruction decoding circuitry be described to handle the opcode gracefully. The remaining arguments are first and second source register indices as former, and a destination register as latter parameter. To use the instructions, we define *cpop1* and *cpop2* macros. (See listing 1.1)

opcode	op3	operation
CPop1	110110	Co-processor operate 1
CPop2	110111	Co-processor operate 2

Suggested Assembly Language Syntax
cpop1 $opc, creg_{rs1}, creg_{rs2}, creg_{rd}$
cpop2 $opc, creg_{rs1}, creg_{rs2}, creg_{rd}$

Format (3):	10 rd 110110 rs1 opc rs2
	10 rd 110111 rs1 opc rs2

Fig. 1. Generic co-processor operate instructions, from [3]. *rs1* and *rs2* denote source registers of the co-processor. *rd* denotes destination register.

3 Examples

A parallel co-processor unit is appealing for using LEON in digital signal processing. A fast DSP oriented co-processor might be employed to operate on streaming audio input. To demonstrate the potential of such a hardware arrangement, we set up a distributed-arithmetic FIR filter as a co-processor operating on a stereo audio stream. The data source and sink was the audio codec which we had attached as a device on the AMBA APB. The data is supplied to and from the codec on periodic basis. Consider an example FIR source code , shown in listing 1.2. For this purpose we are using a custom codec access module.

Listing 1.2. FIR filter software.

```
   #include "codec.h"
2  #define CODEC_BASE 0x800000C0
   volatile long left , right , leftplay , rightplay;
4  int main() {
     cp_en ();
6    codec_control         (CODEC_BASE, 0);
     codec_write_prescale(CODEC_BASE, 1);
8    codec_control         (CODEC_BASE, 1);
     for (;;) {
10     asm("st_%%c4,_%0": "=m" (rightplay));
       asm("st_%%c5,_%0": "=m" (leftplay));
12     codec_write_right ( CODEC_BASE,
                           rightplay>>13 );
14     codec_write_left  ( CODEC_BASE,
                       leftplay >>13 );
16     left  = codec_read_left ( CODEC_BASE);
       right = codec_read_right( CODEC_BASE);
18     asm("ld_%0,_%%c0" : : "m" (right));
       asm("ld_%0,_%%c1" : : "m" (left));
20     asm(cpop1("0x49","0","2","4"));
       asm(cpop1("0x48","1","3","5"));
22   }
     return 0;
24 }
```

Software. The co-processor access must begin with a call to *cp_en*, so we are making it the first statement (line 5) of the program. The following lines (lines 6 up to 8) set up the codec prescaler and enable it. The processing loop is placed in lines 10 to 21. The designer might as well decide to place this code inside an interrupt routine. The longest lasting instructions (filtering, done in lines 20 and 21) are scheduled to execute at the end of the loop, as they might take many clock cycles to complete, depending on the length and type of the FIR chain. In case of interrupt driven processing, this causes the instructions to be scheduled for execution inside the co-processor and the program would resume, in effect using the parallelism of co-processor.

Filter. The FIR filter, which is used in this design is implemented using distributed serial arithmetic. The processing time depends upon the number of bits of the coefficients and the data, as well as the number of independent channels that are processed. Each audio sample is represented by a 32-bit signed integer. Given the two channels of the stereo signal, the filtering is completed in 64 clock cycles. Reading samples and placing them into co-processor registers for processing is performed in lines 16 to 19. Functions *read_codec_left* and *read_codec_right* retrieve samples from the left and right codec input respectively. Processing samples is performed independently, in line 20 for the left, and in line 21 for the right channel.

Instructions. The interface of the FIR filter does elementary instruction decoding. As our FIR processor has only two instructions, *procleft* and *procright*, we use only one, least significant bit of the *opcode* to distinguish between them. Thus, all possible even opcodes will match *procleft*, and all odd opcodes will match *procright*. The *procleft* instruction places an input sample to the left channel filter queue. At the same time, it retrieves the left output channel sample from the filter queue. *procright* does the same for the right channel. The samples output by the co-processor are read in lines 10 to 15. These instructions in fact read the results from the *previous* pass through the filtering loop (or the previous interrupt routine call). Samples first have to be extracted from the co-processor register files to variables *leftplay* and *rightplay* (lines 10, 11). They are then output to the codec (lines 13, 15). The samples have to be shifted to convert to codec's dynamic range, which is represented as 20-bit normalized, signed two's complement. As the number of quantization levels of the FIR filter is 2^{32} due to the 32 bit wide data, the normalization is done by shifting for at least 12 bit positions to the right.

Instruction Format. The first source register field is taken to contain the sample value. The destination field specifies the register which will accept the output of the filter. Note that it was also possible to incorporate both left and right *input* supplying with a single instruction. However, we decided not do proceed this way, as all the co-processor operations are allowed to have only a single result. That way we would have to make separate instructions for reading output channels, which would affect the symmetry of the instruction set.

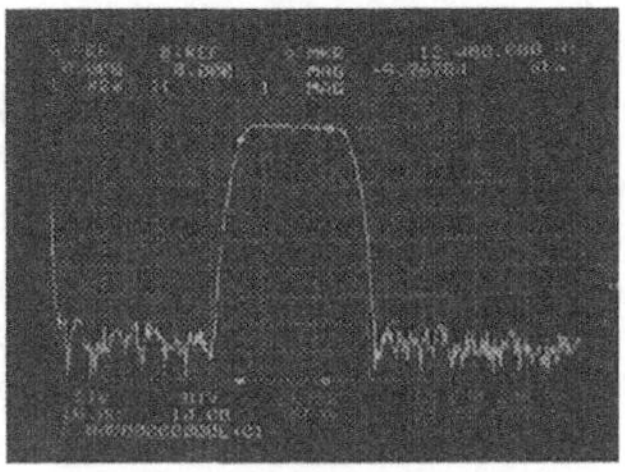

Fig. 2. The FIR filter frequency response, as measured on the actual hardware.

Measurements. The filter was designed using Matlab Signal Processing Toolbox. Its cutoff frequency is at about 13kHz. The obtained frequency response, as measured, is given in figure 2.

4 Conclusion

In this paper we presented a platform which allows for fast prototyping of data processors. It consists of publicly available components: a VHDL model and GNU design tools. We have extended this platform to include an audio interface, a fast serial interface and an infrastructure and methodology to integrate a co-processor quickly. As results we have shown the design of a FIR filter processor.

References

[1] *Leon model*, http://www.gaisler.com.

[2] Filip Miletic Rene van Leuken, Alexander de Graaf, *General purpose prototyping platform for data-processor research and development*, Tech. report, Delft University of Technology, April 2002.

[3] *The sparc architecture manual*, Prentice-Hall, Inc., 1992.

High Speed Computation of Three Dimensional Cellular Automata with FPGA

Tomoyoshi Kobori and Tsutomu Maruyama

Institute of Engineering Mechanics and Systems, University of Tsukuba
1-1-1 Ten-ou-dai Tsukuba Ibaraki 305-8573 JAPAN
kobori@darwin.esys.tsukuba.ac.jp

Abstract. In cellular automata, a single update rule is applied simultaneously to each cell on the lattice. Therefore, many approaches with parallel and distributed systems have been researched. In this paper, we propose a computation method of three dimensional cellular automata for small FPGA systems with limited memory bandwidth. We implemented the method on a FPGA board (Celoxica RC1000 with one Virtex-E XCV2000E). The speed gain for a 3D Life Game and a 3D Forest Fires model with $128 \times 128 \times 128$ lattice is 386 and 79 times compared with Celeron Processor 1.20GHz.

1 Introduction

Cellular Automata are used for simulating various phenomenon and run very efficiently on many platforms. Therefore, many approaches with parallel and distributed systems have been researched [2][3].

The size of FPGAs has been drastically improved in the last several years, and with one latest FPGA, it becomes possible to apply the update rules of the cellular automata to more than one hundreds cells in parallel. However, internal memory size of FPGAs is still too small for storing whole cells and the memory bandwidth of the FPGA becomes the bottleneck for the parallel processing. Therefore, we have proposed a new computation method of two-dimensional cellular automata for small systems with limited memory bandwidth [1]. In this paper, we propose a computation method of three dimensional cellular automata for the small FPGA systems.

2 Computation Method and the Circuit

First, we would explain a basic idea of the computation method, and then describe the strategy for computing three dimensional cellular automata in detail. In order to apply the update rule to one cell on the lattice, we need the status of 27 neighbor cells at the most. Therefore, we have to read nine lines at least from the memories. In practice, however, FPGAs can not read out data of k lines at once, and can not hold whole data for $k \times 3$ lines in the internal memories (the

M. Glesner, P. Zipf, and M. Renovell (Eds.): FPL 2002, LNCS 2438, pp. 1126–1130, 2002.

size of the lattice is much larger than the I/O width and internal memory size of the FPGAs in general).

Figure 1 shows a computation method for three dimensional cellular automata. In the figure, suppose that the FPGA can read out data of $a \times b$ cells at once (a is the number of cells in the direction along y axis, while b is the one along z axis), and hold only the data for $3 \times w \times a \times b$ cells (w is the the depth of distributed RAMs which are used to store the data). Then, the circuit on the FPGA, first, reads $a \times b$ cells (suppose that data of the cells are aligned in the external memory on the FPGA board so that $a \times b$ cells can be read out at once), and stores the data of first $2 \times w \times a \times b$ cells (two vertical plane) in the distributed RAMs by repeating the read operation $2 \times w$ times. When the next $a \times b$ cells are read in, the update rule is applied to $a \times b$ cells on the second vertical plane which are already stored in the FPGA. And, this update cycle is repeated w times. After updating the status of $w \times a \times b$ cells on the plane (w cycles are required), the circuit starts to read next $w \times a \times b$ cells. In this update cycle, however, status of neighbors can not be given on the four edges of the vertical plane. Therefore, only the output results of $(w \times a - 2) \times (b - 2)$ cells become correct (the gray parts of Figure1 (1)).

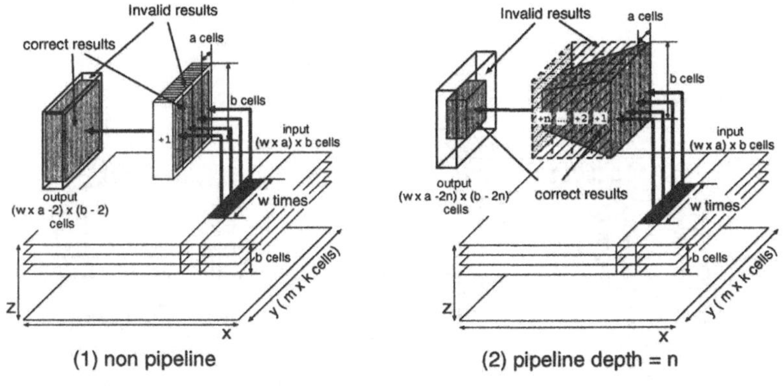

Fig. 1. Computation Method

Suppose that the FPGA can hold data of $n \times 3 \times w \times a \times b$. Then, by pipelining the circuit as shown in Figure 1 (2), we can process $n \times a \times b$ cells at a time (n is the depth of the pipeline). The generation of the outputs by the pipeline processing is the generation of the inputs $+n$. However, in this case, status of i cells on the four edges become incorrect at the i-th stage of the pipeline circuit as shown in Figure 1 (2). Therefore, the number of correct outputs (p) becomes $(w \times a - 2n) \times (b - 2n)$.

The parts which results become invalid have to be processed once more in order to obtain correct new status. Thus, the effective parallelism of this method becomes as follows.

$$q = p \times n/w = (a - 2n/w) \times (b - 2n) \times n \qquad (1)$$

In this method, depth of the distributed RAMs (w) is used to store data along y axis. However, when the bit-width of each cell is very small (namely, data of many cells can be packed in one data word), it gives better performance if the depth (w) is used to store data along z axis. This is because the effective parallelism becomes higher if the figure of the vertical plane ($(w \times a) \times b$ or $a \times (w \times b)$) is closer to a square. In this case, the results of $(a-2) \times (w \times b - 2)$ cells become valid when the circuit is not pipelined, while the number of correct outputs by pipelined circuit becomes $(a - 2n) \times (w \times b - 2n)$. Therefore the effective parallelism in this case becomes as follows.

$$q = p \times n/w = (a - 2n) \times (b - 2n/w) \times n \quad (2)$$

If the circuit can hold whole data along z axis (or y axis) in these strategies, the amount of invalid results can be more decreased, and higher performance can be achieved, because the boundary conditions on upper and lower edges of the lattice are given correctly. In this case, the number of correct outputs can be improved to $(a - 2n) \times w \times b$ and the effective parallelism is also improved as follows.

$$q = (a - 2n) \times b \times n \quad (3)$$

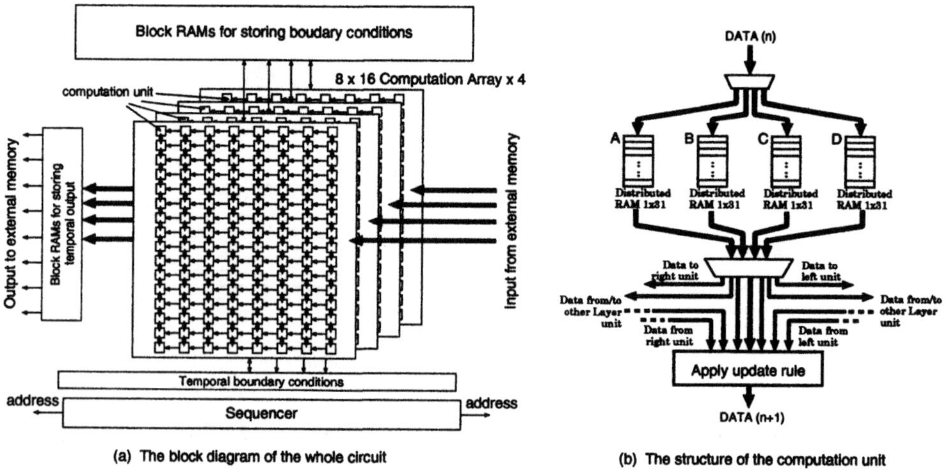

Fig. 2. Overview of the Circuit

Figure 2 (a) shows the block diagram of the circuit for 3-D Lifegame implemented on one Virtex-E XCV2000E. The circuit has $8 \times 16 \times 4$ computation units, and each computation unit computes the next status of one cell. Figure 2 (b) shows the structure of the unit. Each unit has four buffers which consist of distributed RAMs. By preparing four buffers, the unit can process one cell in every clock cycle. The outputs are transferred to its left unit. The width of the outputs by the circuit may not be equal to the width of external memory on the FPGA board (for example, the output width of the 3D Life Game is 8×4 bit). Therefore, the outputs are once stored in the block RAMs and then written to the external memory.

3 Results

Table 1 shows the results of 3D Life Game and 3D Forest Fires model with $128 \times 128 \times 128$ cells. The speed gain for these models is 386 and 79 times compared with Celeron Processor 1.20 GHz. In 3D Life Game, the size of unit array implemented on the FPGA is $8 \times 16 \times 4$. Therefore, the effective parallelism is 256. By comparison, in 3D Forest Fires model, the size of unit array implemented on the FPGA is $8 \times 1 \times 16$, and the effective parallelism is 48.

Table 1. Speed gain for 3D Life Game and 3D Forest Fires

	Software (for 8 generations)	Cellular Automata System	Speed gain
3D Life Game	454×8 (msec)	9.4 (msec)	386
3D Forest Fires	387×8 (msec)	39.3 (msec)	79

The speed gain for 3D Forest Fires is much worse than 3D Life Game because of the two reasons below.

- A lower effective parallelism caused by larger bit-width of cells (four bits).
- Only 6 neighbors are accessed in Forest Fires (these 6 neighbors are accessed in parallel) while 26 neighbors are accessed in 3D Life Game.

4 Conclusions

In this paper, we proposed a new computation method of 3-D cellular automata for small systems with limited memory bandwidth. We implemented the method on a FPGA board (Celoxica RC1000 with one Virtex-E XCV2000E), and the speed gain for a 3D Life Game and a 3D Forest Fores model with $128 \times 128 \times 128$ lattice is 386 and 79 times compared with Celeron Processor 1.20GHz. The method can be used for other 3-D cellular automata. We are now evaluating to more complex models.

However, we can not process all types of three dimensional cellular automata efficiently, because of some problems such as (1) FPGA can not read in several cells at a time because of the large bit-width of cells, and (2) the update rules are very complex, and we can not implement many processing unit on one FPGA. We expect that these problems will be solved by the rapid improvement of the size of the FPGAs.

References

1. Tomoyoshi Kobori, Tsutomu Maruyama and Tsutomu Hoshino. "A Cellular Automata System with FPGA" Proc. FCCM '01, IEEE Computer Soc 2001.
2. C. Adler, B. M. Boghosian, E. G. Flekkoy, N. Margolus and D. H. Rothman, "Simulation Three-Dimensional Hydrodynamics on a Cellular-Automata Machine", Journal of Statistical Physics, 1995
3. Norman Margolus. "An FPGA architecture for DRAM-based systolic computations" Proc. FCCM '97, pp. 2-11, IEEE Computer Soc 1997.
4. U. Frisch, D. d'Humires, B. Hasslacher, P. Lallemand, and Y. Pomeau. "Lattice gas hydrodynamics in two and three dimensions" Complex Systems, 1 PP.649-707 1987.

SOPC-based Embedded Smart Strain Gage Sensor

Sylvain Poussier, Hassan Rabah, and Serge Weber

Laboratoire d'Instrumentation Electronique de Nancy
BP239 - 54506 Vandoeuvre les Nancy - France
{poussier, rabah, sweber}@lien.u-nancy.fr

Abstract. This paper presents a new design of a system on a programmable chip (SOPC) for smart strain gage sensor. The system is designed to meet flexibility and complex computations required in compensation algorithm of strain gage thermal output. To satisfy the real-time processing constraints in one hand, and parameterization in another hand, parts of the algorithm are implemented in hardware and others are implemented in software. This new architecture, consisting of hardware and software functionalities, is implemented on an Altera APEX20K Field Programmable Gate Array (FPGA) including a NIOS core processor. A description of the methodology developed for the temperature compensation of the system is reported and the proposed system architecture is described.

1 Introduction

Strain gage based smart sensor finds numerous industrial applications. More often, calibration and thermal compensation is necessary to scale the system sensitivity. Analog techniques are often used to carry out these operations particularly when the system operates in narrow interval of temperature. However, temperature scale is much often in a wide range, for example, -40^oC to $+180^oC$ in automobile vehicles. Moreover, strain gage can be used to measure shock events [1]; thus, dynamic measurements above 100kHz are necessary. Sometimes, the substrate material composition is unknown, a calibration or an auto calibration is necessary to adapt compensation. In most applications, the strain gage is stick in cramped place; hence the conditioner must be compact and positioned close to the sensors in order to decrease electromagnetic noise and to realize embedded measures. Commercial solutions and techniques are available on the market but don't satisfy all this constraints [2]. They use heavy means of computations and generally operate in deferred time [3], [4]. In the industrial domain, the most important issues in designing a new system is time-to-market, cost, cumbersome size and low energy consumption. Analog digital hardware software co-design allows an adequate partitioning and parallel development of each part of the system. The modern Systems On Programmable Chip (SOPC) has become a good candidate. Besides, the availability of core processors blocks makes the hardware and software co-design more straightforward. In this paper we focus on SOPC implemen-tation on a FPGA including core processor.

M. Glesner, P. Zipf, and M. Renovell (Eds.): FPL 2002, LNCS 2438, pp. 1131–1134, 2002.

2 Thermal Compensation Algorithm

In the strain gage based smart sensors calibration and thermal compensation is necessary to scale the system sensitivity. Equation 1 gives the effective strain S_e.

$$S_e = \frac{\alpha}{F(T)}.S_m - \frac{F^*}{F(T)}.S_{app} \quad (\mu m/m); \tag{1}$$

α is a coefficient depending on the bridge type and the sensor excitation voltage. T is the temperature. S_m is the measured strain. $S_{app}(T)$ represents the apparent strain of the gage and $F(T)$ the gage factor drift. The two quantities are respectively fourth and second order polynomial functions of temperature. F^* is provided by the manufacturer. Polynomial coefficients require a high precision decimal representation that can be satisfied by floating-point format. Analog to digital converters provide the non-compensated strain data, excitation voltage and temperature data. Time constraint for our application is dependent on the data flow: it must be about $3\mu s$ for strain computation but no more than 100 Hz for temperature.

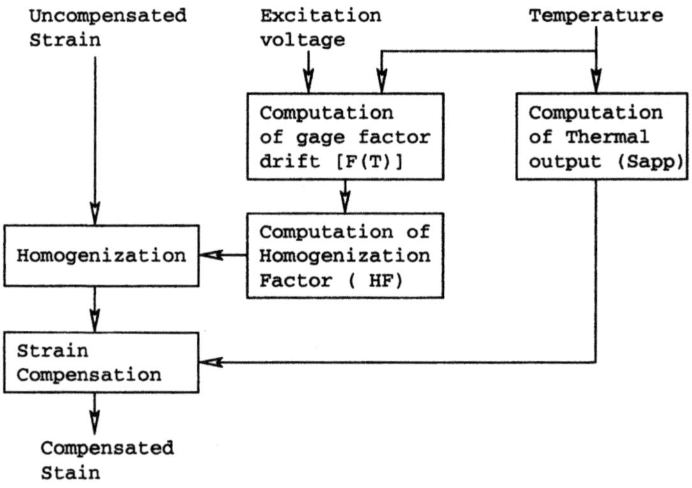

Fig. 1. The multiple data flow graph of the compensation algorithm.

3 Basic Implementation

In all the different implementations, control of the analog parts is done in hardware. An ALTERA Excalibur board, including an FPGA APEX20KEFC484-2X, RAM, EEPROM, a 32 bits core processor and some peripherals to control the ADCs, is used as a target. Three approaches are used: fully software, fully hardware and mixed hardware software. In the fully software approach, the entire compensation algorithm is imlemented as an interrupt routine. The ADC generates an interruption each time that a sample is acquired. All computations must be done between tow interruptions. Computation of S_{app} and α takes much more time than the compensation itself. In the fully hardware approach, to meet the required precision, operators was implemented using floating-point format IEEE's 754 standard. A MAC operator, controlled by a state machine, implements the polynomial computation of thermal output. A timer is used to measure execution time in software implementation. The core processor used has RISC architecture and a four stages pipeline. Software is written in C language and compiled with level two optimization. The implementation results are shown in table 1. The function processing temperature uses 100809 clock cycles. The function processing strain takes 645 clock cycles. Additional hardware blocks and software functions are implemented to manage peripherals and memories. The complete processing is computed in 101454 clock cycles. Using a system clock of 33MHz, the strain signal frequency will be then limited to 300Hz. Temperature processing makes the most important limitations and degrades the acquisition time of the strain. In hardware implementation, the strain data is processed within 86 clock cycles. The temperature processing is realized within 551 clock cycles. In this configuration, temperature and strain can be processed simultaneously. For LEs consummation, fully software implementation uses 3651 LEs including the core processor and peripheral blocks. The fully hardware implementation uses 7693 LEs that represents 92 % of the total surface of the used FPGA (APEX20).

4 Hardware/Software Implementation

In this section, a codesign approach and obtained implementation are presented. Some methodologies are presented in the literature. First, all the algorithm operators must be isolated. Each one is distinguished by its necessary speed and its processing complexity. According to the previous configuration, processing can be divided in two parts, operators used to process strain and those for temperature. The first ones, implemented in hardware, are the multiplication of the stress by α, and subtraction by S_{app}. The second ones, implemented in software, are the computations of α, $F(T)$ and S_{app}. Table 1 shows the execution time and consumption in logic elements results. In the H/S configuration, all operators used to process temperature are implemented in software. They take same number of clock cycles as in fully software configuration. Operators used to process strain take 3 clock cycles which is less than in the fully hardware configuration. In H/S, This difference is explained by the fact that in fully hardware implementation additional blocks are used to convert integer signed format to floating-point format whereas in H/S configuration this transformation is made in software. So, in H/S implementation, using a system clock of 33.3MHz the hardware processing is achieved in 0.1 μs and the software execution time is 3.03 ms.

Table 1. Execution time table (clock cycle) and Logic blocs table (number of LE)

OPERATORS	LOGIC ELEMENT (LE)			EXECUTION TIME		
	Software	Hardware	H/S	Software	Hardware	H/S
Sapp	3651	1994	3343	13695	304	13695
$F(T)$		2057		40256	233	40256
α		2021		46858	14	46858
$Strain * \alpha$		925	60	299	5	3
$Strain - Sapp$		696		346	81	3

The benefit of the use of the H/S implantation is its adaptability to auto-calibration process. This process is running during a special phase used to calibrate the system. Some measurement points are acquired following a strict procedure, and next, factors for compensation are computed according to a classical approximation algorithm. This auto calibration is realized in software. LEs consumption is the same because, only the C programme is modified. The execution time is about several milliseconds but it is not important because this process is realized before the real time compensation.

5 Conclusion

The main goal of our work was to find a configuration that meet time constraints for shock events, where auto calibration is possible, with best surface and development cost for thermal compensation of strain gage in a wide temperature range. Hardware/software co-design was very helpful and using FPGA has confirmed to be very effective in implementing complex system on a chip. Associated with an IP core processor, it provides more flexibility than ASIC implementations and generates higher data rates than equivalent software implementations. Through IP processors and FPGA, we showed that a fully hardware or fully software solutions are not appropriate to our application; whereas a mixed hardware software solution provides flexibility and responds to the specifications. A further advantage is the use of Intellectual Property for interface, for specific processing. All of this characteristics made that this system is a product where measure is fast, the development and the accuracy of compensation for strain gage is high and close to the sensor.

References

1. Knapp, E. Altmann, J. Niemann, K.D. Werner: Measurement of shock events by means of strain gauges and accelerometers. Measurement, Elsevier (1998) 87-96
2. Somat product web site: http://www.somat.com/products/index.shtml
3. H. J. Howland, An integrated software/hardware approach to experimental stress analysis. Experimental stress analysis, Martinus Nijhoff publishers (1986) 263-270
4. Vishay web site: http://www.vishay.com.

Adding Hardware Support to the HotSpot Virtual Machine for Domain Specific Applications

Yajun Ha[1]*, Radovan Hipik[2], Serge Vernalde[1], Diederik Verkest[1]**, Marc Engels[1]***, Rudy Lauwereins[1]***, and Hugo De Man[1]***

[1] IMEC, Kapeldreef 75, Leuven 3001, Belgium,
yjha@imec.be

[2] Department of Microelectronics FEI STU, Ilkovièova 3, 81219 Bratislava, Slovakia

Abstract. Like real general-purpose processors, Java Virtual Machines (JVMs) need hardware acceleration for computationally intensive applications. JVMs however require that platform independence can be maintained while resorting to hardware acceleration. To this end, we invented a scheme to seamlessly add hardware support to Sun's HotSpot JVM. By means of run-time profiling, we select the most heavily used Java methods for execution in Field Programmable Gate Arrays (FPGA) hardware. Methods running in hardware are designed at compile-time, but the bitstreams are generated at run-time to guarantee platform independence. If no method improves the performance by running in hardware, all Java methods still can run in software with trivial run-time overheads. We have implemented this hardware supported JVM. The results show that hardware acceleration for JVMs can be achieved while maintaining platform independence for domain specific applications.

1 Introduction

Java applications doing high-throughput streaming computations require hardware acceleration while maintaining traditional Java platform independent features [1]. Different approaches have been explored in the previous researches. But they are constrained by either the limited parallelism that they can explore or the ignorance of the platform independence issues.

We invented a scheme to seamlessly add hardware support to the current HotSpot JVM, while maintaining the platform independence at the same time. We call this the *Hard-HotSpot JVM* in the remainder of this text. By doing runtime profiling, we use the previously adaptively compiled Java methods as candidates, and select most heavily used Java methods from these candidates to run in FPGA hardware. The bitstreams for those methods are generated at run-time. As a result, we end up with a hardware supported HotSpot JVM, where large portions of bytecodes are executed in the interpreted mode, small portions of bytecodes are executed in the compilation mode, and even smaller portions of heavily used bytecodes are executed in the hardware mode.

* also Ph.D. student at Katholieke Universiteit Leuven

** also Professor at Vrije Universiteit Brussel

*** also Professor at Katholieke Universiteit Leuven

M. Glesner, P. Zipf, and M. Renovell (Eds.): FPL 2002, LNCS 2438, pp. 1135–1138, 2002.

The hardware design for methods in the hardware mode are done at compile-time, but the generation of the bitstreams is delayed until runtime, which guarantees that the same design can be executed on different platforms.

This paper is organized into the following sections. In section 2, we give the overview of the Hard-HotSpot JVM. Section 3 explains the run-time bitstream generation. Finally in section 4, experimental results are given for an application running on the Hard-HotSpot JVM.

2 The Hard-HotSpot JVM

This section gives an overview of the Java method classification, the programming model and the execution sequence of the Hard-HotSpot JVM.

```
......
method_a () {
   boolean is_to_hw;
   if(is_to_hw)
       interface calls to HW
   else {
       SW algorithm A code
   }
}
HW_method_a () {
   JBits codes for SW algorithm A
}
......
```

(a)

is_to_hw = FALSE;
while ($exit! = TRUE$) {
  Execute the software code;
  run-time profiling;
  find H;
  if ($T_{new} < T_{original}$) {
    generate bitstream;
    configure programmable HW;
    $is\_to\_hw = TRUE$;
  }
}
end

(b)

Fig. 1. (a) Example Java code that uses hardware support. (b)Sequence to execute Java codes in the hardware supported HotSpot VM.

Java methods running on the Hard-HotSpot JVM are classified into normal ones and the computationally intensive ones. This classification is done at compile-time with the help of profiling information. No extra work needs to be done for the normal methods. But for the computationally intensive methods, both software and hardware implementations should be provided. To maintain the platform independence feature for the hardware description, the hardware implementation of computationally intensive methods is captured in a platform independent way by using *JBits API*, which is a Java package that can be used to generate FPGA bitstreams at run-time.

The Hard-HotSpot JVM uses a simple programming model. For normal methods, Java programming does not change in any way. But for the computationally intensive methods, some programming style rules should be followed. For example, in Fig. 1(a), if $method\_a()$ is one of the computationally intensive candidates identified at design-time, there should be a corresponding method $HW\_method\_a()$, which contains the

JBits codes that describe the hardware implementation of $method\_a()$. The Hard-HotSpot VM will decide at run-time to execute $HW\_method\_a()$ or not. The Hard-HotSpot JVM will only execute it at run-time if it can gain by running method $method\_a()$ in hardware. is_to_hw is a run-time flag, which is set by the Hard-HotSpot JVM at run-time to switch the control flow from software to hardware.

The Hard-HotSpot JVM executes programs with the algorithm shown in Fig.1(b). It first runs the bytecodes in the interpretation mode, gives the run-time flag *is_to_hw* an initial value of FALSE, and executes the software implementation of the methods. At the same time, the Hard-HotSpot JVM does run-time profiling to identify the candidates to be dynamically compiled to native methods. Based on these native methods, the Hard-HotSpot JVM chooses the most computationally intensive native methods as the candidates to be migrated to HW, and evaluates their SW execution time and HW execution time. If the evaluation shows that HW will gain and all the other run-time conditions are met, the bitstream will be generated from the JBits code. The bitstream is then used to configure the programmable HW. Once the configuration is done, the run-time flag *is_to_hw* is turned to TRUE by the virtual machine. From then on, the method will be executed in hardware. Runtime profiling will continue, and dynamically choose the methods that should be executed in hardware.

3 Run-Time Bitstream Generation

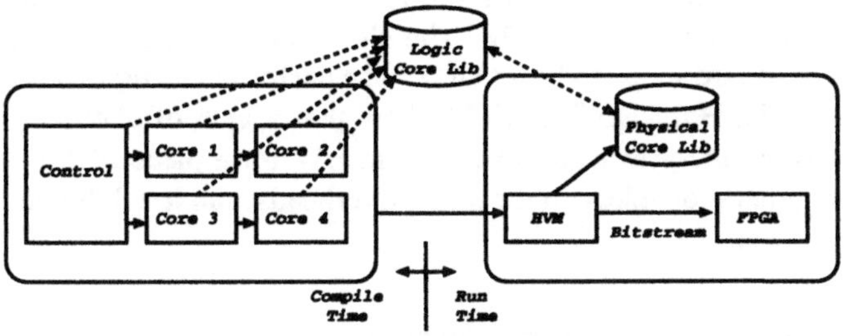

Fig. 2. Runtime bitstream generation.

Run-time bitstream generation is a key step to ensure the platform independence. The Hard-HotSpot JVM implements the run-time bitstream generation in a framework shown in Fig.2. In the framework, various logic cores and physical cores are implemented. The logic cores capture the functionalities of cores like multipliers and FIR filters, while the physical cores give the real platform specific implementation of their corresponding logic cores. The logic cores are developed to give the designers a high level means to capture architectures at compile-time, while the physical cores are developed to give the Hard-HotSpot JVM the executable Java codes to generate bitstreams at run-time. Running Java codes to generate bitstreams is enabled by the JBits Java API developed at Xilinx. It also provides the run-time routing support.

4 Experimental Results

We implemented the Hard-HotSpot JVM based on Sun's HotSpot 1.3.1 community source Linux version. It is a multi-thread C++ implementation. Apart from the existing threads, we added a separate thread *HWCompilerThread* to handle all management work that is related to the hardware support. The Hard-HotSpot VM used the JBits version 2.8 package.

To check the pure overheads of the run-time evaluation to the JVM, part of the benchmarks of size *A* in Java Grande Forum Benchmark Suit[2] have been run on the platform. In this experiment, overhead time is intentionally set to a very high value, thus almost no method will be chosen to run in hardware, and pure run-time evaluation overheads are measured. Figures are shown in table 1, and they prove that the overheads for the run-time decision of the hardware methods are trivial. This result is important, since it shows even in the worst case, all methods can still run in software with low overheads.

	SeriesA	LUFactA	SORA	HeapSortA	CryptA	FFTA	SparseA
HotSpot (s)	60.714	4.422	23.753	5.327	14.027	43.164	25.816
Hard-HotSpot (s)	61.268	4.623	24.078	5.419	14.713	43.335	26.152

Table 1. Pure run-time evaluation overheads for the Java Grande Forum Benchmark.

A grayscale video player applet that converts color video clips to grayscale has also been tested on the Hard-HotSpot JVM. The clock for the bitstream of grayscale filter is simulated with BoardScope to be 98MHZ. The performance figures for the grayscale filter running on the Hard-HotSpot JVM show that a gain of about 11 seconds have been obtained when the grayscale filter runs in HW for a piece of 100 seconds video clip. Bitstream generation takes up the major overheads, and it will be helpful to further reduce this overhead.

5 Conclusions and Acknowledgments

We implemented a new JVM, that enables hardware acceleration and platform independence for Java methods at the same time. As an important feature, the new JVM does not degrade the original JVM performance. Because even in the worst case, all Java methods can still run in software. Experimental results show that the run-time evaluation overheads are trivial. The authors would like to thank Tim Price and Xilinx Labs for providing the Grayscale filter JBits core and allowing us to use it in this paper.

References

1. Y. Ha, S.Vernalde, P. Schaumont, M. Engels, R. Lauwereins and H. De Man: Building a virtual framework for networked reconfigurable hardware and software objects. The Journal of Supercomputing. **21** (2002) 131–144
2. Java Grande Forum Benchmark Suit. (http://www.epcc.ed.ac.uk/javagrande)

An FPGA-based Node Controller for a High Capacity WDM Optical Packet Network

Roberto Gaudino, Vito De Feo, M. Chiaberge, and C. Sansoè

Dipartimento di Elettronica - Politecnico di Torino
Corso Duca degli Abruzzi, 24 - 10129 Torino - Italy
lastname@polito.it

Abstract. We present architecture and experimental results for an high-speed digital node controller developed in the "RINGO" project, a demonstrator of a next-generation ultra-high capacity network based on WDM optical fiber ring. The MAC protocol and other controller functions have been developed on a high capacity FPGA, which supports efficient input queuing and multicast capabilities by handling several concurrent real time processes.

1 Introduction

The challanges of today Terabit core switches/routers are related to their extremely high cost, power consumption and very large dimensions. Thanks to DWDM optical technology, the bandwidth bottleneck for core transport networks is not any more in transmission, but in switching. Many industrial and academic research groups are working on solving this "electronic bottleneck" by moving part of the electronic functions in the optical domain. Fitting in this scenario, we present an innovative proposal developed in the RINGO (RING Optical network) project. RINGO [1] is a consortium of Italian Universities coordinated by the Optical Communication Group at Politecnico di Torino, Italy. The project is focused on experimentally studying the feasibility of a WDM optical packet network based on a ring topology. The key idea in RINGO is keeping the complexity of the network protocol mostly at the electronic level, but at the same time achieving an efficient use of the optical bandwidth by simultaneously multiplexing data in the wavelength domain (with DWDM techniques) and in the time domain (with optical packets). We based our design on a high capacity FPGA because it allows fast prototyping of custom VLSI network controllers without using expensive ASIC's technologies.

2 RINGO Architecture and Protocol

The general architecture of the RINGO network [1] is shown in Fig. 1, while the structure of a node is shown in Fig. 2. RINGO is based on a unidirectional fiber ring with N nodes. Each node queues at the electronic level fixed-size packets to be sent on the ring according to the following rules: (a) packet transmission is

M. Glesner, P. Zipf, and M. Renovell (Eds.): FPL 2002, LNCS 2438, pp. 1139–1143, 2002.

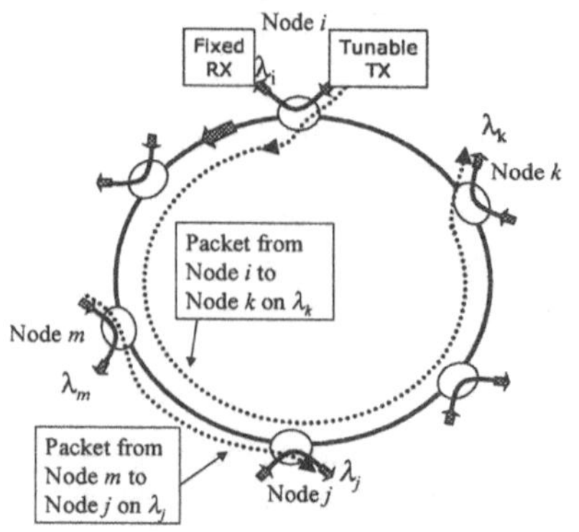

Fig. 1. Architecture of the RINGO network.

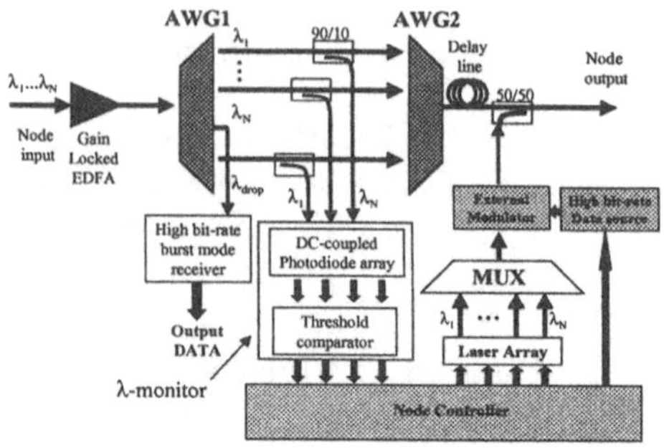

Fig. 2. Structure of a RINGO node.

time-slotted and synchronized on all channels; (b) the number network nodes is equal to the number of wavelengths; (c) each node optical interface is equipped with a tunable transmitter, and with a fixed receiver operating on a given wavelength λ_i that identifies the node itself; in order to communicate to node k, a node tunes its transmitter on λ_k, as shown in Fig. 1; (d) each node check input wavelength occupation on a slot-by-slot basis, and avoid collisions by a generalization of the empty-slot approach, where packets are sent only in those slots that are actually available; (e) input packets are queued using a Virtual Output Queueing (VOQ) [2] algorithm; (f) a packet can be simultaneously sent to multiple destinations for multicasting, by turning on in the same slot more than one wavelength.

3 FPGA Implementation of the Node Logic Controller

The RINGO node logic controller was implemented on a board equipped with a high-performance Altera APEX20KE600-3, a commercial FPGA (600000 gates, 24320 flip-flops, 4 internal PLL's, 588 I/O). A special daughterboard has been developed to interconnect the PROC20KE and the optoelectronic hardware. The main operations of the MAC protocol hardware implementation are shown in Fig. 3. When a packet arrives from the PCI bus, it is stored into an input buffer, which separate the activity of the PCI bus from the on-board logic. The RINGO protocol requires sending a waiting packet on the first available slot, and thus imposes a strict real-time requirement on the controller. Every packet is formatted in a fixed size Protocol Data Unit (PDU) which contains the payload bits (Service Data Unit SDU), and a fan-out set, with the packet destination(s). Since four wavelengths/destinations are currently used, the fan-out set is composed of four bits. Eight FIFO queues (4 unicast and 4 multicast) are used. A simple criterion based on the minimum Hamming distance [2] is used to choose one of the four multicast queues. In the example of Fig. 3, a

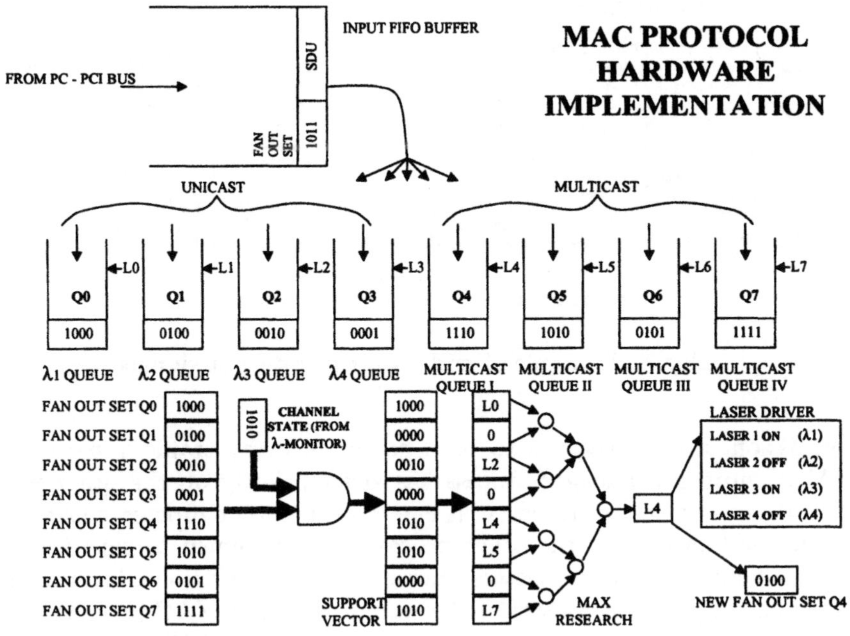

Fig. 3. MAC protocol hardware implementation.

transmission request is coded with a logic "1". The queue lengths are stored in a special register file (L0...L7). On the slot synchronization signal rising edge, channel state is acquired. In the example, an available wavelength is coded by a logic "1". A bitwise AND operation is computed between the channel state vector and the residual fan-out set of the HOL packet of each queue. The result is loaded into a support vector. A queue may not be entitled for transmission (in the example Q1, Q3, Q6) because all the wavelengths of its fan-out set are busy. The next step finds the queue with maximum length among all queues entitled for transmission, using a "tournament algorithm". The transmission requests of the "winner" queue (Q4 in the example), have to be served in accordance with the channel wavelength availability. In the example, the node controller enables laser 1 and laser 3 for transmission, and it sends the PDU of the first packet in queue 4 to the external laser modulator. The last step is to refresh the queue content. In the example, the fan-out set of the first packet in queue 4 has to be changed from 1110 to 0100 because λ_2 is the only transmission request not served. When all transmission requests are served, the packet is removed by the queue head and the queue fan-out restored. Four different concurrent processes work to control the node. Besides the traffic generation process, the others are the buffer manager, the queue manager and the MAC manager. This last process is the core of the system and has been given higher priority. The other processes have to work in transparent mode with respect to this one, meaning that processing time from the rising edge of the synchronization signal to the

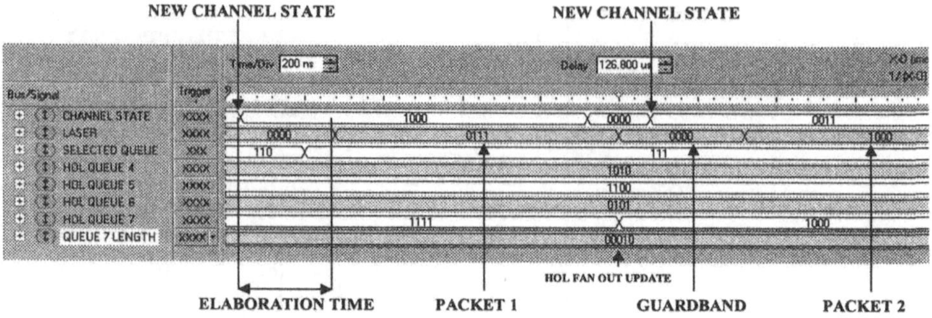

Fig. 4. Example of node controller output signals.

transmission of a packet has to be constant in every traffic situation. Hence the MAC protocol manager process has strict priority on the other processes and, if it needs a shared resource, it can stop the other processes using control signals. For this reason, the other processes are designed to save the current job in dedicated support registers during a single clock cycle, in order to give as soon as possible the control of the resources to the MAC protocol manager process. The RINGO controller logic synthesis required 5% of the total logic elements of the APEX20KE600-3, 99% of the total pins and 11 ESBs cells. The current maximum working frequency is 44.5 MHz, though the next version of the board will work at 100 MHz. All the implemented functionalities have been tested in several experiments [1]. As an example, Fig. 4 shows some internal electrical signals of the node controller logic, acquired by a logic analyzer. The signal CHANNEL STATE is the logic state of the channel at the node input. On the first slot shown in the figure, the master node is sending a packet on λ_1, so that the relative channel state is 1000 (a logic '1' means the channel is busy on the relative wavelength). On the second time slot, a packet is seen on both λ_3 and λ_4. Hence, the relative channel state is 0011. During the guardband between the two packets, the channel state value is 0000. The signal LASER is the logic state of the full node laser array (a logic '1' means that the relative laser is to be turned ON for transmission in the present time slot). The signal SELECTED QUEUE shows the queue qualified for transmission in the present time slot. In the example, the selected queue is the queue 7 (111 in binary). The signal HOL QUEUE is the Head of The Line packet of the queues 4-7 (i.e. the packet at the top of the multicast queues). In the first time slot Fig. 4, the HOL packet of the selected queue (the queue 7) is 1111 (i.e. a broadcast packet). This packet can be transmitted only on λ_2, λ_3 and λ_4 because λ_1 is busy (infact, the signal laser is 0111). After the transmission of this packet, the fan out of the queue7 HOL packet is updated to 1000 (only λ_1 has to be trasmitted). The signal QUEUE 7 LENGTH: it is the length of the queue7 (in the example: 2).

Aknowledgments: this work was partially funded by MURST (Italian Scientific Research and University Ministry), project COFIN 99. A special thanks to VITESSE SEMICONDUCTORS *(www.vitesse.com)* and to GIDEL LTD *(www.gidel.com)*.

References

1. R. Gaudino, A. Carena, V. Ferrero, A. Pozzi, V. De Feo, P. Gigante, F. Neri, and P. Poggiolini, "RINGO: a WDM Ring Optical Packet Network demonstrator", *ECOC 2001*, paper Th.L.2.6, Oct. 2001, Amsterdam, The Netherlands.
2. N. McKeown *et al*, "Achieving 100% throughput in an input-queued switch", *IEEE Transactions on Communications,* Vol. 47, No. 8, pp. 1260-1267, Aug. 1999.

FPGA and Mixed FPGA-DSP Implementations of Electrical Drive Algorithms

F. Calmon [1], M. Fathallah [2], P.J. Viverge, C. Gontrand [1], J. Carrabina [3], P. Foussier

[1] LPM (Laboratoire de Physique de la Matière)
INSA - Building Blaise Pascal
F- 69621 Villeurbanne Cedex – France
Francis.Calmon@insa-lyon.fr
[2] CEGELY (Centre de Génie Electrique de Lyon)
INSA - Building Leonard de Vinci
F- 69621 Villeurbanne Cedex – France
[3] Centre Nacional de Microelectronica
Universitat Autonoma de Barcelona
08193 Bellaterra - Spain

Abstract. This paper deals with the implementation of control algorithms for alternative current (ac) motors using co-design methodology for hard or mixed hardware/software solutions. The authors focus on the design flow and experiments using FPGA / DSP platform. A full FPGA implementation of the well-known field oriented control strategy is presented. In a next step a mixed FPGA / DSP platform is presented associated with preliminary results concerning a mixed implementation of the scalar control algorithm.

1. Introduction

This work is part of study of real-time ac drive control for asynchronous motors (ASM). We present two implementations of the well-known ASM control strategy called "flux oriented control (FOC)". The aim is to optimize the design flow methodology in order to be able to implement much more complicated ASM control algorithms and real-time diagnosis features. We choose firstly, a full hardware implementation which was successfully tested by hand of large programmable device (FPGA), secondly, a mixed approach coupling FPGA and signal processor (DSP) for improved performance. This leads us to develop several parametrical blocks which can be considered as intellectual properties (IPs) as they are described with high level language (VHDL or C-code), they are first of interest when considering future developments based on single chip (SoC or programmable SoC).

The block diagram of the electrical machine drive is shown on Fig. 1. As inputs, the DSP / FPGA digital controller receives the stator currents, the rotor speed, the DC voltage magnitude and finally, the torque or speed order. Two types of control protocol have been studied, both dedicated to electrical vehicle application: the scalar control (opened loop) and the flux vector control [1-2].

M. Glesner, P. Zipf, and M. Renovell (Eds.): FPL 2002, LNCS 2438, pp. 1144-1147, 2002.

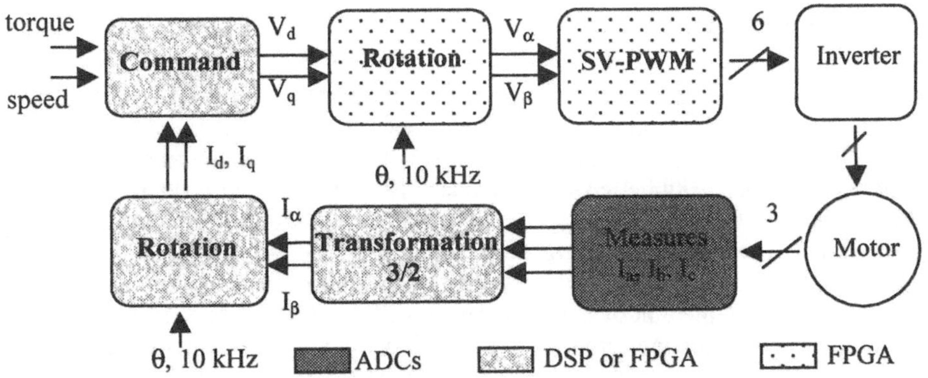

Fig. 1. Block diagram of an AC drive

2. Design Flow and Methodology

The co-design approach is complicated because it involves many different tasks [3-5]. Unify co-design methodology dealing with all kinds of applications is an ultimate goal but associated tools are not available. The proposed design flow (based on [3]) focuses on four main points: system specification, functional verification, hardware / software partitioning and emulation. One major problem is the *system specification* for control applications with a language that can support most tasks of a co-design methodology. We decided to use the Grafcet formalism for functional specification (converted into Matlab scripts). Using the Matlab / Simulink software, we simulate that model coupled with our analog electrical drive model for *functional verification.* We build the comprehensive model at first, and then, the specification model. The first one uses blocks from the Matlab library and our electrical machine model. The specification model is closer to the final implementation as it schedules the operation calculated with the chosen arithmetic (fixed point parameterized format so as to analyze its influence on accuracy and overflow). The *partitioning* step is made manually. We decided to develop firstly, a full hardware implementation with a FPGA device, in parallel we are investigating a mixed one. The *model refinement* and *arithmetic proof* are carried out conjointly in order to reach sufficient precision without overflow. The *hardware (and software) code generation* is done manually. From the Grafcet and the constraints (speed, area ...), we inference the ASIC architecture, that is then described in VHDL code. At this time we build the full hardware implementation. The *formal proof* step which is, in fact, restricted to a system verification consists in simulating the VHDL code (with SYNOPSYS software) for specific sets of input vectors. The simulation results have to be compared to a reference model that could be the specification model. We have also used Cadence-SPW platform and VHDL-AMS language for mixed simulation. The *physical model synthesis* is made with SYNOPSYS software (target: Flex 10K100 device from Altera in our case). The results here are presented in [6-7].

3. Implementations

In order to achieve a space vector pulse width modulation (SV-PWM) driven by a vector or scalar control command, arithmetic operations and rotation computations have to be made with a sufficient accuracy level. To optimize material resources, the choice of fixed-point arithmetic was been made (12/16 fixed-point format).

Fig. 2 depicts the ASIC hardware architecture. In addition to the storage entities (ROM, RAM), two other IPs have been developed: the ALU and the coordinate rotation digital processor (CORDIC [8] [5]). The control unit module is basically made of a state machine that oversees the entire ASIC. RAM module stores command variable during calculation otherwise ROM bloc contains constants and micro-rotations for CORDIC algorithm. High-speed output (HSO) block builds the inverter signals from duty cycles and switching period and clocks the sampling unit (SU) and the control unit. The register bench provides 16-bits registers for dialog operations. Sampling Unit (SU) dialogs to external ADCs. ALU module allows adding, subtracting, shifting and variable to constant multiplication / division operations. CORDIC module computes rotations and variable-to-variable multiplication / division operations. The processor was synthesized and prototyped with an Altera Flex10K100-3 device (100000 gates). Our design area occupation for the FOC algorithm is about 90000 gates and 4100 logical cells. The resulting critical path is less than 240 ns. We have chosen a 4 MHz operating frequency. The total computation time (including ADC) is 76 μs [6]. The FOC control implementation on FPGA device was succesfully tested on test bench platform [6].

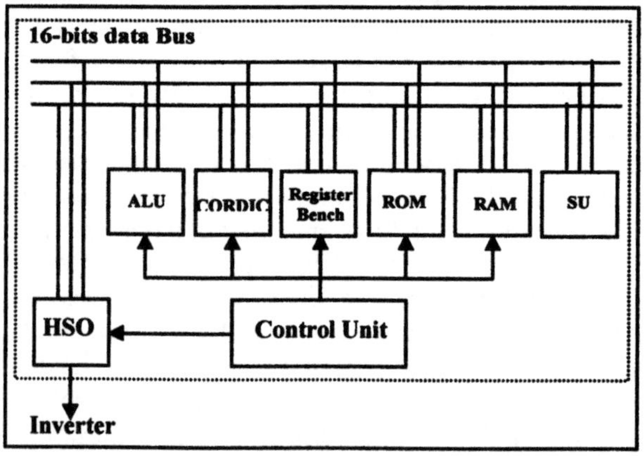

Fig. 2. Full hardware implementation architecture

Our first mixed hardware-software implementation was presented in [9]. In this past work, FPGA only served to build the signal waveforms towards the inverter and this, from the duty cycles calculated by the software part (i.e. DSP). Now, a new mixed hardware / software is currently investigated. Partitioning is made manually (Fig. 1). SV-PWM and rotation (d-q to α-β reference) are implemented in hardware because there are standard functions non-dependant on the control algorithm strategy. Software implementation is dedicated to the control algorithm as it can be rather complicated and can integrate diagnosis routines and parameter observers [10-11]. The mixed hardware/software strategy uses the major modules of the full hardware solution. Some of these IPs are entirely rewritten (ROM, HSO), some of them are preserved (ALU), CORDIC processor was partially modified. The RAM is deleted and replaced by the VME exchange module witch is developed to allow the DSP/FPGA dialogue protocol. As the mixed implementation is much more complicated to finalize due to the communication problems between the hard and soft parts, we decided to test the system with a more simple ac machine drive strategy (e.g. a scalar command - opened-loop).

4. Conclusion

The integration of the whole motor control algorithm within a single chip (FPGA) is very convenient, compact and reliable. This circuit was designed to serve in electrical vehicle applications (field orientation control) and was successfully tested. The use of mixed resource (FPGA and processor) allows higher performances in terms of time calculations. This is particularly adapted to advanced machine drive algorithms including complex algorithm (e.g. direct torque control), parameter observers and real time diagnosis routines. But the design of such systems is extremely difficult due to the communication problems for example. It appears clearly that new generation of logic programmable devices will present a serious alternative to standard solutions (DSP, micro-controller) for electrical drive as these system-on-a-programmable-chips provides functionalities to implement embedded processors.

References

1. Mohan, N. et al.: Power electronics – Converters, applications and design. John Wiley edition, 1995.
2. Jorda, X.: Conception et réalisation d'une commande économique de couple d'une machine asynchrone pour la traction électrique. PhD INSA Lyon, France, 1995.
3. Gajski, D. et al.: Specification and design of embedded systems. Prentice-Hall, 1994.
4. Kalavade, A. et al.: A hardware / software codesign for DSP applications. IEEE Design & Test of Computers, Sept 1993.
5. Foussier, P.: Intégration des systèmes de commande des machines électriques à courant alternatif. PhD INSA Lyon, France, 1998.
6. Fathallah, M. et al.: Design of an optimized IC for control algorithms of ac machines: System testing and application. IEEE IAS conference 2001.
7. Fathallah, M. et al.: Different control strategies for three-phase PWM inverters. EPE conference 2001.
8. Volder, J. E.: The CORDIC trigonometric computing technique. IRE Transactions on Electronics Computers, Sept 1959.
9. Salles, G. et al.: Mixed DSP / ASIC solution for electrical machine drive. PCIM conference, 1999.
10. Kryter, R. C. et al.: Condition monitoring of machinery using motor current signature analysis. Sound and Vibrations, Sept 1989.
11. Salles, G. et al.: Study of monitoring load failure of an actuator system. Eur. Phys. J. AP 4, Nov 1998.

Image Registration of Real-Time Broadcast Video Using the UltraSONIC Reconfigurable Computer

Wim J.C. Melis[1], Peter Y.K. Cheung[1], and Wayne Luk[2]

[1] Department of Electrical & Electronic Engineering, Imperial College, Exhibition Road, London SW7 2BT, England.
[2] Department of Computing, Imperial College, 180 Queen's Gate, London SW7 2BZ, England

Abstract. This paper is concerned with the image registration problem as applied to real-time video. It describes the development of a computationally efficient algorithm to restore broadcast quality video sequences using image registration techniques. A motion vector based approach is used and found to be successful in restoring the video sequence for any global perspective transform based distortion. The algorithm is implemented on a reconfigurable computing platform called UltraSONIC in a hardware/software codesign environment. It is shown that the algorithm can accurately restore video data in real-time.

1 Introduction

Reconfigurable computing platforms are known to be good for implementing applications with a high data throughput and large computational demand. The application this paper is concerned with is image registration for perspective transformed watermarked image and video data.

Image registration has many applications, but in this paper it is used to restore the geometrically distorted watermarked images. It is well known that most watermarking algorithms are not sufficiently robust to deal with geometric distortions [2]. Some approaches to this problem have been proposed [5], though they employ algorithms suited to a general-purpose computer. The authors of this paper reported a computationally efficient algorithm for image registration based on localised motion vectors [6] to overcome affine transformation based distortions. This paper describes the extension to cover the more general perspective transformation based distortions.

2 The SONIC Architecture

The SONIC platform [3] is a reconfigurable computing system designed to cope with the computational power and the high data throughput demanded by real-time video applications. It has plug-in processing elements, and is developed to facilitate design reuse.

A detailed description of the latest implementation of this architecture, UltraSONIC, based around Virtex XCV1000E devices can be found in [4].

M. Glesner, P. Zipf, and M. Renovell (Eds.): FPL 2002, LNCS 2438, pp. 1148–1151, 2002.

3 The Image Registration Problem in Watermarking

The sensitivity problem of watermarking algorithms can, in the case of non-blind watermarking, be solved by comparing the original and corrupted images to find an estimate of the distortion. These parameters can then be used for the registration.

The perspective distortions are assumed to be globally applied, and can be represented using the following matrix representation [7]:

$$(x' \; y' \; z') = (x \; y \; z)T = (x \; y \; z)\begin{pmatrix} a & b & g \\ c & d & h \\ e & f & i \end{pmatrix} \tag{1}$$

where (x, y, z) are the position in the original image in 2D space (with $z = 1$), (x', y', z') are the position to which the pixel is mapped in 3D space and $(a, b, \ldots, i)$ are the parameters of the distortion function T used to restore the image.

4 The Algorithm

The approach used in solving the image registration problem is based on localised motion vectors [1] using the original and distorted image (See Figure 1 a) & b.)). This results in a motion vector map, of which an example is shown in Figure 1 c).

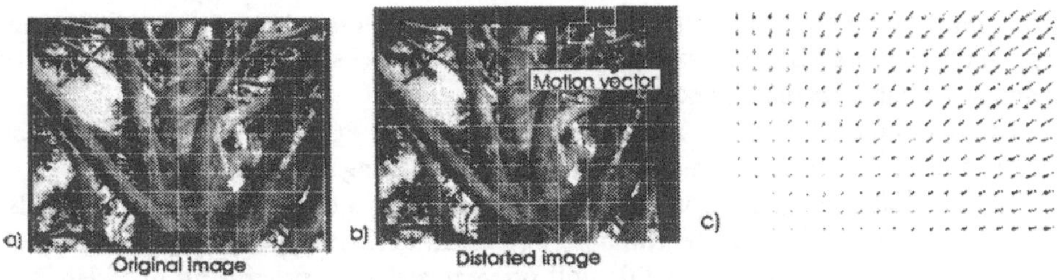

Fig. 1. Motion Vector Estimation a) & b) Division into blocks and determined motion vector; c) Motion vector map for perspective distortion of similar type as shown in b).

As perspective transforms are actually 3D transformations (1), but only 2D images are considered, a conversion is necessary. Combined with the fact that i and z can be set to one (as described in [7]) this leads to (2) in which x'' and y'' are the coordinates in the new image.

$$x'' = \frac{x'}{z'} = \frac{ax + cy + e}{gx + hy + 1}, \quad y'' = \frac{y'}{z'} = \frac{bx + dy + f}{gx + hy + 1} \tag{2}$$

These equations give a relation between the values x and y, for which the centre of the block will be taken, the parameters and the new positions (x'', y''). The new positions are not known, but can be derived from the motion vectors (u, v), using: $x'' = x - u$ and $y'' = y - v$.

The values of x'' and y'' can then be used in a rearranged version of (2) to construct a matrix representation with the parameters as unknown. The least square method is used to improve on the estimated parameters.

$$\begin{pmatrix} x_1 & y_1 & 1 & 0 & 0 & 0 & -x_1x_1'' & -y_1x_1'' \\ \vdots & \vdots & \vdots & \vdots & \vdots & \vdots & \vdots & \vdots \\ x_n & y_n & 1 & 0 & 0 & 0 & -x_nx_n'' & -y_nx_n'' \\ 0 & 0 & 0 & x_1 & y_1 & 1 & -x_1y_1'' & -y_1y_1'' \\ \vdots & \vdots & \vdots & \vdots & \vdots & \vdots & \vdots & \vdots \\ 0 & 0 & 0 & x_n & y_n & 1 & -x_ny_n'' & -y_ny_n'' \end{pmatrix} \begin{pmatrix} a \\ c \\ e \\ b \\ d \\ f \\ g \\ h \end{pmatrix} = Ap = \begin{pmatrix} x_1'' \\ \vdots \\ x_n'' \\ y_1'' \\ \vdots \\ y_n'' \end{pmatrix} \tag{3}$$

To find the parameters, the pseudo inverse of A is needed, and this for each frame as the matrix is dependent on the motion vectors through (x_i'', y_i'').

Once the parameter values are found, they can be used to perform the image registration, making use of the reverse mapping technique.

5 Implementation on UltraSONIC

The hardware implementation of the motion vector calculation is designed to minimise the amount of dataflow such that the data are read only once from the external memory. This is achieved by extensive data buffering made possible by the large amount of memory available on the Virtex device.

The parameter estimation, implemented on the host PC in C++, takes the motion vectors and generates the estimated parameters, by making use of (3).

Since the image registration engine performs linear interpolation (using 4 pixels) and only two memory ports are available, two clock cycles would be required for each pixel to be calculated. However this will prevent real-time processing of video data which arrive at one pixel per clock cycle. This problem is again solved by on-chip data buffering in combination with heavy pipelining and parallelism.

6 Results

Results on the accuracy of the algorithm as well as the successfulness of the watermark extraction for different types of images are shown in Table 1. The detected parameter values for (a, b, c, d, e, f) are accurate, but some of the detected parameters for (g, h) have larger differences. However, this does not affect the final image registration results due to their small absolute values. The test on successfulness of the watermark extraction is based on a figure of merit, called *sim* (similarity) *value*. If this value is above a threshold of 10, then the registration is successful in order for the watermark to be extracted, which is the case for all entries.

Table 1. Accuracy of detecting the parameters and successfulness of extracting the watermark

Source		a	b	c	d	e	f	g	h	Sim-value
Rail	Applied	1.00	0.05	0.05	1.00	-18.00	-14.40	2.30E-06	6.00E-07	30.6
	Detected	1.00	0.05	0.05	1.00	-17.29	-13.56	2.09E-06	1.47E-07	
Susie	Applied	1.00	0.01	-0.01	1.00	3.97	-5.86	5.50E-09	8.90E-10	100.2
	Detected	1.00	0.01	-0.01	1.00	3.81	-5.92	7.03E-08	1.79E-08	

7 Conclusion

An algorithm based on motion vectors to solve the problem of image registration for watermarked video is presented. It is capable of handling all global distortions of the perspective type. By applying the method recursively, the achieved results can be improved slightly.

The hardware implementation is capable of real-time processing for the image registration as well as the motion vector calculation. It has been designed to minimise the data flow by using on-chip data buffering and extensive parallelism and pipelining.

Acknowledgement

The authors would like to thank Jason Pelly, John Stone, Simon Haynes and Henry Epsom from Sony Broadcast and Professional Research Labs. We would also like to thank Mike Brookes for his suggestions.

References

1. Haskell, B. G.: Digital Video: An Introduction to MPEG-2. New York: Chapman and Hall (1996) 118-121
2. Hartung F., Kutter M.: Multimedia Watermarking Techniques. Proceedings of the IEEE, Vol. 87 No. 7 (July 1999) 1079-1107
3. Haynes S. D., Cheung P. Y. K., Luk W., Stone J.: Video Image Processing with the Sonic Architecture. IEEE Computer (April 2000) 50-57
4. Haynes S. D., Epsom H. G., Cooper R. J. McAlpine P. l.: UltraSONIC: A Reconfigurable Architecture for Video Image Processing. Proc. Field Programmable Logic (FPL) (2002)
5. Loo P., Kingsbury N.: Motion Estimation based Registration of Geometrically Distorted Images for Watermark Recovery. Security and Watermarking of Multimedia Contents SPIE Electronic Imaging, Vol. 4314 (Jan 2001)
6. Melis W. J. C., Cheung P. Y. K., Wayne L.: Image Registration of real-time video data using the SONIC reconfigurable computer platform. Proc. IEEE Symposium on Field-Programmable Custom Computing Machines (FCCM) (2002)
7. Wolberg G.: Digital Image Warping. Los Alamitos: IEEE Computer Society Press **3rd ed.** (1994) 52-56

A Novel Watermarking Technique for LUT Based FPGA Designs

Dylan Carline, Paul Coulton

Department of Communication Systems, Lancaster University, Lancaster, Lancashire, U.K., LA1 4YR
d.carline@lancaster.ac.uk, p.coulton@lancaster.ac.uk

Abstract. Although methods for watermarking Field Programmable Gate Arrays (FPGA) have been proposed, they require a high-level design approach whereby additional circuitry, or information embedded in unused logic elements indicate design ownership. The method proposed in this paper is unique in that: it is applied directly to the bit-stream used to configure Look Up Table (LUT) -based FPGAs; has no effect on the operation of the device; can be applied retrospectively to existing designs; attacks require both detailed knowledge of device architecture and direct manipulation of the design at a bit-stream level.

1. Introduction

Techniques used in the watermarking of standard digital information (audio, video and image) predominantly involve the degradation of the contained information. Where hardware is concerned however, no degradation of the configuration data is possible, as *full* functionality must be maintained. Previous methods used for FPGA authentication have involved either the alteration of the whole design [1], or the utilisation of unused LUT components. Although these techniques provide the vendor with authentication of the intellectual property contained within the design, the major disadvantage is that, apart from 'post-process' techniques [2], they require the alteration of a design through high-level design tools.

In this paper a scheme is proposed for FPGA design authentication that is completely transparent and involves no degradation or alteration of the design. Section two explains how auxiliary information is embedded within the configuration files. In section three, an example is given whereby an image is embedded within a configuration file, used to configure the device and extracted again. Section four offers a further use for the auxiliary data by introducing a simple and very novel technique for watermarking FPGA designs to aid authentication and prevent misappropriation of designs.

2. Embedding Auxiliary Data

FPGAs can be considered as an array of configurable logic units attached to input and outputs having their functionality defined through a serial bitstream file. This bitstream relates all aspects of routing, logic and memory to the FPGA device. Pad

M. Glesner, P. Zipf, and M. Renovell (Eds.): FPL 2002, LNCS 2438, pp. 1152-1155, 2002.

bits placed within FPGA configuration data streams, which occur at the end of each frame of information, ensure correct configuration alignment of the device when programmed. and are succeeded by the next configuration frame.

The logical state of these bits is unimportant, which yields the possibility of using these bits to obtain additional functionality. As additional information can be injected into the configuration bitstream in the *post-design* stage, no degradation in performance or alteration of the original FPGA design is required.

2.1 Recalculating the Cyclic Redundancy Check (CRC)

Configuration files fed to the FPGA contain a CRC which is a simple method of ensuring the validity of the configuration file on loading. CRC values are calculated every time data is written to a configuration register. The CRC value at the time of writing is compared to the CRC value upon 'readback'. In the event of these two values being different, an error is generated and the configuration file will fail to program the device. In order to append the configuration data in the *post-design* stage, the CRC must be recalculated and written over the old value.

The bounds of this method are driven only by the amount of data which can be stored in the particular devices. With respect to the Xilinx Virtex® family of devices [3], Table 1 demonstrates the ranges of available data for some common FPGA devices. It is clear that the ranges offered by this family allow large files to be embedded in even the smallest device configuration file. A significant advantage offered by this procedure benefits designers of FPGA configurations in that *any* existing design can have information embedded within it, regardless of its age, as the technique does not affect the data responsible for device-configuration.

Device Name	Available Space in CLB Columns (kb)
Virtex XCV50	8.44
Virtex XCV800	21.65
Virtex XV1000E	33.75
Virtex XV3200E	40.22

Table 1. The available amounts of auxiliary storage data for some common Xilinx Virtex® FPGA devices

The embedding of auxiliary data within the FPGA configuration stream creates possibilities for both FPGA users and design vendors to utilise an increased design functionality and security. In the following sections both of these issues are addressed.

3. FPGA Watermarking

The proposed method of authentication involves the injection of information into the unused 'pad' portion of the configuration bitstream. This means that full operation of the device is maintained with no added design complexity or alteration of the design. Furthermore, the embedded data can be retrieved from the FPGA configuration bitstream quickly as it is a separate entity to the design configuration (the watermark is added to the configuration file *after* the initial design procedure).

The image in figure 1 was embedded within the configuration file of a Xilinx Virtex® XCV50 device. The device was configured with the amended bitstream in order to evince the maintenance of full functionality, after which the image was extracted again. Both original and amended bitstreams demonstrated identical device operation.

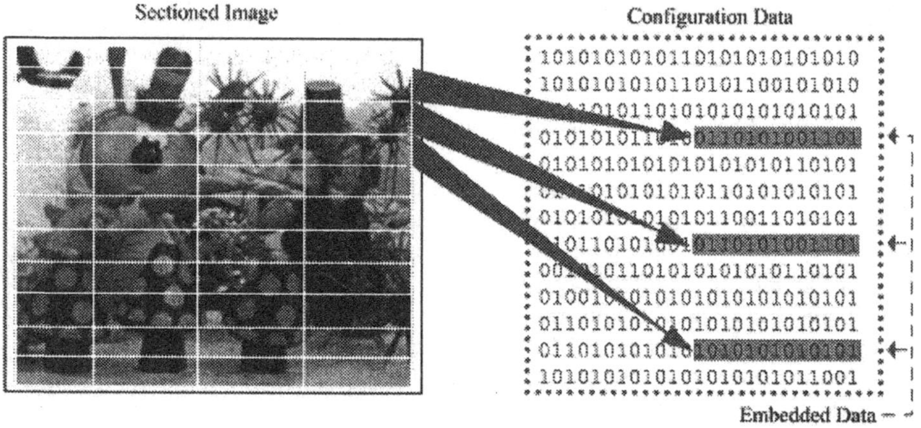

Figure 1. Showing the sectioning procedure of the embedding method upon an image

In order to remove this watermark, a very detailed knowledge of both FPGA architectures an bitstream formats is required. However, it must be argued that if subjected to a sustained attack, any watermarking technique could be removed. As previously stated, the concept of watermarking within hardware is extremely different to the concept of digital watermarking for audio, image and video and so conventional watermark attacking techniques [5] would in this instance be inapplicable.

4. Conclusions

In this paper, a method was proposed allowing auxiliary data to be stored within an FPGA's design file. Section 1 introduced the present techniques used in fingerprinting FPGA designs and the concept of the study. Section 2 went on to detail the methods used to embed data within its redundant areas while section 3 provided an example whereby an image was stored within an FPGA configuration file which was then downloaded to a physical device. Normal device functionality was observed before the image was extracted from the configuration file. This method has great advantages over present techniques, namely that far more space is available within the configuration bitstream's padding area than has previously been available. A further advantage of this method of data embedment is that it can be applied to a wide range of applications besides watermarking.

The prevention of misappropriation of FPGA designs will become increasingly important as reconfigurable-logic systems begin to be implemented at home [6], across multiple-user networks and hostile environments. Without authentication techniques, designs may be misappropriated with ease. The method presented in this paper is relatively robust, offering many possibilities due to the space available whilst allowing existing designs to be protected without reverting to high-level design tools.

References

1. Lach, J., Mangione-Smth, W.H., Potkonjak, M.: Signature Hiding Techniques for FPGA Intellectual Property Protection. Proc. IEEE International Conference on Computer Aided Design, pp 194-198, San Jose, California, U.S.A., November, 1998
2. Kahng, A.B. Lach, J., Mangione-Smith, W.H., Mantik, S., Markoz, L., Potkonjak, M., Tucker, P., Wang, H., Wolfe, G.: Watermarking Techniques for Intellectual Property Protection. Proceedings of the IEEE Design Automation Conference, San Fransisco, California, U.S.A., June 1998
3. Xilinx Inc.: Virtex Series Configuration Architecture User Guide. September, 2000
4. McVeigh, M.: Digital Watermarking FPGA Designs for Copyright Protection. MSc Thesis, Lancaster University, September 2001
5. Voloshynovskiy, S., Pereira, S., Pun, T., Eggers, J.J., Su, J.K.: Attacks on Digital Watermarks: Classification, Estimation-Based Attacks, and Benchmarks. IEEE Communications Magazine, pp 118-126, August, 2001
6. Xilinx Inc.: Introducing Xilinx and Programmable Logic Solutions for Home Networking. March, 2001

Implementing CSAT Local Search on FPGAs

Martin Henz, Edgar Tan, and Roland H.C. Yap

School of Computing, National University of Singapore, Singapore

Abstract. Stochastic local search methods such as GSAT, WalkSAT and their variants have been used successfully at solving propositional satisfiability problems (SAT). The key operation in these local search algorithms is the speed of variable flipping. We present a parallel FPGA designs for CSAT capable of one flip per clock cycle which is achieved by exploiting maximal parallelism and "multi-try" pipelining. Experimental results show that a speedup of two orders of magnitude over software implementations can be achieved.

1 Introduction

Stochastic local search (SLS) methods have been used successfully for solving satisfiability problems (SAT).

The key features of local search SAT algorithms are an initial assignment of variables occurring in the given set of clauses *cnf* followed by local moves, which flip (invert) the truth value of a chosen variable until a satisfying assignment is found. The instances of the algorithm differ in their choice of initial assignment (`INIT_ASSIGN`) and variable choice (`CHOOSE_FLIP`).

In previous work, we show an implementation of the SLS variant GSAT [HTY01], which achieves one flip per clock cycle. Here, we extend this design methodology and approach to the CSAT variant [GW93].

In order to describe and analyze parallel implementations of `GenSAT` algorithms, we use a notation close to the parallel functional language NESL [BHSZ95] explained in [HTY01], which allows an asymptotic complexity analysis with respect to the two factors that concern hardware implementations. The total size of the design can be measured by an abstraction of the number of gates needed to run a program P, denoted by $g(P)$. The analog of time complexity is the depth of program P, denoted by $d(P)$, the number of time units required for execution of P.

Let V be a set of boolean variables $v_1, v_2, \ldots, v_n$. A SAT problem C is a propositional formula in conjunctive normal form (CNF) consisting of a conjunction of m clauses. Each clause c_i is a disjunction of one or more literals where each literal is either a variable v_j or its negation $\neg v_j$. A SAT problem is called a k-SAT problem, if each clause has at most k literals. Without loss of generality, we consider only 3-SAT problems in this paper. The formula C is satisfiable, if there is an assignment of truth values to all variables in V that satisfies all clauses.

2 The CSAT Algorithm

CSAT [GW93] is a variation of GSAT, in which the candidate variables to be flipped are categorized into three groups with decreasing priority: increase in score (downward

M. Glesner, P. Zipf, and M. Renovell (Eds.): FPL 2002, LNCS 2438, pp. 1156–1159, 2002.

Program 1 The CHOOSE_FLIP algorithm for CSAT

```
procedure CHOOSE_FLIP(V, cnf)   returns: variable to be flipped
      U := []; S := []; s := score(cnf, V);
L1 :  for i := 1 to n do /* for all variables */
            s' := score_f(i, cnf, V);
            if s' > s then U := U ∪ [i]
            else if s' = s then S := S ∪ [i]
      end ;
      if U ≠ [] then return CHOOSE(U)
      else if S ≠ [] then return CHOOSE(S)
      else return CHOOSE(V)
end
```

moves), no change in score (sideways moves), and decrease in score. Program 1 shows a sequential implementation; the choice between moves of the same group is done by the macro CHOOSE, which randomly selects an element of a given sequence. The function $score(cnf, V)$ returns the number of clauses satisfied by variable assignment V and $score_{\mathfrak{f}}(i, cnf, V)$ the number of satisfied clauses if variable i is flipped.

Our goal is to exploit the parallelism available in a hardware implementation. There is a trade-off between the degree of parallelism in the implementation and the hardware resource requirements. The time complexity of the sequential implementation of CHOOSE_FLIP for 3-SAT is $\mathcal{O}(nm)$. A direct parallel implementation with the sequential loop *L1* in Program 1 with parallelization of $score_{\mathfrak{f}}$ by evaluating all clauses in parallel gives a time complexity of CHOOSE_FLIP of $\mathcal{O}(n\ log\ m)$ for 3-SAT. A fully parallel implementation can achieve a time complexity of $\mathcal{O}(log\ m)$ at the expense of replicating the scoring circuit n times.

A more realistic hardware implementation hinges on two key observations: (i) the selection of the flip variable can be done on the basis of relative contribution to the score of that variable when flipped; and (ii) the number of clauses which will be affected by a change to one variable is small, typically much less than m. Program 2 shows the resulting CSAT hardware design written in our notation.

This implementation assumes 3-SAT clauses where only the clauses relevant to a variable j are considered in *score*. Furthermore, the incremental score evaluation pre-computes for each of the two possibilities of a variable flip i, a simplified set of clauses. The optimization uses the notation $\mathtt{EVAL}_j^{C(i^+)}(V)$ to denote the evaluation of a new j-th 2-SAT clause formed by deleting variable i from an original clause where variable i occurs positively (respectively $\mathtt{EVAL}_j^{C(i^-)}(V)$ where i is negative). RECEIVE_INITIAL_ASSIGNMENT and SEND_ASSIGNMENT perform the data transfer from and to the external software environment, respectively.

The incremental score computation is done in *s1* and *s2*. The following optimization (not feasible for GSAT), allows to reuse the circuitry for computing the score increments for negative and positive variables. The *Diff* array gives the incremental score for flipping from $0 \rightarrow 1$, and the incremental score for the reverse flip needs a negation. Since CSAT only needs to consider a positive incremental score for downward moves, there are only two cases to consider for a downward move for variable i: (i) $V[i] = 0$ and

Program 2 Instance Specific Implementation of the CSAT Algorithm

program MAIN
    $V :=$ RECEIVE_INITIAL_ASSIGNMENT();
    for $i := 1$ **to** *maxflips* **do**
s1   (**if** SATISFIED(V) **then break** ||
s1 $Dyn0 := \{\mathtt{SUM}(\{\mathtt{EVAL}_j^{C(i^+)}(V) : j \in [1 \ldots |C(i^+)|]\}) : i \in [1 \ldots n]\} \parallel$
s1 $Dyn1 := \{\mathtt{SUM}(\{\mathtt{EVAL}_j^{C(i^-)}(V) : j \in [1 \ldots |C(i^-)|]\}) : i \in [1 \ldots n]\});$
s2 $Diff := \{Dyn1[i] - Dyn0[i] + Static[i] : i \in [1 \ldots n]\};$
s3 $(Side := \{Diff[i] = 0 : i \in [1 \ldots n]\} \parallel$
s3 $Down := \{Diff[i] \neq 0 \wedge \mathtt{ISNEG}(Diff[i]) = V[i] : i \in [1 \ldots n]\});$
s4   **if** SUM($Down$) > 0 **then** $FlipVars := Down$
s4   **else if** SUM($Side$) > 0 **then** $FlipVars := Side$
s4   **else** $FlipVars := \{1 : i \in [1 \ldots n]\};$
s5 $v :=$ CHOOSE_ONE($FlipVars$);
s6 $V[v] := \neg V[v]$
    end ;
    SEND_ASSIGNMENT(V)

$Diff[i] > 0$ for a $0 \rightarrow 1$ flip; (ii) $V[i] = 1$ and $Diff[i] < 0$ for a $1 \rightarrow 0$ flip (note that $Diff[i]$ is negative for variables whose value is currently 1). This is done in *s3* where ISNEG(x) is a macro returning 1 when x is negative and otherwise 0. Finally, to achieve a one flip design, we use multi-try pipelining [HTY01] with pipeline stages labeled as *s1* to *s6*. Assuming each stage is executed in one cycle, this implementation yields a depth complexity of $\mathcal{O}(log\ m + log\ n)$ and gate complexity of $\mathcal{O}(m + n)$ for 3-SAT.

3 Performance Evaluation

The actual FPGA implementation of CSAT (Program 2) was obtained using Handel-C programs,which is compiled into a netlist and then turned into a FPGA bitmap file with Xilinx Foundation Express. The target hardware used was a prototyping board developed by Celoxica Inc, the RC-1000PP board which contains a XCV1000E FPGA from Xilinx with 1.5 million system gates grouped into 6144 CLBs of two slices each.

All designs run at one flip per clock cycle and exploit parallel clause evaluation, parallel score computation and multi-try pipelining. In order to compare the efficiency of FPGA implementations, we measure their *flip rate*, i.e. the number of flips per second (flips/s). Column 4 of Table 1 shows the flip rate of the GSAT41 software by Selman and Kautz running CSAT on a Pentium II-400MHZ machine. The FPGA implementations of CSAT and GSAT are all run at a clock speed of 20MHz, which corresponds to a flip rate of 20,000 K flips/s. Column 5 shows that the FPGA implementation is two orders of magnitude faster than software.

In [HTY01], we developed a performance measure for hardware SAT implementations that takes hardware cost into account. This measure, called *flip density*, divides the flip rate by the number of FPGA slices (*fps/sl*). The last four columns in Table 1 shows that the presented CSAT implementation improves over the GSAT implementation of [HTY01] by a factor of 1.5 with respect to this performance measure.

Table 1 Flip Rate Speedup and Flip Density for Hardware Implementations of CSAT using Selected Benchmarks from SATLIB [SAT]

SAT Problem	Var (n)	Clause (m)	Software K*fps*	Speedup factor	GSAT slices	CSAT slices	GSAT *fps/sl*	CSAT *fps/sl*
uf20-01	20	91	52.7	393	1490	1019	13832	20332
uf50-01	50	218	72.8	287	3170	2062	6521	10131
uf100-01	100	430	71.6	291	5918	3860	3484	5391
aim-50-1_6-yes1-1	50	80	138.0	151	1818	1110	11374	18795
aim-50-3_4-yes1-1	50	170	74.3	281	2464	1667	8386	12521
aim-50-6_0-yes1-1	50	300	40.6	514	3506	2600	5897	8022
aim-100-1_6-yes1-1	100	160	138.4	151	3480	2018	5932	10331
aim-100-3_4-yes1-1	100	340	72.7	287	4712	3080	4381	6773
flat30-1	90	300	96.7	216	3515	2141	5883	9744
rti_k3_n100_m429_0	100	429	71.2	293	5904	3857	3494	5401
bms_k3_n100_m429_0	100	429	107.0	195	4766	2812	4332	7409

4 Conclusion

We show how to achieve a one flip per clock cycle design for the SLS solver CSAT. This design has comparable asymptotic depth and gate complexity to the one flip GSAT design in [HTY01] but improves on the flip density. Thus CSAT has the potential of a smaller implementation compared with GSAT.

The results here also demonstrate the potential hardware acceleration afforded by an FPGA implementation. The software results were taken on a Pentium II running at 400MHz, while the FPGA was only clocked at 20MHz. In this setting, we observe a speed-up of two orders of magnitude. Current work—beyond the scope of this paper—achieves one flip per clock cycle reconfigurable SLS implementations at the expense of a reduction in flip density. Details of the FPGA implementations with the SLS WalkSAT [SKC94] algorithm are reported in [Tan01].

References

[BHSZ95] Guy Blelloch, Jonathan Hardwick, Jay Sipelstein, and Marco Zagha. NESL user's manual, version 3.1. Technical Report CMU-CS-95-169, Carnegie Mellon University, Pittsburgh, PA, 1995.

[GW93] Ian P. Gent and Toby Walsh. Towards an understanding of hill-climbing procedures for SAT. In *Proceedings of AAAI-93*, pages 28–33, 1993.

[HTY01] Martin Henz, Edgar Tan, and Roland Yap. One flip per clock cycle. In Toby Walsh, editor, *Proceedings of the Seventh International Conference on Principles and Practice of Constraint Programming*, Lecture Notes in Computer Science, pages 509–523, Cyprus, 2001. Springer-Verlag, Berlin.

[SAT] SATLIB – The Satisfiability Library, `http://www.satlib.org`.

[SKC94] B. Selman, H. Kautz, and B. Cohen. Noise strategies for improving local search. In *Proceedings of AAAI-94*, pages 337–343, 1994.

[Tan01] Edgar Tan. *Local Search Algorithms for SAT on FPGAs*. Master's thesis, School of Computing, National University of Singapore, 2001.

A Reconfigurable Processor Architecture

Adronis Niyonkuru, Göran Eggers, and Hans Christoph Zeidler

Universität der Bundeswehr Hamburg,
Holstenhofweg 85,
D-22043 Hamburg, Germany
{adronis.niyonkuru, goeran.eggers, h.ch.zeidler}@unibw-hamburg.de

Abstract. Until now, the lack of software and hardware compatibility between existing reconfigurable processors make them less competitive with hard-wired processors for mainstream computing. In this paper we propose a reconfigurable processor architecture based on the von-Neumann computing model, so that software compatibility can be achieved with minimal work. Furthermore, the proposed processor takes advantage of key features of some FPGAs like partial and dynamic reconfiguration to load on-the-fly a variable number of different coarse-grained execution units.

1 Introduction

Since the last decade significant research activities on dynamically reconfigurable processors have been carried out, e.g. [1,2,3,4] with positive results reported. Nevertheless, this type of processor is still failing to be established as an alternative to the conventional hard-wired processors in mainstream computing. One of the main reasons is the lack of software and hardware compatibility between different reconfigurable processor architectures [2,5].

In our project we propose a reconfigurable processor architecture based on the von-Neumann computing model, so that software compatibility can be assured with little effort. The key novelty of this processor is the extensive use of partial and dynamic reconfiguration offered by some FPGA devices to allow a variable number of different execution units. This is performed while a program is executed and according to the software requirements.

In the following section we present some related work. Section 3 describes the processor architecture proposed and discusses some design issues. Section 4 gives an overview of the current implementation process and future work. Finally, the last section contains a short conclusion.

2 Related Work

There is already a wide range of reconfigurable processor architectures that have explored the use of dynamically reconfigurable logic to achieve a better processor performance. Some of them such us DISC [1] implement specialized instructions

M. Glesner, P. Zipf, and M. Renovell (Eds.): FPL 2002, LNCS 2438, pp. 1160–1163, 2002.

as hardware configurations that are dynamically mapped to reconfigurable hardware. Another group of processor architectures including SCORE [2] partition an application in small computing tasks, and corresponding hardware resources are dynamically made available to execute these tasks sequentially or in parallel (e.g. *"operator"* and *"compute page"* for SCORE). The main difference between these architectures and our model is that we make use of hardware techniques to increase the amount of instruction-level parallelism. Furthermore, partial and dynamic reconfiguration of some FPGAs is explored to dynamically optimize the use of hardware resources while implementing standard coarse-grained execution units.

3 A Reconfigurable Processor Architecture

The processor architecture proposed is based on the von-Neumann computing model in order to maintain the mainstream programming model. Since our processor has many execution units, two instructions are simultaneously fetched from a program memory, so that every cycle at least two instructions may be executed. Already decoded instructions are centralized by a dispatcher which issues them to the corresponding execution unit. The main difference between our reconfigurable processor and a conventional super-scalar processor is that our processor has a variable number of execution units. Unlike other super-scalar hard-wired processors which have a fixed number of execution units, the proposed processor takes advantage of partial and dynamic reconfiguration of some FPGAs to determine during program execution what kind of execution units and how many of each of them have to be available in hardware. To achieve this, four basic configurations are designed and stored in a configuration memory: an ALU configuration performing arithmetic and logic operations, a configuration corresponding to a load/store unit (LSU), another one for a multiply-divide unit (MDU) and a fourth one for a floating-point unit (FPU). Each of these execution units operates on 32-bit data.

According to the program requirements, suitable configurations are dynamically loaded to execute the current operations. For example, if a part of the program contains many ALU operations, multiple ALU configurations are loaded into the reconfigurable hardware according to the available hardware resources, so that these operations can be executed in parallel. Configurations corresponding to other execution units which are currently not needed are unloaded to make hardware resources available for the required configuration. If another kind of operation has to be executed later on, the corresponding configuration will be loaded and the kind and the number of hardware-resident execution units will be updated.

There are many design issues that have to be considered when implementing such a reconfigurable processor. To achieve a notable performance gain, a high level of instruction-level parallelism has to be ensured to provide the reconfigurable execution units with instructions which can be executed in parallel. As described in [6], there are many software and hardware techniques that are likely to increase the amount of parallelism among instructions. As long as software aspects imperatively imply modifying either the programming model or the compiler process, only hardware-based techniques will be considered, so that software compatibility at binary level can be guaranteed.

The basic technique adapted for our processor to increase the amount of instruction-level parallelism is the so called hardware-based speculation [6]. It was preferred for two reasons. First, it only requires hardware effort and minimize software adaptation, and second, it combines three techniques: dynamic branch-prediction, speculative execution and dynamic scheduling. Dynamic branch-prediction implies the use of hardware to dynamically predict the outcome of a branch. Doing so, a fetch cycle can be skipped if a branch is predicted and taken. To support this, a branch-prediction buffer with a two-bit prediction scheme, also called branch history table, is added to the processor architecture. Speculation allows instructions to be executed out-of-order but forces them to commit in the correct order. Therefore, a dispatcher issues decoded instructions out-of-order but a reorder-buffer is also introduced that holds the results of operations that finished execution but are still waiting to write back their results. However, these results can be forwarded to serve as source operands for further instructions.

A novel architectural component is introduced in our processor to support dynamic scheduling. The key idea behind dynamic scheduling is to allow multiple instructions to be simultaneously issued. This is possible only if there are many instructions ready to be issued at the same time. In addition to the two instructions fetched per cycle, our processor provides an instruction buffer that holds a sequence of instructions already executed. Only the instructions that are likely to be executed more than once are held in this buffer. According to the kind of instructions traced in this buffer, a configuration manager updates the hardware configurations to get the maximum number of the required execution units activated in the FPGA. The instructions held in the buffer are then executed in parallel after control and data hazards [6] have been eliminated. Execution units that are currently not needed are unloaded, so that all available hardware resources can be used to implement the required configurations.

4 Implementation Process

Since the key features of the proposed processor architecture are hardware-based solutions, we prefer to carry out a hardware implementation of the processor rather than just simulate it. Thus, we can estimate at each stage the feasibility of such a processor architecture model. As shown in the previous section, the reconfigurable processor proposed updates the number of its execution units by run-time reconfiguration according to software requirements. Therefore, such a processor requires a hardware platform supporting partial and dynamic reconfiguration as provided by some FPGAs such as the Xilinx Virtex-II family [7]. A development board including a Virtex-II XC2V1000 with 1 million gates is available, so that the processor implementation can be immediately carried out without any additional hardware effort.

The pipelined RISC processor that has been designed and implemented is based on the ARM Thumb instruction set [8]. This instruction set was chosen because of its simplicity and because it allows to fetch two instructions per cycle by a 32-Bit memory interface since each instruction is encoded using 16-Bit only. In order to be able to test the processor at every implementation stage, a minimal computing system that consists of basic processor components, a small program and data memory and an UART to serve as input/output unit have been designed and implemented on the Virtex-II FPGA. Currently, we are making use of the Modular Design flow and the Partial Reconfiguration flow recommended by Xilinx to find out how far a variable number of different execution units could be dynamically implemented on the FPGA.

Next, we plan to add the hardware components that increase the amount of instruction-level parallelism (dispatcher, branch-prediction logic, reorder-buffer) to the actual processor. Afterwards we will run some real-world applications, so that we could make reports about the performance gain.

5 Conclusions

In this paper we proposed a reconfigurable processor architecture based on the von-Neumann computing model with enhanced instruction level-parallelism. Exploring partial and dynamical reconfiguration of some FPGAs, it may be possible in the future to generate a non-fixed number of different execution units that execute instructions in parallel. To achieve this, intensive hardware design efforts are required. As a result, we expect a notable performance improvement while assuring at least software compatibility with the mainstream programming model.

References

1. M. J. Wirthlin, B. L. Hutchings, "A Dynamic Instruction Set Computer", *Proc. IEEE Work. FPGAs for Custom Computing Machines*, IEEE CS Press, April 1995
2. E. Caspi et al., "Stream Computations Organized for Reconfigurable Execution (SCORE)", *Proc. 10th Int. Conf. Field-Programmable Logic and Applications*, Springer-Verlag, Aug. 2000
3. S.C. Goldstein et al. "PipeRench: A Reconfigurable Architecture and Compiler", *IEEE Computer, Vol. 33, No. 4*, April 2000
4. S. Sawitzki, A. Gratz, R.G. Spallek, "CoMPARE: A simple processor architecture exploiting instruction level parallelism", *Proc. 5th Australasian Conf. Parallel and Real-Time Systems*, Springer-Verlag, 1998
5. M. Dales, "The Proteus Processor - A Conventional CPU with Reconfigurable Functionality", *Proc. 9th Int. Conf. Field-Programmable Logic and Applications*, Springer-Verlag, Sept. 1999
6. J. L. Hennessy, D. A. Patterson, "Computer Architecture: A Quantitative Approach", Morgan Kaufmann Publishers, Inc., Second Edition, 1996
7. Xilinx, Inc. "Virtex-II 1.5V Field-Programmable Gate Arrays", Advance Product Specification, April 2001
8. ARM Limited, "ARM Architecture Reference Manual", 2000

A Reconfigurable System-on-Chip-Based Fast EDM Process Monitor

Sebastian Friebe[1], Steffen Köhler[1], Rainer G. Spallek[1], Henrik Juhr[2], and Klaus Künanz[2]

[1] Institute of Computer Engineering
Department of Computer Science
{friebe,stk,rgs}@ite.inf.tu-dresden.de
[2] Institute of Production Engineering
Department of Mechanical Engineering
{juhr,kuenanz}@mciron.mw.tu-dresden.de
Dresden University of Technology
D-01062 Dresden, Germany

Abstract. This work introduces an innovative concept of a high-speed parameter monitor/classifier for fast electric discharge machining (EDM) process monitoring and feedback control. The proposed architecture enhances the process control system in terms of fast parameterizability through runtime hardware reconfiguration. Additionally, this paper presents a reconfigurable discharge impulse classification prototype, which is based on a Field Programmable System Level Integrated Circuit.

1 Introduction

Reconfigurable system-on-chip-based circuits are increasingly accepted in the embedded control domain. Latest trends in reconfigurable system-on-chip architectures combine a RISC microprocessor core with a reconfigurable hardware block. Their main operational area is located in the network [1] and telecommunications processing [2] domain.This paper presents the advantages of the Atmel FPSLIC [3] reconfigurable SoC as a platform for an impulse classifier, which is applicable for electric discharge machining process monitoring and optimization. Special emphasis is put on fast hardware adoption for process parameter space exploration purposes. Therefore, the FPGA hardware may be software-programmed (short-term adoption) or reconfigured (long-term adoption) to a specific process parameter window. The basic impulse classification functionality, which needs to be performed under high-speed real-time constraints (several μs downto 40ns), has been completely mapped to the FPGA part, whereas process monitoring and feedback can be executed as software in the AVR microcontroller. Hence, we present a generic, parameterizable classifier module for FPGA design hardware synthesis. In contrast to existing FPGA based implementations, our solution is capable of runtime reconfiguration and parameter modification through the on-chip microcontroller. This reduces high-speed bus hardware costs in an EMI sensitive environment.

M. Glesner, P. Zipf, and M. Renovell (Eds.): FPL 2002, LNCS 2438, pp. 1164–1167, 2002.

2 EDM Process Background

The electric discharge machining (EDM) is a spark-erosive manufacturing process for production of complex mechanical structures providing highest precision. It can be performed on any conductive material within a liquid dielectric environment. The material erosion is a result of several thousands of microplasma channel discharge phases between the tool electrode and the workpiece, which are controlled by a complex, high-energy impulse generator. Besides the parameters of the generator (e.g. discharge duration and current), the gap distance between the tool electrode and the workpiece as well as its electric behavior have a significant influence on the process properties. Since the gap distance and its physical consistency cannot be measured directly, process prediction is achieved indirectly through discharge impulse ignition statistics observation. Further details on monitoring the EDM process can be found in [5].

As a part of the machine development effort, every tool electrode/product material pair refers to its own, discrete, manually optimized process parameter set. To perform the EDM process economically, we apply a continuous process model, which allows exploration of the whole parameter space, even at runtime. This raises the demand of a parallel, high-performance impulse monitoring system, which avoids the use of empirically obtained sub-optimal parameters. The monitor has to be configured dependent on the electrical properties of the pulses specific to the material to assure maximum process observation accuracy. According to the proposed impulse monitor, an evaluation framework was created, which allows the implementation of a trend analysis for the process of sinking electric discharge machining over a large number of impulses (several thousands) during a observation period. Several impulse properties are measured and classified including the ignition delay and the voltage fall times. The histograms obtained supply predicates about process conditions. Based on these results, parameter changes for automatic feedback control can be extracted, which will be transfered to the generator and gap control.

Another important feature is the recognition of pulses outside the process parameter window to protect both the tool electrode and the workpiece from destruction.

3 System Architecture

Lookup for a low-power, single-chip solution, we found that a reconfigurable system-on-chip design was feasible and cost-effective. In this project, we chose the Atmel Field Programmable System Level Integrated Circuit (FPSLIC [3]). It consists of an 8-bit AVR RISC microprocessor core and a lookup-table-based FPGA, both coupled by dual-ported SRAM memory. The FPGA can be reconfigured at runtime through a microprocessor interface. Execution of the classification sequence is performed under the control of the AVR microprocessor (master). It performs less time-critical tasks and runs asynchronously to the FPGA part. Fig. 1 shows an overview of our proposed system architecture.

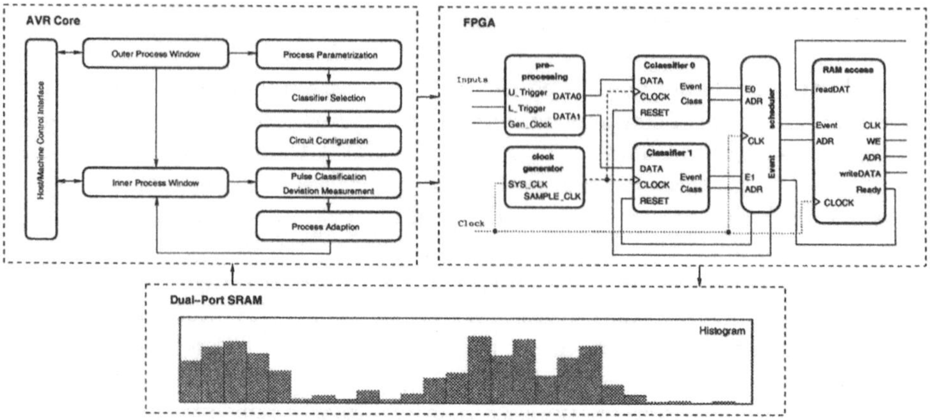

Fig. 1. FPSLIC based classification system

The microcontroller processes the classified impulse data and communicates with the FPGA circuit in the following ways:

- Impulse classification data access through the dual-ported SRAM
- Classifier clock/class property specification through the I/O interface
- Classification circuit reconfiguration

The hardware section is implemented as a parameterizable VHDL model. It can be synthesized, placed and routed for a large set of classifier parameters. The classifiers are parameterizable, non-wrapping counters. Its number is EDM process specific and dimensioned at design time. Although the generic classifier architecture is scalable at design time, the number of classifiers is not only limited by the FPGA logic resources but also by the dual-ported SRAM access bandwidth. To exploit this bandwidth economically, an access scheduler is inserted between the classifiers and the SRAM. The adaptation of the impulse classifiers to the EDM process is performed in two steps. The first step is the selection of an outer, larger impulse classification range for classification hardware design parameterization. Once the FPGA is configured through the AVR configuration interface, inner process window measurements can be achieved by selecting/switching classifier properties (e.g. classification clock, class ranges) through the AVR FPGA-I/O interface without circuit reconfiguration.

4 Results and Conclusions

The described system was implemented on an Atmel FPSLIC evaluation board [4] that is based on an AT94K40 chip with a total capacity of 1638 cells and 207 available I/O pins. The board is serially connected to a host PC system. We chose the Atmel System Designer V2.1 [4] for hardware synthesis and hardware/software co-simulation. The obtained results concerning different impulse classification criteria are summarized in Table 1.

# of classifiers	counter width	values per class	design size (cells)	utilization in %	max. FPGA clock (MHz)
2	8	2	322	14.0	44.21
2	8	4	319	13.8	37.01
2	8	8	315	13.6	44.42
2	8	16	300	13.0	42.52
2	8	32	293	12.7	44.33
2	12	4	364	15.8	40.19
2	12	32	345	15.0	39.43
2	16	32	405	17.6	33.66
4	8	32	328	14.2	53.19
4	12	32	483	21.0	40.19
4	16	32	605	26.3	30.38
6	8	32	371	16.1	51.47
6	12	32	637	27.4	29.03
6	16	64	774	33.6	29.17

Table 1. FPGA utilization

In conjunction with the considered problem of parameterizable impulse classification for the sinking electric discharge machining process our system meets all timing requirements. In contrast, the wire discharge machining process optimization demands a much higher impulse observation accuracy (down to 10ns). Therefore, the clock speed has to be increased by a factor of 2 to 3. Another problem is the monolithic dual-ported RAM interface. As we consider scalability of the classification system, the RAM block should be separable. This provides access from every classification unit to its own dedicated RAM module, avoiding a scheduler-based memory access. The reconfigurable SoC-based architecture provides a power- and area-efficient solution compared to a classic FPGA microcontroller board, where high speed memory access (up to 25 MBytes/s) had to be performed across a parallel bus system and an additional, external dual-ported SRAM chip would be necessary.

References

1. Iliopoulos, M., Antonakopoulos, T.: Reconfigurable Network Processors Based on Field Programmable System Level Integrated Circuits. FPL'2000, LNCS 1896, Springer-Verlag, Aug. 2000, pp. 39–45.
2. Chameleon Systems Inc.: Wireless Base Station Design Using Reconfigurable Communication Processors V1.0-00005, 2000
3. ATMEL Corp.: AT94 Series Field Programmable System Level Integrated Circuit. Advance Information, 2000.
4. ATMEL Corp.: FPSLIC System Designer Programmable System Level Integration. User's Guide and Tutorials, 2000.
5. Wang, W. M., Rajurkar, K. P.: Monitoring, Modeling and Control of EDM. Monitoring and Control for Manufacturing Processes, ASME PED-Vol. 44, 1990, pp. 393–406.

Gene Matching Using JBits*

Steven A. Guccione** and Eric Keller

Xilinx, Inc., 2100 Logic Drive, San Jose, CA 95124 (USA)
{Steven.Guccione ,Eric.Keller}@xilinx.com

Abstract. As the emerging field of bioinformatics continues to expand, the ability to rapidly search large databases of genetic information is becoming increasingly important. Databases containing billions of data elements are routinely compared and searched for matching and near-matching patterns. In this paper we explore the use of run-time reconfiguration using field programmable gate arrays (FPGAs) to provide a compact, high-performance matching solution to accelerate the searching of these genetic databases. This implementation provides approximately an order of magnitude increase in performance while reducing hardware complexity by as much as three orders of magnitude when compared to existing commercial systems.

1 Introduction

One of the fundamental operations in computing is string matching. Here, two linear arrays of characters are compared to determine their similarity. This operation can be found across a wide range of algorithms and applications. One area where string matching has recently received a renewed interest is in the area of bioinformatics, in particular in the area of searching genetic databases.

With the initiation of the Human Genome Project [2] in the early 1990s, the amount of data to be searched, as well as the number of searches being performed on this data has continued to increase. Because of the size and ongoing growth of this problem, specialized systems have been commercially introduced to search these databases of genetic information.

In this paper we present a system used to implement one of the most popular genetic search algorithms, the Smith-Watermann algorithm, using run-time reconfiguration. This approach provides not only smaller, faster circuits, but also reduces the input-output requirements of the system while simplifying hardware / software interfaces.

2 The Smith-Watermann Algorithm

While many applications performing string matching look for an exact match to the searched data, many other applications are interested in finding approximate matches. This requires a somewhat more complex algorithm than the search for exact matches.

* This work was supported in part by DARPA in the Adaptive Computing Systems (ACS) program under contract DABT63-99-3-0004.

** Steven Guccione is now at QuickSilver Technology, Inc. steve.guccione@qstech.com

M. Glesner, P. Zipf, and M. Renovell (Eds.): FPL 2002, LNCS 2438, pp. 1168–1171, 2002.

One area where inexact string matching has become important is in the searching of genetic databases. The optimal algorithm for inexact search in the field of bioinformatics is typically known as *Smith-Watermann*[8] and uses a dynamic programming technique. The algorithm compares two strings S and T by performing a pairwise comparison of each element in the two strings, then computing a score to determine the similarity of the two strings. Figure 1 gives a two-dimensional representation of the algorithm. The two strings S and T are compared and intermediate values a, b and c are used to produce the intermediate result, d. This calculation is repeated once for each pairwise element comparison.

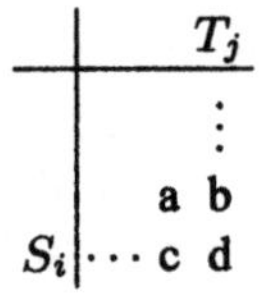

Fig. 1. Pairwise comparisons in the Smith-Watermann matching algorithm.

The matching algorithm itself is given in Equation 1. If the elements being compared are the same, the value a is used to calculate the result value d. If the elements in the two strings are not the same, then the value of a plus some *substitution* penalty is used. The result value d is determined by taking the minimum of this value, the value of b plus some *insertion* penalty and the value of c plus some *deletion* penalty.

$$d = min \begin{cases} \begin{cases} a & \text{if } S_i = T_j \\ a + sub & \text{if } S_i \neq T_j \end{cases} \\ b + ins \\ c + del \end{cases} \tag{1}$$

In the case where string S is of length m and string T is of length n, the algorithm begins by comparing S_0 and T_0 and proceeds onward until a final value of d is calculated at the comparison of S_m and T_n. This value is the *edit distance* between the strings.

3 The JBits™ Implementations

Rather than using the standard VHDL design flow to implement the Smith-Watermann algorithm, the Xilinx® *JBits* toolkit was used [5]. *JBits* was particularly useful in the implementation of this algorithm because there were several opportunities to take advantage of run-time circuit customization.

There are four different opportunities for run-time circuit customization. Three of these are the folding of the constants for the insertion, deletion and substitution penalties into the LUTs. Rather than explicitly feeding a constant into an adder circuit, the constant can be embedded in the circuit, resulting in (in effect) a customized constant adder circuit. Note that these constants can be set at run time and may be parameters to the circuit.

The fourth run-time optimization is the folding of the match elements into the circuit. In genomic databases, a four character alphabet is used to represent the four bases in the DNA molecule. These characters are typically denoted A for adenine, T for thymine, G for guanine and C for cytosine. In this circuit, each character can be encoded with two bits. The circuit used to match S_i and T_j does not require that both strings be stored as data elements. In this implementation, the S string is folded into the circuit as a run-time customization. Note that the string values are not fixed constants and will vary from one run to another. This means that the entire string S is used as a run-time parameter to produce the customized circuit.

This design uses a feature of the algorithm first noted by Lipton and Lopresti [7]. For the commonly used constants, 1 for insert/delete and 2 for substitution, b and c can only differ from a by +1 or -1, and d can only differ from a by either 0 or 2. Because of this, modulo 4 encoding can be used, thus requiring only 2 bits to represent each value. The final output edit distance is calculated by using an up-down counter at the end of the systolic array. The up-down counter is initialized to the match string length which makes zero the minimum value for a perfect match.

Further optimizations were performed to more efficiently map the design to the Virtex™ architecture. These optimizations make use of the Virtex carry-chain, which reduced the delay of the circuit since general routing was not needed internal to the processing element. The optimization is evident in Equation 2 which is equivalent to Equation 1 . The equation is basically a wide or gate which is efficiently implementable with the Virtex carry-chain. Another optimization evident from the transformed equation is the fact that d is equal to a or $a+2$. Because of this, the least significant bits of a and d are always equal. Therefore, only 1 bit is needed to represent d.

$$d = \begin{cases} a & \text{if } b \text{ or } c \text{ equals } a-1 \text{ or } S_i = T_i \\ a+2 & \text{if } b \text{ and } c \text{ equal } a+1 \text{ and } S_i \neq T_i \end{cases} \tag{2}$$

4 Other Current Implementations

As the computing demands of bioinformatics has continued to increase, commercially available solutions to the problem of searching genetic databases have become available. Today, the three major systems used commercially all take different approaches. It should also be noted that these systems all support a variety of matching algorithms in addition to Smith-Watermann. Table 1 gives a comparison of the various technologies currently available to perform Smith-Watermann matching. For a historical comparison, the *Splash 2* work of Hoang has also been included.

5 Conclusions

A gene matching system using run-time reconfiguration and operating on a single FPGA device has been presented. This system is able to perform Smith-Watermann

Table 1. This displays both performance and hardware size for various implementations.

	Processors per Device	Devices	Updates per sec
Celera (Alpha cluster)[1]	1	800	250B
Paracel (ASIC)[3]	192	144	276B
TimeLogic (FPGA)[4]	6	160	50B
Splash 2 (XC4010)[6]	14	272	43B
JBits (XCV1000-6)	4,000	1	757B
JBits (XC2V6000-5)	11,000	1	3,225B

matching at a rate of over three billion matches per second. This compares favorably to the currently available systems used commercially in this field. In the area of performance, the run-time reconfiguration approach provides an order of magnitude increase over both custom ASIC and multiprocessor systems, while reducing the hardware complexity by two to three orders of magnitude.

Such results would often indicate that some system parameter, usually flexibility, has been lost. This, however, is not necessarily true. It is possible to use similar techniques to implement other matching algorithms other than Smith-Watermann using run-time reconfiguration. Interestingly, there may be little or no advantage to implementing sub-optimal matching algorithms using this approach. Because this implementation appears to be limited more by data input / output than by processing power, implementing a faster algorithm may not provide substantial increases in performance. This would make the sub-optimal algorithms much less desirable.

As the field of bioinformatics continues to grow, and various fields from drug design to law enforcement come to rely on this technology, it is expected that interest in high performance matching systems will also grow. Reconfigurable logic and run-time reconfiguration promise to permit faster, less expensive systems to meet these needs.

References

[1] Celera Genomics, Inc. World Wide Web site http://www.celera.com/, 2002.

[2] Human Genome Project Information. World Wide Web http://www.ornl.gov/hgmis/, 2002.

[3] Paracel, Inc. World Wide Web site http://www.paracel.com/, 2002.

[4] TimeLogic, Inc. World Wide Web site http://www.timelogic.com/, 2002.

[5] Steven A. Guccione, Delon Levi, and Prasanna Sundararajan. JBits: A java-based interface for reconfigurable computing. In *Proc. 2nd MAPLD*, 1999.

[6] Dzung T. Hoang. Searching genetic databases on splash 2. In *IEEE Workshop on FPGAs for Custom Computing Machines*, pages 185–191, April 1993.

[7] Richard Lipton and Daniel Lopresti. A systolic array for rapid string comparison. In *Chapel Hill Conference on Very Large Scale Integration*, pages 363–376, 1985.

[8] T. F. Smith and M.S. Waterman. Identification of common molecular subsequences. *Journal of Molecular Biology*, 147:195–197, 1981.

Massively Parallel/Reconfigurable Emulation Model for the D-algorithm

Daniel G. Saab[1], Fatih Kocan[2], and Jacob A. Abraham[2]

[1] Department of EECS, CWRU, Cleveland, Ohio, 44106,
dgs3@po.cwru.edu
[2] Department of CSE, SMU, Dallas, Texas, 75275,
kocan@engr.smu.edu
[3] CERC, University of Texas at Austin, Austin, TX 78712,
jaa@cerc.utexas.edu.

Abstract. In this paper, we propose an approach to test generation based on reconfigurable devices, emulators, and Field Programmable Gate Arrays (FPGA). This approach is based on automatically designing a circuit which implements the D-algorithm specialized for the circuit under test. This approach exploits fine-grain parallelism in the forward/backward implications, and conflict checking. In this paper, we show an implementation with a lower hardware overhead than previous approaches making this technique more attractive.

1 Introduction

As integrated circuit designs continue to increase in size, structural testing that insures against manufacturing fault was and still difficult. Structural testing problem has been formulated as a search for an input pattern that will distinguish between the circuit functions in the presence and absence of the fault. This search process computes input vectors that detect a fault or determining that a fault is redundant when no such vector exists. This process requires a large amount of CPU time and in many cases they abort many of the hard-to-detect faults.

ATPG tools employ a branch-and-bound [1] technique to exhaustively search all input combinations. The D-algorithm, in [9], makes decisions at internal and primary input circuit nodes. The PODEM, in [6], makes decisions only on primary inputs (PI) to reduce the number of nodes appearing in the search tree. The FAN algorithm, in [5], improves to the basic PODEM search by making decisions at some internal nodes (head-lines) in addition to PIs and by tracing back multiple objectives instead of a single objective as used in PODEM. Mandatory assignments based on dominator are introduced in [7] to further improves FAN. In this paper, we exploit hardware to speed-up the ATPG process.

1.1 Related Work

Emulation systems are being used increasingly in the design, verification, and in rapid prototyping of digital systems [3]. In [4], a method is proposed to emulate

M. Glesner, P. Zipf, and M. Renovell (Eds.): FPL 2002, LNCS 2438, pp. 1172–1176, 2002.

serial fault simulation. In [8], a method is proposed to emulate D-algorithm. In [2], a method is proposed to emulate PODEM algorithm with its application to SAT. In all of those algorithms, a significant speed-up was obtained over software-based implementation. In this paper, we present a new method to emulate the D-algorithm on a reconfigurable hardware. Figure 1 illustrates the general data flow of this approach. This paper deals with the ATPG Mapping

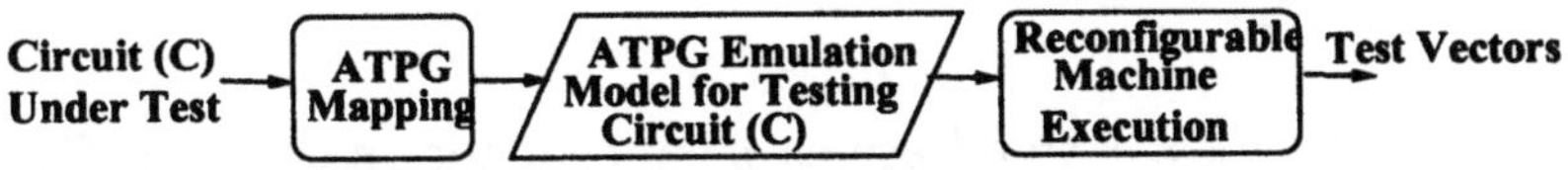

Fig. 1. Approach to ATPG using FPGA

which reads a design generates a model of a new circuit, which executes the Test generation algorithm on the original read design. This newly designed circuit will be used only once, thus it would not be economically feasible to implement it in a conventional way. Using reconfigurable hardware allows one to "virtually" create many circuits; then the algorithm is executed by emulating these circuits. The advantage is that each hardware will run at emulation speed, without incurring the cost of building special-purpose hardware.

2 The D-algorithm

The D-algorithm [9] which is described in [1]. This algorithm operates on two lists: The D- and J-frontiers. The J-frontiers are the set of lines whose implied values are unknown but set to values as the results of decisions. The D-frontiers are the set of gates whose output values are unknown but have faulty value in their input.

The algorithm can be divided into three parts. The first part is the Imply-Check() procedure which computes the logical behavior of the circuit for a given assignment, finds all direct implications, maintains D-frontiers and J-frontiers sets, and check for conflicts. Procedure ImplyCheck() returns FAIL in the case of conflict between signals. In the case when ImplyCheck() returns SUCCESS, the algorithm proceeds to either (the Second part) propagation phase or (the third part) the justification phase depending on whether the effect of faulty values is observed at any primary outputs.

In the propagation phase, a gate is selected from the D-frontiers, and all of its inputs whose values are unknown (X) are set to the inverse of the controlling value of the gate. This propagates the effect of the faulty value to the output of the gate and the D-Algorithm is called recursively to compute the effect of this on the circuit state. This process is repeated until a faulty value is propagated to at least one of the primary outputs. Upon completion of propagation, the program executes the justification procedure.

In the justification code, a gate from the J-frontier set is selected to assign its controlling value to one of its unknown-valued inputs. After assignment, the D-Algorithm is called recursively to compute the effect of the state of the circuit. In case the algorithm returns failures, this assignment is changed to the inverse of the gate's controlling value. This process is repeated until all gates in the J-frontiers are justified.

3 Our Approach

Figure 2 illustrates the essential features of our emulation model. The Emulation model consists of a FaultInjection Network, an Activation Block, a Justification Network, a Propagation Network, an ImplyCheckConflicts, and a Frontier Computation Block. The Emulation model starts by activating a fault which is performed in the the fault FaultInjection Network. The ImplyCheckConflicts block computes the logical behavior of the network in response to a change on any signals and propagates the effects to Primary Outputs (PO's) in both the good and the faulty network. The network, ImplyCheckConflicts, checks for conflicts by propagating an illegal code to the PO. The Frontier Computation block computes for each gate a flag indicating that the gate is active in the D-frontier. The Justification network justifies values assigned to internal nodes at the the primary inputs. It signals a failure if the justification fails or a success by activating DONE. In this case, a test is found otherwise it issues a backtrack to the Propagation network. The Propagation network propagates errors to PO's by selecting a gate from the D-frontier and propagating the error to its output. Once the errors reaches PO's, the Justification Network is activated to justify all the decisions made by the propagation network. If the justification is done, then a test is found. Otherwise, the propagation is activated to produce a new propagation patters. This process is repeated until a test is found or all propagation patterns are tried. In this case, the fault is redundant.

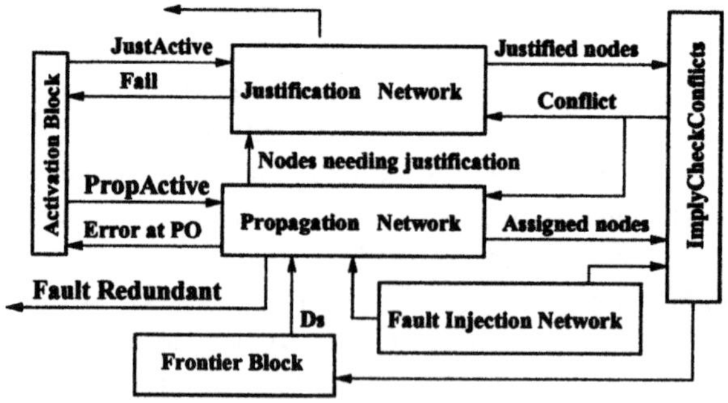

Fig. 2. ATPG Emulation Model

4 Results

The above approach has been implemented in a computer program for test emulation. To demonstrate our system on combinational circuits, we give the hardware overhead for testing the ISCAS 85 benchmarks. The results are shown in Table 1. For example, Circuit C432 has 160 Gates and 524 single stuck-at faults. To emulate the ATPG D-algorithm on this circuit we needs 1227 4-input modeled gates and 2360 modeled flip-flops. which is an overhead of 7 modeled gates for every real gate in the circuit and 14 flip-flop for every gate in the circuit. This is a much better improvement when compared to previous approaches.

Table 1. Hardware Overhead.

Circuit	Original		Emulation Model	
Name	Gate Count	Fault Count	4-in Gate Count	Flip-Flop Count
C432	160	524	1227	2360
C1908	880	1879	7741	9940
C2670	1193	2747	1088	13550
C3540	1669	3428	10975	17900
C5310	2307	5350	22300	26950
C6288	2416	7744	25824	32440
C7552	3512	7550	28435	38760

5 Conclusions

We presented an approach to test generation based on reconfigurable devices, emulators, and Field Programmable Gate Arrays (FPGA). Our approach is based on automatically designing a circuit which implements the D-algorithm specialized for the circuit under test. This approach exploits fine-grain parallelism in the forward/backward implications, conflict checking. Previous published techniques have shown the feasibility of these approaches in terms of speed when compared to software techniques with high hardware overhead. In this paper, we showed an implementation with a reasonable hardware overhead making this approach more attractive.

References

1. M. Abramovici, M. A. Breuer and A. D. Friedman, "Digital Systems Testing and Testable Design," *IEEE Press*, 1994.
2. M. Abramovici and D. G. Saab, "Satisfiability on Reconfigurable Hardware," *Int. Workshop on Field Programmable Logic and Applications*, Sept. 1997.
3. M. Butts, J. Bacheler. and J. Varghese, "An Efficient Logic Emulation System," *Proc. of ICCD*, 1992. pp. 138–141.

4. K-T. Cheng, S-Y. Huang, and W-J. Dai, "Fault Emulation: A New Approach to Fault Grading," *Proc. ICCAD*, 1995. pp. 681–686.
5. H. Fujiwara and T. Shimono, "On the acceleration of test generation algorithms," *IEEE Transaction on Computers*, vol. C-32, pp. 1137-1144, Dec. 1983.
6. P. Goel, "An Implicit Enumeration Algorithm to Generate Tests for Combinational Logic Circuits," *IEEE Trans. On Computers*, Vol. C-30, No.3 pp. 2 15-222, March, 1981.
7. T. Kirkland and M. R. Mercer, "A topological search algorithm for ATPG," *Design Automation Conf*, pp. 502-508, 1987.
8. F. Kocan and D. G. Saab, "Concurrent D-Algorithm on Reconfigurable Hardware," *Proceedings of ICCAD*, pp.152-155, 1999.
9. J. P. Roth, W. G. Bouricius and P. R. Schneider, "Programmed Algorithms to Compute Tests to Detect and Distinguish Between Failures in Logic Circuits," *IEEE Trans. on Electronic Computers*, Vol. EC-16, No. 10, pp. 567-579, October, 1967.

A Placement/Routing Approach for FPGA Accelerators

Akira Miyashita, Toshihito Fujiwara, and Tsutomu Maruyama

Institute of Engineering Mechanics and Systems, University of Tsukuba
1-1-1 Ten-ou-dai Tsukuba Ibaraki 305-8573 JAPAN
maruyama@darwin.esys.tsukuba.ac.jp

Abstract. In this paper, we propose an algorithm of placement and routing for FPGA accelerators. The algorithm is designed to reduce the time for placement and routing of the register transfer level codes generated by a C to HDL compiler. In the codes generated from algorithms written in programming languages, only the limited kinds of operations are used, and they have strong sequentiality from top to bottom. Therefore, in our approach, all circuits for operations in the codes are placed and routed sequentially from top to bottom without finding global optimal placement in order to reduce the computation time. Experiments on some circuits showed good results. The execution time for placement/routing of about 100K gate circuits is a few seconds and more than 70% of CLBs can be utilized.

1 Outline of the Placement/Routing Algorithm

Figure 1 shows examples of data-flow graphs generated from a sequential block and a loop block in programming languages. In the sequential block, all data on the graph flow from top to bottom, while data paths for loop variables (variables which are first read out, and then updated in loops) go back to opposite direction in the loop block.

The features of the data-flow graphs which are generated from programming languages can be summarized as follows.

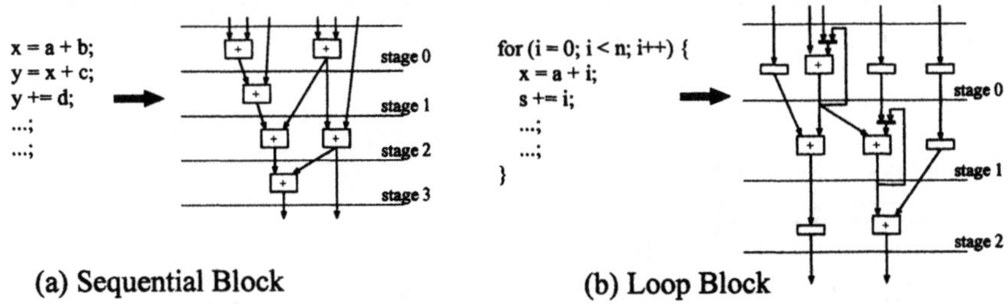

Fig. 1. Examples of Data-Flow Graphs of Blocks

M. Glesner, P. Zipf, and M. Renovell (Eds.): FPL 2002, LNCS 2438, pp. 1177–1181, 2002.

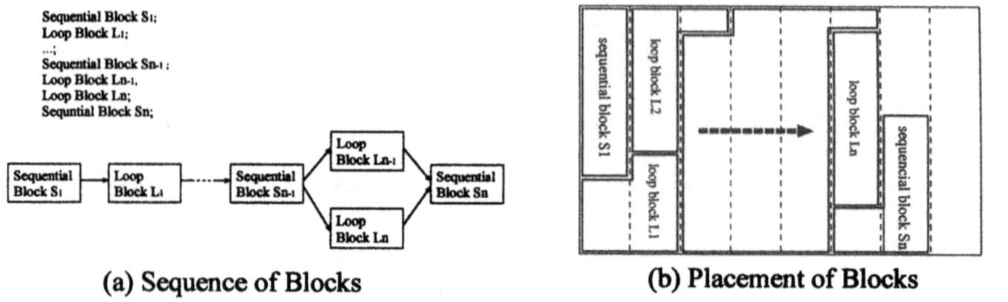

Fig. 2. Sequence of Blocks

1. The graphs have strong sequentiality from top to bottom.
2. The operations used in the data-flow graphs are very limited.
3. Registers are placed between most operations in order to achieve higher operation frequency.

Figure 2 shows an example of sequences of the blocks (blocks with no data dependencies can be processed in parallel), and how the blocks are placed on the area of CLBs. In our approach, the area of CLBs are divided to rectangles ((typical data width of the operations $\times$ (average parallelism of operations in one stage + margin)) $\times$ vertical length of the area), and circuits for operations in the blocks are simply placed sequentially in the rectangles.

Figure 3 shows how the circuits for operations in the data-flow graphs in each block are placed. The left half of the figure shows a data-flow graph which consists of two stages. In the figure, data width of the operation C and X is half of other operations. The operations on the data-flow graphs are placed in the rectangle area as shown in the right half of the figure.

1. First of all, macros for operations which will appear in the data-flow graphs are prepared in advance, and used for each operation.
2. Operations in the same stage are placed with a fixed margin for routing, and then routed.
3. Then, the operations in the next stage are placed and routed. This placement is decided so that the routings between the operations in the two stages are minimized.

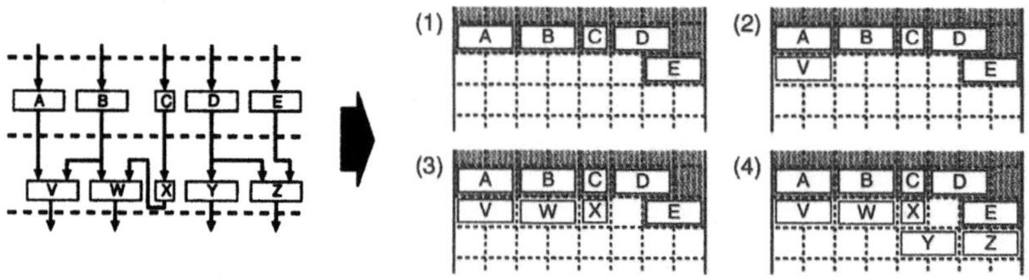

Fig. 3. Placement of Operations

4. When the operations on the stage can not be routed, the operations are replaced with more margins for routing resources.
5. If the operations can not be routed after several trials with larger margins, the operation in stages which are already placed are replaced with more margins.
6. By repeating 2 to 5, all operations in the all stages are placed and routed.

As described above, in our approach, all circuits are placed and routed from top to bottom sequentially. Therefore, the problems in our approach are

1. Routing of data paths to opposite direction (data paths for loop variables),
2. Long routes between blocks, and
3. Routing for memory access operations to access block RAMs or IOBs (to access external RAMs) which are placed on the edges of CLB areas (another kind of long routes).

2 Routing for Data Paths to Opposite Direction

Figure 4 shows how the data paths to opposite direction are routed. In the figure, circuits for operations on a data-flow graph are placed on the rectangle area (from the top), and data for a loop variable is sent back from *Y* to *X*. We first estimate the size of circuits between *X* and *Y*. If the distance between *X* and *Y* is small (figure 4 left), we allocate single routing resources *r0*, *r1* and *r2* in advance. After we place and route all circuits between *X* and *Y*, we place *Y* and connect *Y* to *r2* using *r3*. When the estimation is not accurate, more single routing resources are used to connect *Y* to *r3*.

When the distance is long (figure 4 right), we allocate long routing resources (hex routing resources in the figure) and single routing resources, and place *Y* on the estimated position in advance. In this case, even if the estimation is not accurate, we can not move *Y* afterward, because shorter routing resources can not drive longer routing resources. When the estimation is not accurate, long routing resources (hex routing resources in the figure) are also used to route to input of *Y* as shown in the figure.

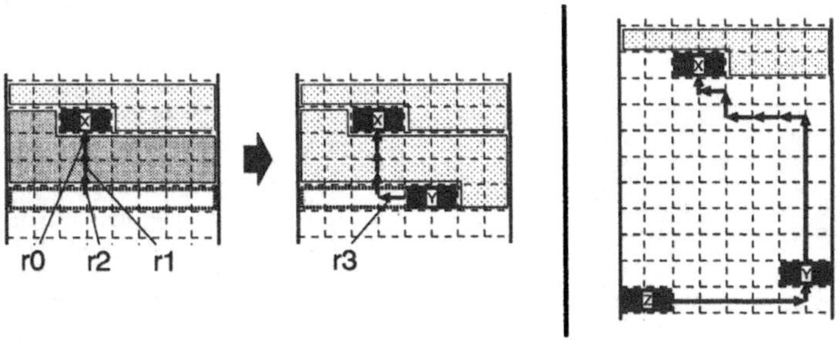

Fig. 4. Allocating Routing Resources for Loop Variables

3 Routing for Long Data Paths

Figure 5 shows how the data paths between two operations (X and Y) in different blocks (namely long data paths) are routed. In the figure, data are sent to the Y in L_n from X in S_1. In order to make long data paths, first, size of all blocks between the two operations (X and Y) is estimated and the position where Y will be placed are calculated. Then, long routing resources to Y are allocated before the placement of all blocks between X and Y. After we place and route all circuits between X and Y, we place Y and route from long routing resources to Y. When the estimation is not accurate, shorter routing resources are connected to the long routing resources. As shown in the figure, we need to allocate longer routing resources first, because shorter routing resources can not drive longer routing resources.

4 Routing for Memory Access Operations

In order to connect circuits for memory access operations to block RAMs or IOBs (to access external RAMs), we need to route two kinds of data paths; paths from circuits for the memory access operations to memories, and paths from memories to the circuits. The basic strategies for these routings are almost same with the routings described above except for that device length resources and tri-state buffers are used to connect CLBs to memories.

5 Experiments

We evaluated our algorithm using three programs on 733 MHz Pentium-III processor. Table 1 shows the results. The target device is XCV1000. Sobel filter is a circuit to extract edges in images, and eight same units are implemented to process 8 pixels in the images in parallel. Pattern matching is a circuit to compare given sequence of alphabets with long text. 4N magic square is a circuit to solve a simple puzzle game. In sobel filter, first, one unit is placed and routed to a certain area, and then, it is copied seven times to different area. Therefore, its execution time is very short. The execution time of 4N magic square is also short,

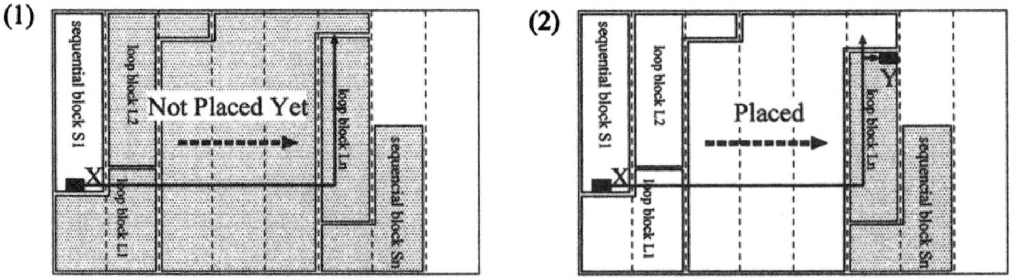

Fig. 5. Routing Between Blocks (Long routing)

because, in this circuit, only a few paths for loop variables and memory accesses are used. On the other hand, in pattern matching, many feed back paths and memory access paths are used, and more computation time is required. In all three programs, our approach can utilize more than 70% of CLBs. Table 1 shows only the time for placement and routing executed in the C programs written by us. We need about 3 seconds to output JBits programs, and 20 seconds to one minutes to compile the JBits program (more than several hundreds Mega Byte main memory is necessary to compile the program in 20 seconds).

Table 1. The result of experiments

Program	CLB areas (K gates)	Used rate of CLBs (%)	Computing time (seconds)
sobel filter	80	77.90	0.23
pattern matching	100	72.21	2.59
4N magic square	140	72.08	0.54

6 Current Status and Future Work

We need to improve details of placement/routing algorithm to achieve higher utilization of CLBs by evaluating more number of circuits. We also need more help by the C to HDL compiler. For example, routing of long wires is the major problems in our program. However, as for the long routes between the blocks, the delay time caused by the routes are not important in most cases. Therefore, the routing can be more simplified by inserting registers between the sources and destinations of the long routes by the compiler.

References

1. T. J. Callahan, et al, "Fast Module Mapping and Placement for Datapaths in FPGAs", International Symposium on Field Programmable Gate Arrays 1998
2. S. W. Gehring, et al, "Fast Integrated Tools for Circuit Design with FPGAs", International Symposium on Field Programmable Gate Arrays 1998
3. J. S. Swartz, et al, "A Fast Routability-Driven Router for FPGAs", International Symposium on Field Programmable Gate Arrays 1998
4. Y. Sankar, and J. Rose, "Trading Quality for Compile Time: Ultra-fast Placement for FPGAs", International Symposium on Field Programmable Gate Arrays 1999
5. C. Mulpuri and S. Hauck, "Runtime and Quality Tradeoffs in FPGA Placement and Routing", International Symposium on Field Programmable Gate Arrays 2001

Author Index

Lecture Notes in Computer Science

For information about Vols. 1–2358
please contact your bookseller or Springer-Verlag

Vol. 2398: K. Miesenberger, J. Klaus, W. Zagler (Eds.), Computers Helping People with Special Needs. Proceedings, 2002. XXII, 794 pages. 2002.

Vol. 2399: H. Hermanns, R. Segala (Eds.), Process Algebra and Probabilistic Methods. Proceedings, 2002. X, 215 pages. 2002.

Vol. 2400: B. Monien, R. Feldmann (Eds.), Euro-Par 2002 – Parallel Processing. Proceedings, 2002. XXIX, 993 pages. 2002.

Vol. 2401: P.J. Stuckey (Ed.), Logic Programming. Proceedings, 2002. XI, 486 pages. 2002.

Vol. 2402: W. Chang (Ed.), Advanced Internet Services and Applications. Proceedings, 2002. XI, 307 pages. 2002.

Vol. 2403: Mark d'Inverno, M. Luck, M. Fisher, C. Preist (Eds.), Foundations and Applications of Multi-Agent Systems. Proceedings, 1996-2000. X, 261 pages. 2002. (Subseries LNAI).

Vol. 2404: E. Brinksma, K.G. Larsen (Eds.), Computer Aided Verification. Proceedings, 2002. XIII, 626 pages. 2002.

Vol. 2405: B. Eaglestone, S. North, A. Poulovassilis (Eds.), Advances in Databases. Proceedings, 2002. XII, 199 pages. 2002.

Vol. 2406: C. Peters, M. Braschler, J. Gonzalo, M. Kluck (Eds.), Evaluation of Cross-Language Information Retrieval Systems. Proceedings, 2001. X, 601 pages. 2002.

Vol. 2407: A.C. Kakas, F. Sadri (Eds.), Computational Logic: Logic Programming and Beyond. Part I. XII, 678 pages. 2002. (Subseries LNAI).

Vol. 2408: A.C. Kakas, F. Sadri (Eds.), Computational Logic: Logic Programming and Beyond. Part II. XII, 628 pages. 2002. (Subseries LNAI).

Vol. 2409: D.M. Mount, C. Stein (Eds.), Algorithm Engineering and Experiments. Proceedings, 2002. VIII, 207 pages. 2002.

Vol. 2410: V.A. Carreño, C.A. Muñoz, S. Tahar (Eds.), Theorem Proving in Higher Order Logics. Proceedings, 2002. X, 349 pages. 2002.

Vol. 2412: H. Yin, N. Allinson, R. Freeman, J. Keane, S. Hubbard (Eds.), Intelligent Data Engineering and Automated Learning – IDEAL 2002. Proceedings, 2002. XV, 597 pages. 2002.

Vol. 2413: K. Kuwabara, J. Lee (Eds.), Intelligent Agents and Multi-Agent Systems. Proceedings, 2002. X, 221 pages. 2002. (Subseries LNAI).

Vol. 2414: F. Mattern, M. Naghshineh (Eds.), Pervasive Computing. Proceedings, 2002. XI, 298 pages. 2002.

Vol. 2415: J.R. Dorronsoro (Ed.), Artificial Neural Networks – ICANN 2002. Proceedings, 2002. XXVIII, 1382 pages. 2002.

Vol. 2417: M. Ishizuka, A. Sattar (Eds.), PRICAI 2002: Trends in Artificial Intelligence. Proceedings, 2002. XX, 623 pages. 2002. (Subseries LNAI).

Vol. 2418: D. Wells, L. Williams (Eds.), Extreme Programming and Agile Methods – XP/Agile Universe 2002. Proceedings, 2002. XII, 292 pages. 2002.

Vol. 2419: X. Meng, J. Su, Y. Wang (Eds.), Advances in Web-Age Information Management. Proceedings, 2002. XV, 446 pages. 2002.

Vol. 2420: K. Diks, W. Rytter (Eds.), Mathematical Foundations of Computer Science 2002. Proceedings, 2002. XII, 652 pages. 2002.

Vol. 2421: L. Brim, P. Jančar, M. Křetínský, A. Kučera (Eds.), CONCUR 2002 – Concurrency Theory. Proceedings, 2002. XII, 611 pages. 2002.

Vol. 2423: D. Lopresti, J. Hu, R. Kashi (Eds.), Document Analysis Systems V. Proceedings, 2002. XIII, 570 pages. 2002.

Vol. 2425: Z. Bellahsene, D. Patel, C. Rolland (Eds.), Object-Oriented Information Systems. Proceedings, 2002. XIII, 550 pages. 2002.

Vol. 2426: J.-M. Bruel, Z. Bellahsene (Eds.), Advances in Object-Oriented Information Systems.Procedings, 2002. IX, 314 pages. 2002.

Vol. 2430: T. Elomaa, H. Mannila, H. Toivonen (Eds.), Machine Learning: ECML 2002. Proceedings, 2002. XIII, 532 pages. 2002. (Subseries LNAI).

Vol. 2431: T. Elomaa, H. Mannila, H. Toivonen (Eds.), Principles of Data Mining and Knowledge Discovery. Proceedings, 2002. XIV, 514 pages. 2002. (Subseries LNAI).

Vol. 2435: Y. Manolopoulos, P. Návrat (Eds.), Advances in Databases and Information Systems. Proceedings, 2002. XIII, 415 pages. 2002.

Vol. 2436: J. Fong, C.T. Cheung, H.V. Leong, Q. Li (Eds.), Advances in Web-Based Learning. Proceedings, 2002. XIII, 434 pages. 2002.

Vol. 2438: M. Glesner, P. Zipf, M. Renovell (Eds.), Field-Programmable Logic and Applications. Proceedings, 2002. XXII, 1187 pages. 2002.

Vol. 2440: J.M. Haake, J.A. Pino (Eds.), Groupware: Design, Implementation and Use. Proceedings, 2002. XII, 285 pages. 2002.

Vol. 2442: M. Yung (Ed.), Advances in Cryptology – CRYPTO 2002. Proceedings, 2002. XIV, 627 pages. 2002.

Vol. 2443: D. Scott (Ed.), Artificial Intelligence: Methodology, Systems, and Applications. Proceedings, 2002. X, 279 pages. 2002. (Subseries LNAI).

Vol. 2444: A. Buchmann, F. Casati, L. Fiege, M.-C. Hsu, M.-C. Shan (Eds.), Technologies for E-Services. Proceedings, 2002. X, 171 pages. 2002.

Vol. 2445: C. Anagnostopoulou, M. Ferrand, A. Smaill (Eds.), Music and Artificial Intelligence. Proceedings, 2002. VIII, 207 pages. 2002. (Subseries LNAI).

Vol. 2447: D.J. Hand, N.M. Adams, R.J. Bolton (Eds.), Pattern Detection and Discovery. Proceedings, 2002. XII, 227 pages. 2002. (Subseries LNAI).

Vol. 2451: B. Hochet, A.J. Acosta, M.J. Bellido (Eds.), Integrated Circuit Design. Proceedings, 2002. XVI, 496 pages. 2002.

Vol. 2453: A. Hameurlain, R. Cicchetti, R. Traunmüller (Eds.), Database and Expert Systems Applications. Proceedings, 2002. XVIII, 951 pages. 2002.

Vol. 2454: Y. Kambayashi, W. Winiwarter, M. Arikawa (Eds.), Data Warehousing and Knowledge Discovery. Proceedings, 2002. XIII, 339 pages. 2002.

Vol. 2455: K. Bauknecht, A M. Tjoa, G. Quirchmayr (Eds.), E-Commerce and Web Technologies. Proceedings, 2002. XIV, 414 pages. 2002.

GPSR Compliance

The European Union's (EU) General Product Safety Regulation (GPSR) is a set of rules that requires consumer products to be safe and our obligations to ensure this.

If you have any concerns about our products, you can contact us on ProductSafety@springernature.com

In case Publisher is established outside the EU, the EU authorized representative is:

Springer Nature Customer Service Center GmbH
Europaplatz 3
69115 Heidelberg, Germany

Batch number: 10704711

Printed by Printforce, the Netherlands

Lecture Notes in Computer Science 2438
Edited by G. Goos, J. Hartmanis, and J. van Leeuwen

Springer-Verlag
Berlin Heidelberg GmbH

Manfred Glesner Peter Zipf
Michel Renovell (Eds.)

Field-Programmable Logic and Applications

Reconfigurable Computing Is Going Mainstream

12th International Conference, FPL 2002
Montpellier, France, September 2-4, 2002
Proceedings

Springer

Volume Editors

Manfred Glesner
Peter Zipf
Technische Universität Darmstadt
Institut für Datentechnik, FG Mikroelektronische Systeme
Karlstraße 15, 64283 Darmstadt, Germany
E-mail: {glesner,zipf}@mes.tu-darmstadt.de

Michel Renovell
LIRMM, Microelectronics Department
161 rue Ada, 34392 Montpellier Cedex, France
E-mail: renovell@lirmm.fr

Cataloging-in-Publication Data applied for

Die Deutsche Bibliothek - CIP-Einheitsaufnahme

Field programmable logic and applications : reconfigurable computing is going mainstream ; 12th international conference ; proceedings / FPL 2002, Montpellier, France, September 2 - 4, 2002. Manfred Glesner ... (ed.).

(Lecture notes in computer science ; Vol. 2438)
ISBN 978-3-540-44108-3 ISBN 978-3-540-46117-3 (eBook)
DOI 10.1007/978-3-540-46117-3

CR Subject Classification (1998): B.6-7, C.2, J.6

ISSN 0302-9743
ISBN 978-3-540-44108-3

http://www.springer.de

Originally published by Springer-Verlag Berlin Heidelberg New York in 2002

Typesetting: Camera-ready by author, data conversion by Boller Mediendesign
Printed on acid-free paper SPIN: 10870229 06/3142 5 4 3 2 1 0

Preface

This book is the proceedings volume of the 12th International Conference on Field-Programmable Logic and Applications (FPL) held on September 2–4, 2002. The conference was hosted by the Laboratoire d'Informatique, de Robotique et de Microélectronique de Montpellier (LIRMM), France. The FPL conference covered areas like reconfigurable logic and reconfigurable computing, as well as their application in various areas like DSP, communication and cryptography. Its subtitle "Reconfigurable Computing Is Going Mainstream" emphasizes the extensive role reconfigurable logic has started to play.

The annual FPL series is the oldest international conference in the world covering configware and all its aspects (also see: http://www.fpl.org). It was founded in 1991 at Oxford University (UK) and is two years older than its two most important competitors, which usually take place in Monterey and Napa. FPL has been held in Oxford (three times), Vienna, Prague, Darmstadt, London, Tallinn, Glasgow, Villach, and Belfast. It brings together experts, users, and newcomers from industry and academia in an informal, social, and productive atmosphere that encourages stimulating and profitable interaction between the participants.

Covered topics. The scope of this conference has been substantially extended over the past years and today also covers evolvable and adaptable systems, coarse-grain reconfigurable (sub)systems, their synthesis methods and applications, and their indispensable role in System-on-a-Chip (SoC) development, as well as reconfigurable computing (RC) as an emerging new paradigm, threatening to shake the general foundations of computer science: computing in space vs. computing in time. The application of field-programmable logic in different areas has gained increasing importance also, and the number of according submissions has grown.

Still growing importance. The size of FPL conferences has grown rapidly from 1991 to 2001. The figure below shows the numbers of submitted and accepted papers, starting in 1996. The 214 papers submitted in 2002 represent

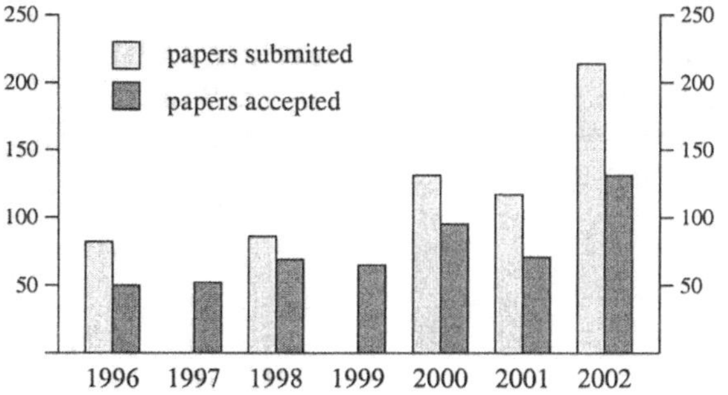

Numbers of submitted and accepted papers by year

an 83% increase compared to the year 2001. The program was assembled from 104 selected regular papers and 27 posters, resulting in a very interesting and attractive book. Another four papers are invited, including three keynotes. Because of the huge number of accepted contributions, this year for the first time the FPL program consisted of three parallel sessions. The selected contributions were submitted by researchers from 26 different countries:

USA:	30	Canada:	5	Ireland:	2	Lebanon:	1
UK:	15	Poland:	5	Portugal:	2	Mexico:	1
Germany:	12	Hong Kong:	4	Slovakia:	2	New Zealand:	1
Japan:	11	The Netherlands:	4	Australia:	1	Switzerland:	1
Spain:	9	Belgium:	3	Brazil:	1	Singapore:	1
France:	6	Czech Republic:	3	Greece:	1		
Italy:	6	Finland:	3	Iran:	1		

We gratefully acknowledge the reviewing work done by the PC members and many additional reviewers who contributed with their expertise to successfully compile the program.

Trends at FPL 2002. The main focus, set by the number of papers, was on the use of field-programmable logic for applications, mainly in the area of DSP (3 sessions), but also in various other areas (7 sessions, including two about arithmetic and two about cryptography). The use of field-programmable logic for communication applications (2 sessions) has been a sustaining field of interest. Reconfiguration and reconfigurable computing remain major points of interest, and are covered by 7 sessions ranging from custom computing engines to reconfigurable processors and issues of dynamic reconfiguration. Finally, low-power issues are receiving growing attention which is reflected in a new session dedicated to that topic.

Acknowledgements. We would like to thank the authors for submitting their first versions and for preparing the final versions of the accepted papers, as well as the members of our Program Committee and all other reviewers listed on the following pages. We also thank Reiner Hartenstein for making the event public on the web. We especially thank Thilo Pionteck and Ralf Ludewig from Darmstadt University of Technology for their help in managing the reviewing process and for their assistance while the proceedings volume was being assembled. We thank as well Alberto Garcia Ortiz, Octavian Mitrea, Juan Jesus Ocampo Hidalgo, Gilles Sassatelli, and Clemens Schlachta for supporting them. We gratefully acknowledge the excellent cooperation with Alfred Hofmann from Springer-Verlag, now FPL's official publisher for the 10th year.

June 2002

Manfred Glesner,
Peter Zipf,
Michel Renovell

Organization Committee

Program Chair:	Manfred Glesner Darmstadt University of Technology, Germany
General Chair:	Michel Renovell LIRMM, University of Montpellier II, France
Publicity Chair:	Reiner Hartenstein University of Kaiserslautern, Germany
Local Chair:	Lionel Torres LIRMM, University of Montpellier II, France
Proceedings:	Peter Zipf Darmstadt University of Technology, Germany
Sponsors:	Pascal Nouet LIRMM, University of Montpellier II, France
Exhibition:	Michel Robert LIRMM, University of Montpellier II, France
Social:	Daniel Auvergne, Nadine Azémard LIRMM, University of Montpellier II, France
Finance:	Marie-Lise Flottes, Denis Deschacht LIRMM, University of Montpellier II, France

Program Committee

Nazeeh Aranki	Jet Propulsion Laboratory/NASA, USA
Peter Athanas	Virginia Tech, USA
Neil Bergman	Queensland University of Technology, Australia
Dinesh Bhatia	University of Texas, USA
Eduardo Boemo	University of Madrid, Spain
Gordon Brebner	University of Edinburgh, UK
Stephen Brown	University of Toronto, Canada
Klaus Buchenrieder	Infineon Technologies AG, Germany
Stephen Casselman	Virtual Computer Corp., USA
Charles Chiang	Synopsys, Inc., USA
André DeHon	California Institute of Technology, USA
Carl Ebeling	University of Washington, USA
Hossam ElGindy	University of New South Wales, Australia
Manfred Glesner	Darmstadt University of Technology, Germany
John Gray	Independent Consultant, UK
Herbert Grünbacher	Carinthia Tech. Institute, Austria
Steven Guccione	QuickSilver Technology, USA
Reiner Hartenstein	University of Kaiserslautern, Germany
Scott Hauck	University of Washington, USA
Brad Hutchings	Brigham Young University, USA

Tom Kean	Algotronix Consulting, UK
Andres Keevallik	Tallinn Technical University, Estonia
Andreas Koch	University of Braunschweig, Germany
Dominique Lavenier	IRISIA and CNRS Univ. of Montpellier II, France
Philip Leong	Chinese University of Hong Kong, China
Jason Lohn	NASA Ames Research Center, USA
Wayne Luk	Imperial College London, UK
Patrick Lysaght	Xilinx, Inc., USA
Bill Mangione-Smith	University of California at Los Angeles, USA
Reinhard Männer	University of Mannheim, Germany
Oskar Mencer	Bell Labs, USA
Georges Milne	University of Western Australia
Toshiaki Miyazaki	NTT Network Innovation Labs, Japan
Fernando Moraes	PUCRS, Brazil
Sebastien Pillement	ENSSAT, France
Viktor Prasanna	University of Southern California, USA
Michel Renovell	LIRMM, University of Montpellier II, France
Jonathan Rose	University of Toronto, Canada
Zoran Salcic	University of Auckland, New Zealand
John Schewel	Virtual Computer Corp., USA
Hartmut Schmeck	University of Karlsruhe, Germany
Rainer Spallek	Dresden University of Technology, Germany
Adrian Stoica	Jet Propulsion Laboratory/NASA, USA
Jürgen Teich	University of Paderborn, Germany
Lothar Thiele	ETH Zürich, Switzerland
Lionel Torres	LIRMM, Univ. of Montpellier II, France
Stephen Trimberger	Xilinx, Inc., USA
Ranga Vemuri	University of Cincinnati, USA
Roger Woods	Queen's University of Belfast, UK

Additional Reviewers

Shailendra Aulakh	University of Texas, USA
Shankar Balachandran	University of Texas, USA
Marcus Bednara	University of Paderborn, Germany
Rajarshee P. Bharadwaj	University of Texas, USA
Elalaheh Bozorgzadeh	University of California at Los Angeles, USA
G.A. Bundell	University of Western Australia, Australia
Ney Calazans	PUCRS, Brazil
Gaston Cambon	LIRMM, Univ. of Montpellier II, France
Daniel Chillet	LASTI, University of Rennes, France
Seonil Choi	University of Southern California, USA
George Constantinides	Imperial College London, UK
Tim Courtney	Queen's University Belfast, UK

Didier Demigny	ETIS/ENSEA, France
Arran Derbyshire	Imperial College London, UK
Dirk Fischer	University of Paderborn, Germany
Thomas Geocaris	Synopsys, Inc., USA
Soheil Ghiasi	University of California at Los Angeles, USA
Herbert Grünbacher	Carinthia Tech. Institute, Austria
Manish Handa	University of Cincinnati, USA
Frank Hannig	University of Paderborn, Germany
Christian Haubelt	University of Paderborn, Germany
Fabiano Hessel	PUCRS, Brazil
Thomas Hollstein	Darmstadt University of Technology, Germany
Lorentz Huelsbergen	Bell Labs, USA
Minoru Inamori	NTT Network Innovation Labs, Japan
Ju-Wook Jang	University of Southern California, USA
Rajeev Jayaraman	Xilinx, Inc., USA
Adam Kaplan	University of California, LA, USA
Ryan Kastner	University of California, LA, USA
Jamil Kawa	Synopsys, Inc., USA
Jawad Khan	University of Cincinnati, USA
Ryusuke Konishi	NTT Network Innovation Labs, Japan
Gareth Lee	University of Western Australia, Australia
Norris Leong	Chinese University of Hong Kong, China
Stan Y. Liao	Synopsys, Inc., USA
Gaye Lightbody	Amphion Semiconductor, UK
Ralf Ludewig	Darmstadt University of Technology, Germany
Reinhard Männer	University of Mannheim, Germany
Chi-Yu Mao	Synopsys, Inc., USA
César Marcon	PUCRS, Brazil
Maire McLoone	Queen's University Belfast, UK
Seda Ogrenci Memik	University of California, LA, USA
Peter Moceyunas	Synopsys, Inc., USA
Sumit Mohanty	University of Southern California, USA
Rolf Fredi Molz	Universidade de Santa Cruz du Sul, Brazil
John Morris	University of Western Australia, Australia
Madhubanti Mukherjee	University of Cincinnati, USA
Takahiro Murooka	NTT Network Innovation Labs, Japan
Kouichi Nagami	NTT Network Innovation Labs, Japan
Ulrich Nageldinger	Infineon Technologies AG, Germany
Yoshiki Nakane	NTT Network Innovation Labs, Japan
Abdulfattah Obeid	Darmstadt University of Technology, Germany
Alberto Garcia Ortiz	Darmstadt University of Technology, Germany
Thilo Pionteck	Darmstadt University of Technology, Germany
Michel Robert	LIRMM, University of Montpellier II, France
Majid Sarrafzadeh	University of California at Los Angeles, USA
Gilles Sassatelli	Darmstadt University of Technology, Germany

Clemens Schlachta	Darmstadt University of Technology, Germany
Ron Scrofano	University of Southern California, USA
Alexander Sedlmeier	Infineon Technologies AG, Germany
Olivier Sentieys	IRISA, University of Rennes, France
Seung Kim	University of California, USA
Tunemichi Shiozawa	NTT Network Innovation Labs, Japan
Shiva Navab	University of California, USA
Reetinder Pal Sidhu	University of Southern California, USA
Subramanyan D. Siva	University of Cincinnati, USA
Frank Slomka	University of Paderborn, Germany
Vijay Sundaresan	University of Cincinnati, USA
Russ Tessier	University of Massachusetts Amherst, USA
Sudhir K. Vaka	University of Texas, USA
Vicky Vrolijk	University of Western Australia, Australia
Wendong Hu	University of California, USA
Ralph Weper	University of Paderborn, Germany
Lyndon While	University of Western Australia, Australia
Cliff Young	Bell Labs, USA
Yumin Zhang	Synopsys, Inc., USA
Peter Zipf	Darmstadt University of Technology, Germany

Michal Servit Award Committee

Gordon Brebner	University of Edinburgh, UK
Manfred Glesner	Darmstadt University of Technology, Germany
Reiner Hartenstein	University of Kaiserslautern, Germany
Wayne Luk	Imperial College London, UK
Paul Master	QuickSilver Technology, USA (sponsor)
Michel Renovell	LIRMM, University of Montpellier II, France
Roger Woods	Queen's University of Belfast, UK

Steering Committee

Manfred Glesner	Darmstadt University of Technology, Germany
John Gray	Independent Consultant, UK
Herbert Grünbacher	Carinthia Tech Institute, Austria
Reiner Hartenstein	University of Kaiserslautern, Germany
Andres Keevallik	Tallinn Technical University, Estonia
Wayne Luk	Imperial College London, UK
Patrick Lysaght	Xilinx, Inc., USA
Michel Renovell	LIRMM, University of Montpellier II, France
Roger Woods	Queen's University of Belfast, UK

Table of Contents

Keynote Address

Trends

Rapid Prototyping

FPGA Synthesis

Custom Computing Engines

DSP Applications 1

Reconfigurable Fabrics

Dynamic Reconfiguration 1

DSP Applications 2

Routing & Placement

Dynamic Reconfiguration 2

Power Estimation

Synthesis Issues

Keynote Address

Communication Applications 1

New Technologies

Reconfigurable Architectures

Image Processing

Crypto Applications 1

Keynote Address

Multitasking

Special Architectures

Crypto Applications 2

Compilation Techniques

DSP Applications 3

Complex Applications

Architecture Implementation

Design Flow

Miscellaneous

Short Papers

The Age of Adaptive Computing Is Here

Paul Master

Chief Technology Officer (CTO)
QuickSilver Technology

Abstract. Adaptive Computing: An advanced processing technology in which dynamic algorithms are directly mapped onto dynamic hardware resources, resulting in the most efficient use of CMOS silicon to enable high performance, low power consumption, reduced silicon area, and low cost. The first instantiation is the Adaptive Computing Machine (ACM).

The age of adaptive computing is upon us and the efforts of the engineering community are about to pay off in a very big way. As the market drivers move from the desktop to ever more portable applications, the demand for wireless devices dramatically increases, as do the requirements for high performance with low power consumption at low cost.

The driving trends for wireless devices are 3G and SDR, which will provide consumers with a vastly improved handset experience, worldphone capability, connectivity to their data anywhere in the world, as well as advanced features, such as multimedia. Additionally, PC and Internet experiences have played a pivotal role in driving consumer expectations for immediate access to information resources and a variety of applications in one mobile device.

Moore's Law has been the bellwether of performance for the semiconductor industry since the invention of the microprocessor. This dictum holds true to the present and is predicted to continue. However, packing more transistors and increasing clock speeds on a chip is no longer the answer for advanced mobile and wireless computing needs of the future.

Furthermore, rapidly changing network standards and the demand for new applications cannot tolerate the limitations of the conventional fixed function and rigid RISC/DSP/ASIC design approach. A more advanced IC architecture is required, one that provides a powerful, flexible processing platform for enabling next-generation wireless and mobile devices to execute a variety of applications, as well as any number of wireless standards and protocols.

The solution lies in adaptive computing, a new processing technology with an IC architecture that changes on demand to perform a much wider variety of functions at high processing speeds, with low power consumption, reduced silicon area, and at very low cost. These attributes are imperatives for next-generation wireless and

M. Glesner, P. Zipf, and M. Renovell (Eds.): FPL 2002, LNCS 2438, pp. 1-3, 2002.

mobile devices, creating a complex design challenge for developers. These problematic criteria are further compounded by the need to adapt to a constantly changing environment, such as consumer fads, new and improving standards, customer requirements, or to simply lengthen a product's life cycle once it's reached the "cash cow" side of the equation.

In the keynote, Mr. Master will address the following:

- Why the time and market are right for adaptive computing

- A comparison of conventional IC technologies to adaptive computing

The advantages and limitations of fixed-function silicon, such as DSPs, ASICs, FPGAs, and microprocessors are compared to an all software-programmable solution of adaptive computing.

- The differences that exist between FPGA-based reconfigurable computing and adaptive computing

There are several distinctions that are causing reconfigurable computing to be supplanted by a highly efficient form of adaptive computing. A few examples include: Adaptive computing has fewer interconnects, lower capacitance, dynamic configuration during run time, and the instantiation of heterogeneous algorithmic elements in hardware, running for as little as one clock cycle. Conversely, reconfigurable architectures are FPGA-based, with massive interconnect and capacitance issues, are static in nature, and make use of homogenous elements, running for an extended length of time.

- Micro and macro levels of adaptability

- Spatial and temporal segmentation SATS, also thought of as time sharing, is a key factor in enabling software defined radio (SDR)

SATS is the process of adapting dynamic hardware resources to rapidly perform various portions of an algorithm in different segments of time (temporal) and in different locations in the adaptive circuitry fabric (spatial) of the adaptive computing architecture.

- The technical aspects of the adaptive computing platform and architecture details of the ACM

What are the unique elements of this processing technology and the structure that enable ASIC-class performance, small silicon area, low power consumption, low cost, and architecture flexibility? This discussion will include adaptive computing's underlying IC architecture – the Adaptive Computing Machine (ACM) – that uses standard CMOS silicon more efficiently, while easing the design risks for developers.

- System scalability

- How this powerful level of processing performance and capability is moving adaptive computing into mainstream computing

- Adaptive computing test chip example with benchmark performance

An adaptive computing benchmark focuses on demanding areas of software defined radio (SDR) wireless-handset applications for two key wireless standards, cdma2000 and WCDMA. The benchmark elements were selected for their emphasis on compute-intensive operations, and for comparing an ACM chip to a known high-performance, fixed function silicon ASIC solution.

- Ultimate benefits for OEMs, developers, and consumers

The advantages are numerous and far reaching, including faster time to market, lower development costs, less design risk, rapid design response to consumer fads and trends, changes at any time during the design cycle, bug-fixes after product shipment, and product customization for markets or individuals, to name a few.

Disruptive Trends by Data-Stream-Based Computing

Invited Presentation

Reiner W. Hartenstein
University of Kaiserslautern
hartenst@rhrk.uni-kl.de

Computing is an extremely conservative science. After about a dozen of technology generations the dominant basic principles have mainly remained the same. Although von Neumann has not invented this mainstream form of computing, he and his co-authors have been in the mid' 40ies the first to clearly describe the strikingly simple machine paradigm which I would like to call the ***von Neumann paradigm.*** Other paradigms, like dataflow machines, reduction engines, or others, have never been commercially significant. Commercial break-throughs mainly stem from the progress of semiconductor technology but have hardly affected the blinders limiting the scope of conference series like ISCA or MICRO, which remained almost 100% von-Neumann-based all the time. Dozens of expired supercomputing companies illustrate, how decades of searching for the universal massively parallel computer architecture finally failed. Von-Neumann-based parallel computing really succeeded only in some special application areas. Not only the area of embedded computing systems, but also PCs demonstrate, that more and more most silicon real estate is occupied by accelerators, prostheses needed by the aging von Neumann processor, now being a methusela after surviving so many technology generations.

The von Neumann paradigm is the driving force behind the success of software industry, by its simplicity helping to focus language design and compilation techniques to a usefully narrow design space, and, by helping to educate zillions of programmers. Prerequisite of this success is the fact, that its operational principles are RAM-based, yielding a seemingly almost unlimited flexibility. But we now have a RAM-based competitor: Reconfigurable Computing, where structure definition is RAM-based, instead of the instruction execution schedules as known from von Neumann principles. It turns out, that von Neumann does not support such soft hardware. This is the basis of a emerging disruptive trend which has (almost) all prerequisites to repeat the success story of the software industry: by a configware industry needing the support of a revolutionary new machine paradigm. However, the new trend is coming along with the challenge to overcome the incising limitations of users' dominant "procedural-only" mind set of computing science in the von Neumann era. The new direction appears like the antimatter of computing. There is a lot of similarities between the worlds of von Neumann and its anti machine paradigm. But like in particle physics, there are asymmetries - making it a bit inconvenient to teach the coming dichotomy of computing sciences. The talk will introduce a more detailed survey.

M. Glesner, P. Zipf, and M. Renovell (Eds.): FPL 2002, LNCS 2438, pp. 4-4, 2002.

Multithreading for Logic-Centric Systems

Gordon Brebner*

Division of Informatics
University of Edinburgh
Mayfield Road
Edinburgh EH9 3JZ
United Kingdom

Abstract. This paper concerns 'logic-centric' systems on chip, that is, systems in which the main computational focus is on logic circuitry — specifically programmable logic circuitry here. In particular, processors have a subordinate role to the logic in such systems. The key idea pursued in the paper is the importation and adaptation of the concept of *multithreading* from the world of the processor into the world of programmable logic, as one element in a higher-level model of logic-centric computation. A general mechanism for implementing time slicing for multithreading, and for dealing with synchronization issues that arise, is presented. Then, an actual case study is described: the implementation of a multi-version IP router on the Xilinx Virtex-II Pro part, where multithreading was profitably introduced into a system design in order to minimize latency when handling packets at gigabit rates.

1 Introduction

System-level integration — system on chip — presents both enormous opportunities and enormous challenges to system designers. The use of field-programmable logic as a first-class system entity looks central to the provision of efficiency and flexibility in the digital electronic aspects of such systems. More generally, overall systems can be viewed as 'chip area networks', involving the rich interconnection of diverse components — not just digital electronics, but analogue electronics, photonics, micromechanics, wetware, etc. In the first instance though, exploring novel options just in digital electronics can help to point the way to more general techniques for chip area networking.

One immediate approach to system-level integration is to treat the chip as a scaled-down board, by mapping down the conventional architecture of computing systems from a board (or several boards connected by a bus). This offers a plausible route to initial progress, allowing a focus on the technological challenges of deep submicron design, using long-established and trusted architectures. Further assistance can then come from a 'platform-based' design methodology, where an

* Part of this research was conducted by the author while visiting Xilinx Inc, 2100 Logic Drive, San Jose, CA 95124, U.S.A.

M. Glesner, P. Zipf, and M. Renovell (Eds.): FPL 2002, LNCS 2438, pp. 5–14, 2002.

on-chip architecture is provided, meaning that just the addition of new IP[1] blocks is needed in order to produce a complete system on chip.

The author's background research agenda is to explore novel architectural approaches that differ from just scaling down Von Neumann computing systems, with a stereotyped view of software and hardware and of partitioning between these two. Here, the focus is on 'logic-centric' systems, that is, systems in which the main computational focus is on logic circuitry — specifically programmable logic circuitry here — with processors, in particular, viewed as additional system components rather than the central system components. Aside from computational differences, there are implied architectural differences, most notably concerning serial data access and shared buses, features both tailored to processor behaviour. The enviromental context will be that of the *reactive system* [2] — a system that reacts to, and is driven by, inputs received over time. In such a model, there is a distinct contrast to the *transformational system* that is typically associated with running programs on a processor, notably that the environment, not the computer, is the controlling force.

The particular idea pursued in this paper is the importation and adaptation of the concept of *multithreading* from the world of the processor into the world of programmable logic, with the intention of supplying one part of a higher-level model of computing in a logic-centric manner. Other important parts of such a model include the notion of virtual circuitry, as explored by the author and several other researchers in recent years (e.g., [4,5,7,8,9]). In fact, the runtime management methods originally developed with virtual circuitry in mind are directly applicable to the instantiation and destruction of threads.

The remainder of the paper is organized as follows. Section 2 supplies a background on threads and multithreading, and how this may be applied in the context of fine-grain parallelism using programmable logic. Section 3 then describes a general mechanism for implementing time slicing for multithreading, and for dealing with synchronization issues that arise. Section 4 describes an actual case study where multithreading was profitably introduced into a system design. Finally, Section 5 draws some conclusions and points to future work.

2 Threads and Multithreading

The notion of a *process* — informally, a program in execution — is well established as a basic unit of work in time-shared operating systems. Conventionally, a process had a single thread of control within its associated program. More recently, however, the notion of multi-threaded processes has been introduced. Here, a *thread* is a lightweight form of process. In processor terms, each thread has a program counter, register set and stack, but all threads share the same program, data, open files, etc. A well-known example is the support for multi-

[1] In this paper, the abbreviation 'IP' is used in both well-known roles: here, meaning 'Intellectual Property', but later, meaning 'Internet Protocol'. In all cases, the intended meaning will be clear from the context.

threading built in at the language level in Java. Benefits of multithreading in processes are summarized by Silberschatz *et al* [12] as:

- *Responsiveness.* One thread can run when another is blocked.
- *Resource sharing.* Threads share memory and other resources.
- *Economy.* Creating and context switching threads is much easier than for processes.
- *Utilization of multiprocessor architectures.* Each thread can run on a different processor.

All of these characteristics make multithreading attractive as a means of efficiently organizing the fine-grain parallelism made available by programmable logic into a coherent higher-level computational entity.

In terms of importing the concept of multithreading into the world of programmable logic, a relatively low-level approach would be just to carry out circuit partitioning, with each member of the partition being regarded as a thread. For example, this might follow some hierarchical structuring in the circuit design, such as each IP block being regarded as a thread, or it might correspond to the results of some automated partitioning process applied to a flattened design. However, while proceeding in this way would allow the expression of coarser-grain parallelism, it is a process already carried out in normal design flows, and so there is no particular gain in tagging this as 'multithreading'.

In order to make multithreading have some real significance, we look here to identify a notion of a single control flow within each thread, in addition to the abundant data flow exhibited by circuitry. In its simplest form, such a flow within a thread corresponds to a finite state machine. Therefore, the context of a thread will be defined by the current state of its machine, and the contents of all registers within its circuitry (the former being a special case of the latter, in implementation terms)[2]. New threads can be instantiated in programmable logic by the configuration of circuitry and initialization of its state.

Overall, the flavour of such multithreaded circuitry has much in common with the Berkeley *Co-design Finite State Machine* (CFSM) model [1], where CFSMs are used for system specification, prior to automated (or semi-automated) partitioning of FSMs into hardware or software. This model has earlier roots in work on communicating finite state machines, for example, the well-known *Statecharts* model of Harel [11]. The two main elaborations here are, first, the specialization of the model to the particular domain of logic circuitry, with a greater emphasis on globally synchronous behaviour, and, second, the dynamic nature of threads. The latter aspect is closely related to prior work on virtual circuitry, and the runtime management of circuitry in general.

In comparison with processor-oriented threads, note that the spatial substrate for logic-oriented threads is analogous to the multiprocessor situation,

[2] In fact, one might stretch the model by regarding the contents of all registers, combined, as being the state. However, the intention here is that the state would normally be represented by the contents of just a single register.

where there is one processor per thread. That is, all registers can be simultaneously present, with no swopping needed (unless the total thread circuitry exceeds the physical resource available, in which case virtual circuitry mechanisms can be used). The subtlety comes in the time domain, reflecting interactions between threads and between threads and the environment. This topic is explored in the next section.

3 Timeslicing and Synchronization

Where threads execute independently of other threads, their state machines can be clocked as desired. In particular, in the reactive system context here, the clocking might be related to external input/output rates. However, greater care is necessary when there is interaction between threads. In the CFSM model, mentioned in the previous section, it is expected that such interaction will be asynchronous, giving a locally-synchronous, globally-asynchronous system.

Such an approach is, of course, possible here. A particular case is where combinational or registered signals, stable over one or more clock cycles, travel between threads. However, in general, reflecting the more integrated nature of the programmable logic substrate, a tighter synchronous approach, likely to carry fewer overheads and hence be more lightweight, is desirable. Central to this approach is the need for apt clocking of communicating threads. This issue is considered first, followed by discussion of downstream implications. Examples follow in the case study in the next section of the paper.

Clocking for Inter-thread Communication

Assuming that edge-triggered logic is used for the finite state machine component of each thread, then reliable communication using a direct signal from one thread to another impacts on mutual clocking. Specifically, the edge for the recipient thread must not occur until the signal from the source thread is stable. This means that there is a type of timeslicing in the system — in this logic-centric case, to synchronize two threads, as opposed to the need to share a processor in the conventional processor-centric case. Following the timeslicing analogy through, a very simple scheme for synchronizing two communicating threads is to clock one on the rising edge of a clock, and to clock the other on the falling edge of the same clock.

While this gives a simple scheme for two threads, using a single clock, it can be generalized, still following the timesliced approach. All that is required is division of a base clock, and delivery of the divided clock at an appropriate number of equally-spaced phases. This is particularly easy for modern FPL devices, e.g. use of the Digital Clock Manager (DCM) modules and dedicated clock routing available on the Xilinx Virtex-II range [13]. Although the use of equally-spaced clocks might not be optimal for a particular set of interacting threads, this scheme is particularly easy for an operating system to provide (just as timeslicing with equal slices is easiest for a processor operating system).

Arbitration between Threads

The above discussion concerned one-to-one communication between threads. Generalizing this to one-to-many communication is straightforward: all recipient threads must obey an appropriate clocking constraint with respect to the clocking of the source thread. In particular, where there is no interaction amongst the recipient threads, they may all have the same clock. As usual, the opposite case — many-to-one communication — is harder to deal with, and arbitration is needed. A typical circumstance for such communication is write access to a shared register. In this case for example, when two threads are clocked on different edges, it is not possible to synthesize the required register directly, since the register's clocking is ambiguous. Aside from this fundamental problem, there is also a need to arbitrate/combine the actual data input to the register.

A particular solution, related to the basic timeslicing concept, is to use time-division multiplexing between threads for many-to-one communication. In a general setting, if there are n source threads, each with the same clock frequency but with equally-spaced clock phases, then the recipient thread should operate at n times the frequency of the source threads, its clock being suitably phased with the source threads' clocks. Data selection from the multiplex is made using a simple counter tracking each clock cycle. In the simple case of two sources only, such a counter is effectively just a one-bit value tracking the recipient thread clock. However, in practice, this should not be implemented just by using the clock signal directly, since this is likely to be an abuse of dedicated clock routing, by its direction to combinational logic.

Resets

The action taken upon resets is one detail following on from the above discussion. Initialization of the state and local registers of a thread must be done with respect to the clock of that thread. In other words, reset actions should be localized to threads. Where time-division multiplexing is used, care is necessary to ensure that the selection counter is correctly initialized to align with the clocks of source threads. The duration of a global reset signal must, of course, exceed the longest clock period over all threads.

Thread Activation/Deactivation

As described so far, a thread is in continuous execution once instantiated, in the sense that its finite state machine is operational. However, viewed at a higher level, a thread can usefully be viewed as having, minimally, two identifiable *idle* and *active* 'metastates', with perhaps further metastates, such as *blocked*; these metastates are conditioned by events outside the thread. The basic inter-thread communication mechanism described so far is adequate to underpin transmission of metastate transition events. For example, suppose that one thread performs a service for another. The server thread can be activated using an input signal from the client thread, and it can in turn supply an output signal denoting completion to the client thread.

4 Case Study: Mixed-version IP Router

In this case study, the application is a Mixed-version IP Router, named MIR, servicing four gigabit ethernet ports. This application would be of use to organizations operating several gigabit ethernet networks, with a mixture of IPv4 and IPv6 hosts and routers attached directly to the networks[3]. The implementation is based on the Xilinx Virtex-II Pro part, launched in Spring 2002 and a member of Xilinx's family of 'platform FPGAs' [13]. Virtex-II Pro chips can have between none and four PowerPC cores, and between 4 and 16 gigabit serial links. Here, a single PowerPC core and four serial links are used.

The intention is that the router's functions can evolve smoothly, maintaining router performance as an organization migrates from IPv4 to IPv6 internally, and also as the Internet migrates externally. The basic aim is to carry out more frequent, and less control intensive, functions in logic, and other functions in the processor. In essence, the PowerPC core on the Virtex-II Pro acts as a slave to the logic, rather than the more common opposite master-slave relationship. The overall system design, and general motivation, was covered in a recent paper by the author [6].

Here, the focus will be on just the multithreaded part of the implementation, in which all of the aspects covered in the previous section feature. The multithreading is concerned with the processing of packets in parallel with their receipt, in order to minimize router latency. The key to minimizing latency is avoiding copying packets between buffers, a well-known cause of inefficiency in packet routers.

In MIR, this is achieved by two mechanisms. First, as a packet is received from a port, it is stored in the correct buffer for onward transmission. To do this precisely would require psychic ability, since the onward path can only be determined after some examination of the packet header. MIR gets round this problem by initially storing a copy of the packet in all possible onward buffers, refining this selection after header analysis. Although an interesting feature in its own right (further details being in [6]), this is not germane to the multithreading discussion.

The main thread interest arises from the second latency-improvement mechanism: the processing and modification of packets during reception, which is necessary in order to support mixed-mode IPv4 and IPv6 operation, in addition to basic packet routing. The most frequent operation of such a mixed-mode router is not conversion between IPv4 and IPv6 formats, which is discouraged (although it is supported by MIR). Rather, the approved action is *encapsulation*: forwarding IPv4 packets inside IPv6 packets, or vice versa. Achieving this is a central concern in the use of multithreading in MIR.

In a typical implementation of a basic IP router, the data flow is likely to be pipelined on the granularity of packets, for example:

[3] IPv4 is version 4 of the Internet Protocol, in general use on the Internet since 1981; IPv6 is version 6, defined since 1994, and gradually coming into service on the Internet.

1. receive gigabit ethernet packet and process MAC header; then
2. process IP header of packet and make routing decision; then
3. construct MAC header and transmit gigabit ethernet packet.

This implies buffering between ethernet and IP protocol modules, regardless of whether the flow is implemented by logic and/or program. This scheme is consistent with a clean layering of protocols, of the sort exemplified by the *network wrappers* of Braun *et al* [3]. There are, however, some alternative systems where there is still pipelining, but handling of different protocol layers is not disjoint, for example, XCoNET [10]. In MIR, multithreading, rather than pipelining, is the key to ensuring that a packet can be forwarded almost immediately after its reception has been completed.

MIR Packet Handling Threads

There is a main thread concerned with receiving packets. This receives 32-bit words from the serial gigabit/second interface, detects gigabit ethernet PHY framing and then stores the words of each recognized PHY frame. This is done under the control of an appropriate finite state machine. For operation at one gigabit/second, the 32-bit interface must be clocked at 31.25 MHz, and words are available on the leading edge of the clock. Therefore, the packet receiving thread is clocked on the trailing edge of this clock, synchronizing the thread with its external environment.

In addition to this main thread, the current MIR prototype has six other resident threads concerned with incoming packet handling:

1. MAC/SNAP header recognition thread;
2. IPv4 header recognition thread;
3. IPv6 header recognition thread;
4. IPv4 address lookup thread;
5. IPv6 encapsulation thread; and
6. MAC header construction thread.

These are activated as appropriate while a packet is being received, in order to handle either incoming header recognition or outgoing header construction. All six threads use the same clocking arrangement, which is in opposite phase to the main thread. That is, they are all clocked on the leading edge of the 31.25 MHz clock, whereas the main thread is clocked on the trailing edge. This arrangement reflects two characteristics:

- interaction amongst the six threads is sufficiently constrained that it is safe to have the recipient of a signal receiving it one full clock cycle later; and
- the six threads can perform computation and buffer writing at times disjoint from the main thread's operations.

Note the simplification of the pure timeslicing scheme introduced in the previous section. Such simplification is not possible in general, but results from particular analysis of thread interaction in this instance.

Activation and Deactivation

Figure 1 shows an example timeline for the threads concerned with packet handling (times not to scale), together with activation/deactivation interactions.

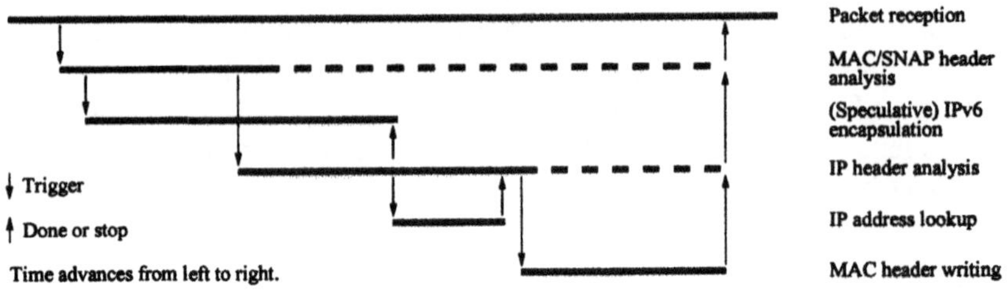

Fig. 1. Example timeline for MIR packet reception threads

The MAC/SNAP header recognition thread is activated by the main thread, as soon as it has recognized the PHY header of a packet. This is done by raising a trigger signal between the threads. Meanwhile, the main thread continues receiving and buffering subsequent words of the packet. As each word is received, it is also placed in a shared register, so that it can be examined by the header recognition threads when they are clocked at the next half-cycle.

The MAC/SNAP header recognition thread makes an initial speculation that the incoming packet will need to be encapsulated inside an IPv6 packet for onward transmission to the Internet. It therefore activates the IPv6 encapsulation thread immediately. Thereafter, its finite state machine tracks each of six MAC/SNAP header words in turn, until the final word reveals the actual type of the enclosed packet: IPv4, IPv6, or something else. It then activates the IPv4 header recognition thread or the IPv6 header recognition thread as appropriate. Finally, it waits until all (if any) of its activated threads are finished, then signals its own completion to the main thread by raising a done signal.

The IPv6 encapsulation thread is rather unusual. Its finite state machine stores a six-word MAC/SNAP header followed by a 10-word IPv6 header in the transmission buffer(s), starting at a point that is 10 words ahead of the first word stored from the incoming packet. Therefore, if the thread runs to completion, it will have constructed a valid encapsulated outgoing packet. This is because it will have overwritten the original MAC/SNAP header, with its own headers now directly preceding the incoming IPv4 packet. The thread may be deactivated prematurely however, by the IPv4 or IPv6 header recognition threads ascertaining that this encapsulation is not required.

The IPv4 header and IPv6 header recognition threads operate in a similar way to the MAC header recognition thread. In fact, in the current prototype, only IPv4 header recognition is implemented fully in logic, IPv6 header recognition (like IPv6 in IPv4 encapsulation) being deemed a 'rarer' occurrence, and left to the processor. The IPv4 header recognition thread can detect when an IPv6 packet is contained within an IPv4 packet, in which case it deactivates itself and activates the other thread. When necessary, it also activates the IPv4 address lookup thread, which carries out a lookup, signalling the availability of its result at a later time. After IPv4 header recognition is complete, and address lookup has finished if necessary, the thread finally activates the MAC header writing thread if IPv6 encapsulation has been deactivated. The MAC header writing thread updates the MAC header for onward transmission. When it signals completion, the IPv4 header recognition thread signals its own completion.

Time Division Multiplexing

From the above description, it can be seen that two threads might be writing to the same buffer simultaneously: the main thread storing incoming words; and either the IPv6 encapsulation thread or the MAC header writing thread. The threads are organized so that that are no conflicts caused by writing to the same place in the buffer. However, synchronization of clocking is needed, and this is an example of simple time division multiplexing. Writing to the buffer is clocked at double the rate of the threads, that is, at 62.5 MHz. The falling edges of the buffer clock are synchronized with both the rising and falling edges of the thread clocks. Thus, the buffer is clocked alternately in the middle of the time slice of the main thread and of the other threads, giving the desired effect.

5 Conclusions and Future Work

The MIR prototype described in the previous section has been fully implemented for the Virtex-II Pro, using Verilog descriptions of the threads and their interactions. It has been successfully tested in simulation and, at the time of writing, initial experiments with real parts were just under way. The multithreaded packet reception allows onward forwarding with minimal latency — just two 31.25 MHz clock cycles, even in the worst case of a minimum-length ethernet packet (when there is least time available for header analysis during packet reception).

The experience gained from the practical case study has been invaluable in extracting some general principles of multithreading. This is a step towards higher-level computational models that accurately reflect the power of programmable logic. The case study has also pointed to several optimizations that are possible when it is known that threads are well behaved in some sense. Examples include clock sharing by related threads, and simplified activation and deactivation.

Future work will include investigation of how these principles can be incorporated into automated tools for assisting in multithreaded designs. One particular aspect will be the automatic generation of appropriate clocking for threads. There will also be investigation of the dynamic instantiation of threads, since the MIR prototype has no support for automated thread configuration. This will integrate well with earlier work on dynamic circuitry management.

Acknowledgements

It is a pleasure to thank Xilinx Inc for hosting the author's visit in July-September 2001, during which much of the practical work was carried out, and for continued support since. Particular thanks to Khang Dao, Matt Dipaolo, Adam Donlin, Hamish Fallside, Doug Pecchenino, Peter Ryser, Steve Trimberger and Steve Trynosky at Xilinx for their invaluable help and support.

References

1. F. Balarin, M. Chiodo, P. Giusto, H. Hsieh, A. Jurecska, L. Lavagno, C. Passerone, A. Sangiovanni-Vincentelli, E. Sentovich, K. Suzuki and B. Tabbara. Hardware-Software Co-Design of Embedded Systems: The Polis Approach. Kluwer Academic Press, 1997.
2. N. Bergmann, G. Brebner and J. Gray. Reconfigurable computing and reactive systems. *Proc. 7th Australasian Conference on Parallel and Real-Time Systems*, Springer, 2000, pages 171–180.
3. F. Braun, J. Lockwood and M. Waldvogel. Reconfigurable router modules using network protocol wrappers. *Proc. 11th International Conference on Field Programmable Logic and Applications*, Springer LNCS 2147, 2001, pages 254–263.
4. G. Brebner. A virtual hardware operating system for the Xilinx XC6200. *Proc. 6th International Workshop on Field Programmable Logic and Applications*, Springer LNCS 1142, 1996, pages 327–336.
5. G .Brebner and O. Diessel. Chip-based reconfigurable task management. *Proc. 11th International Conference on Field Programmable Logic and Applications*, Springer LNCS 2147, 2001, pages 182–191.
6. G. Brebner. Single-chip gigabit mixed-version IP router on Virtex-II Pro. *Proc. 10th Annual IEEE Symposium on FPGAs for Custom Computing Machines*, IEEE, 2002, to appear.
7. J. Burns, A. Donlin, J. Hogg, S. Singh and M. de Wit. A dynamic reconfiguration run-time system. *Proc. 5th Annual IEEE Symposium on FPGAs for Custom Computing Machines*, IEEE, 1997, pages 66 – 75.
8. O. Diessel and H. ElGindy. Run–time compaction of FPGA designs. *Proc. 7th International Workshop on Field Programmable Logic and Applications*, Springer LNCS 1304, 1997, pages 131 – 140.
9. H. ElGindy, M. Middendorf, H. Schmeck and B. Schmidt. Task rearrangement on partially reconfigurable FPGAs with restricted buffer. *Proc. 10th International Workshop on Field Programmable Logic and Applications*, Springer LNCS 1896, 2000, pages 379 – 388.
10. H. Fallside and M. Smith. Internet Connected FPL. *Proc. 10th International Workshop on Field Programmable Logic and Applications*, Springer LNCS 1896, 2000, pages 48 – 57.
11. D. Harel. Statecharts: a visual formalism for complex systems. *Science of Computer Programming*, **8**, June 1987, pages 231–274.
12. A. Silberschatz, P. Galvin and G. Gagne. Applied Operating System Concepts (1st edition). New York:Wiley, 2000.
13. Xilinx Inc. *Platform FPGAs*. `http://www.xilinx.com/products/platform/`

Fast Prototyping with Co-operation of Simulation and Emulation

Siavash Bayat Sarmadi[1], Seyed Ghassem Miremadi[2], Ghazanfar Asadi[1], Ali Reza Ejlali[1]

[1] Sharif University of Technology, Department of Computer Engineering, Azadi Ave., Tehran, IRAN
{bayat, asadi, ejlali}@ce.sharif.edu
[2] Sharif University of Technology, Department of Computer Engineering, Azadi Ave., Tehran, IRAN
miremadi@sharif.edu

Abstract. A method for simulation-emulation co-operation of Verilog and VHDL models is presented. The method is based on using Programming Language Interface (PLI) to achieve speedup in prototyping and to facilitate the communication between an emulator and a simulator. The PLI technique is implemented for both Verilog and VHDL models. The results show that this simulation-emulation co-operation method can significantly reduce the simulation time of a design implemented by VHDL codes as well as Verilog codes.

1 Introduction

Two important approaches for design verification are simulation and logic emulation [16], [17]. Some advantages of the logic emulation as compared with the simulation are as follow:

- The logic emulation is about 10^3 to 10^6 faster than simulation [15].
- An emulator can be connected to the real application environment.

As stated above, logic emulation provides high performance. However, simulators benefit some features, which are not available in emulators; these are:

- The possibility of observing and controlling the signals and values of a circuit during simulation [1].
- Both synthesizable [4] and non-synthesizable models can be simulated.

The above discussion shows that both simulation and emulation have some advantages and disadvantages. Some attempts to incorporate the advantages of both methods have been described in [2], [3], [5], [11], [12] and [13]. The idea presented in [2], uses an emulator to accelerate event-driven simulation of some non-synthesizable behavioral models. In that work, the logic is synthesized into FPGA chips, while a simulator manages events. This removes the event-processing overhead from behavioral simulation. In [3], some parts of a circuit are simulated and the rest parts are emulated. In this work, the TEXTIO package [9] available in the standard VHDL library, is used to establish a communication between the simulator and the emulator. It should be noted that no physical emulator was used in [3]; another simulator was employed instead of the emulator. This method has two notable drawbacks: a) the use

M. Glesner, P. Zipf, and M. Renovell (Eds.): FPL 2002, LNCS 2438, pp. 15-25, 2002.

of text files could be very time-consuming, and b) the method is only applicable to VHDL models. In [11] and [12], some efforts have been taken to combine simulation and emulation in the functional verification as well as functional debugging of designs. In these approaches, the emulator is used to drive test vectors to the design. When a design fault is detected, then a cut-set is transferred from the emulator to the simulator for analysis. A transaction-based layered architecture was presented in [13] to speed up functional verification. In this work, Programming Language Interface (PLI) was utilized to establish a communication between the simulator and the emulator. With this architecture, up to 50 times speedup is reached as compared to the software simulation [5]. In this work, a special simulator as well as a special emulator was used; namely the Specman Elite simulator and the VStation emulator.

In this paper, a Simulation-Emulation Co-OPeration environment, called SECOP, is presented. This environment utilizes a general simulator as well as a general emulator, as compared with other environments that use special emulator and simulator. In addition, a method to invoke the PLI [10], [14] by VHDL processes is also presented. In the SECOP environment, a PCI-based PLDA board [7] is used for the emulation part and the ModelSim simulator (Version 5.5a)[6] is used for the simulation part. To evaluate the SECOP, two example circuits have been used as benchmarks: a simple RISC processor and a 256-point FFT processor. Furthermore, the TEXTIO method proposed in [3], is also experimentally evaluated. The results and speedups obtained from the experiments are reported for both Verilog and VHDL codes.

This paper is organized as follows. In Section 2, the reasons of combining a simulator with an emulator are described. The hardware and the software of the SECOP environment as well as the communication strategy between the simulator and the emulator are presented in Section 3. In Section 4, the method of using Verilog PLI in VHDL is given. The experimental results are presented in Section 5. Finally, the conclusion is given in Section 6.

2 Why Simulation+Emulation?

Some advantages of the simulation methods as well as the logic emulation methods were discussed in the previous section. In this section, some advantages of combining simulation and emulation are discussed. The main advantages of the Simulation+Emulation method as compared with the pure simulation are as follows:

- A prototype of a model, which is not completely synthesizable, can be developed. In this case, the synthesizable part of the model is emulated, while the non-synthesizable part is simulated.
- The time overhead caused by the logic synthesis and technology mapping during the iterations of modification can be removed [3]. In this case, those parts of the circuit that require redesigns are simulated, and the rest parts, which do not need the logic synthesis and the technology mapping in each iteration, are emulated.
- As mentioned in the previous section, an advantage of emulators as compared with simulators is the possibility of connecting an emulator as a prototype to application environments. With the use of the Simulation+Emulation method, simulators can also be connected to the application environment through emulators.

- Some designs may be too large, which need a great deal of FPGA resources. These designs can be emulated with some emulators, such as CoBALT [8]. However, the synthesis and the technology mapping of these designs are very time-consuming. The pure simulation of such designs is also very time-consuming. In such cases, the Simulation+Emulation method can be used to accelerate the simulation of the design.

3 SECOP: Simulation-Emulation Co-OPeration

This section describes the SECOP environment, which consists of two parts: a PCI-based PLDA board and a ModelSim simulator (Version 5.5a). In the experiment, a Pentium III system is used (933 MHz, RAM=256 MB, OS=Windows Me). Figure 1 shows a schematic diagram of the co-operation between simulation and emulation.

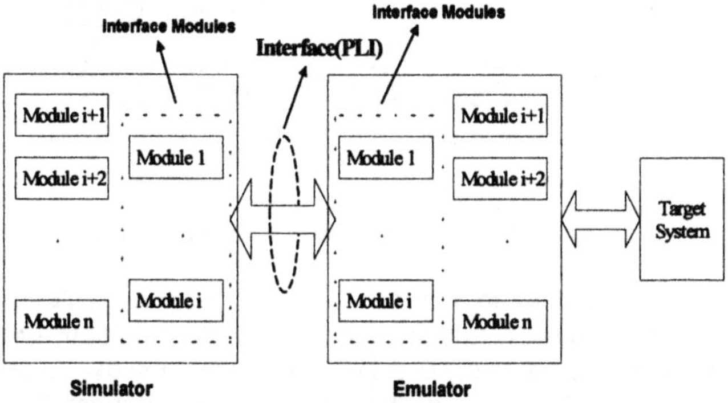

Figure 1. Co-operation between Simulation and Emulation

The PLDA board is connected to the computer via a PCI expansion slot. A FPGA chip, Flex 10K200SFC484-1 [7], is mounted on the board. This FPGA can be configured through the PCI bus. After the configuration, the FPGA can communicate with the computer through the PCI bus. The logic, which is synthesized to the FPGA, consists of two parts: a user-defined logic, and a PCI core. The PCI core automatically handles all bus events. The user-defined logic can communicate with PCI bus only through the PCI core.

The PLDA board can be accessed through memory-mapped I/O technique. It is possible to implement a PLI routine to access memory locations. The simulator can communicate with the FPGA chip by means of this PLI routine.

To evaluate a design by the SECOP method, three file groups must be prepared for compilation: a) codes for emulation, b) codes for simulation, and c) PLI routines. A software tool prepares these files automatically. Figure 2 gives an overview of the SECOP environment.

Some simulators can simulate both VHDL and Verilog codes. Also, some simulators such as ModelSim can simulate a model in which parts of the model are coded in VHDL, while the rest of the model is coded in Verilog. Using such simulators, the Verilog PLI can be employed even in the VHDL codes.

One of the most important issues is the communication mechanism between the emulator and the simulator. This communication should be done in such a manner that SECOP method resembles a unique simulator in results.
In the SECOP environment, the simulator controls and coordinates the activities of the emulator by the PLI routines. A PLI routine is called when the simulator needs information from the emulator.

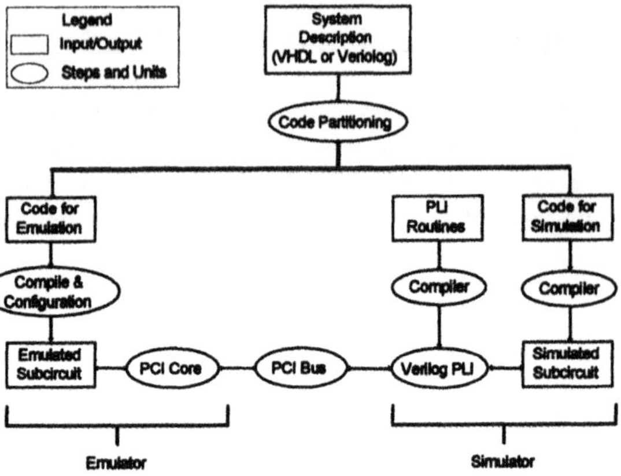

Figure 2. Overview of the SECOP environment

The communication strategy in Verilog is schematically presented in Figure 3. As shown in this figure, when the result of a subcircuit in the emulator is needed, the PLI routine, i.e., the $WriteToEmulator, is called. This routine activates the subcircuit in the emulator. To receive the results of the subcircuit from the emulator, another PLI routine, i.e., the $ReadFromEmulator, is called.

The operation of the emulated subcircuit is concurrent with the execution of the statements which are inserted between $WriteToEmulator() and $ReadFromEmulator().

```
module co_simulate_emulate(inputs,outputs);
  //declaration statements
  always @(inputs)
  begin
    //behavioral statements
    $WriteToEmulator(SubcircuitId, InputV); //PLI routine
    //behavioral statements
    $ReadFromEmulator(SubcircuitId, OutputV); //PLI routine
    // behavioral statements
  end
Endmodule
```

Figure 3. Communication Strategy

Figure 4 shows how the PLI routines are used. Figure 4a shows the code of a half-adder, which is a subcircuit of a design inserted in the emulator. As shown in Figure 4b, the inputs of the HA (a,b) are sent to the emulator by the $WriteToEmulator PLI routine. The results of the HA (s,c) is received from the emulator by the call of the $ReadFromEmulator.

```
module half_adder(a,b,s,c);
  xor(s,a,b);
  and(c,a,b);
Endmodule
```

(a)

```
module half_adder(a,b,s,c);
always @(a,b)
begin
  $WriteToEmulator(HalfAdderId, a,b); //PLI routine
  $ReadFromEmulator(HalfAdderId, s,c); //PLI routine
end
Endmodule
```

(b)

Figure 4. a) A synthesizable gate level model of a half adder **b)** The substituted code for the emulated half adder module

4 Using Verilog PLI in VHDL

PLI is a standard mechanism in Verilog to invoke a C function from a Verilog code. PLI cannot be used in VHDL code directly. To invoke a C function from a VHDL code, a mixed-VHDL-Verilog code can be used. In this way, VHDL part of the mixed code describes the system model and the Verilog part is used only for communication between the simulator and the emulator.

The Verilog module should be instantiated in a proper location (PLI call location) of VHDL codes. If the instantiation occurs in the sequential body, a problem raises. To solve this problem, a mechanism as shown in Figure 5, is used to activate the Verilog module from the VHDL process and to inform the termination of the Verilog module task.

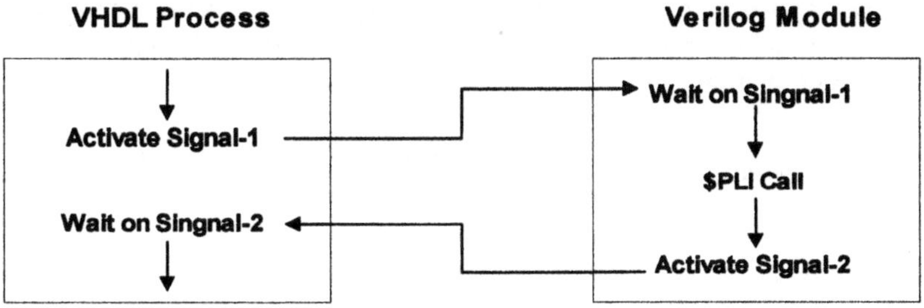

Figure 5. The flow of using Verilog module in VHDL process

In this way, the synchronization between the Verilog module and the VHDL process is done by Signal-1 and Signal-2.

In the VHDL process, if a signal is assigned several times, the last assignment will overwrite all the previous assigned values. So, there may be a problem for multiple PLI routine calls, which require multiple assignments to each of Signal-1 and Signal-2. To use shared variables is a possible solution to avoid this difficulty. As the communication between the VHDL and Verilog codes occurs only through the IO ports of the Verilog module, and shared variables cannot be used in the IO ports, therefore, it is not possible to utilize shared variables instead of Signal-1 and Signal-2. To solve this problem, an intermediate process can be used. Figure 6 shows the synchronization flow between the intermediate process, the main VHDL process and the Verilog module. The synchronization flow shows how a communication between the VHDL and Verilog codes can be performed.

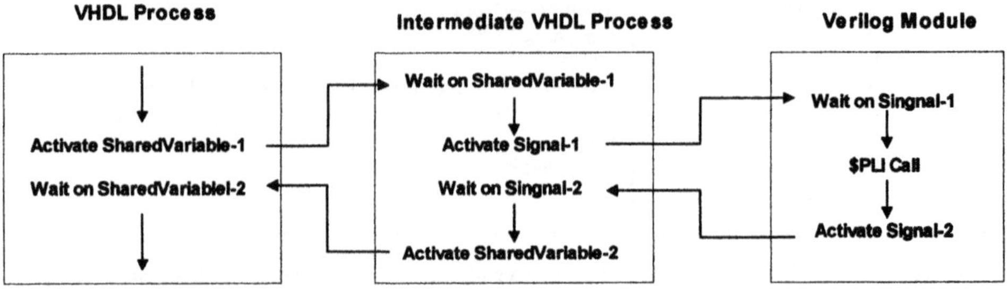

Figure 6. The synchronization flow between the intermediate VHDL process, the Verilog module and the VHDL processes

5 Experimental Evaluation

Two digital circuits are used as benchmarks to evaluate the SECOP approach: 1) a simple RISC processor, and 2) a 256-point FFT processor. The main reasons for using these circuits are:

1. Both of the circuits have parts, which require significant simulation time.
2. Both general purpose and special purpose features of digital systems are examined (the simple RISC processor as general purpose and the 256-point FFT processor as special purpose).

As a general purpose digital system can be programmed, the resulted speedups of a system will depend on the application program. The speedup is computed according to the following relation:

$$Speedup = \frac{Simulation\ time}{Simulation\_emulation\ \ co\_operation\ time} \qquad (1)$$

In subsections 5.1 and 5.2, the experiments are described.

5.1 A Simple Arithmetic RISC Processor

The arithmetic RISC processor (ARP) is coded by both Verilog and VHDL with 530 and 655 lines of code, respectively. This processor can be used as a main part of a typical calculator. The instruction set of this processor is shown in Table 1.

Table 1. The instruction set of the simple arithmetic RISC processor

Arithmetic instructions	Add, Sub, Mul, Div Sqrt	Rd, Rs1, Rs2 Rd, Rs
Logical instructions	And, Or, Xor Not	Rd, Rs1, Rs2 Rd, Rs
Jump and Branch instructions	Jmp, Jz, Jv	Addr

The booth algorithm, restoring division algorithm, and the Newton-Raphson algorithm have been used to implement multiplication, division, and square root operations, respectively.

This processor has sixteen 16-bit user registers, stored in a register file. A 16-bit fixed-point number system is used. Each number consists of two fields: 8-bit integer field, and 8-bit fractional field. Figure 7 shows the architecture of this processor.

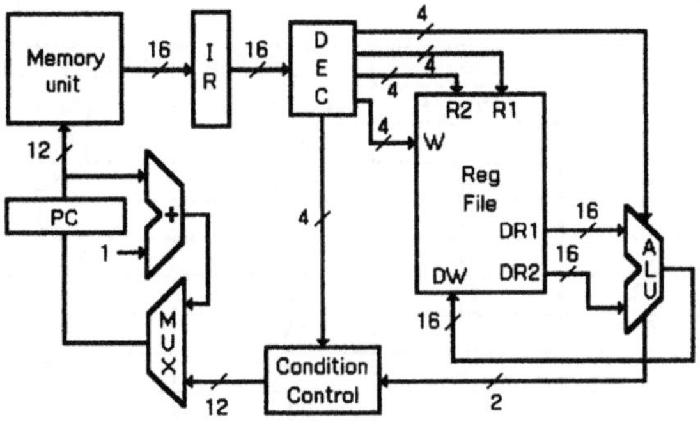

Figure 7. The architecture of the simple arithmetic RISC processor

The ALU and register file of the ARP have been inserted in the emulator (85 percent of the FPGA resources is used) and all other parts are simulated.

As a general purpose system, i.e. the ARP, is used, the speedup of the ARP depends on the executed program. In order to examine the effect of programs on speedup, the instructions are divided into three groups:

1- Group1: Simulated instructions = {Jmp, Jz, Jv}; the execution of these instructions only needs simulated parts of the system. Only ALU and register file have been emulated, and jump and branch instructions do not need these units for their execution.

2- Group2: Emulated time-consuming instructions = {Div, Sqrt}; the execution of these instructions needs emulator because ALU unit and register file have been emulated. If ALU unit and register file are simulated, these instructions will be very time-consuming because of the complex hardware needed for division and square root computing.

3- Group3: Emulated fast instructions = {Add, Sub, Mul, And, Or, Xor, Not}; the execution of these instructions needs emulator, just like Group2 instructions. But, if ALU unit and register file are simulated, these instructions will not be very time-consuming because of the simple hardware needed for their execution.

Several programs with different number of instructions from Group1, Group2 and Group3 have been used. Table 2 shows the resulted speedups when the Verilog model is utilized. To calculate the speedup, each program was run several times. As shown in Table 2, when a program consists of only simulated instructions (i.e. those instructions, which do not need the emulated parts for their execution), the resulted speedup is the highest. The reason is that the code loaded into the simulator of the SECOP, is smaller than what is loaded into the simulator in a pure simulation method. Therefore, despite the emulator is not used, a smaller code in the simulator results in a high speedup. Also, a program consisted of only simulated instructions, need not communicate with the emulator. This is because that it does not consume communication time. However, a program with emulated instructions consumes communication time, which results in a reduction of the speedup in comparison with the speedup resulted from running a program consisted of only simulated instructions.

Table 2. The speedups of the PLI-based SECOP in Verilog vs. pure simulation of the ARP (for 10000 iteration)

Number of Instructions in the Program			Simulation Time (ms)	SECOP Time (ms)	Speedup
Group1	Group2	Group3			
3	2	10	22137	4450	4.97
1	4	0	22080	1540	14.34
2	0	8	9413	3023	3.11
3	0	0	974	42.8	22.76
1	12	42	102900	20033	5.14
22	2	7	25210	3633	6.94
5	2	7	19720	3383	5.83
11	2	7	21363	3493	6.12
4	2	1	19533	3383	5.77

Table 3 shows the resulted speedups when the VHDL model is used. As shown in this table, in contrast to the Verilog case, the speedup decreases when the number of simulated instructions increases. This is because of the simulation time of the VHDL-based ARP versus its Verilog model. The experiments show that the simulation of the VHDL-based ARP is more time-consuming than the simulation time of its Verilog model.

Table 3. The speedups of the PLI-based SECOP in VHDL vs. pure simulation of the ARP (for 100 iteration)

Number of Instructions in the Program			Simulation Time (ms)	SECOP Time (ms)	Speedup
Group1	Group2	Group3			
3	2	10	1682	90	18.7
1	4	0	1729	31	55.8
2	0	8	668	59	11.3
3	0	0	32.48	4	8.1
1	12	42	8110	372	21.8
22	2	7	1675	100	16.8
5	2	7	1459	72	20.3
11	2	7	1532	81	18.9
4	2	1	1442	69	20.9

To compare the SECOP method with the method presented in [3], a similar set of experiments have been performed by TEXTIO package. In these experiments, the method proposed in [3] is used, i.e., a text file have been used to transfer data from the simulator to the emulator, while another text file has been used to transfer data from the emulator to the simulator. Figure 8 shows an overview of this method.

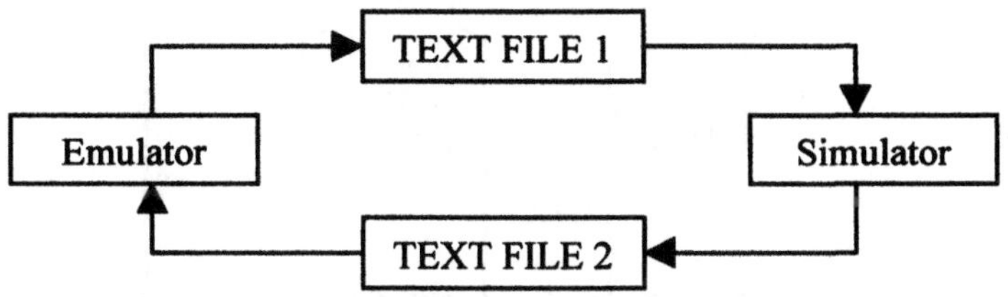

Figure 8. An overview of the TEXTIO method

Table 4 shows the resulted speedups from the TEXTIO method as compared with the pure simulation. As shown in the table, the TEXTIO method has not reduce the simulation time. The reason is that reading from or writing to the text files is very time-consuming.

Table 4. The speedups of the TEXTIO-based SECOP vs. the pure simulation of the ARP (for 100 iteration)

Number of Instructions in the Program			Simulation Time (ms)	SECOP Time(ms)	Speedup
Group1	Group2	Group3			
3	2	10	1682	60432	0.028
1	4	0	1729	19564	0.088
2	0	8	668	40251	0.016
3	0	0	32.48	4887	0.007
1	12	42	8110	263853	0.031
22	2	7	1675	43601	0.038
5	2	7	1459	45978	0.032
11	2	7	1532	45074	0.034
4	2	1	1442	45602	0.032

However, the TEXTIO method does not reduce the simulation time, this method can remove the time overhead caused by the logic synthesis and technology mapping during the iterations of the modification - just like the PLI method. Therefore, like the PLI method, TEXTIO method can reduce turn-around time.

5.2 A 256-Point FFT Processor

Another benchmark is a 256-point FFT processor. The code size of Verilog and VHDL for 256-point FFT processor is 580 and 652 lines, respectively. The processor uses decimation-in-time (DIT) FFT algorithm.

The architecture of this FFT processor is shown in Figure 9. The 256-point FFT processor is made up of a shuffle and twiddle module, a reordering module and 32 16-point FFT modules.

The code describing the 256-point FFT consists of non-synthesizable modules of shuffle and twiddle unit and reordering unit as well as synthesizable modules of 16-point FFT unit.

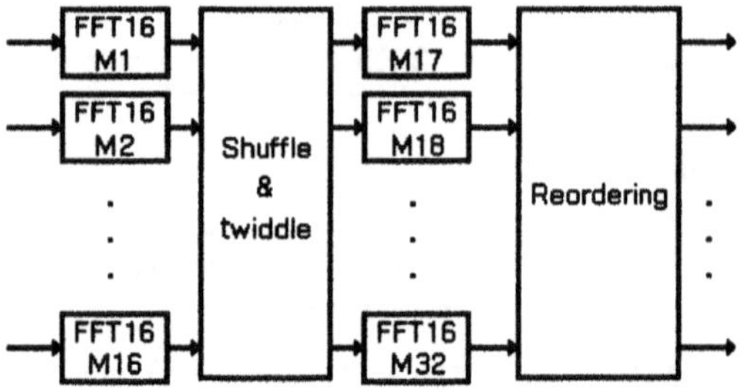

Figure 9. A 256-point FFT processor

A 256-point FFT unit is too big to be synthesized into a Flex 10K200SFC484-1 FPGA. Also, a 16-point FFT unit uses 75 percent of the FPGA resources (This amount of resources is used by the 16-point FFT unit as well as the PCI core). Therefore, only a 16-point FFT unit has been synthesized into the FPGA, and all other parts have been simulated. To compute a 256-point FFT, the simulated part uses the emulated 16-point FFT unit 32 times.

Table 5. The speedups of the PLI-based SECOP in Verilog and VHDL vs. the pure simulation of the FFT processor (for 1000 iteration)

	Simulation time (ms)	SECOP time (ms)	Speedup
Verilog	40520	3179	12.75
VHDL	153120	49994	4.38

As shown in Table 5, the resulted speedup for Verilog description is 12.75 and for VHDL is 4.38. The speedup in VHDL is lower, because, the simulation time of the code, which is in simulator, is rationally larger than Verilog one. Also, the std_logic library [9], which is a nine-valued logic, is used in VHDL code. So, simulation time increases significantly.

6 Conclusion

A Simulation-Emulation Co-OPeration environment, called SECOP, was presented. This method combines the advantages of the simulation and the emulation to achieve speedup as compared with the pure simulation. The SECOP environment utilizes a general simulator as well as a general emulator. In addition, a method to invoke the Programming Language Interface (PLI) by VHDL processes was presented. In the SECOP environment, a PCI-based PLDA board [7] was used for the emulation part and the ModelSim simulator (Version 5.5a) [6] was used for the simulation part. To evaluate the SECOP, two example circuits have been used as benchmarks: a simple RISC processor and a 256-point FFT processor. As the results show, depending on the sample code and the inputs, the speedup of the SECOP varies from 3 to 56 times, as compared with the pure simulation method.

Furthermore, the SECOP has also been compared with the VHDL TEXTIO method. The results show that the SECOP is much faster than the method based on VHDL TEXTIO.

References

1. Abramovici, M., Breuer, M. A., and Friedman, A. D., Digital Systems Testing and Testable Design, Revised edition, IEEE Press, 1995.
2. Bauer, J., Bershteyn, M., Kaplan, I., and Vyedin, P., "A Reconfigurable Logic Machine for Fast Event-Driven Simulation", in Proceedings of ACM/IEEE Design Automation Conf. (DAC), 1998, pp. 668-671.
3. Canellas, N., Moreno, J. M., "Speeding up hardware prototyping by incremental Simulation/Emulation", in Proceedings of 11th International Workshop on Rapid System Prototyping, 2000.
4. De Micheli, G., Synthesis and Optimization of Digital Circuits, McGraw-Hill, 1994.
5. HTTP://www.ikos.com/datasheets/vstation_specmanelite.pdf.
6. HTTP://www.model.com
7. HTTP://www.plda.com/hardware/cpciprod10k.pdf.
8. HTTP://www.quickturn.com/w_new/CoBALTUltra.htm.
9. IEEE Std 1076-1993: IEEE Standard VHDL Language Reference Manual.
10. IEEE Std 1364-1995: IEEE Standard Verilog HDL Language Reference Manual.
11. Kirovski, D., Potkonjak, L, Guerra, M., "Improving the Observability and Controllability of Datapaths for Emulation-Based Debugging", in IEEE trans. CAD of IC and System, 1999.
12. Kirovski, D., Potkonjak, L, Guerra, M., "Cut-Based Functional Debugging for Programmable System-on-Chip," in IEEE trans. on VLSI, 2000.
13. Kudlugi, M. , Hassoun, S., Selvidge, C., Pryor, D., "A Transaction-Based Unified Simulation/Emulation Architecture for Functional Verification," in Proceedings of 38th ACM/IEEE Design Automation Conference, 2001, pp. 623-628.
14. Mittra, S., Principles of Verilog PLI, Kluwer Academic Publishers, 1999.
15. Rowson, J. A., "Hardware/Software Co-Simulation", in Proceedings of 31st ACM/IEEE Design Automation Conference, 1996, pp. 439-440.
16. Varghese, J., Butts, M., and Batcheller, J., "An efficient logic emulation system," IEEE Trans. on VLSI Syst., vol. 1, June 1993, pp. 171-174.
17. Walters, S., "Computer-aided prototyping for ASIC-based system", IEEE Design Test Comput., June 1991, pp. 4-10.

How Fast Is Rapid FPGA-based Prototyping: Lessons and Challenges from the Digital TV Design Prototyping Project

Helena Krupnova[1], Veronique Meurou[2], Christophe Barnichon[3], Carlos Serra[3], and Farid Morsi[4]

[1] ST Microelectronics CMG FVG Grenoble, France, Helena.Krupnova@st.com
[2] ST Microelectronics CR&D Crolles, France, Veronique.Meurou@st.com
[3] ST Microelectronics TVD Grenoble, France, {Christophe.Barnichon, Carlos.Serra}@st.com
[4] Aptix, San Jose, USA, faridm@aptix.com

Abstract. This paper presents a case study targeting the Aptix MP4 board and Xilinx VirtexE FPGAs, for digital TV application prototyping. The difficult FPGA prototyping issues typically encountered by engineers are illustrated on a big industrial example. Due to the increasing ASIC complexity, the basic challenge was to meet the project deadlines. To enable faster FPGA-based prototyping, both the ASIC design practices and the FPGA design tools should be adjusted. The study has led to a number of guidelines for design teams to make designs prototyping friendly and a number of points for the improvement of the FPGA tools.

1 Introduction

Logic emulation is an indispensable technology for hardware debug ([4], [12], [14], [5]). Offering up to 10^5 times faster speed than simulation ([3]), full signal visibility, fast memory load and dump capability and relatively rapid mapping process encapsulating the synthesis, partitioning, place and route, hardware emulation brings a significant contribution to getting working silicon first time. Our verification flow uses extensively the hardware emulation technology based on the Mentor Graphics Celaro.

Having a hardware prototype is also extremely interesting for the SoC software developers, enabling application software development before the first silicon becomes available. Unfortunately, the cost of the big hardware emulators is too high to allow the unlimited use of the emulator by the software development teams. The emulator is usually shared between different projects and the access is possible only within the limited time slots.

Using the less expensive semi-custom hardware prototypes ([2]) is more suitable for software development purposes. For software development, it is even more interesting because it can work about 10 times faster than the large emulation systems.

The hardware platform based validation for the STX design considered in this paper consisted in: (1) using the Celaro emulators for hardware debug; (2)

M. Glesner, P. Zipf, and M. Renovell (Eds.): FPL 2002, LNCS 2438, pp. 26–35, 2002.

using the Aptix MP4 platform ([13]) as a high speed and low cost alternative for the development and validation of the application software. This concurrent engineering approach made possible the software development before the silicon was ready, permitting a real demo just a few days after the chip came back from production. Although the prototyping project was finally successful, the mapping process was extremely difficult due to the large number of problems encountered with FPGA implementation flow.

The semi-custom prototyping technology has been used for many years ([10], [9], [4]) but the actual industry tool status still makes prototyping the large multi-FPGA industrial designs a challenge. This challenge concerns (1) the feasibility: it is not known in advance if a successful FPGA implementation will be possible, since the design size is not the only factor that determines the feasibility; (2) meeting the project time scales: it is not guaranteed that it will be possible to have a working FPGA prototype before the first silicon is available.

In this paper, we present the difficulties encountered during the rapid FPGA prototyping of the STX design. Based on the lessons learned from this project, we outline the guidelines for the design teams to make their designs rapid prototyping-friendly and for the FPGA domain EDA community to make the tools more efficient.

2 Implementation Flow

The following steps are usually required to map an RTL design on FPGAs: (1) synthesis on the selected FPGA technology; (2) partitioning on several FPGAs; (3) FPGA place and route; (4) board place and route. The prototyping flow described here is represented in Fig. 1 .

The input for both Celaro and Aptix mappings is the Synopsys GTECH netlist generated by the design team using Synopsys Design Compiler. The choice to start from the GTECH and not from the RTL is justified by the following reasons: (1) taking the GTECH netlist guarantees that the netlist is synthesiseable and thus saves time for multiple iterations between the design and verification teams; (2) the design team understands the RTL synthesis issues for their design; (3) manipulating a single netlist file is easier than manipulating thousands of RTL files (3000 for the STX design); (4) it is guaranteed that the same netlist is targeted to ASIC, Celaro and Aptix platforms.

The Aptix mapping starts after the design is validated on Celaro and the hardware becomes stable (Fig. 1). Starting from the GTECH netlist, the design is mapped on Xilinx Virtex technology using Design Compiler with the corresponding target FPGA library. The synthesized netlist is partitioned using the Aptix Logic AggreGATER tool. Bus multiplexing is used to fit within the I/O pin constraints on the FPGAs. Then the partitioned and multiplexed netlist is given as input to the Aptix Explorer tool that handles the board placement, routing and encapsulates the FPGA place and route.

As shown in Fig. 1, porting to the Aptix platform can be divided in two steps. The first step corresponds to executing the flow and getting the board

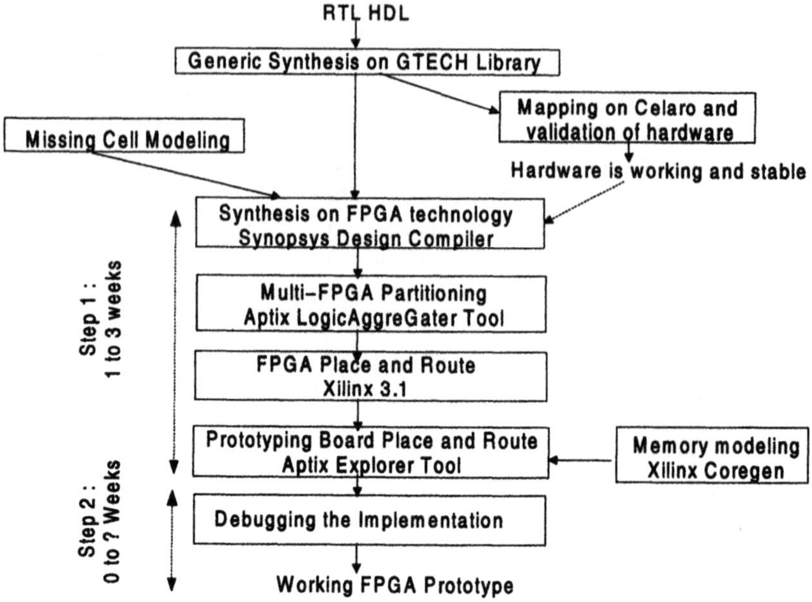

Fig. 1. Prototyping Flow

programmed. The second step is the debugging which consists of getting the design working on the board. The duration of the first step is predictable and can be limited to one or two weeks. This does not include the initial preparation step that may take longer time and includes creation of memory models, decisions about the external memory and clock implementation, interfaces to the external devices, etc. The duration of the second step is not predictable and depends on the number of problems that occur. Considering the restricted probing capability and signal observability of the semi-custom prototyping platforms, the prototyping engineer cannot afford to make errors if he wants to finish the project in time. The ideal case would be to have zero problems and finish the porting in one or two weeks. However in practice, because of the flow complexity, software and hardware bugs, design complexity, a number of tasks to be done manually, the errors always happen. The challenge is to shorten the first step - that implies automating the implementation flow, and to reduce or eliminate the second step - that implies avoiding problems or bugs.

3 Project Data

The Fig. 2 shows the Aptix board configuration for the STX project. The STX design is a digital TV application with a 100MHz system clock, however there is no real time requirement for the FPGA prototyping. The design size is between

1 and 1.5 M real ASIC gates. The Xilinx XCV2000 devices were targeted because they were the biggest available on the market at that moment. The design has 12 clocks. The 100MHz system clock is the fastest one. Some of the other clocks are asynchronous, some of them are synchronous with known phase and frequency relationships. The clock handling inside the design is done with the complex digital clock generation block having some analog parts extracted before prototyping. The XCV2000 FPGAs contain 4 global clock lines. The clock handling was one of the key feasibility constraints for this design.

Fig. 2. Aptix MP4 board view for the STX project

The design includes an ST20 microcontroller. The communication between different system blocks is realized using the protocol called the ST Bus. The ST Bus includes a number of blocks that handle the arbitration and a number of full and partial crossbars that implement the interconnect. These crossbars represent the basic difficulty for the design partitioning. The 8 to 2 arbiter crossbar has 1563 I/Os, the 3 to 1 arbiter crossbar has 636 I/Os and 5 to 1 arbiter crossbar has 838 I/Os. The maximum number of I/Os available on the Aptix adapter module for the XCV2000 FPGA is 480. Aptix provides also the modules with up to 799 I/Os but they require more space on the board and thus reduce the board capacity. Without the bus multiplexing the prototyping of the STX project was not feasible and even with multiplexing it was not a trivial task.

The design was put into 6 Xilinx XCV2000 FPGAs with 70% average filling (Table 1). The image data input/output is done through the National Instruments DIO 6533 acquisition cards installed inside a PC. One additional XCV1000 FPGA was used to realize the 5V connection with the acquisition cards.

The design uses a FLASH memory that was implemented internally inside one of the FPGAs with the reduced size. The 4M x 16bit SDRAM memory was emulated with an SRAM using the dedicated 1M x 64bit Aptix SRAM module.

The stand alone tests aimed at validating the functionality were performed by programming the FLASH with an initial contents corresponding to the test program and then observing the signals using an HP Logic Analyzer. The in-circuit operation was realized through the ST20 JTAG Ethernet Interface (JEI) by loading the application code inside the SDRAM memory through the ST20 software debugger interface. The obtained prototype performance was between 1 and 2 MHz, approximately 10 times faster than on Celaro.

Table 1. FPGA filling data

FPGA	Device	# of used Slices	# of used FFs	I/Os before mult.	I/Os after mult.	# of used BRAMs
FPGA1	XCV2000	18,128 (=94%)	8,457 (=22%)	240	207	38 (=23%)
FPGA2	XCV2000	7,253 (=37%)	5,542 (=14%)	543	315	-
FPGA3	XCV2000	6,541 (=34%)	4,854 (=12%)	437	353	16 (=10%)
FPGA4	XCV2000	16,964 (=88%)	9,958 (=25%)	487	286	41 (=25%)
FPGA5	XCV2000	14,631 (=76%)	8,091 (=21%)	499	357	25 (=15%)
FPGA6	XCV2000	15,666 (=81%)	11,548 (=30%)	871	445	62 (=38%)
FPGA7	XCV1000	111 (=1%)	126 (=1%)	164	164	-

4 Problems and Solutions

4.1 Partitioning

The partitioning was difficult because of two factors: (1) the crossbars composing the ST Bus have a large number of I/Os (1500 for the largest one); (2) the design contains more than 4 clocks which is the limit on the Xilinx XCV2000 devices. The partitioning was driven by the available clock resources. The embedded Xilinx DLLs cannot be used because the required minimum frequency is 25 MHz ([15]) and the system performance is below that. Assigning too many signals to the low skew lines makes the FPGA place and route run forever. The same will happen when constraining a clock that drives a large amount of logic. Thus, the primary objective is to decide which 4 clocks are driving the largest amount of logic to become global.

The first task was to identify which clocks drive which hierarchy blocks. After the identification of clocks, the design was divided into groups of blocks with common clocking. The partitioning was done manually by using the Logic AggreGATER tool provided by Aptix. After analyzing the connectivity matrices, the blocks with the highest connectivity were identified for each ST Bus crossbar. This was done to reduce the number of I/Os on FPGAs connected to the ST Bus. Fortunately, the ST Bus logic was driven by only one clock, and thus we were free to split the ST Bus between several FPGAs.

4.2 Pin Multiplexing

Pin multiplexing is an established technique used to overcome the FPGA pin limitation problem ([3]). This technique can also be used in case of the semi-custom prototyping but it is not completely automated. The multiplexing requires the introduction of an additional multiplexing clock. As we already have 12 clocks, it is desirable to restrict the multiplexing to as few clock domains as possible. We succeeded to limit it to signals driven by a single clock (the system clock). Once the multiplexable signals have been selected, the Aptix multiplexing tool automatically generates the additional logic and clocking, as required. The multiplexing is difficult because of the risk of introducing timing problems where busses have combinational paths inside an FPGA and are multiplexed from both sides (Fig. 3).

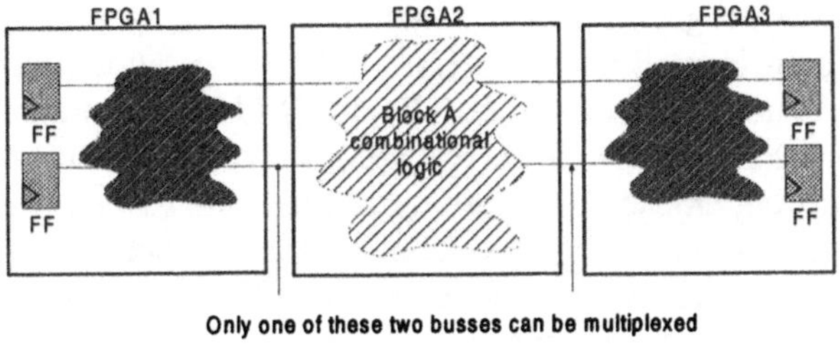

Fig. 3. Multiplexing Combinational Paths

With more FPGAs on the board, the probability of multiplexing combinational paths increases. To avoid such cases, the timing analysis should be performed for all the multiplexed busses. In this case, the major partitioning difficulty was the ST Bus that is built from the combinational logic: we had a number of cases shown in Fig. 3. Eight busses belonged to the combinational paths traversing FPGA6 that contains the biggest crossbar of the ST Bus (Fig. 4). One week was lost tracing functional problems in the design because of the wrong selection of two busses due to the incomplete timing analysis. The final solution was obtained using a 4 to 1 multiplexing that divides the emulation frequency by 6.

4.3 Clock Implementation

The complicated digital clock management block was bypassed and the dedicated simplified clock generation module was built for FPGA implementation (Fig. 5). There is only one source clock coming from an oscillator. This clock corresponds to the multiplexing clock and is divided by 6 to generate the system clock. The other clocks are derived from the system clock adding dividers by 2 and by 4 and additional logic to generate the phase shift. The real frequencies of some clocks were not exactly divisible by 2 and 4 but the design was able to function with the

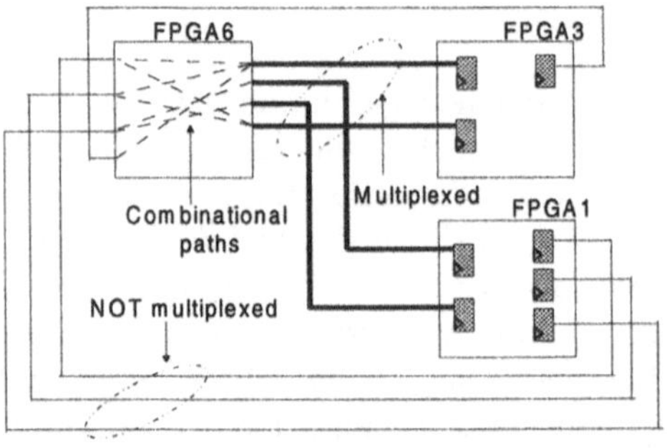

Fig. 4. Combinational Paths

approximated values and this significantly simplified the implementation. Some of the clocks have programmable frequency. In these cases, a multiplexor was added. This was performed inside FPGA3. After that, all the clocks were routed out from FPGA3 and distributed to all the FPGAs, including the FPGA3 to avoid clock skew. Four of the clocks are assigned to the clock lines on the Aptix board, the remaining clocks going into more than one FPGA are assigned to the low skew lines on the board. The decision on which clocks absolutely needed to be global and which ones were feasible with the Virtex low skew lines was done after a number of unsuccessful place and route trials. These trials converged to the final feasible solution.

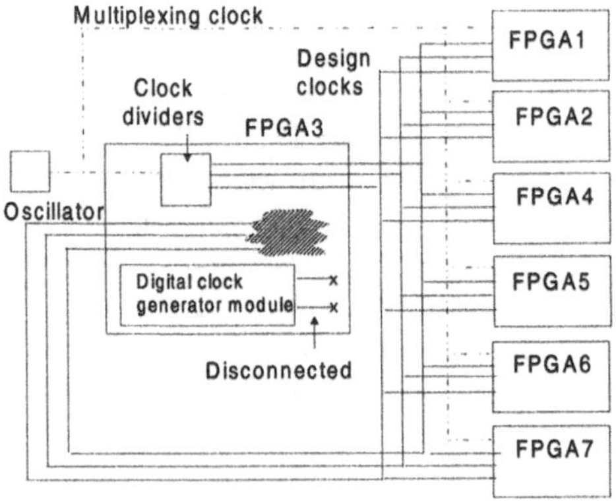

Fig. 5. Clock Implementation on FPGAs

4.4 Gated Clocks

The gated clocks are a big problem for FPGA designs. The signal delays are not predictable, resulting in glitches that may lead to registering the wrong state by a

FF or memory element. Manual modifications transforming the gated clocks into enables were performed. The ST20 core contains a big number of gated clocks. Many problems were encountered with modeling the pad cells which also have gated clocks. Another example is the read and write signals for FIFO models.

4.5 Memory Modeling

The design contains about 20 types of small memories that are implemented with the embedded FPGA memory resources (Xilinx Virtex Block RAMs [16]) using the Xilinx CoreGen tool. To make the correspondence between the Xilinx BlockRAM functionality and required functionality the wrapper models were developed for each memory type. The design contains a 4M x 16bit SDRAM implemented with the Aptix 1M x 64bit SRAM module, using a dedicated wrapper.

4.6 Debugging

The semi-custom prototyping boards have limited observability, for example 256 signals can be observed simultaneously on the Aptix MP4 system. These can be signals present on the FPGA pins and going through FPICs (interconnect chips) or internal FPGA signals. The partitioning should take into account that at least 10 to 20 FPGA pins must remain free for probing. Xilinx incremental probe routing allows to observe the internal FPGA signals provided there are some free pins ([11]). To view different signals, the incremental probe routing must be repeated and it takes at each time 15 to 20 minutes on FPGA filled by 30% for 20 signals and about 40 minutes on FPGA filled by 90% for 32 signals (Sparc Ultra 60 station). The probing is time consuming and that is why the debugging takes time. The netlist for rapid prototyping should be mature, the flow better automated and software and hardware tools reliable and robust.

5 Challenges to the Design Teams

A number of guidelines listed below can assist the rapid prototyping if they are taken into consideration early in the design flow. Some of these guidelines correspond to the Reuse Methodology Manual (RMM) rules ([7]) but are still not completely adopted by the designers community.

- For all the major functional blocks restrict the number of clocks to the maximal available on the FPGA (4 for Virtex, 16 for Virtex II).
- Use pipelining inside the big combinational blocks. This will reduce the probability of having the combinational paths traversing the FPGAs, facilitate the multiplexing and improve the emulation speed.
- Gated clocks should be avoided if not really needed.
- If there are constants applied to some unused block outputs, apply them on the highest hierarchy level. If the partitioning tool does not handle the constant propagation, applying constants to the block outputs introduces additional connectivity in the design.

- Avoid high fanout inside the hierarchy. The high fanout creates the additional connectivity inside the design. If the fanout happens deeply inside the hierarchy, then it is not visible during the partitioning and the same signal can occupy several pins on the FPGA.
- Reduce the number of I/Os on the top level hierarchy blocks. The size of the latest FPGAs allows to fit one or more functional blocks (IPs). In general case, partitioning will be performed inside the top level. As a consequence, the top level connectivity will play the major role in fast and efficient partitioning.
- Avoid having blocks with the number of I/Os exceeding the maximum available FPGA I/O number. If no other hierarchy block can absorb the extra I/Os, the pin multiplexing may be needed. From practice, if the number of FPGA pins exceeds 3* MAX_FPGA_IO, the implementation is not feasible. For easy partitioning, keep the number of I/Os smaller than the maximum available I/O number on the largest FPGA module. For feasible partitioning, avoid blocks with number of I/Os exceeding 2*MAX_FPGA_IO.
- Avoid the feed-throughs. Some nets can traverse the hierarchy blocks and make a feed-through. The feed-throughs are not visible during partitioning and the design can be partitioned in a way that the feed-throughs waste pins on the FPGAs.

6 Challenges to the FPGA Tools

- Run time is a known problem that the EDA tool vendors are constantly working on. Debugging the semi-custom prototypes is a very time-consuming process that requires to iterate on the FPGA place and route step.
- Automatic handling of gated clocks should be provided by the FPGA synthesis tools.
- Up to now, multi-FPGA partitioning was not viewed as a function of the used clocks and available clock resources ([6], [1]). There is no assistance in clock signal detection/tracing even to enhance the manual partitioning. There is no help for deciding about the global clock implementation strategy on the board and inside the FPGAs.
- Increasing the amount of clock resources and providing the better ways to use the existing resources can concern both FPGA and board architectures.
- Another issue is the multi-FPGA partitioning taking into account the pin multiplexing and including the automatic selection of signals to multiplex. This process should include the timing analysis to detect the combinational paths traversing the FPGAs.
- There is no single tool that can encapsulate the entire RTL-to-FPGA flow for complex multi-FPGA designs and thus minimize the number of manual steps and reduce the possibility of human error.
- Having the incremental flow is critical for fast design debugging. It is difficult to work incrementally if the flow consists from the calls of different tools, shell scripts and manual manipulations.

- The debugging can be accelerated if there is a better internal FPGA signal visibility. The improvements may concern the FPGA architectures, tools and hardware architectures.
- Some easier way to load the initial FF (for ex. for the reset) and memory contents will also contribute to speeding up the flow.

7 Conclusions

The semi-custom and custom rapid prototyping with FPGAs is an attractive verification technique due to the relatively low cost and high operation speed. Its viability was proven by the successful implementation of the big multi-FPGA industrial design. But in despite these techniques existing for more than ten years, the implementation flow is not yet mature enough. The implementation is not a push-button and not even a push a number of buttons in a right order. There is a big improvement potential regarding the acceleration of the implementation flow and speed-up the time-to-prototyping.

References

1. C. J. Alpert, A. B. Kahng: Recent directions in netlist partitioning: a survey. INTEGRATION, the VLSI journal, N19 (1995): 1-81.
2. Aptix Home Page, www.aptix.com
3. J. Babb, R. Tessier, M. Dahl, S.Z. Hanono, D. M. Hoki, A. Agrawal: Logic Emulation with Virtual Wires, IEEE Trans. Computer-Aided Design of Integrated Circuits and Systems 16/6 (1997): 609-626.
4. S. Hauck: The Roles of FPGAs in Reprogrammable Systems. Proc. of the IEEE, Vol. 86, No. 4 (1998): 615-639.
5. IKOS Home Page, //www.ikos.com/
6. F. M. Johannes, Partitioning of VLSI Circuits and Systems. Proc. 33rd Design Automation Conference (1996): 83-87.
7. M. Keating, P. Bricaud, Reuse Methodology Manual, Kluwer A. P., 1999
8. H. Krupnova, G. Saucier, FPGA Technology Snapshot: Current Devices and Design Tools, Proc. RSP 2000.
9. H. Krupnova, G. Saucier, FPGA-Based Emulation: Industrial and Custom Prototyping Solutions, Proc. FPL 2000.
10. D. M. Lewis, D. R. Galloway, M. Ierssel, J. Rose, P. Chow: The Transmogrifier-2: A 1 Million Gate Rapid Prototyping System. Proc. ACM/SIGDA Int. Symp. on Field Programmable Gate Arrays (1997): 53-61.
11. D. Lim, Efficient Debugging Using Probe, //www.xilinx.com, xl36_44.pdf
12. Mentor Graphics Accelerated Verification/ Emulation page, //www.mentorgraphics.ca/meta/celaro/oui.html
13. System Explorer MP4 Reference Guide, Aptix, 1999.
14. Quickturn Home Page, //www.quickturn.com
15. Using the Virtex DLL, Xilinx Application Note XAPP132, September 2000.
16. Using the Virtex Block Select RAM+ Features Application Note XAPP130, December 2000.

Implementing Asynchronous Circuits on LUT Based FPGAs

Quoc Thai Ho[1], Jean-Baptiste Rigaud[1], Laurent Fesquet[1], Marc Renaudin[1], and Robin Rolland[2]

[1] TIMA Laboratory, 46 avenue Félix Viallet, 38031 Grenoble, France,
{Quoc-Thai.Ho, Jean-Baptiste.Rigaud, Laurent.Fesquet, Marc.Renaudin}@imag.fr,
http://tima.imag.fr/cis
[2] CIME INPG, 46 avenue Félix Viallet, 38031 Grenoble, France,
rolland@cime.inpg.fr

Abstract. This paper describes a general methodology to rapidly prototype asynchronous circuits on LUT based FPGAs. The main objective is to offer designers the powerfulness of standard synchronous FPGAs to prototype their asynchronous circuits or mixed synchronous/asynchronous circuits. To avoid hazard in FPGAs, the appearance of hazard in configurable logic cells is analyzed. The developed technique is based on the use and the design of a Muller gate library. It is shown how the place and route tools automatically exploit this library. Finally, an asynchronous dual-rail adder is implemented automatically to demonstrate the potential of the methodology. Several FPGA families, like Xilinx X4000, Altera Flex, Xilinx Virtex and uptodate Altera Apex are targeted.

1 Introduction

Asynchronous circuits have shown very interesting potentials in many application areas: processor design, smart-card design, low-power circuit design, low EMI circuit design [9], [8], [9], [10], [13]. Very complex and relevant prototypes have been designed to demonstrate key properties such as speed, power, and noise emission. Most of the time, the design was done by hand. Today, the acceptance of the asynchronous technology by the semi-conductor industry strongly depends on the availability of synthesis tools and the possibility to prototype such circuits especially on standard FPGAs. This work is part of the development of an open design framework, TAST (TIMA Asynchronous Synthesis Tools)[17], [18], dedicated to asynchronous design. It constitutes a first proposition of a very general methodology for the synthesis of asynchronous circuits starting from HDL specifications to ASICs or FPGA prototypes. Today, very complex systems can be mapped on FPGA. This opportunity offers the ability to rapidly prototype VLSIs. Unfortunately, conventional FPGA architectures are exclusively dedicated to clocked systems.

Previous works in this area show that one solution is to design specific FPGA to support asynchronous logic implementation like MONTAGE [5], STACC [7] or PCA-1 [11].

M. Glesner, P. Zipf, and M. Renovell (Eds.): FPL 2002, LNCS 2438, pp. 36–46, 2002.

Researchers from the University of Washington have presented the first FPGA, MONTAGE designed to support explicitly asynchronous implementation, and its mapping software [5]. This FPGA includes many features to improve the implementation of self-timed circuits: arbiters, sequencers, and routing architecture avoiding isochronic forks.

Payne has proposed STACC for implementing self-timed circuits [7]. The difference between STACC and MONTAGE is that MONTAGE targets both synchronous and asynchronous circuits. STACC is completely dedicated to self-timed circuits (especially for bundled data systems). In addition, STACC's architecture does not disrupt the structure of the logical blocks. In fact, the global clock control in conventional FPGA has been replaced by a timing array. Each timing cell is connected to its neighbors by two wires that are used for handshaking. More recently, another fully asynchronous FPGA (PCA-1) has been proposed [11]. Two programmable layers compose the FPGA architecture: the logic layer (named Plastic Part), which consists in an homogeneous sea-of-LUTs, and the Built-in Part, which is designed as self-timed circuits, dedicated to the communication between the LUTs.

Another approach consists in developing specific libraries for the back-end tools or constraining the place and route phase to avoid the problems due to logic hazard.

Brunvand has designed a library of macrocells in 1992 for self-timed circuits using Actel FPGA [1]. The macrocell library uses a two-phase transition signaling protocol for control signals and a bundled protocol for data signals. The hazard behavior of these macrocells has not been characterized. Moreover place and route operations of the macrocells are not controlled in the Actel array. Indeed, there are timing constraints inside the macrocells that must be met to ensure the functionality of the macrocells. In addition, the programming of Actel FPGA is based on anti-fuse architecture. Once programmed, it can not be reusable and is not suitable for prototyping.

Moore and Robinson have proposed a method combining floor and geometry planning tools to solve the problems of isochronic forks and equipotential regions in self-timed circuits [6]. However, the commercial floor-planning tools are not sufficient to avoid hazard. Although the timing constraints of Muller gate are well described within HDL, an automatic timing-driven FPGA implementation can not ensure hazard-free logic.

This work presents an alternative to enforce the mapping in FPGAs to avoid hazard. Moreover, the geometry tools are exploited to automatically map Muller gates onto FPGAs. The approach combines the use of standard FPGAs and the TAST methodology developed at TIMA. The paper is organized as follows. Section 2 addresses general considerations on the principles of asynchronous circuits and its specific constraints like hazard-free logic. The difficulties to map such kind of logic on FPGAs are shown. Section 3 introduces hazard removal in asynchronous circuits and Section 4 introduces the implementation of hazard-free Muller gates on Xilinx FPGAs. Finally, the methodology is validated by the implementation of a dual-rail adder in Section 5.

2 Principles of Asynchronous Logic

While in synchronous circuits a clock globally controls activity, asynchronous circuits activity is locally controlled using communicating channels able to detect the presence of data at their inputs and outputs [2], [8], [9], [12]. This is consistent with the so-called handshaking or request/acknowledge protocol (Fig.1). This communication protocol is the basic of the following sequencing rules of asynchronous circuits [9]:

- a module starts the computation if and only if all the data required for the computation are available,
- as far as the result can be stored, the module releases its input ports,
- it outputs the result in the output port if and only if this port is available.

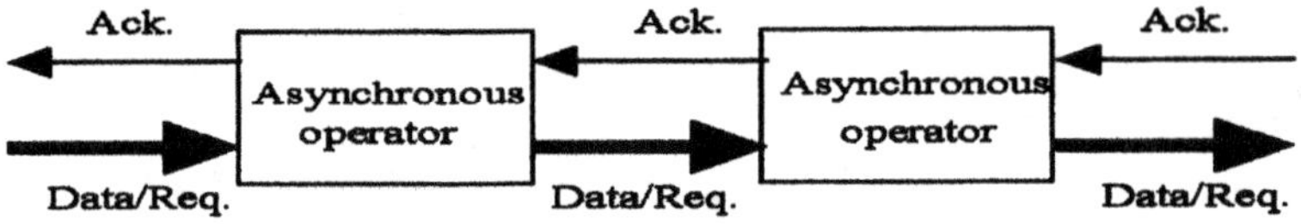

Fig. 1. Request/Acknowledge communication between asynchronous operators to guarantee a timing independent synchronization.

However, asynchronous modules communicate with each other using requests and acknowledges. One transition on a request signal activates another module connected to it. Therefore, signals must be valid all the time. Hazard is not allowed on signals. Asynchronous circuit synthesis must be thereby more strict, i.e. hazard-free. In fact, different timing assumptions are considered for different types of asynchronous circuits. For QDI (Quasi-Delay Insensitive) circuits, for example, the circuit only works correctly in the "isochronic fork" assumption limit. The connection delay must be considered when such a circuit is designed. This is common to expect in ASIC based-on asynchronous designs that the connection delays may be considered negligible. Contrarily, the connection delays can not be considered negligible in FPGA based designs because the connections between two nodes go through one or many programmable connection points. Another drawback is that, in almost all standard FPGA architectures, the feedback signals from outputs to inputs are not routable inside a programmable logic cell. The previous points imply that the mapping of Muller gates must be enforced in one configurable logic block (CLB) and the routing of isochronic fork branches must be balanced to avoid hazard and minimize delays.

3 Hazard Analysis in Muller Gates

Avoiding hazard logic [14] is necessary to properly implement asynchronous circuits. With this aim, the development of a specific asynchronous gate library, based on LUTs, is needed to map asynchronous logic onto FPGAs. This library includes symmetric and asymmetric Muller gates with or without set/reset that implement a "rendezvous" between 2, 3, or 4 input signals. This library is needed because TAST maps HDL specification onto a limited number of Muller gates and logical gates. The Muller gates have monotonous inputs and function in Burst Mode.

3.1 Muller Gates

The symmetric Muller gate with two inputs denoted MULLER2 and described on Fig.2 implements a "rendezvous" of two signals.

Inputs	Output
A=1 and B=1	S=1
A=0 and B=0	S=0
others	Previous state

S / S^{-1}	AB 00	01	11	10
0	0	0	1	0
1	0	1	1	1

Fig. 2. Functional description and symbol of MULLER2

Another example of Muller gate with four inputs denoted MULLER4B is given on Fig.3.

Inputs	Output
A=B=C=D=1	0
A=B=C=D=0	1
Others	Previous state

Fig. 3. Functional description and symbol of MULLER4B

3.2 Eliminating Hazards in Asynchronous Circuits

The standard method [8] for eliminating hazards depends on the assumption that the unexpected changes in the outputs are in response to single-bit changes in the inputs. The technique does not apply when more than one input bit changes at the same time. Close examinations of the K-map in Fig.4 suggest what caused the glitch. When the initial and final inputs are covered by the same prime implicant, no glitch is possible. But when the input change spans prime implicants, a glitch can happen. The hazard-free implementation of MULLER2 is given in Fig.4.

The feedback output signal of the Muller gate is considered as input. The minimization of canonical minterms in three overlapping terms AB, AS^{-1}, BS^{-1} makes possible to avoid static hazard depending on the delay distribution when an input changes. Thus, this implementation is hazard-free when

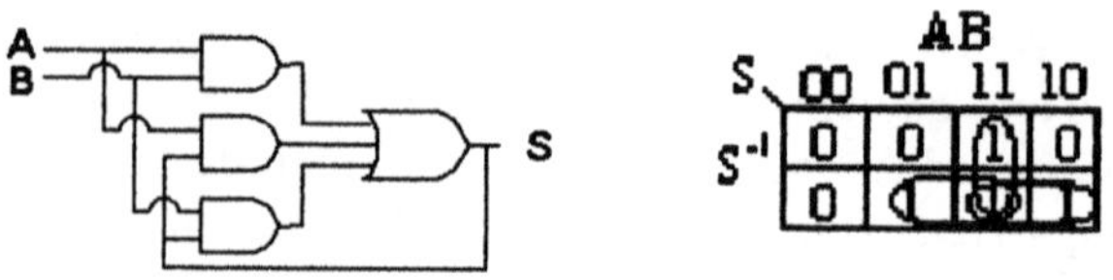

Fig. 4. Hazard-free implementation of MULLER2 with AND and OR gates

one input changes. Multiple input change is allowed, except for the transitions $AB = 01 \rightarrow 10$ and $AB = 10 \rightarrow 01$ which produce a glitch. TAST produces circuits, which do not exhibit such behaviors. Hence simultaneous transitions $AB = 01 \rightarrow 10$ and $AB = 10 \rightarrow 01$ have not to be considered in hazard analysis. This ensures that the circuits are hazard-free.

4 Hazard-Free Implementation on Xilinx Configurable Logic Block (CLB)

In this section, we consider only the Xilinx implementation case. Nevertheless, this study is fully portable to the Altera components. QDI circuits have been implemented on Altera Flex10k and Altera Apex20k. The main difference between the two competitors is the LUT size. Xilinx LUTs are implemented with 4 or 3 inputs while Altera LUTs offer only 3 inputs. Therefore Altera Muller gate libraries do not contain Muller gates with four inputs.

4.1 Hazard-Free Implementation of Muller Gates

A MULLER2 (Muller gate with 2 inputs) can be implemented with a 4 inputs function generator. The truth table of MULLER2 is given bellow.

F1	F2	F3	F4	F
S^{-1}	A	B	X	S
0	0	0	X	0
0	0	1	X	0
0	1	0	X	0
0	1	1	X	1
1	0	0	X	0
1	0	1	X	1
1	1	0	X	1
1	1	1	X	1

The inputs A, B and the output S of the Muller gate are respectively mapped onto F2, F3 and F of a function generator. The feedback signal S-1 is mapped onto F1. The equation of S is the following: F2F3 + F2F1 + F3F1. This logical equation includes only overlapping terms. F1, F2, F3, F4 are the selection inputs of the multiplexer.

In the case of single-bit changes, the properties of Xilinx function generator ensure that there is no decoding glitch when only one selection input changes, even if it is a non-overlapping decoding [16]. There is consequently no hazard when only a single input changes.

Considering the case of multiple input change, the difference of the logical implementation using memory LUT compared with one using AND, OR standard gates is that the output is multiplexed into a configuration bit according to the input coding. Configuration bits of function generator and inputs of Muller gate are respectively used as data inputs and selection inputs of the multiplexer. Therefore the data inputs are only affected by configuration bits, and do not change dynamically. Xilinx LUT (cf. 4.2) was carefully designed so that the delay propagation from its inputs to its output is balanced. The output is retained stable during the change of selection inputs coding to another. If an intermediate code, which may force the output glitch, does not occur, there is no hazard. This assumption is ensured because the inputs of the Muller gate are monotonous.

The previous paragraph explains hazard-free implementation using function generator where the memory behavior of the Muller gate is controlled by feedback signal. Another way to control memory is using a RS latch. In fact, the gate output is set when both inputs go high, and cleared when both inputs go low. For all others input combinations the output is memorized. This functional behavior is indeed similar to a RS latch. Hence, the set and reset of RS can be evaluated such as equations: S=AB and R=!A!B. The RS can be easily programmed from memory element of FPGA logic block. Because R and S of latch are ensured not to be high at the same time by the function of the Muller gate. It does not thereby fall in metastable state. In addition, the MTBF of these latches is reliable [16], [6].

4.2 Hazard Analysis of Transmission Gate Multiplexer

This section clarifies hazard-free implementation using LUTs. An $8 \rightarrow 1$ multiplexer can be designed with transmission gates[1] as shown in the Figure 5. The MULLER2 can be implemented using three inputs LUT as shown in the Figure 6. The input/output mapping is also shown.

Consider a transition from one prime wich are not overlapping, for example: $S0S1S2 = 101 \rightarrow 111$. In this case, only S1 changes from 0 to 1. Thus, only stage 1 changes from P8, P10 ON / P9, P11 OFF to P8, P10 OFF / P9, P11 ON. Because S0 is always connected to "1", the state P12 OFF / P13 ON is always retained. Therefore no hazard appears. In the case of multiple input change, the change from an input selection coding to another may cause one or more intermediate codes. By applying the previous analysis to single input changes, there is no glitch at the output between an input value to another if the logical equation contains only the overlapping terms.

In conclusion, the Muller gate, MULLER2, is hazard-free using LUT based FPGA of Xilinx or Altera if it is mapped onto only one configurable logic cell and its logic equation is optimized for overlapping terms. Finally, a library of

[1] The multiplexers in Xilinx function generators are designed with transmission gates

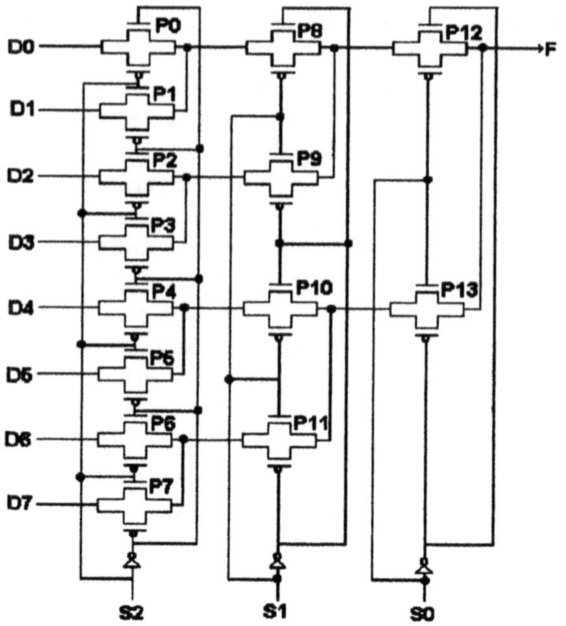

Fig. 5. Structure of the 8 → 1 multiplexer using transmission gates

Muller gates fitting into a CLB was designed. The TAST gate netlist maps onto this Muller gate library.

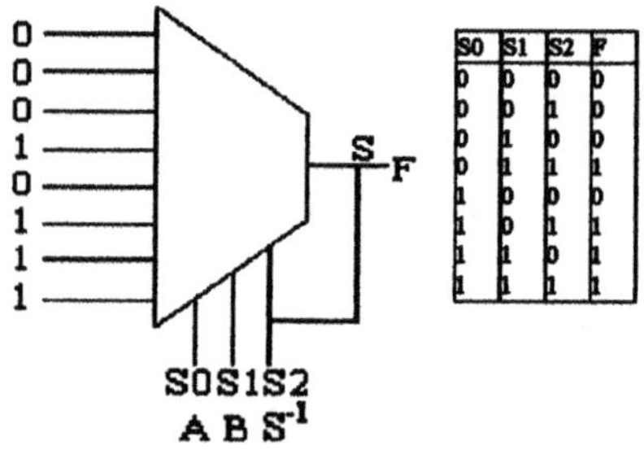

Fig. 6. Implementation of MULLER2 using transmission gate based-on function generator

4.3 Mapping Muller Gates onto Configurable Logic Cells

In this section, Xilinx synthesis and place & route tools are considered. It explains how this gate library is designed to ensure hazard-free behavior and to maximize gate utilization.

Commercial synthesis tools do not allow the automated synthesis of Muller gates. Indeed, it is not ensured that the logic equation is correctly synthesized in terms of hazard onto configurable logic cells (Figure 7). In the Figure 7.a, the MULLER4 (symmetric Muller gate with four inputs and one simple output) is mapped onto 4 LUT-4 (synthesized with Leonardo tool for a Xilinx 4010XL). Its implementation needs two Xilinx CLBs. The memory of the Muller gate is controlled by the feedback signal. Because of delay distribution, hazards may thereby occur when the gate is automatically placed in FPGA even if its logic equation is correctly optimized to overlapping terms. Figure 7.b fits this problem (synthesized by hand). It is mapped onto two LUT-4 and one LUT-3. The global memory is also controlled by feedback signal but the gate occupies only one Xilinx CLB.

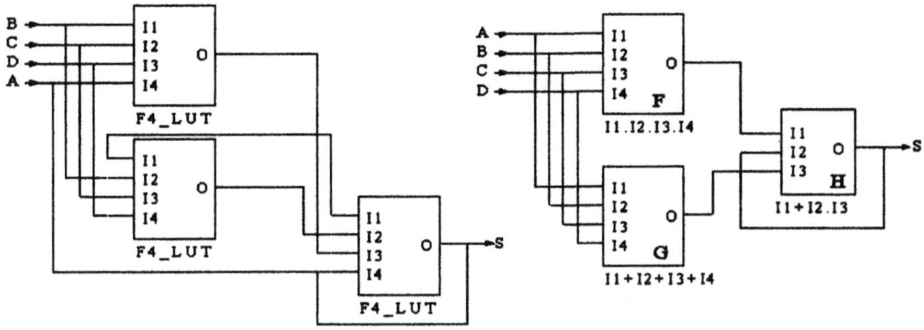

Fig. 7. MULLER4: a. automatic synthesis, b. hazard-free synthesis (by hand)

The place & route tools can remove redundant terms in the logic equation during the optimization phase of floor planning. These tools do not ensure that the Muller equation remains correct. Hence, the traditional FPGA design flow is not applicable. It is first necessary to carefully design a hazard-free Muller gate library. This approach solves two issues. First, the logic equation is hazard-free. Second, because it is mapped into a unique CLB, wire delays are known and cannot introduce hazard. To do so, each gate is modeled using a XNF netlist, which enables us to enforce a given mapping on CLBs.

The following table shows the CLB utilization of the Muller gates library for the Xilinx X4000 family.

Name	Function generator count	Memory element used
2-input Muller gates	1 FG	No
3-input Muller gates	1 FG and 1 H	No
4-input Muller gates without Set/Reset	2 FG and 1 H	No
4-input Muller gates with Set/Reset	2 FG and 1 H	1

Note: FG=LUT-4 and H=LUT-3

5 A Simple Example: A 4-bit QDI Adder

To demonstrate that this library can be automatically used for implementing an asynchronous circuit, this section presents the design of a 4-bit dual-rail adder. Cacasding four 1-bit dual-rail adder constructs a 4-bit adder. The 1-bit adder is decomposed in Muller gates as in the Figure 8 [10], [13]. The 4-bit dual rail adder was mapped on a Xilinx FPGA 4010XLPC84. The Muller gate library is

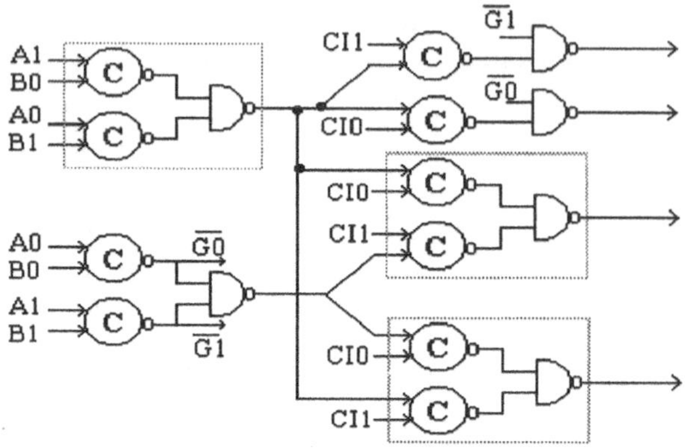

Fig. 8. Dual-rail 1-bit adder using Muller gates

described as primitives in XNF format. The place and route tool uses the library and maps correctly the HDL gate netlist (i.e. Muller gates into one CLB) onto the FPGA. The final generated XNF gate netlist gives a full description of the placed & routed asynchronous circuit. The user constraint file helps geometry planning tool to place the gates, to balance the isochronic forks and to satisfy timing performance of the circuit.

6 Conclusion & Perspectives

The TAST methodology and the associated tools are dedicated to asynchronous circuit design. This general design framework targets the behavioral simulation of HDL models and the synthesis of QDI or micropipeline circuits. The resulting gate netlists from the synthesis is exploited to target ASICs or FPGA prototypes. The mapping on standard FPGAs is quasi-automated (except the generation of the constraint file so far) and does not need specific place & route tools. Only a Muller gate library in XNF format and a user constraint file are necessary (for Xilinx components). Once the location and the mapping of Muller gates are physically enforced to satisfy hazard-free and minimize CLB utilization in FPGA, the place & route tools are able to automatically map asynchronous circuits. This approach is suitable to rapidly prototype asynchronous circuits in QDI style or in micropipeline style. The logic synthesis (by hand) of Muller

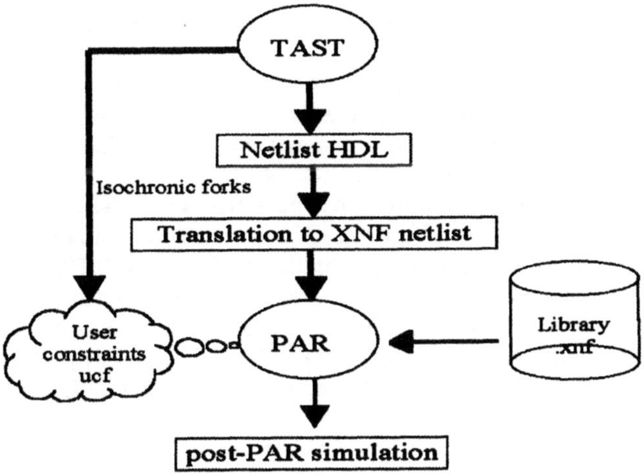

Fig. 9. Design flow using Muller gates library on Xilinx FPGA (HDL description and functional pre-PAR simulation are not shown)

gates requires care but the use of the library is automatic. This methodology was successfully applied to the design of a system including an ADC, a QDI FIR filter and a DAC onto Xilinx X4000 and Altera APEX families. QDI circuits were implemented onto Altera Flex and Xilinx Virtex too.

The experimental results show that the tested asynchronous circuits are fully functional. The TAST methodology, developed at TIMA, is well suited for the rapid prototyping and the evaluation of asynchronous circuits and mixed synchronous/asynchronous circuits on standard FPGAs. Future work will be focused on analyzing the FPGA power consumption of asynchronous designs versus synchronous designs.

References

1. Erik Brunvand, " Using FPGAs to Implement Self-Timed Systems ", University of Utah, January 8, 1992.
2. Al Davis and Steven M. Nowick, " An Introduction to Asynchronous Circurts", UUCS-97-103, September 19, 1997.
3. Laurent Dutrieux et Didier Demigny, " Logique Programmble: Architecture des FPGA et CPLD, Méthode et Conception, le Langage VHDL ", Editions Eyrolles, 1997.
4. Robert J. Francis, " Technology Mapping for Lookup-Table Based Field-Programmable Gate Arrays, Ph.D. Thesis, University of Toronto, 1993.
5. Scott Hauck, Steven Burns, Gaetano Borriello, and Carl Ebeling, " An FPGA for Asynchronous Circuits ", IEEE Design & Test of Computers, Vol.11, No.3, pp. 60-69, Fall, 1994.
6. S. W Moore and P. Robinson, "Rapid Prototping of Self-Timed Circuits", University of Cambridge, Proc. ICCD'98, 5-7 October 1998 in Austin Texas.

7. Robert Payne, " Self-Timed Field Programmable Gate Array Architectures ", Ph.D. thesis, University of Edinburgh, 1997.
8. Marc Renaudin, " Etat de l'art sur la conception des circuits asynchrones: perspectives pour l'intégration des systèmes complexes ", document interne, janvier 2000.
9. Marc Renaudin, " Asynchronous circuits and systems: a promising design alternative ", Microelectronic Engineering 54(2000) p. 133-149.
10. Marc Renaudin, P. Vivet, F. Robin, " ASPRO-216: a standard-cell Q.D.I 16-bit RISC asynchronous microprocessor ", Proc. Of the Fourth International Symposium on Advanced Research in Asynchronous Circuits and Systems, 1998, IEEE, p.22-31.
11. Ryunsuke Konishi, Hideyoki Ito, Hiroshi Nakada, Arika Nagoya, Kiyoshi Oguri, Norbert Imlig, Tsunemich Shiozawa, Minoru Inamori, and Kouichi Nagami, " PCA-1 : A Fully Asynchronous, Self-Reconfigurable LSI ", IEEE, 2001, p.54-61.
12. Ivan E. Sutherland, " Micropipelines ", Communication of ACM, June 1989, Volume32, Number 6.
13. Pascal Vivet, " Une Méthodologie de Conception des Circuits Intégrés Quasi-insensible aux Délais, Application à l'Etude et la Réalisation d'un Processeur RISC 16-bit Asynchrone ", thèse doctorale, l'INPG, 21 juin 2001.
14. K. Maheswaran, V. Akella, " Implementing Self-Timed Circuits in field programmable Gate arrays ", MS Thesis, U.C. Davis, 1995.
15. Xilinx Nelist Format (XNF) Specification, Version 6.2, published by Xilinx June 1, 1995.
16. Data book, Published by Xilinx 1999.
17. Anh Vu Dinh Duc, Jean-Baptiste Rigaud, Amine Rezzag, Antoine Sirianni, Joo Fragoso, Laurent Fesquet, Marc Renaudin, " TAST ", ACiD Workshop, Munich, Germany, Jan 2002.
18. A.V. Dinh Duc, J.B. Rigaud, A. Rezzag, A. Sirianni, J. Fragoso, L. Fesquet, M. Renaudin, "TAST CAD Tools: Tutorial", tutorial given at the International Symposium on Advanced Research in Asynchronous Circuits and Systems ASYNC'02, Manchester, UK, April 8-11, 2002, TIMA internal report ISRN:TIMA-RR-02/04/01-FR, http://tima.imag.fr/cis.

A Technique for FPGA Synthesis Driven by Automatic Source Code Analysis and Transformations

Beniamino Di Martino[1], Nicola Mazzocca[1], Giacinto Paolo Saggese[2], and Antonio G.M. Strollo[2]

[1] Department Of Information Engineering, Second University of Naples, Via Roma 29, 81031 Aversa (CE), Italy
[2] Department of Electronics and Telecommunications Engineering, University of Naples "Federico II", Via Claudio 21, 80125 Napoli, Italy
{beniamino.dimartino, n.mazzocca, saggese, astrollo}@unina.it

Abstract. This paper presents a technique for automatic synthesis of high-performance FPGA-based computing machines from C language source code. It exploits data-parallelism present in source code, and its approach is based on hardware application of techniques for automatic loop transformations, mainly designed in the area of optimizing compilers for parallel and vector computers. Performance aspects are considered in early stage of design, before low-level synthesis process, through a transformation-intensive branch-and-bound approach, that searches design space exploring area-performance tradeoffs. Furthermore optimizations are applied at architectural level, thus achieving higher benefits with respect to gate-level optimizations, also by means of a library of hardware blocks implementing arithmetic and functional primitives. Application of the technique to partial and complete unrolling of a Successive Over-Relaxation code is presented, with results in terms of effectiveness of area-delay estimation, and speed-up for the generated circuit, ranging from 5 and 30 on a Virtex-E 2000-6 with respect to a Intel Pentium 3 1GHz.

1 Introduction

In the last years reconfigurable computing systems, based on FPGAs or other programmable hardware, is gaining more and more interest. This is due to their capability of mapping algorithm execution of compute-intensive calculations to reconfigurable hardware, thus achieving speed-ups up to 3 order of magnitude faster than commercial processors, and performance typical of an ASIC implementation. FPGA Custom Computing Machines (FCCMs) have demonstrated the potential for achieving extremely high performance for many data-intensive tasks, such as data encryption/decryption [9], automatic target recognition [3], string pattern matching and morphological skeletonization [2]. Although significant performance speed-ups for many applications are achieved, main issues with FCCMs are the complexity of their design and the difficulty of integrating use of

M. Glesner, P. Zipf, and M. Renovell (Eds.): FPL 2002, LNCS 2438, pp. 47–58, 2002.

reconfigurable co-processors into traditional PC-based systems. Manual circuit description is a powerful method for the production of high-quality circuit designs, but it requires time effort, expertise in digital systems design and a deep knowledge of the particular reconfigurable system employed. Furthermore it is often hard to highlight and exploit all parallelism present in target applications. We devise in these problems a possible limiting factor for adoption of reconfigurable hardware. In this paper we present the *SUNthesis* (Second University of Naples synthesis) project. Main goal of SUNthesis project is to design and develop an automatic compilation framework, that accepts C language programs and automatically outputs various synthesizable VHDL description of the system, optimized for a FPGA architecture, mainly in terms of throughput. From this description it is straightforward to generate the configuration bitstream for target FPGA, by using commercial synthesis tools. The framework shall in addition automatically interface reconfigurable hardware with PCs, by means of suitable wrapping C functions that take care of communication with the target reconfigurable processor. In this way it is possible to provide the user with hardware acceleration capability, transparently and without any knowledge of the reconfigurable platform employed.

SUNthesis framework exploits results of software optimizing compiler techniques, and is based on a transformation-intensive branch-and-bound methodology, that permits to highlight design trade-offs between area and throughput. SUNthesis VHDL code generator extracts an RTL description that exploits FPGA logic blocks target architecture (for instance multiplexers with many inputs, that are area-consuming, are inferred by means of tristate buffers). Hardware block library contains different implementations of arithmetic operators, described as bit-length parametrized VHDL blocks: for example adders with many operands, are synthesized using carry-save technique, and are specified for actual number and width of operands. SUNthesis can provide high-performance designs by using optimizations at architectural level, usually not employed by gate-level synthesizer: for instance, operators are arranged when possible in tree-like structure (instead of series of blocks) and signals arriving last are assigned to fastest propagation block inputs, by using information derived from critical-paths analysis.

Although synthesis techniques based on repeated and extensive application of data-flow graph transformations were demonstrated in the past to be very time consuming, our synthesis technique is rather fast, because estimation of area-time performances is conducted at an early stage of the design process, before any time consuming process of low level synthesis; this is possible by means of the adoption of a strict interaction with a hardware component library, characterized by propagation delay and silicon area requirement. Pipeline vectorization [2] shares with SUNthesis project some aspects: it uses C language, it copes with automatic parallelization of loops, but considers only inner loops that can be completely unrolled for parallel execution in hardware, in order to build deeply pipelined circuits. Outer loops may not have different iterations executing simultaneously. Any loop re-ordering transformation is left to designer.

In proposed framework of [2] is well-faced also the automatic software/hardware partitioning problem. Cameron project [13] is the closest to our approach, but it uses a language specifically designed for hardware description, named SA-C. The adoption of a dedicated language makes difficult real co-design methodology.

The paper proceeds as follows. In the following section the synthesis technique that exploits application of unrolling and tiling transformations is described. Section 3 shows the application of the technique to a case study, a Successive OverRelaxation code excerpt. In section 5 numerical results are reported and conclusions on the validity of the technique are drawn.

2 The Synthesis Technique

In this paper we focus attention on managing of data-parallelism included in loop nests. It is well known in literature that, in scientific and engineering programs, major fraction of execution time is usually spent in very small parts of the code corresponding to loops. Furthermore loops, especially regular and iterative computations, are likely to achieve high speed-up when implemented on an hardware processors. So our technique is focused on loop analysis and optimisation, and uses as basic building block loop nests. Central problem regards the hardware implementation of a loop nest, using a given number of hardware resources (in FPGA case, we intend CLBs as hardware resources), with the objective of minimizing loop execution time. Proposed technique can cope with perfect loop nest (Fig. 1), which loop bounds can be expressed as linear function of outermost indexes, and which dependence vectors can be expressed as distance vectors[4][7]. These hypothesis are sufficiently general to cover a number of actual programs.

$$
\begin{array}{l}
\mathit{for}\ (i_1 = L_1; i_1 < U_1; i_1 + +) \\
\quad \mathit{for}\ (i_2 = L_2; i_2 < U_2; i_2 + +)\ \cdots \\
\qquad \mathit{for}\ (i_N = L_N; i_N < U_N; i_N + +)\ \{ \\
\qquad\quad S_I :\ a[f_1(i_1, \ldots, i_N), \ldots, f_M(i_1, , i_N)] = \cdots; \\
\qquad\quad S_J :\ \cdots = a[g_1(i_1, \ldots, i_N), \ldots, g_M(i_1, \ldots, i_N)];\ \}
\end{array}
$$

Fig. 1. Perfect N-nested loop model in pseudo-C code.

The choice of transformations to apply, after their legality verification, is driven by purpose of maximizing some cost-function, that is in our case maximize performances, guaranteeing that synthesized circuit can be hosted on target FPGA.

In literature regarding optimizing compiler for multiprocessors, different approaches are presented: some use heuristic search, others as [1] propose a unified framework for unimodular transformations. We combine both, using transformations to expose all available parallelism, and then evaluating effects of loop transformations that exploit parallelism (tiling, unrolling), in order to occupy available area and maximize throughput. Enough accurate estimate of performance parameters, before any gate-level synthesis process, is possible for two reasons: the former is the internal representation of the code that directly corresponds to the synthesized data-path, the latter is the utilization of synthesizable off-the-shelf blocks available into hardware characterized in terms of area and propagation delay.

We intend to present an algorithm to exploit most profitable one between coarse and fine grain parallelism. We use a method similar to [1] in order to detect sequence of unimodular transformations that enable and make useful tiling and wavefront, partial and complete unrolling. By using skewing, it is possible to transform an N-nested loop with lexicographically positive distance vectors in a fully permutable loop (Th. 3.1 in [1]). A nest of N fully permutable loops can be transformed to code containing at least N-1 degrees of parallelism [10], when no dependences are carried by these loops, it can be exposed a degree of parallelism N, otherwise, N-1 parallel loops can be obtained. In the following we consider application of transformations in order to expose finest or coarsest granularity of parallelism making reference to simple algebraic case, and then generalizing.

Finest Granularity of parallelism: finest granularity of parallelism corresponds to a situation where innermost loops are parallel, while outermost loops are constrained to be executed sequentially because of loop-carried dependences [4]. From a fully permutable loop, skewing the innermost loop of the fully permutable nest by each of the remaining loops and moving it to the outermost position (Th. B.2 in [1]), it is possible to place the maximum number of parallelizable loops in the innermost loops, maximizing fine-grain parallelism. This situation involves in hardware presence of counters spanning dimensions of iteration space associated to outermost loops, and possibility to make a complete unrolling (or complete tiling if legal [1]) of innermost loops, allocating multiple active instances of loop body. Supposing that available hardware resources are A_{avail} (number of CLBs), the number of outermost sequential loops are K, area required for one instance of loop body is A_{body} and T_{body} is its propagation delay, then we can calculate approximatively A_{tot}, total area required and T_{elab} total execution time as:

$$\begin{cases} T_{elab} = (U_1 - L_1) \cdot (U_2 - L_2) \cdot \ldots \cdot (U_K - L_K) \cdot (T_{body} + T_Q + T_{set-up}) \\ A_{tot} = (U_{K+1} - L_{K+1}) \cdot \ldots \cdot (U_N - L_N) \cdot A_{body} \end{cases}$$

where T_Q and T_{set-up} are respectively delay and set-up time of registers, needed when results calculated by the loop body are stored in registers. So it is possible to do a *complete* unrolling, exploiting parallelization and exhausting available parallelism, only when $A_{tot} \leq A_{avail}$. In this case, if necessary, it is possible to use other resources to partial unroll sequential loops, at the cost of remarkable increase of area, but with quite performance improvement, by reducing impact of $T_Q + T_{set-up}$ on T_{elab}. Note that we have referred simple case in which loop bounds are constant, and only in this case it is possible use simple expression of T_{elab} reported. However if the loop bounds are linear (as we supposed) it is possible to resort symbolic sum technique [12] or use efficient numerical technique like [11]. If resources required for a complete unrolling exceeds available resources, a *partial* unrolling, or a partial tiling if legal, can be applied. Problem in this case is choice of unrolling/tiling factors $f_{K+1} \dots f_N$ for parallel loops, and can be formalized in following minimization problem if loop bounds are constant:

$$\begin{cases} Minimize\ T_{elab} = (U_1 - L_1) \cdot \ldots \cdot (U_K - L_K) \cdot \lceil (U_{K+1} - L_{K+1})/f_{K+1} \rceil \cdot \\ \qquad \ldots \cdot \lceil (U_N - L_N)/f_N \rceil \cdot (T_{body} + T_Q + T_{set-up}) \\ A_{tot} = f_{K+1} \cdot \ldots \cdot f_N \cdot A_{body} \le A_{avail} \\ 1 \le f_{K+1} < (U_{K+1} - L_{K+1}), 1 \le f_N < (U_N - L_N) \end{cases}$$

In general situation when number of clock ticks are computed with [12] or [11], T_{elab} is function of $f_{K+1} \dots f_N$, and this problem can be solved using an exhaustive enumeration technique with cuts.

Coarsest Granularity of parallelism: coarsest granularity of parallelism corresponds to a situation where outermost loops are parallel, while innermost loops are constrained to be executed accordingly to loop-carried dependences. Theorem and algorithm B.4 in [1] describes an effective method to detect a series of transformations producing the maximal number of parallel loop as outermost loops. The problem can be modeled in a similar way of previous case, and we will describe method to obtain system to solve with an example. In Fig. 2, a 3-nested perfect loop is reported:

```
1.  for(i = 0; j < N; i++)
2.    for(j = 0; j < P; j++)
3.      for(k = 0; k < M; k++)  a[i][j][k] = f(a[i][j][k-1]);
```

Fig. 2. A simple example of application of proposed technique for choice of unrolling factor.

Distance vector is (0,0,1), and so two outermost loops are parallel, while innermost loop has to be serially executed considering loop-carried dependence on loop k with level equal to 1. It is possible to (completely or partially) unroll and parallelize outermost loops, and unroll innermost loop. When considering unrolling of loop body, propagation delay is difficult to analytically estimate, because of the composition of critical paths. In this case it is essential to exploit a critical path analysis of data-flow graph resulting from unrolled loop. In case study section, we prove that our technique of area-time estimation, based on analysis of data-flow graph of loop body, is effective and gives results enough close to actual results obtained through synthesis process. Note that only when unrolling factor is greater than level of loop-carried dependences, dependences are moved into unrolled body of the loop, requiring a data-dependence analysis to be correctly treated (see parallel version of case study). In the case of Fig. 2 applying unrolling (or tiling that is legal in this case) to outermost loops, and unrolling innermost, we obtain the subsequent optimization problem:

$$\begin{cases} Minimize\ T_{elab} = \lceil N/f_1 \rceil \cdot \lceil P/f_2 \rceil \cdot (T_{body}(f_3) + T_Q + T_{set-up}) \\ A_{tot} = f_1 \cdot f_2 \cdot A_{body}(f_3) \le A_{avail} \\ 1 \le f_1 < N,\ 1 \le f_2 < P,\ 1 \le f_3 < K \end{cases}$$

Values of A_{body} and T_{body} are function of unrolling factor f_3 and can be considered as upper bounds respectively $f_3 \cdot A_f$ and $f_3 \cdot t_f$, where A_f and t_f are area and delay of block implementing function f. These inequalities can become equalities when no circuit optimization is possible on data-flow graph obtained from unrolling. If input code corresponds to one reported to Fig. 3 implementing matrix multiplication algorithm between $\underline{A}$ and $\underline{B}$, effects of possible optimization on unrolled data-flow graph is clear, by means of the application of transformation exploiting associativity and commutativity properties of addition. In Fig. 4 we

1. $for(i = 0; j < N; i++)\ \ for(j = 0; j < P; j++)\{$
2. $\quad temp = 0;$
3. $\quad for(k = 0; k < M; k++)\ \ S:\ temp+ = a[i][k] \cdot b[k][j];$
4. $\quad c[i][j] = temp;$

Fig. 3. C-code for Matrix multiplication.

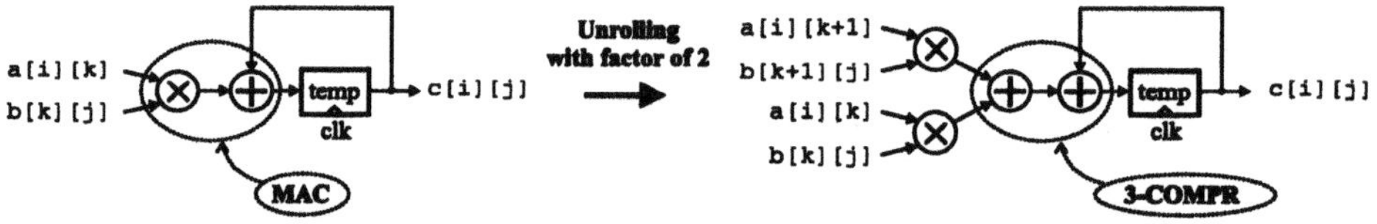

Fig. 4. Data-flow graph generation after application of unrolling with factor 2 on the loop body of matrix multiplication algorithm.

report data-flow graph for loop body S of code in Fig. 3. Using library of hardware components it is possible to implement multiplication and addition with a MAC (multiply-and-accumulate) block. Furthermore, when loop on k is unrolled twice, few other architectural level optimisations can be developed (in Fig. 4 use of 3-compressor instead of cascade of two adders), and so analysis of data-flow graph is essential in order to estimate area requirement and critical path.

3 Application of the Technique to a Case Study

In this section we describe the unrolling transformation and its effects on a case study, in order to prove effectiveness of our technique of area-delay evaluation from data-flow graph. As case study we propose the algorithm known as Successive Over Relaxation (SOR), because, although this is a not straightforward parallelizable algorithm [5], it is a typical example where proper choice and application of sequences of unimodular loop transformations can provide optimal speedups on different target architectures [6]. SOR is a method for the numerical resolution of systems of linear equations, i.e. finding a solution to the vector equation $\widetilde{A} \cdot \underline{x} = \underline{b}$, where $\widetilde{A}$ is the $N \times N$ matrix of linear equation coefficients, and $\underline{x}$ and $\underline{b}$ are N-dimensional vectors. In non-simulaneous methods, value of the generic j-th variable at the (k+1)-th iteration $x_j(k+1)$ is updated in sequence, using the newly obtained j-1 values of the preceding variables for step k+1 and the "old" N-j values of the remaining variables from step k. One of these methods is Successive Over Relaxation:

$$x_j^{(k+1)} = \left(\frac{\omega}{a_{j,j}}\right) \cdot \left(b_j \sum_{i=1}^{j-1} a_{j,i} x_i^{(k+1)} - \sum_{i=j+1}^{N} a_{j,i} x_i^{(k+1)}\right) - (\omega - 1) x_j^{(k)}$$

When the matrix $\widetilde{A}$ is a $(2 \cdot s + 1)$-diagonal matrix $(0 \leq s \leq N)$, computational complexity can be improved by modifying the update expression to:

$$x_j^{(k+1)} = \left(\frac{\omega}{a_{j,j}}\right) \cdot \left(b_j \sum_{i=-s}^{-1} a_{j,(j+i)} x_{j+i}^{(k+1)} - \sum_{i=1}^{+s} a_{j,(j+i)} x_{j+i}^{(k+1)}\right)$$

This paradigm of computation is called a stencil computation, and s is the stencil size, which can vary from N (full range interaction) to 1 (nearest neighbours interaction). The C sequential code to compute reported expressions, assumes the generalized form of the loop nest in Fig. 5. The outer loop on index n represents the iteration for convergence, the intermediate loop on j represents the scanning of the elements of $\underline{x}$, while the inner loop on i represents the update of the jth element of x, based on the value of neighbour elements belonging to the stencil. The + sign in the updating statement can be substituted by any associative operator, while $f_{j,i}$ and g_j are generic functions, which could depend on i and j.

Loop carried dependence relation can be taken in account as set of direction vectors $\{(1,0,<),(0,0,>),(1,0,0)\}$: with reference to conditions enabling parallelizations [1], neither the outermost loop (n) nor the intermediate loop (j) can be parallelized. The innermost loop (i) can be unrolled and it is possible to use a single block that sums together all the inputs, exploiting the associativity and commutativity of the addition. SUNthesis resorts to a tree-organization of adders, reducing the propagation delay of statement 3-4 of Fig. 5 that are just the core of the computation. Loop on i derives from a lack of a summatory operator in C and a lack of correspondent functional block in conventional processors, while in a hardware synthesis process, loop can be substituted by a

```
for (n = 0; n < Niter; n++) for (j = 0; j < N; j++){
  temp = 0;
  for (i = -s; i <= s; i++)
    if ((i + j >= 0)&&(i + j <= N - 1)) temp += f_{j,i}(x[i + j]);
    x[j] = g_j(temp); }
```

Fig. 5. Sequential SOR algorithm in C. It is worth point out that perfect loop model can be adopted.

block directly implementing this arithmetic primitive with a significant gain of performance.

We describe the algorithm for systematic and partial unrolling, making reference to loop j of SOR code in Fig. 5, where, without loss of generality, we assume N = 8, S = 1. Furthermore we suppose that operators $f_{j,i}$ and g_j are multiplication operations respectively by bidimensional array a, and by vector b, including dependences of operator f_j,i and g_j from subscripts j and i. The specified code is reported in Fig. 6.. Function $f_{j,i}$ is substituted with a[j][i+1]

```
int n, i, j; signed_int8 x[8], a[3][8], b[8]; int temp;
  for (n = 0; n < Niter; n++) #pragma clk
    for (j = 0; j < 8; j++) { #pragma unrolling
      for (i = -1; i ≤ 1; i++) #pragma unrolling, partial eval, const folding
        if ((i + j >= 0)&&(i + j <= 7)) temp += a[j][i + 1] * x[i + j];
        x[j] = b[j] * temp;
```

Fig. 6. SOR algorithm in C, specified with described assumptions, with declaration of type variable. The pragma directive clk allows to specify which loop corresponds to the clock, i.e. execution of which loop of the nest is completed in a clock tick.

in order to guarantee that subscripts falls in $[0, 2 \cdot S]$ in according to C syntax. Examples of C code in the following are enhanced with some pragma directives that mean application of transformations by SUNthesis, helping to understand effects of transformations on internal graph structures. The pragma *unrolling* means that unrolling is complete, i.e. all instances of the loop referred by unrolling directive are concurrently active. The pragma directive *clk* implicates that all the hardware blocks corresponding to statements executed in the loop n, must be accommodated in a clock tick, or an iteration of loop n would be executed in a clock period. After application of complete unrolling on loop i, it is possible to apply partial evaluation, constant evaluation (and if necessary redundancies removing), that can simplify the if conditions. In Fig. 7 we report resulting code

During unrolling of j loop the signal temp has been replicated one for each loop instance (*temp_j* where j = 0...7), j and i values have been propagated

```
#pragma partial eval, const folding
if ((-1 + j >= 0)&&(-1 + j <= 7)) temp += a[j][-1 + 1] * x[-1 + j]; //i = -1
if ((j >= 0)&&(j <= 7)) temp += a[j][1] * x[j]; //i = 0
if ((1 + j >= 0)&&(1 + j <= 7) temp+ = a[j][1 + 1] * x[1 + j]; //i = 1
x[j] = b[j] * temp;
```

Fig. 7. Loop i of the SOR algorithm in C after complete unrolling and constant propagation.

through the code. All the if statements with condition not verified are clearly considered dead-code, and hence are discarded with corresponding hardware blocks. A simple data-dependence analysis [4] can point out which values can be forwarded, because they are calculated in the same clock cycle in which other hardware blocks need them. For instance, in our example, updated value of x[j] element is loaded into the register at the end of any clock tick, but it is needed, if j = 1 ...N-1, to calculate new value of x[j+1], so the block corresponding to instances of statement 5 of Fig. 6, can exploit x_new[i]. In Fig. 8 we report the resulting code:

```
for(n = 0; n < Niter; n++) {#pragmaclk
  temp_0 = 0; temp_0+ = a[0][1] * x[0]; //j = 0, i = 0
  temp_0+ = a[0][2] * x[1]; //i = 1
  x_new[0] = b[0] * temp_0;
  ...
   temp_7 = 0; temp_7+ = a[7][0] * x_new[6]; //j = 1, i = 0...
```

Fig. 8. SOR algorithm in C, completely unrolled with respect to j loop and i loop, after partial evaluation, constant propagation of i and j, and dead code elimination.

The algorithm obtained with the above-mentioned sequence of transformations can be translated in a VHDL description with a direct inspection of the annotated graph, and in example of complete unrolled description of Fig. 8, SUNthesis produces the circuit of Fig. 9.

Unrolling of loop i - serial implementation of SOR algorithm: Serial version of SOR algorithm of Fig. 5 (with the same assumptions made in the completely unrolled example) is derived by the code of Fig 6 leaving pragma unrolling of line 3 and substituting it with a pragma clk. It corresponds to datapath depicted in Fig. 10. In this case a decreasing of throughput corresponds to a decrease of area consumed. It is possible to obtain other intermediate implementations of SOR algorithm using a partial unrolling, providing a trade-off between performances and area required.

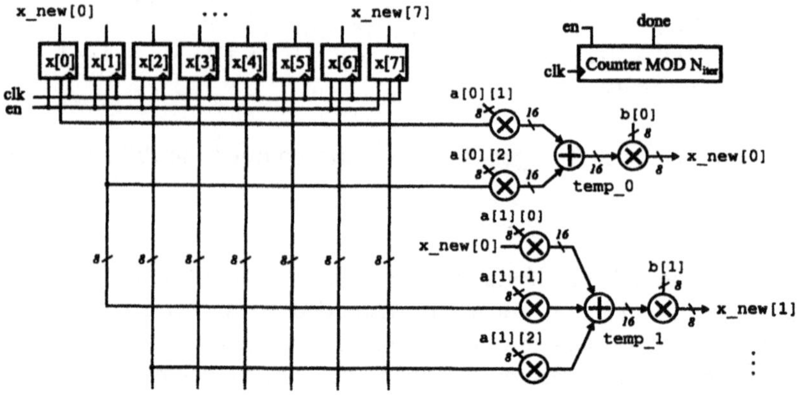

Fig. 9. Circuit corresponding to parallel description of C code of Fig. 8. Counter stores value of number n of iterations, and issues done signal when circuit has completed elaboration, while en started the execution.

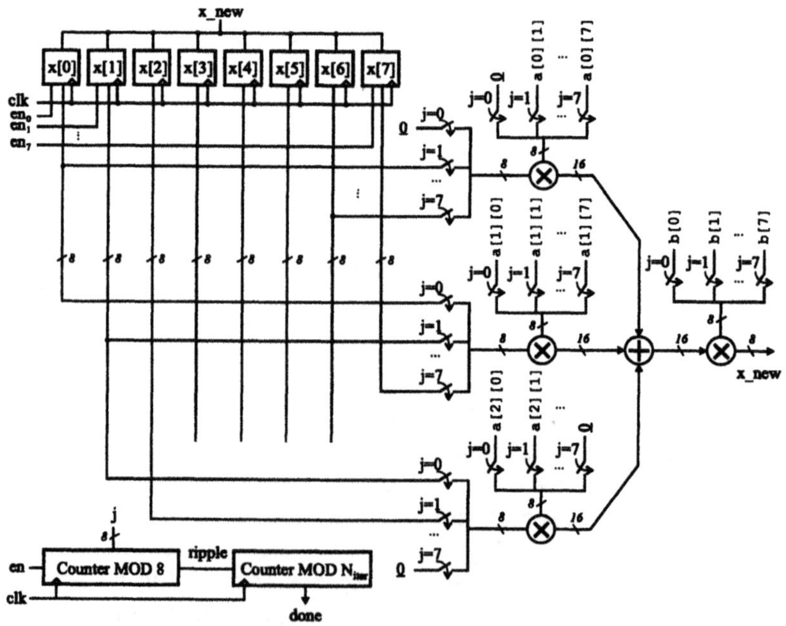

Fig. 10. Serial implementation of SOR. Please note the extended use of tristate buffer, represented as controlled switches, and enable signals for flip-flop, to implement respectively multiplexers and demultiplexers.

Unrolling Factor	Area [slices]	Tristate buffers	Minimum T_{Clock} [ns]	Execution Time Sw [s]	Execution Time Hw [s]	Speedup
U = 1	795 (4%)	1984	46,6	0,373	2,03	5,44
U = 2	1162 (6%)	1984	64,5	0,259	2,03	7,86
U = 4	2048 (11%)	1984	108,3	0,217	2,03	9,37
U = 8	3623 (19%)	0	131,3	0,131	2,03	15,5

Table 1. Results for the case N = 8, S = 7, exploring with different unrolling factor U the design space (U=1 is serial case, and U=8 is parallel). Execution times are referred to 1 million iterations of variables update. Occupation as number of slices used and tristate buffer are also reported.

Unrolling Factor	Area [slices]	Tristate buffers	Minimum T_{Clock} [ns]	Execution Time Sw [s]	Execution Time Hw [s]	Speedup
U = 1	2257 (12%)	8064	56,5	0,904	8,1	8,96
U = 16	9172 (48%)	0	267,5	0,267	8,1	30,3

Table 2. Results for the case N = 16, S = 15, where U = 1 is serial case, while U = 16 parallel

	Xilinx after place&route			SUNthesis estimate		Xilinx estimate after synthesis
Unrolling Factor	Area [slices]	T_{Clock} [ns]	Logic Levels	Area [slices]	T_{Clock} [ns]	T_{Clock} [ns]
U = 1	795	46,6	18	823(+3,5%)	31,4(-32%)	31,5(-32%)
U = 2	1162	64,5	27	1213(+4,4%)	53,8(-17%)	40,4(-37%)
U = 4	2048	108,3	37	2037(-0,5%)	90,8(-16%)	64,1(-40%)
U = 8	3623	131,3	55	3617(-0,2%)	164(+25%)	94,5(-28%)

Table 3. Comparison among estimation of area-time performance for N = 8, S = 7. Values of area-time performance after place&route process, estimation of area-time with SUNthesis (without synthesis), and finally estimation of clock period after synthesis pass. Area estimation is very close to actual results, while minimum operating frequency estimation is less close to actual performances because of route delays.

4 Numerical Results and Conclusions

In this paper, for synthesis of VHDL RTL description, we have targeted a Xilinx Virtex-E 2000-6bg560. Xilinx XCV2000E presents 19200 slices and 19520 tristate buffers. All the synthesis were been realized using Xilinx ISE 4. In Tab. 1 we compared performances of circuits produced by SUNthesis with execution time of an Intel Pentium 3 processor running at 1 GHz. Hardware execution is between 5 and 15 times faster than a P3 1GHz. It is clear that if N and S grow, the speed-up can be higher. This is proven by results reported in Tab. 2 referring to the case N = 16, S = 15, in which parallel version can run 30 times faster than software version. Finally in Tab. 3 we report results of comparison of area-time estimation done by SUNthesis with respect to results of synthesis process. It is worth point out that early SUNthesis estimates are in very good accordance to actual results. Note also that after synthesis pass ISE values worst than SUNthesis minimum period, although it has information about gate netlist not available to SUNthesis, proving effectiveness of our approach. Reported experiments proved validity of its early estimation of impact of transformations on area requirements and performances.

References

1. M.E. Wolf and M.S. Lam: "A loop transformation theory and an algorithm to maximize parallelism", IEEE Trans. Parallel. Distrib. Syst. Vol.2, pp. 452-471, Oct 1991.
2. M. Weinhardt and W. Luk: "Pipeline Vectorization", IEEE Trans. On CAD of Integrated Circuits and Systems, Vol.20, No. 2, Feb 2001.
3. M. Rencher, B. L. Hutchings, "Automated Target Recognition on SPLASH2", IEEE Symposium on Field-Programmable Custom Computing Machines, 1997.
4. H. Zima and B. Chapman: "Supercompilers for Parallel and ", Reading MA: Addison-Wesley, 1991.
5. B. Di Martino, G. Iannello, "Parallelization of Nonsimultaneous...", in: *Parallel Processing*, Lecture Notes in Computer Science n. 854, pp. 253-262, Springer-Verlag, 1994.
6. B. Di Martino, "Algorithmic Concept Recognition Support for Automatic ...", *Journ. of Information Science and Engineering*, Vol. 14, n. 1, pp. 191-203, March 1998.
7. M. J. Wolfe: Optimizing Supercompilers for Supercomputers. Research Monographs in Parallel and Distributed Computing. MIT Press, Cambridge, Mass.
8. M. Girkar and C.D. Polychronopoulos : "Automatic Extraction of Functional Parallelism...", IEEE Trans. On Par. and Distr. Syst. Vol.3, No.2, March 1992, pp. 166-178.
9. A. J. Elbirt, C. Paar, "An FPGA Implementation and Performance Evaluation ...", ACM/SIGDA International Symposium on FPGAs, pp. 33-40, 2000.
10. F. Irigoin and R. Triolet, "Supernode partitioning", In Proc. 15th Annual ACM SIGACT-SIGPLAN Synp Principles Programming Languages, Jan. 1988, pp. 319-329.
11. N. Tawbi : "Estimation of nested loops execution time by integer arithmetic in convex polyhedra", Parallel Processing Symposium, 1994. Proceedings., 1994, Page(s): 217-221
12. D.E. Knuth, "The Art of Computer Programming", Vol. I, Addison-Wesley, 1973
13. R. Rinker et al.: "An Automated Process for Compiling Dataflow Graphs into ...", IEEE Trans. On VLSI Systems, Vol.9, No.1, Feb. 2001, pp. 130-139.

Flexible Routing Architecture Generation for Domain-Specific Reconfigurable Subsystems

Katherine Compton[1], Akshay Sharma[2], Shawn Phillips[2], and Scott Hauck[2]

[1]Northwestern University
Evanston, IL, USA
kati@ece.northwestern.edu
[2]University of Washington
Seattle, WA, USA
{akshay, phillips, hauck}@ee.washington.edu

Abstract. Reconfigurable hardware is ideal for use in Systems-on-a-Chip, as it provides hardware speeds as well as the benefits of post-fabrication modification. However, not all applications are equally suited to any one reconfigurable architecture. Therefore, the Totem Project focuses on the automatic generation of customized reconfigurable hardware. This paper details our first attempts at the design of algorithms for automatic generation of customized flexible routing architectures. We show that these algorithms provide results with a low area overhead compared to the custom-designed RaPiD routing architecture, as well as the flexibility needed to handle some application modifications.

Introduction

Reconfigurable hardware shows great potential for use in systems-on-a-chip (SoCs), as it provides speeds similar to hardware execution, but maintains a level of flexibility not available with more traditional custom circuitry. This flexibility is the key to allowing for both hardware reuse and post-fabrication modification.

A widely available form of reconfigurable hardware is the field-programmable gate array (FPGA), and the structures within an SoC could be patterned after these designs. However, because of their highly flexible nature, FPGAs can incur significant area and speed penalties. If the SoC itself will be custom-fabricated, this presents the opportunity for customization of the reconfigurable hardware based on characteristics of the target application domain. Domain-specific reconfigurable hardware provides only the amount of reconfigurability needed by the applications, which leads to reduced area and increased performance compared to a generic FPGA-style solution.

Manual design of a new reconfigurable architecture for each new application set would be disadvantageous in terms of design time and expertise required. Instead, we focus on the automatic creation of customized reconfigurable architectures, including high-level design, VLSI layout [1], and custom place and route tools creation [2]. This paper focuses on the Totem Project's work towards the automatic creation of reconfigurable architectures that are flexible enough to handle small changes in the application circuits, such as upgrades or bug-fixes, or perhaps even the addition of different circuits entirely.

M. Glesner, P. Zipf, and M. Renovell (Eds.): FPL 2002, LNCS 2438, pp. 59-68, 2002.

Background

Our current architecture generator creates designs in the style of the RaPiD architecture [3][4][5]. The two primary motivations for choosing the RaPiD system as a starting point for our research, apart from its successes in DSP applications, are that it is a one-dimensional architecture, and because a compiler for this system is already in place. The one-dimensional nature of RaPiD simplifies our task significantly, though in future efforts we will extend our techniques to 2D architectures. Also, as is the case for the RaPiD architecture, a 1D design is quite suited to the datapath-style computations that we are initially targeting. The existing compiler is also important because this provides us with a method to generate benchmark application circuits.

RaPiD (shown in Fig. 1) is composed of coarse-grained word-sized computation units such as ALUs, Multipliers, and RAMs, arranged along a 1D axis. Routing is in the form of word-sized busses arranged in tracks running parallel to the axis. Each component contains multiplexers on each of its inputs which choose between the signals of each routing track, as well as demultiplexers on each of the outputs that allow the unit to directly output to any of the routing tracks.

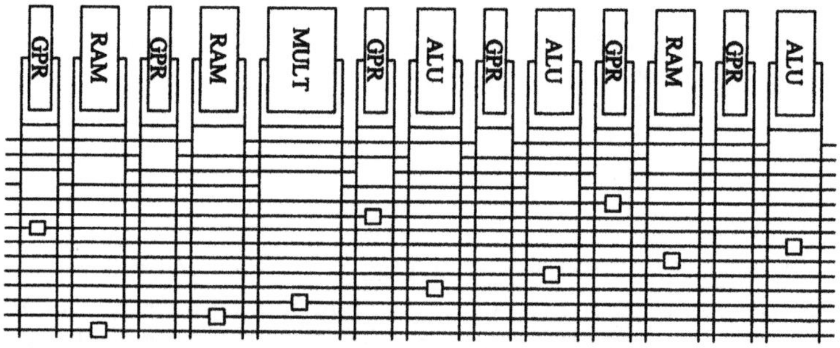

Fig. 1. A single cell from the RaPiD architecture [4][5]. The full architecture is composed of 16 of these cells tiled end-to-end.

RaPiD has proven itself to be a very good architecture for digital signal processing type applications. However, this architecture was manually designed, and does not have enough routing capability for a number of the benchmarks we are using. Furthermore, RaPiD was designed to be suitable for executing a wide variety of circuits. Our goal is to customize an architecture for a given application set, with some extra resources if desired for future flexibility, and to be able to generate this architecture automatically.

Routing Architecture Generation

For this paper we concentrate primarily on the generation of configurable routing architectures. We use a slightly modified version of our previous algorithms for generating logic structures along a 1D axis [6]. The routing architectures are created using a number of heuristics to generate solutions targeting different combinations of area and flexibility goals.

Each of our routing generation algorithms shares several key concepts. The first is the difference between local and distance routing tracks. Local tracks are used for short connections (the top five tracks of RaPiD are of this type). The length of a wire in a track can be determined by subtracting the indices of the furthest units a wire can reach. A special local track contains length 0 "feedback" wires that only route from a unit's outputs to the unit's inputs. Distance routing tracks include the added flexibility that longer wires can be created from shorter ones through the use of bus connectors. Each bus connector can be independently programmed. This allows a great deal of routing flexibility, but adds a delay as a signal passes through the bus connector, and adds an area penalty. The lower eight tracks of RaPiD are of this type.

Another important idea is the "offset" of the track. This offset determines the left-right shifting of the track once its wire length has been determined. Fig. 2 left demonstrates a type of routing architecture where all tracks have the same offset value. The routing choices available to a signal can be very dissimilar (and potentially undesirable) depending on the location of the signal's source and sink components. On the other hand, by carefully choosing our offset values for the tracks, we can achieve an architecture closer to Fig. 2 right. This "distributed" type of routing architecture will provide more flexibility in routing, as it provides a variety of routing choices for signals connecting to each component.

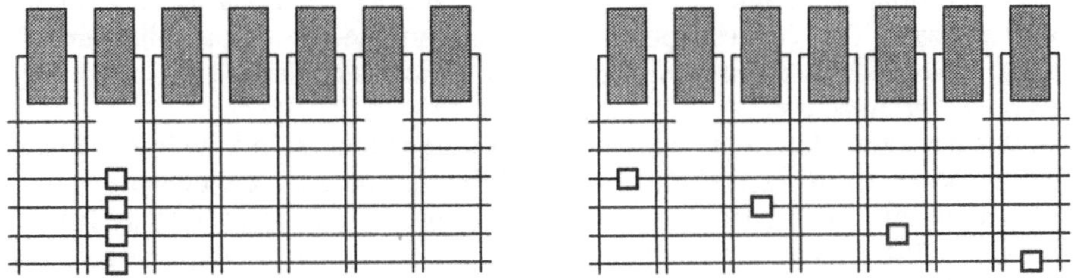

Fig. 2. An extreme example of a non-distributed routing architecture (left). A distributed routing architecture (right).

The cross-section of signals is a concept we use to measure the performance of our algorithms. This is calculated by finding the maximum cross-section at any component location for each individual netlist, then finding the maximum across all netlists. We use this value as a lower bound on the number of tracks needed to implement the source netlists on the architecture generated for them. This lower bound is an improbable solution due to the very high number of bus connectors that would be required in order to use this few tracks. Each of our algorithms also repeatedly determines the cross-section of the signals that cannot yet be routed on the architecture being generated. This computation is used as one of the indicators of whether or not a particular track is providing any "benefit" to the architecture. We try to add tracks that will decrease the unroutable signal cross-section value.

In order to determine the cross-section of the signals that cannot yet be routed, we need to perform a routing operation. Because this is a frequent operation performed within loops, we needed a very fast router (faster than the higher-quality router used for "final" routing) that provides reasonable results. We therefore use a greedy heuristic. Like a left-edge algorithm, we consider signals by increasing left edge. However, rather than routing each signal to the leftmost unassigned wire that can implement it, we also consider how closely the span of the signal matches the span of the wire. Each time an initial wire/signal pair is considered, we examine the other signals which could also be routed onto the wire, and choose the one which is the closest "fit". We mark the chosen signal as "routed", and if we did not choose our original signal, we reconsider that signal on the next iteration. For the routing operation, each netlist is considered a separate problem.

The next few sections describe our three different routing architecture generation algorithms. The first, *Greedy Histogram*, does not attempt to generate distributed routing structure. The remaining two algorithms, *Add Max Once* and *Add Min Loop*, focus on generating a more regular architecture, where these breaks and spaces are very evenly distributed. The details of each algorithm are presented below, followed by a comparison of the results obtained by each.

Greedy Histogram

This algorithm attempts to keep the overall number of tracks low, while encouraging the use of local tracks over distance tracks in order to avoid introducing a large number of bus connectors. Each track has a specific type and wire length used for all segments within that track. However, we make no restrictions as to what offset should be used. This creates a potentially non-distributed routing architecture which may not have uniform connectivity and thus may not be as flexible as a more regular interconnect architecture.

In this algorithm, tracks are added one at a time within an infinite loop. The loop is broken when all of the netlists can be fully routed onto the architecture using the routing algorithm we discussed previously. The algorithm chooses the wire length for a "new" track by looking at largest value in the histogram of the unrouted signal lengths. The actual track creation method depends in part upon the wire length chosen. For lengths smaller than 8, we choose a local routing track to avoid excessive use of bus connectors, and check all possible offsets (from 0 to length-1) to find the best one for that wire length. Otherwise we create a distance track, and we check all wire lengths from 8 to the chosen length, and all offsets for each length to find the track that reduces the histogram the most at the length we chose.

Regular Routing Algorithms

The next two algorithms generate a distributed routing architecture, where not only are the breaks or connectors evenly distributed within a track, but also across tracks. In other words, we choose our track offsets so as to provide a somewhat consistent level of connectivity regardless of location in the architecture. Fig. 2 right shows an example of this type of routing architecture. In order to make the complex task of even break/connector distribution easier to approximate, we have restricted wire lengths to powers of two, where the track possibilities are now local tracks of length 0 (feedback), 2, and 4, and distance tracks of length 8 and 16. Because the Greedy

Histogram method infrequently chose wire lengths greater than 16, we did not include options for lengths 32 or higher.

Add Max Once

This algorithm is fairly simple in organization, much more than the *Greedy Histogram* algorithm. We start from the shortest track length and go to the longest track length, seeing how many tracks of each type we can add while still improving the cross-section of unroutable signals. In other words, we add tracks of the given type until no further cross-section reductions are possible due to the creation additional tracks of the type.

Add Min Loop

The previous algorithm tends to weight towards the use of distance routing tracks because it only considers each wire length and type combination once. It is possible, however, that once a distance track is added, using additional local tracks will once again reduce the unroutable signal cross-section. Therefore, we have created the *Add Min Loop* algorithm in an effort to more accurately generate tracks with local wires.

This algorithm iteratively adds a small number of tracks to the overall routing architecture, until full routeability can be achieved, with only one type of track added per iteration. Within the loop, we repeatedly attempt to add tracks in the following order: length 0 local tracks, length 2 local tracks, length 4 local tracks, length 16 distance tracks, and length 8 distance tracks. In the case of the local routing tracks, we attempt to add as many tracks as the length of the wires in the track (providing potentially the full range of offsets for that particular track type). For distance routing tracks, which we consider to be much more expensive, we only attempt to add a single track of each type. We only keep the tracks we attempt to add if it causes a reduction in the cross-section of unroutable signals. If we keep any tracks, we immediately remove any track containing longer wires than our new track(s). This is done because that once the shorter wire length track is added, the architecture may not need as many longer-type tracks as was earlier computed. After we modify the counts accordingly, we return to the top of the loop.

Algorithm Comparison

Both area and flexibility are important when comparing reconfigurable architectures, as a very small architecture with little flexibility may not meet the needs of the user. Conversely, an architecture that is overly flexible may be able to implement any circuit required, yet the area cost may be prohibitive. In this paper we compare our three different routing generation algorithms first on an area basis, and second on the flexibility of the resulting architectures.

We are using a number of benchmarks from which we choose our various application "sets". These benchmarks have been compiled using the RaPiD compiler [3] into a coarse netlist format. The benchmark sets are:

- Radar – used to observe the atmosphere using FM signals
- Digital Camera – a set of three operations needed for a digital camera
- OFDM – part of a MC-CDMA receiver application that uses a smart antenna
- Image Processing Library – a minimal image processing library
- All DCT/FFT – two different 16-point FFTs and a DCT
- All FIR –six different FIR filters, two of which time-multiplex use of multipliers
- All Matrix Multiply – five different matrix multipliers
- All Sort – two 1D sorting netlists and two 2D sorting netlists

Area

In order to determine area numbers, we used logic component area values as provided by the RaPiD group. All layouts were done in a TSMC .25µm process. To compare to a RaPiD implementation, we assume that RaPiD is easily tileable to any number of cells, but that the routing architecture and logic within each cell is fixed. This represents the obvious hard-macro approach to SoC reconfigurable subsystem design. For each application group, we found the minimum number of RaPiD cells that fit all of the netlists [2]. The individual area results of the comparisons are shown in Fig. 3. If a benchmark set cannot be implemented using tileable RaPiD cells, a "*" appears in the results table. In these cases, the RaPiD routing architecture is simply not large or flexible enough for that particular application set.

For each application set, we show the track count generated by each of the three algorithms, and compare to a lower bound of the maximum of the cross-section of all signals for each netlist. As mentioned earlier, we consider this lower bound to be unrealistic. Note that the lower bound is different for *Greedy Histogram*, since the logic layout is not constrained to be "distributed". The chart then indicates how far from the lower bound each algorithm's routing architecture is. Finally, the total area is given for the architectures, including for the required RaPiD implementation, and each method is compared to the RaPiD implementation for the same application group. These results are summarized in Fig. 4.

The average fraction of the RaPiD solution was .66 for the *Greedy Histogram*, .69 for *Add Max Once*, and .70 for *Add Min Loop*. This is not even including benchmark sets that could not be implemented on RaPiD as the architecture is now. The majority of this benefit is due to using only the necessary logic for each benchmark set – this is where customization can greatly affect overall area results. As these values indicate, the extra routing area overhead introduced by using automatic routing generation (instead of the manual design as used for RaPiD) did not overwhelm the benefits of logic customization. For the cases where a RaPiD implementation was possible, we averaged a factor of nearly 2.5 in logic area reduction. Meanwhile, we only increased routing area by an average of 1.37 times for *Greedy Histogram*, 1.53 times for *Add Max Once*, and 1.57 times for *Add Min Loop*.

Application Group	Method	Tracks (L/D/Tot)			Bound	Factor of Bound	Total Area	Factor of RaPiD
Radar	GH	7	8	15	10	1.50	6879160	0.44
	AMO	1	18	19	13	1.46	10637760	0.68
	AML	5	14	19	13	1.46	10066770	0.64
	RaPiD	5	10	15			15647260	1.00
Digital Camera	GH	9	17	26	14	1.86	26414350	*
	AMO	2	23	25	17	1.47	30348850	*
	AML	11	20	31	17	1.82	33974950	*
	RaPiD	5	10	15			*	*
OFDM	GH	10	23	33	19	1.74	94797900	*
	AMO	1	27	28	22	1.27	88205800	*
	AML	6	25	31	22	1.41	86888800	*
	RaPiD	5	10	15			*	*
Image Proc. Library	GH	7	12	19	11	1.73	12085300	*
	AMO	2	25	27	11	2.45	12974970	*
	AML	5	14	19	11	1.73	12789070	*
	RaPiD	5	10	15			*	*
All DCT/FFT	GH	8	17	25	12	2.08	17737070	0.76
	AMO	3	19	22	14	1.57	15084150	0.64
	AML	6	17	23	14	1.64	14629560	0.62
	RaPiD	5	10	15			23475660	1.00
All FIR	GH	9	11	20	10	2.00	14106060	0.68
	AMO	3	12	15	9	1.67	8991460	0.43
	AML	4	11	15	9	1.67	8857280	0.42
	RaPiD	5	10	15			20857340	1.00
All Matrix Mult	GH	10	7	17	9	1.89	7287170	0.70
	AMO	4	15	19	10	1.90	8127370	0.78
	AML	8	12	20	10	2.00	9547450	0.92
	RaPiD	5	10	15			10426080	1.00
All Sort	GH	7	12	19	10	1.90	11045520	0.71
	AMO	6	14	20	11	1.82	14641540	0.94
	AML	7	13	20	11	1.82	14316820	0.91
	RaPiD	5	10	15			15647780	1.00

Fig. 3. The individual area results for the architectures generated by our three algorithms. Area values are in microns^2. A "*" indicates that no RaPiD implementation was possible. Track count is given by # local tracks / # distance tracks / # total tracks

		Number of Tracks			Factor of Bound	Routing Factor of RaPID	Total Factor of RaPID
Averages	GH	8.38	13.38	21.75	1.84	1.37	0.66
	AMO	2.75	19.13	21.88	1.70	1.53	0.69
	AML	6.50	15.75	22.25	1.69	1.57	0.70

Fig. 4. A summary of the results of Fig. 3. The factor of RaPiD area is separated into total factor, and the factor of the routing area only.

We also compared the areas and track counts between the different routing generation algorithms. We expected that the *Greedy Histogram* method, because it does not require as much regularity as the other algorithms, would perform best in terms of track count and area. In some cases, however, *Greedy Histogram* in fact had the *highest* area of the three algorithms. We feel that this is because in the *Greedy Histogram* algorithm we are really only looking at one signal length at a time, and not considering how signals of multiple lengths can use wires on a single track. These results indicate that the algorithm needs refinement.

The remaining two algorithms have similar area results in general. We expected, however, for the *Add Max Once* algorithm, which in all cases generated more distance routing tracks than *Add Min Loop*, to have higher area results than *Add Min Once*. One case in particular explains why this is not actually the case. For the All Matrix Mult application set the routing area for *Add Min Loop* in this case is actually 27% larger than the *Add Max Once* results with a higher proportion of distance tracks. The root cause of this area jump is actually the multiplexer height required for the track count. These multiplexers increase the total height of the architecture by a somewhat small amount, but this amount multiplied by the width of the architecture is quite significant. Multiplexer size is therefore of more import to area results than the number of bus connectors. Bus connectors do affect the area to some degree, as can be seen by the All FIR results, just not as much as multiplexer size.

Finally, we note that the track count generated by our three different routing generation algorithms is generally within a factor of two of our unrealistic lower bound. Especially in the case of *Add Max Once* and *Add Min Loop*, which require a great deal of routing regularity that we would normally feel would move the results away from the bound. We find this fact to be very encouraging.

A custom hand-designed routing structure by a knowledgeable designer will likely require less area than our generated results in most cases. However, we showed that our generated architectures, even with larger routing structures, are at least comparable to (and for these tests, better than) the custom-designed reconfigurable hardware when potential logic savings is considered. We indicate that the quality of the generated results is quite reasonable even for the cases where the benchmarks can in fact be implemented on a pre-defined RaPiD structure. Furthermore, the fact that some of the benchmark sets would not fit on the fixed RaPiD structure further justifies the assertion that different reconfigurable architectures may be needed depending on the targeted applications. For this case, automatic design tools can provide a fast and efficient solution.

Flexibility

In addition to comparing our algorithms in terms of area and track count, we have also evaluated the flexibility of the architectures that they generate. The tests in this section involve examining architectures that were designed for one benchmark or benchmark set, and attempting to place and route, using our initial place and route tool [2], a different benchmark onto that architecture. The results for these tests are shown in Fig. 5. Here we take each benchmark set used in the previous table of results, and attempt to route all 26 of our benchmarks netlists to the generated architectures. If a benchmark failed placement and/or routing, we also examined versions of the architectures created with a percentage-based increase in logic resources, as indicated in the table.

Naturally, the larger benchmarks tended to generate architectures more capable of implementing the other benchmarks. For example, the Digital Camera application and the minimal Image Processing Library were able to implement far more benchmarks than the All Matrix Multiply or All Sort benchmark sets. The All Sort benchmark set has the added difficulty that absolutely no multiplier units were required by the benchmarks used to create the architectures. Therefore, increasing the logic on a percentage scale does not introduce any multipliers. All benchmarks that "fail" to place and route onto this architecture require at least one multiplier.

In many cases, increasing the logic to the point where a benchmark could be placed also enabled for routing onto the architecture. However, one of the FIR filter benchmarks will place onto the All Matrix Mult architecture generated by the *Greedy Histogram* method with no additional logic resources, but will fail to route. Increasing the logic by 10% allows the circuit instances to be placed in a more routable fashion. Both *Add Max Once* and *Add Min Loop* create distributed routing structures, which may contribute to their ability to implement this benchmark without an increase in logic.

	Radar			Camera			OFDM			Image			DCT/FFT			FIR			Matrix			All Sort		
	GH	AMO	AML	GH	AMO	AML	GH	AMO	AML	GH	AMO	AML	GH	AMO	AML	GH	AMO	AML	GH	AMO	AML	GH	AMO	AML
SRC	3	3	3	3	3	3	2	2	2	5	5	5	3	3	3	6	6	6	5	5	5	4	4	4
0	8	8	8	18	18	18	16	16	16	11	11	11	9	9	9	5	5	5	3	4	4	1	1	1
10	0	0	0	2	2	2	1	1	1	4	4	4	0	0	0	7	7	7	1	0	0	0	0	0
20	0	0	0	1	1	1	0	0	0	0	0	0	3	3	3	0	0	0	0	0	0	0	0	0
Fail	15	15	15	2	2	2	7	7	7	6	6	6	11	11	11	8	8	8	17	17	17	21	21	21

Fig. 5. Flexibility study of the generated architectures. All 26 available benchmarks were tested on all architectures. When necessary, we increase the logic in the architecture on a % basis to attempt to fit the benchmark. The rows of this table indicate how many benchmarks are source netlists for the architectures (SRC), how many will P&R based on a percent increase in logic (0%, 10%, or 20% increase), and how many will fail altogether.

Conclusions

Because of its flexibility and ability to run applications in hardware instead of software, reconfigurable hardware is well-suited for use on Systems-on-a-Chip (SoCs). Although a generic architecture, such as pre-existing FPGA tiles, could be used, the fact that the SoC will be custom fabricated opens the door to another possibility: customized reconfigurable logic. However, the cost in terms of design time and effort to create a new reconfigurable architecture for each type of SoC would be prohibitive. The Totem Project seeks to solve this problem by automating the process of custom reconfigurable architecture creation in order to quickly and easily provide reconfigurable structures for use in systems-on-a-chip.

Our previous work produced a tool that could generate architectures with the minimum amount of flexibility required for the maximum amount of hardware-reuse across benchmark circuits. This resulted in a very ASIC-like architecture, with no real flexibility for future upgrades or changes. The work presented in this paper shifted the focus to the automatic generation of more flexible architectures, concentrating on routing architectures for RaPiD-style 1D reconfigurable architectures.

Using our architecture generation tool, we can provide a custom reconfigurable architecture targeted to specific netlists that uses just over 2/3 of the area of a RaPiD implementation on average. Despite the fact that RaPiD is an efficient architecture targeted to DSP in general, in some cases our generated architectures are even less than half the required RaPiD area. These improvements are due to the automatic customization of reconfigurable architectures according to the actual needs of the netlists that will be used. We have also shown that even with these area savings, we are able to generate routing architectures flexible enough to handle changes to the application netlists, as well as different netlists entirely. Researchers are only beginning to explore this area of study. Our future work will expand our efforts even further, considering algorithm improvements, additional algorithms, and other issues aimed at producing efficient flexible architectures automatically.

Acknowledgements

Thanks to the members of the RaPiD group who provided tools, layouts and particularly advice. Katherine Compton is supported by a UPR grant from Motorola, Inc. Scott Hauck is supported in part by an NSF CAREER Award and a Sloan Research Fellowship. The overall Totem effort is support by grants from NSF.

References

[1] S. Phillips, S. Hauck, "Automatic Layout of Domain-Specific Reconfigurable Subsystems for System-on-a-Chip", *ACM/SIGDA Symposium on Field-Programmable Gate Arrays*, 2002.

[2] A. Sharma, "Development of a Place and Route Tool for the RaPiD Architecture", *Master's Project, University of Washington*, December 2002.

[3] D. C. Cronquist, P. Franklin, S.G. Berg, C. Ebeling, "Specifying and Compiling Applications for RaPiD", *IEEE Symposium on FPGAs for Custom Computing Machines*, 1998.

[4] D. C. Cronquist, P. Franklin, C. Fisher, M. Figueroa, C. Ebeling, "Architecture Design of Reconfigurable Pipelined Datapaths", *Twentieth Anniversary Conference on Advanced Research in VLSI*, 1999.

[5] M. Scott, "The RaPiD Cell Structure", *Personal Communications*, 2001.

[6] K. Compton, S. Hauck, "Totem: Custom Reconfigurable Array Generation", *IEEE Symposium on FPGAs for Custom Computing Machines*, 2001.

iPACE-V1: A Portable Adaptive Computing Engine for Real Time Applications*

Jawad Khan, Manish Handa, and Ranga Vemuri

Department of ECECS, University of Cincinnati, Cincinnati, OH 45221-0030
{jkhan, mhanda, ranga}@ececs.uc.edu

Abstract. The iPACE-V1 (Image Processing Adaptive Computing Engine) is a portable, reconfigurable hardware platform, designed for real time, in-field image processing applications. IPACE-V1 has ample memory and the capability of full or partial reconfiguration without the need of a host computer. This paper describes the architecture of the hardware board along with the software design environment. We shall also discuss a real-time background elimination application for video images implemented on iPACE-V1.

1 Introduction

Adaptive or Reconfigurable Computers (RC) are those that can be programmed to change their hardware configuration and functionality dynamically to suit the application at hand; Field Programmable Gate Arrays (FPGA) are an essential building block of such systems. During the past few years RC systems have reached a remarkable level of maturity [3]. Several commercial and research platforms have been realized; WILDSTAR [1], SLAAC [4] and Rapid [5] are some of the well known reconfigurable platforms available now. However, none of these systems appear to be readily portable: All of them seem to require a host computer that is responsible for configuration of the processing elements and management of input and output data. Since reconfigurable architectures are particularly well suited for applications with repeated compute intensive operations, it is natural to use this technology for image processing applications, [2, 11] which are characterized by a large number of such operations.

We have developed a portable reconfigurable hardware platform, iPACE-V1, along with a CAD environment. Some of the main features of iPACE-V1 are Xilinx Virtex FPGAs, a large memory to capture and store raw image data, standalone dynamic full/partial reconfiguration and portability. We shall demonstrate that iPACE-V1 can achieve significant speedup for compute intensive applications in general and image processing applications in particular. iPACE-V1 can be used to implement in-field face recognition or on-the-go finger print analysis for law enforcement or military applications.

* This work is sponsered by The Dayton Area Graduate Studies Institute (DAGSI) and The Air Force Research Laboratory(AFRL) Research Program under contract number IF-UC-00-07.

M. Glesner, P. Zipf, and M. Renovell (Eds.): FPL 2002, LNCS 2438, pp. 69–78, 2002.

The rest of this paper is organized as follows. Section 2 describes unique features of iPACE-V1 and its architecture. Section 3 discusses the software design flow. In Section 4 we describe a real-time background elimination algorithm implemented on iPACE-V1 to demonstrate its usefulness. We discuss the results in Section 5 and finally, in Section 6 we discuss ongoing work and enhancements.

2 iPACE-V1 Architecture

Some of the currently available RC platforms that can be used for in-field applications, can be described as reconfigurable accelerators that need a host CPU to configure and use them [7, 6, 5, 1, 4]. The CPU to RC board communication is done through a peripheral bus such as PCI (Peripheral Component Interconnect)[10, 1, 4] and the processor-RC communication speed is limited by the effective bandwidth of the peripheral bus. Also a CPU based system tagging along with the RC accelerator makes it cumbersome for portable applications. These boards do not provide mechanisms to achieve partial reconfiguration without a host CPU [1, 4, 5]. iPACE-V1 has some features that make it unique among the line of existing RC boards, which we shall discuss now.

2.1 Design Goals

We developed iPACE-V1 with these design goals in mind:

1. *Dynamic Reconfiguration:* iPACE-V1 has the capability of full and partial dynamic reconfiguration without the need of a host computer. The debug FPGA can program the Main FPGA via the SelectMap Port at anytime during the application execution. The SelectMap port is retained after the Main FPGA is configured and hence we can read back the state of the FPGA too. Two different kinds of memories are provided to store several different configuration bit streams, that can be programmed one after the other. Xilinx XC18V04 serial PROMs provide a simple JTAG based programming solution and the larger 2Mbyte FLASH PROM is used as a configuration cache for several design bit streams.
2. *Portability:* iPACE-V1 is a small board measuring just 6 x 9 inches. All the necessary logic and memory is provided on this eight layer PCB, with components on the both, top and bottom layers. A small battery provides power for this system, which makes it portable. An LCD screen with a touch pad is interfaced, which provides the necessary I/O capabilities; obliterating the need of a bulky CRT monitor and a keyboard. An onboard color camera provides image data frames.
3. *Real-time Video Processing:* The iPACE-V1 has a fast SDRAM (Synchronous Dynamic Random Access Memory) connector, which can have SDRAM DIMMs upto a GigaByte; This memory is large enough to hold several image frames. The SDRAM can run upto 133MHz, therefore, providing a very fast and cheap storage area for data intensive applications. Along with the

SDRAM, the board has 4Mbytes of Zero Bus turnaround (ZBT) SRAM that has the unique feature of having no dead cycles between read and write cycles, therefore improving the effective throughput of the system. This memory can be used as a scratch pad area for storing intermediate values in a computation.

4. *Debug Support:* iPACE-V1 provides excellent debug facilities. A debug environment [14] is being developed targeted exclusively for this board, as a part of this project. We can read and write to any memory in the system. The clock is programmable and can be run in step mode as well. FPGA read-back is available through the retained SelectMap port.
5. *Interface to existing PC Platforms:* Virtex FPGAs are large enough to house a CPU softcore should the need for a processor based computing paradigm arise. However, we provide two mechanisms for interfacing existing PC platforms to iPACE-V1: An RS232 port is available along with a USB port for weak coupling of a processor board with iPACE-V1. For a more tighter coupling, an industry standard PC104 bus is provided.

2.2 Architecture Details

We present iPACE-V1 performance numbers in Table 1. Figure 1 shows the six basic modules of iPACE-V1 and their relationships to each other. Figure 2 illustrates a more detailed system architecture and finally, Figure 3 is a photograph of the actual board. The Basic modules of iPACE-V1 are explained below:

Main Processing Element	XCV 800 Virtex(upgradable)
Maximum Usable Gates	800,000(upgradable)
Programmable Clock Range	138 KHz - 100 MHz
Maximum Clock Frequency	200 MHz
Maximum ZBT SRAM Capacity	4 Mbytes
Maximum ZBT Bandwidth	400 Mbytes / sec
Maximum SDRAM Capacity	1 Gbytes
Maximum SDRAM Bandwidth	114 Mbytes / sec
Maximum FLASH ROM	4 Mbytes
Maximum Dynamic Reconfiguration Rate	400 Mbits / sec

Table 1. *iPACE-V1 Performance Numbers*

The *Debug Module* is responsible for bringing up the system to a known state at start up. It is housed in a XCV50 Virtex FPGA, which is referred to as Debug FPGA in this paper. This module is made up of several controller cores such as the programmable clock core and the configuration core etc.

The *Data Capture Module* is responsible for the initialization of the camera module or any other image acquisition device on board. Once the camera is programmed, this module can start capturing the data and dumping it in the

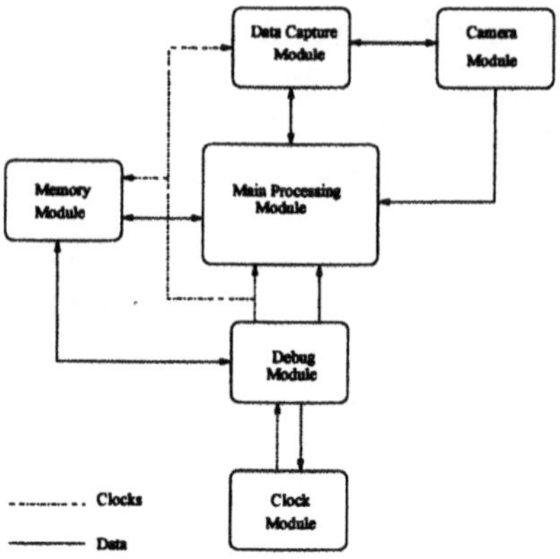

Fig. 1. iPACE-V1 Top Level Hardware Architecture

SDRAM. The data capture module is mapped to a XCV50 Virtex FPGA, which we will refer to as SDRAM FPGA.

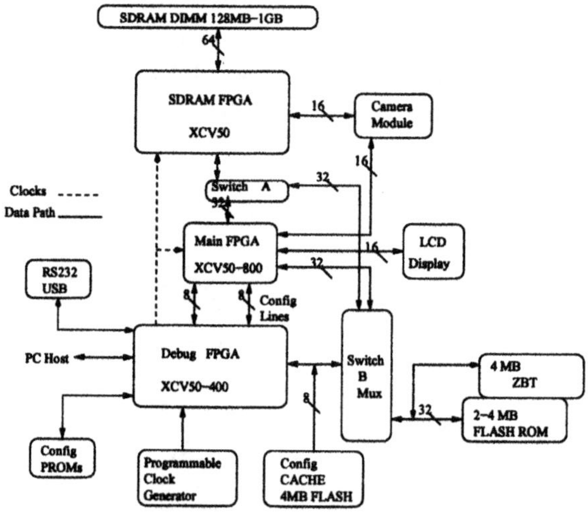

Fig. 2. iPACE-V1 Detailed Architecture

The *Main Processing Module* is the actual workhorse of the system. It can be mapped to any Virtex FPGA ranging from XCV50 (50,000 Gates) to XCV800 (800,000 Gates) [9]. In the current configuration we have a XCV300 FPGA (300,000 Gates). This is called the Main FPGA. The user design is targeted to this module. This module is directly connected to the Data Capture Module for using the data stored in the SDRAM. Further, it is connected to the Memory Module that contains ZBT SRAM and the FLASH PROM. Should the user need to work on the streaming video data without the need to capture it, we have provided a direct link from the camera to the Main FPGA. Sixteen general-purpose input/output lines are provided for interfacing an I/O device to this module. Currently we have a 320x240 LCD (Liquid Crystal Display) unit interfaced to the system.

The *Memory Module* contains the ZBT SRAM and the FLASH PROM, that are accessible from the main FPGA. A switch has been provided which transfers control to the Debug FPGA, to examine the contents of these memories for debugging purpose. In the current configuration, the data path width is 32 bits.

The *Clock Module* consists of a reference crystal oscillator and a programmable clock chip. The programmable clock chip can provide clock with frequencies in the range of 380 KHz up to 100 MHz. The resultant synthesized clock is fed to the Debug FPGA, which provides two final clocks MCLK and PCLK for the system. MCLK is the clock going to the Memory Module as well as to the other two FPGAs and the PCLK is processing clock, which is available to the other FPGAs exclusively.

The *Camera Module* has an OV7620 color camera chip by OmniVision Technologies Inc. This is a 640 X 480 interlaced/progressive scan CMOS digital color camera. This camera supports YCrCb 4:2:2 16 bit or 8 bit format, ZV port output format, RGB raw data format, CCIR601 and CCIR656 formats.

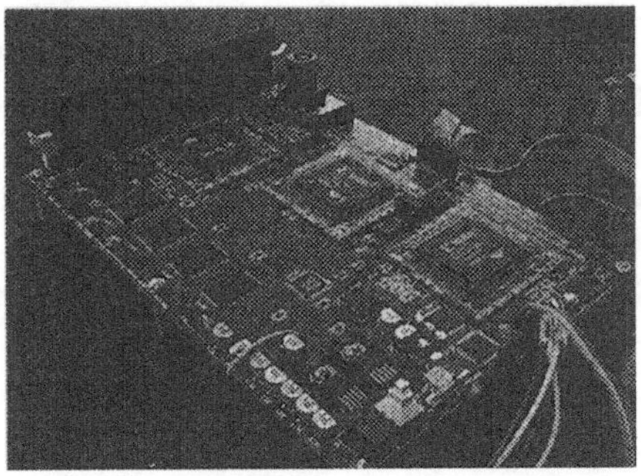

Fig. 3. iPACE-V1 Photograph

3 iPACE-V1 Software Design Environment

An integrated design environment has been developed to map an application to iPACE-V1. The software allows designs to be specified at the behavioral level of abstraction. Further, this environment takes advantage of partial reconfiguration capabilities of Virtex FPGA.

In a conventional FPGA design flow placement and routing of a netlist with a large number of nodes is a time consuming process. Additionally, it is very difficult to find correspondence between signal names in the high level description

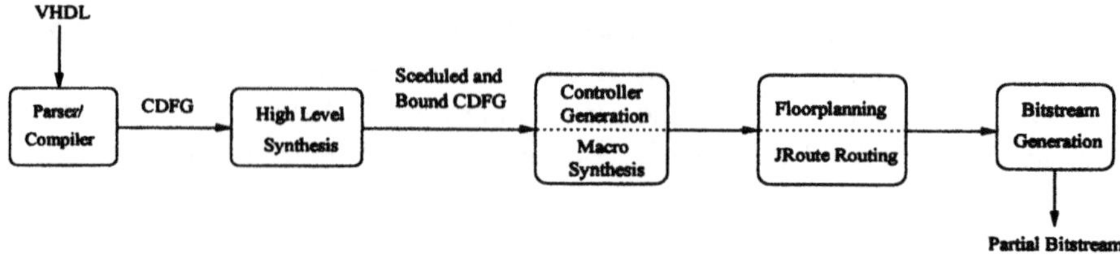

Fig. 4. iPACE-V1 Design Flow

and the signal names in the gate level netlist. We have proposed and implemented a methodology which uses macro synthesis. No logic synthesis is performed on the data path of the design as it is done in a conventional design flow. Macro netlist has a small number of nodes as compared to those of a gate level netlist. Therefore, placement and routing is much faster.

Our design environment is shown in Figure 4. An application is specified using a subset of hardware description language VHDL. We use Asserta [13] for high level synthesis [12]. Scheduled and bound CDFG (control flow data flow graph) is represented in SBlox [15]; SBlox is an uninterpreted operation sequence specification language for high level synthesis systems. SBlox representation specifies the task with a single thread of control. We generate the controller from the information specified implicitly in SBlox. Macro synthesis and interconnect generation is performed on the SBlox representation. Then, the operations in the SBlox descriptions are mapped to the macros specified in the macro library and inter-macro interconnect is generated. Also, the data path and control path macros are mapped to a JBits [8] based macro library: These macros are parameterized and relationally placed and routed. Floorplanning is performed on these macros and these are placed onto a two dimensional grid representing the FPGA. Finally, partial bitstreams are generated.

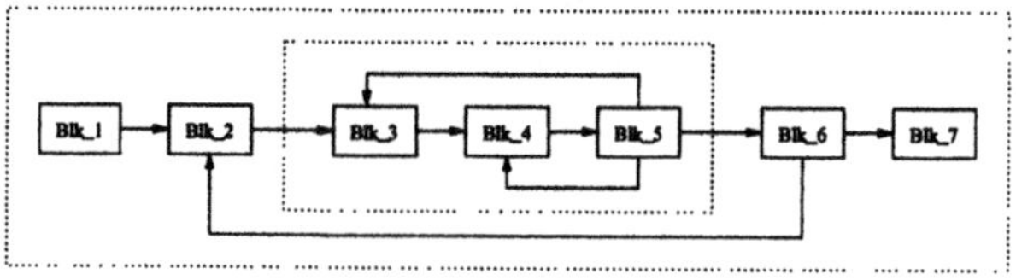

Fig. 5. Basic block partitioning and clustering

Any given task is partitioned into basic blocks, as shown in figure 5. Basic blocks are the entities that are responsible for computation or interaction with environment using ports. Conditional and unconditional control transfer and clustering of the blocks can be done depending upon resources available in the FGPGA. Partial bitstreams are generated for these clusters and the FPGA is configured using these bitstreams.

4 Case Study: Real Time Video Background Elimination

The problem of background elimination [16] can be defined in broad terms as determining whether each pixel in the image belongs to foreground or background and then displaying the pixels on the foreground only and removing the background pixels. This is a very compute intensive application, if done in real-time; It involves several matrix multiplications and matrix inverse calculations. We have implemented this algorithm to demonstrate two things: to show functional correctness of the board and to illustrate its usefulness for image processing in general.

4.1 Algorithm Description

Consider an m x n image. Each pixel in the image has a color value as given by the equation 1.

$$x = (R, G, B)^T \tag{1}$$

In this algorithm, the color of each pixel is assumed to have a normal distribution. We build a background model which consists of the mean value and the covariance matrix for each pixel of a given frame. A few initial frames are analyzed that are known to have only background in them for building the background model. Then the problem of detecting the foreground and the background is reduced to finding the Mahalanobis Distance of every pixel from this model and checking whether it is greater than or less than a given threshold value. If it is greater than the threshold then it is foreground, otherwise, it is background. We now provide the mathematical basis for this algorithm.

4.2 Building the Model

For a given set of k frames that are known to have only background in them, we compute the mean and the covariance of the color at every pixel.

Mean is given by:

$$\mu = 1/k \sum_k x_k \tag{2}$$

Covariance is given by:

$$\Delta = 1/k \sum_k (x_k - \mu_k)(x_k - \mu_k)^T \tag{3}$$

Mean of each pixel is a 3x1 vector and covariance is a 3x3 matrix. After the background model is made we acquire a new image for which we wish to subtract the background. For each frame, we find the Mahalanobis distance of every pixel. That is, for every pixel we compute:

$$d = (x - \mu)^T \Delta^{-1} (x - \mu) \tag{4}$$

If $d > T$ (some threshold), then we mark this pixel as foreground otherwise mark it as background. T is usually in the range of 20-100. We chose a value of 45 for the results presented in this paper. For those pixels in which inverse of the covariance matrix does not exist, we replace the covariance matrix with a 3x3 identity matrix; This, in turn, amounts to just calculation of the Euclidean Distance for that particular pixel.

4.3 Real Time Implementation

For this implementation we chose a frame size of 314 x 208 and a frame rate of 30 frames per second. This algorithm can be divided into two parts: model building and d-Value calculation.

In the first part we analyze 64 frames and keep on updating the mean and covariance values for every pixel in the frame. This operation requires matrix multiplication in (3) and also addition of the result to the previously stored value for each particular pixel. For matrix- multiplication, we instantiate four fast parallel multiplier cores. This allows us to unroll the matrix-multiplication loop in time and in space. As a final step we calculate the inverse of the covariance matrices for each pixel using a similar loop unrolling. We then go on to the second partition of the design in which we analyze any given input frame using this model at runtime and calculate the Mahalanobis distance for every pixel and classify it as foreground or background. This operation entails three matrix-multiplications which are done in a similar fashion. The camera pixel rate is 32bits/296ns where every pixel has 24 bits with 8 bits for each Red, Green and Blue color. This application executes at 27MHz inside the FPGA. The d-value calculation is done in a pipelined fashion and it takes about 7 cycles per pixel, therefore, the system is well within the real-time constraint.

5 Results

We present the preliminary results in Table 2, where we compare the results of the application executing on iPACE-V1 with a similarly coded application in MATLAB. The MATLAB code was running on a Pentium III at 1GHz with 256Mbytes of memory. We are getting a speedup factor of about 8 in the model building part and a speedup factor of about 113 in the d-value calculation part. The reason of disparity between the two is that the model building part is not designed to match the frame rate, since it is only a one-time operation. However, the d-value calculation is done at the frame rate and the result is a significant improvement. Figure 6 shows the background image in the first row, some objects in front of the background are shown in the second row and the last row shows the final background eliminated images[1]. Note that in the background eliminated images some area in the shadow of the object is also detected, albeit incorrectly, as foreground; This is a known limitation of the algorithm used.

[1] These are all color images

	MATLAB (Execution time in sec.)	iPACE-V1 (Execution Time in sec.)	Speedup
Model Building (64 frames)	11.81	1.41	8.34
d-value calculation (per frame)	2.22	0.012	113.60

Table 2. Table of Results

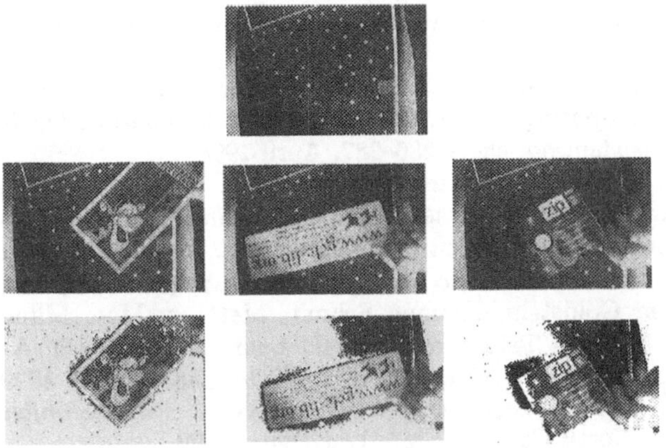

Fig. 6. Images with and without background

6 Conclusion and Ongoing Work

We have provided portability and all the necessary system resources on one RC board, which does not require a host computer to configure itself. We have also presented a software design flow for this system. A case study demonstrates the suitabiilty of this system for image processing applications. We are currently working on iPACE-V2 which will have Xilinx Virtex II platform FPGAs and better memory bandwidth than iPACE-V1. Some other demonstration applications are also underdevelopment.

7 Acknowledgments

We are grateful to Dr. Karen Tomko and Dr. Jack Jeans whose positive criticism of the board was a tremendous help in the design evolution process. We thank Ms. Kerry Hill, Al Scarpelli and Frank Scarpino for their support. Thanks go to Sohaib Khan, at University of Central Florida, Orlando, for help with background elimination application. Special mention must be made of Anna Acevedo in Xilinx Inc., Corninna Provant in Micron Technologies, and people in Texas Instruments, Maxim, Analog Devices and IDT who made the generous donations of IC parts on behalf of their companies.

References

[1] Inc. Annapolis Micro Systems. Wildstar Reference Manual. In *http://www.annapmicro.com/*, 2000.
[2] P. Athanas and A. Abbott. Image Processing on a Custom Computing Platform. In *4th International Workshop on FieldProgrammable Logic and Applications*, pages 156–167, September 1994.
[3] K. Compton and S. Hauck. Reconfigurable Computing: A Survey of Systems and Software, 2000.
[4] S. P. Crago, B. Schott, and R. Parker. SLAAC : A Distributed Architecture for Adaptive Computing. In *FPGA for Custom Computin Machines, Proceedings, IEEE Symposium on*, pages 286–287, April 1998.
[5] C. Fisher, K Rennie, G. Xing, S. G. Berg, K. Bolding, J. Naegle, D. Parshall, D. Portnov, A. Sulejmanpasic, and C. Ebeling. An Emulator for Exploring RaPiD Configurable Computing Architectures. In *11th International Conference on FieldProgrammable Logic and Applications*, pages 17–26, August 2001.
[6] Seth Copen Goldstein, Herman Schmit, Matthew Moe, Mihai Budiu, Srihari Cadambi, R. Reed Taylor, and Ronald Laufer. PipeRench: A Coprocessor for Streaming Multimedia Acceleration. In *ISCA*, pages 28–39, 1999.
[7] John Reid Hauser. *Augmenting a Microprocessor with Reconfigurable Hardware.* PhD thesis, North Carolina State University, 2000.
[8] Xilinx Inc. JBits Reference Manual Release 2.8. http://www.xilinx.com/products/jbits, 2001.
[9] Xilinx Inc. The Programmable Logic Data Book. www.xilinx.com, 2001.
[10] Ronald Laufer, R. Reed Taylor, and Herman Schmit. PCI-PipeRench and the SwordAPI: A system for stream-based reconfigurable computing. In Kenneth L. Pocek and Jeffrey Arnold, editors, *IEEE Symposium on FPGAs for Custom Computing Machines*, pages 200–208, Los Alamitos, CA, 1999. IEEE Computer Society Press.
[11] A. Lecerf, F. Vachon, D. Ouellet, and M. Arias-Estrada. FPGA based Computer Vision Camera. In *Proceedings of the 1999 ACM/SIGDA seventh international symposium on Field programmable gate arrays*, page 248. ACM Press, 1999.
[12] Giovanni De Micheli. *Synthesis and Optimization of Digital Circuits.* McGraw-Hill, Inc., 1994.
[13] N. Narasimhan. *Formal Synthesis: Formal Assertions Based Verification in aHigh-Level Synthesis System.* PhD thesis, University of Cincinnati, 1998.
[14] K. A. Tomko and A. Tiwari. Hardware/Software Co-debugging for Reconfigurable Computing. In *IEEE International High Level Design Validation and Test workshop*, November 2000.
[15] Ranga Vemuri and Rajesh Radhakrishan. SBlox: A Language for Digital System Synthesis. Technical Report No. 258/05/01/ECECS, University of Cincinnati, 2000.
[16] Christopher Wren, Ali Azarbayejani, Trevor Darrell, and Alex Pentland. Pfinder: Real-Time Tracking of the Human Body. In *IEEE Transactions on Pattern Analysis and Machine Intelligence*, pages 780–785, July 1997.

Field-Programmable Custom Computing Machines – A Taxonomy –

Mihai Sima[1,2], Stamatis Vassiliadis[1], Sorin Cotofana[1], Jos T.J. van Eijndhoven[2], and Kees Vissers[3]

[1] Delft University of Technology, Department of Electrical Engineering, PO Box 5031, Mekelweg 4, 2600 GA Delft, The Netherlands, {M.Sima,S.Vassiliadis,S.Cotofana}@et.tudelft.nl

[2] Philips Research Laboratories, Department of Information and Software Technology, Box WDCp-045, Professor Holstlaan 4, 5656 AA Eindhoven, The Netherlands, jos.van.eijndhoven@philips.com

[3] TriMedia Technologies, Inc., 1840 McCarthy Boulevard, Sunnyvale, CA 95035, U.S.A., kees.vissers@trimedia.com

Abstract. The ability for providing a hardware platform which can be customized on a per-application basis under software control has established *Reconfigurable Computing* ($\mathcal{RC}$) as a new computing paradigm. A machine employing the $\mathcal{RC}$ paradigm is referred to as a *Field-Programmable Custom Computing Machine* (FCCM). So far, the FCCMs have been classified according to implementation criteria. For the previous classifications do not reveal the entire meaning of the $\mathcal{RC}$ paradigm, we propose to classify the FCCMs according to architectural criteria. To analyze the phenomena inside FCCMs, we introduce a formalism based on microcode, in which any custom operation performed by a field-programmed computing facility is executed as a microprogram with two basic stages: `SET CONFIGURATION` and `EXECUTE CUSTOM OPERATION`. Based on the `SET/EXECUTE` formalism, we then propose an architectural-based taxonomy of FCCMs.

1 Introduction

The ability of providing a hardware platform which can be transformed under software control has established *Reconfigurable Computing* ($\mathcal{RC}$) [28], [42], [29] as a new computing paradigm in the last ten years. According to this paradigm, the main idea in improving the performance of a computing machine is to define custom computing resources on a per-application basis, and to dynamically configure them onto a *Field-Programmable Gate Array* (FPGA) [11]. As a general view, a computing machine working under the new $\mathcal{RC}$ paradigm typically includes a *General-Purpose Processor* (GPP) which is augmented with an FPGA. The basic idea is to exploit both the GPP flexibility to achieve medium performance for a large class of applications, and FPGA capability to implement application-specific computations. Such a hybrid is referred to as a *Field-Programmable Custom Computing Machine* (FCCM) [7], [16].

Various FCCMs have been proposed in the last decade. Former attempts in classifying FCCMs used implementation criteria [15], [31], [26], [47], [23], [38]. As the user observes only the architecture of a computing machine [4], the previous classifications do not seize well the implications of the new $\mathcal{RC}$ paradigm as perceived

M. Glesner, P. Zipf, and M. Renovell (Eds.): FPL 2002, LNCS 2438, pp. 79–88, 2002.

by the user. For this reason, we propose to classify the FCCMs according to architectural criteria. In order to analyze the phenomena inside FCCMs, yet without reference to a particular instruction set, we introduce a formalism based on microcode, in which any task (operation) to be performed by a field-programmable computing facility models its execution pattern on that of a microprogrammed sequence with two basic stages: `SET CONFIGURATION`, and `EXECUTE CUSTOM OPERATION`. The net effect of this approach is to allow a view on an FCCM at the level defined by the reference of the user, i.e., the architectural level, decoupled from lower implementation and realization hierarchical levels. The reader may note the similarity between the preceding formalism and the *requestor/server* formalism of Flynn [13]. Based on the `SET/EXECUTE` formalism, we propose an architectural-based taxonomy of FCCMs.

The paper is organized as follows. For background purpose, we present the most important issues related to microcode in Section 2, and the basic concepts concerning SRAM-based FPGAs in Section 3. Section 4 introduces a formalism by which the FCCM architectures can be analyzed from the microcode point of view, and Section 5 presents the architectural-based taxonomy of FCCMs. Section 6 concludes the paper.

2 The Microcode Concept

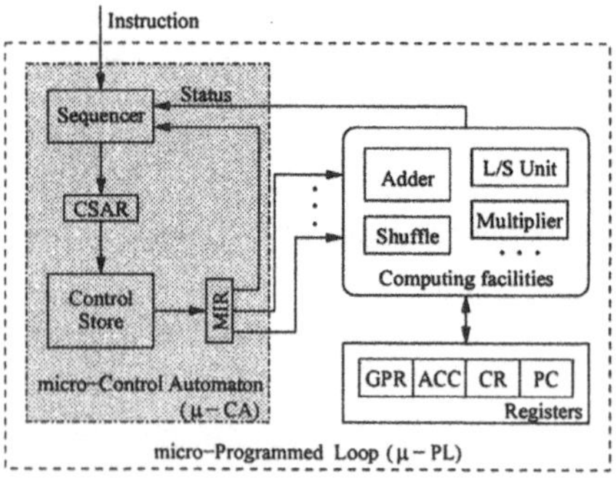

Fig. 1. The basic microprogrammed computer

Figure 1 depicts the organization of a microprogrammed computer as it is described in [32]. In the figure, the following acronyms were used: GPR – General Purpose Registers, ACC – Accumulator, CR – Control Registers, and PC – Program Counter. For such a computer, a microprogram in *Control Store* (CS) is associated with each incoming instruction. This microprogram is to be executed under the control of the *Sequencer*, as follows:

1. The sequencer maps the incoming instruction code into a control store address, and stores this address into the *Control Store Address Register* (CSAR).
2. The microinstruction addressed by CSAR is read from CS into the *MicroInstruction Register* (MIR).
3. The microoperations specified by the microinstruction in MIR are decoded, and the control signals are subsequently generated.
4. The computing resources perform the computation according to control signals.
5. The sequencer uses status information generated by the computing facilities and some information originating from MIR to prepare the address of the next microinstruction. This address is then stored into CSAR.
6. If an *end-of-operation* microinstruction is detected, a jump is executed to a instruction fetch microsubroutine. At the end of this microsubroutine, the new incoming instruction initiates a new cycle of the microprogrammed loop.

The microinstructions may be classified by the number of controlled resources. Given a hardware implementation which provides a number of computing resources (facilities), the amount of explicitly controlled resources during the same time unit (cycle) determines the verticality or horizontality of the microcode as follows:

- **A microinstruction which controls multiple resources in one cycle is *horizontal*.**
- **A microinstruction which controls a single resource is *vertical*.**

Let us assume we have a *Computing Machine* (CM) and its instruction set. An *implementation* of the CM can be formalized by means of the doublet:

$$\mathrm{CM} = \{\mu P\,,\, \mathcal{R}\} \tag{1}$$

where μP is the microprogram which includes all the microroutines for implementing the instruction set, and $\mathcal{R}$ is the set of N *computing (micro-)resources* or *facilities* which are controlled by the microinstructions in the microprogram:

$$\mathcal{R} = \{r_1\,,\, r_2\,,\, \ldots\,,\, r_N\} \tag{2}$$

Let us assume the computing resources are hardwired. If the microcode[1] is exposed to the *user*, i.e., the instruction set is composed of microinstructions, there is no way to adapt the architecture to application but by custom-redesigning the computing facilities set, $\mathcal{R}$. When the microcode is not exposed to the *user*, i.e., a microroutine is associated with each instruction, then the architecture can be adapted by rewriting the microprogram μP.

Since the architecture of the vertical microinstructions associated with hardwired computing facilities is fixed, the adaptation procedure by rewriting the microprogram has a limited efficiency: a new instruction is created by threading the operations of fixed (i.e., inflexible) computing facilities rather than generating a full-custom one.

If the resources themselves are microcoded, the formalism recursively propagates to lower levels. Therefore, the implementation of each resource can be viewed as a doublet composed of a *nanoprogram* (nP) and a *nano-resource set* ($n\mathcal{R}$):

$$r_i = \{nP\,,\, n\mathcal{R}\}\,, \quad i = 1, 2, \ldots, N \tag{3}$$

Now it is the rewriting of the nanocode which is limited by the fixed set of nano-resources.

The presence of the reconfigurable hardware opens up new ways to adapt the architecture. Assuming the resources are implemented on a programmable array, adapting the resources to the application is entire flexible and can be performed on-line. In this situation, the resource set $\mathcal{R}$ metamorphoses into a new one, $\mathcal{R}^*$:

$$\mathcal{R} \longrightarrow \mathcal{R}^* = \{r_1^*\,,\, r_2^*\,,\, \ldots\,,\, r_M^*\}, \tag{4}$$

and so does the set of associated vertical microinstructions. It is obvious that writing new microprograms with application-tuned microinstructions is more effective than with fixed microinstructions.

[1] In this presentation, by *microcode* we will refer to both microinstructions and microprogram. The meaning of the microcode will become obvious from the context.

At this point, we want to stress out that the microcode is a *recursive formalism*. The *micro* and *nano* prefixes should be used against an *implementation reference level*[2] (IRL). Once such a level is set, the operations performed at this level are specified by *instructions*, and are under the explicit control of the *user*. Therefore, the operations below this level are specified by *microinstructions*, those on the subsequent level are specified by *nanoinstructions*, and so on.

3 FPGA Terminology and Concept

A device which can be configured *in the field* by the end user is usually referred to as a *Field-Programmable Device* (FPD) [11], [19], [5]. Generally speaking, the constituents of an FPD are *Raw Hardware* and *Configuration Memory*. The function performed by the raw hardware is defined by the information stored into the configuration memory.

The FPD architectures can be classified in two major classes: *Programmable Logic Devices* (PLD) and *Field-Programmable Gate Arrays* (FPGA). Details on each class can be found for example in [6]. Although both PLD and FPGA devices can be used to implement digital logic circuits, we will pre-eminently above all use the term of *FPGA* hereafter to refer to a programmable device. The higher logic capacity of FPGAs and the attempts to augment FPGAs with PLD-like programmable logic in order to make use of both FPGA and PLD characteristics, support our choice for this terminology.

Some FPGAs can be configured only once, e.g., by burning fuses. Other FPGAs can be reconfigured any number of times, since their configuration is stored in SRAM. Initially considered as a weakness due to the volatility of configuration data, the reprogramming capabilities of SRAM-based FPGAs led to the new $\mathcal{RC}$ paradigm. By reconfiguring the FPGA under software control, application-specific computing facilities can be implemented on-the-fly.

A discussion on choosing the appropriate FPGA architecture is beyond the goal of this paper. More information concerning this problem can be found for example in [19].

4 FPGA to Microcode Mapping

In this section, we will introduce a formalism by which an FCCM architecture can be analyzed from the microcode point of view. This formalism originates in the observation that every custom instruction of an FCCM can be mapped into a microprogram.

As we already mentioned, by making use of the FPGA capability to change its functionality in pursuance of a reconfiguring process, adapting both the functionality of *computing facilities* and *microprogram in the control store* to the application characteristics becomes possible with the new $\mathcal{RC}$ paradigm. For the information stored in FPGA's configuration memory determines the functionality of the raw hardware, the dynamic implementation of an instruction on FPGA can be formalized by means of a microcoded structure. Assuming the FPGA configuration memory is written under the

---

[2] If it will not be specified explicitly, the IRL will be considered as being the level defined by the instruction set. For example, although the microcode is exposed to the *user* in the RISC machines, the RISC operations are specified by *instructions*, rather than by microinstructions.

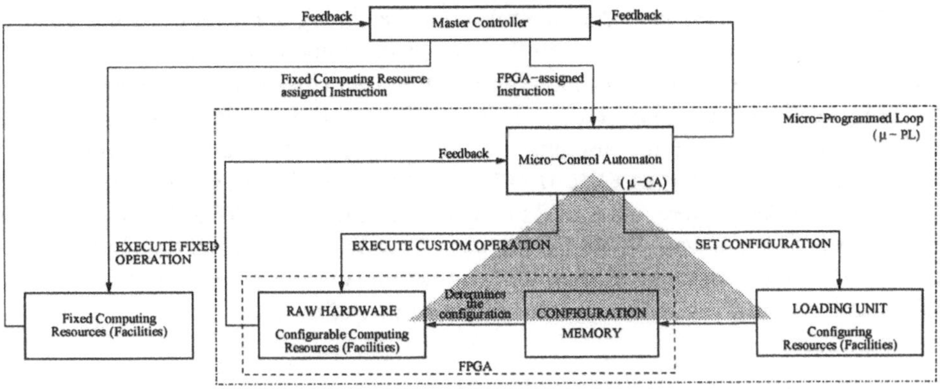

Fig. 2. The microcode concept applied to FCCMs. The Δ arrangement.

control of a *Loading Unit*, the control automaton, the FPGA, and the loading unit may have a Δ arrangement, as depicted in Figure 2. The circuits configured on the raw hardware and the loading unit(s) are all regarded as controlled resources in the proposed formalism. Each of the previously mentioned resources is given a special class of microinstructions: `SET` for the loading unit, which initiates the reconfiguration of the raw hardware, and `EXECUTE` for the circuits configured on raw hardware, which launches the custom operations.

In this way, any custom operation of an FCCM can be executed in a reconfigurable manner, in which the execution pattern models on that of a microprogrammed sequence with two basic stages: `SET CONFIGURATION`, and `EXECUTE CUSTOM OPERATION`. It is the `SET/EXECUTE` formalism we will use in building the taxonomy of FCCMs.

It is worth to specify that only `EXECUTE FIXED OPERATION` microinstructions can be associated with fixed computing facilities, because such facilities cannot be reconfigured. Also, assuming that a multiple-context FPGA [11] is used, activating an idle context is performed by an `ACTIVATE CONFIGURATION` microinstruction, which is actually a flavor of the `SET CONFIGURATION` microinstruction. In the sequel, we will refer to all loading unit(s) and resource(s) for activating the idle context as *Configuring Resources (Facilities)*.

Since an FCCM includes both computing and configuring facilities, the statement regarding the verticality or horizontality of the microcode as defined in Section 2 needs to be adjusted, as follows:

Definition 1. *For an FCCM hardware implementation which provides a number of* computing and configuring facilities, *the amount of explicitly controlled* computing and/or configuring facilities *during the same time unit (cycle) determines the verticality or horizontality of the microcode.*

Therefore, any of the `SET CONFIGURATION`, `EXECUTE CUSTOM OPERATION`, and `EXECUTE FIXED OPERATION` microinstructions can be either vertical or horizontal, and may participate in a horizontal microinstruction.

Let us set the *implementation reference level* as being the level of instructions in Figure 2. In the particular case when the microcode is not exposed to the upper level, an explicit SET instruction is not available to the *user*. Consequently, the system performs by itself the management of the active configuration, i.e., without an explicit control provided by *user*. In this case, the *user* "sees" only the FPGA-assigned instruction which can be regarded as an `EXECUTE CUSTOM OPERATION` microinstruction visible to the instruction level. Here, we would like to note that the `EXECUTE FIXED OPERATION` microinstruction is always visible to the *user*. Conversely, when the microcode is exposed to the upper level, an explicit SET instruction is available, and the management of the active configuration becomes the responsibility of the *user*.

5 A Proposed Taxonomy of FCCMs

Before introducing our taxonomy, we would like to overview the previous work in FCCM classification.

In [15] two parameters for classifying FCCMs are used: *Reconfigurable Processing Unit (RPU) size* (*small* or *large*) and *availability of RPU-dedicated local memory*. Consequently, FCCMs are divided into four classes. Since what exactly means *small* and what exactly means *large* is subject to the complexity of the algorithms being implemented, the differences between classes are rather fuzzy. Also, providing dedicated RPU memory is an issue which belongs to *implementation level* of a machine; consequently, the implications to the *architectural level*, if any, are not clear.

The *Processing Element (PE) granularity*, *RPU integration level* with a host processor, and the *reconfigurability of the external interconnection network* are used as classification criteria in [31]. According to the first criterion, the FCCMs are classified as *fine-*, *medium-*, and *coarse-grain* systems. The second criterion divides the machines into *dynamic* systems that are not controlled by external devices, *closely-coupled static* systems in which the RPUs are coupled on the processor's datapath, and *loosely-coupled static* systems that have RPUs attached to the host as coprocessors. According to the last criterion, the FCCMs have a *reconfigurable* or *fixed* interconnection network.

In order to classify the FCCMs, the *loosely coupling* versus *tightly coupling* criterion is used by other members of the FCCM community, e.g., [26], [47], [23], [38]. In the loosely coupling embodiment, the RPU is connected via a bus to, and operates asynchronously with the host processor. In the tightly coupling embodiment, the RPU is used as a *functional unit*.

We emphasize that all these taxonomies are build using *implementation* criteria. As the user observes only the architecture of a computing machine, classifying the FCCMs according to architectural criteria is more appropriate. Since FCCMs are microcoded machines, we propose to classify the FCCMs according to the following criteria:

- The verticality/horizontality of the microcode.
- The explicit availability of a SET instruction.

While the first criterion is a direct consequence of the proposed formalism, several comments regarding the second criterion are worth to be provided. An user-exposed SET instruction allows the reconfiguration management to be done explicitly in software, thus being subject to deep optimization. The drawback is that a more complex compiler is needed for scheduling the SET instruction at a proper location in time. Conversely, if SET is not exposed to the user, such management will be done in hardware. This time, the compiler is simpler, but at the expense of a higher reconfiguration penalty. With a hardware-based management, the code compatibility between FCCMs with different FPGA size and reconfiguration pattern can be preserved. Since the user has no concern about the reconfiguration, the configuration management is an implementation issue, much like the cache management in a conventional processor is.

In order to describe the classification process, several classification examples will be provided subsequently. We have to mentioned that, for each system, the IRL has been chosen such that as much FCCM-specific information as possible is revealed.

PRISC [33] is a RISC processor augmented with Programmable Functional Unit (PFU). Custom instructions can be implemented on the PFU. The specification of such instruction is done by means of a preamble to the RISC instruction format. When a custom instruction is called, the hardware is responsible for updating the PFU configuration: if a reconfiguration is needed, an exception which stalls the processor is raised, and a long latency reconfiguration process is initiated. Since the reconfiguration is not under the direct control of the user, a dedicated instruction for reconfiguration, i.e., `SET CONFIGURATION`, is not exposed to the user. Only one fixed or programmable functional unit is explicitly controlled per cycle; therefore, the microcode is *vertical*.

The *PipeRench* coprocessor [8] consists of a set of identical physical *Stripes* which can be configured under the supervision of a *Configuration Controller* at run-time. PipeRench also includes a *Configuration Memory* which stores virtual stripe configurations. A single physical stripe can be configured per cycle; therefore, the reconfiguration of a stripe takes place concurrently with execution of the other stripes. Pipelines of arbitrary length can be implemented on PipeRench. A program for this device is a chained list of configuration words, each of which includes three fields: configuration bits for each virtual pipeline stage of the application, a *next-address* field which points to the next virtual stripe, and a set of flags for the configuration controller and four *Data Controllers*. Therefore, the configuration word is a horizontal instruction. Since the configuration controller handles the multiplexing of the application's stripes onto the physical fabric, the scheduling of the stripes, and the management of the on-chip configuration memory, while the user has only to provide the chained list of the configuration words, we can conclude that there is no user-exposed SET instruction.

The (re)configuration of the Nano-Processor [46] or RaPiD [10] is initiated by a master unit at application load-time. Each system may be used, at least theoretically, in a multi-tasking environment, in which the applications are switched on or idle. Since no further details whether the user can or cannot manage the reconfiguration are given, we classify such systems as *not obvious information about an explicit* SET *instruction.*

The Colt/Wormhole FPGA [3] is an array of Reconfigurable Processing Units interconnected through a mesh network. Multiple independent streams can be injected into the fabric. Each stream contains information needed to route the stream through the fabric and to configure all RFUs along the path, as well as data to be processed. In this way, the streams are self-steering, and can simultaneously configure the fabric and initiate the computation. Therefore, SET is explicit and the microcode is horizontal.

Following the above mentioned methodology, the most well known FCCMs can be classified as follows:

1. Vertical microcoded FCCMs
   (a) With explicit SET instruction: PRISM [2], PRISM-II/RASC [43], [44], RISA′ [39], RISA″ [39], MIPS + REMARC [30], MIPS + Garp [21], OneChip-98″ [23], URISC [12], Gilson's FCCM [14], Xputer/rALU [17], Molen vertically-coded processor [41], MorphoSys system [38].
   (b) Without explicit SET instruction: PRISC [33], OneChip [47], ConCISe [25], OneChip-98′ [23], DISC [45], Multiple-RISA [40], Chimaera [20].
   (c) Not obvious information about an explicit SET instruction: Virtual Computer [9], [46], Functional Memory [27], CCSimP (load-time reconfiguration) [35], NAPA [34].
2. Horizontal microcoded FCCMs
   (a) With explicit SET instruction: CoMPARE [36], Alippi's VLIW [1], RISA‴ [39], VEGA [24], Colt/Wormhole FPGA [3], rDPA [18], FPGA-augmented TriMedia/CPU64 [37], Molen horizontally-coded processor [41].
   (b) Without explicit SET instruction: PipeRench [8].
   (c) Not obvious information about an explicit SET instruction: Spyder [22], RaPiD (load-time reconfiguration) [10].

We would like to mention that applying the classification criteria on OneChip-98 machine introduced in [23], we determined that an explicit SET instruction was not provided to the user in one embodiment of OneChip-98, while such an instruction was provided to the user in another embodiment. It seems that two architectures were claimed in the same paper. We referred to them as OneChip-98′ and OneChip-98″. The same ambiguous way to propose multiple architectures under the same name is employed in [39]. For the Reconfigurable Instruction Set Accelerator (RISA), our taxonomy provides three entries (RISA′, RISA″, RISA‴).

6 Conclusions

We proposed a classification of the FCCMs according to architectural criteria. Two classification criteria were extracted from a formalism based on microcode. In terms of the first criterion, the FCCMs were classified in vertical or horizontal microcoded machines. In terms of the second criterion, the FCCMs were classified in machines with or without an explicit SET instruction. The taxonomy we proposed is architectural consistent, and can be easily extended to embed other criteria.

References

1. C. Alippi, W. Fornaciari, L. Pozzi, and M. Sami. A DAG-Based Design Approach for Reconfigurable VLIW Processors. In *IEEE Design and Test Conference in Europe*, Munich, Germany, 1999.
2. P. Athanas and H. Silverman. Processor Reconfiguration through Instruction-Set Metamorphosis. *IEEE Computer*, 26(3):11-18, 1993.

3. R. Bittner, Jr. and P. Athanas. Wormhole Run-time Reconfiguration. In *Proc. Intl. Symp. on FPGAs*, pp. 79-85, Monterey, California, 1997.
4. G.A. Blaauw and F.P. Brooks, Jr. *Computer Architecture. Concepts and Evolution*. Addison-Wesley, Reading, Massachusetts, 1997.
5. G. Brebner. Field-Programmable Logic: Catalyst for New Computing Paradigms. In *Proc. Intl. Workshop FPL'98*, pp. 49-58, Tallin, Estonia, 1998.
6. S. Brown and J. Rose. Architecture of FPGAs and CPLDs: A Tutorial. *IEEE Transactions on Design and Test of Computers*, 13(2):42-57, 1996.
7. D.A. Buell and K.L. Pocek. Custom Computing Machines: An Introduction. *Journal of Supercomputing*, 9(3):219-230, 1995.
8. S. Cadambi et al. Managing Pipeline-Reconfigurable FPGAs. In *Proc. Intl. Symp. on FPGAs*, pp. 55-64, Monterey, California, 1998.
9. S. Casselman. Virtual Computing and the Virtual Computer. In *Proc. IEEE Workshop on FCCMs*, pp. 43-48, Napa Valley, California, 1993.
10. D. Cronquist et al. Architecture Design of Reconfigurable Pipelined Datapaths. *Advanced Research in VLSI*, pp. 23-40, 1999.
11. A. DeHon. Reconfigurable Architectures for General-Purpose Computing. A. I. 1586, Massachusetts Institute of Technology, Cambridge, Massachusetts, 1996.
12. A. Donlin. Self Modifying Circuitry - A Platform for Tractable Virtual Circuitry. In *Proc. Intl. Workshop FPL'98*, pp. 199-208, Tallin, Estonia, 1998.
13. M. J. Flynn. Some Computer Organizations and Their Effectiveness. *IEEE Transactions on Computers*, C-21(9):948-960, September 1972.
14. K.L. Gilson. Integrated Circuit Computing Device Comprising a Dynamically Configurable Gate Array Having a Microprocessor and Reconfigurable Instruction Execution Means and Method Therefor. U.S. Patent No. 5,361,373, 1994.
15. S. Guccione and M. Gonzales. Classification and Performance of Reconfigurable Architectures. In *Proc. Intl. Workshop FPL'95*, pp. 439-448, Oxford, United Kingdom, 1995.
16. R. Hartenstein, Becker, and R. Kress. Custom Computing Machines versus Hardware/Software Co-Design: From a Globalized Point of View. In *Proc. Intl. Workshop FPL'96*, pp. 65-76, Darmstadt, Germany, 1996.
17. R. Hartenstein et al. A Novel Paradigm of Parallel Computation and its Use to Implement Simple High-Performance Hardware. *Future Generation Computer Systems*, (7):181-198, 1991/1992.
18. R. Hartenstein, R. Kress, and H. Reinig. A New FPGA Architecture for Word-Oriented Datapaths. In *Proc. Intl. Workshop FPL'94*, pp. 144-155, Prague, Czech Republic, 1994.
19. S. Hauck. The Roles of FPGA's in Reprogrammable Systems. *Proc. of the IEEE*, 86(4):615-638, 1998.
20. S. Hauck, T.W. Fry, M.M. Hosler, and J.P. Kao. The Chimaera Reconfigurable Functional Unit. In *Proc. IEEE Symp. on FCCMs*, pp. 87-96, Napa Valley, California, 1997.
21. J. Hauser and J. Wawrzynek. Garp: A MIPS Processor with a Reconfigurable Coprocessor. In *Proc. IEEE Symp. on FCCMs*, pp. 12-21, Napa Valley, California, 1997.
22. C. Iseli and E. Sanchez. A Superscalar and Reconfigurable Processor. In *Proc. Intl. Workshop FPL'94*, pp. 168-174, Prague, Czech Republic, 1994.
23. J. Jacob and P. Chow. Memory Interfacing and Instruction Specification for Reconfigurable Processors. In *Proc. Intl. ACM/SIGDA Symp. on FPGAs*, pp. 145-154, Monterey, California, 1999.
24. D. Jones and D. Lewis. A Time-Multiplexed FPGA Architecture for Logic Emulation. In *Proc. IEEE CICC'95*, pp. 487-494, Santa Clara, California, 1995.
25. B. Kastrup, A. Bink, and J. Hoogerbrugge. ConCISe: A Compiler-Driven CPLD-Based Instruction Set Accelerator. In *Proc. IEEE Symp. on FCCMs*, pp. 92-100, Napa Valley, California, 1999.

26. B. Kastrup, J. van Meerbergen, and K. Nowak. Seeking (the right) Problems for the Solutions of Reconfigurable Computing. In *Proc. Intl. Workshop FPL'99*, pp. 520-525, Glasgow, Scotland, 1999.
27. A. Lew and R. Halverson, Jr. A FCCM for Dataflow (Spreadsheet) Programs. In *Proc. IEEE Symp. on FCCMs*, pp. 2-10, Napa Valley, California, 1995.
28. W. Mangione-Smith and B. Hutchings. Reconfigurable Architectures: The Road Ahead. In *Reconfigurable Architectures Workshop*, pp. 81-96, Geneva, Switzerland, 1997.
29. W. Mangione-Smith et al. Seeking Solutions in Configurable Computing. *IEEE Computer*, 30(12):38-43, 1997.
30. T. Miyamori and K. Olukotun. A Quantitative Analysis of Reconfigurable Coprocessors for Multimedia Applications. In *Proc. IEEE Symp. on FCCMs*, pp. 2-11, Napa Valley, California, 1998.
31. B. Radunović and V. Milutinović. A Survey of Reconfigurable Computing Architectures. In *Proc. Intl. Workshop FPL'98*, pp. 376-385, Tallin, Estonia, 1998.
32. T. Rauscher and P. Adams. Microprogramming: A Tutorial and Survey of Recent Developments. *IEEE Transactions on Computers*, C-29(1):2-20, 1980.
33. R. Razdan and M. Smith. A High Performance Microarchitecture with Hardware-Programmable Functional Units. In *Proc. 27th Annual Intl. Symp. on Microarchitecture*, pp. 172-180, San Jose, California, 1994.
34. C. Rupp et al. The NAPA Adaptive Processing Architecture. In *Proc. IEEE Symp. on FCCMs*, pp. 28-37, Napa Valley, California, 1998.
35. Z. Salcic and B. Maunder. CCSimP - An Instruction-Level Custom-Configurable Processor for FPLDs. In *Proc. Intl. Workshop FPL'96*, pp. 280-289, Darmstadt, Germany, 1996.
36. S. Sawitzki, A. Gratz, and R.G. Spallek. Increasing Microprocessor Performance with Tightly-Coupled Reconfigurable Logic Arrays. In *Proc. Intl. Workshop FPL'98*, pp. 411-415, Tallin, Estonia, 1998.
37. M. Sima, S. Cotofana, J.T. van Eijndhoven, S. Vassiliadis, and K. Vissers. 8 × 8 IDCT Implementation on an FPGA-augmented TriMedia. In *Proc. IEEE Symp. on FCCMs*, Rohnert Park, California, 2001.
38. H. Singh et al. MorphoSys: An Integrated Reconfigurable System for Data-Parallel and Computation-Intensive Application. *IEEE Tran. on Computers*, 49(5):465-481, 2000.
39. S. Trimberger. Reprogrammable Instruction Set Accelerator. U.S.Patent No. 5,737,631, 1998.
40. S. Trimberger. Reprogrammable Instruction Set Accelerator Using a Plurality of Programmable Execution Units and an Instruction Page Table. U.S. Patent No. 5,748,979, 1998.
41. S. Vassiliadis, S. Wong, and S. Cotofana. The MOLEN rm-coded Processor. In *Proc. Intl. Workshop FPL-2001*, pp. 275-415, Belfast, N. Ireland, U.K., 2001.
42. J. Villasenor and W. Mangione-Smith. Configurable Computing. *Scientific American*, pp. 55-59, 1997.
43. M. Wazlowski et al. PRISM-II Compiler and Architecture. In *Proc. IEEE Workshop on FCCMs*, pp. 9-16, Napa Valley, California, 1993.
44. M. Wazlowski. *A Reconfigurable Architecture Superscalar Coprocesor*. PhD thesis, Brown University, Providence, Rhode Island, 1996.
45. M. Wirthlin and B. Hutchings. A Dynamic Instruction Set Computer. In *Proc. IEEE Symp. on FCCMs*, pp. 99-109, Napa Valley, California, 1995.
46. M. Wirthlin, B.L. Hutchings, and K.L. Gilson. The Nano Processor: A Low Resource Reconfigurable Processor. In *Proc. IEEE Workshop on FCCMs*, pp. 23-30, Napa Valley, California, 1994.
47. R. Wittig and P. Chow. OneChip: An FPGA Processor With Reconfigurable Logic. In *Proc. IEEE Symp. on FCCMs*, pp. 126-135, Napa Valley, California, 1996.

Embedded Reconfigurable Logic Core for DSP Applications

Katarzyna Leijten-Nowak[1,2] and Jef L. van Meerbergen[1,2]

[1] Philips Research Laboratories, Prof. Holstlaan 4, 5656 AA Eindhoven, The Netherlands
[2] Eindhoven University of Technology, Den Dolech 2, 5600 MB Eindhoven, The Netherlands
knowak@natlab.research.philips.com

Abstract. Reconfigurable Computing (RC) has already been proved as a cost-efficient solution for rapid prototyping and some low-volume applications. Today, RC also gains importance in the context of embedded systems. However, mature and fully developed reconfigurable logic solutions for such systems are still missing. The primary reasons for this are the intrinsic cost of reconfigurable logic, and dedicated process technologies that reconfigurable designs are usually based on. In this paper, we present a novel reconfigurable logic core which addresses these issues. A logic cell architecture of the core has been tuned to a single application domain only (application-specific kernels in DSP applications). This allowed a reduction of the required amount of routing resources by 28% compared with a commercial FPGA architecture. The core has been implemented in a standard CMOS 0.13μm process technology.

1 Introduction

After more than a decade of intensive research, Reconfigurable Computing has already been proved as a cost-efficient solution for rapid prototyping and some low-volume applications. Improvements of system performance [10] and reductions in overall power consumption [22] have been reported.

Today, the ever-increasing mask costs of new process technologies, the continuous increase in the design complexity and frequently changing standards make Reconfigurable Computing an interesting option in the design of embedded systems. Nevertheless, mature and fully developed solutions for embedded reconfigurable logic are still missing.

Firstly, the intrinsic area, delay and power consumption overhead of reconfigurable logic results in one to two orders of magnitude inferior designs compared to traditional ASIC implementations [9]. This is unacceptable for cost-sensitive embedded platforms. Secondly, in spite of the rich general 'know-how' on standalone FPGA devices, there is still no clear methodology for the design of flexible embedded reconfigurable logic cores. Thirdly, most commercial FPGA vendors use dedicated process technologies to improve the efficiency of their current reconfigurable logic architectures [6]. Because using a standard CMOS process may

M. Glesner, P. Zipf, and M. Renovell (Eds.): FPL 2002, LNCS 2438, pp. 89–101, 2002.

mean giving up some essential device features, FPGA vendors are reluctant to do so. Therefore, it is not surprising that major commercial vendors, such as Xilinx, Altera and Atmel, offer their own reconfigurable systems-on-chip that can fully exploit the advantages of their dedicated process technologies.

In this context, we propose an architecture for a novel embedded reconfigurable logic core. Rather than aiming at a broad spectrum of applications, we optimise our logic cell architecture for a single application domain only. The proposed architecture is meant for mapping application specific kernels in DSP applications. A cost reduction is achieved by exploiting characteristic properties of the mapped kernels, and decreasing the flexibility in random logic mapping. The latter enables a reduction in the amount of required routing resources.

This paper has a following structure. In the next section, we briefly describe techniques which are used in DSP-optimised reconfigurable logic architectures. In Section 3, we characterise the DSP application domain and motivate the use of reconfigurable hardware accelerators. Section 4 gives an overview of the basic concepts exploited in our architecture, and Section 5 focuses on the proposed logic cell architecture. An implementation of the proposed reconfigurable logic core is described briefly in Section 6. A comparison of our architecture with several commercial FPGAs is presented in Section 7. Finally, conclusions can be found in Section 8.

2 Previous Work

The need to optimise general-purpose RL architectures for DSP applications is recognised in the FPGA design community. For example, in traditional LUT-based FPGAs, special carry generation/propagation logic is used to reduce critical path delay [24]. In other LUT-based architectures, a look-up table is decomposed in such a way that the logic cell resources are maximally utilised if arithmetic functions are mapped [3][5][4][14]. To improve performance and mapping efficiency even further, fully optimised, dedicated logic based architectures have been proposed as well, e.g. [2]. Although very efficient for DSP functions, they have, however, very restricted flexibility in random logic mapping. A trade-off between these two approaches is offered in architectures in which an ALU is used as a basic computational element, e.g. [19].

Also , hybrid RL architectures, with dedicated components on a global level, e.g. [20], or locally within a logic cell (cluster), e.g. [17], are used. In modern FPGAs, optimised processing units, such as multipliers, are often embedded with other RL resources [25][4]. Additionally, a trend exists towards building coarser, clustered logic cells, e.g. [25].

3 Target Application Domain

Emerging applications, for example, in multimedia and mobile communication systems, rely heavily on signal processing. The computational efficiency (mW/

MIPS) of general-purpose processors (GPPs) and generic DSP processors is often insufficient for high-performance requirements coupled with low power requirements of these applications. Because of this, modern processors are often enhanced with dedicated functional units, so-called Application Specific Units (*ASUs*). The ASUs are used to map critical parts of the application code which are implemented inefficiently by standard processor resources.

3.1 ASU Motivation Example

Fig. 1 shows the results of the design space exploration for the implementation of a GSM Viterbi decoder [1]. The decoder has been implemented as a micro-coded VLIW processor using a high-level synthesis tool. A default solution and four optimisation steps were considered. As shown in Fig. 1, the introduction of four application specific units to the processor results not only in the increased performance, but also in a very large reduction (a factor of 72) of power consumption. The complexity of the mapped ASU is very low, as shown in Fig. 2. Thus, their introduction to the system leads to only a slight increase in the total silicon area.

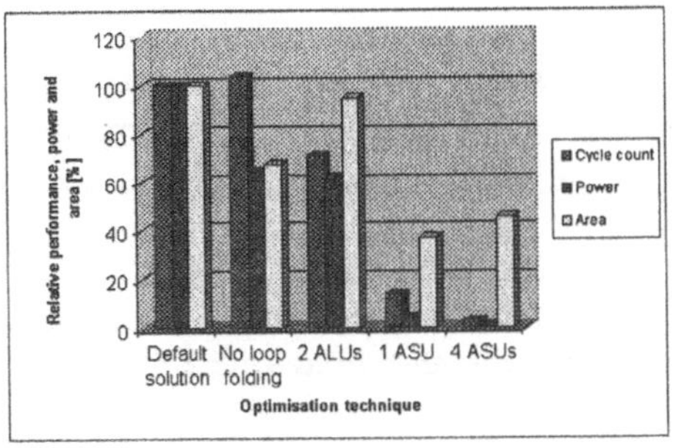

Fig. 1. Performance improvement and power consumption reduction in a programmable processor with hard-wired ASUs. Results obtained for the Viterbi decoder application.

Fig. 2. Function implemented as a hard-wired application specific unit in a Viterbi decoder implementation.

Because of the diversity in DSP applications, support of all possible critical kernels by a means of dedicated hardwired units does not make sense. For this reason, we propose an implementation of critical kernels in reconfigurable logic. Reconfigurable logic can implement one or multiple Application Specific Units at the same time. Furthermore, unused ASUs can be replaced by new ones simply by loading a new configuration memory context.

4 Basic Architectural Concepts

4.1 Multi-functionality

In application-specific DSP kernels, a mix of arithmetic, random logic and small memory functions is required. For example, arithmetic (carry propagation based) operations dominate many DSP algorithms. Random logic functions implement the decision making (conditions), small control units (e.g. in a divider) or bit-level manipulations. The memory functionality is required to implement look-up tables, shift registers, small data memories or dedicated register file units. Therefore, to implement a wide class of DSP kernels in reconfigurable logic, a reconfigurable logic architecture must efficiently support datapath (arithmetic), random logic and small memory functions. We refer to this requirement as *multi-functionality.*

4.2 Homogeneous Structure

The complexity of Application Specific Units in DSP applications is usually much lower than the complexity of typical applications mapped onto stand-alone FPGA architectures. Thus, in contrast to such FPGAs, there is no need to integrate large memory blocks with embedded reconfigurable logic resources. As a consequence, an architecture of an embedded reconfigurable logic core can be made homogeneous. Next to the reduction in the logic core complexity, this also simplifies the mapping tools. This is because of the absence of extra mapping constraints which are usually raised by a fix physical location of specific blocks (e.g. memories) in the core.

A homogeneous architecture implies that the multi-functionality requirement, as discussed in Section 4.1, must be fulfilled locally, i.e. in every logic cell. The potential area overhead is avoided by the maximal reuse of already existing logic cell resources.

4.3 Multi-output Look-Up Table with Inverting Property

To guarantee flexibility in random logic mapping, a look-up table (LUT) is chosen as a basic computational element of a logic cell in a reconfigurable logic core. In contrast to traditional, single-output, look-up tables [8], the look-up table proposed here is implemented as a multi-output LUT. This means that several logic outputs are generated based on one set of inputs.

The choice of a multi-output LUT is dictated by the fact that many DSP functions generate a multi-bit result. Exploiting this feature allows a reduction in the number of logic cell pins and, consequently, in the amount of required routing resources. Since reconfigurable routing resources and their associated configuration memory dominate the reconfigurable device area [9], the area reduction can be substantial. An additional benefit is that the multi-output LUT structure can be almost directly reused to implement small storage functions. This matches the multi-functionality requirement very well. Furthermore, only a single LUT decoder is required to address all LUT memory columns in this case, in contrast to two decoders (for reading and writing) needed to address a single-output LUT with memory functionality in a standard implementation [24].

In arithmetic functions, the generation of consecutive bits of a final result often depends on carry propagation between basic arithmetic components. This potentially complicates the use of the proposed multi-output LUT for the implementation of arithmetic functions. This is because including such a dependence requires the LUT to be made very large. To avoid this, we exploit the adder inverting property [21][18], and we build a multi-output LUT in the way suggested in [18].

The multi-bit output LUT, as described here, reflects the nature of DSP functions and allows some cost reduction due to this fact. At the same time, however, it reduces flexibility in random logic mapping. Nevertheless, results of experiments mentioned in [6] and [17] show that 50-60% of all logic functions produce more than one output based on one set of inputs. Furthermore, a 5-input LUT which can be obtained in the implemented multi-output LUT is found to provide the most performance-optimised mapping [23].

4.4 Granularity

In most DSP applications datapath functions require wide, i.e. multi-bit, operands. To fulfil this requirement and improve performance of the mapped functions, a nibble-level granularity has been chosen for a single logic cell. This means that datapath functions with 4-bit arguments and maximally a 4-bit output can be implemented in one logic cell.

However, this granularity is too coarse for typical random logic functions. For this reason, the structure of the logic cell has been divided into two identical slices, each with 2-bit granularity. In this way, a trade-off between flexibility and performance has been achieved.

5 Logic Cell Architecture

The structure of our logic cell is shown in Fig. 3. The cell consists of two identical logic slices which can be used independently or be combined together to offer richer functionality. Each slice contains a multi-output LUT (see Section 4.3) which has 4-inputs and 2-outputs (4/2-LUT). The LUT is implemented in a memory-like way, i.e. it has only one decoder. The 4:16 decoder present in our architecture addresses memory cells in two memory columns of the LUT, and it is used during read and write operations if the LUT is configured for the memory mode. Moreover, the same decoder is reused to address bits of the configuration memory which, similarly to the LUT, are organised in columns. This technique simplifies the configuration memory architecture and allows partial reconfiguration of the core.

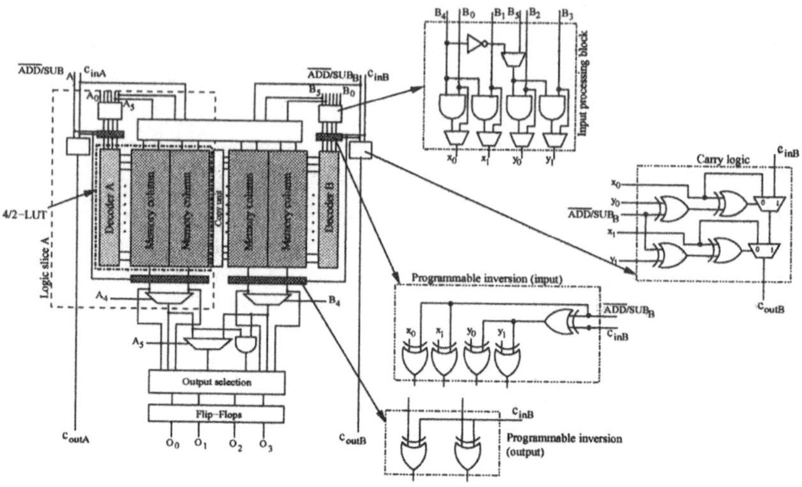

Fig. 3. Logic cell architecture.

The *programmable inversion blocks* placed at the LUT inputs and outputs, and implemented by means of XOR gates, realise the adder inverting property, as discussed in Section 4.3. The change in the polarisation of inputs is determined by two signals: carry input signal c_{in} and the $\overline{ADD}/SUB$ control signal. The latter signal determines the type of operation that the LUT performs. To reduce critical path delay, the carry signal in arithmetic operation is generated by dedicated carry logic.

The outputs of the 4/2-LUTs in both slices are combined in 2:1 multiplexers. Each multiplexer is controlled by a signal from a logic cell pin. Such a structure allows an implementation of 5-input logic functions in each slice. A third multiplexer and extra AND gate, which use outputs of the multiplexers from a higher level as inputs, extend random logic functionality of the cell. They allow mapping of 6-input logic functions and wide AND and OR functions up to 10 inputs.

The output multiplexers together with the *memory inputs processing block* are utilised also if the LUTs are configured as memory units (one big, or two independent of a smaller size). They determine, based on the most significant address bits of the mapped memory, to which memory columns input bits are written, and from which memory column bits are taken to the output. To allow an implementation of a dual-port memory, a special copy unit is placed between the LUTs of both slices. The task of this unit is to copy data being written to the LUT memory columns of the first slice, updating in this way the data stored in the second slice. This is necessary because of the limited number of the decoder inputs[1].

[1] The dual-port memory functionality assumes that in a memory one write and two read ports are available.

The *output selection block* determines how many signals are connected to the logic cell output pins. Each of the output signals can be registered using a dedicated flip-flop. To allow deep pipelining of arithmetic functions, the carry output signals can be registered as well.

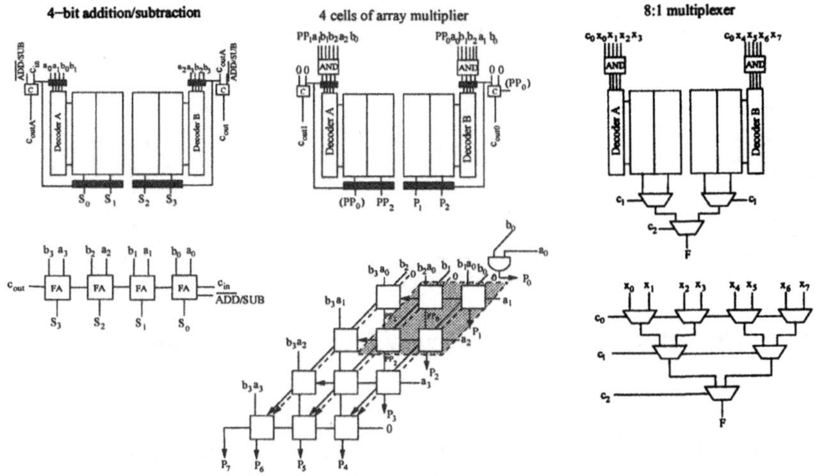

Fig. 4. Implementation of basic datapath functions in the proposed logic cell.

The proposed logic cell can operate in three different modes: datapath mode, random logic mode and memory mode. In the *datapath mode* (see Fig. 4), 4-bit addition/subtraction operations, four cells of an array multiplier (unsigned or two's complement) and wide multiplexers (up to a 8:1 multiplexer) can be implemented. In *random logic mode*, each logic cell slice implements maximally 4-input/2-output logic functions or 5-input/1-output logic functions. If the LUTs of both slices are combined, a 6-input/1-output logic function or partial logic functions with a much higher number of inputs can be implemented as well. In this mode, an efficient implementation of binary counters is possible as well. In the *memory mode* (see Fig. 5), the LUT resources are used to implement memory functionality. Various memory configurations with the output data width of 1, 2 or 4 bits are possible. A dual-port memory with maximally a 2-bit output can be also implemented. Furthermore, implementations of variable-length shift registers with a 1-, 2- or 4- bit output are possible as well.

6 VLSI Implementation

The reconfigurable logic core presented here has been implemented as a 4x4 array of logic cells using a TSMC CMOS 0.13μm process technology with six metal layers and copper interconnects. Due to a limited time budget, the core has been implemented using a standard cell library enhanced with a dedicated

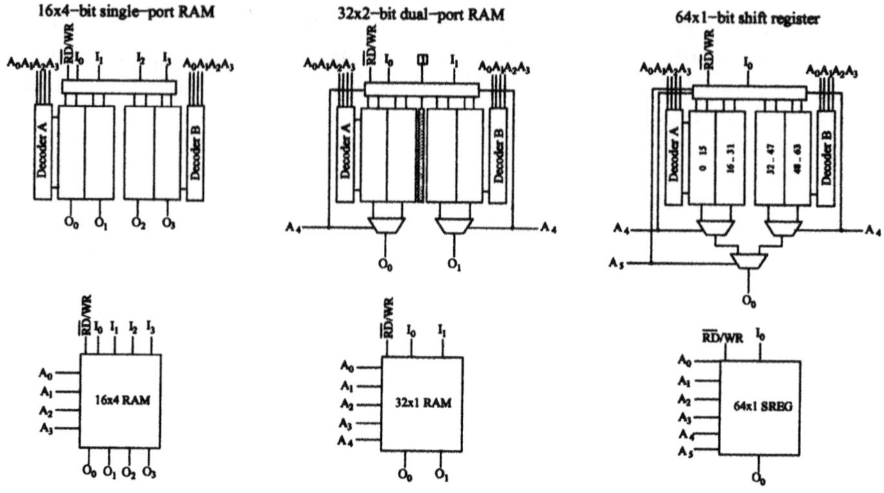

Fig. 5. Implementation of basic memory functions in the proposed logic cell.

reconfigurable logic cell library. The cells of the reconfigurable cell library were designed to have the same height as the standard cells. This approach allowed us to considerably reduce design effort since standard placement and routing tools (Cadence Silicon Ensemble) could be used. At the same time, however, a much less dense layout than possible using a custom design style, as done for all commercial FPGAs [8], was obtained.

One of the crucial issues was the implementation of the look-up table. It has been designed in a memory-like way with a 7-transistor memory cell, a single bit line and without a precharging mechanism. A special regeneration circuitry in the form of an inverter and bus keeper was placed at the end of the bit line to deal with the voltage drop behind the pass transistor. A different, 5-transistor memory cell was used for the configuration memory part.

The routing architecture has been determined through routing experiments using the open-source VPR placement and routing tool [12]. A complementary pass gate was chosen as a programmable switch because it minimises the power-delay product and scales better with new technologies. To reduce the load on the routing tracks, buffers were placed at the inputs of the multiplexers of the input connection box. Furthermore, programmable switches were used to separate those tracks from the load of the logic cell output pins.

A strictly modular design approach has been followed to implement the core. Three types of basic blocks: a logic tile, an input/output tile and input/output tile with routing have been used for this purpose.

In Fig. 6, details of the logic cell layout with marked configuration memory areas, and in Fig. 7 the final layout of the core, are shown. The dimensions of the tile are $227 \times 134 \mu m$. The tile layout area is dominated by configuration memory (39%) and interconnect (33%).

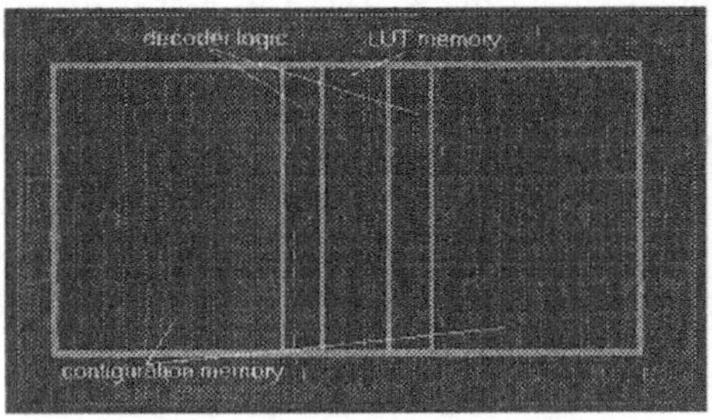

Fig. 6. The logic cell layout.

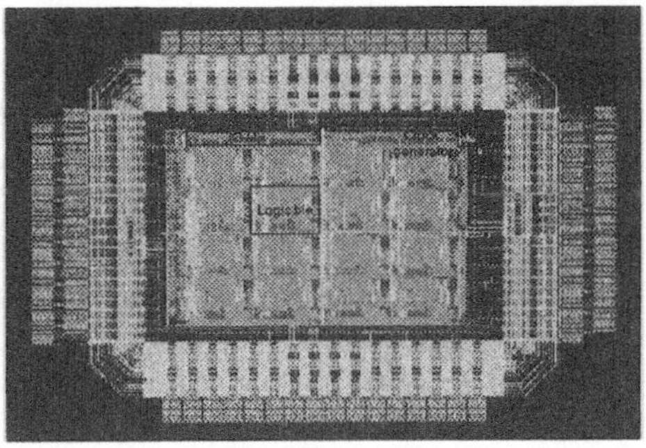

Fig. 7. The final layout of the test chip (4×4 array of logic tiles).

7 Comparison and Cost Analysis

The most fair way of comparing different RL architectures is by establishing their mapping efficiency. The mapping efficiency can be calculated as $N_{LC} \times A_{LC}$, where N_{LC} is the number of logic cells (tiles) required to map a benchmark function, and A_{LC} is the cost function of the logic cell (tile) architecture, expressed in terms of its silicon area. Because of its proprietary nature, the information on the complexity of commercial FPGAs is, however, not available. At the same time, the commonly used models, such as [7] and [9], are rather inaccurate and do not take into account the differences in the LUT implementation styles. The model proposed in [6], in which logic cell area is estimated based on the minimum width transistor area calculation, requires details of the logic cell structure. Furthermore, results are influenced by transistor sizing, and this by the chosen optimisation criterion (e.g. area or performance).

Because of this, we propose a new cost model, which is based on the assumption from [15]. According to this assumption, simple measures such the total number of configuration bits of a logic cell (tile) and the total number of logic cell pins are good estimates of the logic cell (tile) area and its associated routing resources, respectively. We extended this model to capture the information on the LUT implementation style and the final silicon requirements. The model is described by the following equations:

$$A_{LC} = A_{LM} + A_{DE}, \tag{1}$$

$$A_{LM} = TD_M \times N_{lmb} \times C_{lmb}, \tag{2}$$

$$A_{DE} = TD_L \times (C_{dec} + C_{ex}). \tag{3}$$

The logic cell area A_{LC} is calculated as the sum of the area taken by all LUT configuration memory bits A_{LM}, and the total area required by the LUT decoders and the LUT extra logic A_{DE} (Eq. 1). The area of the LUT configuration memory A_{LM} (Eq. 2) is calculated as the product of the total number of LUT memory bits N_{lmb} and the complexity of a single bit (C_{lmb}), expressed in the number of transistors required to implement a single LUT memory cell. A 10-transistors memory cell is used for a Xilinx Virtex device [11], and 6-transistors cells for Atmel and Altera memory bits[2]. For our architecture, a 7-transistor LUT memory cell is used, and the factor '1.5' is introduced to capture the presence of the copy unit (see Section 5). The transistor density factor for memory TD_M is used to scale results and express them in the normalised $\lambda^2/trans.$ units. λ is a measure for the transistor feature size [9]. The TD_M is calculated as an average transistor density in a compact FPGA memory cell, the size of which has been reported in [7], and equals $222\lambda^2/trans.$

Table 1. Comparison of the logic cell implementation cost and the amount of required routing resources for different FPGA architectures.

Logic cell type	N_{cb} [–]	C_{lmb} [#trans.]	A_{LM} [$k\lambda^2$]	C_{dec} [#trans.]	C_{ex} [#trans.]	A_{DE} [$k\lambda^2$]	A_{LC} [$k\lambda^2$]	N_{pins} [-]
Xilinx Virtex	64	10	138.7	768	132	406	544.8	28
Atmel AT40K	16	6	20.8	92	12	46.9	67.7	6
Altera FLEX10K	16	6	20.8	92	12	46.9	67.7	9
Proposed	64	7+1.5	117.9	272	356	283.3	401.2	20

The area of the LUT decoders and extra logic A_{DE} (Eq. 3) is calculated based on the total LUT decoders complexity C_{dec}, and the complexity of extra logic C_{ex}. The latter captures the cost of LUT multiplexers (e.g. multiplexers which combine LUT outputs [5]) and the dedicated carry circuitry. In case of our logic cell architecture, all extra XOR gates are taken into account. Both C_{dec} and C_{ex} are expressed in the number of transistors, and are calculated assuming the complexity of basic logic gates as in the TSMC library [13]. The transistor density factor for logic TD_L is used to express results in terms of the required silicon area. It is calculated as an average transistor density in a $0.13\mu m$ process technology, and equals $462\lambda^2/trans.$

The intermediate and final results of the logic cells area estimation, and the required amount of routing resources (A_{LC} and N_{pins}) are shown in Table 2. In Table 2, the results of mapping basic arithmetic, logic and memory functions onto three commercial FPGA architectures and the architecture proposed in this paper are shown. The mapping onto commercial architectures is done using macro-block generators to assure that specific properties of these architectures are exploited. For our architecture, manual mapping is done. In each case, two parameters are reported: N_{LC} which expresses the number of logic cells required to map a benchmark function, and WC which is a weighted cost measure and expresses the area required by the benchmark function including the logic cell complexity estimates from Table 2. The WC is described by a pair of numbers. The first number indicates the total complexity of a logic cell ($N_{LC} \times A_{LC}$),

[2] Due to no available information on the memory cell implementation, a memory cell structure, as suggested in [6], is assumed.

Table 2. Results of mapping basic arithmetic, logic and memory functions onto logic cells of different FPGA architectures.

Benchmark function	Xilinx Virtex		Atmel AT40K		Altera FLEX10K		**Proposed**	
	N_{LC} [-]	WC [$(M\lambda^2$,-)]	N_{LC} [-]	WC [$(M\lambda^2$,-)]	N_{LC} [-]	WC [$(M\lambda^2$,-)]	N_{LC} [-]	WC [$(M\lambda^2$,-)]
8-bit add./sub.	2	(1.06,56)	8	(0.53,48)	8	(0.53,72)	2	(0.78,40)
16×16 mult. un.	68	(36.18,1904)	256	(16.92,1536)	730	(48.26,6570)	65	(25.47,1300)
8:1 mux	1	(0.53,28)	7	(0.46,42)	6	(0.40,54)	1	(0.39,20)
16:1 mux	2.25	(1.20,63)	15	(0.99,90)	13	(0.86,117)	2.5	(0.98,50)
10-input AND	0.75	(0.40,21)	3	(0.20,18)	3	(0.20,27)	1	(0.39,20)
4:16 decod.	4	(2.13,112)	16	(1.06,96)	16	(1.06,144)	4	(1.57,80)
mod 15 count.	1	(0.53,28)	4	(0.26,24)	4	(0.26,36)	1	(0.39,20)
16×8 RAM	2	(1.06,56)	-	-	-	-	2	(0.78,40)
16×4 shift reg.	1	(0.53,28)	-	-	-	-	1	(0.39,20)

and the second about the total complexity of the associated routing resources ($N_{LC} \times N_{pins}$ [15]).

The analysis of results from Table 2 shows that the proposed architecture is 23% smaller than the logic cell used in Xilinx Virtex devices, because of the chosen LUT implementation style (the LUT decoder sharing). Nevertheless, it is 38% and 29% larger than logic cells used in Atmel devices and Altera devices, respectively. However, these logic cells do not support memory functionality. Because of the reduced number of logic cell pins (the input sharing), our architecture also reduces considerably the amount of required routing resources. The saving because of this fact depends on the compared architecture and equals 28% for the Xilinx Virtex devices, 22% for Atmel and 58% for Altera. Since reconfigurable interconnect and its associated configuration memory strongly dominate the area of reconfigurable logic devices, saving due to the routing resource reduction is assumed to be dominant. Furthermore, it may diminish the area overhead of our cell compared to logic cells without memory functionality (Atmel and Altera).

8 Conclusions

We have presented an embedded reconfigurable logic core based on an architecture that has been tuned to cost-efficiently map application specific kernels of DSP applications. The multi-functionality required by these kernels has been guaranteed by the use of a logic cell that includes a novel look-up table implemented in a memory-style. In this way, the support for datapath, random logic and memory functions can be achieved at virtually no extra cost. We also showed that our approach is 23% more area efficient than a comparable commercial approache. Furthermore, flexibility in random logic mapping has been partially traded for a reduction of 28% in the cost of routing resources. Since the reconfigurable interconnect and associated configuration memory dominate the area of reconfigurable logic devices, and also indirectly influence their performance and power consumption, such a saving is essential.

We have implemented our reconfigurable logic core in $0.13\mu m$ technology using standard cells. Using a new cost model we showed that the proposed architecture compares favourably to commercial FPGAs for various mapped benchmark functions. We are confident that our architecture will be competitive, assuming a full-custom implementation style. Detailed motivations for this will be given in a forthcoming paper.

In the future, we will focus on optimisation of the proposed architecture to further minimise the area overhead. We also plan a thorough benchmarking of the new architecture, including performance and power consumption comparison. For this purpose, we are going to adapt existing mapping tools.

References

1. Adelante Technologies, *"DSP" Hardware Implementation using Behavioural Synthesis*, Internal presentation, www.adelantetech.com.
2. Agarwala M., Balsara P.T., *An Architecture for a DSP Field-Programmable Gate Array*, IEEE Transactions on VLSI, Vol. 3, No. 1, March 1995.
3. Altera, *Embedded Programmable Logic Family. FLEX 10K*, Data sheet, September 2000, ver. 2.10.
4. Altera, *Stratix Programmable Logic Device Family* , Data sheet, February 2002, ver.1.0.
5. Atmel, *AT40K FPGAs with FreeRAM*, Data sheet, January 1999.
6. Betz V., Rose J., Marquardt A., *Architecture and CAD for Deep-submicron FPGAs*, Kluwer Academic Publisher, 1999.
7. Brown S.D., Francis R.J., Rose J., Vranesic Z.G., *Field-Programmable Gate Arrays*, Kluwer Academic Publishers, 1992.
8. Chow P., Seo S.O., Rose J., Chung K., Páez-Monzón G., Rahardja I., *The Design of an SRAM-Based Field-Programmable Gate Array, Part II: Circuit Design and Layout*, IEEE Transactions on VLSI, Vol. 7, No. 3, September 1999.
9. Dehon A., *Reconfigurable Architectures for General-Purpose Computing*, AI Technical Report 1586, MIT Artificial Intelligence Laboratory, 545 Technology Sq., Cambridge, MA 02139, September 1996.
10. DeHon A., *The Density Advantage of Configurable Computing*, Special Issue of IEEE Design and Test, April 2000.
11. Bauer T.J., *Lookup Tables which Doubles as Shift Registers*, Patent Application No. 754 421, Xilinx, Filed November 1996.
12. Betz V., Rose J., *VPR: A New Packing, Placement and Routing Tool for FPGA Research*, International Workshop on Field Programmable Logic and Applications, 1997.
13. *gcorelib. CMOS Cell Library*, Philips Semiconductors, November 2001, rev. 1.1.
14. George V., *Low Energy Field-Programmable Gate Array*, Ph.D. Thesis, University of California, Berkeley, 2000.
15. He J., Rose J., *Advantages of Heterogeneous Logic Block Architectures for FPGAs*, IEEE Custom Integrated Circuits Conference, San Diego, May 1993.
16. Kaviani A., Vranesic D., Brown S., *Computational Field Programmable Architecture*, IEEE Custom Integrated Circuits Conference, May 1998.

17. Kaviani A., *Novel Architectures and Synthesis Methods for High Capacity Field Programmable Devices*, Ph. D. Thesis, University of Toronto, Canada, 1999.
18. Leijten-Nowak K., van Meerbergen J. L., *Applying the Adder Inverting Property in the Design of Cost-Efficient Reconfigurable Logic*, IEEE Midwest Symposium on Circuits and Systems, Dayton, USA, August 2001.
19. Marshall A., Stansfield T., Kostarnov I., Vuillemin J., Hutchings B., *A Reconfigurable Arithmetic Array for Multimedia Applications*, ACM/SIGDA International Symposium on FPGAs, Monterey, February 1999.
20. Miller N.L., Quigley S.F., *A Reconfigurable Integrated Circuit for High Performance Computer Arithmetic* , IEE, 1998.
21. Rabaey J., *Digital Integrated Circuits. A Design Perspective*, Prentice Hall, 1996.
22. Rabaey J., *Reconfigurable Processing: The Solution to Low-Power Programmable DSP*, IEEE International Conference on Acoustic, Speech and Signal Processing, April 1997.
23. Singh S., Rose J., Lewis D., Chung K., Chow P., *Optimisation of Field-Programmable Gate Array Logic Block Architecture for Speed*, IEEE Custom Integrated Circuits Conference, May 1990.
24. Xilinx, *XC4000E and XC4000X Series Field Programmable Gate Arrays*, Data sheet, January 1999.
25. Xilinx, *Virtex 2.5V Field Programmable Gate Arrays*, Data sheet, January 2000.

Efficient FPGA-based QPSK Demodulation Loops: Application to the DVB Standard*

Francisco Cardells-Tormo[1], Javier Valls-Coquillat[2], Vicenc Almenar-Terre[3], and Vicente Torres-Carot[2]

[1] R&D Dept., Hewlett-Packard InkJet Commercial Division (ICD)
08190 Sant Cugat del Valles, Barcelona, Spain
fcardell@bpo.hp.com
[2] Department of Electronic Engineering, Polytechnic University of Valencia (UPV),
Camino de Vera s/n, 46022 Valencia, Spain
{jvalls,vtorres}@eln.upv.es
[3] Department of Telecommunications, Polytechnic University of Valencia (UPV),
Camino de Vera s/n, 46022 Valencia, Spain
valmenar@dcom.upv.es

Abstract. This paper deals with the optimized implementation of high performance coherent demodulators in FPGAs for the DVB standard. This work provides design guidelines in order to optimize fixed-point demodulation loops in terms of symbol rate. Several schemes are evaluated such as ROM partitioning techniques and the CORDIC algorithm. We go through the whole design process from simulation to timing analysis for a particular case study. For each architecture we propose the most efficient design for Virtex FPGAs in terms of area and throughput. Finally we will compare them in order to establish the most suitable de-rotator scheme for each transmission bandwidth, and for transmission rates up to 25.8 Mbauds.

1 Introduction

Reconfigurability is compulsory in software defined radios because of this technology being multi-system and multi-standard. Digital signal processing is performed closer and closer to the antenna [1, 2, 3] thus requiring high sampling rates. At this point FPGAs become the only reconfigurable devices capable of attaining a speed of several hundred megasamples per second (MSPS). But in order to get the most from these devices, designs must be conceived having in mind the target technology. Throughout this paper we will study and design high performance Quadrature Phase Shift Keying (QPSK) digital demodulators. The principles of digital communications can be found in [4].

There are several ways to perform QPSK coherent demodulation which have been very successful in VLSI designs [5]. From all these possibilities, we have

* This work was supported by Generalitat Valenciana under grant number GV00-93-14. Francisco Cardells-Tormo acknowledges the support of Hewlett-Packard ICD in the preparation of his Ph.D. thesis

M. Glesner, P. Zipf, and M. Renovell (Eds.): FPL 2002, LNCS 2438, pp. 102–111, 2002.

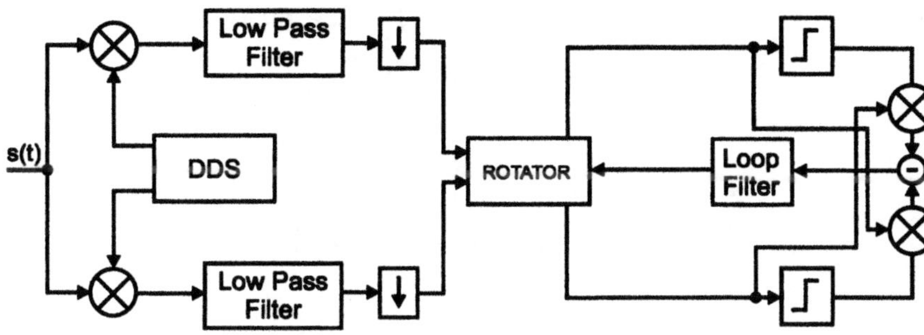

Fig. 1. Building Blocks of a QPSK Demodulation Loop

chosen the architecture shown in figure 1. Because of stability requirements, pipelined operators must be avoided inside the loop. The speed required to process the intermediate frequency (IF) signals, e.g. 200 MSPS, can only be achieved in FPGAs with pipelining. This fact rules out the remaining architectures such as the Costas loop and therefore designs like those presented in [6] are unrealistic.

The demodulator shown in figure 1 consists of a free-runnning down-converter, low pass filters, down-samplers and a non-pipelined demodulation loop for phase and frequency recovery. The demodulation loop consists of a quadrature de-rotator, a loop filter and a phase-error detector. This loop obtains the phase-error signal by measuring the phase difference between the actual space vector and a symbol estimation. The phase error is used to correct the frequency control word of a direct digital frequency synthesizer (DDS) by means of a loop filter, thus removing any shifting in phase or frequency. Conventional quadrature rotators (figure 2) consist of four digital multipliers and a quadrature direct digital synthesizer [7]. There are several DDS architectures, they are all summarized in [8]. An alternative method to perform the digital mixing uses the CORDIC algorithm [9, 10]. The CORDIC-based mixer generates the quadrature waveforms and computes the complex-number multiplication at the same time, thus avoiding the extra multipliers used in the conventional case [11, 12].

The FPGA-optimization of DDS has already been covered in [13]. So we will focus on the optimization of the demodulation loop. It should be able to produce a sequence of symbols with a certain accuracy given by the Bit-Error-Rate (BER). As we reduce loop precision we should expect the BER to worsen. There is no closed-form expression and the design procedure for this optimization has not been dealt in the literature. Therefore we will spend a whole section going through this process.

The FPGA technology we are aiming at is the Xilinx Virtex/E family [14]. The cores presented in this paper have been developed by instantiating the target technology components in our code. Besides we have specified their relative position in the FPGA. We have used Synplify as synthesis tool and vendor-supplied software for FPGA placement and routing.

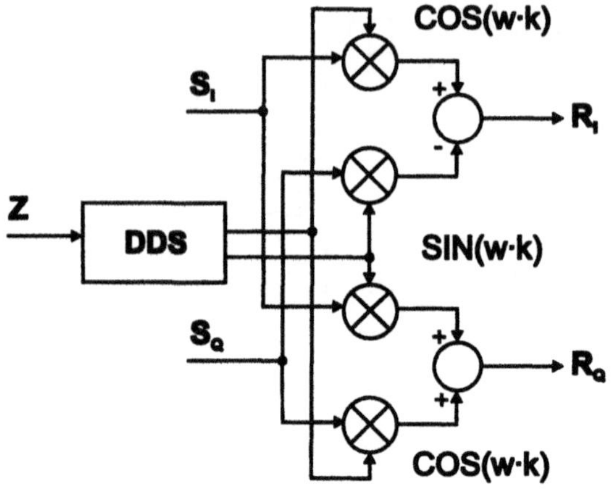

Fig. 2. Building Blocks of a DDS-based Rotator

The structure of this paper is as follows. First of all we will examine the effect that finite precision has on the demodulation loop performance. Secondly we will profit from this study and we will design a demodulation loop with the smallest, and therefore fastest, components using several de-rotating techniques. In the third place we will compare their performance in terms of area and speed. Finally we will use these results to establish the most suitable working range for each technique.

2 Fixed-Point Loop Optimization: A Case Study

Let us begin with a study of the loop requirements. Our goal is to maximize the throughput of the loop in order to obtain the maximum symbol rate. On the other hand we would like to minimize area. This optimization relies on the behaviour the loop presents for fixed-point operation. Our goal is to find out the optimum phase resolution, de-rotator precision and the wordlength of the filter coefficients. We have carried out this study with Matlab and the fixed-point blockset.

The loop is designed to comply with the Digital Video Broadcasting (DVB) standard [15], an European standard protocol for satellite communications. We will focus on a satellite transponder bandwidth-symbol rate ratio (BW/Rs) of 1.28. The standard shows that for this transmission capacity we require a symbol rate between 20.3 and 42.2 Mbauds, and a BER before decoding of at least 10^{-1} for a Signal-to-Noise Ratio (SNR) of 4 dBs. In the first place, we have chosen the loop filter parameters, i.e. normalized natural frequency ($\omega_n \cdot T$) and damping factor ξ, so as to be DVB standard compliant. Simulations show that the optimum values are: $(\omega_n \cdot T) = 10^{-3}$ and $\xi = 0.8$. Secondly, we have carried out a study to find the sensitivity of the Bit-Error-Rate (BER) with the loop filter parameters. The results of this study do not show a strong correlation, which

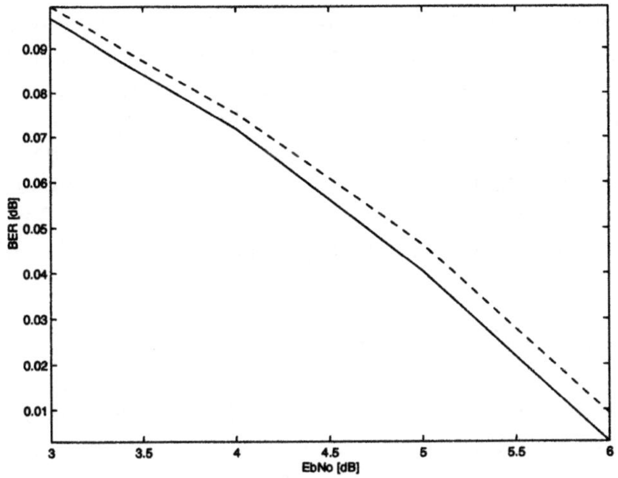

Fig. 3. The figure shows the BER in dBs versus SNR for floating point operation (solid line), and for fixed point operation (dashed line)

means that the pole placement of the loop filter is not that critical. Finally, we have performed fixed-point simulations where we have changed the precision of the de-rotator and the loop filter. As it was expected, the fact of working with finite precision worsens the ability of the loop to attain the required BER (figure 3). Nevertheless it may happen that for a particular precision, the BER is so close to the ideal value that the fact of increasing the wordlength has a negligible effect. We translate this to our study by using the lowest possible precision which only makes the BER drop in 1 dB.

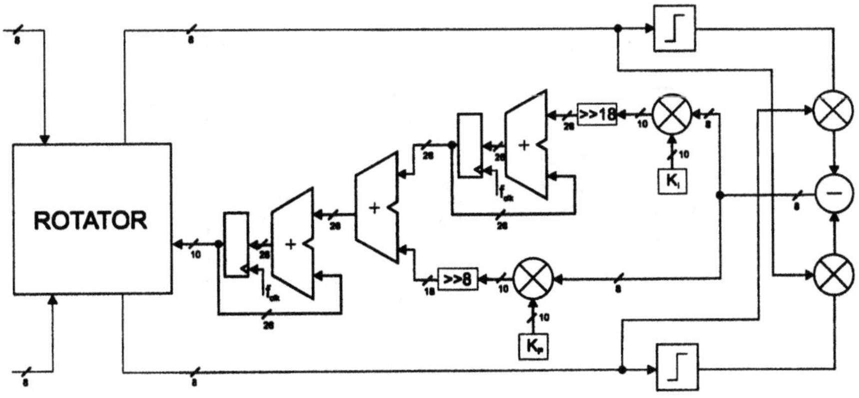

Fig. 4. Fixed-point optimization of the demodulation loop

Simulations revealed which components of the loop require the highest resolution. It has helped us determine the fact that for our case study the bottle neck is to be found in the loop filter. In actual fact, the rotator's precision can be lowered as much as to 7 fractional bits and the rotating angle phase resolution, i.e. either the DDS phase resolution or the CORDIC angle datapath precision, can be reduced to 10 bits. Yet, the loop filter must use an inner precision of 28 bits. A more detailed description can be found in figure 4. This configuration allows for hardware savings without significantly affecting the BER.

3 QPSK Demodulation Cores

Speed in FPGA combinational circuits depends on the logic depth, i.e. the number of LUTs the signal has to go through, and on the routing delays. It is of our interest to find architectures in which this logic depth is minimized. The block in figure 4 labelled as rotator performs combinational complex rotation. Rotator architectures are going to be based on CORDIC or ROM partitioning techniques.

3.1 QPSK Loop with a ROM-based Rotator

In addition to a combinational DDS, ROM-based rotators need four multipliers and two adders to perform complex multiplication as in figure 2. There is of course another solution for performing this operation which uses three multipliers and three adders instead, but even though it lowers area requirements it increases logic depth, and that is what we are avoiding. There are several architectures for ROM-based DDS and each one relies on a compression algorithm, i.e. [8, 16, 17]. Their efficient implementation has been discussed in [13].

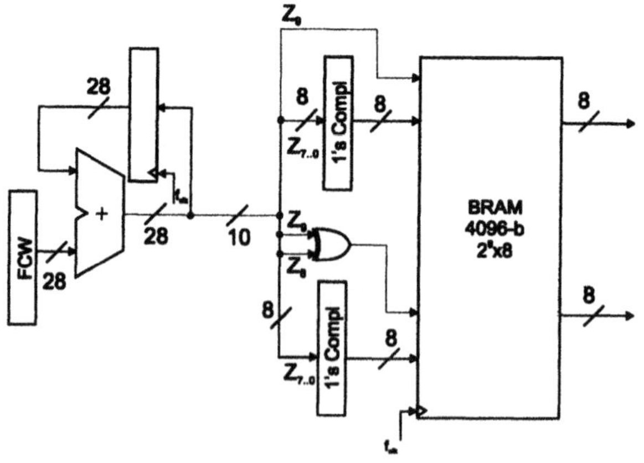

Fig. 5. ROM-based DDS

In the first place we have considered keeping the same precision for all the components in the demodulation loop, i.e. 14 bits. Because of this phase resolution the most suitable technique to perform the phase-to-amplitude conversion is the Nicholas architecture [17]. The implementation results are 727 slices, 2 BRAMs and a maximum clock frequency of 19.5 MHz.

Nevertheless, the fixed-point optimization may provide the same functionality at a much lower hardware cost. The study of the demodulation loop that we performed in section 2 has revealed that we need a DDS with a phase resolution of 10 bits and a sample resolution of 8 bits. A whole period can be fitted in two BRAMs, thus making any compression technique unnecessary. Nevertheless we still need a logic stage to build the cosine function out of the phase accumulator. Due to this fact we could still reduce memory requirements to a single BRAM as in figure 5. We have stored two quarters of the sine function, quarter I and quarter III. The phase word is mapped into the first quarter. The 8 least significant bits of the phase word are used to look-up the corresponding amplitude. An additional bit establishes whether the output belongs to the first quarter or the third.

BRAMs are synchronous memories, therefore in order to avoid extra delays, re-timing must be applied to the accumulator as in figure 5. Each of the four combinational multipliers is a tree multiplier with a precision of 8 bits. We obtain the following implementation results for a XCV300E-8 device: area 337 slices and a single BRAM, and a maximum clock rate of 27 MHz.

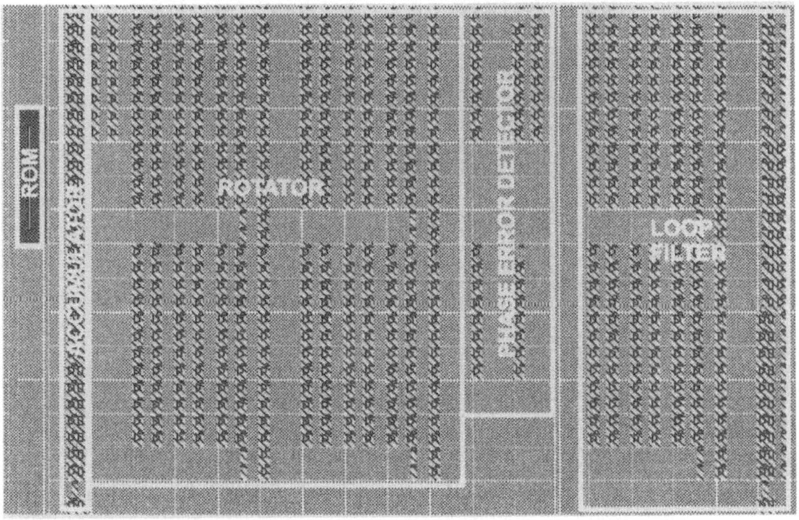

Fig. 6. Floorplan of the placed and routed core: QPSK loop with a ROM-based rotator. Device: Virtex XCV300

3.2 QPSK Loop with a CORDIC-based Rotator

The rotator could be realized using a CORDIC processor as in [12], but with a first-order loop filter instead. On the other hand there are several CORDIC architectures [8, 18, 19, 20]. Nevertheless these designs have been optimized for VLSI. Let us have a close look at the design guidelines that we must follow in order to make the most of FPGA devices. It has been shown in [13] that the architecture presented in [20] is the most efficient in terms of precision. On the other hand it was shown that it is the most appropriate for FPGAs in terms of both area and speed. The architecture corresponds to a conventional CORDIC in rotation-mode driven by a signed accumulator. The Z datapath is shortened as iterations progress. In addition, in order to reduce fan-out we will extend the sign bit of the Z datapath, as suggested in [21]. The embedded registers are left without use.

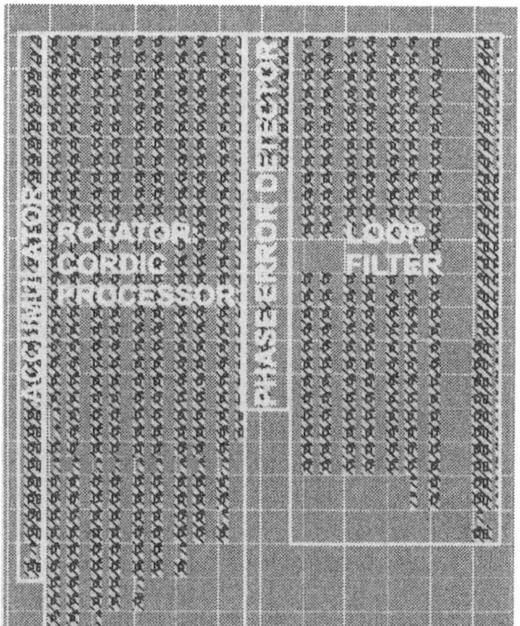

Fig. 7. Floorplan of the placed and routed core: QPSK loop with a CORDIC-based rotator. Device: Virtex XCV300

In a first implementation of this loop we did not make use of the fixed-point optimization results. We have kept a 14-bit precision. For a XCV300E-8 device we require 648 slices and the maximum frequency is 12.7 MHz. Next we have implemented the loop as in figure 4. We find that area requirements drop to 308 slices and that the speed rises to 20.3 MHz.

3.3 Summary of Results

In order to make a direct comparison, we have summarized in table 1 the main implementation results. The area is evaluated both in terms of slices and BRAMs. The symbol rate is equivalent to the loop clock rate.

Rotator	Area Slices/BRAMs	Clock rate MHz
CORDIC	648/0	12.7
CORDIC (Fixed-Point Optimization)	308/0	20.3
Memory Compression	727/2	19.5
Memory Compression (Fixed-Point Optimization)	337/1	27.0

Table 1. Coherent demodulators in FPGA. Device XCV400E-8

We must now compare the symbol rate values that we have obtained with those found in the DVB standard for our case study conditions, i.e. $BW/Rs = 1.28$. In table 2 we have listed the symbol rate requirements for different transmission bandwidths. The lowest bandwidth, i.e. 26 MHz, could be covered by any technique after optimization. The range from 26 MHz up to 33 MHz can only be covered by memory compression techniques after optimization. Looking back at table 1, we see that the loop based on a CORDIC rotator has the minimum area requirements and complies with the speed requirements of the lowest bandwidth. Therefore it should be selected rather than a demodulation loop based on memory compression techniques. Besides we must highlight the additional benefits of using CORDIC-based demodulation loops: they could easily be resized for other design constraints.

BW [MHz]	Rs [MBaud]	Technique
54	42.2	none
46	35.9	none
40	31.2	none
36	28.1	none
33	25.8	Memory Compression
30	23.4	Memory Compression
27	21.1	Memory Compression
26	20.3	CORDIC

Table 2. Suitable technique for each transponder bandwidth ($BW/Rs = 1.28$). Device XCV400E-8

4 Conclusions

In this paper we have established the design process of a fixed-point demodulation loop for reconfigurable devices. For instance, we have carried out the design of a QPSK demodulation loop compliant with the DVB standard. The loop was based on a de-rotating scheme instead of a Costas loop for it provides a higher symbol rate. We have performed floating point simulations in order to design the loop filter. Next we have carried out fixed-point simulations in order to optimize the size of the combinational blocks inside the demodulation loop. They have revealed that the most demanding component is the loop filter and that the phase resolution can be kept low enough to avoid the use of complex compression algorithms. We have considered rotating schemes based on memory compression techniques and CORDIC, and we have adapted them in order to satisfy the simulation requirements.

Finally we have obtained area and speed results. Optimized demodulators present hardware savings and higher speeds. When compared to CORDIC-based loops, BRAM-based loops could be run by a faster clock but at the expense of more area. Nevertheless CORDIC-based loops have the advantage that they can be easily redesigned with minor changes. In addition, memory-based loops can be applied to higher bandwidths within a range up to 25.8 Mbauds. This work will be continued in order to achieve the remaining frequencies in FPGAs by evaluating the use of other synchronization algorithms, such as feed-forward synchronization and the application of VLSI architectural transforms such as look-ahead pipelining.

References

[1] Cummings, M., Haruyama, S.: FPGA in the software radio. IEEE Communications Magazine (1999) 108–112

[2] Hentschel, T., Henker, M., Fettweis, G.: The digital fron-end of software radio terminals. IEEE Personal Communications (1999) 40–46

[3] Dick, C., Harris, F.: Configurable logic for digital communications: Some signal processing perspectives. IEEE Communications Magazine (1999)

[4] Proakis, J.G.: Digital Communications. McGraw-Hill (2000)

[5] Hinedi, S., Shah, B.: Acquisition performance of various QPSK carrier tracking loops. IEEE Transactions on Communications **40** (1992) 1426–1429

[6] Dick, C., Harris, F., Rice, M.: Synchronization in software radios - carrier and timing recovery using FPGAs. In: IEEE Symposium on Field-Programmable Custom Computing Machines. (2000)

[7] Tierney, J., Rader, C.M., Gold, B.: A digital frequency synthesizer. IEEE Transactions on Audio and Electroacoustics **19** (1971) 48–57

[8] Vankka, J.: Methods of mapping from phase to sine amplitude in direct digital synthesis. IEEE Transactions on Ultrasonics, Ferroelectrics, and Frequency Control **44** (1997) 526–534

[9] Volder, J.E.: The CORDIC trigonometric computing technique. IRE Transactions on Electronics and Computers (1959) 330–334

[10] Walther, J.S.: A unified algorithm for elementary functions. (1971) 379–385

[11] Loehning, M., Hentschel, T., Fettweis, G.: Digital down conversion in software radio terminals. In: 10th European Signal Processing Conference (EUSIPCO).Tampere, Finland. Volume 3. (2000)

[12] Vuori, J.: Implementation of a digital phase-locked loop using cordic algorithm. In: Proceedings of the IEEE International Symposium on Circuits and Systems. Volume 4. (1996) 164–167

[13] Cardells-Tormo, F., Valls-Coquillat, J.: Optimized FPGA-implementation of quadrature dds. In: IEEE International Symposium on Circuits and Systems. (2002)

[14] Xilinx: The programmable logic data book (2001)

[15] E.T.S.I.: Digital Video Broadcasting (DVB). framing structure, channel coding and modulation for 11/12 Ghz satellite services. European Standard EN 300 421 (1997)

[16] Bellaouar, A., O'brecht, M.S., Fahim, A.M., Elmasry, M.I.: Low-power direct digital frequency synthesis for wireless communications. IEEE Journal of Solid-State Circuits **35** (2000) 385–390

[17] Nicholas, H.T., Samueli, H.: An analysis of the output spectrum of direct digital frequency synthesizers in the presence of phase-accumulator truncation. In: Proceedings 41st Annual Frequency Control Symposium 1987. (1987) 495–502

[18] Gielis, G.C., van de Plassche, R., van Valburg, J.: A 540-MHz 10-b polar-to-cartesian converter. IEEE Journal of Solid-State Circuits **26** (1991) 1645–1650

[19] Madisetti, A., Kwentus, A.Y., Willson, Jr., A.N.: A 100-MHz, 16-b, direct digital frequency synthesizer with a 100-dBc spurious-free dynamic range. IEEE Journal of Solid-State Circuits **34** (1999) 1034–1043

[20] Cardells, F., Valls, J.: Optimization of direct digital frequency synthesizer based on CORDIC. IEE Electronics Letters **37** (2001) 1278–1280

[21] Valls, J., Kuhlmann, M., Parhi, K.K.: Evaluation of CORDIC Algorithms for FPGA design. To be published in the Journal of VLSI Signal Processing (2002)

FPGA QAM Demodulator Design

Chris Dick[1] and Fred Harris[2]

[1] Xilinx Inc., Signal Processing Group, 2100 Logic Drive,
San Jose, CA 95124, USA
chris.dick@xilinx.com

[2] CUBIC Signal Processing Chair, College of Engineering, San Diego State University
San Diego, CA 92182, USA
fred.harris@sdsu.edu

Abstract. Bandwidth efficient communication systems employ high-order modulation schemes like M-ary QAM modulation for reasons of spectral efficiency. Many sophisticated signal processing algorithms are implemented in a QAM demodulator, including adaptive equalization, timing recovery, carrier recovery, automatic gain control and digital down conversion to name a few. This paper examines the FPGA implementation of the adaptive equalizer and carrier recovery loop for a 50 Mbps 16-QAM receiver.

1 Introduction

Digital signal processing (DSP) is the most important technology of our time. It has changed the way humans communicate, are serviced by medical procedures, do business, are entertained, travel, protect countries, explore our planet as well as others, and understand and predict nature. The driving requirement for DSP is high performance arithmetics. While instruction set architectures such as DSP processors and application specific integrated circuits (ASICs) have served this need adequately in the past, these outdated modes of computation will not be the dominant implementation vehicles for many current generation DSP systems, and they will certainly not be the primary DSP technology in the future. Rapidly increasing processing requirements, coupled with fiscal considerations, decreasing product market windows and the challenges of deep submicron fabrication all favor the use of reconfigurable technology as the cornerstone of complex DSP systems.

Field programmable gate arrays (FPGAs) have achieved high levels of success in many signal processing systems, in particular in the area of digital communications. Combining high-performance with enormous memory and input/output (I/O) bandwidth, FPGA signal processing platforms can service the many complex tasks performed in a modern communication transmitter and receiver. And of course we recognize that this solution maintains flexibility, a key requirement as communication technology moves forward to an era that will be dominated by the software defined radio (SDR).

This paper examines what could be considered one personality of a soft radio - an equalized 50 Mega-bit-per-second (Mbps)16-QAM receiver. The focus of the

M. Glesner, P. Zipf, and M. Renovell (Eds.): FPL 2002, LNCS 2438, pp. 112–121, 2002.

paper is the FPGA realization of the adaptive channel equalizer and the carrier tracking loop. Software and intellectual property (IP) is becoming *harder* than the supporting hardware platforms. Interlaced through the paper we emphasize the use of an efficient FPGA design methodology based on a visual dataflow paradigm called *System Generator for DSP*^{TM} [1] [2] (hereafter simply referred to as *System Generator*) for realizing our designs.

The first section of the paper introduces the demodulator architecture and provides a high-level overview of the topology. Next, we examine the adaptive equalizer, present some implementation considerations and describe its realization using System Generator. Performance plots and FPGA benchmarking data are provided. Finally, the carrier recovery loop (CRL) is described before concluding.

2 QAM Demodulator Architecture

The design space is rich when considering solutions to most signal processing applications, and nowhere is this more evident than in the design of digital communication systems. In the case of a QAM demodulator, although there are many opportunities for architectural innovation, the tasks of digital down conversion, matched filtering, automatic gain control (AGC), timing recovery, adaptive equalization, carrier tracking, source decoding and forward error control (FEC) will all generally be required.

Most modern bandwidth efficient communication systems use quadrature amplitude modulation. The input data stream is partitioned into sets of N bits. These bits are used to select one of 2^N possible waveforms that are both amplitude and phase modulated. The waveforms are directed to the channel, each with the same shape and bandwidth.

The basic operations required by an all digital QPSK or QAM receiver are illustrated in Fig. 1. The signal from the antenna is conditioned using analog signal processing, translated to a suitable analog intermediate frequency (IF) and then sampled. Indicated in the diagram is the symbol timing recovery process, adaptive equalizer, carrier recovery synchronizer and FEC.

2.1 Adaptive Channel Equalizer

Adaptive equalizers operate in a receiver to minimize intersymbol interference (ISI), due to channel-induced distortion, of the received signal. The equalizer operates in cascade with a matched filter (MF), synchronous sampler, and decision device (slicer) operating at the symbol rate. A gradient descent process such as the least-mean square (LMS) algorithm [3] adjusts the equalizer weights to minimize the difference between the input and output of the decision device. In modern receivers the sampling process precedes the matched filter, and in order to satisfy the Nyquist criterion for the matched filter, the sample rate is greater than the symbol rate by a ratio of small integers p-to-q such as 3-to-2 or 4-to-3 and often is 2-to-1 to simplify the subsequent task of down sampling prior to the

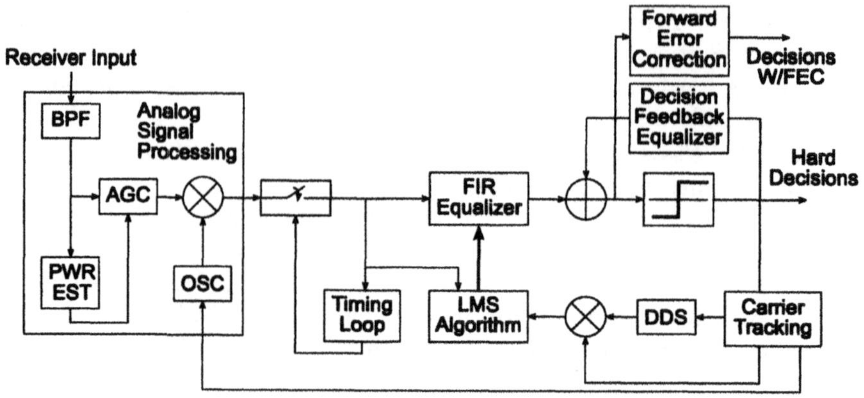

Fig. 1. Generic QAM demodulator.

slicer. If the down sampling occurs prior to the equalizer, the equalizer operates at 1-sample per symbol and it is termed a symbol-rate equalizer, and if the down sampling occurs after the equalizer, the equalizer operates on p/q-samples per symbol and it is termed a fractionally-spaced equalizer (FSE).

There are many options for realizing adaptive filters, including FIR, IIR lattice and transform domain architectures. There are also a large number of algorithmic choices for implementing the coefficient update process - least-mean-square, fast Kalman, conventional Kalman, square-root Kalman and recursive-least-square (RLS) lattice to name a few. One of the most successful, because of its simplicity and excellent behavior under finite arithmetic conditions, is the least-mean-square (LMS) algorithm.

In the case of an adaptive decision directed (DD) channel equalizer the desired signal is produced by utilizing the known structure of the system alphabet. A 4-tap decision directed equalizer using an LMS coefficient update is shown in Fig. 2. The input samples are complex valued quantities as are the filter weights and the output signal.

Further, in order to avoid aliasing, we will employ a fractionally spaced equalizer that samples at a rate of two samples per symbol. The equalizer result is of course generated at the baud rate T. The equalizer is a multirate structure that is most efficiently implemented using a polyphase decimator architecture.

2.2 Equalizer Implementation

The receiver was implemented in two stages. First the equalizer was designed and verified, then the carrier recovery loop, and finally the two designs were combined to produce the completed system. An 8-tap equalizer is to be employed in our system. Each polyphase segment will comprise a 4-tap filter. Each symbol in the 16-QAM alphabet carries 4 bits of information. To achieve the required 50 Mbps data rate the symbol rate must be 12.5 Mbaud. Each polyphase segment in the equalizer will operate at the low output symbol rate in contrast to the

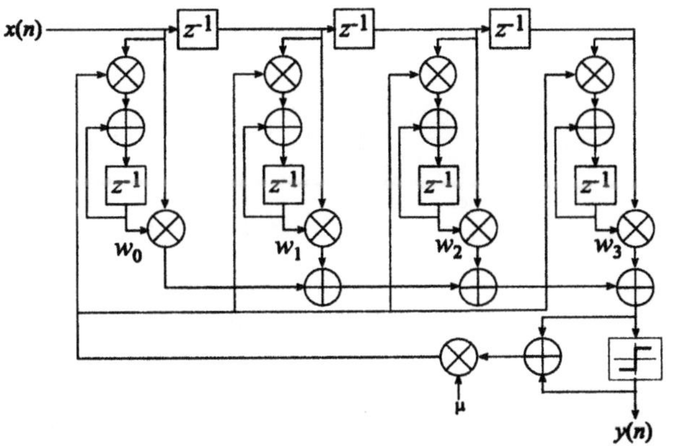

Fig. 2. Decision directed fractionally spaced equalizer employing LMS coefficient update.

higher input sample rate. That is, the equalizer must generate a new output at a sample rate of 12.5 MHz. We will assume that the coefficients need to be updated at the symbol rate. The equalizer architecture must now be defined. There are many options. For example, a fully parallel design consisting of 8 FIR processing elements (PE) and 8 LMS processors could be employed. In this case the system would only be required to support a clock frequency of 12.5 MHz. Since this is a very modest operating point for current generation FPGAs, a folded design is considered that runs at a higher clock rate and uses only a small number of functional units to service all of the operations. This in turn minimizes the FPGA device utilization. The performance objective can be achieved using a single FIR and LMS PE in each of the two polyphase arms. This only requires a clock frequency of 50 MHz. In each polyphase segment, the four filter operations will be scheduled onto a single complex multiply-accumulate (MAC) engine. Similarly, the 4 coefficient updates will be folded onto a single LMS PE. The System Generator implementation of the equalizer is shown in Fig. 3. Subsystem $F1$ contains the polyphase filter (Fig. 4) and LMS processors. $F2$ is the symbol de-mapping circuit consisting primarily of several comparators and a small look-up table. The error signal is generated using the complex subtractor comprising $A0$ and $A1$. $F3$ weights the error signal by the adaption rate constant.

The heart of both the FIR and LMS PE is a complex MAC. This was implemented using 4 multipliers and 2 additions. The multipliers are realized using the embedded multipliers in the Virtex-II^{TM} (and Virtex-II Pro^{TM}) FPGA family. The LMS PE is shown in Fig. 5. $F0$ is the address generator that accesses data from the two (one for each of the in-phase and quadrature signals) regressor vector memories $M0$ and $M1$. This data, along with the coefficients from the preceeding time-step, stored in buffers $C0$ and $C1$, are presented to the complex MAC consisting of the complex multiplier $CMPY$ and the accumulators $A1$ and $A2$. The equalizer error signal is also required to perform the update, and this is

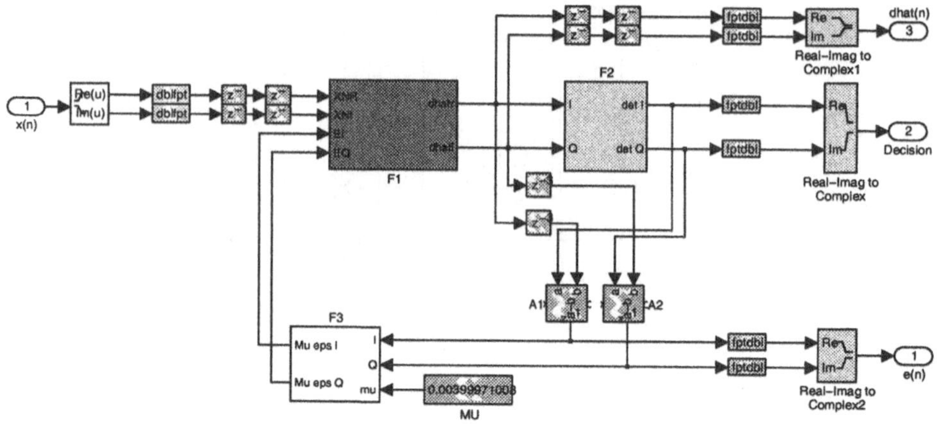

Fig. 3. System Generator implementation of the adaptive equalizer. Top level design.

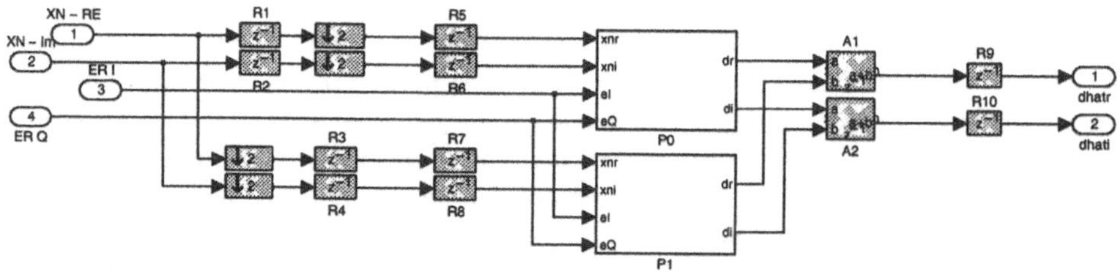

Fig. 4. System Generator implementation of the equalizer polyphase filter. Input samples are presented at a rate of 2 samples/symbol while the output samples are generated at the baud rate T.

represented in the figure as terminals 3 (error signal in-phase component) and 4 (error signal quadrature component).

What may not be obvious from the previous description and the associated figures is that the FIR and LMS PEs each have their own local copy of the complex channel data. Why has this architectural choice been made when the filter computation and the LMS coefficient update process each use the same data? [3] The reason is hardware performance related, and in particular associated with the desire to pipeline the design to achieve a suitable clock frequency. The memory systems in the FIR and LMS processors are skewed in time with respect to each other. This effectively decouples the processes and permits the filter and LMS engines to be heavily pipelined. In looking ahead to the integration of the equalizer and carrier recovery loop, the symbol decisions required to drive the coefficient adjustment will no longer be derived from the detector within the equalizer, but from the carrier recovery loop. The relative timing between the

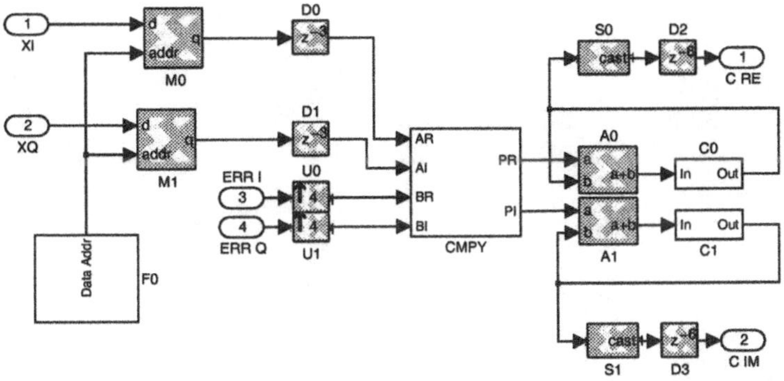

Fig. 5. System Generator implementation of the LMS coefficient update processor.

decisions and the regressor vector samples needs to be handled carefully, and the decoupled memory architecture meets this objective.

The equalizer was tested using an exponentially weighted multipath channel model. A 16-QAM alphabet was generated, waveform encoded and upsampled using an interpolation factor of 4 before being applied to the channel. The channel output samples were re-timed, done manually in this case since timing recovery is not in the design under consideration, decimated by 2 and presented at a rate of 2 samples/symbol to the equalizer.

The next question that arises is related to quantizing the design, or defining suitable bit-precisions for the various nodes in the circuit. Because System Generator employs the Simulink(R) kernel and has access to all of the flexibility offered by Matlab, it is straightforward to establish a test and verification procedure that permits rapid design exploration. In the System Generator design, the data format of each functional unit is specified symbolically. The references are resolved by executing a Matlab script that allocates workspace variables. Each equalizer customization is defined by unique script. When the simulation is run, various signals are logged to the workspace and used in post-simulation analysis. Fig. 6 shows the received signal with ISI, the instantaneous equalization error, the constellation diagram in the initial acquisition phase, and then the constellation again with the startup transient removed for 12- (subplots (a) to (d)), 18- (subplots (e) to (h))and 24-bit (subplots (i) to (l))precision arithmetic. Plots (c), (g) and (k) for each precision presents symbols 1 to 4000 of the simulation while plots (d), (h) and (l) in each case shows symbols 4000 to 5000. For all cases the adaption rate constant is 0.004. From Fig. 6 we note that a 12-bit precision design does not provide the required performance. The equalized constellation has a residual phase rotation due to the low-precision calculations and the error vector magnitude will be large as is evident from the significant dispersion of the constellation points. The 18-bit datapath in Fig. 6 provides adequate performance. As shown in Fig. 6(j), (k) and (l), increasing the datapath precision to 24-bits provides little improvement. An additional point to note from the plots is

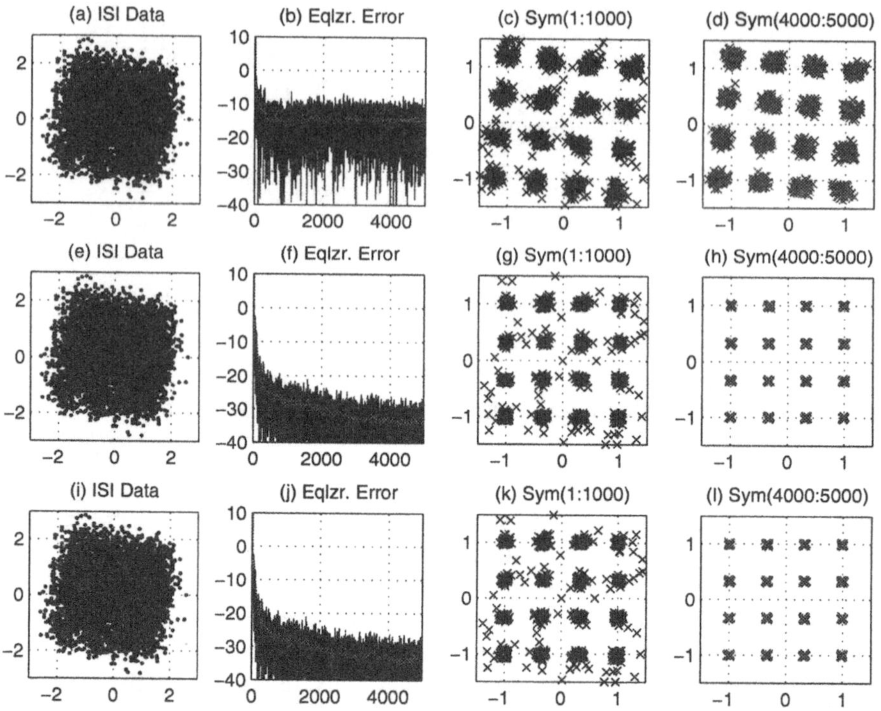

Fig. 6. Adaptive equalizer simulation. (a),(b),(c),(d) 12-bit precision datapath. (e),(f),(g),(h) 18-bit precision datapath. (i),(j),(k),(l) 24-bit precision datapath.

the comparatively large value of the equalizer error for the low-precision design, compared to the 18b and 24b designs that exhibit a 20dB improvement after convergence.

The design was implemented using version 4.2i (speed-file version 1.96) of the Xilinx tool suite. The 50 MHz clock frequency was achieved using a -5 speed grade Virtex-II device. The utilization data is: 1808 logic slices and 18 embedded multipliers. Place-and-route was run with the switches `par -ol 5 -xe 2`.

2.3 16-QAM Carrier Recovery

There are many options for implementing carrier phase and frequency synchronization in a digital communication system, but at the heart of all synchronizers is the digital phase-locked loop (DPLL). Fig. 7 shows the CRL architecture used in our design. This DPLL employs a proportional plus integral loop filter formed by a scaled digital integrator and a scaled direct path. The filter coefficients K_p and K_i control the DPLL bandwidth and damping factor. The phase detector is implemented using the arctangent operation suggested by the *Atan* block.

The most complex component in the loop is the phase detector. Since the phase of QPSK or QAM signals is data dependent, the phase detector must strip

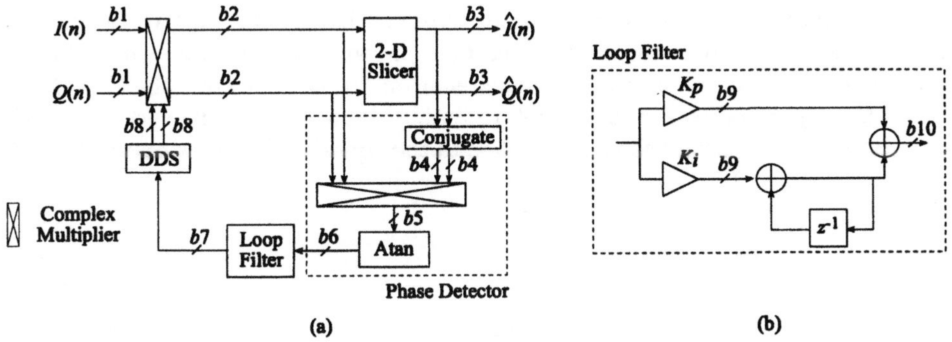

Fig. 7. 16-QAM carrier recovery loop. (a) Top-level architecture. (b) Loop filter.

the modulation from the received signal and produce a signal proportional to the phase difference between the locally generated quadrature carriers and those of the received signal. The CORDIC [5] algorithm was used to compute the arctangent operation. Fig. 8(a),(b),(c) and (d) show respectively the rotating constellation (0.001 Hz Doppler frequency, sample rate = 1 Hz) used to test the CRL, the CRL phase error, the CRL DDS waveform and the derotated constellation. The CORDIC processor was a fully unfolded architecture, using 5 iterations and 11-bit precision input samples. Bit-growth to the final output precision of 16-bits was permitted in the CORDIC algorithm. Observe from the figures that the loop achieved lock in approximately 20 symbols.

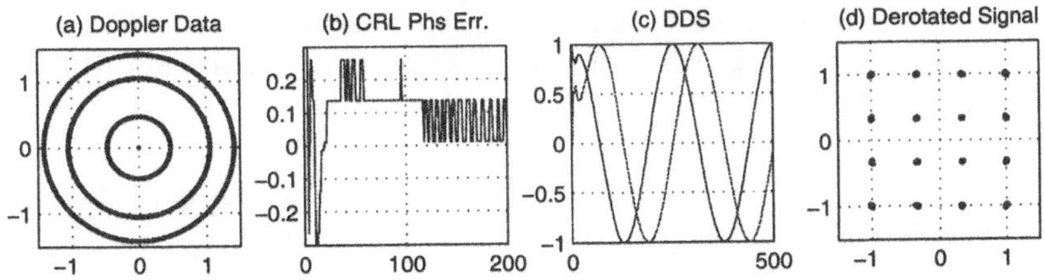

Fig. 8. (a) Data with Doppler. (b) CRL phase error. (c) CRL DDS. (d) Derotated constellation.

2.4 Equalized and Carrier-Locked Demodulator

After independent verification, the equalizer and CRL were integrated to produce the final design. The top-level System Generator specification of the system is shown in Fig. 9. The design includes a data source, channel model, Doppler source, adaptive equalizer, carrier loop and various virtual instruments to observe critical nodes in the circuit. The Doppler content of the signal means that the equalizer slicer cannot be used to drive the decision directed LMS coefficient update. The required decisions must be supplied by the detector in the carrier recovery loop. Further, these decisions must be available at the same rotation rate, and direction, as the received constellation. To achieve this, the CRL DDS cisoid is conjugated to produce a heterodyning signal that up-converts the CRL hard decisions. This waveform is supplied to the equalizer LMS processor. Fig. 10

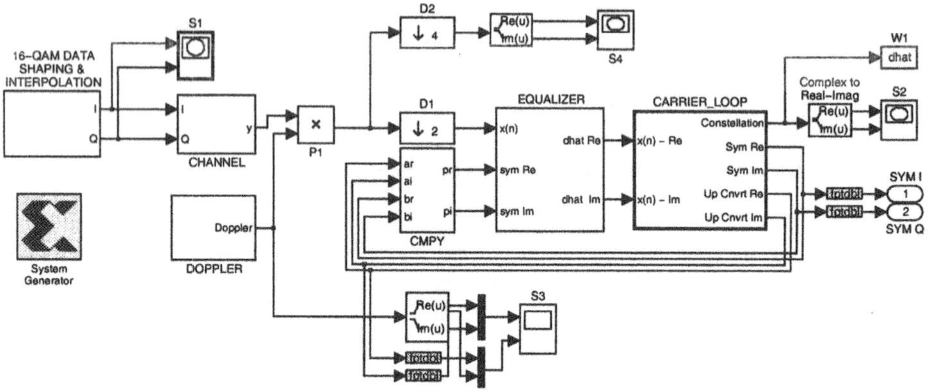

Fig. 9. System Generator implementation of QAM demodulator with equalizer and carrier recovery loop.

shows the equalized and carrier locked baseband data. Fig. 10(a), (b),(c) and (d) show respectively the received data with ISI and Doppler shift, initial acquisition phase, the constellation a short time after the transient response and finally the constellation after the channel induced ISI has been removed and the Doppler rotation accounted for.

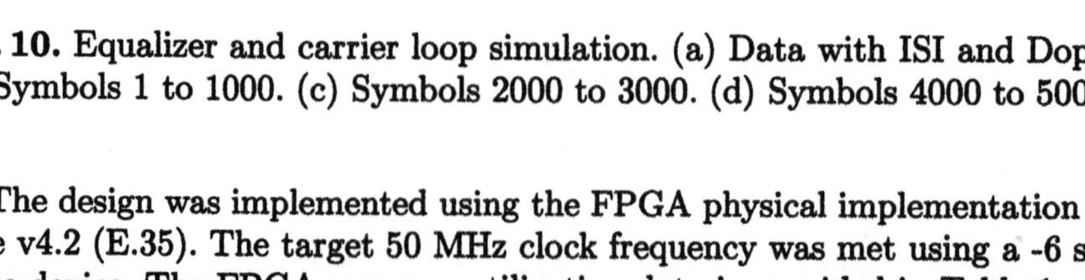

Fig. 10. Equalizer and carrier loop simulation. (a) Data with ISI and Doppler. (b) Symbols 1 to 1000. (c) Symbols 2000 to 3000. (d) Symbols 4000 to 5000.

The design was implemented using the FPGA physical implementation software v4.2 (E.35). The target 50 MHz clock frequency was met using a -6 speed grade device. The FPGA resource utilization data is provided in Table 1.

Function	Slice Count	Block RAMs	Embedded Multipliers
Equalizer	1808	0	18
Carrier Recovery Loop	523	1	8
Symbol Rotate	58	0	3
Total	2389	1	29

Table 1. FPGA resource utilization for the equalizer and carrier recovery loop.

3 Conclusion

The continuing evolution of communication standards and competitive pressure in the market-place dictate that communication system architects must start the engineering design and development cycle while standards are still in a fluid state. Third and future generation communication infrastructure must support multiple modulation formats and air interface standards. FPGAs provide the flexibility to achieve this goal, while simultaneously providing high levels of performance.

We have reviewed several key functions required in a QAM demodulator. This topic is of interest in the context of soft radios because bandwidth efficient modulation schemes, like M-ary QAM, are important radio personalities for configurable communication platforms. The keystone of the FPGA is flexibility. This attribute enables a large number of implementation alternatives for a given datapath.

As signal processing systems increase in complexity, software and intellectual property development become harder than the implementation of the target hardware itself. The equalized receiver described here was implemented using the System Generator [1] system level design tool. This approach provided a rapid development cycle, while providing a useful environment to explore and quantify the performance of different quantized versions of the system. The benefit of this approach from a hardware development perspective, is that the simulation model is also the FPGA source specification.

References

1. Xilinx Inc.:
   http://www.xilinx.com/xlnx/xil_prodcat_product.jsp?title=system_generator
2. Hwang, J., Milne, B., Shirazi, N., and Stroomer, J.: System Level Tools for DSP in FPGAs, Field-Programmable Logic and Applications, FPL 2001, Springer Lecture Notes in Computer Science, 2001 pp 534-543
3. Haykin, S.: Adaptive Filter Theory, Prentice Hall, New Jersey, 1996
4. The Mathworks Inc, Simulink, Dynamic System Simulation for Matlab, Using Simulink, Natick, Massachusetts, U.S.A, 1999
5. Hen Hu, Y.: CORDIC-Based VLSI Architectures for Digital Signal Processing, IEEE Signal Processing Magazine, July 1992 16-35

Analytical Framework for Switch Block Design

Guy G. Lemieux and David M. Lewis

Edward S. Rogers Sr. Dept. of Electrical and Computer Engineering
University of Toronto, Toronto, Ontario, Canada
{Lemieux, Lewis}@eecg.utoronto.ca

Abstract. One popular FPGA interconnection network is based on the island-style model, where rows and columns of logic blocks are separated by channels containing routing wires. Switch blocks are placed at the intersections of the horizontal and vertical channels to allow the wires to be connected together. Previous switch block design has focused on the analysis of individual switch blocks or the use of ad hoc design with experimental evaluation. This paper presents an analytical framework which considers the design of a continuous fabric of switch blocks containing wire segments of any length. The framework is used to design new switch blocks which are experimentally shown to be as effective as the best ones known to date. With this framework, we hope to inspire new ways of looking at switch block design.

1 Introduction

Over the past several years, a number of different switch block designs have been proposed such as those shown in Figure 1. FPGAs such as the Xilinx XC4000-series [1] use a switch block style known as *disjoint*. Some alternatives to this style, known as *universal* [2] and *Wilton* [3], require fewer routing tracks and use less transistor area with interconnect of single-length wires. However, with longer wire segments they use more switches per track and often require more transistor area overall [4]. The *Imran* block [5] addresses this overhead by modifying the *Wilton* pattern to use the same number of switches as the *disjoint* pattern.

These switch blocks are designed using different methodologies. The *universal* switch block is analytically designed to be independently routable for all two-point nets. Recently, the *hyperuniversal* switch block [6] extends this for multi-point nets. These blocks rely on reordering nets at every switch block, so their local optimality does not extend to the entire routing fabric. In comparison, the *Wilton* and *Imran* switch blocks are examples of ad hoc design with experimental validation. The *Wilton* block changes the track number assigned to a net as it turns. This way, two different global routes may reach two different tracks at the same destination channel. This forms two disjoint paths, a feature we call the *diversity* of a network. The *Wilton* and *Imran* designs introduce the notion that a switch block must consider its role as part of a larger switching fabric.

The above methods have produced switch blocks that perform well, but there is no formal method to design a switch block while considering the overall routing fabric. In pursuit of this goal, this paper introduces an analytical framework which considers

M. Glesner, P. Zipf, and M. Renovell (Eds.): FPL 2002, LNCS 2438, pp. 122–131, 2002.

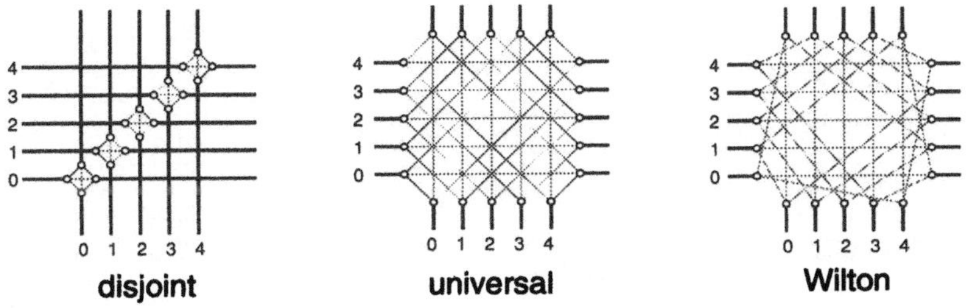

Fig. 1. Different switch block styles.

both long wire segments and the interaction of many switch blocks connected together. This framework includes a restricted switch block model which allows us to analyse the diversity of the network. The framework is used to design an ad hoc switch block named *shifty* and two analytic ones named *diverse* and *diverse-clique*. These new switch blocks are very diverse, and routing experiments show they are as effective as the others.

2 Design Framework

This section describes the switch block framework being composed of a switch block model, permutation mapping functions, and simplifying assumptions and properties.

2.1 Switch Block Model

The traditional model of a switch block draws a large box around the intersection of a horizontal and vertical routing channel. Within the box, switches connect a wire on one side to any wires on the other three sides. Long wire segments pass straight across the switch block, but some track shifting is necessary to implement fixed length wires with one layout tile. Figure 2a) presents this model in a new way by partitioning the switch block into three subblocks: ***endpoint*** **(f_e)**, ***midpoint*** **(f_m)**, and ***midpoint-endpoint*** **(f_{me})** subblocks. The endpoint (midpoint) subblock is the region where the ends (midpoints) of wire segments connect to the ends (midpoints) of other wire segments. The f_{me} subblock connects the middle regions of some wires to the ends of others. A switch placed between two sides always falls into one of these subblocks.

The traditional model in Figure 2a) is too general for simple diversity analysis, so we propose restricting the permissible switch locations. One restriction is to prohibit f_{me} switches; this was done in the *Imran* block [5]. We propose to further constrain the f_m switch locations to lie within smaller subblocks called $f_{m,i}$, as shown in Figure 2b) for length-four wires. This *track group model* is a key component to the framework.

The track group model partitions wires into *track groups* according to their wire length and starting points. The midpoint subblocks are labeled $f_{m,i}$, where i is a position between 1 and $L-1$ along a wire of length L. This model is somewhat restrictive, but it can still represent many switch blocks, *e.g.*, *Imran*, and we will show that it performs well. As well, early experiments we conducted without the $f_{m,i}$ subblock restric-

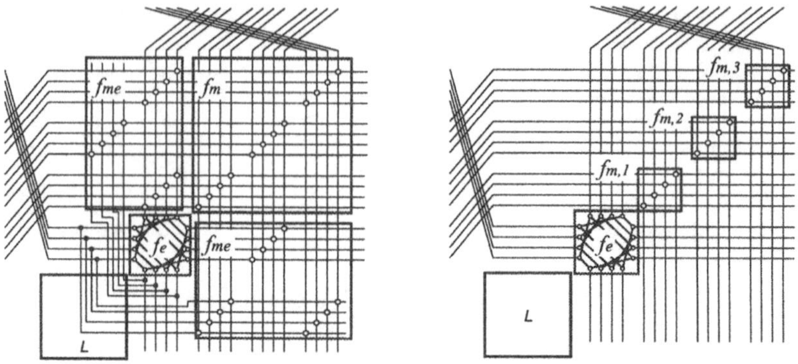

Fig. 2. Switch block models with subblocks, a) traditional and b) track group model.

tions did not produce better results. However, the $f_{m,i}$ subblocks explicitly force track groups to be in separate routing domains so each group can be treated independently.

2.2 Permutation Mapping Functions

Previous work suggests only a small number of switches need to be placed within a switch block. Early work [7] defined switch block flexibility, F_s, as the number of other wires connecting to each wire in this block. They found that $F_s = 3$ is the lowest that is routable with single-length wire segments. Other work [4, 5] has used $F_s = 3$ at wire endpoints and $F_s = 1$ at wire midpoints when long wire segments are used. As well, our experience with $F_s < 3$ is that a few more tracks but less transistor area is needed [8]. This suggests $6W$ and W are reasonable upper bounds for the number of switches in endpoint and midpoint subblocks, respectively.

Given these upper bounds, switch locations can be represented by a *permutation mapping function* between each pair of sides. The different mapping functions and their implied forward direction are shown in Figure 3. In this figure, $f_{e,i}(t)$, or simply $f_{e,i}$, represents an endpoint turn of type i. A switch connects the wire originating at track t to track $f_{e,i}(t)$ on the destination side. Turns in the reverse direction to those indicated are represented as $f_{e,i}^{-1}$ such that $f^{-1}(f(t)) = t$.

Similarly, $f_{m,i}$ is a mapping function for a midpoint turn at position i along the length of a wire, with the most South/West endpoint being the origin at position $i = 0$. Figure 3b) illustrates the different midpoint subblocks in a fabric of 2×4 logic blocks (L) for a single track group. The other three track groups are independent, but they would be similar and have staggered starting locations. There are no connections between the track groups.

Examples of mapping functions for various switch blocks are shown in Table 1. Each of these functions are modulo W, where W is the track group width. Also, note that it is common for connections straight across a switch block (E–W or N–S) to stay in the same track, so it is usually assumed that $f_{e,5} = f_{e,6} = t$.

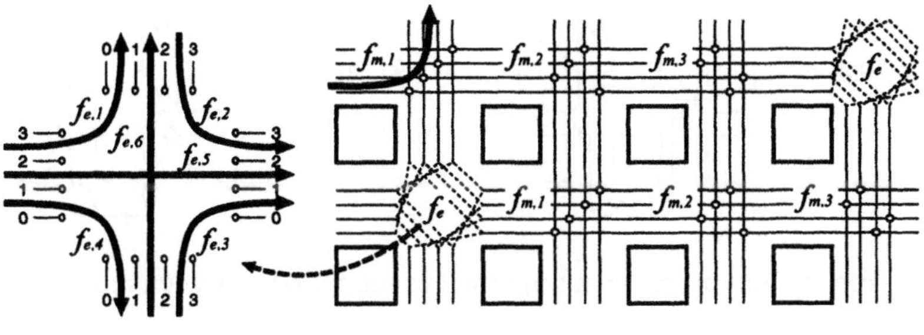

Fig. 3. Mapping functions for a) endpoint and b) midpoint subblock turns.

2.3 Additional Assumptions

In addition to the explicit assumptions above, there are a few implicit ones being made as well. It is assumed that the subblocks are square with W tracks on each side and there is a one-to-one correspondence between the originating track and the destination track. Since $f^{-1}(f(t)) = t$, it is also presumed that each switch is bidirectional. Additionally, we assume a track group contains only one wire length and switch type.

2.4 Commutative Switch Blocks

The mapping functions of the *universal* and *Imran* switch blocks involve *twists* where the function is of the form $f(t) = W - t + c$. Unfortunately, these functions are difficult to analyse because the twist is not commutative. Using commutative functions simplifies the model because the order in which turns are made becomes unimportant. Paths with an arbitrary number or sequence of turns can be reduced to a canonical permutation which uniquely determines the destination track. Later in Section 3.2, this will allow us to significantly reduce the search space. We define a switch block to be *commutative* if all of its mapping functions are commutative.

Consider the example shown in Figure 4, where two paths are compared in two different architectures. The left architecture uses commutative switch blocks, but the right one does not. The destination track of the upper path is $f_{e,2}(f_{e,4}(f_{e,3}(f_{e,1}(t))))$, while the lower path is $f_{e,3}(f_{e,1}(f_{e,2}(f_{e,4}(t))))$. In a commutative architecture, both paths can be rewritten as $f_{e,1}(f_{e,2}(f_{e,3}(f_{e,4}(t))))$. These necessarily reach the same track. In a non-commutative architecture, the operations cannot be reordered and the paths may reach different tracks. This example suggests that commutative architectures are less diverse. However, results will demonstrate that commutative switch blocks are very diverse and as routable as the non-commutative *Imran* block.

3 Framework Applications

To illustrate the use of the new framework, two approaches will be used to determine a set of permutation mapping functions. The first, named *shifty*, is an ad hoc commutative switch block. The second creates two switch blocks, named *diverse* and

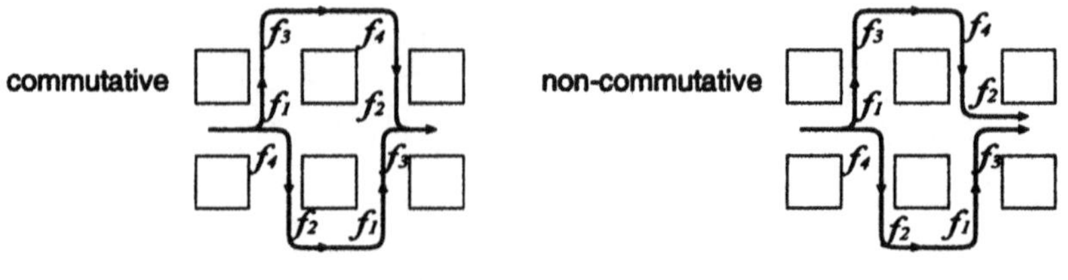

Fig. 4. Turn order is not important in commutative switch blocks.

diverse-clique, by optimizing diversity. Both of these approaches assume length-four interconnect wires. As well, they will assume that two separate layout tiles can be used in a checkered fashion to further increase diversity.

3.1 Application: *shifty* and *universal-TG* Designs

The first application of the new framework is the design of a commutative switch block similar to *Imran* but without the non-commutative twists. The following mapping functions describe the new switch block: $f_{e,1} = t-1$, $f_{e,2} = t-3$, $f_{e,3} = t-2$, $f_{e,4} = t-4$, and $f_{m,i} = t \pmod W$. This block is named *shifty* because each turn involves a shift from one track number to another by a constant amount. The constant values are chosen to be small because the arithmetic is always done modulo W. This avoids $f_{e,1}$ from being equivalent to $f_{e,4}$, for example, except with certain small W values.

Other switch blocks can also be adopted within this framework. For example, the *disjoint* and *Imran* switch blocks naturally conform to the track group model already. As well, suppose the *universal* pattern is applied only at endpoint subblocks and the identity mapping $f_{m,i} = t$ is used at midpoint subblocks. This new pattern, *universal-TG*, is similar to the original in that *each subblock* can connect any set of two-point nets that obey basic bandwidth constraints. It also requires less transistor area with long wire segments in the same way that *Imran* improves *Wilton* by reducing the number of switches per track.

To create additional diversity, it is possible to use two different switch block designs arranged in a checkerboard pattern. If the above switch blocks are assigned to the white square locations, a modified one can be used on the black square locations. These black switch blocks are characterized by their own mapping functions, g. Ad hoc designs for various g switch blocks, which are chosen to be slightly different from their f counterparts, are shown in Table 1. In choosing the specific g_e functions for the *disjoint* and *universal-TG* blocks, care is taken to preserve their layout structures by merely re-ordering the horizontal tracks.

3.2 Application: *diverse* and *diverse-clique* Designs

This section will use the design framework to develop commutative switch blocks that are maximally diverse for all possible two-turn paths. Two different switch blocks will be designed, *diverse* and *diverse-clique*. The latter design is more restricted because its endpoint subblock uses the 4-wire clique layout structure of the *disjoint* switch block.

Table 1. Complete switch block mappings used for white (f) and black (g) squares

	White Square Switch Block					Black Square Switch Block			
Turn	*disjoint*	*universal-TG*	*Imran*	*shifty*	Turn	*disjoint*	*universal-TG*	*Imran*	*shifty*
$f_{e,1}$	t	$W-t-1$	$W-t$	$t-1$	$g_{e,1}$	$t-1$	$W-t-2$	$W-t+3$	$t-8$
$f_{e,2}$	t	t	$t+1$	$t-3$	$g_{e,2}$	$t+1$	$t+1$	$t+3$	$t-7$
$f_{e,3}$	t	$W-t-1$	$W-t-2$	$t-2$	$g_{e,3}$	$t+1$	$W-t$	$W-t+2$	$t-9$
$f_{e,4}$	t	t	$t-1$	$t-4$	$g_{e,4}$	$t-1$	$t-1$	$t+1$	$t-6$
$f_{m,i}$	t	t	t	t	$g_{m,i}$	$t+1$	$t+1$	$t+1$	$t+1$

This design approach is repeated for an architecture containing two layout tiles, f and g, arranged in a checkered pattern.

Design Space Let each switch block mapping function be represented by the equations $f_i(t) = t + a_i \bmod W$ or $g_i(t) = t + b_i \bmod W$, where i represents one of the endpoint or midpoint turn types. The a_i and b_i values are constants which can be summarized in vector form as:

$$\boldsymbol{x}_W = \left[a_{e,1}\ a_{e,2}\ a_{e,3}\ a_{e,4}\ a_{m,1}\ a_{m,2}\ a_{m,3}\ b_{e,1}\ b_{e,2}\ b_{e,3}\ b_{e,4}\ b_{m,1}\ b_{m,2}\ b_{m,3}\right]^T.$$

Note that a solution $\boldsymbol{x}_W$ is only valid for a specific value of W. Constraining f and g in this way explores only a portion the design space. However, this is sufficient to develop very diverse switch blocks.

Enumerating the Path-Pairs Before counting diversity, we enumerate all paths containing two turns and the pairs of these paths that should be diverse.

The six basic two-turn paths created by $\binom{4}{2} = 6$ pairs of single turns are: ENE, ESE, ENW, WNE, NES and SEN, where N, S, E, or W refer to compass directions. For example, two different ENE paths, using columns A and B to reach row *out1*, are shown in Figure 5. In general, the commutative property allows all ENE paths (or ESE paths, etc.) of an infinite routing fabric to be enumerated using the 8×8 grid or *supertile* in Figure 5. The size of the supertile arises from the length-four wires and two (checkerboard) layout tiles. Within it, each subblock is labeled with the mapping functions from one track group.

A number of isomorphic paths can be eliminated using the supertile and commutative property. Longer horizontal or vertical distances would reach another supertile and turn at a switch block equivalent to one in this supertile. Similarly, other input rows can be disregarded. Since NEN and SES paths are commutatively equivalent to ENE and ESE paths, they are also ignored.

For maximum diversity, each *pair of paths* that reach the same output row must reach different tracks. With 8 possible routes (columns A–H), there are $\binom{8}{2} = 28$ pairs of paths to be compared. Hence, for all turn types and all output rows, there are $6 \times 7 \times 28 = 1176$ *path-pairs* to be compared.

Counting Diversity To detect diversity between a pair of paths, first compute the difference between the two permutation mappings, $y = f_{pathA} - f_{pathB}$. The path-pair is

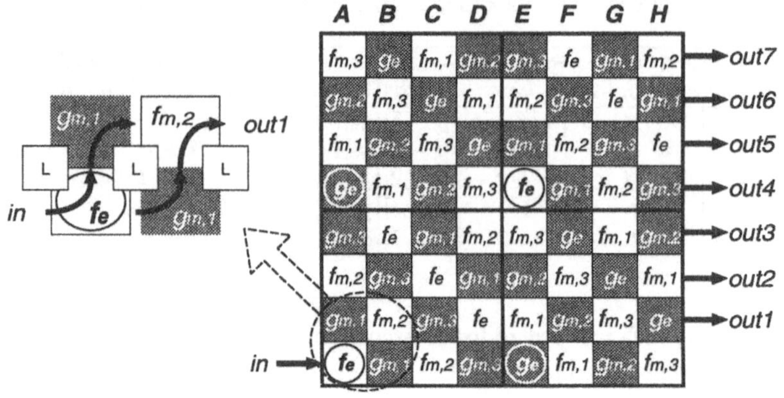

Fig. 5. An 8 × 8 grid or supertile used for enumerating all two-turn paths.

diverse if y is non-zero. This can be written in matrix form as $\boldsymbol{y} = \boldsymbol{A} \cdot \boldsymbol{x}_W$ where each row in $\boldsymbol{A}$ is predetermined based on the path-pair being considered, and each row in $\boldsymbol{y}$ is the corresponding diversity test result.The number of rows has been considerably reduced by the large number of equivalent paths eliminated earlier. Additional types of path-pairs (not only those with two turns) can be represented by adding more rows to $\boldsymbol{A}$ and $\boldsymbol{y}$.

Diversity of a given switch block $\boldsymbol{x}_W$ is measured by counting the number of non-zero entries in $\boldsymbol{y}$. For our architecture, the maximum diversity is 1176.

Searching Design Space Rather than solve large matrix equations to maximize the number of non-zero values in $\boldsymbol{y}$, we performed various random and brute-force searches of $\boldsymbol{x}_W$ for W ranging from 2 to 18. Typically, an exhaustive search produced the best results in about one CPU-day (1 GHz Pentium) even though it wasn't allowed to run to completion.

Switch Blocks Created Using the above procedure, switch blocks named *diverse* are designed for a variety of track group widths, $W \leq 18$. For each W, a solution set $\boldsymbol{x}_W$ is found. Similarly, we designed a *diverse-clique* switch block which preserves the 4-wire clique structure at endpoint subblocks. A layout strategy for these cliques is given in [9]. The precise solution sets obtained for these two switch blocks can be found in [8].

4 Results

The new switch blocks are evaluated below by counting diversity and computing the minimum channel width and area from numerous routing experiments.

Diversity Results The diversity of various switch blocks is shown in Figure 7. The *disjoint* switch block has no diversity but its checkered version has considerably more.

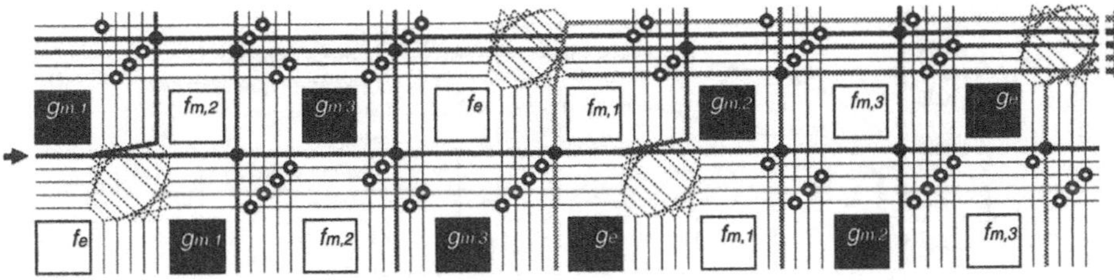

Fig. 6. Checkered layout showing diversity of a $W = 5$ *diverse-clique* switch block.

The *shifty* switch block and its checkered version provide even more diversity. However, the *diverse* and *diverse-clique* checkered switch blocks reach the highest levels of diversity. For $W > 10$, these are within 99% of the maximum possible. However, note that it is impossible to attain maximum diversity when $W < 8$ because some of the 8 global routes necessarily map to the same track. Considering this, the *diverse* and *diverse-clique* switch blocks perform very well at being diverse.

Routing Results The experimental environment is similar to the one used in [4]. Benchmark circuits are mapped into 4, 5, and 6-input LUTs, clustered into groups of 6, and placed once. The new switch blocks are evaluated using a modified version [8] of the VPR router [4]. Routing experiments use only length four wires in the interconnect. Half of all tracks use pass transistors 16x minimum width, and the other half use buffers of size 6x minimum [10]. Although not shown, similar results are obtained if all wiring tracks contain buffers.

The routability performance of the new switch blocks is presented in Figures 8 and 9. The former plots the minimum number of tracks required to route, W_{min}, while the latter plots the transistor area of the FPGA at the low-stress point of $1.2 \times W_{min}$ tracks. The graphs on the left compare *shifty* to the older switch blocks, and the graphs on the right compare *disjoint* to the newer switch blocks. A number of different curves are drawn in the graphs, corresponding to different LUT sizes (as labeled) and whether one layout tile is used (**bold** curves) or two tiles are checkered (thin curves). Delay results have been omitted because there is no apparent correlation with switch block style.

The area and W_{min} results exhibit only small variations across the designs, so conclusions might be sensitive to noise and must be carefully drawn. Each data point is an arithmetic average of the twenty largest MCNC circuits, so large variations should not be expected unless many circuits are affected. To mitigate the influence of noise, it is important to identify trends in the results, *e.g.*, across all of the different LUT sizes.

Analysis One clear trend in the routing results is that the plain *disjoint* switch block performs worse than any perturbation of it (including its own checkered version). Beyond this, the ranking of specific switch blocks is difficult. It appears that *shifty* is the best, followed by *universal-TG* and *Imran*, then *disjoint*. The diversity-optimized switch blocks are better than *disjoint*, but worse than *shifty*.

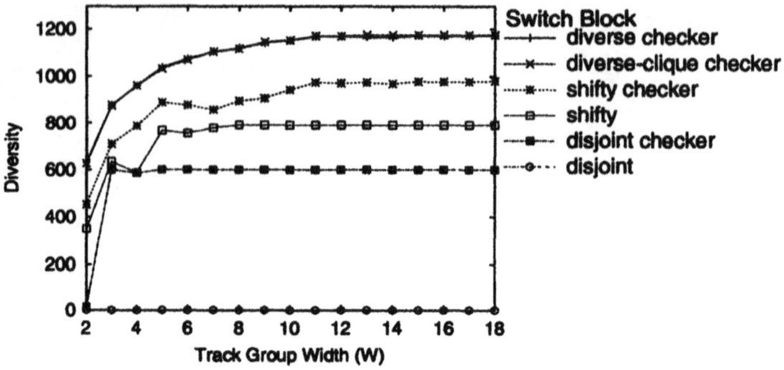

Fig. 7. Diversity of various commutative switch blocks.

In addition to *shifty*, a variety of other ad hoc switch blocks (both commutative and not) were explored. The *shifty* design gives better results, but the differences are small. These experiments did not clearly suggest that one particular design is significantly better. The effectiveness of *shifty* demonstrates that the twist or non-commutative features of the *universal-TG* and *Imran* blocks is not likely the key factor to their good performance. However, it makes us ask why is track shifting effective? Is it because of increased diversity?

The diverse switch blocks always require fewer routing tracks than the *disjoint* baseline. However, *shifty* always outperforms the diversity-optimized ones. This suggests that it is **not** the diverse property that makes *shifty* effective. It also counters the belief that the *Imran* and *Wilton* switch blocks are effective because they add some diversity.

Why do the diversity-optimized switch blocks not perform as well as anticipated? One conjecture is that negotiated-congestion type CAD tools, like the VPR router, might have difficulty with diversity. This seems plausible because a local re-routing near the source of a net would force most downstream connections to use a new track, even if they continue using the same routing channels. With less diversity, it may be easier for a net to resume using the previous routing tracks. This difficulty might increase the number of router iterations, but our experiments show little increase. Diversity adds a new degree of freedom to routing, but CAD tools must be able to efficiently utilise it.

5 Conclusions

This paper presents an analytical framework for the design of switch blocks. It is the first known framework to consider the switch block as part of an infinite switching fabric that easily works with long wire segments. The most fundamental component of this framework is the new track group switch block model.By separating wiring tracks into independent groups, each can be considered separately. Using permutation mapping functions to model switch block turns adds a mathematical representation to the framework. With commutative switch blocks, the order in which a net executes turns becomes unimportant and the network is easier to analyse. This framework can design diverse switch blocks, but it is not clear the router is utilising this diversity.

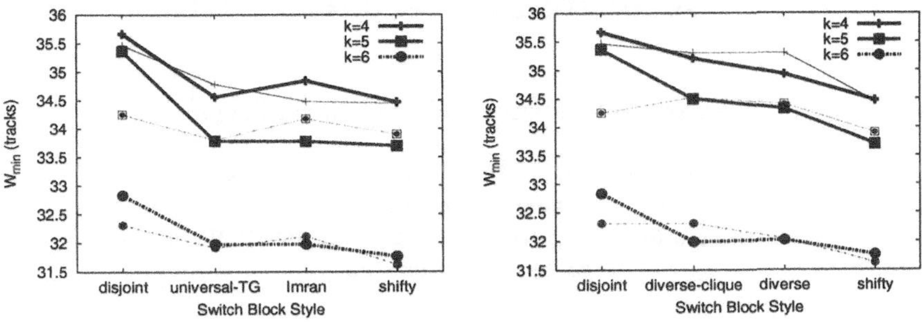

Fig. 8. Minimum channel width results using the new switch blocks.

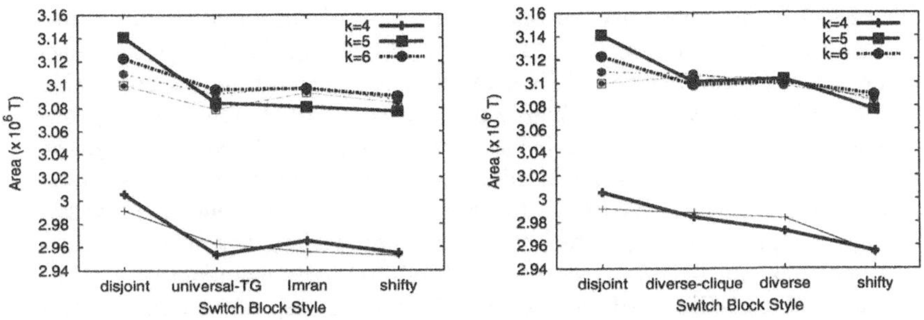

Fig. 9. Area results using the new switch blocks.

References

[1] Xilinx, San Jose, CA, *Online Databook*, 2002. `www.xilinx.com/partinfo/databook.htm`.

[2] Y.-W. Chang, D. F. Wong, and C. K. Wong, "Universal switch-module design for symmetric-array-based FPGAs," *ACM Transactions on Design Automation of Electronic Systems*, vol. 1, pp. 80–101, January 1996.

[3] S. J. Wilton, *Architectures and Algorithms for Field-Programmable Gate Arrays with Embedded Memories*. PhD thesis, Dept. of ECE, Univ. of Toronto, 1997.

[4] V. Betz, J. Rose, and A. Marquardt, *Architecture and CAD for Deep-Submicron FPGAs*. Boston: Kluwer Academic Publishers, 1999.

[5] M. I. Masud and S. Wilton, "A new switch block for segmented FPGAs," in *Field Programmable Logic*, August 1999.

[6] H. Fan, J. Liu, Y.-L. Wu, and C.-C. Cheung, "On optimum switch box designs for 2-D FPGAs," in *ACM/IEEE Design Automation Conference*, June 2001.

[7] J. Rose and S. Brown, "Flexibility of interconnection structures in field-programmable gate arrays," *IEEE J of Solid State Ccts*, vol. 26, pp. 277–282, March 1991.

[8] G. Lemieux, *In preparation*. PhD thesis, Dept. of ECE, Univ. of Toronto, 2002.

[9] H. Schmit and V. Chandra, "FPGA switch block layout and evaluation," in *Int. Symp. on FPGAs*, (Monterey, CA), pp. 11–18, February 2002.

[10] G. Lemieux and D. Lewis, "Circuit design of routing switches," in *Int. Symp. on FPGAs*, (Monterey, CA), pp. 19–28, Feb. 2002.

Modular, Fabric-Specific Synthesis for Programmable Architectures

Aneesh Koorapaty[1] and Lawrence Pileggi[2]

[1] Carnegie Mellon University, Pittsburgh PA 15213, USA
aneeshk@ece.cmu.edu
[2] Carnegie Mellon University, Pittsburgh PA 15213, USA
pileggi@ece.cmu.edu

Abstract. Traditionally, programmable fabrics consist of look up table (LUT) based programmable logic blocks (PLBs). Typically, the PLBs are either homogeneous (consisting of LUTs of the same size), or heterogeneous (consisting of LUTs of varying sizes). To bridge the cost-performance gap between ASICs and FPGAs, several new programmable logic fabrics are employing highly heterogeneous PLB architectures, consisting of a combination of LUTs of varying sizes, MUXes, logic gates, and versatile local routing architectures. Currently, there are two possible approaches to Synthesis for such fabrics. In the generic Synthesis approach, the first step of technology mapping generates a netlist of functions that can be implemented by individual logic elements of a PLB, like LUTs, MUXes and logic gates. The second step of packing clusters these functions into groups of logic that can fit in a single PLB. The second approach constructs a library of certain PLB configurations (like a standard cell library) and performs library based technology mapping, followed by packing. In this paper, we show that both these approaches result in sub-optimal and uneven fabric utilization for two reasons: (a) a lack of fabric-specific knowledge; (b) a lack of integration between mapping and packing. We present a new, modular, Synthesis approach, consisting of a fabric-specific technology mapping algorithm which maps directly to the entire PLB, rather than individual logic elements. In this manner, the new approach integrates the steps of mapping and packing, resulting in higher fabric utilization. Using the highly heterogeneous eASIC PLB as an example, we demonstrate that our approach requires 22% and 24% fewer PLBs than the generic and library based Synthesis approaches, across a standard benchmark set. We also demonstrate the modularity of our approach, by comparing three PLB architectures. Our results show that highly heterogeneous PLBs are much more area efficient than homogeneous PLBs.

1 Introduction

Driven by the economics of design and manufacturing of integrated circuits, an emphasis is being placed on developing new, regular fabrics that: (a) simplify the design process; (b) amortize the exorbitant design cost over multiple design

M. Glesner, P. Zipf, and M. Renovell (Eds.): FPL 2002, LNCS 2438, pp. 132–141, 2002.

volumes. To meet these objectives, several new programmable fabrics are taking advantage of the speed and density benefits resulting from highly heterogeneous PLB architectures, consisting of a combination of LUTs of various sizes, MUXes, logic gates, and versatile local routing architectures. One commercial example of such a fabric is the eASIC fabric shown in Figure 1. From the PLB diagram in

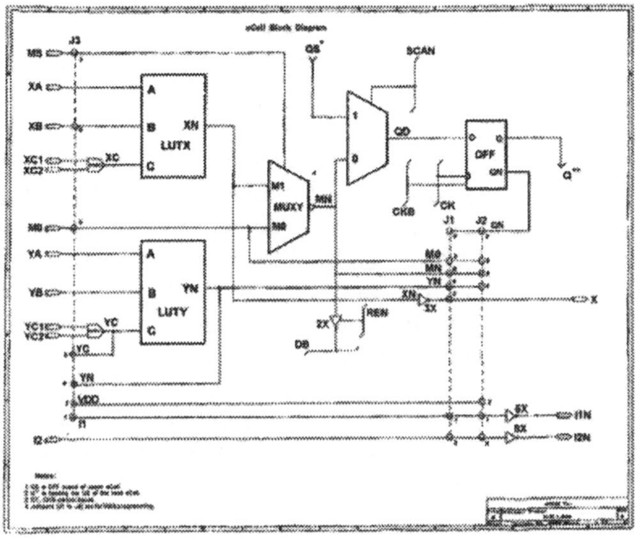

Fig. 1. eASIC PLB Architecture

Figure 1, we observe that the local interconnect architecture, consisting of configurable jumpers J1, J2 and J3 enables this PLB to implement various functions ranging from two up to nine inputs. For example, the Nand gate (NANDY) driving the bottom LUT (LUTY) can be made to drive the upper LUT (LUTX), by using jumper J3. This enables LUTX to implement a 5-feasible function. Also, the output of LUTY can be connected to the M0 input of the MUX using jumper J2 or J1, or to the MS input of the MUX using jumper J3. Since the inputs and output of the MUX can be generated in any polarity, it can implement all 2-feasible functions. Similarly, the inputs and outputs of the Nand gates can also be generated in any polarity, enabling the Nand gates to implement any 2-feasible function, except XOR and XNOR functions.

The generic Synthesis approach for programmable fabrics consists of two independent and sequential steps: (a) technology mapping; (b) packing. During technology mapping, algorithms like [1][2] and [3] generate a netlist of K-feasible (fewer than or equal to K inputs) functions, where K is defined by the size of the various LUTs in the PLB. During packing, the functions in the mapped netlist are clustered into larger single PLB feasible functions, which can be packed into a single PLB of the target fabric.

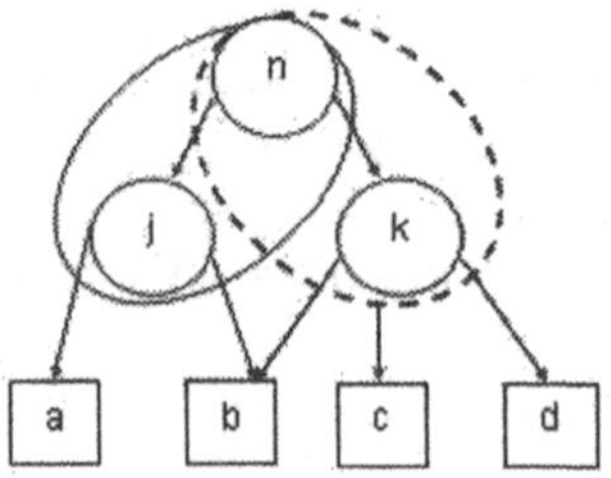

Fig. 2. K-feasible supernodes

Figure 2 illustrates the concept of supernodes. The cluster of logic covered by the solid line in Figure 2 is an example of a 3-feasible supernode, since it has three unique inputs (a, b, k). Similarly, the cluster of logic covered by the dashed line is an example of a 4-feasible supernode. Both of these supernodes are rooted at the node n.

For highly heterogeneous cells like the eASIC PLB, the K-feasible functions illustrated in Figure 2 only consume individual components of the cell, like the K-input LUTs, or the Nand gates. It is left to the packing step to efficiently combine these components into single PLB feasible clusters that consume a larger percentage of the PLB. However, as discussed in [4], many packing algorithms cannot easily incorporate simultaneous constraints on the maximum number of inputs, number of clocks, and the number of LUTs and registers in a logic block. For highly heterogeneous architectures these constraints are even more difficult to capture. For example, in the eASIC PLB, the output of LUTX always drives the M1 input of the MUX, and is always available as the X output of the PLB. Therefore, if a multiple fanout function is packed into LUTX, it need not be duplicated during mapping. Similarly, a multiple fanout 2-input function packed into NANDY, also need not be duplicated, since the output of NANDY can be tied to a PLB output, using jumper J3. Without such fabric-specific knowledge, the generic Synthesis approach cannot take advantage of the diverse capabilities of emerging programmable fabrics, resulting in uneven and sub-optimal fabric utilization.

A second approach to Synthesis for programmable fabrics is to construct a library of certain PLB configurations and perform library based technology mapping, followed by packing. However, for a sufficiently complex PLB like the eASIC fabric, the number of elements required to represent all possible logic configurations is extremely large. As discussed in [6], the size of the library grows as a double exponential. Since the complexity of library based mapping is proportional to the total number of patterns in the library, this approach is not scalable, as the complexity of logic blocks increases with the integration scale.

In this paper, we present a new, fabric-specific Synthesis approach which integrates the steps of mapping and packing, and captures particular features of PLB and routing architectures. This approach is also modular in design, to enable a systematic analysis of new, highly heterogeneous PLB and routing architectures. Such an analysis is necessary to design new programmable fabrics that can offer a combined cost and performance advantage. Although [4] and more recently [5] analyzed the area and delay effect of various LUT and cluster sizes, these studies excluded heterogeneous logic blocks. Also, these studies depended on general routing models, and excluded over the cell routing.

The rest of this paper is organized as follows. Section 2 presents the new, modular, fabric-specific Synthesis approach. Using the eASIC fabric as an example, Section 3 illustrates the benefits of the new approach. Section 4 demonstrates the modularity of our approach, and presents some results on fabric exploration. Section 5 concludes the paper.

2 Fabric-Specific Synthesis

In this section, we present a new, modular, fabric-specific Synthesis approach for emerging programmable architectures. The main component of this approach is a new technology mapping algorithm called FSMaP (Fabric-specific Map and Pack) which: (a) considers fabric-specific information about PLB logic clusters and local routing features; (b) integrates the steps of mapping and packing by mapping directly to single PLB feasible functions.

2.1 Single-PLB Feasible Functions

To illustrate the concept of single PLB feasible functions, we define the following types of single PLB feasible functions for the eASIC PLB from Figure 1. These single PLB feasible functions can be thought of as pre-packed clusters of logic.

- 2-feasible functions packed into the MUX, or the Nand gates driving the LUTs
- 3-feasible functions packed into the LUTs
- 4-feasible functions packed into a LUT, and the Nand gate feeding it
- 5-feasible functions packed in the upper LUT, and the two Nand gates (both can drive the upper LUT)
- A 2-feasible function packed into the MUX, driven by a 3-feasible, or 4-feasible function packed into the upper LUT
- A 2-feasible function packed into the MUX, driven by a 5-feasible function packed into the upper LUT
- A 2-feasible function packed into the MUX, driven by two, 3 or 4-feasible functions, packed into the lower and upper LUT and Nand gates

The single PLB feasible functions defined above are provided as an input to the FSMaP algorithm via a logic template.

2.2 FSMaP Algorithm

The FSMaP algorithm can operate in two modes: (a) generic; (b) fabric-specific. In the generic mode, it only maps to K-feasible functions, which are clustered into larger single PLB feasible functions during packing. In the fabric-specific mode it maps directly to single PLB feasible functions, thus integrating the steps of mapping and packing. Since not all the single PLB feasible functions cover the entire PLB, a packing step is still required. However, a significant amount of the work typically reserved for the packing step is already done during mapping.

The inputs to the FSMaP algorithm are a boolean network N in the BLIF netlist format, and in the fabric-specific mode, a logic template defining the single PLB feasible functions for the target fabric. Given the input netlist, FSMaP constructs a directed acyclic graph (DAG) representing the network, then partitions the network into logic cones. For each cone of logic, the first phase of the algorithm determines all possible matches rooted at each non-primary input node in the cone, using the flow network technique outlined in [6]. In the generic mode, a match is defined only as a K-feasible supernode. In the fabric-specific mode, a match is defined as either a K-feasible supernode or a single PLB feasible function. The second phase of the algorithm traverses the cone from primary outputs to primary inputs, and covers the cone in a greedy manner, by picking the supernode or single PLB feasible function with the lowest cost at each node.

Unlike the Hetero-Map [2] or Flowmap [3] algorithms which optimize primarily for depth, with post-mapping area recovery, FSMaP considers area, depth, wiring, and logic duplication factors in its cost function. In both generic and fabric-specific modes of operation, the cost for each match is computed as the sum of three terms. The first term is the inverse of the product of the number of inputs to the match, and the number of nodes covered by the match. This term gives larger matches a lower cost. The second term is the inverse of the number of wires re-used by the match. The number of re-used wires is computed by counting the number of inputs to the match that are already available as outputs of previously chosen matches. If the number of re-used wires is zero or one, this component is set to 1 or 0.75, respectively. By including this component, the algorithm attempts to minimize the number of nets in the mapped netlist. Finally, the third term computes the ratio of multiple fanout nodes in the match to total number of nodes in the match. This component attempts to limit logic duplication by increasing the cost for supernodes or single PLB feasible functions that have a large percentage of multiple-fanout nodes.

To demonstrate the effectiveness of the FSMaP algorithm, we map a standard set of MCNC benchmarks to the eASIC PLB with the FSMaP algorithm in generic mode (map only to K-feasible functions) and the Flowmap algorithm (with area recovery). After mapping, we pack the mapped netlists for both algorithms using the same packing strategy, and compare the number of PLBs required. Since the FSMaP algorithm is operated in generic mode, it cannot benefit from any fabric-specific information in this comparison. Furthermore, since the same packing strategy is employed, any differences in results for the two algorithms can only be attributed to the technology mapping step. Table 1 summarizes the results of this comparison.

From Table 1 we observe that FSMaP requires fewer PLBs on all but four benchmarks. Across the benchmark set, FSMaP requires 10.54% fewer PLBs. These results confirm that even with a greedy mapping strategy, and no fabric-specific information, the FSMaP algorithm achieves significantly better results than Flowmap. Optimizing the FSMaP algorithm further can only produce an improvement in these results.

Table 1. Comparison of Block Counts for Generic FSMaP and Flowmap

Circuit	FSMaP	Flowmap	Circuit	FSMaP	Flowmap
rd84	7	9	clip	66	73
decod	13	12	C1908	67	74
misex1	13	15	C880	68	87
b12	22	25	alu2	84	91
f51m	23	21	i6	107	106
misex2	20	24	duke2	107	115
cht	40	39	2large	111	125
5xp1	28	30	vda	129	147
sao2	34	37	apex6	149	186
ttt2	37	42	alu4	167	179
C1355	59	66	table3	210	241
i2	39	70	des	834	912
bw	52	53	**Total**	**2486**	**2779**

3 Benefits of Fabric-Specific Synthesis

To illustrate the benefits of fabric-specific Synthesis, we map an example netlist with Flowmap (with area recovery), and the fabric-specific version of FSMaP. Again, we use the eASIC PLB as the target architecture, with the single PLB feasible functions defined in Section 2.1. Figure 3 illustrates the final mapping solutions for both approaches.

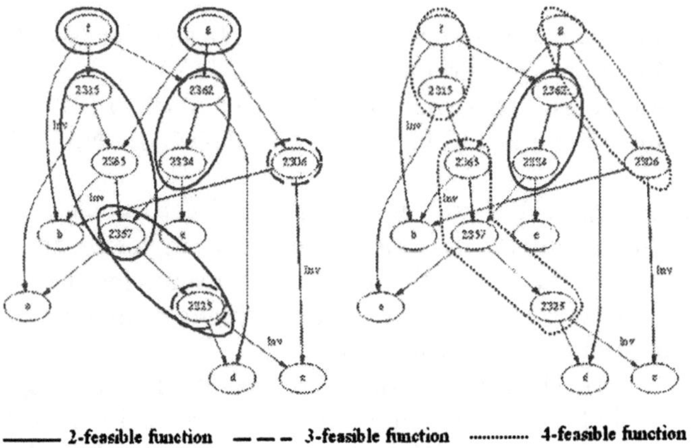

Fig. 3. Example Netlist: Flowmap and Fabric-specific FSMaP Solutions

The Flowmap solution in Figure 3 (shown on the left) consists of five 3-feasible (3-input) functions, and two 2-feasible functions. A minimum of three

PLBs is required to implement this solution. On the other hand, the fabric-specific solution (shown on the right in Figure 3) consists of three 4-feasible functions and one 3-feasible function. The 4-feasible function 2365 consists of a multiple fanout 2-feasible function (2365), driven by a multiple fanout 3-feasible function (nodes 2357 and 2325 combined). These functions can be packed into the MUX, and LUTX of an eASIC PLB, respectively. Since both the MUX and LUTX outputs are available as cell outputs, neither multiple fanout function needs to be duplicated. With a half of the first PLB still available, only one extra PLB is required, resulting in a total of only two PLBs.

This example illustrates that packing algorithms are constrained by the structure of the netlist produced by the technology mapping step. Although some of the 3-feasible and 2-feasible functions in the Flowmap solution from Figure 3 can be combined during packing, no packing solution can be found with fewer than three PLBs unless the structure of the mapped netlist is altered.

3.1 Block Count Analysis

In this section, we compare the fabric-specific Synthesis approach to the generic Synthesis approach for programmable fabrics, and a library based approach, on a standard set of MCNC benchmarks. First, we map each netlist with fabric-specific FSMaP, with the single PLB feasible functions for the eASIC fabric from section 2.1. For the generic approach, we map each netlist with Flowmap (with area recovery). For the library based approach, we map with Synopsys Design Analyzer to a library (called eLibrary) consisting of only the following kinds of functions (to keep the size manageable):

- 2-feasible functions (packed into the MUX, NANDX or NANDY)
- 3-feasible functions (packed into LUTX or LUTY)
- 4-feasible functions (packed into LUTX and NANDX, or LUTY and NANDY)
- 5-feasible functions (packed into LUTX, NANDX and NANDY)

For all three approaches, we pack the mapped netlists with the same packing algorithm, and compare the block counts. By employing the same packing algorithm we ensure that any differences in the results for the three Synthesis approaches, can only be attributed to the technology mapping step. Table 2 summarizes the results of this comparison.

From Table 2 we observe that the fabric-specific FSMaP algorithm always has lower or equal block counts than both the generic and library based Synthesis approaches. Furthermore, FSMaP requires 22% fewer PLBs than the generic approach, and 24% fewer PLBs than the library based approach across the benchmark set. The large reduction in block counts with FSMaP translates to a large reduction in layout area. For example, the Flowmap solution for the benchmark des has a layout area of 440232 micron squared (663 x 663 micron), as opposed to 317622 micron squared (563 x 563 micron) for the fabric-specific FSMaP solution. This represents a 28% reduction in layout area.

Table 2. Total Area for three PLB architectures

Circuit	FSMaP	Flowmap	eLibrary	Circuit	FSMaP	Flowmap	eLibrary
rd84	4	9	8	clip	59	73	76
decod	12	12	19	C1908	66	74	88
misex1	13	15	18	C880	72	87	99
b12	20	25	26	alu2	81	91	99
f51m	20	21	28	i6	91	106	109
misex2	20	24	25	duke2	97	115	132
cht	24	39	34	2large	106	125	143
5xp1	27	30	36	vda	117	147	160
sao2	34	37	46	apex6	142	186	187
ttt2	34	42	45	alu4	161	179	186
C1355	39	66	94	table3	186	241	261
i2	39	70	74	des	658	912	837
bw	45	53	56	**Total**	**2167**	**2779**	**2886**

3.2 Fabric Utilization Analysis

For benchmark C1355, the fabric-specific approach requires only 39 PLBs, as opposed to 66 PLBs for the generic approach (Flowmap), and 94 PLBs for the library based approach. To explain this result, we compare the utilization of the various PLB components for the three different mapping solutions. Figure 4 shows the percentage utilization of each of the PLB logic elements for the three Synthesis approaches.

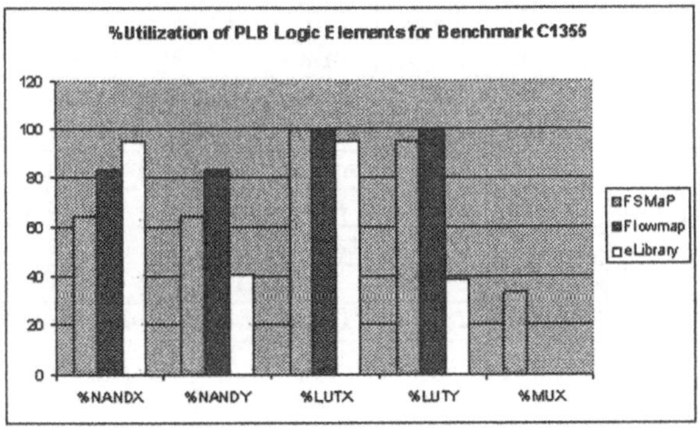

Fig. 4. Comparison of Fabric Utilization for fabric-specific FSMaP and Flowmap

From Figure 4 we observe that both the library based and the generic Synthesis approach do not utilize the MUX at all. Furthermore, the library based approach has 95% utilization of LUTX and NANDX, and only 40% utilization of LUTY and NANDY. On the other hand, the generic Synthesis approach has 100% utilization of both LUTX and LUTY, and 84% utilization of NANDX and

NANDY. This difference in the cell utilization profiles accounts for the large difference in total number of PLBs for the library based and generic Synthesis approaches. Similarly, the large difference in PLB counts for the Flowmap and FSMaP algorithms is due to the higher, and more even PLB utilization of the fabric-specific approach. The increased MUX utilization for the fabric-specific approach (33% as opposed to 0%) is due to the fact that the FSMaP algorithm maps directly to the entire PLB, rather than individual logic elements.

4 Fabric Exploration

An important feature of the FSMaP algorithm is its modularity. By considering fabric-specific PLB features, FSMaP can target a wide range of PLB architectures. In this section, we illustrate the modularity of the FSMaP algorithm by comparing three different PLB architectures. The first architecture is homogeneous, with four 4-LUTs and one D Flip Flop. The second is a heterogeneous PLB, consisting of two 3-LUTs, one 2-LUT, and one D Flip Flop. The third is the highly heterogeneous eASIC PLB.

Table 3. Total Area for three PLB architectures

Circuit	PLB1	PLB2	PLB3	Circuit	PLB1	PLB2	PLB3
rd84	1725	1000	525	clip	15525	10000	10150
decod	2875	2000	2100	C1908	16100	10000	10850
misex1	4025	2400	2275	C880	18400	11400	11725
b12	5175	3400	3500	alu2	20700	11800	13650
f51m	5750	3200	3500	i6	17825	17400	15925
misex2	5750	3800	3500	duke2	27600	15800	16800
cht	6900	6800	4200	2large	26450	17400	18550
5xp1	6325	4400	4725	vda	40250	23000	20300
sao2	8050	5600	5950	apex6	37375	25400	24850
ttt2	9200	5800	5950	alu4	37950	25400	27125
C1355	12075	9600	6825	table3	51175	39000	32550
i2	18975	9400	6825	des	177100	134400	114625
bw	12650	9200	7875	**Total**	**585925**	**407600**	**374850**

To compare the total logic block area for these architectures, we use the area model in [4]. Based on this model, we estimate the total logic block area for the homogeneous, heterogeneous, and highly heterogeneous PLB in this analysis to be 575, 200, and 175 units respectively. In [4] a combination of a K-LUT and a D Flip Flop is defined as a K-input basic logic element (BLE). With our model, we estimate the area of a 4-input, 3-input and 2-input BLE, as 155, 90 and 50 units respectively. These numbers follow a very similar curve to the one presented in [5]. Using our area estimates, we run FSMaP on a set of benchmark circuits, and compare the block count and total area for each of these PLB architectures.

Table 3 presents these results. The total area values in Table 3 are computed as the product of the number of logic blocks and the area per logic block.

From Table 3, we observe that the heterogeneous PLB, consisting of two 3-LUTs and one 2-LUT consumes about 30% less area than the homogeneous cell, with four 4-input LUTs. However, the highly heterogeneous eASIC PLB does even better, consuming 36% less area than the homogeneous cell, and 8% less area than the heterogeneous cell. From this analysis, we conclude that highly heterogeneous architectures are worth further exploration.

5 Conclusion

In this paper, we have shown that the generic Synthesis approach for programmable fabrics, and library based Synthesis techniques are not suitable for new, increasingly complex programmable architectures. We have presented a new modular, fabric-specific, Synthesis approach for programmable fabrics which takes PLB-specific logic configurations and routing constraints into account, and maps directly to the entire PLB, thus integrating the steps of mapping and packing. Using the eASIC fabric as an example, we demonstrated that the fabric-specific Synthesis approach achieves higher, and more even fabric utilization, resulting in significant reductions in block count across a standard benchmark set. This reduction translates into a large reduction in layout area, an advantage that is particularly important for embedded programmable logic cores like the eASIC fabric. Finally, we demonstrated the modularity of our Synthesis approach, and showed that highly heterogeneous PLBs are significantly more area efficient than conventional homogeneous PLB architectures. Our work enables a systematic analysis of such architectures. Such an analysis is necessary to design new programmable fabrics which can offer a combined cost and performance advantage. In future work, we expect to show that the fabric-specific Synthesis approach also results in better congestion and routability.

References

1. J. He, J. Rose: Technology Mapping for Heterogenous FPGAs ACM International Workshop, FPGA, Monterey CA, Feb. 1994
2. Cong, J., Xu, S.: Performance-Driven Technology Mapping for Heterogeneous FPGAs IEEE Transactions on Computer-aided Design of Integrated Circuits and Systems, vol. 19, no. 11, pp. 1268-1281, November 2000
3. Cong, J., Ding, Y.: Flowmap: An optimal technology mapping algorithm for delay optimization in lookup-table based FPGA designs IEEE Trans. Computer Aided Design, vol. 13, pp. 1-12, Jan. 1994
4. Betz, V., Rose, J., Marquardt, A.: Architecture and CAD for Deep-Submicron FPGAs Kluwer Academic Publishers, 1999
5. Ahmed, E., Rose, J.: The effect of LUT and Cluster Size on Deep-Submicron FPGA Performance and Density ACM/SIGDA Workshop on FPGAs (FPGA 00), Monterey, CA
6. Murgai, R., Brayton, R. K., Vincentelli, A. S.: Logic Synthesis for Field-Programmable Gate Arrays Kluwer Academic Publishers, 1995

On Optimum Designs of Universal Switch Blocks

Hongbing Fan[1], Jiping Liu[2*], Yu-Liang Wu[3**], and Chak-Chung Cheung[3]

[1] University of Victoria, Victoria, BC. Canada V8W 3P6
hfan@csr.uvic.ca

[2] The University of Lethbridge, Lethbridge, AB. Canada T1K 3M4
liu@cs.uleth.ca

[3] The Chinese University of Hong Kong, Shatin, N.T., Hong Kong
ylw, cccheung@cse.cuhk.edu.hk

Abstract. This paper presents a breakthrough decomposition theorem on routing topology and its applications in the designing of universal switch blocks. A switch block of k sides and W terminals on each side is said to be universal (a (k, W)-USB) if it is routable for every set of 2-pin nets with channel density at most W. The optimum USB design problem is to design a (k, W)-USB with the minimum number of switches for every pair of (k, W). The problem was originated from designing better k sides switch modules for 2D-FPGAs, such as Xilinx XC4000-type FPGAs, where $k \leq 4$. The interests in the generic USBs come from their potential usages in multi-dimensional and some non-conventional 2D-FPGA architectures, and as an individual switch components. The optimum (k, W)-USB was solved previously for even W, but left open for odd W. Our new decomposition theorem states that when W $(> \frac{k+3-i}{3})$, a (k, W) routing requirement ((k, W)-RR) can be decomposed into one $(k, \frac{k+3-i}{3})$-RR and $\frac{3W-k+i-3}{6}$ $(k, 2)$-RRs, where $1 \leq i \leq 6$ and $k \equiv i$ (mod 6). By this theorem and the previously established reduction design scheme, the USB design problem is reduced to its minimum kernel designs, that enables us to design the best approximated (k, W)-USBs for all odd W. We also run extensive routing experiments using the currently best known FPGA router VPR, and the MCNC circuits with the conventional disjoint switch blocks and two kinds of universal switch blocks. The experimental results show that both kinds of USBs consistently improve the entire chip routability by over 6% than the conventional switch blocks.

Keywords. FPGA architecture, routing, universal switch block

1 Introduction

Switch blocks are critical reconfigurable components in Field Programmable Gate Arrays (FPGAs); they have great effects on the area and time efficiency

* This research was partially supported by the Natural Sciences and Engineering Research Council of Canada.

** Research partially supported by a Hong Kong Government RGC Earmarked Grant, Ref. No. CUHK4236/01E, and Direct Grant CUHK2050244

M. Glesner, P. Zipf, and M. Renovell (Eds.): FPL 2002, LNCS 2438, pp. 142–151, 2002.

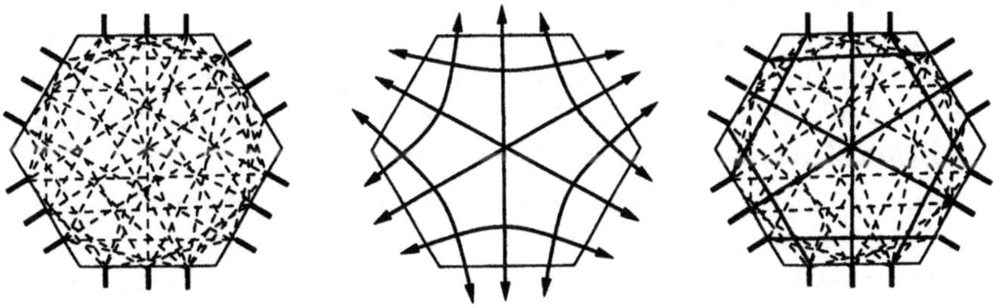

(a) (6, 3)–SB (b) a (6, 3)–RR (c) a detailed routing

Fig. 1. Examples of (k, 3)-SBs,(k, 3)-RRs and the corresponding detailed routings.

and routability of FPGA chips. Many kinds of switch blocks have been studied, designed and used in various kinds of FPGA architectures [3, 2]. We here consider the (k, W) switch block ((k, W)-SB for short), in which terminals are grouped into k sides, each side has W terminals, and non-direct configurable switches connect pairs of terminals from different sides. The $(4, W)$-SBs are typical switch modules used in two dimensional FPGA architectures such as Xilinx XC4000-type FPGAs [3, 4, 10, 12, 13].

The routability and area efficiency are the foremost two issues in switch block designs. But the high routability and high area efficiency are two conflicting goals. It is easy to see that an FPGA with complete switch blocks, namely having a switch between every pair of terminals from different sides, will have the highest routability of the same channel density. But it has the lowest area efficiency and it is impractical when the channel density is high.

To balanced the two goals, Rose and Brown [10] introduced an important concept called the *flexibility*, denoted by F_s, which is the maximum number of switches in a switch block from a terminal to others. They investigated the effects of flexibility on the global routability, and observed that $(4, W)$-SBs with $F_s = 3$ result in a sufficiently high global routability, which is an acceptable tradeoff between global routability and area efficiency. However, there are various designs with the same flexibility. This raises the interests of designing switch blocks with a high routing capacity, a small flexibility and the minimum number of switches.

To achieve high routing capacity, Chang et al. [4] proposed the significant concept of universal switch modules. A (k, W)-SB is said to be universal (a (k, W)-USB) if it is routable for every set of nets satisfying the routing constraint, i.e., the number of nets on each side is at most W. The net used in the definition of universal switch blocks is actually 2-pin net. Fan et al. [5] generalized the concept of USB to hyper-universal switch blocks (HUSB) by allowing multi-pin nets. The main contribution of [5] is the discovery of the decomposition property and the reduction design scheme for switch block designs.

The first optimum $(4, W)$-USB was given in [4], called a symmetric switch module. It has $6W$ switches with $F_s = 3$. The symmetric universal switch modules were generalized to genetic symmetric (k, W)-SB in [11]. However, the generalized symmetric switch blocks are not universal for odd W (≥ 3) when $k \geq 7$. This was firmly proved in [7]. Consequently, the optimum design USB problem for $k \geq 7$ and odd W is still open. This paper continues the investigation on the unsolved part of the optimum USB design problem.

To avoid ambiguity, we next specify the terms net, detailed routing, and routing requirement (called global routing in [5]) with respect to a (k, W)-SB. By a *net* we mean an indication of two sides of the switch block in which two terminals should be connected by a switch. A *detailed routing of a net* is an exact assignment of a switch whose two terminals are in the sides indicated by the net. A (k, W)-routing requirement ((k, W)-RR for short) is a set of nets such that the number of nets that connect each side is no more than W. A *detailed routing of a (k, W)-RR in a (k, W)-SB* is an assignment of switches in the switch block such that each net in the routing requirement corresponds to a switch, and the switches corresponding to different nets are not incident. For example, Fig. 1(a), (b), (c) depict a $(6, 3)$-SB, a $(6, 3)$-RR, and a detailed routing of (b) in (a). Thus a (k, W)-SB is *universal* if it has a detailed routing for every (k, W)-RR. The optimum USB design problem can be described as: *for any given pair of k and W, design a (k, W)-USB with the minimum number of switches.*

The difficulty of the optimum USB design problem is due to the verification of a design. That is, to prove a (k, W)-SB has a detailed routing for every (k, W)-RR. The verification involves two subproblems: (a) to generate all testing routing requirements, and (b) to find a detailed routing algorithm.

In the case of W being even, the two problems were solved precisely by a strong decomposition property of $(k, 2m)$-RRs: a $(k, 2m)$-RR can be decomposed into m $(k, 2)$-RRs. Thus a union of m $(k, 2)$-USBs forms a $(k, 2m)$-USB, and the design job is reduced to compute all $(k, 2)$-RRs and to design a $(k, 2)$-USB. All $(k, 2)$-RRs and optimum $(k, 2)$-USBs are given in [11, 7], and the union of m optimum $(k, 2)$-USBs forms an optimum $(k, 2m)$-USB. For a $(k, 2m)$-USB formed by union of m $(k, 2)$-USBs, a detailed routing of a $(k, 2m)$-RR can be easily done by first decomposing the $(k, 2m)$-RR into m $(k, 2)$-RRs and then accommodating them in the m $(k, 2)$-USBs. This outlines the so called reduction design scheme.

For odd W, it is known that there is a minimum integer $f_2(k)$ such that a (k, W)-RR can be decomposed into a $(k, f_2(k))$-RR and some $(k, 2)$-RRs [6]; $f_2(k)$ is the maximum value w such that there is a non-decomposable (k, w)-RR. The value of $f_2(k)$ is important in the generation of all (k, W)-RRs and (k, W)-USB design as well.

In Section 2, we will introduce a breakthrough result on $f_2(k)$: $f_2(k) = \frac{k+3-i}{3}$ where k and i satisfy $k \geq 7$ and $1 \leq i \leq 6$ and $k \equiv i \pmod 6$. This result gives the best decomposition theorem, which makes it possible to generate all $(k, 2m+1)$-RRs, and to design the best approximated $(k, 2m+1)$-USBs using the reduction design scheme.

The routability of 2D-FPGA with USBs was tested in [4]. We further perform the experimental justification using VPR [1] with the commonly used disjoint switch block, the symmetric USB [4] and an alternative USB. The setting and results are presented in Section 4.

2 The Extreme Decomposition Theorems

We use the combinatorial and graph models to represent routing requirements, switch blocks and detailed routing as in [5]. For convenience, we describe the modeling briefly as the following.

We label the sides of a (k, W)-SB by $1, 2, \ldots, k$, respectively, then a 2-pin net can be represented as a size 2 subset of $\{1, 2, \ldots, k\}$. For example, a net that connects two terminals on sides 1 and 2 can be represented by $\{1, 2\}$. A (k, W)-RR is a collection (multiple set) of size 2 subsets (also called nets) of $\{1, 2, \ldots, k\}$, such that each $i \in \{1, 2, \ldots, k\}$ is contained in no more than W subsets in the collection. A (k, W)-SB can be modeled as a graph: represent the jth terminal on side i by a vertex $v_{i,j}$ and a switch connecting $v_{i,j}$ and $v_{i',j'}$ by an edge $v_{i,j}v_{i',j'}$, then a (k, W)-SB corresponds to a k-partite graph G with vertex partition $(V_1, \ldots, V_k)$, where $V_i = \{v_{i,j} | j = 1, \ldots, W\}, i = 1, \ldots, k$. We also call such a graph a (k, W)-SB. Two (k, W)-SBs are isomorphic if there is an isomorphism which preserves the vertex partitions. A detailed routing of a net $\{i, j\}$ can be represented by an edge connecting a vertex in part V_i and a vertex in part V_j. A detailed routing of a (k, W)-RR in a (k, W)-SB corresponds to a subgraph consisting of independent edges.

The verification of USBs can be simplified by using formalized routing requirements. First of all, add some singletons (nets of size one) to a (k, W)-RR such that each element appears W times; called a *balanced routing requirement* (*(k, W)-BRR)*, or k-way BRR (k-BRR) with density W. Second, pair up the non-equal singletons until no two different singletons are left; such a BRR is called a *primitive* BRR (PBRR). It can be seen that a (k, W)-SB is universal if and only if it has a detailed routing for every (k, W)-PBRR. We need to compute all (k, W)-PBRRs.

The decomposition property of PBRRs provides an efficient way to compute all (k, W)-PBRRs. Let R be a (k, d)-PBRR and R' be a subset of R. If R' is a (k, d')-PBRR with $d' < d$, then we say R' is a *sub-routing requirement* of R. A PBRR is said to be a *minimal* (PMBRR for short) (or *non-decomposable*) if it contains no sub-routing requirement. A (k, W)-PBRRs can be decomposed into k-PMBRRs, so that, if all k-PMBRRs are known, then we can use them construct all (k, W)-PBRRs. The following is the fundamental decomposition theorem.

Theorem 2.1. [6] *For any given integer k, the number of k-PMBRRs is finite and every (k, W)-PBRR can be decomposed into k-PMBRRs with densities at most $f_2(k)$, where $f_2(k)$ equals the maximum density of all k-PMBRRs.*

The function $f_2(k)$ is important in the computation of the complete list of k-PMBRRs. If we know the value of $f_2(k)$, we can at least enumerate all k-PBRRs with densities no more than $f_2(k)$ and check each of them see if it is a k-PMBRR.

It was known that $f_2(k) = 1$ for $k = 1, 2$, and $f_2(k) = 2$ for $3 \le k \le 6$ [6], and $f_2(k) = 3$ for $k = 7, 8$; and that the complete lists of k-PMBRRs for $k \ge 8$. It was conjectured that $f_2(k) = \frac{k+3-i}{3}$. This conjecture is proved recently by employing the graph theory. Let R be a (k, W)-PBRR. Then R corresponds to a W-regular 2-graph with vertex set $\{1, \dots, k\}$ and edge set R. Note that 2-graphs allow edges with one vertex. An r-factor of a graph is a spanning regular subgraph of the graph. So in terms of graph theory, a (k, W)-PMBRR corresponds to a W-regular 2-graph without proper regular factors. The following result is proved, the detail is omitted.

Theorem 2.2. *A $(2r+1)$-regular G has no proper regular factor if and only if G has a 2-factor free block which is incident to at least $(2r+1)$ cut edges.*

The significance of the theorem is, (a) it gives a characterization for (k, W)-PMBRRs, which makes it possible to generate all k-PMBRRs efficiently, and (b) it leads to the following result on $f_2(k)$.

Theorem 2.3. *Let $k \ge 7$ be an integer. Then $f_2(k) = \frac{k+3-i}{3}$, where $1 \le i \le 6$ and $k \equiv i \pmod 6$.*

Proof. $f_2(k) \ge \frac{k+3-i}{3}$ follows from the examples in [7]. Now we show $f_2(k) \le \frac{k+3-i}{3}$. Let D be the 2-graph of a $(k, f_2(k))$-PMBRR. If D contains singletons (edge of size one), we transform D into a $f_2(k)$-regular graph R as follows.

Let x be the vertex of D such that $\{x\}$ is a singleton of D, and let p be the multiplicity of $\{x\}$ in D. If $p = f_2(k)$, then x is an isolated vertex, delete x from D; if $p = 2m$ for some m, then add in vertices y, z, and m copies of xy, m copies of xz, $f_2(k) - m$ copies of yz; else we have $p = 2m + 1 < f_2(k)$, then add in new vertices y, z, w, and $2m + 1$ copies of the edge xy, $\frac{f_2(k)-2m-1}{2}$ copies of yz and yw, $2m+1$ copies of zw. Let R be the graph obtained by the above construction, then R is minimal for otherwise D would be not minimal. Note that $|R| \le k+3$.

By Theorem 2.2, R has a 2-factor free block C which is incident to at least $f_2(k)$ cut edges. Each such cut edge joins a component of R with at least 3 vertices because R is a $f_2(k)$-regular graph and $f_2(k) \ge 3$ is odd. It follows that $3f_2(k) + |C| \le |R|$ and

$$f_2(k) \le \frac{|R| - |C|}{3} \le \frac{k+3-1}{3} = \frac{k+2}{3}.$$

Let $k = 6r+i$, where $r \ge 1$ and $1 \le i \le 6$. Then we have $f_2(k) \le \frac{k+2}{3} = \frac{6r+i+2}{3} = 2r + 1 + \frac{i-1}{3}$. Since $\lfloor \frac{i-1}{3} \rfloor = 0$ and $f_2(k)$ is odd, $f_2(k) \le 2r + 1 = \frac{k+3-i}{3}$. □

As an immediate consequence of Theorem 2.3, we have the following new extreme decomposition theorem of (k, W)-PBRRs.

Theorem 2.4. *Let $k \ge 7$ and $1 \le i \le 6$ with $i \equiv k \pmod 6$, and W be odd. Then the following statements hold:*
(i) If $W > \frac{k+3-i}{3}$, then every (k, W)-PBRR can be decomposed into a $(k, \frac{k+3-i}{3})$-PBRR and $\frac{3W-k-3+i}{6}$ $(k, 2)$-PBRRs.
(ii) There are (k, W)-PMBRRs for every $W \le \frac{k+3-i}{3}$.

By the above decomposition theorem, we know, when W is odd and $W > \frac{k+3-i}{3}$, the disjoint union of one $(k, \frac{k+3-i}{3})$-USB and $\frac{3W-k-3+i}{6}$ $(k, 2)$-USBs forms a (k, W)-USB; when W is odd and $W \leq \frac{k+3-i}{3}$, no (k, W)-USB is the disjoint union of smaller USBs. Therefore by the reduction scheme, for any fixed k, we need to design the basic (k, r)-USBs for $r = 1, 2, 3, 5, \ldots, \frac{k+3-i}{3}$. Once these basic USB has been designed, then we can combine m $(k, 2)$-USB to obtain a $(k, 2m)$-USB, and combine one $(k, \frac{k+3-i}{3})$-USB and $\frac{6m-k+i}{6}$ $(k, 2)$-USBs to obtain a $(k, 2m+1)$-USB. The SBs obtained in this way is scalable, and detailed routing can be done efficiently.

3 The Design Scheme for Basic USBs

The USB design problem has been reduced to the designing of the basic (k, r)-USBs for $r = 1, 2, 3, 5, \ldots, \frac{k+3-i}{3}$. Designing the basic USBs is the problem kernel, and it is a real tough task except for $r = 1, 2$. The optimum $(k, 1)$-USB and $(k, 2)$-USB were designed in [11, 7]. But for $k \geq 7$ and odd r $(3 \leq r \leq \frac{k+3-i}{3})$, no optimum (k, r)-USB is known yet. However, we can design approximated basic (k, r)-USBs by the following inductive design scheme.

Let $U(k, 1)$ and $U(k, 2)$ be optimum $(k, 1)$-USB and $(k, 2)$-USB, respectively. Construct a $(k, 3)$-USB $U(k, 3)$ by, first making a copy of $U(k, 1)$ and a $U(k, 2)$, and then adding some switches between them such that the resulting switch block is routable for all $(k, 3)$-PMBRRs. A $(k, 5)$-USB $U(k, 5)$ can then be constructed by combining a copy of $U(k, 3)$ and $U(k, 2)$ and adding some switches such that it is routable for all $(k, 5)$-PMBRRs. Continue this construction until a $U(k, \frac{k+3-i}{3})$-USB is constructed.

Note that in the universalbility verification of $U(k, r)$, we only check detailed routings for (k, r)-PMBRRs, not for all (k, r)-PBRRs. This is because that those decomposable (k, r)-PBRRs are routable in the union of $U(k, r-2)$ and $U(k, 2)$.

Next we illustrate this method in detail for $k = 7$. Since $f_2(7) = 3$, we need only construct a $(7, 3)$-USB. Denote by $U(7, 1) + U(7, 2)$ the disjoint union of $U(7, 1)$ and $U(7, 2)$. We next consider adding the minimum number edges between $U(7, 1)$ and $U(7, 2)$ (called cross edges) so that the resulting graph $\bar{U}(7, 3)$ is routable for every $(7, 3)$-PMBRRs. By Theorem 2.2, a $(7, 3)$-PMBRR must be isomorphic to the 2-graph shown in Fig. 2(a). Let R be a $(7, 3)$-PMBRR. Then to be routable in $\bar{U}(7, 3)$, there is at least one cross edge which will be used in the detailed routing. We consider a detailed routing of R which uses exact one of the cross edges. Suppose we use one cross edge to detailed route $\{i_1, i_2\}$ and i_1 corresponds to a vertex v in $U(7, 1)$. Then we must use three independent edges in $U(7, 1) - \{v\}$ to implement three independent pairs in $R - \{i_1, i_2\}$. Therefore, we should select $\{i_1, i_2\}$ in R such that $R - \{i_1\}$ contains three disjoint pairs. It is easy to see that such a $\{i_1, i_2\}$ must be an edge in a triangle of R.

A smallest (in terms of number of edges) graph on seven vertices which will always contain a triangle edge of any $(7, 3)$-PMBRR is given in Fig. 2-(b). We call it a connection pattern. The labels of the vertices and the orientation of edges in the pattern are arbitrary. A directed edge (i, j) in the pattern corresponds

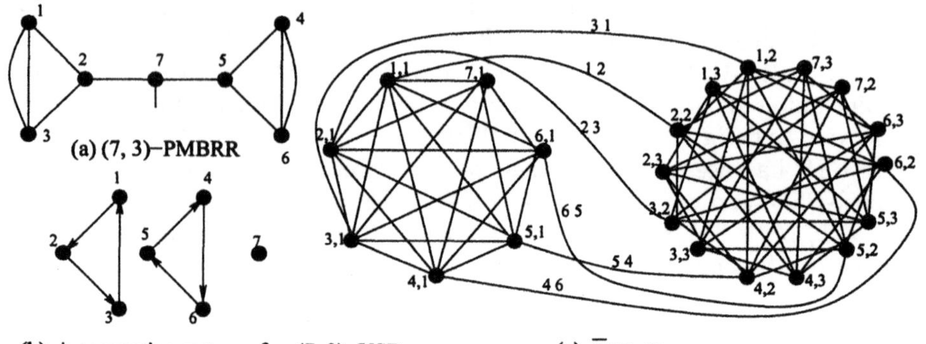

Fig. 2. A (7,3)-USB.

to a cross edge joining the i-th side of $U(7,1)$ and the j-th side of $U(7,2)$ (the joining of the cross edge is not unique; it depends on only the label of the sides). With this pattern, we obtain a (7,3)-USB $\bar{U}(7,3)$ as shown in Fig. 2(c).

We next consider the $(7,2h+1)$-USB obtained by combining $\bar{U}(7,3)$ and $U(7,2)$s. Let $\bar{U}(7,2h+1) = \bar{U}(7,3) + \sum_{i=1}^{h-1} U(7,2)$.

Note that the number of switches in an optimum (k,W)-USB, denoted by $e_2(k,W)$, is bounded below by $\binom{k}{2}W$ because there must be at least W switches between any two sides of a (k,W)-USB.

Theorem 3.1. *Let W (≥ 3) be an odd integer, then $\bar{U}(7,W)$ is a USB with approximation ratio $\frac{|E(\bar{U}(7,W))|}{e_2(7,W)} \leq 1 + \frac{6}{21W}$ and flexibility $F_s = 7$.*

Proof. By our construction, we see that $\bar{U}(7,3)$ is a $(7,3)$-USB. By Theorem 2.4, every $(7,W)$-PBRR can be decomposed into a $(7,3)$-PBRR and $\frac{W-3}{2}$ $(7,2)$-PBRRs. The $(7,3)$-PBRR have detailed routing in $\bar{U}(7,3)$, and each $(7,2)$-PBRR has a detailed routing in one of the $\frac{W-3}{2}$ $U(7,2)$. Therefore, $\bar{U}(7,W)$ is universal. $|E(\bar{U}(7,W))| = \binom{7}{2}W + 6 = 21W + 6$ and $e_2(7,W) \geq \binom{7}{2}W = 21W$. Therefore, $\frac{|E(\bar{U}(7,W))|}{e_2(7,W)} \leq 1 + \frac{6}{21W}$. □

By the above theorem, we see when W is large, the ratio is close to 1. Hence $\bar{U}(7,W)$ is nearly optimal when W is large. Since $f_2(k) = 3$ for $k = 8, 9, 10, 11, 12$, therefore, $\bar{U}(k,W)$ can be constructed similarly for these ks.

Finally we provide an alternative design of k sides switch block which is routable for every (k,W)-RRs. Let $\underline{U}(k,W) = \sum_{i=1}^{\lceil \frac{W}{2} \rceil} U(k,2)$.

Theorem 3.2. *If W is even, the $\underline{U}(k,W)$ is an optimum (k,W)-USB. If W is odd, $\underline{U}(k,W)$ is a $(k,W+1)$-SB routable for every (k,W)-RRs, and has approximation ratio $\frac{|E(\underline{U}(k,W))|}{e_2(k,W)} \leq 1 + \frac{1}{W}$ and flexibility $F_s = k-1$.*

Proof. This is clearly true when W is even. For odd W, we need to show that any (k,W)-RR R is routable in $\underline{U}(k,W)$. Let R_1 be any $(k,1)$-RR and let $R' = R \cup R_1$. Then R' is a $(k, W+1)$-RR. Since $W+1$ is even, R' can be decomposed into $\frac{W+1}{2} = \lceil \frac{W}{2} \rceil$ $(k,2)$-RRs. Each of these $(k,2)$-RRs can be detail-routed in one $U(k,2)$, therefore, R' is routable in $\underline{U}(k,W)$. Simply remove the detailed routing for R_1 yields a detailed routing of R in $\underline{U}(k,W)$. Therefore, $\underline{U}(k,W)$ is routable for every(k,W)-RR.

If W is even, $|E(\underline{U}(k,W))| = \binom{k}{2}W$; otherwise $|E(\underline{U}(k,W))| = \binom{k}{2}(W+1)$. Therefore, $\frac{|E(\underline{U}(k,W))|}{e_2(k,W)} \leq 1 + \frac{1}{W}$. □

4 Experimental Results

As we can see, USB is defined to have highest local routing capacity. There is no theoretical proof that USB can lead to a high global routability, however we can test the routing behavior by experiments. Universal property is an isomorphic property. Two isomorphic USB designs may have different layouts. The routing network in FPGA is determined by the settings of each switch blocks. If all switch blocks use the the same layout, then we have a disjoint grid routing networks. However, no analytical model for global routing is well-established. Lemieux and Lewis [8] proposed an analytical framework for overall routings. We use the probabilistic model [3] and experiment to justify the entire chip routability by USBs with different layouts.

We adopt the well-known FPGA router VPR [1] for our experiment. The logic block structure for our VPR runs is set to contain one 4-input LUT and one flip-flop. The input or output pin of the logic block is able to connect to any track in the adjacent channels ($F_c = W$). Inside the switch box, each input wire segment can connect to three other output wire segments of other channels ($F_s = 3$).

The results in [4] shown a notable improvement on global routability of symmetric USB against the disjoint type and antisymmetric type in [10]. Their experiments were done by using the modified CGE router [10] and CGE benchmark circuits. In our experiment, we conduct a vast experiment on 21 large benchmark circuits with Disjoint switch-blocks, symmetric USBs and an alternative USBs of different channel widths.

Fig. 3(a), Fig. 3(b) and Fig. 3(c) show the actual connection of the Disjoint switch-block, the symmetric USB and the alternative USB of channel width 8. The alternative $(4,8)$-USB is a union of 4 $(4,2)$-USBs, which is isomorphic to the symmetric $(4,8)$-USB but has different layout.

Table 1 shows the results on the number of tracks required to route some larger MCNC benchmark circuits [14] by FPGAs with the three SBs respectively. Overall, the routing results of the symmetric USB and our proposed USB FPGAs both use about 6% less tracks than that by Disjoint SBs. There is no big differences between the symmetric USBs and the proposed ones; this indicates that the global routability depends largely on the topological structures of the switch blocks rather than their layouts.

Table 1. Channel widths required for different benchmark circuits $F_C = W$, $F_S = 3$.

	Disjoint	Symmetric USB	Alternative USB
alu4	10	10 (-0%)	10 (-8.3%)
apex2	12	11 (-8.3%)	11 (-8.3%)
apex4	13	12 (-7.7%)	13 (-0%)
bigkey	7	7 (-0%)	6 (-14.3%)
clma	13	11 (-15.4%)	12 (-7.7%)
des	8	7 (-12.5%)	7 (-12.5%)
diffeq	8	7 (-12.5%)	7 (-12.5%)
dsip	7	7 (-0%)	7 (-0%)
elliptic	11	10 (-9.1%)	10 (-9.1%)
ex1010	11	10 (-9.1%)	10 (-9.1%)
ex5p	14	13 (-7.1%)	13 (-7.1%)
frisc	13	12 (-7.7%)	12 (-7.7%)
misex3	11	11 (-0%)	11 (-0%)
pdc	17	16 (-5.9%)	16 (-5.9%)
s298	8	7 (-12.5%)	7 (-12.5%)
s38417	8	7 (-12.5%)	8 (-0%)
s38584.1	8	8 (-0%)	8 (-0%)
seq	12	11 (-8.3%)	11 (-8.3%)
spla	14	14 (-0%)	13 (-7.1%)
tseng	7	6 (-14.3%)	6 (-14.3%)
e64	8	8 (-0%)	8 (-0%)
Total	220	205 (-6.8%)	206 (-6.3%)

5 Conclusions

We have addressed the open USB design problems on odd densities. We have provided an extreme decomposition theorem, reduced the USB design problem to the basic USB design problem, and outlined an inductive design scheme for designing the basic USBs. We have shown two types of universal switch blocks for all (k, W)-RRs. The first are (k, W)-USBs with higher approximation ratio, but have higher flexibility. The second uses one more track on each side, but with the minimum flexibility $k-1$. Our extensive experimental results further justify that, under the same hardware cost, the USBs can bring the global routability improvement of over 6% on the 2-D FPGA entire chip routings.

References

[1] V. Betz and J. Rose. “A New Packing, Placement and Routing Tool for FPGA Research”. *Seventh International Workshop on Field-Programmable Logic and Applications (Available for download from http://www.eecg.toronto.edu/~jayar/software.html)*, pages 213–222, 1997.

[2] V. Betz, J. Rose, and A. Morquardt. *Architecure and CAD for Deep-Submicron FPGAs.* Kluwer-Academic Publisher, Boston MA, 1999.

[3] S. Brown, R. J. Francise, J. Rose, and Z. G. Vranesic. *Field-Programmable Gate Arrays.* Kluwer-Academic Publisher, Boston MA, 1992.

[4] Y. W. Chang, D. F. Wong, and C. K. Wong. “Universal switch models for FPGA”. *ACM Trans. on Design Automation of Electronic Systems*, 1(1):80–101, January 1996.

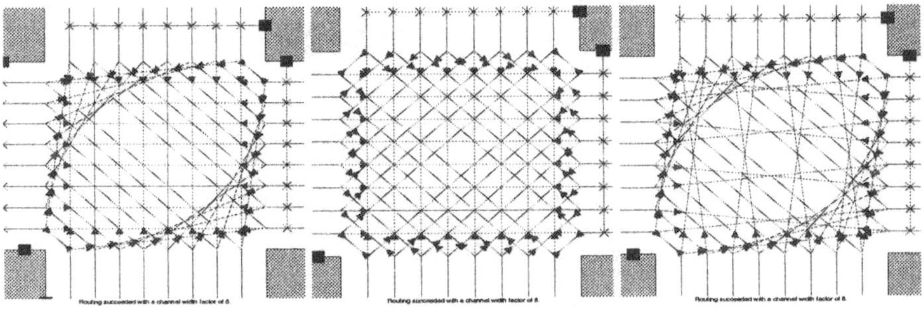

(a) Disjoint (4, 8)-SB (b) Symmetric (4, 8)-USB (c) Alternative (4, 8)-USB

Fig. 3. Structures of switch blocks.

[5] H. Fan, J. Liu, and Y. L. Wu. "General Models for Optimum Arbitrary-Dimension FPGA Switch Box Designs". *Proc. IEEE International Conference on Computer-Aided Design (ICCAD)*, Nov. 2000.

[6] H. Fan, J. Liu, and Y. L. Wu. "Combinatorial routing analysis and design of universal switch blocks". *Proceedings of the ASP-DAC 2001*, 2001.

[7] H.B. Fan, Y.L. Wu, and Y.W. Chang. "Comment on General Universal Switch Blocks". *IEEE Transactions on Computers*, 51(1):93–95, Jan. 2002.

[8] G. G. Lemieux and D. M. Lewis. "Analytical Framework for Switch Block Design". *12th International Conference on Field Programmable Logic and Application*, 2002.

[9] E. C. Milner. "Basic wqo- and bqo-theory". *Graphs and Order (Banff, 1984), NATO Adv. Sci. Inst. Ser. C: Math. Phys. Sci. 147, Reidel, Dordrecht-Boston*, pages 487–502, 1985.

[10] J. Rose and S. Brown. "Flexibility of interconnection structures for field-programmable gate arrays". *IEEE J. Solid-State Circuits*, 26(3):277–282, 1991.

[11] M. Shyu, G. M. Wu, Y. D. Chang, and Y. W. Chang. "Generic Universal Switch Blocks". *IEEE Trans. on Computers*, pages 348–359, April 2000.

[12] Y. L. Wu and M. Marek-Sadowska. "Routing for array type FPGAs". *IEEE Trans. on Computer-Aided Design of Integrated Circuits and Systems*, 16(5):506–518, May 1997.

[13] Y. L. Wu, S. Tsukiyama, and M. Marek-Sadowska. "Graph based analysis of 2-D FPGA routing". *IEEE Trans. on Computer-Aided Design*, 15(1):33–44, 1996.

[14] S. Yang. "Logic Synthesis and Optimization Benchmarks, Version 3.0". *Tech. Report, Microelectronics Centre of North Carolina*, 1991.

Improved Functional Simulation of Dynamically Reconfigurable Logic

Ian Robertson[1], James Irvine[1], Patrick Lysaght[1], and David Robinson[2]

[1]EEE Department, University of Strathclyde,
204 George St., Glasgow, G1-1XW, UK
i.robertson@eee.strath.ac.uk
[2]Verilab, Willow House, Strathclyde Business Park,
Bellshill, ML4-3PB, UK

Abstract. Several techniques to simulate dynamically reconfigurable logic (DRL) have been published during the last decade. These methods each have their own strengths and weaknesses, and perform well when used under particular circumstances. This paper introduces a revised version of dynamic circuit switching (DCS), a DRL simulation technique reported previously, which improves the accuracy of the simulation models and extends the range of situations to which they can be applied. The internal state of dynamic tasks that contain memory elements can change when they are reconfigured. Modelling this presents a further simulation requirement. The paper indicates how this can be achieved by including the ideas behind another simulation technique, clock morphing, in the methodology. Finally, the run-time overheads introduced by the technique are analysed.

1. Introduction

Creating dynamically reconfigurable designs poses additional design problems, over and above those of conventional logic design. Given such complexity, it is vital to verify the design's operation early in the design flow, thus eliminating errors quickly. As the design's logic circuits are reconfigured over time, its behaviour is altered. Conventional simulation techniques do not provide any mechanism by which the design can be altered during the simulation. To simulate reconfigurable designs, therefore, either a specialist simulator or a method of mimicking the reconfigurations within a conventional simulator is required. The robustness and maturity of conventional simulation technology, combined with the complexity of implementing a new simulator make the second option more attractive.

Several methods have been reported for using conventional simulation tools to model the behaviour of DRL designs, ranging from low-level models of FPGAs to high-level abstract simulators [1-10]. Low-level device models [1,2] achieve accurate simulation results, since they model the device's behaviour throughout its operation, including the reconfiguration periods. This sort of simulation can only be performed at the end of the design flow when partial configurations are available. To simulate system behaviour earlier in the design flow, more abstract simulation techniques must be used, based on generic approximations of the actual device behaviour.

M. Glesner, P. Zipf, and M. Renovell (Eds.): FPL 2002, LNCS 2438, pp. 152-161, 2002.

Abstract simulations therefore rely on certain assumptions about the behaviour of the target FPGA and the design they are simulating. The accuracy of the simulation depends on the validity of these assumptions. This paper examines a set of cases that are not accurately modelled by previously reported simulation techniques. These cases occur when the dynamic tasks in a set of mutually exclusive tasks do not all drive exactly the same output lines. We present improvements to dynamic circuit switching (DCS) [3], that allow these cases to be simulated accurately.

One persistent problem is that of simulating changes in the state of dynamic tasks during reconfiguration intervals. This issue was discussed by Vasilko who introduced a technique called clock morphing (CM) for simulating DRL. CM can model changes in task state during reconfigurations; however, it is less accurate when applied to other areas of the simulation model and requires more effort to port it to other FPGA families. In addition, CM assumes that all dynamic tasks contain synchronous elements. Consequently, a tool is required to simulate any purely combinatorial tasks in a set of dynamic tasks. A simulation consisting of the new DCS approach combined with CM can tackle this remaining problem, while resolving many of CM's limitations.

In the next section, a review of high-level approaches to simulating DRL is presented. The review considers only techniques for applying conventional simulation technology to DRL simulation. Therefore, simulation using specialist languages such as JHDL [5] or Lava [6] is excluded, along with custom computing machine simulation tools such as DRIVE [7]. In section 3, the difficult cases are introduced, followed by the improved DCS technique in section 4. Section 5 discusses the task state issue and how DCS can be combined with CM, with little additional simulation overhead. The run-time overheads of the DCS technique are investigated in section 6. Future research possibilities and conclusions are discussed in sections 7 and 8.

2. Previous Work

A *mutex set* is a set of dynamic tasks which are mutually exclusive either for algorithmic reasons or because they share areas of the logic array. Most abstract simulation methods are based on the concept of activating one dynamic task from a mutex set by allowing it to receive inputs and drive outputs. The other inactive tasks (which are not present on the logic array) need to be isolated from the simulation in some way, to prevent them altering the system's behaviour.

In [8] Luk presented a method of modelling DRL based on virtual multiplexers. A reconfiguration can be simulated by switching the selected input to the virtual multiplexers. This allows functional verification of a task's behaviour and sequencing, but does not give any insight into a design's behaviour during a reconfiguration interval. Gibson [9] proposed dynamic generic mapping (DGM), in which VHDL *generics* are used to parameterise components. A design's behaviour can be altered by modifying the values of the appropriate generics. Again, this technique does not provide any insight into the reconfiguration behaviour, as the tasks are swapped instantly. As VHDL does not support changing generic values during simulation, these changes have to be made manually or using custom scripts.

In [4] Vasilko proposed clock morphing (CM) in which a new signal value, 'V', is added to the VHDL std_logic package. 'V' is specified as the weakest driver level in the new std_logic package. When a signal carries the new 'V' value, it indicates that its associated circuitry is not present on the logic array. The 'V' value is introduced to a dynamic task via its clock line. The sequential elements in the design are modified to propagate any 'V' clock inputs to their output. To ensure 'V' signals propagate to all areas of the dynamic task, the combinatorial logic functions are altered to propagate any 'V' input regardless of the other inputs. So, for example, in the case of the logical AND function, '0' AND 'V' = 'V'. When a task is activated after being inactive for a while, all the internal memory elements will be set to 'V'. A more appropriate value may be 'U'. To achieve this, the sequential elements in the design are further modified to reset to 'U' whenever a valid clock signal replaces a 'V' input. This is the correct result as the task's state is usually unknown at this stage. The reconfiguration interval can be simulated by holding all the dynamic tasks in the inactive state for the reconfiguration period, resulting in an output of 'V' on all lines driven by a dynamic task. Since 'V' is the weakest driver level in the new std_logic package, task selection is performed by active task outputs overwriting the 'V' signals driven by inactive tasks. This approach is similar to that used in DCS, except that there the signal is driven to 'Z' [3].

In FPGAs such as the XC6200, a reconfiguration does not alter the contents of registers within the area affected. Successive dynamic tasks can therefore share the contents of registers. This can be modelled using a "global technology register array" [4], which stores the values of all registers on the logic array. The technique therefore depends on the availability of placement information early on in the design flow. Otherwise, the technique is generic and independent of CM. It can therefore be applied alongside other simulation techniques such as DCS.

CM suffers from a few issues that limit its applicability to general DRL simulation situations:

- Tasks containing no synchronous components cannot be simulated. An alternative technique such as DCS must be used with such tasks.
- When 'V' is driven onto a task output (e.g. if a task is reconfiguring or there is no task currently driving the output) it will propagate through all the combinatorial logic in the static task corrupting its operation due to the 'V' propagation rules. This is a pessimistic result, as an AND operation with a '0' input could be used to isolate the static circuits from a reconfiguring task.
- The technique requires a new version of the std_logic_1164 package and new versions of any VITAL libraries used in the simulation. The basic IEEE VITAL libraries also need to be ported.
- CM cannot be ported to Verilog as it does not allow new signal values to be created. This rules out a large amount of current intellectual property and legacy designs.

Lysaght and Stockwood [3] introduced dynamic circuit switching (DCS), a simulation technique for DRL used with the Viewlogic schematic design tools. Robinson [10] updated DCS make use of the greater flexibility offered by VHDL. The method relies on the insertion of a set of simulation artefacts into the design prior

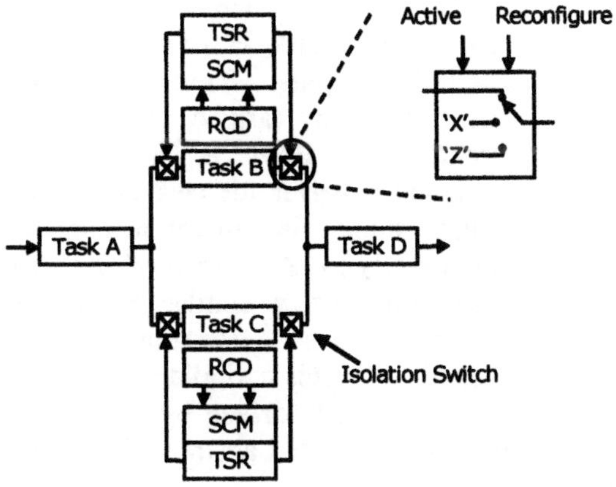

Fig. 1. DCS simulation artefacts added to a simple design consisting of two static tasks, A and D and two dynamic tasks, B and C.

to simulation, fig. 1. The components are reconfiguration condition detectors (RCDs), schedule control modules (SCMs), task status registers (TSRs) and isolation switches. The RCDs monitor designer selected signals to detect the conditions under which tasks should be activated or deactivated. These *reconfiguration requests* are passed to the SCMs, which collectively form a simple configuration controller. The SCMs manipulate the TSRs to reflect the current configuration status of the dynamic tasks. Details of the TSRs were published in [11]. Isolation switches are attached to the inputs and outputs of dynamic tasks.

The behaviour of the isolation switches is controlled by the TSRs. When a task is inactive (not configured), its isolation switches output 'Z', the weakest driver value in std_logic. When reconfiguring they output 'X' and when active (configured) they output their input, effectively forming a wire. The result of this behaviour is that the stronger drivers of reconfiguring or active tasks overwrite the values driven by inactive circuits, effectively isolating them from the design. Hence, the design's changes over time are mimicked in the simulation. DCS assumes that the designer will take responsibility for modelling changes in a task's state, unlike CM. However, it is portable to Verilog, has no technology dependencies and models the dynamic task's external effects on the circuit more accurately than comparable techniques. Accurate modelling of the possible effects of a reconfiguration on the surrounding circuitry is its key advantage over comparable simulators.

3. Problematic Cases

Previous simulation techniques have assumed that all the dynamic tasks in a mutex set receive the same inputs and drive identical outputs, as suggested by the use of multiplexers in [8]. Indeed, in DGM, the same component is used to represent different tasks, so it would be difficult to model tasks with differing connectivity. While this will often be the case, there is no reason why it should apply in all cases. Fig. 2 shows a simple DRL design in which two dynamic tasks are members of the same mutex set but do not drive an identical set of outputs. Tasks A and B are dynamic tasks and C and D are static. When task A is active, it drives the input to task C, while the input to task D is not driven. This un-driven signal should be indicated by feeding 'X' or 'U' into task D's input.

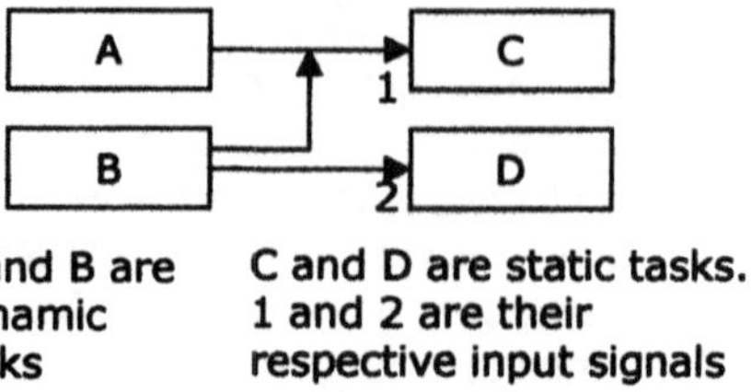

Fig. 2. Two mutually exclusive dynamic tasks that do not drive the same output signals. B drives signals 1 and 2, while A only drives 1.

In DCS, the isolation switches surrounding task B drive 'Z' onto both its outputs. This is correctly overwritten by task A to form the input to C. However, there is no alternative driver for task D's input. This input is therefore driven incorrectly to 'Z' instead of 'X'. As CM relies on a similar system of stronger drivers overwriting the 'V' signals, it yields a similar result of 1 being correctly driven by A while 2 is erroneously driven to 'V'. Therefore, no previously reported abstract simulation techniques can accurately simulate this situation.

4. Improved DCS Technique

The original DCS fails in these situations because the isolation switches attempt to perform both circuit isolation and dynamic task modelling. CM also uses one technique to perform both functions and has the same limitations. The accuracy of the simulation can be improved by splitting the roles between two new components: dynamic task modellers (DTMs) and dynamic task selectors (DTSs). Fig. 3 shows the new arrangement of components applied to the example in fig. 2. DTMs are instantiated in the same places as isolation switches. However, their functionality is simpler; they output either the input, when the task is active, or 'X' in all other circumstances. There is no longer any need for the 'Z' output as task selection is now performed by DTSs. One DTS is instantiated on each line that is driven by one or more tasks in the mutex set. These components select a DTM output from the list of tasks that can drive the signal based on the TSRs corresponding to those tasks. If none of the valid driver tasks is active, 'X' is output by the DTS. DCSim [10] has been updated to automate this revised technique.

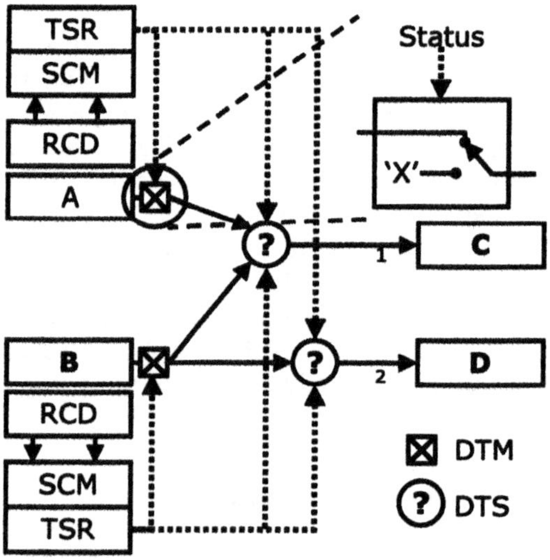

Fig. 3. An improved DCS simulation model of the system illustrated in fig. 2. Dynamic task modellers (DTMs) and dynamic task selectors (DTSs) replace the isolation switches in the original DCS. The DTSs select an appropriate driver for their output signal based on the status of the tasks within the mutex set.

The results of a simulation of this example are shown in fig. 4. Initially, both tasks are inactive. Both DTMs therefore drive 'X' and the DTSs, making a random selection, drive 'X' onto both 1 and 2. At 85ns task B completes its activation. The DTMs on its output switch to propagating its input and the DTSs for 1 and 2 select the input from task B. The signal values on 1 and 2 therefore change to '1'. At 165ns task B deactivates and task A begins to activate. It completes its activation at 255 ns, at which time 1 is driven by task A's output. Since there is no valid driver for 2, it continues to be driven with 'X'.

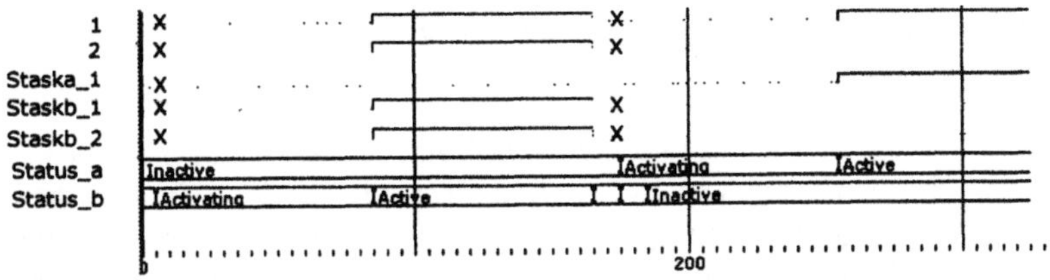

Fig. 4. Simulation results from a short run of the model in fig. 3. For simplicity, tasks A and B are both pull-ups. The signal staska_1 represents the input from task A's DTM to the DTS for signal 1, staskb_2 represents the signal from B's DTM to the DTS for signal 2, etc. The two waveforms at the bottom indicate the reconfiguration status of tasks A and B respectively.

5. Accurate Simulation of Circuit State During Reconfiguration

At this stage, we have achieved a simulation that models the external interactions of reconfiguring circuitry accurately at an abstract level. The changes that can occur in the internal state of dynamic tasks have not been considered. In some cases the designer may decide that the task's initial state does not affect the design's behaviour. In such cases, no modelling of the task's state is required. However, in many cases, it will be relevant. Task state is an issue of some complexity, as it depends on a number of factors. The first is technology dependent. Some FPGA architectures reset the memory elements within the reconfigured area whenever a new configuration is loaded. In such cases, the resulting state may be random, or all the elements may be set to a default value. Other architectures, such as the XC6200 leave the registers unchanged. Therefore, the initial state of the task depends on what tasks occupied the array prior to the current task's activation, their final state when their operation completed and the exact placement of their registers. To generate an accurate simulation, therefore, the exact layout of the task is required.

At a more abstract level, however, three generic cases can be considered:

1. The initial state of the task should not affect the system's behaviour, but the designer wishes to test this. In this case, the initial state should be set to unknown (i.e. all 'X' or 'U') in order to check that the initialisation operates correctly. In CM, the task's state can be initialised in this way, by altering the functionality of the model's synchronous elements.
2. The task is to return to the array with the same state as it left the array. In most cases, this would involve reloading the state values into its registers from some memory in which they were stored (unless an XC6200-type FPGA is used and

no other task has occupied the dynamic task's area while it was inactive). The DCS CAD framework supports this situation via the pre-emption interface in its configuration controllers [12]. In simulation, simply cutting off the clock while the task is inactive will achieve the desired result.

3. The designer intends dynamic tasks to share register contents. One dynamic task is initialised by values left behind on the array by another dynamic task. To simulate this, a mechanism to transfer values between dynamic tasks is required. Vasliko [4] suggests the use of a global technology register. This is intended for use after the design has been placed. A similar idea, in which the designer specifies the values to be shared instead of relying on the register's placement, can be used earlier in the design flow.

Initially DCS supported option 2 by modifying the DTM on the task's clock input (i.e. output '0' while the task is inactive, instead of 'X'). It was the designer's responsibility to model the required behaviour for cases 1 or 3. However, CM supports case 1 by default and uses the global technology register array [4] extension to cover case 3. This extension is simulator independent, however, and can be applied alongside other simulation techniques. DCS and CM can be combined to create a simulation method capable of automatically modelling both the task state issues and the interactions of dynamic tasks with surrounding logic accurately. CM can be introduced into a DCS based simulation with little additional runtime overhead by using a modified DTM to introduce the 'V' value to a task's clock input (a simple matter of interchanging the 'X' with a 'V'). All other task I/O is connected to conventional DTMs. The DTMs block 'V' signals and convert them to 'X's. This prevents 'V' outputs overwriting other signals in combinatorial logic outwith the dynamic task and corrupting the system's operation.

A simple example of a combined CM/DCS simulation is shown in fig. 5. It consists of a reconfigurable up/down counter constructed from an up counter and a down counter. Initially, neither counter is activated; therefore, the value on both counters is "VVV". At 100 ns, the up counter activates and counts until 600 ns, when the down counter begins activation. Note that the internal state of the up counter becomes "VVV" at this stage. By 700 ns, the down counter is activated. However, its initial state is unknown. Therefore, it cannot begin counting until its reset is applied. The `Count` signal shows the actual output of the counter, while the signals `Downcount_dtm` and `Upcount_dtm` show the outputs of the dynamic task modellers. It can be seen that all the 'V' values are blocked, as required.

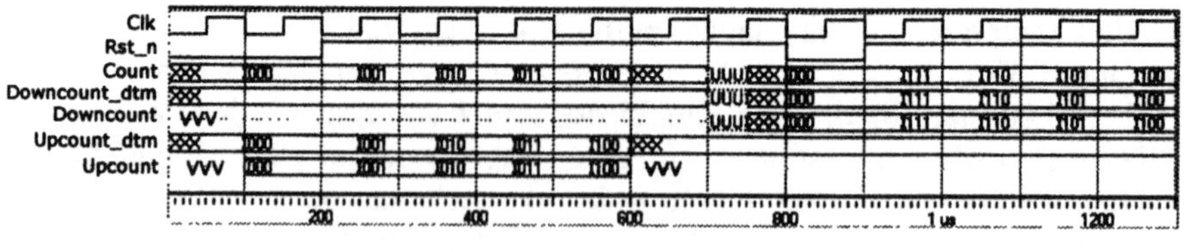

Fig. 5. A reconfigurable up/down counter simulated using a combination of the new DCS and CM techniques. Count represents the output of the counter, while Downcount and Upcount are the internal states of the two counters. Downcount_dtm and Upcount_dtm show the individual task's counts after they have been 'filtered' by the DTMs

By combining the new DCS and CM simulation techniques, we solve the task state issue in DCS and improve the modelling of situations where the constituent tasks in a mutex set do not drive exactly the same lines. The combined technique does not suffer from CM's limitations when applied to combinatorial tasks or modelling of the configuration interval. However, whereas DCS was completely portable across FPGA families without modification, new libraries in which the components have been modified to correctly handle the 'V' signal value are required for CM. Therefore, the portability has been reduced. Vasilko [4] states that only minor modifications were required to port the standard XACT6000 technology libraries for use with CM, however as FPGAs become more complex, the associated increase in the complexity of their technology libraries will also increase the porting effort. In addition, the combined technique will not port to verilog. More portable simulation techniques are under investigation.

6. Simulation Overheads and Scalability

As fig. 3 shows, the simulation model of a DRL system contains artefacts that will reduce the speed of simulation. In general the number of simulation artefacts scales linearly with the number of dynamic tasks, where each task has a similar number of input and output ports. It is also linear with the number of ports in each dynamic task. On average, therefore, the time taken to execute the simulation artefacts will scale linearly with the complexity of the system. The time taken to execute the system's logic will also increase. This increase is less than linear, because the level of switching activity (and hence simulation effort) is very low in tasks that are inactive, since the DTMs cut off their inputs. The total simulation time will therefore scale in a sub-linear fashion against system complexity, as will the runtime overheads.

To measure the run-time overheads introduced by the simulation technique, three designs, of varying complexity, were simulated. The first design contained two communicating UARTs and had no simulation overhead. The second design treated the two UARTs as dynamic tasks and had some 109 simulation artefacts added to it. Finally, to examine how the overheads scale with design complexity, a third design containing 100 UARTs arranged into two mutex sets of 50 UARTs each was created. The times taken to complete the simulations are shown in table 1.

The DRL design ran approximately one third slower than the static design. As the design proceeds through the implementation process, and gate-level models are used instead of RTL (as used in this example), the proportion of the time the simulator expends on running the simulation components will decrease. The additional run-time will be insignificant in such cases. Simulation of the large design, which contained 50 times the hardware of the simple design and over 5000 simulation artefacts, took less than six times longer than the simple design, a sub-liner increase. We conclude that large systems can be simulated without prohibitive run-time overheads.

Table 1. Execution times for simulation of three designs of different complexity.

Simulation	Run-time(s)	Increase
Static design (2 UARTs)	312	0%
Dynamic design (2 UARTs)	421	35%
Dynamic design (100 UARTs)	1751	461%

7. Future Work

A major recent focus of attention in CAD research has been into languages to ease the high-level modelling of systems-on-a-chip (SoC) designs. The design of such SoCs is a complex hardware/software co-design problem, typically involving the use of pre-verified intellectual property (IP) blocks. IP is typically associated with hardware, but the concept also applies to software and testbenches. SoC design languages therefore must be capable of representing hardware designs at multiple levels of abstraction (behavioural, RTL, netlist) and allow hardware/software co-simulation. As many DRL designs are created through a similar hardware/software co-design process, many of the language features are likely to be applicable to DRL design. We intend to investigate how our simulation techniques can be ported to a language such as SystemC and what modelling flexibility this provides.

A verification technique that is increasingly being applied to large designs, as simulation becomes more complex and time consuming, is formal verification. Formal verification of a full DRL design is a complex problem. Some work has been published in the literature [13-15] in which formal methods have been applied to certain DRL systems or situations. No generic approach for applying it to a broad range of systems at design time has been reported. However, equivalence checking between a reference design and a design that has been through some transformation, such as synthesis, may be more easily applied. In [16] we described a design flow for applying conventional synthesis and APR tools to DRL designs. One of the outputs of this process is a gate-level representation of the input RTL design. Equivalence checking between these two designs is therefore little different from conventional equivalence checking in an SoC.

8. Conclusions

This paper has illustrated that previously published simulation methods cannot accurately model some types of dynamic reconfiguration. It introduced a revision of DCS that resolves these issues. We then showed how the principles behind another simulation technique, CM, could be used to further improve the accuracy and applicability of the simulations at the cost of reduced portability. Finally, we illustrated that the run-time overheads of the technique scale at a rate below system complexity so that it can be used effectively with larger designs.

9. References

[1] K. Kwiat and W. Debany, "Reconfigurable Logic Modelling", in Integrated System Design, 1996, http://www.isdmag.com/Editorial/1996/CoverStory9612.html

[2] S. McMillan, B. Blodget and S. Guccione, "VirtexDS: A Device Simulator for Virtex", Reconfigurable Technology: FPGAs for Computing and Applications II, Proc SPIE 4212, Bellingham, WA, November 2000.

[3] P. Lysaght and J. Stockwood, "A Simulation Tool for Dynamically Reconfigurable Field Programmable Gate Arrays", in IEEE Transactions on VLSI Systems, Vol. 4, No. 3, pp. 381 – 390, 1996.

[4] M. Vasilko and D. Cabanis, "A Technique for Modelling Dynamic Reconfiguration with Improved Simulation Accuracy", in IEICE Transactions on Fundamentals of Electronics, Communications and Computer Sciences, November 1999.

[5] B. Hutchings and P. Bellows, "JHDL – An HDL for Reconfigurable Systems", Proceedings of the IEEE Symposium on Field-Programmable Custom Computing Machines, California, USA, April 1998.

[6] S. Singh and M. Sheeran, "Designing FPGA Circuits in Lava", Unpublished paper, http://www.gla.ac.uk/~satnam/lava/lava_intro.pdf.

[7] K. Bondalapati and V. K. Prasanna, "DRIVE: An Interpretive Simulation and Visualisation Environment for Dynamically Reconfigurable Systems", Field Programmable Logic and Applications, Glasgow, UK, August 1999.

[8] W. Luk, N. Shirazi and P. Y. K. Cheung, "Compilation tools for run-time reconfigurable designs", Proc. IEEE Symposium on Field-Programmable Custom Computing Machines, Napa, California, USA, April 1997.

[9] D. Gibson, M. Vasilko and D. Long, "Virtual Prototyping for Dynamically Reconfigurable Architectures using Dynamic Generic Mapping", Proceedings of VIUF Fall' 98, Orlando, Florida, USA, October 1998.

[10] D. Robinson and P. Lysaght, "Methods of Exploiting Simulation Technology for Simulating the Timing of Dynamically Reconfigurable Logic", in IEE Proceedings Computer and Digital Techniques – Special Issue on Reconfigurable Systems, G. Brebner and B. Hutchings (Eds.), Vol. 147, No. 3 May 2000.

[11] D. Robinson and P. Lysaght, "Verification of Dynamically Reconfigurable Logic", in Field Programmable Logic and Applications, Villach, Austria, August 2000.

[12] D. Robinson and P. Lysaght, "Modelling and Synthesis of Configuration Controllers for Dynamically Reconfigurable Logic Systems Using the DCS CAD Framework", Field Programmable Logic and Applications, Glasgow, UK, August 1999.

[13] S. Singh and C. J. Lillieroth, "Formal Verification of Reconfigurable Cores", in IEEE Symposium on FPGAs for Custom Computing Machines, Napa, California, USA, April 1999.

[14] K. W. Susanto and T. Melham, "Formally Analysed Dynamic Synthesis of Hardware", Theorem Proving and Higher Order Logics: Emerging Trends: 11th International Conference, Canberra, September – October 1998.

[15] N. McKay and S. Singh, "Dynamic Specialisation of XC6200 FPGAs by Partial Evaluation", Field-Programmable Logic and Applications, Tallinn, Estonia, 1998.

[16] I. Robertson, J. Irvine, P. Lysaght and D. Robinson, "Timing Verification of Dynamically Reconfigurable Logic for the Xilinx Virtex FPGA Series", Tenth ACM International Symposium on Field-Programmable Gate Arrays, Monterey, California, USA, February 2002.

Run-Time Reconfiguration to Check Temperature in Custom Computers: An Application of JBits Technology

S. Lopez-Buedo[1], P. Riviere[2], P. Pernas[2] and E. Boemo[1]

[1] School of Computer and Telecommunication Engineering
Universidad Autonoma de Madrid, Spain
{sergio.lopez-buedo, eduardo.boemo}@uam.es

[2] Applied Physics Department, Universidad Autonoma de Madrid, Spain
{paula.riviere, pablo.pernas}@uam.es

Abstract.- This paper is a progress report of a novel application of JBits technology. The capability of handling run-time reconfiguration is utilized to add an array of temperature sensors into a working circuit. The thermal map thus obtained provides information not only of the overall chip temperature, but also about the power consumption of each block of the design. The sensors utilized need no external components, and, by means of the partial reprogrammability of the Virtex FPGA family, no permanent occupation of any resources is made. Several experiments are summarized to illustrate the feasibility of the technique.

1. Introduction

JBits [1] can be defined as an API (application program interface) that permits describing FPGA designs entirely in Java. One of the merits of JBits is that it fully integrates the hardware specification into Java code, thus becoming a powerful tool for HW/SW codesign. But its main advantage is that it gives access to all the partial reconfiguration features of the Virtex family of FPGAs. Not only JBits allows reconfigurations to be made, but it also opens a way to generate run-time parameterizable designs. That is, circuits that are created at run-time according to the current situation of the FPGA (resources availability, input data rate, current temperature, etc.)

JBits technology also is useful to study the thermal aspects of FPGA-based computer machines. In a previous work, we demonstrated the feasibility of measuring FPGA temperature by adding several fixed ring-oscillators in different circuit zones [3], [4]. But this solution makes permanent use of both internal resources (CLBs and routing) and I/O pads (required to output the signals and control the sensors). On the contrary, a resource-free alternative can be accomplished by using dynamic reconfiguration. First, the main application circuit is downloaded into the FPGA, for example, a system-on-chip composed by a processor and associated peripherals. Each time a thermal analysis is required, a second configuration bitstream with an array of thermal sensors is loaded. In few microseconds they record the FPGA temperature in different parts of the die. After that, their measurements are processed using standard

M. Glesner, P. Zipf, and M. Renovell (Eds.): FPL 2002, LNCS 2438, pp. 162-170, 2002.

bitstream read back Then, the first configuration can be reloaded again, to resume the normal operation in the FPGA.

All this actions are done via the Virtex configuration port, so that no dedicated I/O pads are consumed. For the chips utilized in our experiment, the reconfiguration takes few milliseconds, so that the temperature variation respect to the normal function can be neglected. The thermal information not only reveals the average temperature of the die, but also points out the elements that produce hot-spots. For instance, in the previous example the designer could know if an anomalous chip temperature is caused by the code running in the microprocessor, o by a particular peripheral.

But the JBits capacity of handling run-time parameterizable designs also permits more powerful approaches to be materialized. First, it is not necessary to stop the currently running design to add the array of sensors. JBits can be used to find free spaces in the configuration where to add them using run-time reconfiguration. After the measurement has been made, the sensors can be eliminated using another reconfiguration.

Additionally, if the application running in the FPGA is also run-time parameterizable, the information retrieved from the sensors can be used to adapt it to the current thermal situation. For example, if the temperature surpasses a certain limit, the design running in the FPGA can be reconfigured into a low-power mode, in order to put it back into safe margins. Another application could be reorganizing the location of the different elements of the design in order to minimize the thermal gradients (and thus, silicon stress) in the chip.

2. Thermal Sensors in Virtex

Ring-oscillators can be utilized to measure die temperature [2]. Particularly, in the area of programmable logic devices, they represent a simple and efficient alternative for thermal analysis [3], [4]. They can be implemented on all FPGA architectures, and its fully digital output makes them a good alternative to the dedicated temperature-sensing diode included in the Virtex series. While diodes have the advantage of being immune to power supply variations, they require some external analog circuitry [5].

In this paper, each sensor is basically composed by two 14-bit counters, and a ring-oscillator that provides a temperature-dependent frequency output. The counters are combined to construct a custom frequency meter. The first counter (timebase) generates a fixed measuring window, meanwhile the second just records the number of pulses in the interval fixed by the timebase.

The sensor block diagram is shown in Fig.1a. The ring-oscillator was constructed using 7 inverters, each one implemented in a 4-input LUT. The LUTs were placed separated, leaving a minimum space of a 1 CLB between them, in order to increase the routing delay. Unusually in digital design, a high frequency operation is not desirable: It implies both a higher counter size and extra self-heating. The final sensor layout can be observed in Fig. 1b. The size is 8 CLBs tall by 2 CLBs wide. That is, less than 0.4% of the total area of an XCV800 Virtex FPGA. This fact makes the sensor suitable for thermal mapping. Two chip samples have been utilized during the experiments: one XCV800PQ240-4 and one XCV50PQ240-4 [6]. A typical thermal response of the sensor is shown in Fig. 2.

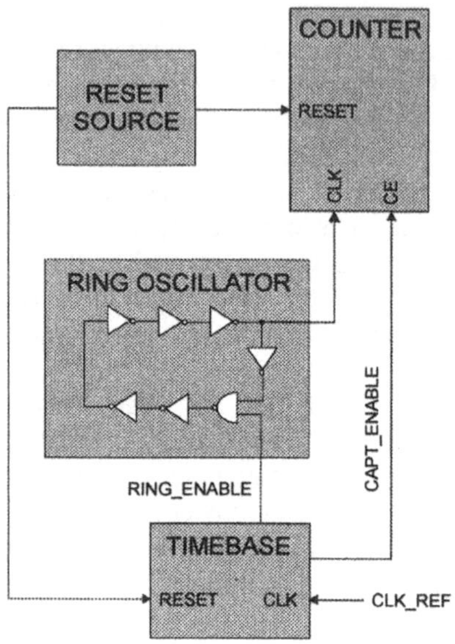

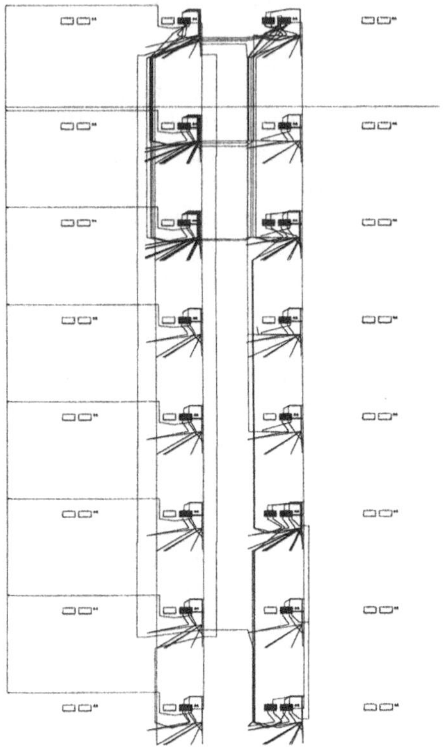

Fig.1a (left). Block diagram for the temperature sensor. **Fig. 1b (right).** Sensor layout

2.1 Design Methodology

The sensor circuitry was written following the CoreTemplate JBits API [7] for RTP (run-time parameterizable) cores. The only external pin utilized is the clock reference of the timebase counter, which should be connected to one of the main FPGA clock lines. Three enable signals are generated from the four most significant bits of this counter. The first, `Ring_Enable`, allows the ring-oscillator to start running. The second, `Capt_Enable`, establishes the interval during which the ring-oscillator frequency output will be counted. Finally, `Time_Enable` disables the timebase counter when the measurement is completed, to avoid spurious power dissipation.

The timing values have been empirically adjusted, taking advantage of the FPGA reprogramability. In the final arrangement, the ring-oscillator runs during 555 μs in each temperature sampling. This corresponds to 2048 cycles of the 3.6864 MHz clock reference. The capture counter is enabled during the second half of that time (277 μs), leaving the first 1024 cycles as a safe margin for oscillation start-up.

Once the measurement has been made, the capture counter stores a value that is proportional to the frequency output of the ring-oscillator, and therefore, to the die temperature. This count is read back by the host processor, where the actual temperature is calculated. Thus, the use of I/O pads to transfer the data is eliminated.

The sensor was designed as a primitive core, directly accessing to the low-level CLB configuration using the `jbits.set` function. All the routing was done automatically, using JRoute. The Java code has near 500 lines. Three parameters define the circuit: the timings of the enable signals, expressed as the contents of the LUTs that generate them.

3. Operation of a Run-Time Configurable Sensor

The use of the thermal strategy proposed in this work requires a system composed by one or many FPGAs, and a host microprocessor running a Java Virtual Machine (JVM). During the initialization, the host microprocessor configures the FPGAs, and the system starts working. Whenever the host checks the thermal status of the board, the following steps are executed:

- The current bitstream is inspected to find a free space where to insert the sensor. This operation can be made statically, providing a free space to insert the sensor at design time. But JBits also allows the designer made it dynamically, finding a place where to insert the sensor. This alternative is useful in evolvable and adaptive systems where the designer could ignore what circuit will be running in the FPGA at a certain time.
- Once a possible location for the sensor is found, its elements are inserted and routed.
- The new bitstream (with the sensor embedded in it) is generated by JBits, and the FPGA is partially reconfigured: only the modified frames are updated. That is, the sensor is inserted in the FPGA meanwhile the system continues its normal operation.
- As the FPGA is only partially reconfigured, the state of the registers of the sensor is unknown (the global reset signal will not be asserted to permit the normal operation of the circuit that is already running in the FPGA). To solve this problem, first the circuit will be downloaded with its reset signals activated, so that the count will be initialized at zero. Since the reset signal is enabled, no activity will be present. Immediately after that, the sensor is reconfigured again with the reset signals de-asserted (only one LUT needs to be changed). Thus, the oscillator runs and the counting begins.
- Finally, once the measurement has been made, the state of the sensor is read back to obtain the frequency of the ring-oscillator. Then, the host microprocessor translates this count into the actual temperature, using a pre-calculated table.

In order to verify the feasibility of the strategy, two Xilinx AFX PQ240-100 prototyping boards with XCV50PQ240-4 and XCV800PQ240-4 FPGAs were utilized. They were connected via a custom interface to a MS-Windows host running JBits. The link was implemented through the parallel port of the PC. This option lead to a simple, yet full connectivity to the FPGA, at a moderate configuration speed (around hundreds of KB per second).

To calibrate the sensors, the boards were placed in a temperature-controlled oven. An iron–constantan (Fe–CuNi) thermocouple was positioned in the center of the package to measure chip temperature. The sensor outputs were measured for different temperatures and power supply voltages. One sensor was measured for the XCV50, located in the bottom left corner of the chip, and five sensors for the XCV800, located in the four corners and in the center of the die.

Fig. 2 shows the output of the sensor versus the die temperature, and Fig. 3 its dependence to power supply variations. The two graphics are normalized respectively at 17 °C and 2.5 V. It is worth noting that, once normalized, the thermal characteristics of the sensors are completely similar, independently of its location or device type. This simplifies the process of calibration, because the data obtained for a sensor can be safely extrapolated to other locations or even different device models. Unfortunately, the correlation between Vcc and the output frequency appears to be more device-dependent. The figures also show that severe increments of the chip temperature (such as those caused by serious circuit errors) cannot be masked by moderate (±5%) power supply variations.

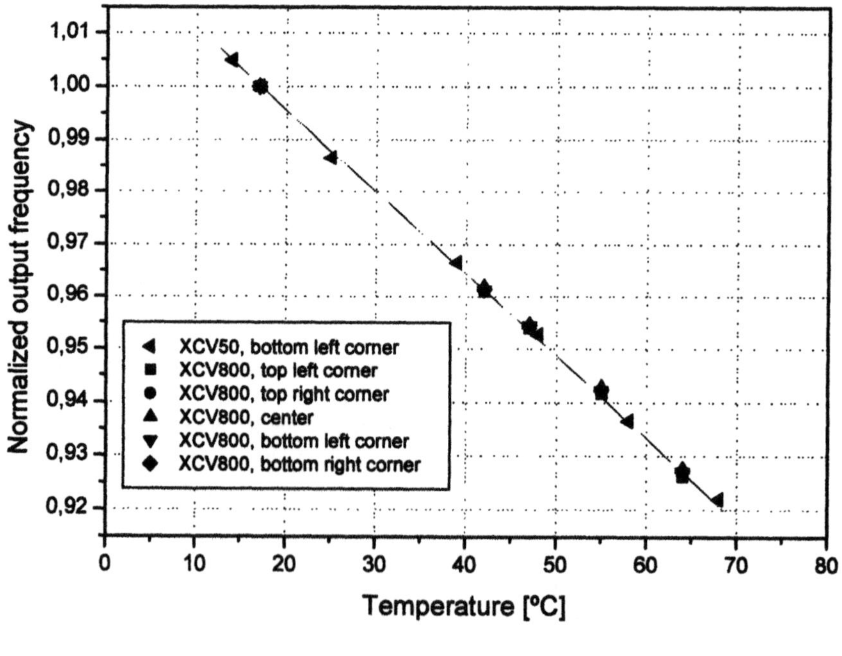

Fig. 2. Normalized ring-oscillator frequency response versus die temperature.

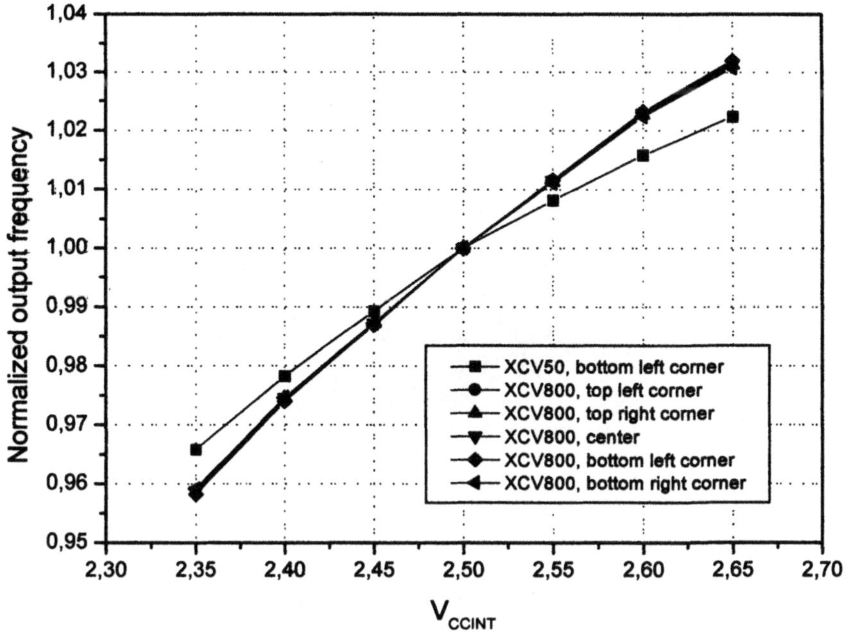

Fig. 3. Normalized ring-oscillator frequency response versus power supply voltage.

Additionally, the viability of obtaining a thermal map of the FPGA has also been confirmed. Using the XCV800 FPGA, a small hot spot was situated in several locations of the die. It consisted of 64 flip-flops and 4-input LUTs arranged in a 4 by 4 CLB square. Toggling at 100 MHz, they consumed 100 mW. To obtain the temperature map, an array of 4 by 10 temperature sensors was added and measured using JBits and the methodology described above. Figs. 4 to 7 show the map of the temperature increments in several locations of the chip due to the activity of this hot spot. The actual locations of the hot spot are: Fig. 4, top left corner (FPGA rows 1-4, cols 4-7). Fig. 5, middle of the upper side (rows 1-4, cols 41-44). Fig. 6, center of the die (rows 27-50, cols 41-44). Fig. 7, halfway between the center and the top left corner (rows 10-13, cols 27-30).

In every map there is a clear correlation between the hottest point of the die and the location of the hot spot. It should also be noted that some configurations caused significant temperature gradients, reaching 3.5 °C. Only the temperature increments after the activation of the hot spot are shown, because the actual temperature of the chip is dominated by the clock buffer, which at 200 MHz consumes about 500 mW. Finally, it is clearly visible an anisotropy in the heat distribution; it is dissipated much faster in the up-down direction than in the left-right one. This effect could be caused by the unknown dimensions of the FPGA (here, rows and columns are supposed to be similar), or by some other undisclosed physical characteristics of the chip.

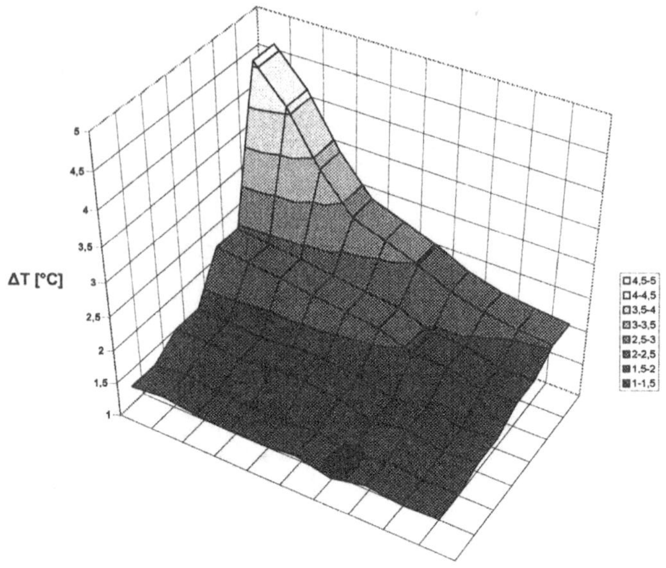

Fig. 4. Map of the temperature increments due to a hot spot in the top left corner of the die.

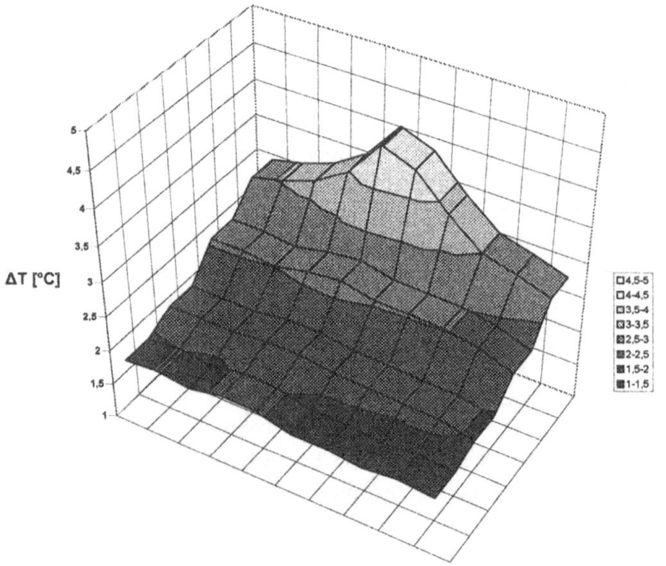

Fig. 5. Map of the temperature increments due to a hot spot in the upper side of the die.

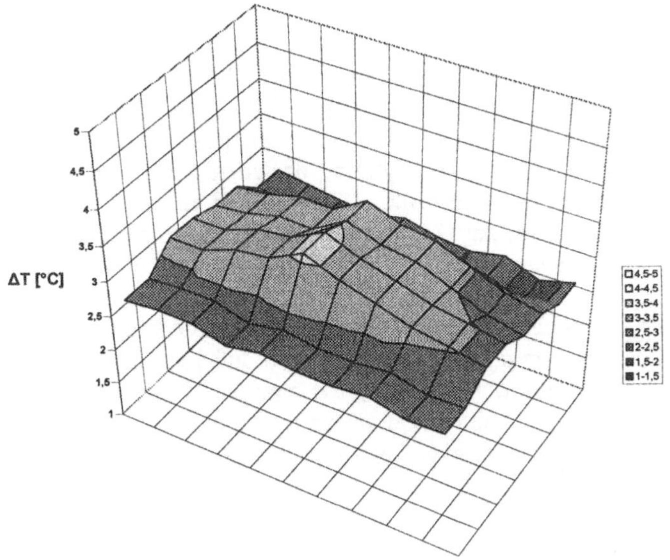

Fig. 6. Map of the temperature increments due to a hot spot in the middle of the die.

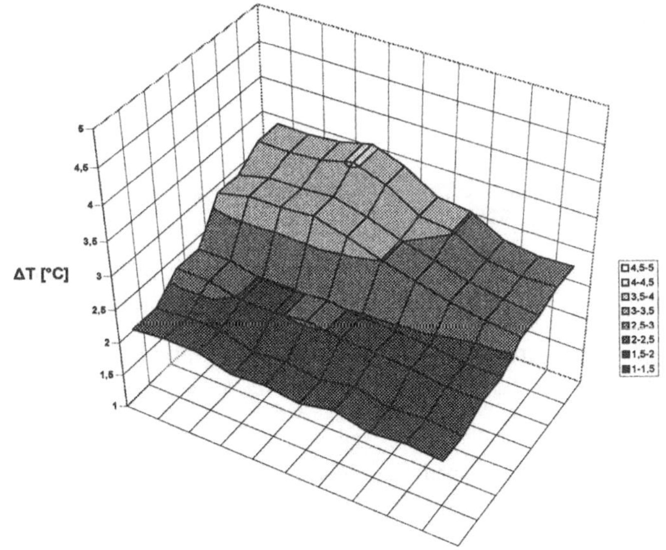

Fig. 7. Map of the temperature increments due to a hot spot in an arbitrary location of the die.

4. Conclusions

The thermal verification proposed in this paper allows the designer to check the correct status of the machine. Not only is possible to know if some elements of the circuit are causing excessive power dissipation: the position of hot-spots can be also determined. Thus, FPGA-based system designers can incorporate reliability considerations to the design trade-offs. The required circuitry is fully digital and it makes no permanent use of any FPGA resource. As the thermal transient time of the integrated circuits is several order of magnitude greater than current reprogramming periods, dynamic reconfiguration can be utilized to replace the main application by an array of sensors. JBits also makes possible to measure the temperature using run-time partial reconfiguration, employing the free spaces left by the main design. Thus, the sensors can be added without interrupting the function of the circuit. As a conclusion, thermal monitoring is one application where run-time reconfiguration is completely effective. Several experiments have been presented to illustrate the feasibility of the technique.

Acknowledges

The authors wish to thank E. Ruiz and P. Rodriguez for their help in the setup of the experiments, and S. Ocaña and G. Cutillas of Silica for their careful support. Spanish Ministry of Science, under contract TIC2001-2688-C03-03, has supported this work. Additional funds were obtained from project 658001 of the FGUAM.

References

1. S. A. Guccione and D. Levi, *"JBits: A Java-Based Interface to FPGA Hardware"*, Xilinx Inc., San Jose, California, 1998.

2. G. Quenot, N. Paris and B. Zavidovique, "A temperature and voltage measurement cell for VLSI circuits", *Proc. 1991 EURO ASIC Conf.*, pp-334-338, IEEE Press, 1991.

3. E. Boemo and S. Lopez-Buedo, "Themal Monitoring on FPGAs using Ring-Oscillators", *Proc. FLP'97 Workshop, Lecture Notes in Computer Science, No.1304*, pp.69-78, Berlin: Springer-Verlag, 1997.

4. S. Lopez-Buedo, J. Garrido and E. Boemo, "Thermal Testing on Reconfigurable Computers", *IEEE Design & Test of Computers*, pp.84-90, January-March 2000.

5. Xilinx Inc., *Application Note XAPP155*, 2000.

6. Xilinx Inc., *Virtex 2.5V Field Programmable Gate Arrays Data Sheet*, 2001

7. S. A. Guccione and D. Levi, *"Run-Time Parameterizable Cores"*, Xilinx Inc., San Jose, California, 1998.

Dynamic Reconfiguration in Mobile Systems

Gerard J.M. Smit, Paul J.M. Havinga, Lodewijk T. Smit, Paul M. Heysters, Michel A.J. Rosien

University of Twente
Department of Computer Science
Enschede, The Netherlands
{smit, havinga, smitl, heysters, rosien}@cs.utwente.nl

Abstract. Dynamically reconfigurable systems have the potential of realising efficient systems as well as providing adaptability to changing system requirements. Such systems are suitable for future mobile multimedia systems that have limited battery resources, must handle diverse data types, and must operate in dynamic application and communication environments. We propose an approach in which reconfiguration is applied dynamically at various levels of a mobile system, whereas traditionally, reconfigurable systems mainly focus at the gate level only. The research performed in the CHAMELEON project [1] aims at designing such a heterogeneous reconfigurable mobile system. The two main motivations for the system are 1) to have an energy-efficient system, while 2) achieving an adequate Quality of Service for applications.

1. Introduction

We are currently experiencing an explosive growth in the use of handheld mobile devices, such as cell phones, personal digital assistants (PDAs), digital cameras, global positioning systems, and so forth. Advances in technology enable portable computers to be equipped with wireless interfaces, allowing networked communication even while on the move. *Personal mobile computing* (often also referred to as *ubiquitous computing*) will play a significant role in driving technology in the next decade. In this paradigm, the basic personal computing and communication device will be an integrated, battery-operated device, small enough to carry along all the time. This device will be used as a replacement of many items the modern human being carries around. It will incorporate various functions like a pager, cellular phone, laptop computer, diary, digital camera, video game, calculator and remote control. To enable this, the device will support multimedia tasks like speech recognition, video and audio. Whereas today's notebook computers and personal digital assistants (PDAs) are self contained, tomorrow's networked mobile computers are part of a greater computing infrastructure. Furthermore, consumers of these devices are demanding ever-more sophisticated features, which in turn require tremendous amounts of additional resources.

---

[1] This research is supported by the PROGram for Research on Embedded Systems & Software (PROGRESS) of the Dutch organization for Scientific Research NWO, the Dutch Ministry of Economic Affairs and the technology foundation STW.

M. Glesner, P. Zipf, and M. Renovell (Eds.): FPL 2002, LNCS 2438, pp. 171-181, 2002.

The technological challenges to establishing this paradigm of personal mobile computing are non-trivial. In particular, these devices have limited battery resources, must handle diverse data types, and must operate in environments that are insecure, unplanned, and show different characteristics over time [2].

Traditionally, (embedded) systems that have demanding applications – e.g., driven by portability, performance, or cost – lead to the development of one or more custom processors or application-specific integrated circuits (ASICs) to meet the design objectives. However, the development of ASICs is expensive in time, manpower and money. In a world now running on 'Internet time', where product life cycles are down to months, and personalization trends are fragmenting markets, this inertia is no longer tolerable. Existing design methodologies and integrated circuit technologies are finding it increasingly difficult to keep pace with today's requirements. An ASIC-based solution would require multiple design teams running simultaneously just to keep up with evolving standards and techniques.

Another way to solve the problems has been to use general-purpose processors, i.e., trying to solve all kinds of applications running on a very high speed processor. A major drawback of using these general-purpose devices is that they are extremely inefficient in terms of utilising their resources.

To match the required computation with the architecture, we apply in the CHAMELEON project an alternative approach in order to meet the requirements of future low-power hand-held systems. We propose a heterogeneous reconfiguration architecture in combination with a QoS driven operating system, in which the granularity of reconfiguration is chosen in accordance with the computation model of the task to be performed. In the CHAMELEON project we apply reconfiguration at multiple levels of granularity. The main philosophy used is that operations on data should be done at the place where it is most energy efficient and where it minimises the required communication. Partitioning is an important architectural decision, which dictates where applications can run, where data can be stored, the complexity of the mobile and the cost of communication services. Our approach is based on a dynamic (i.e. at run-time) matching of the architecture and the application. Partitioning an application between various hardware platforms is generally known as hardware/software co-design. In our approach we investigate whether it is possible and useful to make this partitioning at run-time, adapting to the current environment of the mobile device.

The key issue in the design of portable multimedia systems is to find a good balance between flexibility and high-processing power on one side, and area and energy-efficiency of the implementation on the other side. In this paper we give a state-of-the-art report of the ongoing CHAMELEON project. First we give an overview of the hardware architecture (section 2) and the design flow (section 3) and after that a typical application will be presented in the field of wireless communication (section 4).

1.1. Reconfiguration in Mobile Systems

A key challenge of mobile computing is that many attributes of the environment vary dynamically. Mobile devices operate in a dynamically changing environment and must be able to adapt to a new environment. For example, a mobile computer will have to deal with unpredicted network outage or should be able to switch to a different network, without changing the application. Therefore it should have the *flexibility* to handle a variety of multimedia services and standards (like different video decompression schemes and security mechanisms) and the *adaptability* to accommodate the nomadic environment, required level of security, and available resources. Mobile devices need to be able to operate in environments that can change drastically in short term as well as long term in available resources and available services. Some short-term variations can be handled by adaptive communication protocols that vary their parameters according to the current condition. Other, more long-term variations generally require a much larger degree of adaptation. They might require another air interface, other network protocols, and so forth. A *software defined radio* that allows flexible and programmable transceiver operations is expected to be a key technology for wireless communication. Reconfigurable systems have the potential to operate efficiently in these dynamic environments.

Until recently only a few reconfigurable architectures have been proposed for wireless devices. There are a few exceptions, for example, the Maia chip from Berkeley [1][4]. Most reconfigurable architectures were targeted at simple glue logic or at dedicated high-performance computing. Moreover, conventional reconfigurable processors are bit-level reconfigurable and are far from energy efficient.

However, there are quite a number of good reasons for using reconfigurable architectures in future wireless terminals:

- New emerging multimedia standards such as JPEG2000 and MPEG-4 have many adaptivity features. This implies that the processing entities of future wireless terminals have to support the adaptivity needed for these new standards.
- Although reconfigurable systems are known to be less efficient compared to ASIC implementations they can have considerable energy benefits. For example: depending on the distance of the receiver and transmitter or cell occupation more or less processing power is needed. When the system can adapt - at run-time - to the environment significant power-saving can be obtained [7].
- Standards evolve quickly; this means that future systems have to have the flexibility and adaptivity to adapt to slight changes in the standards. By using reconfigurable architectures instead of ASICs costly re-designs can be avoided.
- The cost of designing complex ASICs is growing rapidly, in particular the mask costs of these chips are very high. With reconfigurable processors it is expected that less chips have to be designed, so companies can save on mask costs.

Dynamically reconfigurable architectures allow to experiment with new concepts such as software-defined radios, multi-standard terminals, adaptive turbo decoding, adaptive equalizer modules and adaptive interference rejection modules.

Reconfigurability also has another more economic motivation: it will be important to have a fast track from sparkling ideas to the final design. Time to market is crucial. If the design process takes too long, the return on investment will be less.

2. Heterogeneous Reconfigurable Computing

In the CHAMELEON project we are designing a heterogeneous reconfigurable System-On-a-Chip (SOC). This SOC contains a general-purpose processor (ARM core), a bit-level reconfigurable part (FPGA) and several word-level reconfigurable parts (FPFA tiles; see Section 2.3) (see Figure 1).

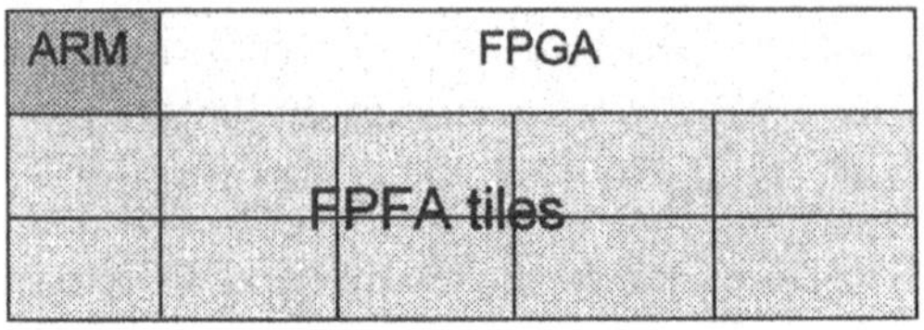

Figure 1: Chameleon heterogeneous architecture

We believe that in future 3G/4G terminals heterogeneous architectures are needed. The main reason is that the efficiency (in terms of performance or energy) of the system can be improved significantly by mapping application tasks (or kernels) onto the most suitable processing entity. Basically we distinguish three processor types in our heterogeneous reconfigurable system: bit-level reconfigurable units, word-level reconfigurable units, and general-purpose programmable units. The programmability of the architecture enables the system to be targeted at multiple applications. The architecture and firmware can be upgraded at any time (even when the system is already installed). In the following sections we will discuss the three processing entities in more detail.

2.1. General-Purpose Processor

While general-purpose processors and conventional system architectures can be programmed to perform virtually any computational task, they have to pay for this flexibility with a high energy consumption and significant overhead of fetching, decoding and executing a stream of instructions on complex general-purpose data paths. The energy overhead in making the architecture programmable most often dominates the energy dissipation of the intended computation. However, general-purpose processors are very good in control type of applications; e.g. applications with frequent control constructs (if-then-else or while loops).

2.2. Bit-Level Reconfigurable Unit

Today, *Field Programmable Gate Arrays* (FPGAs) are the common devices for reconfigurable computing. FPGAs present the abstraction of gate arrays, allowing developers to manipulate flip-flops, small amounts of memory, and logic gates. Currently, many reconfigurable computing systems are based on FPGAs. FPGAs are particularly useful for applications with bit-level operations. Typical examples are PNcode generation and Turbo encoding.

2.3. Word-Level Reconfigurable Units

Many DSP-like algorithms (like FIR and FFT) call for a word-level (reconfigurable) datapath. In the CHAMELEON project we have defined a word-level reconfigurable datapath, the so called Field-Programmable Function Array (FPFA) [3] [8].

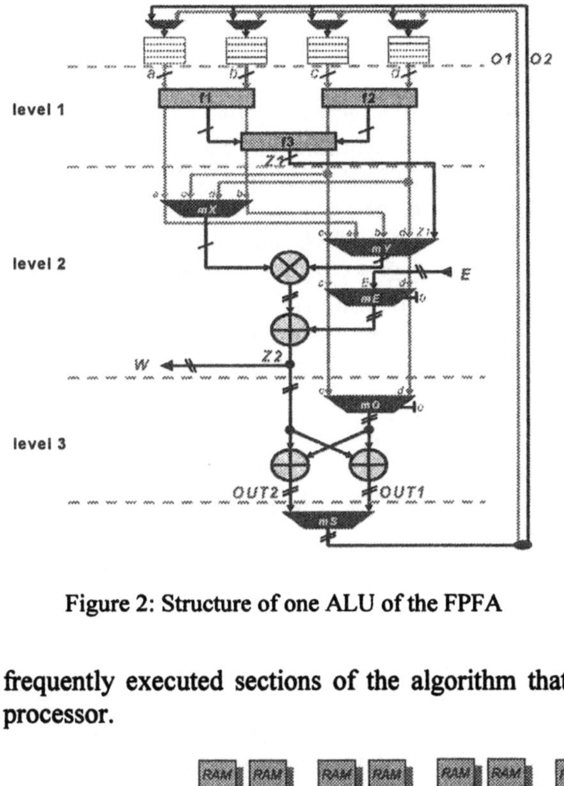

Figure 2: Structure of one ALU of the FPFA

It consists of multiple interconnected processor tiles. Within a tile multiple data streams can be processed in parallel in a VLIW manner. Multiple processes can coexist in parallel on different tiles. Each processor tile contains five reconfigurable ALUs, 10 local memories, a control unit and a communication unit. Figure 3 shows a FPFA tile with the five ALUs. Each FPFA can execute a fine grain computational intensive process. We call the inner loops of a computation, where most time is spent during execution, *computational kernels*. A computational kernel can be mapped onto an FPFA tile and interfaces with the less frequently executed sections of the algorithm that may run on the general-purpose processor.

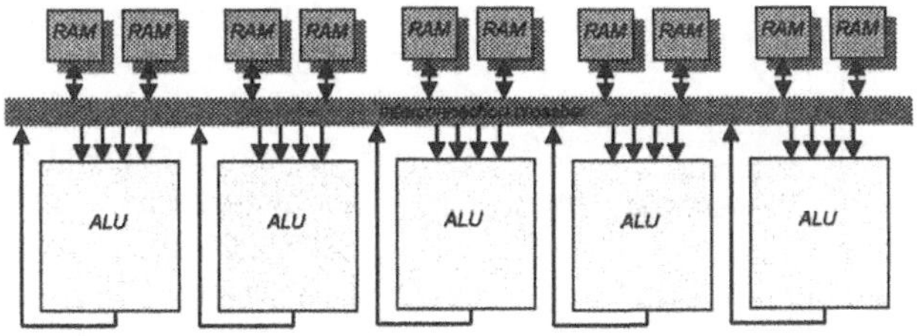

Figure 3: FPFA tile with five ALUs.

FPFAs have resemblance to FPGAs, but have a matrix of word-level reconfigurable units (e.g. ALUs and lookup tables) instead of Configurable Logic Blocks (CLBs). Basically the FPFA is a low power, reconfigurable accelerator for an application specific domain. Low power is mainly achieved by exploiting locality of reference. High performance is obtained by exploiting parallelism.

The ALUs on a processor tile are tightly interconnected and are designed to execute the (highly regular) inner loops of an application domain. ALUs on the same tile share a control unit and a communication unit. The ALUs use the locality of reference principle extensively: an ALU loads its operands from neighbouring ALU outputs, or from (input) values stored in lookup tables or local registers. Each memory has 256 20-bit entries. A crossbar-switch allows flexible routing between the ALUs, registers and memories. The ALUs are relatively complex (see Figure 2), for instance they can perform a multiply-add operation, a complex multiplication or a butterfly operation for a complex FFT in one cycle.

2.4. Implementation Results

The FPFA has been designed and implemented. The FPFA architecture is specified in a high-level description language (VHDL). Logic synthesis has been performed and a one FPFA tile design fits on a Xilinx Virtex XCV1000. In CMOS .18 one (un-optimized) FPFA tile is predicted to have an area of 2.6 mm^2 and it can run at least at 23 MHz. In this technology we can have approx. 20 FPFA tiles in the same area as an embedded PowerPC. For the prototype we probably will use CMOS .13 technology. Several often-used DSP algorithms for SDR have been mapped successfully onto one FPFA tile: e.g. linear interpolation, FIR, correlation, 512-point FFT and Turbo/SISO decoding. Of course, these are only a few of the algorithms that the FPFA should be able to handle.

3. CHAMELEON System Modeling

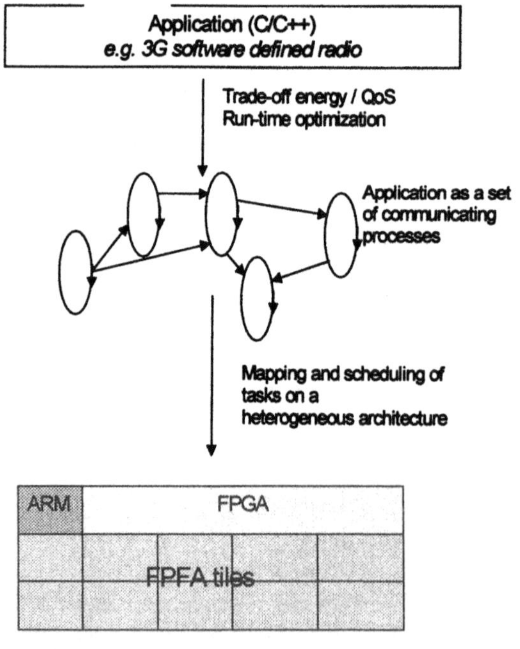

Figure 4: Chameleon design flow

The design of the above-mentioned architecture is useless without a proper tool chain supported by a solid design methodology. At various levels of abstraction, modern computing systems are defined in terms of processes and communication (or, at least, synchronisation) between processes. Many applications can be structured as a set of processes or threads that communicate via channels. These threads can be executed on various platforms (e.g. general purpose CPU, FPFA, FPGA, etc).

We use a Kahn based *process graph* model, which abstracts system functionality into a set of *processes* represented as nodes in a graph, and represents functional dependencies among processes (channels) with graph edges. The functionality of a process graph will be referred to as *task*. This model emphasizes communica-tion and concurrency between system processes. Edge and node labeling are used to enrich the semantics of the model. For instance, edge labels are used to represent communication band-width requirements, while state labels may store a measure of process computational requirements. Process graph models may include hierarchical models, which describe systems as an assembly of tasks. The root of such a hierarchy of tasks is called the *application.*

The costs associated with a process graph in the context of reconfiguration can be divided into *communication* costs between the processes, *computational* costs of the processes and *initialization* costs of the task. The costs can be expressed in energy consumption, resource usage, and aspects of time (latency, jitter, etc).

The mapping of applications (a set of communicating tasks) is done in two phases. In the first phase (macro-mapping) for each task the most- (or near) optimal processing entity is determined. This phase defines what is processed where and when. This phase is supported by a number of profiling tools. In the second phase (micro-mapping) for each task a detailed mapping is derived to the platform of choice.

3.1. Macro-mapping

In practice, most complex systems are realized using libraries of components. In a reconfigurable system, application instantiation consists first of all of finding a suitable partition of the system specification into parts that can be mapped onto the most appropriate resources of the system (processors, memories, reconfigurable entities). Because of the dynamics of the mobile environment we would like to perform the macro-mapping *at run-time.* In Section 4 we will show an example how macro-mapping can be used to save energy.

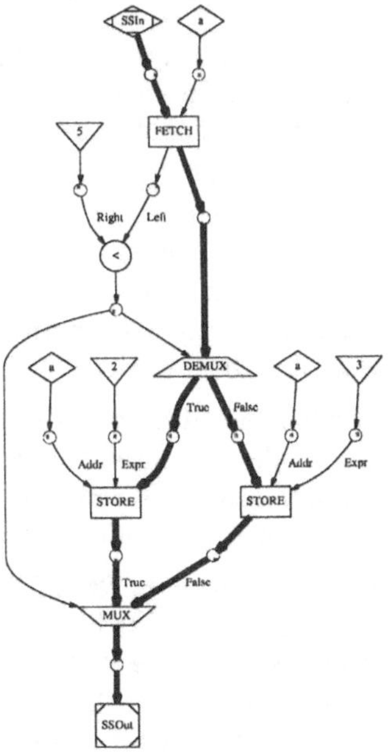

Figure 5: DFGC of a C statement

The traditional allocation of system functions into hardware and software during the design phase is already a complex task, doing it dynamically at run time, in response to the changed environment, available resources, or demands from the user, is an even more challenging task. The search of the 'best' mapping is typically a very hard problem, due to the size of the search space. Moreover, the costs associated with the mapping cannot be ignored.
Macro-mapping and algorithm selection assumes the existence of a library with multiple implementations for the computation of some (commonly used) processes or adequate profiling tools. Furthermore, it is assumed that the characteristics (e.g. energy consumption and performance) of the library elements on a given architecture are known beforehand.

3.2. Micro-mapping

Once the designer has decided what to map where, the micro-mapping comes into play. This is normally done at design-time, as this is a quite time-consuming operation. We assume that all processes are written in C. The mapping of C processes to the general-purpose processor is straightforward; we use the standard GNU tools for that. In this paper we concentrated on mapping C tasks to the FPFA.

We first translate C to a Control Data-Flow Graph (CDFG). In this graph control (order of execution) and data are modeled in the same way. As an example Figure 5 shows the automatically generated CDFG graph of a simple C statement (IF (A<5) A=2; ELSE A=3;). The bold arrows in the figure indicate the State-Space of the architecture, where the State-Space denotes the mathematical representation of the C memory model. Store and fetch are operations on the State-Space. We have defined several behavior-preserving transformations on these graphs e.g. constant propagation, loop unrolling and removing of intermediate variables. The FPFA tile can also be described in terms of a CDFG graph; the *architecture graph*. With the help of these transformations we can derive a 'simple' CDFG that is suitable for mapping onto an architecture graph. In general the mapping of algorithm graphs to an architecture graph is NP complete. Fortunately, the size of the algorithms tasks is usually quite small (no more than two nested loops). We have performed several mappings by hand, and currently we are implementing a method to automate this process.

4. Sample Application: Reconfiguration in a Wireless Terminal

In this section we show how a reconfigurable architecture and macro-mapping can be used to save energy in wireless terminals. As said before, in a mobile multimedia system many trade-offs can be made concerning the required functionality of a certain mechanism, its actual implementation, and values of the required parameters.

In contrast to ASIC implementations reconfigurable architectures offer the possibility to tune the settings of a software-defined radio (SDR) *at run-time* to the current wireless environment, even in continuously changing conditions. In this way overkill is avoided, which can be translated in a reduction in energy consumption for a mobile, or savings in the necessary computing resources for a base station.

To support this run-time adaptive behavior, trade-offs between different parameter sets should be made to determine the most optimal set for the current situation. We introduced a control system, which is based on a model that selects at run-time a set of parameters that minimizes the cost, while satisfying the requested quality.

In our initial approach, we reduce the set of performance indicators for a SDR to two: the *quality* and the *required effort*. Figure 6 depicts the relationship between the quality and the required effort. The dots represent a certain setting of the system in the quality/cost space. Due to the dynamic external environment of a SDR, the wireless link conditions change constantly and therefore the quality of the output of the SDR will change. In Figure 6, this implies that the dots will move in horizontal direction as a function of time. If the conditions of the external environment become worse, then a dot will move to the right and if the conditions become better, the dots will move to the left.

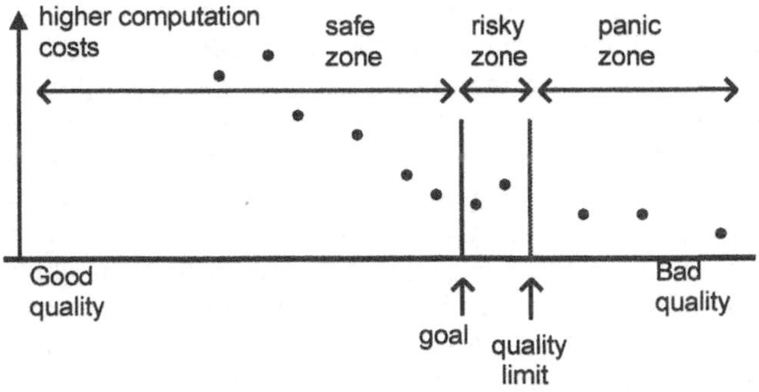

Figure 6: Quality vs cost trade-off

Given a specific application, a certain minimum quality limit will apply. A quality worse than this quality limit is not acceptable. Furthermore, a certain area left of the quality limit will be considered as a risky zone in the sense that the system is not allowed to stay too long in this area.

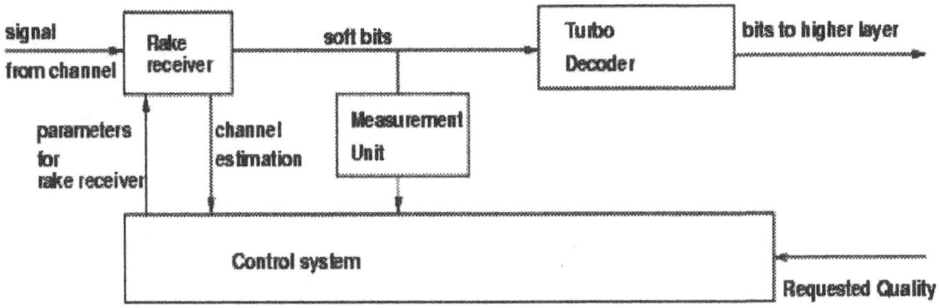

Figure 7: Rake receiver Turbo decoder combination

Therefore, when an optimal setting is determined, the optimization goal for the quality is left of the risky zone to maintain a certain 'safety margin', because otherwise a quality violation may occur, when the external environment changes only slightly. The optimal parameter setting in Figure 6 is the first dot on the left side of the goal line: it has the lowest costs (e.g. energy consumption) that satisfies the required quality of service. The quality limit is mainly dictated by the application and cannot be changed. For a specific application, the 'goal' line is at a fixed distance from the quality limit. Currently, the design of most SDR ensures that worst-case situations are handled well, which provides overkill in 'normal' situations. So, these SDRs operate almost always in the left most part of the safe zone that is mentioned in Figure 6. The added value of our approach is that we provide a run-time optimization to minimize the operation costs.

4.1. Example in Detail

Our control system will be demonstrated with a wideband code division multiple access (WCDMA) RAKE receiver [5], in combination with a turbo decoder [6], as shown in Figure 7. This combination can be used in an UMTS terminal or base station. For an in-depth discussion about the simulation of this system, see [7]. The quality is expressed in bit error rate (BER) and the costs are expressed in number of operations needed for the datapath (excluding control costs). In our current implementation input samples are 6 bits wide and 5 fingers can be executed in one single tile. The main part of the Turbo-decoder, (SISO module) can also be executed in one tile. We built a control system that adapts the system at run-time to the dynamic external environment. The goal is to operate with minimum use of resources and energy consumption, while satisfying an adequate quality of service. The control system is based on a model, which selects the most optimal configuration based on off-line gathered information and on-line measurements.

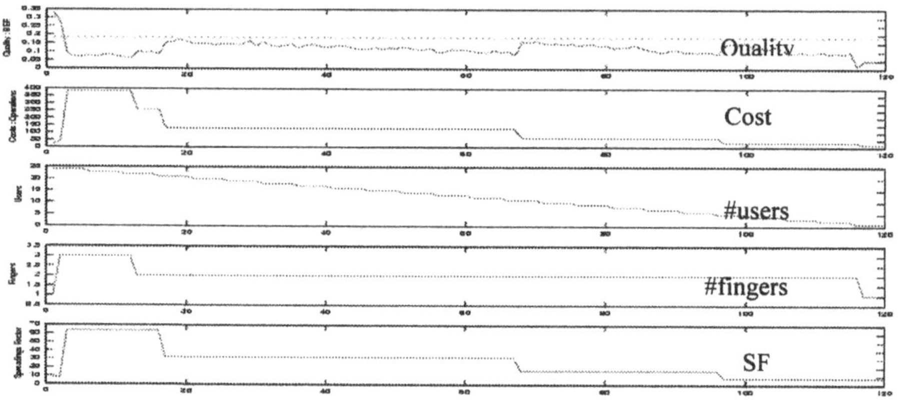

Figure 8: Simulation results

Figure 8 shows simulation results of the behaviour of the control system, when the number of users decreases. In this situation, the external environment becomes better. The five graphs in this figure represent (top - down): the quality of the output of the RAKE receiver expressed in BER, the costs of the RAKE receiver expressed in number of operations, the number of simultaneously transmitting users, the number of fingers of the RAKE receiver and the spreadingsfactor used by the RAKE receiver. On the horizontal axis the sequence number of the transmitted block is shown. Blocks contain 1000 bits.

As can be seen from the figure, the number of fingers and the spreadingsfactor are decreased as soon as possible, whereas the quality is maintained below the BER quality limit of 0.18. Note that the costs for the worst-case situation are much higher than the average costs, which indicates a considerable energy saving.

4.2. Evaluation

Compared to a system that is optimized for the worst-case situation, substantial savings can be achieved. In our simulations, savings of a factor three were no exception. The control system presented here has been applied to a specific RAKE/turbo case. The data required by the control system were: the quality limit (application dependent), the width of the risky zone (application dependent), and per parameter the: the range and the estimated gain when a parameter changes. The control system can be used as a general framework. For example, the turbo decoder can very easy be replaced by another kind of forward error decoder (e.g. Viterbi). The presented control system has a number of attractive properties: it is able to handle an unpredictable time-variant changing environment with a lot of parameters, it is simple and therefore possible to compute at run-time, it is suitable for a dynamically reconfigurable mobile terminal with scarce energy resources, it is fast enough (within tenths of ms) to react to a fast changing environment.

5. Conclusion

Reconfigurable systems are suitable for the dynamic application and communication environment of wireless multimedia devices. Reconfigurable systems provides flexibility to design new equipment that can adapt to changing standards and algorithms once/year, add new features once/month or adaptively modify the algorithm once/millisecond based on the contents of the data stream.

Central in our approach is the matching between granularity of computation and architecture. This by necessity leads to a heterogeneous reconfigurable system that spans many levels of the system. A hierarchical system model is used in which Quality of Service and energy consumption play a crucial role. This model is used to dynamically partition tasks of an application such that an energy efficient configuration is established while achieving a sufficient Quality of Service of the running applications.

References

[1] Abnous A., Rabaey J.: "Ultra-low-power domain-specific multimedia processors", *VLSI Signal processing IX*, ed. W. Burleson et al., IEEE Press, pp. 459-468, November 1996.

[2] Havinga P.J.M., "Mobile Multimedia Systems", *Ph.D. thesis University of Twente*, February 2000, ISBN 90-365-1406-1, www.cs.utwente.nl/~havinga/thesis.

[3] Heysters P.M., Smit J., Smit G.J.M., Havinga P.J.M.: "Mapping of DSP algorithms on Field Programmable Function Arrays", *FPL '2000 (Tenth International Workshop on Field Programmable Logic and Applications)*, Villach, Austria, August 28 - 30, 2000.

[4] Rabaey Jan M., "Reconfigurable Computing: The Solution to Low Power Programmable DSP", *Proceedings 1997 ICASSP Conference*, Munich, April 1997.

[5] G. L. Turin. "Introduction to spread-spectrum anti-multipath techniques and their application to urban digital radio", *Proc. of the IEEE, 68(3)*:328–353, Mar. 1980.

[6] C. Berrou and A. Glavieux. "Near optimum error correcting coding and decoding: Turbo-codes", *IEEE Transactions on Communications, 44*(10):1261–1271, Oct. 1996.

[7] L. T. Smit, G. J. Smit, P. J. Havinga, J. L. Hurink, and H. J. Broersma. "Influences of rake receiver/turbo decoder parameters on energy consumption and quality" *2002 International Conference On Third Generation Wireless and Beyond*, pp. 175-180, May 2002.

[8] P.M. Heysters, H. Bouma, J. Smit, G.J.M. Smit, P.J.M. Havinga, "A reconfigurable function array architecture for 3G and 4G wireless terminals, *2002 International Conference On Third Generation Wireless and Beyond*, pp. 399-404, May 2002.

Using PARBIT to Implement Partial Run-Time Reconfigurable Systems

Edson L. Horta[1], John W. Lockwood[2], and Sérgio T. Kofuji[1]

[1] Department of Electronic Engineering, Laboratory of Integrated Systems, Escola Politécnica da Universidade de São Paulo, Av. Prof. Luciano Gualberto, trav. 3, 158. CEP 05508-900 - São Paulo, SP, Brazil, edson-horta@ieee.org,

[2] Department of Computer Science, Applied Research Lab, Washington University, 1 Brookings Drive, Saint Louis, MO 63130, lockwood@arl.wustl.edu, http://www.arl.wustl.edu/arl/projects/fpx/parbit

Abstract. Field Programmable Gate Arrays (FPGAs) can be used to implement partial run-time reconfigurable (RTR) systems. A tool called PARBIT has been developed that transforms FPGA configuration bitstreams into partial bitstreams. With this tool it is possible to define a partial reconfigurable area inside the FPGA and download it into a specified region of the FPGA device. This paper presents PARBIT, the methodology used to design the partial RTR system, and three application examples.

1 Introduction

Field Programmable Gate Arrays (FPGAs) enable hardware circuits to be reconfigured an unlimited number of times. The implementation of a system that uses reconfigurability can be done in two ways: Compile-Time and Run-Time Reconfiguration [1]. For Compile-Time Reconfiguration (CTR) the FPGA does not change configuration during the application lifetime. Each application has specific functions that are loaded when the FPGA is started. Some examples of CTR systems are SPLASH [2] and PAM [3]. For Run-Time Reconfiguration (RTR), the FPGA changes configuration while it is operating. RTR can be total (all the device is reprogrammed) or partial (only part of the device is reprogrammed). Existing platforms have focused on reconfiguration of entire FPGA devices [4] [5] [6]. Some recent work has considered partial reconfiguration [7] [8].

Partial reconfiguration is a difficult task, especially in systems that require both partial reprogramming and run-time reconfiguration. In order to partially reconfigure a FPGA, it is necessary to isolate an specific area inside the FPGA and download the configuration bits related to that area. A tool called PARBIT (PARtial BItfile Transformer) [9] has been developed to easily transform and restructure bitstreams to implement dynamically loadable hardware modules.

M. Glesner, P. Zipf, and M. Renovell (Eds.): FPL 2002, LNCS 2438, pp. 182–191, 2002.

To restructure the configuration bitstream, the tool utilizes the original bitstream, a target bitstream (when needed) and parameters given by the user. These parameters include the block coordinates of the logic implemented on a source FPGA, the coordinates of the area for a partially programmed target FPGA, and the programming options.

Section 2 describes the architecture and configuration issues of the Xilinx FPGAs used to implement the partial RTR. Section 3 describes PARBIT, along with the design methodology used to generate the bitstreams employed by the tool. Section 4 describes three application examples of partial RTR systems. The last section summarizes the results obtained until now, with the utilization of PARBIT.

2 VIRTEX FPGA

The Xilinx VIRTEX [10] family of FPGA combines the features of partial reconfiguration with high density. A single VIRTEX device can hold more than 3 million system gates and permits a partial reconfiguration of frames, which are a fraction of the logic found on a column of the FPGA.

A simplified floorplan of this device family can be seen in Figure 1. Programmable Input/Output Blocks (IOBs) around the edge of the array are used to interface to off-chip resources. The interior consists of a matrix of Configurable Logic Blocks (CLBs) containing, lookup tables, flip-flops and programmable interconnect. The lookup tables in the CLB can be used as function generators, small distributed RAMs or programmable-length shift registers. A number of columns in the CLB matrix are replaced with Block SelectRAMs, which are dedicated dual-ported memories. Not shown in Figure 1 is a central column of clock drivers used for global clock distribution.

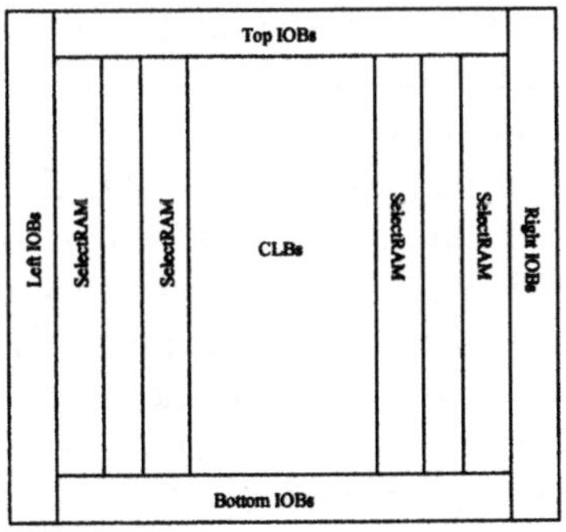

Fig. 1. VIRTEX Architecture

To configure each resource on the VIRTEX, a series of bits, divided into fields of commands and data, are loaded into the device. The configuration file is called bitstream and it can be loaded into the device through three different ways: Master/Slave Serial, SelectMAP [11], and Boundary Scan [12]. The SelectMAP is an 8-bit parallel interface and the others are one-bit serial interface. One can write the configuration memory through one of these three interfaces, but only SelectMAP and Boundary Scan allows reading this memory.

VIRTEX-E configuration bits are organized in columns corresponding to a column of the FPGA's logic resources.The Center Column controls the global clock pins. The IOB Columns control the configuration for the left and right side IOBs. Each CLB Column controls one column of CLBs and two IOBs above and bellow these CLBs. Each column has n rows, with one CLB per row. The Block SelectRAM Interconnect Columns define the interconnection of each RAM column. The Block SelectRAM Content Columns define the contents of each RAM column.

3 PARBIT

In order to generate the partial bitstream file, PARBIT reads the configuration frames from the original bitstream and copies to the partial bitstream only the configuration bits related to the area defined by the user. It then generates new values to the configuration address registers, according to the partial reconfigurable area.

There are two main operation modes defined by the user parameters. In the first, called **Slice Mode**, the user specifies a slice containing one or more CLB columns. The slice includes the control bits for the top and bottom IOBs. The tool generates the partial bitstream with these columns, in the same position they were in the original bitstream file. In the second, **Block Mode**, rows and columns of a rectangular area inside the FPGA are specified. The block is then targeted to be located at a specific region in a target FPGA. The tool generates the partial bitstream file containing the logic in the user specified region from the original bitstream and configuration data from the target device at the top and bottom rows of the selected columns.

There are three types of files used by the PARBIT tool. The **Original** bitstream file is generated by Xilinx tools. This file contains the reconfigurable area that is extracted by PARBIT and transformed in a partial bitstream file. The **Target** bitstream file is also generated by Xilinx tools. When operating in Block Mode, this file contains the fixed configuration for the FPGA, plus an empty area reserved to receive the reconfigurable area generated by PARBIT. Finally, the **Partial** bitstream file is generated by PARBIT, containing data from the original bitstream file and, in Block Mode, data from the target bistream file.

If the block mode is used, the tool also reads the target bitstream file to copy the configuration bits that are inside a column specified by the user, but outside the partial reconfigurable area. This happens due to the fact that one frame occupies all the rows of a column and, in block mode, the partial reconfigurable area is smaller than a whole column. Another task performed by PARBIT is the reallocation of the partial reconfigurable area: the tool calculates new frame addresses according to the new coordinates chosen by the user.

The design flow with PARBIT depends on the configuration mode chosen by the user. The following sections describe two design flows using the slice mode and one using the block mode.

3.1 Design Flow - Start-End Column (Slice Mode)

In the "Slice Mode", the user has to define only the start and end columns of the design to be reconfigured in the chip. The location of this design is always the same (see Figure 2). The only file needed is the original bitstream, containing the partial reconfigurable area that will be extracted by PARBIT.

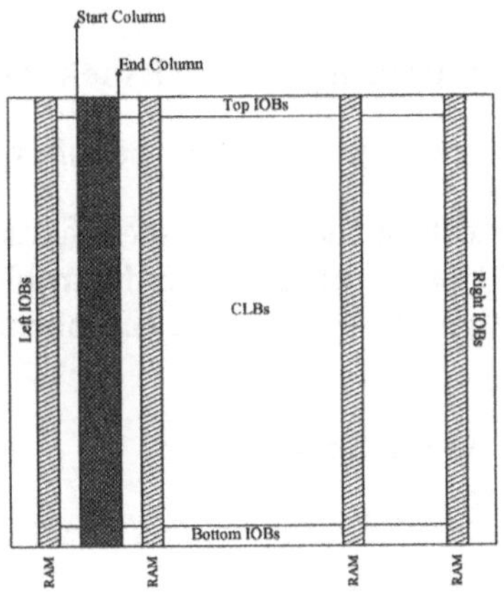

Fig. 2. Slice Mode - Original Bitstream Device

In this mode, all the I/O pins controlled by the CLB columns of the partial bitstream change according to the new design. It is important to keep these pins in the same location, when generating a new partial design.

3.2 Design Flow - Left-Right Sides (Slice Mode)

This mode is a special condition of Slice Mode. The user has to choose only between the left and right sides of the chip, to be reconfigured. PARBIT then generates the partial bitstream containing only the configuration bits from the side chosen. It calculates automatically the amount of columns that are necessary to reconfigure only one half of the chip.

The original bitstream is the only one needed, and must have the desired half of the chip that will be extracted by PARBIT (see Figure 3).

Using this mode it is possible to change the configuration of half a chip, while the other half keeps working.

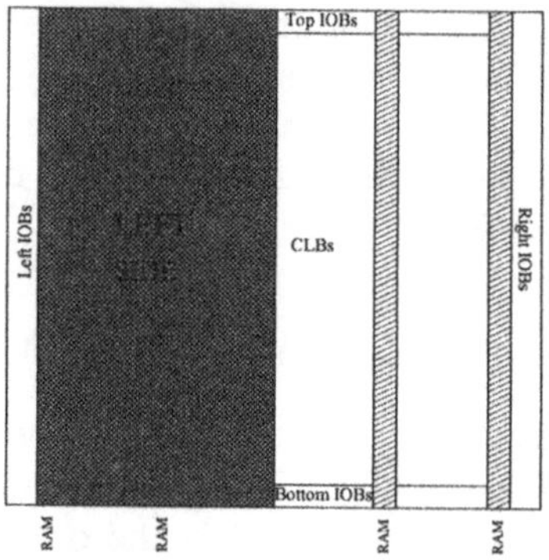

Fig. 3. Left-Right Mode - Original Bitstream Device

3.3 Design Flow - Relocatable Area (Block Mode)

In the "Block Mode", the user has to define the following variables:

- Start/end columns: width of the partial reconfigurable area;
- Start/end rows: height of the partial reconfigurable area;
- Target row/column: the new location of the partial reconfigurable area, in the target project;

These values can be seen on Figure 4.

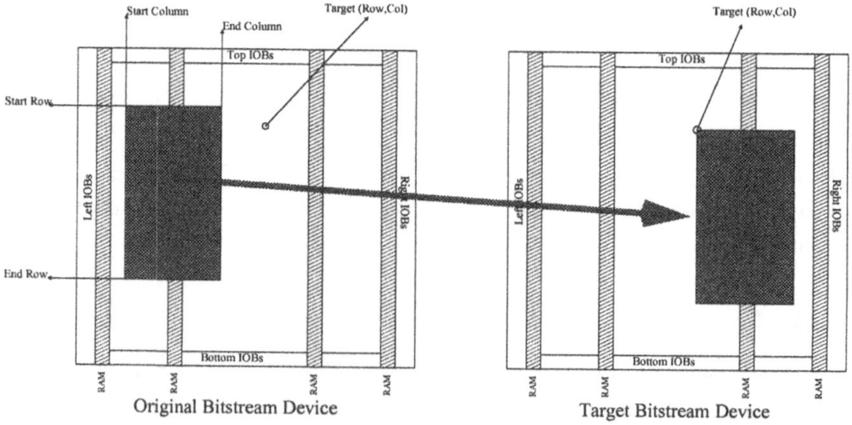

Fig. 4. Block Mode

The tool needs the original bitstream and the target bitstream to generate the partial bitstream. After loading the new design into the target device, it will be like the one shown on the left side of Figure 4.

The I/O pins from the target device do not change after the partial bitstream is loaded.

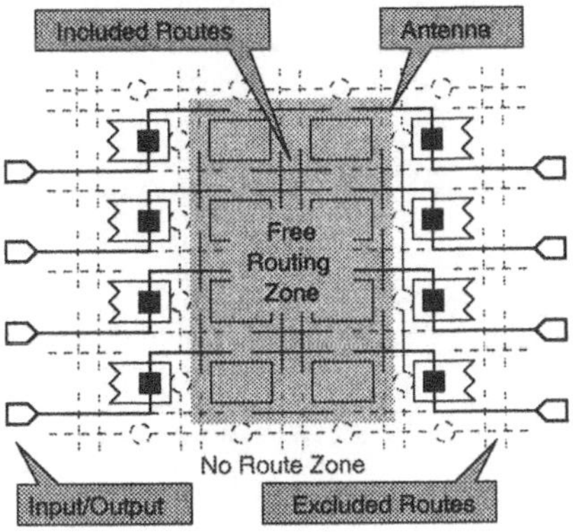

Fig. 5. GASKET Antennas

The user module that will be downloaded into the FPGA needs fixed interconnection points to communicate with the static logic region of the device. These points are connected by special wires, called antennas. The interface formed by the interconnection points and the antennas is called Gasket interface.

The key to implementing the partial reconfigurable area is that the existing CAD tools, with little modification, can be used to implement the routed-and-placed logic for the antennas. The Figure 5 shows the routing resources for the VIRTEX-E FPGA.

When building a partial reconfigurable area, PAR (Place And Route) is made to limit routing to only included routes. It may not use excluded routes. By placing the antennas between the user module logic and the static logic region, the routing through the gasket is fixed.

4 Applications

Using PARBIT and the methodology detailed on the previous sections, it is possible to implement a partial run-time reconfigurable system. The following subsections presents three examples of such systems. The first one is a practical system used to prove the concepts and validate the tool. The next ones are more complex systems used in network packet processing applications.

4.1 Small Example - LEDs Controller

In this example, PARBIT is used, in the Block Mode, to generate partial bitstreams to reconfigure a small area inside an XCV1000E FPGA. It also makes possible to reallocate this area inside the FPGA.

The first step is to generate the original bitstream. There are two reconfigurable areas in each side of the FPGA. Each one controls 2 LEDs connected to the left and right sides of the chip. The left reconfigurable area makes the LEDs blinking in a alternating pattern. The right side makes them blinking together. The floorplanning for this design is show on Figure 6.

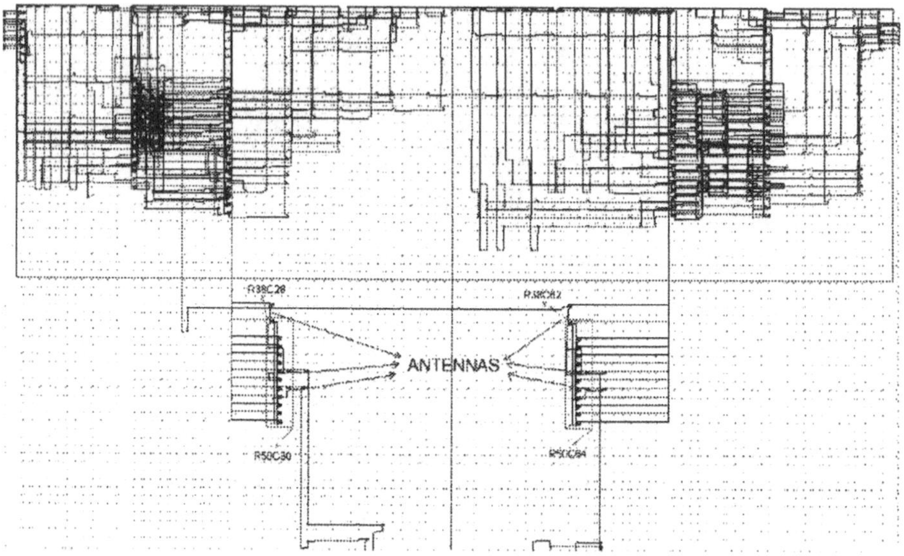

Fig. 6. LEDs Example - Floorplanning

As shown in this figure, the partial reconfigurable area is confined in the rectangle defined by the following coordinates:

- Left Side: (Row 38, Column 28; Row 50, Column 30);
- Right Side: (Row 38, Column 62; Row 50, Column 64);

In this figure one can see the Gasket interface, denoted by the antennas signals. These signals are kept in the same position, for the original and the target bitstreams. They are located in the same relative position, for both modules.

In this example, the target bitstream will be the same as the original one, and PARBIT will extract the left module and generate the partial bitstream to realocate it to the position of the right module, making both LEDs blinking with the alternating pattern.

With the partial bitstream generated it is possible to see the right LEDs changing their blinking pattern "on-the-fly" while the left LEDs don't stop blinking.

4.2 Dynamic Hardware Plugin (DHP)

One of the applications for PARBIT is the generation of the DHP [13] partial bitstream that is loaded in the FPX [14] board.

The design methodology for build DHP modules on the FPX is to use standard tools to compile, place, and route logic into a fixed region of an XCV1000E or XCV2000E FPGA. After generating the source bitstreams, PARBIT is run to transform the source file into a partial bitstream file.

The first step is the generation of the original bitstream file. This file contains the partial reconfigurable area, that will be loaded into the device. It must have always the same location for the partial reconfigurable area. The user must confine the block between these coordinates (for XCV1000E device):

- start column=8, end column=29;
- start row=7, end row=58.

The original bitstream has the format shown in Figure 7.

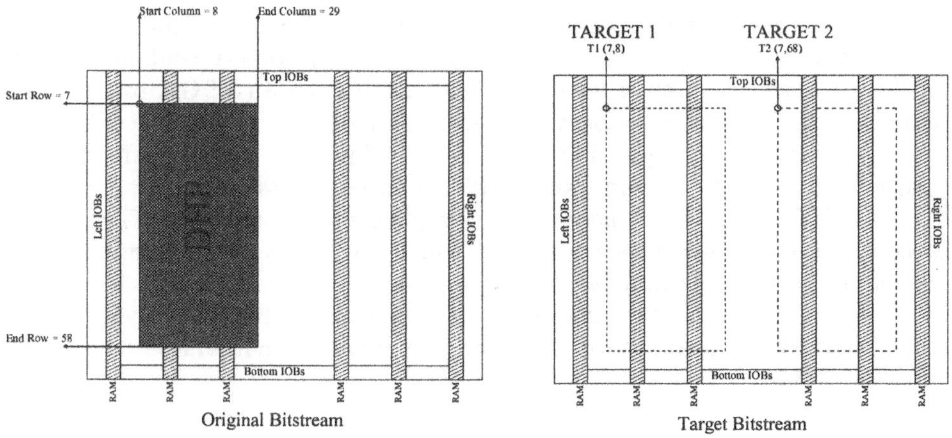

Fig. 7. DHP - XCV1000E

The target design has to provide some specific empty areas to load the block design generated in the previous step. Each one of these areas is defined by two coordinates (Row, Col), as shown in Figure 7.

4.3 Reconfigurable ATM Switch (RECATS)

RECATS [15] is a reconfigurable switch that has been implemented in a single FPGA device. It is based on the ATLAS [16] chip, with some simplifications in the original structure and the inclusion of partial Run-Time Reconfiguration (RTR) feature. It contains a Partial Reconfigurable (PR) module, that will be located always in the same position inside the FPGA.

Using PARBIT, in the slice mode, it is possible to generate the new partial bitstreams for each one of the new PR modules defined by the user.

The original bitstream used by PARBIT must have the new PR module confined in the same position. In order to generate the full bitstreams, commercial tools can be used, provided that they can confine the PR module in a rectangular area inside the CLB columns of the FPGA. After generating the full bitstream with available commercial tools, PARBIT is run to generate the partial bitstream containing only the PR module.

The partial bitstream is then stored in an external memory, making use of a control module, that receives it inside the payload of the ATM cells and writes it to the memory.

The control module is responsible also by downloading the partial bitstream into the FPGA. It reads the external memory and sends its contents to the SelectMAP port of the FPGA.

5 Conclusions

A tool called PARBIT has been developed that transforms and combines multiple bitstreams into files that can be used for partial run-time reconfiguration (P-RTR). It allows regions of logic to be extracted from an FPGA bitstream. It enables this logic to be relocated to another region of the device. Finally, it allows a partial reconfiguration block to reconfigure an FPGA even when the target block shares common frames with the original bitstream.

PARBIT enables DHP modules to be implemented on the FPX. The program accepts options to generate a bitstream which can load a DHP module into any region of the Reprogrammable Application Device on the FPX.

It also enables the implementation of a Reconfigurable ATM Switch, using the slice mode to generate the new hardware modules that will be downloaded into the FPGA.

References

[1] Hutchings, B.L., Wirthlin, M.J.: Implementation approaches for reconfigurable logic applications. In Moore, W., Luk, W., eds.: Field-Programmable Logic and Applications (FPL'1995), Oxford, England, Springer-Verlag, Berlin (1995) 419–428

[2] Hoang, D.T.: Searching genetic databases on splash 2. In Buell, D.A., Pocek, K.L., eds.: IEEE Workshop on FPGAs for Custom Computing Machines, Los Alamitos, CA, IEEE Computer Society Press (1993) 185–191

[3] Bertin, P., Touati, H., Lagnese, E.: PAM programming environments: Practice and experience. In Buell, D.A., Pocek, K.L., eds.: IEEE Workshop on FPGAs for Custom Computing Machines, Los Alamitos, CA, IEEE Computer Society Press (1994) 133–138

[4] Ditmar, J.M.: A Dynamically Reconfigurable FPGA-based Content Addressable Memory for IP Characterization. Master's thesis, KTH- Royal Institute of Technology, Stockholm, Sweden (2000)

[5] Hadley, J.D., Hutchings, B.L.: Designing a partially reconfigured system. In Schewel, J., ed.: Field Programmable Gate Arrays (FPGAs) for Fast Board Development and Reconfigurable Computing, Proc. SPIE 2607, Bellingham, WA, SPIE - The International Society for Optical Engineering (1995) 210–220
[6] Ross, D., Vellacott, O., Turner, M.: An FPGA-based Hardware Accelerator for Image Processing. In Moore, W., Luk, W., eds.: More FPGAs: Proceedings of the 1993 International workshop on field-programmable logic and applications, Oxford, England (1993) 299–306
[7] McMillan, S., Guccione, S.: Partial run-time reconfiguration using JRTR. In: Field-Programmable Logic and Applications / The Roadmap to Reconfigurable Computing (FPL'2000), Villach, Austria (2000) 352–360
[8] Horta, E.L., Kofuji, S.T.: The architecture of a reconfigurable ATM switch (RECATS). In: Workshop de Computação Reconfigurável, Marília, SP, Brazil (2000)
[9] Horta, E., Lockwood, J.W.: PARBIT: a tool to transform bitfiles to implement partial reconfiguration of field programmable gate arrays (FPGAs). Technical Report WUCS-01-13, Washington University in Saint Louis, Department of Computer Science (July 6, 2001)
[10] Xilinx Inc.: Virtex-E 1.8V Field Programmable Gate Arrays. Xilinx DS022 (2001)
[11] Carmichael, C.: Virtex configuration and readback. Xilinx XAPP138 (1999)
[12] Xilinx Inc.: Configuration and readback of Virtex FPGAs using (JTAG) boundary scan. Xilinx XAPP139 (2000)
[13] Taylor, D.E., Turner, J.S., Lockwood, J.W.: Dynamic Hardware Plugins (DHP): Exploiting reconfigurable hardware for high-performance programmable routers. In: IEEE OPENARCH 2001: 4th IEEE Conference on Open Architectures and Network Programming, Anchorage, AK (2001)
[14] Lockwood, J.W., Naufel, N., Turner, J.S., Taylor, D.E.: Reprogrammable Network Packet Processing on the Field Programmable Port Extender (FPX). In: ACM International Symposium on Field Programmable Gate Arrays (FPGA'2001), Monterey, CA, USA (2001) 87–93
[15] Horta, E.L., Kofuji, S.T., Martins, C.A.P.S.: (RECATS): A Reconfigurable ATM Switch Proposal. In: Workshop em Arquiteturas Reconfiguráveis - IX Simpósio Brasileiro de Arquiteturas de Computadores-Processamento de Alto Desempenho, Campos do Jordão, SP, Brazil (1997)
[16] Katevenis, M., Serpanos, D., Vatsolaki, P.: ATLAS I: A General-Purpose, Single-Chip ATM Switch with Credit-Based Flow Control. In: Proceedings of the Hot Interconnects IV Symposium, Stanford, CA (1996) 63–73

Multiplier-less Realization of a Poly-phase Filter Using LUT-based FPGAs

R.H. Turner, R. Woods, and T. Courtney

Programmable Systems Laboratory, School of Electrical and Electronic Engg.
Queen's University Belfast, Stranmillis Road, Belfast BT9 5AH, N. Ireland
Tel: +44 2890 274081 Fax: +44 2890 274417
{r.h.turner, r.woods, t.courtney}@ee.qub.ac.uk

Abstract. In DSP applications such as fixed transforms and filtering, the full flexibility of a general-purpose multiplier is not required and only a limited range of values is needed on one of the multiplier inputs. A new design technique has been developed for deriving multipliers that operate on a limited range of multiplicands. This can be used to produce FPGA implementations of DSP systems where area is dramatically improved. The paper describes the technique and its application to the design of a poly-phase filter on a Virtex FPGA. A 62% area reduction and 7% speed increase is gained when compared to an equivalent design using general purpose multipliers. It is also compared favourably to other known fixed coefficient approaches.

1. Introduction

In many DSP algorithms, the flexibility of a general purpose multiplier may not be required as one of multiplier inputs can be fixed or use a limited range of values [1,2]. For example, in the case of an 8-point Discrete Cosine Transform, the coefficients used in the transform are derived from cosine values related to the point size of the transform and only 7-8 separate coefficient values are needed. In these cases, the multiplication can be implemented by a series of shifts, additions and/or subtractions. Multipliers used to implement such functions have been referred to as constant coefficient multipliers or KCMs.

A number of mechanisms exist to perform constant coefficient multiplication including Distributed Arithmetic (DA) [3], string encoding [4] and common sub-expression elimination [5]. In DA, several multiplication and addition operations are performed in a single block on a bit-by-bit basis in either a serial or parallel fashion [3]. When the multiplicands of these computations are fixed, the system can be efficiently implemented by pre-computing all the possible outcomes and storing these in ROM. Goslin [3] showed how LUT-based FPGAs are ideal for computing these operations.

In string encoding, the number of additions used to perform the multiplication can be reduced by allowing subtraction. This is particularly useful where multiplicands have long numbers of ones. For example, the string 0111110_2 can either be implemented at the cost of 4 adders or at the cost of one subtractor if number is represented as 2^6 - 2^1 (64_{10} - 2_{10}). A third less adders/subtractors are needed to implement fixed coefficient multipliers when compared to standard binary representations [1].

M. Glesner, P. Zipf, and M. Renovell (Eds.): FPL 2002, LNCS 2438, pp. 192-201, 2002.

Common sub-expression elimination can also be used to reduce the size of the KCM by developing hardware to perform a number of operations. Figure 1(a) shows how three adders can be used to perform a multiplication by 45_{10} ($101101_2 = 2^5+2^3+2^2+2^0$) by factorising it as 5*9 i.e. $(2^2+2^0) * (2^3+2^0)$. In figure 1(a), the value P is the number to be multiplied and can represent a bit or word and the expressions $*2^n$ represent an n shift performed in the routing of the FPGA. As the adders in the first column are effectively performing the same multiplication by 5, they can be combined to produce figure 1(b). Whilst this example is trivial, the aim of the *multiplier-less realization* technique [1,2,5-8] has been to represent the factorisation of the number in such a way that the sharing possibilities are enhanced, thereby resulting in a minimal adder implementation.

In this paper, the use of multiplier-less realization is applied to the design of DSP circuits in FPGAs. The key issue is the implementation of the multiplexers which are necessary to implement the sub-expression sharing. These would usually require additional LUTs. This paper presents a technique for the efficient implementation of the multiplier-less realization resulting in the design of circuits that perform only the multiplications necessary for the application required. Using a clever implementation of the multiplexer, application-specific multipliers are developed that are optimized in terms of area and speed. The technique is applied to the design of a poly-phase filter and is compared to other constant coefficient approaches.

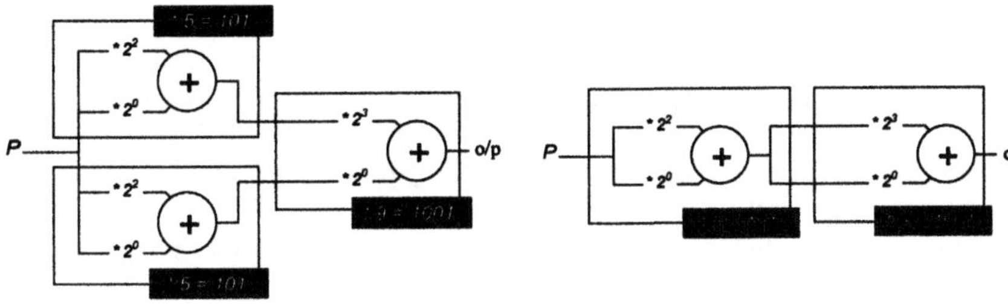

(a) (b)

Figure 1. Circuit implementation for performing fixed multiplication by 45_{10}

2. Poly-phase Filter

Sample rate conversion is a key DSP operation required in many systems. In down-sampling process, decimation by a factor of M is achieved by discarding ($M-1$) out of every M samples of a digital signal. As this will lower the Nyquist frequency the signal must be low-pass filtered to remove higher frequency components before removing the samples. Interpolation by L is accomplished by inserting $L-1$ equidistant zero-valued samples between each input sample. As this introduces spectral replicas between the original Nyquist frequency and the higher interpolated Nyquist frequency, the signal must be low-pass filtered after increasing the samples.

Interpolators and decimators are examples of sample rate converters that change the rate by integer factors. In practice, a converter is required to alter the rate by an arbitrary rational factor, L/M, so that the output rate is related to the input rate by:

$$f_s' = \frac{L}{M} f_s \tag{1}$$

The rate conversion can be accomplished by increasing the rate by a factor of L to the higher rate $f_s''(= L.f_s)$ using an L-fold interpolator, and then decreasing the rate by M down to f_s' $(= f_s''/M = L.f_s/M)$ using an M-fold decimator (figure 2). As both the interpolation and decimation low-pass filters are operating at the same frequency and are cascaded, they can be combined to give the second structure.

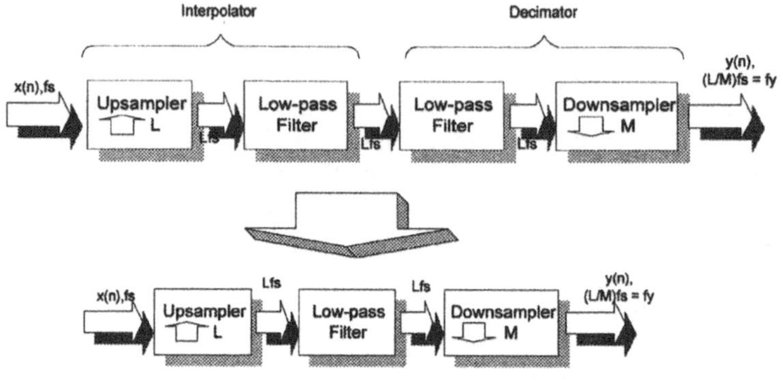

Figure 2. Sample Rate Converter with a factor of L/M.

A popular means of implementing sampling rate conversion is through the use of a poly-phase filter. Poly-phase filters are used to reduce the large filtering length (e.g. N taps) into a set of smaller filtering length K (where K is defined as N/L and N is a multiple of the integer L). Since the up-sampling process inserts L-1 zeros between consecutive samples, only K out of N input values in the FIR filter are non-zero. At any one time, these non-zero values coincide and are multiplied by filter coefficient $h(0)$, $h(1)$, … , $h(N\text{-}L)$. This gives the poly-phase unit sample responses as:

$$p_k(n) = h(k + nL) \tag{6}$$

where $k = 0,1,\ldots,L\text{-}1$ and $n = 0,1,\ldots,K\text{-}1$.

The poly-phase filter in figure 3 has an interpolation of 1:3. Circuit details were determined from a design in [9] and backed up by detailed Matlab™ simulations (This paper describes the filter but does not give any implementation details). A Hamming window was selected to act as the anti-filtering process providing a suppression of the sidelobes by at least 40dB. Filter lengths were examined up to 150 taps and a filter length of 55 was identified. As the filter is linear phase, this corresponded to 27 different coefficient values. The input wordlength was also determined from simulation carried out using 8, 12, 16 and 24 bits wordlengths. This revealed that a 16-bit wordlength gave the best compromise between performance and area. The non-zero sample of $x(n)$ data is fed into the circuit every 3 clock cycles and produces an output data sample value, $y(n)$, at every sample of the $x(n)$ input. The three coefficient values are cycled and repeated every three cycles - a process represented by the multiplexer. For this design, the circuit comprises 18 multipliers and 18 adders. This filter was used as a design example because not all the filter taps are used in the computation of each output sample. Therefore a number of taps time-share a resource.

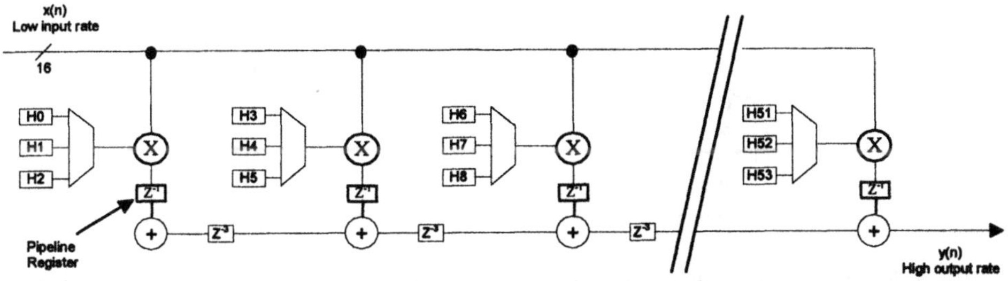

Figure 3. Transformed poly-phase design

3. Efficient FPGA Implementation of Multiplier-less DSP Circuits

A number of ways of achieving a multiplier-less realization of DSP systems such as the poly-phase filter, have been presented [1,2,5-8]. In these papers, the authors use optimized adder tree structures to implement DSP functions. In all references except [6,7], the structures involve static coefficient values and do not involve circuits where a number of coefficients would need to be implemented on the same resource as presented here. In addition, these techniques are not particularly suitable for FPGA implementation as the fixed hardware resource has not been taken into consideration in synthesizing the circuit description. The way that the programmable shifts and muxes in [2,6] must be implemented in FPGA technology means that there is little advantage in using these methods.

3.1 Novel FPGA Design Approach

FPGAs such as the Virtex I and II families and 4000 families use a four input LUT and fast carry logic to implement adders. These structures are implemented using the mux-based adder implementation shown in figure 4. In the Virtex FPGA, the carry propagation and sum generation is implemented using dedicated fast carry logic circuitry comprising of an EXOR gate (CY XOR) and a multiplexer (CY MUX) as shown in figure 5. The additional two input EXOR function is implemented using two inputs of the LUT. An interesting feature of this design mapping is that the two other inputs are unused. In our approach, these additional inputs have been used to implement additional logic thereby allowing the cells functionality to be increased. In essence this broadens the functionality of the cell from a single bit adder to a variety of cells descriptions some of which are shown in figure 6. This allows a number of different functions/circuits in the same logic without having to increase the area of the design and without having to reconfigure the hardware. In order to fully utilize this approach, the circuit architecture must be derived in terms of these cells.

The process of mapping different fixed coefficient multiplications is illustrated in figure 7. The adder circuit on the left in figure 7 performs the multiplication by 5 as previously illustrated in figure 1(b). With the additional multiplexer, either 3 or 9 can be selected for the second adder, thereby allowing multiplication by 45 or 15. Therefore by factorizing the multiplication into various smaller computations, different fixed coefficient multiplications can be mapped into the same hardware.

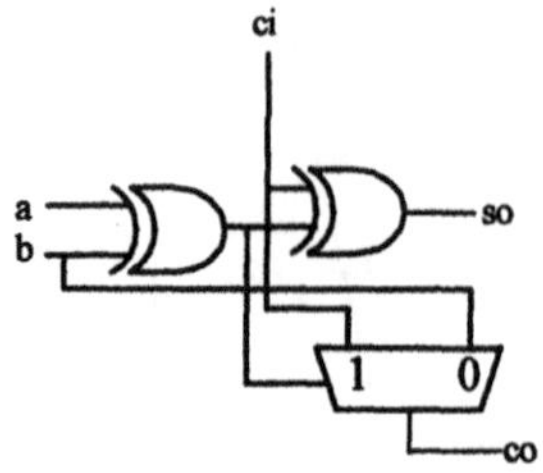

Figure 4. Mux-based adder implementation

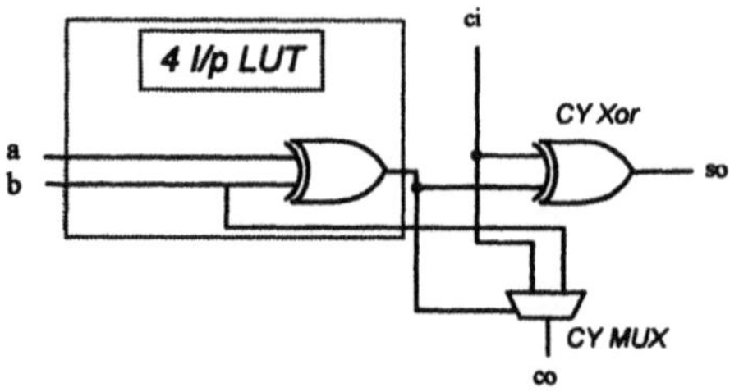

Figure 5. Adder implementation on Virtex

To show that this technique is not limited to numbers with common factors, figure 8 demonstrates how prime number values can be implemented by adding a shifted version of the product. In this case the multiplication by 45 is implemented by a multiplication by 15 followed by multiplication by 3. This allows 23 to be implemented by a multiplication of 15 and the addition of a shifted product, 8*P. This illustrates how important the factorisation is in achieving an efficient implementation. In many cases, the same circuit area can be used to realize several coefficient multiplications particularly as shifts can be implemented for free in the routing. The signals for changing the coefficients (i.e. controls to the MUXes) are implemented via the FPGA configuration MUXes and are also effectively free.

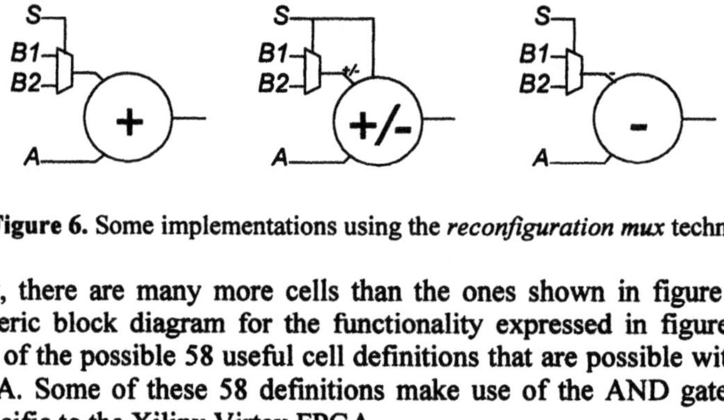

Figure 6. Some implementations using the *reconfiguration mux* technique

In reality, there are many more cells than the ones shown in figure 6. Figure 9 gives a generic block diagram for the functionality expressed in figure 6. Table 1 highlights 7 of the possible 58 useful cell definitions that are possible with the Xilinx Virtex FPGA. Some of these 58 definitions make use of the AND gate (figure 10) which is specific to the Xilinx Virtex FPGA.

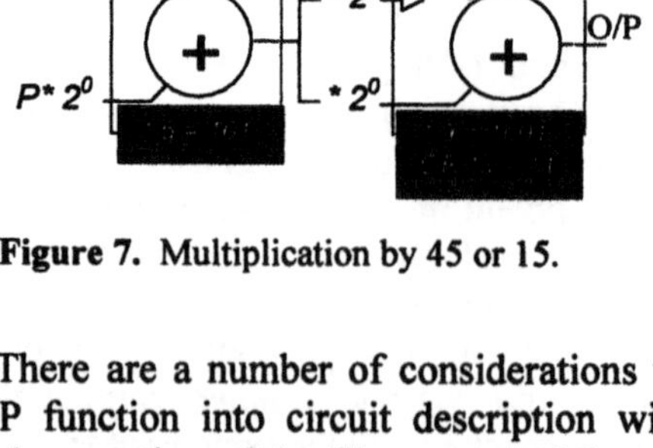

Figure 7. Multiplication by 45 or 15.

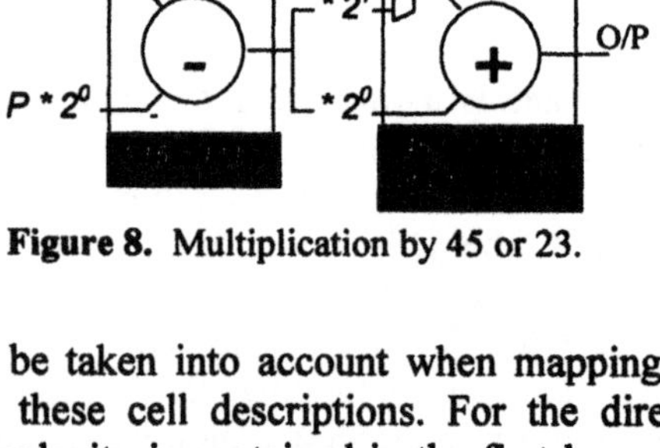

Figure 8. Multiplication by 45 or 23.

There are a number of considerations to be taken into account when mapping a DSP function into circuit description with these cell descriptions. For the direct implementation of the filter, most of the complexity is contained in the first layer of the multipliers, namely the generation of the partial products and the first stage of addition. After this, the rest of the circuit involves only additions. In the Virtex FPGA, two partial products and an adder can be implemented in each cell as shown in figure 10. This requires the full resource of the LUT. Subsequent adders do not use all the inputs of the LUT. Therefore part of the multiplier-less design flow is to move control logic from the first stage of the multiplier through to the subsequent adders including the final adder chain. This technique is demonstrated in the next section in the design of a poly-phase filter.

	Cells input for single select cell (figure 7(a))						
Function	A+B A+C	A−B A−C	A+B A−C	B A+C	−B A−C	B A−C	−B A+C

Table 1. Various useful functionalities possible for a Virtex FU.

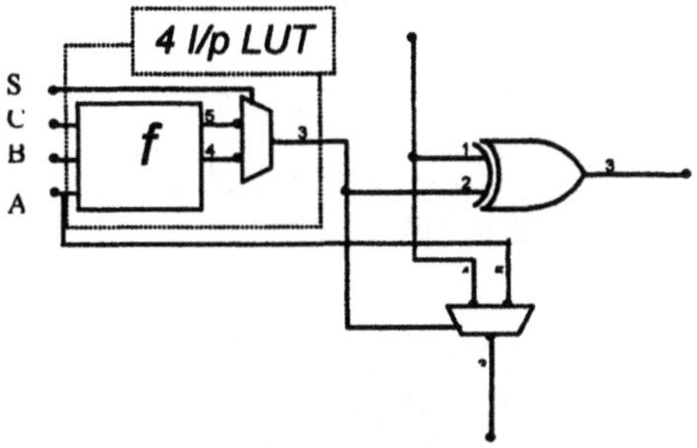

Figure 9. Function models for the Xilinx Virtex FPGA

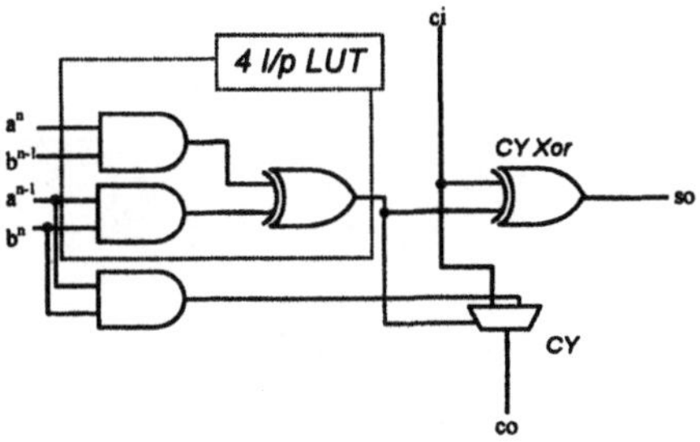

Figure 10. Cell implementation of two partial products and one addition

4. Implementation

Four separate implementations were investigated: a general-purpose design; the new design technique; a Hybrid ROM/Adder KCM and; a bit serial DA implementation produced from Xilinx's CoreGen software. The last two designs were chosen as they were ROM-based which usually results in good implementations.

4.1 Reduced Coefficient Multiplier (RCM)

There are a number of issues in applying the design technique described earlier in the implementation of the poly-phase filter.

- The design flow was restricted to cells used in figure 6. This ensures that the resulting design has wider applicability than Xilinx Virtex implementations.
- The cell definition mean that the design process must be applied in such a way that one input to the cell must be fixed (as shown by input A in figure 6). This will impact the design process and selection of terms to be shared.
- A concentrated effort is required to share terms between the three multiplications to be implemented in order to minimize hardware.

It was determined that a combination of using signed digit encoding and common sub-expression elimination resulted in an efficient implementation – as demonstrated in this section. The implementation of one of the blocks representing coefficients *h13-h21* as shown in figure 11, is implemented as given in figure 12. The circuit has coefficients *h13- h21*and produces three outputs in parallel. Firstly, the pattern of bits in the coefficient representations that can be shared, are identified. In figure 11, data-set ① can cover the bits streams in *h20* and *h21* as well as *h17* and *h18*. It is possible to implement this functionality using one of the cells given earlier as shown in figure 12. The functionality in cell ① needs either multiplication by 101_2 or 110_2. This is formed by $A=100_2$, $B1=001_2$ and $B2=010_2$ giving the relevant outputs. In the ② term, the string 0111_2 is implemented as (1000_2-0001_2) giving $A=1000_2$ and $B1=0001_2$ and the term 101_2 is implemented by $A=1000_2$ and $B2=0010_2$ giving 1010_2 which is shifted by 2 to give 101_2. In such a way the terms ③ and ④ are formed. The next two columns in the circuit then combine these common terms together. For example the term h14 is constructed by shifting the ④ by 5 and adding zero to it (see ⑦ in figure 12). The shifting is performed in the routing. In this way, the various outputs are constructed.

h13	0	0	0	0	0	0	0	0	0	0	0	0	0	0	0	0
h14	0	0	0	0	0	0	1	1	1	1	1	0	0	0	0	0
h15	0	0	0	0	0	1	0	0	1	0	0	1	1	1	1	0

h16	0	0	0	0	0	0	0	0	0	0	0	0	0	0	0	0
h17	1	1	1	1	1	0	0	1	1	0	0	0	1	0	1	0
h18	1	1	1	1	1	0	0	0	0	1	0	1	1	1	0	0

h19	0	0	0	0	0	0	0	0	0	0	0	0	0	0	0	0
h20	0	0	0	0	1	0	1	0	1	1	0	0	0	1	1	1
h21	0	0	0	0	1	1	0	0	1	1	1	1	0	0	0	0

Figure 11. The coefficient representations for h13-h21

4.2 Hybrid ROM/Adder Tree

In order to allow a fair comparison with other approaches, the filter was designed based on hybrid ROM/adder KCM blocks (Figure 13) [10]. The KCM performs a 16-bit constant coefficient multiplication. As the four ROMs perform the same function and are area-intensive, it was determined to share this resource as shown in figure 14. This circuit now takes 4 cycles to complete the multiplication. There are 33 non-zero coefficients in the poly-phase filter [9] and so 33 of these multipliers are required. These are implemented as 3 rows of multipliers (16 in the first, 16 in the second amd 1 in the third) one row of which is shown in figure 15. Only one version of the MUXing circuitry is used as shown. Any zero coefficients are simply implemented using flip-flops. An extra section is included at the input to handle signed inputs. The bit width of the adder chain was optimised to match word growth requirements. We believe that this is a very efficient implementation and represents a fair comparison to the RCM implementation described earlier.

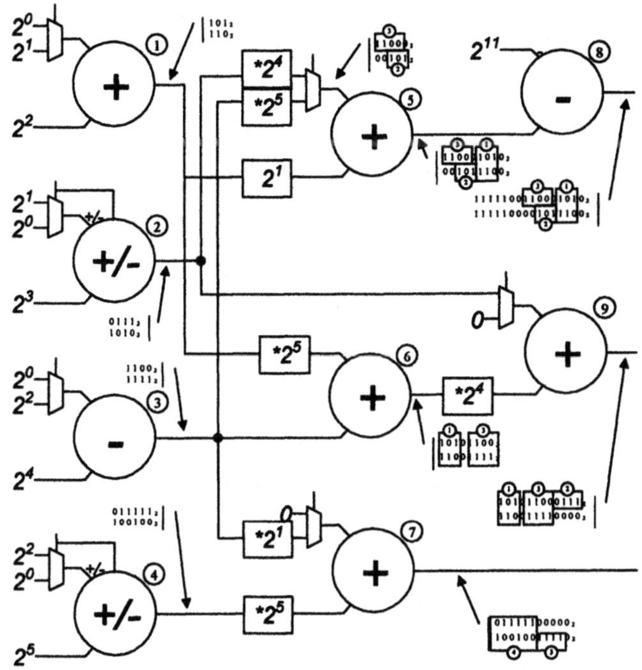

Figure 12. An example of one of the multiplier blocks which implements *h13-h21*

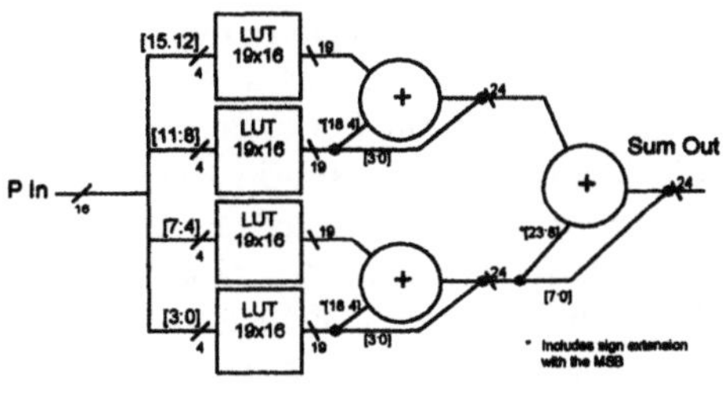

Figure 13. Hybrid ROM/Adder multiplier

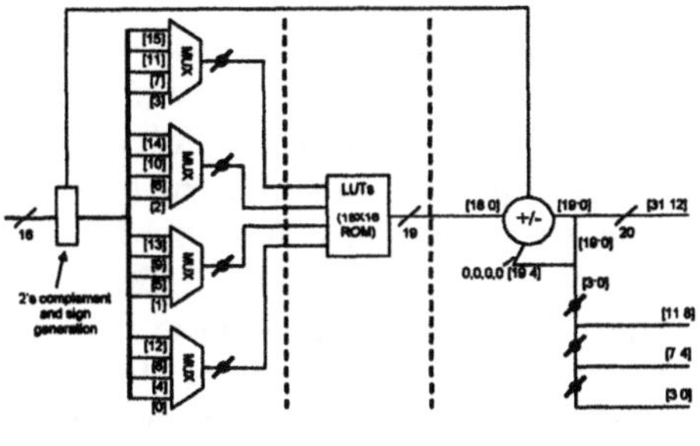

Figure 14. The multi cycle KCM

5. Results

The performance of the four implementations is shown in Table 2. The general purpose design was synthesized using the Synplify tools. In the poly-phase filter, there were 55 coefficients of which 33 were non-zero. In the RCM technique, there were five blocks of 9 coefficients (with 3 each equal to 0), one block of 3 coefficients and the two remaining blocks of 3 coefficients were 0. The hybrid ROM design was as described in the previous section and the DA design was implemented using the Coregen compiler from Xilinx. It can be seen that the RCM implementation has resulted in improved performance both in area and speed. As the multipliers dominate the area of the filter, the area gain has been substantial.

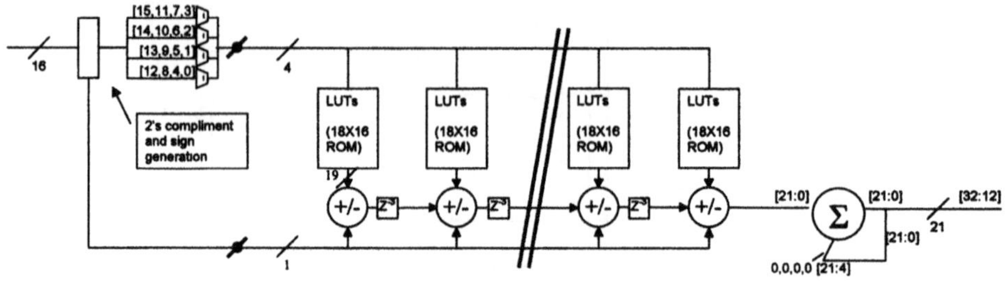

Figure 15. Full KCM filter implementation

Design Style	Clock Rate (CR) (MHz)	Throughput (TR) (Megasample/s)	Area (Luts/Slices)	TR/Area (Samples/s/LUT)
General-purpose	26.2	26.2	(5599/4123)	4500
RCM	28·0	28.0	(1661/ 1583)	16857
Hybrid ROM/adder	37·3	28.0*	(2199/1528)	12733
CoreGen poly-phase filter (Bit serial DA)	44·5	2.6**	(416/235)	6250

* Produces a result every 4 cycles but operate 3 block in parallel
** Produces a result after 17 clock cycles

Table 2: Performance of four design approaches

The Hybrid ROM produced the next best set of results. From initial analysis, the DA and Hybrid ROM designs should have produced a similar result as they both should have used the ROM efficiently. A possible reason for the difference is that there are optimisations that the tools can only identify in the Hybrid ROM design which are not possible with the DA implementation as it is a fixed generator. An important design point with RCM is that zero coefficients cause the circuitry to be wasted. The tools can pick these zero coefficients out from the ROM-based design by removing the unused circuitry. In the RCM approach, this reduces to a scheduling problem. By scheduling the circuit such that only non-zero data is fed to the multipliers ensures that the design does not encompass '0' coefficients

6. Conclusions

By extending techniques that have been explored for constant coefficient structures and utilising spare inputs to the LUT, multipliers have been developed that are well suited for situations where the number of coefficients is small and known. This technique results in a superior use of LUTs and carry logic resulting in a 62% area saving and a 7% speed increase over a general purpose solution. Whilst this design was synthesized for one set of poly-phase coefficients, it is clear that the technique has wider application and will produce consistent results across a number of designs. For example, the concept has already been explored for implementing the Discrete Cosine Transform resulting in similar savings [11].

7. Acknowledgements

The authors gratefully acknowledge financial support from the Department of Education and Learning, Industrial Research and Technology Unit, Nortel Networks and the Engineering and Physical Sciences Research Council.

8. References

1. A. Yurdakul, G. Dundar, "Multiplierless Realization of linear DSP transforms by using common two-term expressions", Journal of VLSI Signal Processing, No. 22, pp163-172, 1999.
2. Dempster, A.G. and M.D. Macleod, "Use of minimum-adder multiplier blocks in FIR digital filters", IEEE Trans Circuits & Systems II - Digital & Analog Signal Processing, vol. 42(8), no. 9, pp. 569-577, September 1995.
3. G. R. Goslin, "Using Xilinx FPGAs to design custom Digital Signal Processing Devices", Proceedings of the DSPX 1995, Jan 1995, pp565-604.
4. A R. Omondi, "Computer Arithmetic Systems", Prentice Hall Int., New York, 1994.
5. B. Feher "Efficient Synthesis of Distributed Vector Multipliers", Proc Euromicro '93, 19th Symp. on Microprocessing and Microprogramming, pp345-350, 1993.
6. D. Li, "Minimum Number of adders for implementing a multiplier and its application to the design of Multiplierless Digital Filters", IEEE Trans. on Circuits and Systems II, vol. 42, pp 451-460, July 1995.
7. A Chatterjee, R. K. Roy and M. A. d'Adreu, "Greedy Hardware Optimization for linear Digital Circuits using Number splitting and Refactorization", IEEE Trans. on VLSI Systems, Vol. 1, No. 4, pp423-431, Dec. 1993.
8. A.G. Dempster and M.D.Macleod "Comments on 'Minmum Number of adders for implementing a multiplier and its application to the design of Multiplierless Digital Filters'", IEEE Trans. on Circuits and Systems II, vol. 45, No. 2, pp242-243, February 1998.
9. C. N. Ang, R. H. Turner, T Courtney and R Woods, "Virtex FPGA implementation of a polyphase filter for sample rate conversion", 34th Asilomar Conference on Signals, Systems and Computers, Asilomar, USA, IEEE Computer Society, pp365-369, Oct. 2000.
10. T. Kean, B. New and B. Slous, "A Fast Constant Coefficient Multiplier for the XC6200", Field Programmable Logic and Applications, Darmstadt, Springer LNCS 1142, pp230-241, 1996.
11. R. H. Turner, T Courtney and R Woods, "Implementation of fixed DSP functions using the reduced coefficient -multiplier", ICASSP, ISBN 0-7803-7043-0, Salt Lake City, USA, Volume II, SPEC-L3, May 2001.

Speech Recognition on an FPGA Using Discrete and Continuous Hidden Markov Models

Stephen J. Melnikoff, Steven F. Quigley & Martin J. Russell

Electronic, Electrical and Computer Engineering, University of Birmingham, Edgbaston, Birmingham, B15 2TT, United Kingdom
S.J.Melnikoff@iee.org, S.F.Quigley@bham.ac.uk, M.J.Russell@bham.ac.uk

Abstract. Speech recognition is a computationally demanding task, particularly the stage which uses Viterbi decoding for converting pre-processed speech data into words or sub-word units. Any device that can reduce the load on, for example, a PC's processor, is advantageous. Hence we present FPGA implementations of the decoder based alternately on discrete and continuous hidden Markov models (HMMs) representing monophones, and demonstrate that the discrete version can process speech nearly 5,000 times real time, using just 12% of the slices of a Xilinx Virtex XCV1000, but with a lower recognition rate than the continuous implementation, which is 75 times faster than real time, and occupies 45% of the same device.

1 Introduction

Real time continuous speech recognition is a computationally demanding task, and one which tends to benefit from increasing the available computing resources.

A typical speech recognition system starts with a pre-processing stage, which takes a speech waveform as its input, and extracts from it feature vectors or observations which represent the information required to perform recognition. The second stage is recognition, or decoding, which is performed using a set of phoneme-level statistical models called hidden Markov models (HMMs). In most systems, several context-sensitive phone-level HMMs are used, in order to accommodate context-induced variation in the acoustic realisation of the phone. Word-level acoustic models are formed by concatenating phone-level models according to a pronunciation dictionary. The word models are then combined with a language model, which constrains the recogniser to recognise only valid word sequences.

For small- to medium-sized vocabularies the word and language models are compiled into a single, integrated model. Recognition is performed using the Viterbi algorithm to find the route through this model which best explains the data. For large vocabulary systems this approach is not viable, and some form of heuristic search strategy, such as stack-decoding, is used instead [11].

The pre- and post-processing stages can be performed efficiently enough in software. The decoder, however, places a particularly high load on the processor, and so it is this part of the system that has been the subject of implementations in hardware.

M. Glesner, P. Zipf, and M. Renovell (Eds.): FPL 2002, LNCS 2438, pp. 202-211, 2002.

Research has been carried out in the past on such implementations, generally using custom hardware, as described in section 4. However, with ever more powerful programmable logic devices being available, such chips appear to offer an attractive alternative.

Accordingly, in this paper we describe our implementation of an HMM-based speech recognition system, with separate discrete and continuous HMM versions, which makes use of an FPGA for the decoder stage. This work follows on from that introduced in [4,5].

The paper is organised as follows. Section 2 explains the motivation behind the research; this is followed in section 3 by an overview of speech recognition theory. In section 4, we look at other hardware speech recognition systems, including implementations on FPGAs, custom hardware, ASICs and cores. We describe the structure of our system in section 5, followed by details of the implementations and discussion of the results in section 6. Section 7 summarises the conclusions drawn so far, and describes ideas to be incorporated into future implementations.

2 Motivation

The ultimate aim of this work is to produce a hardware implementation of a speech recognition system, with an FPGA acting as a co-processor that is capable of performing recognition at a much higher rate than software.

For most speech recognition applications, it is sufficient to produce results in real time, and software solutions that perform recognition in real time already exist. However, there are several scenarios that require much higher recognition rates which can benefit from hardware acceleration.

For example, there are telephony-based applications used for call centres (e.g. the AT&T "How may I help you?" system [2]), where the speech recogniser is required to process a large number of spoken queries in parallel. There are also analogous non-real time applications, such as off-line transcription of dictation, where the ability of a single system to process multiple speech streams at high speed may offer a significant financial advantage.

Alternatively, the additional processing power offered by an FPGA might be used for real-time implementation of the "next generation" of speech recognition algorithms, which are currently being developed in laboratories. For example, improved recognition of fluent, conversational speech may require multiple-level acoustic models which incorporate a representation of the speech production process, and are able to accommodate the production strategies which individuals employ in fluent speech. Such models are much more complex than conventional HMMs and, if successful, will inevitably lead to a substantial increase in demand for computing power for speech recognition applications.

3 Speech Recognition Theory

The most widespread and successful approach to speech recognition is based on the Hidden Markov Model (HMM), which is a probabilistic process that models spoken

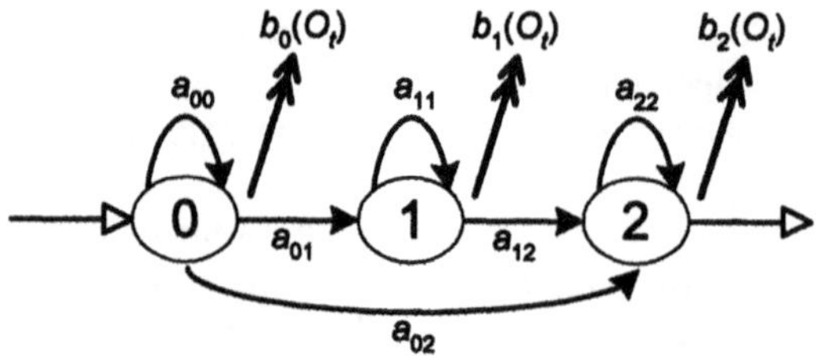

Fig. 1. Finite state machine for a Hidden Markov Model, showing the paths between states within the HMM (*filled arrows*), and paths between HMMs (*unfilled arrows*). The probability of a transition from state i to state j (transition probability a_{ij}) is shown, as is the probability of each state emitting the observation corresponding to time t (observation probability $b_j(O_t)$ for each state j) (*double-headed arrows*)

utterances as the outputs of finite state machines. A very brief outline is given below. For a more detailed description of HMM theory, see [7], or for an overview of the theory as it relates to this implementation, see our previous paper [5]. The notation here is based on [7].

3.1 Hidden Markov Models

The underlying problem is as follows. Given an observation sequence $O = O_0, O_1 \ldots O_{T-1}$, where each O_t is data representing speech which has been sampled at fixed intervals, and a number of potential models, each of which is a representation of a particular spoken utterance (e.g. word or sub-word unit), we would like to find the sequence of models which is the most likely to have produced O. These models are based on HMMs.

An N-state Markov Model is completely defined by a set of N states forming a finite state machine, and an $N \times N$ stochastic matrix defining transitions between states, whose elements $a_{ij} = P(\text{state } j \text{ at time } t \mid \text{state } i \text{ at time } t{-}1)$ are the *transition probabilities*.

With a Hidden Markov Model (Fig. 1), each state additionally has associated with it a probability density function $b_j(O_t)$ which determines the probability that state j emits a particular observation O_t at time t (the model is "hidden" because any state could have emitted the current observation). The p.d.f. can be continuous or discrete; accordingly the pre-processed speech data can be a multi-dimensional vector or a single quantised value. $b_j(O_t)$ is known as the *observation probability*.

Such a model can only generate an observation sequence $O = O_0, O_1 \ldots O_{T-1}$ via a state sequence of length T, as a state only emits one observation at each time t. Our aim is to find the state sequence which has the highest probability of producing the observation sequence O. This can be approximated efficiently using Viterbi decoding.

3.2 Viterbi Decoding

We define the value $\delta_t(j)$, which is the maximum probability that the HMM is in state j at time t. It is equal to the probability of the most likely partial state sequence which emits observation sequence $O = O_0, O_1 \ldots O_t$, and which ends in state j. It can be shown that this value can be computed iteratively as:

$$\delta_t(j) = \max_{0 \le i \le N-1} [\delta_{t-1}(i) a_{ij}] \cdot b_j(O_t), \tag{1}$$

where i is the previous state (i.e. at time $t-1$).

This value determines the most likely predecessor state $\psi_t(j)$, for the current state j at time t, given by:

$$\psi_t(j) = \arg\max_{0 \le i \le N-1} [\delta_{t-1}(i) a_{ij}]. \tag{2}$$

At the end of the observation sequence, we backtrack through the most likely predecessor states in order to find the most likely state sequence. Each utterance has an HMM representing it, and so this sequence not only describes the most likely route through a particular HMM, but by concatenation provides the most likely sequence of HMMs, and hence the most likely sequence of words or sub-word units uttered.

Implementing equations (1) and (2) in hardware can be made more efficient by performing all calculations in the log domain, reducing the process to additions and comparisons only - ideal when applied to an FPGA.

3.3 Computation of Observation Probabilities

For discrete HMMs, the probability density function for the observation probability $b_j(O_t)$ is implemented as a look-up table, with quantised data computed from the input speech waveform used as the address for the look-up. The probabilities are evaluated when the model is trained, and during recognition can simply be read from memory.

Continuous HMMs, however, compute their observation probabilities based on feature vectors extracted from the speech waveform. The computation is typically based on uncorrelated multivariate Gaussian distributions [3], but can be further complicated by using Gaussian mixtures, where the final probability is the sum of a number of individually weighted Gaussian values.

As with Viterbi decoding, we can perform these calculations in the log domain, resulting in the following equation:

$$\ln(N(\mathbf{O}_t; \boldsymbol{\mu}_j, \boldsymbol{\sigma}_j)) = \left[-\frac{L}{2}\ln(2\pi) - \sum_{l=0}^{L-1} \ln(\sigma_{jl}) \right] - \sum_{l=0}^{L-1} (O_{tl} - \mu_{jl})^2 \cdot \left[\frac{1}{2\sigma_{jl}^2} \right], \tag{3}$$

where $\mathbf{O}_t$ is a vector of observation values at time t; $\boldsymbol{\mu}_j$ and $\boldsymbol{\sigma}_j$ are mean and variance vectors respectively for state j; O_{tl}, μ_{jl} and σ_{jl} are the elements of the aforementioned vectors, enumerated from 0 to $L-1$.

Note that the values in square brackets are dependent only on the current state, not the current observation, so can be computed in advance. For each vector element of each state, we now require a subtraction, a square and a multiplication. Because each of these calculations is independent of any other at time t, they can be performed in parallel if sufficient resources are available.

4 Speech Recognition in Hardware

4.1 FPGAs

The work most closely related to our research is that done by Stogiannos, Dollas and Digalakis [10]. They use discrete-mixture HMMs, in which the elements of the observation vector are quantised in advance, allowing the probability associated with each element to be looked up, rather than calculated. These values (in the log domain) are then summed, converted to the normal domain using another look-up, and further summation takes place (as for Gaussian mixtures).

Their speech model uses 10,900 states grouped into 1,100 "genones," with each genone being represented by 32 Gaussians. Discrete-mixture HMMs are described as being capable of recognition accuracy above 85%.

The system is designed for an Altera FLEX 10KE running at 66 MHz, and is capable of a speedup of up to 7.74 times real-time.

This approach relies mainly on using RAM for table look-ups. We instead compute these values on the FPGA, greatly reducing the large storage and bandwidth requirements inherent in such an implementation, while taking advantage of more recent devices which are faster and have more resources available.

4.2 Custom Hardware

Non-FPGA-based parallel implementations of speech recognition systems have also been produced before, most using HMMs. In contrast to the systems described in our previous paper [5], which were based on parallel architectures employing multiple processing elements of varying sophistication, newer implementations typically use a single processor or ASIC for the bulk for the calculations.

Recent examples include monophone recogniser ASICs [1,6], with [6] also using an FPGA for training the speech model; a speaker-dependent small vocabulary system based on an 8051 microcontroller, which uses dynamic time warping to achieve an accuracy above 90% [8]; and a multilingual recognition chip incorporating DSP and microcontroller cores, capable of accuracy above 87% [9].

4.3 Commercial Products

A small number of commercial speech recognition ASICs exist, such as Sensory's RSC-300 & RSC-364 [14], which use a RISC microprocessor with a pre-trained neural network; their Voice Direct 364 which is also based on a neural network; and Philips' HelloIC [15], which is based on a DSP. All three are designed for applications requiring a small vocabulary (typically 60 words or less), and boast a speaker-independent recognition accuracy of 97% or more. (Further performance comparisons with our system are not possible due to a lack of suitable information).

There are no FPGA cores designed specifically for speech recognition. However, cores do exist for performing Viterbi decoding for signal processing, such as those produced by TILAB and Xilinx. In addition, some DSPs have dedicated logic for Viterbi decoding, for example, the Texas Instruments TMS320C6416 [12], and the TMS320C54x family.

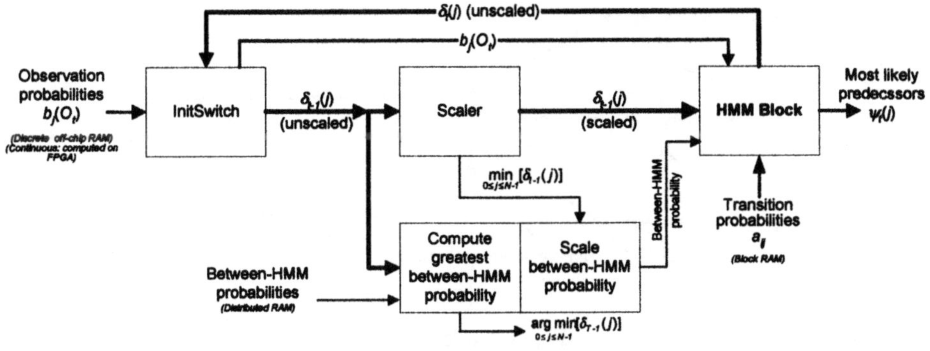

Fig. 2. Viterbi decoder core structure

In both cases, however, these decoders are designed for signal processing applications, which have different requirements from speech recognition, including narrower data widths, different data formats, and fewer states.

5 System Design

The complete system consists of a PC, and an FPGA on a development board inside it. For this implementation, the speech waveforms are processed in advance, in order to extract the observation data used for the decoding. This pre-processing is performed using the HTK speech recognition toolkit [11]. HTK was also used in order to verify the outputs of our system.

The speech data is sent to the FPGA, which performs the decoding, outputting the set of most likely predecessor states. This is sent back to the PC, which performs the backtracking process in software.

5.1 FPGA Implementation Structure

The structure of the Viterbi decoder core is shown in Fig. 2. This core is virtually identical for both the discrete and continuous HMM versions, differing only in the data widths and the small on-chip data tables.

The HMM Block contains the processing elements (or nodes) which compute $\delta_t(j)$. Each node processes the data corresponding to one state of an HMM, as shown in Fig. 3. As every node depends only on data produced by nodes in the previous time frame (i.e. at time $t-1$), and not the current one, as many nodes can be implemented in parallel as resources and bandwidth allow.

InitSwitch is used at initialisation to set the values of $\delta_0(j)$. Thereafter, $\delta_t(j)$ is passed to the Scaler, which scales the data in order to reduce the required precision, and discards values which have caused an overflow.

In order to keep the design as simple as possible, no language model is being used. As a result, the probability of the most likely transition from any HMM's exit state to another's entry state is the same for all HMMs, and is computed and scaled with dedicated blocks as shown.

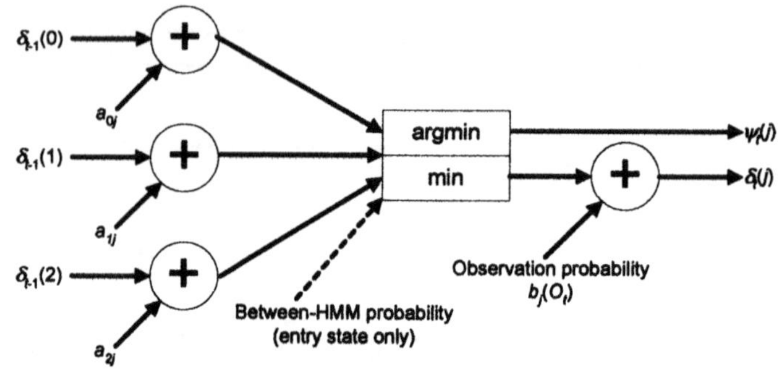

Fig. 3. Node structure

5.2 Observation Probability Computation

The block which computes the observation probabilities for continuous HMMs processes each observation's 39 elements one at a time, using a fully pipelined architecture. A floating point subtractor, squarer and multiplier are used, with the resulting value sent to an accumulator. The output probability is converted to a fixed point value, and is stored in a FIFO until all of the probabilities corresponding to a single HMM are computed; these values are then sent to the Viterbi decoder core.

The observation, mean and variance values are read from off-chip RAM, one of each per clock cycle. However, because the same observation data is used in the calculations for each state, the observation values need only be read in once for each time frame, freeing up part of the data bus for other uses. A buffer stores the values when they are read, then cycles through them for each HMM.

6 Implementation and Results

6.1 System Hardware and Software

The design was implemented on a Xilinx Virtex XCV1000 FPGA, sitting on Celoxica's RC1000-PP development board. The RC1000 is a PCI card, whose features include the FPGA, and 8 Mb of RAM accessible by both it and the host PC. The RC1000 was used within a PC with a Pentium III 450 MHz processor.

In order to ensure uniformity of data between HTK and our software and hardware, our software used the same data files as HTK, and produced VHDL code for parts of the design and for testbenches.

6.2 Speech Data

The speech waveforms used for the testing and training of both implementations were taken from the TIMIT database [13], a collection of speech data designed for the development of speech recognition systems. Both the test and training groups contained 160 waveforms, consisting of 10 male and 10 female samples from each of 8 American English dialect regions.

For these implementations, we used 49 monophone models of 3 states each, with no language model.

6.3 Discrete HMM Implementation

For the discrete implementation, the pre-processed speech observations consisted of quantised 8-bit values, treated as addresses into 256-entry, 15-bit-wide look-up tables, one for each state, and stored in off-chip RAM. Internally, scaled probabilities were stored as 16-bit log-domain values, with overflows detected as necessary. The software used the same bit widths.

This design was successfully implemented, requiring 1,600 slices, equal to 12% of the XCV1000's resources. It operated at 55 MHz, with a 62-stage pipeline. Most of this latency was due to the Scaler and between-HMM probability block requiring the data for all 49 HMMs to pass through them before they could produce a result.

One consequence of processing just one HMM at a time was that the effective delay due to RAM accesses was reduced, as data from RAM could enter the pipeline as soon as it was read, rather than being buffered first as was done in a previous, more parallel, implementation. Hence a complete observation cycle took 1.13 μs.

As the pipeline was circular, all of the HMM data had to pass through it before new data could be processed, but since the pipeline depth was longer than the data length, 11 cycles out of every 62 were wasted.

While this implementation had less of a problem with RAM-FPGA bandwidth than more parallel versions, the system had to pause from time to time while predecessor state data was written to RAM. This was aided by queuing the data in the FPGA while it was waiting to be written. A consequence of this was that data was written to RAM continually, including during the cycles wasted while processing was taking place.

Taking this into account, the average observation time went up to around 1.8 μs per 10 ms observation - more than 5,500 times real time.

6.4 Continuous HMM Implementation

We implemented in software and hardware a continuous HMM-based speech recogniser, which involved computing the observation probabilities as defined in equation (3). As before, the software was written so as to be as functionally similar as possible to the hardware implementation.

The continuous observation vectors extracted from the speech waveforms, and the mean and variance vectors for each state, consisted of 39 single-precision floating-point values. The observation probabilities calculated from these tended to be one or two orders of magnitude smaller than their discrete HMM counterparts, so it was necessary to increase the fixed point, log-domain, representation from 16 bits to 24.

The design occupied 5,590 of the XCV1000's slices, equal to 45%, and was capable of running at 47 MHz, though the speed of the off-chip RAM allowed a maximum clock rate of 44 MHz. (We used 1-cycle reads for this implementation, whereas for the discrete one we used 2-cycles reads, allowing a higher clock speed; in both cases, we were limited to using 2-cycle writes).

The slowest part of the system was the observation probability computation block, which produced a single value every 40 cycles. Consequently, the Viterbi decoder core sat idle for most of the 133.6 μs which, according to the simulation, the system took to compute all of the observation probabilities for each observation, and then produce the predecessor information. This did at least remove the bottleneck in writing this information to RAM.

6.5 Results

The results for the two implementations are shown in Table 1. Time per observation for the hardware is defined as the time between the PC releasing the shared RAM banks after writing the observation data, and the FPGA releasing the banks after writing all the predecessor information.

For both implementations, our software and hardware produced the same results as each other, while having a very small number of discrepancies compared to HTK, due to scaling and differences in the representation of data.

The times per observation for both hardware implementations are slightly larger than those found from their simulations, probably due to the additional time taken in dealing with the RAM arbitration.

The accuracy of these implementations are clearly lower than those found in commercial products (typically above 97%) - but such products use significantly more complex models. It is our intention to move on to more complex models in due course.

Comparing the speedups vs. real time for discrete and continuous, the gulf in the hardware speedups is mainly due to the fact that the discrete implementation takes 1 clock cycle to produce 3 observation probabilities in parallel, whereas the continuous one takes 120 clock cycles to do the same. This is not echoed in the software, where we replace serial memory look-ups with floating point calculations.

In addition, while the speedup of the discrete HMM hardware implementation over its software counterpart is much higher than for the continuous version, it is likely that future research will focus on continuous HMMs, as for speech recognition, accuracy takes precedence over speed.

7 Conclusions and Future Work

We have implemented a speech recognition system on an FPGA development board, comparing versions based on discrete HMMs and continuous HMMs, and using a simple monophone model. We have demonstrated that both are capable of processing speech data faster than equivalent software, and faster than real time, but that speed has to be sacrificed if greater recognition accuracy is required.

Table 1. Results from discrete and continuous HMM implementations. Accuracy is (N-D-S-I)/N; correctness is (N-D-S)/N; where N is number of phones, and D, S and I are deletion, substitution and insertion errors, respectively

	FPGA resources	Acc. (%)	Corr. (%)	Time/obs (μs)	Speedup v S/W	Speedup v real time
Disc. S/W	-	28.3	31.7	887	-	11.3
Disc. H/W	12%	28.3	31.7	2.03	437	4930
Cont. S/W	-	49.5	52.1	5390	-	1.86
Cont. H/W	45%	49.5	52.1	134	40.2	74.6

The next step is to generate and implement models based on biphones and triphones (combinations of 2 and 3 monophones respectively), which can contain 500 or more HMMs, but result in greater recognition accuracy.

As a way of utilising the small amount of spare bandwidth available to the continuous HMM implementation, and the large number of wasted cycles in the decoder core, multiple speech streams could be interleaved within the FPGA. Each one would require its own observation probability computation block, but would share the decoder core.

References

1. Burchard, B. & Romer, R., "A single chip phoneme based HMM speech recognition system for consumer applications," *IEEE Trans. Consumer Elec.*, **46**, No.3, 2000, pp.914-919.
2. Gorin, A.L., Riccardi, G. & Wright, J.H., "How may I help you?" *Speech Communication*, **23**, 1997, pp.113-127.
3. Holmes, J. N. & Holmes WJ, "Speech synthesis and recognition," Taylor & Francis, 2001
4. Melnikoff, S.J., James-Roxby, P.B., Quigley, S.F. & Russell, M.J., "Reconfigurable computing for speech recognition: preliminary findings," *FPL 2000, LNCS #1896*, 2000, pp.495-504.
5. Melnikoff, S.J., Quigley, S.F. & Russell, M.J., "Implementing a hidden Markov model speech recognition system in programmable logic," *FPL 2001, LNCS #2147*, 2001, pp.81-90.
6. Nakamura K. *et al*, "Speech recognition chip for monosyllables," *Proc. Asia and South Pacific Design Automation Conference (ASP-DAC 2001)*, IEEE, 2001, pp.396-399.
7. Rabiner, L.R., "A tutorial on hidden Markov models and selected applications in speech recognition," *Proceedings of the IEEE*, **77**, No.2, 1989, pp.257-286.
8. Shi Y.Y., Liu J. & Liu R.S., "Single-chip speech recognition system based on 8051 microcontroller core," *IEEE Trans. Consumer Elec.*, **47**, No.1, 2001, pp.149-153._.
9. Shozakai, M., "Speech interface VLSI for car applications", *ICASSP '99*, 1999, pp.141-144.
10. Stogiannos, P., Dollas, A. & Digalakis, V., "A configurable logic based architecture for real-time continuous speech recognition using hidden Markov models," *Journal of VLSI Signal Processing Systems*, 2000, **24**, No.2-3, pp.223-240.
11. Woodland, P.C., Odell, J.J., Valtchev, V. & Young, S.J. "Large vocabulary continuous speech recognition using HTK," *ICASSP '94*, 1994, pp.125-128.
12. http://dspvillage.ti.com/docs/dspproducthome.jhtml
13. http://www.ldc.upenn.edu/Catalog/LDC93S1.html
14. http://www.sensoryinc.com/
15. http://www.speech.philips.com/

FPGA Implementation of the Wavelet Packet Transform for High Speed Communications

Antony Jamin and Petri Mähönen

Center for Wireless Communications
University of Oulu, Finland
{antony.jamin,petri.mahonen}@ee.oulu.fi

Abstract. Recent work has shown interest in wavelet-packet based modulation (WPM). This scheme is implemented with an architecture similar to orthogonal frequency division multiplex (OFDM), except for using the wavelet packet transform (WPT) in place of the Fourier transform.
In this article, we study the implementation complexity of a WPT suitable for such a modulation scheme. A speed optimized implementation of the Mallat algorithm based on a generic reconfigurable filter structure is proposed. Measured complexity results of the designed transform implemented in FPGA using VHDL are reported and commented.

1 Introduction

With the success of OFDM in providing high data rates over wireless [1], the interest in multicarrier systems has grown rapidly in the past decade. OFDM has reached the consumer market for some time now, and research on competitive multicarrier schemes is being carried out. Wavelet packet modulation is among the most promising schemes, its main advantages being flexibility and the potential of lower implementation complexity.

We focus in this article on issues related to the design of a wavelet packet transform suited for use in transceivers for this new modulation scheme. Since the aim is to support future wireless local area networks, the sustainable data rate of our system must range from 10 to 100 Msymbols/sec. This obviously implies that speed is the largest constraint on the design of the transform core. This is not however the only one, since the need for flexibility of wireless communication at the link layer required a certain degree of reconfigurability in the transform. In the case of the core transform, the reconfigurability is actually three fold. First, the length of the wavelet filters and their coefficients must be programmable. Second, the transform size must be configurable. And last, any wavelet packet tree structure must be realisable.

This paper is divided as follows. First, the iterative algorithm implementing the WPT is recalled. The corresponding generic architecture is derived, and its theoretical complexity is given. The scheme proposed in order to take advantage of the fastest speed supported by the implementation technology is then described. We pursue in studying the modifications required to allow for our architecture to support transforms with a non fully pruned tree structure. Finally,

M. Glesner, P. Zipf, and M. Renovell (Eds.): FPL 2002, LNCS 2438, pp. 212–221, 2002.

implementation complexity results obtained after the synthesis of our VHDL design are reported and commented.

2 Wavelet Packet Transform Algorithm

In this article, we limit our analysis to discrete WPT that can be defined through a pair of length L FIR filters denoted (h, g). The wavelet packet transform can be efficiently implemented through the Mallat recursive algorithm. Denoting $\omega_{j,i}$ the wavelet coefficient of branch i at decomposition level $j = 1 \dots J$, we can calculate the wavelet coefficients recursively through the relations

$$\omega_{j+1,2i}[k] = \sum_{l=0}^{L-1} \omega_{j,i}[2k-l]\, h[l] \tag{1}$$

$$\omega_{j+1,2i+1}[k] = \sum_{l=0}^{L-1} \omega_{j,i}[2k-l]\, g[l] \tag{2}$$

with $i = 0 \dots (2^j - 1)$. The recursion starts with $\omega_{0,0}$ which is the signal to be decomposed. The inverse wavelet packet transform (IWPT) can similarly reconstruct the signal from its coefficients by iteration, i.e.

$$\omega_{j,i}[k] = \sum_{l=0}^{L-1} \tilde{\omega}_{j-1,2i}[(k-l)/2]\, \tilde{h}[l] + \sum_{l=0}^{L-1} \tilde{\omega}_{j-1,2i+1}[(k-l)/2]\, \tilde{g}[l] \tag{3}$$

with $i = 0 \dots (2^j - 1)$ and where $\tilde{\omega}_{j,i}[k]$ denotes the upsampled-by-two version of $\omega_{j,i}[k]$, i.e. $\tilde{\omega}_{j,i}[k] = \omega_{j,i}[k]$ if $k \in \mathbb{N}$, and 0 otherwise. The recursion ends with $\omega_{0,0}$ which is the reconstructed signal. Eq. (2) and (3) correspond to upsampling and filtering operations as depicted on the left and right side of Figure 1 respectively. The reconstruction makes use of another filter pair $(\tilde{g}, \tilde{h})$, and we refer the reader to [2, 3] for further characteristics on their inter-relations.

A rough estimate of the fast discrete wavelet packet transform gives a complexity of order $Mlog(M)$, thus of similar order to what is required for DFT. This complexity analysis can be further refined by calculating the number of operations required by the elementary blocks composing a complete transform. For the decomposition block (WPT), the amount of operations per input sample is

$$C_{WPT} = \begin{cases} 2\,(L-1) & \text{ADD} \\ 2\,L & \text{MULT} \end{cases} \tag{4}$$

Note that the reconstruction block is using one extra addition to combine the two filters output samples. Considering now the full transform, there are J stages, each composed of $N(j) = 2^{j-1}$ elementary blocks running at the rate $R(j) = 2^{1-j}$. We thus obtain the total number of operation for each M-point transform with $M = 2^J$ as

$$\mathcal{N}_{WPT}(J) = \mathcal{C}_{WPT} \sum_{j=1}^{J} N(j)\, R(j) \tag{5}$$
$$= \begin{cases} (2^{J+1}-1)\,(L-1) & \text{ADD} \\ (2^{J+1}-1)\,L & \text{MULT} \end{cases}$$

The total number of memory word $\mathcal{P}$ required by the transform can be similarly derived, i.e.

$$\mathcal{P}_{IWPT}(J) = L \sum_{j=1}^{J} N(j) = (2^{J+1}-1)\,L \tag{6}$$

3 Proposed WPT Architecture

The iterative structure of the WPT is in fact very well suited to hardware implementation. For each stage of the transform, the product of the number of elementary blocks by their processing rate is constant and equal to 1. Thus, for each transform period, the number of output samples to produce is constant and equal to the transform size. Both forward and reverse transforms can therefore be built by successive stages, each operating synchronously and at an identical rate. This is illustrated in Figure 3 for the forward transform. The reverse transform is identical except for the stage indexes which are in reverse order. This simple structure has the advantage that J_{max} stages can be instantiated in a programmable logic device, leading to a transform of size $M_{max} = 2^{J_{max}}$ maximum. If a lower size transform is needed, the corresponding higher order stages can be bypassed, and eventually put in standby mode if low power consumption is of interest.

Our design work is thus reduced to the implementation of the J stages. An interesting architecture has been proposed in [4]. In this scheme, the input samples of stage j are written in cyclic buffers of size 2^j. They are then read by generating successively the addresses corresponding to the $2 \times L/2$ samples required to calculate the output sample of each elementary block. Each sample read from memory is multiplied by the corresponding filter coefficient, and the results feed an accumulator. After L clock cycles, the accumulator contains the

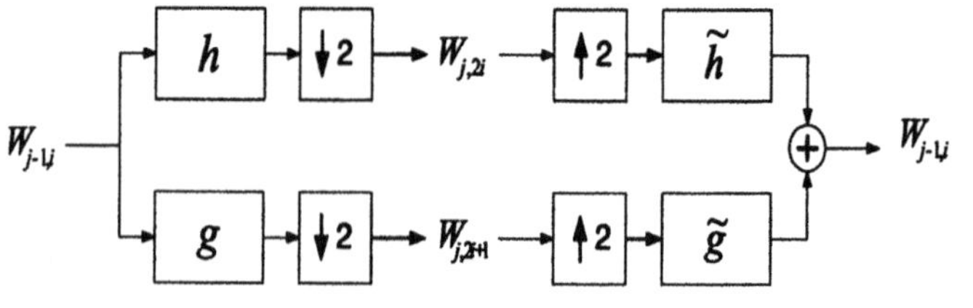

Fig. 1. Wavelet packet elementary block decomposition and reconstruction

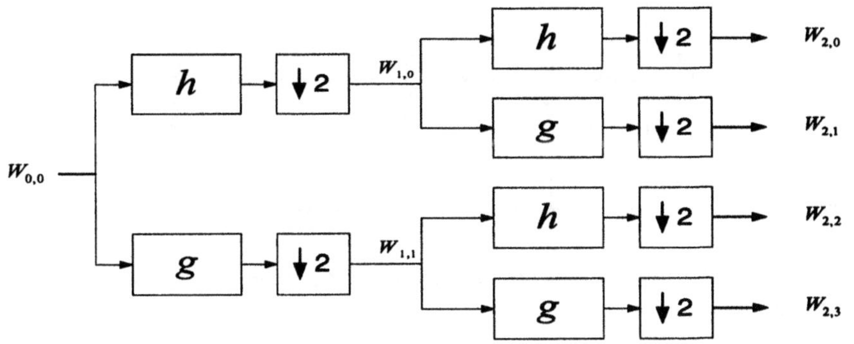

Fig. 2. Forward wavelet packet transform (decomposition operation)

elementary block output to be transmitted to the next stage input. This method benefits from a rather simple architecture since only one memory block, one multiplier, one accumulator, and two address generators are needed for each stage. The major limitation is obviously its speed, since L clock periods are required per output sample. With current technology, such a method is thus not capable of reaching the bit rate our application is targeting, and thus a slightly different architecture must be derived.

In the given example, the speed limitation is obviously bound to the filter implementation. We must therefore parallelize the filter implementation in order to reach a rate of one cycle per output sample. This can be achieved by making use of L multipliers fed at each clock cycle with its data samples and corresponding filter coefficients. The L resulting products are then added in a pipelined adder with L inputs. This last block can be built from $log_2(L)$ adders and thus have a delay of $log_2(L)$ clock cycles as well. We choose an intermediate approach, using only $L/2$ multipliers. With current technology, a data rate of half of the clock frequency is sufficient for our application, and the 50% complexity reduction allows a doubling of the maximum transform size.

We study in the following the sequencing of an overall period for both the forward and reverse transforms. In particular, we must review the combination data-filter coefficients that must be provided at each clock cycle to every multiplier.

3.1 IWPT Architecture

Since we assumed a data rate equal to half the clock frequency, each stage receives a new data sample every two clock cycles. For the IWPT, the upsampler imposes a division of the transform period in two. In the first half-period, we calculate the even output samples $\omega_{j,i}[2k]$, and in the second, the odd ones $\omega_{j,i}[2k+1]$. On the other hand, every other input sample of the h and g filters is null, thanks to the preceding upsampler. Thus only the even coefficients of the filters are

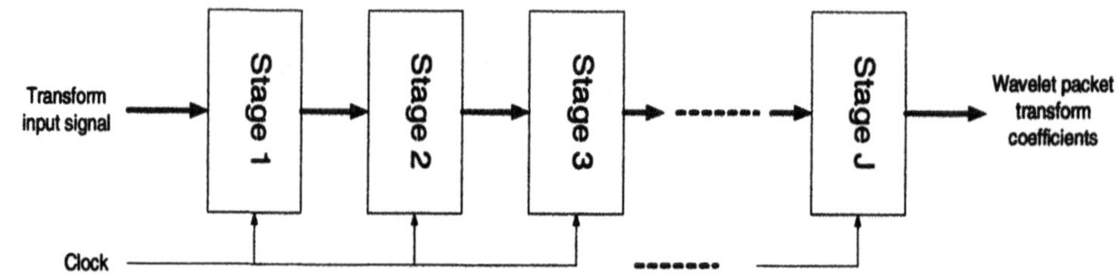

Fig. 3. Forward wavelet packet transform implementation through J synchronous stages

used to calculate $\omega_{j,i}[2k]$, and the odd ones are used for $\omega_{j,i}[2k+1]$. Processing successively every $w_{j,i}[k]$ in increasing order of i, we calculate alternatively the output of filter $\tilde{h}$ or $\tilde{g}$ depending on if i is even or odd. The output of filter $\tilde{h}$ is stored for one clock cycle, and added to the output of filter $\tilde{g}$ during the next clock cycle to form the stage output. The usage of the processing elements is of 100%, and the output data rate of the stage is half the clock rate.

One problem arising in this architecture is the need of providing $L/2$ input samples at every clock cycle. This can not easily be achieved with one single memory block. However, using one memory block of size 2^j per multiplier leads to a very simple address generation architecture, and this is the approach we choose to take here. During the first half-period, 2^j samples coming from the previous memory block are simultaneously feeding the multiplier and written in memory. The multiplier coefficients are then the even coefficients of the filters $\tilde{h}$ and $\tilde{g}$, alternatively. During the second half-period, the 2^j data samples are read from the memory and sent again to the multipliers, whose coefficients are now the odd coefficients of the filters $\tilde{h}$ and $\tilde{g}$ alternatively.

Overall, this results in the architecture shown in Figure 4. In addition to the structure we described, a FIFO is inserted between the first memory block and the stage input. This is required due to the fact that the 2^j input samples are input in 2^{j+1} clock cycles, but must be available from memory after the first half of that period. The introduction of the FIFO of depth 2^{j-1} in thus necessary, though it leads to an increase in overall processing delay.

3.2 WPT Architecture

We deduce from Eq. (2) that only every other filter output is needed. We can therefore calculate the output filter in two cycles, each calculating half of the products needed for the whole filter. Processing again the wavelet coefficients $\omega_{j,i}[k]$ in increasing order of the index value i, we use the filters h and g alternatively. For each filter output, we first calculate the even terms of the filter summation. In the next cycle, we calculate the odd terms and add the result to the partial result previously obtained. Thus, one output sample is again calculated every two clock cycles.

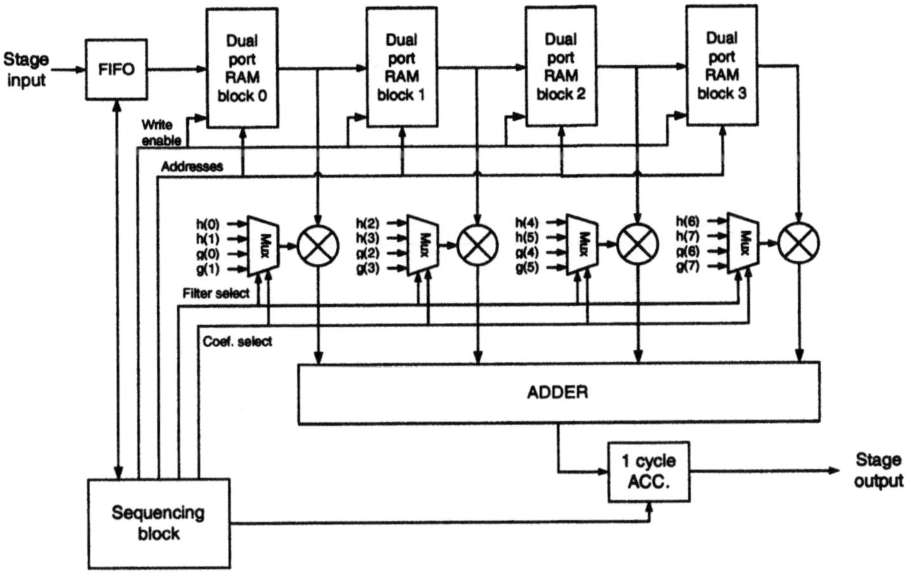

Fig. 4. Architecture of one IWPT stage with filter of length $L = 8$

In this operational sequencing, the elementary cycle is four clock cycles long. In the first (resp. second), each multiplier has to be feed by an even (resp. odd) sample of each elementary block input stream, together with the corresponding even (resp. odd) coefficient of filter h. In the two remaining clock cycles, the same input samples are multiplied by the even and odd coefficients of filter g consecutively.

3.3 Configurable Forward/Reverse Transform

It can be easily noticed that the structures described for forward and reverse transforms are almost identical. The only differences are essentially in filter coefficient selection and in the memory reading/writing address generators. It is therefore interesting to study the possibility to build a configurable forward/reverse WPT. For a given stage, the differences mentioned can be easily overcome by selecting one out of the two address generators for either direction of the transform. Similarly, doubling the size of the multiplexers selecting the suitable filter coefficients allow access to the coefficient of the four filters h, g, $\tilde{h}$, and $\tilde{g}$. The remaining issue is the inter-stage connections, since the transform requires them in increasing or decreasing order of their index j. Moreover for any stage j, both transforms require memory block sizes of 2^j words and thus stages are not interchangeable. It is nevertheless possible to build a configurable forward/reverse transform by using bidirectional links between blocks. This solution is illustrated in Figure 5.

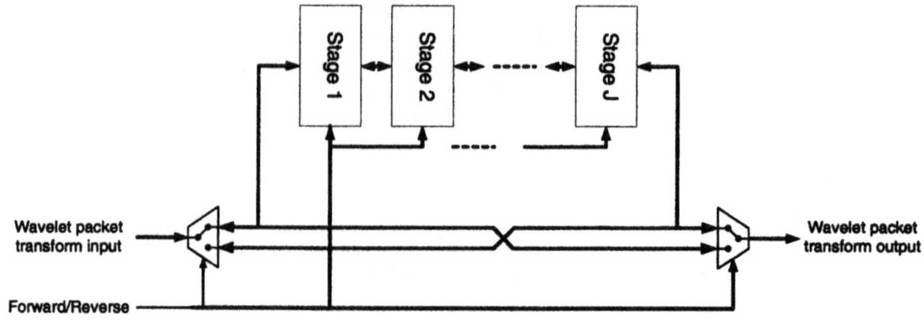

Fig. 5. Architecture of a configurable bi-directional wavelet packet transform

3.4 Non-regular Transform

We considered until now only a fully pruned transform. We show here that some rather simple modifications allow our architecture to support non-fully pruned transforms as well. From an implementation point of view, we start with an architecture with a depth equal to the maximal depth of the non-regular transform. Focusing only on the inverse transform fo the moment, we assume without loss of generality that the elementary block i_0 of the higher index stage J is not implemented. Thus, the transform input coefficients $\omega_{J,2i_0}$ and $\omega_{J,2i_0+1}$ of the bypassed elementary block are no longer required. On the other hand, we need to provide the coefficients $\omega_{J-1,i_0}[k]$ and $\omega_{J-1,i_0}[k+1]$ to the next stage. An simple way to achieved this without modifying the input and output format of the transform is to substitute the second pair of coefficients for the first one. In a such situation, the input coefficients are passing through the stage unmodified and are provided to the input of the next stage. Similar reasoning can be applied to any stage.

From an implementation point of view, this can be done easily using a binary flag for each input coefficient of every stage. If the flag is not set, then *normal* processing is performed, and otherwise the elementary block is bypassed. The actual bypassing operation can be done by providing an alternative path from input to output with the required number of clock cycle delays[1]. Another possibility is to switch to an alternate pair of specific filters. It can be easily verified that a filter pair $h[k] = \delta[k]$ and $g[k] = \delta[k-1]$ leads to the expected result. This latter solution has the advantage of not requiring the implementation of an alternative data path.

4 Performance and Complexity of the Implemented Transform

The architecture proposed has been developed using VHDL. At the time where this article is written, complete results are only available for the inverse transform

[1] The total delay is equal to $log2(L) + 3$ and thus dependent of the filter length L.

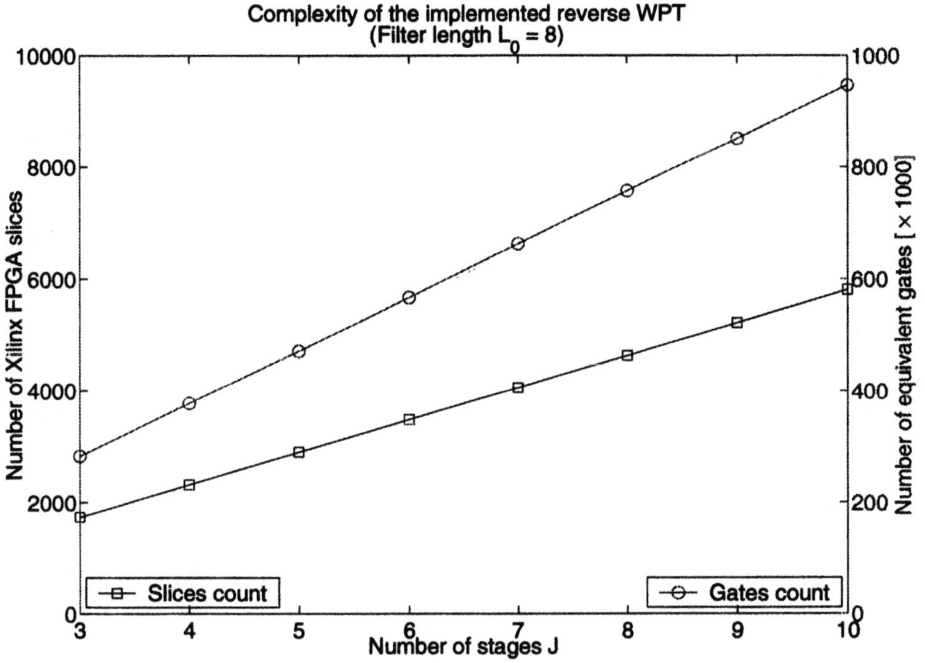

Fig. 6. Complexity of our synthesized IWPT for different transform sizes (in number of stages) for a filter length L_0 of 8

without support for fully pruned reconstruction tree. The functionality of the configurable bi-directional and arbitrary tree transforms has been completed, but the corresponding VHDL implementations are still under developments.

We intend to implement the developed core in a transceiver testbed based on FPGA devices from Xilinx Virtex-E family. Consequently, most of the elementary blocks have been taken from the manufacturer provided VHDL library. Those blocks are in particular the input FIFO, dual-port memory, multipliers and adders.

For modularity reason, the read and write address generators have been instantiated separately for each memory block. This differs slightly from our reference architecture where only one pair of address generators was used for each stage. This has only a minor impact on overall system complexity and furthermore, later versions of our model could remove this non optimal design. Similar duplications appear in the registers holding the filter coefficients: there is one pair of registers per stage, while one per transform would actually be sufficient.

Our design has been synthesized with an inter-stage data path and filter coefficients resolution of 16 bits. Subsequently, the multiplier operates at the same resolution, which provides a 32 bit wide result. This value is truncated the first time to 16 bits before reaching the adder input, and a second time before the stage output. Those data path widths have been chosen arbitrary for

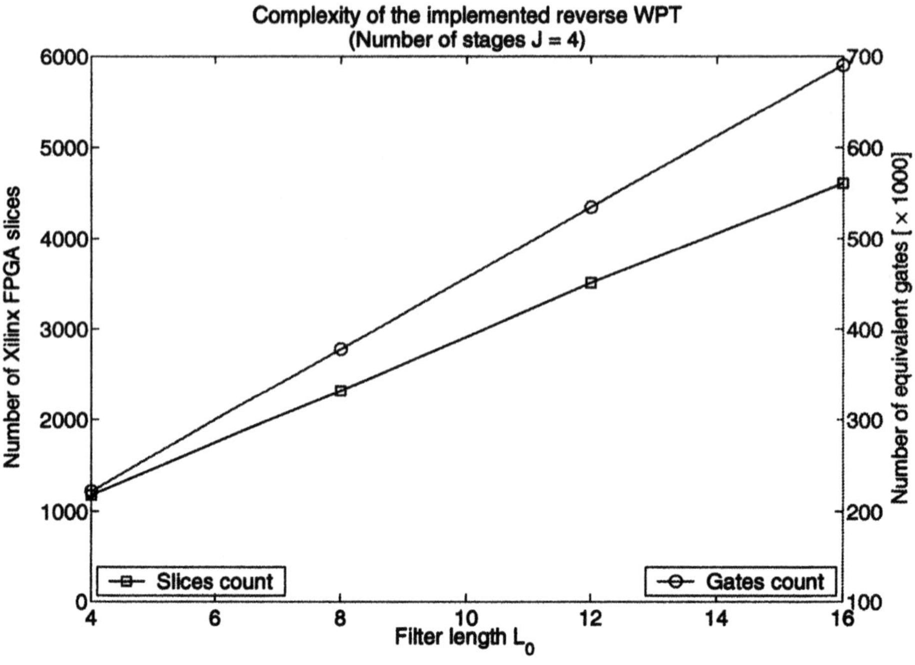

Fig. 7. Complexity of the synthesized IWPT as a function of the filter length for a transform size J of 4.

testing purposes only and other values would most probably better suit a given application in terms of overall complexity versus overall round-off error.

Our design has been synthesized with Xilinx development tools with the assumptions mentioned above. Figure 6 plots the complexity of the implemented inverse transform as a function of its size. The filter length L_0 is equal to 8 in this case. Both the number of slices and equivalent number of gates are displayed for transform sizes between 8 ($J = 3$) and 1024 ($J = 10$). The influence of the filter length on the overall complexity is illustrated in Figure 7 for a 4-stage transform size. The XCV1000-E device used has 12288 slices in total. Thus, a 512-point, 8-tap filter based IWPT requires only about 43% of the whole device. For this particular configuration and a device speed grade of "-6", the post-synthesis timing analysis indicates a maximum clock frequency of 125 MHz when default constraints are used. Well setup additional constraints should permit to keep this value higher than 100 MHz, thus allowing to fulfill the highest initial requirement.

5 Conclusion

This article has proposed an architecture to implement very fast, largely configurable forward and inverse wavelet packet transforms. Though high speed has been preferred to a reduced silicon area, it has been underlined that the proposed architecture permits to trade complexity for speed. A complete implementation has been done in order to validate the expected performance and obtain exact complexity measurements. The results are matching the initial speed requirement and our design can therefore be used as the core of an multicarrier transceiver running at up to 100 Msymbols/sec. Further work nevertheless remains to be carried out to complete the design a workable WPM transceiver.

Acknowledgments

This work has been supported in part by the Academy of Finland (Grants for project 50624 and 50618).

References

[1] van Nee, R., Prasad, R.: OFDM wireless multimedia communications. Artech house (2000)
[2] Mallat, S.: A wavelet tour of signal processing. Academic Press (1997)
[3] Chui, C.K.: An introduction to wavelets. Volume 1. Academic Press (1992)
[4] Trenas, M.A., López, J., Zapata, E.L.: FPGA implementation of wavelet packet transform with reconfigurable tree structure. In: EUROMICRO conference proceedings. (2000) 916–919

A Method for Implementing Bit-Serial Finite Impulse Response Digital Filters in FPGAs Using JBits™

A. Carreira, T.W. Fox, and L.E. Turner

Department of Electrical and Computer Engineering, University of Calgary,
2500 University Drive N.W., Calgary, Alberta, Canada, T2N 1N4
turner@enel.ucalgary.ca

Abstract. A method for implementing bit-serial Finite Impulse Response (FIR) filters in Field Programmable Gate Arrays (FPGA) using JBits™ to generate FPGA configuration bitstreams is presented. Traditional general-purpose placement tools have been bypassed with a bit-serial FIR filter placement method that uses JBits to generate FPGA configuration bitstreams. The JBits™ based bit-serial FIR filter placement method takes advantage of next-neighbor connectivity of bit-serial arithmetic cores to reduce the length of interconnections between cores and increase packing density of the cores in the FPGA. A design example for a filter with finite-precision coefficients generated by a Peak-Constrained Least-Squares filter design method is presented.

1 Introduction

Finite duration Impulse Response (FIR) digital filters perform many functions in Digital Signal Processing (DSP) systems. Example uses include: signal preconditioning, anti-aliasing, band selection, decimation/interpolation, matched filtering, and image processing convolution functions [1][2].

System architectures that trade sample-rate performance for additional area-efficiency, such as bit-serial architectures, can be used to implement filters in FPGA based DSP systems [3]. Bit-serial FIR filter architectures [4] used in DSP systems require less hardware to perform similar arithmetic to bit-parallel architectures at the expense of reduced sample-rate performance.

The Java™ language is used in conjunction with the JBits™ Application Program Interface (API) and JBits™ Run-Time Parameterizable (RTP) Cores [5] to implement a bit-serial FIR filter core and the bit-serial core library that the filter core is based on. A core is a pre-designed logic module that removes the need to implement an entire design in low-level detail [5]. JBits™ is a set of Java(tm) classes that provide an interface into the Xilinx Virtex FPGA configuration bitstream, allowing the user to directly modify the configuration bitstream [6].

Bit-serial arithmetic cores are compact and can be created with identical hardware width, resulting in simplified core alignment when placing a design. The identical hardware width and compactness of the cores result in less wasted hardware due to gaps or irregular fit between adjacent bit-serial library cores in a placement. Fewer

M. Glesner, P. Zipf, and M. Renovell (Eds.): FPL 2002, LNCS 2438, pp. 222-231, 2002.

interconnection resources are required in bit-serial implementations because the bit-serial hardware is smaller than a bit-parallel implementation.

Further hardware cost reduction results from an application specific mapping and placement method that is similar to the linear layout of cells in a chip described in [4], which is presented in this paper. Effective hardware packing is achieved by the placement method while avoiding the time consuming general-purpose placement processes used in conventional tools that synthesize FPGA configuration bitstreams. The application-specific placement method takes advantage of the next-neighbor connectivity of bit-serial arithmetic cores to reduce the length of interconnect between cores and increase the packing density of the cores in the FPGA.

2 Filter Architecture

Hardware cost and the number of control signals can be reduced by using a transposed FIR filter architecture [4] instead of the direct form FIR filter architecture [4].

A benefit of the transposed architecture is the absence of the direct form FIR filter architecture's adder tree, which requires additional control signals for each adder layer in the tree and results in increased latency of the filter. (The time between data arriving at the input of a bit-serial component and the corresponding processed data leaving the output is the latency of a bit-serial component.)

Hardware cost can be reduced further in the transposed FIR filter architecture if multipliers for duplicate coefficients in the coefficient set are shared. Multiplier sharing leads to the use of a single multiplier for each unique coefficient. The output of the shared multiplier is connected to the appropriate tap adders in the filter. Multiplier sharing in the transposed FIR filter architecture for the coefficient set {1, 5, 5, 2, 2, 4} is shown in Figure 1.

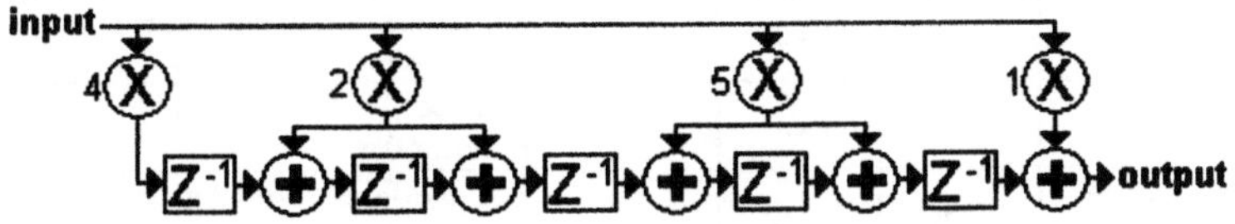

Fig. 1. Sharing coefficient multipliers in the transposed FIR filter architecture for the coefficient set {1, 5, 5, 2, 2, 4}.

3 Bit-Serial Component Library

To construct a bit-serial FIR filter core, a bit-serial core library is required. Bit-serial arithmetic cores are compact and can be created with identical width dimensions, resulting in simplified core alignment when placing a design. The identical width and compactness of the cores reduces wasted hardware due to gaps or empty spaces between bit-serial library cores in a placement. Each core in the pipelined bit-serial core library is pre-coded in the Java™ programming language as an RTP Core.

RTP Cores are an extension of the traditional static core model that can be created at run-time and support run-time parameterization of designs [5]. One example of parameterization is a register core that uses a parameter to define its data-width, thereby creating a register of varying data-width depending on the value of the parameter. The core library described in this paper is implemented as parameterizable static cores. That is, the cores are not instantiated during run-time, but during creation of the FPGA configuration bitstream. Traditional FPGA design tools provide a library of predefined cores, for example flip-flops, AND gates, adders, inverters and other cores that are not parameterized [5].

The pipelined bit-serial library we have built is similar to the library described in [7], but has been extended to simplify construction of serial by parallel multipliers [7] for constant coefficients. Additional cores for negative Most Significant Bit (MSB), positive MSB, zero, and one-bit values in coefficients have been created. For instance, there is a core exclusively for a one-bit in a coefficient and another core for a zero-bit. This reduces the hardware cost of implementing zero-bits in coefficients, because a zero bit can be implemented as a flip-flop (with inverted synchronous reset), which is smaller than a pipelined bit-serial carry-save adder. Table 1 gives the dimensions (in Xilinx Virtex FPGA LEs and Slices), the latency and a brief description for each core in the library.

Logic Elements (LE) and Slices are related to the Combinational Logic Blocks (CLB) that form the interior columns in Xilinx Virtex FPGAs. A Slice is a column of two LEs and a CLB is a row of two Slices [8]. Each logic element contains a four-input look-up table and a flip-flop [8].

Table 1. Summary of data for pipelined bit-serial core library

Component	Width	Height	Latency (cycles)	Functionality
FD (one-bit register)	1 Slice	1 LE	1	Positive coefficient MSB in a coefficient multiplier.
FDIRSlice	1 Slice	1 LE	1	A coefficient "zero-bit" in a coefficient multiplier.
CarrySaveAdder-Slice	1 Slice	2 LEs	1	A coefficient "one-bit" in a coefficient multiplier (carry-save adder [7]).
TapAdderSlice	1 Slice	2 LEs	1	Adder for delay and coefficient multiplier outputs (carry-save adder [7]).
TapDelaySlice	1 Slice	2 LEs	1-32	Unit sample delay [7].
TwosComplement-Slice	1 Slice	2 LEs	1	Negative MSB bit in a coefficient multiplier (two's complement [7]).

The CarrySaveAdderSlice is used to create a one-valued coefficient bit in the multiplier and differs from a TapAdderSlice in name to distinguish between carry-save adders used in coefficient multipliers and carry-save adders used to add up tap outputs in the delay line of Figure 1. An FDIRSlice is a one-bit register with inverted synchronous reset that can be used to create zero valued coefficient bits in the multiplier.

4 Constant Coefficient Serial by Parallel Multiplier

A serial by parallel multiplier architecture [7] with signed two's complement constant coefficient coding can be implemented from the bit-serial component library presented in Table 1. To build a serial by parallel coefficient multiplier, a finite precision coefficient must be converted to a binary number. The binary number is used to select cores to implement the multiplier according to the functionality column of Table 1.

Figure 2 shows a constant coefficient serial by parallel multiplier signal flow diagram and corresponding core diagram for a finite precision constant coefficient value of five. In Figure 2(b), cores are placed vertically adjacent to each other to shorten interconnections between adjacent cores. The LSB first serial input data is applied to each core in the multiplier, while processed output is received one bit-time later from the core corresponding to the LSB of the binary coefficient.

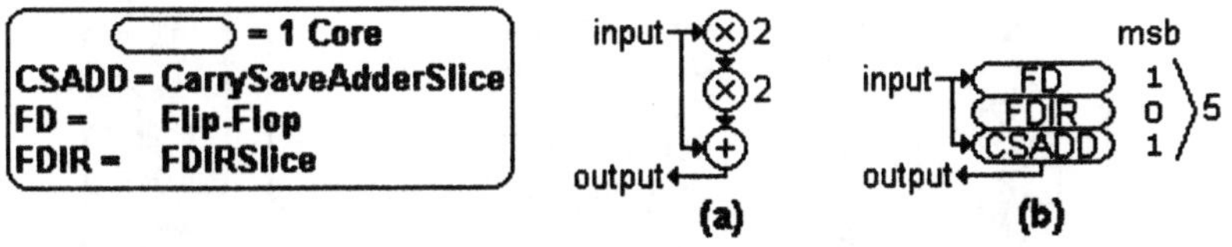

Fig. 2. (a) Constant coefficient serial by parallel multiplier signal flow diagram for a coefficient value five. **(b)** Constant coefficient serial by parallel multiplier core diagram for coefficient value five. Clock, control, and inter-core connections have not been shown for simplicity.

The constant coefficient multiplier pictured in Figure 2(a) and 2(b) performs the shift-add algorithm: the constant coefficient parallel bits are multiplied in turn by each bit of the serial input as it is presented, and each of those partial products is added to the shifted accumulation of the previous products [7].

5 Placement Method

A placement method similar to the linear layout of cells in a chip described in [4] has been created for the construction of a bit-serial FIR digital filter core in an FPGA and is presented in this section. This method provides fast generation of the FPGA configuration bitstream using the bit-serial FIR filter placement method in conjunction with JBits™ to avoid time-consuming general-purpose placement tools. Designing placement methods for constructing cores based on specific structures requires additional designer input initially when contrasted with the use of general-purpose placement tools.

A finite-precision coefficient set is converted into hardware in the Bit-Serial Filter RTP Core. This process is divided into mapping, placement, and routing subtasks. Each subtask is described in more detail in sub-sections 5.1, 5.2 and 5.3.

5.1 Mapping

The Bit-Serial Filter core is the top level in a hierarchy of cores. Sub-cores within the Bit-Serial Filter core are the bit-serial library cores described in Table 1. Mapping is accomplished by the Serial Mapper, which is a data structure that maps the position of each sub-core relative to the other sub-cores in the filter. Two one-dimensional lists (or serial maps), are contained in the data structure: a symbolic serial map that is a column of all cores in the filter and a physical serial map that is a column of all LEs used to construct the cores in the filter. Figure 3 shows the filter architecture of Figure 1 rearranged into a column, and a column of cores for the coefficient set {1, 5, 5, 2, 2, 4} as well as the corresponding serial maps.

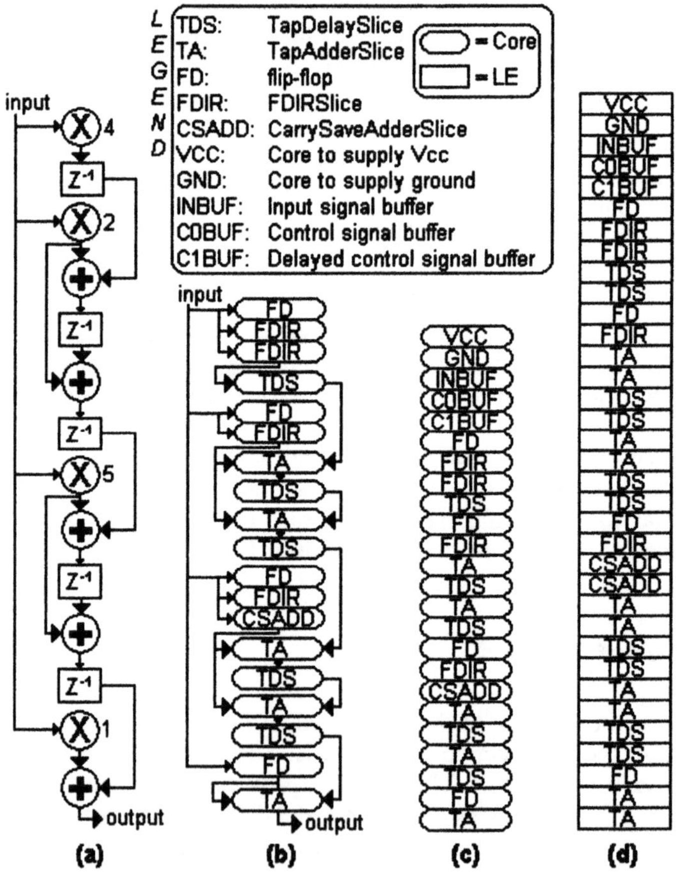

Fig. 3. (a) Transposed FIR filter architecture rearranged into a column for coefficient set {1, 5, 5, 2, 2, 4}. (b) Cores substituted into column rearrangement of transposed FIR filter architecture. (c) Symbolic serial map corresponding to (a) and (b). (d) Physical serial map corresponding to (a) and (b).

Figure 3(a) is a transposed FIR filter for the coefficient set {1, 5, 5, 2, 2, 4} that has been rearranged into a column to illustrate how the serial maps of the Serial Mapper are created. Figure 3(b) shows the result of substituting cores into the column of Figure 3(a). Note that constant coefficient multipliers of Figure 3(b) are constructed according to the method described in Section 4.

Figure 3(c) and Figure 3(d) are maps generated by the Serial Mapper for the coefficient set {1, 5, 5, 2, 2, 4}. Figure 3(c) is the symbolic serial map and is a column of cores that must be implemented to create the filter in Figure 3(a). After the first five cores at the top of the symbolic serial map of Figure 3(c), the remaining cores correspond exactly to the cores presented in Figure 3(b). The first five cores are used to buffer the serial data input and control signal and to provide Vcc and ground signals required in implementation.

The physical serial map of Figure 3(d) is constructed by converting each core in the symbolic serial map of Figure 3(c) to the appropriate number of LE's of FPGA hardware. For example: the VCC core requires one LE of FPGA hardware, represented by one block in the physical serial map. The CSADD core requires two LEs of FPGA hardware and is represented by two blocks in the physical serial map of Figure 3(d).

The sharing of coefficient multipliers is evident in Figure 3(a) and leads to a reduction in the number of LEs that compose the physical serial map of Figure 3(d). If coefficient multipliers were not shared, additional multipliers for coefficients five and two would be required. The additional hardware cost would be an additional six LEs to the 35 already present in the physical serial map. As the size and number of duplicate coefficients increase, hardware savings from sharing coefficient multipliers also increases.

5.1.1 Increased Hardware Utilization by Reducing Fan-Out

Input fan-out is a problem when implementing the transposed filter architecture of Figure 1. Loading from input fan-out reduces the rate that the system clock can operate at, and must be compensated for in situations of excessive fan-out. Recall that within an FPGA each additional input connected to an output signal increases the capacitive loading on the output signal driver in addition to the loading already present from the interconnect. The chosen constant coefficient serial by parallel multiplier architecture also contributes to the input fan-out problem because the input is connected to each core in the multiplier. Input fan-out in the constant coefficient serial by parallel multiplier increases with the size of coefficients because additional cores will be required for the implementation. The problem of input fan-out is less severe in the direct form architecture, where the registers in the delay line serve to insulate the input signal from the effects of fan-out.

A bit-serial FIR filter implementation presents additional fan-out problems because of the need for additional framing control signals. In a filter with many coefficients or very large coefficients, the control signal fan out rises considerably and can be a factor in the overall system performance because of the aforementioned loading problem.

To solve the fan-out problem described above, the control and input signals are applied to the filter implementation through a layer of flip-flops that buffer the signals against the effects of fan-out. The limit of a signal's fan-out can be controlled through the parameterization feature of RTP Cores [5]. This feature allows the Serial

Mapper to insert flip-flops into the symbolic serial map when the fan-out limit of signals is reached. The signal is connected to the input of the flip-flop and new connections are made to that flip-flop until the fan-out limit is reached again, at which point the process is repeated. Because of this fan out compensation, the latency of the filter is increased by one bit-time unit.

It is possible to increase hardware utilization in the implementation by placing fan-out buffer flip-flops as spacers for instances of the TapDelaySlice core when required. The Tap-Delay Slice core reserves both LEs within a slice because it is implemented with 16-bit Shift Register Look-up tables (SRL16) [9]. SRL16s are unique to Xilinx Virtex™ devices and require that the slice be placed in a special mode. A slice that is in the special mode cannot implement ordinary 4-input look-up tables, both look-up tables in the slice can only be used as SRL16s. As a result, it is sometimes necessary to insert a core of one LE in height into the design prior to the Tap-Delay Slice core. The inserted core positions the Tap-Delay Slice core for construction within one slice, thereby averting complications in the construction of Tap-Delay Slice cores.

If the inserted core is an empty, placeholder core, hardware density and area efficiency are reduced. Inserting a fan-out buffer flip-flop instead of an empty core allows hardware that would otherwise be unused to be purposeful. This is possible because the flip-flops within the slices that are used to buffer the input and control signals are unaffected by the special mode required for implementing SRL16s.

5.2 Placement

If the rectangle formed by adjacent columns of LEs within an FPGA are thought of as adjacent folded segments of one line, it is possible to fold the column of LEs in a physical serial map into a rectangular bounding-box within the FPGA. A bounding-box is a rectangular area reserved by an RTP Core within an FPGA that can be of arbitrary size. It can have LE, Slice, or CLB granularities depending upon the dimension (JBits™ does not allow Slice vertical granularity or LE horizontal granularity). Granularity is the unit of measure (LE, Slice, or CLB) used to describe the height and width dimensions of a core or bounding box. The column folding methodology appears in Figure 4; the vertical line represents the physical serial map, the folded line represents the map folded to fit inside of a rectangular bounding-box within an FPGA.

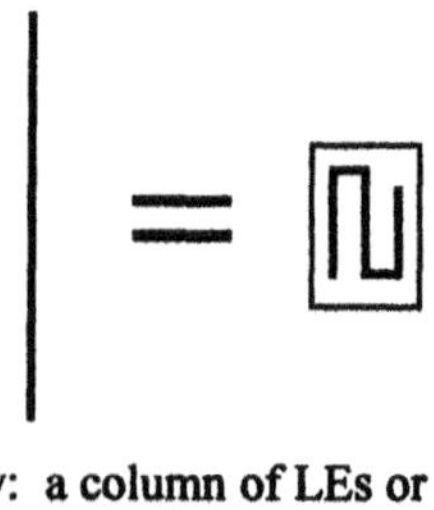

Fig. 4. Column folding methodology: a column of LEs or physical serial map is represented by the line, which is folded to fit within a bounding box that lies within an FPGA.

Folding is possible because all cores in the bit-serial core library are implemented with the same width. Any library width can be used with the folding process as long as all cores in the library are the same width. If different core widths were to be used, the placement problem would be more complex because gaps in the placement would be difficult to fill without resorting to methods used by conventional general-purpose placement tools.

The folding process starts with the first column on the left edge of the bounding-box, which is filled bottom to top with LEs from the physical serial map until the top is reached. Then placement moves right one column and proceeds from the top to the bottom until the bottom is reached. Then placement will move right another column and continue until all the cores in the physical serial map are placed in the bounding box.

The placement director is responsible for implementing the folding process. A column height and a starting coordinate corresponding to the bottom left corner of the bounding-box must be specified for the placement director to work. The director is then called to generate a coordinate for each core placement based on the size of the core and the current coordinate location.

5.3 Routing

Routing is the process of assigning wires within the FPGA to create interconnections between cores. The routing process is accomplished using the JRoute tool included with JBits™. For further information, refer to [10].

6 Design Example

A filter design method that can be used to control minimum stopband attenuation, Passband to Stopband energy Ratio (PSR), and hardware cost is presented in [11]. This method generates finite precision coefficients directly, which avoids degrading the frequency response performance due to quantization of floating point precision coefficients. This design procedure has been extended to support the design of bit serial FIR filters using the exact hardware cost, measured in LEs, from the Serial Mapper described in Section 5.1. This new design procedure provides the ability to trade PSR performance for reduced hardware cost in the filter core without altering the minimum stopband attenuation.

Table 2. Hardware cost and PSR results for Adams' filter [12] (95 taps, passband ripple=1dB, passband cutoff=0.125π rad, stopband cutoff=0.1608π rad, minimum stopband attenuation=43.22dB).

Hardware Cost (LEs)	PSR (dB)
1144	49.9
865	48.6
668	41.7

Table 2 shows the tradeoff between the PSR and the hardware cost (the number of LEs required to implement the bit-serial FIR filter core) for a 95-tap filter with 1dB passband ripple, 0.125π rad passband cutoff, 0.1608π rad stopband cutoff, and 43.22dB stopband attenuation [12]. Each entry in Table 2 satisfies these frequency response constraints.

Tolerating a slight reduction of 1.3dB in the PSR results in a 24% reduction in hardware cost. If the filtering application does not require a high PSR then the filter core requiring 668 LEs can be used. This filter core is 42% smaller than the filter core requiring 1144 LEs.

7 Implementation

It is possible to visualize the implementation of a Bit-Serial FIR filter core in the JBits™ BoardScope tool [13]. Operational simulation and verification of the core is also possible in the Boardscope environment using the Virtex Device Simulator (VirtexDS) [14].

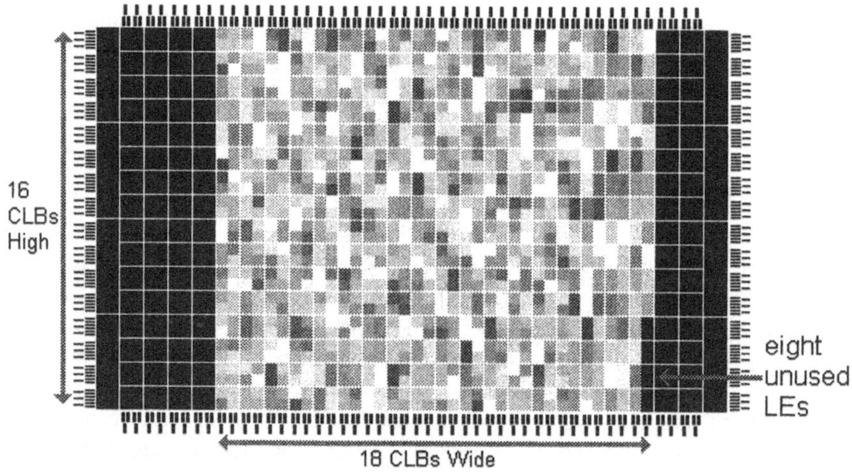

Fig. 5. Visualization of bit-serial component library sub-cores placed within the bounding box of a Bit-Serial FIR Filter core (95 taps, PSR of 49.9dB).

The core pictured in Figure 5 occupies 1071 LEs if fan-out buffers are not counted. The bounding box of the core is 18 CLBs wide by 16 CLBs high. The fan out for the core pictured has been limited to a maximum of 25 input nets for any output signal resulting in 73 additional LEs for fan-out buffers. The bounding box contains 1152 LEs, including fan-out buffers, the filter occupies 1144 LEs (eight LEs are allocated but are unused in this implementation). The only unused area of the FPGA within the bounding box is the eight LEs at the bottom right corner of the box

References

1 H. Lee and G.E. Sobelman: "FPGA-Based FIR Filters Using Digit-Serial Arithmetic", Proc. IEEE International ASIC Conference and Exhibit, pp. 225-228, 1997.

2 A. Antoniou, Digital filters, analysis, design, and applications. New York, NY: McGraw-Hill Inc., 1993.

3 J. Valls, M. M. Peiro, T. Sansaloni, and E. Boemo: "Design and FPGA implementation of Digit-Serial FIR filters" , ", Proc. 1998 IEEE ICECS'98 (5th IEEE International Conference on Electronics, Circuits and Systems), Vol.2, pp.191-194, Lisboa, 7-10 Sept. 1998.

4 R.I. Hartley and K.K. Parhi, Digit-serial computation. Boston, MA: Kluwer Academic, 1995.

5 S. A. Guccione and D. Levi: "Run-Time Parameterizable Cores", Proc. of FPL99, Glasgow, UK, pp 215-222, 1999.

6 S. A. Guccione, D. Levi, and P. Sundararajan: "JBits™: java based interface for reconfigurable computing." Proc. Second Annual Military and Aerospace Applications of Programmable Devices and Technologies (MAPLD '99), The Johns Hopkins University, Laurel, Maryland, Sep. 1999.

7 R. J. Andraka: "FIR Filter Fits in an FPGA using a Bit Serial Approach", Proc. 3rd Annual PLD Conference, Manhasset, NY, 1993.

8 Virtex(tm) 2.5 V Field Programmable Gate Arrays - Final Product Specification, http://www.xilinx.com/partinfo/ds003.pdf, DS003 (v2.2) May 23, 2000.

9 Libraries Guide, Xilinx, http://toolbox.xilinx.com/docsan/xilinx4/manuals.htm

10 E. Keller, "JRoute: A run-time routing API for FPGA hardware," in Parallel and Distributed Processing, J. Romlin et al., ed., pp. 874-881, Springer-Verlag, Berlin, May 2000. 7th Reconfigurable ArchitecturesWorkshop (RAW), Proc. of the 15th International Parallel and Distributed Processing Symposium (IPDPS) Workshops 2000, Cancun, Mexico May 1-5, 2000. (Published in the series Lecture Notes in Computer Science 1800.)

11 T.W. Fox and L.E. Turner, "The design of peak constrained least squares FIR filters with low complexity finite precision coefficients," IEEE Trans. Circuits and Systems II, vol. 49, pp. 151-154, Feb. 2002.

12 J.W. Adams, "FIR digital filters with least-squares stopbands subject to peak-gain constraints," IEEE Trans. Circuits Syst., vol. 39, pp. 376-388, Apr. 1991.

13 D. Levi and S. A. Guccione, "BoardScope: A Debug Tool for Reconfigurable Systems", Configurable Computing Technology and its uses in High Performance Computing, DSP and Systems Engineering, Proc. SPIE Photonics East, J. Schewel (Ed.), Bellingham, WA, November 1998.

14 S. McMillan, B. Blodget, and S. Guccione, "VirtexDS: A Device Simulator for Virtex," Reconfigurable Technology: FPGAs for Computing and Applications II, Proc. SPIE 4212, pp. 50-56, Bellingham, WA, November 2000, November 2000.

Automatic Partitioning for Improved Placement and Routing in Complex Programmable Logic Devices

Valavan Manohararajah, Terry Borer, Stephen D. Brown, and Zvonko Vranesic

Altera Corporation
Toronto Technology Center
151 Bloor St. West, Suite 200
Toronto, ON
CANADA M4Y 1R5
vmanohar@altera.com, tborer@altera.com,
sbrown@altera.com, zvonko@altera.com

Abstract. This work explores the effect of adding a new partitioning step into the traditional complex programmable logic device (CPLD) CAD flow. A novel algorithm based on Rent's rule and simulated annealing partitions a design before it enters the place and route stage in CPLD CAD. The resulting partitions are then placed using an enhanced placement tool. Experiments conducted on Altera'a APEX20K chips indicate that a partitioned placement can provide an average performance gain of 7% over flat placements.

1 Introduction

An incremental design methodology called LogicLock [1] was introduced in version 1.1 of Altera's Quartus II software. LogicLock offers users an alternative to the traditional "flat" place and route steps in CPLD CAD. In traditional CPLD CAD, the design being compiled is represented as one large netlist as it enters the place and route steps. This allows a global view that is beneficial for some circuits. However, for many large circuits it is difficult for a placement tool to ensure that tightly connected components in the design are not separated by large distances. With the LogicLock feature, users can create *partitions* (referred to as *regions* in Quartus II terminology) of logic which are kept together during the place and route stages. A partition may contain both logic and any smaller child partitions. Feedback from LogicLock users has indicated that the ability to keep components together during placement and routing helped increase the overall speed of several designs. This work considers a natural extension to the LogicLock feature. When the user has not specified a set of partitions, a partitioner within Quartus II is run to determine a set of good partitions for the design. To operate without any user assistance, the partitioner automatically determines both the number of partitions as well as the partitioning itself. The partitioning procedure may not be beneficial for all circuits therefore we also

M. Glesner, P. Zipf, and M. Renovell (Eds.): FPL 2002, LNCS 2438, pp. 232–241, 2002.

consider the problem of determining when the automatically created partitions are to be used.

2 Previous Work

An excellent survey of previous work in netlist partitioning was presented by Alpert and Kahng [4]. In their work, partitioning approaches are classified into four categories: move-based approaches, geometric representations, combinatorial formulations and clustering approaches. Our work uses a move-based approach with some elements of the clustering approach. During a single iteration of the proposed algorithm, a move-based approach is used within a simulated annealing framework to generate a set of partitions. Bigger partitions are created out of smaller partitions discovered during earlier passes of the algorithm in a process that is similar to many bottom-up clustering approaches [7] [8].

Roy and Sechen [5] explored the use of a simulated annealing approach within a timing-driven FPGA partitioner. In their work, the netlist is clustered to create a smaller problem for the partitioning tool. In another simulated annealing approach described by Sun and Sechen[6], the circuit to be placed is clustered in a preprocessing step and the clustering information is used during placement.

Our work uses a cost function based on Rent's rule [16]. A clustering algorithm based on Rent's rule was previously described by Ng et al [9]. Hagen et al. [10] described a spectra-based ratio cut partitioning scheme that creates partitions with the lowest observed Rent's parameter. Recently, Rent's rule has found several uses in interconnection prediction and congestion estimation during placement [11] [12] [13] [14].

3 The APEX Architecture

In this work, Altera's APEX chips were the target of the partitioning experiments. A simplified internal view of an APEX chip is presented in Figure 1. At the highest level, the chip is organized into four quadrants. Each quadrant contains an array of *MEGALABs* arranged into set of columns and rows. A *MEGALAB* contains a number of *LABs* and a single *ESB*. Each LAB contains a set of *LEs*. An LE is the basic logic element in the APEX architecture. It consists of a four-input LUT (4-LUT), a programmable register, carry and cascade logic. The ESB can be used to realize memory functions in the design. For a detailed description of the internal structure and interconnect arrangement in the APEX chips see [2].

4 The CAD Flow

The CAD flow used in our work is illustrated in Figure 2. Once technology mapping is complete an optional partitioning step is executed to discover a set of partitions for the design. Following partitioning, a partition aware clustering

Fig. 1. The APEX architecture.

step is performed. The partition aware clusterer decomposes the logic within a partition into LABs. It also ensures that logic from one partition is not mixed with logic from another partition. The partition aware placement step is much more complicated than the normal placement step found in the traditional flow. First, each partition in the design is assigned a rectangular shape large enough to hold its contents. After shape assignment, the new placement step has to determine a position for each of the rectangular shapes in the design as well a position for each of its contents. A detailed description of the placement tool is beyond the scope of this paper. A description can be found in [3]. The final step, routing, requires no changes and is identical to the one used in an unpartitioned CAD flow.

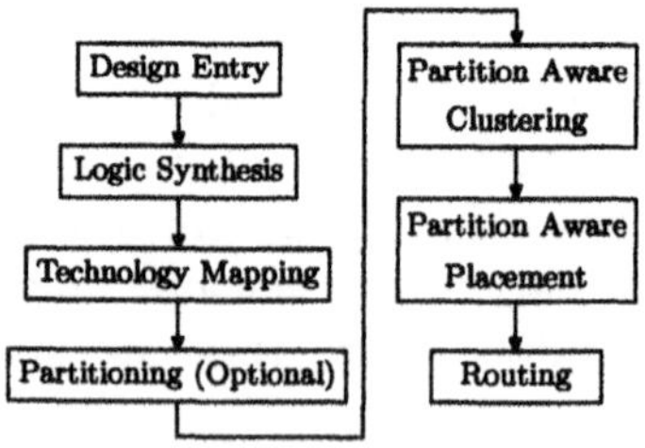

Fig. 2. A CAD flow that incorporates a partitioning step.

5 Partitioning

The input to the partitioning step is a netlist that consists of memory elements, LEs and IOs. The partitioning step produces a set of partitions for the netlist as output. A partition may contain both LEs and smaller partitions. Memory elements and IOs do not participate in the partitioning process because their placement is quite restricted. Both memory elements and IOs can only be placed at select locations on the chip whereas the possibilities for the placement of LEs is numerous. The placement tool is left the task of discovering the best spots for both memory elements and IOs.

5.1 Overview

An overview of the partitioning algorithm is presented in Figure 3. First, a timing analysis routine is executed to determine a weight for each wire in the design. Interconnect delays are required in order to perform a timing analysis but they only become available after placement and routing have completed. An experiment was performed with 25 small to medium sized industrial circuits to determine if a net's delay could be related to its fanout. Each circuit was placed and the delay of the fastest path (using general interconnect) between each source-sink pair was obtained. This data allows for some rough estimation of wire delays. A rough estimate for the delay (in picoseconds) of a source-sink connection on a net with fanout of f is given by $(1141 \log f + 733)$. Now that a model for interconnect delay is available, timing analysis can be performed. Timing analysis determines a slack s_{uv} [15] for each source-sink pair (u, v). We define the criticality, c_{uv}, of each source-sink pair (u, v) as

$$c_{uv} = 1 - \frac{s_{uv}}{\max_{\forall ij} s_{ij}} \tag{1}$$

The criticality provides an indication of the relative importance of each source-sink connection and is used as the weight when the cost function is computed.

The main partitioning loop consists of block formation and partitioning steps. Block formation behaves differently depending on the value of h. During the first call to block formation ($h = 0$), blocks will be created out of the LEs in the design. Most blocks will contain a single LE. However, if there is logic in the design that uses the specialized carry or cascade chain routing, then all LEs that are a part of the carry or cascade chain will become a part of a single block. During the subsequent calls to block formation ($h > 0$), blocks are created out of the partitions discovered during the previous pass. Each partition discovered during the previous call to PARTITION is transformed into a block. In this manner, larger partitions can be built out of smaller ones. The partitioning step, PARTITION, uses a simulated annealing based optimization algorithm to divide the blocks into partitions. The main loop terminates whenever new partitions are not being discovered or when the number of levels in the hierarchy discovered so far exceeds the prespecified limit, *hlimit*. In the experiments, *hlimit* was set to 4.

```
TimingAnalysis()
h ← 0
do
    BlockFormation(h)
    Partition()
    h ← h + 1
while NewPartitionsFormed() = true
        and h < hlimit
```

Fig. 3. Overview of the partitioning process.

5.2 Cost Function

Rent's Rule The partitioning cost function is based on Rent's rule [16]. The rule relates the number of blocks in a partition, B, to the number of external connections, P, emanating from the partition. Rent's rule is given by

$$P = T_b B^r \tag{2}$$

where T_b denotes the average number of interconnections for a block in the partition and r is Rent's exponent. Rent's exponent, r, is a value in the range $[0, 1]$. A value close to 1 indicates that most of the connections in the partition are external and a value near 0 indicates that almost all connections are internal.

Weighted Rent's Rule Rent's rule as stated in Equation 2 treats all connections equally. However, to account for the fact that some connections may be more critical than the others, each connection is weighted using the criticality value obtained through timing analysis (Section 5.1). The terms in Equation 2 were revised slightly to account for weighted connections. The number of external connections, P, now denotes the total weight of all external connections. Similarly, the average number of interconnections for a block in the partition, T_b, now denotes the average weight of interconnections for a block in the partition.

Cost of a Partitioning Solution A solution to the partitioning problem consists of a set of partitions each containing a number of blocks. The cost of the partitioning is given by

$$C = \frac{\sum B_i r_i}{\sum B_i} \tag{3}$$

where B_i is the number of blocks in region i and r_i is Rent's exponent for region i. Like Rent's exponent, the cost, C, is also a value in the range $[0, 1]$. A value closer to 0 is indicative of a good partitioning and a value closer to 1 is indicative of a bad partitioning.

Effect of Partition Size Consider two extreme solutions to the partitioning problem. In one case, all blocks may be placed in a single partition. In the other case, every partition contains a single block. Both cases cannot improve the quality of the placement that is obtained. A lower and upper limit on partition size was established to prevent the creation of partitions that are either too small or too large. If some solution to the partitioning problem has partitions that are smaller than the lower limit or bigger than the upper limit, the cost, C, is pulled towards 1.

5.3 Optimization

The main partitioning procedure, referred to as PARTITION in Figure 3, starts with a random partitioning solution and iteratively improves it using simulated annealing [17].

The starting temperature for the anneal, is obtained using a method similar to that described in [18] [19]. A set of m moves is randomly generated. Each move is then evaluated and the change in score is observed. The initial temperature is computed to be 20 times the standard deviation of the set of scoring changes.

At each temperature in the anneal, m moves are generated and evaluated. The value of m is equal to the total number of external connections of the blocks participating in the partitioning process. During the first pass of partitioning, most blocks will contain a single LE. A four-input LUT is the primary component within an LE therefore, on average, each block is expected to have four input connections and one output connection. If n is the number of LEs in the circuit then m is approximately equal to $5n$ during the first pass of partitioning. During the subsequent passes, blocks are formed from the partitions discovered during the preceding pass. A block that is formed in this manner will contain highly "localized" connections. The value of m will be greatly reduced because very few connections will be external to the newly formed blocks.

The move generation routine used by the simulated annealer generates two types of moves: *directed* and *random*. To generate a directed move, a block with at least one connection crossing a partition boundary is picked at random. The directed move that is generated moves the block into a partition containing one of its endpoints. A random move may be further classified into two types: *empty* and *non-empty*. An empty random move picks a block at random and creates a new partition to contain the block. A non-empty random move picks a block at random and moves it into a randomly selected partition that already contains a number of blocks. The move generation routine generates directed moves with a probability of 0.75 and random moves with a probability of 0.25. During random move generation, empty moves are generated with a probability of 0.25 and non-empty moves are generated with a probability of 0.75.

Once all moves at a particular temperature have been generated and evaluated, the temperature is reduced for the next iteration in the anneal. The new temperature, t_{new}, is given by

$$t_{new} = t_{old} \cdot \gamma \cdot \left(\beta + (1-\beta)e^{-(\alpha-0.45)^2/4}\right) \tag{4}$$

Here, t_{old} is the current temperature and α is the accept ratio observed during the iteration. The accept ratio is defined to be the ratio of the number of moves accepted to the total number of moves tried. The multiplier, γ, controls the basic rate at which the temperature decreases. The fraction, β, controls whether the full multiplier or a scaled down version of the multiplier is used in determining the next temperature value. A Gaussian function which depends on the accept ratio, α, generates the scale factor used to reduce the multiplier. The function reaches its maximum value of 1 when the accept ratio is 0.45. Previous research has indicated the benefit of keeping the temperature hovering around an accept ratio of 0.45 [20]. Note that the full multiplier is used when the accept ratio is close to 0.45 or when β is close to 1. A value for β is computed by observing the improvement in score obtained during the pass that just completed. If there was a large improvement in score and if the accept ratio is low enough to ensure that the improvement cannot be attributed to random behavior, β is given a value close to 1. This allows the search to spend more time at those temperatures that seem to produce large improvements in the score.

Simulated annealing stops when the exit criterion is met. The exit criterion used here is similar to that described in [18]. The exit criterion is true if the current temperature is lower than the exit temperature, t_{exit}. A value for t_{exit} is computed based on the current cost, C, and the total number of external connections of all blocks in the design, n_{ext}:

$$t_{exit} = \epsilon \frac{C}{n_{ext}} \tag{5}$$

Here, ϵ is a small constant which was set to 0.05 during the experiments. Any move performed during the anneal is likely to affect several external connections. If the temperature drops below a fraction of the average cost of an external connection, it is unlikely that any move which increases the cost will be accepted and the annealing process can be terminated.

6 Experimental Results

In the first experiment, the performance of the partitioned flow was compared to the flat flow on 20 industrial circuits (Table 1). The partitioned flow produces an average speedup of 6.81% over the flat flow. Note that the partitioning algorithm produces a wide variety of partitions — circuit "ccta16" was partitioned into 6 partitions while "ccta14" was partitioned into 118 partitions.

In the second experiment, the performance of the automatic partitioning algorithm was compared to the performance of user created partitions (Table 2). The user partitions were created by Altera's field application engineers and design engineers working on the LogicLock feature. The user partitioned flow obtained a speedup of 9.3% over the flat flow whereas the automatically partitioned flow obtained a speedup of 7.82%. Apart from the results observed for circuits "cctb2" and "cctb3", the automatic partitioning is competitive with the user created partitions. In fact, for circuits "cctb1", "cctb4", "cctb5", "cctb7", "cctb9", "cctb11" and "cctb12", the automatically generated partitions outperformed the user created partitions.

Combining the results observed for both experiments, the automatically generated partitioning improved the overall speed of the 32 circuits by 7.04%.

Compared to the flat flow, the automatically partitioned flow increases the overall compile time by 25.26% for the 32 circuits. However, most of this time is spent within the partition aware placer rather than in the partitioner. The partitioning procedure itself consumes 7.67% of the total compile time. Most of the increase in compile time is due to the increased cost of performing partition moves (the normal placer deals with LAB moves only) in the placer. Given a circuit of size n, the complexity of the partitioning procedure is $O(n)$ (see Section 5.3) whereas the complexity of the placer is $O(n^{\frac{4}{3}})$. As circuits grow larger, the time spent within the partitioner will be a smaller fraction of the overall compile time.

Circuit		*Flat*	*Partitioned*					
Name	*Size (LEs)*	*Speed (Mhz)*	*Speed (Mhz)*	*Partitions*	*Speedup (%)*	*C*	*R*	*U*
ccta1	9027	60.93	60.38	26	-0.90	0.36	3.27	1
ccta2	5357	126.58	153.73	33	21.45	0.31	12.44	1
ccta3	5828	39.02	43.08	34	10.40	0.54	5.38	1
ccta4	11304	52.87	52.89	23	0.04	0.51	2.86	1
ccta5	11273	38.02	46.43	16	22.12	0.52	4.39	1
ccta6	5593	41.47	43.45	43	4.77	0.55	4.45	1
ccta7	5455	99.03	109.06	30	10.13	0.09	2.80	1
ccta8	10824	42.57	43.83	46	2.96	0.32	17.79	1
ccta9	5380	57.51	56.36	15	-2.00	0.37	8.90	1
ccta10	7147	157.16	177.97	20	13.24	0.42	7.30	1
ccta11	6145	45.54	41.72	84	-8.39	0.76	1.48	0
ccta12	5086	95.19	110.14	10	15.71	0.41	27.22	1
ccta13	6789	30.16	29.47	28	-2.29	0.63	1.00	0
ccta14	9565	25.49	26.18	118	2.71	0.36	1.25	1
ccta15	4720	105.94	124.19	14	17.23	0.38	2.13	1
ccta16	3640	70.88	70.92	6	0.06	0.22	18.61	1
ccta17	12064	43.61	41.12	21	-5.71	0.58	4.86	0
ccta18	8940	12.43	12.46	16	0.24	0.67	2.98	0
ccta19	3403	71.57	78.29	16	9.39	0.37	9.76	1
ccta20	3378	43.14	51.84	35	20.17	0.34	16.09	1
Average					6.57			

Table 1. Comparing flat compilations with partitioned compilations.

7 Auto On/Off

There are instances where automatic partitioning does not improve the performance of the circuit. For example, in Table 1, when automatic partitioning is used, the performance of "ccta11" drops by 8.39% and the performance of "ccta17" drops by 5.71%. Similarly, in Table 2, the performance of "cctb2" drops by 12.84% with automatic partitioning. A natural question to ask is if situations like this can be prevented by using some statistics generated by the partitioner. First, we define the *crossing ratio*, R, as

$$R = \frac{c_{AvgAll}}{c_{AvgCross}} \quad (6)$$

Circuit		*Flat*	*User Partitioned*			*Auto Partitioned*					
Name	*Size (LEs)*	*Speed (Mhz)*	*Speed (Mhz)*	*Part-itions*	*Speedup (%)*	*Speed (Mhz)*	*Part-itions*	*Speedup (%)*	*C*	*R*	*U*
cctb1	4514	85.59	93.61	5	9.37	104.25	29	21.80	0.42	3.31	1
cctb2	10460	58.87	72.63	32	23.37	51.31	16	-12.84	0.61	2.33	0
cctb3	4999	26.76	30.47	17	13.86	26.97	79	0.78	0.48	4.82	1
cctb4	10630	98.65	109.84	11	11.34	113.07	2	14.62	0.31	16.50	1
cctb5	13405	92.82	94.28	22	1.57	96.99	64	4.49	0.31	17.29	1
cctb6	14149	20.85	21.38	23	2.54	20.60	13	-1.20	0.47	8.61	1
cctb7	20532	29.18	32.14	4	10.14	33.57	12	15.04	0.48	6.34	1
cctb8	8300	72.21	80.28	9	11.18	77.92	24	7.91	0.39	2.51	1
cctb9	10914	44.26	46.69	16	5.49	47.40	44	7.09	0.40	5.42	1
cctb10	4385	129.25	134.32	11	3.92	127.06	11	-1.69	0.09	3.60	1
cctb11	4936	79.81	87.02	16	9.03	101.33	136	26.96	0.40	1.68	1
cctb12	4425	107.97	118.57	25	9.82	119.75	4	10.91	0.17	13.10	1
Average					9.30			7.82			

Table 2. Comparing flat compilations, user partitioned compilations and automatically partitioned compilations.

Here, c_{AvgAll} is the average criticality of all connections in the circuit and $c_{AvgCross}$ is the average criticality of all connections that cross a partition boundary. Intuitively, a good set of partitions would have a low cost (see Section 5.2) and a high crossing ratio. Now, consider the following rule

$$Useful = \begin{cases} 1 \text{ if } C < 0.56 \text{ or } R > 5 \\ 0 \text{ otherwise} \end{cases} \tag{7}$$

The rightmost three columns of Tables 1 and 2 summarize the C, R and *Useful* values for each circuit. This simple rule could help eliminate the use of the automatically created partitions on circuits "ccta11", "ccta13", "ccta17" and "cctb2". However, it does not eliminate circuit "ccta9" which has a low cost and a high crossing ratio. More experimentation with a wide variety of circuits is necessary to determine whether rules such as this could be used to determine when the automatically created partitioning is useful.

8 Conclusions

This work introduced a new partitioning algorithm that can be used to improve the quality of CPLD placements. The algorithm used simulated annealing to optimize a cost function based on Rent's rule. An average performance improvement of 7% was observed for a set of 32 industrial circuits. The automatically created partitions were found to be competitive with partitions created by experienced users. This work also considered the possibility of using some of the statistics available to the automatic partitioner to determine if the automatically generated partitions would help or hurt a circuit's performance.

References

1. Altera. "LogicLock Methodology White Paper". Available at: http://www.altera.com/literature/wp/wp_logiclock.pdf.
2. Altera. *Altera 2000 Databook*. Available at: http://www.altera.com/html/literature/lds.html.
3. D. P. Singh, T. P. Borer and S. D. Brown. "Constrained FPGA Placement Algorithms for Timing Optimization". *ACM Intl. Conf. FPGAs*, submitted, 2003.
4. C. J. Alpert and A. B. Kahng. "Recent Directions in Netlist Partitioning: A Survey". *Integration: The VLSI Journal*, 19:1–81, 1995.
5. K. Roy and C. Sechen. "A Timing-Driven *n*-way Chip and Multi-Chip Partitioner". In *Proc. IEEE/ACM Intl. Conf. Computer-Aided Design*, pages 240–247, 1993.
6. W. Sun and C. Sechen. "Efficient and Effective Placement for Very Large Circuits". In *Proc. IEEE/ACM Intl. Conf. Computer-Aided Design*, pages 170–177, 1993.
7. D. M. Schuler and E. G. Ulrich. "Clustering and Linear Placement". In *Proc. IEEE/ACM Design Automation Conf.*, pages 50–56, 1972.
8. H. Shin and C. Kim. "A Simple Yet Effective Technique for Partitioning". *IEEE Trans. VLSI Systems*, 1(3): 380–386, September 1993.
9. T.-K. Ng, J. Oldfield and V. Pitchumani. "Improvements of a Mincut Partition Algorithm". In *Proc. IEEE/ACM Intl. Conf. Computer-Aided Design*, pages 470–473, 1987.
10. L. Hagen, A. B. Kahng, F. J. Kurdahi and C. Ramachandran. "On the Intrinsic Rent Parameter and Spectra-Based Partitioning Methodologies". *IEEE Trans. Computer-Aided Design*, 13(1):27–37, 1994.
11. A. Singh, G. Parthasarathy and M. Marek-Sadowska. "Interconnect Resource-Aware Placement for Hierarchical FPGAs". In *Proc. IEEE/ACM Intl. Conf. Computer-Aided Design*, pages 132–136, 2001.
12. J. Dambre, P. Verplaetse, D. Stroobandt and J. Van Campenhout. "On Rent's Rule for Rectangular Regions". In *Proc. IEEE/ACM Intl. Workshop on System-Level Interconnect Prediction*, pages 49–56, 2001.
13. X. Yang, R. Kastner and M. Sarrafzadeh. "Congestion Estimation During Top-Down Placement". In *Proc. Intl. Symp. on Physical Design*, pages 164–169, 2001.
14. D. Stroobandt. "A Priori System-Level Interconnect Prediction: Rent's Rule and Wire Length Distribution Models". In *Proc. IEEE/ACM Intl. Workshop on System-Level Interconnect Prediction*, pages 3–21, 2001.
15. R. B. Hitchcock, G. L. Smith and D. D. Cheng. "Timing Analysis of Computer Hardware". *IBM Journal of Research and Development*, 26(1):100–105, January 1982.
16. B. Landman and R. Russo. "On a Pin Versus Block Relationship for Partitions of Logic Graphs". *IEEE Transactions on Computers*, c-20:1469–1479, 1971.
17. S. Kirkpatrick, C.D. Gelatt and M.P. Vecchi. "Optimization by Simulated Annealing". *Science*, 220:671–680, 1983.
18. V. Betz, J. Rose and A. Marquardt. "Architecture and CAD for Deep-Submicron FPGAs". Kluwer Academic Publishers, 1999.
19. M. Huang, F. Romeo and A. Sangiovanni-Vincentelli. "An Efficient General Cooling Schedule for Simulated Annealing". In *Proc. IEEE/ACM Intl. Conf. Computer-Aided Design*, pages 381–384, 1986.
20. J. Lam and J.-M. Delosme. "Performance of a New Annealing Schedule". In *Proc. IEEE/ACM Intl. Design Automation Conf.*, pages 306–311, 1988.

Rapid and Reliable Routability Estimation for FPGAs

Parivallal Kannan, Shankar Balachandran, and Dinesh Bhatia

Center for Integrated Circuits and Systems
Erik Jonsson School of Engineering and Computer Science
University of Texas at Dallas
PO Box 830688, Richardson, TX 75083, USA
{parik, shankars, dinesh}@utdallas.edu

Abstract. Modern large scale FPGA designs require interconnect estimation for cutting down the design cycle times. Most of the available estimation techniques use empirical methods to estimate routability. These methods lack the ability to accurately model back-end routers and the estimation results produced are not very reliable. We recently proposed a fast and generic routability estimation method, fGREP [1], that predicts the peak routing demand and the channel occupancies in a given FPGA architecture. The peak demands are within 3 to 4% of actual detailed routing results produced by the well known physical design suite, VPR [2]. In this paper, we observe that, fGREP spends a significant portion of its execution time in estimating the demands for nets with large number of terminals. We propose a new routability estimation method based on fGREP which offers significant speedups over fGREP, while maintaining the same high levels of accuracy. The new method is up to $36X$ faster than fGREP, and on an average is about $102X$ faster than VPR's detailed router.

1 Introduction

Interconnect prediction is taking center stage in the current design cycles. With ever-increasing design and device sizes, the design cycles are becoming long and repetitive. The main reason for this iterative process is the lack of sufficient interaction between the different stages, especially between placement and routing. Reliable interconnect prediction is required at all stages of physical design to ensure quick design closure.

Most of the recent work in interconnect prediction and routability estimation is based on the Rent's rule [3]. Van Marck et. al. [4] used Rent's rule to describe local variations in interconnect complexity. Sadowska et. al. [5] used Van Marck's results and modified the VPR placement cost function (originally linear wirelength based) to account for interconnection complexity. Wei [6] has used Rent's rule to arrive at a statistical model for predicting routability for hierarchical FPGAs prior to placement. Sarrafzadeh et.al. [7] used Rent's rule to estimate global and local routing requirements and compare their result with a primitive L-shaped global router. El Gamal [8] proposed a stochastic model for estimating the channel densities in mask programmable gate arrays. The model assumes a normal distribution of interconnection within channels. Brown [9] et. al. extended this model by taking into account the FPGA routing architecture and various flexibilities associated with programmable switching elements.

M. Glesner, P. Zipf, and M. Renovell (Eds.): FPL 2002, LNCS 2438, pp. 242–252, 2002.

Lou et.al. [10] proposed a new method for estimating routing requirements for standard cell designs. Multi-terminal nets were decomposed to 2-terminal segments and routing demands were estimated using a probabilistic approach that involved path enumeration. This method was adopted for FPGAs in [11] and was shown to be fast but not very accurate when compared to actual detailed routers.

Most of the routability estimation methods are not able to produce estimates at fine levels of detail and also do not model the characteristics of the routers that are commonly used. The result is that incomplete estimates are produced and/or the estimates do not comply with the routing produced by standard routers [12] [13]. We recently proposed a routability estimation method, fGREP [1], which produced reliable results over a large set of standard benchmarks. We observe that the execution times for fGREP are very high for nets with large number of terminals. In this paper, we analyze the fGREP formulation and propose a new routability estimation method based on fGREP that has significantly lesser computation times, without any sacrifice in the estimation quality and reliability.

2 Motivation

The fGREP [1] methodology introduced a new routability estimation method for FPGAs that is reliable, fast and FPGA architecture independent. The methodology produced routing demand values in terms of tracks, on a channel by channel basis and also produced the global channel width required to route a given placed circuit. The peak routing demand estimates for fGREP are within 3 to 4% of the actual detailed routes produced by the well known FPGA physical design suite VPR [2]. fGREP's estimates correlate very well with VPR's detailed route results on a channel by channel basis also. The mean of the differences between fGREP's estimates and VPR's detailed routes over all the channels are about 1.5 tracks and the standard deviation is about 1 track, for all the benchmarks. This high level of reliability makes fGREP ideal for routability estimation inside other physical design processes like placement, global routing and detailed routing, where accuracy of the estimation is of concern.

For any net N_i, the routing estimation time for fGREP, as per [1], is proportional to $E_i \times T_i$, where E_i is the number of routing elements in the bounding box of the net N_i, and T_i is the number of terminals. The number of terminals versus the number of nets is plotted in log-log scale for a few large benchmark circuits in Figure 1(a). We can observe that a vast majority of nets have small number of terminals (2-25), and there are a few nets that have very large number of terminals (> 1000). Since the fGREP method's runtime complexity is proportional to the total number of terminals, large runtimes are incurred when large nets are considered. This observation is clearly highlighted by the Fig 1(b), which plots the distribution of the average runtime per net of the fGREP method with respect to the number of terminals per net.

From the above discussions it is apparent that a few high-fanout nets collectively bring down the performance of the fGREP method by increasing the total runtime. In this paper we analyze the fGREP method to identify the problem areas and propose two new formulations that overcome these problems and compare the results with fGREP [1] and VPR [2]. The new formulations are derived from the first principles

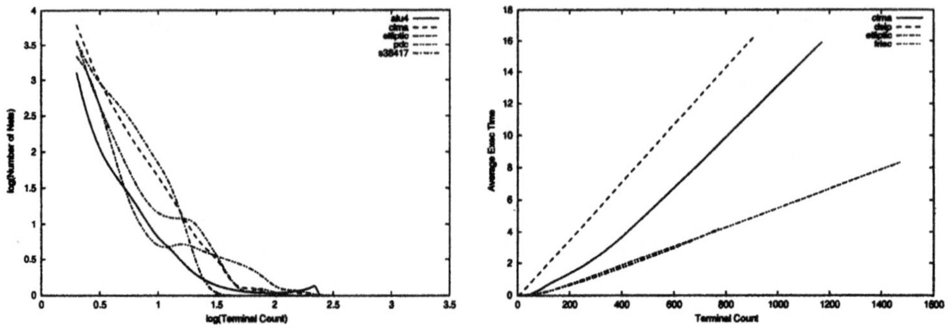

Terminal Count Vs Number of Nets

Terminal Count Vs Avg. Execution time

Fig. 1. Distribution of nets (a) and avg. execution time (b) with respect to the number of terminals

of fGREP and are not simple extensions to it. Based on these new formulations we propose a new method that is far superior to fGREP with respect to runtime while producing similar estimates.

3 fGREP Methodology

fGREP is a theoretical routability estimation method based on the concept of *routing flexibility* over the routing elements. The routing fabric of the FPGA is modeled as a graph $G(V, E)$, where V represents the channels in the FPGA and E represents the switchboxes. For each $v_i, v_j \in V$, there exists an edge $< v_i, v_j > \in E$ iff channel v_i and channel v_j share a switch box between them. fGREP defines routing flexibility as the number of alternative paths available for routing a net. If P^k is the set of all possible paths for a net $n_k \in N$, where N is the netlist and $P_i^k \subseteq P^k$ is the set of paths that are incident on a routing element e_i, then according to fGREP, the routing demand on e_i due to n_k is,

$$D_k^i = \frac{|P_k^i|}{|P^i|} \tag{1}$$

fGREP proposes that this routing demand is proportional to a quantity defined as the *terminal demand*. Using this, fGREP calculates the routing demand of a net without actually enumerating all the paths. This is explained below.

A net $n_k \in N$, is made up of a set of terminals $T_k \in V$. Every terminal $t_k^i \in T_k$, exacts a certain routing demand called the *terminal-demand*, on all the routing elements inside the net bounding box. According to fGREP, this terminal-demand on a routing element at a distance of $l = q$ from the terminal is proportional to the total number of elements at the same distance l from the terminal. The distance metric is measured on a breadth-first search tree on the routing graph, with the terminal as the root. The set of equidistant ($l = q$) routing elements from a terminal t_k^i, is defined as the level set,

$$LS_k^{iq} = \{v_j \in V | l_{ij} = q\} \tag{2}$$

The terminal-demand on the routing element v_j is then,

$$TD_k^{ij} = \frac{1}{|LS_k^{iq}|}; where, l_{ij} = q \tag{3}$$

fGREP then derives a quantity called the *net-demand* for all routing elements inside the net bounding box. The net-demand of v_j is defined as the terminal-demand due to the terminal with the lowest value for the distance metric l_{ij}.

$$ND_k^j = TD_k^{ij} | l_{ij} = min(\forall_i l_{ij}) \tag{4}$$

The final *routing-demand* on the routing element v_j due to all the nets in the netlist is then defined as,

$$D^j = \sum_{k=1}^{\#nets} ND_k^j \tag{5}$$

3.1 Illustration of fGREP

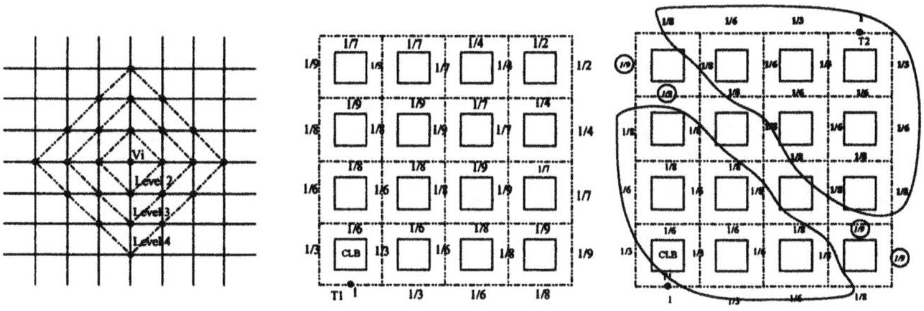

a) Levels In a Routing Graph b) Demands due to a terminal T1 c) Interaction of Multiple Terminals

Fig. 2. fGREP - Illustration of Level and Demands

Fig 2(a) shows a hypothetical routing graph, on which v_i is the current root vertex. The vertices at the same level from v_i are all shown to be connected by dotted lines. Fig 2(b) shows a terminal of a two terminal net, on the FPGA layout. The routing demands on the channels due to the terminal are also shown. All the channels at the same level q get the same demand value $1/|LS_{iq}|$. Fig 2(c) shows the interaction of the terminals of a two terminal net. The demand entries in regular typeface are those due to terminal v_1 and those in boldface are due to terminal v_2. The entries with circles on them are equidistant from both the terminals, and are on the border of regions of influence of both the terminals. The maximum of the demands due to two terminals is assigned for them, which in this case happens to have the same value of $1/9$.

4 New Formulation

It can be observed that the operation of calculating the net demand as described in Eqn 4, partitions the net bounding box into *Zones* of influence, around each terminal. These zones correspond to the voronoi regions of the terminals. Fig 2(c) shows the zoning effect for a two terminal net and Fig 3 shows the zoning effect for a generic multi-terminal net. Inside a zone, only one terminal, called the *Master-Terminal* exacts the maximum demand and is responsible for the routing demand. In other zones, its contribution to the routing demand value is zero. Hence, the search space for a terminal can theoretically be limited to within its zone alone, instead of the entire bounding box. If this were possible, the runtime complexity per net will become $O(|E|)$ instead of $O(|E| \times |T|)$, thereby providing tremendous speedup over fGREP for high-fanout nets.

4.1 Clipping and Fragmenting of the Search Wavefront

The zone limited search technique cannot be directly applied to the fGREP method. fGREP relies on the enumeration of the level set as explained in Eqn 2. The level sets are identified by starting a breadth-first search from the terminal. At each step of the search, the current elements form a wavefront, which expands outwards with each step of the breadth-first search. By limiting the search to within the terminal's zone alone, fragmenting and clipping of the wavefront can occur. This has the effect of reducing the level set size and produce artificially high demand values.

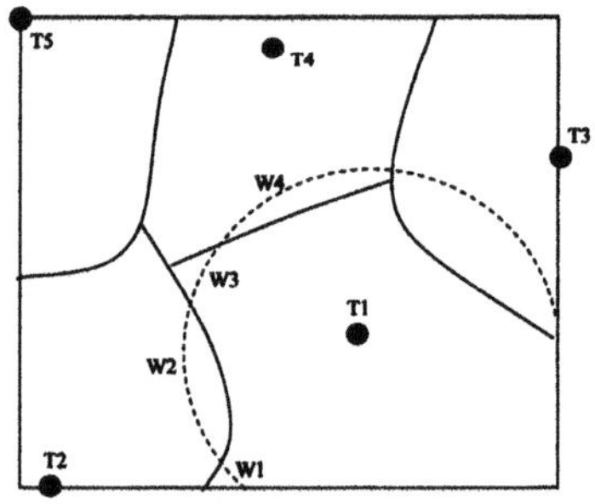

Fig. 3. Illustration of Zones, Wavefront Clipping and Fragmentation

Fig 3 illustrates the clipping and fragmenting of the search wavefront. The wavefront for the terminal T_1 is shown by the dotted line. The zones are marked by solid lines. It can be seen that the wavefront W of T_1 is divided into 4 arcs, two of which (W_1 and W_3) are inside T_1's zone while the other two (W_2 and W_4) are outside the zone. According to fGREP, the cardinality of the level set at this distance will be $|W_1|+|W_3|$, which is far less than that of the complete wavefront. This will produce very high demands for the routing elements on this wavefront, which is clearly erroneous.

Any method that attempts to use the zone limitation technique must handle this scenario. To use zone limited search, first the zones of all the terminals have to be identified. Parallel breadth-first search from all the terminals of a net can be used to identify the zones in a cost effective manner. In the following sections, we propose two methods that calculate the routing element demands along with zone limiting while taking care of the clipping effect.

5 fGREP-P : Zone Limited Path Enumeration

The first method is based on the fundamental principle of the fGREP method, as explained by Eqn 1. fGREP attempts to find the ratio of the number of paths incident on a routing element to the total number of possible paths. But, fGREP did not enumerate the actual paths and used a key result, whereby the *level-set* served the purpose. The second method for routing demand estimation with zone limited search uses this underlying principle.

For a net n_k, the zone z_i of each terminal t_i is first identified. The routing elements in the zone constitute a graph G_i, which is a sub-graph of the routing graph G. The number of paths incident on each vertex $v_j \in G_i$ and the total number of paths are calculated. This is done by performing a depth first traversal from the terminal to the boundaries of the zone. All traversals are performed in only one direction - outwards from the terminal and towards the zone boundary. The routing element demand is then calculated as per Eqn 1. By not using the level-sets, this method is free from the clipping & fragmenting effects and also performs true zone limited search.

5.1 Algorithm and Complexity Analysis

The runtime complexity of the algorithm is of the order of the number of paths present from the root vertex of the DFS traversal to the boundary of the zone. The number of paths can grow exponentially with the distance from the root vertex to the boundary. So, this method is suitable only for small zones. For large nets with high-fanout, the number of terminals are very high and the zones are very small, of the order of a few CLBs. But for low fan-out nets with big bounding box sizes, the runtime will be very high.

6 fGREP-U : Parallel Search with Unclipped Wavefront

In this method, we perform parallel breadth first traversal from all terminals of a net. The terminals are assigned as the root vertices for the traversal and individual waves are propagated from all terminals simultaneously, one step at a time. The effects of wavefront clipping and fragmenting are removed by maintaining the complete wavefront for all terminals as long as at least one routing element is still contained in its zone. If at any stage, no part of the wavefront is inside the terminal's zone, then further search for that terminal is halted. The whole process comes to an end when all terminals get dropped out in this manner. This method performs zone identification and demand calculation simultaneously.

```
Procedure fGREP-P (netlist N, target architecture A, placement):
  Build routing graph G(V, E) from target architecture A;
  Read Netlist and Placement information;
  for each net n_k ∈ N do
    Calculate the bounding box of the net;
    Identify the zones Z of all terminals T;
    for each terminal T_i ∈ T;
      set dfs_que = vertex v_i corresponding to T_i;
      while dfs_que not empty, do;
        pop dfs_que front and find its children C ∈ Z_i;
        if branching occurs
          increment num_of_incident_paths for all predecessors and increment total_paths;
        end if;
        add children to dfs_que;
      end while; –end of dfs traversal
      for all routing elements in Z_i
        routing_element_demand = number_of_incident_paths / total_paths;
      end for;
    end for; –end of all terminals
    Add demand_for_net to global_demand;
  end for; –end of all nets
  return global_demand;
End Procedure fGREP-P
```

Fig. 4. fGREP-P : Routing Demand Estimation Procedure using Zone Limited Path Enumeration

6.1 Unclipped Search Wavefront

The routing elements in the wavefront of a terminal v_i can be either inside or outside the zone z_i of v_i. The elements inside the zone are called in-zone elements and those that are outside the zone are called out-zone elements. For the next stage generation, all routing elements in the wavefront are used, irrespective of their zones. Similarly, the level set is composed of all the elements in the wavefront and the routing element demand is calculated from the complete level set. However, the routing elements not in the zone z_i, do not get a demand value.

$$LS_{iq} = LS_{iq}^{in-zone} \cup LS_{iq}^{out-zone} \tag{6}$$

$$D_{ij} = \begin{cases} 0 & ; v_j \notin z_i \\ \frac{1}{|LS_{iq}|} & ; v_j \in z_i \end{cases} \tag{7}$$

6.2 Algorithm and Complexity Analysis

The runtime complexity is not strictly of the order of $O(|E|)$. The wavefronts have to be maintained in their entirety, as long as at least one element is inside the zone, and

```
Procedure fGREP-U (netlist N, target architecture A, placement):
    Build routing graph G(V, E) from target architecture A;
    Read Netlist and Placement information;
    for each net n_i ∈ N do
        Calculate the bounding box of the net;
        Create a BFS que for each terminal v_i and add v_i as the root;
        while at least a single terminal has in-zone children, do;
            for each terminal v_i, do
              Find the number of children C in the next level
              If all children are out-zone (visited from other terminals), drop terminal v_i;
              Calculate routing element demand due to v_i as 1/|C|;
              for each in-zone child
                 Update demand_for_net;
              end for; -end of update demand
            end for; -end of one bfs step for one terminal
        end while; -end of bfs search for all terminals
        Add demand_for_net to global_demand;
    end for; -end of all nets
    return global_demand;
End Procedure fGREP_U
```

Fig. 5. fGREP-U : Routing Demand Estimation Procedure using Unclipped Search Wavefront method

hence there is an overshoot beyond the zone boundaries. The worst case occurs when two terminals are on the opposite sides of the bounding box. In this case, the wavefront of either terminal has to propagate to the other side, incurring an extra runtime penalty of $|E|/2$, per terminal. However, the average case is much better, especially for large high-fanout nets. Higher the number of terminals, the smaller the zones and lesser is the overshoot.

7 Observation

The Table 1 compares the estimation quality of the two newly proposed methods with fGREP and VPR's detailed route results. The maximum channel width W is the comparison factor. The fGREP-U method produces estimates identical to the original fGREP estimates. The table also shows that the estimation quality of the fGREP-P (zone limited path enumeration) is very bad when compared with fGREP. This unexpected behavior can be attributed to the following reason. fGREP-P calculates the routing demand using the Eqn 1, by enumerating all the paths within a terminal's zone of influence. Depending on the shape of the zones, routing elements near the boundary may be used by very few paths leading to very high demands. This results in overall routing demands that are significantly higher than fGREP's. Unless this side-effect can be countered, the fGREP-P method is not very usable.

Ckt	W_{vpr}	W_f	W_{f-U}	W_{f-P}
alu4	11	9.686	9.686	14.671
apex2	12	10.916	10.916	15.557
apex4	13	12.008	12.008	16.369
diffeq	8	8.873	8.873	13.322
dsip	7	7.550	7.550	10.265
elliptic	11	10.519	10.519	17.606
ex5p	14	12.876	12.876	17.806
misex3	11	10.673	10.673	14.611
s298	8	8.292	8.292	12.466
seq	12	10.978	10.978	15.352

Table 1. *Estimation Quality : Channel Width*

8 Experimentation

We have implemented fGREP, fGREP-U and fGREP-P methods for a generic FPGA architecture as defined in VPR [2]. The implementation was done in C and was executed on a standard Pentium 800MHz system running Linux. To evaluate the quality of the estimation, we use the FPGA physical design suite VPR. Most of the runtime options to VPR were set to their default values. The only changes made were to set the number of I/O pads per row(column) to 1 (*io_rat = 1*) in the FPGA architecture description file, 4lut_sanitized.arch and set the router option to search for routes only inside the bounding box (*bb_fac = 0*). The FPGA architecture has 4-input LUTs, switch-box flexibility $F_s = 3$, and connection-box flexibility $F_c = 1$. VPR is first run in *place_only* mode for all the circuits to get the placement. The estimation methods use the placed circuits and produce routing demand estimation on a channel by channel basis. Then, VPR is run in the *route_only* mode with breadth_first router algorithm to produce actual global and detailed routes. The fGREP estimates and the VPR's routed results are compared on a channel-by-channel basis and the mean and standard deviation of the differences, over all the channels are calculated.

9 Results

We used 20 largest circuits from the ISCAS-89 benchmark set. The benchmarks, their characteristics and the results are tabulated in the Table 2. W_v, W_f, W_{f-U} are respectively the peak channel width predicted by VPR, fGREP, and fGREP-U. T_f and T_{f-U} are the runtimes in seconds for fGREP and fGREP-U respectively. T_v is the runtime for VPR's detailed router to route on a device with a maximum channel width of W_v. The column headed by μ lists the mean of the difference between routing demand of fGREP-U and that of VPR's detailed router, over all the channels. The column headed by σ lists the standard deviation of the differences. This reporting method is consistent with that reported in [14]. The estimation results produced by fGREP-U are same as those of fGREP and hence W_{f-U} is not tabulated.

The results highlight the fact that *fGREP-U*, the newly proposed method of estimating FPGA routability is very fast compared to fGREP and also very close to the actual detailed route results from VPR. Overall, *fGREP-U* is approximately 17 times faster than fGREP and 102 times faster than VPR's detailed router.

Name	Cells	Nets	W_v	W_f	μ	σ	T_v	T_f	T_{f-U}
alu4	1523	1536	11	9.686	1.4896	1.1180	38	5.2472	0.2677
apex2	1879	1916	12	10.916	1.7240	1.3199	59	4.9357	0.4845
apex4	1263	1271	13	12.008	1.9701	1.4474	43	2.6261	0.2514
bigkey	1708	1935	9	7.720	0.5762	0.7338	101	49.7068	2.7890
clma	8384	8444	13	11.910	1.7633	1.2846	549	121.3537	6.2520
des	1592	1847	8	8.070	0.5905	0.6482	76	27.5926	3.7043
diffeq	1498	1560	8	8.873	1.1213	0.8172	23	2.4776	0.2023
dsip	1371	1598	7	7.550	0.4243	0.6808	181	56.9334	2.8054
elliptic	3605	3734	11	10.519	1.4145	1.0699	237	20.2369	0.9475
ex1010	4599	4608	12	11.261	1.6783	1.2393	131	35.3223	1.4693
ex5p	1065	1072	14	12.876	1.9141	1.4937	35	1.9600	0.2028
frisc	3557	3575	14	12.331	1.7388	1.3249	150	15.2451	1.0821
misex3	1398	1411	11	10.673	1.5866	1.1978	45	3.3300	0.0563
pdc	4576	4591	16	16.236	2.1965	1.5740	460	36.5067	2.5079
s298	1932	1934	8	8.292	1.1876	0.8572	60	10.0832	0.2777
s38417	6407	6434	8	8.747	1.1100	0.8204	203	28.3561	1.3714
s38584.1	6448	6484	9	8.725	1.1156	0.8526	248	45.0922	1.4954
seq	1751	1791	12	10.978	1.7512	1.3048	53	4.1382	0.3900
spla	3691	3706	15	12.838	2.0554	1.4984	132	20.3293	1.4919
tseng	1048	1098	6	7.407	0.9336	0.7322	28	2.4219	0.1484

Table 2. *Results for the 20 largest ISCAS-89 Circuits*

10 Conclusion

In this paper we analyzed our earlier routability estimation method called fGREP, identified the causes for its high execution times for large designs and proposed two solutions to alleviate the problem. One of the solutions, the fGREP-U method turned out to be very useful. On an average, it is 17 times faster than fGREP and 102 times faster than VPR, while producing estimates that are within 4% of actual detailed routes produced by VPR. In most cases our method is correctly able to predict the peak (local) routing demand (also called as channel width) and the routing demand for each and every channel in the FPGA. The *Mean* and *Std.Deviation* gives even greater confidence that our prediction is very close to how the overall routing would be performed.

References

[1] Parivallal Kannan, Shankar Balachandran, and Dinesh Bhatia, "fGREP - Fast Generic routing Demand Estimation for Placed FPGA Circuits," in *11th International Workshop on Field-Programmable Logic and Applications, FPL.* August 2001, Springer-Verlag, Berlin.
[2] Vaughn Betz and Jonathan Rose, "VPR: A New Packing, Placement and Routing Tool for FPGA research," in *Field-Programmable Logic and Applications.* Sep 1997, pp. 213–222, Springer-Verlag, Berlin.
[3] H. B. Bakoglu, *Circuits, Interconnections, and Packaging for VLSI,* Addison Wesley, Reading, MA, 1990.
[4] H. Van Marck, D. Stroobandt, and J. Van Campenhout, "Toward an Extension of Rent's Rule for Describing Local Variations in Interconnection Complexity," in *Proceedings of the 4th International Conference for Young Computer Scientists,* 1995, pp. 136–141.
[5] G. Parthasarathy, M. Marek-Sadaowska, and A. Mukherjee, "Interconnect Complexity-aware FPGA Placement Using Rent's Rule," in *Proc. Intl. Workshop on System Level Interconnect Prediction (SLIP),* April 2001.
[6] Wei Li, "Routability Prediction for Hierarchical FPGAs," in *Proc. Great Lakes Symposium on VLSI,* 1999.
[7] R. Kastner X. Yang and M. Sarrafzadeh, "Congestion Estimation During Top-down Placement," in *Proceedings of the 2001 International Symposium on Physical Design (ISPD),* 2001.
[8] Abbas A. El Gamal, "Two-Dimensional Stochastic Model for Interconnections in Master Slice Integrated Circuits," *IEEE Trans. CAS.,* Feb 1981.
[9] S.Brown, J.Rose, and Z.G.Vranesic, "A Stochastic Model to Predict the Routability of Field Programmable Gate Arrays," *IEEE Transactions on CAD,* pp. 1827–1838, Dec 1993.
[10] S. Krishnamoorthy J. Lou and H.S. Sheng, "Estimating Routing Congestion using Probabilistic Analysis," in *Proceedings of the 2001 International Symposium on Physical Design (ISPD),* 2001.
[11] Shankar Balachandran, Parivallal Kannan, and Dinesh Bhatia, "On Routing Demand and Congestion Estimation for FPGAs," in *Proc. 15th Intl. Conf. on VLSI Design and 7th ASP-DAC,* January 2002.
[12] S. Mantik A.B. Kahng and D. Stroobandt, "Requirements for Models of Achievable Routing," in *Proceedings of the 2000 International Symposium on Physical Design (ISPD),* 2000.
[13] L. Scheffer and E. Nequist, "Why Interconnect Prediction doesnt Work," in *Proc. Intl. Workshop on System Level Interconnect Prediction (SLIP),* April 2000.
[14] Parivallal Kannan, Shankar Balachandran, and Dinesh Bhatia, "On Metrics for Comparing Routability Estimation Methods for FPGAs," in *Proc. 39th DAC,* June 2002.

Integrated Iterative Approach to FPGA Placement*

Martin Daněk and Zdeněk Muzikář

Dept. of Computer Science and Engineering, Czech Technical University in Prague
Karlovo nám. 13,
121 35 Praha 2, Czech Republic
{danek,muzikar}@fel.cvut.cz

Abstract. This paper describes a new iterative method based on an integrated timing-driven approach to the FPGA layout synthesis. The method uses a global routing to assess the quality of a placement. The placement and routing algorithms use a unified nonlinear cost function that takes into account both area and delay constraints imposed by a design, and eliminates effects of different signal net routing orders.

1 Introduction

Field-programmable gate arrays (FPGAs) provide a flexible and efficient way of synthesizing complex logic. Their drawback is that the performance of implemented circuits is rather poor when compared to ASICs. New performance-driven design algorithms are one way to improve this situation. This paper presents an iterative method that is based on an integrated design style that merges together the placement and global routing phases.

The rest of the paper is organized as follows: the traditional design cycle is briefly described in Section 2, Section 3 contains problem analysis, Section 4 describes the solution proposed, and experimental results are presented in Section 5.

2 Traditional Design Cycle

The input to the physical design cycle is an abstract logical description of a circuit (a netlist) and the output is its layout (locations of all blocks and detailed routes of all nets). Typically, physical design proceeds in several steps [3]: technology mapping – placement – global routing – detailed routing. Further we will focus our attention on placement and global routing.

The aim of *placement* is to determine legal locations of all blocks in the FPGA while optimizing routability (and/or delay, power). The placement problem can be solved either by *constructive methods*, which build up a legal placement from

* This research has been partially supported by the Czech Technical University under grant no. CTU0210413

M. Glesner, P. Zipf, and M. Renovell (Eds.): FPL 2002, LNCS 2438, pp. 253–262, 2002.

scratch by optimizing a cost function that takes into account previously placed blocks, or by *iterative methods*, which repeatedly modify a given placement while improving a cost function based on an estimation of the total wire length and/or local density of wires [3]. In practice, a combination of both approaches is often used. First, an *initial placement* is generated using a constructive algorithm. Next, a sequence of *replacements* is applied in order to improve the quality of the initial placement.

Global routing is a preliminary planning stage for detailed routing. It deals with a *global model* [3] of routing resources that consist of segmented wire *channels*. The primary objective is to avoid channel overflow.

The classical decomposition of the design process to a sequence of independent subproblems doesn't reduce the problem complexity, because all these subproblems are still NP-hard [3]. This leads to suboptimality, even if all the subproblems are solved optimally. Moreover, the rigid and quite complex structure of routing resources of current FPGAs is not usually taken into account in the placement and global routing phases of common algorithms. Placement algorithms usually work with a bounding box, or some other pre-computed approximation of a future routing, and routing algorithms have limited possibilities to optimize wiring paths within the fixed placement [3]. As a result, the delay and routability constraints cannot be treated properly.

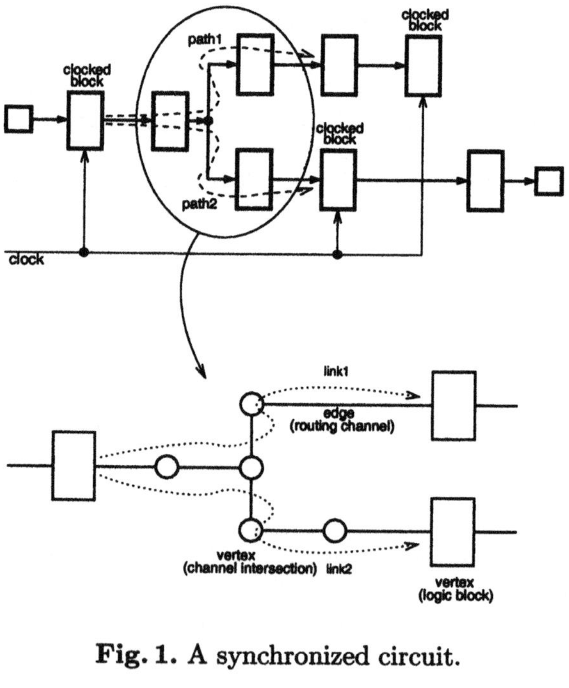

Fig. 1. A synchronized circuit.

3 Problem Analysis

In order to avoid disadvantages of the traditional approach, [2] proposed to integrate placement and global routing into one compound problem. The main idea is to generate an initial placement using a method described in [5], and then to further improve it by iterative replacements, where the quality of each partial result is measured by a cost function. The cost function originates from a relatively precise estimation of a detailed topology of all nets via global routing. This allows us to take into account both routability and timing issues.

3.1 Timing Analysis

The performance of the chip is determined partly by the delays of the blocks used and partly by the delays of the interconnecting wires. One of the characteristics of FPGAs is the dominating influence of wire delays rather than logic block delays [1]. Obviously, the placement and routing may influence wire delays substantially.

The performance of synchronized circuits is determined by the clock frequency. The upper part of Fig.1 shows an example of such a circuit. A preliminary timing analysis can identify all *paths* between a clocked source block and clocked target blocks. Then the maximum signal delays for all paths can be derived from the required clock frequency.

The lower part of Fig.1 shows a representation of one net in the environment of a *global model*. The net is formed by a set of *links*. A link is a collection of edges (channel segments) and vertices (channel segment crossings) that interconnect two logic blocks.

The delay of each link and path can be estimated with a relatively good precision [4]. This allows us to control the process of placement and global routing so that a detailed router has a good chance to meet all timing requirements expressed in terms of maximum delays for all signal paths.

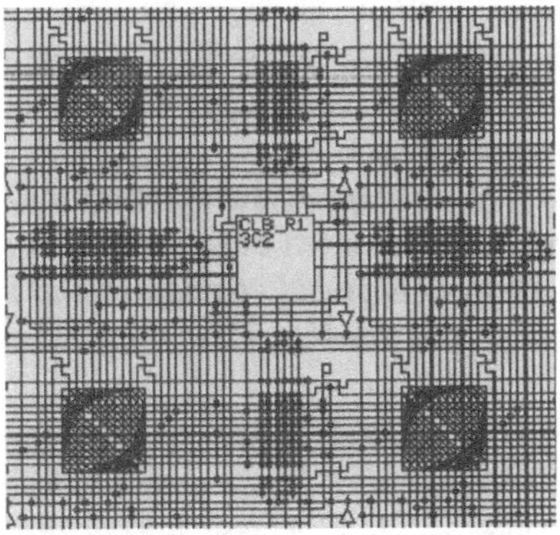

Fig. 2. XC4000 - internal structure.

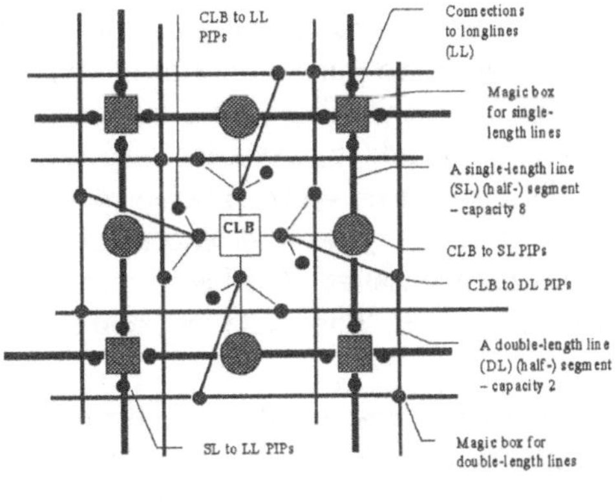

Fig. 3. XC4000 - global routing graph [4].

3.2 Problem Formulation

A circuit to be designed is represented by a set of *blocks* $B = \{B_1, B_2, ..., B_b\}$, and a set of *nets* $N = \{N_1, N_2, ..., N_k\}$, where $N_i \subseteq B$. Each block B_i is labeled by its type T_j.

An FPGA environment is modelled by a *global graph* $G = (V, E)$, where vertices in V represent FPGA logic blocks and certain routing resources, e.g. channel intersections (see Figures 1, 2, 3, and [4]). The remaining routing resources (typically routing channel segments) are represented by edges from E. Each vertex and edge of G is labeled by its capacity C_i and delay Y_i. Each net $N_i \in N$ is modelled by a connected subgraph S_i of G containing all vertices from $V_i \subset V_B$, i.e. by the corresponding Steiner tree.

A placement $P : B \rightarrow V_B$ is a mapping of blocks, and a corresponding global routing $R = (S_1, S_2, ..., S_k)$ is a set of Steiner trees for placement P. A solution of a timing-driven placement and global routing problem is any pair (P, R) where P represents admissible (compatible and not overlapping) placement.

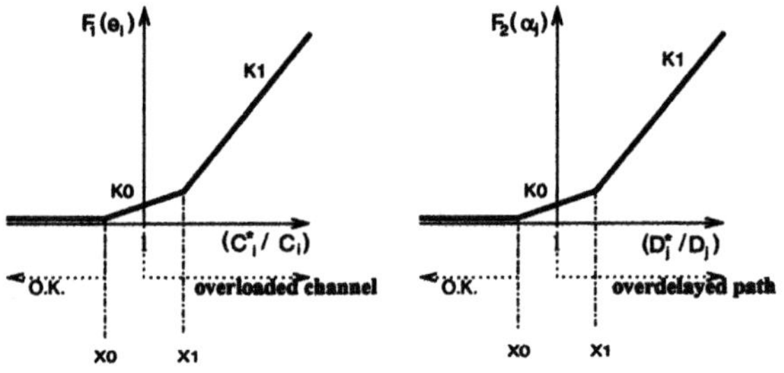

Fig. 4. The integrated cost function, capacity and delay constituents.

3.3 Integrated Cost Function

The primary objective of placement and global routing tasks in an FPGAs environment is to guarantee *routability*, which means that restrictions determined by predefined routing resources must be satisfied. The secondary objective is to guarantee (and/or maximize) the required *performance*.

[5] introduced an integrated cost function $c(P, R)$ to measure the quality of a constructively generated placement. The function considers both routability and performance issues. It is based on a construction of a *global routing sketch* R for a placement P. The same function is used here to control iterative replacements.

Routability Issues If a global routing sketch R has been constructed, then for each edge $e_i \in E$ (each routing channel) with capacity C_i it is possible to compute a *demand* C_i^* as the number of Steiner trees $S_1, S_2, ...S_k$ containing the edge e_i. A given routing sketch is considered as routable if $C_i^* \leq C_i$ for any edge e_i [3].

Performance Issues A net $N_i \in N$ consists of a set of blocks $\{B_0, B_1, ..., B_n\}$, where $n \geq 1$. Let the block B_0 be a signal source, the others are targets. A net can be decomposed into a collection $L = l_1, l_2, ..., l_n$ of source–target connections, called *links* (see Fig.1): $l_1 = (B_0, B_1), l_2 = (B_0, B_2), \ldots, l_n = (B_0, B_n)$.

During a preliminary timing analysis maximal delays D_j for all *paths* $\mathcal{L}_j$ are generated. Let $\mathcal{P} = \{\mathcal{L}_1, \mathcal{L}_2, ..., \mathcal{L}_n\}$ be a set of all paths. Let the path $\mathcal{L}_j$ be formed by a sequence $B_{j0}, l_{j1}, B_{j1}, l_{j2}, ..., l_{jk}, B_{jk}$ of links and blocks where B_{j0} is a clocked source block and B_{jk} is a clocked target block (see Fig. 1).

The actual delay d^*_{ji} of a link $l_{ji} \in \mathcal{L}_j$ for a given routing sketch R can be estimated using a linear or an Elmore model [4]. The actual delay D^*_j of a path $\mathcal{L}_j$ is then estimated as a sum of delays of links and blocks that form the path. A given routing sketch R is considered admissible from the performance point of view if $D^*_j \leq D_j$ for any path $\mathcal{L}_j$.

The above observations lead to the following cost function [2]:

$$c(P,R) = \sum_{e_i \in E} F_1(e_i) + \alpha \sum_{\mathcal{L}_j \in \mathcal{P}} F_2(\mathcal{L}_j), \tag{1}$$

where α is a constant and $F_1 = f(C_i, C^*_i), F_2 = g(D_j, D^*_j)$ are nonlinear functions. Notice that F_1, or F_2, should grow rapidly when the demand C^*_i is greater than the channel capacity C_i, or when the delay estimation D^*_j is greater than the given limit D_j (see Figure 4), respectively.

4 Integrated Placement and Global Routing Algorithm

The integrated approach [2] is based on measuring the quality of a placement by a cost function that captures the properties of future topology of signal nets. The cost function is used for controlling iterative replacements.

4.1 Initial Placement and Initial Global Routing

The first phase of the algorithm is an initial placement together with its initial global routing [5]. As the final solution quality and the time complexity of iterative algorithms depend on the initial solution, a good initial phase is required.

Initial Placement The aim of this step is to construct an admissible placement in a short time. A constructive cluster-growth algorithm [3] is used. The task is decomposed into two steps: *block sorting* and *consecutive placement.*

Initial Global Routing Global routing [3] is a fundamental part of the approach because it allows to measure the quality of a given placement reliably. It is based on a Steiner tree construction performed sequentially for each net. This process consists of two phases [2]: initial routing and rerouting. The cost function used in the *first phase* minimizes only the total delay, channel capacities are not taken into account. This means that *the order of net routing does not* *influence the result* and that the minimum delay paths are constructed. However, the resulting routing sketch need not be routable.

The *second phase* takes all previously routed nets into account in order to balance routability and performance issues. The nets are sorted in an ascending order according to their costs (i.e. delays) and then for each net, the corresponding Steiner tree $S_j = (V_j, E_j)$, $V_j \subseteq V$, $E_j \subseteq E$ for net N_j is removed and again constructed while the following cost function is minimized:

$$c(S_j) = k_1 \sum_{e_i \in E_j} F_1(e_i) + k_2 \sum_{l_i \in L_j} d_i^* + k_3 \sum_{e_i \in E_j, v_i \in V_j} F_3(e_i, v_i) \,, \tag{2}$$

F_1 reflects the available capacity of edges used for the Steiner tree construction, d_i^* is the actual delay of the link l_i and F_3 adds a penalty for unnecessary usage of especially "precious" routing resources (such as longlines).

4.2 Replacement and Rerouting

The global routing provides an evaluation of the previously performed placement according to the function (1) which becomes a guideline for the replacement process. The replacement uses *generalized pairwise interchanges* to generate new, possibly better placements. To speed up the process, only the appropriate nets that are affected by the replacement process are rerouted (according to Equation 2), and affected signal path delays are adjusted. Currently we are testing a greedy approach that accepts new placements only if they are better than previous ones.

The replacement and rerouting is repeated until no improvement in the value of the cost function (1) can be reached.

Mnemonics	Value	Comment
F1 X0	0.60	First breaking point
F1 K0	3	Tangent after the first breaking point
F1 X1	1.1	Second breaking point
F1 K1	5	Tangent after the second breaking point
F2 X0	0.6	First breaking point
F2 K0	3.578	Tangent after the first breaking point
F2 X1	1.1	Second breaking point
F2 K1	7.4	Tangent after the second breaking point

Table 1. Definition of the cost function - F1 and F2 approximations by partially linear functions.

5 Experimental Evaluation

In order to be able to perform experiments in a real world environment, we decided to use Xilinx XC4000 family FPGAs and the tools from the Xilinx

Name	Type	Chip	#Blks	#Nets	#Pins	#Paths	CLBs/IOs
cu	Comb	4003	41	30	116	76	16 / 41 %
dk16	Seq	4003	107	121	640	696	99 / 9 %
ex1	Seq	4003	121	114	635	1127	92 / 46 %
keyb	Seq	4003	112	151	816	1156	100 / 16 %
minm	Seq	4003	77	107	451	29612	63 / 19 %
mux	Comb	4003	38	37	124	141	16 / 36 %
s1a	Seq	4003	117	141	782	942	100 / 24 %
top	Seq	4003	125	177	777	13164	100 / 37 %
ttt2	Comb	4003	145	158	726	987	100 / 73 %
alu2	Comb	4005	172	215	1009	31021	79 / 26 %
alu4	Comb	4005	218	344	1655	94154	100 / 36 %
planet	Seq	4005	224	251	1445	3174	99 / 44 %
sand	Seq	4005	218	250	1455	2776	99 / 34 %
styr	Seq	4005	206	216	1314	2168	93 / 32 %
term1	Comb	4005	193	194	904	1591	76 / 72 %

Table 2. Benchmark circuits used in experiments. Column 3 shows the size of the target device (XC400xPC84-5). Columns 4-8 show the number of gates and flip-flops, number of signal nets, number of pins over all nets, number of combinational paths, and FPGA utilisation.

XACT 5.2.1 system to perform mapping and detailed routing. Unfortunately, we were unable to fully guide the Xilinx detailed router by the recommendations provided by our global router (we were only able to lock block placements) - this is a clear disadvantage. On the other hand, a comparison to a commercially available tool is, in our opinion, more convincing than a comparison to other experimental algorithms/tools described elsewhere.

5.1 Strategy of Testing

The experiments consisted of processing and implementing a subset of standard MCNC benchmarks (see Table 2). Each benchmark was implemented in the smallest XC4000 chip that was able to contain it in order to deal with dense problems.

First, all benchmarks were implemented using just the standard XACT design tools, this way we got reference values. Then we processed the benchmarks with our tool, and fed the results to the XACT system to get real routability and delay data. We were interested in results after performing initial placement, and after each iteration performed by our tool to check how our critical signal path estimation corresponded to the one pinpointed by XACT.

The cost function (1) used in the experiments was defined as follows:

$$c(P,R) = 0.2 \sum_{e_i \in E} F_1(e_i) + 30 \max_{\mathcal{L}_j \in \mathcal{P}} (D_j^*) \qquad (3)$$

where F_1, F_2 were defined according to Table 1 (also see Figure 4).

The cost function (2) used for the construction of the Steiner tree was defined as follows:

$$c(S_j) = 2 \sum_{e_i \in E_j} F_1(e_i) + \sum_{l_i \in L_j} d_i^* + \sum_{e_i \in E_j, v_i \in V_j} F_3(e_i, v_i) \ , \qquad (4)$$

where $F_1(e_i)$ is the same function as in (3) and $F_3 = 4$ for longlines, otherwise $F_3 = 0$. The iterative replacement phase ended when no improvement was found, or when 42 iterations were performed, whichever appeared first.

Name	XACT	Timed				Delay estimation	
		INIT	END	Performance	Improvement	END	Error
	[ns]	[ns]	[ns]	[%]	[%]	[ns]	[%]
cu	37.90	37.70	35.10	-7.40	-6.90	31.41	-10.51
dk16	55.60	58.80	56.60	1.80	-3.70	67.63	19.49
ex1	55.50	59.40	56.10	1.10	-5.60	59.83	6.65
keyb	51.80	58.20	54.60	5.40	-6.20	68.18	24.87
minm	88.10	99.40	89.90	2.00	-9.60	115.25	28.20
mux	62.20	64.20	62.90	1.10	-2.00	66.15	5.17
s1a	51.80	54.50	49.00	-5.40	-10.10	56.01	14.31
top	109.20	118.80	109.30	0.10	-8.00	114.70	4.94
ttt2	62.70	74.20	65.30	4.10	-12.00	69.82	6.92
alu2	166.10	234.60	182.90	10.10	-22.00	164.46	-10.08
alu4	187.10	269.70	252.20	34.80	-6.50	185.14	-26.59
planet	68.30	74.60	72.10	5.60	-3.40	72.55	0.62
sand	64.60	70.60	68.90	6.70	-2.40	72.59	5.36
styr	65.90	69.00	66.70	1.20	-3.30	68.19	2.23
term1	99.90	127.20	114.70	14.80	-9.80	96.35	-16.00
Average	Excluding ALU4			2.94	-7.5		5.87
Average	All			5.07	-7.43		3.71

Table 3. Results of the integrated iterative algorithm. Negative values in columns 5,6 mean improvement.

5.2 Results

Table 3 shows results of our algorithm. All placements have been routed *successfully* by the XACT detailed router and timed by XDelay. Column 2 gives the maximum path delay (in ns) for pure XACT placements measured by XDelay, the rest of the table shows results of the integrated approach. Detailed results for the initial placement phase can be found in [5], a summary of values is provided in column 3, column 4 shows a delay value after 42 iterative replacements.

Column 5 shows that maximum path delays measured by *XDelay* for placements generated by our tool were, on average, by 2.94% (or 5.07% including ALU4) worse than the delays of XACT placements. Column 6 shows that the iterative heuristic improved the initial placements by 7.5% on average. We attribute this to the simplicity of the greedy scheme used to control the iterative process, and to a possible weakness of a pairwise interchange used for generation of new placements. Column 8 shows how the delay estimations of the final placements corresponed to the *XDelay* values.

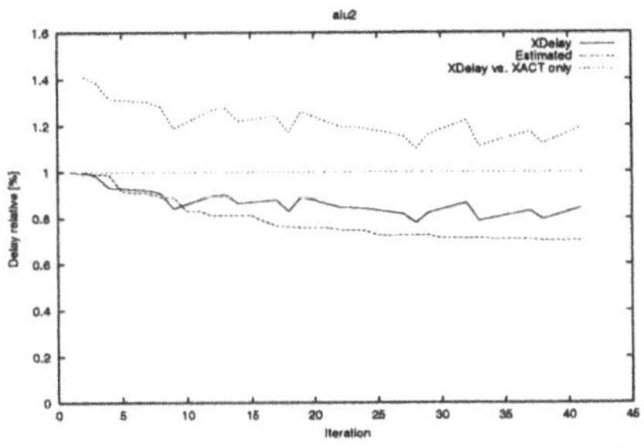

Fig. 5. Iterative improvements - trends shown for ALU2.

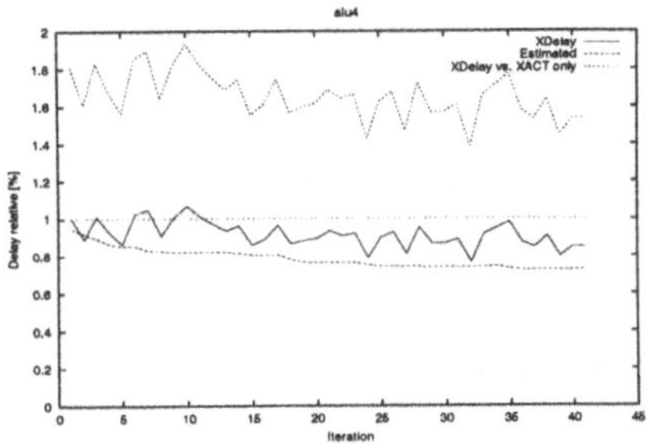

Fig. 6. Iterative improvements - trends shown for ALU4.

Although as diverse values as -26.6% to 28.2% may seem disappointing, one has to realise that rather than the absolute values, a trend of the estimation (with respect to more realistic delay values provided by *XDelay*) is critical for a correct performance of the algorithm. Typical observed trends are shown in Figures 5, 6, 7, 8.

The figures were chosen so as to demonstrate all major trends of our delay estimator. Figures 5 and 7 show a desired trend, where the estimated critical signal delay decreases almost monotonously in the same fashion as the delay calculated for the same design after detailed routing by *XDelay*.

Figure 8 shows a situation where the trend does not correspond exactly to the *XDelay* values, but is roughly the same. A similar situation is shown in Figure 6, but there the estimated delay corresponds to the lower "peaks" of the *XDelay* values. Both situations are not desirable, since there is a danger that our tool could identify signal paths that are not identical with those addressed by the detailed router.

The disagreement of trends is most probably caused by different topologies of signal networks routed by the global and detailed routers. It is highly probable that the detailed router uses some bounding-box based metrics, which would certainly result in different topologies given the integrated function used in the global router. On the other hand, it may be possible that many network topologies generated by the cost function are routed with a substantial detour (since they are not critical), which may not be desirable.

Currently we are checking this possibility by restricting the routing (using the integrated cost function) to a bounding box. Initial results support the above interpretation.

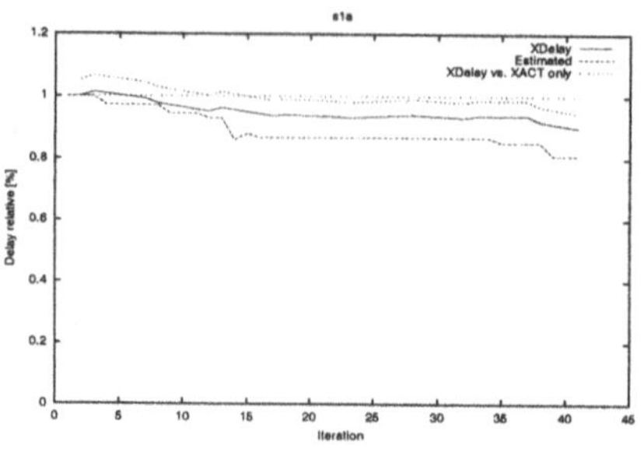

Fig. 7. Iterative improvements - trends shown for S1A.

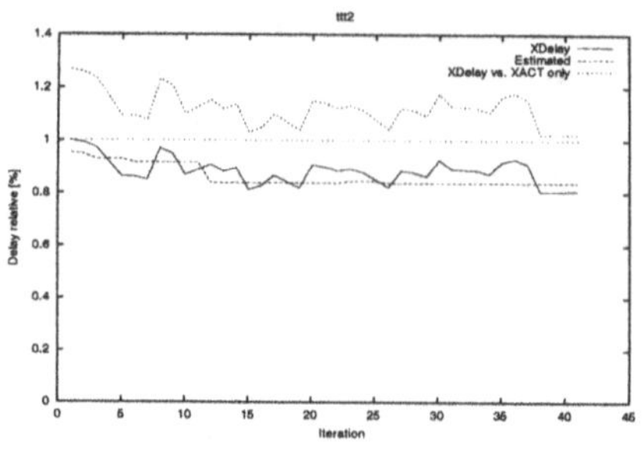

Fig. 8. Iterative improvements - trends shown for TTT2.

6 Conclusions

Common approaches to placement and routing for FPGAs usually deal with cost functions based either on a wirelength estimation by a bounding box metrics, or on architectural issues such as the maximum channel capacity needed to route a design.

This paper presents a new integrated iterative approach to layout synthesis that is based on assessing a placement by a quality of the induced routing. The routing algorithm uses a nonlinear cost function that takes into account both channel capacities and estimated signal delays. The nonlinear cost function allows situations where channel capacities are exceeded (although such cases are heavily penalised). This way it eliminates the problems of unroutable designs and routing orders present in other approaches. Real-world results have been presented for an application of the method to several benchmark circuits.

References

1. Lee,Y.S., Wu,A.C.H.: *A Performance and Routability-Driven Router for FPGA's Considering Path Delays.* IEEE Transactions on Computer Aided Design, Vol.16, No.2, February 1997, pp. 179-185.
2. Servít,M., Muzikář,Z.: *Integrated Layout Synthesis for FPGAs.* In: Field-Programmable Logic, Springer-Verlag, 1994, pp. 23-33.
3. Sherwani,N.A.: *Algorithms for VLSI Physical Design Automation.* Kluwer, Boston, 1993.
4. Daněk,M., Servít,M.: *Xilinx XC4000 Global Routing Model and Signal Delay Estimation.* In: DMMS'97 Proceedings, PANEM, 1997, pp. 213-222.
5. Daněk,M., Muzikář,Z.: *Integrated Timing-Driven Approach to the FPGA Layout.* To appear in: ICECS 2002 Proceedings, IEEE Press, 2002.

TDR: A Distributed-Memory Parallel Routing Algorithm for FPGAs

Lucídio A.F. Cabral[1], Júlio S. Aude[2](in memorium), and Nelson Maculan[3]

[1] Statistics Department, Federal University of Paraíba
Cidade Universitária, João Pessoa, PB, Brazil
lucidio@de.ufpb.br
[2] NCE/IM, Federal University of Rio de Janeiro
Ilha do Fundão, Rio de Janeiro, RJ, Brazil
[3] Systems Engineering and Computing Program, Federal University of Rio de Janeiro
Ilha do Fundão, Rio de Janeiro, RJ, Brazil
maculan@cos.ufrj.br

Abstract. This paper proposes a distributed-memory parallel routing algorithm for FPGAs based on the partitioning of the routing graph under special FPGA architectural constraints. Coarse-grain parallelism is adopted by assigning different processors to the routing of nets within different partitions of the routing graph. The experimental results have demonstrated that TDR can achieve linear and superlinear speedups in relation to the state-of-art VPR router even when it is running on an Ethernet cluster of workstations. However, it usually requires more tracks than VPR for routing the same circuit.

1 Introduction

Despite the rapid growth of FPGA circuit integration level and the computational power that can be delivered by networks of workstations or powerful parallel machines, few works have been previously reported in the literature [1], [2], [3] that tackle the FPGA routing problem by using a parallel approach. In fact, the problem complexity limits the application of any obvious parallel approach because the routing channels have fixed width and the interdependency among nets implies that net ordering is important for a successful routing process.

In this paper we present an approach that exploits parallelism under the distributed-memory paradigm as an attempt to accelerate an FPGA router. It is based on a natural decomposition of the routing graph associated with the architecture model of a class of FPGA architectures. As a result, the netlist can be divided into partitions that can be routed independently by the processors after the removal of potential conflicts in the use of logic block input pins. The resulting TDR (Track Domain Router) distributed-memory parallel algorithm [4] has produced almost linear and, in some cases, superlinear speed-ups in relation to the state-of-art VPR router on an Ethernet cluster of workstations.

This paper is organized as follows. Initially the 2D-array FPGA architecture model is described and the behavior of negotiation-based routers is briefly reviewed. Following, the TDR parallel algorithm is detailed. Then, experimental results with

M. Glesner, P. Zipf, and M. Renovell (Eds.): FPL 2002, LNCS 2438, pp. 263-270, 2002.

MCNC benchmark [5] circuits are presented and discussed. Finally, the main conclusions of the paper are summarized and some suggestions for future work are presented.

2 FPGA Architecture Model

The FPGA model is shown in Figure 1(a). It is a two-dimensional array of logic cells and routing resources. Each logic cell (L) can be configured to be an LUT (Look-Up-Table), a flip-flop, etc [6]. Wire segments for connecting logic cell pins run between the cells in vertical and horizontal channels and are aligned into tracks. In the example shown in Figure 1, there are 4 tracks per channel and each logic block has 2 pins on each side. Therefore, a vertical (horizontal) channel is a set of tracks between two consecutive columns (rows) of cells. Since wire segments are prefabricated, customization of routing resources is achieved through a proper programming of switches. Routing switches are grouped into connection (C) boxes and switch (S) boxes (Figures 1(b) and 1(c)). The C boxes contain routing switches that can be programmed to connect logic cell pins to wire segments. The termination points of wire segments are inside S boxes which contain switches that allow the connection of two wire segments. In this paper, all wire segments are assumed to have the same length (that is, every wire segment spans only one logic block). This architecture is called a *2-D (array) FPGA* [7]. All vertical and horizontal channels are assumed to have the same number of tracks, W. The tracks are numbered from top to bottom in each horizontal channel and from right to left in each vertical channel. A number assigned to each track defines the *track id*.

The flexibility of a C box, F_c, is the number of tracks a logic pin can connect to. For example, in Figure 1(b) there are three logic pins in the C box, and each pin can be connected to any of the 4 tracks in the C box. Thus, the C box flexibility is 4. The flexibility of an S box, F_s, is the number of wire segments that each segment can connect to. For example, in Figure 1(c), all possible connections for the right wire segment on track 1 are shown. It can be connected to the top segment on track 4, or bottom segment on track 1, or left segment on track 3. Suppose that all other wire segments adjacent to this S box can also connect to other 3 wire segments. In this case, the S box flexibility is 3.

In our study, the S box topology is assumed to be disjoint. This means that the wiring tracks are isolated onto disjoint domains by the switch organization. So, if all S box switches are turned on, a number of unconnected wiring groups, called *track domains*, is created. For example, a signal beginning on track 1 is restricted to have wire segments on track 1, no matter which S box switches it goes through. So, the flexibility of such S box will also be 3, but its topology will be different from the one shown in Figure 1(c). In [8] the impact of the flexibility of S and C boxes is well-studied.

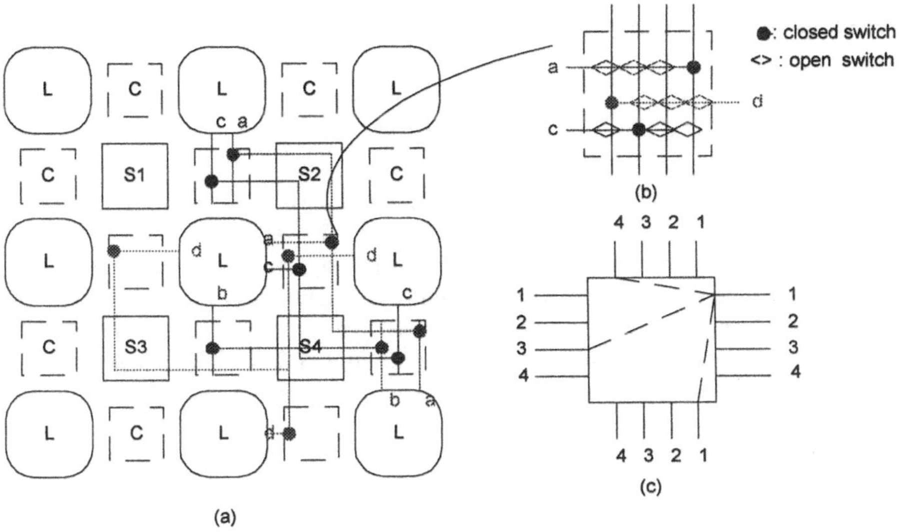

Fig. 1. (a) The routing model. (b) The C-box. (c) The S-box.

3 Negotiation-Based Routers

In order to route all the nets in a netlist it is necessary to assign a set of different routing resources to each net such that there is a Steiner tree connecting its source to all its sinks. When the set of nets is routed sequentially, the order in which the nets are routed may be critical since nets that are routed earlier may occupy some routing resources needed by another net. The main idea of the negotiation algorithm is to initially allow unlimited sharing of routing resources and repeatedly reroute nets until no resources are shared. By assigning congestion costs to the shared routing resources and by increasing these costs with each iteration through the nets, the routing algorithm encourages the use of alternative routes to be explored until all conflicts are resolved.

The negotiation-based routing paradigm was originally developed by McMurchie and Ebeling [9] and has been successfully used in a number of field-programmable FPGA routers [10], [11], [12]. Acceleration of this paradigm with the use of A* search [11], [12] and its parallelization [1] have been reported. In [2] the convergence of this paradigm is studied in detail. If we consider a parallel approach based on this paradigm, the main issue that needs to be addressed is how the maximum fidelity of the congestion costs in each channel (Connection Blocks) of the FPGA can be guaranteed. The solution to this problem requires the occupation of each Connection Block in each processor to be added up. Therefore, as the amount of communication increases better quality results may be achieved. Unfortunately, it is widely known that by increasing the amount of communication, the performance of parallel algorithms become poorer. Nowadays the state-of-art algorithm based on this paradigm is the VPR (Versatile Place and Route) algorithm [10].

4 The Track Domain Parallel Router

Since routing is a time-consuming phase of the synthesis process, it is an attractive problem to be tackled with the use of parallelism. In fact, there have been many attempts to develop parallel routers for some design styles, like standard-cell designs [13] but not as much for FPGAs. Recently, however, Chan et al [2] have presented an interesting work in which a parallel based-negotiation router has been developed for a distributed memory environment. However, their approach leads to a high amount of communication for updating the routing resource costs in each processor, particularly when large designs are considered.

Within TDR parallel approach [4], there is no need to exchange congestion costs among processors due to the complete separation of the routing graph in track domains. Therefore, the algorithm can produce considerable speedups even when the routing graph has several thousands of edges.

Let us consider the FPGA architecture model described above where the topology of the S boxes partitions the routing graph into track domains. Figure 2(a) shows a 2x2 FPGA having the channel width equal to 2. The respective track domains are illustrated in Figure 2(b) and the associated routing graph is shown in Figure 2(c).

TDR parallel routing approach consists of assigning one or more track domains and disjoint subsets of nets to each processor. Therefore, as each track domain is allocated to only one processor, the routing of a net by any particular processor does not depend on information sent by the other processors on congestion costs of routing resources. Unfortunately, routes of nets established by different processors can still conflict because logic block input pins are logically equivalent. Therefore, two or more nets connected to the inputs of a particular logic block may be routed to the same physical input pin of that logic block by different processors.

To solve this problem the routing graph is divided in as many partitions as the number of processors by assigning net_i to processor j if $i \bmod n = j$, where n is the number of processors available. Based on this partitioning, a list of forbidden logic block input pins is initially built by the master task by considering the sequence of nets assigned to the processors in the different partitions. The master task then sends this list to all slave tasks. With this approach any possibility of conflicting routes in relation to logic block input pins is eliminated.

Coarse-grain parallelism is achieved by having several processors routing different netlist partitions in their private track domains. Routing is completed when the last processor finishes the routing of nets in its partition. Only a small number of track domains is initially assigned to each processor. The number of track domains is increased for each processor when its routing resources are saturated. In each processor the VPR [10] algorithm is used to route the netlist partition assigned to it.

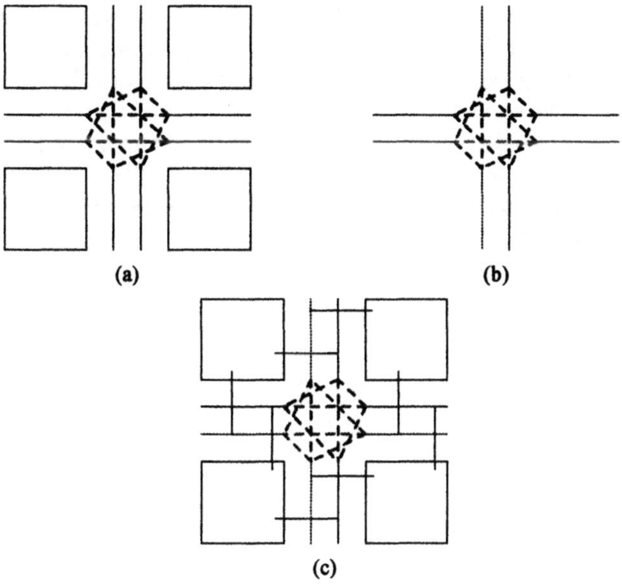

Fig. 2. (a) A 2x2 FPGA, (b) two track domains, (c) routing graph

TDR has been written in C and uses the MPI library [14] to implement the required message-passing functions. TDR communication cost is very low because only a few messages are exchanged among the processors just after the netlist partitioning. However, TDR performance strongly depends on the load balancing which results from the netlist partitioning since the last processor to complete the routing process defines the overall routing time. Even when balanced partitions in the amount of nets are generated, there is no guarantee of good load balancing among the processors, since the routing times for each netlist partition can be very different.

5 Experimental Results

All experiments have been performed on a network of 200MHz IBM RS 6000 43P workstations each with 64 Mb of RAM. The four circuits apex4 (1262 logic blocks), alu4 (1522 logic blocks), s38417 (6406 logic blocks) and clma (8383 logic blocks) used in the experiments have been extracted from the MCNC benchmark [5]. They have been chosen to illustrate the behavior of TDR when circuits consisting of small, medium and large numbers of logic blocks are considered. The routing experiments on these circuits have been performed with both VPR and the proposed TDR algorithm.

Figure 3 shows the speedup achieved by TDR with the use of up to 8 processors in the network. The speedup is measured in relation to the sequential VPR execution time associated with just the iteration using the minimum number of track domains found by the algorithm for each circuit. The results show that TDR achieves good speedups and displays an almost linear behavior for the biggest circuits, clma and s38417. In addition, TDR achieves a superlinear speedup for the alu4 and apex4 (both small circuits) circuits for some configurations of the number of processors. This is due to the very low TDR communication cost and the big reduction of the maze router expansion phase performed by VPR, which needs to expand, for instance, a logic block output pin to all segments in the adjacent channel. Within TDR, each processor needs to perform this expansion just on its limited set of track domains. Therefore, the maze router computational effort is greatly reduced.

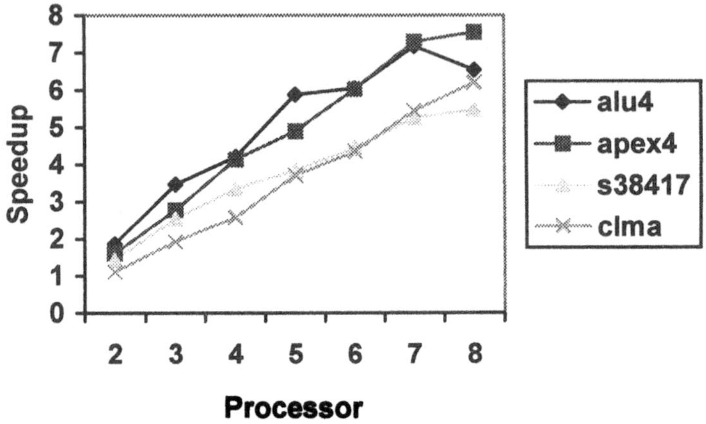

Fig. 3. TDR Speedup

Two additional issues need to be considered as well in the analysis of the results. The first one is concerned with the observation that most of the routing time is spent on the routing of nets with high fanout. Therefore, it is crucial to assign these nets to the processors in a balanced way. The second issue is concerned with the importance of net ordering for the routing result. No effort has been put into trying the routing with different net orderings. However, as the number of processors involved in the routing process changes, a different ordering is produced at each processor as a result of the new netlist partitioning. These two aspects may also explain some superlinear speedup results shown in Figure 3 for some configurations as well as the speedup degradation that has been observed with the alu4 circuit when the number of processors changed from 7 to 8.

In Figure 4, the effect of the initial number of tracks assigned to each processor on the routing time (in seconds) is illustrated for circuits alu4 and apex4. It can be seen that up to a certain threshold value, the routing time tends to decrease as the number of initial tracks increases because less additional track domains tend to be required by the set of processors. However, for each circuit, if the initial number of tracks is above a certain threshold value, the routing time tends to increase again since the routing graph, which is handled by the VPR algorithm, becomes too large.

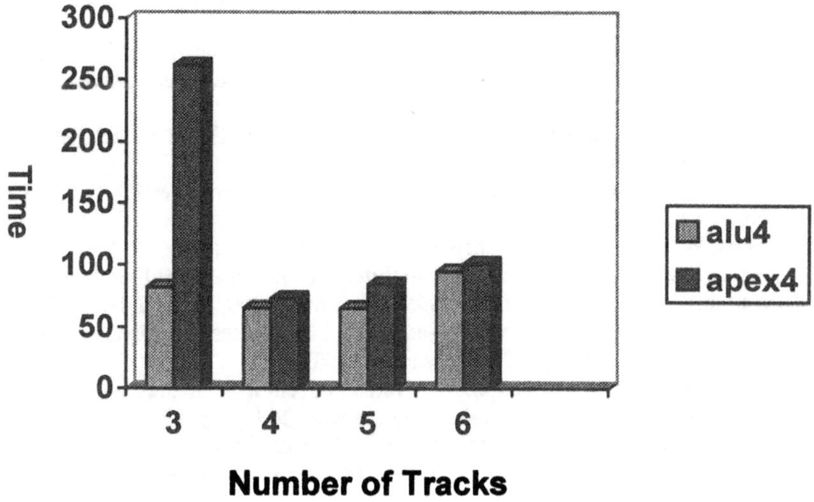

Fig. 4. Routing Time x Initial Number of Track Domains.

For the alu4 circuit, when 3 tracks are initially assigned, TDR uses 2 more tracks than the minimum number of tracks required by VPR but achieves a speedup of 3.32. For the apex circuit when 3 or 4 tracks are initially assigned, TDR uses 4 more tracks than the the minimum number of tracks required by VPR but achieves a speedup of 1.15 and 4.12, respectively. This shows that TDR runs much faster than VPR while producing still good solutions in terms of area.

6 Conclusions and Future Work

The experimental results have demonstrated that TDR, a parallel router based on the partitioning of the routing graph under special FPGA architectural constraints, can achieve linear and superlinear speedups in relation to the state-of-art VPR router even when it is running on an Ethernet cluster of workstations. However, it usually requires more tracks than VPR for routing the same circuit. As future work we intend to change the maze router encapsuled in VPR by a new Steiner tree heuristic in order to improve the quality of TDR solutions in terms of the average net length and to reduce the minimum number of tracks required to completion of routing.

References

1 P. K. Chan and M. Schlag, " Acceleration of an FPGA router," in *Proc. 1997 IEEE Workshop FPGAs for Custom Computing Machines*, 1997, pp. 175-181.

2 P. K. Chan, M. Schlag, C. Ebeling and L. McMurchie, "Distributed-Memory Parallel Routing for Field-Programmable Gate Arrays", *IEEE Trans. on CAD*, Vol. 19, No. 8,pp. 850-862, August 2000.
3 L. A. F. Cabral, J. S. Aude and N. Maculan, "FPGA Routing: A Brief Survey and a Parallel Strategy", in *Proc. Brazilian Symp. of Operational Research*, Brazil, pp. 1624-1633, October 1999.
4 L. A. F. Cabral, "Paralleling Routing Phase of Circuits Based on FPGAs", *Ph.D Thesis*, Federal University of Rio de Janeiro, 2001.
5 S. Yang, "Logic Synthesis and Optimization Benchmark, version 3.0", Tech. Report, MCNC, USA, 1991.
6 H. Hsieh, W. Carter , J. Ja, E. Cheung, S. Schreifels, C. Erickson, P. Freidin, L. Tinkey and R. Kanazawa, " Third-Generation Architecture Boosts Speed and density of Field-Programmable Gate Arrays", *Proc. 1990 CICC*, May 1990, pp. 31.2.1-31.2.7.
7 Y.-L. Wu, S. Tsukiyama, M. Marek-Sadowska, "Graph Based Analysis of FPGA Routing", *IEEE Trans. CAD*, 15(1), pp. 33-44, January 1996.
8 J. Rose and S. Brown, "Flexibility of Interconnection Structures in Field-Programmable Gate Arrays", *IEEE Journal of Solid State Circuits*, 26 (3), pp. 277-282, March 1991.
9 L. McMurchie and C. Ebeling, "Pathfinder: A Negotiation-based Perfomance Driven router for FPGAs", in *Proc. 3rd Int ACM/SIGDA Symp. Field-Programmable Gate Arrays*, Monterey, CA, Feb. 1995, pp. 111-117.
10 V. Betz and J. Rose, "VPR: A New Packing, Placement and Routing Tool for FPGA Research", in *7th Int'l Workshop on Field Programmable Logic and Applic.*, London, 1997, pp.213-222.
11 J. Swartz, V. Betz and J. Rose, "A Fast Routability-Driven for FPGA", in *ACM/SIGDA Int'l Symp. on Field-Programmable Gate Arrays*, Monterey, CA, 1998, pp. 140-149.
12 R. Tessier, "Negotiated A^* routing for FPGAs", presented at the *Proc. the Fifth Canadian Workshop on Field-Programmable Devices*, Quebec, Canada, June, 1998.
13 Z. Xing, J. Chandy, and P. Banerjee," Parallel global routing for standard cell", in Proc. IPPS-97, Apr. 1997, pp. 527-532.
14 M. Snir, S. Otto, S. Huss-Lederman, D. Walker and J. Dongarra," MPI The Complete Reference", The MIT Press, 1997.

High-Level Partitioning of Digital Systems Based on Dynamically Reconfigurable Devices

Rafal Kielbik[1], Juan Manuel Moreno[2], Andrzej Napieralski[1], Grzegorz Jablonski[1], and Tomasz Szymanski[1]

[1] Department of Microelectronics and Computer Science, Technical University of Lodz
Al. Politechniki 11, 93-590 Lodz, Poland
{rkielbik, napier, gwj, szyman}@dmcs.p.lodz.pl
Department of Electronics Engineering, Technical University of Catalunya
c/ Gran Capita s/n, 08034 Barcelona, Spain
moreno@eel.upc.es

Abstract. This paper presents a high-level temporal partitioning algorithm, which is able to split the VHDL description of a digital system into two equivalent subdescriptions. The primary goal of the algorithm is to obtain two area-balanced, time-independent partitions. The descriptions of these partitions can be separately simulated, synthesized and implemented as different configurations of a dynamically reconfigurable device. The partitioning principle is based on a directed task hypergraph. Each vertex of this hypergraph corresponds to one concurrent assignment of the description being analysed. The resources required for the physical implementation of each vertex are calculated by means of a simplified resource estimator. Time dependencies between vertices are denoted by hyperedges representing signals connecting appropriate concurrent assignments.

1 Introduction

The fast evolution of programmable devices which can be nowadays observed generates new demands for tools supporting the efficient use of modern chips, as well as their resources and reconfiguration techniques. The explicit example of this tendency can be observed in the case of Dynamically Reconfigurable FPGA (DRFPGA) architectures [6,7,8,9,10]. For these devices the expression "partitioning" has a completely new meaning and common partitioning techniques are ineffective. Traditional partitioning algorithms divide the design in two (bipartition) or more (multiway partition) circuits. The algorithms try to balance the size of the partitions, while ensuring that they are not larger then the capacity of the target devices [1]. The goal of these algorithms is to minimise the amount of communication signals (cutsize) between partitions. Since in the case of dynamic reconfigurable programmable logic the most important aspect to be guaranteed is the time dependencies between partitions [2,3,4,5], traditional algorithms are not in charge of exploiting dynamic the reconfiguration capabilities of novel programmable devices.

This paper will propose a new concept of partitioning suitable for dynamic reconfigurable devices.

M. Glesner, P. Zipf, and M. Renovell (Eds.): FPL 2002, LNCS 2438, pp. 271-280, 2002.

2 Assumptions

The general assumption of the presented algorithm is that it must operate on the high abstraction level of the system description. Therefore this description should be first of all given using a high-level Hardware Description Language (HDL). Among the many HDLs which fulfil this criterion VHDL was chosen as one of the most popular and representative ways of specifying hardware by means of its functionality.

The assumption of the high-level approach to the partitioning entails also the fact that each concurrent assignment of the given system description is treated as the smallest, indivisible part called "code element".

Furthermore, it is important to bear in mind that dynamically reconfigurable devices allow for a multiple use of their resources by means of fast reconfiguration mechanisms. Therefore the presented algorithm must perform partitioning in the time domain – not in the resource domain, like traditional partitioning algorithms.

Our algorithm will also try to keep balanced the resources required by the descriptions resulting from the partitioning process. In this way it will be possible to minimise the overall resource requirements of the system.

The next assumptions concern the architecture to be divided. First of all, it should be relatively complex. But not because partitioning of a small architecture is not necessary, since small designs can also be optimised. The most important advantage resulting from the partition of a complex architecture can be observed during the estimation of the resource requirements for the subsystems resulting from the partitioning process. Some parts of these subsystems can be overestimated, but others can be underestimated, so that the global estimation error can be compensated. Complex architectures, composed of many smaller elements, can be also more easily divided as far as the balance of resource requirements is concerned. The architectures being exposed to the partitioning process should be also described as optimally as possible. The assignments should not be redundant too often. This assumption permits the use of simplified estimation algorithms, without common term simplification.

3 Algorithm Environment

The general concept of the high-level partitioning algorithm presented in this paper is depicted in Fig. 1. It results directly from the assumptions presented the previous section. Both the input and output of the algorithm are a VHDL description of a digital system. The Input description is first pre-processed by the extractor of the time dependencies between code elements and the estimator of the size of these elements. The size of each code element should be understood as the number of resources required for implementing this code element in a given technology.

The mentioned time dependencies are unambiguously defined and can be easily extracted from the description. But the size of the code elements is closely connected with the structure of the synthesis target. Therefore the code size estimator needs some guidelines given by the user. These guidelines constitute a kind of database including basic information about primitives available in the synthesis target. The more accurate is this information, the more exact is the result of the estimation.

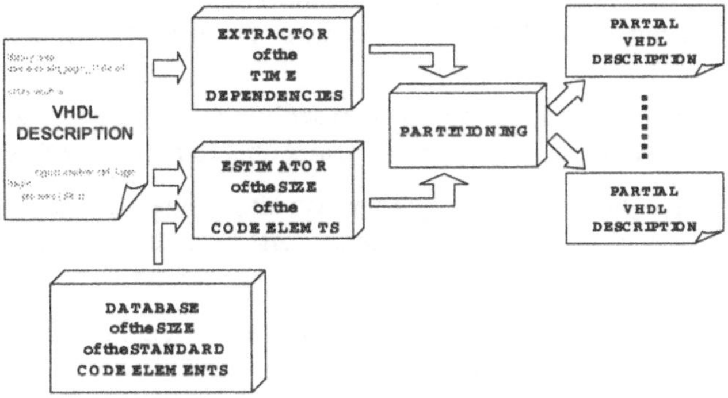

Fig. 1. Environment of the partitioning algorithm

The main task of the time dependencies extractor is to build a directed hypergraph *G(V,E)* [1], which constitutes the base for the partitioning algorithm. The vertices of this graph (set *V*) correspond to code elements. The Edges (set *E*) correspond to the signals which connect these vertices.

4 Resources Estimation

The estimator of the size of the code elements (resource estimator) assigns to each vertex of the set *V* an estimated weight which describes the resources (vertex resources) required to implement this vertex in the chosen technology [12,13]. Of course, the implementation of the vertex should be understood as the implementation of the code element corresponding to this vertex.

The estimated weights have the form of a record. There is one record assigned to each vertex. It keeps the number of 4-input LUTs and flip-flops demanded to accomplish the physical realization of the structure corresponding to this vertex.

Flip-flops and 4-input LUTs have been chosen as the most representative components of any FPGA technology. This approach allows for treating the result as general enough to permit the adaptation of the proposed algorithm to any device family.

The chosen components can also be easily replaced or extended by other technology specific elements to estimate more accurately the required vertex resources.

5 Hypergraph Generation

The extractor of the time dependencies sets vertices of the hypergraph in the order that illustrates the sequence of operations being represented by these vertices. This process is based on the analysis of edges connecting individual vertices.

As it was already stated, the edges of the hypergraph $G(V,E)$ represent signals connecting concurrent statements. Therefore three types of edges sets can be identified:

Target edges ($E_{TRG}(v)$) – set of edges representing all signals that are the target of at least one assignment in the statement corresponding to a given vertex.

Source edges ($E_{SRC}(v)$) – set of edges representing signals being a source of at least one assignment or being at least once tested or compared in the statement corresponding to a given vertex.

Activating edges ($E_{ACT}(v)$) – set of edges representing signals capable of activating the statement corresponding to a given vertex.

The introduced definitions can be easily understood on the following examples:

```
P1: process(a)
begin
     if (a'event and a = '1') then
       b <= c and d;
     end if;
end process;
```

$E_{TRG}(P1) = \{b\}$
$E_{SRC}(P1) = \{a, c, d\}$
$E_{ACT}(P1) = \{a\}$

```
P2: process(e,f,g)
begin
     if (e = '1') then
       h <= f and g;
     end if;
end process;
```

$E_{TRG}(P2) = \{h\}$
$E_{SRC}(P2) = \{e, f, g\}$
$E_{ACT}(P2) = \{e, f, g\}$

```
A1: j <= '1' when (i = '1') else
           k;
```

$E_{TRG}(A1) = \{j\}$
$E_{SRC}(A1) = \{i, k\}$
$E_{ACT}(A1) = \{i, k\}$

```
A2: p <= (n and m) when (r = '1') else
           n;
```

$E_{TRG}(A2) = \{p\}$
$E_{SRC}(A2) = \{n, m, r\}$
$E_{ACT}(A2) = \{n, m, r\}$

As it can be observed in the case of process $P1$, the edges corresponding to signal c and signal d are source edges only. Neither of them can activate the process $P1$. This can be done only by signal a. In general, for each vertex v_A representing concurrent assignment $E_{ACT}(v_A) = E_{SRC}(v_A)$ and for each vertex v_P corresponding to a process $E_{ACT}(v_P) \subseteq E_{SRC}(v_P)$.

It must be stressed that the introduced classification is closely connected with vertices. The same edge can be the target edge for one vertex and the source or activating edge for other vertices.

On the basis of the presented classification, analogous definitions can be introduced:

Source vertex: $v_{SRC}(e) = v : e \in E_{TRG}(v)$

Target vertex: $v_{TRG}(e) = v : e \in E_{SRC}(v)$

A sample usage of the definitions introduced previously is presented in Fig.2. To simplify the first approach to the partitioning algorithm, each edge *e* can have only one source vertex $v_{SRC}(e)$.

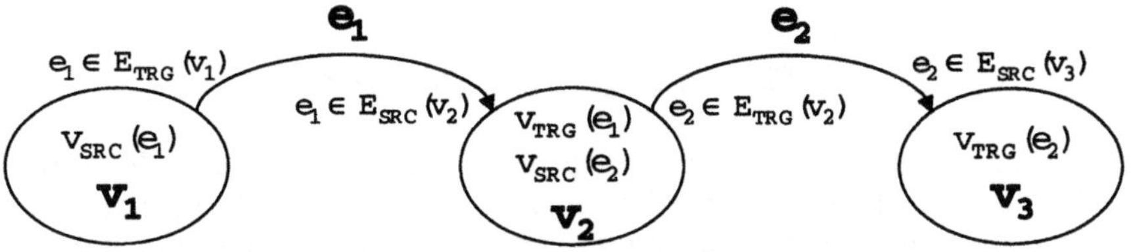

Fig. 2. Dependencies between edges and vertices

For further analysis additional definitions must be introduced:

Input edges (E_{IN}) – set of edges representing all signals declared as entity input ports.

Output edges (E_{OUT}) – set of edges representing all signals declared as entity output ports.

Sequential edges (E_{SEQ}) – set of edges corresponding to output signals of latches or flip-flops estimated by the resource estimator.

Combinational edges (E_{CMB}) – set of edges that are not sequential.

The distinction between sequential and combinational edges is particularly important when the partitioning process is performed. As a result of the partitioning, some edges are cut (cut edges) and the vertices of these edges are placed in different partitions. The values of the signals represented by cut edges (cut signals values) and evaluated by first partition must be stored to be used by the second partition. In some reprogrammable devices there are special buffers devoted for keeping cut signals values (Dharma [6], DPGA [7], Xilinx TMFPGA [8]). In other architectures general-purpose memory elements must be used to this end (FIPSOC [9,10]). In some cases of DRFPGAs only the values of cut signals corresponding to combinational edges must be stored in additional buffers. The values of signals represented by sequential edges are held in their native memory elements, which are not affected by the reconfiguration process (FIPSOC).

Additional buffers, keeping values of cut signals (cut resources), must be introduced during the partitioning process. Therefore, a weight $W(e)$ is assigned to each edge e . This weight determines the number of memory elements, which would be required to store the value of the signal corresponding to the edge e if it is a cut edge.

It should be mentioned that the edges discussed in this paper are actually hyperedges. They can connect more than two vertices. Nevertheless they can be easily split into simple edges connecting two vertices only. This is equivalent to the transformation from hypergraph to graph (Fig. 3). In fact partitioning is performed on the result of this transformation. Therefore only edges are considered in this paper.

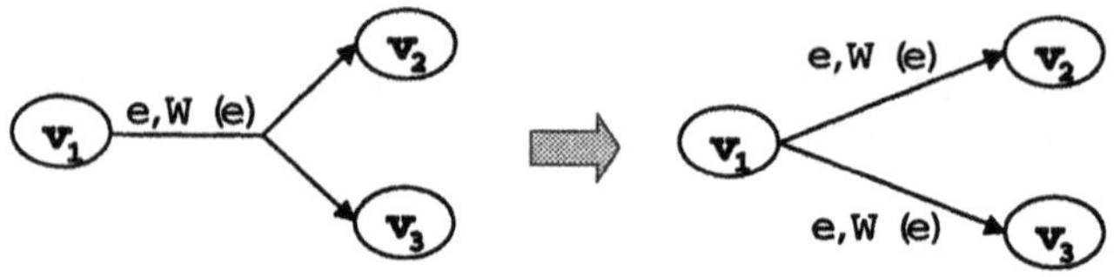

Fig. 3. Hypergraph to graph conversion

Each simple edge obtained during hyperedge splitting must have the same label and weight as the hyperedge from which it is derived (Fig. 3). When the cut resources are calculated, weights of non-cut edges are not taken into account (Fig. 4a). But if a few cut edges have the same label, the weight of only one of them has to be considered (Fig. 4b).

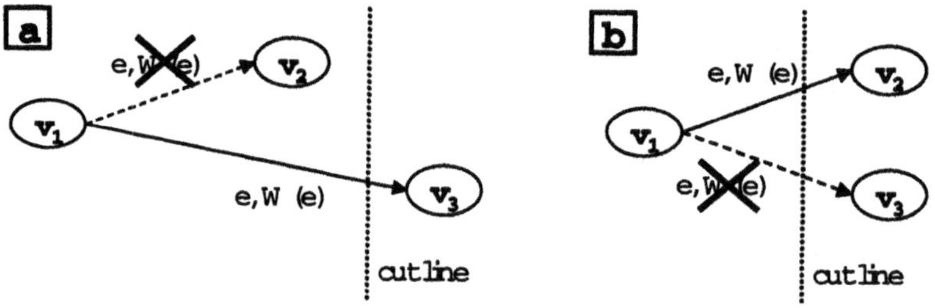

Fig. 4. Omission of multiple edge weights

Hypergraph generation (Fig. 5) consists in choosing the proper vertices from an unordered set V_N and adding them to the ordered set V. The set V_N is being generated during the syntactical analysis of the architecture which is being partitioned. The Set V is empty before the hypergraph generation process. When the hypergraph is already constructed the set V constitutes a sum of subsets (columns): $V = C_0 \cup C_1 \cup \ldots \cup C_{K-1}$, where K is a number of columns. Each column corresponds to a certain period of time, in which all operations represented by vertices included in this column must be performed. If two vertices are in consecutive columns, the mentioned operations can share the same resources in successive periods of time.

Generating column C_k ($k \in N$, $K > k \geq 0$) demands some steps (Loop 1) constituting a separated *k-th* stage of the whole hypergraph generation process. The first step of each *k-th* stage consists in determining the set of initial edges $E_{INIT}(k)$:

$$E_{INIT}(k) = \begin{cases} E_{IN} & when \quad k = 0 \\ \{e : e \in (E_{TRG}(v) - E_{OUT})\big|_{v \in C_{k-1}}\} & when \quad k \geq 0 \end{cases} \tag{1}$$

The edges included in $E_{INIT}(k)$ are responsible for adding new vertices to the *k-th* column. If $E_{INIT}(k)$ is empty, the previous stage of the hypergraph generation was the last one. If not, each vertex $v \in V_N$, fulfilling relationship:

$$\exists e \in E_{INIT}(k): \quad e \in E_{ACT}(v) \tag{2}$$

must be removed from set V_N and added to column C_k (Loop 2).

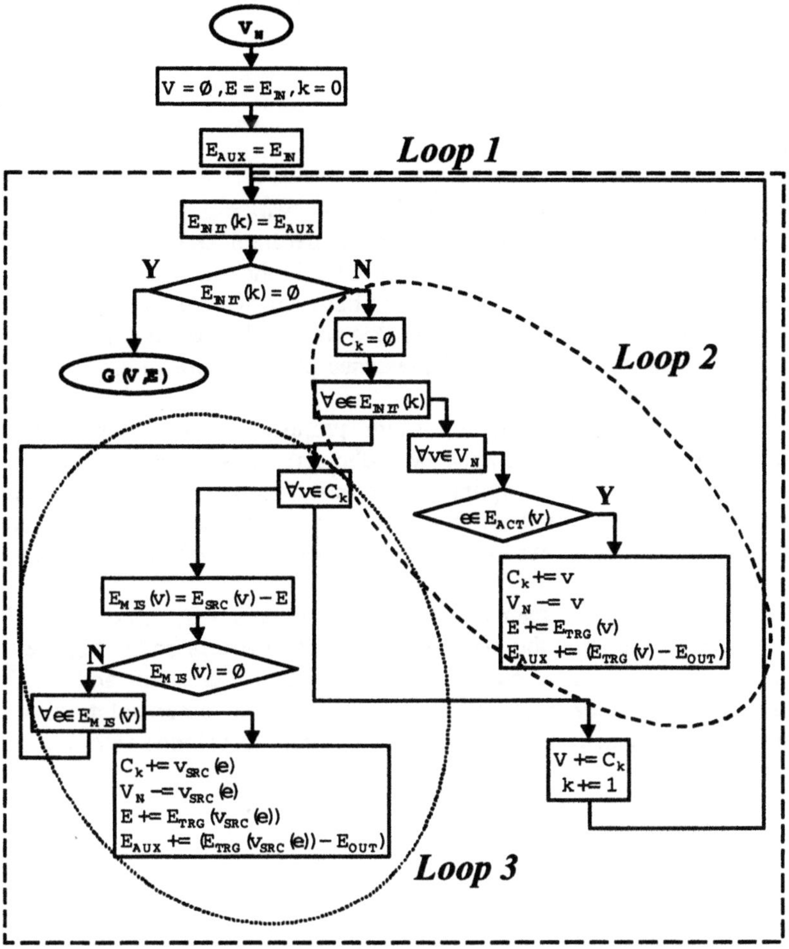

Fig. 5. Hypergraph constructing algorithm

All target edges of the moved vertices must be added to the set *E*, which initially includes input edges only. When the next edges are added, they can be used as source edges of vertices, which will be placed in the next columns, as well as vertices that have been added to the current column.

When the set *E* is already extended the following relationship has to be tested (Loop 3):

$$\forall v \in C_k \quad E_{MIS}(v) = E_{SRC}(v) - E = \emptyset \tag{3}$$

The set $E_{MIS}(v)$ consists of missing (not in included in the set *E*) source edges of vertex $v \in C_k$. If $E_{MIS}(v)$ is not empty, the missing edges must be added to set *E*. This can be done by moving appropriate vertices from V_N to C_k and extending the set E with the target edges of the moved vertices (like in the previous step). Of course, some or even all the source edges of the moved vertices can be not included in set *E*.

Therefore the action of moving next vertices has to be performed until each vertex of column C_k meets relationship (3).

6 Bipartitioning

The simplest idea of the bipartitioning algorithm, which is the crucial point of this paper, results directly from the structure of the hypergraph *G(V,E)* described above. In general, to meet the assumption of the partitioning in the time domain, the hypergraph can be divided along the straight boundaries between two columns. But this solution is not efficient. In some cases, certain vertices can be shifted from one column to the next one preserving the temporal independence principle but reducing the resource requirements of the obtained partitions.

As the fist approach to the algorithm proposed in this paper all possible partitioning boundaries (between each two columns), for all possible shifts of vertices are tested in order to find the optimal partitions. This boundary, which assures the best balance of partitions as far as the resources requirements are being concerned (taking into consideration cut resources mentioned above), determines the final partitioning result.

The proposed approach seems to be inefficient and very time-consuming. But bearing in mind the fact that the presented algorithm operates on the high-level of the system description, it can be recognised as acceptable for small and medium size digital systems. For very big and complex description other solutions are being considered (e.g., modifications of the algorithm developed by Fiduccia and Mattheyses [11]).

7 Results

On the basis of the partitioned hypergraph three separate VHDL entities are automatically generated. The explanation of this process is depicted in Fig. 6.

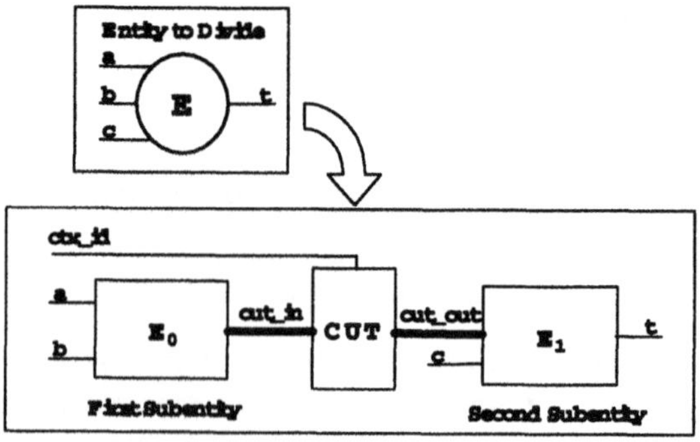

Fig. 6. Transition from one description to subdescriptions

The hypothetical entity *E*, which is divided, has three input ports (*a*, *b*, *c*) and one output port (*t*). Subentities E_1 and E_2 correspond to the partitions that are obtained for entity *E*. The third entity (*CUT*) constitutes the connection between the subentities E_1 and E_2. This connection is achieved by mapping the output ports of the first subentity onto input ports of the second subentity. These output ports of E_1, which do not have to be latched, are mapped by means of unconditional concurrent assignments. The remaining ones are mapped using processes defining additional flip-flops. The signal *ctx_id* indicates the active context of the dynamically reprogrammable device and is used as a clock signal of these flip-flops. In this way all the signals that have to be propagated from E_1 to E_2 are latched before chip reconfiguration. It is necessary to highlight that the reconfiguration process can not be applied to latches and flip-flops storing communication signals between partitions.

8 Conclusions

First tests performed on the high-level partitioning algorithm presented in this paper show that it can constitute an effective tool for supporting dynamically programmable devices. The subdescriptions obtained from this algorithm can be synthesised separately. Thus total synthesis time can be much shorter than in case of synthesis of the original, not-partitioned description.

Furthermore, partitioning before synthesis has also another, very important advantage. The synthesis of each subdescription can be performed under different constrains. In this way the obtained result can be better optimised.

Since the presented algorithm manipulates concurrent statements of VHDL description, it is relatively fast and the result obtained is readable for the user. Therefore it can be easily examined and simulated by means of standard simulation tools.

Acknowledgements

This work has been partially funded by the European Union within the IST Programme (Contract IST - 2001 - 34016 - RECONF2)

References

1. de Micheli, G.: Synthesis and Optimisation of Digital Circuits. McGraw-Hill, 1994
2. Canto, E., Moreno, J.M., Cabestany, J., Lacadena, I., Insenser, J.M.: A Temporal Bipartitioning Algorithm for Dynamically Reconfigurable FPGAs. IEEE Transactions on Very Large Scale Integration (VLSI) systems, Vol. 9, No. 1., pp. 210-218, February 2001
3. Canto, E.: Temporal Bipartitioning Techniques for Multi-context FPGAs. Ph.D. Thesis, Universitat Politecnica de Catalunya, July 2001
4. Kaul, M., Vemuri, R.: Temporal Partitioning combined with Design Space Exploration for Latency Minimization of Run-Time Reconfigured Designs. Proceedings on Design,

Automation and Test in Europe (DATE'99), IEEE Computer Society Press, pp. 202-209, March 1999
5. Maestre, R., Kurdahi, F.J., Fernandes, M., Hermida, R., Bagherzadeh, N., Singh, H.: A Framework for Reconfigurable Computing: Task Scheduling and Context Management. IEEE Transactions on Very Large Scale Integration (VLSI) Systems, Vol. 9, No. 6, pp. 858-873, December 2001
6. Bhat, N.B., Chaudhary, K., Kuh, E.S.: Performance-Oriented Fully Routable Dynamic Architecture for a Field Programmable Logic Device. UCB/ERL M93/42, University of California, Berkley, June 1993
7. DeHon, A.: Reconfigurable Architectures for General-Purpose Computing. Ph.D. Thesis, Massachusetts Institute of Technology, October 1996
8. Trimberger, S.: A Time Multiplexed FPGA. Proceedings FPGAs for Custom Computing Machines (FCCM'97), IEEE Computer Society, 1997
9. Faura, J., Horton, C., van Doung, P., Madrenas, J., Insenser, J.M.: A Novel Mixed Signal Programmable Device with On-Chip Microprocessor. Proceedings of the IEEE 1997 Custom Integrated Circuits Conference, pp.103-106
10. Faura, J., Moreno, J.M., Aguirre, M-A., van Doung, P., Insenser, J.M.: FIPSOC: A Filed Programmable System On a Chip. Proceedings of the XII Design of Circuits and Integrated Systems Conference (DCIS'97), pp. 597-602, Sevilla, November 1997
11. Fiduccia, C.M., Mattheyses, R.M.: A Linear-Time Heuristic Procedure for Improved Network Partitions. Proceedings on Design Automation Conference, pp. 241-247, 1982
12. Enzler, R., Jeger, T., Cottet, D., Tröster, G.: High-Level Area and Performance Estimation of Hardware Building Blocks on FPGAs. Proceedings of FPL 2000, pp. 525-534, Springer-Verlag, 2000
13. Machado, F., Torroja, Y., Casado, F., Riesgo, T., de la Torre, E., Uceda, J.: A Simple Method to Estimate the Area of VHDL RTL descriptions. Proceedings of the XV Design of Circuits and Integrated Systems Conference (DCIS 2000), Montpellier, November 2000

High Speed Homology Search Using Run-Time Reconfiguration*

Yoshiki Yamaguchi[1], Yosuke Miyajima[1], Tsutomu Maruyama[1], and Akihiko Konagaya[2,3]

[1] Institute of Engineering Mechanics and Systems, University of Tsukuba 1-1-1 Ten-ou-dai Tsukuba Ibaraki 305-8573, JAPAN
{yoshiki, miyajima, maruyama}@darwin.esys.tsukuba.ac.jp
[2] Japan Advanced Institute of Science and Technology 1-1 Asahidai Tatsunokuchi Ishikawa 923-1292, JAPAN
kona@jaist.ac.jp
[3] Japan Riken Genomic Sciences Center 1-7-22 Suehiro Tsurumi Yokohama Kanagawa 230-0045, JAPAN

Abstract. In this paper, we show a new approach for homology search based on run-time reconfiguration. In our approach, the search consists of two phases, and different circuits are configured on demand during the search to make up for the limited memory bandwidth of off-the-shelf FPGA boards. Experiments with an off-the-shelf FPGA (Xilinx XCV2000E) board showed good results. The time for comparing a query sequence of 2,048 elements with a database sequence of 64 million elements by the Smith-Waterman algorithm is about 34 sec, which is about 330 times faster than a desktop computer with a 1GHz Pentium-III.

1 Introduction

Human genome sequencing has been accelerating rapidly since 1995 [1,2,3], and the whole sequence will be determined in the near future. At present, the main focus in the Human Genome Project is functional analysis of whole genes of the human genome [4]. In the functional analysis, sequence homology searches are probably the most commonly used techniques.

In the homology search, a given sequence (query sequence) is compared with database sequences, and fragments which are similar to the query sequence are searched. Well-known approaches to this search problem include Smith-Waterman algorithm [5, 6] (based on dynamic programming), FASTA [7] and BLAST [8, 9]. The Smith-Waterman algorithm can find any fragment which generates good score between any two sequences. However, the computation order is $O(MN)$ when the lengths of a database sequence and a query sequence are

* This work was supported by Grant-in-Aid for Scientific Research on Priority Areas (C) "Genome Information Science" from the Ministry of Education, Culture, Sports, Science and Technology of Japan, and Japan Society for the Promotion of Science (JSPS) Research Fellowships for Young Scientists (#5304).

M. Glesner, P. Zipf, and M. Renovell (Eds.): FPL 2002, LNCS 2438, pp. 281–291, 2002.

M and N respectively. Since this approach is extremely time consuming, heuristic algorithms have been developed. The most common heuristic algorithms are BLAST and FASTA, and these programs can find most fragments in a reasonable time. However, they can not find some fragments which are containing many gaps or posttranslational modifications (posttranslational modifications are chemical reactions that change the biological activity and/or localization of a protein).

With dedicated hardware systems [10, 11, 12], the computation time of dynamic programming can be dramatically improved, because the algorithms have a lot of parallelism. Therefore, all possibilities can be checked in reasonable time. However, the cost of the systems is very expensive. In order to accelerate functional analysis of genes, reasonably-priced high speed homology search systems are necessary.

In this paper, we propose a FPGA-based system for the dynamic programming. Our system consists of only off-the-shelf components. Therefore, personal users can easily obtain all the parts and update each part. However, off-the-shelf FPGA boards have not enough hardware resources (especially memory bandwidth). In order to make up for these problems, the search consists of two phases, and different configuration data are downloaded to FPGA during the search.

With this run-time reconfiguration [13, 14, 15], the system can achieve high performance. In the first phase, fragments that are similar to the query sequence are searched and only their scores and positions are output. When the fragment is found, the FPGA is reconfigured from the first phase to the second phase. Then, the details of the matching are output. In many cases, each database sequence includes a small number of fragments that are similar to the query sequence. Therefore, the reconfiguration does not happen many times. When the second phase is finished, the first phase is started again by reconfiguring the FPGA to the first phase.

This paper is organized as follows. Section 2 gives a brief overview of the dynamic programming. Section 3 introduces the system overview of our approach, and the details are given in Section 4. Section 5 presents experimental results. Section 6 describes scalability of the system. Finally, Section 7 concludes this paper including aspects of our future works.

2 Homology Search with Hardware

2.1 Dynamic Programming

In the dynamic programming, a query sequence and a database sequence are compared inserting gaps as shown in Figure 1. Scores for each matching of the elements and inserting gaps are given by score matrices [16, 17]. The computation order by dynamic programming is $O(MN)$ when the length of the database sequence and query sequence are M and N respectively. The length of database sequence (M) is often more than several hundreds mega bytes. Therefore, it is unrealistic to use dynamic programming algorithm against long database sequences on desktop computer systems.

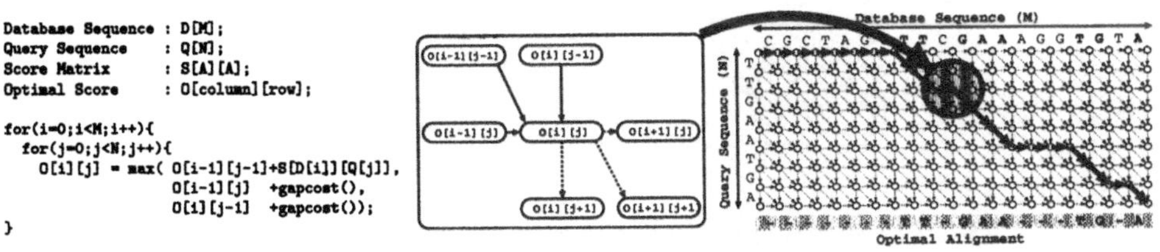

Fig. 1. Finding Similar Fragments by Dynamic Programming

With dedicated hardware systems, or reconfigurable devices such as FPGAs, we can process matching of elements in parallel. Figure 2 shows how the matching of the elements is processed in parallel. In the right-hand side part in Figure 2, elements on each diagonal line are processed at once. Therefore, the order of the computation can be reduced to $O(M+N)$ from $O(MN)$ if N elements can be processed in parallel. If the size of the hardware is not large enough to compare N elements at once, the first p elements (suppose that the hardware process p elements in parallel) of the query sequence are compared with the database sequence at once, and the scores of all p-th elements are stored in temporal memory. Then, the next p elements of the query sequence are compared with the database sequence using the scores stored in the temporal memory.

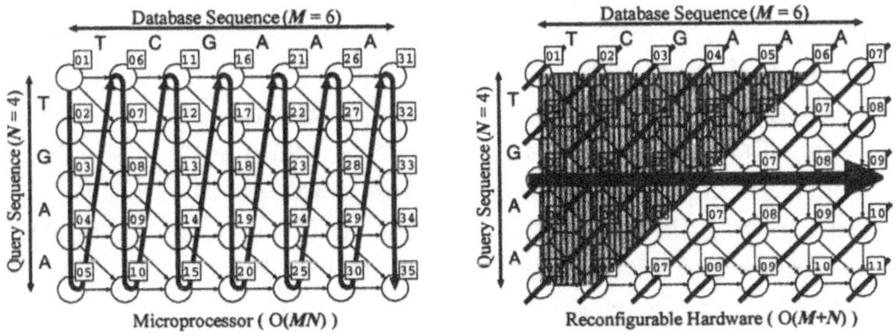

Fig. 2. Difference between Software and Hardware

However, we can not implement the dynamic programming simply onto hardware. Figure 3 shows the output data width by dynamic programming. In order to hold the route information of the sequence matching (including gap), the output data width becomes $k + 2p$ (bit/clock-cycle) when the score and the route information are k and $2p$ respectively.

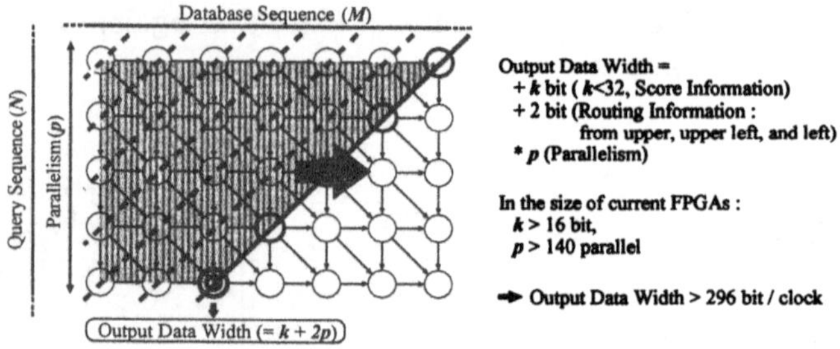

Fig. 3. Relationship between Parallelism and Data Width

2.2 Smith-Waterman Algorithm

In our approach, the Smith-Waterman algorithm [5] and affine gap function [6] are used. The Smith-Waterman algorithm is based on dynamic programming, and a query sequence is compared to a database sequence inserting gap if it gives better score. Gap cost is calculated as "*-a-bt*", where a is the creation penalty (namely opening gap cost), b is the extension penalty (namely extend gap cost), and t is the gap length. In this gap function, a is typically larger than b.

The goal of the Smith-Waterman algorithm is not simply to compare the two sequences, but to find fragments which are similar to the query sequence from the database sequence. For this purpose, all scores on upper edges in Figure 1 is always set to zero.

2.3 Previous Approach

In the homology search, many algorithms [5, 6, 8, 7, 9] and dedicated hardware systems [10,11,12] have been developed. The results obtained there is a trade-off of quality, time and cost.

With desktop personal computer systems, it is unrealistic to check all pattern matching possibilities within a reasonable time using some algorithms based on dynamic programming. Simplified algorithm, such as BLAST and FASTA, can not find some fragments which are containing many gaps or posttranslational modifications, although they realized dramatically improvement in the speed.

With dedicated hardware systems, the computation time is dramatically improved, because most of the pattern matching problems have many parallelism in them. However, since the cost of the systems are very expensive, it is very difficult for many users to purchase the systems.

Since the genome databases have been published on the many Web site at present, many users want to do search in their local environment. Therefore, high speed homology search systems with reasonable cost are required.

2.4 Our Approach

Our system consists of only off-the-shelf components which are one Pentium based computer and one off-the-shelf FPGA board. Therefore, personal users can easily obtain all the parts and update each part. However, the off-the-shelf FPGA boards do not have enough hardware resources, especially memory bandwidth, for the dynamic programming. In order to make up for the limited hardware resources, in our approach, the search consists of two phases and different circuits are downloaded from the host computer in each phase using run-time reconfiguration.

The performance is almost proportional to the size of the FPGA because the performance of the first phase dominates the computation time, and the performance does not depend on memory band width of the FPGA board. FPGAs are becoming larger and larger following Moore's law. The high performance of the system can be easily maintained by exchanging the FPGA board if necessary.

3 System Overview

3.1 Target Problems

Our current target problems in homology search are shown in Table 1. In our approach, the Smith-Waterman algorithm [5] is used in all comparisons of sequences shown in Table 1.

Table 1. Target Problems in Homology Search

Query sequence	Database sequence
amino acid	amino acid
amino acid	translated nucleotide
nucleotide	nucleotide

3.2 Requisites of the System

Our approach requires the followings :

1. one off-the-shelf FPGA board (with PCI bus interface), and
2. one host computer

In our approach, two memory banks to transfer data between the FPGA and the one host computer are assumed. Most off-the-shelf FPGA boards have at least two memory banks in order to receive data from the host computer while the FPGA is running using another memory bank. We also need DMA functions for data transfer.

3.3 Run-Time Reconfiguration

In our approach, the homology search consists of two phases in order to make up for the limited memory bandwidth, and different configuration data are downloaded from the host computer for each phase. Figure 4 shows a timing diagram of the reconfiguration.

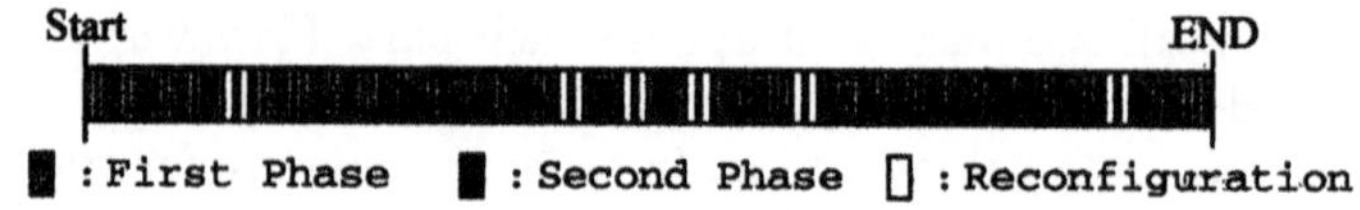

Fig. 4. Timing Diagram using Run-time Reconfiguration

In the first phase, positions of fragments that are similar to the query sequence are searched, and scores of the fragments are output. When the fragment is found, the FPGA is reconfigured from the first phase to the second phase as shown in Figure 4. In the second phase, the details of the pattern matching with the fragment is output. When the search of second phase is finished, the first phase search are started again by reconfiguring to the first phase.

In many cases, most database sequences include a small number of fragments that are similar to the query sequence. Therefore, the reconfiguration does not happen many times, and the total performance follows the performance of the first phase. If a database sequence includes a lot of similar fragment to the query sequence, the reconfiguration time becomes fatal overhead. In this case, the host computer stops the reconfiguration, and makes the search of the first phase completed. Then, search of the second phase is started without any reconfiguration.

4 Details of the System

4.1 Structure of Processing Unit and Multi-thread Computation

Figure 5 shows the structure of one processing unit for Smith-Waterman algorithm. It consists of four stages, and takes four clock cycles to compute scores on each cell on the dynamic programming array (Figure 1). However, by overlapping the computation, we can start to compute the scores of elements on the next diagonal line (Figure 1) in every two clock cycles.

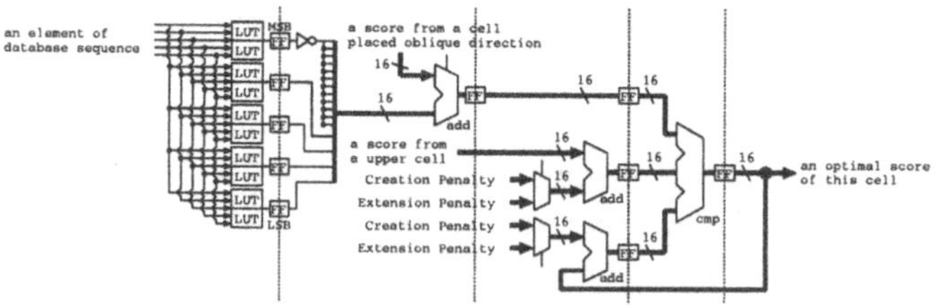

Fig. 5. Implementation of a Processing Unit

Figure 6 shows how a database sequence whose length is M, is compared with a query sequence whose length is N. In the figure, each circle represents a processing unit. If the length of the query sequence (N) is not larger than the number of processing elements (p) on the FPGA, the query sequence can be processed at once as shown in Figure 6. In this case, the computation order is O($2M$), because the processing units have to wait for one clock cycle to compare elements on the next diagonal lines as described above, and $M \gg N$ in general.

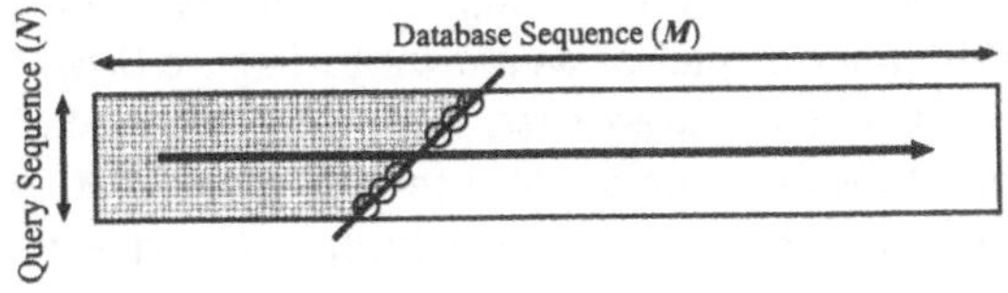

Fig. 6. Sequential Execution, ($p \geq N$, O($2M$))

Suppose that the length of the query sequence (N) is longer than the number of processing units (p) on the FPGA. In this case, we can reduce the computation time by the multi-thread computation method. In this computation :

1. first, p elements on the diagonal line in upper half in Figure 7(b) are processed, and the score of p-th element is stored on temporal registers, and
2. then, the next p elements on the diagonal line in lower half are processed without waiting for one clock cycle using the intermediate result.
3. the multi-thread computation is repeated w times when the number of thread (N/p) is w. In this case, when the first $2p$ elements in the query sequence are processed, scores of all $2p$-th elements are stored in memories (all M scores are stored in total), and used for the computation of the next $2p$ elements.

By interleaving the processing of elements in upper half and lower half, we can eliminate the idle cycles of the processing elements. The computation order can be reduced from O($2wM$) to O(wM).

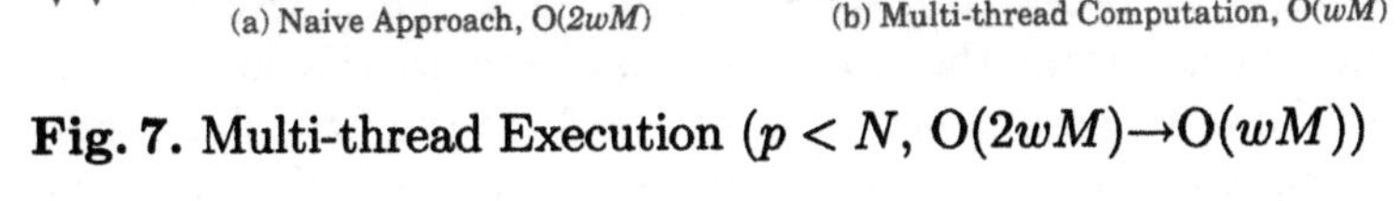

Fig. 7. Multi-thread Execution ($p < N$, O($2wM$)$\rightarrow$O(wM))

4.2 Two Phase Search

First Phase In the first phase, database sequences are divided into sub-sequences, because the size of the intermediate results described above is very large, and can not be stored in the temporal memory (namely the memory banks on the FPGA board) at once.

Figure 8(a) shows how a long database sequence (M) is compared with the query sequence (N). The database sequence is divided into sub-sequences of size s (s is decided based on the size of the temporal memory), and each sub-sequence is compared with the query sequence as shown in Figure 8(a). Figure 8(b) shows how a sub-sequence (s) is compared with the query sequence (N) by the multi-thread computation. In this division to the sub-sequences, some parts whose length is $p \times l$ are overlapped in order to compare the query sequence with all sub-sequences (Figure 8(a)). These parts are compared twice, and become the major overhead in the first phase. The length of the overlapped area is decided based on the length of the query sequence in general. We assume that the length of the overlapped parts ($p \times l$) is from twice to four times of the query sequence (N). Therefore, this overhead is almost proportional to the length of the query sequence.

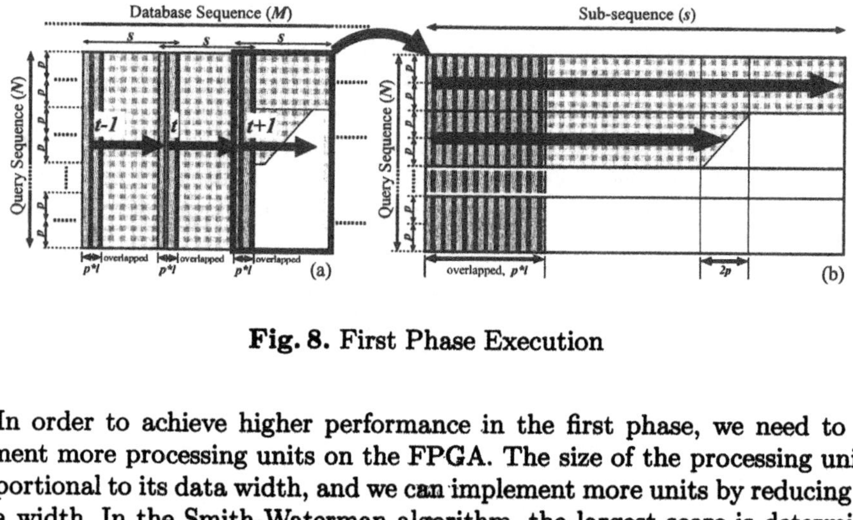

Fig. 8. First Phase Execution

In order to achieve higher performance in the first phase, we need to implement more processing units on the FPGA. The size of the processing unit is proportional to its data width, and we can implement more units by reducing the data width. In the Smith-Waterman algorithm, the largest score is determined by the length of query sequence. Therefore, we can achieve higher performance if the length of the query sequence is shorter.

Second Phase In order to display optimal alignments, we need to find the routing information from the upper left position to the lower right position which gives the best score as shown in Figure 1 (in the first phase, only the best score is computed, and all the information about the path is discarded during the computation).

For the routing information, we need 2 bits for each cell on the array in Figure 3 to distinguish where the path comes from (from upper, upper left or left). Therefore, the number of elements which can be processed in parallel (namely the performance of the second phase) is decided by the FPGA's data width to the memory banks on the FPGA board, not by the size of the FPGA.

If the width is $2 \times p$, p elements can be processed in parallel. In the second phase, only the routing information about the path is output, because the score is already obtained in the first phase. However, the number of the fragments that we need to display their alignments, is not so many and the performance of this phase is not so important. If the length of the query sequence is less than a few thousand, we can obtain the optical alignments against one fragment within one second by a desktop computer.

5 Experiments

The system performance depends on the number of the fragments which are similar to the query sequence, because the performances of the first phase and the second phase are considerably different. According to our experiments, however, the number of the fragments are not so many in most cases, and the performance of the first phase almost decides the total performance. Therefore, we evaluate the performance of each phase respectively.

We have tested the performance of our approach using a Pentium-based desktop computer with one FPGA board (RC1000-PP by Celoxica) [18]. The board has four memory banks, and two of them are used for data transfer between the FPGA board and the host computer. The FPGA (Xilinx XCV2000E) on the board is one of the latest FPGAs that we can obtain now. We could implement 144 processing elements for the first phase of the homology search, and they run at 40 MHz. The overhead for the reconfiguring the FPGA is very small [18,19,20].

Figure 9 shows the relationship between the time of the first phase and the length of the query sequence, when the length of the database sequence is 64 million. The slope of the search time becomes slightly larger as the length of the query sequence becomes larger, because the percentage of the overhead by the overlapped area will gradually increase. The speedup compared with a Pentium-III 1 GHz under Linux and gcc-2.91.66 is 327 times when the length of the query sequence is 2048.

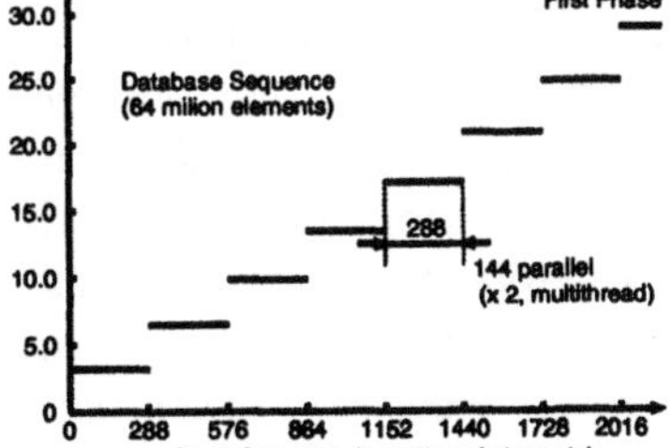

Fig. 9. Computation time of the First Phase

As for the second phase, we can process 32 elements in parallel, because we can write 64 bits to the memory banks on the board at once. The computation time for a query sequence of 2048 elements and a fragment of 8192 elements is about 13 msec. This is about 102 times faster than the Pentium-III 1GHz.

6 Scalability

In our approach, the performance is propotional to the size of the FPGA. Therefore, the high performance of the system can be easily maintained by exchanging the PCI board with the latest FPGA.

The performance is also almost proportional to the number of the FPGA boards when :

1. the query sequence is compared with many database sequences which are stored in different hard disks, or
2. each database sequence is divided into sub-sequences which are stored in different hard disks,

because the database sequences or the sub-sequences can be compared with the query sequence independently. However, the data transfer rate of the PCI bus is limited, and many FPGA boards can not be added to one host computer. We have not evaluated the performance when we use more than one FPGA board, but according to our estimation, more than two boards should not be added to one host computer.

By connecting more hardware platforms by Ethernet, we can easily accelerate the performance furthermore. The performance is almost proportional to the number of the hardware platforms. Then, the total performance can be comparable with large class dedicated hardware systems.

7 Current Status and Future Works

In this paper, we proposed an approach to realize high speed homology search using run-time reconfiguration. With the approach, we demonstrated that we can achieve high performance using off-the-shelf FPGA boards. The performance is almost comparable with small to middle class dedicated hardware systems when we use one board with one of the latest FPGAs (Xilinx XCV2000E). The time for comparing a query sequence of 2048 elements with a database sequence of 64 million elements by the Smith-Waterman algorithm is about 34 sec, which is about 330 times faster than a desktop computer with a 1GHz Pentium-III.

We are now developing software for parallel processing of the homology search with more number of pairs of FPGAs and host computers connected by Ethernet. We are also planning to accelerate other pattern matching problems in bioinformatics with FPGAs.

References

1. http://www.gene.ucl.ac.uk/hugo/
2. http://www.nhgri.nih.gov/HGP/

3. http://www.celera.com/
4. http://www.sciencemag.org/cgi/content/full/282/5389/682/
5. Smith, T.F. and Waterman, M.S.: *Identification of common molecular subsequences*, Journal of Molecular Biology 147, pp.195-197, (1981).
6. Gotoh, O.: *An improved algorithm for matching biological sequences*, Journal of Molecular Biology 162, pp.705-708, (1982).
7. Pearson, W.R.: *Searching Protein Sequence Libraries: Comparison of the Sensitivity of the Smith-Waterman and FASTA Algorithms*, Genomics 11(3), pp.635-650, (1991).
8. Altschul, S.F., et al: *Basic Local Alignment Search Tool*, Journal of Molecular Biology 215, pp.403-410, (1990).
9. Altschul, S.F., et al: *Gapped BLAST and PSI-BLAST: a new generation of protein database search programs*, Nucleic Acids Research 25, pp.3389-3402, (1997).
10. http://www.compugen.com
11. http://www.paracel.com/index.html
12. http://www.timelogic.com
13. Styles, H., and Luk, W.: *Customizing Graphics Applications: Techniques and Programming Interface*, FCCM'00, pp.77-87, (2000).
14. Simmler, H., et al: *Multitasking on FPGA Coprocessors*, FPL2000, pp.121-130, (2000).
15. Yamaguchi, Y., et al: *A Co-processor System with a Virtex FPGA for Evolutionary Computation*, FPL2000, pp.240-249, (2000).
16. Henikoff, S. and Henikoff, J.G.: *Amino Acid Substitution Matrices from Protein Blocks*, Proc. Natl. Acad. Sci. 89, pp.10915-10919, (1992).
17. Jones, D.T. Jones, et al: *The Rapid Generation of Mutation Data Matrices from Protein Sequences*, CABIOS 8, pp.275-282, (1992).
18. Celoxica, Limited.: *RC1000 Hardware Reference Manual*, Ver. 2.3, (2001).
19. Xilinx, Inc.: *Vietex Series Configuration Architecture User Guide*, Ver. 1.5, (2000).
20. Xilinx, Inc.: *Vietex^{TM}-E 1.8V Field Programmable Gate Array*, Ver. 2.2, (2001).

Partially Reconfigurable Cores for Xilinx Virtex*

Matthias Dyer, Christian Plessl, and Marco Platzner

Computer Engineering and Networks Lab,
Swiss Federal Institute of Technology, ETH Zurich, Switzerland
(dyer|plessl|platzner)@tik.ee.ethz.ch

Abstract. Recent generations of high-density and high-speed FPGAs provide a sufficient capacity for implementing complete configurable systems on a chip (CSoCs). *Hybrid CPUs* that combine standard CPU cores with reconfigurable coprocessors are an important subclass of CSoCs. With *partially reconfigurable* FPGAs, coprocessors can be loaded on demand while the CPU remains running. However, the lack of high-level design tools for partial reconfiguration makes practical implementations a challenging task.
In this paper, we introduce a design flow to implement hybrid processors on Xilinx Virtex. The design flow is based on two techniques, *virtual sockets* and *feed-through components*, and can efficiently generate partial configurations from industry-quality cores. We discuss the design flow and present a fully operational audio streaming prototype to demonstrate its feasibility.

1 Introduction

In the last years, many custom computing machines have been presented that achieve high performance by coupling general-purpose CPUs with field-programmable logic. These computers map the runtime-intensive parts of algorithms to application-specific coprocessors implemented in reconfigurable hardware. Many of the early custom computing machines attached one or several FPGAs to a processor via the memory bus or a coprocessor interface. In such a coupling, the processor architecture largely dictates the interface between CPU and coprocessor which often results in speedups that are far from the optimum. Usually, these interfaces lack bandwidth and flexibility, i.e., they cannot be adapted to match the coprocessor's data and control flows.

Hybrid CPUs integrate CPU cores and reconfigurable logic in form of a Configurable System on a Chip (CSoC) and thus potentially overcome the interface limitations. Hybrid CPUs come in two flavors: hybrids using *hard* CPU cores and hybrids based on *soft* CPU cores. Hard CPU cores, e.g., PowerPC core in Virtex-II Pro [15] or ARM7 core in Triscend A7[13], are built-in dedicated CPUs, whereas soft CPU cores, e.g., LEON [5] or OpenRISC 1200 [10] are fully

* This work is partially supported by the Swiss National Science Foundation (SNF) under the NCCR MICS.

M. Glesner, P. Zipf, and M. Renovell (Eds.): FPL 2002, LNCS 2438, pp. 292–301, 2002.

synthesizable blocks of intellectual property (IP). Soft CPU cores are of particular interest for building custom computing machines as they not only allow the modification of the interface between CPU and coprocessors, but also facilitate adaptations to the CPU core itself. Soft cores enable the rapid exploration of different couplings between CPU and coprocessors. The interface can be tailored specifically to the applications need, ranging from memory mapped interfaces over FIFOs to more sophisticated structures such as memory prefetch buffers and DMA controllers.

Recent generations of high-density and high-speed FPGAs, e.g., the Xilinx Virtex series, provide a sufficient capacity for implementing or prototyping complete configurable systems on a chip. Virtex devices are *partially* reconfigurable, i.e., the reconfiguration affects only a part of the FPGA while other parts remain working. Although many authors proposed and described partially reconfigurable systems, the reduction to practice for Virtex devices lags behind. The major hurdle is the lack of high-level design tools that support partial reconfiguration. The Xilinx Java class-library JBits [6] is a prominent example for a design tool at a somewhat lower level. JBits allows to create circuits basically by structural description and to manipulate and generate full and partial configurations. Currently, JBits does not offer synthesis, optimization, or timing analysis capabilities. This restricts the usability of JBits for designing complex hybrid processors. Developers of high-quality cores will resort to hardware description languages and proven synthesis and FPGA design implementation tools.

To facilitate the development of partially reconfigurable coprocessors, we introduce a new design flow that combines industry-quality design tools with JBits' ability of creating partial configurations. The main contributions of this work are:

- a design flow to implement hybrid processors on Virtex FPGAs
- a technique to create partial configurations from optimized cores
- an audio streaming prototype to prove the feasibility of the design flow

Section 2 of this paper reviews different design flows and related work for generating partial reconfigurable cores. Section 3 presents detail of our design flow; Section 4 discusses a hybrid CPU prototype implementation. Finally, Section 5 concludes the paper.

2 Design Flows for Partial Virtex Configurations

A Virtex configuration bitstream contains an integer number of so-called *frames*. Frames are the basic units of reconfiguration and determine the settings of all FPGA resources in the vertical dimension. If the reconfigured frame contains only stateless elements, i.e., no flip-flops or LUTs used as RAM, there will be no transient effects. Elements with state, however, are overwritten with their initial values. A procedure to avoid this is to stop the clock and read back the current state values prior to reconfiguration. The retrieved state data must be included in the reconfiguration bitstream. After reconfiguration, the clock is enabled again. Although Xilinx Virtex FPGAs support partial reconfiguration, an integrated design flow that allows to develop complex partially reconfigurable systems is missing so far. Currently, developers have the choice between two basic design tool flows: direct bitstream manipulation based on standard FPGA design implementation tools, and bitstream generation and manipulation with JBits.

2.1 Direct Bitstream Manipulation

Standard design implementation tools for FPGAs generate full configuration bitstreams. The structure of Virtex bitstreams is partly open to the public, which allows to directly manipulate such bitstreams.

A rather simple manipulation is to change the contents of LUTs and BlockRAMs [14] in a bitstream. Such a technique has been used, for example, to customize logic functions at download time for instance-specific SAT solvers [11]. By extracting the relevant frames from a full configuration, partial bitstreams are generated. In combination with LUT modifications, runtime customization of FPGA cores becomes feasible. This technique could be used, for example, to dynamically change coefficients of a digital filter. In principle, this technique can also be used to generate partial configurations for reconfigurable coprocessors. Figure 1 shows two full configurations, each containing a static core and a dynamic core. The set of frames containing the dynamic core can be extracted directly from the full bitstream to form a partial configuration. At runtime, the partial configuration is loaded on demand.

The main advantage of direct bitstream manipulation is that it bases on full configuration bitstreams that can come from arbitrary standard FPGA synthesis and design implementation tools. These tools are laid out to optimize circuit qualities, such as speed and area. Further, when the partial configurations modify only the contents of LUTs and BlockRAMs, the direct bitstream manipulation is quite simple and efficiently implemented.

Direct bitstream manipulation shows two limitations. First, for more complex designs the low-level manipulation of bits in a monolithic bitstream becomes extremely tedious. Second, as the routing cannot be changed, different coprocessor cores must occupy exactly the same subarea of the FPGA, and the interface between the CPU and coprocessors must be bound to a fixed location. Moreover, it must be ensured that the routes for the CPU core do not run through the partially reconfigured area and vice versa. Because current design implementation tools do not allow to pose location constraints on routing resources, constraining the routing becomes more or less a trial-and-error process, involving manual intervention (see Section 3). Nonetheless, direct bitstream manipulation has been used for generating partial reconfigurations in [8] [7]. A comprehensive study of the technique can be found in [7].

2.2 Bitstream Generation and Manipulation with JBits

The Xilinx JBits SDK [6] provides access to most of the Virtex resources through a Java class library. JBits starts operating on an initial configuration. All Vir-

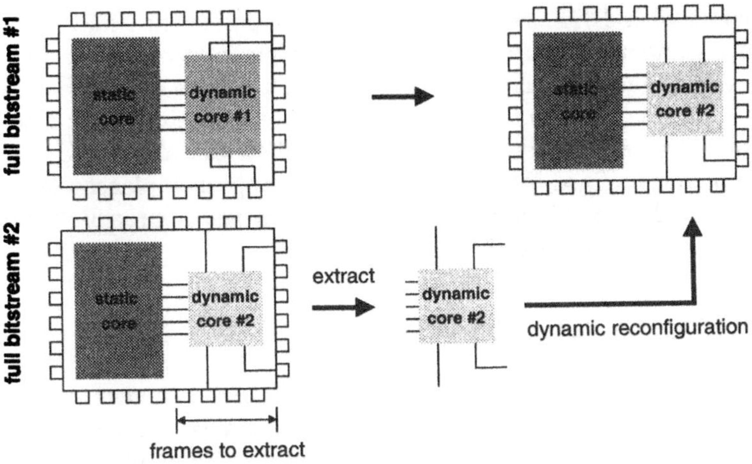

Fig. 1. Extracting a partial bitstream from a full bitstream.

tex resources can be instantiated and configured. At any time, JBits can save changes to the design as partial bitstreams. Up to now, JBits supports structural circuit design only, but it enables hierarchical designs by grouping subcircuits into modules or cores. JBits also includes an automatic router, which can dynamically route and unroute connections. In the design flow described in [12], JBits manipulates designs, given as EDIF netlists, that have been fully mapped and placed by synthesis tools. JBits adds the routing and generates configuration bitstreams. JBits development is still in flux. For example, currently the abilities of the autorouter are still limited and some Virtex resources cannot be manipulated, e.g., long lines.

JBits offers two advantages over direct bitstream manipulation. First, JBits introduces a higher level of abstraction as it operates on CLBs, routes, etc., rather than on raw bits in a bitstream. This feature also opens up future dynamic applications, where tasks can be relocated and connections can be re-routed online. Second, JBits includes versatile functions for full and partial bitstream manipulation.

The limitation of JBits stems from the fact that it does not yet provide support for combinatorial and sequential synthesis, timing-driven placement and advanced routing. Currently, a pure JBits design flow seems only applicable for smaller or data flow oriented applications. Developers of more complex designs, such a coprocessors, prefer synthesis from RTL specifications in hardware description languages and corresponding optimization tools.

2.3 Combining High-Quality Synthesis with JBits

To get the best features from both worlds, standard design flows and JBits can be combined. We experimented with two different ways to combine complex, high-quality cores with JBits. Both design flows synthesize the static and dynamic cores with standard synthesis and design implementation tools, and generate the partial configuration bitstreams with JBits. The first approach uses JBits to merge the cores but does not dynamically re-route the connections. The locations for the reconfigurable cores and the interface between static and reconfigured cores are bound to fixed locations. The second approach places and routes the cores dynamically. In this paper, we focus on the first approach. The details of this technique are described in the next section.

3 Merging Cores with JBits

This section presents our design tool flow that allows to generate an initial full configuration and a number of subsequent partial configurations. We discuss the details of the tool flow on the example of a soft CPU core plus one coprocessor as initial configuration, and coprocessor cores as partial configurations. The tool flow relies on two techniques: the *virtual socket*, a fixed-location interface between the CPU and the coprocessor cores, and *feed-through components* to constrain routing.

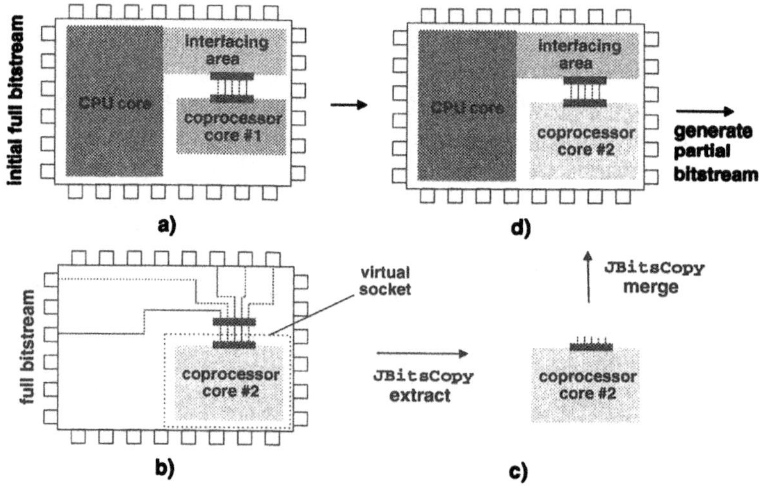

Fig. 2. Generation of initial full and partial bitstreams.

3.1 Overall Tool Flow

The overall FPGA area is divided into two non-overlapping parts, one part for the CPU core and the other one for the reconfigurable coprocessors. The generation of the initial full configuration involves following steps (shown in Figure 2a)):

1. Create an initial design which consists of the CPU core and a coprocessor component. Any synthesis tool or core generator can be used to derive high-quality designs.
2. Insert the virtual socket, a predefined interface component. Connect the CPU and coprocessor via the virtual socket.
3. Run FPGA back-end tools with constraints on the locations of the CPU, the coprocessor, and the virtual socket. This generates the initial full bitstream.

The tool flow respects the characteristics of the Virtex frame-based configuration mechanism. The part of the CPU core that is located in the same (vertical) frames as the coprocessor area, denoted as *interfacing area* in Figure 2, contains only stateless resources. A partial bitstream for a coprocessor is generated as follows:

1. Create the coprocessor design with any front-end tool.
2. Connect the coprocessor to the predefined virtual socket. The CPU-bound signals of the virtual socket are connected to unused I/O pins to prevent the optimizer from removing the socket component.
3. Run FPGA back-end tools with constraints on the locations of the coprocessor and the virtual socket. This generates a full bitstream (shown in Figure 2b).
4. Use the tool *JBitsCopy* to i) extract the coprocessor from the full bitstream (shown in Figure 2c)), and ii) merge the coprocessor with the initial full bitstream (shown in Figure 2d)). By this, the initial coprocessor area is overwritten with the new coprocessor. The new coprocessor fits seamless into the initial design, provided the location constraints for the coprocessors and the virtual socket have been respected. JBits is then used to generate a partial configuration bitstream that reflects the coprocessor area.

3.2 Virtual Socket

The virtual socket is a component that provides fixed locations for a set of predefined signals. All signals from the CPU or the I/O pins to the coprocessor and vice versa are routed through this interface. The only exceptions are the global nets for clock and set/reset signals. Because the interface is static, new coprocessors can be developed without having access to the CPU design.

3.3 Constraining the Design

The Xilinx back-end tools allow to put placement constraints on a design's logic resources, but not on the routing. On the other hand we have to make sure that routing from one core, CPU or coprocessor, does not cross the area occupied by the other core. Such routes could potentially be destroyed when a different core is reconfigured. The same holds for connections between the CPU and coprocessor cores and any specific resources, such as the BlockRAM, external memory, or I/O devices. We use floorplanning by location constraints to separate the CPU and coprocessor areas. Routing is constrained by following techniques:

- *Local routing:* We define connections between logic blocks that belong to the same core as local routing. Cores are constrained to rectangular areas on the FPGA. Depending on the size of the bounding-box and the core's requirements, some routes can cross the rectangle. Obviously, the rectangle can be enlarged to include the routing as well. Increasing the rectangle's dimensions by only a few CLBs proved to work well since the delay-based router prefers short local routes. Our experiments show that separating the initial areas for CPU and coprocessor cores by a *safety border* of 3-6 CLBs successfully prevents the unintentional overlapping of routes from the two cores. This was also confirmed in [7].

- *Disturbing lines:* External devices, such as memories, are connected to the CPU core via I/O pins. We denote such non-local routes that cross the coprocessor area as disturbing lines, see Figure 3a). To control non-local routing, we introduce *feed-through* components. A feed-through component is a CLB with its LUT programmed to the identity function. Being a logic resource, a feed-through component can be constrained to any location on the FPGA. Disturbing lines are routed through one or more feed-through components that are placed such that the disturbing lines keep out of the coprocessor area, shown in Figure 3b). Placing the right number of feed-through components at the right locations is a manual process. However, this is needed only once for the initial full configuration.

- *Virtual Sockets:* The virtual socket is also built from feed-through components to allow the placement of the interface. The routing of signals around the CLBs that form the virtual socket is critical, as the virtual socket defines a border between static and reconfigured parts. Using a single feed-through CLB does not guarantee a sufficient safety margin. Therefore we have designed a special hard macro, the *2-CLB feed-through* component, using the Xilinx FPGA editor. The macro consists of two feed-through CLBs connected by a local, straight route. Figure 4 displays a block diagram of our prototype, which uses the 2-CLB feed-through macros to connect the coprocessor core.

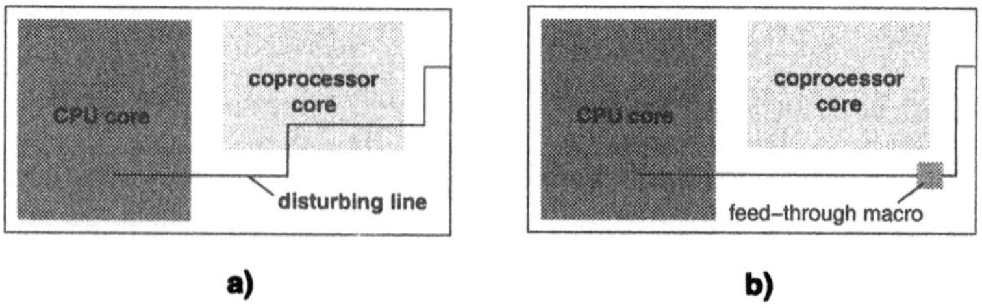

Fig. 3. Insertion of feed-through macros to avoid disturbing lines.

3.4 JBitsCopy

We have developed a JBits-based tool called *JBitsCopy*, that extracts fully synthesized circuits out of configuration bitstreams. JBitsCopy grabs all the FPGA resources, logic and routing, within a definable bounding box of an existing configuration and inserts it into another configuration. Additionally, JBitsCopy can relocate the grabbed design to different vertical and horizontal positions. The functionality of JBitsCopy is similar to the *JBitsRipper* tool described in [9], which targets Xilinx XC4000 series. JBitsRipper allows to grab the configuration within a bounding-box and creates a Java program that reproduces this configuration.

4 Prototype Implementation: Audio Streaming

As case study and proof of concept for the proposed design flow, we have implemented a complete and fully operational audio decoding application [3]. The prototype consists of a minimal embedded computer based on a general-purpose CPU core, memories, network interface, and several coprocessors for hardware-accelerated playback of audio streams.

The CPU receives UDP packets containing encoded audio data from a network via an Ethernet interface. The CPU unpacks the audio data and sends it to the audio coprocessor's input FIFO via the virtual socket. The coprocessor decodes the audio stream and sends the raw audio data to the on-board digital-to-analog converter. Different formats for the encoding of audio data require different coprocessors. Depending on the audio format currently used, the audio decoders are dynamically configured into the prototype. The technical details of the prototype are:

- *Prototyping Platform*
  The prototype has been implemented on a XESS XCV800 board which consists of a Xilinx Virtex XCV800-4 FPGA and a multitude of I/O interfaces. A block diagram of the prototyping board is given in Figure 4.

The cores were designed in VHDL, synthesized and implemented using Synopsys FPGA Express 3.6.0 and Xilinx Foundation 4.1i tools, respectively.

- *CPU core*
  The soft CPU core is the SPARC V8 compatible 32bit LEON CPU [5]. The CPU was configured with 2kB separated data- and instruction-cache (implemented in internal BlockRAM), a 256 byte internal boot-ROM (implemented in internal distributed RAM) and an external 32bit memory interface. The CPU core requires 3865 Virtex slices which amounts to 41% of the XCV800's logic resources, and 14 BlockRAMs which equals 50% of the memory resources. Without any optimization, the CPU runs at 25 MHz. Applications for the LEON core run on top of the RTEMS [2] real-time operating system and are compiled using the GNU C based LECCS cross-compiler kit [4].

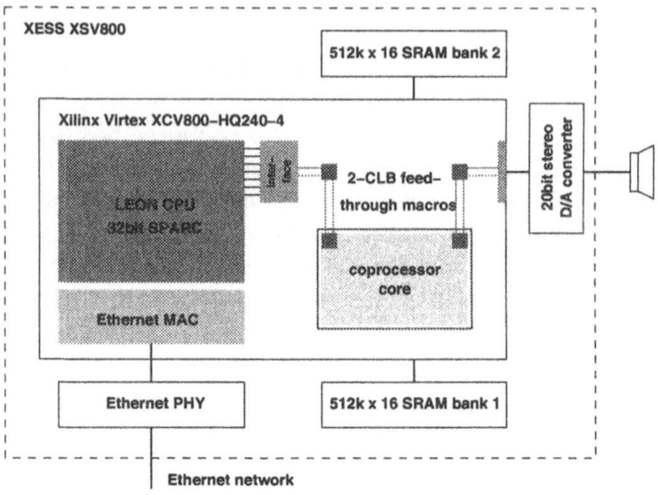

Fig. 4. Block diagram of the audio streaming prototype.

- *Coprocessor cores*
  We have implemented two audio decoding coprocessors, a PCM and an Intel/DVI compliant ADPCM decoder. The ADPCM core uses 430 Virtex slices, or 4.5% of the XCV800 resources; the PCM decoder fits into 35 slices, or 0.4% of the resources.

We envision the prototype application as a typical scenario for future embedded networked systems that load hardware functions on demand. The current limitations of our prototype are that the reconfiguration has to be initiated by the user and that the partial configurations are loaded onto the FPGA from a host computer via a configuration port. We are working to extend the prototype to perform fully autonomous reconfiguration. There, the configuration bitstreams are stored locally in the prototype and CPU software recognizes the audio format used and initiates reconfiguration. A straight-forward implementation uses a small controller in the system to control reconfiguration. However, recent advances in Virtex technology, i.e., internal configuration access port in Virtex-II, seem to make a reconfiguration controlled by the FPGA itself feasible. Our goal is to construct such an embedded networked reconfigurable system prototype.

5 Conclusions and Future Work

In this paper, we have discussed a design flow to implement hybrid CPUs and demonstrated it on the working example of one CPU and two coprocessor cores. The design flow is, however, not restricted to one single static and one single reconfigurable part. Extensions to several partial reconfigurable subareas are straight-forward. In such a system, interfaces can be established by on-chip busses to which the reconfigurable modules connect [1].

We plan to extend our work in the following directions:

- Construction of a prototype with fully autonomous reconfiguration.
- Development of hybrid CPUs employing multiple reconfigurable coprocessors connected via on-chip busses.

6 Acknowledgements

We would like to thank Marco Wirz for his work on the prototype, including the design of the network subsystem, and Herbert Walder for the JBitsCopy tool and for sharing his JBits experience.

References

[1] G. Brebner and O. Diessel. Chip-Based Reconfigurable Task Management. In *Proceedings of the International Conference on Field-Programmable Logic and Applications (FPL)*, pages 182–191, 2001.

[2] O. Corp. RTEMS Homepage. http://www.rtems.com.

[3] M. Dyer and M. Wirz. Reconfigurable System on FPGA. Master's thesis, Computer Engineering and Networks Lab, ETH Zurich, March 2002.

[4] J. Gaisler. LECCS: LEON/ERC32 Cross Compilation System. http://www.gaisler.com/leccs.html.

[5] J. Gaisler. *The LEON Processor User's Manual.* Gaisler Research, version 2.3.7 edition, August 2001.

[6] S. A. Guccione, D. Levi, and P. Sundararajan. JBits: A Java-based Interface for Reconfigurable Computing. In *Proceedings of the 2nd Annual Military and Aerospace Applications of Programmable Devices and Technologies Conference (MAPLD)*, 2000.

[7] A. Haase. Untersuchungen zur dynamischen Rekonfigurierbarkeit von FPGA. Master's thesis, TU Chemnitz-Zwickau, Germany, September 2001. (in German).

[8] E. L. Horta and J. W. Lockwood. PARBIT: A Tool to Transform Bitfiles to Implement Partial Reconfiguration of Field Programmable Gate Arrays (FPGAs). Technical report, Department of Computer Science, Applied Research Lab, Washington University, Saint Louis, July 2001.

[9] P. James-Roxby, E. Cerro-Prada, and S. Charlwood. A Core-based Design Method for Reconfigurable Computing Applications. In *Proceedings of the IEE Colloquium on Reconfigurable Systems*, Glasgow, March 1999. IEE Informatics.

[10] D. Lampret. *OpenRISC 1200 IP Core specification.* www.opencores.org, 2001.

[11] P. Leong, C. Sham, W. Wong, W. Yuen, and M. Leong. A Bitstream Reconfigurable FPGA Implementation of the WSAT Algorithm. *IEEE Transactions on VLSI Systems*, 9(1):197–201, February 2001.

[12] S. Singh and P. James-Roxby. Lava and JBits: From HDL to Bitstream in Seconds. In *Proceedings of the IEEE Symposium on FPGAs for Custom Computing Machines (FCCM)*, 2001.

[13] Triscend Corp. *Triscend A7 Datasheet*, 2001.

[14] Xilinx Inc. *Xilinx Application Note XAPP151: Virtex Series Configuration Architecture User Guide*, v1.5 edition, 9 2000.

[15] Xilinx, Inc. *Virtex-II Pro Platform FPGA Handbook*, January 2002.

On-line Defragmentation for Run-Time Partially Reconfigurable FPGAs

Manuel G. Gericota[1], Gustavo R. Alves[1], Miguel L. Silva[2], José M. Ferreira[2]

[1] Department of Electrical Engineering – DEE/ISEP
Rua Dr. António Bernardino de Almeida, 4200-072 Porto – PORTUGAL
{mgg, galves}@dee.isep.ipp.pt
http://www.dee.isep.ipp.pt/~mgg/indexe.htm
[2] Dep. of Electrical and Computers Engineering – DEEC/FEUP
Rua Dr. Roberto Frias, 4200-465 Porto – PORTUGAL
{mlms, jmf}@fe.up.pt

Abstract. Dynamically reconfigurable systems have benefited from a new class of FPGAs recently introduced into the market, which allow partial and dynamic reconfiguration at run-time, enabling multiple independent functions from different applications to share the same device, swapping resources as needed. When the sequence of tasks to be performed is not predictable, resource allocation decisions have to be made on-line, fragmenting the FPGA logic space. A rearrangement may be necessary to get enough contiguous space to efficiently implement incoming functions, to avoid spreading their components and, as a result, degrading their performance. This paper presents a novel active replication mechanism for configurable logic blocks (CLBs), able to implement on-line rearrangements, defragmenting the available FPGA resources without disturbing those functions that are currently running.

1 Introduction

Reconfigurable logic devices, namely Field Programmable Gate Arrays (FPGAs), experienced a considerable expansion in the last few years, due in part to an increase in its size and complexity, with gains in board space and flexibility. With the advent of a new kind of SRAM-based FPGAs, capable of implementing fast run-time partial reconfiguration (e. g. the Virtex family from Xilinx used to validate this work), the advantages of these devices were considerably reinforced, wide-spreading their usage as a base for reconfigurable computing platforms.

The new features offered by these devices enabled the concept of "virtual hardware", where resources are supposed to be unlimited and those implementations that exceed the reconfigurable area are resolved by temporal partitioning. The static implementation of a circuit is separated in two or more independent hardware contexts, which may be swapped during runtime [1]. Extensive work is under way to improve the capability of these devices to handle multi-context, by storing several

• This work is supported by the Portuguese Foundation for Science and Technology (FCT), under contract POCTI/33842/ESE/2000.

M. Glesner, P. Zipf, and M. Renovell (Eds.): FPL 2002, LNCS 2438, pp. 302-311, 2002.

configurations and enabling quick context switching [2, 3]. The main objective is to improve the execution time by minimising external memory transfers, assuming that some amount of on-chip data storage is available in the reconfigurable architecture. However, this solution is only viable if the functions implemented on hardware are mutually exclusive on the temporal domain; otherwise, the length of reconfiguration intervals would imply delays unacceptable to most applications.

An application comprises a set of functions that are frequently executed sequentially, or with a low degree of parallelism, in which case their simultaneous availability is not required. On the other hand, the reconfiguration intervals offered by new FPGAs, are sufficiently small to enable functions to be swapped in real time. If a proper floorplanning schedule is devised, it becomes feasible to use a single device to run a set of applications, which in total require more than 100% of the FPGA resources, by swapping functions in and out of the FPGA as needed.

Partial reconfiguration times are in the order of microseconds, depending on the configuration interface and on the complexity (and thus on the size) of the function being implemented. However, the reconfiguration time overhead may be reduced to zero, if new functions are swapped in advance with those already out of use, as illustrated in figure 1. The reconfiguration interval (r_t) refers to the period where the configuration of a new function may be performed in order to be available when required by the application flow (and should therefore not be mistaken by the reconfiguration time). Notice that an increase in the degree of parallelism may retard the reconfiguration of incoming functions, due to lack of space in the FPGA. Delays will therefore be introduced in the application execution, systematically or not, depending on the application flow.

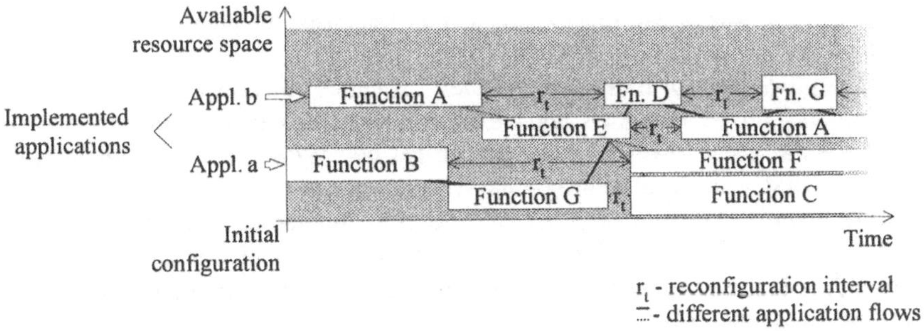

Fig. 1. Temporal scheduling of functions.

The FPGA logic space comprises three types of elements:

- Configurable Logic Blocks (CLBs);
- Input/Output Blocks (IOBs);
- Routing resources.

All these resources may be shared in the spatial and/or temporal domains. The goal is to allocate to each function as much resources as it needs to execute independently of all the others, as if it were the sole application running on a chip just large enough to support it. The partitioning of the FPGA logic space in a three-dimensional basis, two spatial dimensions and one temporal, is addressed in [4]. The resources are shared among multiple independent functions, each having its own spatial and temporal requirements. As the resources are allocated to functions and later released, many small areas of free resources are created. These portions of unallocated resources tend to become so small that they fail to satisfy any request and so remain unused – the FPGA logic space gets fragmented. This problem is illustrated in figure 2 in the form of a 3-D floorplan and function schedule [5], where each shadow area corresponds to the optimal space occupied by the implementation of a single function.

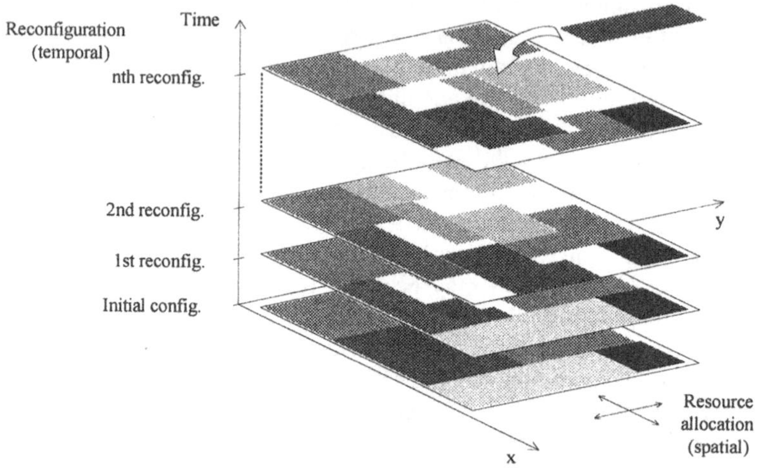

Fig. 2. 3-D representation of the fragmentation problem.

If the requirements of functions and their sequence are known in advance, suitable arrangements can be designed and sufficient resources can be provided to handle them in parallel [6]. However, when placement decisions need to be made on-line, it is possible that a lack of contiguous free resources will prevent functions from executing, even if the total number of resources available is sufficient. Notice that spreading the components of incoming functions by the available resources would lead to a degradation of its performance, delaying tasks from completion and reducing the utilisation of the FPGA.

When a new function cannot be allocated immediately due to lack of contiguous resources, a suitable rearrangement of a subset of the executing functions might solve the problem. Three methods are proposed in [4] to find such (partial) rearrangements, with the goal to increase the rate at which waiting functions are allocated, while minimising disruptions to executing functions that are to be moved. However, the physical execution of these rearrangements implies halting currently running functions and consequently halting their respective applications. A mechanism to implement the rearrangements without disturbing the running functions is presented in this paper. To address this problem, a new concept is introduced – the active replication –, which enables the relocation of each FPGA CLB (and therefore of its associated routing) even if it is active, i.e. the CLB is part of an implemented function that is actually being used by an application [7]. This concept enables the defragmentation of the FPGA logic space on-line, without introducing time overheads.

We start by describing the active CLB replication and releasing mechanism, followed by a summary of its limitations, be it due to the FPGA architecture or to the particular configuration mechanism used.

2 Resource Replication and Release

Conceptually, an FPGA could be described as an array of uncommitted CLBs, surrounded by a periphery of IOBs, which are interconnectable by configurable routing resources, whose configuration is controlled by a set of memory cells that lies beneath.

The implementation of an on-line defragmentation strategy implies the use of a dynamic replication mechanism, where CLBs currently being used by a given function have their functionality relocated to other CLBs, without disturbing function execution. The replicated CLBs are then free to be allocated to new functions. One of the major problems facing the implementation of such replication mechanism is the dynamic replication of active elements, be it CLBs or routing resources. Dynamically replicating an active CLB is not just a matter of relocating its functional specification: the corresponding interconnections with the rest of the circuit have to be established; additionally, internal state information also has to be copied, depending on the functionality it is implementing. All these actions must be carried out without interfering with its normal operation. The same happens when dealing with routing resources, although their replication is a simpler job.

The transparent release of active CLBs it is not trivial, due to two major issues: i) configuration memory organization and ii) internal state information.

The configuration memory can be visualized as a rectangular array of bits, which are grouped into one-bit wide vertical frames extending from the top to the bottom of the array. One frame is the smallest unit of configuration that can be written to or read from the configuration memory. These frames are grouped together into larger units called columns. Each CLB column corresponds to a configuration column with multiple frames, mixing internal CLB configuration and state information, and column routing and interconnect information. The partitioning of the entire FPGA configuration memory into frames enables on-line concurrent partial reconfiguration, facilitating the implementation of on-line rearrangement procedures.

The configuration procedure is a sequential mechanism that spans through some (or eventually all) CLB configuration columns. When replicating an active CLB more than one column may be affected, since its input and output signals (as well as those in its replica) may cross several columns before reaching its source or destination. Any reconfiguration action must therefore ensure that the signals from the replicated CLB are not broken before being totally re-established from its replica, otherwise its operation will be disturbed or even halted. It is also important to ensure that the functionality of the CLB replica must be perfectly stable before its outputs are connected to the system, so as to avoid output glitches.

A set of experiments performed with a XCV200 from Xilinx demonstrated that the only possible solution is to divide the replication procedure in two phases, as illustrated in figure 3.

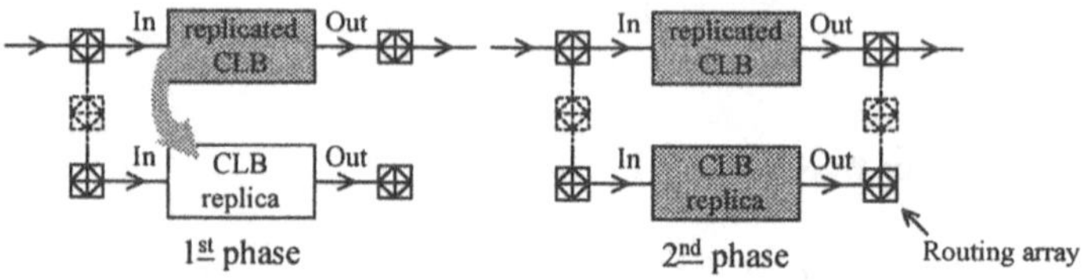

Fig. 3. Two-phase CLB replication procedure.

In the first phase, the internal configuration of the CLB is replicated and the inputs of both CLBs are placed in parallel. Due to the slowness of the reconfiguration procedure, when compared with the application speed of operation, the outputs of the CLB replica are already perfectly stable when they are connected to the circuit, in the second phase. To avoid output glitches, both CLBs (replicated and replica) must remain in parallel for at least one clock cycle. Notice that rewriting the same configuration data does not generate any transient signals, so this procedure does not affect the remaining resources covered by the rewriting of the configuration frames that are needed to carry out the replication procedure.

Another major requirement for the success of the replication procedure is the correct transfer of state information. If the current CLB function is purely combinational, a simple read-modify-write configuration procedure will suffice to accomplish the replication. However, in the case of a sequential function, the internal state information must be preserved and no writes could be lost during the copying procedure. The solution to this problem depends on the type of implementation. In this paper we shall consider three implementation cases: synchronous free–running clock circuits; synchronous gated–clock circuits, and; asynchronous circuits.

When dealing with synchronous free-running clock circuits, the two-phase replication procedure described earlier is a good solution. Between the first and the second phase, the CLB replica has the same inputs as the replicated CLB, and all its four flip-flops acquire the state information. Several experiments made using this class of circuits have shown the effectiveness of this method in the replication of active CLBs. No loss of state information or the presence of output glitches was observed.

Despite the effectiveness of this solution, its restriction to synchronous free--running clock circuits is a serious limitation. A broad range of circuits uses gated--clocks, where input acquisition by the flip-flop is controlled by the state of the clock enable signal. As we cannot ensure that this signal will be active between the first and the second phase of the replication procedure, it is uncertain that the CLB replica will capture the state information. On the other hand, it is not feasible to set this signal as part of the replication procedure, because the value present at the input of the replica flip-flops may change in the meantime, and a coherency problem will then occur.

A replication aid block was used to solve this problem, which manages the transfer of the state information from the replicated flip-flops to the replica flip-flops, while enabling their update by the circuit at any instant, without delaying the replication procedure. The whole replication scheme is represented in figure 4, where only one logic cell is shown, for reasons of simplicity. Each CLB comprises four of these cells, which can be considered individually for the purpose of implementing this procedure. The temporary transfer paths established between the replicated cells and their replica do not affect their functionality, since they use only free routing resources and do not modify their structure.

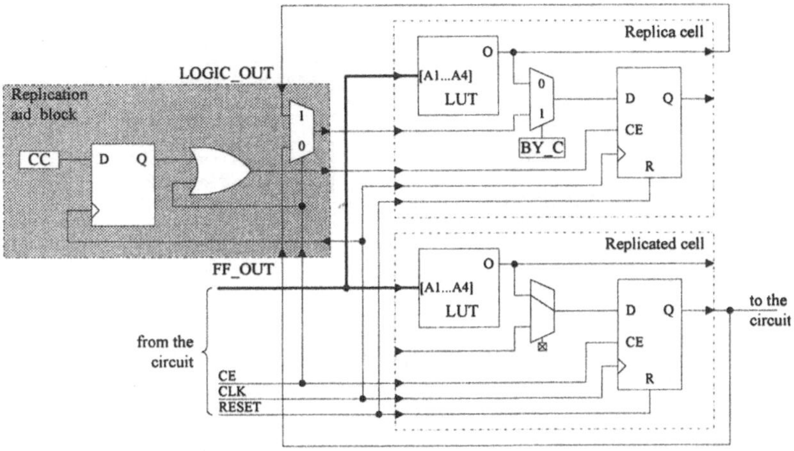

Fig. 4. Implementation of the gated-clock flip-flop replication scheme.

The inputs of the 2:1 multiplexer present in the replication aid block receive one temporary transfer path from the output of the replicated flip-flop (FF_OUT), and another one, in this example, from the output of the Look-Up Table (LUT) in the replica logic cell (LOGIC_OUT), which is normally applied to the flip-flop. If the LUT in the logic cell being replicated is not used by the current implementation, the input of the flip-flop cell will be directly connected to one of the cell inputs. In this case, LOGIC_OUT will be connected to that input. The multiplexer is controlled by the clock enable signal (CE) of the replicated flip-flop. If this signal is not active, the output of the replicated flip-flop (FF_OUT) is applied to the input of the replica flip--flop. A clock enable signal, generated by the replication aid block (capture control signal - CC), forces the replica flip-flop to hold the transferred value. The replica flip--flop acquires the state information present in the replicated flip-flop. If the CE signal is active or is activated during this procedure, the multiplexer selects the LOGIC_OUT signal and applies it to the input of the replica flip-flop, which is updated at the same time and with the same value as the replicated flip-flop, guaranteeing state coherency. Figure 5 represents the flow diagram describing the replication procedure, while figure 6 shows the waveform simulation of state transfer and update operations during the replication procedure. No loss of information or functional disturbance was observed during the execution of the procedure.

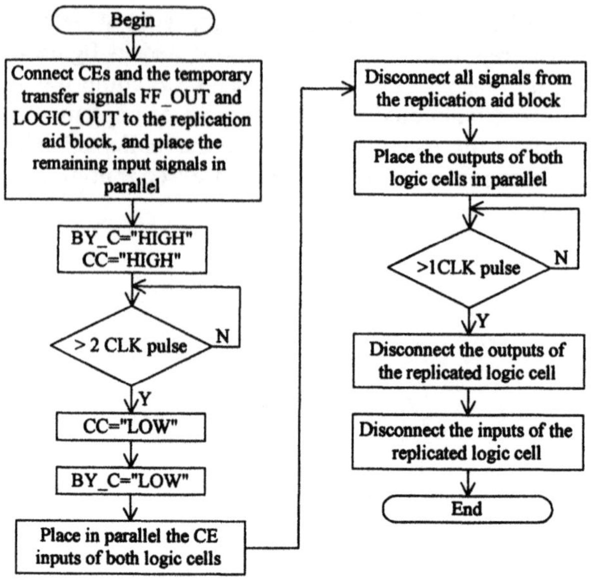

Fig. 5. Replication procedure flow.

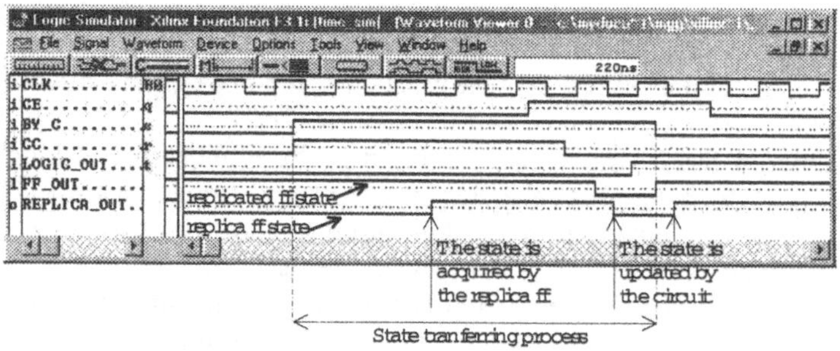

Fig. 6. Simulation of a state transfer and update during the replication procedure.

The control signals CC and BY_C are configuration memory bits whose values are driven through reconfiguration of the configuration memory. BY_C directs the state signal to the input of the replica flip-flop, while CC enables its acquisition. It is therefore possible to control the whole replication procedure through the configuration interface used, and as such no extra FPGA pins are required.

Each replication aid block makes use of one CLB slice. Since four of these blocks are required to replicate the four logic cells of a CLB, two extra CLBs will be required to implement this procedure. However, this overhead is only apparent, since the occupancy of those CLBs takes place only during the replication procedure. After the replication they become free to be used by new functions.

Since we decided to control all signals through the configuration memory, so as not to use extra FPGA pins, the CC net includes the flip-flop shown in figure 4. However, it is there simply as a consequence of the structure of the CLB slice, and does not play any role in the implementation of the procedure that was described.

After the state has been transferred, the input signals involved in the execution of the replication procedure are placed in parallel, all the signals to and from the replication aid block are disconnected (and consequently the occupied CLBs are free), and the outputs are also placed in parallel. After at least one function clock cycle the replicated block is disconnected and becomes free.

Practical experiments performed over the ITC'99 Benchmark Circuits from the Politécnico di Torino [8] implemented in a Virtex XCV200 proved the effectiveness of our approach. These circuits are purely synchronous with only one single-phase clock signal present. However, this approach is also applicable to multiple clock/multiple phase applications, since CLB replication is performed individually. Only one clock signal is involved in the replication of each CLB, even if many of these blocks were processed simultaneously.

Using the Boundary Scan [9] interface to perform the reconfiguration, the average replication time of each CLB implementing synchronous gated-clock circuits is about 22,6 ms, for a 20 MHz frequency of the test clock.

This method is also effective when dealing with asynchronous circuits, if transparent data latches are used instead of flip-flops. In this case, the CE signal is replaced in the latch by the input control signal G. Data present in the D input is stored when the control input G changes from '1' to '0'. The same replication aid block is used and the same replication sequence is followed. The register present in the replication aid block may be configured as a latch, instead as a flip-flop, if this is preferred or if no adequate clock signal is available.

In the Virtex family of FPGAs, LUTs can be configured as Distributed RAMs. However, the extension of this on-line replication concept to the replication of those LUT/RAMs is not viable. The content of the LUT/RAMs could be read and written through the configuration memory, but there is no feasible way, other than to stop the function, capable of ensuring data coherency, if there is a write attempt during the replication interval, as stated in [10]. Furthermore, since frames span an entire column of CLB slices, the same LUT bit in all of them is updated with a single write command. We must ensure that either all the remaining data in the slice is constant, or it is also modified externally through partial reconfiguration. Even if not being replicated, LUT/RAMs should not lie in any column that could be affected by the replication procedure.

3 Reconfiguring Routing Resources

Each CLB comprises, in addition to its logic resources, three routing arrays: two local (input and output) and one global. The routing resources in these arrays may be unidirectional or bi-directional, as indicated in figure 7. No routing resources are available in the local arrays to establish direct interconnections with other CLBs, so those required by the replication procedure can only be established through the global routing array. Between local and global routing arrays, only unidirectional routing resources are available, as seen in figure 7.

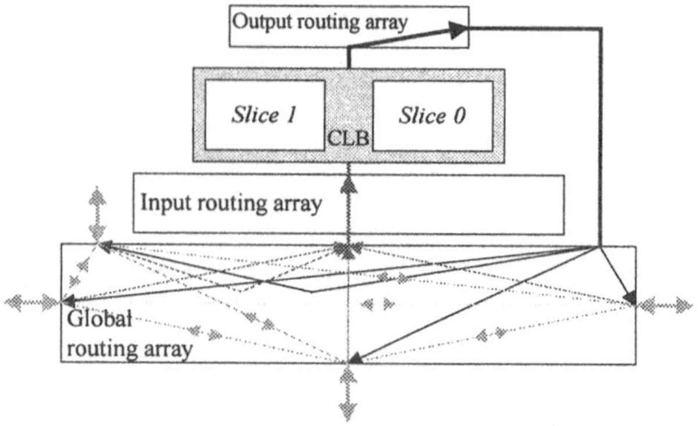

Fig. 7. CLB routing arrays resources.

To place the inputs in parallel, interconnection segments between global arrays may be unidirectional (from the replicated CLB inputs towards the CLB replica inputs), or bi-directional. Concerning the outputs, interconnection segments between global arrays may also be unidirectional (from the CLB replica outputs towards the replicated CLB output), or bi-directional. Otherwise, since signals do not propagate backwards, no signals will exist at the inputs of the CLB replica, and the outputs of both CLBs will not be in parallel. As a result, output glitches will occur when the outputs of the replicated CLB are disconnected from the system, and no signals will be propagated to the rest of the circuit.

As mentioned before, the relocation of functional active CLBs should have a minimum influence (preferably none) in the system operation, as well as a reduced overhead in terms of reconfiguration cost. This cost depends on the number of reconfiguration frames needed to replicate and free each CLB, since a great number of frames would imply a longer rearrangement time. The impact of the replication procedure in the running functions is mainly related to the delays imposed by re--routed paths, since the relocation procedure might imply a longer path, thus diminishing their maximum frequency of operation (the longest path delay determines the maximum frequency of operation).

The placement algorithms (in an attempt to reduce path delays) gather in the same area the logic that is needed to implement the components of a given function. It is unwise to disperse it, since it would generate longer paths (and hence, an increase in path delays). On the other hand, it would also put too much stress in the limited routing resources. Therefore, the relocation of the CLBs should be performed to nearby CLBs. If necessary, the relocation of a complete function may take place in several stages, in order to avoid an excessive increase in path delays.

The replication of routing resources – in order to rearrange their positioning and to free some segments to be used in incoming functions – posed no problems. The same two-phase replication procedure is effective on the replication and release of local and global active interconnections. The interconnections involved are first duplicated in order to establish an alternative path, and then disconnected, becoming available to be reused. Notice that due to the lack of routing resources following the replication of the CLB, it might be necessary to perform a rearrangement of the routing interconnections, in order to optimize them or to increase the availability of routing resources to incoming functions.

4 Conclusion

This paper presented a novel replication procedure able to replicate active CLBs without halting their operation. The proposed procedure enables the implementation of a truly on-line non-intrusive FPGA logic space defragmentation, which allows the dynamic scheduling of tasks in the spatial and temporal domains. It is therefore possible that several applications share the same hardware platform, with their respective functions running and being swapped in and out of the FPGA without generating any time overhead to the running applications, or disturbing their operation.

References

1. Cardoso, J. M. P, Neto, H. C.: An Enhanced Static-List Scheduling Algorithm for Temporal Partitioning onto RPUs. *Proc. of the 10th Intl. Conf. on Very Large Scale Integration*, Lisbon, Portugal, 1999, pp. 485-496.
2. Maestre, R., Kurdahi, F. J., Hermida, R., Bagherzadeh, N., Singh, H., A Formal Approach to Context Scheduling for Multicontext Reconfigurable Architectures. *IEEE Transactions on Very Large Scale Integration Systems*, Vol. 9, No. 1, February 2001, pp. 173-185.
3. Sanchez-Elez, M., Fernandez, M., Maestre, R., Hermida, R., Bagherzadeh, N., Kurdahi, F. J.: A Complete Data Scheduler for Multi-Context Reconfigurable Architectures. *Proc. of the Design, Automation and Test in Europe*, Paris, France, 2002, pp. 547-552.
4. Diessel, O., ElGindy, H., Middendorf, M., Schmeck, H., Schmidt, B.: Dynamic scheduling of tasks on partially reconfigurable FPGAs. *IEE Proc.-Computer Digital Technology*, Vol. 147, No. 3, May 2000, pp. 181-188.
5. Vasilko, M.: DYNASTY: A Temporal Floorplanning Based CAD Framework for Dynamically Reconfigurable Logic Systems. *Proc. of the 9th International Workshop on Field-Programmable Logic and Applications*, Glasgow, Scotland, 1999, pp.124-133.
6. Teich, M., Fekete, S., Schepers, J.: Compile-time optimization of dynamic hardware reconfigurations. *Proc. of the Intl. Conf. on Parallel and Distributed Processing Techniques and Applications*, Las Vegas, USA, 1999.
7. Gericota, M. G., Alves, G. R., Silva, M. L., Ferreira, J. M.: Dynamic Replication: The Core of a Truly Non-Intrusive SRAM-based FPGA Structural Concurrent Test Methodology. *3rd IEEE Latin-American Test Workshop Digest of Papers*, Montevideo, Uruguay, 2002, pp. 70-75.
8. Politécnico di Torino ITC'99 benchmarks. *http://www.cad.polito.it/tools/itc99.html*
9. *IEEE Standard Test Access Port and Boundary Scan Architecture (IEEE Std 1149.1)*, IEEE Std. Board, May 1990.
10. Huang, W., McCluskey, E. J.: A Memory Coherence Technique for Online Transient Error Recovery of FPGA Configurations. *Proc. of the 9th ACM Int. Symposium on Field-Programmable Gate Arrays*, Monterey, California, 2001, pp. 183-192.

A Flexible Power Model for FPGAs*

Kara K.W. Poon, Andy Yan, and Steven J.E. Wilton

Department of Electrical and Computer Engineering,
University of British Columbia, Vancouver, BC, Canada
{karap,ayan,stevew}@ece.ubc.ca
http://www.ece.ubc.ca/~stevew

Abstract. This paper describes a flexible power model for FPGAs. The model estimates the dynamic, short circuit, and leakage power for a wide variety of FPGA architectures. Such a model will be essential in the design and research of next-generation FPGAs, where power will be one of the primary optimization goals. The model has been integrated into the VPR CAD flow, and is available to the research community for use in FPGA architectural and CAD tool experimentation.

1 Introduction

Power dissipation is becoming a major concern for semiconductor vendors and customers [1]. According to [2], if current design trends continue, a typical microprocessor (MPU) will consume 50 times more power than that can be supported by cost-effective packaging techniques by 2016. A study in [3] indicates that power will become one of the two most serious design concerns (along with design complexity) in coming process generations. FPGAs will not escape this trend; already, FPGA vendors report that power consumption is one of the primary concerns of their customers. Compared to ASICs and other custom chips, FPGAs contain long routing tracks with significant parasitic capacitance; during high speed operations, the switching activity on these long routing tracks causes significant power dissipation.

There have been several low-power architectures described in previous works [4] [5] [6]. However, these papers present "point solutions," in that each only considers a single architecture. In order to migrate these low-power techniques to commercial FPGAs, it is critical that researchers be able to estimate power for a wide variety of architectural parameters. To do this, a power model that is flexible enough to target many different FPGA architectures is required.

There have also been numerous CAD algorithms that target low power [7] [8] [9]. Often, these studies rely primarily on reducing switching activity to result in a low-power solution; although reducing switching activity does lower the power, power also depends on the architecture, the lengths of critical signal routes, the rise and fall times of the signals, and the amount of static power.

* This work was supported by Micronet, the British Columbia Advanced Systems Institute, and the Natural Sciences and Engineering Research Council of Canada

M. Glesner, P. Zipf, and M. Renovell (Eds.): FPL 2002, LNCS 2438, pp. 312–321, 2002.

Though neglected in the past, static power is expected to become an increasingly important part of the total power. In order to adequately evaluate these new CAD algorithms and techniques, a detailed power model is needed to take all these factors into account.

This paper presents a detailed and flexible power model for FPGAs, which includes terms for dynamic power, short-circuit power, and leakage power. Although the techniques we employ have been used before, the integration of these techniques into a flexible power model for FPGAs is a novel approach. The model is flexible enough to target FPGAs with different look-up table (LUT) sizes, different interconnect strategies (segment length, switch block type, connection flexibility), different cluster sizes (for a hierarchical FPGA), and different process technologies. As described above, a model such as the one in this paper will become an essential part of any FPGA architect's and CAD tool designer's arsenal.

The power model has been integrated into the widely-used VPR CAD tool, which already contains detailed area and delay models [10]. Section 2 describes this framework. The model itself is described in Section 3. Section 4 shows how the model can be used to evaluate FPGA architectures. The model is publicly available for use by the FPGA research community (refer to appendix A).

2 Frameworks

The model has been integrated into the VPR CAD tool, which is commonly used by the FPGA research community [11]. As shown in figure 1, VPR contains a place and route tool, and detailed area and delay models. The place and route tool maps a benchmark circuit to an FPGA architecture, using estimates from the area and delay model to guide the tool. A description of the architecture is provided to the tool using an architecture file; the architecture file contains information such as segment length, connection topologies, logic block size and composition, and process parameters. The flexibility of this architecture file is key to VPR; the CAD tool is flexible enough to target any architecture that can be specified in the architecture file. The area and delay models are also used to estimate the area and critical path delay of the circuit after placement and routing has completed.

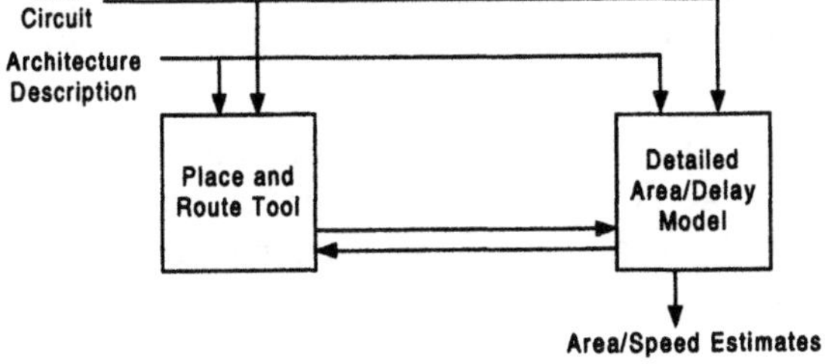

Fig. 1. Original VPR Framework

Figure 2 shows how we have included the power model in the VPR framework. An activity estimator was developed which estimates the switching frequencies of all nodes in the circuit; the activity estimator will be described in section 3.1. The detailed power model was integrated into the area/delay model. This model is described in sections 3.2 to 3.4. In our current implementation, the activity estimator and the power model are not used to guide the placement and routing; the model is only used to estimate the power after placement and routing has occurred. It is possible using this framework, however, to use power estimates during placement and routing to optimize the implementation for power.

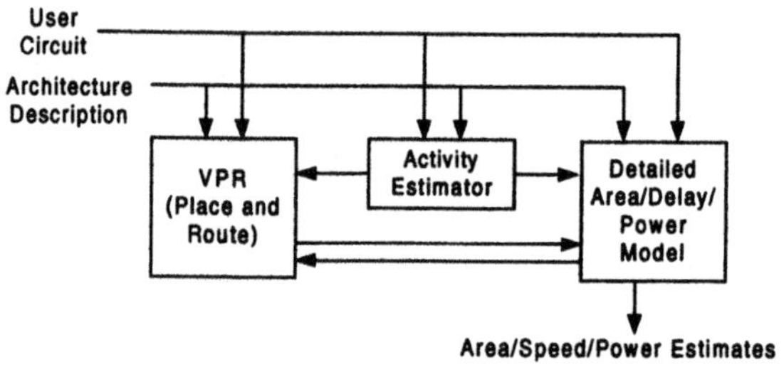

Fig. 2. VPR Framework with Power Model

3 Power Model

Our power model is aimed at the island-style FPGA architectures. Figure 3(a) shows a typical island-style FPGA architecture, which has logic blocks, switch blocks, connection blocks, and routing. We also assume that an H-tree clock network is employed, as illustrated in figure 3(b).

3.1 Activity Generation

Our power model uses the transition density signal model to determine signal activities within the FPGA [12] [13]. The transition density of a signal is the expected number of toggles for the signal in each clock cycle. It is calculated as follows:

For each LUT in the circuit, the function implemented by that LUT can be expressed as a function $f(x)$. For each input, x_i, two new boolean functions $f(x_i)$ and $f(\bar{x}_i)$ can be generated from $f(x)$ by setting input x_i to 1 and 0 respectively. To illustrate, consider the following example:

Example 1. If $f(x) = x_1x_2 + \bar{x}_1x_3$, then $f(x_1) = x_2$ and $f(\bar{x}_1) = x_3$. where x_1, x_2, and x_3 are inputs and $f(x)$ represents the output of the LUT.

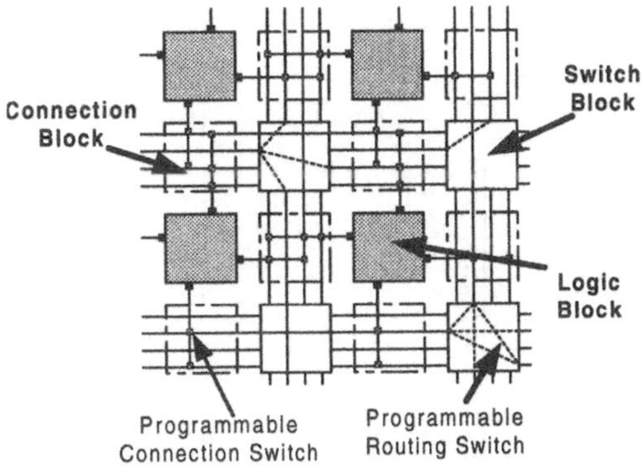

a) An Island-Style FPGA (from [10])

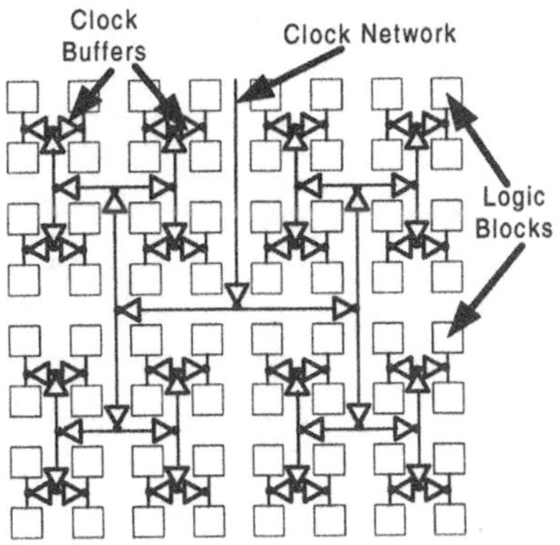

b) Clock Distribution Network

Fig. 3. Assumed Architectural Model for FPGAs

A *boolean difference* of the output with respect to an input, x_i, is then calculated [13]:

$$\frac{df(x)}{dx_i} = f(x_i) \oplus f(\bar{x_i}) \tag{1}$$

The probability of the *boolean difference* , $P(df(x)/dx_i)$, is then the static probability that a change in x_i causes a change at the output . Because of the uncorrelated input assumption of the transition density signal model, each input contributes a static probability, $P(df(x)/dx_i)$, and a transition density, $D(x_i)$, to the total density, $D(y)$, at the output [13].

$$D(y) = \sum_{\text{all inputs}} P\left(\frac{df(x)}{dx}\right) D(x) \tag{2}$$

We assume that the primary inputs to our circuits are random; all primary inputs have a static probability of 0.5 and a transition density of 0.5. These values can be adjusted to reflect other user inputs.

The extension of the transition density model to sequential circuits is straightforward. For each D flip-flop, the output probability is the same as the input probability. The transition density of the output, $D(y)$, of the flip-flop can be written as:

$$D(y) = 2P(x)(1 - P(x)) \tag{3}$$

where $P(x)$ represents the input probability. For the sequential feedback loops, we first determine the static probability at the output of the LUT by iterations, and then apply (3) for the transition density at the output.

3.2 Dynamic Power

Dynamic power is dissipated every time when a signal changes due to the charging and discharging of the load and parasitic capacitance associated with the

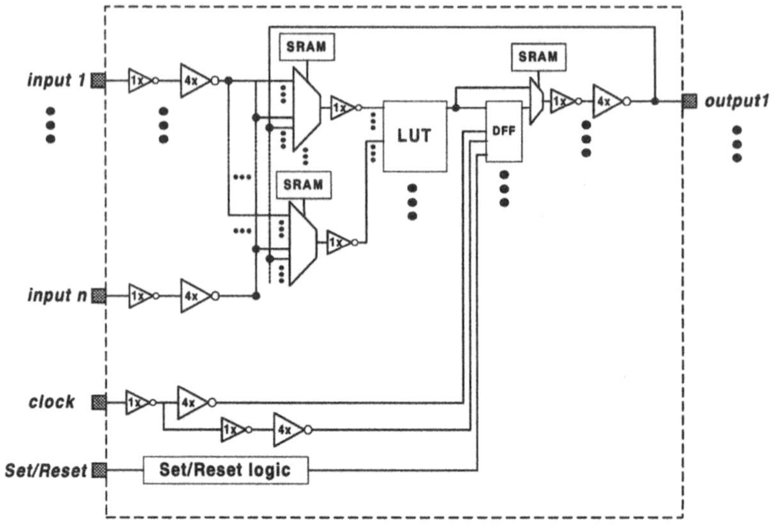

Fig. 4. Schematic of a logic block (from [10])

signal. The dynamic power is the dominant portion of the total power in today's technologies. Using the transition density model [13], the total power dissipation is:

$$\text{Dynamic Power} = \sum_{\text{all nodes}} 0.5 C_y V^2 D(y) f_{\text{clk}} \tag{4}$$

where V is the swinging voltage of each node; C_y is the capacitance being charged and discharged during each transition; $D(y)$ is the individual transition density at each node, and f_{clk} is the clock frequency of the circuit. For each signal, we can apply this equation using the transition density calculated in section 3.1 and the node capacitance estimated by VPR. The clock frequency can be determined by the critical path of the circuit.

We estimate the power dissipated both within the logic blocks and in the global routing network. The assumed logic block structure is shown in figure 4 [10]; the model is flexible enough to account for any number of LUTs and any number of internal routing wires. The length of each internal routing wire is calculated based on the number of LUTs within the logic block; this length is then used to estimate the parasitic capacitance of each internal routing wire. The structure of the LUTs and multiplexers significantly affects the power estimates; we assume the LUTs and multiplexers are implemented using a tree of 2-input multiplexers, as shown in figure 5. We estimate the transition density and parasitic capacitance of each node in figures 5(a) and 5(b) using the transistor sizes in [10] and layout assumptions in [14], and use these results to estimate the power within each LUT and multiplexer.

Note that the internal nodes of each local routing multiplexer swing between the power supply voltage and ground because the gate voltage of the pass transis-

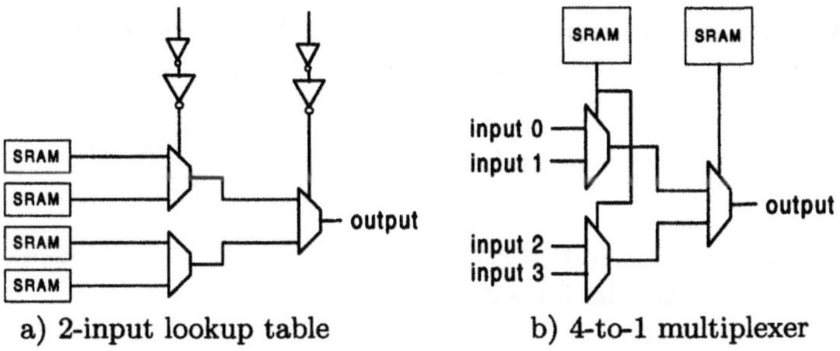

Fig. 5. Implementation of a LUT and MUX using 2-input multiplexers

tors in the SRAM cells has been boosted to overcome the body effect. However, the internal nodes of the LUT toggle at a smaller voltage range since the body effect is applied to the pass transistors inside the multiplexers. We verified our results using HSPICE by simulating different sizes of LUTs and multiplexers with inputs toggling from 5Mhz to 50Mhz. By shifting the delay of each input to model the inputs with different input correlation, we gathered the minimum, average, and maximum values of the average dynamic power dissipation for each size of LUT and multiplexer. From our analysis, the power dissipation calculated by our model matches the maximum values of our simulation results. This is because the transition density signal model that we used assumes uncorrelated inputs. The power dissipated in the global routing network was calculated using the transition densities of each network node, and the capacitance of each node from [10]. For the clock network, we assume a metal-5 H-tree network, as shown in figure 3(b). For very large FPGAs, this results in long wire segments between the clock buffers. FPGA vendors can add buffers to shorten wire segments. However, since we want our model to apply to FPGAs of any size, we need a way, within the model, to estimate an appropriate number of buffers, and to use this number of buffers in the power estimation. To do this, we use a distributed RC model, find the delay as a function of the number of clock buffers, and differentiate the function to find the optimum clock buffer size. This ensures that we have a realistic clock network for any given architecture.

3.3 Short-Circuit Power

Short-circuit power is the power dissipated through a direct current path formed between the power supply and the ground during the rise and fall times of each transition. Short circuit power is a function of the rise and fall time and the load capacitance [15]. Based on calculations using Altera and Xilinx datasheets [16] [17], we assume that short-circuit power is 10% of dynamic power.

3.4 Leakage Power

The leakage power dissipation comes from two sources: reverse-bias leakage power and sub-threshold leakage power. As the majority of the leakage power is from the sub-threshold current [18], we assume the reverse bias leakage current to be negligible. To estimate the sub-threshold current, we use [18]:

$$I_{\mathrm{drain}}(\text{weak inversion}) = I_{\mathrm{on}} \exp\left[\frac{(V_{\mathrm{gs}} - V_{\mathrm{on}})q}{nkT}\right] \tag{5}$$

V_{on} is defined as the boundary between the weak and strong inversion regions. To calculate V_{on}, we use the following equations [18]:

$$V_{\mathrm{on}} = V_{\mathrm{t}} + \frac{nkT}{q} \tag{6}$$

where

$$n = 1 + \left(\frac{qN_{\mathrm{FS}}}{C_{\mathrm{ox}}}\right) + \left(\frac{C_{\mathrm{d}}}{C_{\mathrm{ox}}}\right) \tag{7}$$

I_{on} is the drain current at the boundary when V_{gs} is equal to V_{on}. We apply the velocity saturation model [20] to calculate I_{on}.

$$I_{on} = \frac{W v_{sat} C_{ox} (V_{gs} - V_{\mathrm{t}})^2}{(V_{gs} - V_{\mathrm{t}}) + E_{\mathrm{c}} L_{\mathrm{eff}}} \tag{8}$$

where W is the device width, v_{sat} is electron velocity, E_{c} is the piecewise carrier drift velocity, L_{eff} is the effective source-drain channel length, V_{gs} is the gate-source voltage, V_{t} is the threshold voltage, and C_{d} is the drain capacitance. The constants k and q are Boltzman's constant and elementary charge, respectively. T is the temperature in Kelvins.

N_{FS} is defined as the number of fast superficial states; it is a current fitting parameter that determines the slope of the sub-threshold current-voltage characteristic [18]. To determine the N_{FS} values of NMOS and PMOS, we have run HSPICE simulations for both NMOS and PMOS transistors which operate within the junction temperature range, from -40 to 100 °C [16] [17]. All the inactive transistors, including unused switches, SRAM cells, and inactive pass transistors in the LUTs and multiplexers, contribute to the leakage power for the FPGA. In our model, we assume the gate-source voltage of these inactive transistors to be half of their threshold voltages.

4 Experimental Results

To illustrate an application of our model, we investigated how the values of various architectural parameters affect the power dissipation. We used 36 MCNC benchmark circuits, and varied the segment length [1], the cluster size[2], and the LUT size. Energy rather than power is used for comparing our results to avoid bias from the circuits' clock frequencies.

[1] Segment length is defined as the number of logic blocks spanned by a wire segment.
[2] Cluster size is defined as the number of LUTs contained in a logic block.

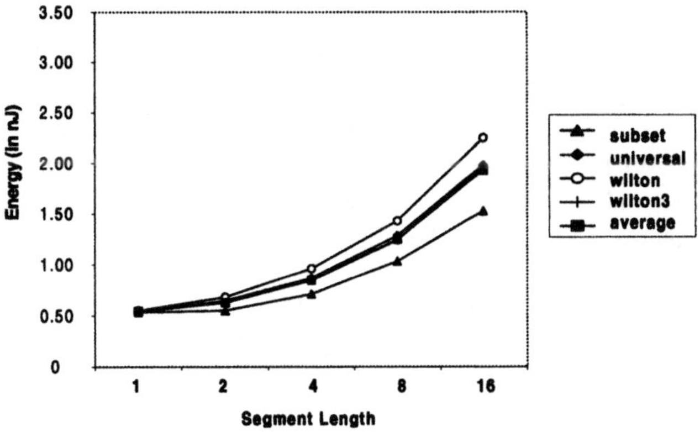

Fig. 6. Routing energy versus segment length

Figure 6 illustrates the relationship between the routing energy and the segment length, using four previously published switch blocks [19]. The graph shows that the longer the global routing wire, the more routing energy is dissipated. This result indicates that short wires are more favorable to reduce power consumption on FPGA interconnects.

Figures 7(a) and 7(b) show how the LUT and cluster sizes affect total energy. As figure 7(a) shows, increasing cluster size does not cause any significant changes on the routing energy, but it slightly increases the logic block energy and significantly decreases the clock energy dissipation. This is because as more LUTs are included in a logic block, more internal wires for local connections and longer routing wires for block-to-block connections are required, but each logic block can implement more complicated functions. As a result, the total number of logic blocks required decreases, and therefore, reduces the number of clock branches and routing branches.

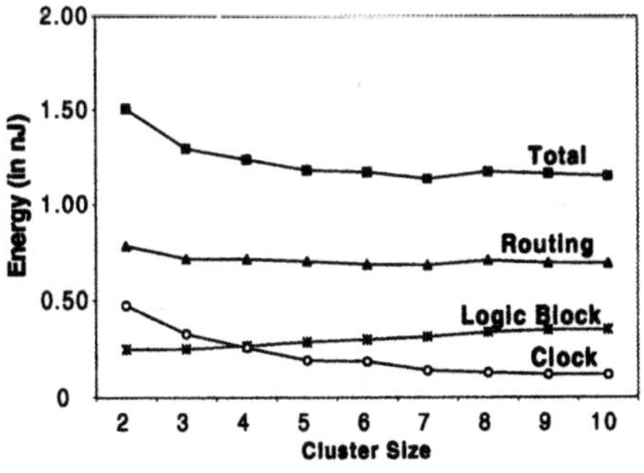

a) different cluster sizes

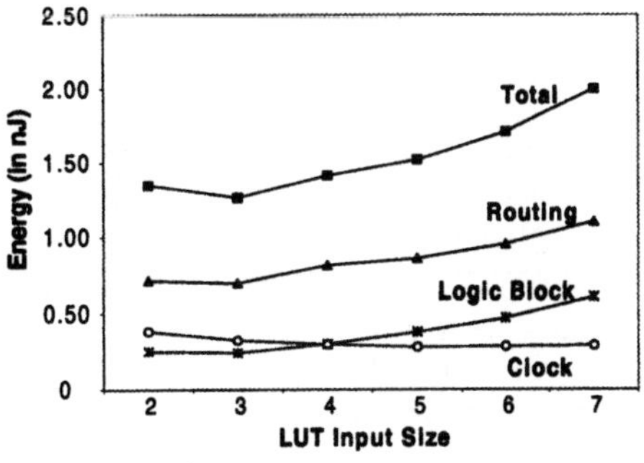

b) different LUT sizes

Fig. 7. Energy versus cluster and LUT sizes

As shown in figure 7(b), energy consumed by the logic blocks and routing fabric increase with the LUT size. This is because a larger LUT contains more internal nodes, and results in longer global wiring segments. The behavior of the clock energy is the result of two competing factors: smaller LUTs means more LUTs are required to implement a circuit, and hence, more clock branches are required; on the other hand, the length of each clock branch increases as the LUT size increases. Overall, a three-input lookup table appears to be a good choice.

Our results show that approximately 57% of the total energy consumption is due to the routing fabric, 24% is due to the logic blocks, and 19% is due to the clock distribution network.

5 Conclusions

In this paper, we have presented a detailed power model that is flexible enough to estimate the power dissipation on a wide variety of island-style FPGA architectures. The power model is available to the research community, and has been integrated into the popular VPR CAD tool suite. We have shown how the model can be used to investigate architectural tradeoffs; the model can also be used to estimate the effectiveness of CAD tools that attempt to minimize power.

Acknowledgments

The authors would like to thank Dr. Resve Saleh for his helpful discussions and Dr. Vaughn Betz for supplying us with the VPR place and route tool.

References

1. The International Technology Roadmap for Semiconductors, 2001 Edition, International Sematech, Austin, Texas, 2001.
2. A. Allan, D. Edenfeld, W. Joyner Jr, A. Khang, M. Rogers, Y. Zorian: "2001 Technology Roadmap for Semiconductors". Computer, Vol. 35, Issue 1, Jan 2002, pp. 42 -53
3. G. Lim, R. Saleh, "Trends in Low Power Digital Systems on Chip Design", in International Symposium on Quality of Electronic Design, March 2002.
4. V. George, H. Zhang, J. Rabaey, "The design of a low energy FPGA", in proceedings of the Low Power Electronics and Design, August 1999.
5. L. Shang, A. S. Kaviani, K. Bathala, "Dynamic Power Consumption in Virtex-II FPGA Family", ACM/SIGDA International Symposium on Field-Programmable Gate Arrays, February 2002.
6. F. G. Wolff, M. J. Knieser, D. J. Weyer, C. A. Papachristou, "High-level low power FPGA design methodology"National Aerospace and Electronics Conference, October 2000.
7. A. Garcia, W. Burleson, J. Danger, "Power Modelling in Field Programmable Gate Arrays (FPGA)",in Proceeding of Field-Programmable Logic and Applications, pp. 396-404, September 1999.

8. L. Shang, N. K. Jha, "High-level power modeling of CPLDs and FPGAs", International Conference on Computer Design, September 2001.
9. K. Roy, "Power-Dissipation Driven FPGA Place and Route Under Timing Constraints", IEEE Transactions on Circuits and Systems: Fundamental Theory and Applications, Vol 46, No 5 May 1999
10. V. Betz, Architectures and CAD for Speed and Area Optimizations of FPGAs. PhD thesis, University of Toronto, 1998.
11. V. Betz , VPR and T-VPack User's Manual. version 4.30, March 2000.
12. F. N. Najm, "A Survey of Power Estimation Techniques in VLSI Circuits", IEEE Trans. on Very Large Scale Integration (VLSI) Systems, Vol 2, No 4, pp 446-455, December 1994.
13. G. Yeap, Practical Low Power Digital VLSI Design. Kluwer Academic Publishers, 1998
14. S. J. E. Wilton, N. P. Jouppi, "CACTI: An Enhanced Cache Access and Cycle Time Model", in IEEE Journal of Solid-State Circuits, Vol 31, No 5, pp 677-687, May 1996.
15. D. Eckerbert, P.L. Edefors, "Interconnect-Driven Short-Circuit Power Modeling", in Proceedings of Euromicro Symposium on Digital Systems, September 2001.
16. Altera. APEX 20K Programmable Logic Device Family Data Sheet. version 4.1. Altera Corporation. September 2001.
17. Xilinx. Virtex-E 1.8V Field Programmable Gate Arrays Data Sheet. version 2.2. Xilinx Corporation. November 2001.
18. S.M. Kang, Y. Leblebici, CMOS Digital Integated Circuits: Analysis and Design. 1999
19. M. I. Masud, S. J. E. Wilton, "A New Switch Block for Segmented FPGAs", in Proceeding of Field-Programmable Logic and Applications, pp. 396-404, Se ptember 1999.
20. K.Y. Toh, P.K. Ko, R.G. Meyer, "An Engineering Model for Short-Channel MOS Devices", IEEE Journal of Solid-State Circuits, Vol. 23, No. 4, August 1988.

Appendix A

The model can be downloaded free for non-commercial use by the research community. Instructions and a download link are available from
http://www.ece.ubc.ca/~ stevew/powermodel.html

A Clocking Technique with Power Savings in Virtex-Based Pipelined Designs

Oswaldo Cadenas and Graham Megson

University of Reading,
Department of Computer Science, Cybernetics and Electronic Engineering
PO Box 225 Whitenights, RG6 6AY, Reading, UK
{o.cadenas,g.m.megson}@reading.ac.uk

Abstract. This paper presents the evaluation in power consumption of a clocking technique for pipelined designs. The technique shows a dynamic power consumption saving of around 30% over a conventional global clocking mechanism. The results were obtained from a series of experiments of a systolic circuit implemented in Virtex-II devices. The conversion from a global-clocked pipelined design to the proposed technique is straightforward, preserving the original datapath design. The savings can be used immediately either as a power reduction benefit or to increase the frequency of operation of a design for the same power consumption.

1 Introduction

Low-power design has become crucial in both field programmable logic (FPL) and VLSI due to increasing design size and increasing demand for battery-powered devices [1,2]. Power savings can be used in many ways such as to extend battery life, reduce heat dissipation and cooling requirements. Low power is so important that it is now presented as a key marketing feature in the processor market such as in the Transmeta's Crusoe processor [3].
CMOS is the most common technology in FPGAs [4] and therefore FPGA power dissipation study is similar to the study in CMOS ASIC devices [5]. Dynamic power in CMOS technology is proportional to CV^2f [4] (parasitic capacitance, voltage and frequency of operation) and consequently a common recommendation of designing for low-power consumption is to minimize all three factors [6]. For example, the StrongARM processor reduced its supply voltage operation in order to obtain power reduction while in the Crusoe processor frequency and power supply are conveniently adjusted for less power consumption [1].
Clock gating is a technique that can be used to reduce power consumption by temporarily disabling inactive elements dynamically in the circuitry [7]. For instance, it is used effectively for low power consumption in the PAX250 processor [8]. This technique and other more general practices are mostly orientated to VLSI design and not to FPGAs [1]. In order to apply clock gating in FPGA designs, specifically tailored HDL code at the RTL level is required [9]. This code is produced either by a lengthy and costly manual process or by automatic but expensive commercial tools [9,10].

M. Glesner, P. Zipf, and M. Renovell (Eds.): FPL 2002, LNCS 2438, pp. 322–331, 2002.

FPGA power evaluation is also important early in the design process, thus manufacturers provide models to estimate the power consumption for their devices [5,11]. But, techniques for reducing power in FPGAs are commonly given by general guidelines [12] or design tricks [13]. An option is to move the design to lower power family of devices [14]. This frequently has a negative impact in performance.

More general proposals for lower power consumption in FPGAs are based on optimizations of the combinational logic [15], or re-synthesis after some logic manipulations [16]. However, most of them are not orientated to pipelined designs or some require a large amount of changes at the logic level.

A pipeline with a clocking mechanism to recreate asynchronous-like operation more suitable to FPGA resources was proposed in [17], referred to here as PP-technique. In this paper, power consumption using this clocking PP-technique is experimentally evaluated in Virtex-II FPGA family of devices [18]. The results show dynamic power reduction for the case of a systolic circuit used as an example. The PP-technique allows migrating from a global-clocked pipelined datapath into an equivalent PP-clocked pipeline. No changes in the datapath are required at the HDL RTL description level. Additionally the new PP-clocked designs can run at a faster clock than the original design after place-and-route on the same device.

The paper is organized as follows: Section 2 gives a brief review of power calculation in FPGAs. The PP-clocking technique is presented in Section 3 followed by the methodology to evaluate its power in Section 4. The main results are summarized in Section 5. A discussion of results and general conclusions are finally given in Sections 6 and 7 respectively.

2 FPGA Power Dissipation

Power estimation in SRAM-based FPGAs has been carried out in [19]. FPGA power estimation is similar to CMOS ASIC devices [5]. Dynamic power dissipation is CMOS ASIC devices is due to switching current for charging and discharging parasitic capacitance, and short circuit current [4]. Most of the dynamic power dissipation arises from the switching current; it is proportional to $P = CV^2f$, capacitance, voltage and frequency. The total power is the sum of static power and dynamic power.

The power results in our study use the XPower tool from Xilinx [20]. XPower calculates dynamic power as a summation of the power consumed by each element in the design given by: $P = CV^2f \times E \times 1000$ mW, where E is the switching activity on each element in the design. Determining the switching rate, or frequency of an element can be done by a post-fit simulation in HDL to generate a file containing the simulation data for each signal. This file is used by XPower to set the activity rate of all the nodes in the design. XPower breaks down the dynamic power into Logic, Signals, and Outputs components. The total power from XPower is the sum of a constant or quiescent power and the dynamic power.

3 The Clocking Technique

A PP-clocked circuit version from a global-clocked pipelined circuit is obtained after applying the conversion diagram on the left of Fig. 1. The basic idea is to replace the global clock to the pipe stages with local clocks coming from a PP-controller. The PP-controller takes a global clock and delivers local signals to clock the pipe stages. The PP-controller in turn is an interconnection of PP-modules, it is shown in the upper right part of the figure. The internal circuitry of each PP-module is given in the lower right part of Fig. 1. The conversion is straightforward and the main datapath of a pipelined design is preserved. The original idea of the technique was presented in [17] for a more general case of handling asynchronous pipelines. Here, the idea has been simplified to the case of a fully synchronous operation. In essence, a local clock is generated at an stage $i+1$ after the stage i has generated a clock (one clock cycle) and no new local clock at stage i is generated until the local clock at stage $i+1$ has been generated (second clock cycle). This ensures the correct forward operation of the pipeline flow. Each pipeline stage is clocked at half the global clock speed to the PP-controller. This means that in order to have a new PP-design running at the same clock speed of the original one, the PP-controller needs to take a clock at twice the speed, as depicted in Fig. 1 (left). It was shown in [17] that the regularity and the simplicity of the PP-module allows the PP-controller to achieve this speed for most practical cases. The timing constraint of the original datapath is also preserved.

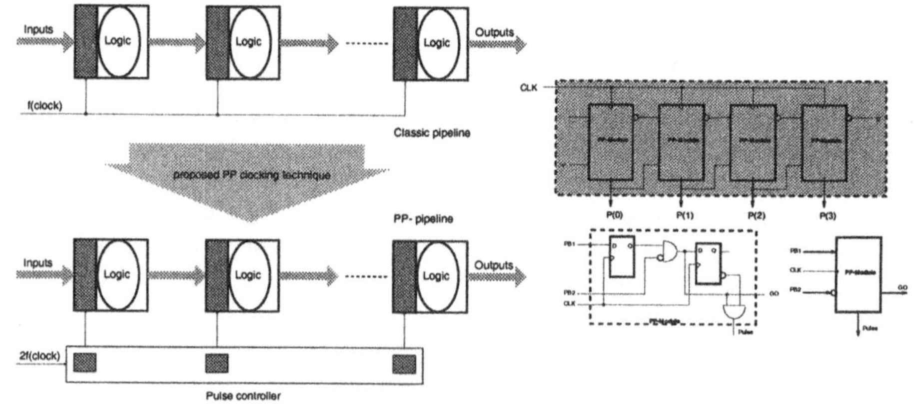

Fig. 1. Left: Conversion from a global-clocked pipelined circuit to a PP-clocked pipeline. Upper Right: A PP-controller array of four PP-modules. Lower Right: Internal circuity and block diagram of a PP-module.

4 Methodology

The methodology followed in this paper is straightforward. For a given pipelined design using a classic global clock, the PP-clocking technique can be applied to the main datapath of the design to obtain a PP-clocked design. This can be done following the description in Section 3. Each design can be then place-and-routed and information of its power behavior derived from the power analysis of the XPower tool for the case of Virtex-II devices. The switching rate activity are obtained from simulations of the design using appropriate data sets. In our case, the simulation tool was ModelSim XE 5.5b embedded into the Xilinx ISE 4.1 development tool.

4.1 The Data Sets

Three data sets were used for obtaining the switching activity rate needed in the XPower power evaluation tool. The first is a collection of eight test gray-scale images presented in [21]. This data set is later referred to as Images. The second data set is a 64K data set generated randomly. This is referred to as the Random data set. The third is a Pattern data set composed of an alternate data pattern of $(AA \ldots A)_{16}$ and $(55 \ldots 5)_{16}$. This pattern creates the maximum switching activity rate in the main data path of the pipelined example.

4.2 The Pipelined Design

A simple pipelined design where RTL code, simulations, FPGA mapping were readily available was chosen for the initial study of the PP-clocking technique. An example of such a design is a systolic scalar quantization solution [22]. An FPGA implementation of this solution called DIQ was presented in [23]. Each stage of the design (DIQ element) is shown on the left of Fig. 2. Any number of stages can be interconnected by arranging a linear array of DIQ elements as shown on the right of the figure. The datapath can be easily varied in data width and number of pipe stages. All this is controlled from a parameterized VHDL specification.

5 Results

5.1 Power Consumption Vs. Frequency

In this experiment the purpose was to tune our methodology and validate that the results obtained were consistent. As it is known from Section 2 the power consumption is linear with respect to frequency of operation. In Fig. 3 the results of dynamic power consumption vs. frequency for both the global classic clocking and the PP-clocking on the DIQ implementation is shown. The DIQ circuit was implemented for the case of eight pipe stages handling 8-bit of input data. The device used was the XCV2000 with a quiescent current consumption of 225 mW. In Tab. 1 the total power savings of PP-clocking over global clocking both in dynamic and total power for the XC2V2000 device are given.

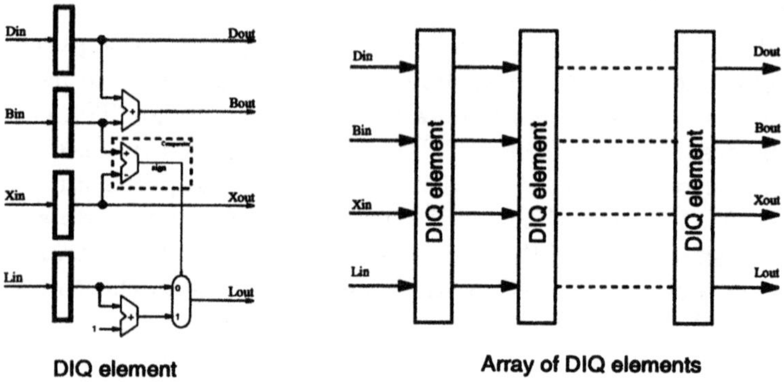

Fig. 2. Left: A DIQ systolic element and Right: A linear array of DIQ elements

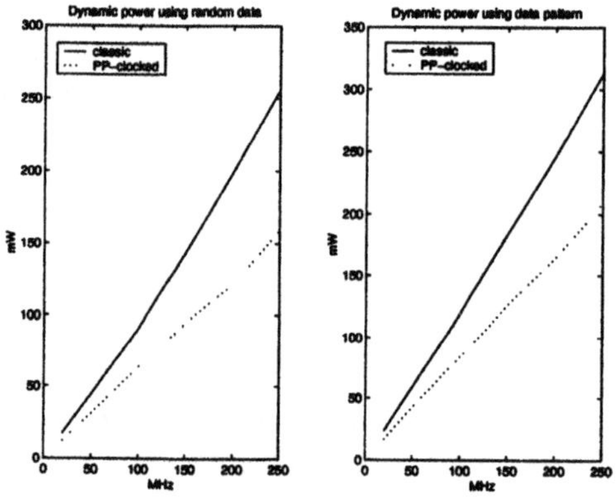

Fig. 3. Dynamic power consumption

Table 1. Savings in dynamic and total power of PP-cloking over global clocking for different frequencies. The design is an 8-stage DIQ implementation on Virtex XC2V2000.

% Savings of PP-clocking over classic clocking				
Frequency in MHz	Random data		Data pattern	
	Dynamic	Total	Dynamic	Total
20	29.9	2.2	29.8	2.8
50	30.3	5.0	27.7	5.8
100	30.3	8.7	30.2	10.5
150	33.9	13.2	31.4	14.1
250	37.7	20.1	33.3	19.3

5.2 Varying the Data-Width

Keeping the stages of the DIQ quantizer to eight, power consumption for different data widths were conducted for a constant frequency of 50 MHz. Due to the nature of the example, practical variations of the data width are relevant from 4 to 16 bits. The power savings results of PP-clocking are presented in Tab. 2.

Table 2. Savings in dynamic and total power of PP-clocking over classic clocking for different data widths. The design is an 8-stages DIQ implementation on Virtex XC2V2000.

% Savings of PP-clocking over classic clocking				
Data-width	Random data		Data pattern	
in bits	Dynamic	Total	Dynamic	Total
4	34.2	3.4	21.4	3.1
8	29.5	4.9	29.5	6.1
12	34.9	7.3	27.8	7.4
16	33.9	7.1	25.0	7.8

5.3 Varying the Pipeline Depth

Keeping the DIQ implementation data-width constant to 8-bits, and the frequency at 50 MHz, power consumption was measured as a function of the pipeline depth. The main results are presented in Tab. 3. Due to the nature of the example, the number of pipeline stages was varied in a practical range of four to 12.

Table 3. Savings of dynamic and total power of PP-clocking over global clocking for different pipe depths. The design is an 8-bit DIQ implementation on Virtex XC2V2000.

% Savings of PP-clocking over classic clocking				
Pipeline	Images		Random data	
depth	Dynamic	Total	Dynamic	Total
4	83.6	5.0	18.2	2.4
5	83.5	5.3	28.9	3.8
8	83.1	7.4	34.5	5.7
12	80.9	8.5	35.9	6.1

5.4 Power Consumption on the Virtex II Family

Power consumption was measured in most members of the Virtex II family. The main purpose of this experiment is to re-validate the results. Dynamic power was also broken down into their components. For each device the whole circuit was re-placed and re-routed and new simulations carried out to obtain the switching information on which the power consumption is calculated. For this experiment, it was used the DIQ implementation for eight pipe stages, handling 8-bit data at 50 MHz. The two main data sets used is the images data sets and the random data set. The savings results are given in Tab. 4.

Table 4. Savings of dynamic and total power of the PP-clocking mechanism over global clocking for different members of the Virtex-II family.

% Savings of PP-clocking over classic clocking				
Family member	Images		Random data	
	Dynamic	Total	Dynamic	Total
XC2V250	81.5	12.3	25.3	6.8
XC2V500	75.6	8.7	23.8	5.2
XC2V1000	82.4	9.8	35.2	7.8
XC2V1500	77.7	9.4	27.1	6.1
XC2v2000	82.1	7.2	26.2	4.3
XC2V3000	80.1	6.6	26.5	4.2
XC2V4000	76.5	5.5	25.4	3.4
XC2V6000	77.5	5.1	27.6	3.5
XC2V8000	80.2	3.8	33.4	3.0

The fraction of Logic, Signal and Output of the dynamic power for each clocking mechanism is presented in Tab. 5. In the same table, it is given the percentage of savings of the clocking mechanism compared to the global clock in both data sets. This results are derived from the detailed dynamic power consumption of the results shown in Table 4.

Table 5. Percentages of Logic, Signals and Output of dynamic power consumption and the savings of PP-clocking compared to global clocking for the same fractions

Dynamic power	Images data set			Random data set		
	Logic	Signal	Output	Logic	Signal	Output
% fraction of	46.6	47.7	5.7	26.5	24.7	48.8
% savings of PP	81	84	10	67	73	-15

6 Discussion

Results from Table 1 and Table 4 can be taken as a validation of the results. Table 1 shows the linearity of the power consumption vs. frequency of operation. The PP-clocking mechanism shows around 30% saving in dynamic power consumption for the worst possible case of activity rate in the DIQ circuit. Table 4 shows a consistent and repetitive dynamic power savings of the PP-clocking mechanism of around 30% over most of the Virtex II family of devices. All the results were carried out after individual re-place-and-route and simulations for each case. This explains the minor differences on common implementations across the tables of Section 5.

A similar power saving of around 25%-30% is shown in Table 2. In this case, the data width used as a parameter varies the amount of logic in both the storage elements and in the logic of the pipeline; the saving remains.

When a more common data set for the nature of the DIQ design is used, such as data of still images, the power savings of the PP-clocking mechanism over the global clocking was counted in the order of over 80%. This is shown in Table 3. For a random data set the dynamic power savings are of around 30%.

Table 5 shows details of dynamic power consumption of Table 4 in its portions of logic,signal and output. As both the global clocking and the PP-clocking pipeline circuits run at the same pipe frequency, no power savings in the output portion is expected. All the savings of the technique come from saving in the operation of internal nodes and logic. It is observed from the table, that the lower the percentage of the output portion to the dynamic power, the more benefit can be obtained from the PP-cloking mechanism. It is not clear why and how the power reduction operates, it is left to further analysis and study. From all the tables it is shown that the total power consumption of the PP-clocking mechanism is in the order of 5%-10%. However, this savings depends on the percentage of dynamic power relative to the the quiescent power of the device.

The power savings of the PP-mechanism can be used as such or to run a faster pipeline with the same power consumption to the global clocking one. For the case of the systolic quantizer, around a 30% faster PP-clocked DIQ can consume the same power of a global-clocked DIQ.

7 Conclusions

The power savings of dynamic power consumption of the proposed PP-clocking mechanism over a global clock for pipelined designs showed a reduction of around 30%. The reduction was consistent for the example of a systolic circuit mapped into Virtex-II devices when different parameters were used in the power evaluation such as: variation in the data width, variation in the pipe depth, variation in frequency, variation of the family of devices.

A PP-clocked pipelined design is obtained from a f_{gclk} global clocked pipelined design in a straightforward way. A PP-controller is inserted taking a clock twice as fast as the original clock to generate local clocks to the pipe stages of the PP-design at f_{gclk}. Any existing datapath of the original design is preserved.

The technique gives better results for lower proportion of output power to the dynamic power, because the power savings are mostly of internal signals and logic power. The actual mechanism of how the power reduction operates is not clear and it is left open to further research. Evaluation of the technique in applications such as processors, DSP-orientated arithmetic functions needs to be conducted to put the technique in a more general context.

References

1. L. Benini, G. De Micheli, and E. Macii, "Designing for Low-power Circuits: Practical Recipes", *IEEE Circuits & Systems Magazine*, Vol. 1, No. 1, Q1, 2001, pp. 6-25.
2. S. Wenande and R. Chidester, "Xilinx Takes Power Analysis to New Levels with Xpower", *Xcell Journal*, Issue 41, Xilinx Inc., Fall/Winter 2001., pp. 26-27.
3. http://www.transmeta.com/why/index.html
4. M. Smith, *Application-specific Integrated Circuits*, Reading, Mas: Addison-Wesley, 1997.
5. Actel Corp., "Predicting the Power Dissipation of Actel FPGAs" *Application Note*, April 1996.
6. P. Alfke, "Evolution, Revolution and Convolution", Tutorial at *11th Int. Conf. on Field Programmable Logic and Applications*, Belfast, Norhtern Ireland, 2001.
7. L. Benini, P. Siegel, and G. De Micheli, "Automatic Synthesis of Gated Clocks for Power Reduction in Sequential Circuits", *IEEE DEsign and Test of Computers*, Vol. 11, No. 4, pp.32-40, December 1994.
8. Intel Corp., "The Intel PXA250 Applications Processors", White Paper, February 2002.
9. P. J. Schoenmakers, and J. F. M. Theeuwen, "Clock gating on RT-level VHDL", *Proc. of the Int. Workshop on Logic Synthesis*, Tahoe City, CA, June 7-10, 1998, pp. 387-391.
10. http://www.offis.de/
11. Altera Corp., *Evaluating Power for Altera Devices*, Application Note 74, Version 3.1, July 2001.
12. J. Jenkins, "Reducing CPLD Power Consupmtion" *Xcell Journal*, Xilinx Inc., Q4 1998. http://www.xilinx.com/apps/3volt.htm
13. P. Alfke, "Low Power FPGA Achieves 400 MHz Performance" *Xcell Journal*, Xilinx Inc., Q2, 1998. http://www.xilinx.com/apps/3volt.htm
14. Xilinx, Inc. "CoolRunner XPLA3 CPLD", DS012 V1.5, January 7, 2002.
15. B. Kumthekar. L. Benini, E. Macii, and F. Somenzi, "In-Place Power Optimization for LUT-Based FPGAs", *Proc. of the 31st Design Automation Conference*, June 15-18, San Francisco, 1998.
16. J. Hwang, F. Chiang and T. Hwang, "A Re-engineering Approach to Low Power FPGA Design Using SPFD", *Proc. of the 31st Design Automation Conference*, June 15-18, San Francisco, 1998.
17. O. Cadenas and G. Megson, "Pipelining considerations for an FPGA case",*Proc. of Euromicro Symposium on Digital Systems Design (DSD 2001)* Warsaw, Poland, September 4th-6th, 2001, pp.276-283.
18. http://www.xilinx.com/partinfo/ds031-2.pdf

19. K. Weiβ, C. Oetker, I. Katchan, T. Steckstor, and W. Rosentiel *Power estimation approach for SRAM-based FPGAs*, Proceedings of the 2000 ACM/SIGDA eighth international symposium on Field programmable gate arrays February 10 - 11, 2000, Monterey, CA USA, pp. 195 - 202.
20. Xilinx Inc, *XPower Tutorial: FPGA Design*, May 11, 2001.
21. K. Sayood. *Introduction to Data Compression*. San Francisco, CA: Morgan Kaufmann Publishers, 1996.
22. Megson, G.M. and Diemoz E., 1997. "Scalar Quantisation Using a Fast Systolic Array," in *Electronics Letters*, 1997, Vol. 33, No. 17, pp.1435-1437.
23. J. O. Cadenas, G. M. Megson, *An n-bit reconfigurable scalar quantiser*. Field Programmable Logic and Applications, FPL2001, LNCS 2147, Gordon Brebner and Roger Woods (Eds.) Springer, Belfast, UK. 2001 , pp.420-429.

Energy Evaluation on a Reconfigurable, Multimedia-Oriented Wireless Sensor*

Maurizio Martina, Guido Masera, Gianluca Piccinini, Fabrizio Vacca, and Maurizio Zamboni

Dipartimento di Elettronica
Politecnico di Torino
C.so Duca degli Abruzzi, 24
10129 TORINO – ITALY
{maurizio.martina, masera, piccinini, fabrizio.vacca, zamboni}@polito.it
http://www.vlsilab.polito.it

Abstract. This paper aims to evaluate the energy required on an integrated, reconfigurable wireless sensor node with basic multimedia capabilities. Recently a growing interest is gathered by the development of wireless network made of small, self-consistent sensors with embedded processing capabilities. While the first generation of these devices will deal with small bandwidth signals, it is forecastable that distributed image processing algorithms should be soon needed. Moreover, in order to guarantee a widespread deployment of these sensors, they ought to rely on reconfigurable radio paradigm. Nevertheless energy related constraints should seriously tackle the sensor feasibility. The analysis proposed in this paper relies on the development of a very low-complexity, parametric wavelet transform IP. Starting from an high level description, different implementation on different physical layers have been pursued. The experimental results show that very interesting reduced energy figures can be achieved on modern CPLD devices.

1 Introduction

The interest towards wireless networks has widely increased in the last years mainly due to cellular market explosion. In particular several emerging technologies such as UMTS and BlueTooth have shaken not only industrial interests but even many researcher's activities with new challenges. Besides, the growth of research in the field of wireless networks has opened perspectives never previously investigated. The possibility to create very small devices, able to communicate together in a wireless network scenario, is currently one of the most challenging topics in the design of wireless embedded systems. It would be desirable to obtain a small network node with on board sensors and processing [1]. However behind these goals there are many critical factors as limited power

* This project is partially supported by CERCOM (Center for Multimedia Radio Communications).

M. Glesner, P. Zipf, and M. Renovell (Eds.): FPL 2002, LNCS 2438, pp. 332–339, 2002.

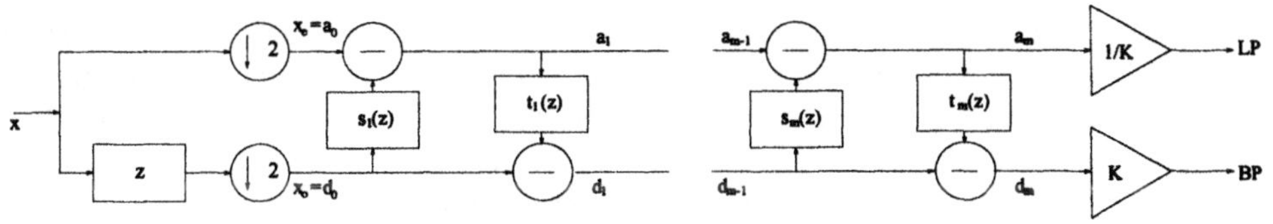

Fig. 1. Lifting scheme structure

budgets and reduced resources availability which should be faced taking into account the need for high reconfigurability. This paper investigates the feasibility of a Discrete Wavelet Transform (DWT) in a node for a wireless sensor network. In particular this work tries to find a very low complexity implementation with good performance in terms of decorrelation capability. Since the developed Intellectual Property (IP) has to grant high flexibility, it has been designed posing very much care to assure fine reconfigurability. Finally different physical layers have been compared to prove how they can meet different system requirements.

The paper is organized as follows: section 2 briefly summarizes how a very low complexity wavelet transform can be achieved; section 3 is devoted to explain wireless sensor network scenario introduced above. In section 4 the proposed IP architecture is described, emphasizing how its regular structure can be exploited; section 5 shows the results obtained mapping the proposed IP on different physical layers and provides interesting comparisons and trade-offs. Finally in section 6 some conclusions and future work directions are driven.

2 Theoretical Framework

Excellent decorrelation properties shown by the Discrete Wavelet Transform have been widely addressed yet [2]. Nevertheless, DWT main bottleneck seems to be its computational toughness. In the last few years the Lifting Scheme (LS) [3] has demonstrated that the number of operations required for the evaluation of wavelet coefficients can be reduced of about a factor of two. In fact, as described in [3], the LS can be obtained from the polyphase matrix of wavelet filters through a decomposition based on the Euclidean algorithm. The decomposition can be represented as depicted in figure 1 where $s_i(z)$ and $t_i(z)$ are simple and short FIR filters called respectively *primal* and *dual* lifting steps. Besides the LS has been successfully employed in different image compression frameworks such as JPEG2000 [4] as an efficient mode to implement the wavelet transform. A further improvement can be achieved resorting to the joint benefits offered by the Integer Wavelet Transform (IWT) [5] and the employment of filters with integer lifting coefficients. While the integer wavelet transform maps integers to integers, enabling true lossless reversible transformations, filters with integer lifting coefficients have the great advantage of reducing $s_i(z)$ and $t_i(z)$ multiplications into simple shifts. In particular the LeGall(5,3) filter, which is the default one for lossless compression in JPEG2000, grants very good decorrelation among samples with a very simple structure. As shown in figure 2 the IWT–LS, based on the (5,3) filter, is able to easily map integer samples into integer coefficients. For the sake of completeness it must be stated that IWT performance are slightly inferior with respect to DWT ones. However, the (5,3) filter structure greatly relaxes computational requirements being an ideal choice in low energy systems.

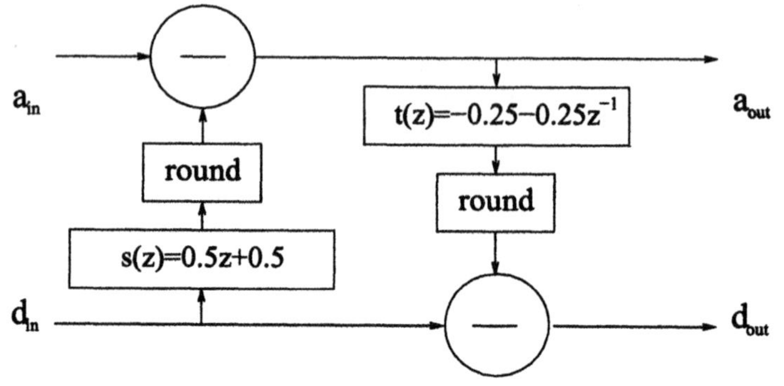

Fig. 2. LeGall(5,3) filter LS structure

3 Possible Scenarios

Wireless sensor networks are currently on the cutting-edge of international research. In fact they involve heterogeneous competences in different research fields: network protocols, signal processing, analog RF, digital architectures design and MicroElectroMechanical Systems are just few examples. In order to keep system's complexity as reduced as possible and to grant high flexibility, reconfigurable supports have to be employed. In fact every network node will embed both fixed and flexible blocks: the formers will be made mainly by analog parts, the latters mainly by the digital ones. In particular the flexible blocks are usually made of software programmable cores such as DSP or embedded microcontrollers and reconfigurable blocks such as CPLDs or FPGAs. This flexibility is needed to bring on sensor nodes software defined radio methodologies, which are crucial to assure ubiquitous nodes deployment.

However, in wireless scenarios, the limited energy budget bounds the possibility to employ effective algorithms such as the wavelet transform. Currently it is not clear if off-the-shelf programmable devices, which grant fine reconfigurability degrees, are able to satisfy power budgets and performance requirements. Since image compression algorithms are usually tough, from computational complexity point of view, it is our belief that they are among the most demanding tasks which will run on the network nodes.

The LS based (5,3) wavelet transform seems to be an ideal candidate for embedded image compression issues, due to its simple structure and good decorrelation properties; besides it enables the possibility to benchmark different physical layers. Several research groups as [6] [7] are working on distributed image compression tasks, resorting to the "make-or-buy" paradigm. In fact it is yet unclear how and when it is energy-convenient to compress sensor's data instead of sending them uncompressed across the net. The solution to this problem seems to be not unique since it is strongly correlated to sensors position and network state.

This work aims to preliminary characterize the wavelet transform stage, in order to prove its actual feasibility in sensor wireless networks.

4 The Proposed IP

In a scenario as the one described in section 3 there are many critical parameters which make difficult to port an efficient transform stage, as the wavelet, in a framework with both reduced power budget and high reconfigurability requirements. In order to have the possibility to explore different solutions the need for an easily re-targettable and fully parametric IP is felt. To better fit different possible requirements, the implementation of a (5,3) LS based integer wavelet transform should be as modular as possible. The proposed intellectual property has been designed as a single lifting step soft IP (see figure 3) which can be reconfigured to compute either primal or dual lifting steps both for direct and inverse transform. Figure 3 can be described starting from figure 2 analysis:

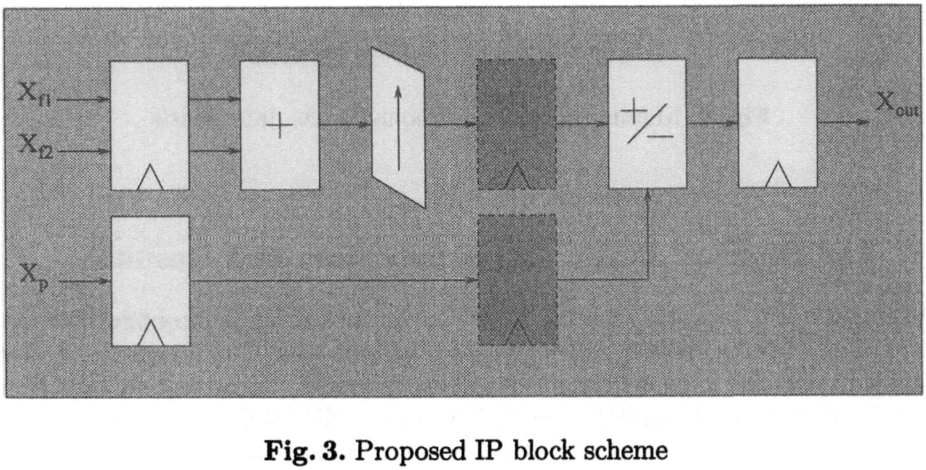

Fig. 3. Proposed IP block scheme

since $s(z) = 0.5z + 0.5$ and $t(z) = -0.25 - 0.25z^{-1}$ the two samples involved in the filtering processes have to be multiplied (shifted) by the same value (0.5 for predict, −0.25 for update), it is more convenient first to add the two samples and then to shift them. The value the samples have to be shifted by and the selection of the final addition or subtraction depend on the lifting step type (predict or update). Finally the shaded dashed registers can be placed or removed to better tune the maximum affordable combinational path.

As far as resources required are concerned it is interesting to note how only two adders and three registers are needed. Since the shift operations will be carried out through fixed coefficients, no complex shifter blocks are required. As an example the proposed IP, configured using 10 bits data width, synthesized on a Xilinx XCV50E, shows an area occupation of just 73 CLBs.

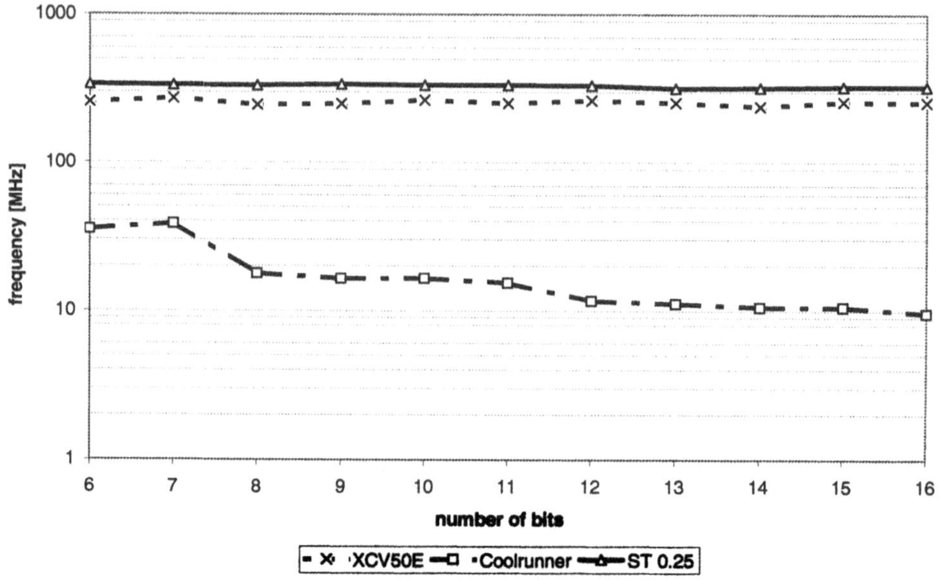

Fig. 4. Maximum clocking frequency vs. data width

5 The Physical Layer: Implementation and Results

As stated in the previous sections, a growing interest towards reconfigurable sensor nodes is felt. In order to prove wavelet transform feasibility on wireless nodes, different physical implementation have been pursued. Three targets have been investigated: an high-performance FPGA device (XCV50E from Xilinx), a low-power CPLD (CoolRunner XPLA3 from Xilinx again) and a 0.25 μm standard cell library from STMicroelectronics.

The measures have been carried out as follows: given a physical target, different data width as well as internal pipeline levels have been investigated. For every configuration the resulting area, the maximum clock frequency and the total power dissipation have been extracted. It is important to note that it is quite difficult to fairly compare area occupation results due to the significant

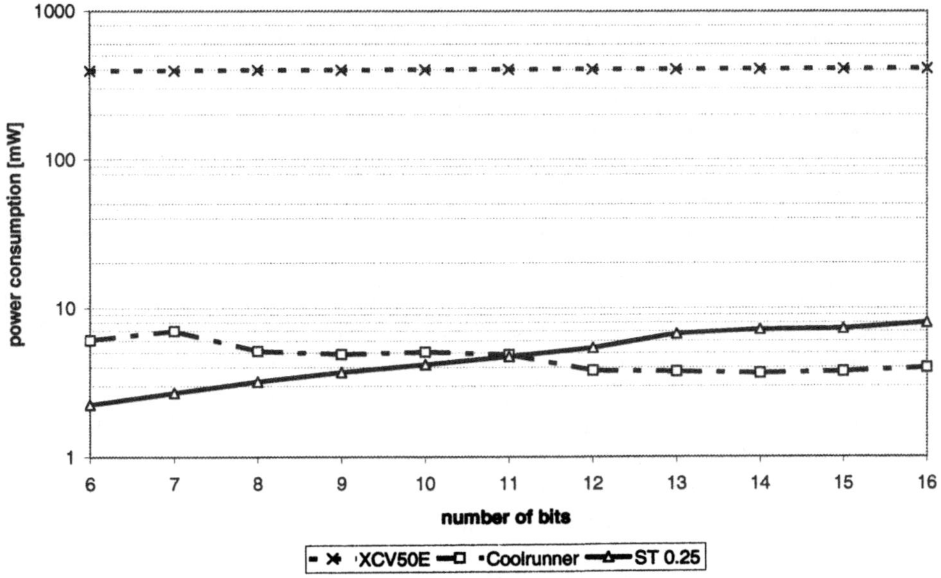

Fig. 5. Overall power dissipation vs. data width

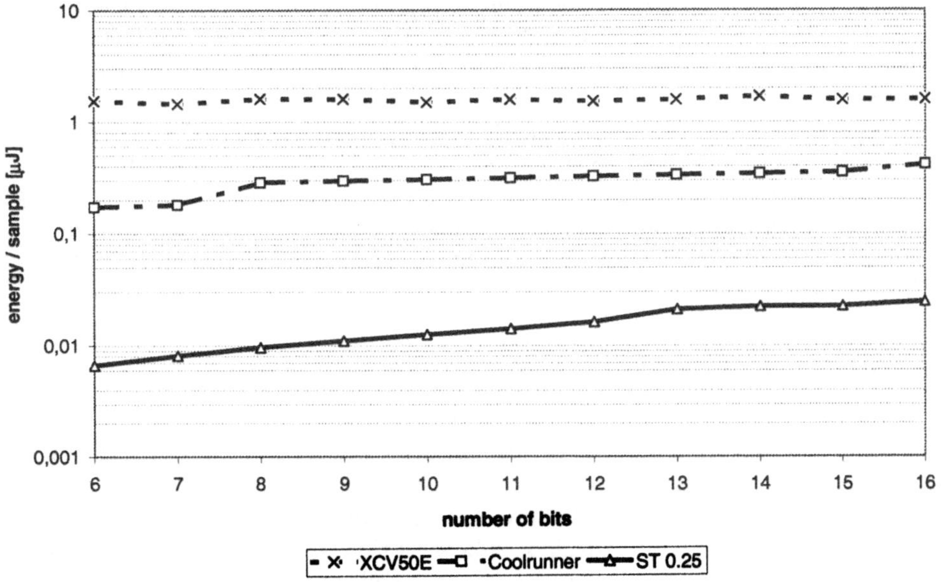

Fig. 6. Energy required per sample vs. data width

difference among the different targets. Moreover, as it can be forecast examining the proposed IP architecture, area occupation tends to be limited. This figure is appreciable both in terms of programmable device's logical blocks and standard cells.

Frequency and power values exhibit more significant dependencies on the physical layer as well as on the chosen IP structure. Generally it has been noted that increasing the internal pipeline leans to an overall power dissipation increase. Starting from this consideration the slowest version has been taken as a reference. In figures 4, 5 and 6 the measured values for clock frequency, power dissipation and energy consumption versus data width are depicted. Looking at figure 4 it is possible to note that silicon implementation slightly outperforms the FPGA based one: in fact, using 16 bits for IWT samples, the standard cell solution achieves a frequency of 326 MHz while the FPGA runs at 257 MHz (26% less than ASIC). On the other hand, FPGA grants an higher degree of reconfigurability that can completely fill this existent performance gap. The CPLD based solution suffers from lower performance offered by this platform: in this case a frequency of just 9.6 MHz has been reached. In figure 5 the power dissipation of the three implementations is compared. In this case the situation abruptly changes since the most promising solution seems to be the CoolRunner based one. On the contrary, XCV50E requires a remarkable amount of power making its use not suitable for power dominated applications. However, it must be noted how more than the 88% of the FPGA power dissipation is directly imputable to static contributions: probably significant reductions will be available with future technological improvements. Ultimately, in figure 6 the energy per sample versus the data size is depicted. It is interesting to observe how the Virtex energy requirement is one order of magnitude greater than the CPLD's one; another order of magnitude should be taken into account if the 0.25 μm implementation is considered.

As far as the performance are concerned, the proposed IP is able to reach very interesting analysis / synthesis rates. As an example, employing 8 bits for data representation, it is possible to achieve a 25 frame-per-second throughput with QCIF images (176×144 pixel elements). The processing of each frame requires an energy of 109 μJ, 20.4 μJ and 0.84 μJ on XCV50E, CoolRunner and STM 0.25 μm respectively.

6 Conclusions

In this paper a novel IP suited for wireless sensor network is proposed. Moreover, exploiting the parametric architecture of this core, different measures has been taken out in order to evaluate how the reconfigurability requirement can be conjugated with low-energy design. Following this methodology the IWT IP has been completely characterized varying its data width as well as its pipeline depth. From the obtained results it has been possible to ascertain an optimal physical layer for an image processing oriented sensor network. While the traditional ASIC solution is able to achieve the better power/delay figure, it completely lacks of the required reconfigurability. On the other hand, the high performance FPGA has shown to be only slightly inferior with respect to STM 0.25 μm in terms of maximum clocking frequency. Anyway it completely misses tight power budget constraints imposed by wireless environment. Only the CPLD seems to be a reasonable trade-off between efficiency and reconfigurability needs.

As far as future developments are concerned, two distinct research lines will be pursued: the former will concentrate on network and communication related issues while the latter will focus on high-level design methodologies and on reconfigurable IP characterization.

Acknowledgment

The authors would like to thank Dr. Carla Fabiana Chiasserini from Politecnico di Torino for her precious introduction to wireless integrated sensor networks and Prof. Gabriella Olmo, Dr. Enrico Magli and Dr. Marco Grangetto for their fruitful collaboration into image processing related research topics.

References

[1] Pottie, G.J., Kaiser, W.J.: Wireless Integrated Network Sensors. Communications of the ACM **43** (2000) 51–58
[2] Grangetto, M., Magli, E., Olmo, G.: Finite Precision Wavelets for Image Coding: Lossy and Lossless Compression Performance Evaluation. In: Proceedings of the 1999 International Conference on Image Processing (ICIP 2000), Vancouver, Canada, IEEE (2000)
[3] Daubechies, I., Sweldens, W.: Factoring wavelet transforms into lifting steps. Technical report, Bell Laboratories, Lucent Technologies (1996)
[4] Boliek, M.: JPEG 2000 Final Committee Draft. ISO/IEC FCD15444-1 (2000)
[5] Calderbank, R., Daubechies, I., Sweldens, W., Yeo, B.L.: Wavelet transforms that map integers to integers. Appl. Comput. Harmon. Anal. **5** (1998) 332–369
[6] WEB: http://bwrc.eecs.berkeley.edu/Research/Pico_Radio (2002)
[7] WEB: http://www-mtl.mit.edu/research/icsystems/uamps (2002)

A Tool for Activity Estimation in FPGAs

E. Todorovich[1], M. Gilabert[1], G. Sutter[1], S. Lopez-Buedo[2], and E. Boemo[2]

[1] INCA, Universidad Nacional del Centro, Tandil, Argentina
{etodorov, gsutter}@exa.unicen.edu.ar

[2] Computer Engineering School, Universidad Autonoma de Madrid, España
{eduardo.boemo, sergio.lopez-buedo}@uam.es

Abstract. In this paper, an activity estimation tool for FPGA-based combinational circuits is presented. The current version is able to estimate average activity for individual nodes. The tool is statistical-based, allowing the user to specify the tolerated error at a given confidence level. The tunable properties of the implemented technique have been carefully tested, demonstrating how the designer can control the accuracy-speed trade-off. The importance of a realistic input pattern characterization has also been verified.

1 Introduction

The main problem in power estimation for CMOS circuits is the activity measurement. Node activity is hard to estimate because it depends on the values at the primary inputs, the logical function of the circuit and finally, the temporal and spatial correlations among the inputs. Additionally, the so-called *pattern-dependence* problem is present: In actual circuits, is practically impossible to evaluate all possible input vector combinations, as well as to consider the effect of glitches, the other source of activity [1]. Thus, power estimation algorithms lead to an important computational effort.

Several techniques have been developed to estimate the power consumption of digital circuits. Each technique proposes a different approache to solve the pattern-dependence problem. Comprehensive surveys about power estimation can be found in [2]-[4]. In the FPGA arena, a coarse approximation to power estimation in Xilinx FPGAs is developed in [5]-[8]. Other estimation technique applicable to FPGAs is implemented in [9]. It is based on the propagation of probabilistic parameters from primary inputs to all the internal circuit nodes. Finally, in the latest *Integrated Software Environment (ISE),* a power estimation tool, called *XPower* [10], [11] is presented. However, the user still must to provide an arbitrary input vector sets. So, the tool cannot guarantee that simulated activity really converges to the average values. Also, the current version of *XPower* does not support all Xilinx FPGA families.

This work tries to contribute to the previous research lines by the development of a new FPGA-oriented activity estimator. Its main features are: integration with commercial design tools, automatic generation of input vectors according to user

M. Glesner, P. Zipf, and M. Renovell (Eds.): FPL 2002, LNCS 2438, pp. 340-349, 2002.

specifications, and finally, applicability to any FPGA device. The current version of the tool can be integrated in the Xilinx *Foundation* suite.

2 Statistical Activity Estimation

The statistical approach for power estimation is based on the Monte Carlo simulation technique. It minimizes the pattern dependence problem: randomly generated input patterns are applied at the circuit inputs whilst the activity per time interval T is monitored by a simulator. The process continues until a *stopping criterion* is reached.

The first work applying a Monte Carlo technique for total average power estimation is [12]. In [13], and later [14], the technique is extended, providing both the total and individual-gate power values. Other works made use of the statistical approach on sequential circuits. For example, a warm-up period and Markov chain theory are utilized in [15]. A statistical technique for large sequential circuits like microprocessors is presented in [16].

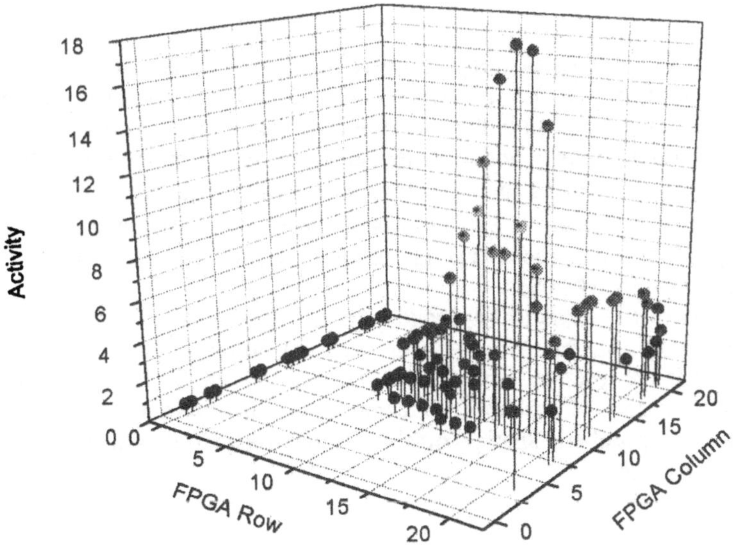

Fig. 1. 8-bit multiplier activity over a 20 × 20 CLB XC4010E FPGA. Node activities belonging to a single CLB are added

If the power consumed by a circuit over a period T has a distribution very close to normal, and if the successive input patterns are independently generated, it can be demonstrated that the required number, N, of random samples is:

$$N \geq \left(\frac{t_{\alpha/2} s}{p \varepsilon} \right)^2 . \quad (1)$$

This equation defines a stopping criterion where p is the average of the random power (activity) samples over a period T, s is the standard deviation of the random sample, $(1 - \alpha) \times 100\%$ is the confidence level that error ε in the measurement is less than a specified value. Finally, $t_{\alpha/2}$ is obtained from a t-distribution with $(N - 1)$ degrees of freedom.

Eq.1 leads to the so-called *slow convergence* problem. That means that this stopping criterion cannot be used to estimate individual gate activity: the lower is p, the larger is N. But individual gate estimations are useful to diagnose high consumption problems, and also to find the circuit nodes that consume more energy. For example, Fig.1 shows how the average activity increases at internal nodes in a FPGA from the inputs to the outputs.

In order to solve the slow convergence problem, a partition of the circuit nodes in two sets is proposed in [13] and [14]. If n is the measured average activity over a period T, and s is its standard deviation, the user defines an activity threshold n_{min} that classifies the nodes into regular and low density ones.

$$N \geq \left(\frac{z_{\alpha/2} s}{\bar{n} \varepsilon_1} \right)^2 \text{ . (a)} \qquad N \geq \left(\frac{z_{\alpha/2} s}{n_{\min} \varepsilon} \right)^2 \text{ . (b)} \qquad (2)$$

Eq. 2a and 2b are used as stopping criterion for the regular nodes ($n > n_{min}$) and low-density nodes ($n < n_{min}$) respectively. It bounds the maximum number of samples tolerated by the algorithm. In both cases, the stopping criterion is tested after $N > 30$. Considering that low-density nodes have a negligible effect on the power figure of the circuit, this strategy reduces the execution time with a little penalty. ε_l is an upper bound of the percentage error, ε is the user specified error tolerance ($\varepsilon = \varepsilon_l / (1-\varepsilon_l)$). Thus, the product $n_{min}\varepsilon$ represents an absolute error limit that characterizes the accuracy for low-density nodes.

The benefits of the statistical approach are: a) any standard simulator can be used in the inner loop of the Monte-Carlo program making the technique easy to implement; b) if the tolerated error is not selected too small, the execution time can compete with the ones of probabilistic techniques; c) a simple input specification can be defined; d) temporal and spatial correlations are considered; and finally, e) glitches are taked into account.

3 Implementation Details

The described technique can be implemented using any simulator that reports the circuit activity, provided that it is able to interact with an external program that controls the simulation. Active-HDL [17] fulfills these conditions. Basically, a wrapper over the simulator was developed to implement the estimation technique.

Before using the tool, some steps must be done: The *ncd* file, generated after the place and route stages, must be used to produce the associated VHDL model and the *sdf* files (Standard Delay Format) [18]. For this purpose, Xilinx Foundation provides two commands: *ngdanno* and *ngd2vhdl*. The obtained VHDL model takes into account the actual layout for the selected device, and the *sdf* file gives the simulator an accurate delay model.

The implementation of the software that governs the simulator is based on *Tcl-Tk* scripts. These scripts can execute external programs and Active-HDL macros that run simulator commands. The main procedure performs the following actions: 1) Call the program (Fig. 2) that shows the user interface, 2) Call the *Tk* interface with feedback about the estimation progress, 3) Initialize the simulator, 4) Execute the core script that actually runs the estimation algorithm, and 5) Build a report based on the resultant switching activity.

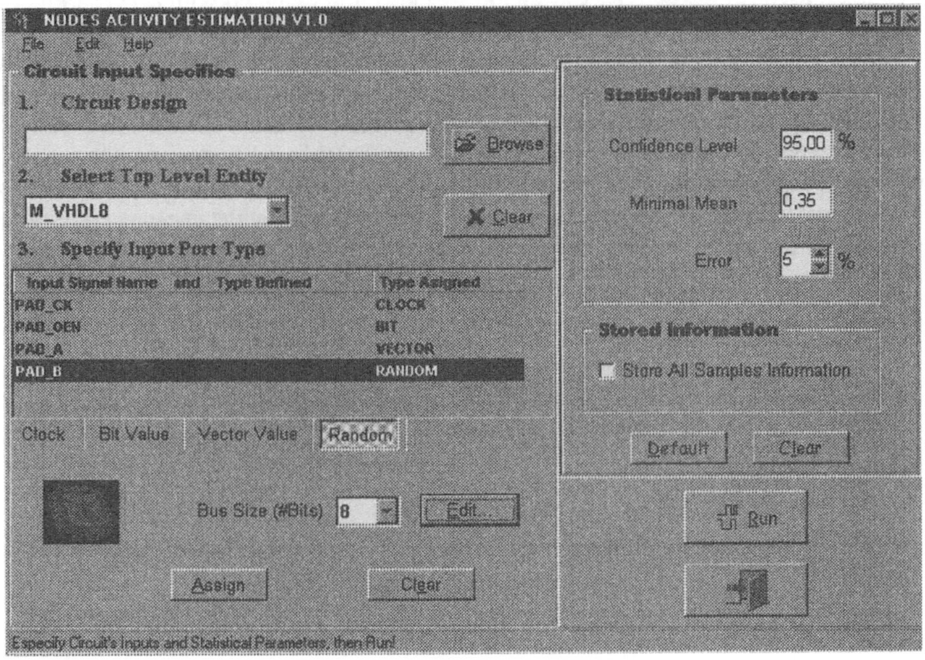

Fig. 2. Activity estimation tool: User interface

3.1 User Configuration - Input Specification

User configuration is divided in two parts: the statistical parameter settings, and the activity specification on the primary inputs.

The first ones are necessary to perform the individual nodes activity estimation, applying a Monte Carlo simulation according to Eq. 2. In the other hand, the file containing the VHDL model must be specified, and the top-level entity must be selected. For this entity, all the port descriptions are loaded. Then, the user must choose the activity type for each port: Clock, Bit Value, Vector Value, or Random (Fig. 2). An alternative way to configure the tool is loading a previously defined configuration file.

By default, each line x_i of an input port specified as Random has a signal probability 0.5 and an average transition count per clock cycle 0.5. This is equivalent to assume temporal independence. But users can set each input signal to any signal probability $P_s(x)$ or transition density $D(x)$. Any individual input line of type Random can also be defined as connected to a counter or to a fixed logical signal. This allows the user to specify complex activity configurations at primary inputs.

3.2 The Monte Carlo Implementation

The main loop for the activity estimation was also implemented with a Tcl script. This script iteratively calls several programs until the stopping criterion is met for all the nodes. The iteration body is made of the following steps: 1) Call the program that generates a set of input vectors according to user specifications; 2) The simulator run the generated command file with these input vectors; 3) Other Active-HDL script of macros saves the resulting activity; 4) The executable core analyzes the activity reported by the simulator. This module keeps the necessary data in a simple database. Finally two executable programs are called to: 5) To update the mean activity and standard deviation for each node, and 6) To evaluate if the stopping criteria is reached for all nodes.

Table 1. Test circuits

Circuit	# Inputs	# Outputs	# Nodes	Device	# CLBs
C1: Behavioral VHDL Multiplier	16	16	769	XC4010E PC84 -4C	54
C2: Hatamian-Cash Multiplier	16	16	1447	XC4010E PC84 -4C	96

Table 2. Long simulation results. For these runs, 99% confidence and 1% error was specified. The minimum mean varies between 0.1 and 2 transitions per clock cycle

	VHDL Behavioral Multiplier		Hatamian-Cash Multiplier	
Min. Mean	# Samples	Total Av. Trans. per clock cycle	# Samples	Total Av. Trans. per clock cycle
0.10	364900	981	-	-
0.35	367750	979	509450	1226
0.50	347950	979	378950	1225
1.00	225050	980	244600	1224
1.50	180050	981	159550	1229
2.00	116400	978	116750	1229

4 Results

In order to evaluate the tool, two combinational multipliers whose main characteristics are listed in Table 1 were analyzed.

First, a set of long simulations was run to obtain values to compare with. The number of samples for each run, and the total average number of circuit transitions are shown in Table 2.

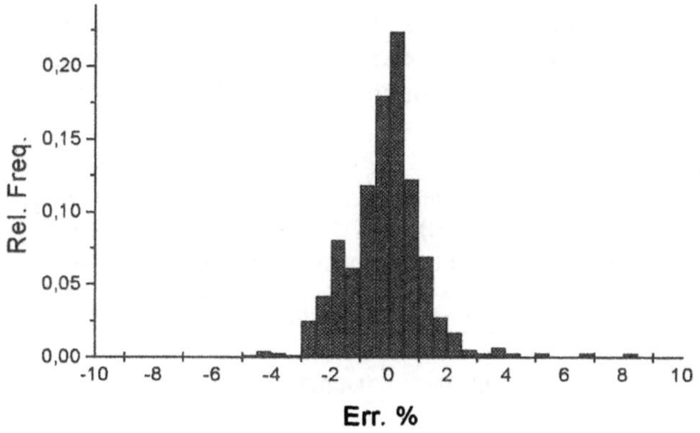

Fig. 3. Error in activity for individual nodes in circuit C1

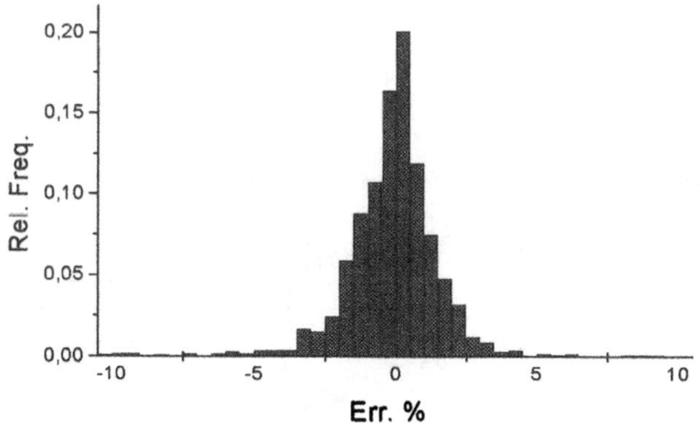

Fig. 4. Error in activity for individual nodes in circuit C2

In order to check if the error is within the specified values, several simulations were run with 95% confidence, 5% error and 0.35 minimum mean. Fig. 3 and 4 show the relative error on the average number of transitions per clock cycle for individual nodes, compared with the corresponding long simulation values. It is observed that more than 95% of the nodes is within the 5% error, while the nodes with the highest relative errors are also low activity nodes, with negligible absolute error. For both test circuits, more than 98% of the nodes have an error less than 5%. In fact, more than 86% of the nodes have an error less than 2%. This is due to the highest activity nodes, which converge earlier in the estimation process, and are over-analyzed.

The tunable accuracy-execution time properties of the technique implemented in this work was studied in a second test. Fig. 5 shows the results of different runs with 95% confidence and 5% error, varying the minimum mean. For all the experiments mentioned in this paragraph, the input signals were specified as time independent, with probability 0.5 and 0.5 transitions per clock cycle. As expected, the required number of samples monotonically increases as the minimum mean decreases. Nevertheless, a low impact on the estimation error is observed, as stated in [14]. In fact, the correlation between the minimum mean and the relative error is very low as shown in Table 3.

Table 3. Correlation between minimum mean and error for individual nodes. The selected nodes are the most active (named C1H), the 10th most active (C1M), and a low regular- but near the threshold- active node (C1L). Values extracted from simulations of C1

Node	Correlation
C1H	0.3405
C1M	0.4402
C1L	0.1262

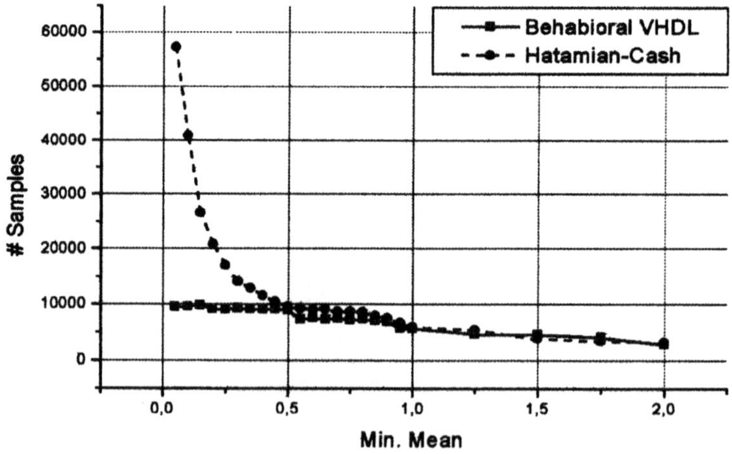

Fig. 5. Tunable property for the user defined threshold in nodes activity

The same tunable property has been checked with respect to the pair error-confidence: as error decreases and confidence level increases, the number of samples monotonically increases (Fig. 6).

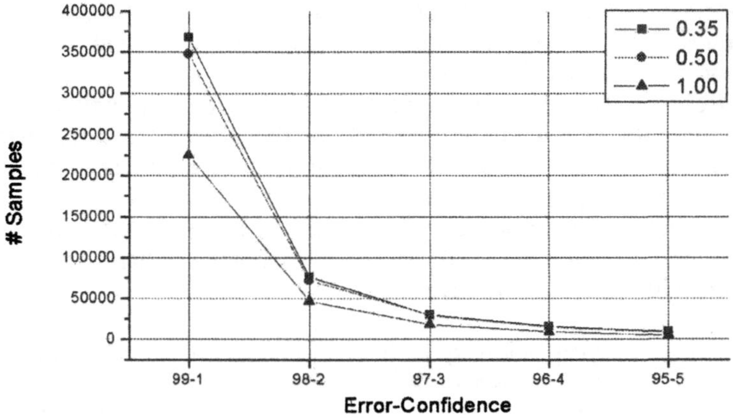

Fig. 6. Error-Confidence tunable property. Values extracted from simulations of C1. Inputs defined as independent

In order to show how the activity can fluctuate in both individual nodes and the whole circuit, the cases defined in Table 4 have been simulated. The different execution times are shown in Fig. 7. It has also been verified the variation in the activities for individual nodes as shown in Table 5.

Table 4. User defined input patterns.

	Input Pattern
1	All primary inputs are independent random patterns
2	The activity of the MSB is set to 0.05 and is increased linearly to 0.95 for the LSB
3	The activity of the MSB is set to 0.95 and is decreased linearly to 0.05 for the LSB
4	The activity is set to 0.75 for the 4 MSBs and 0.25 for the LSBs
5	The activity is set to 0.25 for the 4 MSBs and 0.75 for the LSBs
6	The signal probability is set to 0.75 for the 4 MSBs and 0.25 for the LSBs
7	The signal probability is set to 0.25 for the 4 MSBs and 0.75 for the LSBs
8	The 4 MSBs of the pattern are independent random patterns and the remaining bits are connected to a counter
9	The 4 MSBs of the pattern are connected to a counter and the remaining bits are independent random patterns

5 Conclusions

A statistical-based power estimation tool oriented to FPGA devices has been presented. The experiments confirm the robustness of the technique, allowing a tunable accuracy. According to the precision required at each moment in the design process, appropriate values can be set for both the minimum mean activity and the error-confidence pair. The execution time of the tool grows with the required precision. For instance, running the tool on the C1 multiplier, and selecting 1 as the minimum mean, the execution times are 20 minutes for 95% confidence and 5% error, and 60 minutes for 97% confidence and 3% error, using a PC with a 1-GHz AMD processor with 256 MB RAM memory.

It has also been verified that the actual relative error for individual nodes is bounded by the one specified by the user. As predicted by Eq.2, nodes with higher activity have less error than the specified one: they converge earlier in the estimation process and are over-analyzed according to the specified tolerated error.

Finally, the importance of properly defined input pattern characteristics is pointed out. The use of this tool with a default or arbitrary input pattern, can result in an activity figure with unpredictable error.

Table 5. Maximum variation on activity for individual nodes and the different user specified input patterns. The shown values are extracted from simulations of C1

C1H		C1M		C1L	
#Pattern	Activity	#Pattern	Activity	#Pattern	Activity
3	6.7032	7	0.7916	8	0.5178
6	4.7383	6	4.5503	6	0.0958

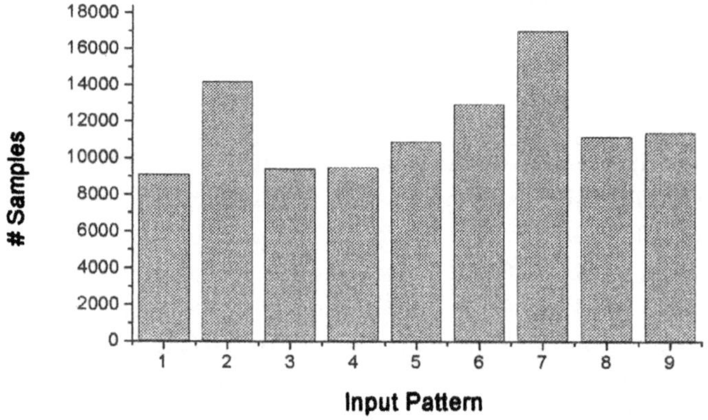

Fig. 7. Execution time for several user defined input patterns. Values extracted from simulations of C1

Acknowledgments

Spanish Ministry of Science and Technology has supported this work, under Contract TIC2001-2688-C03-03. Additional funds have been obtained from Project 658001 of the *Fundación General de la Universidad Autónoma de Madrid.* G. Sutter and E. Todorovich are granted by CONICET of Argentine.

References

1. Boemo, E., Gonzalez de Rivera, G., Lopez-Buedo, S., Meneses, J.: Some Notes on Power Management on FPGAs. Lecture Notes in Computer Science, No. *975*, Springer-Verlag, Berlin (1995) 149-157
2. Najm, F.: Estimating Power Dissipation in VLSI Circuits. IEEE Circuits and Devices Magazine, Vol 10, No 4 (1994) 11-19
3. Pedram, M.: Design technologies for Low Power VLSI. In Encyclopedia of Computer Science and Technology, Vol. 36, Marcel Dekker, Inc. (1997) 73-96
4. Macii, E., Pedram, M., Somenzi, F.: High-Level Power Modeling, Estimation, and Optimization. Computer-Aided Design of Integrated Circuits and Systems (1998)
5. Fawcett, B.: FPGAs, Power and Packages. *XCELL* (1997)
6. Xilinx Press: A Simple Method of Estimating Power in XC4000XL/EX/E FPGAs. Application Brief, XBRF 014 (1997)
7. Tan, J: Virtex Power Estimator User Guide. XAPP 152 (1999)
8. Xilinx Inc.: XC4000XL Power Calculation. XCELL, N°27 (2000) pp 29
9. Osmulski, T., Muehring, J.T., Veale, B., West, J. M., Li, H., Vanichayobon, S., Ko, S-H, Antonio, J.K, Dhall, S.K: A Probabilistic Power Prediction Tool for the Xilinx 4000-Series FPGA. Proc. of the 5th International Workshop on Embedded/Distributed HPC Systems and Applications (EHPC 2000), Cancun, Mexico (2000) 776-783
10. Xilinx Inc.: ISE 4 User Guide. http://www.xilinx.com
11. Xilinx Inc.: XPower Tutorial: FPGA Design, XPower (v1.1). (2001) http://www.xilinx.com.
12. Burch, R., Najm, F. N., Yang, P., Trick, T.: A Monte Carlo approach for power estimation. IEEE Transactions on VLSI Systems, 1(1) (1993) 63–71
13. Xakellis, M., Najm, F.: Statistical Estimation of the Switching Activity in Digital Circuits. 31st ACM/IEEE Design Automation Conference, San Diego, CA (1994) 728-733
14. Najm, F. N., Xakellis, M. G.: Statistical estimation of the switching activity in VLSI circuits. VLSI Design, vol. 7, no. 3 (1998) 243-254
15. Chou, T., Roy, K.: Accurate Power Estimation of CMOS Sequential Circuits. IEEE Trans. on VLSI, Vol.4, n°3 (1996) 369-380
16. Kozhaya, J., Najm, F. N.: Accurate power estimation for large sequential circuits. IEEE/ACM International Conference on Computer-Aided Design (1997) 488-493
17. See On-line documentation at http://www.aldec.com
18. P1497 DRAFT Standard for Standard Delay Format (SDF) for the Electronic Design Process. IEEE SDF P1497 Draft 0.10 Specification, June 7, 2000, http://www.eda.org/sdf/

FSM Decomposition for Low Power in FPGA

Gustavo Sutter[1], Elias Todorovich[1], Sergio Lopez-Buedo[2], and Eduardo Boemo[2]

1. INCA, Universidad Nacional del Centro, Tandil, Argentine
{gsutter, etodorov}@exa.unicen.edu.ar
2. School of Computer and Telecommunication Engineering
Universidad Autonoma de Madrid, Spain
{sergio.lopez-buedo, eduardo.boemo}@uam.es

Abstract. In this paper, the realization of low power finite state machines (FSMs) on FPGAs using decomposition techniques is addressed. The original FSM is divided into two submachines using a probabilistic criterion. Only one submachine is active at a time, meanwhile the other is disabled to save power. Different deactivation alternatives and state encoding have been studied. For each option, actual measurements of power consumption have been done using the MCNC and the PREP benchmark circuits. A Xilinx XC4K device has been utilized as technological framework. The proposed technique fits well with big FSM, where power reductions up to 46% are obtained.

I. Introduction

In this work, the problem of optimising FPGA-based finite state machines (FSM) circuits for low power is addressed. Several techniques for state assignment have been proposed in the past for cell-based or gate array technology. The main idea has been to lower the average switching activity in two ways: either by disabling the input data to the FSM, or by blocking the state registers. The cost is an extra hardware to detect certain conditions to stop parts of the machine.

The experiments presented in this paper are based on the ideas proposed in [7][15][6][3][4], adapted or modified to suit well with the technological target: LUT-based FPGAs. The original FSM is divided into two sub-FSMs. Each submachine must to have roughly the same amount of states. A probabilistic approach is utilised to determine an optimal partition that guarantees a minimum interaction between the submachines. The hardware overhead associated with the decomposition technique makes this method neither effective for FSMs with small numbers of states (under 10) nor applicable for circuits whose decomposition has a highly transition probability between submachines. However, for large machines, an improvement in power consumption up to 46% can be obtained.

The paper is organized as follows. Section II reviews the basic definitions and highlights the main aspects of the traditional approaches to FSM decomposition. The FSM architecture proposed in this paper is described in Section III. In the next section, the characteristics of the benchmark circuits are exhibited. Finally, in Section VI, the main experimental results are summarized.

M. Glesner, P. Zipf, and M. Renovell (Eds.): FPL 2002, LNCS 2438, pp. 350-359, 2002.

II. Background

A finite state machines is defined by a 6-tuple $M = (\Sigma, \sigma, Q, q_0, \delta, \lambda)$, where Σ is a finite set of input symbols, $\sigma \neq \varnothing$ is a finite set of output symbols, $Q \neq \varnothing$ is a finite set of states, $q_0 \in Q$ is the "reset" state, $\delta(q, a)$: $Q \times \Sigma \rightarrow Q$ is the transition function, and λ (q, a): $Q \times \Sigma \rightarrow \sigma$ is the output function.

The 6-tuple M can be described by a state transition graph (STG). Nodes represent the states, and directed edges (labeled with input and output values), describe the transition relation between states. In hardware materializations, each state corresponds to a binary vector stored in registers. From the current state and input values, the combinational logic computes the next state and the output function.

The decomposition for low-power FSM requires first calculating the transitions probabilities in order to divide the machine. Thus, the activity can be reduced. Then, these submachines must be efficiently mapped in a FPGA, so that the hardware overhead does not compensate the power saving of a lower node activity.

II.a. Calculating Probabilities

In order to decide the submachine partitioning, a probabilistic model [24] must be utilized. To compute the transition probabilities for a given STG, it is first necessary to know the probability distribution for the inputs. Those values can be obtained by a higher-level simulation of FSM in a context close to the actual environment of the design. Then, the transition probability for each edge in the STG can be determined by modeling the STG as a Markov chain. A Markov chain is a stochastic process whose dynamic behavior is such that the probabilistic distribution for its future behavior depends only on the present state, without taking into account how the process arrived in that state.

The steady state probability for a state q_i is defined as the chance of the FSM to remain in q_i. This value is not time dependent. That is, as the time increases, it converges to constant real numbers. Let **P** be the conditional transition probability matrix, and **v** be the steady state probability vector (whose components are the state probabilities). Then, the steady state probabilities can be compute by solving the following system of $n+1$ equations: $v \cdot P = v$ and $\sum_{i=0}^{n-1} P_i = 1$;

where $v = [P_0 P_1 \ldots P_{n-1}]$ and $$P = \begin{bmatrix} p_{0,0} & p_{0,1} & \cdots & p_{0,n-1} \\ p_{1,0} & p_{1,1} & \cdots & p_{1,n-1} \\ \cdots & \cdots & \cdots & \cdots \\ p_{n-1,0} & p_{n-1,1} & \cdots & p_{n-1,n-1} \end{bmatrix}$$

Here, **P** is a stochastic matrix (i.e. all the entries are non-negative and the sum of each row is one) whose entries are the conditional transition probabilities. The total transition probabilities $\mathbf{P_{i,j}}$ can be calculated as: $P_{i,j} = p_{i,j} \cdot P_i$

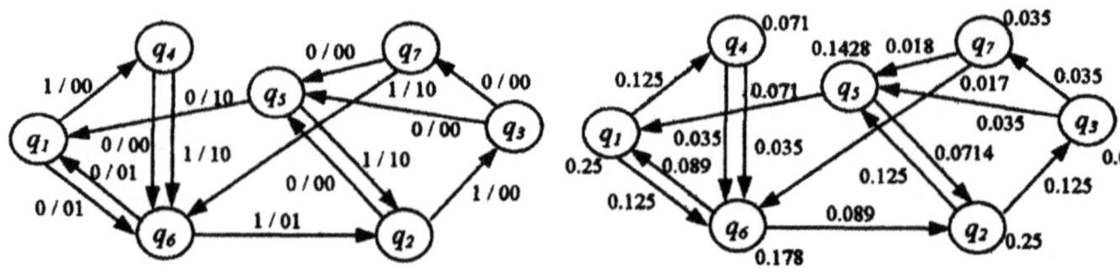

Fig. 1. a) State Transition Graph (STG), b) steady state probabilities and total transition probability

II.b. Low-Power Design of FSM

The most popular technique to reduce power in FSM is to modify the state encoding [27][4][16][28][14]. These works are focused on the Hamming distance minimization of the most probable state transitions. However, this solution usually increases the required logic to decode the next state. Then, a tradeoff between switching reduction and extra capacitance exists.

In the area of FPGAs, the most utilized state encoding technique is one-hot [25][9]. Nevertheless, empirical measurements indicate that binary state encoding is better for low power [21], [8] in these FSMs that have less than eight states.

Other idea for low-power FSMs is the use of power management. That is, to shutdown the blocks of hardware in these periods where they are not producing useful data. Shutdown can be fulfilled in three ways: by turning off the power supply, by disabling the clock signal, or finally by "freezing" (blocking) the input data.

Under the last category, fall methods like precomputation, gated clock, selectively clocked systems, and decomposition. In the gated-clock technique [3][5], the clocking of a FSM is stopped when the machine is in self-loops and the outputs do not change. In precomputation [1], a simple combinational block is added to the original circuit. Under certain input conditions, the precomputation logic disables the loading of the input registers. This paper is focused mainly on the decomposition approach, detailed in the following paragraphs.

II.c. Decomposition Architectures

Several researchers addressed the decomposition o partitioning of FSM. First, the goal is to reduce the complexity of the combinational block to be mapped in a fixed logic [2][11]. The FSM is divided in two (or more) interacting machines (fig.2), where each submachine knows in which state is the other. This strategy adds an idle state to each sub-FSM.

Other scheme is the orthogonal partition [20]. In this case, the number of states in the partition its not $n_1+n_2 = n$, but its approximately $\sqrt{n}$ in each partition. Let consider $Q = \{q_1,q_2,\ldots,q_n\}$ the original state set. Two partitions $\Pi_A = \{A_1, A_2, \ldots, A_m\}$ and $\Pi_B = \{B_1, B_2, \ldots, B_k\}$ of Q are *orthogonal* if, for $i \leq m, j \leq k$, either $A_i \cap B_j = \emptyset$ or $A_i \cap B_j = \{q_i\}$. Thus, in order to represent an original q_t state, this method uses a combination of an A_i and a B_j.

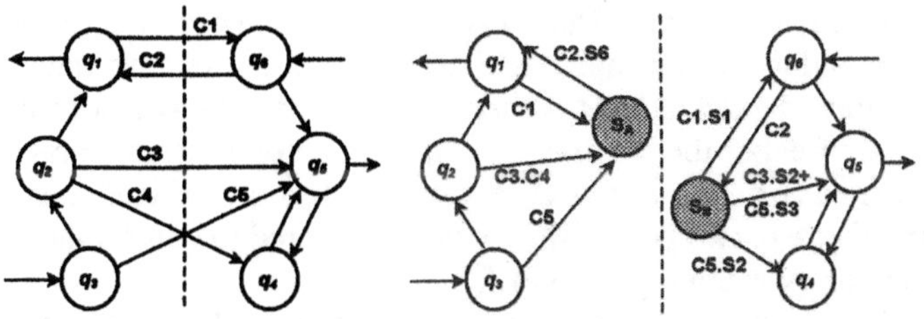

Fig. 2. State diagram of a FSM and the partitioned diagram in the traditional approach.

II.d. Decomposition Techniques for Low Power

The basic low-power idea of decomposition is to disable the inactive part of a FSM. The deactivation is reached either by blocking the inputs (using latches, ANDs or tri-estates buffers) or power-down the part of the circuit that is not used (by clock gating). In [15][6], the FSM is partitioned into several pieces, that are implemented as a separate machine with an extra wait state (idle state). In this case, only one of the sub-machines is active, meanwhile the others are idle. Therefore, the clock for inactive sub-machines can be gated and primary inputs can be disabled. This reduces switching activity and hence, the total power dissipation. In [15], the STG is partitioned into two unbalanced sub-machines: a small one that is active most of the time, and a large submachine that is usually disabled.

An interesting disjoint encoding schema is proposed in [7]. The resulting partition not follows strictly the standard structure of FSM decomposition. In this method, the STG is partitioned in two (or more) sets of states. All the states of a given set are encoded with the MSB (most significant bit) at 0, meanwhile the states of the other sets are encoded with the MSB at 1. Thus, the combinational logic can be broken into two separate blocks: one that is active when the first state bit is 0, and other that is active when the first state bit is 1. In this way, the power consumption can be potentially reduced.

Other technique is to use an orthogonal partitioning together with gated clock mechanism [19]. An N state machine is decomposed into two interacting machines with N_1 and N_2 states, such that $N \leq N_1 \times N_2$. In each sub-FSM, the partition tries to maximize the number of self-edges (where the machine remains in the same state after the clock edge). For all the self-edge conditions, the inputs and clock signal are disabled.

III. A Decomposition Architecture Suitable for FPGAs

In this paper, a decomposition architecture based on [7] have been constructed and evaluated in terms of area-time-power. The structure fits well with LUT-based FPGAs. The same codes are utilized in both submachines, but only one is active. To point the active machine, an extra bit called *ActiveFSM* is set. The first architectural option is shown in Fig.3a. The original FSM is decomposed in two combinational circuits (machines A and B) that compute both outputs and next state. Only one submachine is active at a time. The transference of the control between the machines is based on the values of the inputs and actual state. If the next state corresponds to the other machine, the *activeFSM* is asserted. The shaded blocks of the Fig.3 indicate the circuits that "freeze" the inactive machine. A second architectural option has also been implemented (fig 3.b). In this case, two registers are utilized to stop the machine evolution. In this case, two possibilities can be explored to control the registers: via an enabled signal, or by using a gated-clock.

For both architectures, the same design flow must be followed. First, an algorithm to decompose the FSM in two or more sub-machines must be selected. Second, one of the blocking methods must be implemented. Finally, a synthesizable code of the circuit must be written.

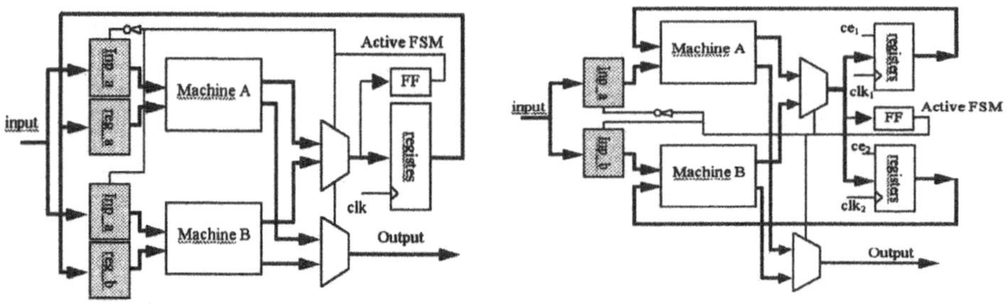

Fig. 3. Two options for decomposition FSM. a) Architecture I, b) Architecture II.

III.a. Partitioning a FSM into Submachines

The technique separates the FSM into two or more submachines so that the probabilities of state transitions inside each submachine are maximized, meanwhile the interaction with the other submachines is low.

First, the transition probability over the STG is calculated (as is shown in fig 1.b). Then, a partition with equal cardinality in subFSMs is achieved. For instance, let consider the two partitions $\Pi_A = \{S_{a1}, S_{a2}, \ldots S_{an}\}$ and $\Pi_B = \{S_{b1}, S_{b2}, \ldots S_{bn}\}$, with a transition probability *p(i,j)* between state S_i and S_j . In this case, the algorithm minimizes sum of transition probabilities between submachines. That is:

$\min(\sum p(i,j)), \quad \forall i \in \Pi_A, j \in \Pi_B$.

No greedy algorithm is necessary, because a backtracking technique with an effective prune is fast enough.

III.b Blocking Method

In order to eliminate the activity in the idle FSM, the best alternative in Fig.3.a machines is to latch the data (*Blocking Latches*). Other possibilities like the use of ANDs, or buffers have been tested and discarded: they are more expensive in both area and time. For FSMs like the described in Fig.3.b, the alternatives are to implement a gate-clock or use the clock enable signal. In the second alternative the clock lines continue consuming power.

III.c. Synthesis of the Final Machine

In this work, a tool that automatically generates a set of benchmark FSMs has been developed. The inputs are the FSM description in a KISS2 format [18], and some extra parameters like the blocking scheme, and the state encoding technique. The tool calculates the steady state probability, divides the machine as described in section IIIa, and finally, writes a synthezable VHDL code. The file contains the entity of the machine, and three processes: one for the combinatorial logic, other for the blocking data circuitry, and the last one to incorporate tri-states buffers at the outputs pads to separately measure the off-chip power.

IV. Experiments

In this paper, the benchmark circuits have been implemented in several ways: First, in the original form with both binary and One Hot state encoding. Then, each machine was partitioned in two ways: one corresponding to the *architecture I* and other for the *architecture II* scheme (fig. 3). Once again, binary and One Hot encoding was the applied in each submachine. Additionally, the option named *architecture I*, was tested using different blocking techniques.

All the experiments use the MCNC91 benchmark set [13]. In addition, a large FSMs extracted from the PREP consortium [17] was utilized. Each FSM was first minimized with STAMINA [12]. Number of inputs, outputs, next state rules (arcs in the STG), and number of states of the benchmark machines are summarized in Table 1. Additionally the probability of transition and the number of arcs between submachines is reported.

The resulting VHDL code was compiled into a XC4010EPC84-1 FPGA sample, using the FPGA Express [10] and the Xilinx Foundation tools [26]. This circuit model does not have latches, so they were constructed using LUTs. All circuits has been implemented and tested under identical conditions. That is, all the measurements are related to the same FPGA sample, output pins, tool settings, printed circuit board, input vectors, clock frequency, and logic analyzer probes. Random vectors were utilized to stimulate the circuit. At the output, each pad supported the load of the logic analyzer, lower than 3pf [22].

Each circuit was measured at 100 Hz, 2 MHz, and 4 MHz to extrapolate the static power consumption. All prototypes include a tri-state buffer at the output pads to measure the off-chip power [23].

Example	Original FSM				Partition	
	$\|\Sigma\|$	$\|\sigma\|$	$\|Q\|$	$\|\delta\|$	Prob	Arcs
Bbsse	7	7	13	208	0,024	52
Cse	7	7	16	91	0,017	36
Dk16	2	3	27	108	0,247	28
Dk512	1	3	15	30	0,175	7
Ex1	9	19	18	233	0,022	53
Ex2	2	2	14	56	0,218	25
Keyb	7	2	19	170	0,004	63
Kirkman	12	6	16	370	0,002	46
Mark1	5	16	12	180	0,037	79
Planet	7	19	48	115	0,052	14
Prep4	8	8	16	78	0,041	9
S386	7	7	13	69	0,024	27
S820	18	19	24	254	0,006	138
S832c	18	19	24	243	0,006	118

Table 1. Original FSM data, number of inputs, outputs, states and arcs. In adition partition information is provided (probability and arcs between partitions)

V. Experimental Results

The slope of the power consumption, expressed in mW/MHz, is depicted in Table II. The first columns show the value for the original FSM coded in One Hot (OH) and binary (bin). Then, the results for the partitioned circuits (encoded in One Hot and binary), are listed for the four different forms: *Architecture 1* (*Arch1*), *Architecture 2* (*Arch2*), *Architecture* 1 without blocking method (*No Blk*), and finally, *Architecture 1* with blocking ANDs (*Blk and*). A power improvement factor is defined: it express the relationship between the power consumption of the best original FSM respect the best-partitioned one.

Power Improvement: For most of the FSM, a power saving is obtained. It can be up to the 42,4%. However, in five circuits, no improvement or negative results can be observed. This is caused by a high transition probability between submachines in these circuits (Table 3).

Binary vs. One Hot encoding in submachines: In accordance with previous results related to non-partitioned states machines [sut02], one hot encoding provides better results in FSMs with more than 16 states. On the contrary, for machines equal or smaller than 8 states, binary state encoding is better.

Blocking method: Latches are better in most of the cases. The improvement respect to the AND gates can be up to the 30%). Only in two benchmark FSMs, the blocking AND gates resulted better, because the low activity of the machines.

Sample	Original FSM		Partitioned One Hot Encoded				Partitioned Binary Encoded				Power Improvement
	OH	Bin	Arch1	Arch2	No Blk	Blk and	Arch1	Arch2	No Blk	Blk and	
Bbsse	3,90	4,70	3,80	3,95	4,04	4,34	3,55	3,76	4,23	3,91	9,0%
Cse	3,85	4,10	3,24	3,46	4,29	5,30	3,00	2,88	3,83	3,59	25,3%
Dk16	3,88	10,00	5,80	5,76	5,81	6,34	7,50	7,01	9,09	9,96	-32,8%
Dk512	1,84	2,80	2,46	2,79	2,44	2,14	2,24	2,51	2,16	1,94	-5,2%
Ex1	7,09	8,56	6,73	6,53	8,11	8,16	6,53	6,11	7,90	7,79	13,8%
Ex2	2,51	4,10	3,40	3,09	2,69	3,26	3,09	2,88	3,58	3,46	-6,5%
Keyb	5,50	7,06	4,73	4,31	7,88	7,69	3,66	4,65	5,25	6,81	33,4%
Kirkman	4,50	4,61	4,90	4,66	4,49	4,50	4,80	4,49	4,83	4,80	0,3%
Mark1	2,70	3,30	3,01	3,01	3,31	3,09	2,66	2,78	2,63	2,88	2,8%
Planet	8,04	16,80	9,18	9,29	10,23	10,01	10,88	11,81	15,18	16,99	-12,4%
Prep4	4,66	5,71	5,44	5,38	6,86	7,55	5,11	4,66	6,86	6,44	0,0%
S386	4,23	4,84	4,08	4,45	4,98	4,98	4,21	4,21	5,55	4,59	3,6%
S820	7,84	9,28	5,81	5,44	8,43	7,98	4,51	4,65	8,83	7,30	42,4%
S832c	7,01	10,21	5,08	5,00	7,64	6,60	4,73	5,04	7,55	6,75	32,6%

Table 2. Power consumption expressed in mW / MHz.

Area penalty: Both the synchronization and the partition circuitry add extra logic to the FSM. This overheard depends on the number of inputs, outputs and states. Each input signal requires 2 LUTs to implement the latches, and each output an extra LUT to implement the output multiplexer. Finally, each state add 2 extra LUTs to implement the latches in *architecture I* (*architecture II* not need extra logic to implement the blocking states). In terms of power, *Architecture I* its slightly better than *Architecture II.*

Sample	$\|\Sigma\|$	$\|\sigma\|$	$\|Q\|$	$\|\delta\|$	Arcs bet. part	% arcs bet. part.	Prob	Power Improv.
Dk16	2	3	27	108	28	26 %	0,247	-32,8 %
Ex2	2	2	14	56	25	45 %	0,218	-6,5 %
Dk512	1	3	15	30	7	23 %	0,175	-5,2 %
Planet	7	19	48	115	14	12 %	0,052	-12,4 %
Prep4	8	8	16	78	9	12 %	0,041	0,0 %

Table 3. Circuits where no improvement its possible due the highly probability of transition between submachines.

Clock period penalty: The synchronization scheme produces speed degradation. Table 4 shows the maximum frequency in MHz in each case. The influence of latches is remarkable nevertheless the partitioned *architecture* with blocking *and gates* shows a better performance.

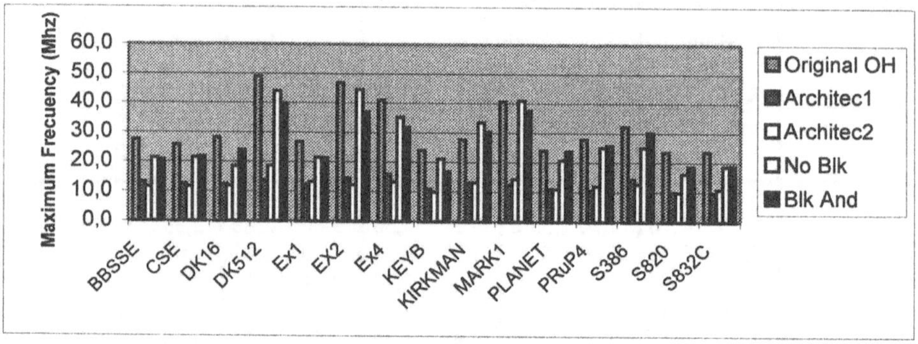

Fig. 4. Frequency chart, where the negative impact of the blocking latches can be observed.

VI. Conclusions

This paper explores partitioning methods to reduce power in FPGA-based FSMs. The main conclusions are that classical decomposition techniques developed for cell-based circuits can be adapted to FPGA. A significant power reduction in big FSMs (up to the 46%) can be obtained. These results should be more significant in devices that have embedded latches (Xilinx XC4000EX or the Virtex and Spartan 2). The state-encoding scheme of each submachine plays an important role: Binary based state encoding works better for small submachines (up to eight), meanwhile one hot is the best option in big FSMs. Finally, the achievement of a low activity between submachines is essential to get full advantage of the technique.

Acknowledgments

Spanish Ministry of Science and tecnology of Spain has supported this work, under Contract TIC2001-2688-C03-03. Additional funds have been obtained from Project 658001 of *the Fundación General de la Universidad Autónoma de Madrid.*

References

[1] M.Alidina, J.Monteiro, S.Devadas, A.Gosh, M.Papaefthymiou, Precomputation-Based sequential logic optimization for Low-Power, *IEEE VLSI, V.2,n°4,pp.426-435,* Dec 1994.

[2] P.Ashar, S.Devadas, and A.Newton. Optimum and heuristic algorithms for an approach to fsm decomposition. *IEEE Trans.Computer-Aided Design,* 10(3):296-310, March 1991.

[3] L.Benini P.Siegel and G.De Micheli. Automatic synthesis of low-power gated-clock finite-state machines. *IEEE Trans.on CAD of IC, vol.15, Issue6,* June 1996, pp. 630–643.

[4] L.Benini and G. De Micheli. State Assignment for Low Power Dissipation. *IEEE Journ. of Solid State Circuits,* Vol. 30, No. 3, pp. 258-268, March 1995.

[5] L. Benini, and G. De Micheli, Transformation and Synthesis of FSMs for Low Power Gated Clock Implementation, *ISLP'95 International Symposium on Low Power Design, ACM-SIGDA and IEEE-CAS*, April 23-26, 1995.

[6] L. Benini, G. De Micheli, and F. Vermeulen, Finite-state machine partitioning for low power. *In Proc. IEEE Int'l Symposium on Circuits and Systems (ISCAS '98), volume 2, pages 5-8*, Monterey, California, May31-June3, 1998.

[7] S-H.Chow, Y-C.Ho, and T.Hwang. Low Power Realization of Finite State Machines Decomposition Approach. *ACM Trans on Design Aut. Elec. Systems*, 315-340, July 1996.

[8] J.Dunoyer, F.Pétrot, L.Jacomme. Intrinsic limitations of logarithmic encodingsfor low power finite state machines. *Mixed Des of VLSI Circ Conf, p 613-618*, Pologne, 1997.

[9] FPGA Compiler II / FPGA Express VHDL Reference Manual, Version 1999.05, Synopsys, Inc.,May 1999

[10] FPGA Express home page. Synopsis, inc.; http://www.synopsys.com/products/fpga/fpga_express.htm

[11] M.Geiger T.Müller-Wipperfürth, FSM Decomposition Revisited: Algebraic Structure Theory Applied to MCNC Benchmark FSMs. *28th ACM/IEEE DAC Conference*, 1991

[12] G.Hachtel, J.Rho, F.Somenzi, R.Jacoby. Exact and Heuristic Alg. for the Minimization of Incompletely Specified State Machines. *Europ. DAC, pp 184–191*, Amsterdam, feb 1991.

[13] Bob Lisanke. "Logic synthesis and optimization benchmarks". *Technical report, MCNC, Research Triangle Park*, North Carolina, December 1988.

[14] M. Martínez, M. J. Avedillo, J. M. Quintana, M. Koegst, ST. Rulke, and H. Susse: Low Power State Assignment Algorithm, *DCIS'00 conf*, pp. 181-187, 2000.

[15] J. Monteiro, A. Oliviera, Finite State Machine Decomposition for Low Power, *Proceedings 35th Design Automation Conference* , San Franscisco, 1998, pp. 758-763.

[16] Winfried Nöth and Reiner Kolla. Spanning Tree Based State Encoding for Low Power Dissipation". *In Proc of Date99, pp 168-174*, Munich, Germany, March 1999.

[17] PREP Benchmarks (Programmable Elect. Performance Company), http://www.prep.org.

[18] E. Sentovich, K. Singh, L. Lavagno, C. Moon, R. Murgai, A. Saldanha, P. Stephan, R. Brayton, and A. Sangiovanni-Vincentelli. SIS: A System for Seq. Circuit Synthesis. *Tech. Report Mem. No. UCB/ ERL M92/41*, Univ. of California, Berkeley, 1992.

[19] R.Shelar, H.Narayanan, M.Desai, Orthogonal Partitioning and Gated Clock Architecture for Low Power Realization of FSMs, *IEEE Int ASIC/SOC conf*, Sep 2000, pp. 266-270.

[20] R.Shelar, M.P. Desai, H.Narayanan, "Decomposition of Finite State Machines for Area, Delay Minimization", *IEEE ICCD99* Austin, 10-13 Oct. 99, pp. 620-625.

[21] G. Sutter and E. Boemo Low Power Finite state machines in FPGA: Bynary vs One hot encoding. *VIII Workshop Iberchip*, Guadalajara, Mexico, April 2002.

[22] Tektronix inc., *"TLA 700 Series Logic Analyzer User Manual"*, http://www.tektronix.com.

[23] E. Todorovich, G. Sutter, N. Acosta, E. Boemo and S. López-Buedo, "End-user low-power alternatives at topological and physical levels. Some examples on FPGAs", *Proc. DCIS'2000*, Montpellier, France, November 2000.

[24] C-Y Tsui, M.Pedram, A. Despain, Exact and Approximate Methods for Calculating Signal and Transition Probabilities in FSMs, *31st Design Autom. Conf.*, pp. 18-23, 1994.

[25] Xilinx software manual, Synth. and Sim. Design Guide: Encoding State. *Xilinx Inc*, 2000

[26] Xilinx Foundation Tools F3.1i, www.xilinx.com/ support/library.htm

[27] C.Tsui, M.Pedram, C.Chen, A.Despain, "Low Power State Assignment Targeting Two-and Multi-level Logic Implement., *ACM/IEEE Inter.Conf. of CAD*, pp. 82-87, Nov.1994

[28] X. Wu, M. Pedram, and L. Wang, "Multi-code state assignment for low power design,", *IEEE Proc. Circuits, Dev. and Systems*, Vol. 147, No. 5, Oct. 2000, pp. 271-275.

Hybrid Routing for FPGAs by Integrating Boolean Satisfiability with Geometric Search

Gi-Joon Nam[1], Karem Sakallah[2] and Rob Rutenbar[3]
[1]IBM Austin Research Lab, 11400 Burnet Road, Austin TX 78758, USA
gnam@us.ibm.com
[2]EECS, University of Michigan, 1301 Beal Avenue, Ann Arbor MI 48109, USA
karem@eecs.umich.edu
[3]ECE, Carnegie Mellon University, Pittsburgh, PA 15213, USA
rutenbar@ece.cmu.edu

Abstract: Boolean Satisfiability (SAT)-based routing has unique advantages over conventional one-net-at-a-time approaches such as simultaneous net embedding or routability decision. Yet SAT-based routing has been criticized for scalability issues. On the other hand, geometric search routing algorithms, even with extensive rip-up-reroute capabilities, have difficulty achieving routing solution convergence when a problem has tight routing constraints. In this paper, we revisit the SAT-based routing idea for FPGA routing, and propose a new hybrid algorithm that integrates SAT-based FPGA routing with a conventional geometric search FPGA router. The advantages of such a combination are two-fold: 1) the scalability handicap of SAT-based routing is overcome due to the path pruning techniques of the geometric search algorithm, and 2) more concrete routability decisions can be made thus achieving the convergence, because the SAT-based technique considers simultaneously any paths in the history of iterative routings. The proposed algorithm named *search-SAT* is implemented and applied to real-world industry circuits. Preliminary experimental results show "search-SAT" is a more viable routing technique than any earlier SAT-based routing approach.

1 Introduction

The Boolean Satisfiability problem (in short SAT) involves finding an assignment to binary variables that satisfies a given set of Boolean constraints. Boolean SAT has been drawing significant attention during the last decade because of its remarkable contributions to various EDA fields including logic synthesis, ATPG (automatic test pattern generation), verifications etc. Naturally, the SAT community becomes surprisingly large and vigorous. Yet it has not been picked up actively in the physical design domain, especially routing area, mainly because of the doubt that a Boolean formulation in routing would generate an tractable size of problem. Although it is true in general, we still argue that the carefully devised Boolean SAT-based formulation can be an efficient method in routing which can provide unattainable information with conventional approaches.

SAT-based routing is a concurrent method which is able to embed nets simultaneously. That is, this approach is independent of net-ordering unlike conventional *one-net-at-a-*

M. Glesner, P. Zipf, and M. Renovell (Eds.): FPL 2002, LNCS 2438, pp. 360-369, 2002.

time routing algorithms. More interesting is that a Boolean SAT-based layout approach is an "exact" method; once we create a Boolean formula which expresses all the possible layout constraints, any satisfying Boolean assignment of values to variables represents a legal layout solution. Furthermore, by demonstrating the absence of such assignments, no existence of layout solutions can be proven, which seems to be a very rare feature in layout domains. In fact, the routability decision under a given placement could be very desirable. For example, at the placement level, the ability to estimate the routability of each placement configuration can be very helpful in producing a better placement solution. Conventional one-net-at-a-time routing algorithms (such as maze routers [5], VPR [1], CGE [2], SEGA [6], PathFinder [8] etc.) are unable to decide routability because of their direct/indirect dependence on net ordering. In spite of these unique advantages, *pure* Boolean SAT-based layout approach has a fundamental limitation. The manageable size of problems by SAT-based routing is far smaller than that by conventional routing approaches. This is why most of SAT-based routing is applied only a small set of carefully selected layout problems such as channel routing instances and FPGAs.

In this paper, we revisit the SAT-based routing idea and provide a new hybrid algorithm that integrates Boolean SAT-based FPGA routing with a state-of-the-art conventional FPGA router, PathFinder [8]. By doing this, we are able to not only overcome the major disadvantage of Boolean SAT-based FPGA routing, namely the scalability issue, but also offset the typical drawbacks of conventional routers: net-ordering dependence and the inability to prove unroutability. In other words, these two methods can complement each other. To validate this approach, the result of applying the combined tool to real-world benchmarks is provided.

The organization of this paper as follows. We first review the most efficient SAT-based FPGA routing formulation in Section 2. In Section 3, we provide the first attempt to combine SAT idea with conventional routing algorithm and in Section 4, the experimental results of the combined algorithm will be presented. Finally, conclusive remarks will follow in Section 5.

2 SAT-based FPGA Routing Formulation

The target FPGA routing architecture model is the typical *island-style* which was adopted in CGE [2], SEGA [6] and VPR [1]. An island-style FPGA is comprised of a two-dimensional array of *Configurable Logic Blocks (CLBs), Connection Blocks (C-blocks)* and *Switching Blocks (S-blocks)*. The routing capacity of this FPGA architecture is conveniently expressed by 3 parameters, W, F_c, F_s. For the detailed description of routing architecture, please refer to [3].

The typical criticisms of SAT-based routing formulation are the limitations of tractable problem size and rather long runtime compared to conventional routing methods. To overcome these, Nam *et al* [11] proposed an efficient routing formulation called *route-based routing formulation*. In this formulation, the FPGA detailed routing is reduced to a *routability checking* problem with a set of explicitly enumerated detailed routes per net. In contrast, the FPGA detailed routing was transformed into a *net-to-track* assignment problem in precedent SAT-based formulations [10, 12]. The key observation is that each net has only a finite number of detailed routes admissible within routing regions specified by a global router. Each detailed route in this set is called a *route candidate*. Once a set of admissible route candidates is identified for each net, a Boolean variable is assigned to each route candidate. These Boolean variables are referred to as *route variables* and act as selection variables. A particular route candidate is included in the final routing solution only if its corresponding route variable is assigned "true". Otherwise it is excluded from a routing option.

To guarantee that this formulation generates an actual FPGA detailed routing solution, they defined two types of routing constraints: *Liveness constraints* and *Exclusive constraints*. Liveness constraints ensure that at least one route candidate is selected in the final routing solution. Exclusivity constraints guarantee that electrically distinct nets with overlapping vertical or horizontal spans in the same channel are assigned to different tracks. Exclusivity constraints are semantically similar to those in [10, 12], but it was demonstrated that they can be more efficiently and compactly represented in a route-based formulation [11].

An illustration of this new formulation is shown in Figure 1 and Figure 2 with the architectural assumption $W = F_c = F_s = 3$. With the global routing solution as in Figure 1-a, three detailed route candidates for two-pin connections *TP1* and *TP2* are enumerated in Figure 1-b and -c, respectively. A Boolean variable is now assigned to represent each of these detailed routes; for example, *TP1R2* represents the detailed route of *TP1* using track 2. As shown in this example, the liveness constraint is simply an OR function over corresponding routes variables. The construction of exclusivity constraints is illustrated in Figure 2. Resource is a track segment in a routing channel. As shown in Figure 2-a, there are 3 two-pin connections that can be routed on the track *k* in C-block (*i*, *j*). The route variables A_k, B_k and C_k are assigned for these nets, respectively and the corresponding exclusivity constraint for track *k* is shown in Figure 2-b. The meaning of this constraint is that if the track *k* is assigned to one of net *A*, *B* or *C*, then it cannot be assigned to the others at the same time.

The routability of a netlist for a given placement and global routing configuration is expressed by a single Boolean function formed from the conjunction of all liveness and exclusivity constraints:

$$Routable(X) = \left[\bigcap_{1 \le i \le n} Live_i(X) \wedge \bigcap_{1 \le j \le r} Excl_j(X) \right]$$

where $Live_i(X)$ is a liveness constraint of two-pin connection *i*, $Excl_j(X)$ is an exclusivity constraint of resource *j* and X is a vector of Boolean route variables that represent the possible detailed routes for each of the nets.

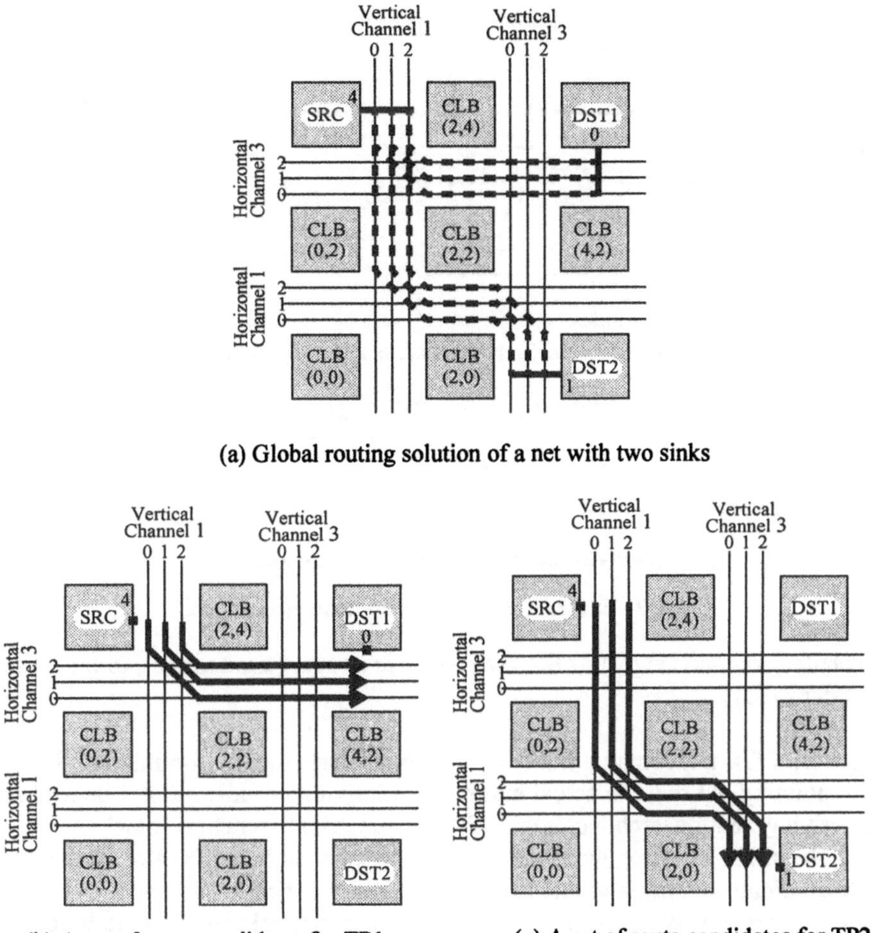

(a) Global routing solution of a net with two sinks

(b) A set of route candidates for TP1

(c) A set of route candidates for TP2

Boolean route variables for TP1 = $\{TP1R0, TP1R1, TP1R2\}$

Boolean route variables for TP2 = $\{TP2R0, TP2R1, TP2R3\}$

$$Live(TP1) = [TP1R0 \vee TP1R1 \vee TP1R2]$$

$$Live(TP2) = [TP1R0 \vee TP1R1 \vee TP1R2]$$

(d) Liveness constraints for TP1 and TP2.

Figure 1. Liveness Constraint Example in Route-based Formulation.

This route-based formulation is, again, a SAT-based routing approach and preserves all the advantages such as simultaneous net embedding and routability decision. In addition, for most circuits it required fewer variables and is expressed in terms of a simpler set of CNF constraints than those generated from track-based formulation of [10]. For

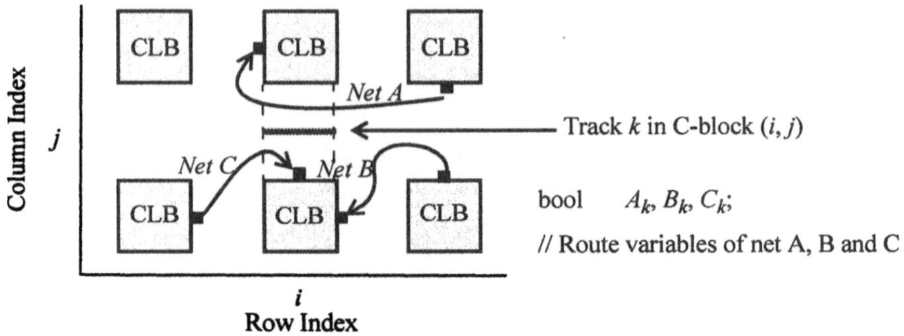

(a) Three nets using a track resource k in C-block (i, j)

$$(A_k \rightarrow \overline{B_k} \cdot \overline{C_k}) \cdot (B_k \rightarrow \overline{A_k} \cdot \overline{C_k}) \cdot (C_k \rightarrow \overline{A_k} \cdot \overline{B_k})$$
$$= (\overline{A_k} \vee \overline{B_k}) \cdot (\overline{A_k} \vee \overline{C_k}) \cdot (\overline{B_k} \vee \overline{A_k}) \cdot (\overline{B_k} \vee \overline{C_k}) \cdot (\overline{C_k} \vee \overline{A_k}) \cdot (\overline{C_k} \vee \overline{B_k})$$
$$= (\overline{A_k} \vee \overline{B_k}) \cdot (\overline{A_k} \vee \overline{C_k}) \cdot (\overline{B_k} \vee \overline{C_k})$$

(b) Exclusivity constraint for track k in C-block (i, j)

Figure 2. Exclusivity constraint formulation example.

more detailed comparison results between track- and route-based routing formulations, please refer to [11].

Yet there are a few unavoidable limitations in route-based routing formulation. First, it is worth pointing out that the actual number of admissible detailed routes depends on the underlying routing architecture. With a symmetrical switching block $F_s = 3$ -- which is one of the most popular routing architectures in modern FPGAs--, the number of route candidates within a global routing path is a constant W. When $F_s > 3$, however, the number of feasible detailed routes grows exponential and the route-based formulation is simply unable to include all of them. That is, the route-based formulation is not an architecture-general method. Second, because a route-based SAT formulation is a detailed routing formulation, if a global router somehow delivers an undesirable global routing solution, there is no way to escape from this bad upper level decision. Finally, due to the nature of Boolean SAT-based routing approach, i.e. concurrent routing characteristics, the route-based formulation was not able to compete over scalability issue with conventional routers such as VPR [1].

3 Integration of SAT-based Routing to PathFinder

In this section, as an effort of overcoming the scalability handicap of pure Boolean SAT-based routing formulations, we provide a hybrid algorithm called *search-SAT* [9] which integrates SAT-based routing into a conventional routing algorithm, PathFinder [8]. The advantages of such a combination are two-fold: 1) it is more scalable than the pure Boolean SAT-based routing enabling search-SAT to attack far larger, practical-sized circuits, and 2) the notorious convergence drawback of most conventional routers--i.e., lack of routability decision-- can be resolved. In addition, the combined algorithm maintains a small set of quality detailed route candidates from various global routing paths essentially removing the dependence on a single global routing configuration.

PathFinder is one of the most advanced FPGA routers reported in the literature. It uses an iterative framework to achieve eliminating congestions and minimizing delay of critical paths simultaneously. Unlike the typical two step routing approaches, this algorithm tries both global and detailed routing at the same time. It starts by constructing a routing graph whose topology mirrors the complete FPGA routing architecture. Thus, paths in this graph correspond to feasible routes in the FPGA. Using this graph, PathFinder uses sophisticated cost functions to search for routing solutions (i.e., paths in the graph) for all the nets in a circuit. Although routing resources are initially allowed to be shared among nets, these are eventually assigned to most demanding signals in subsequent iterations. The negotiation process through cost functions on congested routing resources determines which net needs the corresponding routing resource most. This iteration is repeated until no shared routing resource exists. A timing analysis is also performed at every iteration to set a higher priority for more timely critical nets. In spite of the fact that all the routes are rerouted in every iteration, the reported results were excellent achieving a higher degree of routability as well as shorter critical paths on commercial circuits.

If a routing solution exists for a given circuit and placement, Pathfinder will eventually converge toward it after a sufficient number of iterations. If the problem is unroutable, however, the algorithm may not converge and execution must be aborted after a suitable time limit. This convergence problem is inherent to all heuristic one-net-at-a-time routing algorithms: these algorithms cannot decide the routability of the given circuit placement. Even when only a few nets are not routed in a circuit, these algorithms must resort to time-consuming rip-up-reroute procedures which may or may not lead to a routing solution. The key observation of the hybrid algorithm *search-SAT* is that by combining the PathFinder algorithm with a Boolean SAT-based routing formulation, the convergence drawback of PathFinder can be corrected and the applicable circuit size is not limited to small-scaled instances.

3.1. Combined Algorithm: Search-SAT

At a certain iteration, PathFinder considers only a single route for each connection. The route considered is regarded as the best one for the connection based on the latest congestion and delay cost metrics. As the iteration advances, more routing options (possibly along different global routing paths) are explored for each connection. The core idea of the combined algorithm search-SAT is that at each iteration of the PathFinder algorithm, we can enumerate all detailed routes explored for each connection until the current iteration and examine them all simultaneously via the Boolean SAT technique. The basic rationale behind this approach is that since only the best quality route for a two-pin connection is generated at each iteration, it is worth considering them all concurrently if no routing solution is found at some point. Please note that these detailed routes explored by PathFinder are not limited to a single global routing path as in the route-based formulation [11]. This

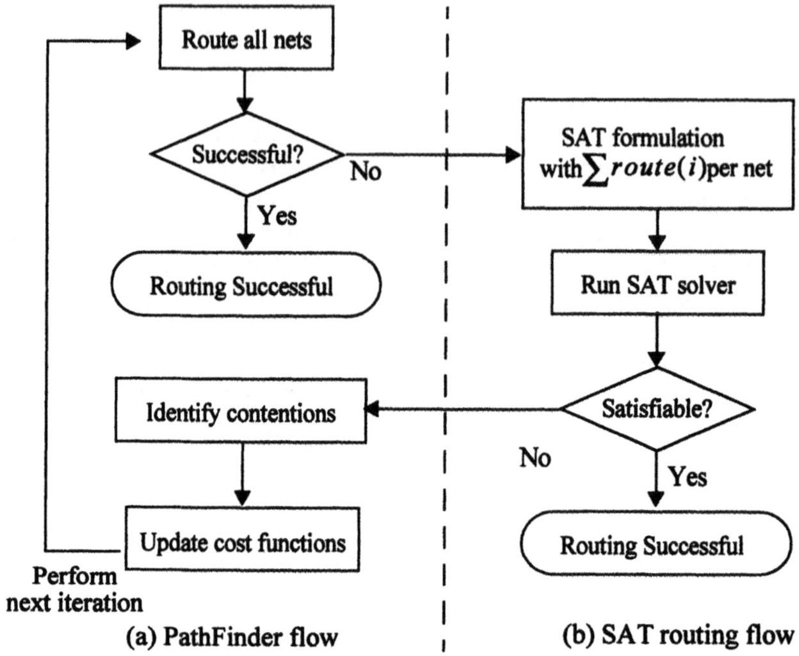

Figure 3. Overall flow diagram of *search-SAT.*

idea has immediate advantages: 1) the escape from a bad global routing decision is inherently provided and 2) the size of detailed route candidates is in under control regardless of the underlying FPGA routing architecture.

Figure 3 presents the simplified overall flow diagram of search-SAT. The left half represents the basic PathFinder flow and the right half corresponds to the SAT-based routing flow. For SAT-based routing formulation, we used the formulation method from [11]. In fact, it is not necessary to run the SAT-based flow for every iteration because of the (small) overhead to transform a routing problem into a Boolean SAT instance. Instead, it is most effective to run the SAT-based routing flow after a sufficient number of new detailed routes are accumulated for each signal without any routing solution found. However, for the experiment that will be presented in Section 4, we employed the SAT routing flow in every PathFinder iteration. In other words, at the *i-th* iteration, at most *i* different detailed routes are considered simultaneously for each two-pin connection. This Boolean function is evaluated with a Boolean SAT solver. If any routing solution is found, the algorithm returns the solution. Otherwise the next iteration of PathFinder algorithm is executed. The new method is able to deliver a firm routability decision via Boolean SAT technology. Once the SAT solution is found, the solution can be easily interpreted as a routing solution. If the SAT instance is unsatisfiable, it implies that there is no routing solution with the current placement configuration and the current accumulated set of detailed routes explored for each two-pin connection thus far. We expect that the information from the unroutable instance could be very valuable for a future rerouting procedure.

Table 1. Experimental results on industry FPGA designs.

Circuit	Nets	Vars	Clauses	Dec.	Con.	CPU	R?
industry1	852	1739	4427	1	0	0.061	No
		1789	4742	537	24	0.111	Yes
industry2	3285	7862	30539	1	0	0.402	No
		7879	31598	2525	423	0.949	Yes
industry3	6573	16880	58924	1252	127	1.34	No
		16888	60640	4057	250	1.57	Yes
industry4	9423	24883	106775	1233	174	3.478	No
		24884	106777	5889	346	2.806	Yes
industry5	12229	21320	32641	1	0	0.611	No
		21323	32644	4679	201	1.233	Yes
industry6		28088	65918	2247	449	1.08	No
	14615	28095	65946	7692	1214	2.53	Yes
industry7	11654	31342	180809	530	267	5.414	No
		31378	181407	10170	1448	8.223	Yes

4 Experimental Results

PathFinder keeps exploring different detailed routes for each net until it finds a legal routing solution, and each rip-up and reroute process of all nets forms a single iteration. Our experimental scenario is to apply a SAT-based routing flow after every PathFinder iteration with the accumulated detailed routes explored upto that point. The goal in this experiment is to find a feasible detailed routing solution *before* the original negotiation-based router PathFinder converges to a final routing solution, or to concretely prove the unroutability with the considered set of detailed routes in a design. With this experimental plan, Table 1 shows the routability checking performance of the combined algorithm for a set of FPGA designs from industry. These designs were targeted to the Xilinx Virtex FPGA architecture [13], and range in size from 852 nets for *industry1* to 14615 nets for *industry6*. All experiments were conducted on a SUN Ultra 2 running SunOS with 1 Gb of physical memory. The GRASP SAT solver [7] was employed as a Boolean SAT search engine to evaluate the routing constraint Boolean function.

The table shows only the last two iterations (unroutable and routable) for each circuit. In other words, all the previous iterations were proven to be unroutable by the SAT-based flow. The first two columns show the name of the circuit and the number of multiple-pin nets in it. Column 3 and 4 are the number of Boolean variables and CNF clauses in the final routing constraint Boolean function. In column 5 and 6, the number of decisions and conflicts made during the SAT solving search are presented and column 7 specifies only the SAT search runtime in seconds. Finally, column 9 gives the routability decisions. For 4 cases out of 7, the combined algorithm was able to find a routing solution at earlier iteration than PathFinder saving one or two iterations. For 3 cases, however, it found the solution at the same iteration. Since our original intention was not to invoke SAT flow every iteration, we didn't include the time for the generation of routing constraint Boolean function. In general, the SAT generation time was order of minutes and took longer than SAT solving time. The observed SAT solution times are very low--less than 2 seconds in all cases-- implying that these routability checking Boolean SAT problems are very easy SAT instances. Regardless of results of routability, the number of decisions and conflicts made during the SAT search procedure is very low. One very interesting observation here is when the routability decision is "no", it took usually only a handful of decisions and conflicts to determine unroutability (infeasibility). This is because the SAT approach is a very quick and efficient method for detecting a critical routing resource which is shared by multiple nets. Obviously this information can be utilized for a future rip-up-rerouting stage; once a critical resource is detected, the rip-up and reroute procedure is performed with only those nets which are using the detected critical resource with more complex detouring net-paths, and this procedure can be repeated again until the routing problem becomes routable.

Another promising plan to generate the set of candidate routes for each connection within an iteration is to generate a set of route alternatives for each net based on only *timing delay*. In other words, regardless of congestion and overusage of routing resources, we can pick the top *m* route alternatives which have the best timing delays for performance. The goal is to find the best timing performance routing solution without violating any resource sharing if there is any or to prove the unroutability with the given route alternative information. If no routing solution exists among route alternatives considered, then at least it tells us that the given timing constraints cannot be met with the considered set of detailed routes. In other words the proposed approach can determine whether the given timing constraints can be satisfied for a set of timing-critical nets. This approach helps to keep the number of feasible detailed route alternatives of each connection small. This is all possible in FPGAs because there is only a finite number of connection patterns and for each detailed route an accurate timing delay can be calculated. This seems to be a favorable approach to guarantee that the final layout meets a certain *hard timing constraint*.

5 Conclusion

In this paper, we described a new hybrid strategy for the routability checking algorithm via Boolean Satisfiability. This work differs from the previous Boolean SAT-based FPGA routing approaches in the sense that the SAT-based FPGA routing algorithm was integrated into a conventional FPGA router. The immediate benefits of this new approach are: 1) the combined method is more scalable than the pure Boolean SAT-based routing approaches described in [10, 11], and 2) it solves the convergence problem of conventional FPGA routers by firmly determining the routability via Boolean SAT techniques. In other words the combined algorithms (PathFinder and route-based formulation) complement each other.

From the perspective of Boolean SAT-based routing, route-based formulation has the ability of considering multiple detailed routes concurrently per two-pin connection to determine the feasibility of routing tasks. The question is how to generate a promising set of detailed routes per two-pin connection to check for routability. Pathfinder produces a small number of high quality detailed routes for each connection via its excellent congestion metrics. An alternative would be to generate routes using a timing-driven router, especially for timing-critical nets.

6 References

1. V. Betz and J. Rose, "VPR: A New Packing, Placement and Routing Tool for FPGA Research," *the Seventh Annual Workshop on Field Programmable Logic and Applications*, pp.213-222, 1997.
2. S. Brown, J. Rose, and Z. G. Vranesic, "A Detailed Router for Field Programmable Gate Arrays," *IEEE Transactions on CAD*, pp. 620-628, vol. 11, no. 5, May 1992.
3. S. D. Brown, R.J. Francis, J. Rose, and Z.G.Vranesic, *Field Programmable Gate Arrays*, Boston, Kluwer Acad. Publishers, 1992.
4. M. R. Garey and D. S. Johnson, *Computers and Intractability: A Guide to the Theory of NP-Completeness*, W.H.Freeman and Company, 1979.
5. A. Hashimoto and J. Stevens, "Wire Routing by Optimizing Channel Assignment within Large Apertures", *Proceedings of 8th Design Automation Conference*, pp. 155 - 169, 1971.
6. G. Lemieux and S. Brown, "A Detailed Router for Allocating Wire Segments in FPGAs," *Proc. ACM Physical Design Workshop*, California, Apr. 1993.
7. J. P. Marques-Silva and K. A. Sakallah, "GRASP: A Search Algorithm for Propositional Satisfiability", *IEEE Transactions on Computers*, vol. 48, no. 5, May 1999.
8. L. E. McMurchie and C. Ebeling, "PathFinder: A Negotiation-Based Path-Driven Router for FPGAs," Proc. *ACM/IEEE Intl' Symposium on Field Programmable Gate Arrays*, Feb. 1995.
9. G.-J Nam, S. Kalman, J. Anderson, R. Jayaraman, S. Nag and J. Zhuang, "A Method and Apparatus for Testing Routability", *U.S. patent pending*.
10. G.-J Nam, K. A. Sakallah, and R. A. Rutenbar, "Satisfiability-Based Layout Revisited: Detailed Routing of Complex FPGAs Via Search-Based Boolean SAT", *Intl' Sym. on FPGAs*, Feb. 1999.
11. G.-J Nam, F. Aloul, K. A. Sakallah and R. A. Rutenbar, "A Comparative Study of Two Boolean Formulations of FPGA Detailed Routing Constraints", *Intl' Symp. on Physical Design*, April 2001.
12. R. G. Wood and R. A. Rutenbar, "FPGA Routing and Routability Estimation Via Boolean Satisfiability," *IEEE Transactions on VLSI Systems*, pp. 222 - 231, June 1998.
13. http://www.xilinx.com

A Prolog-Based Hardware Development Environment

K. Benkrid, D. Crookes, A. Benkrid, and S. Belkacemi

School of Computer Science, The Queen's University of Belfast, Belfast BT7 1NN, UK
(k.benkrid, d.crookes)@qub.ac.uk

Abstract. This paper presents a Hardware Development Environment based on the logic programming language Prolog. Central to this environment are a hardware description notation called HIDE, and a high level generator, which takes an application specific, high level algorithm description, and translates it into a HIDE description. The latter describes scaleable and parameterised architectures using a small set of Prolog constructors. EDIF netlists can be automatically generated from HIDE descriptions. The high-level algorithm descriptions are based on a library of reusable Hardware Skeletons. A hardware skeleton is a parameterised description of a task-specific architecture, to which the user can supply parameters such as values, functions or even other skeletons. A skeleton contains built-in rules, written in Prolog that will apply optimisations specific to the target hardware at the implementation phase. This is the key towards the satisfaction of the dual requirement of high-level abstract hardware design and hardware efficiency.

1 Introduction

Electronic Design Automation (EDA) tools play a crucial role in increasing the productivity of hardware designers. This crucial role is accentuated by the ever-increasing levels of integrations in today's ICs. The advent of System-On-a-Chip (SoC) technology poses enormous challenges to the EDA industry.

Throughout the years, EDA tools have made an enormous improvement. Indeed, hardware designers have moved on from gate level design to register transfer level (RTL) design, to behavioural design. Hardware Description Languages such as VHDL and Verilog were developed. These offer many advantages over schematic design entry since they can use language constructs like repetition and data abstraction. Moreover, many behavioural synthesis tools [1][2] have been developed to allow the user to program at a high level (e.g. in a C-like syntax) without having to deal with low-level hardware details (e.g. scheduling, allocation, pipelining etc.). However, although behavioural synthesis tools have developed enormously, structural design techniques often still result in circuits that are substantially smaller and faster than those developed using only behavioural synthesis tools [3][4]. One problem with the well-established hardware description languages such as VHDL is that they are not very suitable for describing structural circuits. Indeed, structured circuits described in VHDL tend to be very cumbersome, as detailed wiring has to be explicitly specified even for the most trivial connections. Moreover, in order to describe placement information in VHDL, vendors add proprietary extensions, which are not part of standard VHDL.

M. Glesner, P. Zipf, and M. Renovell (Eds.): FPL 2002, LNCS 2438, pp. 370-380, 2002.

There has been a trend towards the use of high level Hardware Description Notations based on existing high level languages [3][5] for structural circuit design. Lava [6] for instance is a language based on the lazy functional programming language Haskell, and allows for rapid generation of regular structures (rows, columns, trees etc.) using function composition. Despite the clear advantages of these notations over VHDL, they are still hardware descriptions and not application descriptions (i.e. the user has to construct a circuit from the assembly of low level primitives). There is a need for bridging the gap between the application level and the hardware level.

In this paper we present a Hardware Development Environment that has been developed since 1996 at The Queen's University of Belfast, which is aimed at bridging this gap. The environment is based on the logic programming language Prolog [7]. We argue that Prolog is a very suitable language for describing hardware composition. Prolog, after all, was designed for expressing logic, and it supports the representation of knowledge (e.g. of common sense placement and routing heuristics) using *rules*. Other features of Prolog include:

- Built-in pattern-recognition facility - the way it unifies objects.
- Built-in automatic backtracking mechanism useful in optimal searching.
- The concept of unbound variables for representing uncommitted details.

Instead of building just from hardware blocks, we build also from reusable frameworks or *hardware skeletons* [8]. In graphical terms, these can be visualised as a library of *sub-graphs*. Users can tailor hardware skeletons to their own application by supplying parameters. These can be variable values, functions or even other skeletons (the latter are called higher order skeletons). A skeleton contains built-in rules, written in Prolog that will apply optimisations specific to the target hardware.

Based on a library of hardware skeletons, a Prolog based compiler will generate optimised hardware configurations in EDIF format.

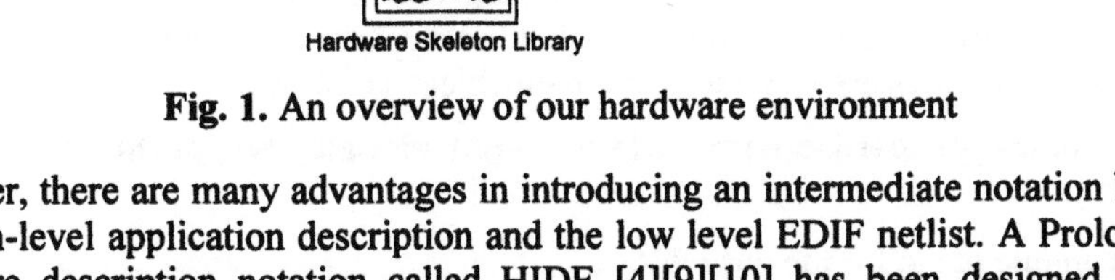

Fig. 1. An overview of our hardware environment

However, there are many advantages in introducing an intermediate notation between the high-level application description and the low level EDIF netlist. A Prolog based hardware description notation called HIDE [4][9][10] has been designed for that purpose. HIDE describes scaleable and parameterised architectures using a small set of Prolog constructors. EDIF netlists can be automatically generated from these intermediate descriptions. Our hardware environment will then consist of a hardware description notation (HIDE) and a high level generator, which takes an application specific, high level algorithm description, and translates it into a HIDE hardware description. In this context, HIDE is a bit analogous to p-code in software compilation.

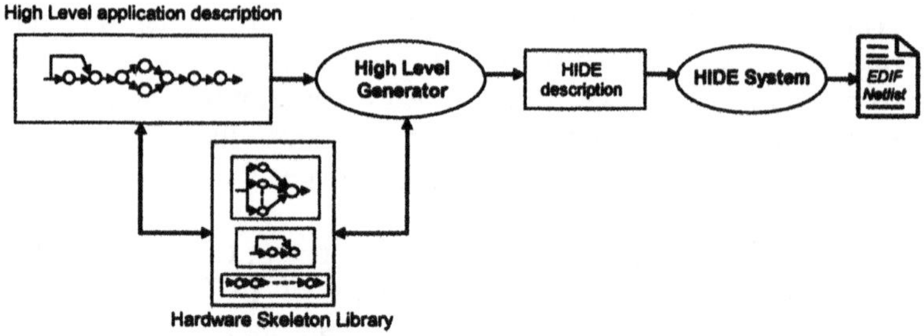

Fig. 2. A refined overview of our hardware environment

Although our approach is not tied to a particular target technology, it has mostly been used on FPGAs with implementations on Xilinx XC4000 and XC6000 chips [4][8].

The remainder of the paper will first present the HIDE notation. Then, the high level programming approach will be illustrated in the particular context of image processing applications. The structure of the hardware skeleton library will then be presented with application examples.

2 Essentials of the HIDE Notation

Rather than invent a brand new notation, Prolog has been used as the base notation for describing and composing basic building blocks in order to build chip configurations. The HIDE notation has a simple and small set of constructors for putting sub-blocks together in order to build a chip configuration.

2.1 HIDE Configuration Description

The main component of a HIDE configuration description is a ***block***. A ***block*** is either:

- ***A basic block***: an individual component, or
- ***A compound block***: a hierarchical composition of sub-components.

A ***basic block*** is a rectangular, non-overlapping block, which completely contains a predefined circuit. At the outer edges of this block, there are input and output ***ports***. Basic block properties are expressed as a data object as follows:

block_properties(name, width, height, signals_list , ports_list)

where

name: a unique name for the basic block.

width and **height**: *width* is the number of logic cells occupied on the chip by the basic block on the **X** (horizontal) axis, while *height* is the number of logic cells on the **Y** (vertical) axis. Both width and height are computed from the basic block origin (0,0) which is assumed to be the bottom left hand corner of the basic block.

signals_list: a list of clock and clear signals used in the block.

ports_list: a list of input/output ports to/from the block located at the perimeter cells of the block.

The decision to limit blocks to be rectangular and non-overlapping was taken to simplify subsequent block assembly. The above attributes are illustrated in Figure 3.

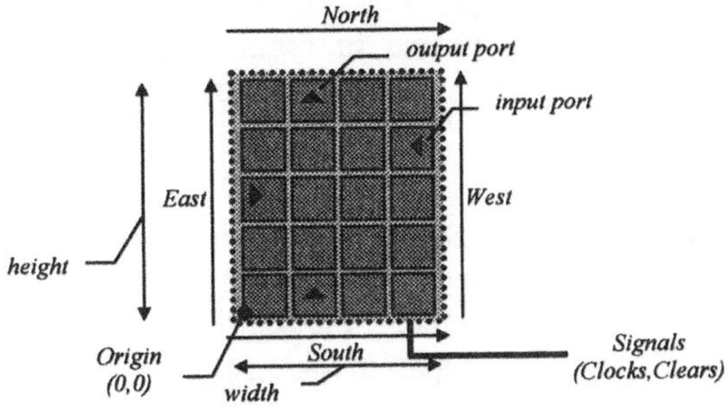

Fig. 3. HIDE Basic block properties

2.2 Compound Blocks

A compound block is obtained by hierarchical composition of sub-blocks using a simple set of five constructors (see Figure 4):

- **vertical([B_1, B_2,..., B_n])** used to compose the supplied sub-blocks (B_1, B_2, ...B_n) together vertically.
- **horizontal([B_1, B_2, ..., B_n])** used to compose the supplied sub-blocks (B_1, B_2, ..., B_n) together horizontally.
- **v_seq(N, B)** used to replicate the supplied block 'B', N times vertically.
- **h_seq(N, B)** used to replicate the supplied block 'B', N times horizontally.
- **offset(B, X, Y)** used to offset the supplied block 'B' by 'X' cell positions horizontally and 'Y' cell positions vertically.

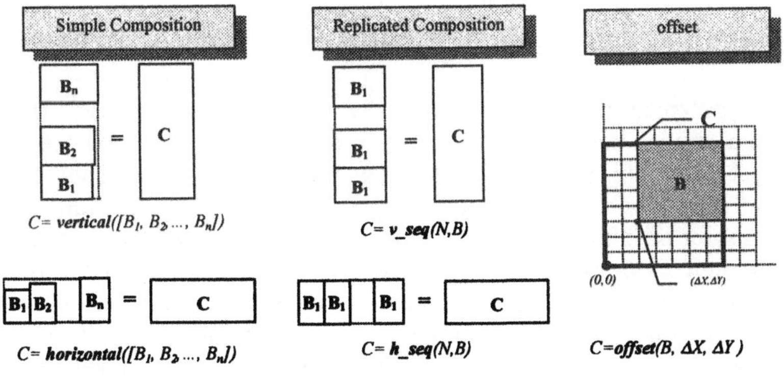

Fig. 4. HIDE's five basic constructors

In addition to these constructors, HIDE provides a facility for generalising **v_seq** and **h_seq** constructors to generate indexed block descriptions useful for describing systolic architectures [4].

2.3 Block Interconnection

During sub-block composition, the ports on the corresponding sides of adjacent sub-blocks are connected together. These corresponding sides are: *north_of(B_1)* and *south_of(B_2)* in case of vertical composition, and *east_of(B_1)* and *west_of(B_2)* in case of horizontal composition. These ports are connected automatically by HIDE in the increasing direction of ports as shown in Figure 5.a. Alternatively, the user can connect the ports explicitly by giving a network connection (**nc**), which specifies all logical port connections (see Figure 5.b):

$$\text{nc([(i, j), ...])} \qquad i > 0,\ j > 0$$

i, j : are the port sequence numbers on the first and second sides respectively.
In the case of Xilinx XC6000, actual logic cells were used for the routing (the network connection was in fact a network block). In the XC4000 (and Virtex) series, however, the routing resources are separate logic resources and hence do not consume any cells (CLBs and slices).

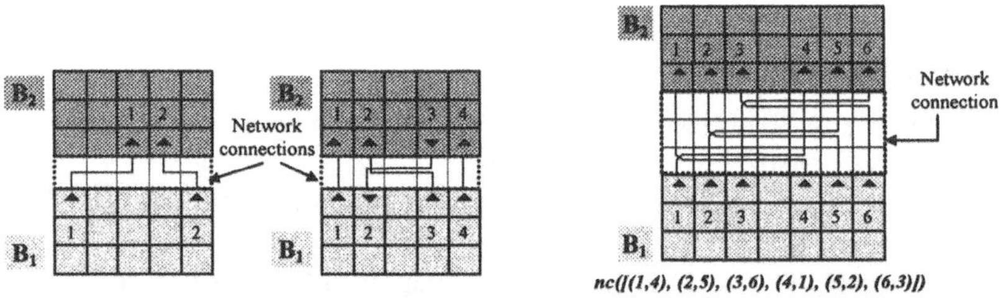

(a) HIDE automatic port matching (b) User-defined network connection

Fig. 5. Examples of ports connectivity in HIDE

In addition to this, HIDE provides extra facilities for routing especially for irregular routing [4]. These are not presented here for the sake of simplicity.

3 Towards an Application Oriented Hardware Environment

The work presented in this paper emerged from research in the field of high performance Image Processing (IP) in the School of Computer Science at Queen's University Belfast. This research developed an FPGA based Image Coprocessor based on the abstractions of Image Algebra [4][11]. From this work, it emerged that an important subset of image algebra operations can be described by a small number of reusable framework or *skeletons* [8]. These are reusable, parameterised fragments to which the user can supply parameters such as values, functions or even other skeletons. Skeleton-based descriptions are independent of the underlying hardware implementation details, thus leading to algorithm-oriented high level programming. The latter, however, need not come at the expense of performance. Indeed, skeletons contain built-in rules that will apply optimisations specific to the target hardware at the implementation phase. The following will illustrate the hardware skeleton approach and its implementation for Image Processing. We will start by presenting an application oriented image processing programming model. Then we will describe our implementation of an IP hardware environment based on a hierarchical library of hardware skeletons. In particular we will describe a small set of high-level skeletons, sufficient for the description of a useful subset of Image Algebra operations.

3.1 A High Level-Programming Model for IP Operations

In our environment, IP application developers describe their IP algorithm in terms of a *Directed Acyclic Graph* (DAG), where *vertices* represent IP tasks, and the *directed edges* represent the data flow.

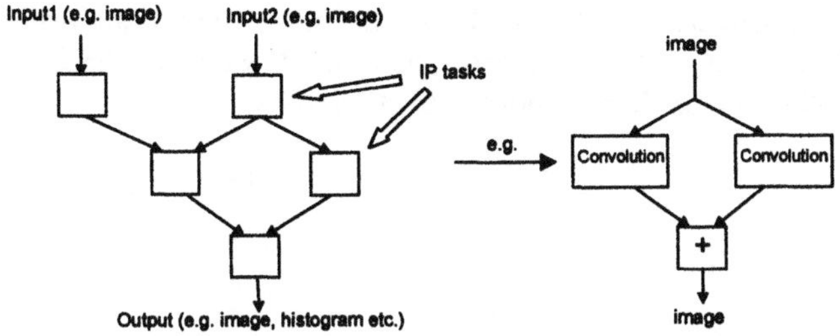

Fig. 6. A hypothetical image processing algorithm modelled as a DAG graph

Nodes are typically simple tasks such as adding two input images, or an image convolution. The IP tasks (DAG nodes) can be classified in terms of the locality of their data access requirements into three categories:

- **Point operations**: The same operation is applied to each individual pixel of one or many source images (e.g. look up tables, '+', '-', '*', '+' etc).
- **Neighbourhood operations**: A Neighbourhood operation is completely defined by a two-stage operation: first the *local* operation between corresponding pixels and window values (e.g. multiplication), then a *global* operation (e.g. accumulation) which reduces the window of intermediate results to a single result pixel. There is a basic set of five neighbourhood operations in Image Algebra: convolution, Multiplicative Maximum, Multiplicative Minimum, Additive Maximum and Additive Minimum [12].
- **Global operations**: These operations operate globally on the whole image (e.g. *count, global maximum, global minimum, histogramming* etc.).

The properties of an item of data (represented by an edge in the DAG) are of two kinds: a *data type* (e.g. integer, boolean) and *a data representation* (e.g. bit serial two's complement).

3.2 Implementation Strategy

Having defined the high level programming model, the question is: how are we going to generate efficient FPGA configurations from such high level descriptions?

Our solution to this problem is based on a hierarchical library of hardware skeletons and a Prolog based high-level generator that takes a high level application description (image processing in this case) and translates it into a HIDE description. This can then be transformed into EDIF netlist using the HIDE system. The HIDE notation was chosen as an intermediate notation between the high level algorithmic description and the low level FPGA configuration. This is a bit analogous to p-code in software compilation.

3.3 Hardware Skeletons Library

We implemented our Hardware Skeleton Library as a hierarchy of three levels of hardware blocks. At the bottom level lies the arithmetic cores library (see Figure 7). This provides arithmetic units (e.g. adders, multipliers) parameterised for different number representations (e.g. bit serial, bit parallel, 2's complement, unsigned etc.). Immediately on the top of this level, we find the basic image operations library. The latter provides implementations for the basic image operations presented in section 3.1 above (e.g. basic neighbourhood operations). Finally, the top level provides implementations for high level (compound) skeletons.

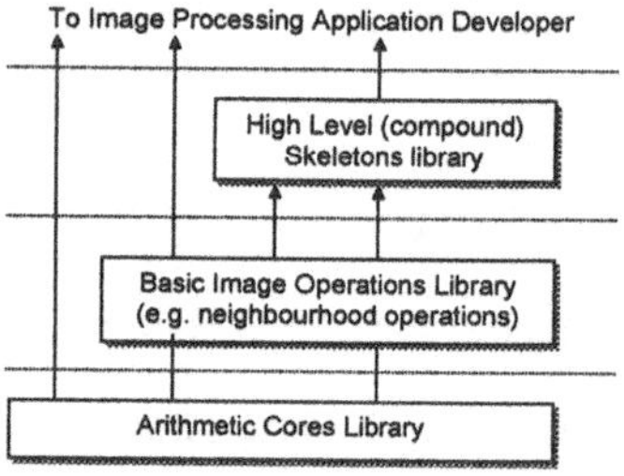

Fig. 7. Hierarchical implementation of the Hardware Skeleton Library

Users supply a library item name with the desired parameters (e.g. arithmetic type, window coefficients, pixel word length etc.) in a query, and the search of the library is performed by Prolog's pattern matching mechanism. The following will present each of these three levels in more details.

Arithmetic Cores Library. This library provides the basic building blocks required for signal processing operations. It includes adders, delays, multipliers etc. Versions of these cores are provided for different number representations. Their implementation is optimised for specific target hardware architecture. The core descriptions are held in HIDE with rules for core-specific optimisations as part of the core. For instance, a constant coefficient multiplication will apply CSD coding of the multiplier coefficient to reduce the consumed hardware [8].

Basic Image Operations Library. This library provides implementations of the basic image operations presented in section 3.1. Consider the case of basic neighbourhood operations. The following figure gives the architecture of a generic PxQ neighbourhood operation with a local operation *Local* and a global one *Global*.

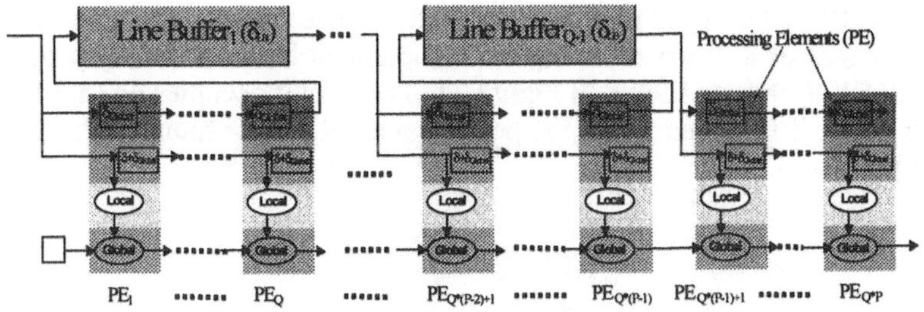

Fig. 8. Architecture of a generic PxQ neighbourhood operation

This architecture is parameterisable, or scaleable, in terms of the window size (PxQ), the window coefficients, the image size (line buffer size δ_{LB}), the pixel wordlength, the local and global operations (*Local* and *Global*) and the number representation (arithmetic type). Our system is capable of generating pre-placed FPGA configurations in EDIF format from generic descriptions of these architectures in 1~2 sec, using HIDE notation as an intermediate level.

High Level Skeletons Library. This library contains efficient implementations of a set of compound skeletons. These compound skeletons result from the process of identifying, by experience, common ways of assembling primitive operations and providing optimised implementations of these. The following will present a small set of such skeletons sufficient for a useful subset of Image Algebra.

3.4. A Collection of High Level Skeletons

The following presents three fundamental high level skeletons which are sufficient for a useful subset of Image Algebra operators.

Pipeline Skeleton. This skeleton consists of a cascade of other IP operations as shown in Figure 9.

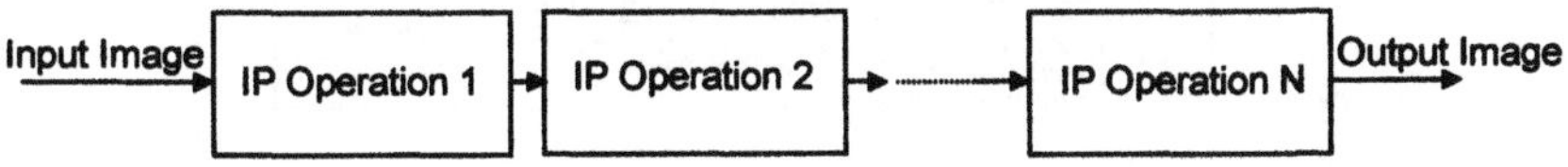

Fig. 9. Pipeline Skeleton

Data type conversions, wordlength conversions and synchronisation issues are handled automatically by the skeleton underlying implementation.
An 'Open' operation is an instance of such skeleton [4][8]:

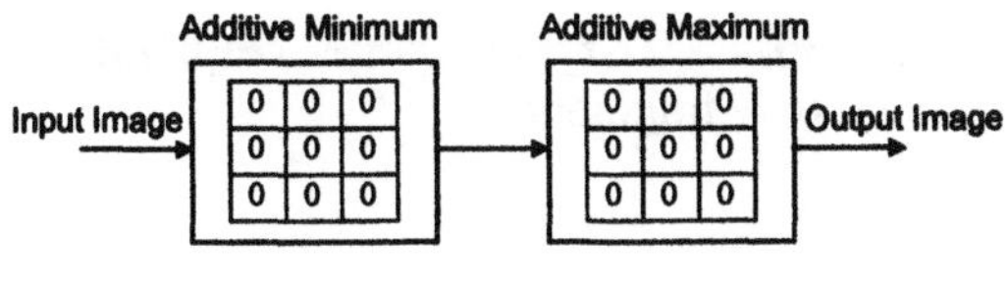

Fig. 10. 'Open' Skeleton

The FPGA floorplan produced automatically for an open operation applied to 256x256 images of 8-bits/pixel using 2's complement bit serial MSBF arithmetic on an XC4036EX-2 chip, is shown in Figure 11. The circuit occupies 443 CLBs and can run at 75 MHz. This speed rivals the performance of a corresponding hand-designed circuit [4].

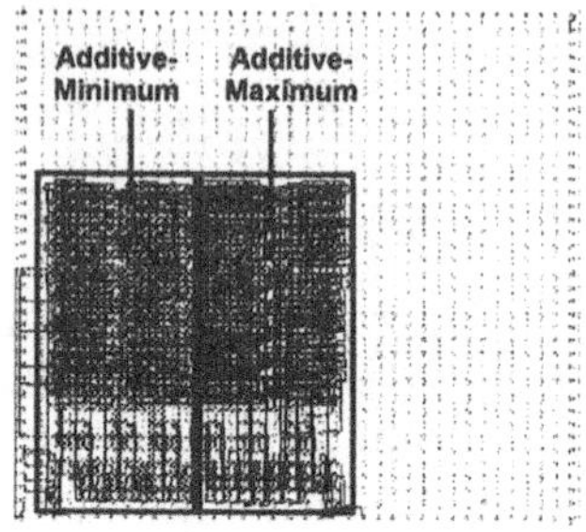

Fig. 11. Physical configuration of an 'Open' operation on XC4036EX-2

Parallel Neighbourhood Operations Skeleton. In this skeleton 'N' neighbourhood operations having the same window size (followed by zero or more point operations) are performed in parallel before they are reduced by a tree of (Image-Image)-Image (II-I_Op) operations as shown in Figure 12. Sobel, Prewitt, Roberts and Kirsch edge detectors [4][8], are all instances of this skeleton.

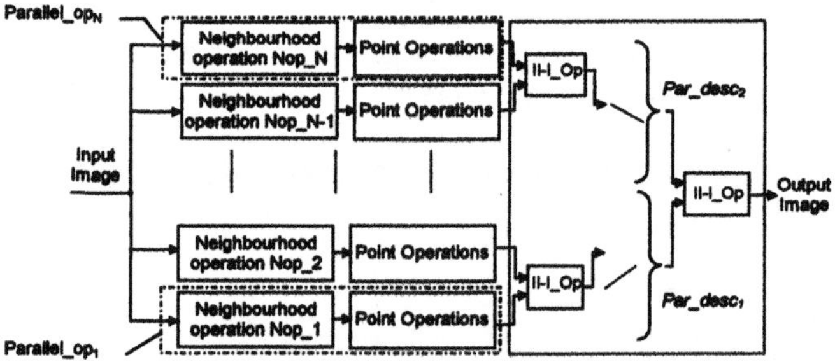

Fig. 12. Parallel neighbourhood operations skeleton

In this case, instead of allocating separate line buffers for each neighbourhood operation to synchronise the supply of pixels for all operations, only one set of line buffers is needed. This and all the resulting synchronisation issues are handled automatically by the skeleton's underlying implementation [4].

Another Compound Skeleton: '*II-I_Op*(Image, Nop(Image))'. This skeleton is described by the following DAG fragment:

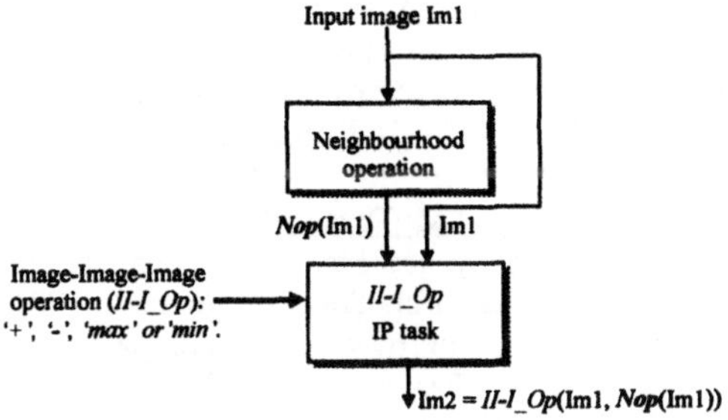

Fig. 13. The *III_Op*(Image, *Nop*(Image)) skeleton

where II-I_Op is a point operation that operates on two images input and produces another image. The skeleton implementation takes care of synchronisation issues automatically [4].

4 Conclusion

In this paper, we have presented a new Hardware Description Environment based on the logic programming language Prolog. The environment is based on a hardware description notation called HIDE. The latter allows for very concise descriptions of scaleable and parameterisable architectures using a small set of Prolog constructors. EDIF netlist with optional placement information can be generated from such descriptions. On top of the HIDE notation lies a Prolog based high level generator that takes an application specific, high level algorithm description, and translates it into a HIDE hardware description. The generator is based on a hierarchical library of hardware skeletons. The bottom layer of this library contains core arithmetic units such as adders and delays. On top of this layer lie the application specific basic units, which in the case of Image Processing would be the basic operators of Image Algebra. At the top of the hierarchy lie the high-level hardware skeletons, which represent complete frameworks to which the user can supply parameters such as values, functions, or even other skeletons. Optimisations are applied at each layer using Prolog rules. The level of abstraction increases from bottom to top. Ultimately at the high-level skeletons layer, the user thinks in terms of algorithms rather than hardware. This approach has been illustrated for the special case of Image Processing applications. However, the approach is not tied to a specific application area or a particular hardware technology (FPGAs or VLSI). In particular, any application area where there is an established algebra (e.g. numerical processing) can benefit from this approach. We foresee that our approach will have more relevance as we enter the system-on-a-chip era.

References

[1] Synopsys Inc., 'Behavioural Compiler', Software documentation, 1998. http://www.synopsys.com/products/beh_syn/
[2] Celoxica Limited, 'Handel C information sheets', 1999 http://www.celoxica.com/

[3] Hutchings, B., Bellows, P., Hawkins, J., Hemmert, S., Nelson, B. and Rytting, M., 'A CAD suite for High-Performance FPGA design', FCCM'99, Preliminary Proceedings.
[4] Benkrid, K., 'Design and Implementation of a High Level FPGA Based Coprocessor for Image and Video Processing', PhD Thesis, Department of Computer Science, The Queen's University of Belfast, 2000.
http://www.cs.qub.ac.uk/~K.Benkrid/MyThesis.html
[5] Bjesse, P., Claessen, K., Sheeran, M. and Singh, S., 'Lava: Hardware Design in Haskell', International Conference on Lisp and Functional Programming 98. Springer-Verlag 1998.
[6] The Xilinx Lava HDL Homepage, http://www.xilinx.com/labs/lava/index.htm
[7] Clocksin, W. F., and Melish, C. S., 'Programming in Prolog', Springer-Verlag, 1994.
[8] Benkrid, K., Crookes, D., Smith J. and Benkrid, A., 'High Level Programming for FPGA Based Image and Video Processing using Hardware Skeletons', FCCM'2001, April 2001, Preliminary Proceedings.
[9] Crookes, D., Alotaibi, K., Bouridane, A., Donachy, P., and Benkrid, A., 'An Environment for Generating FPGA Architectures for Image Algebra-based Algorithms', ICIP98, Vol.3, pp. 990-994, 1998.
[10] Crookes, D., Benkrid, K., Bouridane, A., Alotaibi, K. and Benkrid, A., 'Design and Implementation of a High Level Programming Environment for FPGA Based Image Processing', IEE proceedings: Vision, Image and Signal Processing, Vol. 147, No. 7, pp. 377-384.
[11] Benkrid, K., Crookes, D., Smith, J. and Benkrid, A., 'High Level Programming for Real Time FPGA Based Video Programming', Proceedings of ICASSP'2000, Istanbul, June 2000. Volume VI, pp. 3227-3231.
[12] Ritter, G., X., Wilson, J., N. and Davidson, J., L., 'Image Algebra: an overview', Computer Vision, Graphics and Image Processing, No 49, pp 297-331, 1990.

Fly – A Modifiable Hardware Compiler

C.H. Ho[1], P.H.W. Leong[1], K.H. Tsoi[1], R. Ludewig[2], P. Zipf[2], A.G. Ortiz[2], and M. Glesner[2]

[1] Department of Computer Science and Engineering
The Chinese University of Hong Kong, Shatin NT HK.
{chho2,phwl,khtsoi}@cse.cuhk.edu.hk
[2] Institute of Microelectronic Systems
Darmstadt University of Technology, Germany.
{ludewig,zipf,agarcia,glesner}@mes.tu-darmstadt.de

Abstract. In this paper we present the "fly" hardware compiler for rapid system prototyping research. *Fly* takes a C-like program as input and produces a synthesizable VHDL description of a one-hot state machine and the associated data path elements as output. Furthermore, it is tightly integrated with the hardware design environment and implementation platform, and is able to hide issues associated with these tools from the user. Unlike previous tools, *fly* encourages modification of the compiler for research in rapid system prototyping and code generation, and the full source code to the compiler is presented in the paper. Case studies involving the implementation of an FPGA based greatest common divisor (GCD) coprocessor as well as the extension of the basic *fly* compiler to solve a differential equation using floating point arithmetic are presented.

1 Introduction

With the rapid advancements in FPGA technology and the constant need to improve designer productivity, increasingly higher levels of abstraction are desired. We have found that using a RTL based design methodology results in low productivity compared, for example, with software development in C. It is believed that this is due to the following issues:

- Hardware designs are parallel in nature while most of the people think in von-Neumann patterns.
- The standard technique of decomposing a hardware design into datapath and control adds complexity to the task.
- Designers must develop a hardware interface for the FPGA board as well as a software/hardware interface between a host system and the FPGA.

The above issues serve to significantly increase the design complexity, with an associated increase in design time and debugging. Furthermore, the time spent in the above process restricts the amount of time which can be spent on dealing with higher level issues such as evaluating different algorithms and architectures for the system.

M. Glesner, P. Zipf, and M. Renovell (Eds.): FPL 2002, LNCS 2438, pp. 381–390, 2002.

Hardware description languages (HDL) have been proposed to address some of the issues above, notable examples being VHDL, SystemC, Handel-C [1], Pebble [2] and Lola [3]. For asynchronous circuits, Brunvand [4] has detailed a similar methodology. All of the HDLs above allow the user to describe a circuit using a behavioural model. Tools are used to translate from this higher level of abstraction into either a netlist or a register transfer language (RTL) code in a HDL such as VHDL or Verilog. With the exception of Lola which is written in Oberon, a programming language which is not in widespread usage, none of the above are available in source code form.

In order to facilitate research in high level synthesis and backend code generation, a compiler for the translation of a new language called *fly*, a small subset of Perl, was developed. The full source code to the compiler is included in Appendix A of this paper. Key differences between our approach and that of previous work are that:

- Fly's implementation has an open source license and can be easily understood, and modified by other users. We hope that other researchers will use this tool for research in high level synthesis, language design and circuit generation architectures and techniques.
- *Fly* supports a simple memory mapped interface between a host processor and the FPGA, serving to hide the details of the host interface from the designer.

The rest of the paper is organized as follows, in Section 2, the *fly* programming language, its implementation and development environment is presented. In Section 3, the application of *fly* in developing a greatest common divisor coprocessor is described. In Section 4, the extension of *fly* to operate on floating point numbers, and the application of this new system to the solution of differential equations is given. A discussion and conclusions are given in Sections 5 and 6.

2 The Fly Programming Language

The syntax of the *fly* programming language is modelled on Perl and C, with extensions for parallel statements and the host/FPGA interface. The language is minimal in nature and supports while loops, if-else branches, integer arithmetic, parallel statements and register assignment. Table 1 shows the main elements of the *fly* language with simple examples. The formal grammar definition can be found in the parser (see Appendix A).

2.1 Compilation Technique

Programs in the *fly* language are automatically mapped to hardware using the technique described by Page [1, 3]. In order to facilitate the support of control structures, Page's technique assigns a `start` and end signal to each statement which specifies when its execution begins and ends. By connecting the `start`

Construct	Elements	Example
assignment	var = expr;	$var1 = tempvar;$
parallel statement	[{ ... } { ... } ...]	$[\ \{a = b;\}\ \{\ b = a * c;\}\ ]$
expression	val op expr; valid ops: ∗,/,+,−	$a = b * c;$
loop	while (condition) { ... }	while $(x < y)$ { $a = a + b; y = y + 1;\}$

if-else	if (condition) { ... } else { ... }
	
	if (condition) { ... }
		if $(i <= j)$ $\{\ a = b;\}$
		else $\{a = c;\}$
		if $(i > j)$ $\{i = i + 1;\}$

condition	expr rel expr valid rels: >,<,<=,>=,==,! =	$i >= c$

Table 1. Main elements of the *fly* language.

and **end** signals of adjacent statements together, a one-hot state machine is constructed that serves as the control flow of the hardware.

The *fly* compiler generates synthesizable VHDL code instead of a netlist, simplifying code generation and making the output portable to many different FPGA and ASIC design tools. Furthermore, using VHDL as an intermediate language enables the logic optimization of the synthesis tool to be included in the design flow.

2.2 Implementation Details

Fly is written in the Perl programming language [5]. Perl is a language with very good portability, string handling facilities and libraries. We feel that the *fly* system's source code is made simpler and concise as a result of using Perl. Development of the *fly* compiler was also facilitated using a parser generator called `Parse::RecDescent` [6] which generates a Perl based recursive descent parser from a description of the grammar of the target language.

2.3 Host Interface

Although the interface is easily adaptable to any reconfigurable computing card, the *fly* system currently only supports the Pilchard reconfigurable computing platform [7]. Pilchard uses a DIMM memory bus interface instead of a conventional PCI bus. The advantage of the memory bus is that it achieves much improved latency and bandwidth over the standard PCI bus.

The translated output of a *fly* program is interfaced with a generic Pilchard core written in VHDL. A shell script includes all of the required libraries and invokes all of the programs required to compile the VHDL representation of the user's program to a bitstream. The bitstream is then downloaded to the FPGA and the host interface program invoked. By automating the process of synthesis, implementation and downloading using shell scripts, the specifics of the compilation and execution process are hidden from the user.

Registers are used to transfer data between the FPGA and host. In normal operation, the host processor would initialize values in \$din[1] to \$din[x], and then start execution of the FPGA based coprocessor by performing a write cycle to the \$din[0] register. The write cycle causes the start signal of the first statement in the FPGA to be asserted. The software then polls the least significant bit of \$din[0] which is connected to the end signal of the last statement. When execution on the FPGA finishes, the least significant bit of \$din[0] is set and the program can read values returned by the hardware by reading the appropriate registers.

3 A GCD Processor

The *fly* program for a greatest common divisor (GCD) coprocessor is given below:

```
{
    $s = $din[1]; $l = $din[2];
    while ($s != $l) {
        $a = $l - $s;
        if ($a > 0) {
            $l = $a;
        }
        else {
            [ {$s = $l;} {$l = $s;} ]
        }
    }
    $dout[1] = $l;
}
```

The GCD coprocessor design was synthesized for a Xilinx XCV300E-8 and the design tools reported a maximum frequency of 126 MHz. The design, including interfacing circuitry, occupied 135 out of 3,072 slices.

The following perl subroutine tests the GCD coprocessor using randomly generated 15-bit inputs.

```
for (my $i = 0; $i < $cnt ; $i++) {
    $a = rand(0x7fff) & 0x7fff;
    $b = rand(0x7fff) & 0x7fff;

    &pilchard_write64(0, $a, 1);     # write a
    &pilchard_write64(0, $b, 2);     # write b
    &pilchard_write64(0, 0, 0);      # start coprocessor

    do {
        &pilchard_read64($data_hi, $data_lo, 0);
    } while ($data_lo  == 0);         # poll for finish
    &pilchard_read64($data_hi, $data_lo, 1);

    print ("gcd $a, $b = $data_lo\n");
}
```

The GCD coprocessor was successfully tested at 100 MHz by calling the FPGA-based GCD implementation with random numbers and checking the result against a software version. For randomized input test program above, the resulting system had an average execution time of 1.63μs per GCD iteration, which includes all interfacing overheads but excludes random number generation, checking and Perl looping overheads (Perl overheads were avoided by using inlined C in critical sections).

4 Floating Point Extension

As an example of how the *fly* system can be extended, floating point operators were added. Firstly, a parameterised module library which implemented floating point adders and multipliers, similar to that of Jaenicke and Luk[8] was developed [9]. In the library, numbers are represented in IEEE 754 format with arbitrary sized mantissa and exponent [10]. Rounding modes and denormalized numbers were not supported. The performance of the library is summarized in Table 2. The adder is not yet fully optimized and the maximum frequency was 58 MHz.

Table 2. Area and speed of the floating point library (a Virtex XCV1000E-6 device was used). One sign bit and an 8-bit exponent was used in all cases.

Fraction Size (bits)	Circuit Size (slices)	Frequency (MHz)	Latency (cycles)
Multiplication			
7	178	103	8
15	375	102	8
23	598	100	8
31	694	100	8
Addition			
7	120	58	4
15	225	46	4
23	336	41	4
31	455	40	4

The following modifications were then made to the floating point module library and *fly* in order to utilize this library:

- `start` and `end` signals were added to the floating point operators.
- A dual-ported block RAM interface to the host processor via `read_host()` and `write_host()` was added. This interface works in a manner analogous to the register based host interface described in Section 2.3 and allows data between the host and FPGA to be buffered.

- Three new floating point operators ".+", ".-" and ".*" were added to the parser to invoke floating point addition, subtraction and multiplication respectively.
- The parser was changed to enforce operator precedence and to instantiate the floating point operators appropriately.

4.1 Application to Solving Differential Equations

The modified *fly* compiler was used to solve the ordinary differential equation $\frac{dy}{dt} = \frac{(t-y)}{2}$ over $t \in [0, 3]$ with $y(0) = 1$ [11]. The Euler method was used so the evolution of y is computed by $y_{k+1} = y_k + h\frac{(t_k - y_k)}{2}$ and $t_{k+1} = t_k + h$ where h is the step size.

The following *fly* program implements the scheme, where h is a parameter sent by the host:

```
{
     $h = &read_host(1);
     [
       {$t = 0.0;} {$y = 1.0;} {$dy = 0.0;}
       {$onehalf = 0.5;} {$index = 0;}
     ]
     while ($t < 3.0) {
          [ {$t1 = $h .* $onehalf;} {$t2 = $t .- $y;} ]
          [ {$dy = $t1 .* $t2;} {$t = $t .+ $h;} ]
          [
            {$y = $y .+ $dy;}
            {$index = $index + 1;}
          ]

          $void = &write_host($y, $index);
     }
}
```

In each iteration of the program, the evolution of y is written to the block RAM via a `write_host()` function call and a floating point format with 1 sign bit, 8-bit exponent and 23-bit fraction was used throughout. The floating point format can, of course, be easily changed. Parallel statements in the main loop achieve a 1.43 speedup over a straightforward serial description.

The differential equation solver was synthesized for a Xilinx XCV300E-8 and the design tools reported a maximum frequency of 53.9 MHz. The design, including interfacing circuitry, occupied 2,439 out of 3,072 slices. The outputs shown in Table 4.1 were obtained from the hardware implementation at 50 MHz using different h values. The resulting system ($h = \frac{1}{16}$) took 28.7μs for an execution including all interfacing overheads.

t_k	$h=1$	$h=\frac{1}{2}$	$h=\frac{1}{4}$	$h=\frac{1}{8}$	$h=\frac{1}{16}$	$y(t_k)$ Exact
0	1.0	1.0	1.0	1.0	1.0	1.0
0.125				0.9375	0.940430	0.943239
0.25			0.875	0.886719	0.892215	0.897491
0.375				0.846924	0.854657	0.862087
0.50		0.75	0.796875	0.817429	0.827100	0.836402
0.75			0.759766	0.786802	0.799566	0.811868
1.00	0.5	0.6875	0.758545	0.790158	0.805131	0.819592
1.5		0.765625	0.846386	0.882855	0.900240	0.917100
2.00	0.75	0.949219	1.030827	1.068222	1.086166	1.103638
2.50		1.211914	1.289227	1.325176	1.342538	1.359514
3.00	1.375	1.533936	1.604252	1.637429	1.653556	1.669390

Table 3. Results generated by the differential equation solver for different values of h.

5 Discussion

There are certain limitations associated with the compilation method used in this paper. The compiler produces only one-hot state machines which may be inefficient in certain cases. In addition, the language only supports simple constructs and may be awkward for describing certain types of parallel programs. Finally, unless the designer fully understands the translation process and can explicitly describe the parallelism, the resulting hardware is mostly sequential in nature and would not be very efficient. Despite these limitations, we feel that the benefits in productivity and flexibility that are gained from this approach would outweigh the cons for many applications.

The compiler in Appendix A generates a fixed point bit parallel implementation, and it was shown how this could be extended to a floating point implementation. If, for example, a digit serial operator library were available, it could be easily modified to use digit serial arithmetic. Similarly, both fixed point and floating point implementations of the same algorithm could be generated from the same *fly* description. In the future, we will experiment with more code generation strategies. Many designs could be developed from the same program, and different *fly* based code generators could serve to decouple the algorithmic descriptions from the back-end implementation. In the case of using a digit serial library, users could select the digit size, or produce a number of implementations and choose the one which best meets their area/time requirements.

It is also possible to modify the compiler to produce code for different HDLs, program proving tools, and programming languages. Having an easily understandable and easily modifiable compiler allows the easy integration of the *fly* language to many other tools.

6 Conclusions

In this paper, the Perl programming language was used to develop a powerful yet simple hardware compiler for FPGA design. Unlike previous compilers, *fly* was designed to be easily modifiable to facilitate research in hardware languages and code generation. Since *fly* is tighly integrated with the hardware design tools and implementation platform, designers can operate with a higher level of abstraction than they might be accustomed to if they used VHDL. Examples involving a GCD coprocessor and the solution of differential equations in floating point were given.

Acknowledgements

The work described in this paper was supported by a direct grant from the Chinese University of Hong Kong (Project code 2050240), the German Academic Exchange Service DAAD (Projekt-Nr.: D/0008347) and the Research Grants Council of Hong Kong Joint Research Scheme (Project no. G_HK010/00).

References

[1] Page, I.: Constructing hardware-software systems from a single description. Journal of VLSI Signal Processing **12** (1996) 87–107

[2] Luk, W., McKeever, S.: Pebble: a language for parametrised and reconfigurable hardware design. In: Field-Programmable Logic and Applications. Volume LNCS 1482., Springer (1998) 9–18

[3] Wirth, N.: Hardware compilation: Translating programs into circuits. IEEE Computer **31** (1998) 25–31

[4] Brunvand, E.: Translating Concurrent Communicating Programs into Asynchronous Circuits. Carnegie Mellon University, Ph.D thesis (http://www.cs.utah.edu/~elb/diss.html) (1991)

[5] Wall, L., Christianson, T., Orwant, J.: Programming Perl. 3rd edn. O'Reilly (2000)

[6] Conway, D.: Parse::RecDescent Perl module. In: http://www.cpan.org/modules/by-module/Parse/DCONWAY/Parse-RecDescent-1.80.tar.gz. (2001)

[7] Leong, P., Leong, M., Cheung, O., Tung, T., Kwok, C., Wong, M., Lee, K.: Pilchard - a reconfigurable computing platform with memory slot interface. In: Proceedings of the IEEE Symposium on FCCM. (2001)

[8] Jaenicke, A., Luk, W.: Parameterised floating-point arithmetic on FPGAs. In: Proceedings of the IEEE International Conference on Acoustics, Speech and Signal Processing. (2001) 897–900

[9] Ho, C., Leong, M., Leong, P., Becker, J., Glesner, M.: Rapid prototyping of fpga based floating point dsp systems. In: Proceedings of the 13th IEEE Workshop on Rapid System Prototyping (to appear). (2002)

[10] Hennessy, J.L., Patterson, D.A.: Computer Architecture: A Quantitative Approach 2nd Edition. Morgan Kaufmann (1999)

[11] Mathews, J., Fink, K.: Numerical Methods Using MATLAB. 3rd edn. Prentice Hall (1999)

A Fly Source Code

In this appendix, the entire source code for the *fly* system used to compile the GCD coprocessor is given. Updates to this program and the modified *fly* compiler which supports floating point operations are available from: http://www.cse.cuhk.edu.hk/~phwl/fly/fly.html.

```
package main;
use Parse::RecDescent;

my $grammar = q {
{ my ($seq, $comb, $aux, $paux, $s, %sigs) =
        ("", "", 0, 0, "signal"); }

prog: stmtlist /^$/  {
  print "library ieee;\n";
  print "use ieee.std_logic_1164.all;\n";
  print "use ieee.std_logic_arith.all;\n\n";
  print "package hc_pack is \n";
  print "  subtype word is integer;\n";
  print "  type   words is array(integer ";
  print "range <>) of word;\nend hc_pack;\n\n";
  print "library ieee;\n";
  print "use ieee.std_logic_1164.all;\n";
  print "use ieee.std_logic_arith.all;\n";
  print "use work.hc_pack.all;\n\n";


  print "--type words is array (integer range <>) ";
  print "of word;\nentity arith_core is\nport(\n";
  print "\tclk: in std_logic;\n";
  print "\trst: in std_logic;\n";
  print "\tstart: in std_logic;\n";
  print "\tdin : in words( $sigs{din} ";
  print "downto 1);\n\tfinish: out std_logic;\n";
  print "\tdout: out words( $sigs{dout} ";
  print "downto 1));\nend arith_core;\n";
  print "architecture rtl of arith_core is\n";

  foreach my $k (keys %sigs) {
    if ($sigs{$k}) {
      print "$s  $k :\t words($sigs{$k}  " .
        "downto 0);\n"
      if !($k eq "din")
        and !($k eq "dout") ;
    }
    else {
      print "$s  $k :\t word; \n";
    }
  }
  for (my $i=1; $i<$aux; $i++) {
    print "$s s$i, f$i :\t boolean; ";
    print "--std_logic;\n";
  };
  for (my $i=1; $i<=$paux; $i++) {
    print "$s p$i, q$i :\t boolean; ";
    print "--std_logic;\n";
  };

  print "$s s$item[1], f$item[1] :\t boolean; ";
  print "--std_logic;\nbegin --architecture\n";
  print " s$item[1] <= TRUE when start='1' ";
  print "else FALSE ;--start;\n finish <= '1' ";
  print "when f$item[1] else '0'; --f$item[1];\n";
  print "process(clk)\nbegin\n";
  print "if rising_edge(clk) then\n";
  print $seq;
  print "end if;\nend process;\n";
  print "--combinational part\n$comb";
  print "end rtl;\n";
}

stmtlist: stmt | '{' stmt(s) '}' {
  my $fst_in = shift(@{$item[2]});
  my $int_in = $fst_in;
  $aux += 1 ;
  $comb .= "s$int_in <= s$aux; \n";
  foreach $int_in (@{$item[2]}) {
    $comb .= "s$int_in <= f$fst_in;\n";
    $fst_in = $int_in;
  }
  $comb .= "f$aux <= f$fst_in;\n";
  $aux;
}

stmt: asgn | ifelse | if  | while |
      pstmtlist | <error>

pstmtlist:  '[' stmtlist(s) ']' {
  $aux += 1;
  my $int_in;
  my @plist = ();
  foreach $int_in (@{$item[2]}) {
    $comb .=sprintf("s%d<=s%d;--pstmtlist\n",
                     $int_in, $aux);
    $paux += 1;
    push (@plist, $paux);

    $seq .= "if f$aux then --pstmtlist\n\t";
    $seq .= "q$paux <= false;\n";
    $seq .= "else\n\t";
    $seq .= "q$paux <= p$paux; \n";
    $seq .= "end if; \n";

    $comb .= "p$paux <= f$int_in or q$paux;";
    $comb .= " --pstmtlist\n";
  }
  my $pend ="f$aux <= p".join("and p",@plist)
    . "; --pstmt end\n";
  $comb .= $pend;
  $aux;
}

asgn: var '=' expr ';' {
  $aux = $aux + 1;
  $seq .= "if s$aux then\n\t";
  $seq .= "$item[1] <= $item[3];\n";
  $seq .= "end if;\n";
  $seq .= "f$aux <= s$aux;\n\n";
  $aux;
}

expr: val op expr{"$item[1]$item[2]$item[3]"}
    | val

op: '*' | '/' | '+' | '-'

val: /\d+/ | var

var: /\$[a-z][\w\[\]]*/  {
 $item[1] =~ s/^\$//;
 my $sig = $item[1];
 $sig =~ s/\[(\d+)\]//;
 $sigs{"$sig"} = ($sigs{"$sig"} &&
```

```
    ($sigs{"$sig"} > $1) ) ? $sigs{"$sig"} : $1;
  $item[1] =~ tr/\[\]/\(\)/;
  $item[1];
}

while: 'while' '(' cond ')' stmtlist {
  $aux += 1;
  $comb .= "s$item[5] <= ($item[3]) and " .
           "(s$aux or f$item[5]);\n";
  $comb .= "f$aux <= (not ($item[3])) and " .
           "(s$aux or f$item[5]);\n";
  $aux;
}

ifelse: 'if' '(' cond ')' stmtlist 'else' stmtlist {
  $aux += 1;
  $comb .= "s$item[5] <= ($item[3]) and s$aux;\n";
  $comb .= "s$item[7] <= (not ($item[3])) and s$aux;\n";
  $comb .= "f$aux <= f$item[5] or f$item[7];\n";
  $aux;
}

if: 'if' '(' cond ')' stmtlist {
  $aux += 1;
  $comb .= "s$item[5] <= ($item[3]) and s$aux;\n";
  $comb .= "f$aux <= (not ($item[3]) and s$aux) or f$item[5];\n";
  $aux;
}

cond: expr rel expr  { "$item[1] $item[2] $item[3]" }

rel: '>' | '<' | '<=' | '>=' | '!=' { "/=" } | '==' { "=" }

varlist: var ',' varlist  { "$item[1] $item[3]" } | var
};

$::RD_HINT = 0;
$::RD_AUTOACTION = q { $item[1] };
my $parser = Parse::RecDescent->new($grammar)
  or die "Bad grammar";

local $/;
my $script = <>;
my $tree = $parser->prog($script) or die "Bad script";
```

Challenges and Opportunities for FPGA Platforms

Ivo Bolsens

Xilinx, San Jose, CA
ivo@xilinx.com

Abstract

Today, FPGA devices contain up to 10 million system gates [1] and within three to four years processing technology will allow us to build 50 million gate devices, i.e. enough logic to build very complex , high performance systems. In addition, these devices operate at internal clock speeds, the equal of most ASIC's. Although the opportunities for building complex systems with these FPGA platforms are unprecedented, new breakthroughs will be required to solve

- the design productivity,
- the scalability of the architectures,
- the power requirements of embedded computing applications,
- the ease of use

As device densities keep increasing, a wide variety of hard and soft intellectual property cores are being made available on these platforms. Hardware processors and DSP datapaths are combined with softcores and large embedded memories. Moreover, demand of high performant systems requires the integration of gigabit-per-second serial I/O capability for interconnecting devices, backplanes and systems. These FPGA platforms will have to be accompanied by high level design tools that allow to capture the growing complexity, heterogeneity and flexibility (in time and space) of these components
New modeling languages, HW/SW co-design flows, verification techniques and IP-re-use strategies will be required. Research teams from different fields have to join forces to master the problem of such large complexity. [2]

In order to further ride the wave of Moore's law, advanced FPGA architectures will have to focus on innovative interconnect strategies to further guarantee scalability, flexibility and performance improvements. Whereas today, in case of 0.13 μm process technology, the transfer of a signal over a 1mm wire takes already twice as long as the execution of a 32-bit ALU operation, for a 0.05μm technology the relative interconnect delay will be a factor 9 higher. Moreover, transporting a signal over a 1mm wire, in a 0.05 μm technology will require more than 50 times the energy of a 32 bit ALU operation in the same technology and the off-chip interconnect will consume more than 1000 times the energy of a 32-bit ALU operation. Hence, novel circuit techniques such as overdrive, low-swing signaling as well as new architectures and 3D interconnect/packaging techniques will become essential to mitigate effects of slow wires. [3]

M. Glesner, P. Zipf, and M. Renovell (Eds.): FPL 2002, LNCS 2438, pp. 391-392, 2002.

Deeply embedded devices make up an emerging market that comes with stringent requirements for power consumption. Extrapolating the current trends in power consumption of FPGA's leads to a 5 times increase in dynamic power consumption and 30 times increase in static power consumption by 2010. This will result in components where 65% of the total power will be dynamic power and 35% will be static. Optimizing the power consumption requires a holistic view that encompasses all aspects of the design flow from manufacturing technology to design tools and architecture optimizations. [4]

The ubiquitous access to networked multimedia services will require end-to-end system solutions that can cope with very dynamic data requirements, additional functionality downloads and different security levels. This Quality of Service (QoS) adaptation process has to be performed at run-time over all parts of the system i.e. server, network and user terminal. Software implementations do not offer the best solution in terms of cost, speed and power. FPGA platforms can create a good compromise between high performance and maintaining the capability of reconfiguration. The challenge lays in providing a development environment that offers the same end-user experience for run-time reconfiguration as software based systems. The main target is to devise a programming environment that will enable a 'software-like' use of reconfigurable platforms consisting of instruction set processor(s) and reconfigurable hardware [5].

[1] Xilinx, http://www.xilinx.com/products/platform/

[2] Celoxica, http://www.celoxica.com/products/technical_papers/

[3] William Dally, Interconnect Focus Centre, http://marco.stanford.edu/

[4] L. Shang, A. Kaviani, K. Bathala, "Dynamic Power in the Virtex-II FPGA Family", Proceedings FPGA 2002, Monterey, CA, February 2002

[5] S. Guccione, D. Verkest, I.Bolsens, " Design technology for Networked Reconfigurable FPGA Platforms", Proceedings Design Automation and Test in Europe, Paris, France, March 2002

Design and Implementation of FPGA Circuits for High Speed Network Monitors

Masayuki Kirimura[1], Yoshifumi Takamoto[1], Takanori Mori[1], Keiichi Yasumoto[2], Akio Nakata[1], and Teruo Higashino[1]

[1] Graduate School of Info. Sci. & Tech., Osaka Univ.,
Toyonaka, Osaka 560-8531, Japan
{nakata,higashino}@ist.osaka-u.ac.jp
[2] Graduate School of Info. Sci., Nara Inst. of Sci. & Tech.
Ikoma, Nara 630-0101, Japan
yasumoto@is.aist-nara.ac.jp

Abstract. Due to the recent progress of the Internet, we need high-speed network monitors which can observe millions of packets per second. Since several types of network attacks occur, we need to modify monitoring facilities and their capacities depending on monitoring items and network speed. In this paper, we propose (1) a methodology for designing and implementing such network monitors flexibly and (2) a high-level synthesis technique which automatically synthesizes FPGA circuits from specifications of network monitors in a model called concurrent synchronous EFSMs. The proposed technique makes it possible to synthesize an FPGA circuit suitable for given monitoring items and parameters where the designer need not consider about how pipe-line processing and parallel processing should be adopted. We have developed a tool to automatically derive FPGA circuits and evaluated the speed and size of derived circuits.

keywords: high-level synthesis, design methodology, passive network monitor, multi-way synchronization, concurrent EFSMs

1 Introduction

With the rapid progress of the Internet and high-speed networks, vicious acts for attacking networks such as DoS attack and flooding are also increased[4,8,12]. It is very important to prevent such network attacks and protect our computers. There are some systems/software for detecting network intruders (for example, see[7,9,10]). Ref. [10] proposes a passive real-time network monitor for FDDI networks. Refs. [7,9] propose techniques of distributed DoS attack prevention. There are also some commercial products. Among them, real-time network monitors receive much attention recently since (1) they can detect network attacks in real-time, (2) network intruders cannot know the existence of passive monitors, and (3) it is relatively easy to add facilities for detecting new types of network attacks.

Until now, such network monitors have usually been developed as software since we often modify/add the monitoring items. However, as wide-band networks such as Gigabit Ethernet become popular, we need higher-speed network monitors if we want to monitor and notify the network attacks in real-time [2]. Although some high-speed

M. Glesner, P. Zipf, and M. Renovell (Eds.): FPL 2002, LNCS 2438, pp. 393–403, 2002.

network monitors have been developed as hardware[3,14], we need more flexibility so that we can cope with the modification/addition of monitoring items easily. One way for improving the flexibility is that we use reconfigurable circuits such as FPGAs and adopt speed-up techniques such as parallel and pipe-line processing.

In Refs. [6,15], we have defined a model called concurrent synchronous EFSMs to specify concurrent processes where multi-way synchronization in LOTOS [5] is used for data transmission among EFSMs. In this paper, using this model, we propose (1) a methodology for designing and implementing such network monitors flexibly and (2) a high-level synthesis technique to synthesize a FPGA circuit automatically from a specification of a network monitor.

Here, we focus on the design and implementation of two of the most basic monitoring facilities : (1) the module for detecting IP addresses whose hosts are attacked by IP flooding [4,12], and (2) the module for detecting SYN flood [4,12]. IP flooding is that an extremely lot of IP packets are sent to a host (a set of hosts in a LAN) called victim in a short time interval. SYN flood is an attack for TCP based communication between two hosts in the network where all communication ports of the victim's host are obstructed. Depending on the types of network attacks and the bandwidth of the monitoring communication link, we must designate a suitable threshold and check whether the number of IP packets per second passed through the monitoring communication link exceeds the designated threshold in order to detect that some flooding has occurred. There are some statistics about the number of IP packets for deciding whether DoS attacks have occurred [1,2,8]. Using those data, we can designate the suitable threshold about IP flooding. In our library, such threshold can be specified as a parameter. Depending on the specified threshold and the network speed, we can decide the required number of parallel processing in the derived FPGA circuit using our synthesis tool. Based on those results, our tool synthesizes the corresponding FPGA circuit automatically.

Through some experiments to synthesize circuits for a network monitor, we have confirmed that our tool makes it possible to derive reasonable sized FPGA circuits with enough speed for handling millions of IP packets per second.

2 Outline of Hardware Synthesis

2.1 Concurrent Synchronous EFSMs

In the concurrent synchronous EFSMs model (hereafter, called *S-EFSMs* model), we suppose that each EFSM has a finite number of registers (variables), that an execution condition called the *guard* expression can be specified to each transition, and that each transition can input/output several values via a gate as an I/O action. Each transition is denoted by $g\ v\ [f]$ where g is a gate, v is a sequence consisting of input variables ($?x : t$) and output expressions ($!E$) on gate g, and f is a guard expression of the transition.

In S-EFSMs model, any subset of concurrent EFSMs can communicate with each other via gates by multi-way synchronization. For the purpose, we borrow the parallel operators used in LOTOS [5] where S-EFSMs are described by the following notation.

$$S ::= S\,|[gate\_list]|\,S \;\mid\; S\,|||\,S \;\mid\; EFSM$$

($EFSM$ denotes an EFSM. $gate\_list$ indicates the gates whose events have to be synchronized between its operands. $|||$ is an independent parallel operator, and it is defined as the special case of the parallel operator such that $gate\_list = \emptyset$.)

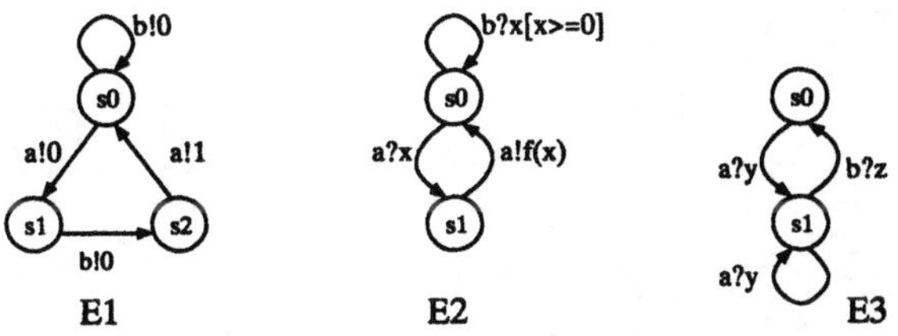

Fig. 1. Example system in S-EFSMs model

	E_1	E_2	E_3
p_1	$(a!0,$	$a?x$	$a?y)$
p_2	$(a!0,$	$a!f(x)$	$a?y)$
p_3	$(a!1,$	$a?x$	$a?y)$
p_4	$(a!1,$	$a!f(x)$	$a?y)$
p_5	$(b!0$	$b?x[x \geq 0])$	
p_6	$(b!0$		$b?z)$

Table 1. Possible instances

	E_1	E_2	E_3
r_1	$(\{a!0\},$	$\{a?x, a!f(x)\},$	$\{a?y\})$
r_2	$(\{a!1\},$	$\{a?x, a!f(x)\},$	$\{a?y\})$
r_3	$(\{b!0\},$	$\{b?x[x \geq 0]\})$	
r_4	$(\{b!0\},$		$\{b?z\})$

Table 2. Multi-rendezvous table

We can also specify one-to-many or many-to-many synchronization like $E_1|[a]|(E_2|[a]|E_3)$. This is useful to specify multi-point communication such as multi-cast data distribution and/or a mutual exclusion mechanism for avoiding simultaneous access to common resources among multiple EFSMs.

In $E_1|[a,b]|(E_2|[a]|E_3)$ of Fig. 1, events with gate a have to be executed synchronously among E_1, E_2 and E_3. For example, when E_1, E_2 and E_3 execute $a!0$, $a?x$ and $a?y$, respectively, the output value "0" of $a!0$ must be assigned to the input variables x and y (the variable types of x and y must match the type of "0"). When E_1 and E_3 execute $a!1$ and $a?y$, and E_2 executes $a!f(x)$, the value $f(x)$ must be equal to the output value "1". When multiple synchronizations become executable simultaneously, one of them must be selected and executed exclusively. For example, in the example of Fig. 1, when E_1 executes $b!0$ for $E_1|[a,b]|(E_2|[a]|E_3)$, either E_2 or E_3 can execute the event with gate b ($b?x[x >= 0]$ or $b?z$).

2.2 Outline of Our Synthesis Technique

Control of Multi-way Synchronizations For implementation of S-EFSMs model, we statically derive the following information about synchronizations to simplify the dynamic evaluation : (1) all possible tuples of synchronizing events and the corresponding tuples of EFSM names, (2) the execution condition (guard) for each tuple. For the example of Fig. 1, we show all possible instances of synchronization tuples in Table 1. Here, $p1-p4$ show the possible instances on gate a, and $p5-p6$ show those on gate b.

Since the number of all possible instances of synchronization tuples may become large in general, we adopt a compressed notation where multiple instances are repre-

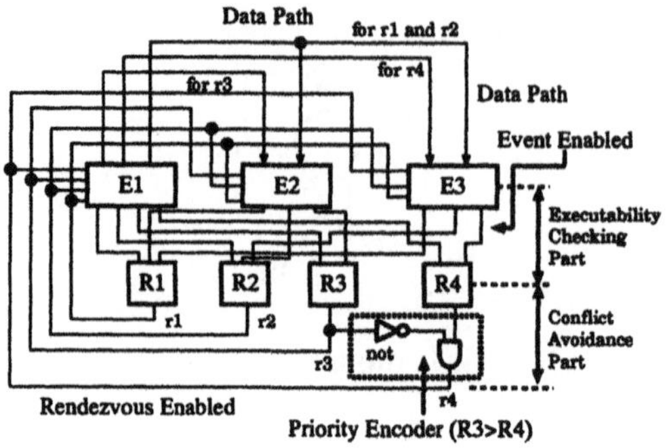

Fig. 2. Architecture of the whole circuit

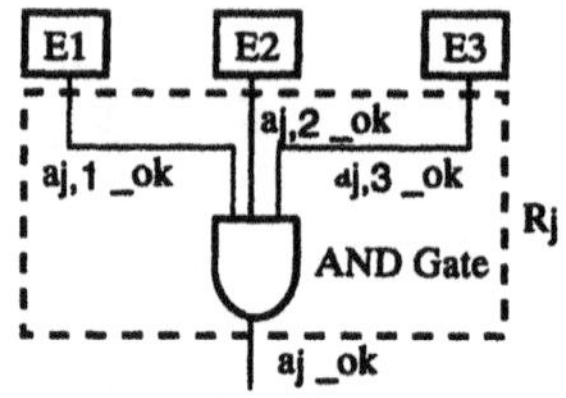

Fig. 3. Executability checking part R_j

sented as one tuple called *rendezvous indication*. Each rendezvous indication consists of (1) a tuple of EFSMs/event sets where each set includes events executed in each EFSM and (2) the execution condition. Here note that we compose each tuple so that any combination of events from the event sets can satisfy the synchronization condition and guard. The set of all rendezvous indications is called *multi-rendezvous table*. Table 2 is the multi-rendezvous table for the example of Fig. 1. The details about S-EFSMs model and the multi-rendezvous table can be found in [6,15].

Architecture of Derived Circuits We compose the final circuits of two components: (1) sequential circuits corresponding to EFSMs with the same clock and (2) a multi-way synchronization controller. Each EFSM executes one of events outgoing from the current state at each clock cycle if it is executable. Otherwise, it stays in the same state. Fig. 2 shows the architecture of the circuits synthesized from the specification of Fig. 1.

The multi-way synchronization controller is constructed as (i) the executability checking part for checking whether each tuple of synchronous events (in each rendezvous indication) is executable or not in each clock cycle, and (ii) the conflict avoidance part for selecting one of tuples which become executable but cannot be executed simultaneously. The above part (i) is constructed for each synchronous event tuple (see R_1 to R_4 in Fig. 2). Since each tuple becomes executable when all events in the tuple becomes executable, it is implemented as an AND gate with n inputs where each input connects to the signal from each EFSM in the tuple (n is the number of events in the tuple). The executability checking part for the example of Fig. 1 and Table 2 is constructed as shown in Fig. 3. Here, when $a!1$ becomes executable in E_1, the signal $a_{j,1}\_ok$ to each R_j (j = 1..4) becomes "1" and it is transfered to the AND gate of R_j. Similarly, when $a?x$ and $a?y$ become executable in E_2 and E_3, the signals $a_{j,2}\_ok$ and $a_{j,3}\_ok$ become "1"(signal "Event Enabled" in Fig.2). Since the output signal a_j_ok of the AND gate of R_j becomes "1"(signal "Rendezvous Enabled" in Fig. 2) when all inputs are "1", EFSMs E_1, E_2 and E_3 receive this signal and execute the event "a", respectively. For (ii), we can use a priority encoder when we select the tuple with the highest priority.

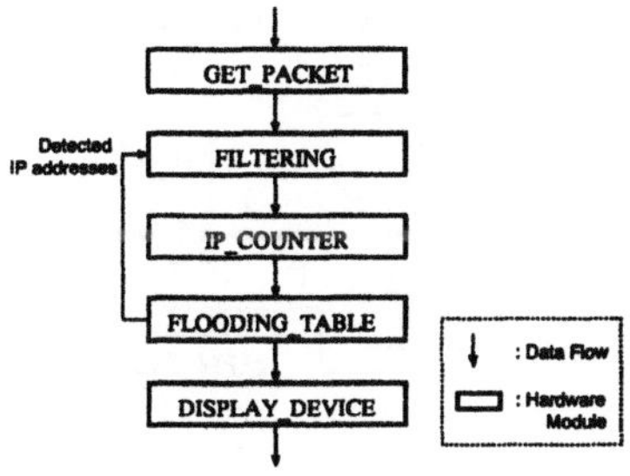

Fig. 4. IP Flooding Detection Module

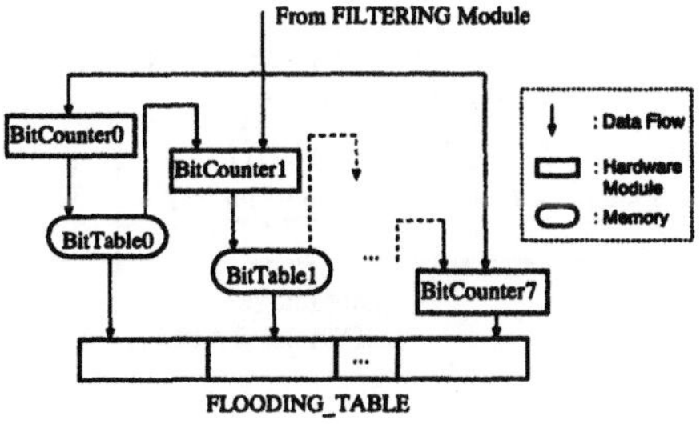

Fig. 5. IP_COUNTER module

3 Network Monitoring Circuits

The passive network monitor observes the IP packets by probing the target communication line. Usually it is constructed with two modules : **Header Information Capturing Module** and **Network Monitoring Module**. In the proposed method, we assume that we can use Header Information Capturing Module as an existing module [3,14]. The acquired header information is a bit sequence about the control fields in the IP packets such as "From IP address" and "To IP address" and types of the packets and so on.

Also in our method, in order to reduce the size of the FPGA circuit and to maximize its clock frequency (performance), we elaborate a way to construct network monitoring circuits which use as small amount of memory as possible (we do not use external memory modules but use only registers in the FPGA circuit for speed-up).

3.1 IP Flooding Detection Module

Smurf is an attack that a lot of packets are sent to the specific IP address. So, the main objective of our IP flooding detection module is to detect the IP address whose host is being attacked by flooding.

IP Flooding Detection Module Fig. 4 shows the whole architecture of the IP flooding detection module which we suppose. The input of this module is the packet header information, which is acquired from the header information capturing module.

At first, GET_PACKET module acquires "From (To) IP address" from the packet header information. FILTERING module stores and keeps in a table a fixed number of IP addresses which have been judged as being attacked by IP flooding, and forwards data with IP addresses not included in the table to IP_COUNTER module. In IP_COUNTER module, each 32 bit IP address is divided into several partitions with the same number of bits (called *partition size*). If the partition size is 4, the number of partitions is 8 and the number of bit patterns for each partition is 16. For each partition, we invoke the same number of counter modules in parallel as the number of bit patterns so that each counter module can count the arrived packets with the specified bit pattern. When a counter exceeds a certain threshold during a specified time period, we regard that the corresponding bit pattern is a part of the IP address of the attacker/victim of

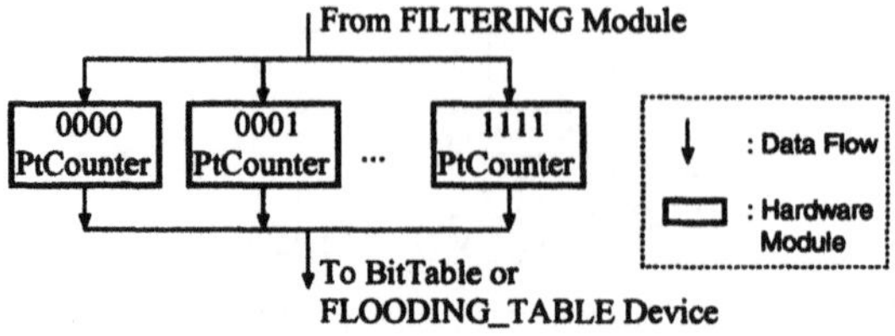

Fig. 6. BitCounter module

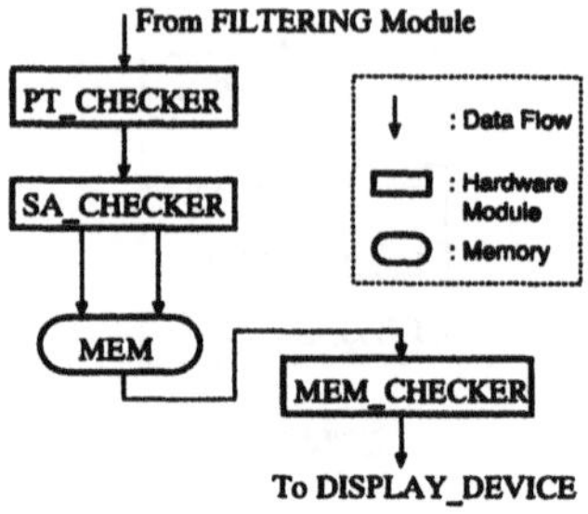

Fig. 7. SYN_COUNTER

the IP flooding. The same operation is repeated until the bit patterns of all partitions are determined. Thus we can detect the whole IP address of the attacker/victim of the IP flooding. The IP address detected by the above steps is stored in a table by FLOODING_TABLE module. The detected IP addresses are sent to FILTERING module to filter the detected IP addresses.

Fig. 5 shows the detailed architecture of IP_COUNTER module. Here since the partition size is 4, the whole module consists of (i) 8 sub-modules BitCounter0-BitCounter7 which count packets for the corresponding partitions in parallel and (ii) 8 tables BitTable0-BitTable7 which store the IP addresses where the IP flooding was detected.

In the figure, at first, BitCounter0 which is responsible for the first 4 bits of each IP address, counts packets for each bit pattern for a time period, and detects the bit pattern which has appeared most frequently and its counter value has exceeded a threshold. Then it regards the bit pattern as the first 4 bits of the IP address which causes flooding. The detected bit pattern is stored in BitTable0. BitCounter1 is responsible for the next 4 bits of each IP address. BitCounter1 counts only packets whose first 4 bits match the bit pattern stored in BitTable0, and similarly it detects the bit pattern which appeared most frequently and whose counter exceeded a threshold, and stores it in BitTable1. IP_COUNTER module repeats the above steps until BitCounter7 finishes its operations, and finally determines the 32 bit IP address which seems to cause flooding by concatenating the bit patterns in BitTable0 to BitTable7.

In this way, we detect the IP address by incrementally determining the bit pattern for each partition. By composing these 8 BitCounters and 7 BitTables as shown in Fig. 5, lots of IP packets can efficiently be processed in pipe-line manner.

Architecture of BitCounter Fig. 6 shows the architecture of BitCounter module. If the partition size is 4, each BitCounter module has 2^4 PtCounters which are responsible to bit patterns 0000 to 1111, respectively. The arrows in Fig. 6 show the data flow, where data exchange between modules are done by multi-way synchronization. Each PtCounter module just inputs a bit pattern and increments its counter if the bit pattern matches the pattern for which it is responsible. This is done during a given time period. If there is a counter which has exceeded a threshold during the period, BitCounter module outputs the corresponding bit pattern.

3.2 SYN Flood Detection Module

SYN Flood Detection Circuit In SYN flood detection module, similarly to IP flooding detection module, at first, GET_PACKET module acquires the necessary packet information from the header information capturing module. The necessary information consists of (1) From IP address, (2) To IP address, and (3) Flag bit sequence in the TCP header. Both of From and To IP addresses are the 32 bit sequence. Flag bit sequence consists of the six bits which specify the type of the packet. This bit sequence includes two flag bits: SYN and ACK.

FILTERING module picks out only SYN+ACK and ACK packets by checking the bit sequence (SYN,ACK) in the acquired information. Furthermore, to detect the IP address of the host which is being attacked by SYN flood, FILTERING module extracts (1) To IP address from the information if the packet is a SYN+ACK packet and (2) From IP address if the packet is an ACK packet. For example, if we need to detect the 4 bits from the victim's IP address, FILTERING module sends the packet information to 2^4 SYN_COUNTER modules which are responsible to bit patterns 0000 to 1111, respectively so that each SYN_COUNTER module counts the number of packets whose bit pattern matches its responsible bit pattern.

Architecture of SYN_COUNTER Module Fig. 7 shows the architecture of SYN_COUNTER module. At first, PT_CHECKER module extracts the necessary bit sequence from the packet information, and checks whether it matches its responsible bit pattern. If it matches, PT_CHECKER module transfers the extracted bit sequence to SA_CHECKER module. SA_CHECKER module checks whether the extracted bit sequence is SYN+ACK or ACK packet by watching (SYN,ACK) bits. If it is SYN+ACK packet, then the counter MEM is incremented. If it is ACK packet, then MEM is decremented. Consequently, the difference between the number of SYN+ACK packet and that of ACK ($MEM = \#(SYN + ACK) - \#(ACK)$) is kept in the counter MEM. If SYN flood occurs, the difference (the value of MEM) will increase rapidly. So, MEM_CHECKER module checks whether the value of MEM exceeds a threshold. When the value has exceeded the threshold, MEM_CHECKER module judges the corresponding bit pattern as a part of the IP address being attacked by SYN flood. After the judgment, MEM_CHECKER module sends the bit pattern to a display device, and resets the counter MEM.

4 Evaluation

We have developed a tool for generating the corresponding VHDL description in RT level from a given S-EFSM specification[6,15]. We can synthesize the hardware circuit in FPGA level from the generated VHDL description using commercial tools.

4.1 Experimental Results

In order to evaluate our network monitoring circuits, we have synthesized circuits for the IP flooding detection module (IP-FLOOD) in the previous section and the SYN

Component Type	IP-FLOOD	SYN-FLOOD
Num. of EFSMs	156	67
Time for Synthesis(sec)	1048	123
Max. Clock Freq.(MHz)	12.45	12.45
Size(gate)	14181	3392

Table 3. Circuit size for two modules

Steps	Dummy	Branches	Gates	Clocks(MHz)
1	0	64	7062	11.51
2	2	32	7171	12.45
2	4	16	7410	14.90

(Here, "Steps" is the number of steps, "Dummy" is the number of dummy modules, and "Branches" is the number of branches from each dummy module (or the FILTERING module))

Table 4. Performance improvement by reducing the number of branches (5 bit partition)

Name	Bit	EFSMs	Gates	Clocks(MHz)
SYN2	2	19	843	13.37
SYN3	3	35	1700	13.37
SYN4	4	67	3392	12.45
SYN5	5	131	7062	11.51
SYN6	6	259	14680	10.55
SYN7	7	515	30848	9.63
SYN8	8	1027	64598	8.67

Table 5. Performance variation depending on the number of bits

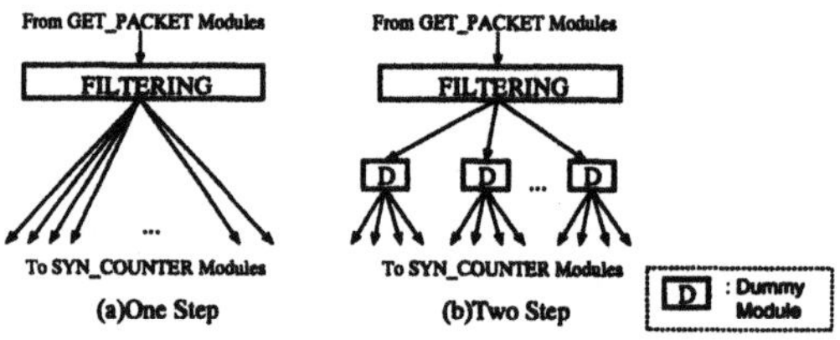

Fig. 8. Distribution of IP counter processing

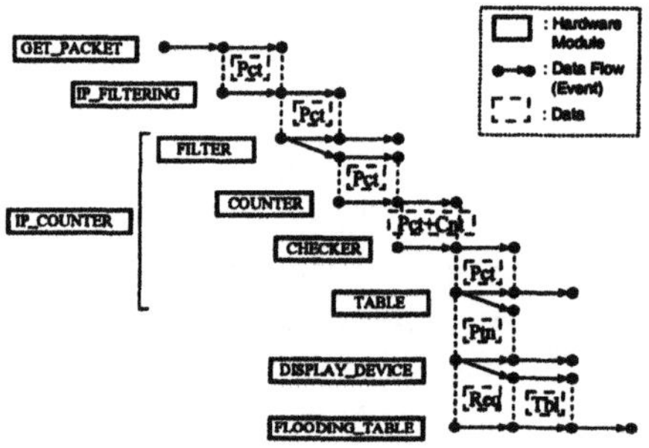

Fig. 9. Processing stages of IP flooding detecting component

flood detection module (SYN-FLOOD). Here, we used FPGA Express as a synthesis tool and FLEX10K of ALTERA Corp. as a FPGA chip-set. In both modules, we have used 4 bit partition for counting IP addresses. The characteristics of the synthesized circuits are shown in Table 3.

For the IP-FLOOD circuit, the time for synthesis was about 17 min., the size was about 14,000 logic gates, and the maximum clock frequency was about 12.5 MHz. For the SYN-FLOOD circuit, the time, the size and the max. clock frequency were about two min., 3,300 logic gates and 12.5 MHz, respectively.

We have investigated the performance variation (in the max. clock frequency) depending on the partition size in the SYN-FLOOD circuit. The result is shown in Table 5. Since the number of required counter registers is doubled when the partition size (Bit) increases by one, the sizes of resulting circuits (Gates) are increasing in proportion to the power of two. In the circuits, since the operations to all counter registers are executed in parallel, the performance reduction does not occur in this part. However, due to increase of the number of synchronizing EFSMs, the maximum clock frequency is reduced as the partition size increases.

In the SYN-FLOOD specification, as shown in Fig. 8(a), we make the FILTERING module transfer each packet information to all of the SYN_COUNTER modules by multi-way synchronization. When the number of the SYN_COUNTER modules is larger than a threshold, data cannot be transfered to all the SYN_COUNTER modules at one time due to the restriction of fan-out. Therefore, the synthesis tool automatically inserts extra logic gates for relaying data to the modules so that data transfer is carried out in a clock cycle. In order to improve performance, we modified the specification so that data transfer to SYN_COUNTER modules is done in several clock cycles by inserting dummy modules "D" as shown in Fig. 8(b). We show the performance improvement in Table 4. In the table, we see that the size of the circuits is increasing as the numbers of steps and dummy modules increase. However, when we increase the number of steps by one, the maximum clock frequency was improved by one to three MHz.

We show the packet flow on the series of the sub-modules in Fig. 9. As we see in Fig. 9, the number of events executed in each sub-module (EFSM) for processing a packet is at most three where each EFSM returns to its initial state after executing these events. Since all sub-modules work in parallel, they proceed in pipe-line manner. We suppose that each event can be executed in a clock cycle. Therefore, the number of packets the circuits can process per second is $12.45(MHz)\ /\ 3\ = 4.15$ million.

4.2 Criteria to Decide Threshold for Given Network Environment

In both of the IP-FLOOD and SYN_FLOOD modules, each counter module increases its counter when the specified bit pattern appears in the obtained IP address. Each counter module regards that the flooding has occurred when the counter exceeds a certain threshold. Here, we discuss about the dependency between the appropriate threshold and the number of packets per second processed at each counter.

In Ref. [2], it is reported that about 200 to 300 thousands packets per second as the maximum have been transmitted in a backbone between U.S. and U.K. The number of packets may be increased. Here, we assume the maximum number of packets to be treated is one million packets per second. In such a backbone network, small sized flooding such as 1,000 packets per second may not be treated as IP flooding. On the other hand, if such a backbone network with heavy traffic has additional 5-10% flooding packets (50-100 thousands packets/sec.), then the network will be more congested. It may cause some trouble to the network. Here, we would like to detect such IP flooding.

Now, we assume that there are 100 thousands flooding packets per second to some specific IP address. If we assume that we use 4 bit partition, that is, 8 IP_COUNTER modules, then each IP_COUNTER module is supposed to process about 63 thousands packets per second (1 $million$ / 16 = 63 $thousands$). Here, we have to consider deviation in the bit patterns of IP addresses. If we suppose there is at most 50% deviation, each IP_COUNTER module may have to process at most 95 thousands packets per second (63 thousands plus 50% is 95 thousands). In this case, we suppose that we use 98 thousands packets per second as the threshold of each IP_COUNTER module. When the number of flooding packets for the specific IP address exceeds 100 thousands per second, the counter at an IP_COUNTER module always exceeds the threshold (98 thousands packets/sec) independently of deviation of IP addresses (minimum $zero$ +

100 *thousands* > 98 *thousands packets*/*sec*). So, we can detect such flooding with 4 bit partition (8 IP_COUNTER modules).

If we want to detect the flooding of 6,000 packets per second, IP_COUNTER module cannot detect the flooding since minimum *zero* + 6,000 < 98 *thousands packets*/*sec* holds. If we use the 8 bit partition, that is, 4 IP_COUNTER modules, each IP_COUNTER module is supposed to receive one million / 256 = 3,906 packets per second. Even if we assume that additional 50% packets are transmitted for some specific IP address depending on deviation of IP addresses, the number of packets to the specific IP address does not exceed 6,000 packets/sec since 3,906 plus 50% is 5,940 packets/sec. So, in this case, we can detect the flooding with the threshold of 6,000 packets/sec independently of deviation of IP addresses, although the size of the resulting circuit becomes large.

When (1) the maximum number of packets per second, (2) the maximum deviation in the bit patterns of IP addresses, and (3) the flooding size (packets/sec) which we would like to detect are given, we can mechanically decide the partition size and the number of IP_COUNTER modules. Also, we can automatically derive the corresponding FPGA circuits of IP_COUNTER modules from the partition size and the number of IP_COUNTER modules. On the other hand, Ref. [8] has reported that the amount of SYN+ACK and ACK packets is about 5 % of all traffic in the Internet backbone networks. Using such information, the SYN-FLOOD module can also be automatically derived using our tools.

5 Conclusion

In this paper, we have proposed a method for synthesizing network monitor circuits. We have been investigating the applicability of our method for real backbone traffic, such as traffic logs in [13]. From our experimental results, we have expected that our method has enough applicability for practical backbone traffic. We have also confirmed that the performance and the size of the generated FPGA circuits are practically sufficient for monitoring a few millions of IP packets per second.

Since our network monitoring circuits can observe a lot of IP packets in real-time, their monitoring speed is sufficient for passive monitoring of high-speed networks such as Gigabit Ethernet. They may be used for detecting various types of DoS attacks. More precise evaluation of the proposed method through actual network monitoring of the Internet backbone is part of our future work.

Acknowledgements This work is partly supported by Semiconductor Technology Academic Research Center (STARC) and KDDI R&D Labs.

References

1. J. Apisdorf, K. Claffy and K. Thompson: "OC3MON:Flexible, Affordable, High-Performance Statistics Collection", Proc. of INET'97 (1997), http://www.isoc.org/isoc/whatis/conferences/inet/97/proceedings/F1/F1_2.HTM

2. K. Claffy, G. J. Miller and K. Thompson: "the nature of the beast: recent traffic measurements from an Internet backbone", Proc. of INET'98 (1998), http://www.caida.org/outreach/papers/1998/Inet98/
3. Z. D. Ditta, J. R. Cox Jr and G. M. Parulkar: "Design of the APIC: A High Performance ATM Host-Network Interface Chip", Proc. of IEEE INFOCOM'95, pp. 179-187 (1995).
4. L. Garber: "Denial-of-Service Attacks Rip the Internet", Proc. of IEEE Computer, pp. 12-17 (2000).
5. ISO : "Information Processing System, Open Systems Interconnection, LOTOS - A Formal Description Technique Based on the Temporal Ordering of Observational Behavior", ISO 8807 (1989).
6. H. Katagiri, K. Yasumoto, A. Kitajima, T. Higashino and K. Taniguchi: "Hardware Implementation of Communication Protocols Modeled by Concurrent EFSMs with Multi-Way Synchronization", 37th IEEE/ACM Design Automation Conference (DAC-2000), pp. 762-767 (2000).
7. G. Mansfield et. al: "Towards Trapping Wily Intruders in the Large", Computer Networks, Vol. 34, pp. 659-670 (2000).
8. D. Moore, G. M. Voelker and S. Savage: "Inferring Internet Denial-of-Service Activity", USENIX Security Symposium (2001).
9. K. Park and H. Kee: "On the Effectiveness of Route-Based Packet Filtering for Distributed DoS Attack Prevention in Power-Law Internets", Proc. of ACM SIGCOMM2001, pp. 15-26 (2001).
10. V. Paxson: "Bro: A System for Detecting Network Intruders in Real-Time", Computer Networks, Vol. 31, No.23-24, pp. 2435-2463 (1999).
11. SYNOPSYS, Inc. : http://www.synopsys.com
12. A. S. Tanenbaum: "Computer Networks, Third Edition ". Prentice-Hall Inc. (1996).
13. WIDE Project: "Packet traces from WIDE backbone", http://tracer.csl.sony.co.jp/mawi/
14. S. Yagi, T. Ogura, T. Kawano, M. Maruyama and N. Takahashi: "METAMONITOR: An Adaptive Network-traffic Monitor", Journal of Information Processing Society of Japan, Vol.41, No.2, pp. 444-451 (2000) (in Japanese).
15. K. Yasumoto, A. Kitajima, T. Higashino and K. Taniguchi: "Hardware Synthesis from Protocol Specifications in LOTOS", Proc. of Joint Intl. Conf. on 11th Formal Description Techniques and 18th Protocol Specification, Testing, and Verification (FORTE/PSTV'98), pp. 405-420 (1998).

Granidt: Towards Gigabit Rate Network Intrusion Detection Technology

Maya Gokhale, Dave Dubois, Andy Dubois, Mike Boorman, Steve Poole, and Vic Hogsett

Los Alamos National Laboratory
Los Alamos, NM, U.S.A. 87545

Abstract. We describe a novel application of reconfigurable computing to the problem of computer network security. By filtering network packets with customized logic circuits, we can search headers as well as packet content for specific signatures at Gigabit Ethernet line rate. Input to our system is a set of filter rule descriptions in the format of the public domain "snort" databases. These descriptions are used by the hardware circuits on two Xilinx Virtex 1000 FPGAs on a SLAAC1V [9]board. Packets are read from a Gigabit Ethernet interface card, the GRIP [8], and flow directly through the packet filtering circuits. A vector describing matching packet headers and content are returned to the host program, which relates matches back to the rule database, so that logs or alerts can be generated. The hardware runs at 66 MHz with 32-bit data, giving an effective line rate of 2 Gb/s. The granidt combination software/hardware runs at 24.9X the speed of snort 1.8.

1 Introduction

As digital network technologies become more advanced, the security issues related to these technologies become more complex [1], [4]. To protect public and private networks, software-based intrusion detection systems have become the norm, with the goal of protecting against compromise to the network's integrity, the machines that form the network, and the information contained within it. However, with the widespread availability of 1 Gb/s Local Area Networks and 10Gb/s links, it has become clear that current software-based intrusion detection systems cannot process packets at those line rates, resulting in inadequate monitoring of network traffic and increasing the probability of an undetected attack. Available software-only systems can monitor, at the very most, 100Mb/s rate, which is an order of magnitude less than required. Parallel processing solutions are appearing in the marketplace (for example, see [6]), and reconfigurable hardware assist for ATM firewall [5] as well as regular expression matching [2] have been proposed.

In this paper, we present a novel use of reconfigurable computing to filter GigE network packets for network security applications. Our hardware platform consists of the SLAAC1V[9] card, a reconfigurable computer containing three Xilinx Virtex XCV1000 FPGAs, ten 256KBx36 SRAM memory modules, and a

M. Glesner, P. Zipf, and M. Renovell (Eds.): FPL 2002, LNCS 2438, pp. 404–413, 2002.

daughter Gigabit Ethernet card, the GRIP[8]. Packets pass from the line directly into the logic circuits programmed into the FPGAs. One set of logic circuits compare header fields from the packet with known attack features according to a "snort"-format rule database. A second set of circuits compares packet content to desired content strings. The patterns to be matched are loaded into the FPGAs on start-up, and new patterns can be easily accomodated without re-compiling the hardware.

Positive matches from comparisons on both circuits are processed in software, where more complex analysis can be performed. By filtering packet headers and content in hardware, we greatly reduce the burden of software processing. The software can log the packet or generate an alert after examining the hardware match results.

In the next section, we describe the network intrusion detection application and summarize current capabilities of these systems. Next, we describe our hardware/software approach, and the system we have built, "granidt," that filters Gigabit rate Ethernet packets. We report area/clock-speed/throughput performance statistics of the system. We end with conclusions and directions for future work.

2 Network Intrusion Detection Systems

The purpose of network intrusion detection systems (NIDS) [7] is to protect a Local Area computer network from unauthorized access and malicious interference. A NIDS must scan every packet in order to monitor network traffic for pre-defined patterns that might indicate suspicious activity. Basic NIDS operations include scanning for particular patterns with packet headers, checking message content for suspicious patterns, and monitoring the interchange of related messages in a session. NIDS typically operate in passive receive-only mode, sniffing all packets coming over the wire and reporting results over a different channel.

These systems are often rules-based, as illustrated in Figure 1. This rule language is used by snort, a light-weight public domain network intrusion detection. The rules specify actions to perform when a packet contains certain combinations of protocol, IP addresses, port address ranges, IP option values, content strings, etc. The action might be to log the packet, log summary information about the packet, or to alert an operator. The packet log can be used by backend analysis tools to determine post-facto intrusions.

More sophisticated techniques analyze entire TCP messages and perform session-level analysis in "real-time" as packets are being received. However, all of these approaches share the need to scan and process packets at line speed. If a packet is dropped, the fidelity of downstream processing is reduced, and network security is potentially compromised. In the current state of the practice, all these functions are carried out in software, with a combination of kernel-level and application-level code. Software-only NIDS that we have measured operate in the 100Mb/s regime. As the complexity of the software processing increases,

```
alert tcp $EXTERNAL_NET any -> $HOME_NET 23
  (msg:"BACKDOOR Telnet Solaris StoogR";
 flags: A+; content: "StoogR";
  reference: arachnids,526;)

alert tcp any any -> $HOME_NET 139
  (msg:"WORM - Possible QAZ Worm Infection";
   flags:A; content: "/71 61 7a 77 73 78 2e 68 73 71/";
  reference:MCAFEE,98775;)
```

Fig. 1. Examples of Intrusion Detection Rules from snort Data Base

software methods drop packets at even 100Mb/s, compromising the effectiveness of the network security application.

3 A Software/Hardware Approach to Packet Scanning

Our software/hardware co-processing approach combines flexible software with reconfigurable hardware circuits as illustrated in Figure 2.

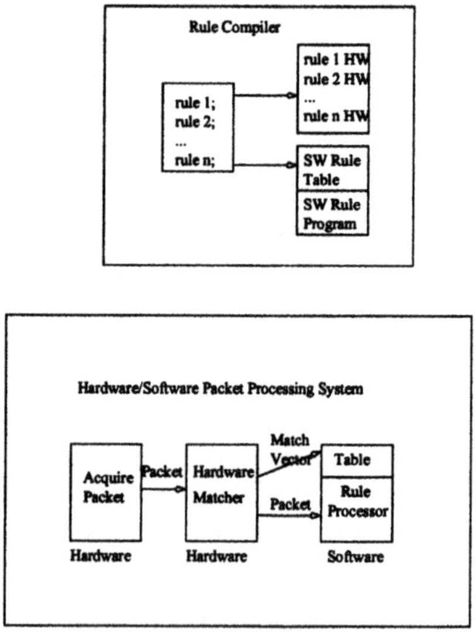

Fig. 2. Hardware/Software Co-Processing

To partition between hardware and software, the rule compiler (a modified snort rule parser) reads a snort format database (see Figure 1) and creates entries for Content Addressable Memories (CAMs). If rules are updated, the rule compiler simply creates new CAM entries – no FPGA reconfiguration is required. Our modified snort loads the hardware configurations and CAM entries and then initiates packet processing. The software then receives each packet, to which a "Match Vector" is appended by the hardware, and performs the appropriate action as dictated by the rule(s) that match the packet. The hardware reads packets from a GigaBit Ethernet Network Interface Card (NIC) and matches the packet to CAM entries, creating the Match Vector.

3.1 Software Processing

The software consists of two components, the Rule Compiler, and Rule Processor. The rule compiler reads a rule file in snort database format. It creates

- a hardware representation of the rule fields to be matched, and
- a software representation of the rules, which is input to the Rule Program.

The rule compiler accepts a subset of snort rule syntax, including the snort header, and the content and message fields of the snort options. Fields in the packet header such as protocol, source and destination IP addresses, and port address ranges may also be specified in a rule. For example, in Figure 1, the first rule specifies TCP protocol; the source IP address of "EXTERNAL_NET," which is a snort variable initialized elsewhere; any source port; the destination IP address of "HOME_NET;" and destination port 23. The relevant options are the content string "StoogR," the flags, and the message to be generated if a packet matches the rule. The action to be taken is an alert.

The rule compiler creates several tables that are used to initialize hardware CAMs. These include a protocol table; source and destination IP addresses, possibly with subnet masks and possibly negated; specific source and destination ports; source and destination port range tables; and content strings.

In addition, the rule compiler creates an internal representation of the rules that links fields specified by the rules to the hardware CAM tables and range tables. This data structure is used by the Rule Processor. The Rule Processor initializes the hardware CAMs and initiates packet processing. It receives each packet scanned by the hardware. Appended to the packet is a Match Vector generated by the hardware that records which CAM entries matched the packet. The Rule Processor correlates the Match Vector to the internal rule database and determines an action for each rule, such as alert or log.

3.2 Alternative Rule Processor

In the above design, the Rule Processor compares Match Vector results to the rule database for each rule in order to generate the appropriate action for that rule. This incurs a software overhead that moderates the hardware pattern match speedup.

We have also designed an alternative rule processor in which the hardware automatically uses match vector output to identify matching rules, and returns a Rule Vector to the software. A "1" bit in the Rule Vector indicates that the corresponding rule matched, and the software then merely performs the actions associated with the matching rules. In this approach, the Rule Compiler, in addition to the CAM and Range Tables, generates VHDL statements that set the Rule Vector.

As an example, suppose we have three fields. Field A is 32 bits wide and has a CAM that is 64 slots deep. It does not require any Range Table (RT) entries. Field B is 16 bits wide and has a CAM with 16 slots, and uses 4 RTs. Field C is 8 bits wide and has a CAM with 128 slots. We have the following rules:

Rule 1: A = X'00001234 and B= Range X'1000 downto X'0005 and C = X'CB
Rule 2: A = X'00001234 and B= Range X'1000 downto X'0007 and C = X'01
Rule 3: A = X'abcd1234 and B= X'0050 and C = EXCEPT X'CB

The software registers A= X'00001234 to slot 7 of field A CAM. It registers B= Range X'1000 downto X'0005 to RT 2, and C= X'CB to slot 127 of C CAM.

VHDL code will be generated for rule 1:
Rule(1) <= CAM_A(7) AND RT(2) AND CAM_C(127)
Software detects A=X'00001234 is registered to slot 7 of CAM_A. Software registers B=RANGE X'1000 downto X'0007 t0 RV 3. Software registers C=X'01 to slot 0 of CAM_C

VHDL code will be generated for rule 2:
Rule(2) <= CAM_A(7) AND RT(3) and CAM_C(0)
Software registers A=X'abcd1234 to slot 63 of CAM_A. Software registers B= X'0050 to slot 7. Software detects C=X'CB is registered to slot 127 of CAM_C.

VHDL code will be generated for rule 3:
Rule(3) <= CAM_A(63) AND CAM_B(7) AND not(CAM_C(127))

The generated VHDL is compiled into the part along with the fixed part of the design and then the bit stream down loaded. This approach improves overall system performance but suffers the limitation that the design must be re-synthesized each time the rules change. Since we foresee having to add or delete rules dynamically, we have focused on the technique of Section 3.1, which does not require FPGA reconfiguration to accomodate rule update.

3.3 Hardware Processing

The hardware processing flow is illustrated in Figure 3. For this work, we have used the SLAAC1V PCI board, which contains three Xilinx Virtex 1000 FPGAs and ten banks of ZBT SRAM. each 36x256K. A daughter card, the GRIP, is a Gigabit Ethernet card that accepts a serial bit stream from the Ethernet and creates Ethernet packets. The packets are streamed in 32-bit chunks into X0, using a FIFO protocol.

In our application, a packet is collected on X1. Relevant header fields – protocol, address, ports – are extracted and pipelined through the header CAMs, creating the header portion of the Match Vector. The packet is simultaneously forwarded to X2, where the content portion of the packet is matched to the content CAMs. The header and content components of the Match Vector are appended to the packet. The augmented packet then flows back through X0 to the host and is received by the software Rule Processor. Each block in Figure 3 is described below.

General Mux Demux Module (GMDM) This block creates a 72-bit bus interface. It supplies two 32-bit wide FIFO interfaces, one for each direction, with byte enables and a control bit. It also contains out-of-band FIFOs in both directions, and the designer can specify how to implement each FIFO (block ram or LUT-based) and the depth of each FIFO. Our design used the in-band 32-bit FIFO portion in one direction only.

IP Detector/Flag Processor This block checks if incoming Ethernet frames carry IP datagrams, and if so, it sets the start and end of packet flags. This logic also determined if the upper-layer protocol is ICMP, UDP or TCP, and sets the start of content field at the correct word location. The flags are carried in parallel with the packet data.

Packet Queue FIFO This block consists of two FIFOs. The 512 x 41-bit packet data FIFO is used to queue the packet data, while a smaller 16 x 4-bit control FIFO is used to buffer packet information and indicates when a fully queued packet is available in the packet data FIFO. Queuing complete packets guarantees no gaps to the down-stream CAM blocks.

Content Addressable Memory (CAM) Our CAM design utilizes the shift register primitives built into a Virtex slice. A reconfigurable LUT (two LUTs per slice) is used to implement a single clock cycle read CAM. Writes to the CAM cells require 16 clock cycles. The base design was modified to add a "don't care" state to the CAM, giving limited regular expression match capability. The design is fully parameterized for depth and width expansion.

Header Field CAMs The design is flow though in nature. As packets are presented a full header is built in the Data Pipeline section. Once a complete header is built, the data is presented to five separate CAMs. A one cycle read operation is performed and the resulting match vectors are generated for each CAM. When the packet end is detected the match vectors are injected immediately after the packet. There is an assumption made here that there is enough of an inter-packet gap to accommodate the match vectors.

The header fields and CAM sizes are:

– Protocol (8 bits x 16 entries)
– Source IP Address (32 bits x 16 entries)

- Destination IP Address (32 bits x 16 entries)
- Source Port (16 bits x 64 entries)
- Destination Port (16 bits x 128 entries)

For both the Source Port and Destination Port fields we have also constructed range checking circuits. For the Source Port there are 11 of these Range Table circuits available. The Destination Port has 6 Range Tables available. Configuration is done using the external SRAM on the SLAAC1V card. Out of the card reset built in state machines read from the external memory and configure the CAM and range checking circuits.

Content CAMs This design is once again flow through. As the content portion of the packet is passed through the circuit we check for string matches on each clock cycle for patterns up to 20 bytes in length. These patterns are case sensitive; however, it would be relatively simple to generate a case insensitive checker.

Configuration is done in a manner similar to the Header Field CAM (see section 3.3).

3.4 CAM Design Alternatives

We considered three ways of implementing CAM designs in Virtex devices. These designs are based upon Virtex-specific device features including fast dedicated carry chains, distributed RAM, Virtex Block SelectRAM+ memory, and built-in shift registers (SRL16E).

Our design called for single cycle read operation of the CAM which ruled out the distributed RAM case since it requires multiple cycles per read. The Block SelectRAM+ approach offered single cycle reads and writes, however, it is limited in size. The maximum CAM size in this case is 12,288 bits and uses all of the available Block SelectRAM+.

This leaves the shift register (SRL16E) with fast carry chains (MUXCY) CAM structure. With this approach we have single cycle reads but 16 cycle writes. Using the Virtex slice shift register primitives we can implement two reconfigurable LUTs. A 4-bit CAM word fits into each LUT. Each Virtex CLB contains two slices; therefore we can implement a 16-bit CAM word per CLB.[1]

The CLB Array for the XCV1000E is 64x96. This could be configured as a 512-bit CAM word. CAM depth is defined in multiples of 16 word blocks. This seemingly large capacity is limited by routing: to build a large CAM block we use up routing resources quite quickly. Thus in our design, the Content CAM section is configured as 160 bits (20 bytes) by 32 deep. This utilizes 20x32 CLB's which is approximately 10% of the available CLB resource. Efforts to increase the depth have resulted in unacceptable operational frequency.

We also mapped the CAM designs onto an Altera APEX part. In contrast to the Virtex, Altera utilizes dedicated resources to implement CAM. The Altera

[1] The CAM implementation suggested in a Xilinx application note was not used due to our requirement for "don't care" positions in the CAM fields.

Embedded system blocks (ESBs) directly implement tertiary CAM. A similar sized device to the Virtex1000E, the EP20KE600C contains 152 ESBs each of which can implement a 32-bit x 32 deep CAM. The Content CAM section (20 bytes by 32 deep) of our design takes 40 ESBs to implement on the Altera.

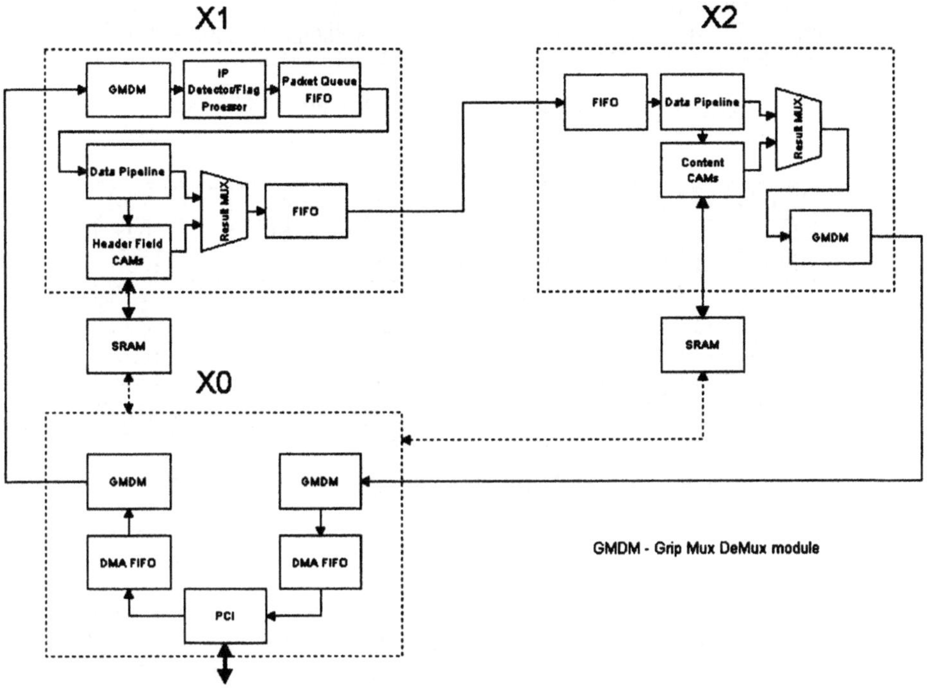

Fig. 3. Header and Content CAMs

4 Results

For our hardware design environment, we used Mentor Graphics' FPGA Advantage HDL/block diagram schematic entry tool, Xilinx's CORE generation tool, ModelTech's Modelsim Simulator, Synplicity's Synplify synthesis tool, and Xilinx's Alliance Series Place and Route tool.

Device utilization for the Header (X1) and Content (X2) matching hardware is summarized in Figures 4 and 5. The header comparison circuit occupies 34% of the on-chip Block RAM and uses 28% of the logic slices. The content comparison circuit uses 18% of the on-chip memory and 39% of the slices. The circuits operate at >66 MHz.

We have measured communication to the host program at 33 MHz, with 32-bit data. The measured bandwidth is 87MB/s bandwidth between the SLAAC1V

Number of External GCLKIOBs	3 out of 4	75%
Number of External IOBs	357 out of 512	69%
Number of LOCed External IOBs	357 out of 357	100%
Number of BLOCKRAMs	11 out of 32	34%
Number of SLICEs	3535 out of 12288	28%
Number of CAPTUREs	1 out of 1	100%
Number of STARTUPs	1 out of 1	100%
Min period/Max frequency :	14.486ns	69.032MHz

Fig. 4. Device Utilization on Header FPGA X1

Number of External GCLKIOBs	3 out of 4	75%
Number of External IOBs	325 out of 512	63%
Number of LOCed External IOBs	325 out of 325	100%
Number of BLOCKRAMs	6 out of 32	18%
Number of SLICEs	4861 out of 12288	39%
Number of CAPTUREs	1 out of 1	100%
Number of STARTUPs	1 out of 1	100%
Min period/Max Freq:	14.67ns	68.148MHz

Fig. 5. Device Utilization on Content FPGA X2

board and PC using DMA. Thus the circuits can process 2Gb/s, and the PCI bandwidth for the 32/33 bus limits bandwidth to 696Mb/s. When the SLAAC1V's 66MHz PCI interface becomes operational, this will double the bandwidth.

In addition we have compared wall clock time between our software/hardware granidt approach vs. snort 1.8. For our experiments, we used a 733 MHz Pentium PIII with Linux 2.4.7-10 Operating System (non-SMP kernel). We measured approximately 24.9X speedup of granidt over snort using Match Vector processing in software. Compared to a 1GHz PowerPC G4 running snort, our hardware/software system was 8.9X the speed of snort on the PPC. For these experiments, we used the Lincoln Labs Intrusion Detection data ([3]).

5 Conclusions

In this paper, we have described granidt, a software/hardware method for processing network packets. Our approach uses the same interface as the public domain snort tool, and exploits reconfigurable hardware to accelerate IP header and content matching. Our circuits operate at 66 MHz, giving 2 Gb/s bandwidth through the hardware. Granidt achieves 24.9X over snort on the same input data.

Our future work is directed at extending the granidt capabilities to process messages rather than individual packets and to increase to Gigabyte rates.

References

[1] William Cheswick and Steven Bellovin. *Firewalls and Internet Security*. Addison-Wesley, 1994.

[2] R. Franklin et al. Assisting network intrusion detection with reconfigurable hardware. *IEEE FCCM 2002*, 2002.

[3] Joshua W. Haines, Richard P. Lippmann, David J. Fried, et al. 1999 darpa intrusion detection system evaluation: Design and procedures. *MIT Lincoln Laboratory Technical Report*, 2001.

[4] Steven McCanne and Van Jacobson. The BSD packet filter: A new architecture for user-level packet capture. In *USENIX Winter*, pages 259–270, 1993.

[5] J. McHenry et al. An fpga-based co-processor for atm firewalls. *IEEE FCCM 2002*, 1997.

[6] IntruVert Networks. www.intruvert.com. 2002.

[7] Martin Roesch. Snort: The open source network intrusion detection system. *www.snort.org*, 2002.

[8] USC/ISI. Grip project. *www.east.isi.edu/projects/GRIP*, 2002.

[9] USC/ISI. Slaac project. *www.east.isi.edu/projects/SLAAC*, 2002.

Fast SiGe HBT BiCMOS FPGAs with New Architecture and Power Saving Techniques

Kuan Zhou*[1], Channakeshav*[1], Jong-Ru Guo[1], Chao You[1], Bryan S. Goda[2], Russell P. Kraft[1], and John F. McDonald[1]

[1] Rensselaer Polytechnic Institute, Troy, NY 12180, USA
{zhouk, chann}@rpi.edu, mcdonald@unix.cie.rpi.edu
[2] US Military Academy, West Point, NY 10996, USA
db9416@exmail.usma.army.mil

Abstract. Field Programmable Gate Arrays (FPGAs) have always been used for applications like signal processing, rapid prototyping etc. With the advent of SiGe HBT devices, FPGAs have found new applications in high-speed digital-system design. Since SiGe HBTs can be used along with CMOS, it has made SiGe devices very popular. This paper elaborates new ideas in designing high-speed SiGe BiCMOS FPGAs. The architecture is based on Xilinx 6200. The paper explains new methods to cut down the number of trees in the circuit. Selective tree shutdown has been used to reduce power consumption. A new decoding logic has been developed where the address and data lines are shared. These ideas have improved the performance of SiGe FPGAs. The operating frequencies of the new Configuration Logic Block (CLB) is in the range of 1-20 GHz.

1 Introduction

Field programmable Gate Arrays (FPGAs) have gained more and more popularity. An FPGA consists of multiple copies of a basic programmable logic element or cell. Logic cells are arranged in a column or matrix on the chip. To perform more complex operations, logic cells can be automatically connected to other logic elements on the chip using a programmable interconnection network. The operating speeds of current CMOS FPGAs are around 70-250 MHz. These slow operating speeds prevent their use in high-speed digital system applications. In order to achieve higher speeds, we design FPGAs using Silicon Germanium (SiGe) Heterojunction Bipolar Transistors (HBTs). These are high speed transistors with cutoff frequencies around 50 GHz [1].

High speed FPGAs find applications in many research and commercial fields such as Digital Signal Processing, where digital filters need fast multipliers, adders, subtractors, flip-flops etc [2]. They can also be used in applications which involve high-speed broadband networks [3], high-speed inline processing, rapid prototyping of microprocessors and in the area of image recognition.

---

* Both the authors have equal contribution to this paper.

M. Glesner, P. Zipf, and M. Renovell (Eds.): FPL 2002, LNCS 2438, pp. 414–423, 2002.

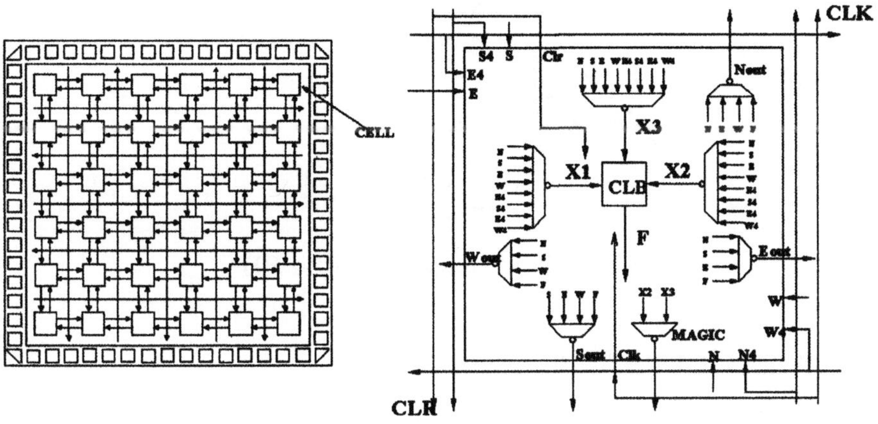

Fig. 1. (a) Top level architecture of the SiGe FPGA (b) Schematic of a logic cell - CLB + Routing Multiplexers

The top-level architecture of a SiGe FPGA is shown in Fig. 1(a). The block diagram of a single logic cell is shown in Fig. 1(b). It consists of a Configuration Logic Block (CLB) and routing multiplexers [4]. This paper describes SiGe FPGA design (with new features) which is bitwise compatible with Xilinx 6200 architecture. Changes have been made to make it work optimally in the design environment. Inspite of operating at high frequencies, the switching noise is less because Current Mode Logic (CML) has been selected for the logic cell design. All the signal lines are differential.

2 The SiGe HBT Structure and Its Advantages

We live in a "silicon world". Currently there is no semiconductor as mature as Si. Si may be an ideal semiconductor for fabrication but is hardly ideal from a device designer's point of view. It doesn't have the advantages offered by some HBTs designed using compound semiconductors. In order to achieve an improved performance a small quantity of Germanium (Ge) is added to the base of a bipolar junction transistor. The Ge mole fraction varies linearly from 3-8% in the base region. From Fig. 2, it can be seen that there exists a drift field in the base, which aids the faster movement of minority carriers. This reduces the base transit time and hence increases the cutoff frequency. SiGe HBT and Si CMOS can be grown over the same substrate and this technology is referred to as BiCMOS technology. The high current gain and low input capacitance of bipolar transistors makes it an attractive replacement for CMOS in some high performance applications. SiGe HBT is by far the most mature Si-based bandgap engineered electronic device [5]. Due to all these advantages, we chose the SiGe 5HP technology (provided by IBM) for our FPGA design.

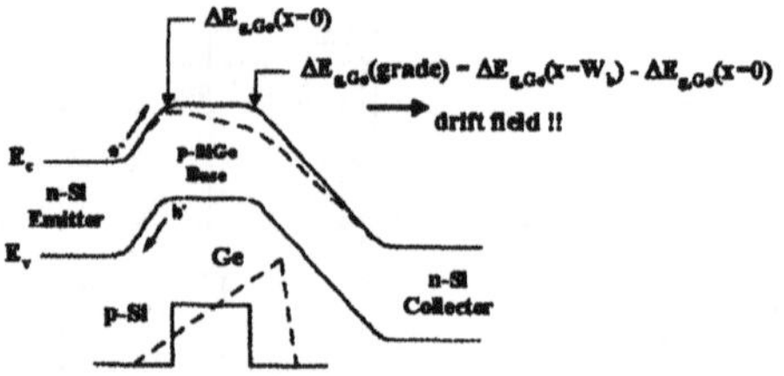

Fig. 2. Band Diagram of SiGe HBT

3 Design Description

Changes from the original Xilinx 6200 design were required to increase the clock rate and improve the flexibility in configuration storage. A fast switching logic design scheme that uses differential and 250 mV peak-to-peak signals was found to be appropriate (CML).

3.1 Current Mode Logic

CML is very similar to Emitter Coupled Logic (ECL). The only difference being that differential pairs are used for all signals and there is no need for a reference voltage. Fig. 3 shows a simple CML buffer with the input and output waveforms [6]. The rise and fall times of this buffer are 19.16 ps and 14.05 ps respectively. The total current is maintained constant using a Widlar current mirror at the bottom of the tree structure. The current can flow through any of the branches of the tree. There can be 3 transistors in every branch of the tree. Therefore there should be 3 levels of logic, (0 to -0.25 V), (-0.95 to -1.2 V) and (-1.9 to -2.15 V) (Power supply is 0 and -3.4 V).

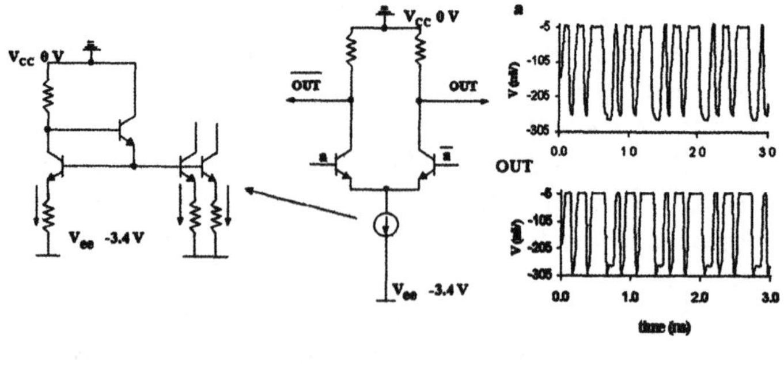

Fig. 3. A CML buffer with input and output waveforms

3.2 Power Saving Techniques

In CML designs, there is a constant current flowing in all the trees, so there is always a constant power dissipation even if a tree is not being used. So power saving techniques play an important role in all CML designs. Each logic cell has a combinational part and a sequential part. A cell can be programmed to be either combinational or sequential. So the trees which are not being used must be shut down. Fig. 4(a) shows the circuit for implementing this power saving mechanism.

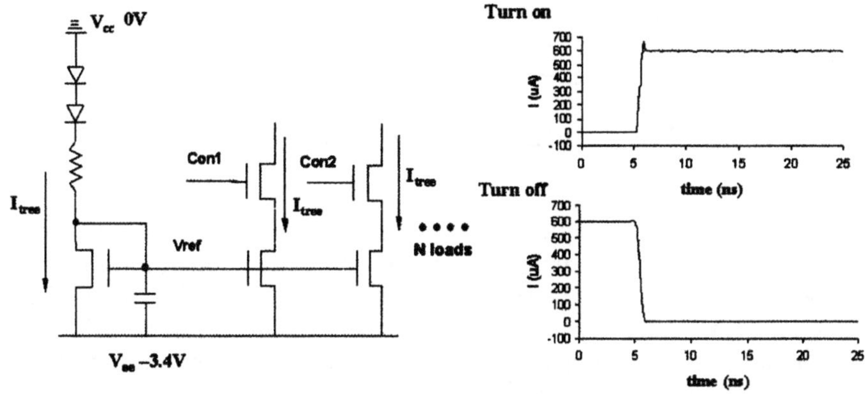

Fig. 4. (a) CML tree structure with control bits to save power and with an improvised current mirror (b) Current response of the tree structure when the control bit is switched

There is an additional NMOS device in the tree structure which is controlled by a configuration memory bit. This NMOS device conducts only when the tree is being used, otherwise it is switched off. The routing multiplexers can also be shutdown by this mechanism. The control bit can be programmed initially or it can also be programmed during run-time. Fig. 4(b) shows the response of a tree when the control bit is switched. The switching speed is very high and is in the order of 400 ps. The Widlar current mirror shown in Fig. 3 has been replaced by a NMOS current mirror. Since all the devices are NMOSFETs, this current mirror is able to maintain a constant current in more trees than a Widlar current mirror. The MOS current mirror is able to drive more than 25 loads which is surely an advantage.

3.3 The CLB Structure

Fig. 5 shows the CLB structure in Xilinx 6200. There are 2 paths in the structure. They are,

1. The sequential path that passes through the input multiplexers and then through the flip-flop.
2. The combinational path that involves only the input multiplexers.

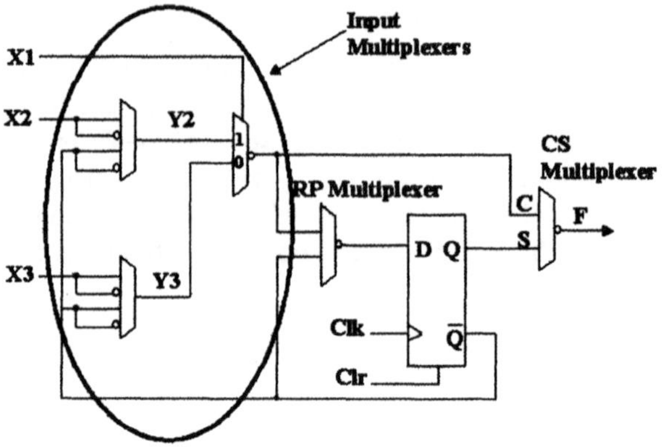

Fig. 5. Original Xilinx 6200 structure [4]

The Chip Select (CS) multiplexer selects the path based on the programming. The select bits for all the multiplexers come from the configuration memory. The original structure has been modified to make it suitable for CML. The objective is to achieve the same logic using lesser number of trees in order to reduce the power and propagation delay. A simple implementation would be to design each multiplexer separately and then join them. The power dissipation in such an implementation is large. Fig. 6 shows the redesigned structure. Since

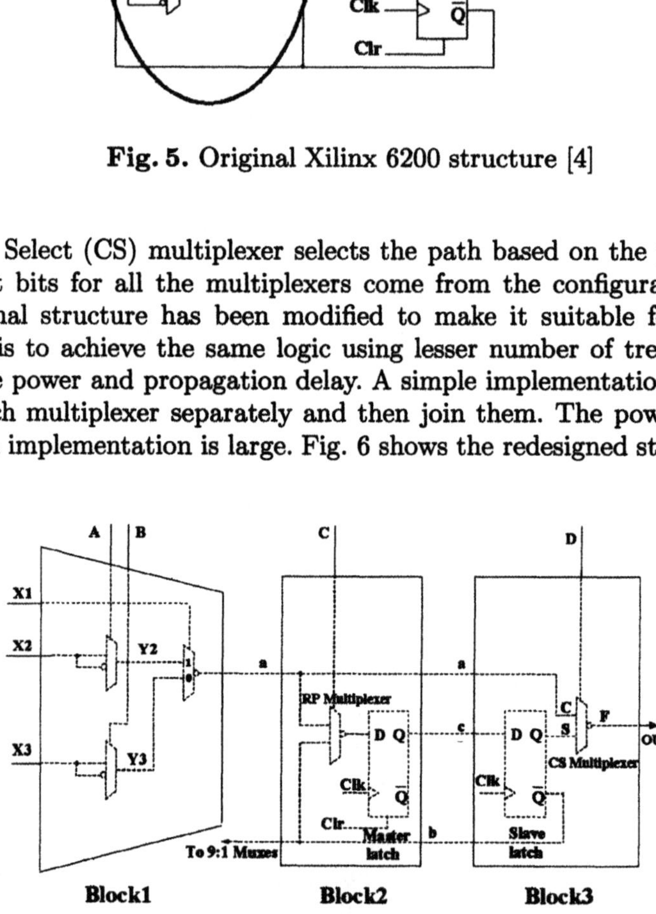

Fig. 6. Redesigned CLB structure

this is already a fast FPGA, the fast logic present in Xilinx 6200 is redundant. Hence, there is no feedback from $\bar{Q}$ in Block3 to Block1. This structure can be implemented in just 5 trees (3-logic with 2-emitter followers), whereas the original structure required 11 trees. This 55% reduction in the number of trees leads to at least a 55% reduction in power dissipation. Fig. 7 shows the schematics of all the three blocks. Since the number of trees in both the combinational and sequential paths have been reduced, the propagation delay is also reduced.

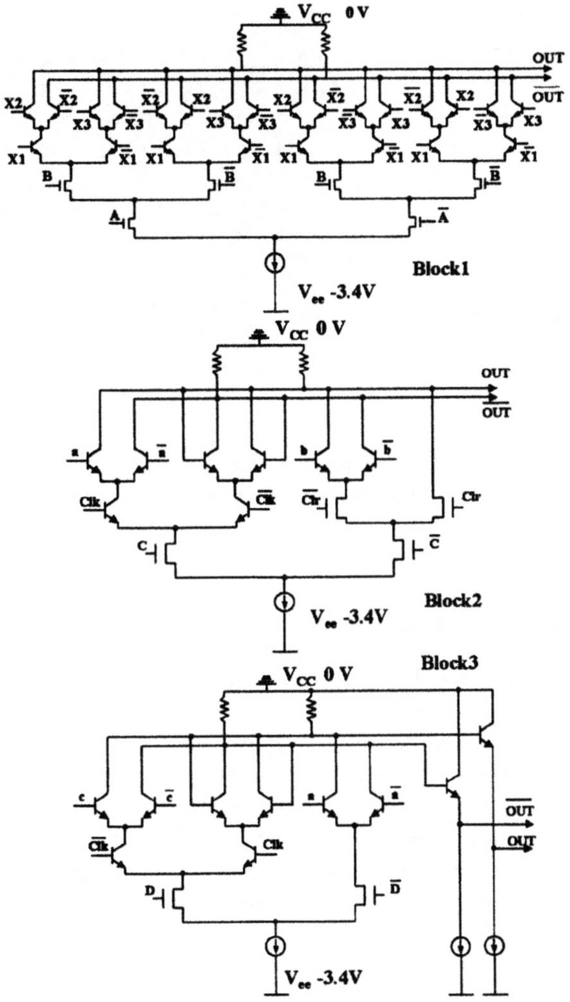

Fig. 7. Schematic of all the three blocks in the new structure

Fig. 8(a) shows the waveforms obtained from the new CLB architecture. The propagation delay for the earlier CLB was 100 ps [7] and that of the new CLB is around 52 ps. The new architecture has better performance in terms of speed and power. Fig. 8(b) shows the layout of the redesigned CLB.

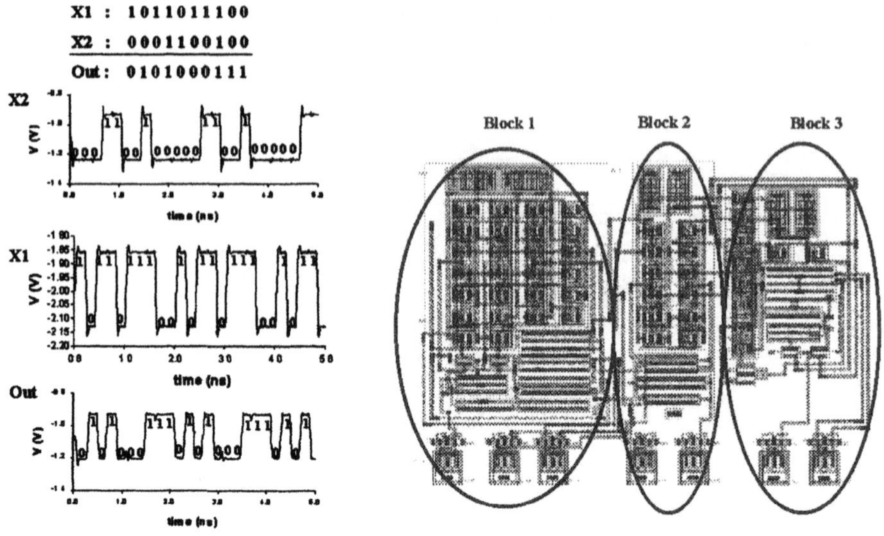

Fig. 8. (a) Input and Output waveforms from new CLB architecture - XNOR functionality has been implemented (b) Layout of the new CLB (79 μm $\times$ 126 μm)

3.4 Configuration Memory

The configuration memory is similar to the previous generation SiGe FPGA [7] [8] [9]. The FPGA has 2 memory planes for the configuration data. Each memory plane contains a different configuration for the FPGA as well as the state of the latch in the CLB. The CLB can change functionality by loading in a different set of configuration bits. The only difference in the new design is that a CMOS to CML buffer interface is not required because a differential SRAM is being used. Each memory plane has 32-bits to program the logic cell (18-bits for Routing multiplexers, 4-bits for CLB functionality and 10-bits for selective tree shutdown).

3.5 X Pattern Decoding

A CAD software generates the binary data to configure the FPGA. This configuration is stored into the memory, which in turn makes every cell behave as desired. Unless an efficient decoding scheme is in place, programming may result in many long address and data lines. Long address/data lines will increase congestion. Fig. 9 shows a new decoding scheme which is more symmetric and has shared address and data lines. For a 4 $\times$ 4 FPGA design in Fig. 9(a), there is one main-decoder and four sub-decoders. When the global enable line is set, the main decoder enables one of the sub-decoders based on the least significant 2-bits of the control signals. The enabled sub-decoder in turn enables one of

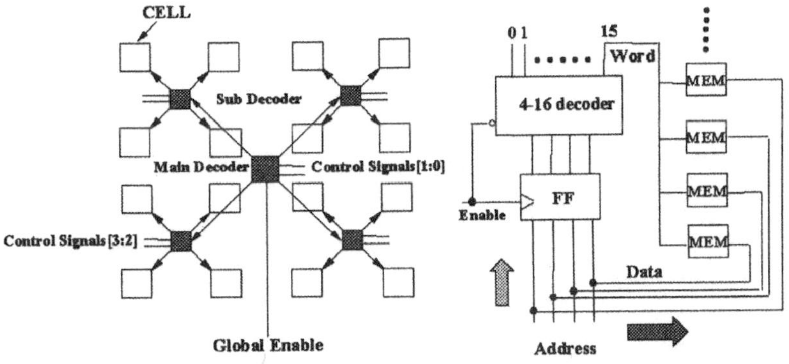

Fig. 9. (a) X-pattern decoding (b) Cell decoder structure inside a single cell

the cell decoders based on the most significant 2-bits of the control signals. The cell whose decoder is enabled will get programmed by the data coming on the address/data lines. This is shown in Fig. 9(b). There are four address/data lines reaching each cell decoder. The address of the memory location into which the data has to be written is sent first over the address/data bus. The address is registered by the rising edge of the enable signal. Each decoded address enables 4 SRAMs simultaneously. Next, the data which is to be written into the 4 enabled SRAMs is sent over the shared bus. By this method, it is possible to write into $2^4 * 4 = 64$ memory locations by using only 4 lines. By using a straightforward decoding scheme, it requires 6 address lines and 1 data line. The new decoding scheme reduces the number of lines. This reduction is significant because all the address/data lines go through all the logic cells in the FPGA. Moreover, the normal decoding scheme would require a 6-64 decoder for each cell, which is pretty complex. Apart from this, there are 64 lines going into the memory, which makes the layout more dense. The decoding logic has been implemented in CMOS.

4 Test Structures

Fig. 10 shows the testing mechanism. The Linear Frequency Shift Register (LFSR) generates random bit patterns which are given as an input to the CLB i.e. X1, X2 and X3. A Voltage Controlled Oscillator (VCO) is used to generate varying frequency clock which is given to the clock input of the CLB. This is used for testing the sequential path in the CLB. The CLB may be programmed to any desired function by writing the correct bits into the configuration memory.

5 Performance

The performance for major parts of the SiGe FPGA have been summarized in Table 1. It is obvious from the table that this is a very high speed FPGA with

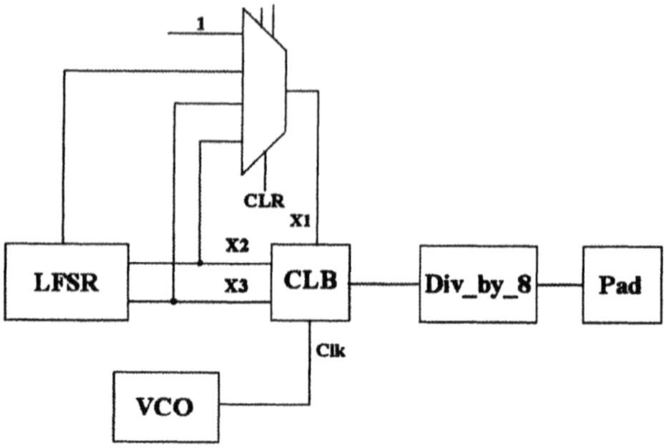

Fig. 10. Test Structure

very less propagation delay. The main consideration for a bipolar FPGA is power dissipation. By using new strategies, which were discussed earlier, up to 63% of the power can be conserved. According to simulations, the operating frequency of the CLB is 6.8 GHz, which is higher than the 5.1 GHz reported in [8].

Table 1. SiGe HBT FPGA performance at 25°C under no load

Circuit type	Buffer	2-level CML gate	CLB
Propagation delay(ps)	13	21	52
Rise time(ps)	19.16	29	43.89
Fall time(ps)	14.05	12.5	29.49
Number of trees	1	1	3-seq. (2-comb.)
Current(mA)	0.6	0.6	1.8-seq. (1.2-comb.)
Power(mW)	2.04	2.04	6.12-seq. (4.08-comb.)

6 Conclusion

Demand for high-speed FPGAs is surely on a rise. This demand can be met only by using the latest devices which offer speed as well as easy processing. SiGe is the obvious solution. The long turn-around time faced by high-speed circuits can now be reduced by using SiGe FPGAs for prototyping. The new FPGA design effectively combines high-speed SiGe with low-power CMOS. Hence, it has a better performance in terms of speed and power. New ideas like "selective tree shutdown" and "reduction in number of trees" will go a long way in reducing power. The main argument given against CML is power consumption. As new circuits using BiCMOS technology start emerging, power consumption will surely be reduced. New techniques to conserve power are being studied by our group. The number of global lines have been reduced by the new decoding scheme. The idea of sharing some signal lines with the data/address lines is being explored.

References

1. 'SiGeHP (BiCMOS 5HP) Design Manual', IBM, May 2001.
2. Herzen, B.: 'Signal Processing at 250 MHz Using High-Performance FPGAs', IEEE Transactions on VLSI Systems, Vol. 6, No. 2, June 1998, 238-246.
3. McHenry, J., Dowd, P., et al.: 'An FPGA-Based Coprocessor for ATM Firewalls', IEEE Symposium on FPGAs for Custom Computing Machines, April 1997, Napa, CA, 30-39.
4. 'Xilinx Series 6000 User Guide', Xilinx Inc. San Jose, CA., 1997.
5. Cressler, J.: 'SiGe HBT Technology: A new Contender for Si-Based RF and Microwave Circuit Applications', IEEE Transactions on Microwave Theory and techniques, Vol. 46, No. 5, May 1998, 572-589.
6. Greub, H., McDonald, J., Yamaguchi, T.: 'High Performance Standard Cell Library and Modeling Technique for Differential Advanced Bipolar Current Tree Logic', IEEE Journal of Solid-State Circuits, Vol. 26, No. 5, May 1991, 749-762.
7. Goda, B., McDonald, J., Carlough, S., Krawczyk, T., Kraft, R.: 'SiGe HBT BiCMOS for fast reconfigurable computing', IEE Proceedings of Computers and Digital Techniques, Vol. 147, No. 3, May 2000, 189-194
8. Goda, B., McDonald, J., Kraft, R., Carlough, S., Kwawczyk, T.: 'Gigahetz Reconfigurable Computing using SiGe HBT BiCMOS FPGAs', International Conference on Field Programmable Logic and Applications, 2001.
9. Weste, N., Eshraghian, K.: 'Principles of CMOS VLSI Design: A Systems Perspective', 2nd Edition, Addison Wesley, Oct. 1994.

Field–Programmable Analog Arrays: A Floating–Gate Approach

Tyson S. Hall, Paul Hasler, and David V. Anderson

Georgia Institute of Technology, Atlanta, GA 30332-0250

Abstract. Floating-gate analog circuits are being used to implement advanced signal processing functions and are very useful for processing analog signals prior to analog to digital conversion. We present an architecture analogous to FPGA architectures for rapid prototyping of analog signal processing systems. These systems go beyond simple programmable amplifiers and filters to include programmable and adaptive filters, multipliers, gains, winner-take-all circuits, and matrix–array signal operations. We discuss architecture as well as details such as switching characteristics and interfacing to digital circuits or FPGAs.

1 Introduction

For creating extremely low-power signal processing systems, it is often necessary to implement substantial portions of the processing in analog circuits [1]. The process of designing, fabricating, and testing an analog chip requires certain expertise and is often long and expensive. The process is not unlike designing digital ASICs (application specific integrated circuits) except there are fewer tools and libraries available to the designer. The difficulties in digital ASIC design are largely ameliorated by using FPGAs that, for digital circuits, provide a fast, simple way to implement, test, and eventually compile custom circuits.

Field-programmable digital circuits have made a large impact on the development of custom digital chips by enabling a designer to try custom designs on easily reconfigurable hardware. These integrated circuits have programmable logic elements and programmable interconnects between the logic elements. Using these programmable devices greatly reduce the design time and cost for custom circuits.

Programmable floating–gate analog devices have benefits and design similar to FPGAs. Like FPGAs, the analog arrays, dubbed field–programmable analog arrays or FPAAs, are not optimal for all solutions. They are, however, very useful for many situations, and a solution can be found for many problems not requiring full functionality.

Relative to custom-designed analog circuits, a design implemented on an FPAA results in higher parasitics as well as increased die area for a given design; therefore, the design always possesses some inefficiencies (measured in lower bandwidth and higher consumed power). On the other hand, since analog circuit design is often time-consuming, these adverse tradeoffs are well balanced by decreased time to market.

M. Glesner, P. Zipf, and M. Renovell (Eds.): FPL 2002, LNCS 2438, pp. 424–433, 2002.

The proposed FPAA chips are mixed-mode chips. While the computational and switching logic is all based on analog floating-gate transistors, the programming control and interface logic to the analog devices is all digital.

Some related devices have been developed for analog circuit design, but historically, these devices have very few programmable elements and limited interconnect capabilities, making them limited in their usefulness and versatility. Currently available commercial and academic FPAAs are typically based on op-amp circuits with only relatively few op-amps per chip [2, 3, 4, 5, 6, 7, 8, 9].

2 Power and Resolution in Analog Signal Processing

As embedded computing becomes mainstream, a significant market has emerged for feature–rich signal processing devices that consume very little power. While digital processors can perform the desired functions, there are many cases where an analog design could offer the same functionality at a fraction of the power required for the digital solution. For example, the analog multiplier presented later in this paper requires only two floating-gate transistors and two small DIBL transistors operating in the subthreshold region. Kucic, et. al. [10] show that this kind of multiplier can easily provide 10 bits of resolution. Now, consider a digital 10-bit multiplier requiring thousands of transistors. In this case, the power savings of the analog version are at least three orders of magnitude over the digital implementation.

Another primary concern in signal processing is the resolution. Sarpeskar [11] showed that an analog computation can have significant advantages over a digital solution when the resolution of the inputs is around 10 bits or less. Experiments with the floating-gate devices done at the Goergia Institute of Technology have confirmed that analog implementations work well within this resolution range.

3 Floating-Gate Transistors

The floating-gate transistors used in these FPAAs are standard pFET devices whose gate terminals are not connected to signals except through capacitors (e.g., no DC path to a fixed potential) [12]. Because the gate terminal is well insulated from external signals, it can maintain a permanent charge, and thus, it is an analog memory cell similar to an EEPROM cell. With a floating gate, the current through the pFET channel is dependent on the charge of the floating-gate node. By using hot-electron injection to decrease the charge on the floating-gate node and electron tunneling to increase the charge on the floating-gate node, the current flow through the pFET channel can be accurately controlled [12, 10].

3.1 Floating-Gate Switches

Using a floating-gate transistor as a switch requires that the device be turned "on" or turn "off." Ideally, the "on" state corresponds to the free flow of current

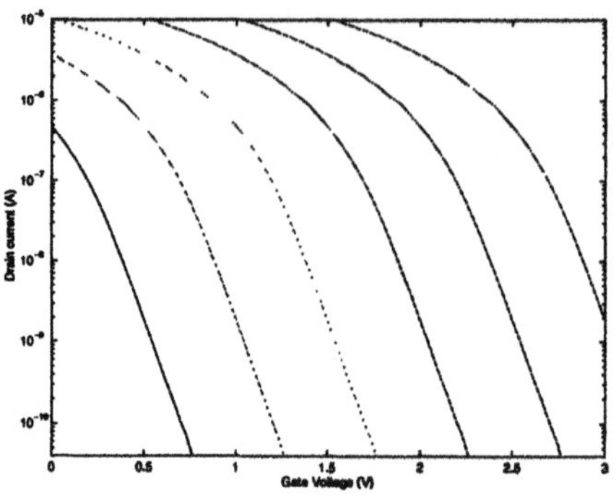

(a)

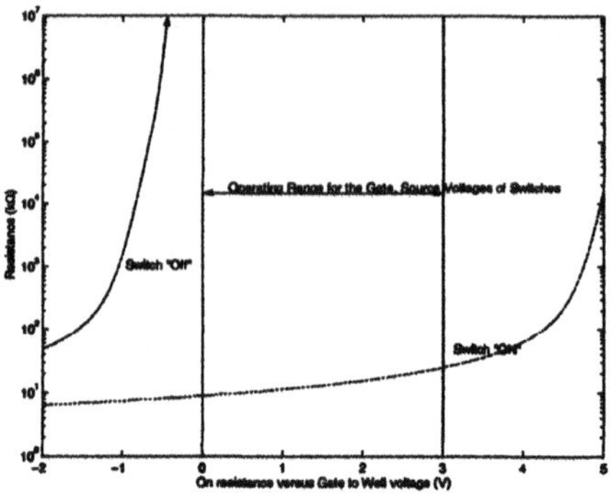

(b)

Fig. 1. (a) This is a current–voltage plot of a single floating–gate transistor programmed to different levels of floating–gate charge. The floating–gate transistors can be programmed over a wide range of currents. (b) This plot shows the resistance versus gate voltage for a single floating–gate transistor programed to the "on" level and to the "off" level.

through the device or equivalently, zero impedance between the source and the drain. Likewise, the "off" state is characterized by zero current flowing through the device – an infinite impendance between the source and the drain nodes. A floating-gate transistor, however, will not act as a perfect switch. The "on" state will be characterized by an impedance greater than zero, and the "off" state will have an impedance less than infinity. Therefore, the quality of a floating-gate transistor as a switch will be determined by measuring the "on" and "off" impedances.

The quality of the switches is an important factor in determining the final architecture. The main concern is that routing a signal through multiple switches could degragate data as the cummulative impedance of the switches becomes prohibitive.

The impedance of the floating-gate transistor is a function of the charge on the floating-gate node allowing it to be set using hot-electron injection and electron tunneling. Figure 1(a) shows the relative I-V curves for a floating-gate transistor as it is programmed from "off" to "on." Ideally, each transistor would be programmed to the extreme ends of the graph, but programming floating-gate transistors is a time-comsuming task. The desired quality of the switch will have to be choosen with regard to the time it will take to program the device.

Choosing a reasonable time scale for programming leads to a compromise in the quality of the switch.. Also, note that the operating voltage of the gate node is not fixed. Due to the parasitic capacitances between the gate and drain/source nodes, the gate voltage–and thus the switch's impedance–will vary as a function of the signal current. This variation must be minimized. The final selection of "on" and "off" impedances is shown in Figure 1(b). This choice takes into account the trade-offs between programming time and switch quality.

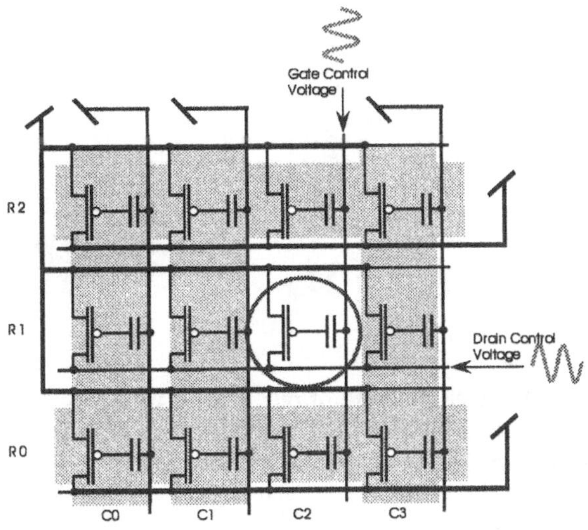

Fig. 2. By selectively setting the gate and drain voltages of the columns and rows, a single floating–gate transistor can be programmed using hot-electron injection without affecting the neighboring devices.

3.2 Switch as Computational Element

When used as a switch, the floating-gate should be as transparent a part of the circuit as possible. However, Figure 1 shows that the floating-gate transistor can be used as an in-circuit element [13, 14]. By adjusting the charge on the floating-gate node between the extremes used for "on" and "off", the impedance of the switch can be varied over several orders of magnitude.

Using the floating-gate switches as in-circuit elements allows for a very compact architecture. The physical area needed for the CABs is reduced greatly, because resistors, which consume relatively large amounts of space on CMOS processes, are not needed as separate components. By reducing the number of individual circuit elements, signal routing is simplified, while not loosing functionality.

4 Programmability

By using floating-gate devices as the only programmable element on the chip, configuring the chip is greatly simplified. Additionally, all of the floating–gate transistors are clustered together to aid in the programming logic and signal routing. Decoders on the periphery of the circuit are connected to the drain, source, and gate (through a capacitor) terminals of the floating-gate matrix. During programming mode, these decoders allow each floating-gate transistor to be individually programmed using hot-electron injection (see Figure 2) [10].

Part of our previous effort was to develop a systematic method for programming arrays of floating-gate transistors [10, 13, 15]. A microprocessor-based board has been built to interface a PC to these analog floating-gate arrays for the purposes of programming and testing. With a PC controlling the programming of these devices, the details of using hot-electron injection and tunneling to

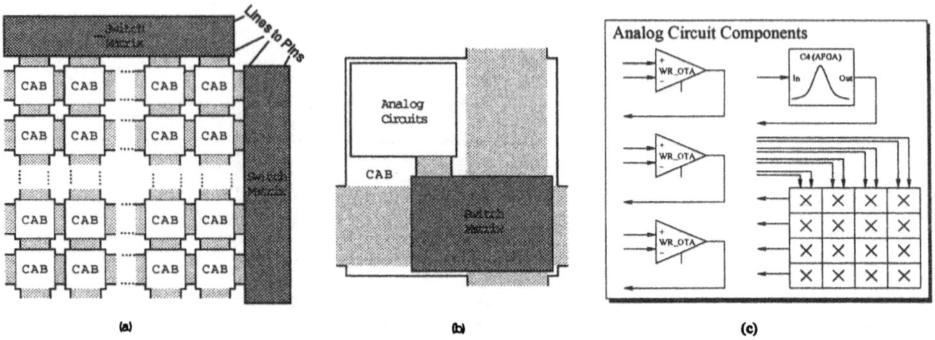

Fig. 3. Block diagram of our generic FPAA chip. (a) Architecture diagram of analog programmable computing blocks. Future FPAAs will have 100 or more Computational Analog Blocks (CAB) each with 23 ports to the mesh switching matrix. (b) Signal flow in a single CAB. (c) Each Computational Analog Block (CAB) has a four-by-four matrix multiplier, three wide-range operational transconductance amplifiers (OTAs), and a capcatively coupled current conveyor (C4). The input and output signals shown in this figure are routed to the rows of the switch matrix.

program individual floating-gate switches have been abstracted away from the end-user. The programming algorithms have been optimized for accuracy and speed, while giving the end-user an easy-to-use interface for configuring arrays of floating-gate devices.

5 FPAA Architecture

Large signal processing systems will require a chip with many (100 or more) computational analog blocks (CABs) on it. However, before such a chip can be successfully designed, a number of implementation details need to be tested on a smaller scale. Specifically, the switching characteristics of floating-gate transistors have not been studied in detail before.

We have developed RASP (Reconfigurable Analog Signal Processor) as a testbed integrated circuit (IC) to study the floating-gate switches, and the interaction between the CAB components and the switch matrix. It was determined that two CABs would be adequate for a first run. Once favorable results are shown on RASP, a larger chip will be fabricated by replicating the basic blocks found on this chip.

5.1 CABs

The computational logic is organized into a compact computational analog block (CAB) providing a naturally scalable architecture. CABs can be tiled across the chip with busses and local interconnects in-between as shown in Figure 3.

Each CAB is comprised of components critical to signal processing applications including a four-by-four matrix-vector multiplier, three wide-range operational transconductance amplifiers (OTAs), and a transistor-only version of the autozeroing floating-gate amplifier (AFGA) or capacitively coupled current conveyor (C4) [16]. The CAB architecture is shown in Figure 3(c).

5.2 Analog Circuit Components

Selecting the types of analog components to include in a general-purpose FPAA is a difficult task. To be as universal as possible, one must consider adding a number of basic linear and nonlinear functions including integration, summation, gain amplification, logarithmic and exponential operations, and more [17]. Because these elements are so basic, constructing larger systems can become very complex because of the routing resources required. Also, as discussed earlier, as the number of switches involved in a circuit increases the cummulative effects of the switches on the circuit may seriously degrade the performance and/or results. To mitigate these challenges, RASP was constrained to be a signal-processing FPAA with specific functions such as adaptive filtering and Fourier (frequency domain) processing in mind. A limited number of basic elements were also included for completeness; however, the focus was placed on selecting an appropriate mix of higher-level components that could facilitate the prototyping of a wide range of problems.

Basic Analog Elements The basic analog functions such as summation, integration, and gain amplification can be included in the FPAA with only a few analog components. In the case of summation, only the switch matrix is needed. Figure 4a shows that if the input signals are currents, summation is achieved by simply connecting the input signals together (Kirchoff's current law).

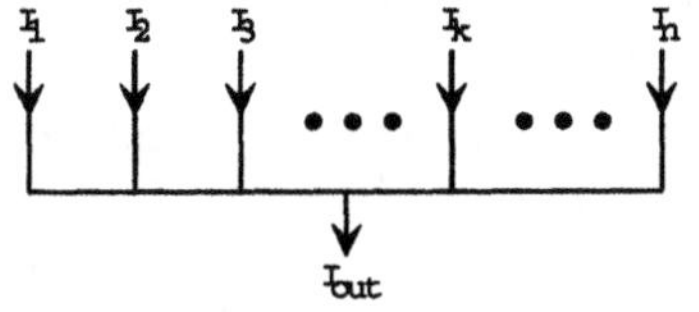

$$I_{out} = \sum_{k=1}^{N} I_k$$

Fig. 4. The output current of a node is equal to the sum of the input currents (Kirchoff's current law).

By adding several configurable operational transductance amplifiers (OTAs) to each CAB, one can configure the FPAA to perform integration, differentiation, gain amplification and more. Also, by including op-amps in the computational logic, RASP can compete with current commercial offerings that are based solely on programmable op-amps.

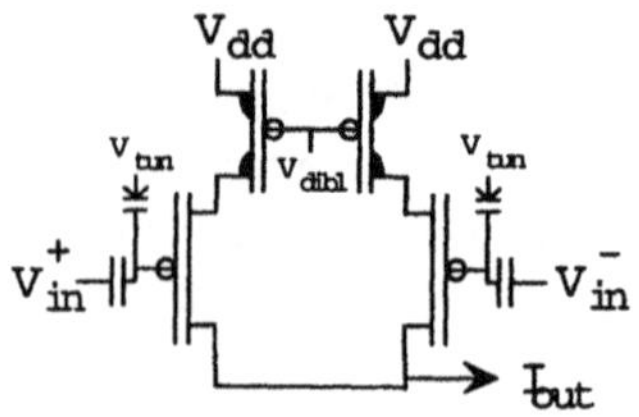

$$I_{out} = I_{bias} + W\left(V_{in}^{+} - V_{in}^{+}\right)$$

Fig. 5. Multiplication of a signed (differential) input by a stored weight can be achieved using two floating-gate transistors. Since the weight is stored as the charge of the floating-gate node it is both programmble and adaptable.

Matrix-Vector Multiplication Multiplication is an important element in many signal processing applications. Figure 5 shows a basic multiplier using two floating-gate transistors. The differential voltage input allows signed numbers to be represented. The multiplier's functionality can be extended by cascading them together to form a matrix-vector multiplier. Each CAB on RASP has a four-by-four matrix multiplier in which four signed (differential) inputs are mutliplied by a four-by-four matrix of programmable weights. Of course, by setting the appropriate weights to zero a single multipy, or a four-by-one, four-by-two, or four-by-three matrix-vector multiply can also be accomplished.

Filtering and Fourier Processing In the near future, FPAA devices based the Matix II's floating-gate architecture will have as many as 100 or more CABs on a single chip. At this level of complexity a number of interesting signal processing systems can be implemented using a Fourier processor. An analog Fourier processor decomposes an incoming signal into its frequency components (sub–bands). Each sub–band is then operated on before reconstructing the output signal by summing the sub–bands together. This is analagous to digitally taking an FFT, operating on each frequency component, and then taking an IFT to generate the time-domain output signal.

In RASP, the frequency decomposition is done by using capacitively coupled current conveyor (C4) circuits to band-pass filter the incoming signal. A C4 circuit is built using two floating-gate transistors and several capacitors as shown in [18, 10]. This method allows the band-pass filters to be programmbly placed at the desired frequencies (e.g., some applications prefer linear spacing while others prefer logarithmic spacing of the sub–bands). When used in combination with the floating-gate multiplier, a wide range of filters, including adaptive filters, can be achieved [12].

5.3 Switch Matrix

RASP has one 16 by 64 switching matrix that provides local interconnects between the two CABs and connections to the external input/output signal lines.

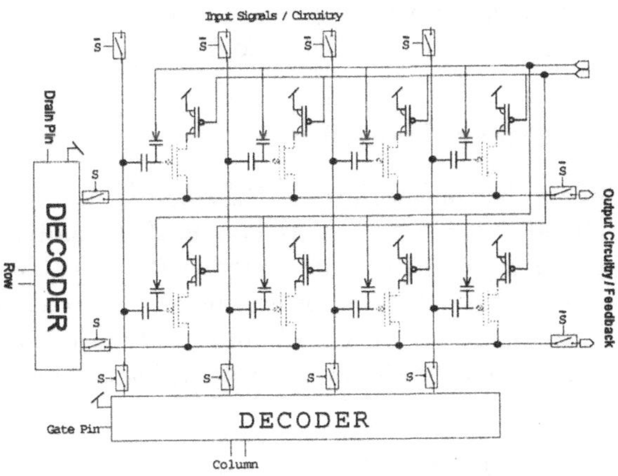

Fig. 6. The switching matrix is built with floating-gate transistors. The charge of the floating-gate node can be adjusted to allow current to flow through the channel ("on") or to restrict current flow ("off"). When in programming mode, T gates connect the floating-gate transistors to the decoders, and when in operational mode, the decoders are unconnected and the output signals are switched on.

The switching matrix uses floating-gate transistors as the switches as shown in Figure 6.

The digital decoders on the outside of the the switch matrix provide access to the individual floating-gate transistors for programming. After programming is complete the decoders are disconnected (using t-gate switches) and external bus lines are connected to start the operation of the chip.

The source lines of the 16 floating-gate switches in each row are connected together; likewise, the drain lines of the 64 floating-gate switches in each column are tied together. Programming a switch to "on" allows current to flow in the source-drain channel and connects a row with a column. Programming a switch to "off" restricts the current flow in the channel creating a very high impedance betweenthe row and column.

The input/output signals from each CAB are connected to the sources nodes of the floating-gate switches. The drain nodes (columns) are either connected to external busses or are used for internal connections only. By doing this, any input/output signal from the CABs can be connected to an external bus by turning on one floating-gate switch. Similarly, it can be connected to another signal in the same CAB or to a signal in an adacent CAB by turning on two switches in the same column.

6 Digital Control and Interface

Today, signal processing is a largely digital domain. Similarly, even if a given algorithm can be implemented in analog alone, the results will more than likely need to be accessed by a digital processor. To make this technology more flexible and more useful to signal processing engineers, this FPAA has a completely digital interface. From programming to operation, all communication to and from these FPAAs is digital. On-chip analog-commercial and academic settingsto-digital (A/D) and digital-to-analog (D/A) converters provide the domain conversions for input and output signals. Likewise, programming operations are turned on and off using digital control logic.

6.1 System Integration

With a digital interface, FPAAs can be easily connected to FPGAs, PCs, and embedded devices such as handheld computers and cell phones. In this way, rapid prototyping of mixed-mode systems can easily be accomplished. A mixed-mode prototyping station is the natural outcome of this technology. A single board with both an FPAA and an FPGA mounted on it will be a significant advancement for the rapid prototyping of mixed-mode systems.

6.2 Programming

The programming of FPAAs is achieved through a digital interface. Digital switches control the tunneling and injection voltages and the digital decoders provide individual access to the floating-gate transistors. An on-chip, specialized A/D converter provides feedback to the programmer by outputting a digital signal with a pulse width that is proportional to the drain current of the floating-gate transistor currently being programmed. To avoid additional hardware on the prototyping station, the FPGA that is used to implement the digital part of the system in operational mode is used to implement the programming algorithms in configuration mode.

7 Conclusion

An FPAA architecture has been proposed for use in the rapid prototyping of analog signal processing. Programmable floating-gate transistors are used to provide both the switching logic and the computational elements. This results in a compact, expandable switch matrix design as well as a functionally rich compational analog block (CAB). FPAAs using this architecture will be albe to prototype complex signal processing systems including programmable and adaptive filters, multipliers, gain amplification, matrix–array signal operations, and Fourier processing.

References

[1] Paul Hasler and David V. Anderson, "Cooperative analog-digital signal processing," in *Proceedings of the IEEE International Conference on Acoustics, Speech, and Signal Processing*, Orlando, FL, May 2002, Invited Paper, *to appear.*

[2] Massimo A. Sivilotti, *Wiring Considerations in Analog VLSI Systems, with Application to Field-Programmable Networks (VLSI)*, Ph.D. thesis, California Institute of Technology, Pasadena, CA, 1991.

[3] K.F.E. Lee and P.G. Gulak, "A transconductor-based field-programmable analog array," in *ISSCC Digest of Technical Papers*, Feb. 1995, pp. 198–199.

[4] K.F.E. Lee and P.G. Gulak, "A cmos field-programmable analog array," in *ISSCC Digest of Technical Papers*, Feb. 1991, pp. 186–188.
[5] S.T. Chang, B.R. Hayes-Gill, and C.J. Paul, "Multi-function block for a switched current field programmable analog array," in *1996 Midwest Symposium on Circuits and Systems*, Aug. 1996.
[6] D. Anderson, C. Marcjan, D. Bersch, H. Anderson, P. Hu, O. Palusinski, D. Gettman, I. Macbeth, and A. Bratt, "A field programmable analog array and its application," in *CICC'97*, May 1997.
[7] Lattice Semiconductor Corporation, Hillsboro, OR, *ispPAC Overview*, Sept. 1999.
[8] X. Quan, S.H.K. Embabi, and E. Sanchez-Sinencio, "A current-mode based field programmable analog array architecture for signal processing applications," in *IEEE 1998 Custom Integrated Circuits Conference*, Santa Clara, CA, May 1998, pp. 277–280.
[9] Fast Analog Solutions, Ltd., Oldham, UK, *Totally re-configurable analog circuit–TRAC*, Mar. 1999, Issue 2.
[10] Matt Kucic, AiChen Low, Paul Hasler, and Joe Neff, "A programmable continuous-time floating-gate fourier processor," *IEEE Transactions on Circuits and Systems II*, vol. 48, no. 1, pp. 90–99, Jan. 2001.
[11] Rahul Sarpeshkar, *Efficient precise computation with noisy components: extrapolating from an electronic cochlea to the brain*, PhD thesis, California Institute of Technology, Pasadena, CA, 1997.
[12] P. Hasler, B. A. Minch, and C. Diorio, "Adaptive circuits using pfet floating-gate devices," in *Proceedings of the 20th Anniversary Conference on Advnaced Research in VLSI*, Atlanta, GA, March 1999, pp. 215–229.
[13] Matt Kucic, Paul Hasler, Jeff Dugger, and David V. Anderson, "Programmable and adaptive analog filters using arrays of floating-gate circuits," in *2001 Conference on Advanced Research in VLSI*, Erik Brunvand and Chris Myers, Eds. IEEE Computer Society, March 2001, pp. 148–162.
[14] P. Hasler and B. A. Minch, *Floating-gate Devices, Circuits, and Systems*, in press, 2002.
[15] P. Smith, M. Kucic, and P. Hasler, "Accurate programming of analog floating-gate arrays," in *Proceedings of the 2002 International Symposium on Circuits and Systems*, Phoenix, AZ, May May, p. to appear.
[16] P. Hasler, M. Kucic, and B. A. Minch, "A transistor-only circuit model of the autozeroing floating-gate amplifier," in *Midwest Conference on Circuits and Systems*, Las Cruces, NM, 1999.
[17] Sree Ganesan and Ranga Vemuri, "Technology mapping and retargeting for field–programmable analog arrays," in *DATE 2000 Proceedings: Design, Automation and Test in Europe Conference 2000*, Mar. 2000.
[18] P. Hasler, B. A. Minch, and C. Diorio, "An autozeroing floating-gate amplifier," *IEEE Transactions on Circuits and Systems II*, vol. 48, no. 1, pp. 74–82, Jan. 2001.

A Generalized Execution Model for Programming on Reconfigurable Architectures and an Architecture Supporting the Model

Kazuya Tanigawa[1], Tetsuo Hironaka[2], Akira Kojima[2], and Noriyoshi Yoshida[2]

[1] Graduate School of Information Sciences, Hiroshima City University
3-4-1, Ozuka-higashi, Asaminami-ku, Hiroshima 731-3194, JAPAN,
kazuya@csys.ce.hiroshima-cu.ac.jp
[2] Faculty of Information Sciences, Hiroshima City University

Abstract. In this paper, we consider the possibility of using a reconfigurable architecture as a general-purpose computer. Many reconfigurable architectures have been proposed. However, these architectures are hard to use as a general-purpose computer because their architectures have no explicit execution model for software developments. Therefore, in this paper, we propose an Ideal PARallel Structure (*I-PARS*) execution model. To make software developments easily, the program based on the *I-PARS* execution model has no limitation depending on the hardware structure of the processor based on any reconfigurable architectures. Also, we propose a *PARS* architecture to execute programs based on the *I-PARS* execution model effectively. Further, we implement a prototype processor based on the *PARS* architecture and estimated its performance. From the implementation and the estimation, we show the feasibility of programming on the *I-PARS* execution model and executing it on the *PARS* architecture.

1 Introduction

Reconfigurable architectures are focused to achieve high performance as special-purpose circuits with the advantage of ability to reconfigure the circuits by software at runtime. In this paper, we consider the possibility of using the reconfigurable architecture as a general-purpose computer, by extending the advantage of the architecture.

Many reconfigurable architectures such as MorphoSys[1], Garp[2] have been proposed in recent years. However, these architectures are difficult to use as a general-purpose computer because their architectures have no explicit execution model. This causes the following issues. 1) On programming, you always have to consider the limitation depending on the specific hardware structure (e.g. the number of function units), which causes difficulty of programming. 2) Therefore you have to re-develop the software whenever the detail structure of the architecture is changed. This means not only less portability but also difficulty on developing software assets for reconfigurable architectures.

M. Glesner, P. Zipf, and M. Renovell (Eds.): FPL 2002, LNCS 2438, pp. 434–443, 2002.

To solve these issues, PipeRench[3] has been working on hardware virtualization of the number of elements included in their hardware structure. However, the PipeRench mainly keeps its interests on the virtualization, not on providing a general execution model for programming on reconfigurable architectures. Therefore, in the PipeRench, software assets have been developed only for their specific architectures, not for other variations of reconfigurable architectures.

To enable developing software assets for variable architectures, SCORE[4] introduces not only virtualization but also model for programming. In the model of SCORE, programmers can use the unlimited memory space. However, the memory space is divided into fixed size memory block for execution on reconfigurable architectures, and only the partition of program are allowed to access the fixed size memory blocks, which causes unefficient execution in case of dealing large amount of data.

In our research, we have proposed an *I-PARS* (Ideal PARallel Structure) execution model [5]. As the *I-PARS* execution model is based on an ideal reconfigurable architecture, programs based on our model have no limitation depending on the hardware structure. Next, our model doesn't cause unefficient execution such as SCORE because our proposed architecture has only one memory with enough large size. In addition, the *I-PARS* execution model is a simple execution model, so we can convert the other execution model to the our proposal model easily. In fact, I-PARS execution model is a super set of SCORE's computation model.

Also, we have proposed a *PARS* architecture so that the processors based on the architecture can execute programs based on the *I-PARS* execution model [6]. The processor execute the programs by folding down the program to match the size of hardware structure of the processor. Moreover, we implement a prototype processor based on the *PARS* architecture and estimate its performance by using some benchmark programs.

The organization of this paper is as follows. Section 2 introduces the *I-PARS* execution model and Section 3 introduces the *PARS* architecture. In Section 4, we present results of performance estimation of the *PARS* architecture and give the conclusions in Section 5.

2 *I-PARS* Execution Model

2.1 Requirements

The required execution model has an ideal hardware structure of reconfigurable architectures for software programming and play a role of interface between software and hardware.

So the requirements are to satisfy the following two items.

- No limitation depending on the size of hardware to limit ease of software programming.
- No difficulty in implementing hardware which can support the execution of the program based on the model.

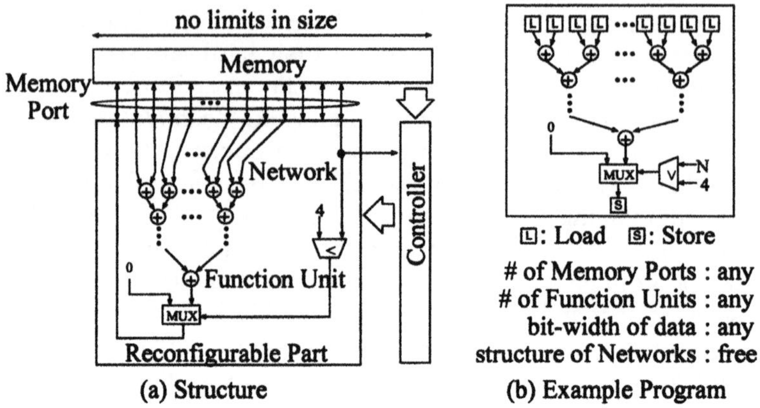

Fig. 1. *I-PARS* Execution Model

For the traditional processors, the execution model which satisfies the requirements is the Von Neumann execution model. The Von Neumann execution model is independent from the hardware structure of the processor, so that the model realizes the following two items.

(1) Portability among different architectures
Even if a new hardware architecture is developed, as long as it supports the model, we can reuse the software developed at past.

(2) Developments of software assets
Even if a new programming language is developed, as long as it supports the model, we can use the same algorithm for programming.

However, to make the hardware implementation easily, the Von Neumann execution model has only one function unit and is limited to serial execution. From these reasons, it is difficult to develop such a software that is expected to run in parallel on the Von Neumann execution model.

2.2 Proposal of *I-PARS* Execution Model

In this subsection, we present an *I-PARS* execution model which satisfies the requirements and solves the issues described in the former subsection.

Fig. 1.(a) shows the structure of *I-PARS* execution model. The *I-PARS* execution model consists of a *Reconfigurable Part*, a *Memory*, and a *Controller*. The *Reconfigurable Part* consists of a sea of *Function Units* and *Networks* which transfer data among the *Function Units*. The *Memory* stores data used in the program and also programs organized by some configuration data. Data transfers between the *Memory* and the *Reconfigurable Part* are done through *Memory Ports*.

The features of the *I-PARS* execution model are the following:

(1) Parallel Execution
Executions of *Function Units* are all done in parallel, when there is no special restriction due to the software, a potential parallelism of an application can be easily described on the *I-PARS* execution model.

(2) Dynamic Reconfiguration
In the *I-PARS* execution model, the *Controller* creates a specific circuit for executing the program on the *Reconfigurable Part.* To create the unique circuit according to the value specified at run time, the *Reconfigurable Part* supports dynamic reconfiguration.

(3) Easy Programming
In the *I-PARS* execution model, there is no limitation to the size of its components. Further, programmers don't have to consider the reconfiguration overhead and reconfiguration timing.

(4) Feasibility to Implement on Hardware by Folding
In the *I-PARS* execution model, mapping the model to the limited hardware structure is also well considered. For example, the Von Neumann execution model is a special case of the *I-PARS* execution model, when the *I-PARS* execution model was folded down to one function unit.

Next we explain how the programs based on the *I-PARS* execution model are executed. As a sample, we use the program described below (in this case, we use C language grammar).

```
if( N > 4 ) {
  sum = 0;
  for( i = 0; i < N; i++ )
    sum = sum + in[i];
} else { sum = 0; }
```

In this program, i, N, sum and in is a variable. In case when $N > 4$, on serial execution model, the number of computational step is $O(N)$.

The same program described on *I-PARS* execution model is shown in Fig. 1.(b) and execution of the program is shown Fig. 1.(a). In the figure, load/store instructions are replaced to the actual memory access and, the MUX stands for multiplexer function. In case of $N \leqq 4$, the result is stored before the calculation of sum is finished, because the calculation result is not required and not selected by MUX. In case of $N > 4$, the number of computational step is $O(logN)$.

Thus, in the *I-PARS* execution model, *Function Unit* is executed when the required data arrive. Further, the parallel execution of *Function Units* makes the number of computational step decrease.

3 *PARS* Architecture

In this section, we present a *PARS* architecture which can execute the program based on the *I-PARS* execution model by folding it down. In addition, we present

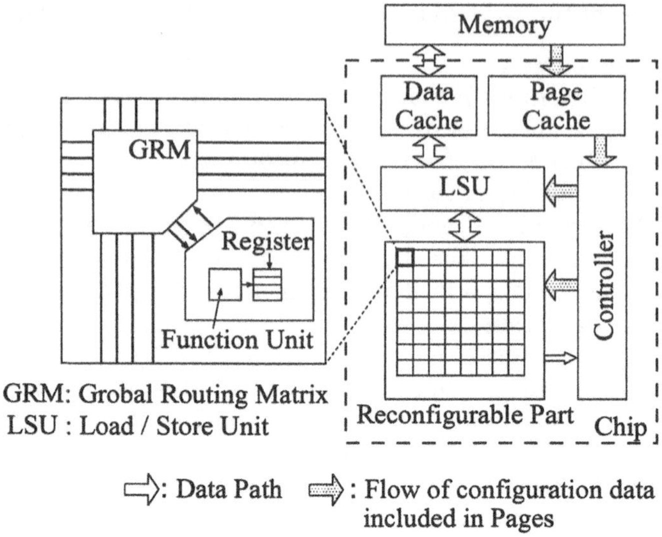

Fig. 2. Structure of *PARS* Architecture

the implemented chip of the prototype processor based on the *PARS* architecture and its estimation compared with UltraSPARC-III 750MHz processor.

3.1 Proposal of *PARS* Architecture

To execute the program based on the *I-PARS* execution model efficiently, the *PARS* architecture supports branch instruction to introduce control flow on execution and has a large *Reconfigurable Part* for highly parallel execution. Further, the *PARS* architecture has ability of every-cycle reconfiguration and execution to make the reconfiguration overhead decreasing as much as possible, because there is no reconfiguration overhead in the *I-PARS* execution model.

Fig. 2. shows the structure of the *PARS* architecture, and the details of components included in the architecture are described below.

Memory stores data and configuration data in it. We recommend that the *Memory* is implemented as a multi-port memory to provide high memory throughput for supporting the *I-PARS* execution model efficiently.

Data Cache is implemented on the chip to provide the required data memory bandwidth.

Page Cache is implemented on the chip to provide the required bandwidth for fetching configuration data. In the *PARS* architecture, we call the smallest unit of reconfiguration data a *Page*.

Controller fetches *Pages* from the *Page Cache*. The *Controller* can also select the next *Page* dynamically by using branch instructions. The action of branch instruction is defined by the information in the *Page*.

Reconfigurable Part consists of *Function Units*, *GRMs*, and *Registers* placed on a two-dimensional array, and all *Function Units* can be executed in parallel.

Function Unit provides functions such as adder, multiplexer. The output of a *Function Unit* must be stored in a *Register*.

***GRM* (Global Routing Matrix)** transfers data among *Function Units*.

***LSU* (Load Store Unit)** transfers data between *Reconfigurable Part* and the *Memory*.

3.2 Mapping from *I-PARS* Execution Model

One example algorithm for mapping the program based on the *I-PARS* execution model to that for the processor based on the *PARS* architecture is shown below.

Step 1 : First, *Function Block* is extracted from the program based on the *I-PARS* execution model. The *Function Block* is a group of *Function Units* and load/store instructions as a basic block in a traditional program.

Step 2 : The *Function Block* is divided into groups of *Function Units* and load/store instructions which can be executed in parallel. Then each group is temporally mapped to a *Page*.

Step 3 : If the number of *Function Units* in a *Page* is larger than the number of *Function Units* available in the processor, the *Page* is divided into several *Pages* until it matches with the number of the *Function Units* in the processor.

Step 4 : If the number of *Memory Ports* required in a *Page* is larger than the number of *Memory Ports* available in the processor, the *Page* is divided into several *Pages* until it matches with the number of the *Memory Ports* in the processor.

Step 5 : If necessary, the MUX function is replaced to proper branch instruction. The decision to replace or not may need many consideration, for example, hardware resources, critical path, and so on. Then the branch instruction is added to proper *Page*.

3.3 Execution of Program

As an example of program execution, we show Fig. 3. which is mapped from Fig. 1.(b) according to above algorithm. In this example, the MUX function in Fig. 1.(b) is replaced to proper branch instruction, and we assume that the number of *Function Units* and *Memory Ports* is four in the processor. As the execution and reconfiguration of a *Page* is done at one cycle in the *PARS* architecture, when $N \leqq 4$, the *PARS* architecture executes this program at three cycles. When $N = 8$, the *PARS* architecture executes it at seven cycles. Thus, in the *PARS* architecture, using the branch instruction makes the length of critical path in the program changed dynamically.

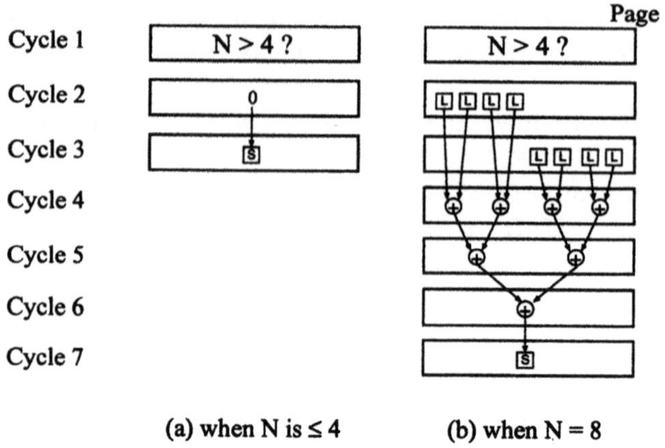

Fig. 3. Example: Execution of Program

Table 1. Specification of Prototype Processor

# of memory ports	1
Data Cache	-
Page Cache	1120 bits × 8
# of *Function Units*	4× 5
bit width of a *Function Unit*	8 bits

3.4 Implementation of Prototype Processor

To estimate the feasibility, the chip size, transistor counts, and the performance of the *PARS* architecture, we designed a prototype processor.

Table 1 shows the specification of the prototype processor. In this implementation, multi-port memory was not implemented. Fig. 4. shows the layout design with 0.18 μm CMOS technology, Table 2 summarizes the feature of the prototype processor. The clock frequency in Table 2 is confirmed by simulation because the chip is currently under fabrication.

From Table 2 summarizing the feature of the prototype processor, transistor count of the processor is about 420,000 transistors. We compare this result with UltraSPARC-III 750 MHz processor implemented in 0.15 μm technology. The transistor count of UltraSPARC-III 750 MHz processor is about 11,000,000 transistors except on-chip cache memory[7]. Comparing the transistor count, we can say that the prototype processor is implemented with only 3.8% of the number of transistors used in the UltraSPARC-III 750 MHz processor. From the results, we can see that the reconfigurable architecture supporting the *I-PARS* execution model can be implemented with transistor count available on one chip.

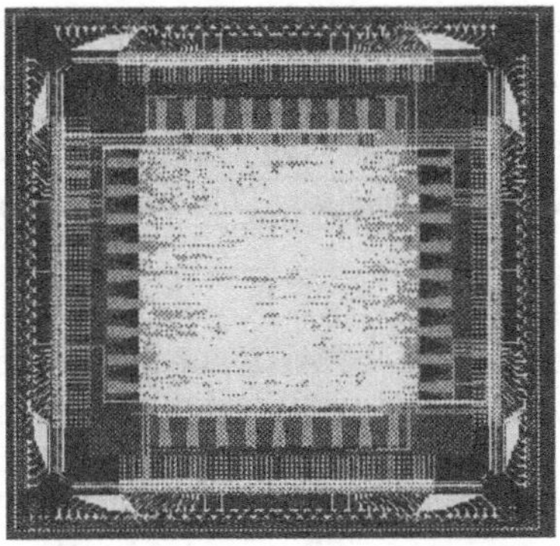

Fig. 4. Layout of Prototype Processor with 0.18 μm CMOS Technology

Table 2. Feature of Prototype Processor

<table>
<tr><td colspan="2">Process technology</td><td>HITACHI CMOS, 0.18 μm, five layer metal</td></tr>
<tr><td colspan="2">Core size</td><td>$17.6mm^2$ (4.2 mm × 4.2 mm)</td></tr>
<tr><td rowspan="3">Transistor count</td><td>logic</td><td>420,377</td></tr>
<tr><td>RAM</td><td>115,704</td></tr>
<tr><td>total</td><td>536,081</td></tr>
<tr><td colspan="2">Clock frequency</td><td>200 MHz</td></tr>
</table>

4 Performance Estimation

In this section, we estimate the performance of the implemented prototype processor by using FEAL cipher algorithm [8] mapped to the *I-PARS* execution model as a benchmark. Further we compare its performance with that of a traditional general-purpose processor.

4.1 FEAL Cipher Algorithm

In the FEAL cipher algorithm, only 8-bits operation is used to achieve fast data encipherment. The prototype processor has 8-bit width *Function Units*to prevent configuration data of a *Page* from increasing. Therefore the program of the FEAL cipher algorithm suits very well with the execution on the prototype processor.

4.2 Estimation Details

We estimate the performance of the prototype processor by comparing the execution time of the benchmark program.

The execution time on the prototype processor is estimated by logic simulation using Cadence Verilog-XL 3.2. At first, the program of a FEAL cipher

Table 3. Result of Performance Estimation

	Execution time
Prototype processor (200 MHz)	4905 ns
UltraSPARC-III processor (750 MHz)	4020 ns

algorithm is programmed on the *I-PARS* execution model, and then it maps to the program for prototype processor by using the algorithm introduced on subsection 3.2. The FEAL cipher algorithm used as a benchmark program for the prototype processor is the same as that for the UltraSPARC-III 750 MHz, but the execution models are not same. The model for the prototype processor is the *I-PARS* execution model, and the model for UltraSPARC-III 750MHz processor is the Von Neumann execution model. In this estimation, we assume there are no miss hits in *Page Cache* and *Data Cache*. Also, the clock frequency of the prototype processor is set to 200 MHz, from the result of Table 2.

The executable program for UltraSPARC-III 750MHz processor is generated by the C-Language compiler "Sun WorkShop 6". In the execution on the UltraSPARC-III 750 MHz processor, there was no effect caused by the miss hit penalty from the instruction cache and data cache.

4.3 Result of Performance Comparison

Table 3 shows the results of performance estimation. From Table 3, the prototype processor achieves 82 % of the performance of UltraSPARC-III 750MHz processor. This is exciting results considering the less hardware resources of the prototype processor (implemented by using only 3.8 % of the transistors counts compared with UltraSPARC-III 750 MHz processor).

The performance of the prototype processor can be increased by optimizing the program. In detail, the number of *Function Units* used in this program is eight at max, but the available number of *Function Units* on the prototype processor is twenty. By adding extra optimizing algorithm which increase the parallelism in the program such as loop unrolling, it is possible to extend its performance of the prototype processor drastically.

As another benchmark program, we use a program of discrete cosine transform (DCT). In this estimation result, with 3.8 % of transistor counts, the prototype processor achieves 29 % of the performance of UltraSPARC-III 750 MHz processor.

5 Conclusion and Future Works

In this paper, we proposed an *I-PARS* execution model to make it possible to develop software assets for variations of reconfigurable architectures.

Also, we proposed a *PARS* architecture supporting execution of programs based on the *I-PARS* execution model. To enable the execution, the programs are folded down to match the size of specified hardware structure of the processor based on the *PARS* architecture.

By implementation of the prototype processor based on the *PARS* architecture, we found out that the reconfigurable architecture supporting the *I-PARS* execution model can be implemented with transistor counts available on current LSI technology.

Further, from the performance estimation by using a program of a FEAL cipher algorithm as a benchmark, we found out that the prototype processor can achieve nearly the same performance (82 %) with the UltraSPARC-III 750 MHz processor, and it was implemented with only using 3.8% of the number of transistors compared with the UltraSPARC-III 750 MHz. By further program optimization to increase the amount of parallelisms, the prototype processor can achieve further more high-performance drastically.

Our future works will include to estimate the performance of the prototype processor by using various programs, and to develop the compiler for better optimization on mapping the *I-PARS* execution model to the *PARS* architecture.

Acknowledgements This research has benefited from comments by Dr. Ochi (Hiroshima City University). The VLSI chip in this study has been fabricated in the chip fabrication program of VLSI Design and Education Center (VDEC), the University of Tokyo with the collaboration by HITACHI Ltd. The VLSI chip in this study is designed with Avant! CAD tools. Part of this research work is funded by The Takeda Foundation.

References

1. H. Singh, M. Lee, G. Lu, F. J. Kurdahi, N. Bagherzadeh, E. M. C. Filho, "MorphoSys: An Integrated Reconfigurable System for Data-Parallel Computation-Intensive Applications," IEEE Transactions on Computer, Vol. 49, No.5, pp.465-481, May 2000.
2. T. J. Callahan, J. R. Hauser, J. Wawrzynek, "The Garp Architecture and C Compiler, " IEEE Computer, pp62-69, Vol.33, No. 4, April 2000.
3. S. C. Goldstein, H. Scbmit, M. Budiu, S. Cadambi M. Moe, R. R. Taylor, "PipeRench: A Reconfigurable Architecture and Compiler," IEEE Computer, pp. 70-77, April 2000.
4. E. Caspi, M. Chu, R. Huang, J. Yeh, J. Wawrzynek, and A. DeHon, "Stream Computations Organized for Reconfigurable Execution (SCORE): Introduction and Tutorial," `http://brass.cs.berkeley.edu/documents/score_tutorial.pdf` .
5. K. Tanigawa, T. Hironaka, N. Yoshida, "PARS Programming Model and PARS Architecture," Information Processing Society of Japan, Tech. Rep. 2000-ARC-140, pp.37-42, 2000 (in Japanese).
6. K. Tanigawa, T. Yoshida, A. Kojima, T. Hironaka, N. Yoshida, "The Detailed Design of the PARS Architecture" Information Processing Society of Japan, Tech. Rep. 2001-ARC-144, pp.31-36, 2001 (in Japanese).
7. http://www.sun.com/processors/UltraSPARC-III/specs.html
8. Akihiro Shimizu, Shoji Miyaguchi, "Fast Data Encipherment Algorithm FEAL," In David Chaum and Wyn L. Price, editors, Advances in Cryptology — EUROCRYPT'87, volume 304 of Lecture Notes in Computer Science, pp. 267-278. Springer-Verlag, Berlin, Heidelberg, New York, 1988.

A Framework for Teaching (Re)Configurable Architectures in Student Projects

T. Pionteck, P. Zipf, L.D. Kabulepa, and M. Glesner

Darmstadt University of Technology
Institute of Microelectronic Systems
Karlstr. 15, 64283 Darmstadt, Germany
pionteck@mes.tu-darmstadt.de

Abstract. Due to the increasing complexity of integrated circuits it is becoming more difficult to teach all design steps on the basis of real-world examples submitted to realistic constraints. This turns out to be a problem especially in the design of reconfigurable architectures since they will often be integrated with other components. Therefore we developed a framework which gives students the opportunity to test any desired design in a realistic environment. This framework is based on TTAs (Transport Triggers Architectures) which enables the design of simple but universal processors.

1 Motivation

The advances in technology and CAD tools in the last years enable chip designers to implement ever increasing designs on a single chip. This development has strong influence on the way universities have to teach students so that they are able to make use of these technological advances [1][2]. Student design courses have to be up to with this development in order to provide students with an adequate education. It no longer suffices to teach them the classical gate level design, it is also required to train them in high level design methodologies like IP (Intellectual Property) based chip design [3]. Here the problem emerges how to integrate these different demands in one single student project. A good student project should cover all design steps of actual chip design flows and should also provide one topic where a student can focus on.

Especially design projects with (re)configurable hardware architectures require the demands mentioned before. In the last years it has turned out that reconfigurable architectures will only be used in conjunction with standard components like DSPs and microprocessors or with application specific components. This complicates the effort to provide students a realistic test environment for their designs. Even though it is desirable that students should work in teams which allow them to work on bigger tasks, experiences show that it is desirable to cut down the problem size. For example in [4] a dynamically reconfigurable architecture for mobile communication systems was realized with the help of student projects. During this project we observed that students were motivated

M. Glesner, P. Zipf, and M. Renovell (Eds.): FPL 2002, LNCS 2438, pp. 444–451, 2002.

to work in such a design project but that this motivation decreased by the end of the project. This was mainly caused by the fact that it was not possible for them to test their components with the other parts of the design as not all students finished at the same time.

Thus there are two contrary motivations. On one side, design projects should cover all aspects of actual design flows and on the other side student projects should be small enough so that students can finish them in the scheduled time. The best way to solve this problem consists in finding a simple hardware architecture which easily allows to integrate different modules in a complex environment. Such an architecture should be scalable, easily to be programmed and easily to be prototyped on a FPGA. TTAs (Transport Triggered Architectures)[5] represent an alternative concept that can allow to fulfill the mentioned requirements. In the following we describe how we successfully used this architecture concept in student projects.

In section II a short overview about transport triggered architectures is provided. After this, the design framework is introduced in section III. Section IV gives an example of the usage of this framework in student projects. The paper ends with a conclusion in section V.

2 Transport Triggered Architectures

The main idea behind transport triggered architectures is to separate the data transport from the data manipulation [5]. In normal GGPs (General Purpose Processors) the data transport is a result of an operation. For example, if an addition is required the operation *add r3, r1 ,r2* results in three data transports. First, *r1* and *r2* are transported from registers to the ALU and after the computation the result is transported from the ALU to register *r3*. Such architectures are called OTA (Operation Triggered Architectures). The main drawback of OTAs is that the different processor components depend heavily on each other. For instance the IF (Instruction Fetch) unit has to know all required data transports for each operation. Thus the IF unit has to be redesigned if a functional unit is added to the processor. In transport triggered architectures this dependence of the processor units among each other is eliminated.

For a TTA processor, the addition example will result in three separate data transport operations, as can be seen below. *r1*, *r2* and *r3* are the registers where the operands, respectively the result are stored. *add_o*, *add_t* and *add_r* are registers of the ALU where the operands of the addition are stored, respectively the result of the operation is provided. By writing in a special register of the ALU (*add_t*) the operation is started. Thus a TTA processor requires only one operation for data transports, which does not need to be coded.

$$\texttt{add r3,r1,r2} \Rightarrow \begin{array}{l} \texttt{r1} \rightarrow \texttt{add\_o} \\ \texttt{r2} \rightarrow \texttt{add\_t} \\ \texttt{add\_r} \rightarrow \texttt{r3} \end{array}$$

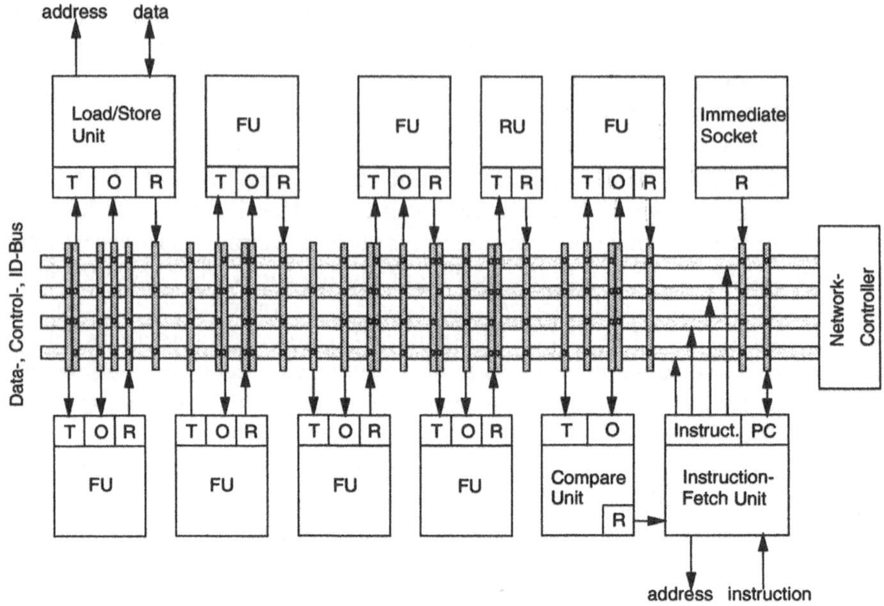

Fig. 1. Block Diagram of a TTA processor [5]

Figure 1 shows a block diagram of a TTA processor. A TTA processor consists of functional units (FUs), an instruction fetch unit and interconnection busses. Functional units can realize any function, for example a simple adder, a memory access unit, a register bank and even other processors as well as reconfigurable architectures. The functional units have three different types of registers. First, there is the *operand register (o)*. The data required for computation in the functional unit are stored in the operand register. Secondly there is the *trigger register (T)*. By writing data in this register the FU knows that all data in the operand registers are valid and that the FU can start its operation. The result is provided in the *result register(R)*. If the FU offers more than one operation, then the bit code for the selection of the operation is also transmitted to the trigger register, where the data is splitted in the actual data and the operation code which is passed to the control logic of the module.

The FUs are connected to the interconnection network with the help of sockets. Figure 2 shows the principle structure of the connection of the FUs to the bus. There are input and output sockets which write or read to the registers in the FUs. The interconnect network itself consists of three sub-busses. The *Data-Bus* transmits the actual data while on the *ID-bus* the address of the source / destination of the data transport is transmitted. The *Control-Bus* is responsible for signalizing the validity of the data on the other busses.

A TTA processor comprises of several busses as the system has to handle a huge amount of data transports. The exact amount of busses does not influence the functionality of the FU or of the IF unit, only the connection sockets of the FUs and of the IF unit have to be changed. Thus a TTA architecture provides a huge scalability.

The only drawback of TTA processors is the effort to program them. As for every data transport the source and destination address has to be declared, the program code is very large. On the other side it is quite simple to generate the program code. With the help of a simple compiler program code can be written which can be used for several designs.

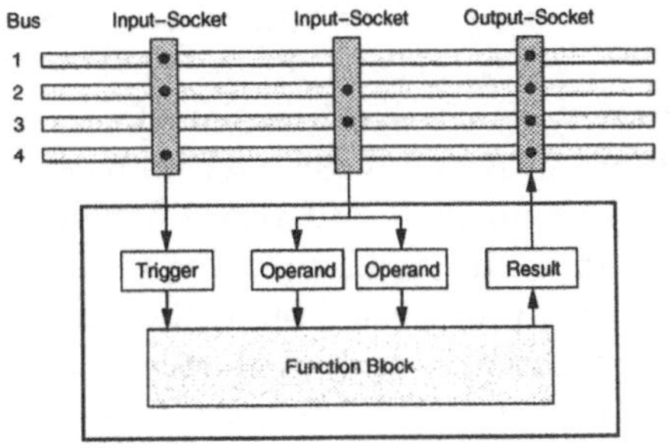

Fig. 2. Connection of FUs to the busses

3 Design Framework

The flexibility and modularity of TTAs make them promising for the integration in student design projects. The structure of TTAs offers the arrangement of the processor components in two categories. On one side there are the core components. The behavior of these components should not be changed as otherwise the compatibility of the components among each other is not given. These include the bus structure, the instruction fetch unit and the input / output sockets. All other components of the processor can be changed as desired. For student projects this means that students can either work on the improvement of the core components (processor design) or that they can make use of a TTA based platform as a fast and simple test environment for their modules.

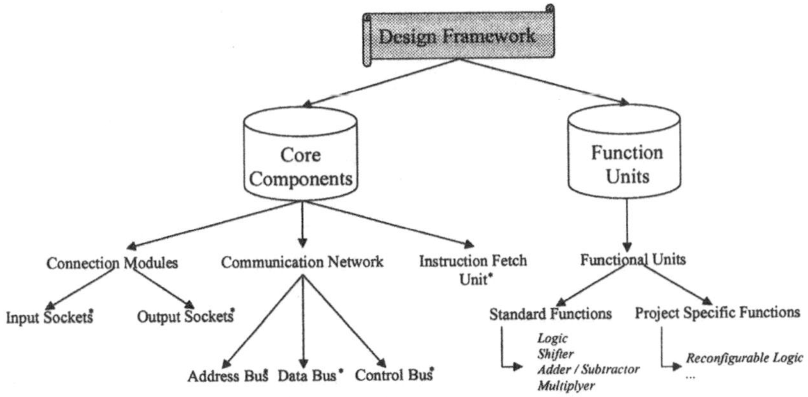

Fig. 3. Library Structure

The actual design framework consists of two libraries, one includes the core components of the processor and the other one includes function units. With these libraries students can easily compose a TTA processor by means of IP based design. For each component a functional description with information about timing and hardware structure is provided. The actual design is available for several target platforms. First of all there is the VHDL code of the module. Secondly synthesized versions for a standard cell process and FPGA prototyping are provided which can be used by the students as a black box. For some components there are also different implementations, depending on the target platform. The organization of the libraries is shown in figure 3.

For a processor design, the different processor components have simply to be instantiated and connected. There is no need for glue logic or any other additional coding. The main design choices for TTAs are the amount of busses and the bus width. These parameters influence all core components and also the structure of the program code. Therefore all components in figure 3 which are marked with a * are designed in such a way that these settings can be made with the help of generic parameters.

The programming of the designs realized with the design framework is supported by a simple assembler. This assembler allows the usage of symbols for the source/destination address of data transports. Thus programs or program parts can be reused as the real addresses of the sockets are inserted during compile time. As the compiler and the top-level VHDL file chiefly need the same information, the addresses for the different sockets and the design parameters for the busses are isolated in a single file. Figure 4 shows the file organization of a project.

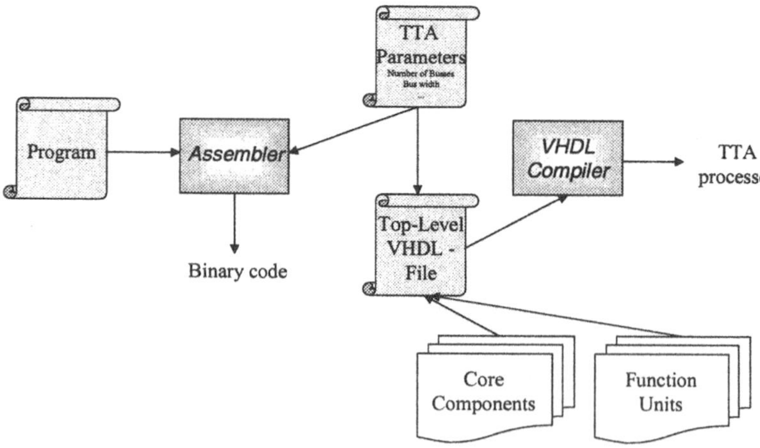

Fig. 4. File structure of a project

4 Design Example: Reconfigurable Logic

In the following the usage of the design framework in a student project is presented. The main focus of this project was the design and test of a reconfigurable module which should be able to perform several operations required in mobile communication transceivers. In previous design projects about reconfigurable architectures [4] we have learnt that the most problematic task in such project is the final test of the unit. As the reconfigurable unit is not designed to operate alone, there is the problem of how realistic test pattern can be generated. Most often test pattern are generated by hand which does not lead to a sufficient test. This is neither desired by the supervisor nor by the student who wants to know whether his design is functional correct.

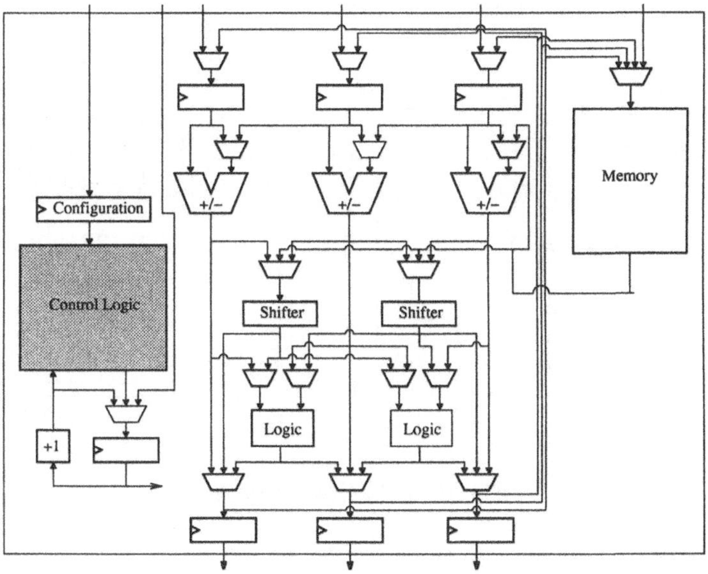

Fig. 5. Test Unit

The reconfigurable unit of this exemplary student project is shown in figure 5. It is designed to provide hardware acceleration for a software based solution for the realization of receiver algorithms for mobile communication systems. The starting point of the design was a folded CORDIC (COordinate Rotation DIgital Computer) architecture. The CORDIC algorithm offers a hardware efficient solution for the rotation of vectors. Vector rotation is often required in OFDM systems, for example for the synchronization or channel estimation. It was also tried to implement some support for CDMA systems. Hence the spreading operation of a CDMA Rake receiver can be supported by the architecture. Besides this, several other operations can be mapped onto the architecture which, however, are out of the scope of this paper.

For test purposes the unit was integrated with standard functional units of the framework library. The final test processor is shown in figure 6. It consists of the actual UUT (Unit Under Test), two multipliers, two adders/substractors and a logic module. These units emulate a general purpose processor which is designated in a final system for the UUT. In addition to the functional units there is an instruction fetch unit and a memory access unit. The memory access unit is required for reading test data out of the memory which are processed by the UUT.

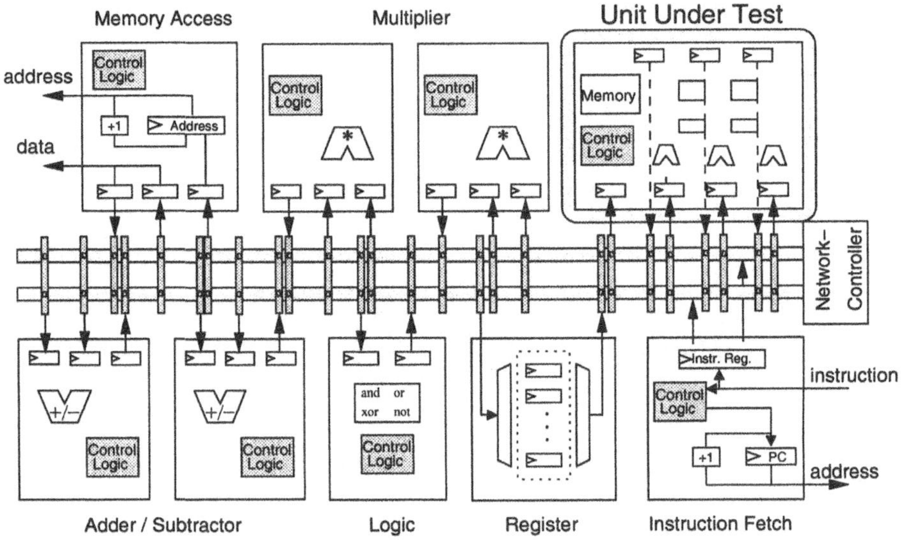

Fig. 6. TTA Test Processor

After a rudimentary test with the VHDL simulator the complete processor was synthesized and mapped onto a FPGA. In the student design project a XCV800-Virtex FPGA from Xilinx was used. It is placed on a XSV-800 Virtex Prototyping Board from XESS. Besides several interfaces the board has two memory banks which were used to store the test data and the program code [6].

For the final test of the UUT an OFDM equalizer was realized with the test processor. Therefore an assembler program was written and compiled with the framework assembler. The test data was generated with the help of an OFDM simulation chain which was realized in a different project. In the simulation chain dump-modules were inserted before and after the equalizer. These modules wrote the data into files which were used as input stimuli and reference data.

Thus it was possible to test the UUT in a realistic environment. The time needed for the realization of the test processor was quite short as the framework contains everything which is needed for building a complete processor. Students can focus on their actual hardware design tasks but they are also involved in all design steps till the FPGA prototyping.

5 Conclusion

This paper introduced a design framework for student projects. Its goal was to provide students the possibility of testing their hardware design in a realistic environment with as less effort as possible. Especially in design courses for reconfigurable architectures the problem emerges how architectures can be tested, as most reconfigurable architectures are not designed to work as a stand alone application. With the framework introduced it is possible to emulate the later environment on the bases of function modules which are available in a library. All modules are synthesizable and therefore it is quite easy to implement a test system on a FPGA. Besides the educational effect that students are now involved in every design step the students will be much more motivated when they know that they will not only test their unit stand alone in a simulator but together with other components in real hardware.

References

1. P. Khosla, H. Schmidt, M.J. Irwin, N. Vijaykrishnan, T. Cain, S. Levitan, D. Landis: *SoC Design Skills: Collaboration Builds a Stronger SoC Design Team.* IEEE International Conference on Microelectronic Systems Education, 2001, Pages: 42-43
2. H. Tenhunen, E. Dubrova: *SoC Master: An International M.Sc. Program in System-On-Chip Design at KTH.* IEEE International Conference on Microelectronic Systems Education, 2001, Pages: 64-66
3. H. De Man: *System-on-Chip Design: Impact on Education and Research.* IEEE Design & Test of Computers, 1999, Volume:16 Issue 3, Pages:78-83
4. J. Becker, T. Pionteck, C. Habermann, M. Glesner: *Design and Implementation of a Coarse-Grained Dynamically Reconfigurable Hardware Architecture.* Workshop on VLSI, Orlando, Florida, 2001
5. H. Corporaal: *Microprocessor Architectures from VLIW to TTA.* John Wiley & Sons, 1998
6. http://www.xess.com

Specialized Hardware for Deep Network Packet Filtering

Young H. Cho, Shiva Navab, and William H. Mangione-Smith

The University of California, Los Angeles, CA 91311
{young, shiva_n, billms}@ee.ucla.edu
http://cares.icsl.ucla.edu

Abstract. Many computer network provide limited security through simple firewall feature in router and switch. Some networks that require higher security use deep packet filter to capture packets that can not be detected by simple firewall. Deep packet filters use list of rules for determining safety of packets. There is a high degree of parallelism in processing these rules because each rule represent independent pattern matching process. We find that the underlying architecture for existing software and hardware firewalls do not fully take advantage of this parallelism. Thus, we design a deep packet filtering firewall on a field programmable gate array (FPGA) to take advantage of the parallelism while retaining its programmability. Our implementation is capable of processing over 2.88 gigabits per second of network stream on an Altera EP20K series FPGA without manual optimization.

1 Introduction

The purpose of a Network Intrusion Detection System (NIDS) is to help protect computer network users from malicious attacks [1]. Today, firewalls with limited capabilities are built into many commercial network switch and router. Simple firewalls usually examine packet headers for specific information to determine whether to block or allow packet passage.

As computer networks grow faster, it becomes easier for the hackers to release malicious packets into a network without being detected. Simple firewalls may be able to protect networks from certain intrusion; but busy packet traffic and smart attacking schemes (e.g. Code Red) can easily by-pass such firewalls [2].

In order to identify such attacks, methods such as stateful multi-layer inspection are used in more advanced firewalls. A multi-layer inspection unit searches for a number of patterns in packet header. They furthermore perform computationally intensive pattern searches on the application level payload. A system with a multi-layer inspection unit offers a higher level of security than a traditional firewall. However, due to their complexity, such systems are slower and require better administration [3].

M. Glesner, P. Zipf, and M. Renovell (Eds.): FPL 2002, LNCS 2438, pp. 452–461, 2002.

1.1 Motivation

There are several rule based multi-layer inspection firewall software packages available today. Most of these systems use one or more general purpose processors running rule-based packet filtering software. Due to exhaustive pattern detection algorithm, software system running on single general-purpose processor may not be able to inspect all network traffic [5,6,7].

On the other hand, there are some custom hardware chips (i.e. ClassiPi [9] and Strata II [10,11]) that support faster network. However, the underlying sequential algorithm running on a Von Neuman architecture eventually leads to performance bottleneck as number of necessary pattern checks increase.

Therefore, we have designed a rule based multi-layer inspection firewall system based on a parallel architecture. We customize our hardware to process each rule separately in parallel.

Because network threats are constantly changing, it is very important to be able to change the rule set. In order to build a fast gate-level design that can be updated frequently, we choose FPGA as our design platform. In addition to speed and flexibility, FPGA tools allow quick extraction of realistic performance and resource costs.

1.2 Related Work

Research in reconfigurable network hardware assess the possibility of using reconfigurable hardware as a network processors [12], switches [13], routers [14,15], and network protocol wrappers [16,17,18,19]. Projects such as PLATO of Technical University of Crete [13] and FPX of Washington University are reconfigurable network hardware design platform on which above application can be configured [14,15,17].

Reconfigurable packet filtering projects mentioned above are pattern matching units that make decision based on TCP and IP header information. Like most ASIC packet classification co-processors, the FPGA is configured to function as a co-processor to reduce the processing time for packet classification in few research projects [18,19]. The reconfigurable nature of the FPGA adds additional flexibility in filtering mechanisms compared to ASIC solutions.

Firewalls which are limited to header processing can only partially satisfy the inspection requirements involved in deep packet search process. In deep packet search algorithm, many strings must be matched over application level payload as well as packet header. More thorough string pattern searches are required once the packet header analysis is complete. The performance cost in Von Neuman architecture of such pattern search is directly proportional to number of search pattern rules.

Sidhu and Prasanna mapped Non-deterministic Finite Automata (NFA) into FPGAs to perform fast pattern matching [20]. Using this method, Carver et. al compiled patterns for an open-source NIDS system into JHDL [21]. Due to parallel nature of the hardware design, the pattern matching engine maintain high performance regardless the size of the string.

1.3 Summary

Our implementation uses high-level rule description from the open-source firewall software Snort to build a complete stand alone NIDS. Therefore, the description of our NIDS begins with software architecture of Snort system in section 2. The algorithm and data structure of Snort becomes our high-level model for the hardware implementation. After understanding the software model, we describe the hardware implementation and its performance in section 3. Then we conclude in section 4 with a summary of our research.

2 Software Firewall

Several software based firewall units provide complex rule-based multi-layer inspection routine in addition to other security protocols. These firewall units can detect malicious packets that are not filtered out by simple header inspection [3]. In this section we describe the design structure of software stateful multi-layer firewall package.

2.1 Libcap Based System

Libcap is a portable library of functions that can capture network packets and examine their length, contents, and header information. The result from the library function can be used to filter or classify network packets. Advanced software security application running on general purpose processor would use libcap or similar filtering library.

Snort is an open source lightweight network intrusion detection system that uses libcap [5]. Snort can perform traffic analysis and packet logging on IP networks, protocol analysis, and payload content searching. Furthermore Snort can be configured to detect a variety of abnormal packet behaviors, such as buffer overflows, stealth port scans, CGI attacks, SMB probes, and OS fingerprinting attempts. The packet payload inspection is the key mechanism for detecting these malicious behaviors.

Hogwash is a software package that wraps around Snort to filter and forward packets between 2 networks [6]. This tool has the ability to generate alerts as well as packet drops and modification. Accordingly, the software can run on top of the network driver to stop attacks that cannot be blocked by a simple firewall. Although the rule format is slightly different between Hogwash and Snort, the underlying technology is the same.

2.2 Rule Based System

Snort uses a list of rules to filter incoming packets. As the number of attacks grow, most commonly occurring attack patterns or dangerous patterns are turned into signatures which Snort parses. A simple rule structure and options allow flexibility and convenience in configuring the NIDS. However, as we will describe in later section, there are performance disadvantages of having a long list of filter rules.

Snort uses a flexible rule language to describe traffic classification. It uses a detection engine that utilizes modular plug-in architecture. There are three primary subsystems that make up Snort: the packet decoder, the detection engine, and the logging and alerting subsystem. Snort maintain its detection rules in a two dimensional linked list of what are termed chain headers and chain options.

These rule chains are searched for each packet incident on the network. The detection engine checks only those chain options that have been set by the rule parser at run-time. The first rule that matches a decoded packet in the detection engine triggers the action specified in the rule definition and returns.

The structure of a rule consists of a command keyword for handling the matching packet, header information signature, and various options for other patterns including the content string search for the payload. Snort can use one or more rule files as its input. Each rule file can contain more than one rule signature consistent with the format shown as following.

```
Action Protocol SrcIPAddr/Port Direction DstIPAddr/Port Options
```

The first part of the rule corresponds to the packet header information. The second part corresponds to the pattern search options applied to the application level packet payload. The most computationally intensive option is called 'content.' This option is the key to better packet filtering in multi-layer inspection firewall.

Following rule is a signature that is used by Snort to detect one type of 'Code Red' worm.

```
alert TCP $EXTERNAL any -> $INTERNAL 80 (msg: "IDS552/web-iis_IIS
ISAPI Overflow ida"; dsize: >239; flags: A+; uricontent: ".ida?";
classtype: system-or-info-attempt; reference: arachnids,552;)
```

2.3 Experimentation

According to the documentation, a Hogwash system running on a celeron 733 with a moderate rule set can keep pace with a 100 Mbps network. We experimented with Hogwash and Snort on our computers to determine achieved performance in the field.

We ran Hogwash with 105 rules to filter the network traffic over a 100 Mbps fast Ethernet. With non-malicious traffic, the benchmark yielded a total throughput range of 39.2 to 58.82 Mbps. Then the test was repeated using malicious packets. As expected, throughput of the network was lower to range of 25.59 and 50.15 Mbps.

Accordingly, the results from our experiment suggested that Hogwash was not able maintain the full bandwidth on fast Ethernet. Although a software implementation is flexible and simple to implement, such a system running on single processor would not be able to accommodate network speeds above 100 Mbps.

3 Our Implementation

Hogwash is designed to block out about 95 percent of all the known Internet attacks using 105 signature rules of most common attacks. Thus, we decided to use these rule set to build our FPGA based NIDS.

The rules contain information to search through packet layers 2 through 4 first. If the packet header information matches the rule criteria, an exhaustive pattern search is performed on the payload (layers 5-7). Such a pattern search is done for all the rules with matching header information [5].

In our approach, each pattern matching component is automatically translated into structural VHDL. The components are then synthesized and mapped on to the FPGA with a vendor CAD tool set. Through the CAD tools, the design functionality is tested and the estimates for the resource requirement and performance are obtained.

3.1 Parallel Design

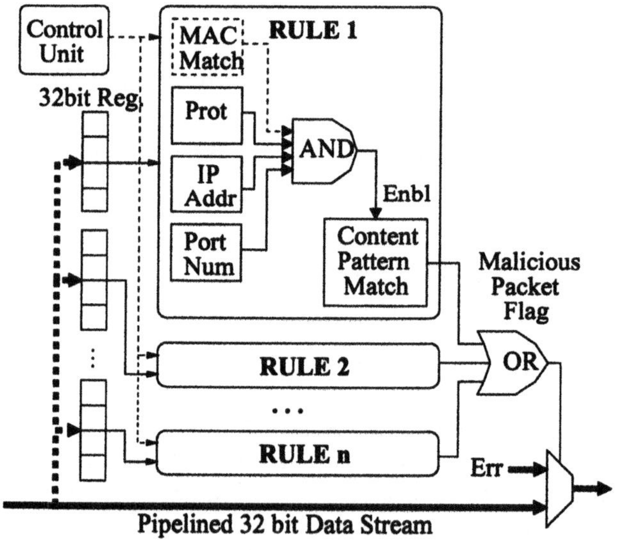

Fig. 1. Parallel Datapath of NIDS in Reconfigurable Hardware

Figure 1 is a block diagram of our architecture. Each rule unit implements the logic for a single Snort rule signature. Packet data is passed to the units through a 32-bit bus. Effective use of the hardware pipeline with optimized combinational logic between each stage shortened the critical path of the design.

The simplicity of the design easily shows its resemblance with the software execution path of Hogwash. The header information of each packet is compared with the predefined header data. If the header information matches the rule, the payload is sent to the content pattern match unit where the predefine pattern is searched. However, unlike the software implementation, all the rule chains are matched in parallel to achieve predictable high performance.

In addition to parallel layout of the rule units, four bytes of data are matched in each stage of the pipeline to increase its throughput. Therefore, four instances of the search string are compared in parallel on every cycle to match through all the byte offsets of the 4-byte input stream.

If a given packet is detected to be malicious, a flag is raised. In a system with sufficient buffer memory, the flag can be used to drop the packet. However, without any external memory, this flag can be used to corrupt the rest of the packet payload going through the pipeline; thereby causing the packet to be dropped at the receiving node.

3.2 Content Pattern Match Unit

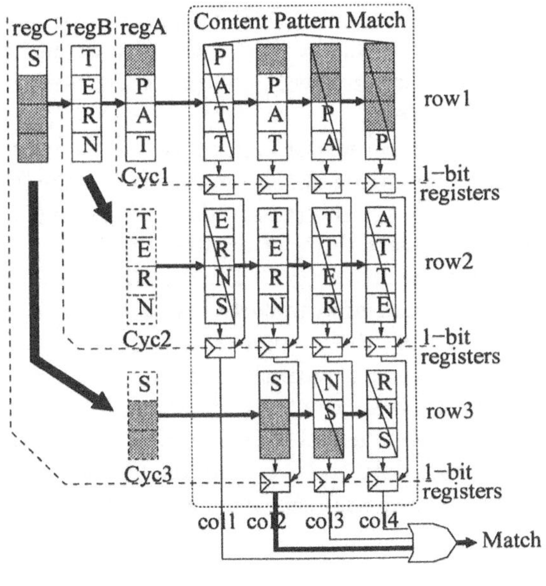

Fig. 2. Pattern Match Example

The content pattern match unit is the main work horse of the design. In order to clarify its functionality, we discuss an example of its operation.

We will first define the structure of the example diagram shown in figure 2. The squares outside of the content match unit are 8-bit register. The solid lined square shows their initial state while the dotted lined squares are the subsequent future states of the registers. The shaded squares represent don't care values while the rest of the squares contain ASCII characters.

The squares within content match unit represent 8-bit comparators. The four 8-bit comparators work together to match four consecutive bytes of data simultaneously. The match results are passed to the 1-bit registers located below all the comparators. Output from 1-bit register control the subsequent 1-bit comparison result.

The content of the register A, B, and C represent the string stream 'PATTERNS.' Since the registers are pipelined, we can separately observe different parts of the design during each clock period. The matching stages are indicated as clock cycles 1, 2, and 3.

During cycle 1, substring 'PAT' is compared against four different strings with different byte offsets in row 1. Since all of the 1-bit registers are initialized as 0, the result will not be latched even if there is a matching pattern in rows 2 and 3. For our example, the comparator in row 1, column 2, produces 1. This value is latched through the 1-bit register to enable the next row of 1-bit registers.

In cycle 2, the substring in register B is latched into register A. The substring is then matched with all the patterns. However, only comparator results that can be latched are all the comparators in row 1 and the comparator in row 2, column 2. The purpose behind enabling all the row 1 registers is because of a possibility that the pattern may have actually started with the content in register B during cycle 1. The matching pattern in row 2, column 2, enables the 1-bit register in row 3, column 2 for the cycle 3.

Finally, with the content of register C in register A in cycle 3, substring 'S' is compared with comparators in row 3. The match in column 2 comparator sends 1 to the OR gate which indicate the match of the substring 'PATTERNS.' This signal then can be used to alert the user or drop the packet.

All contents for the rules are compared in parallel. Although such construction suggests growth of design area linearly proportional to the number of the rules, the performance of the filter is maintained as a constant.

Since all the comparators compare the incoming stream of data with fixed value, it is unnecessary to keep the pattern values in a register. Rather, the effect of comparator can be achieved by using 32-bit AND gate with inversion in the input lines corresponding the zero bits of the bit pattern. Therefore the hardware requirement is much smaller than implementing comparators.

3.3 Methodology

In a production environment, we need to continually update the rule set to guard against new attacks. Thus, flexibility of updating the rules is valuable, if not essential. Consequently, we choose FPGAs as our development platform. Efficient pipeline structure and simplicity of our design algorithm also allows FPGA to perform well.

In order to efficiently update the design upon changes in the rule set, we automate the design process. We extract templates from the optimized structural VHDL files. Then the Hogwash rule file is pre-processed and converted to VHDL files based on the template.

The resulting structural VHDL files are highly pipelined and optimized with user-defined parameter because of the efficient design templates. These VHDL designs can be inserted into the common datapath to complete the system.

FPGA code is produced with the net list of the design. The net list is processed and mapped on to a specified FPGA with a place and route tool. In most cases, the larger match rules cause slower place and route and low performance design. However, due to highly pipelined and parallel architecture, there is more freedom for place and route tool to produce efficient implementation in shorter amount of time.

3.4 Performance

In a large FPGA design, in addition to correct functionality, the critical path and the resource usage information are main concerns. These results are only available at the end of place and route step of the FPGA design process.

Many commercial place and route programs support optimization options. For this paper, we do not use these options. Thus, all our results are based on an FPGA implementation without any timing or resource optimization.

Our implementation use Quartus II FPGA tool from Altera to obtain the final design as well as timing and resource information for single rule implementation of Hogwash.

Our NIDS design is mapped on to the Altera EP20K series FPGA chips. The basic construction units are called "logic elements" (LE) ranging from hundreds of LE on smaller devices up to fifty-two thousand LE on the largest of the series. There are also larger and faster FPGA series available but we found this series more than suitable [22].

The design is placed and routed without invoking any optional timing restriction allowed in the tool. Therefore, the critical paths are not optimized. With the longest clock to signal delay of 11.685 ns for reset signal, the system can run at 90 MHz. At 90 MHz, the system can filter 2.88 Gbps of data regardless of the size of the patterns or the packet length. This is in contrast to the work by Craver et. al which achieved approximately 6.4 Mbps (800 Kilobytes/sec).

With some timing optimizations, the implementation should be able to run at a faster clock rate. However, such optimization would require longer time for place and routing process. Although timing restrictions can take longer place and route time, it maybe necessary to achieve higher throughput. Design time for new reconfiguration may be acceptable in most cases; this is because of the infrequent updates to the Hogwash rule set.

3.5 Resource Requirement

Resource requirement for content pattern matching units vary according to the length of each string. The resource usage report from the Altera place and route tool indicate that up to 10 logic elements are required to implement 1-byte comparator on EP20K series chip. This resource requirement is proportional to the total number of characters defined in the content option of all the rules.

Most of the current rules for Hogwash does not examine IP addresses and source port number. Therefore, the logic resources required for the header comparator, with exception of destination port inspection for each rule, is negligible.

Since a fixed number of logic elements are required for the control and datapath (approximately 250 LE) Hogwash rules requiring a total of 1611 byte comparison from 105 rules may be implemented with roughly 17,000 logic elements. Therefore, we estimate that the current Hogwash rule set can be mapped on a mid-size Altera EP20K FPGA with 20,000 LE.

3.6 Limitations

For the sake of simplicity, some features of Snort were not implemented in our design. One simple option would be case insensitivity in string comparisons. One way to implement case sensitivity in hardware is by checking the range of the characters and simply subtracting the case offset before sending the data to the content pattern match unit. This will require an additional twelve 8-bit comparators for each rule with the nocase option. In such manner, this limitation can be addressed.

A more difficult limitation to overcome is handling packet fragmentation. To overcome this limitation, the implementation requires buffers to store all the packets in a stream until they can be reassembled. Defragmentation is currently addressed in software.

4 Conclusion

The benchmark details of current multi-layer inspection packages reveal performance and functional shortcomings. The performance slow down is due to the sequential execution of a large set of pattern matching rules on each packets. Therefore, existing software or hardware may not be fast enough to filter out the complex malicious attack for the networks with bandwidth above 100 Mbps.

Our parallel implementation can filter network traffic at 2.88 Gbps. By examining the critical path information, we hypothesize that our implementation can filter network traffic with bandwidth of 6 Gbps by turning on some timing constraints on the place and router of the FPGA.

Given sufficient amount of hardware resource, all the filter rules can process the packet in parallel. A highly pipelined design gives fixed high performance for even the most complex pattern search rule. Accordingly, our experimental results indicate full filtering capability on a data bandwidth of several gigabits per second.

References

1. J. McHugh, A. Christie, J. Allen, "Defending Yourself: The Role of Intrusion Detection Systems," IEEE Software Magazine, Sept./Oct. 2000.

2. CERT/CC, "CERT Advisory CA-2001-19 Code Red Worm Exploiting Buffer Overflow In IIS Indexing Service DLL", Carnegie Mellon Software Engineering Institute, August 23, 2001.
3. Viacom Inc., "Firewall Q&A", 2001.
4. J. Allen, A. Christie, W. Fithen, J. McHugh, J. Pickel, E. Stoner, "State of the Practice of Intrusion Detection Technologies,"Technical Report, Carnegie Mellon Software Engineering Institute, Jan. 2000.
5. M. Roesch, "Snort - Lightweight Intrusion Detection for Networks", USENIX LISA '99 conference, Nov. 1999.
6. M. Karagiannis, "How to create a Stealth Packet Scrubber using Hogwash," Application Notes for Hogwash, 2001.
7. Netperf.org, "Netperf documentation", 1997.
8. SonicWall Inc.,"Denial of Service Attacks - An Emerging Vulnerability of "Connected" Network," White paper, 2001.
9. Broadcom Inc., "Strada Switch II BCM5616 - Integrated Multi-layer Switch,"Product Brief, 2001.
10. PMC Sierra Inc., "PM2329 ClassiPi Network Classification Processor Datasheet,"Product Datasheet, PMC-2010146, Issue 4, 2001.
11. PMC Sierra Inc., "Preliminary PM2329 ClassiPi Wire-speed Performance Application Note,"Application Note, PMC-2010258, Issue 1, October 2001.
12. M. Iliopoulos, T. Antonakopoulos, "Reconfigurable network processors based on field programmable system level integrated circuits," 10th Conference on Field Programmable Logic and Applications, pp. 39-47, 2000.
13. A. Dollas, D. Pnevmatikatos, N. Aslanides, et al., "Rapid prototyping of a reusable 4x4 active ATM switch core with the PCI pamette," 12th International Workshop on Rapid Prototyping, pp. 17-23, 2001.
14. J.W. Lockwood, "Evolvable Internet hardware platforms," Proceedings of the 3rd NASA/DoD Workshop on Evolvable Hardware, pp. 271-279, 2001.
15. F. Braun, J. Lockwood, M. Waldvogel,"Reconfigurable router modules using network protocol wrappers," 11th Conference on Field Programmable Logic and Applications (FPL01), pp. 254-263, 2001.
16. H. Fallside, M.J.S. Smith, "Internet connected FPL," 10th Conference on Field Programmable Logic and Applications, pp. 48-57, 2000.
17. F. Braun, J. Lockwood, M. Waldvogel, "Protocol wrappers for layered network packet processing in reconfigurable hardware,"IEEE Micro, Vol. 22, Issue 1, pp. 66-74, Jan.-Feb. 2002.
18. P.W. Dowd, J.T. McHenry, F.A. Pellegrino, T.M. Carrozzi and W.B. Cocks, "An FPGA-Based Coprocessor for ATM Firewalls,"Proceedings of the IEEE Symposium on FPGA's for Custom Computing Machines (FCCM97), April 1997.
19. R. Sinnappan and S. Hazelhurst, "A Reconfigurable Approach to Packet Filtering,"In Proceedings of FPL 2001: 11th International Conference on Field Programmable Logic and Applications, Belfast, United Kingdom, August 2001.
20. R. Sidhu and V. K. Prasanna, "Fast Regular Expression Matching using FPGAs,"IEEE Symposium on Field-Programmable Custom Computing Machines (FCCM01), April 2001.
21. D. Carver, R. Franklin, B.L. Hutchings, "Assisting Network Intrusion Detection with Reconfigurable Hardware,"Proceedings of the IEEE Symposium on FPGA's for Custom Computing Machines (FCCM02), April 2002.
22. Altera Inc., "Altera Quartus II Development Software Manual", 2001.

Implementation of a Successive Erasure BCH*(16,7,6) Decoder and Performance Simulation by Rapid Prototyping

Thomas Buerner

Institute for Computer Aided Circuit Design,
University of Erlangen, Paul-Gordan-Str. 5, 91052 Erlangen, Germany
buerner@lrs.e-technik.uni-erlangen.de

Abstract. A major problem in simulating communication systems is that, below a certain error rate, software simulation is too slow. Also software often does not allow to simulate the real system but only a somehow simplified version. Rapid prototyping can help to execute a hardware emulation of the system that is fast and represents the real behaviour too. As an example this paper describes the software simulation and hardware emulation of an extended BCH(16,7) code over an additive white Gaussian noise(AWGN) channel using binary phase shift keying (BPSK). Successive erasure decoding(SED) shows an additional gain of about 1 dB at a bit error rate of 10^{-6} and below, compared to a standard Berlekamp-Massey algorithm(BMA).
The first two sections present the theoretical coding background, section three deals with implementation issues and section four discusses simulation and emulation results.[1]

1 Introduction

When decoding BCH codes (or Reed-Solomon codes) the first and obvious choice is the Berlekamp-Massey algorithm (BMA). This algorithm is a so called hard decision decoder that corrects up to $t = \lfloor \frac{d-1}{2} \rfloor$ errors, d the minimum distance of the code. Above this bound the decoder either finds out that it cannot decode or performs invalid corrections. So how to get beyond the t-limit?

Data transmissions are not digital. They are based on analogue signals. Therefore the signal received is not a zero or one, but a real value. This real value combines the hard decision (zero or one) and also a reliability measure: less distance to the hard decision threshold value means less reliable than a longer distance. Decoding using these real values is called soft decision decoding. Koetter and Vardy found a way to decode these soft values on symbol level algebraically [7]. This was a great breakthrough in channel coding, particularly

* Bose-Chaudhuri-Hochquenghem

[1] For an exhaustive introduction to coding theory in general refer to Blahut [1] or any other coding theory textbook.

M. Glesner, P. Zipf, and M. Renovell (Eds.): FPL 2002, LNCS 2438, pp. 462–471, 2002.

in Reed-Solomon and BCH soft decision decoding achieving an additional coding gain of several dB. Unfortunately the complexity of this algorithm is much bigger than the standard BMA making hardware implementation difficult.

Another well known method to utilize soft information is the Generalized Minimum Distance Decoding introduced by Forney already in 1966 [4], a means of bridging the gap between hard and soft decision decoding. Generalized Minimum Distance Decoding generates a list of candidate decoding outputs by errors and erasure decoding[2], that are tested against an acceptance criterion. This means that many decoding runs have to be made to get such a list: decode with no erasures, decode with the two least reliable symbols erased, decode with the four least reliable symbols erased, and so on. Sorger succeeded in reducing all these runs to just one using Newton's interpolation [9]. But Newton's interpolation is much more expensive than interpolation by a Fourier transform in terms of memory and calculations. Koetter further decreased the effort by eliminating Newton's Interpolation what made hardware implementation feasible [6]. The architecture presented in this paper is based on Koetter's idea. The applied acceptance criterion is very simple: introduce erasures until the allowed number of erasures is exceeded or until the decoder signals a successful decoding. The number of erasures has to be chosen carefully, because the probability of miscorrection increases with more erasures. For Reed-Solomon codes Swanson and McEliece give an upper bound for the probability of miscorrection when more than t errors are received by $1/t!$ [8].

Binary codes binary signaled are best suited to show the additional gain of SED against pure hard decision decoding, because SED is asymptotically optimum there [3]. As a consequence soft decision by SED approaches Maximum-Likelihood performance at high SNR. So the main focus in this presentation lies in transmissions with relatively high SNR i.e. the code works far below its capabilities. Software simulation is inappropriate to get performance results in this SNR region as it takes a too long time and even does not reflect the behaviour of the hardware implementation.

2 Decoding Algorithm for BCH and Reed-Solomon Codes

Let us suppose α a primitive n-th root in GF(2^m) and d the minimum distance of the code. Then a generator polynomial is given by

$$g(X) = \text{LCM}\left\{\phi(\alpha), \ldots, \phi(\alpha^{d-1})\right\}. \tag{1}$$

and $\phi(x)$ terms the minimal polynomial of x in either the extension field GF(2^m) for RS codes or the base field GF(2) in case of BCH codes. By definition the code polynomial $c(x) = \sum_{i=0}^{n-1} c_i X^i$ associated with the codeword $c = (c_0, \ldots, c_{n-1})$ is a multiple of $g(x)$. During transmission an error vector $e = (e_0, \ldots, e_{n-1})$ is

[2] An errors and erasure decoder can correct eo errors and ea erasures, provided that $2eo + ea < d$ holds.

added to the codeword c and forms the received vector $r = (r_0, \ldots, r_{n-1}) = c+e$. Note: $c, r, e \in \{0,1\}^n$ for BCH and $c, r, e \in (GF(2^m))^n$ for Reed-Solomon codes.

2.1 Syndrome Generation

The vector r is mapped onto the received polynomial $r(X) = \sum_{i=0}^{n-1} r_i X^i$. The syndrome values are calculated via a Fourier transform [1].

$$S_{d-1-i} = r(\alpha^i) = c(\alpha^i) + e(\alpha^i) = e(\alpha^i) \qquad i \in \{1, \ldots, d-1\}. \tag{2}$$

The evaluation of $r(X)$ in these points can efficiently be implemented by a Horner scheme

$$r(\alpha^i) = (\ldots(r_{n-1}\alpha^i + r_{n-2})\alpha^i + \ldots)\alpha^i + r_1)\alpha^i + r_0 \qquad i \in \{1, \ldots, d-1\}. \tag{3}$$

The resulting hardware structure for the syndrome coefficient S_{d-1-i} is depicted in Fig. 1 (j starts with $n-1$ and goes down to 0). After the last multiplication and addition step with r_0 the syndrome calculation is finished. The syndrome coefficients define the syndrome polynomial

$$S(X) = S_0 + S_1 X + \ldots + S_{d-3}X^{d-3} + S_{d-2}X^{d-2}. \tag{4}$$

When the code is extended by a parity bit or parity symbol r_n for BCH and Reed-Solomon codes respectively the syndrome polynomial becomes

$$S(X) = S_0 + S_1 X + \ldots + S_{d-3}X^{d-3} + S_{d-2}X^{d-2} + S_{d-1}X^{d-1} \tag{5}$$

and $S_{d-1} = \sum_{i=0}^{n} r_i$. The extension increases the minimum distance d by one.

2.2 Berlekamp-Massey Algorithm

The BMA's task is to locate the error positions in the received word r. Therefore it solves the key equation

$$\Lambda(X)S(X) \equiv \Omega(X) \mod X^{d-1} \tag{6}$$

with degree of $\Lambda(X)$ less than $\lfloor \frac{d}{2} \rfloor$ and degree of $\Omega(X)$ less than the degree of $\Lambda(X)$. The polynomial $\Lambda(X)$ is called *error locator* and vanishes in the error locations, $\Omega(X)$ is called *error evaluator* and only needed for the error value calculation. There are several versions of this algorithm. One according to Sorger[10] is given in Fig. 2. Note that $(P(X))[i]$ picks the coefficient of X^i in the polynomial $P(X)$.

This version is not optimal for implementing a pure BMA, but in the context of the next subsection the necessary changes will prove to be very small. A more convenient algorithm for a standard implementation can be found for instance in Clark and Cain [2].

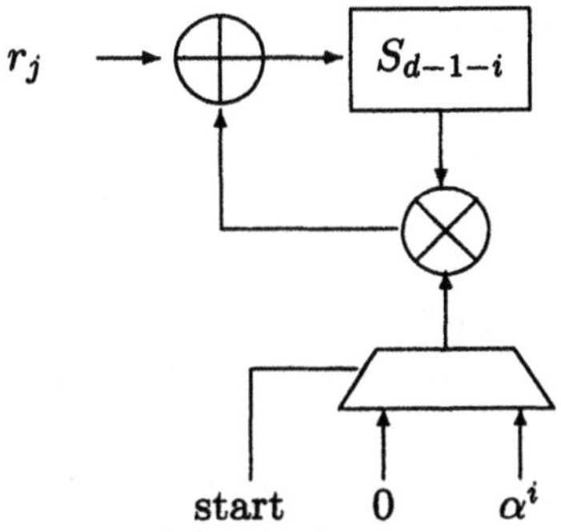

Fig. 1. Syndrome Generator

$S(X) \leftarrow S_0 + S_1X + \ldots + S_{d-2}X^{d-2}$
  $l \leftarrow \min\{i \in \{0,\ldots,d-2\} | S_i \neq 0\}$
$\Lambda(X) \leftarrow X \quad g \leftarrow 1$
$\tilde{\Lambda}(X) \leftarrow S_l \quad \tilde{g} \leftarrow l+1$
FOR $i = l$ TO $d-2$
  $f \leftarrow (\Lambda(X)S(X))[i]$
  $\tilde{f} \leftarrow (\tilde{\Lambda}(X)S(X))[i]$
  IF $f \neq 0$ THEN
    $\tilde{\Lambda}(X) \leftarrow f\tilde{\Lambda}(X) - \tilde{f}\Lambda(X)$
    $\Lambda(X) \leftarrow X\Lambda(X)$
    $g \leftarrow g+1$
    IF $\tilde{g} < g$ THEN
      $\Lambda(X) \leftrightarrow \tilde{\Lambda}(X)$
      $g \leftrightarrow \tilde{g}$
    END IF
  ELSE
    $\tilde{\Lambda}(X) \leftarrow X\tilde{\Lambda}(X)$
    $\tilde{g} \leftarrow \tilde{g}+1$
  END IF
END FOR

Fig. 2. Modified BMA

Remark 1 (Computing $(\Lambda(X)S(X))[i]$). A closer look to $(\Lambda(X)S(X))[i]$ reveals

$$\Lambda(X)S(X) = \sum_{i=0}^{d-2+deg(\Lambda)} \left(\sum_{j=0}^{i} \Lambda_j S_{i-j} \right) X^i \tag{7}$$

and the coefficient of X^i is given by

$$\Lambda(X)S(X)[i] = \sum_{j=0}^{i} \Lambda_j S_{i-j}. \tag{8}$$

This suggests an implementation by a shift register as can be seen in Fig. 3.

2.3 Successive Erasure Decoding

The standard algorithm's result for $\Lambda(X)$ is invalid when the given calculated degree g differs from the number of zeros of $\Lambda(X)$ for $X \in \{\alpha^0, \ldots, \alpha^{n-1}\}$ ($X \in \{\alpha^0, \ldots, \alpha^{n-1}, 0\}$ in case of the extended code) or from the actual polynomial degree $\deg(\Lambda(X))$. In this situation the reliability information is used to generate a vector of erasure positions $(x_1, \ldots, x_{\max})$ arranged in order of rising reliability. x_1 is the position of the least reliable symbol. It should be mentioned that the received vector $r = (r_0, \ldots, r_{n-1})$ corresponds to the position vector

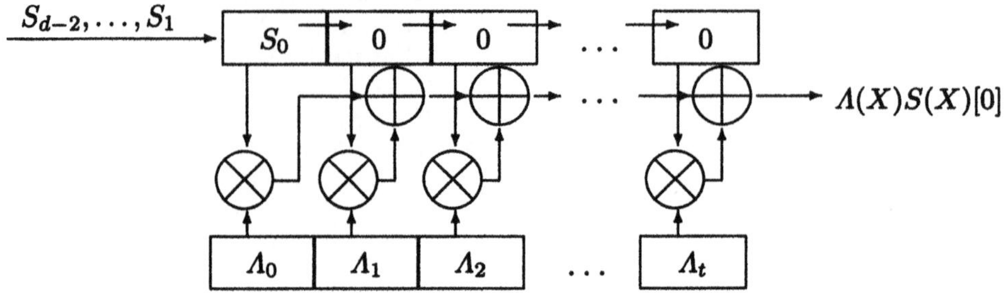

Fig. 3. Coefficient Calculation

$(\alpha^0, \ldots, \alpha^{n-1})$ and when an extension parity symbol/bit is added, this position corresponds to $x = 0$. This is not obvious but can be concluded from the original definition of Reed-Solomon codes [11]. If $\Lambda(X)$ is invalid and there are still erasure positions to be processed, an erasure step for an erasure in position x_e is calculated according to Fig. 4 [6]. The SED step has an apparent analogy to the modified BMA in Fig. 2. The only difference is the calculation of the discrepancies f and $\tilde{f}$. So the two parts can perfectly be merged into one algorithm depicted in Fig. 5 (without initialization because it is the same as in Fig. 2).

Example 1 (RS(6,2) in GF(7)). Let $\alpha = 5$ be the primitive element in GF(7). A (6,2) Reed-Solomon code is chosen, that can correct up to two errors. The generator polynomial consists of four linear factors $g(X) = \prod_{i=1}^{4}(X - 5^i) = X^4+4X^3+6X^2+5X+2$. Let the codeword be $c = (2,5,6,4,1,0)$. The polynomial $c(X) = \sum_{i=0}^{5} c_i X^i$ is obviously divided by $g(X)$. Suppose the received word is $r = (2,5,0,0,0,0)$. This is one error more than can be corrected. An errors only decoder will decode to the all zeros word. Afterwards we will employ erasures for r_3 and r_4, corresponding to erasure positions $x_0 = \alpha^3 = 6$ and $x_1 = \alpha^4 = 2$ and see that the third error is detected.

Syndrome values are calculated to $(S_4, S_3, S_2, S_1) = (2,3,6,1)$ with which the BMA is initialized: $S(X) = 2 + 3X + 6X^2 + 1X^3, l = 0, \Lambda(X) = X, g = 1, \tilde{\Lambda}(X) = 2, \tilde{g} = 1$.

1. $i = 1$: $f \leftarrow 2$ $\tilde{f} \leftarrow 6$.
   $\tilde{\Lambda}(X) \leftarrow 2\tilde{\Lambda}(X) - 6\Lambda(X) = 4 + X$, $\Lambda(X) \leftarrow X^2$,$g \leftarrow 2$. Now $\tilde{g}$ is less than g so exchange register contents: $\Lambda(X) \leftarrow 4 + X$,$\tilde{\Lambda}(X) \leftarrow X^2$, $g \leftarrow 1$, $\tilde{g} = 2$.
2. $i = 2$: $f \leftarrow 6$ $\tilde{f} \leftarrow 2$.
   $\tilde{\Lambda}(X) \leftarrow 6\tilde{\Lambda}(X) - 2\Lambda(X) = 6X^2 + 5X + 6$, $\Lambda(X) \leftarrow X^2 + 4X$,$g \leftarrow 2$.
3. $i = 3$: $f \leftarrow 6$ $\tilde{f} \leftarrow 5$.
   $\tilde{\Lambda}(X) \leftarrow 6\tilde{\Lambda}(X) - 5\Lambda(X) = 3X^2 + 3X + 1$, $\Lambda(X) \leftarrow X^3 + 4X^2$,$g \leftarrow 3$. Now $\tilde{g}$ is less than g so exchange register contents: $\Lambda(X) \leftarrow 3X^2 + 3X + 1$,$\tilde{\Lambda}(X) \leftarrow X^3 + 4X^2$, $g \leftarrow 2$, $\tilde{g} \leftarrow 3$.

```
f ← Λ(x_e)
f̃ ← Λ̃(x_e)
IF f ≠ 0 THEN
   Λ̃(X) ← fΛ̃(X) − f̃Λ(X)
   Λ(X) ← (X − x_e)Λ(X)
   g      ← g + 1
   IF g̃ < g THEN
      Λ(X) ↔ Λ̃(X)
      g      ↔ g̃
   END IF
ELSE
   Λ̃(X) ← (X − x_e)Λ̃(X)
   g̃      ← g̃ + 1
END IF
```

Fig. 4. Erasure Step

```
x^e ← 0
(x_1, ..., x_max) ← least reliable positions
FOR i = l TO d − 2+ max
   IF i > d − 2 THEN
      x^e ← x_{i−d+2}
      f ← Λ(x^e)   f̃ ← Λ̃(x^e)
   ELSE
      f ← (Λ(X)S(X))[i]
      f̃ ← (Λ̃(X)S(X))[i]
   END IF
   IF f ≠ 0 THEN
      Λ̃(X) ← fΛ̃(X) − f̃Λ(X)
      Λ(X) ← (X − x^e)Λ(X)
      g      ← g + 1
      IF g̃ < g THEN
         Λ(X) ↔ Λ̃(X)   g ↔ g̃
      END IF
   ELSE
      Λ̃(X) ← (X − x^e)Λ̃(X)
      g̃      ← g̃ + 1
   END IF
END FOR
```

Fig. 5. Successive Erasure Algorithm

$\Lambda(X) = 3X^2 + 3X + 1$ evaluates to zero for $X = 1$ and $X = 5$, i.e. positions r_0 and r_1, and the all zeros word would be the decoding result. In the next steps two erasures are introduced:

1. first erasure in $X = 6$, $f \leftarrow \Lambda(6) = 1$, $\tilde{f} \leftarrow \tilde{\Lambda}(6) = 3$, $\tilde{\Lambda}(X) \leftarrow 1\tilde{\Lambda}(X) - 3\Lambda(X) = X^3 + 2X^2 + 5X + 4$, $\Lambda(X) \leftarrow 3X^3 + 6X^2 + 4X + 1$,$g \leftarrow 3$.
2. second erasure in $X = 2$,$f \leftarrow \Lambda(2) = 1$, $\tilde{f} \leftarrow \tilde{\Lambda}(6) = 2$, $\tilde{\Lambda}(X) \leftarrow \tilde{\Lambda}(X) - 2\Lambda(X) = 2X^3+4X^2+4X+2$, $\Lambda(X) \leftarrow (3X^3+6X^2+4X+1)(X-2)$,$g \leftarrow 4$. Now $\tilde{g}$ is less than g so exchange register contents: $\Lambda(X) \leftarrow 2X^3 + 4X^2 + 4X + 2$

We get $\Lambda(X) = 2(X - 4)(X - 6)(X - 2)$ and the error location $X = 2$.

3 Implementation

In this section the implementation of a SED is described, based on the extended BCH(16,7). The emulation strategy is to send the all zeros codeword over an AWGN channel model and count the ones after the decoder. Each one in the decoder's output stream is an erroneous bit. Figure 6 shows an overview of the SED architecture and how the design is divided into two XILINX XC4010XL FPGAs. The FPGAs are placed on XS-40XL boards by XESS Corp. The shaded boxes indicate that the according parts are only needed for SED. In the following a brief description of the modules is given.

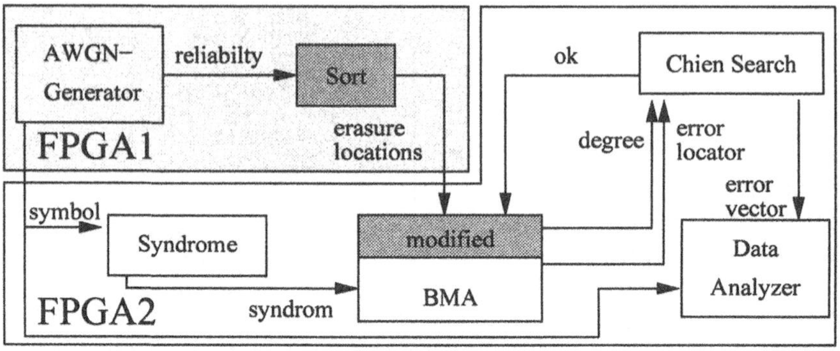

Fig. 6. Architecture Overview

3.1 LFSR Based AWGN Generator

To get an approximation Y of a Gaussian distributed random variable by exploiting the central limit theorem twelve uniformly distributed random variables Y_i $i = 1, \ldots, 12$ are added. For the implementation the variables Y_i are built by eight LFSR bits each. Variance and expectation value of Y is

$$\mathrm{VAR}(Y) = \sum_{i=1}^{12} \mathrm{VAR}(Y_i), \qquad \mu(Y) = \sum_{i=1}^{12} \mu(Y_i). \tag{9}$$

The Gaussian distributed random variable Y with variance $\mathrm{VAR}(Y)$ and expectation value $\mu(Y)$ is transformed to a Gaussian distributed random variable G with variance $\mathrm{VAR}(G) = v$ and expectation value $\mu(G) = 0$ by

$$G = (Y - \mu(Y))\sqrt{\frac{v}{\mathrm{VAR}(Y)}}. \tag{10}$$

3.2 Sort

Sort produces a list of the most unreliable symbols in each code word and transfers this list to the modified BMA for erasing.

3.3 Syndrome

The syndrome coefficients are calculated according to Fig. 1.

3.4 Chien Search

The error locator polynomial $\Lambda(X)$ is checked in this module, whether the number of zeros match the given degree or not. If they match, an 'ok' signal will be given to the BMA and the error vector will be updated. $\Lambda(X)$ has to be evaluated in all symbol positions of the codeword. As the result must be available after one clock cycle, a brute force implementation is inevitable, i.e. an evaluation circuit $\Lambda(\beta) = \Lambda_0 + \Lambda_1\beta + \ldots + \Lambda_t\beta^t$ is necessary for all possible positions β. For further details refer to Clark and Cain [2].

3.5 Modified BMA

An architecture draft of the calculations, disregarding control paths and shifting parts, is illustrated in Fig. 7. The position going to be erased is denoted by β. Thick lines indicate a whole vector, thin lines represent a single Galois Field element. A vector-vector multiplication is to be interpreted componentwise. An element-vector multiplication means that each vector component is multiplied by this element. The summation sums up all vector elements resulting in a single Galois Field element. The multiplexer switches the shift register vector to the output for the standard BMA and the erasure vector for the erasing part of the algorithm. Figure 8 shows the multiplication of a polynomial $A(X) = \sum_{i=0}^{t} A_i X^i$

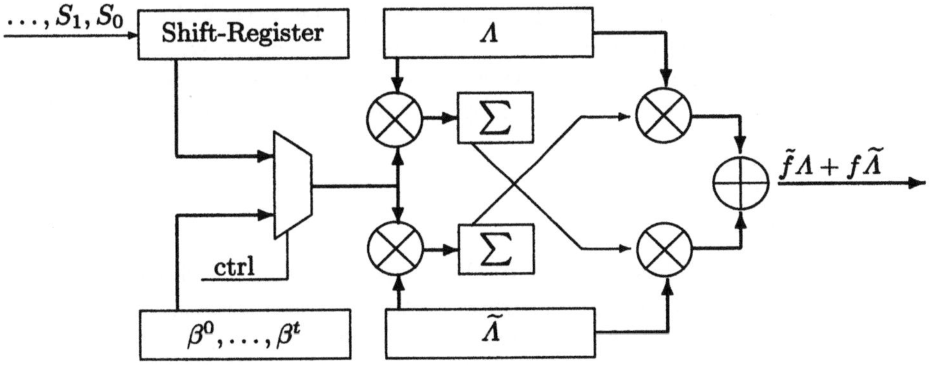

Fig. 7. BMA Calculations

of degree t with a linear factor $(X - \beta)$. After $t + 1$ cycles the result is present in the right $t + 1$ registers. The polynomial will be truncated to degree t.

3.6 Data Analyzer

The analyzer's only task is to compare the correct output stream, i.e. all zeros, to the decoded stream and count all appearing ones, as these are the errors.

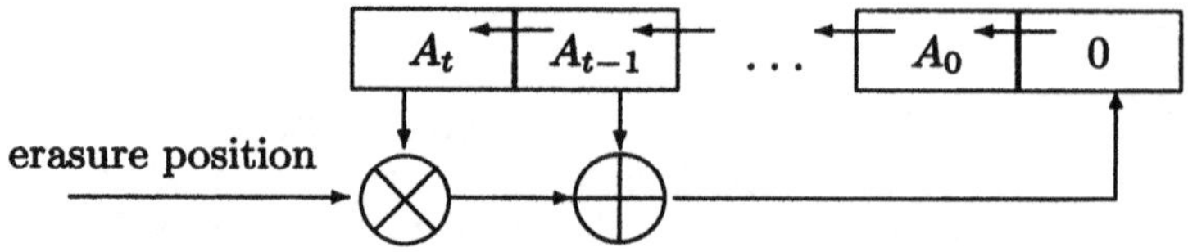

Fig. 8. Shift Operation

4 Performance Comparison

For the hard decision BMA the extended bit is only used to increase the minimum distance thus reducing the probability of miscorrection. For the SED one erasure is introduced, when hard decision decoding failed. This single erasure enhances the correction capability of the code by one error. The software simulation is simplified in so far that miscorrection is neglected for hard decision as well as for SED. The Box-Muller method is used in the software implementation to transform a uniformly distributed random variable to a Gaussian distributed one [5]. The bit error rates are shown without decoding, with hard decision decoding and with SED in Fig. 9. In the hardware emulation the summation of uniformly distributed random variables is applied to model an AWGN channel. Due to limited hardware resources the Box-Muller method is not applicable, although it is well known that there are unfavorable characteristics of this approach at the sides of the distribution. This also constitutes the reason why the hardware emulated bit error rates in Fig. 9 do not match the software simulated points. Nevertheless the achieved performance gain is the same for both AWGN models.

5 Conclusions

A successive erasure decoder was implemented and compared to a standard Berlekamp-Massey decoder with regard to the accessible coding gain. It was shown that an additional coding gain of about 1 dB is achieved by SED in the case of an extBCH(16,7). The SED for this code and one erasure is four times bigger than the standard implementation.For only one erasure two parallel decoders are less hardware consuming than the SED. But the relation flips when more erasures are to be processed. So SED makes sense in applications where hardware resources do not play a major role but coding gain does and of course soft information is available. It was also shown that rapid prototyping is a means of investigating codes in very low SNR regions. The time needed for simulating 10^9 codewords on a SUN UltraSparcII 450MHz is about 17 hours, when emulated on the XC4010XL running with 12.5 MHz this takes 22 minutes. So hardware emulation speeds up simulation by a factor of roughly 45. Not to forget that the hardware used for this project is rather old fashioned and using up to date hardware can even speed it up by another factor of at least 5.

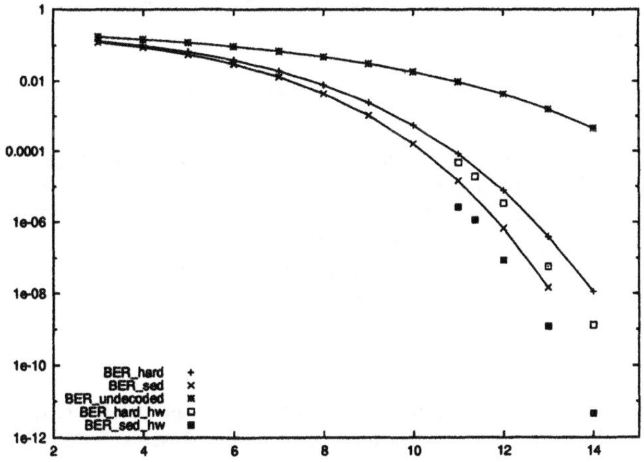

Fig. 9. extBCH(16,7): BER over SNR/dB

6 Acknowledgment

The hardware for this work was kindly sponsored by Xilinx Inc. .

References

1. Blahut R.E., *Theory and Practice of Error Control Codes,* Addison-Wesley Publishing Company, 1983
2. Clark G.C., Cain J.B., *Error Correction Coding for Digital Communications,* Plenum Publishing Corporation, 1981
3. Einarsson G., Sundberg C.-E., *A Note on Soft Decision Decoding with Successive Erasures,* IEEE Transactions on Information Theory, Vol.IT-22, No.1, pp. 88–96, January 1976
4. Forney G. David, *Generalized Minimum Distance Decoding* IEEE Transactions on Information Theory, Vol.IT-12, No.2, pp. 125–131, April 1966
5. Knuth, Donald E., *The Art of Computer Programming* Addison-Wesley, 1998
6. Koetter R., *Fast Generalized Minimum-Distance Decoding of Algebraic-Geometry and Reed-Solomon Codes,* IEEE Transactions on Information Theory, Vol.IT-42, No.3, pp. 721–737, May 1996
7. Koetter R., Vardy A., *Algebraic Soft-Decision Decoding of Reed-Solomon Codes,* IEEE Transactions on Information Theory, submitted for publication, August 2001
8. McEliece R.J., Swanson L., *On the Decoding Error Probability for Reed-Solomon Codes,* IEEE Transactions on Information Theory, Vol.IT-42, No.3, pp. 721–737, May 1996
9. Sorger U., *A New Reed Solomon Codes Decoding Algorithm Based on Newton's Interpolation,* IEEE Transactions on Information Theory, Vol.IT-39, No.2, pp. 358–366, March 1993
10. Sorger U., *Reed Solomon Codes und Newton Interpolation,* VDI Verlag, Reihe 10: Informatik/ Kommunikationstechnik, Nr.343, 1995
11. Wicker S.B. & Bhargava V.K., *Reed–Solomon Codes and Their Applications,* IEEE Press, New York 1994

Fast RNS FPL-based Communications Receiver Design and Implementation

J. Ramírez [(1)], A. García [(1)], U. Meyer-Baese [(2)] and A. Lloris [(1)]

[(1)] Dept. of Electronics and Computer Technology,
Campus Universitario Fuentenueva, 18071 Granada, Spain
{jramirez, agarcia, lloris}@ditec.ugr.es
[(2)] Dept. of Electrical and Computer Engineering,
Florida State University, Tallahassee, USA
umb@eng.fsu.edu

Abstract. Currently, several design barriers inhibit the implementation of high-precision digital signal processing (DSP) systems with field programmable logic (FPL) devices. A new demonstration of the synergy between the residue number system (RNS) and FPL technology is presented in this paper. The quantifiable benefits of this approach are studied in the context of a high-end communications digital receiver. A new RNS-based direct digital synthesizer (DDS) that does not need a scaler circuit is introduced. The programmable decimation FIR filter is based on the arithmetic benefits associated with Galois fields and supports tuning the IF frequency as well as its bandwidth. Results show the proposed methodology requires fewer resources than classical designs, while throughput advantage is about 65%.

1. Introduction

Digital receivers have revolutionized communication systems offering remarkable benefits when compared to their analog counterparts. During the last decade, Direct Digital Synthesizer (DDS) techniques have become increasingly popular methods in digital receiver designs and many ASIC vendors, such as Graychip [1], Intersil [2] or Pentek [3], are providing semiconductor solutions for digital communication systems. These systems yield significant benefits in performance, density and cost as well as provide high frequency resolution, fast and phase-continuous frequency switching, exceptional linearity and excellent temperature and aging stability.

With the advent of the new Field-Programmable Logic (FPL) device families, such as the Altera APEX 20K [4] or the Xilinx Virtex [5], and their increasing speed and density, many new benefits are becoming available to radio frequencies for the design of digital communication systems using these devices. Digital receiver chips perform down conversion, lowpass filtering and decimation of the sampled RF signal. The resulting bandwidth and sample rate reduction makes it possible to perform real-time processing of narrow and wide band radio signals.

Traditional numbering systems are commonly used to build DSP systems with commercially available FPL technology. Although the two's complement (2C) system has been adopted for a wide range of real-time applications including digital

M. Glesner, P. Zipf, and M. Renovell (Eds.): FPL 2002, LNCS 2438, pp. 472-481, 2002.

communications, image, video and speech processing, multimedia systems, networking, etc, a review of the FPL vendor supplied application notes [6, 7] shows that these devices suffer from weak arithmetic performance when compared to carefully designed standard-cell based ASICs. While FPL vendors champion their technology as a provider of *system-on-a-chip* (SOC) DSP solutions, engineers have historically viewed FPL as a prototyping technology. In order for FPL to begin to compete in areas currently controlled by low-end standard-cell ICs, a means must be found to more efficiently implement DSP objects.

An arithmetic system capable of surmounting these barriers is the residue number system, or RNS [8]. This paper develops a mechanism of achieving synergy within an FPL-defined environment to implement arithmetic intensive DSP solutions. FPL devices are organized in channels (typically 8-bits wide). Within these channels are found short delay propagation paths and dedicated memory blocks with programmable address and data spaces, which are commonly used to synthesize small RAM and ROM functions. Performance rapidly suffers when carry bits and/or data have to propagate across channel boundaries. We call this the channel barrier problem [9]. Existing 2C designs encounter the channel barrier problem whenever precision exceeds the channel width. An alternative design paradigm is advocated in this paper. The advantage is gained by reducing arithmetic to a set of concurrent operations that reside in small wordlength non-communicating channels. The quantifiable benefits of this approach are studied in the context of a design example, an RNS-based digital receiver design. This work will build upon previous works [10, 11, 12] and previous RNS-FPL design experience [13].

2. Background

There is emerging evidence that an arithmetic technology, called the RNS [8], can avoid the throughput degradation with the increase in precision and become a custom IC enabling technology. Computer arithmeticians have long held that the RNS offers the best MAC speed-area advantage [14].

In the RNS, numbers are represented in terms of a relatively prime basis set (*moduli* set) $P=\{m_1, m_2..., m_L\}$. Any number $X\in Z_M=\{0, 1, ..., M-1\}$, where $M=m_1\cdot m_2\cdot\ldots\cdot m_L$, has a unique RNS representation $X\leftrightarrow\{X_1, X_2..., X_L\}$, where $X_l=X \bmod m_l$ ($l= 1, 2, \ldots, L$). Mapping from the RNS back to the integer domain is defined by the Chinese Remainder Theorem (CRT) [8].

RNS arithmetic is defined by pair-wise modular operations:

$$\begin{aligned} Z = X \pm Y \leftrightarrow \left[\left|X_{m_1} \pm Y_{m_1}\right|_{m_1}, \left|X_{m_2} \pm Y_{m_2}\right|_{m_2}, \ \ldots \ , \left|X_{m_L} \pm Y_{m_L}\right|_{m_L} \right] \\ Z = X \times Y \leftrightarrow \left[\left|X_{m_1} \times Y_{m_1}\right|_{m_1}, \left|X_{m_2} \times Y_{m_2}\right|_{m_2}, \ \ldots \ , \left|X_{m_L} \times Y_{m_L}\right|_{m_L} \right] \end{aligned} \quad (1)$$

where $|Q|_{m_l}$ denotes Q mod m_l. The individual modular arithmetic operations are typically performed as LUT calls to small memories, the usual core block of today FPL devices.

Index arithmetic [15, 16] constitutes an efficient means for designing high performance, reduced complexity DSP systems. It is based on the mathematical properties associated with Galois fields, denoted GF(p), with p being a prime. All the non-zero elements in a Galois field can be generated exponentiating a primitive element, denoted g_l. This property can be exploited for multiplication in GF(m_l) through the use of the well known isomorphism between the multiplicative group Q= {1, 2, ..., m_l-1}, with multiplication modulo m_l, and the additive group I= {0, 1, ..., m_l-2}, with addition modulo m_l-1. The mapping is given by:

$$q = \Phi_l^{-1}(i) = g_l^i \bmod m_l \qquad l = 1, 2, ..., L \tag{2}$$

$q \in Q$, $i \in I$ and multiplication is based on:

$$\left|q_1 q_2\right|_{m_l} = g^{\left|i_1+i_2\right|_{m_l-1}} \qquad l = 1, 2, ..., L \tag{3}$$

Thus, multiplication of two operands, say q_1 and q_2, can be performed by adding exponents in a modular sense. The exponents, or indexes, i_1 and i_2, can be pre-computed and stored in a look-up table. Adding the indexes can be performed with a modulo m_l-1 adder, and the inverse index transformation can be performed again using a LUT.

3. Digital Receiver RNS Design

In its simplest form, a superheterodyne receiver filters the radio frequency (RF) signal and converts it to a lower intermediate frequency (IF) by mixing with an offset local-oscillator as shown in Figure 1, with many vendors offering digital receiver chips. On the other hand, FPL chips can take advantage of the built-in device resources as well as their low-cost and low development time to meet the continuous evolving market requirements. However, FPL technology suffers from weak arithmetic capabilities when compared to a well designed ASIC. A RNS-based digital receiver FPL design able to surmount inherent technology barriers is presented below. The design consist of an RNS-based DDS and a high throughput programmable decimation FIR filter.

3.1. Direct Digital Frequency Synthesizer

DDS, or Numerically Controlled Oscillators (NCO), are important components in many digital communication systems. Their applications are numerous in down and up converters, demodulators and various types of modulation schemes, including PSK (Phase Shift Keying), FSK (Frequency Shift Keying) and MSK (Minimum Shift Keying) [17]. A common method for building such a system makes use of an integrator and look-up tables (LUTs) that store uniformly spaced samples of cosine and sine waves. Several properties of the DDS design determine its performance. Traditionally, for most practical applications, a quantizer reduces the precision of the phase angle presented to the LUT address space port, thus reducing the memory requirements of the system [17]. In addition, for an area-efficient design, quarter wave

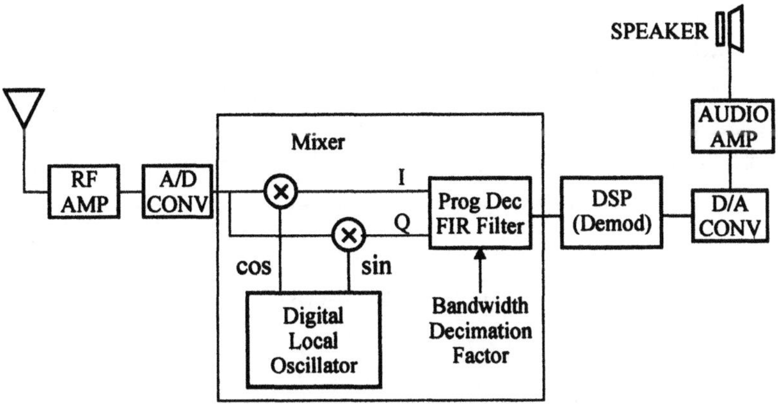

Fig. 1. Digital receiver architecture.

symmetry is exploited, so the two most significant bits of the quantized phase angle are used to perform quadrant mapping. The signal phase and amplitude resolution are affected by the length and width of the LUT, respectively. In this section, an RNS-based DDS for a digital receiver is presented.

A design of a RNS DDS consisting of an RNS Phase Accumulator and a number of LUTs storing the residue digits of sine and cosine waves was presented in [10]. The Phase Accumulator consists of a modulo M adder that increments in $\Delta\theta$ (phase resolution) units the count value each clock cycle. This operation is performed in parallel over the L residue digits, with $\Delta\theta_l = \Delta\theta \bmod m_l$ ($l = 1, 2, \ldots, L$). A clear advantage of this design when compared to traditional structures [17] is that the LUT address space is reduced to the modulus width and the phase accumulation is performed in parallel over low-delay, modular RNS channels. However, most of the RNS-based DDSs often require a complex RNS scaler circuit [10, 11]. In this paper a new RNS-based DDS not requiring scaling is proposed. Moreover, RNS scaler circuits often eliminate two or more RNS channels of the system, thus limiting the digital receiver dynamic range since RNS base extension methods introduce excessive hardware complexity.

Figure 2 shows the design of a low-complexity RNS DDS designed for a high performance FPL programmable digital receiver. Notice that an output RNS engine processes the first quadrant LUT outcomes:

$$c_l(n) = \left(K\cos\left(\frac{2\pi}{N}\theta(n)\right)\right) \bmod m_l \qquad s_l(n) = \left(K\sin\left(\frac{2\pi}{N}\theta(n)\right)\right) \bmod m_l \tag{4}$$

to produce the cosine and sine waves given by:

$$\begin{array}{llll} uv = 00 & \cos_l(n) = c_l(n) & \sin_l(n) = \Phi(s_l(n)) & 0 \le \theta < \pi/2 \\ uv = 01 & \cos_l(n) = -s_l(n) & \sin_l(n) = \Phi(c_l(n)) & \pi/2 \le \theta < \pi \\ uv = 10 & \cos_l(n) = -c_l(n) & \sin_l(n) = \Phi(-s_l(n)) & \pi \le \theta < 3\pi/2 \\ uv = 11 & \cos_l(n) = s_l(n) & \sin_l(n) = \Phi(-c_l(n)) & 3\pi/2 \le \theta < 2\pi \end{array} \tag{5}$$

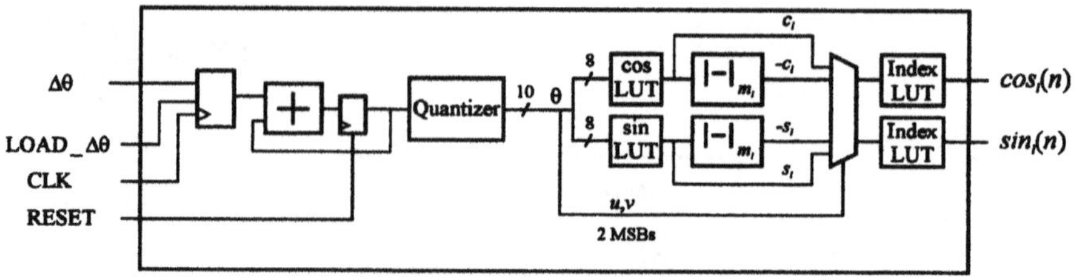

Fig. 2. RNS-based DDS.

where K and N are the precision and depth of the LUTs and Φ is a function that provides the RNS index representation. The proposed design avoids the use of complex RNS scaling hardware and benefits from the sine and cosine symmetry to reduce the LUT address space depth N from 10 to 8 bits, thus fitting the built-in target technology memory resources [4]. For the phase accumulator a carry-chain conventional accumulator was selected. The multiplexer, located at the DDS output, selects the $c_l(n)$, $s_l(n)$, $-c_l(n)$ or $-s_l(n)$ depending on the value of the 2 MSBs of the phase θ. To compute $-c_l(n)$ and $-s_l(n)$, a two-stage modular subtractor was used according to:

$$-c_l(n) = (-c_l(n)) \bmod m_l = (m_l - c_l(n)) \bmod m_l \tag{6}$$
$$-s_l(n) = (-s_l(n)) \bmod m_l = (m_l - s_l(n)) \bmod m_l \qquad l = 1, 2, \ldots, L$$

The DDS generates sine and cosine waves with a frequency given by:

$$f_{\text{out}} = \frac{\Delta\theta}{N} f_{\text{CLK}} \tag{7}$$

where f_{CLK} is the phase accumulator frequency. The frequency resolution Δf of the synthesizer is a function of the clock frequency f_{CLK} and the phase accumulator precision L_{ACC}, and can be determined using the following equation:

$$\Delta f = \frac{f_{CLK}}{2^{L_{ACC}}} \tag{8}$$

Finally, the sine and cosine waves $\sin_l(n)$ and $\cos_l(n)$ are the index representations of the waveforms as shown in Equation 5 and Figure 2.

3.2. Programmable Decimation FIR Filter

The digital receiver is intended to work externally in a 2C format. The programmable decimation FIR filter consists of L index-based parallel RNS channels and a final RNS-to-2C output converter. The main parameters (number of taps, input and output precisions) of the FIR filter are programmable. The filter has a COEFF/$\overline{\text{DATA}}$ input that is used to store the filterbank coefficients serially.

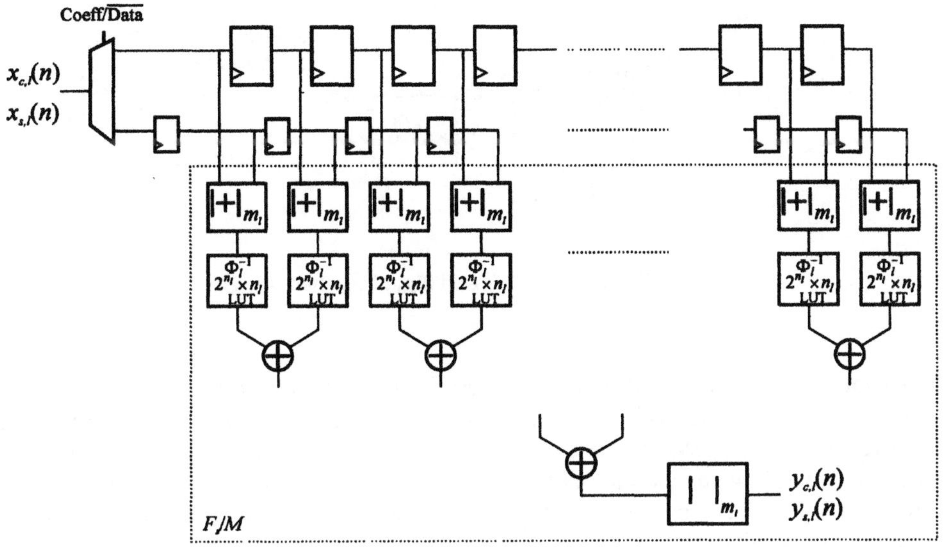

Fig. 3. RNS-based programmable decimation filter design.

To convert the received RF signal to the index domain, a special design of a 2C-to-index converter was used. A B-bit 2C input RF signal $x(n)$ is assumed. The input converter is used to map the B-bit input signal $x(n)$ (or the coefficients sequentially loaded) to an index RNS representation. Its design assumes decomposing the input word into p b-bit blocks: x_0, x_1, …, x_{p-1}, and uses p-1 look-up tables (LUTs) storing the functions $\Phi_k(x_k) = (2^{n_l-1+(k-1)b}x_k) \bmod m_l$ (k= 1, 2, …, p-2) where $n_l = \lceil \log_2(m_l) \rceil$, and $\Phi_{p-1}(x_{p-1}) = (2^{B-q}x_p) \bmod m_l$, with q being the size of the signed x_{p-1} block. Finally, a modular adder tree followed of a LUT provides the index representation modulo m_l (l=1, 2, …, L), denoted by $x_l(n)$. Notice that a LUT is saved since x_0 can be selected as a (n_l-1)-bit block and is directly routed to the modular adder tree.

Once the received RF signal is converted to the index domain, the receiver mixes it with the DDS synthesizer signal using an index domain multiplier and routes the mixed signal to the programmable decimation filter.

Figure 3 shows the internal modular processing engine of the proposed programmable decimation FIR filter. A multiplexer enables loading the coefficient sequentially or distributing the input signal to the index-based multipliers across the register chain. Products are computed by means of a modulo m_l–1 adder modified to correctly compute multiplication by zero [18]. Thus, the modified adder produces a "11…11" value when one input is 0, and a zero value is stored in the $2^{n_l}-1$ LUT address. An inverse index LUT stores the final residue digit given by: $\Phi_l^{-1}(i) = g_l^i \bmod m_l$. The filter product summation is efficiently implemented by means of an enhanced modulo m_l adder tree consisting of conventional adders (with precision extension) followed by a modulo m_l reduction stage implemented by block decomposition [18]. This method leads to an important reduction in resources

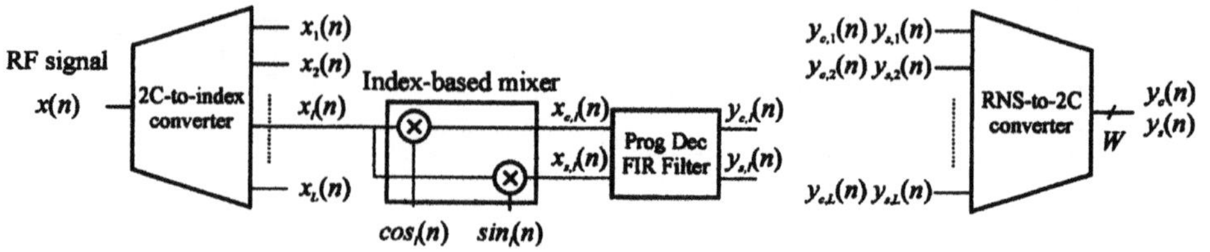

Fig. 4. Complete RNS-based digital receiver design.

(especially for longer filters) and an increase in the system performance. A saving in resources is achieved with a binary MOMA structure when the filter products summation is computed by means of a conventional adder stage (with precision extension) along with a final reduction stage. Notice that the binary adder tree is optimal for FPL devices, in opposition to the use of carry save adders [19], better suited for an ASIC design.

The practical implementation of RNS-based systems encounters a difficulty in the conversion stage. Different solutions has been used to overcome the conversion barrier [18] in FPL-centric designs. In this paper, two solutions were explored for the final index-to-2C output converter. The CRT converter makes use of L LUTs storing $\Theta_l(i) = \hat{m}_l \langle i/\hat{m}_l \rangle \mathrm{mod}\, m_l$, with $\hat{m}_l = M/m_l$, conventional adders and a modulo $M = m_1 \cdot m_2 \cdot \ldots \cdot m_L$ reduction stage. Notice that a subtractor and a multiplexer is needed to map the modulo M output to 2C. A more efficient design is based on the well-known ε-CRT algorithm [20] that maps the L residue digits directly to a scaled W-bit 2C representation. This converter uses smaller LUTs storing the functions $\hat{\Theta}_l(i) = \lfloor 2^{W+b}/m_l \cdot \langle i/\hat{m}_l \rangle \mathrm{mod}\, m_l \rfloor$ and replaces modulo adders by conventional adders. Notice that the $b = \lceil \log_2(L) \rceil$ extra bits are introduced to correct the scaling error, $0 \le \varepsilon < L$, by truncating the final output to W bits.

4. Complexity and Performance Comparisons

Implementations of the proposed communication digital receiver using Altera APEX20K [4] devices were carried out and are presented in the following. The entire RNS-based communication receiver design is shown in Figure 4. Hardware complexity of individual RNS channels was assessed before building the complete systems. The modulus set was selected to ensure the dynamic range of the system, reduce the complexity and maximize the throughput of the system. Prime moduli of up to 5-bit wide as well as a power-of-two modulus of up to 6-bits were found to be the best choice. Thus, the programmable decimation FIR filter was synthesized using only LEs, while ESBs were only required for the DDS sine and cosine LUTs.

The DDS consists of a conventional phase accumulator, 2 LUTs storing the sine and cosine functions and additional logic to exploit quarter wave symmetry. LUTs are mapped directly to 2K-bit ESBs. These blocks can be configured either as $2^7 \times 16$,

$2^8{\times}8$, $2^9{\times}4$, $2^{10}{\times}2$ or $2^{11}{\times}1$. A compromise between hardware requirements and DDS performance is necessary. Thus, for good signal phase and amplitude resolutions larger tables are necessary. However, the number of ESBs increases since a single ESBs can not allocate the whole word of the output residue digits. In this paper we have selected a hardware efficient implementation of the DDS with a 10 bit phase resolution and $2^8{\times}n_l$ sine and cosine LUTs, with each LUT being mapped on a single ESB. The additional logic to deal with the quarter wave symmetry is built with two modular subtracters and two multiplexers.

The programmable decimation FIR filters are based on the design shown in figure 3 and replace slow and complex 2C multipliers with highly efficient FPL-optimized index multipliers [18], thus yielding a sustained increase in system performance.

The proposed design was evaluated using 2C classical receiver benchmarks. The design parameters were: *i*) 8-bit RF signal, *ii*) 8-bit wide sine and cosine LUTs, *iii*) the programmable decimation FIR filters accept 16-bit mixed signals and the filter coefficients are assumed to be 16-bit wide. 2C- and RNS-based digital receivers were modeled using VHDL and synthesized using speed grade –1 Altera APEX 20K devices. The models are parametric and suitable of being modified easily if the system requirements are modified. On the other hand, both systems allow the filter coefficients to be run-time programmable for maximum flexibility.

	2C-based DDS	RNS-based DDS			
		Phase acc.	LUT (quarter wave symmetry)		
			$n_l=3$	$n_l=4$	$n_l=5$
#LEs	94	30	36	46	58
#ESBs	2	30	1	1	2

Table 1. DDS LE and ESB requirement comparisson.

N	*W*	2C FIR		Proposed RNS-based programmable decimation FIR filter CRT/ε-CRT					
		LEs	*F* (MHz)	LEs	Resource reduction	*F* (MHz)	Speed-up	Modulus set
8	34	3892	91	5338/ 4089	-37% -5%	130/ 149	43% 64%	11,13,17,19, 23,29,31,32
16	35	7786	84	9087/ 7365	-16% 5%	128/ 137	52% 63%	11,13,17,19, 23,29,31,64
32	36	15591	79	16828/ 14331	-7% 8%	119/ 131	51% 66%	7,11,13,17, 19,23,29,31,32
64	37	31235	75	32026/ 28173	-2% 10%	116/ 127	55% 69%	7,11,13,17, 19,23,29,31,64

Table 2. Resource reduction and speed-up provided by programmable FIR decimation filters.

Table 1 and Table 2 show the hardware requirements and the maximum operating frequency obtained for the DDS and the programmable decimation FIR filter, respectively. Table 1 quantifies the resources required for a 2C-based DDS and the proposed 2C-RNS merged DDS. The table includes implementation data for different wordwidth RNS moduli since for an entire RNS-based digital receiver design, different wordwidth RNS channels are needed. Table 2 compares 2C FIR filters ranging from 8 to 64 taps with the filters proposed in this paper. Input signal and coefficients are 16-bit wide and, for the 2C design, the 16×16-bit multipliers are designed using five pipeline stages. The table shows the number of taps (N), the system dynamic range (W), the number of LEs, the maximum frequency and the modulus set. Results reveal the proposed filter to have a complexity comparable or even lower than a 2C design, while performance increase is about 65%.

The hardware penalty introduced by the conversion stages was carefully assessed. A CRT-based converter only required between 28% and 7% of the the system total resources for filters ranging from 8 to 64 taps. However, if an ε-CRT converter is used, output conversion only requires from 12% to 2% the of the LEs in the entire system.

5. Conclusions

RNS has been shown as an enabling tool for fast FPL implementation of communication digital receivers. The paper explored building a complete system including the DDS and the programmable bandwidth decimation filter. A new DDS that avoids the problems associated with previous proposals has been presented. Its design exploits the quarter wave symmetry, thus reducing the DDS memory requirements. On the other hand, the programmable decimation filter has shown a reduction in hardware complexity and a throughput improvement over a classical 2C design. Thus, the proposed system introduces clear advantages over previous proposals and meets the performance requirements of modern DSP technology.

Acknowledgements

The authors were supported by the Comisión Interministerial de Ciencia y Tecnología (CICYT, Spain) under project PB98-1354. CAD tools and supporting material were provided by Altera Corp., San Jose CA, under the Altera University Program.

References

[1] Graychip, Inc., "GC1012A Digital Tuner Data Sheet", http://www-s.ti.com/sc/psheets/slws128/slws128.pdf, Feb. 1998.
[2] Intersil, Corp., "HSP50306 Digital QPSK Demodulator", http://www.intersil.com/data/FN/FN4/FN4162/FN4162.pdf, 1998.
[3] Pentek, Inc., "Model 4272 - Multiband Digital Receiver", http://www.pentek.com/products/GetDS.cfm/4272.PDF?Filename=ACF405.pdf.

[4] Altera, Corp., "APEX 20K Programmable Logic Device Family Data Sheet", `http://www.altera.com/literature/ds/apex.pdf`, Dec. 2001, v. 4.2.
[5] Xilinx, Inc., "Virtex 2.5V Field Programmable Gate Arrays Data Sheet" `http://www.xilinx.com/partinfo/ds003-2.pdf`, Jul. 2001, v. 2.6.
[6] Altera, Corp., "Implementing FIR Filters in FLEX Devices", `http://www.altera.com/literature/an/an073.pdf`, Feb. 1998, v.1.01.
[7] Xilinx Inc., "Transposed Form FIR Filters", `http://www.xilinx.com/xapp/xapp219.pdf`, Oct. 2001, v. 1.2.
[8] N. S. Szabo and R. I. Tanaka, *Residue Arithmetic and Its Applications to Computer Technology*, McGraw-Hill, NY, 1967.
[9] J. Ramírez, A. García, P. G. Fernández, L. Parrilla and A. Lloris, "RNS-FPL Merged Architectures for Orthogonal DWT", *Electronics Letters*, vol. 36, no. 14, pp. 1198-1199, Jul. 2000.
[10] W. A. Chren, "RNS-Based Enhancements for Direct Digital Frequency Synthesis", *IEEE Transactions on Circuits and Systems II*, vol. 42. no. 8, pp. 516-524, Aug. 1995.
[11] P. V. A. Mohan, "On RNS-based enhancements for direct digital frequency synthesis", *IEEE Transactions on Circuits and Systems II: Analog and Digital Signal Processing*, vol. 48, no. 10, pp. 988-990, Oct. 2001.
[12] W. Namgoong, T. H. Meng, "Direct-Conversion RF Receiver Design", *IEEE Transactions on Communications*, vol. 49, no. 3, pp. 518-529, Mar. 2001.
[13] J. Ramírez, A. García, P. G. Fernández, L. Parrilla, A. Lloris, "Analysis of RNS-FPL Synergy for High Throughput DSP Applications: Discrete Wavelet Transform", in *Lecture Notes in Computers Science. Field Programmable Logic: The Roadmap to Reconfigurable Computing*, Springer Verlag, págs. 342-351. 2000.
[14] M. A. Soderstrand, W. K. Jenkins, G. A. Jullien and F. J. Taylor, *Residue Number System Arithmetic: Modern Applications in Digital Signal Processing*, IEEE Press, 1986.
[15] G. A. Jullien, "Implementation of Multiplication, Modulo a Prime Number, with Applications to Number Theoretic Transforms", *IEEE Transactions on Computers*, vol. C-29, no. 10, pp. 899-905, Oct. 1980.
[16] D. Radhakrishnan, Y. Yuan, "Fast and Highly Compact RNS Multipliers", *International Journal of Electronics*, 70, pp. 281-293, 1991.
[17] Xilinx, Inc., "Direct Digital Synthesizer (DDS) V2.0", `http://www.xilinx.com/ipcenter/catalog/logicore/docs/dds.pdf`, Nov. 2000.
[18] J. Ramírez, U. Meyer-Bäse, "Benchmarks for Programmable FIR Filters Built in RNS-FPL Technology", accepted in *2002 SPIE's 16th Annual International Symposium on Aerospace/Defense Sensing, Simulation, and Controls.*
[19] S. Piestrak, "Design of Residue Generators and Multi-Operand Modular Adders using Carry-Save Adders", *Proc. of the 10th IEEE Symposium on Computer Arithmetic*, 1991.
[20] M. Griffin, M. Sousa, F. Taylor, "Efficient Scaling in the Residue Number System", *Proc. of the International Conference on Acoustics, Speech and Signal Processing*, pp. 1075-1078, 1989.

UltraSONIC: A Reconfigurable Architecture for Video Image Processing

Simon D. Haynes, Henry G. Epsom, Richard J. Cooper, Paul L. McAlpine

Sony Broadcast & Professional Research Labs, Basingstoke, Hampshire, UK
{simon.haynes, henry.epsom, richard.cooper, paul.mcalpine}@adv.sonybpe.com

Abstract. The UltraSONIC architecture enables rapid development of video processing solutions. This is achieved through a flexible architecture that is tailored for real-time standard and high definition video image processing. This paper shows how solutions for new applications can be implemented quickly using hardware based on reconfigurable logic. We also explain how the software interface abstracts the hardware to simplify hardware/software co-design, permitting parallel development of hardware and software. Dynamic reconfiguration is exploited by the UltraSONIC architecture to allow applications to share hardware resources. A novel method for abstracting the reconfigurable designs from the system level hardware allows the same design to be used for real-time processing and off-line software acceleration. We demonstrate how the UltraSONIC architecture has benefited Sony Broadcast & Professional Research Labs through several examples including: real-time encryption of video, compressed video capture and play-back from a computer, and MPEG Compression/Decompression.

1 Introduction

The professional broadcast industry is traditionally one of huge bandwidths and large processing requirements. Until fairly recently, specialised hardware was used at nearly every stage from video acquisition to display. Any processing required was well defined and had deterministic processing times – in short well suited to a custom-hardware solution.

In recent years the industry has begun to move towards a more computer-centric approach. Computers are used to store, locate and retrieve the increasing volume of archive material, for which *metadata*[1] [1] is becoming more and more important. Computers are also used for such tasks as non-linear editing, video effects, and the compositing of computer-generated and natural images. All these applications require the seamless integration of computers into the broadcast environment; video must be easily transferred between traditional studio equipment and computers in a variety of formats. Standards such as the emerging MXF [2] are helping the convergence of these two domains.

---

[1] Metadata is extra information about the video – what it is about, where it was shot etc

M. Glesner, P. Zipf, and M. Renovell (Eds.): FPL 2002, LNCS 2438, pp. 482-491, 2002.

The result is that a situation now exists in which hardware must be tightly coupled with software running on a computer. We must be able to move large amounts of video data efficiently between the computer and other equipment such as VTRs, cameras and monitors each of which might have it's own I/O requirements. Algorithms that do not fit the classical data flow model are becoming more common, such as face detection and recognition for automatic metadata extraction. Hardware may have to work on real-time video streams, or off-line to accelerate software processing.

The UltraSONIC architecture is designed to meet all of these requirements. It interfaces the computer environment to the professional broadcast world in a flexible way. Hardware resources are provided to allow real-time and off-line video processing. Reconfigurable hardware is exploited to increase the flexibility of UltraSONIC. In this paper we explain the novel features of the UltraSONIC architecture that make this possible.

2 UltraSONIC Architecture

The UltraSONIC architecture, shown in Fig. 1, is based on the earlier Sonic architecture [3]. It consists of a number of Plug-In Processing Elements (PIPEs) connected by PIPEflow buses and a PIPE bus. The PIPEs contain hardware for processing and/or interfacing to external hardware.

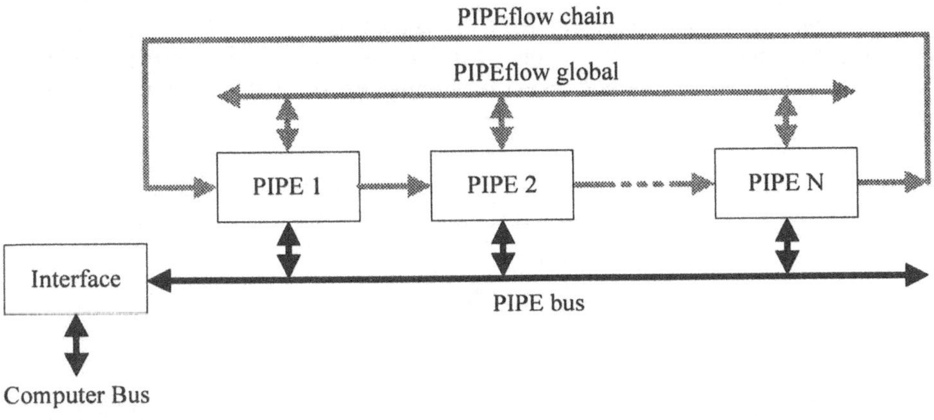

Fig. 1. The UltraSONIC Architecture; the PIPEflow buses are used for the transport of real-time video. The PIPE bus interfaces the PIPEs to the Host Computer

2.1 Bus Architecture

The UltraSONIC bus architecture consists of a shared global bus combined with flexible pipeline buses between PIPEs.

The PIPE bus provides a method for transferring data between the host computer and the PIPEs, matching the bandwidth of the host computer bus. This bus is used for fast transfer of video and control data.

The PIPEflow buses are used for the synchronous transfer of video between PIPEs. Individual PIPEflow buses connect adjacent PIPEs, with the last PIPE connected to the first, forming a loop. Low-latency pipelined processing is possible using the PIPEflow buses, where a video stream is passed using deterministic raster-scan method from PIPE to PIPE. The PIPEflow global bus provides a mechanism for processing multiple video streams and implementing algorithms requiring feedback.

Each PIPE has several unique signals that control configuration, interrupt signalling and PIPE selection. There is also a Parameter bus (not shown in Fig. 1) that provides low bandwidth communication between PIPEs.

2.2 PIPEs

There are two families of PIPEs used in the UltraSONIC architecture: *Processing* and *I/O*. Processing PIPEs contain hardware used to implement the algorithms. I/O PIPEs allow the UltraSONIC architecture to interface to external hardware. A key feature of the UltraSONIC architecture is the flexible way that different types of I/O PIPEs and processing PIPEs can be integrated in a common framework to meet the requirements of different applications.

Processing PIPEs

The architecture of a processing PIPE is shown in Fig. 2. It consists of three conceptual elements: the PIPE engine, PIPE router, and PIPE memory. 'PIPEflow left' is the PIPEflow bus coming form the previous PIPE, 'PIPEflow right' goes to the next.

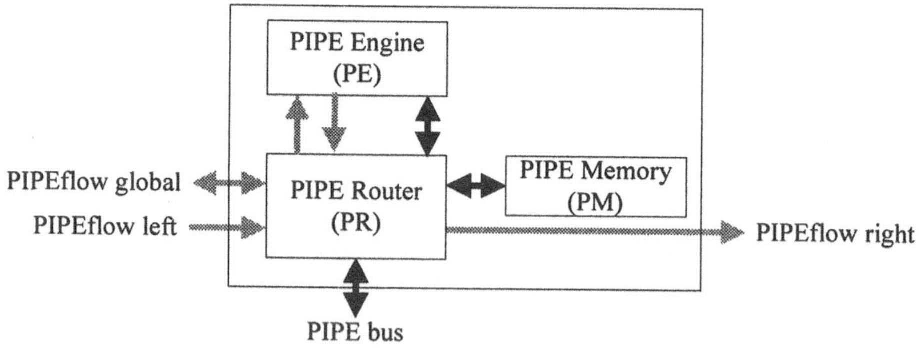

Fig. 2. Processing PIPE architecture. The PIPE engine implements the algorithm, the PIPE Memory acts as an image store, and the PIPE router formats and moves the data

The PIPE engine is responsible for implementing the required algorithm. Depending on the type of PIPE this could be a fixed function (such as an off-the-shelf codec device) or programmable (in the case of an FPGA or DSP processor).

The PIPE memory is used to store images and/or other data. Many image processing algorithms require one or more entire fields to work with, and can not operate using data supplied in a raster-scan fashion. The PIPE memory is designed for use by these types of algorithms.

The PIPE router makes UltraSONIC unique among reconfigurable computing platforms. The PIPE router provides a number of fixed functions that gives the PIPE engine a level of abstraction. The PIPE router can transfer image data to the PIPE engine from any of the PIPEflow buses or from an image held in the PIPE memory: this enables the PIPE engine to operate in the same way regardless of whether the video comes from the computer (software acceleration) or from an I/O PIPE (real-time processing).

I/O PIPEs

The architecture of an I/O PIPE is shown in Fig. 3. It consists of the same three conceptual elements as the processing PIPE, but also has provision for external video input and output.

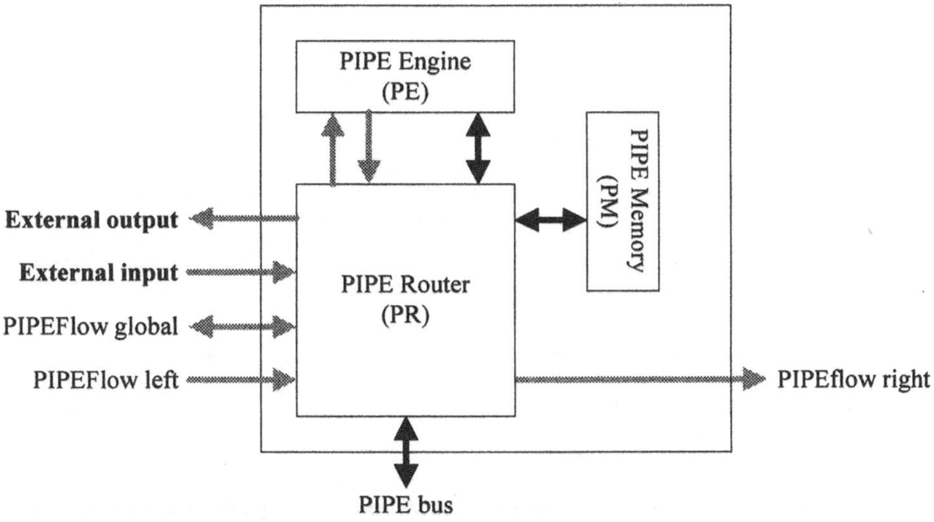

Fig. 3. I/O PIPE architecture. In addition to the elements of a processing PIPE, there are external inputs and output

All external video I/O in the UltraSONIC architecture is implemented using I/O PIPEs. This allows many I/O standards to be supported through the design of different I/O PIPEs. The number of I/O PIPEs required is dictated by the individual requirements of the application. The PIPE engine may not be present in an I/O PIPE (The PIPE may simply route the external video to anther PIPE). The PIPE router implements the same functions as the processing PIPE router with the extra capability of routing external I/O.

3 Reconfiguration in the UltraSONIC Architecture

The UltraSONIC architecture supports reconfiguration on three levels. First, the physical PIPEs can be interchanged to support different I/O standards and functionality; we will refer to this as the *system configuration*. Second, if the PIPE contains a configurable PIPE engine (such as an FPGA), it is possible for a given system configuration to be used in many ways by reconfiguring it for each new application; this is *application configuration*. Third, it is possible for a configurable PIPE to be *dynamically reconfigured* during the course of a given application to perform many sub operations. For example, a PIPE containing an FPGA may be reconfigured many times for each frame of video.

Fig. 4 shows an example system configuration for the real-time processing of video. Assuming that the processing PIPEs are implemented using FPGAs, it will be shown how this system configuration can be used for two different applications: an image rotation and a logo insertion followed by an image rotation.

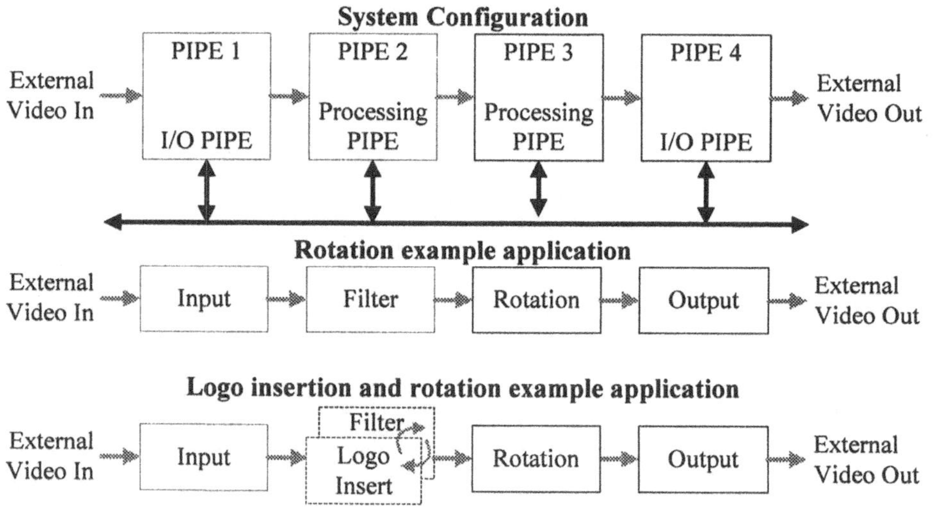

Fig. 4. Example system configuration for real-time video processing and how it could be used in two examples

Three algorithms are used in these examples: a *filter* to remove aliasing artifacts, a *logo inserter* that puts a small logo graphic on each frame, and *rotation* to rotate each frame.

Each algorithm has an associated design for the particular type of processing PIPE used (an FPGA configuration file, in this case).

For the rotation example, PIPE 2 is configured with the filter design and PIPE 3 is configured with the rotation design. After the system has set up the PIPE routers to route the video data from the input to the output, the system is left alone to continue processing until a new application is required. It is interesting to note that, although we are using real-time video in this example, by exploiting the functionality of the

PIPE router, it is also possible for this setup to be used for processing video stored on the computer *without changing the designs for the filter and rotation.*

If the application is now changed to include a logo insertion on the output video, there are now more sub-tasks than physical processing PIPEs. One solution would be to change the system configuration to one using 3 processing PIPEs. However this would require changing the hardware (and spending more money!). A better solution, supported by the UltraSONIC architecture, is to exploit dynamic reconfiguration to provide 'virtual' processing PIPEs. This works as follows: At the beginning of each frame, PIPE 2 is configured for a logo insertion, and PIPE 3 for a rotation. The video data is first run through PIPE 2, and then stored in PIPE 2's memory (remember that the PIPE router can do this without any changes to the logo insertion design). PIPE 2 is then reconfigured to perform a filter operation. The PIPE router passes the stored video data once again to the PIPE engine from the *PIPE memory* and the output to PIPE 3, which performs the rotation. PIPE 2 is then reconfigured to perform a logo insertion operation and the whole process is repeated for each frame.

4 Physical Implementation

The implementation of the UltraSONIC architecture contains a number features making it suitable for a wide variety of applications, whilst providing a high degree of extensibility. The UltraSONIC platform consists of a host board that implements a universal 66Mhz 64bit PCI interface and supporting functions, plus a number of PIPE daughter cards, which implement the PIPEs. The host board is a standard full-length PCI card and the modules are approximately 90mm x 70mm. The UltraSONIC platform has four PIPE slots, although it is possible for the host board to support up to sixteen PIPEs, through a novel system of PIPE 'stacking'. Fig. 5 shows a photograph of the UltraSONIC main board with three PIPEs.

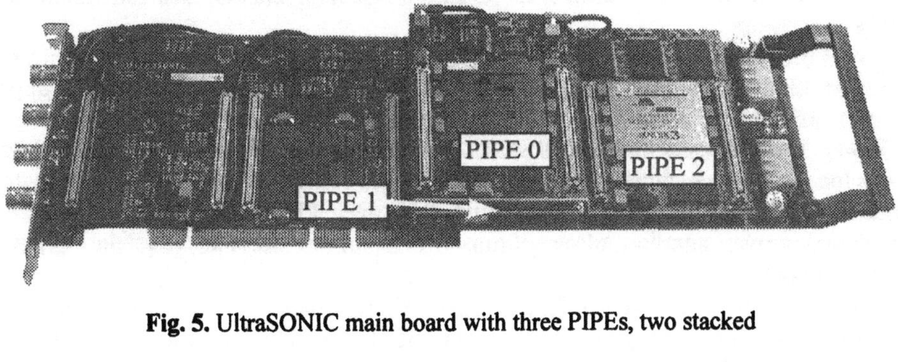

Fig. 5. UltraSONIC main board with three PIPEs, two stacked

Our goal during implementation was to meet the requirements for real-time high definition video processing.

The PIPEflow buses have a bandwidth of 264Mbytes/sec and are designed to support the streaming of high definition video between PIPEs; a data throughput of 249MBytes/sec[2].

[2] The data throughput for 1080p HD video at 30Hz with 4 bytes per pixel = 249MBytes/sec

The 64bit 66MHz PCI interface is the fastest interface to the host PC commonly available. The PIPE Bus has been designed to match this transfer rate, with a peak transfer rate of 528MBytes/sec.

4.1 PIPEs

The PIPE modules are attached to the host board via two connectors on the underside. PIPEs also have connectors on top, forming a new PIPE slot on top of every PIPE; enabling the PIPEs to be stacked. PIPEs can be stacked four deep allowing the board to be populated with up to sixteen PIPEs. With a single layer of PIPEs, the UltraSONIC platform meets the PCI physical specification.

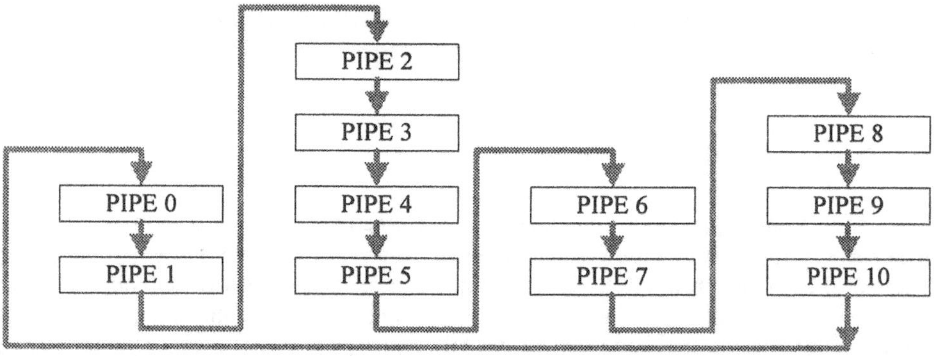

Fig. 6. Implementation of the PIPEflow bus with stacking PIPEs. The global PIPE bus and PIPEflow bus are not shown for clarity.

Fig. 6 shows how PIPEs can be stacked on top of one another, whilst maintaining the PIPEflow chain. It also shows the logical numbering scheme used for identifying PIPEs in software.

Our implementation also solves two power related problems: how to ensure every PIPE has all the voltage levels it requires (3.3V, 2.5V, 1.8V etc.), and how to supply power to all the PIPEs without drawing excessive current.

Power is distributed to all PIPEs at 12V and converted to the required voltage levels locally using switched mode power supplies. The use of high efficiency switch mode supplies reduces the current required by each PIPE. Additionally, the use of distributed power supplies allows future PIPEs to use devices requiring different supply voltages.

Currently there are seven different types of PIPE modules. Examples include the UltraPIPE, the Serial Digital Interface [4] (SDI) I/O PIPE and the MPEG encoder PIPE. The UltraPIPE is a processing PIPE consisting of a Xilinx Virtex 1000E FPGA with 8Mbytes of external memory. The SDI I/O PIPE provides an interface to external video equipment using Serial Digital Interfaces. The MPEG Encoder is an I/O PIPE incorporating dedicated hardware for encoding MPEG-2 video streams.

5 The UltraSONIC API

In the same manner that the PIPE Router abstracts the design of the video processing hardware from the UltraSonic Platform architecture, the Application Program Interface (API) and a dedicated driver abstracts the task of writing software from the low level interactions with the physical hardware. The driver abstracts the hardware resources of UltraSONIC and allows the API to present them to the user in form of easy to understand functions. The programmer links to the API library using a single Dynamically Linked Library (DLL) file.

To ensure the API is portable and backwards compatible, it must have a clearly defined and unchanging interface. However, at the same time it must provide the flexibility required to accommodate new system configurations, PIPE architectures and PIPE Engine Designs. In addition, the API Interface should be implemented at the highest possible level of abstraction. Unfortunately, these requirements are to some extent conflicting.

The UltraSONIC API solves these problems in two ways. First, the API consists of a set of very low level functions (which allows extensibility to new PIPE architectures and designs without the need to alter the interface) dressed up to resemble high level function calls (to facilitate high level programming techniques) through the use of constants defined in header files. Second, the structure of the API is designed as a hierarchy that mimics the hierarchy of the UltraSONIC hardware, allowing the API to be seamlessly extended to support new hardware and PIPE engine designs.

Using the model described above, the basic low-level functions provided by the API may be extended to support future PIPE Architectures and PIPE Engine designs by adding appropriately to the sets of constants defining the register addresses and values. These constants are defined in a hierarchy of separate header files that mirror the hierarchy of the UltraSONIC architecture. This is shown in Fig. 7.

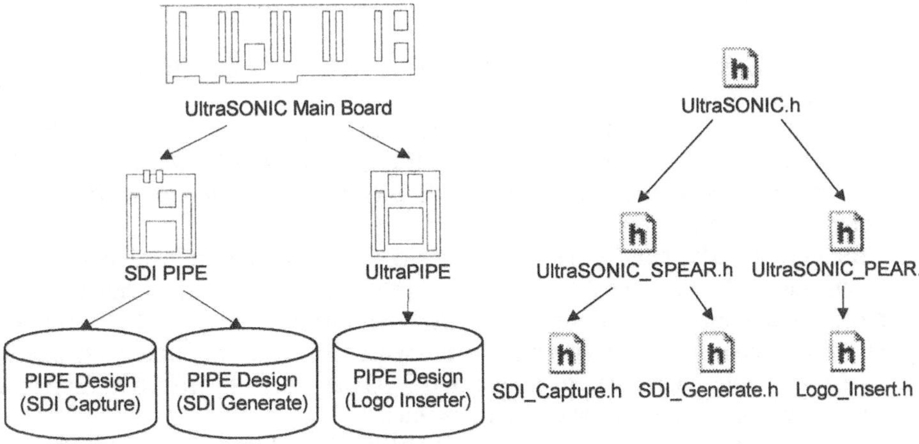

Fig. 7. The relationship between the hardware and configurable designs and the header files

Every application that uses UltraSONIC must include the main API header file, UltraSONIC.h. This file contains the prototypes for the API functions, along with any constants related to the UltraSONIC host board. At the next level of the hierarchy, any combination of PIPE architectures may be used with UltraSONIC. For each architecture an associated header file must be included defining the registers and logical partitions relevant to that type of PIPE. Whenever a new PIPE Architecture is created, an associated header file will also be provided. Finally, each FPGA based PIPE Architecture may be configured with a potentially limitless number of PIPE Engine Designs. Each PIPE design is also supplied with an associated header file defining any registers or constants specific to that PIPE Engine. A simple example showing the low-level functions with high-level constants is given below: An FPGA on PIPE PipeNum is configured with a design. It then writes to a register in the FPGA design to start the processing. Then the resultant image is read back.

```
SonicInit();

SonicConfigure(PipeNum,"LogoDesign.ucd");

SonicWrite(PipeNum, S2_TARGET_PEAR_PE,
          S2_LOGO_REGISTER_CONTROL,
          S2_LOGO_REGISTER_CONTROL_START);

SonicBurstRead(PipeNum, S2_TARGET_PEAR_PM,
            S2_LOGO_IMAGE,
            &ImageData);
```

For a given software application, a set of header files will be included which mirrors the potential hardware that will be used by that application. In this way, the design of the API allows the API to grow and evolve as the UltraSONIC hardware grows and evolves.

6 Applications

UltraSONIC has been used successfully for a wide variety of applications, a selection of which are shown in Table 1.

SDTI-CP [5] is a standard for transferring data packets over the Serial Digital Interface [4]. SDTI-CP capture and playback PIPE Engines have been used to transfer MPEG compressed data embedded in SDTI-CP between a VTR and an MXF [2] file on a computer's hard disk drive.

UltraSONIC has also been applied to a video-conferencing system, which uses four MPEG encoder PIPEs to ingest and compress four standard definition video steams for transfer via a network. Four MPEG decoder PIPEs at each of the receiving stations then decode the video streams to re-create the other conference attendees. Both these examples demonstrate UltraSONIC operating as an effective interface between the computer and broadcast environments.

Conversely, the shear processing power of UltraSONIC is demonstrated by the Rijndael encryption application, which is highly computationally intensive: The design is able to encrypt data at rates exceeding 2Gbits/sec. The Rijndael encryption [6] application has also been designed so it may be used for both real-time video processing and off-line software acceleration, the level of encryption for a given throughput being designed to scale with the number of PIPEs available.

Table 1. Example applications implemented using UltraSONIC

Application	Description	PIPEs used
SDTI-CP Capture & Playback	Real-time capture and playback of MPEG data from a VTR to/from a file on the PC's harddrive.	SDI I/O PIPE
MPEG Encoding & Decoding	Real-time encoding and decoding of 4 video streams for a video conferencing application.	4 x MPEG Encoder 4 x MPEG Decoder
Rijndael Encryption/Decryption	Real-time encryption/decryption of real-time video using the Rijndael encryption algorithm.	2 x FPGA PIPE 2 x SDI I/O PIPE

7 Conclusions

The UltraSONIC architecture is a powerful, flexible architecture well suited to video processing applications. The abstraction provided by the PIPE router allows a hardware design to be used for either real-time processing, or off-line software acceleration. The powerful software API also abstracts the hardware from the programmer, allowing parallel development of hardware and software designs. The physical modular design and extensible software API allows the platform to support new FPGA technology and different PIPE types. The UltraSONIC architecture has proved highly successful within Sony Broadcast & Professional Research Labs for implementing the next generation of solutions requiring the integration of computers into the broadcast environment.

References

1. Jain, R., Hampapur, A.: Metadata in Video Databases, SIGMOD Record, Vol. 23, Num. 4, (1994) 27-33
2. Material Exchange Format File Specification, Proposed SMPTE Standard, January 2002
3. Haynes, S.D., Stone, J., Cheung, P.Y.K, Luk, W.: Video Image Processing with the Sonic Architecture. IEEE Computer, April (2000) 50-57
4. 10-Bit 4:2:2 Component and 4fsc Composite Digital Signals – Serial Digital Interface, SMPTE Standard, ANSI/SMPTE 259M-1997, September 25, 1997
5. SDTI Content Package Format (SDTI-CP), SMPTE Standard SMPTE 326M-2000, January 31, 2000
6. Daemen, J., Rijmen, V.: AES Proposal: Rijndael, NIST AES Proposal, 1998.

Implementing the Discrete Cosine Transform Using the Xilinx Virtex FPGA

Trevor W. Fox and Laurence E. Turner*

University of Calgary
fox@enel.ucalgary.ca

Abstract. A method for the design of low-cost near-exact Discrete Cosine Transform (DCT) approximations on the Xilinx Virtex FPGA is presented. This method can be used to control the coding gain, Mean Square Error (MSE), quantization noise, hardware cost, and power consumption of the DCT approximation. The Xilinx Place-And-Route (PAR) process and XPWR are used to gauge the hardware cost and the power consumption respectively. It is shown that it is possible to generate FPGA based DCT approximations with near optimal coding gains that meet the Mean Square Error (MSE), hardware cost, quantization noise, and power consumption requirements.

1 Introduction

The Discrete Cosine Transform (DCT) has found wide application in audio, image, and video compression and has been incorporated in the popular JPEG, MPEG, and H.26x standards[1]. The phenomenal growth in demand for products that use these compression standards has increased the need to develop methodologies for the design of Field Programmable Gate Array (FPGA) based DCT approximations. A method is proposed in this paper that can be used to generate DCT approximations for the Xilinx Virtex FPGA. This method can be used to control the quality of the DCT approximation, the exact hardware cost, quantization noise, and power consumption by choosing both the data path wordlengths (the number of bits used to represent the signal) and the coefficient values. Optimization based design methods can now use the PAR process to gauge the exact hardware cost because the PAR runtimes have dropped from hours to minutes for small to midrange designs. The Xilinx FPGA Place-And-Route (PAR) process is used to gauge the exact hardware cost. XPWR (a power estimation program provided in the Xilinx ISE Foundation toolset[2]) is used to estimate the power consumption. Previously data path wordlength and coefficient optimization have been considered separately [3][4]. Optimizing both simultaneously produces superior designs because the hardware cost, power consumption, and quantization noise are related to both the data path wordlengths and coefficient values.

* This work was supported in part by the Natural Sciences and Engineering Research Council of Canada

M. Glesner, P. Zipf, and M. Renovell (Eds.): FPL 2002, LNCS 2438, pp. 492–502, 2002.

A method for the design of fixed point DCT approximations has recently been introduced[5], but it does not specifically target FPGAs or Application Specific Integrated Circuits (ASICs). This design method can be used to control the quality of the DCT approximation and an estimate of the hardware cost (the number of adders and subtractors required to implement the coefficient multipliers) by choosing the coefficient values. Unfortunately this method only estimates the hardware cost, ignores power consumption and quantization noise, and cannot be used to control the data path wordlengths.

The proposed design method uses Loeffler's factorization with the lifting scheme [6] to implement the DCT (see Figure 1). This class of DCT approximation can be used in lossless compression applications despite using finite precision arithmetic because the product of the forward and inverse transform matrices equals the identity matrix[6].

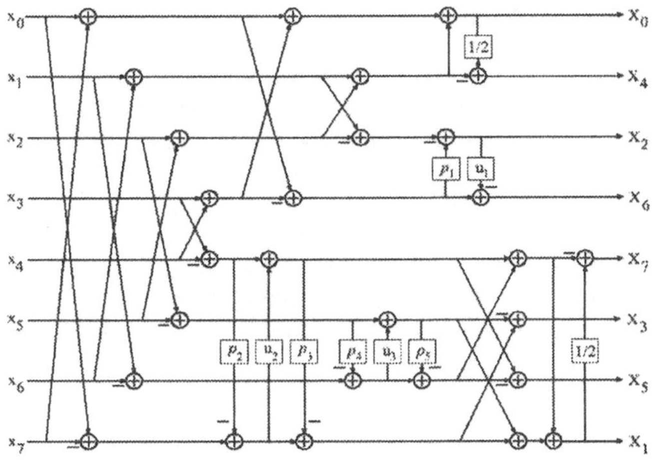

Fig. 1. Signal flow graph of Loeffler's factorization with the lifting structure [6].

2 Performance Measures for FPGA Based DCT Approximations

The DCT maps an input signal into a linear combination of weighted basis functions. The quality of an FPGA based DCT approximation can be measured by five performance measures: Coding gain, Mean Square Error (MSE), hardware cost, quantization noise, and power consumption.

2.1 Coding Gain

The coding gain (a measure of the degree of energy compaction offered by a transform[1]) is important in compression applications because it is proportional to the Peak Signal to Noise Ratio (PSNR). Transforms with high coding gains can be used to create faithful reproductions of the original image with little error. The biorthogonal coding gain is defined as[7]:

$$CodingGain = 10log_{10}\frac{\sigma_x^2}{\left(\Pi_{i=0}^{N-1}\sigma_{x_i}^2 \,||f_i||_2^2\right)^{\frac{1}{N}}} \tag{1}$$

Where $||f_i||_2^2$ is the norm of the ith basis function, N is the number of subbands ($N = 8$ for an eight point DCT), $\sigma_{x_i}^2$ is the variance of the signal at the ith subband, and σ_x^2 is the variance of the input signal.

A zero mean unit variance Autoregressive Process of order one (AR(1)) with correlation coefficient $\rho = 0.95$ is an accurate approximation of natural images[6] and is used in our numerical experiments.

2.2 Mean Square Error

The Mean Square Error (MSE) between the transformed data generated by the exact and approximate DCTs quantifies the accuracy of the DCT approximation. The MSE can be calculated deterministically by the expression[6]:

$$MSE = \frac{1}{N}Trace\left(DR_{xx}D^T\right) \tag{2}$$

Where D is the difference between the forward transform matrix of the exact and approximate DCTs. R_{xx} is the autocorrelation matrix of the input signal. It is advantageous to have a low MSE value to ensure a near ideal DCT approximation.

2.3 Hardware Cost

Hardware cost is the quantity of logic required to implement a DCT approximation. On the Xilinx Virtex series of FPGAs the hardware cost is measured as the number of slices (a slice contains two D type flip flops and two four input lookup tables) required to implement a design and is determined by the Place-And-Route (PAR) process (the assignment of logic functions and interconnect to the slices). In recent years the PAR runtimes have dropped from hours to minutes for small to midrange designs. Consequently, PARs can now be used directly by an optimization method to gauge the exact hardware cost of a design. This paper presents a design method for FPGA based DCT approximations that relies on the PAR to provide the exact hardware cost of a design.

2.4 Quantization Noise

The DCT is a linear operation under infinite precision arithmetic. However floating point arithmetic can be expensive in terms of hardware cost. Instead fixed point arithmetic can be more practical for FPGA designs because it permits fast implementations that require small amounts of FPGA hardware resources. Unfortunately fixed point arithmetic can introduce severe nonlinearities which must be controlled or compensated for to ensure near ideal performance.

A fixed point multiplier can be implemented as the cascade of an integer multiplier followed by a power-of-two division. The power-of-two division truncates the product. This is a nonlinear operation called quantization. The quantization nonlinearity can be modeled as the summation of the signal with a noise source[8]. Assuming the binary point is in the right most position (all signal are represented by integers values) then the maximum error introduced in a multiplication is one for twos complement truncation arithmetic. A worst case bound on the quantization noise introduced by a coefficient multiplication at the ith subband ($|N_{a_i}|$) is given by [5]:

$$|N_{a_i}| \leq \Sigma_{j=1}^{L} |g_{ji}| \tag{3}$$

where g_{ji} is the feed forward gain from the output of the jth multiplier to the ith subband output, and L is the number of multipliers present in the transform.

Quantization through data path wordlength truncation can be arbitrarily introduced at any node (data path) in a DCT approximation to reduce hardware cost at the expense of injected noise as demonstrated in [3][4]. A worst case bound on the quantization noise introduced through data path wordlength truncation at the ith subband ($|N_{b_i}|$) is given by:

$$|N_{b_i}| \leq \Sigma_{j=1}^{L_{qnode}} |h_{ji}| \left(2^{m_j} - 1\right) \tag{4}$$

where h_{ji} is the feed forward gain from jth quantized node to the ith subband output, m is the number of bits truncated from the LSB side of the wordlength, and L_{qnode} is the number of quantized data path wordlengths present in the transform. The total noise at the ith subband output ($|N_{tot_i}|$) is the sum of all scaled noise sources as given by:

$$|N_{tot_i}| = |N_{a_i}| + |N_{b_i}| \tag{5}$$

2.5 Power Consumption

The power consumption of a CMOS circuit due to switching activity can be approximated using [9]:

$$P = C_{tot} f V^2 \tag{6}$$

where C_{tot} is the total charging capacitance of the interconnect and transistors used in the design, f is the clock frequency, and V is the voltage level. The power consumption can be reduced by lowering the clock frequency. However a reduced clock rate reduces throughput and is not preferred for high performance systems that must process large amounts of data. Lowering the voltage level can reduce the power consumption at the expense of a reduction in the maximum clock frequency. An alternative method to reduce power consumption is the reduction of the total charging capacitance of the circuit. The total charging capacitance can be reduced by the use of fewer circuit elements and shorter interconnect paths (fewer slices when dealing with Xilinx FPGAs). The proposed method controls the hardware cost as the means to control the power consumption.

The Xilinx ISE tool set includes a command line program called XPWR and a Graphical User Interface (GUI) program called XPOWER that can both be used to estimate the power consumption of a design on Xilinx FPGAs. XPWR is executed directly by the proposed method to gauge the power consumption of the design.

3 Problem Statement and Formulation

The design of FPGA based DCT approximations requires that a set of coefficients and data path wordlengths, h, must be found such that the DCT approximation has a high coding gain and the MSE, quantization noise, hardware cost, and power consumption specifications are satisfied. This problem can be formulated as a discrete constrained optimization problem:

minimize:

$$-\,CodingGain \tag{7}$$

subject to:

$$g_1(h) = MSE(h) - MSE_{max} \leq 0 \tag{8}$$

$$g_2(h) = SlicesRequired(h) - MaxSlices \leq 0 \tag{9}$$

$$g_3(h) = EstimatedPower(h) - MaxPower \leq 0 \tag{10}$$

$$g_{4_i}(h) = |N_{tot_i}| - MaxNoise_i \leq 0 \quad \text{for } i = 0 \ldots 7 \tag{11}$$

Where the constants MSE_{max}, $MaxPower$, and $MaxSlices$ are the largest permissible MSE, power consumption, and hardware cost values respectively. The functions $SlicesRequired(h)$ and $EstimatedPower(h)$ yield the hardware cost and the estimated power consumption respectively. The constant $MaxNoise_i$ is the largest permissible quantization noise value in the ith subband. A one dimensional DCT approximation with eight subbands (which is used in the JPEG and MPEG standards[1]) requires eight constraints ($i = 0 \ldots 7$) to control the quantization noise in each subband. Little if any quantization noise should contaminate the low frequency subbands in compression applications because these subbands contain most of the signal energy. The high frequency subbands can tolerate more quantization noise since little signal energy is present in these subbands. It is therefore advantageous to set differing quantization noise constraints for each individual subband.

The above problem is difficult to solve analytically or numerically because analytic derivatives of the objective function and constraints cannot be determined. Instead discrete Lagrange multipliers can be used[10]. The constraints (8) to (11) can be combined to form a discrete Lagrangian function with the introduction of a positive valued scaling constant ϵ_{weight} and the discrete Lagrange multipliers λ_1, λ_2, λ_3, and λ_{4_i}:

$$\begin{aligned} L_d = -\epsilon_{weight} CodingGain + \lambda_1 max(0, g_1(h)) + \lambda_2 max(0, g_2(h)) \\ + \lambda_3 max(0, g_3(h)) + \Sigma_{i=0}^{7} \lambda_{4_i} max(0, g_{4_i}(h)) \end{aligned} \tag{12}$$

4 The DCT Local Search Method

The discrete Lagrangian local search was introduced in [10] and later applied to filter bank design in [11] and Peak Constrained Least Squares (PCLS) FIR design in [12][13]. The discrete Lagrangian local search method presented here (see Procedure 1) is adapted from the local search method presented in [12][13] and can be used to solve the FPGA based DCT design problem. Procedure 1 has been implemented using the C++ programming language.

Initialize the algorithmic parameters as described in [12][13]:
  $\lambda_{1_{weight}}$, $\lambda_{2_{weight}}$, $\lambda_{3_{weight}}$, $\lambda_{4_{weight_i}}$, ϵ_{weight}, and $MaxIteration$
Initialize the discrete Lagrange multipliers:
  $\lambda_1 = 0$, $\lambda_2 = 0$, $\lambda_3 = 0$, and $\lambda_{4_i} = 0$ for $i = 0 \ldots 7$
Initialize the variables of optimization
  h = Quantized DCT coefficients and full precision data path wordlengths
While(not converged and not executed $MaxIterations$) do
  Change the current variable by ± 1 to obtain h'
  Generate the DCT VHDL design files
  Perform the Place-And-Route
  Use XPWR to estimate the power consumption
  Calculate $L_d(h')$
  if $L_d(h') < L_d(h)$ then accept proposed change ($h = h'$)
  Update the following discrete Lagrange multipliers once every three iterations
    $\lambda_1 \leftarrow \lambda_1 + \lambda_{1_{weight}} \max(0, g_1(h))$
    $\lambda_2 \leftarrow \lambda_2 + \lambda_{2_{weight}} \max(0, g_2(h))$
    $\lambda_3 \leftarrow \lambda_3 + \lambda_{3_{weight}} \max(0, g_3(h))$
    $\lambda_{4_i} \leftarrow \lambda_{4_i} + \lambda_{4_{weight_i}} \max(0, g_{4_i}(h))$ for $i = 0 \ldots 7$
end

Procedure 1: The DCT Local Search Method

The variables of optimization, h, are composed of the coefficient values and the data path wordlengths. The coefficient values are rational values of the form

$\frac{x}{2^y}$ where x is an integer value that is determined during optimization and y sets the magnitude of the right shift. The data path wordlength is the number of bits used to represent the signal in the data path. The binary point position of input values to the DCT approximation can be arbitrarily set[3]. The discussion in [3] places the binary point to the left of the Most Significant Bit (MSB) of the data path wordlength (all input values are less than one). In this paper the binary point is placed in the right most position (all input values represent integers) which is consistent with the literature on DCT based compression[1].

The coefficients are initially set equal to the floating point precision DCT coefficients rounded to the nearest value permitted by fixed point arithmetic. The data path wordlengths are set wide enough to prevent overflow. The largest possible value at the kth data path wordlength in the DCT approximation is bounded by:

$$|Max_k| \leq \Sigma_{j=0}^{N-1} |f_{jk}| M \tag{13}$$

where N is the number of DCT inputs, f_{jk} is the gain from the jth DCT input to the kth data path, and M is the largest possible input value (255 for the JPEG standard [1]). The bit position of the Most Significant Bit (MSB) and the number of bits required to fully represent the signal (excluding the sign bit) at the kth datapath is:

$$MSB_k = \lceil \log_2(Max_k) \rceil \tag{14}$$

A data path wordlength with more than MSB_k bits is wasteful and should not be used because the magnitude of the maximum signal value can represented using MSB_k bits.

Each variable in h is changed by ± 1 (the quantization step) in a round robin fashion, and each change is accepted if the discrete Lagrangian function decreases in value. Altering a coefficient value changes the gains from the inputs to the internal nodes that feed from the changed coefficient. Consequently, equations (13) and (14) must be used to update the MSB positions at all data paths.

A reduction or increase in the data path wordlength occurs at the Least Significant Bit (LSB) side of the data path wordlength. The binary point position (and hence the value represented by the MSB) does not change despite any changes in the data path wordlength. The possibility of overflow is therefore excluded because the maximum value represented by the MSB of the data path still exceeds the magnitude of the largest possible signal value even though the data path precision may be reduced.

If a constraint is not satisfied then the respective discrete Lagrange multiplier grows in value once every three iterations as shown in Procedure 1.

4.1 The Measurement of Hardware Cost and Power Consumption

A set of VHDL design files that implement the DCT approximation are generated automatically before each PAR. Each adder, subtractor, and multiplier is implemented by a custom VHDL entity because the data path wordlengths are unequal throughout the DCT approximation. A batch file, which automatically runs the PAR process and XPWR, is then executed by the local search method. The hardware cost is parsed from the map report (the .mrp text file) and the power consumption is parsed from the power report (the .pwr text file).

Ideally the proposed method should perform a PAR every iteration. Although the runtimes for PARs have dropped dramatically, they still require several minutes for designs presented in this paper. A typical runtime for the proposed method requires hours of computation if a PAR is performed every iteration. To reduce the run time without hindering convergence, it is possible to perform a PAR every N iterations $2 \leq N \leq 50$ and estimate the hardware cost in between the PARs. A hardware cost estimate, *SlicesRequired*(h), can be obtained based on the number of full adders required by the current DCT approximation, $FullAdders(h)$, the number of full adders required by the DCT approximation during the last PAR, $FullAdders_{par}$, and the number of slices produced at the last PAR, $Slices_{par}$:

$$SlicesRequired(h) = \frac{Slices_{par}}{FullAdders_{par}} FullAdders(h) \tag{15}$$

This provides a local estimate of the number of slices required to implement the DCT approximation.

In a similar fashion, a local estimate for the required power, *PowerEstimate*(h), can be obtained based on the power reported at the last PAR, $Power_{par}$, and the previously defined $FullAdders_{par}$ and $FullAdders_{par}$:

$$PowerEstimate(h) = \frac{Power_{par}}{FullAdders_{par}} FullAdders(h) \tag{16}$$

The local search terminates when all of the constraints are satisfied, the discrete Lagrangian function cannot be further minimized, and $FullAdders_{par} = FullAdders(h)$. This ensures that the hardware cost and power consumption at a discrete constrained local minimum is exact.

The use of the local estimators, equations (15) and (16), have been found to decrease the run time of the proposed method by a factor of twenty-four (using $N = 45$) without hindering convergence.

The rate of convergence varies according to the design specifications. Design problems with tight constraints require at most 1000 iterations to converge. Design problems with no constraints on hardware cost and power consumption require as few as 50 iterations to converge.

5 Coding Gain and Hardware Cost Tradeoff

Table 1 shows a family of FPGA based eight point DCT approximations with eight bit inputs designed using the method described in this paper. Relaxing the constraint on hardware cost (setting $MaxSlices$ to a large number) produces a nearly ideal DCT approximation. Entry 1 in Table 1 shows a near ideal DCT approximation that produces low amounts of quantization noise since no data wordlength truncation was required to satisfy the hardware cost constraint. A method that can be used to reduce the quantization noise at the output subbands to only corrupt the LSB in the worst case for fixed point DCT approximations was presented in [5]. The input signal is scaled above the worst case bound on quantization noise and output signal is reduced by the same factor. A power-of-two shift that exceeds the value of the worst case bound on quantization noise is an inexpensive factor for scaling because no additions or subtractions are required. This method was used to reduce the quantization noise to only corrupt the LSB in the worst case for all subbands except the DC subband. The DC subband does not suffer from any quantization noise since no multipliers feed this subband.

The hardware cost for nearly eliminating quantization noise is high and may not be practical if only a limited amount of computational resources are available for the DCT implementation. A tradeoff between the coding gain and hardware cost is useful in designing small DCT cores with high coding gain values that must share limited space on a FPGA with other cores. The coding gain varies as a direct result of varying *MaxSlices*. The remaining constraints are set to values suiting the application. Entries 2 to 5 in table 1 demonstrates the tradeoff between the coding gain and hardware cost for DCT approximations targeted for the XCV300-6 part when power consumption is ignored, MSE_{max}=1e-3, $MaxNoise_0$=8, $MaxNoise_1$=16, $MaxNoise_j$=32 for $j = 2 \ldots 6$, and $MaxNoise_7$=64. This family of DCT approximations has small MSE values and produces little quantization noise in the low frequency subbands making these designs suitable for low hardware cost compression applications.

Entry 2 in Table 1 shows a high quality DCT approximation with a significantly reduced hardware cost compared to Entry 1. If coding gain is critical to the application then this DCT approximation may be satisfactory. By tolerating a slight reduction in coding gain, the hardware cost can be reduced further. The DCT approximation of Entry 5 in Table 1 requires 208 fewer slices (a reduction of thirty percent) than the DCT approximation of Entry 2 in Table 1 and requires 438 fewer slices (a reduction of forty-eight percent) than the DCT approximation of Entry 1 in Table 1. If coding gain is not critical then this DCT approximation may be appropriate. It is therefore possible to use the proposed design method to find a suitable DCT approximation for the hardware cost/performance requirements of the application. Entry 6 in Table 1 demonstrates that the proposed method can produce extremely small DCT approximations at the expense of significantly more quantization noise (the worst case bound on quantization noise in each subband for Entry 6 in Table 1 is 128).

6 Coding Gain and Power Consumption Tradeoff

A tradeoff between the coding gain and power consumption is possible and is useful in designing low power DCT cores with acceptable coding gain values. Table 2 shows the coding gain, MSE, hardware cost, and the estimated and measured power consumption results. Entries 2 to 4 of Table 2 show the tradeoff between

Table 1. Coding gain, MSE, hardware cost, and maximum clock frequency results (using $N = 45$) for DCT approximations based on Loeffler's factorization using the lifting structure implemented on the XCV300-6 FPGA.

Entry Number	*Coding Gain (dB)*	*MSE*	*Hardware Cost (Slices)*	*Maximum Clock Frequency (MHz)*
1	8.8259	1.80e-8	912	117
2	8.8257	8.00e-6	682	129
3	8.8207	4.00e-5	600	135
4	8.7877	6.02e-4	530	142
5	8.7856	6.22e-4	474	135
6	7.8292	2.03e-2	313	142

Table 2. Coding gain, coefficient complexity, MSE, and power consumption results for DCT approximations based on Loeffler's factorization using the lifting structure implemented on the XCV300-6 FPGA with a clock rate of 100MHz.

Entry Number	*Coding Gain (dB)*	*MSE*	*Hardware Cost (Slices)*	*Estimated Power Consumption (W)*	*Measured Power Consumption (W)*
1	8.8259	1.80e-8	912	1.12	0.98
2	8.8257	8.00e-6	682	0.90	0.83
3	8.8201	2.70e-5	552	0.78	0.76
4	8.7856	6.22e-4	474	0.70	0.61
5	7.8292	2.03e-4	313	0.53	0.42

the coding gain and power consumption when MSE_{max}=1e-3, $MaxNoise_0$=8, $MaxNoise_1$=16, $MaxNoise_j$=32 for $j = 2 \ldots 6$, and $MaxNoise_7$=64. The coding gain varies as a direct result of varying $MaxPower$. Entry 1 in Table 2 shows the power consumption of a near ideal DCT approximation discussed in the previous section. Low power DCT approximations result from a slight decrease in coding gain (compare entries 2 to 4 in Table 2). Entry 5 in Table 2 shows a low power DCT approximation obtained at the expense of significantly increased quantization noise (the worst case bound on quantization noise in each subband is 128).

References

1. K. Sayood, *Introduction to data compression.* Boston, MA: Morgan Kauffmann Publishers, 2000.
2. *ISE 4 User Guide*, Xilinx Inc., 2001.

3. G.A. Constantinides, P.Y.K. Cheung, W. Luk, "Heuristic Datapath Allocation for Multiple Wordlength Systems", *Proc. Design Automation and Test in Europe (DATE)*, Munich, Germany, pp.791-796, March 2001.
4. W. Sung and K.I. Kum, "Simulation-based word-length optimization method for fixed-point digital signal processing systems," *IEEE Trans. Sig. Pro.*, vol. 43, pp. 3087-3090, Dec. 1995.
5. T.W. Fox and L.E. Turner, "Low coefficient complexity approximations of the one dimensional discrete cosine transform," *Proc. IEEE International Symposium on Circuits and Syst.*, Scottsdale, Arizona, vol. 1, pp. 285-288, May 2002.
6. J. Liang and T.D. Tran, "Fast multiplierless approximations of the DCT with the lifting scheme," *IEEE Trans. Sig. Pro.*, vol. 49, pp. 3032-3044, Dec. 2001.
7. J. Katto and Y. Yashuda, "Performance evaluation of subband coding and optimization of its filter coefficients," *SPIE Proc. Visual Commun. Image Process.*, pp. 95-106, Boston, MA, Nov. 1991.
8. L.B. Jackson, "On the interaction of roundoff noise and dynamic range in digital filters," *Bell Syst. Tech. Journal*, vol. 49, pp 159-184, Feb. 1970.
9. K.K. Parhi, *VLSI digital signal processing systems.* New York, NY: John Wiley and Sons, Inc., 1999.
10. B.W. Wah and Z. Wu, "The Theory of Discrete Lagrange Multipliers for Nonlinear Discrete Optimization," *Proc. Principles and Practice of Constraint Programming,* Springer-verlag, pp. 28-42, Oct. 1999.
11. B.W. Wah, Y. Shang, and Z. Wu, "Discrete Lagrangian methods for optimizing the design of multiplierless QMF banks," *IEEE Trans. Circuits Syst. II*, vol. 46, pp. 1179-1191, Sept. 1999.
12. T.W. Fox and L.E. Turner, "The design of peak constrained least squares FIR filters with low complexity finite precision coefficients," *Proc. IEEE International Symp. Circuits Syst.*, vol. 2, pp. 605-608, Sydney, Australia, May 2001.
13. T.W. Fox and L.E. Turner, "The design of peak constrained least squares FIR filters with low complexity finite precision coefficients," *IEEE Transactions on Circuits and Systems II*, vol. 49, pp. 151-154, Feb. 2002.

Implementation of the JPEG 2000 Standard on a Virtex 1000 FPGA

Alexander Staller, Peter Dillinger, and Reinhard Männer

Universität Mannheim, Informatik V, B6, 26, 68131 Mannheim, GERMANY
{staller,dillinger,maenner}@ti.uni-mannheim.de

Abstract. The JPEG 2000 is a well known standard and has some important changes to the former JPEG standard. The use of wavelet transformation and arithmetic entropy encoding improves the image quality and compression ratio significantly. This paper enlightens how this standard can be implemented on a Virtex 1000 FPGA processor and where the drawbacks and compromises between quality and efficiency are. An implementation without the entropy encoder is shown that uses less than half of the resources of the FPGA and operates at high frame rates.

1 Introduction

The new JPEG 2000 image compression standard will supersede the old JPEG standard. A new tranformation algorithm, a complex coefficient bit modelling, and the choice of a binary adaptive arithmetic codec enhance the compression ratio and image quality. The standard also includes the feature to code regions of interest (ROI), the possibility to add content–based descriptions, and it allows to search and extract data without decoding the whole image.

The core of the standard is the discrete wavelet transformation (DWT). Encouraged by the work in [5,6], which showed efficient implementations of the DWT on an FPGA processor, we improved some limitations/restrictions of these former versions and started to add the component transformation, DC level shift, quantization, and entropy coding to complete the standard.

2 The JPEG 2000 Standard

The Joint Photographic Experts Group (JPEG) 2000 standard is a ITU-T (International Telecommunication Union — Telecommunication Standardization Sector) recommendation [4] for lossless and lossy compression of still images. The basic architecture of the standard is depicted in Figure 1. First, the discrete transformation is performed on the original image data, followed by the quantization and the entropy encoding stage. The decoding process is the reverse of the encoding process.

At the beginning of each encoding process, the source image will be separated into equally sized, non overlapping tiles. The dimensions of a tile are not specified in the standard. Tiling reduces the amount of memory required to encode the

M. Glesner, P. Zipf, and M. Renovell (Eds.): FPL 2002, LNCS 2438, pp. 503–512, 2002.

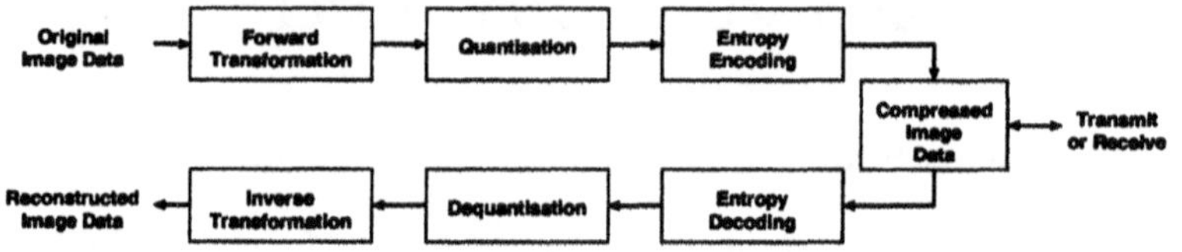

Fig. 1. The basic encoding and decoding block diagram of the JPEG 2000 standard.

image. However, the tile size influences the quality of the reconstructed image (see section 3).

If the source image consists of multiple components, e.g. an RGB image, the tiles will consist of multiple components, too. In order to decorrelate the components from each other, the standard supports two different component transformations. The irreversible component transformation (ICT) for lossy coding and the reversible component transformation (RCT, Eq. 1) for lossy and lossless coding. A block diagram of the JPEG 2000 component transformation is depicted in Figure 2, which shows only the three RGB components. The standard allows up to 16,348 components.

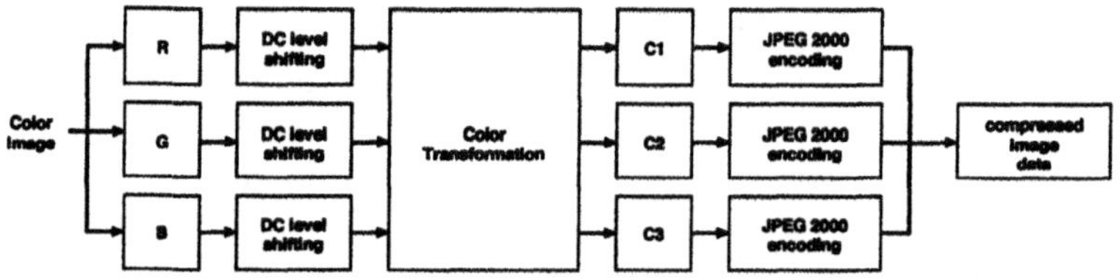

Fig. 2. Block diagram of the JPEG 2000 component transformation.

The advantages of these transformations are a reasonable color space with respect to the Human Visual System (HVS, [7]) for quantization (subsampling) and color decorrelation. During the whole coding process, the ICT/RCT is the only place where the components of an image are directly related to each other. Everywhere else, each component is coded independently.

$$\begin{pmatrix} Y_r \\ U_r \\ V_r \end{pmatrix} = \begin{pmatrix} \lfloor \frac{R+2G+B}{4} \rfloor \\ R-G \\ B-G \end{pmatrix} \tag{1}$$

If the component consists of unsigned samples, a DC level shift is performed prior to the component transformation. This operation subtracts or adds the same quantity of each sample,

$$S(x,y) = I(x,y) - 2^{Ssiz^i - 1} \tag{2}$$

where $I(x, y)$ stands for the original sample at column x and row y, $S(x, y)$ for the shifted sample within the image area, and $Ssiz^i$ is the bit depth of the sample.

After tiling, DC level shifting and, if desired, component transformation, each tile is wavelet transformed. To do so, the tile is decomposed into different decomposition levels using the appropriate wavelet transformation. These decomposition levels consist of coefficients that describe the horizontal and vertical spatial frequency characteristics of the original tile component. The standard specifies the use of a dyadic decomposition, which divides the original image into four equally sized areas, also called subbands. The low–low pass filtered coefficients can be described as the down–sampled original image. The high–low pass filtered coefficients correspond to the horizontal frequencies of the image and the low–high pass filtered samples to the vertical frequencies. Finally, the high–high pass filtered samples stand for the high frequency parts of the image.

The irreversible transformation for lossy coding is implemented by means of the Daubechies 9–tap/7–tap filter [2] and the reversible transformation for lossy and lossless coding is implemented by means of a 5–tap/3–tap filter (Table 1).

	5/3 Filter	
i	Lowpass Filter $h_L(i)$	Highpass Filter $h_H(i)$
0	6/8	1
±1	2/8	-1/2
±2	-1/8	

Table 1. The 5/3 tap analysis filter coefficients.

The decomposition requires to extend the signal periodically as shown in Figure 3, to ensure that the original signal exists beyond the tile boundaries.

Fig. 3. The periodic symmetric extension of the original signal.

A lifting-based filtering [1] is used, which is a very simple filtering operation to calculate the filtered signal values (see Equation 5 and 6). It calculates all odd coefficients of the extended signal by a weighted sum of even sample values and calculates all even coefficients as weighted sum of the odd coefficients. If the encoding process runs in lossless mode, the results are rounded to integer values.

After the DWT, these coefficients are fed into a quantization stage. Quantization of the coefficients is used to achieve a better compression of the image data by losing precision unless the quantization value (Δ_b) is 1. Each coefficient $c_b(u,v)$ of subband b is quantized to the value $q_b(u,v)$ as follows:

$$q_b(u,v) = sign(c_b(u,v))\lfloor\frac{|c_b(u,v)|}{\Delta_b}\rfloor \tag{3}$$

The specified binary arithmetic entropy coder (AEC) in the last encoding stage is based on the recursive probability interval subdivision of Elias coding [3]. An arithmetic coder is able to code much closer to the signal entropy than a Huffman coder. The coding style used within JPEG 2000 is based on a binary adaptive arithmetic coder (MQ-Coder) with context modelling. The encoder gets the data to be coded and the current context from a previous coefficient bit modelling stage and generates the appropriate coded data.

3 The Hardware Design

The following restrictions apply for the design implementation because of the limited amount of hardware resources available on the Xilinx Virtex XCV1000 FPGA.

1. The image data can be any gray–scale image (one image component only).
2. The pixel depth has to be between 8 and 12 bpp.
3. The tile size is set to 64 × 64 pixels (this does not limit the image size).

The first two limitations are due to the fact, that it was intented to use gray–scale cameras only with a maximum of 12 bits per pixel.

The fixed tile size of 64 × 64 pixel is chosen as a trade-off between resource consumption and blocking artifacts visible on the decoded image. In order to verify the subjective impression of the effect that the tile size has on the image quality of the decoded image, the Peak Signal to Noise Ratio (PSNR) was calculated on different images with different tile sizes,

$$PSNR = 10 * log\frac{max[f(x,y)]}{\frac{1}{N*M}\sum_{i=0}^{N-1}\sum_{j=0}^{M-1}(f(x_i,y_j) - \tilde{f}(x_i,y_j))^2} \tag{4}$$

where N and M are the width and the height of the image, $f(x,y)$ is the original pixel at position (x,y), and $\tilde{f}(x,y)$ is the encoded and decoded pixel at position (x,y). The improvement from a tile size of 32×32 to 64×64 was satisfying enough (about 5 average PSNR points, see Table 2), while the smaller improvement (only 3 points) to the next tile size did not justify the larger memory requirements.

The VHDL modules are built up with generics and are responsible for all delay stages and FIFO lengths, which allow an adjustment to other tile sizes.

For the implementation of the encoder a completely pipelined design structure is used. Each tile is read line by line, beginning at the top left pixel, and is fed into the pipeline. The whole encoding pipeline is depicted in Figure 4. Every block passes its results to the next block until the whole tile has been processed.

Image Name	Whole Image	256x256	128x128	64x64	32x32
Lena	34.9029	34.6613	30.603	28.1372	22.472
Monarch	13.6893	11.0974	9.13419	6.95229	3.14556
Sail	42.3201	40.4682	36.482	31.7515	24.3468
Serrano	16.7826	16.0076	13.6017	10.2526	5.96475

Table 2. The PSNR [dB] values for different images coded using different tile sizes. A higher value means a better image quality.

All decomposition levels are calculated without storing the low–low pass filtered coefficients separately by using FIFOs within the DWT unit (see section 4). The Virtex architecture allows a very efficient way to implement FIFOs with look–up–tables.

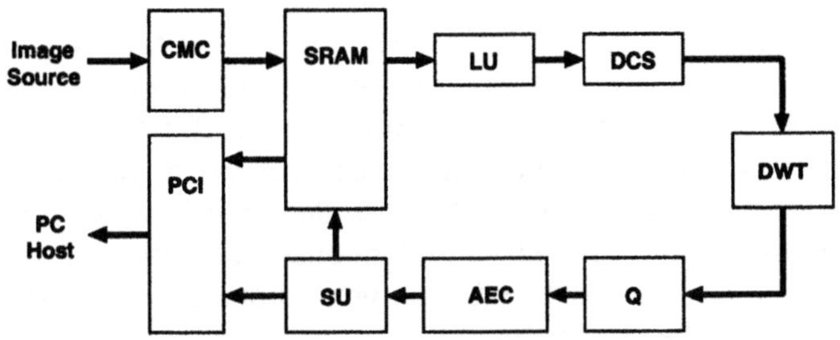

Fig. 4. Schematic view of the pipeline design.

The load unit (LU) is responsible for reading the encoding parameters from the SRAM, for tiling the original image, for providing the bit per pixel and the quantization mode information to other modules, and for starting the encoding process on a tile–by–tile, line–by–line basis. It is only possible to stop the encoding at the end of the tiles. It will be signaled by the arithmetic entropy coding unit whether to stop or to proceed with the next tile.

The DC level shift unit (DCS) implements Equation 2. It receives the pixel depth and the pixel to be DC level shifted. If a control signal is set, the pixel will be DC level shifted, otherwise, the tile samples are already signed.

The implemented quantization unit (Q) is able to work in two different quantization modes: with or without quantization for strictly lossless coding of the DWT coefficients. The real quantization mode quantizises all coefficients with an appropriate dynamic range according to the subband of occurrence. The low–low pass filtered coefficients will be quantized to 8 bit, the low–high and high–low pass filtered coefficients to 7 bit, and the high–high pass filtered coefficients to 6 bit, with respect to the Human Visual System (HVS, [7]).

The store unit (SU) is the last module in the encoding pipeline. It receives byte vectors from the arithmetic entropy coding unit to be stored in the SRAM of the FPGA board. A signal indicates that the current byte input vector is the last byte of the image. When the last write into the SRAM has been performed, it signals the termination of the encoding by setting an encoding finished register, so that the host PC can upload the encoded data.

4 The DWT Module

The discrete wavelet transformation (DWT) is the mathematical core of the JPEG 2000 standard. We decided to implement the 5/3 lifting based filter method because it was proved that the amount of memory used by the lifting based implementation is always smaller than the equivalent convolution based implementation [1]. However, due to the modular design structure, the concentration on one wavelet transformation only is not a penalty, because the DWT module can easily be replaced by other filter banks.

The DWT module gets the pixel depth and the sequence of pixels on a line–by–line basis and calculates the wavelet transformation on these pixels for up to five decomposition levels which is determined by the tile size.

In order to calculate the different decomposition levels, each level has its own wavelet transformation unit. The data flow inside of the DWT module is shown in Figure 5. The first DWT submodule calculates the subbands LL_0, HL_0, LH_0, HH_0 and passes LL_0 to the next submodule. The other subbands build the output of the DWT module.

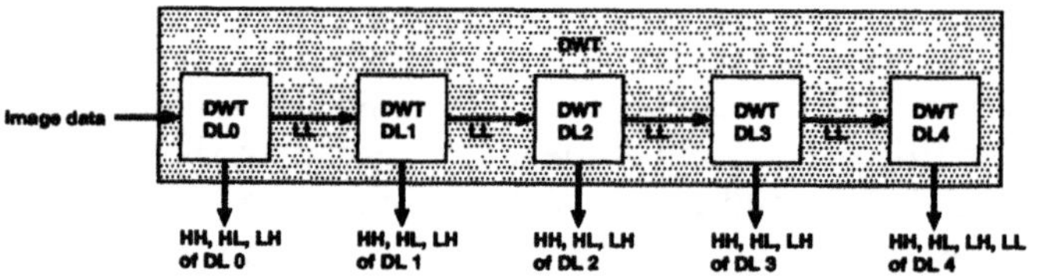

Fig. 5. The five DWT decomposition levels are calculated using one DWT submodule per level.

The submodules inside the DWT module differ only in the internal FIFO length because each submodule receives a quarter of the samples of the previous one. The structure of a DWT submodule is shown in Figure 6. It calculates two 1D-DWTs, one for the the rows (DWT_row) and the other for the columns (DWT_col).

The DWT_row and the DWT_col modules perform four basic operations: the *clipp*, the *addclipp*, the *addshift* and the *addshiftshift* operation. Equation 5 and 6 which correspond to the 5/3 tap filter coefficients (Table 1) illustrate which part of the wavelet transformation is done by which basic operation.

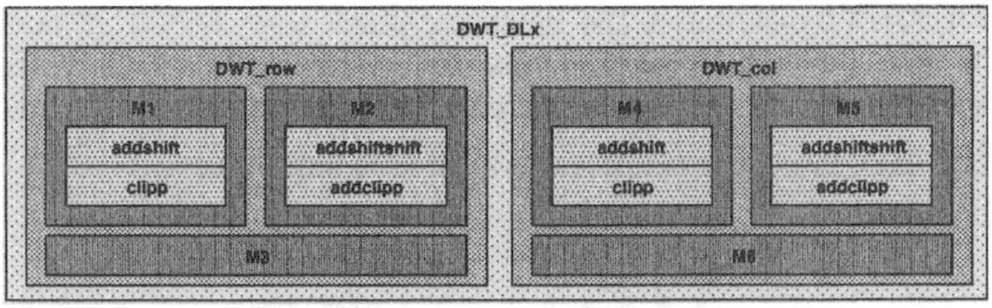

Fig. 6. The structure of the wavelet transformation subunit for one decomposition level.

$$y(2n+1) = \underbrace{x_{ext}(2n+1) - \lfloor \underbrace{\frac{x_{ext}(2n) + x_{ext}(2n+2)}{2}}_{addshift} \rfloor}_{clipp} \tag{5}$$

$$y(2n) = \underbrace{x_{ext}(2n) + \lfloor \underbrace{\frac{y(2n-1) + y(2n+1) + 2}{4}}_{addshiftshift} \rfloor}_{addclipp} \tag{6}$$

The basic operations are combined to six modules. Module *M1* calculates all odd coefficients, module *M2* all even coefficients. Module *M4* and *M5* perform the same operations as *M1* and *M2*, respectively, but for the rows instead for the columns of the image samples.

The coefficients calculated by module *DWT_row* are passed to module *DWT_col*. As can be seen in Equation 5 and 6 all odd coefficients have to be calculated prior to even coefficients. Therefore, module *M3* serves as buffer and interleaves the even and odd coefficients correctly and passes them to the *DWT_col* module, which calculates the 1D-DWT for the columns.

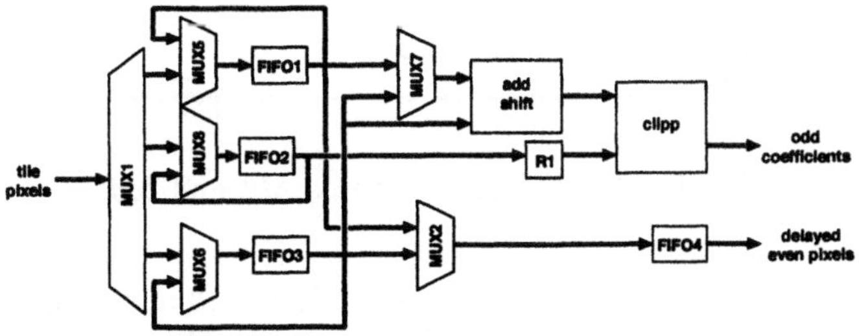

Fig. 7. The set–up of module *M1* and *M4*.

In the following, the structure of the modules will be explained in detail. Module *M1* (Figure 7) gets the tile samples line–by–line, pixel–by–pixel. The multiplexer *MUX1* distributes the incoming pixels over *FIFO1, 2* and *3*. Once the FIFOs hold three valid samples, one odd coefficient is calculated every second clock cycle. *MUX7* is required to handle the right boundary of a tile (see Figure 8).

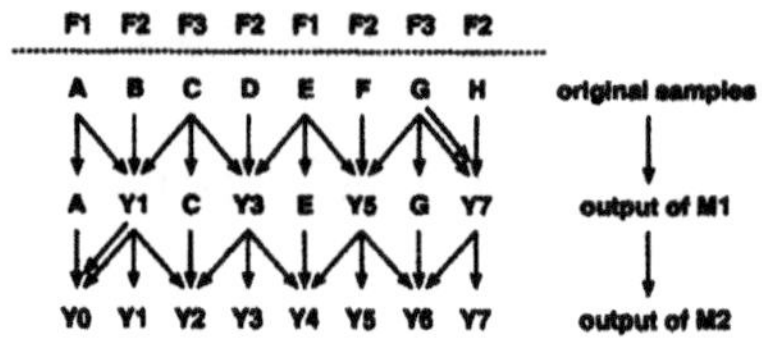

Fig. 8. The calculation of wavelet coefficients. The illustration shows one line of 8 samples fed into module *M1* and their distribution over the input FIFOs.

MUX2 and *FIFO4* store all even samples which will be used by the next module (*M2*). Module *M4* provides the same functionality, but differs in its FIFO length and in the algorithm for *MUX1, 2* and *7*. In order to calculate the DWT coefficients by module *M4*, the FIFOs *1, 2* and *3* need to hold all previously calculated coefficients for one whole line (see Table 3 for the FIFO lengths). Finally, *MUX1, 2* and *7* switch on a line–by–line basis instead of a pixel–by–pixel basis.

Module *M2* gets the odd coefficients as well as the delayed even samples of the tile component in parallel from *M1* (Figure 9). When a new line of the tile starts, the left boundary has to be handled by *MUX3*, according to Figure 8.

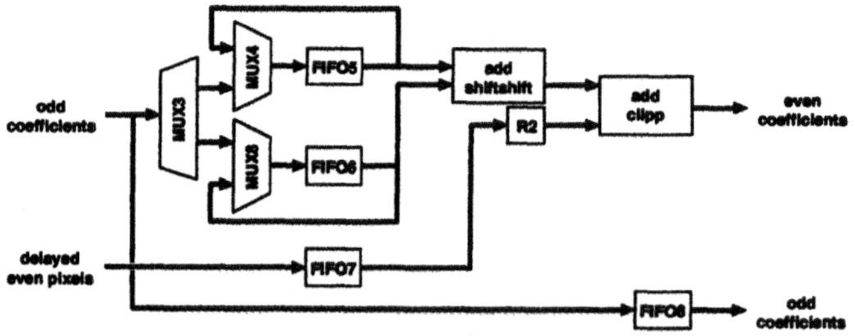

Fig. 9. The set–up of module *M2* and *M5*.

Module *M3* receives the pair of coefficients from *M2* and makes sure that its output alternates between even and odd coefficients. At this stage, a row based 1D–DWT has been successfully performed.

Module *M5* uses the generics of Table 3 to adjust the FIFO lengths appropriately and the multiplexer *MUX3* works with lines of coefficients rather than single coefficients. Furthermore, *M5* passes its results to module *M6* which is depicted in Figure 10. This module is introduced because the next decomposition level needs all *LL* subband coefficients at each clock cycle. *M6* stores the *LL* subband coefficients in one of the two *F1* FIFOs until all coefficients have been received. Then it passes one coefficient per clock cycle to the next decomposition level. Meanwhile, the other *F1* FIFO is used to store the next *LL* subband from module *M5*. All other coefficients — associated to subband *HH*, *HL* or *LH* — are passed to the quantization unit, immediately.

Module	DWT_DL0	DWT_DL1	DWT_DL2	DWT_DL3	DWT_DL4
SRD	64	32	16	8	4

Table 3. The generics for different decomposition levels of the DWT submodules. The shift register depth (SRD) gives the amount of samples that can be stored.

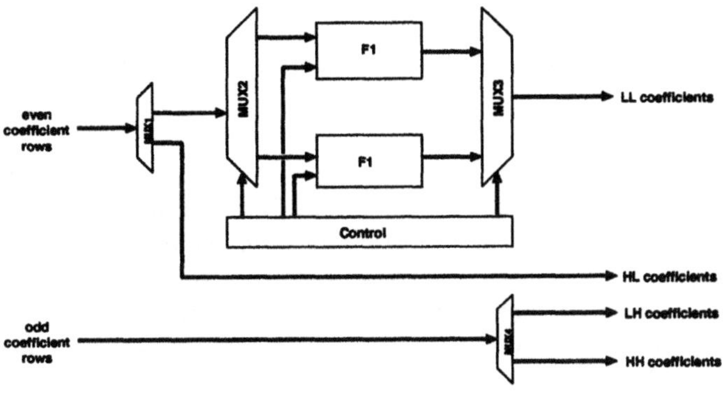

Fig. 10. The interior of the *M6* module.

5 Performance

The design is placed&routed for the Xilinx Virtex XCV1000-4bg560 FPGA and uses 43% of its resources. User constrains are defined prior to the routing process in order to guarantee a minimum clock frequency of 50 MHz for all modules. The maximum allowed clock frequency for each module, calculated by the routing software, is listed in Table 4.

Module	LU	SU	Quant	DCS	DWT
Maximum Clock Frequency	62.3 MHz	85.4 MHz	60.3 MHz	98.1 MHz	52.8 MHz

Table 4. The maximum clock frequency for each module calculated by the Xilinx place&route tool for a Virtex XCV1000-4bg560 FPGA.

Obviously, the most complex module is the module which runs with the lowest clock frequency. Due to the fact that the whole encoder is built of all the modules listed in Table 4, the highest allowed design frequency is 52.8 MHz. The performance of the encoder can be determined by investigating the depth of each module when processing an image of 512 × 512 pixels from the used camera.

Together with a tile size of 64 × 64 samples the required amount of clock cylces to encode the whole tile is 1,942 for filling the pipeline and 4,096 clock cycles for processing each sample. This makes a total of 6,031 clock cycles per tile. Assuming a design frequency of 50 MHz, the tile is encoded completely after 120.62 μs. For a total image size of 512 × 512 samples, the design needs to calculate the coefficients for 64 tiles which is equivalent to 7.7 ms of processing time. This leads to a total encoding performance of 130 images (512 × 512 pixels, 50 MHz design clock frequency) per second.

The performance is independent of the pixel depth of the image. The load unit (LU) is designed to address the SRAM in a way to get one coefficient every clock cycle even at the intented maximum bit depth (12 bpp, see section 3).

A comparison showed that this FPGA approach is similar to a 1 GHz standard micro processor (a Pentium needs about 8 ms for a 512 × 512 image).

6 Conclusion

The standard is not fully implemented, yet. The missing part is the arithmetic coder unit (AEC), for which there are many implementations with various complexity and different clock cycles to process one bit [8]. The performance of 130 frames per second is calculated without it, so the design is allowed to be slowed down by more than a factor of two. Because the design so far does not use any of the BlockRAM of the Virtex FPGA and only about 43% of the slides, it is fair to assume that the remaining resources and the BlockRAM are sufficient for an implementation of the coefficient bit modelling and the entropy encoder.

References

1. C. Chrysafis, A. Ortega, *Minimum Memory Implementations of the Lifting Scheme*, contact chrysafi@hpl.hp.com or ortega@sipi.usc.edu for the paper.
2. I. Daubechies, *Ten Lectures on Wavelets*, SIAM, Philadelphia PA, 1992
3. P. Elias, *Universal Codeword Sets and Representations of the Integers*, IEEE Trans. Inform. Theory 21, 2(Mar.), 194–203
4. ISO/IEC FCD15444-1, *Information technology – JPEG 2000 Image Coding System*, JPEG 2000 Final Committe Draft Version 1.0, 16 March 2000
5. M. Nibouche, A. Bouridane, F. Murtagh, O. Nibouche, *FPGA-Based Discrete Wavelet Transforms System*, FPL 2001, LNCS 2147, pp. 607-612, Springer 2001
6. J. Ritter, P. Molitor, *A Pipelined Architecture for Partitioned DWT Based Lossy Image Compression using FPGA's*, FPGA 2001, February 11-13, 2001, Monterey
7. J. G. Robson, *Spatial and Temporal Contrast–Sensitivity Functions of the Visual System*, Physiological Laboratory, Cambridge, England, March 1966
8. R. Stefo, J.L. Núñez et al., *FPGA-Based Modelling Unit for High Speed Lossless Arithmetic Coding*, FPL 2001, LNCS 2147, pp. 643-647, Springer 2001

Small Multiplier-Based Multiplication and Division Operators for Virtex-II Devices

Jean-Luc Beuchat[1] and Arnaud Tisserand[1,2]

[1] Laboratoire de l'Informatique du Parallélisme
Ecole Normale Supérieure de Lyon
46, Allée d'Italie, F–69364 Lyon Cedex 07
[2] INRIA – Institut National de Recherche en Informatique et Automatique

Abstract. This paper presents integer multiplication and division operators dedicated to Virtex-II FPGAs from Xilinx. Those operators are based on small 18×18 multiplier blocks available in the Virtex-II device family. Various trade-offs are explored (computation decomposition, radix, digit sets ...) using specific VHDL generators. The obtained operators lead to speed improvements up to 18% for multiplication and 40% for division compared to standard solutions only based on CLBs.

1 Introduction

Many algorithms and architectures have been developed for implementing multiplication and division in FPGAs. Those algorithms mainly use solutions proposed for standard integrated circuits. They are based on very low-level basic elements such as full adder and NAND/XOR gates.

Some recent FPGAs embed hardwired small multipliers blocks. For instance, Virtex-II devices from Xilinx include many 18×18 multipliers. ORCA Series 4 from Lattice or Stratix from Altera FPGAs also embed small multipliers. These new basic elements may lead to more efficient arithmetic operators.

This paper deals with the design and the optimization of integer multiplication and division operators based on a combination of small multiplier blocks and configurable logic blocks for the Virtex-II devices. Section 2 briefly describes Virtex-II features used in this work. The multiplication algorithms, operators and implementation results are described in Section 3, and Section 4 deals with division. Finally, Section 5 presents some conclusions and future prospects.

2 The Virtex-II Family

Virtex-II configurable logic blocks (CLBs) provide functional elements for synchronous and combinatorial logic. Each CLB includes four slices containing basically two 4-input look-up tables (LUT), two storage elements, and fast carry logic dedicated to addition and subtraction. A CLB has two separate carry chains, whose height is two bits per slice, running upward (Figure 1a).

M. Glesner, P. Zipf, and M. Renovell (Eds.): FPL 2002, LNCS 2438, pp. 513–522, 2002.

Virtex-II circuits embed many 18×18 two's complement multipliers (the MULT18x18 blocks), each of them supporting two input ports 18-bit signed or 17-bit unsigned wide (Figure 1b). Furthermore, each multiplier has an internal pipeline stage. Surprisingly, this feature is poorly documented in the Virtex-II data sheet[1] and synthesis tools seem unable to automatically deal with it. The MULT18x18S component, available in the library of Synplify Pro, allows us to write multipliers that take advantage of this characteristic (Figure 1c).

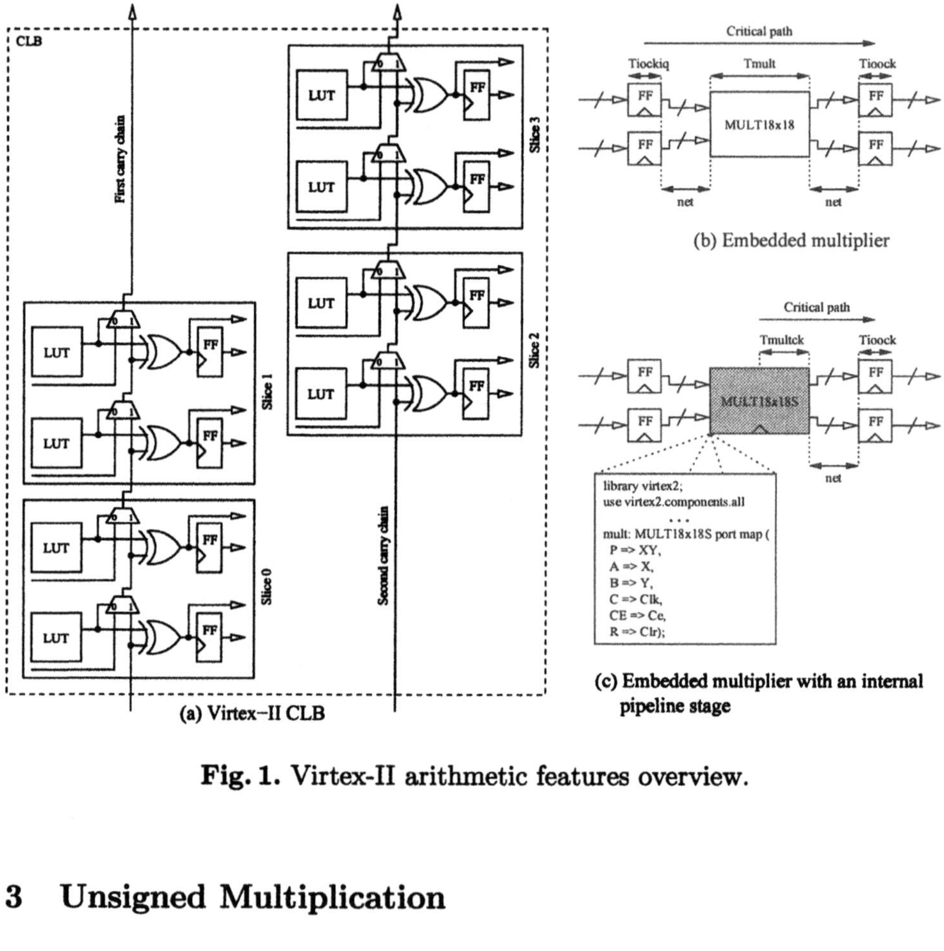

Fig. 1. Virtex-II arithmetic features overview.

3 Unsigned Multiplication

This section presents the design of efficient unsigned integer multipliers based on the MULT18x18 blocks available in Virtex-II devices. The algorithms studied here involve splitting the operands into two parts. A m-bit integer X is decomposed into a lower part X_0 and a higher part X_1 such that

[1] There is only one table with the switching characteristics of a pipelined MULT18x18 block.

$$X = X_0 + 2^n X_1 = \sum_{i=0}^{n-1} x_i 2^i + 2^n \sum_{i=0}^{m-n-1} x_{n+i} 2^i,$$

where $n < m$. Paragraphs 3.1, 3.2, and 3.3 describe three architectures requiring from one to four MULT18x18 blocks. Evaluation and comparison of these methods are summarized in paragraph 3.4.

3.1 Divide-and-Conquer Approach (4 MULT18x18 Blocks)

The well-known divide-and-conquer approach (see for example [1]) requires four small multiplications and two additions to compute the product XY (Figure 2) and is based on the following equation:

$$(X_1 k + X_0)(Y_1 k + Y_0) = X_1 Y_1 k^2 + (X_1 Y_0 + X_0 Y_1)k + X_0 Y_0,$$

where $k = 2^n$. Note that the n least significant bits are obtained directly from a MULT18x18 block. Synplify Pro uses this method to synthesize a multiplier that is larger than the MULT18x18 width. However, X_0 and Y_0 respectively contain the 17 least significant bits of X and Y. Our experiments will demonstrate that this choice does not always lead to the fastest circuit. Therefore, we have written a VHDL generator allowing the user to specify the width of X_0, X_1, Y_0, and Y_1.

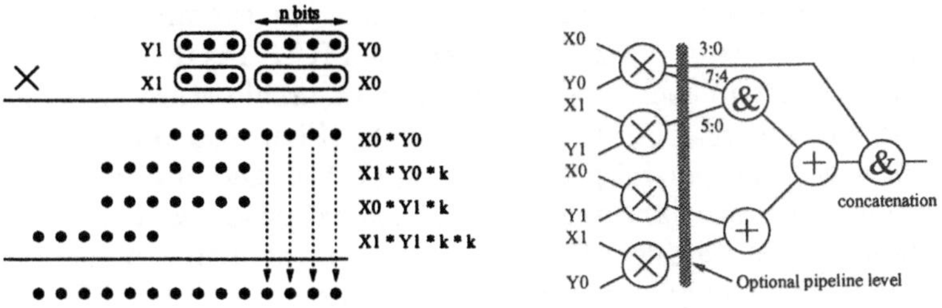

Fig. 2. The divide-and-conquer method (4 MULT18x18 blocks).

3.2 Two-Way Method (3 MULT18x18 Blocks)

The two-way method, originally proposed by Karatsuba and Ofman [2], allows us to spare a MULT18x18 block and is based on the rewriting:

$$(X_1 k + X_0)(Y_1 k + Y_0) = X_1 Y_1 (k^2 - k) + (X_1 + X_0)(Y_1 + Y_0)k + X_0 Y_0 (1 - k).$$

It involves three multipliers, namely $X_1 Y_1$, $(X_1 + X_0)(Y_1 + Y_0)$, and $X_0 Y_0$, three adders, and two subtracters (Figure 3). However, this method has a small drawback in that $(X_1 + X_0)$ and $(Y_1 + Y_0)$ require $n + 1$ bits. In [3], Knuth suggested an improvement by writing:

$$(X_1 k + X_0)(Y_1 k + Y_0) = X_1 Y_1 (k^2 + k) - (X_1 - X_0)(Y_1 - Y_0)k + X_0 Y_0 (1 + k).$$

Knuth was able to replace $X_1 + X_0$ by $X_1 - X_0$. At the price of a few additional logic, we can always subtract the lesser from the greater and save the extra bit [4]. However, we will not consider this option in the following.

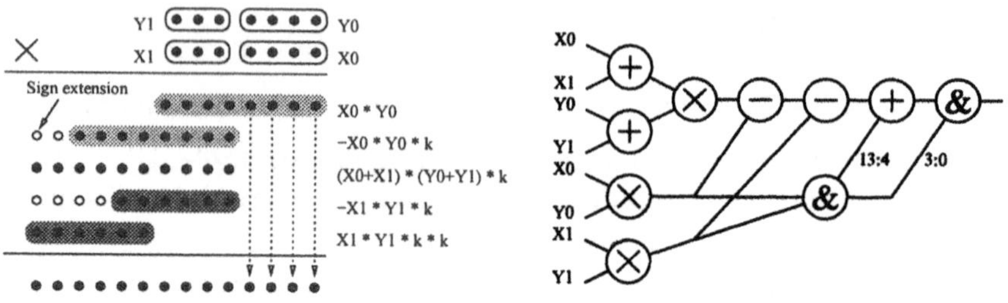

Fig. 3. The two-way method (3 MULT18x18 blocks).

3.3 Using a Single MULT18x18 Block

When the size m of the operands is slightly greater than 17, the divide-and-conquer approach leads to a waste of resources. For example, if X and Y are 20-bit unsigned integers, Synplify allocates a MULT18x18 block for the 3×3 multiplication X_1Y_1. In such cases, we suggest an architecture involving a single MULT18x18 which carries out the product X_1Y_0 (Figure 4a) and some additional logic for the few other partial products computation and addition. We combine the remaining x_iy_j terms and build $m-17$ partial products as depicted in Figure 4a. These partial products PP_i are summed using a tree of carry-propagate adders (Figure 4b). Carry-save adders are not useful in Virtex FPGAs because of the fast carry logic. Formally, PP_i is a $(2m-i-1)$-bit integer defined by:

$$\mathrm{PP}_i = \sum_{j=0}^{m-1-i} x_i y_j 2^{i+j} + \sum_{j=i+1}^{m-1} x_j y_{m-1-i} 2^{j+m-i-1}.$$

The difficulty lies in the determination of the width of the intermediate sums. Let us notice that

$$\begin{aligned}\max(\mathrm{PP}_i) &= \sum_{j=0}^{m-1-i} 2^{i+j} + \sum_{j=i+1}^{m-1} 2^{j+m-i-1} \\ &= \sum_{j=0}^{m-1-i} 2^{i+j} + \sum_{j=m-i}^{2m-2i-2} 2^{i+j} = 2^i\left(2^{2m-2i-1}-1\right).\end{aligned}$$

Therefore,

$$\begin{aligned}\max(\mathrm{PP}_i + \mathrm{PP}_{i+1}) &= 2^{2m-i-1} + 2^{2m-i-2} - 2^{i+1} - 2^i &(1)\\ &= 10\,\underbrace{11\cdots11}_{2m-2i-4\times}\,01\underbrace{0\cdots0}_{i\times} &(2)\end{aligned}$$

and $PP_i + PP_{i+1}$ is a $(2m - i)$-bit integer. Assume that $m = 21$ and consider the sum $(PP_0 + PP_1) + (PP_2 + PP_3)$. From (2), we deduce

$$\max\big(\underbrace{(PP_0 + PP_1)}_{42\text{ bits}} + \underbrace{(PP_2 + PP_3)}_{40\text{ bits}}\big) = 10\underbrace{11\cdots11}_{38\times}01 + 10\underbrace{11\cdots11}_{34\times}0100.$$

Hence, the sum is a 42-bit integer. We have written a VHDL generator that uses such rules to compute the sum of the PP_i terms. While the solution illustrated in Figure 4c seems easier to implement, it leads to larger and slower design. The synthesis tools can not guess the properties of the partial products and allocate full-adders whose inputs remain equal to zero.

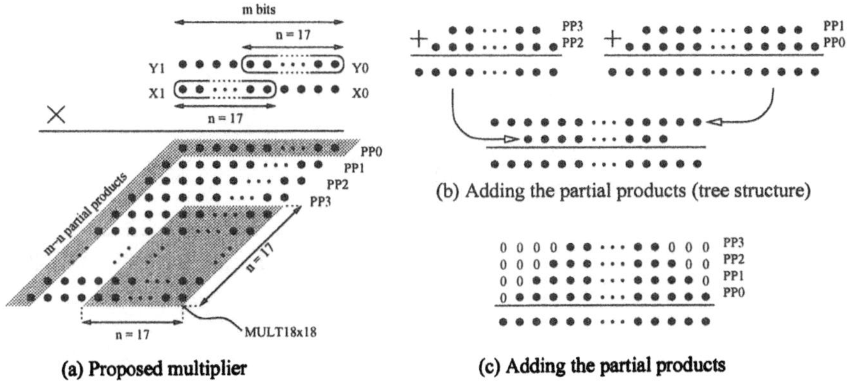

Fig. 4. Multiplication with a single MULT18x18 block.

3.4 Implementation Results

We have written a C library which generates VHDL descriptions of the architectures described above. The VHDL code was synthesized with Synplify Pro 7.0.3 and implemented on a Virtex-II XC2V500-6 device using Xilinx Alliance Series 4.1.03i. In the following, m and n respectively denote the total size of the operands and the size of their lower part.

The first experiment compares the three solutions (Figure 5). The divide-and-conquer strategy leads to the smallest circuits in terms of slices number, except for $m = 18$ and $m = 19$ where the single MULT18x18 architecture is smaller. The two-way method is disappointing: though it spares a small multiplier, it is slower and the additional logic is twice bigger than the divide-and-conquer approach. Finally, the architecture described in paragraph 3.3 is a good trade-off between size and period when m is close to 17.

An interesting point is that the proposed single MULT18x18 architecture is still efficient for $m = 23$, which is the mantissa size in IEEE standard floating-point numbers (a survey on floating-point can be found in [5]). We have implemented two versions of the 23×23 unsigned multiplier involved in the floating-point multiplication with two pipeline stages and the MULT18x18S primitive. The divide-and-conquer approach implies 50 slices, four MULT18x18S blocks, and has a period τ equal to 6 ns. Our algorithm needs 182 slices, a single MULT18x18S block and is a little bit slower ($\tau = 8$ ns). We plan to study floating-point arithmetic on FPGAs.

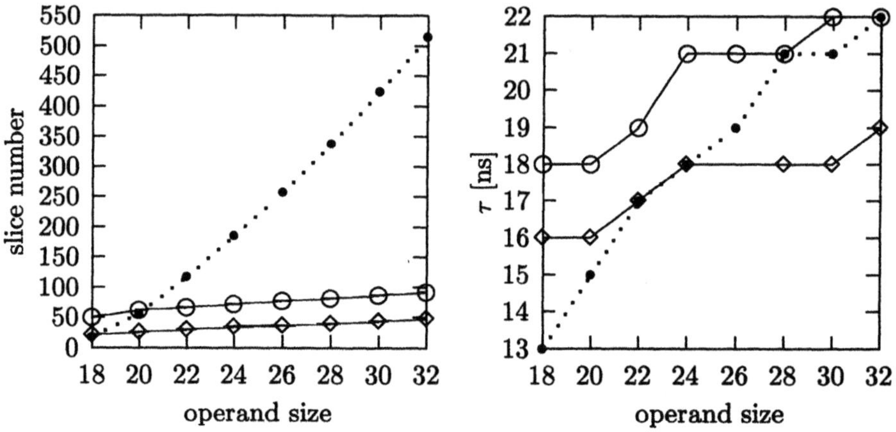

Fig. 5. Number of slices and period τ of various unsigned multipliers on a XC2V500-6 device; ◇: divide-and-conquer algorithm; X_0 and Y_0 are 17-bit integers (4 MULT18x18 blocks); ○: two-way method (3 MULT18x18 blocks); •: algorithm described in paragraph 3.3 (1 MULT18x18 block).

Let us now study the impact of n on the divide-and-conquer method. We obtain the smallest circuits when $n = 17$ (Figure 6). This result is not surprising: remember that the n least significant bits come directly from a MULT18x18 block. Consequently, the larger n is, the smaller the last adder of Figure 2 becomes. For a combinatorial circuit, choosing $n = m/2$ leads however to a faster circuit. When we introduce a pipeline stage by replacing all MULT18x18 blocks by MULT18x18S, our experiments show that $n = 17$ is the best solution: the size is exactly the same one that in the combinatorial case (that's why it is not plotted in Figure 6) and the period doesn't depend anymore on the value of n.

The architectures described in this section only need limited changes so as to perform signed multiplication. The use of MULT18x18 blocks can lead to waste resources for small operand width (i.e. $n << 17$). For the specific case of very small operand width (up to 5 bits), two multiplications can be shared in the same MULT18x18 block.

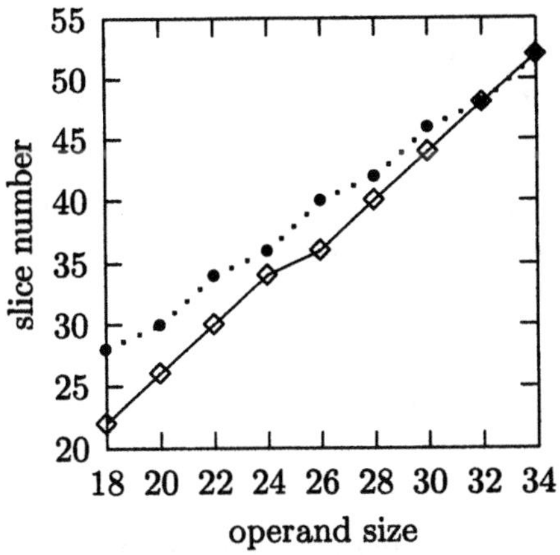

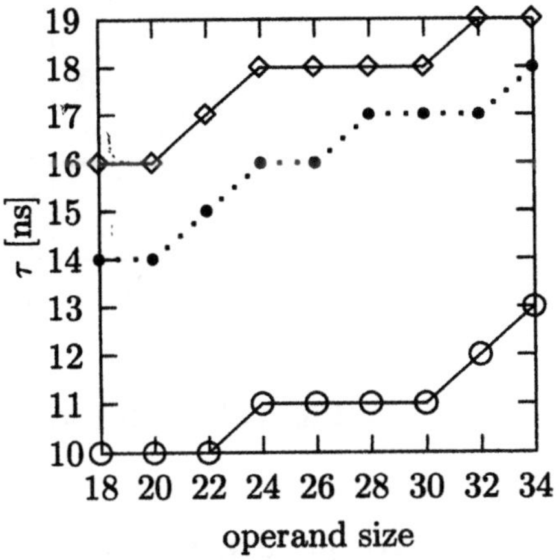

Fig. 6. Impact of the choice of n on the divide-and-conquer method; ◇: $n = 17$; •: $n = m/2$; ○: $n = 17$ with MULT18x18S.

4 Unsigned Division

The most common division implementation in processors is the digit-recurrence algorithm named SRT from the initials of Sweeney, Robertson, and Tocher. SRT and other division algorithms and implementations can be found in a complete survey [6]. Digit-recurrence algorithms retire a fixed number of quotient bits in every iteration. SRT dividers are similar to the "paper-and-pencil" method, but they only use limited comparisons to speed-up the quotient selection. SRT dividers are typically of low complexity, utilize small area, but have relatively large latencies. A complete book is devoted to digit-recurrence algorithms [7].

Figure 7 presents a standard radix-r SRT iteration architecture ($r = 2^k$). There are $t = \lceil n/k \rceil$ iterations in the division of n-bit integers. Two additional cycles are required (1 before and 1 after the iterations) to check input values (division by zero and scaling) and to convert the signed-digit quotient to a standard radix-2 notation. The division x/d produces k bits of the quotient q at every iteration. The quotient digit q_j is represented using a radix-r notation. The first residual w_0 is initialized to x. At iteration j, the residual w_j is shifted by k bits left (it produces rw_j). Based on a few most significant bits of rw_j and d (n_r and n_d-bit large respectively), one can deduce the next quotient digit q_{j+1} using the quotient digit selection table (Qsel). Finally, the product $q_{j+1} \times d$ is subtracted to rw_j to form the next residual w_{j+1}.

4.1 Virtex-II SRT Dividers Implementations

A SRT dividers generator was developed in C++. Based on the operator parameters (operands width, radix, quotient and residual representations), the program checks the parameters combination, generates the quotient digit selection table

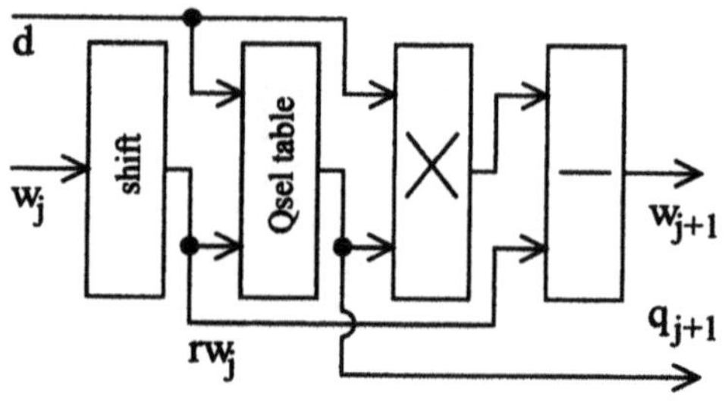

Fig. 7. SRT division iteration architecture.

and the synthesizable VHDL code of the complete operator description. There is no pipeline level inside the generated iteration description.

There are several important parameters in a SRT divider. The radix $r = 2^k$ plays a major role. For large values of k the iteration number t is small but each iteration is complex (large Qsel tables, complex product $q_{j+1} \times d$). High radices (larger than 16 in our case) lead to very huge quotient digit selection tables and seem to be impracticable.

The radix-2^k quotient is represented using a signed-digit redundant number system to ensure that next quotient digit determination is possible only based on a few most significant n_r and n_d bits of the residual and divisor respectively. Several digit sets $\{-\alpha, -\alpha+1, \ldots, 0, \ldots, \alpha-1, \alpha\}$ can be used for radix-2^k notation depending on the values of k and α. For instance, with a radix-4 representation, the minimally redundant digit set is $\{-2, -1, 0, 1, 2\}$ ($\alpha = 2$) and the maximally redundant digit set is $\{-3, -2, -1, 0, 1, 2, 3\}$ ($\alpha = 3$). The digit set used for the quotient is an important design decision. High values of α lead to simpler quotient digit selection (smaller values of $n_r + n_d$ as the address width of the Qsel table) but also to more complex product $q_{j+1} \times d$. In this work, we only use distributed RAM (based on the LUTs inside the CLBs) for the implementation of the selection tables. Furthermore, the specific RAM blocks (called BRAM in Virtex devices) can be used for the Qsel tables.

Usually, another important parameter is the residual w_j representation. For VLSI implementation, a redundant number system such as carry-save is used for w_j to accelerate the $q_{j+1} \times d - rw_j$ subtraction. For Xilinx FPGAs implementation, a non-redundant number system such as the two's complement is sufficient for the residual because of the fast-carry logic available in Virtex-II devices.

In this work we compare a standard radix-2 division (noticed "std r2") and several SRT dividers based on MULT18x18 blocks (noticed "r?/?"). Radix 4, 8 and 16 have been investigated with several quotient digit sets. For each solution, 16, 24, 32 and 40-bit operands operators have been generated. The different solutions investigated in this work are summarized in Table 1.

A radix-16 iteration architecture has been generated but it leads to a huge area (the quotient digit selection table is then a 14-bit address table). It requires

solution name	std r2	r4/2	r4/3	r8/5	r8/6	r16/12
radix	2	4	4	8	8	16
α	1	2	3	5	6	12
MULT18x18 blocks	no	yes	yes	yes	yes	yes
n_r, n_d	na	4,3	6,3	7,4	6,4	7,7

Table 1. Summary of the generated and tested division operators.

more 2 700 slices of the XC2V500-6 (more than 70% of the slice count). So, we limited our study to radices smaller or equal to 8.

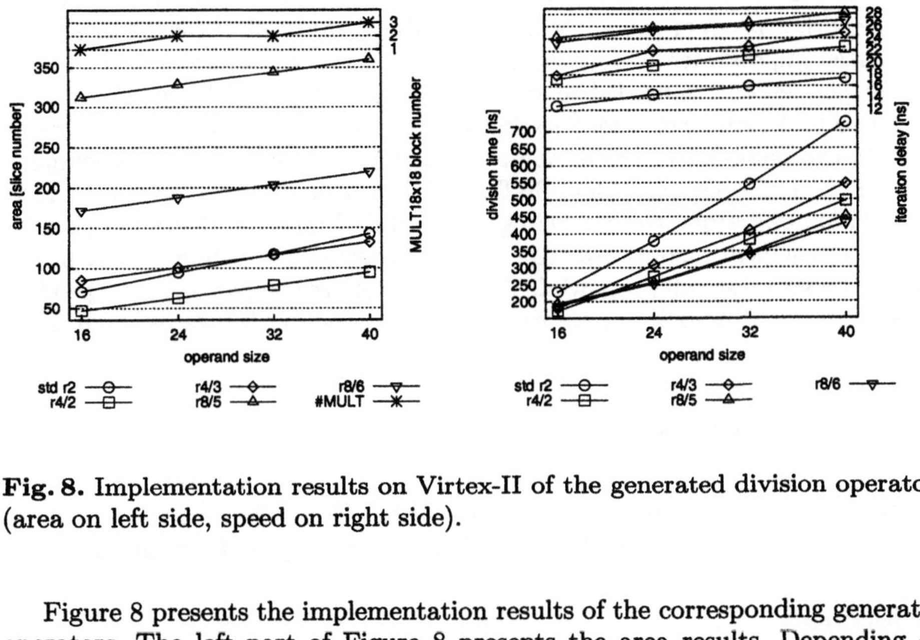

Fig. 8. Implementation results on Virtex-II of the generated division operators (area on left side, speed on right side).

Figure 8 presents the implementation results of the corresponding generated operators. The left part of Figure 8 presents the area results. Depending on the solution ("std r2" or "r?/?") and the operands width, the total area used in the device is the sum of the slice number and the number of MULT18x18 blocks reported on the figure. For instance, a radix-8 and α=6 solution leads to 172 slices and 1 MULT18x18 block for 16-bit operands and to 204 slices and 2 MULT18x18 blocks for 32-bit operands. The standard radix-2 solution does not use any MULT18x18 block. Speed achievements are presented on the right part of Figure 8. There are two curves sets. The five lower ones represent the total division time while the five upper ones represent one iteration delay. All delays have a linear growth with the operand size n. Significant speed improvements are achieved using MULT18x18 blocks for the $q_{j+1} \times d$ product. Indeed, for 40-bit operands a radix-8 solution based on 3 MULT18x18 blocks is more than 40% faster than the standard radix-2 solution.

5 Conclusion

In this paper, improved architectures and implementations of integer multiplication and division operators for Virtex-II FPGAs have been presented. Those operators are based on a combination of small hardwired 18x18 multipliers and CLBs. Dedicated VHDL generators have been developed to provide a wide parameter space exploration. Various trade-offs between speed and area have been explored. A significant speed improvement is possible using MULT18x18 blocks. Cunningly using a few MULT18x18 blocks combined to a few additional logic leads to very efficient operators.

For unsigned multiplication, a computation decomposition based on a single MULT18x18 and some additional logic can lead to faster designs than with 4 blocks. For operands size slightly larger than 17, the single MULT18x18 block solution leads to smaller and faster multipliers. A radix-8 SRT division architecture with a product generator based on MULT18x18 blocks leads to a up to 40% speed improvement compared to a standard radix-2 solution.

Further research is needed to explore other parameters. The presented solutions and tools will be extended to signed integers. The presented multiplication solution can be derived to close operators such as multiplication and accumulation and square operators while SRT division can be extended to square-root. For division operators various coding of the signed quotient digits are possible (two's complement, sign-magnitude, one-hot codings ...). Some codings will reduce the selection table size while they require more complex $q_{j+1} \times d$ product generation. Floating-point operators will also be another future research direction.

Acknowledgments

The authors would like to thank the "Ministère Français de la Recherche" (grant # 1048 CDR 1 "ACI jeunes chercheurs"), the "Fonds National Suisse de la Recherche Scientifique", and the Xilinx University Program for their support.

References

[1] B. Parhami. *Computer Arithmetic.* Oxford University Press, 2000.
[2] A. Karatsuba and Y. Ofman. Multiplication of Multidigit Numbers on Automata. *Soviet Phys. Doklady*, 7(7):595–596, January 1963.
[3] D. E. Knuth. *The Art of Computer Programming*, volume 2. Addison-Wesley, 2nd edition, 1981.
[4] D. Zuras. More On Squaring and Multiplying Large Integers. *IEEE Transactions on Computers*, 43(8):899–908, August 1994.
[5] D. Goldberg. What every computer scientist should know about floating point arithmetic. *ACM Computing Surveys*, 23(1):5–47, 1991.
[6] S.F. Oberman and M.J. Flynn. Division algorithms and implementations. *IEEE Transactions on Computers*, 46(8):833–854, August 1997.
[7] M.D. Ercegovac and T. Lang. *Division and Square-Root Algorithms: Digit-Recurrence Algorithms and Implementations.* Kluwer Academic, 1994.

Automating Customisation of Floating-Point Designs

Altaf Abdul Gaffar[1], Wayne Luk[1], Peter Y.K. Cheung[2], Nabeel Shirazi[3], and James Hwang[3]

[1] Department of Computing, Imperial College, 180 Queen's Gate, London, England
[2] Department of EEE, Imperial College, Exhibition Road, London, England
[3] Xilinx, Inc. 2100 Logic Drive, San Jose, USA

Abstract. This paper describes a method for customising the representation of floating-point numbers that exploits the flexibility of reconfigurable hardware. The method determines the appropriate size of mantissa and exponent for each operation in a design, so that a cost function with a given error specification for the output relative to a reference representation can be satisfied. We adopt an iterative implementation of this method, which supports IEEE single-precision or double-precision floating-point representation as the reference representation. This implementation produces customised floating-point formats with arbitrary-sized mantissa and exponent. The tool follows a generic framework designed to cover a variety of arithmetic representations and their hardware implementations; both combinational and pipelined designs can be developed. Results show that, particularly for calculations involving large dynamic ranges, our tool can produce hardware that is smaller and faster when compared with a design adopting the reference representation.

1 Introduction

Custom data representation is a promising method for optimising designs for a given application. Recent work has focused on developing reconfigurable designs with optimised bitwidth for each operation. Such methods are based on static analysis [1], [5], [11], dynamic analysis [2], [8], [10], or a combination [9]. They generate designs adopting custom integer or fixed-point formats, possibly conforming to user-defined error criteria with respect to a reference representation.

Many reconfigurable hardware devices are now large enough to accommodate floating-point operations. Most existing implementations, however, are based on IEEE single-precision format [7], [14]. The purpose of this paper is to present a tool that automatically customises floating-point arithmetic formats according to user-given accuracy criteria. The resulting implementations are often smaller and faster than those adopting the corresponding standard format, since each operation can be individually customised to have the most appropriate mantissa and exponent sizes as well as other characteristics, such as overflow and underflow protection. Our work is particularly useful for optimising hardware computations involving large dynamic ranges, which can be found in many scientific and medical applications.

M. Glesner, P. Zipf, and M. Renovell (Eds.): FPL 2002, LNCS 2438, pp. 523–533, 2002.

The unique features in this research are summarised below:

- it provides a tool for exploring automatically the trade-offs between speed, size and accuracy for floating-point designs;
- the tool supports various input formats, including languages such as C and block diagram descriptions such as the Simulink dataflow description;
- the tool follows a generic framework designed to cover a variety of arithmetic representations and their hardware implementations; currently it is capable of dealing with both fixed-point and floating-point designs, and their combinational and pipelined implementations.

Our long-term goal is to develop a unified and extensible framework for customising data representations for hardware implementations. The framework would facilitate investigation of: (a) less common forms of data representation such as exact arithmetic [16], (b) multiple data representations, and methods and cost of converting between them, (c) new data representations and their hardware implementation for application-specific or domain-specific systems. The framework would also support different analysis and optimisation methods, so that the most appropriate ones can be used for a given application.

In contrast, many methods for precision optimisation can only deal with integer or fixed-point representations using a specific analysis method. For instance, the BitValue tool [3] is based on detecting and removing unused or constant bits of variables, particularly the most-significant bits, in C programs. This method is currently focused on arbitrary-precision integer data types. The Bitwise tool [15], on the other hand, is based on interval analysis involving the ranges of the data values as they propagate through a design. This method is focused on fixed-point arithmetic, bit manipulation and Boolean operations. As a further example, the Synoptix tool [5] supports custom fixed-point representation by an analytical method for optimising average performance; its applicability is currently limited to linear time-invariant systems. We hope that our framework can combine the advantages of these tools while minimising their limitations.

2 Approach

This section describes our approach for automating the customisation of number representations. A prototype tool based on this approach will be presented in the next section. The basic idea is to customise the bit width of each operation in a design while meeting user-defined output error conditions.

We use a method based on simulating a design to study the effects of customisation. Initially we use the maximum precision for all the operations in the design, and then iteratively reduce these data widths while checking that the final output error condition is met. The customisation terminates when it is no longer possible to reduce the data widths without violating the cost function.

Our approach supports both static analysis and dynamic analysis. While dataflow analysis can be used for determining the number of bits required for a given data representation, the resulting bounds on precision are often higher than necessary. This inefficiency can be addressed by dynamic analysis. Rounding error for a particular operation depends on the exponent of the intermediate result. Actual input data values used for a design enable us to obtain much tighter bounds on precision by taking into account the particular exponents and dependencies at run time. The effectiveness of dynamic analysis, however, depends on the selection of representative input data.

The specification of output accuracy is given by the error between the customised data representation and the reference representation. The reference representation must support higher accuracy than the custom representation. For instance, the reference representation is in exact computation format [16], while the custom representation is in custom floating-point; or the reference representation is in single-precision format, while the custom representation is in custom floating-point format up to 23 bits mantissa and 8 bits exponent. Other number representations, such as redundant or logarithmic representations, can also be customised with suitable reference representations.

Our approach contains three steps: flow analysis, customisation management, and termination analysis (Figure 1).

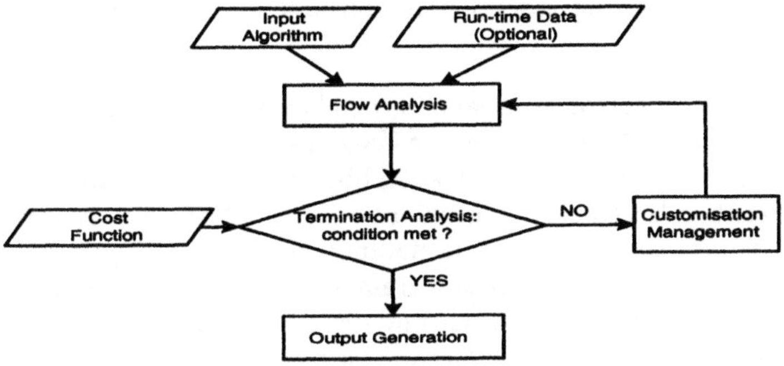

Fig. 1. The main steps in our approach.

Flow analysis evaluates the effects of a specific customisation on a design and the output. It usually involves two steps: forward propagation and backward propagation. In forward propagation, range and error information is propagated through the design. During dynamic analysis, the effect of run-time sample data is also assessed. In backward propagation, the acceptable error in the output is propagated back to the nodes of the dataflow graph to further refine the bit widths identified by forward propagation.

Customisation management controls the selection and parameters of custom number representations. Three ways can be used. In uniform customisation, we reduce the data widths of all the nodes in a single iteration. In non-uniform customisation, we analyse each node separately while keeping the bit widths of the other nodes unchanged. Non-uniform customisation takes longer to complete, but gives a better result than uniform customisation. It is possible to group operations together so that uniform customisation applies to members of each group, while non-uniform customisation applies to different groups. When reducing the bit widths, both the forward and backward propagated bit widths are considered and the smaller is chosen as the final bit width for the node.

Termination analysis determines whether the best customisation has been achieved. An objective function is used to capture the desired emphasis on size, performance or accuracy. For instance, a greedy strategy will begin another iteration if the current customisation results in a more optimal design. If this is not the case, then the tool terminates and outputs the best design obtained so far.

3 Tool Overview

The main components of our prototype tool are shown in Figure 2. The tool is based on a C++ operator overloaded library, and a collection of plug-in modules which interact with each other via interfaces. This method allows replacing one module without affecting the other modules. The tool is designed to have the following features:

- Since we use operator overloaded type classes, it is relatively simple to convert a design in ANSI-C, C++ or Handel-C [4] for analysis by our tool.
- While the C++ operator overloaded library provides a convenient front end, other front ends can also be used; an example alternative is a front end that we develop to support Simulink dataflow description [5], [6].
- the module structure provides a framework for developing new modules to support reference representations in addition to single-precision and double-precision floating-point arithmetic, and customisable representations in addition to floating-point and fixed-point arithmetic.

The tool operates iteratively with multiple passes. During the initialisation step, an annotated dataflow graph of the design is created. The nodes of this dataflow graph represent the variables in the design. The nodes store information about the variables, such as their bit widths and the maximum error with respect to the reference representation. This graph is used in the subsequent operation of the tool. Each pass includes the three steps described in Section 2: flow analysis, termination analysis, and customisation management.

When analysing floating-point arithmetic designs, the analyser operates on the mantissa and exponent components of the floating-point values separately. The mantissa represents the precision of the floating-point value, while the exponent represents the range. Currently the tool uses either IEEE standard double-precision or single-precision floating-point arithmetic for the reference value calculation, and the designer can choose between these two. The internal data structure of our tool can also support customisation of integer and fixed-point representations.

In the following two sections, we focus on our implementation of the three steps for customising floating-point representations: flow analysis, termination analysis, and customisation management. The area and speed of our hardware designs for floating-point operations will also be described.

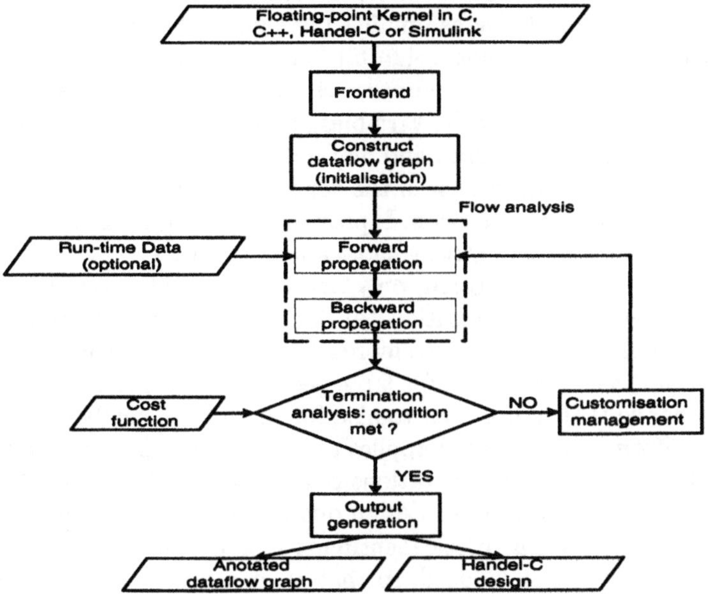

Fig. 2. Main components in our tool.

4 Flow Analysis and Customisation Management

Our tool implements the forward and backward propagation steps for flow analysis (Section 2). In forward propagation, bit-width information based on the reference representation or representative data values are propagated through the dataflow graph. Processing the exponent involves range analysis to determine appropriate minimum and maximum values that satisfy user requirement. Processing the mantissa involves precision analysis to assess the impact of reducing the mantissa on other nodes and the error at the output.

During the flow analysis step, the tool detects overflow or underflow. If they occur, a specific flag would be set in the node. This enables the designer to decide whether it is necessary to include underflow or overflow protection.

The effect of a particular customisation, derived from initial user-defined parameters or from the customisation management step of a previous pass, is evaluated by computing the error between the custom number representation and the reference number representation for given input values. Minimisation of the errors can be included in a cost function in the termination analysis step.

Although flow analysis and customisation management have been introduced as separate steps, our implementation interleaves them for efficiency reasons. As an example, consider range estimation. In addition to computing the error, each node also collects range information by observing the maximum and minimum exponents passing through it. This information is then used in the customisation management step to determine the appropriate exponent data width for that particular node. Similarly by examining the sign of the values propagated, the tool can decide whether or not a sign bit is required for the design.

We now describe our implementation of the customisation management step. In this step, the bitwidths of the variables are adjusted according to the propagated error values. Both uniform and non-uniform customisation are supported. Uniform customisation makes use of the dependencies generated by the dataflow graph to perform the size reduction. It provides the designer an idea of how much reduction is possible in a relatively short amount of time.

In non-uniform customisation, only one node is customised at one time so that the effect of the customisation can be analysed, and different nodes can have different customisation; hence more optimised designs can be produced but the process can take a long time for large designs. A compromise is to group the nodes together so that uniform customisation applies to members of each group, while non-uniform customisation applies to different groups. Heuristics are being developed to decide how the operations of a design can be grouped together to achieve a good trade-off between design quality and optimisation time.

We also make use of a heuristic identifying signals that would give the greatest benefit when their size is reduced, so that we can target these specific signals. For example, reducing the size of the smaller input in an adder would usually have no improvement in speed when compared with reducing the size of the larger input. This significantly reduces the overall analysis time.

Attention is paid to the cost function during the customisation of nodes in the dataflow graph. For instance, the user can specify the rounding mode to be used while the bit widths of variables are reduced. When the cost function involves performance or area, the variables chosen for reduction would be those that yield the largest performance or area benefit. For example, reducing the size of a multiplier would have a greater impact on performance and area than reducing the size of an adder. The analysis time can be reduced by focusing on areas which give the best improvement on cost.

5 Termination Analysis and Output Generation

In termination analysis, we check whether the user-defined termination criteria specified by the cost function are met by the design. This is done by checking the optimisation results using the user-supplied cost function.

Cost Function. The cost function can be described in terms of the area or operating speed of the hardware. should operate in hardware. To calculate the cost function, the system is provided with a cost matrix related to the specific hardware technology of the implementation.

When the termination criteria are met, the analysis terminates and moves on to the output generation stage. If these are not met, it returns to the customisation management stage to refine the design before performing another flow analysis. Possible termination criteria include the final output error, and desirable design size and performance.

Output error calculation. Given simulated output s and reference output r, the normalised output error is $(s-r)/r \times 100\%$.

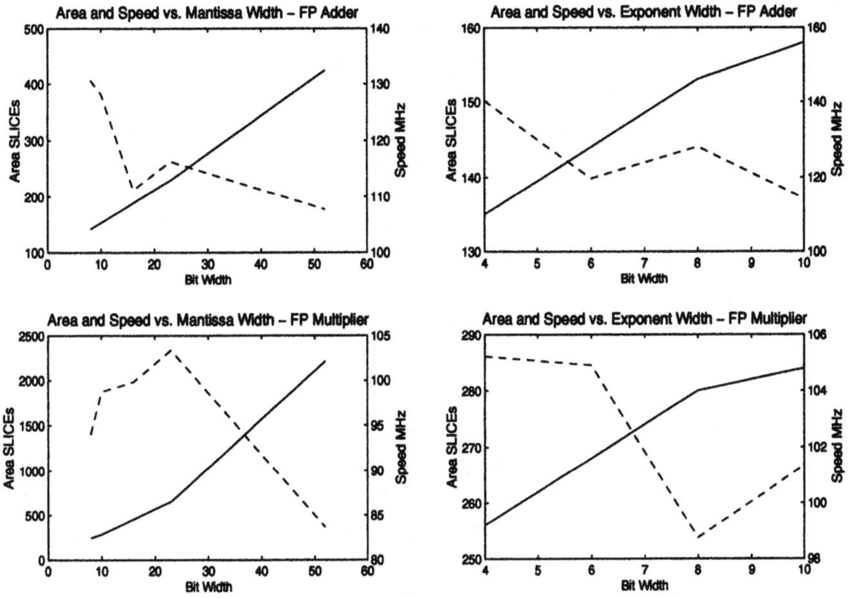

Fig. 3. Area (solid lines) and speed (dashed lines) characteristics as a function of mantissa and exponent bit widths. The mantissa area and speed variation is derived while keeping the exponent fixed at 8 bits, and the exponent area and speed variation is derived while keeping the mantissa fixed at 10 bits. The results are obtained for a Xilinx XC2V1000 FPGA.

Area and speed characteristics. The implementations in custom floating-point format are based on a floating-point library designed by us in Handel-C [4] utilising Xilinx core generator modules. Since the core generator modules are highly optimised with respect to area and speed, they are used as the default implementation in our floating-point libraries. For Xilinx Virtex II devices, designers can also choose to use embedded multiplier blocks which provide a compact implementation at the expense of speed, since long routing is often involved in connecting the multiplier blocks and other components such as shifters.

The graphs in Figure 3 illustrate the variation in area and speed as a function of the bit widths of the mantissa and the exponent. The results are obtained for a Xilinx Virtex XC2V1000 FPGA using only slices in our implementation. It can be seen that, for both the floating-point adder and multiplier, the area variation is largely linear with respect to the mantissa and exponent bit width. The speed variation, on the other hand, is less predictable; in some situations the speed increases with the bit width possibly due to the routing structure. Information in Figure 3 can help designers or tools to achieve the best area-speed trade-offs.

The current output of our tool is a dataflow graph with the nodes annotated with the bit width requirements. We use this information in the implementation phase of the design. When the current customisation results in a worse design as defined by the cost function, such as having output errors exceeding the given values, the iteration will terminate and the tool will proceed to the implementation phase, where bit-width information for implementing floating-point or fixed-point representation is produced.

Our current tool uses the Handel-C language as the main route to implementation [4]. At present we use parametrised floating-point libraries that we develop in Handel-C. The libraries are available for both non-pipelined and pipelined versions [7]. Other hardware description formats, such as VHDL and Pebble [12], can also be supported by our tool.

6 Results

Two experiments are presented to illustrate our analysis tool. In the first experiment, we explore various implementations of an inner product computation module and a 4-tap FIR filter in custom floating-point for a Xilinx XC2V1000 FPGA, which has 5120 slices. We start from a reference representation in IEEE single-precision format. A set of 1000 random floating-point numbers are generated as representative run-time data for our tool.

The result is shown in Figure 4. The variation in resource utilisation and operating speed as a function of output error are plotted. The graphs illustrate that if increased error tolerance is acceptable at the output, it is possible to gain improvement in resource utilisation and operation speed.

As evident from the graphs, the reduction in area becomes less significant beyond an error of 1%. Also the increase in speed is less significant beyond an error of 5%. Any further increase in error beyond 5% does not significantly increase the circuit speed as the interconnect delays become dominant at this point onwards.

In the second experiment, we compare the resource utilisation and the maximum operation speed for fixed-point and floating-point designs of a 4-tap FIR filter in a Xilinx XC2V3000 FPGA, which has 14336 slices.

The results are shown in Table 1. R1 and R2 are designs adopting IEEE single-precision format as the reference representation. F1 and F2 adopt custom floating-point format obtained from our tool, with a 1% maximum output error specification. F3 adopts a custom floating-point format which covers the same precision as R2. R1 and F1 are unpipelined, while R2, F2 and F3 are pipelined.

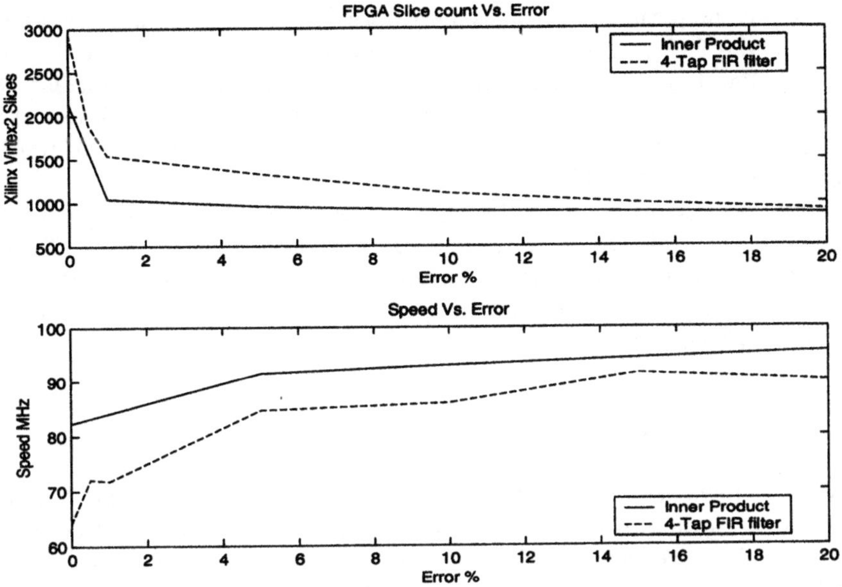

Fig. 4. Variation in design size and speed with output percentage error for inner product and 4-tap FIR filtering.

As expected, the custom floating-point designs are significantly faster and smaller than the corresponding reference designs, at the expense of a 1% maximum output error. In the unpipelined case, the custom design is 53% faster than the reference design, using 38% of the resources. In the pipelined case, the custom design is 45% faster than the reference design, using 39% of the resources. It should be clear that IEEE single-precision format is not required in this case, since F3 can be used without losing precision.

Design	Arith. type	Pipelined	% Error	Format	Virtex slices	Speed (MHz)
R1	Floating-Point	No	0.0	M 23, E 8	2394	25
F1	Floating-Point	No	1.0	M 10, E 6	916	38
R2	Floating-Point	Yes	0.0	M 23, E 8	2925	56
F2	Floating-Point	Yes	1.0	M 10, E 6	1155	81
F3	Floating-Point	Yes	0.0	M 23, E 6	2866	52
X1	Fixed-Point	Yes	0.0	Int 61, Frac 3	5525	49
X2	Fixed-Point	Yes	1.0	Int 57, Frac 0	4882	53

Table 1. Various implementations for a 4-tap FIR filter. For floating-point format, M represents Mantissa and E Exponent. R1, R2 are reference designs, F1, F2 and F3 adopt custom floating-point, and X1, X2 adopt custom fixed-point.

To put the performance of the hardware designs into perspective, we estimate that for the FIR computation a Pentium 3 at 800 MHz performs 31 MFLOPS, while a Pentium 4 at 1600 MHz performs 61 MFLOPS. In contrast, a single-precision design with the same accuracy on a Xilinx XC2V3000 device at 57 MHz performs 400 MFLOPS, and if we can tolerate 1% error, we can improve the performance to 570 MFLOPS at 81 MHz.

It is interesting to note that, for a custom fixed-point design X1 to cover the same dynamic range as the custom floating-point design F2, X1 needs to be almost 5 times larger and 40% slower. If the application can cope with a 1% maximum output error specification, we can use X2, which is 4 times the size of F2 and 34% slower.

7 Concluding Remarks

We have presented an approach for automatically customising floating-point formats according to user-given accuracy criteria. An inner product module and an FIR filter are used to illustrate its applicability. Current and future work includes improving our floating-point hardware implementations [13], supporting useful analytical methods [5] in our tool, and extending it to cover run-time precision management [2].

Acknowledgements. Many thanks to George Constantinides, Jun Jiang and Seng Shay Ping for their comments and assistance. The support of Xilinx, Inc., Celoxica Limited, the ORS Award Scheme and the UK Engineering and Physical Sciences Research Council (Grant number GR/N 66599) is gratefully acknowledged.

References

1. Benedetti, A. and Perona, P., "Bit-width optimisation for configurable DSP's by multi-interval analysis", *Proc. Signals, Systems and Computers*, IEEE, 2000.
2. Bondalapati, K. and Prasanna, V.K., "Dynamic precision management for loop computations on reconfigurable architectures", *Proc. FCCM* , IEEE, 1999.
3. Budiu, M. et. al. "BitValue inference: detecting and exploiting narrow bitwidth compilations", *Proc. EuroPar Conf.*, 2000.
4. Celoxica Limited, http://www.celoxica.com.
5. Constantinides, G.A., Cheung, P.Y.K. and Luk, W., "The multiple wordlength paradigm", *Proc. FCCM*, IEEE, 2001.
6. Hwang, J., Milne, B., Shirazi, N. and Stroomer, D., "System level tools for DSP in FPGAs", *Proc. FPL*, LNCS 2147, Springer, 2001.
7. Jaenicke, A. and Luk, W., "Parameterised floating-point arithmetic on FPGAs", *Proc. Acoustics, Speech, and Signal Processing*, IEEE, 2001.
8. Kim, S., Kum, K. and Sung, S., "Fixed point optimization utility for C and C++ based digital signal programs", *IEEE Trans. on Circuits and Systems II*, 1998.
9. Kum, K.I. and Sung, W., "Combined word-length Optimization and high-level synthesis of digital signal processing systems", *IEEE Trans. on CAD*, Aug. 2001.
10. Leong, M.P. et. al., "Automatic floating to fixed point translation and its application to post-rendering 3D warping", *Proc. FCCM* , IEEE, 1999.

11. Lethje, O. et. al., "A novel approach to code analysis of digital signal processors", *Proc. Compilers, Architecture, and Synthesis for Embedded Systems*, ACM, 2001.
12. Luk, W. and McKeever, S., "Pebble: a language for parametrised and reconfigurable hardware design", *FPL*, LNCS 1482, Springer, 1998.
13. Luo, Z. and Martonosi, M. "Accelerating pipelined integer nt accumulations in configurable hardware with delayed addition techniques", *IEEE Trans. on Computers*, Vol. 49, No. 3, 2000.
14. Shirazi, N., Walters, A. and Athanas, P. "Quantitative analysis of floating-point arithmetic on FPGA based custom computing machines", *Proc. FCCM*, IEEE, 1995.
15. Stephenson, M., Babb, J. and Amarasinghe, S., "Bitwidth analysis with application to silicon compilation", *Proc. Prog. Language Design and Imple.*, ACM, 2000.
16. Yap, C. and Dube, T., "The exact computation paradigm", *Computing in Euclidean Geometry*, 2nd Ed., World Scientific Press, 1995.

Energy-Efficient Matrix Multiplication on FPGAs*

Ju-wook Jang[1], Seonil Choi[2], and Viktor K. Prasanna[2]

[1] Electronic Engineering,
Sogang University, Seoul, Korea
jjang@sogang.ac.kr
http://eeca2.sogang.ac.kr/
[2] Electrical Engineering-Systems,
University of Southern California, Los Angeles, USA
{seonilch, prasanna}@usc.edu
http://ceng.usc.edu/~prasanna

Abstract. We develop new algorithms and architectures for matrix multiplication on configurable devices. These designs significantly reduce the energy dissipation and latency compared with the state-of-the-art FPGA-based designs. We derive functions to represent the impact of algorithmic level design choices on the system-wide energy dissipation, latency, and area by capturing algorithm and architecture details including features of the target FPGA. The functions are used to optimize energy performance under latency and area constraints for a family of candidate algorithms and architectures. As a result, our designs improve the energy performance of the optimized design from the recent Xilinx library by 32% to 88% without any increase in area-latency product. In terms of comprehensive metrics such as EAT (Energy-Area-Time) and E/AT (Energy/Area-Time), our designs offer superior performance compared with the Xilinx design by 50%-79% and 13%-44%, respectively. We also address how to exploit further increases in density of future FPGA devices for asymptotic improvement in latency and energy dissipation for multiplication of larger size matrices.

1 Introduction

Dramatic increases in the density and speed of FPGAs make them attractive as flexible and high-speed alternative to DSPs and ASICs [3][7]. Indeed, FPGAs have become an attractive fabric for implementing computationally intensive applications such as signal and image processing used in mobile devices [8]. Since mobile devices typically operate in multi-mode and energy constrained

* This work is supported by the DARPA Power Aware Computing and Communication Program under contract F33615-C-00-1633 monitored by Wright Patterson Air Force Base and in part by the National Science Foundation under award No. 99000613. Ju-wook Jang's work is supported by Ministry of Information and Communication, Korea.

M. Glesner, P. Zipf, and M. Renovell (Eds.): FPL 2002, LNCS 2438, pp. 534–544, 2002.

environments, energy is a key performance metric in addition to latency and throughput.

Matrix multiplication is a frequently used kernel operation in a wide variety of graphic, image, robotics, and signal processing applications. Several signal and image processing operations can be reduced to matrix multiplication. Most previous work for matrix multiplication on FPGAs focuses on latency optimization [1]. In this paper we develop designs which minimize the energy dissipation and offer trade-offs for performing matrix multiplication on commercially available FPGA devices. Our effort is focused on algorithmic techniques to improve energy-performance instead of low level (implementation level) optimizations. Many parameters affect energy dissipation, area, and latency of FPGA-based designs. These parameters depend on the algorithm and the architecture used and the target FPGA features. These parameters give rise to a large design space.

In our approach we narrow down the design space by devising latency-optimal algorithms on "minimal" architectures (in the sense of hardware resources used) which provide trade-offs among energy dissipation, latency, and area. Closed form functions representing system-wide energy dissipation, area, and latency are derived by incorporating architecture and algorithm details, low level power simulation of individual modules, and FPGA vendors' specifications. A module is a configured block in an FPGA for data processing or storage. The characteristics of power consumption of the modules and the number of configurable logic blocks (CLBs) needed for individual modules are captured in the functions to obtain reasonably accurate estimates.

The functions provide us a high level picture about where we should look for possible savings in energy and area and allow us to make trade-offs to meet the constraints. Using the energy function, algorithm and architecture level optimizations are made. Low level power simulation using XPower from Xilinx is performed to verify accuracy of the energy and latency estimated by the functions. Our experiments show that the estimation of energy dissipation and area using the functions is within 3.8% to 7.8% of the actual values based on low level simulation.

The rest of the paper is organized as follows. An energy model specific to our implementation is described in Section 2. Algorithms and architectures for energy-efficient implementation are presented in Section 3. Section 4 derives functions for energy, latency, and area and illustrates various trade-offs. Section 5 concludes the paper.

2 Energy Model and Design Space

Our family of architectures and algorithms for matrix multiplication forms a domain and we limit algorithm-level exploration for energy optimization to the design space spanned by this domain. The family of architectures in Figure 1 and the parameters in Table 1 represent the design space. In the off-chip model, the storage for input matrices is assumed to be outside the FPGA. I/O ports are used for data access. The on-chip model uses on-chip storage such as BSRAM (Block Select RAM) in the Xilinx FPGA devices. Choosing specific values for the parameters in Table 1 results in a design point in the design space. For example, $n = 24$, $p = 6$, $r = 4$, $m = 1$, $s = 1$, $K_b = 2$, and $K_{io} = 0$ represents a design where 24×24 matrix multiplication is implemented by 6 PEs with 4 registers, one multiplier, and one SRAM (Select RAMs in the Xilinx devices) per PE. The input matrices are stored in two ($\lceil 2 \times 24 \times 24/1024 \rceil = 2$) BSRAMs (on-chip memory banks) of the device and no I/O ports are used.

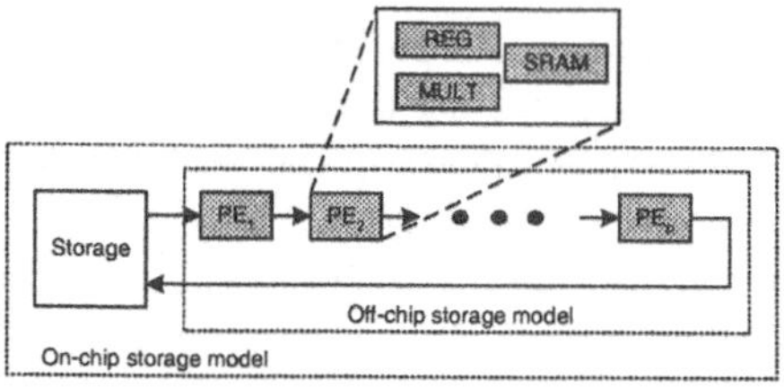

Fig. 1. Family of architectures

An energy model specific to the domain is constructed at the module level by assuming that each module of a given type (register, multiplier, SRAM, BSRAM, or I/O port) dissipates the same power independent of its location on the chip. This model simplifies the derivation of system-wide energy dissipation functions. Energy dissipation for each module can be determined by the number of cycles the module stays in each power state and low level estimation of the power consumed by the module in the power state assuming average switching activity. Additional details of the model can be found in [4].

Table 1. Range of parameters for Xilinx XC2V1500

Parameter	Range	FPGA constraints
Problem size (n)	$2, 3, 4, ...$	
Number of PEs (p)	n/l, n is divisible by l	
Number of registers per PE (r)	$b^{2k+2}, b = 2, 3, 4, ...$ $(0 \leq k \leq \log_b n)$	8/16 bit registers
Number of multipliers per PE (m)	b^{2k}	2-stage dedicated pipeline
Number of SRAMs per PE (s)	$\lceil nb^k/16 \rceil$	16 words minimum
Number of BSRAMs (K_b) (On-chip model)	$\lceil 2n^2/1024 \rceil$	1024 16-bit words minimum
Number of I/O ports (K_{io}) (Off-chip model)	$2b^k$	8/16 bits

3 Energy-Efficient Algorithms for Matrix Multiplication

We present our algorithms and architectures in two theorems and one corollary. Pseudo-code for cycle-specific data movement, the detailed architectures, and a snapshot of an example computation are also shown. Theorem 1 improves the best known algorithm for matrix multiplication [10]. This leads to optimal time complexity with leading coefficient of 1 for matrix multiplication on linear array. Theorem 1 is extended for trade-offs among energy dissipation, latency, and area (Corollary 1). Corollary 1 is used to identify energy-efficient designs under latency and area constraints.

The second algorithm can be used to exploit future increases in the density of FPGA devices to realize improvements in energy dissipation and latency as larger devices become available (Theorem 2). It uses more multipliers and I/O ports. The state-of-the-art design for matrix multiplication from Xilinx reference design uses only 180 slices while a XC2V1500 device can hold upto $10,000$ slices in addition to memory banks (BSRAMs) and I/O ports.

Theorem 1. *$n \times n$ matrix multiplication can be performed in n^2+2n cycles using the architecture in Figures 1 and 2 (b) with the number of processing elements, $p = n$.*

Proof. The algorithm in Figure 2 (a) and the architecture in Figure 1 and Figure 2 (b) are devised to compute $c_{ij} = \sum_{k=1}^{n} a_{ik} \times b_{kj}$ for all i, j. a_{ik}, b_{kj}, and c_{ij} represent an element of $n \times n$ matrices A, B, and C. PE_j denotes the j-th PE from the left in Figure 1, $j = 1, 2, .., n$. It computes the $c_{1j}, c_{2j}, ..., c_{nj}$. Matrix B is fed to the lower I/O port of PE_1 in row major order $(b_{11}, b_{12}, b_{13}, ..., b_{1n}, b_{21}, b_{22}, ...)$. Matrix A is fed to the upper I/O port of PE_1 in column major order $(a_{11}, a_{21}, a_{31}, ..., a_{n1}, a_{12}, a_{22}, ...)$, n *cycles* behind the matrix B. For example, a_{11} is fed to the upper I/O port of PE_1 at the same cycle as the b_{21} is fed to the lower I/O port of PE_1. At the end of the processing, c_{ij} is in the SRAM or registers in PE_j, for $1 \le i \le n$. The a_{ik} traverses the $PE_1, PE_2, PE_3, ..., PE_n$ in order and allows PE_j to update $c'_{ij} = c'_{ij} + a_{ik} \times b_{kj}$ where c'_{ij} represents the intermediate value of c_{ij}. Since a_{ik} stays at each PE_j for just one cycle, it is essential to ensure that b_{kj} arrives at PE_j no later than a_{ik}. We show how the algorithm in Figure 2 (a) satisfies this requirement. The number of cycles needed for b_{kj} to arrive at PE_j is $(k-1)n + 2j - 1$. a_{ik} needs $n + (k-1)n + i + j - 1$ cycles to arrive at PE_j. The requirement is satisfied since $2j - 1 \le n + i + j - 1$ for all i, j. Next we show why two registers (denoted BM and BL in Figure 2 (b)) are enough to hold $b_{kj} (k = 1, 2, .., n)$ until they are no longer needed. b_{kj} is needed until a_{nk} arrives at PE_j in the $\{n + (k-1)n + n + j - 1\}$-th cycle. $b_{(k+2)j}$ arrives at PE_j in the $\{(k+1)n + 2j - 1\}$-th cycle. Since $(k+1)n + 2j - 1 > n + (k-1)n + n + j - 1$ for all j, k,and n, b_{kj} can be replaced when $b_{(k+2)j}$ arrives at PE_j. This proves that PE_j needs only two temporary registers (denoted as BM, BL in Figure 2 (b)) to hold $b_{kj} (k = 1, 2, .., n)$. Now we show $n^2 + 2n$ cycles are needed to complete the matrix multiplication. The computation finishes one cycle after a_{nn} arrives at PE_n, which is the $\{n + (n-1)n + n + n - 1\}$-th or $\{n^2 + 2n - 1\}$-th cycle.□

```
For t=1 to n do
For all j, 1 j n, do in parallel
    PE_j shifts data in BU right to PE_j+1
    If (BU=b_kj), copy it into BM
For t=n+1 to n^2+n do
For all j, 1 j n, do in parallel
    PE_j shifts data in A, BU right to PE_j+1
    If (BU=b_kj), copy it into BL or BM (alternately)
    If (A=a_ik), c_ij := c_ij + a_ik x b_kj
        (b_kj is in either BM or BL)
```

(a)

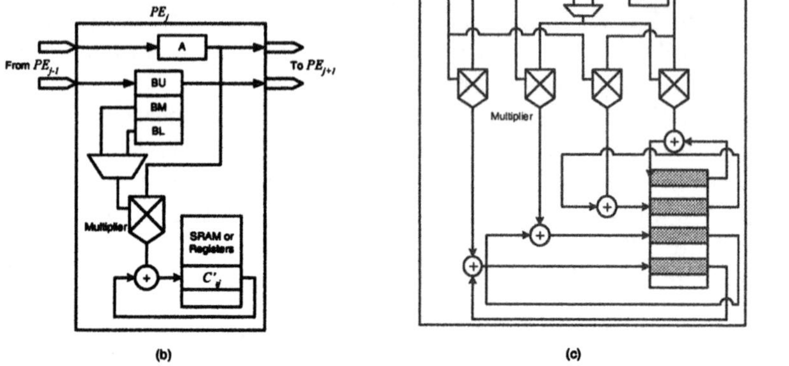

Fig. 2. (a) Algorithm used in the proof of Theorem 1, (b) Architecture of PE_j used in the proof of Theorem 1, and (c) Architecture of PE_j used in the proof of Theorem 2

Corollary 1. *$n \times n$ matrix multiplication can be performed in $(n/p)^3(p^2 + 2p)$ cycles using the architecture in Figure 2 (b), where p is the number of processing elements and $p \le n$.*

Proof Sketch. $n \times n$ matrix multiplication can be decomposed into n^3/p^3 $p \times p$ matrix multiplications. Using Theorem 1 with n replaced by p, the result follows.□

Corollary 1 provides trade-offs between area and latency. Smaller values for p reduces the number of PEs, resulting in less area. But it increases the number of cycles to complete the matrix multiplication. Combined together with power estimation of modules, Corollary 1 provides trade-offs among energy dissipation, latency, and area.

Theorem 2. *$n \times n$ matrix multiplication can be performed in $(n^2/b^k + 2n/b^k)$ cycles using b^k PEs in Figure 2 (c), where b is the block size for block multiplication, n divisible by b^k, and $k \le \log_b n$.*

Proof Sketch. The proof follows from recursive application of the idea in Theorem 1. In general, an $n \times n$ matrix multiplication requires b^{2k} multipliers per PE, and $2b^k$ I/O ports. Local storage of b^{2k} words is used to store intermediate results of the output matrix. Figure 2 (c) shows our architecture for the case $k = 1$ and $b = 2$. An $n \times n$ matrix multiplication is decomposed into 8 $n/2 \times n/2$ matrix multiplications. Let A_{ij}, B_{ij}, and $C_{ij}, 1 \le i, j \le 2$ denote a submatrix of size

$n/2 \times n/2$, respectively. In the first phase, $C'_{ij} = A_{i1} \times B_{1j}, 1 \le i,j \le 2$ are computed simultaneously using the idea in Theorem 1 by feeding A_{11}, A_{21}, B_{11} and B_{12} into the 4 input ports. In the second phase, $C'_{ij} = C'_{ij} + A_{i2} \times B_{2j}, 1 \le i,j \le 2$ are performed. Each phase takes $n^2/4 + n$ cycles from Theorem 1. Since overlapping is possible between the end of the first phase and the start of the second phase, the total number of cycles is $n^2/2+n$. For other values of k and b, the proof follows from successive recursion using the same idea. Detailed proof is omitted due to space limitations. □

4 Performance Analysis

4.1 Functions to Estimate Energy, Area, and Latency

Functions to represent energy dissipation, area, and latency are derived for Theorem 1, Corollary 1, and Theorem 2. Energy function of a design is obtained by $\sum_i t_i P_i$, where t_i and P_i represent the number of active cycles and average power per cycle for module i. For example, P_{MULT} denotes the average power dissipation of the multiplier module. The average power is obtained from low level power simulation of the module. The area function is given by $\sum_i A_i$ where A_i represents the area used for module i. In general, these simplified energy and area functions may not be able to capture all the implementation details needed for accurate estimation. However, we are concerned with algorithmic level comparison, rather than accurate estimation. Since our architectures are simple and have regular interconnection, the error between these functions and the actual values based on low level simulation is expected to be small. In Section 4.4 we confirm the accuracy of the energy and area functions.

Table 2. Number of modules used and the latency of various designs (note: 1 cycle delay added for flushing the 2-cycle multiplier pipeline)

Design	Number of multipliers	Number of registers	Size of SRAMs	Size of BSRAMs	I/O	Latency(cycles)
Xilinx	1	14 (8 *bits*), 5 (16 *bits*)	0	$\lceil 3n^2/1024 \rceil$	3	$(n/3)^3 \times 45$
[10]	n^2/m, $1 \le m \le n$	n^2(16 *bits*), $n^2 + 6n^2/m$ (8 *bits*)	0	$\lceil 2n^2/1024 \rceil$	4	$n^2+2n^2/m+n/m$
Theorem 1	n	$4n$ (8 *bits*)	$n\lceil n/16 \rceil$	$\lceil 2n^2/1024 \rceil$	2	n^2+2n+1
Corollary 1	p	$4p$ (8 *bits*)	$p\lceil p/16 \rceil$	$\lceil 2n^2/1024 \rceil$	2	$(n/p)^3(p^2+2p+1)$
Theorem 2	$b^k n$	$4n$ (8 *bits*)	$n/b^k \lceil b^k n/16 \rceil$	$\lceil 2n^2/1024 \rceil$	$2b^k$	$(n^2/b^k+2n/b^k+1)$

Table 2 shows the number of modules to be used by the designs for $n \times n$ matrix multiplication with 8-bit elements. For the off-chip model, I/O ports are used to fetch elements from outside the FPGA. In the on-chip model, BSRAMs of 16-bit 1024 words are used for on-chip storage of input matrices. The SRAMs are CLB-based memory blocks used for storing intermediate results. Using Table 2, functions to represent energy, area, and latency for Corollary 1 are shown in Table 3. Functions for other designs can be obtained in the same way. An average switching activity of 25% at running frequency of 166MHz is assumed. Dedicated multipliers available in the device are used. A_{offset} denotes the difference between the area of a PE and $\sum_i A_i$ for a PE and accounts for glue logic.

Table 3. Functions to represent energy, area, and latency for $n \times n$ 8-bit matrix multiplication using p PEs. They are based on Corollary 1 with 166MHz

Metric		Functions
Energy (J)	on-chip	$(n^3/p^3) \cdot (p^2+2p+1)\{pP_{MULT} + p\lceil p/16\rceil P_{SRAM}$ $+4pP_{R8} + \lceil 2n^2/1024\rceil P_{BSRAM}\}/(166 \times 10^6)$
	off-chip	$(n^3/p^3) \cdot (p^2+2p+1)\{pP_{MULT} + p\lceil p/16\rceil P_{SRAM}$ $+4pP_{R8} + 2P_{IO}\}/(166 \times 10^6)$
Area (slices)	on-chip	$pA_{MULT} + p\lceil p/16\rceil A_{SRAM} + 4pA_{R8} + pA_{offset}$ and $\lceil 2n^2/1024\rceil$ BSRAMs
	off-chip	$pA_{MULT} + p\lceil p/16\rceil A_{SRAM} + 4pA_{R8} + pA_{offset}$ and 2 8-bit I/O ports
Latency (cycles)		$(n^3/p^3)(p^2+2p+1)$

4.2 Trade-Offs among Energy, Latency, and Area

The functions in Table 3 are used to identify trade-offs among energy, latency, and area. For example, Figure 3 illustrates the trade-offs among energy, latency, and area for 24×24 matrix multiplication for the off-chip model. It can be used to choose energy-efficient designs to meet given area and latency constraints. For example, if 800 slices are available and latency should be less than 6,000 cycles ($36\mu s$), an energy-efficient design is obtained using $p = 4$. Energy dissipation, area, and latency evaluated using the functions in Table 3 are $6.85\mu J$, 524 slices, and 5400 cycles ($32.4\mu s$), respectively. Actual values for energy and area were found to be $7.37\mu J$ and 559 slices based on low level simulation. The simulation was based on a VHDL code of the design and XPower tool. Compared with the Xilinx design, energy dissipation and latency are reduced by 44% and 77%, while the area increases 3.4x. The resulting design occupies 5% of the slices available in a XC2V1500 device. The largest reduction in energy dissipation is 70% and can be obtained using $p = 12$. Trade-off analysis for the on-chip model also shows similar behavior and is omitted due to space limitations.

4.3 Performance Comparison

Using the functions in Table 3, energy-efficient designs are identified for various sizes of matrices under (an arbitrary) area constraint of 1,800 slices. Thus the

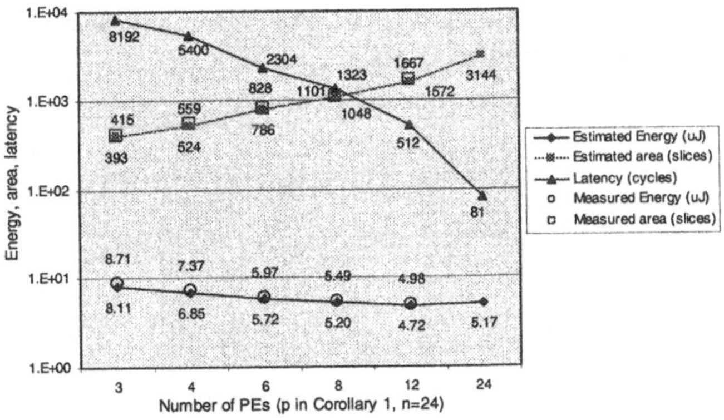

Fig. 3. Trade-offs among energy, latency, and area for 24 × 24 matrix multiplication. Estimated values from functions are plotted along with measured values in empty circles and boxes

area does not necessarily increase with the size of input matrices. Actual values for energy and area based on low level simulation involving VHDL coding and Xilinx XPower tool are obtained for each size of input matrices. Energy is obtained by multiplying the average power (averaged over 1,000 cycles) by the latency. The average power is obtained by XPower. Table 4 compares the performance of our designs against the Xilinx design and a best known latency-optimal design [10] on a linear array for various sizes of matrices. The area and energy are obtained by using synthesized designs and XPower. Xilinx provides an optimized design for 3×3 matrix multiplication only; block matrix multiplication is employed for larger sizes. These comparisons are based on individual metrics as well as more comprehensive metrics of energy×area×latency (EAT) product [2] and energy/(area×latency) (E/AT). Note that the E/AT metric is the average power density of the design.

Our designs improve the performance of the Xilinx reference design by 32%-66% with respect to energy and 2.8-17x with respect to latency while increasing the area by 2.8x to 9.3x. The designs based on [10] with the same latency as ours fail to reduce the energy dissipation compared with the Xilinx reference design. Analysis of energy and area functions reveal that our designs improve the Xilinx design due to reduction in latency.

In terms of EAT (Energy-Area-Time) and E/AT (Energy/Area-Time), our designs based on Corollary 1 offer superior performance compared with the Xilinx design by 50%-79% and 13%-44%, respectively.

Theorem 2 provides asymptotic improvement in energy and latency performance for the on-chip model in Figure 1. From Table 2, for large problems, energy dissipated in BSRAMs and the latency of the Xilinx reference design increase as $O(n^5)$ and $O(n^3)$, respectively, assuming a unit of energy is consumed per cycle for retaining a word in the BSRAM. Energy dissipation and latency for

Table 4. Performance comparison of various designs against the Xilinx design. Reduction in energy is represented in %. The reduction in latency and the increase in area are represented as times

Design	Metric	Matrix size						
		3×3	6×6	9×9	12×12	15×15	24×24	48×48
Xilinx	energy(nJ)	25	201	680	1,612	3,150	12,902	103,219
	latency(cycles)	45	360	1,215	2,880	5,625	23,040	184,320
	area(slices)	180	180	180	180	180	180	180
	$EAT/10^6$	0.2	13	148	836	3200	53×10^3	3.4×10^6
	$(E/AT)\times10^3$	3	3	3	3	3	3	3
Proposed (Corollary 1)	energy(nJ)	17	93	228	622	1,598	5,952	39,808
	(reduction, %)	(32%)	(53%)	(66%)	(61%)	(49%)	(53%)	(61%)
	latency(cycles)	16	49	103	172	972	3,136	11,008
	(speedup, times)	(2.8)	(7.3)	(12)	(17)	(5.8)	(7.3)	(17)
	area(slices)	415	828	1,279	1,667	708	828	1,667
	(increase, times)	(2.3)	(4.6)	(7.1)	(9.3)	(3.9)	(4.6)	(7.1)
	$EAT/10^6$	0.1	3.7	30	178	1100	15	700×10^3
	$(E/AT)\times10^3$	2.5	2.3	1.7	2.2	2.3	2.3	2.2
Design based on [10]	energy(nJ)	25.6	185	721	1,943	2,970	11,904	124,532
	(reduction, %)	(-2%)	(8%)	(-6%)	(-20%)	(6%)	(8%)	(-20%)
	latency(cycles)	16	49	103	172	972	3,136	11,008
	(speedup, times)	(2.8)	(7.3)	(11.8)	(17)	(5.8)	(7.3)	(17)
	area(slices)	487	1,260	2,359	3,683	975	1,260	3,683
	(increase, times)	(2.7)	(7)	(13)	(20)	(5.4)	(7)	(20)
	$EAT/10^6$	0.2	11	175	1230	2800	47×10^3	5×10^6
	$(E/AT)\times10^3$	3	3	3	3	3	3	3

designs based on Theorem 1 and [10] increase as $O(n^4)$ and $O(n^2)$, respectively under similar assumptions. Theorem 2 improves these complexities to $O(n^4/b^k)$ and $O(n^2/b^k)$, respectively. b is the basic block size for block multiplication and n divisible by b^k with $k \leq \log_b n$. Future increase in the density of FPGAs can be used to increase the number of multipliers and hence b^k, leading to asymptotic reduction in energy dissipation and latency. Details of performance improvements and trade-off analysis are omitted due to space limitations.

4.4 Accuracy of Energy and Area Functions

To test the accuracy of the energy and area functions in Table 4, we compared estimates from the functions against actual values based on synthesized designs and low level simulation. The low level simulation involved VHDL coding of designs in Section 4.3. These designs were synthesized using Synopsys FPGA Express and XST (Xilinx Synthesis Technology) in Xilinx ISE 4.1i. The place-and-route file (.ncd file) was obtained for Virtex-II XC2V1500 FPGA. Mentor Graphics ModelSim 5.5e was used to simulate the module and generate simulation results (.vcd file). These two files are then provided to the Xilinx XPower tool to evaluate the average power dissipation. Energy dissipation is obtained by multiplying the average power by the latency. We observed that the estimation error using our functions (see Table 3) is 3.8% to 7% for energy dissipation and 4.1% to 7.8% for area, respectively.

To address the dependency of energy dissipation on input matrices, matrices were randomly generated and fed as input to our design and the Xilinx design for 3×3 matrix multiplication. Equation 1 is employed to estimate the confidence interval for our simulation. The confidence interval is the interval into which the real average (over all possible input matrices in this example) falls with certain probability(confidence) [6]. $\overline{x}$, $z_{\alpha/2}$, s, and M represent the average energy over (randomly generated) sample input matrices, a given constant, standard deviation, and number of sample matrices, respectively [6]. The probability that the real average energy dissipation belongs to the interval in Equation 1 is $1-\alpha$.

$$\overline{x} \pm z_{\alpha/2}\frac{s}{\sqrt{M}} \tag{1}$$

Figure 4 (a) compares the energy dissipation over 50 randomly generated 3×3 input matrices for our design and the Xilinx design. The 95% confidence intervals are compared in Figure 4 (b). Based on 95% confidence intervals, the average energy dissipation of our design for 3×3 input matrices is 7.81 nJ (32%) less than that of the Xilinx design.

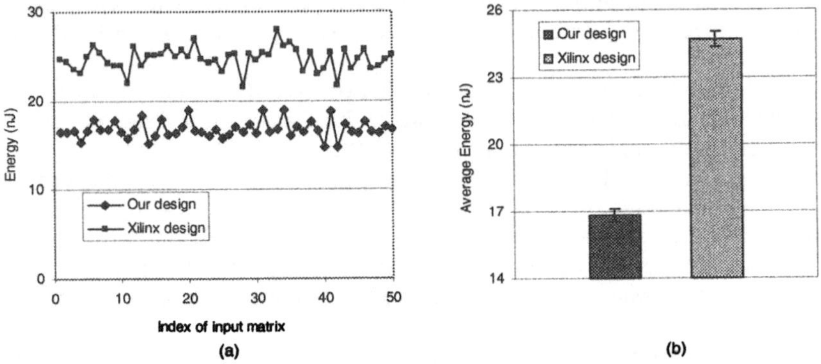

Fig. 4. Comparison between our design (based on Theorem 1) and Xilinx design for 3×3 matrix multiplication: (a) Energy dissipation for randomly generated matrices and (b) Average energy dissipation with confidence intervals

5 Conclusions

New algorithms and architectures were developed for matrix multiplication to significantly reduce the energy dissipation and latency compared with the state-of-the-art FPGA-based designs. These improve the best known design and provide trade-offs among energy dissipation, latency, and area. In our methodology, "energy hot spots," which consume most of the energy, are identified through energy estimation functions. Algorithm level optimizations are performed to reduce "energy hot spots" without increase in latency. Low level simulation using Xilinx ISE 4.1i and Mentor Graphics ModelSim 5.5e and recent Xilinx XC2V1500 as a target FPGA were performed to evaluate the chosen designs. XPower, a low level power estimation tool for FPGAs from Xilinx, was employed for accurate energy estimation. Additional details can be found in [5].

References

1. Amira A., Bouridane A., Milligan P.: Accelerating Matrix Product on Reconfigurable Hardware for Signal Processing. Field-Programmable Logic and Applications (FPL) (2001) 101-111
2. Bass B.: A Low-Power, High-Performance, 1024-Point FFT Processor. IEEE Journal of Solid-State Circuits, Vol. 34, No. 3 (1999) 380-387
3. Brebner G., Bergman N.: Reconfigurable Computing in Remote and Harsh Environments. Field-Programmable Logic and Applications (FPL) (1999)
4. Choi S., Jang J., Mohanty S., Prasanna V. K.: Domain-Specific Modeling for Rapid System-Level Energy Estimation of Reconfigurable Architectures. To appear in ERSA 2002 conference (2002)
5. Choi S., Jang J., Prasanna V. K.: Domain-Specific Modeling and Energy-Efficient Designs for Matrix Multiplication. Technical Report in preparation, Department of Electrical Engineering-Systems, University of Southern California (2002)
6. Hogg R., Tanis E.: Probability and Statistical Inference. 6th Eds. Prentice Hall (2001) 656-657
7. Luk W., Andreou P., Derbyshire A., Dupont-De-Dinechin F., Rice J., Shirazi N., Siganos D.: A Reconfigurable Engine for Real-time Video Processing. Field-Programmable Logic and Applications (FPL) (1998) 169-178
8. Master P., Athanas P. M.: Reconfigurable Computing Offers Options For 3G. Wireless Systems Design. (1999) 20-23
9. Model-based Integrated Simulation. http://milan.usc.edu
10. Prasanna Kumar V. K., Tsai Y.: On Synthesizing Optimal Family of Linear Systolic Arrays for Matrix Multiplication. IEEE Transactions on Computers. Vol. 40, No. 6 (1991)
11. Xilinx Application Note: Virtex-II Series and Xilinx ISE 4.1i Design Environment. http://www.xilinx.com (2001)

Run-Time Adaptive Flexible Instruction Processors

Shay Seng[1], Wayne Luk[1], and Peter Y.K. Cheung[2]

[1] Department of Computing, Imperial College, London, UK.
[2] Department of EEE, Imperial College, London, UK.

Abstract. This paper explores run-time adaptation of Flexible Instruction Processors (FIPs), a method for parametrising descriptions and development of instruction processors. The run-time adaptability of a FIP system allows it to evolve to suit the requirements of the user, by requesting automatic refinement based on instruction usage patterns. The techniques and tools that we have developed include: (a) a run-time environment that manages the reconfiguration of the FIP so that it can execute a given application as efficiently as possible; (b) mechanisms to accumulate run-time metrics, and analysis of the metrics to allow the run-time environment to request for automatic refinements; (c) techniques to automatically customise a FIP to an application.

1 Introduction

This paper explores adapting Flexible Instruction Processors (FIPs) [7] at run time. Previously we concentrated on compile-time issues and described the use of FIPs for the systematic customisation of instruction processor design and implementation. The features of our approach include: a modular framework based on "processor templates" that capture various instruction processor styles, such as stack-based or register-based styles; enhancements of this framework to improve functionality and performance, such as hybrid processor templates and superscalar operation; compilation strategies involving standard compilers and FIP-specific compilers, and the associated design flow; technology-independent and technology-specific optimisations, such as techniques for efficient resource sharing in FPGA implementations.

Our research helps designers to tune hardware implementations to the run-time characteristics of a system over a period of time. Factors such as keeping to power consumption or area constraints have to be traded-off with better performance and the ability to perform a wider range of functions. For instance, in an embedded communications device, we might wish to encrypt, compress and compute a checksum before transmission. A fast solution involves chaining three pieces of hardware that perform these functions together. However, it is likely that further control hardware will be required, for instance to negotiate the transmission protocols or control other peripherals. A flexible and small design is to utilise an instruction processor, and in order to achieve acceptable performance, we may have to run the processor at a high clock speed.

M. Glesner, P. Zipf, and M. Renovell (Eds.): FPL 2002, LNCS 2438, pp. 545–555, 2002.

The FIP approach enables incorporation, at design time, of instructions that will accelerate encryption, compression and checksum generation, thereby improving performance by doing more per cycle, instead of increasing the clock speed. Our design-time system allows easy customisation of various styles of processors and executable code to be compiled for application-specific processors. A FIP can be further improved based on run-time characteristics. For example, an embedded device might be used in an area with high interference, requiring frequent retransmission of the data. In this case, the FIP could evolve to incorporate a more robust error correction code capable of detecting and correcting more error bits, while maintaining similar performance and size, by trading off general functionality for more targeted functionality.

Run-time reconfiguration is often used to gain either functionality or performance. Unfortunately, the time taken for reconfiguration often incurs performance penalty. The increasing density of FPGAs further exacerbate this penalty. The FIP approach provides a way to tune the frequency of reconfiguration. If long reconfiguration time is unacceptable, the application can be executed less efficiently with the instruction processor; otherwise we can reconfigure to a different FIP to run more efficiently.

To summarise, the main contributions of our approach include: (a) a run-time environment that manages the reconfiguration of the FIP so that it can execute a given application as efficiently as possible; (b) mechanisms to accumulate run-time metrics and analysis of the metrics to allow the run-time environment to request for automatic refinements; (c) techniques to automatically customise a FIP to an application.

The rest of the paper is organised as follows. Section 2 describes FIPs and motivates their run-time adaptation. Section 3 addresses point (a) and outlines our design and run-time flow. Section 4 deals with run-time optimisations and addresses (b). Section 5 introduces ideas for custom instruction generation which covers (c). We then use the AES algorithm as an example in Section 6.

2 FIPs and Run-Time Adaptation

Flexible Instruction Processors, or FIPs, consist of a processor template and a set of parameters [7]. Different processor implementations can be produced by varying the template parameters. FIP templates provide a general structure for creating processors of different styles: e.g. stack- or register-based processors. The processor templates can be further enhanced with features found in high performance processors, such as superscalar architectures and pipelining. Various Java Virtual Machines and MIPS style processors have been implemented.

Our FIP generation tool allows us to explore FIP designs with different speed, area and functionality trade-offs. FIPs provide a well-defined control structure that facilitates varying the degree of sharing of resources. FIPs also provide a systematic method for supporting customisation by allowing user-designed hardware to be accommodated as new instructions. By adding customisations or eliminating unused resources, we can tune an instruction processor to make use of available area efficiently and provide a good range of functionality.

Run-time adaptation allows us to further fine tune our FIPs to run-time changes by exploiting the upgradability of FPGAs. Our framework simplifies the process by providing a means of adapting a FIP and creating its executable code at compile and run time.

Hand-crafted implementations provide fast performance but once it has been manufactured and deployed, there is little scope for improvement. Instruction processors, on the other hand, provide a solution that is easily upgradable and flexible. However this flexibility is often provided at the expense of performance. FIPs provide a way to explore the design space between these two extremes. For instance, custom instructions can be included into a design to speed up their operation at the expense of increasing area and power consumption.

The ability for a FIP system to adapt to changing behaviour of applications is a powerful feature, but there are significant challenges involved. Such challenges include: (a) creating a collection of FIP designs at compile time or at run time, (b) managing these FIPs and (c) ensuring that performance of the system is not degraded by its flexibility. To meet these challenges, we develop an approach that contains the following components: (1) a design tool to facilitate the creation of customised FIPs at compile time, (2) a scheme to keep track of available FIP designs and machine code, (3) a run-time system to manage FIP state and configuration, (4) a metric used to decide if reconfiguration is a suitable option at a given time, (5) a specification of what run-time statistics are needed for refinement analysis, (6) a monitor to accumulate run-time statistics, (7) techniques for generating custom instructions.

Component (1) is outlined in [7]. Components (2) and (3) will be described in Section 3, while components (4), (5),(6) and (7) will be discussed in Section 4 and 5.

3 Design and Run-Time Flow

This section describes our proposed framework. Figure 1 shows the design flow and the run-time flow. The flow diagram is essentially divided into two parts: the design environment and the run-time environment.

Details of the design environment is covered in a previous paper [7]. During design time, source code is profiled to extract information that can help in customising the FIP. FIP generation includes producing domain-specific FIPs and the corresponding FIP-specific compiler to generate executable code. The design environment also produces the run-time environment. Users can determine the capability of the run-time environment at compile time. For example, the user can decide whether reconfiguration or automatic adaptation is required. This will affect the complexity of the run-time environment.

The run-time environment is responsible for the execution and management of the system and maintains a database of available FIPs, their associated executable code and a decision condition library, which contains information about

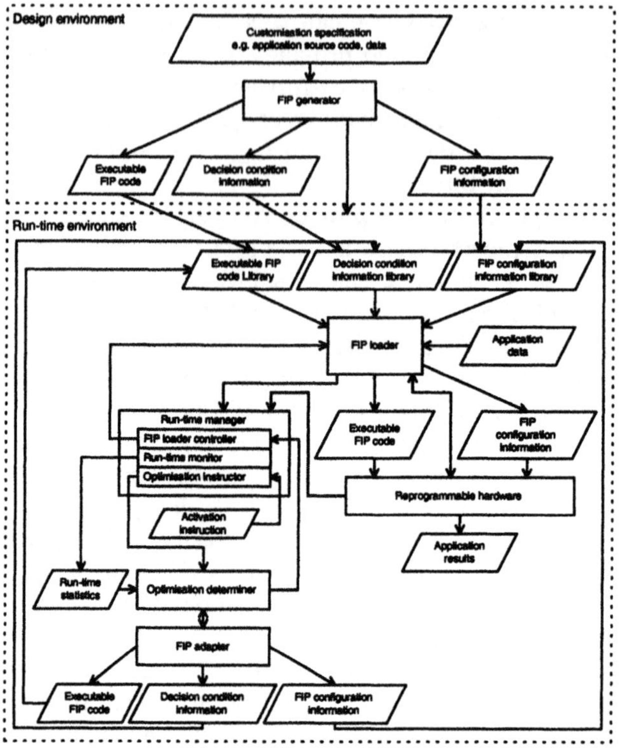

Fig. 1. Design flow and run-time flow. Optimisation analysis and automatic refinement steps are optional and are included when their overheads can be tolerated. The run-time environment is generated by the FIP generator. The run-time manager within the run-time environment can be run locally or on an external server.

when certain FIPs should be loaded. When an application is required, the FIP loader loads the appropriate executable from the code library and if necessary, a new FIP configuration. During execution, a FIP can keep track of run-time statistics, such as the number of times functions are called or the most frequently used opcodes. These run-time statistics can be sent to the run-time manager.

The run-time manager does not have to be local to the run-time environment. Run-time statistics can be uploaded to a central server where a run-time manager may reside. Based on run-time statistics, the optimisation determiner (Figure 1) can decide to dedicate more resources to functions that are used most frequently, by creating custom instructions for these functions. It can also suggest various optimisations, such as using faster operations for more frequently-used instructions, or changing instruction cache size or stack depth. Further issues regarding the optimisation determiner will be discussed in Section 4.2.

The FIP adapter creates a new FIP, executable code and decision condition information. The run-time environment's databases are updated and the new

FIP can be used next time the application is executed. Sections 4.3 and 5 will detail more of the reconfiguration analysis and automatic refinement process.

4 Run-Time Optimisation of FIPs

Several issues have to be addressed in order for a system to be able to dynamically optimise implementations for performance, and to request and perform upgrades via reconfiguration. We need to: (1) decide what statistics to collect, (2) set how frequently to sample the statistics collected, (3) collect the statistics from the application, (4) analyse the collected statistics and decide what to optimise, (5) perform the optimisation, (6) decide when to reconfigure the implementation.

Should data collection and analysis take place during run time, their impact on performance can be reduced if they run concurrently with the FIP. Such activities can be implemented in software, on a PC or on a programmable system-on-chip device.

4.1 Collection and Analysis of Data

There has been research addressing issue (1) and (2) above [8]. The frequency with which such statistics is collected, is pertinent. If statistics are recorded frequently, the available data will more accurately describe run-time characteristics, although this is at the expense of design area. If statistics are analysed frequently, the area required for the storage of these statistics can be reduced. However, frequent analysis may affect the performance of the FIP by either taking processing cycles to analyse the data, or consuming bandwidth involved in downloading the data off-line to be analysed. Furthermore, a short sampling of data before analysis may yield results that do not accurately reflect the run-time characteristics. A full analysis of these issues is beyond the scope of this paper.

Our FIP templates allow users to easily incorporate statistic monitors into their FIP designs. In our implementation, we collect information on the frequency of procedure calls, sampled over an application's run time.

Analysis of the data will depend on the statistics collected. The user could choose to monitor the frequency of use, for certain native or custom instructions. Based on this information we can, for example, increase the performance of a frequently-used multiplier circuit, while reducing the area and performance of the less frequently-used operations. We provide a level of flexibility in the optimisation analysis because of the domain specificity.

Custom instructions are created according to the results of the above analysis. The techniques used in creating custom instructions will be discussed in Section 4.2. Once custom instructions have been generated, the optimisation analyser (Figure 1) performs analysis similar to that done in the design environment. Optimisations based on analysis of congestion and constraints satisfaction of speed, area and latency can also be carried out.

This analysis is necessary because the original request for customisations may contain too many new custom instructions, and may not satisfy area or latency constraints. In that case, the optimisation analyser can decide to remove custom instructions, reduce the number of native opcodes supported, or downgrade the performance of opcodes that are not used frequently.

4.2 Reconfiguration

If configuration occurs too frequently, the overall performance of the system can suffer. The FIP approach provides a way to fine tune the frequency of reconfiguration by allowing an application to run less efficiently with the instruction processor if the reconfiguration time is unacceptable. A metric can be used to decide if it is beneficial to reconfigure. For instance, if we aim to improve performance, then a new, faster FIP should only be adopted if the reduction in run time is greater than the reconfiguration time involved in replacing the old FIP by the new one.

Consider a software function $f()$ which takes C_{sw} clock cycles with time for each cycle T_{sw}. As a custom instruction, it takes C_{ci} cycles with cycle time T_{ci}. The function $f()$ is called F times over the time period we are investigating, in this case one execution of the application. The reconfiguration time for the device is T_r, which includes time for collecting and analysing data. The time spent executing the software function (t_{sw}) can be shown to be $C_{sw}T_{sw}F$ and the time spent executing the custom instruction (t_{ci}) to be $C_{ci}T_{ci}F$. We define the reconfiguration ratio R as follows:

$$R = \frac{t_{sw}}{t_{ci} + T_r} = \frac{C_{sw}T_{sw}F}{C_{ci}T_{ci}F + T_r} \tag{1}$$

More generally, with n custom instructions, R becomes:

$$R = \left(T_{sw} \sum_{j=1}^{n} C_{sw,j}F_j \right) / \left(T_{ci} \sum_{j=1}^{n} (C_{ci,j}F_j) + T_r \right) \tag{2}$$

The point where $R = 1$ is the threshold: if $R > 1$, reconfiguration will be beneficial. Figure 2 demonstrates the effect of varying different parameters R on our designs. The horizontal axis measures the number of times an application is executed. The vertical axis shows R values. The curve with the circular disks corresponds to the base FIP, the R values of which is calculated by making $C_{ci}T_{ci} = C_{sw}T_{sw}$. The value of R for the base FIP will never reach 1, unless reconfiguration time is less than or equal to zero. The following discusses the effects of various FIP features on R.

Number of Custom Instructions. The general form of R, as shown in equation 2, shows that as we include more custom instructions, the reconfiguration threshold can be reached with fewer execution of the application. This is demonstrated by the two dashed curves in Figure 2. As more custom instructions are added and generic instructions are removed, the shape of the reconfiguration

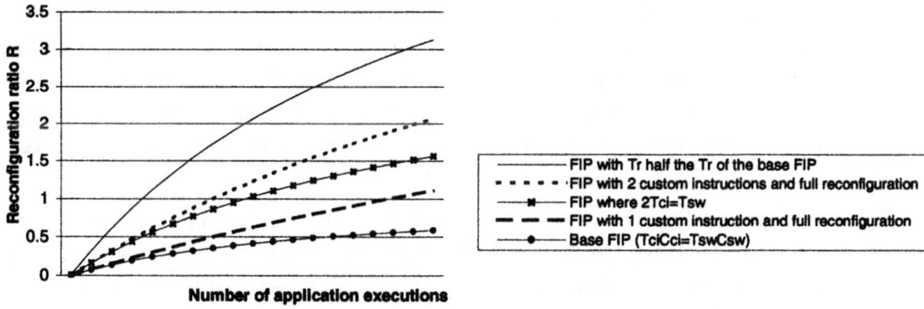

Fig. 2. This graph shows the effects of varying different parameters in the general reconfiguration ratio equation. When $R > 1$ reconfiguration should be attempted. Here we see the effects of increasing the number of custom instructions, reducing the cycle time of the custom instruction FIP and the reconfiguration time.

curve will tend towards that of a direct hardware implementation. The rate of this improvement is expected to decrease as more custom instructions are added.

Changing FIP cycle time. FIPs with custom instructions often require fewer clock cycles to complete an operation, but they may operate at a lower clock speed. The curve with crosses shows the reconfiguration ratio of a FIP with two custom instructions operating at half the clock speed of the base FIP. Although the performance is still better than the design with one custom instruction, the gain is not as much as one would expect.

Changing reconfiguration time. Changing the value of T_r may also affect R. The topmost curve shows a FIP with two custom instructions and half the reconfiguration time of the base FIP. Halving the reconfiguration time increases the initial gradient of the curve and reduces the number of application execution required to reach the threshold.

We have assumed the use of full reconfiguration until now. The reconfiguration time, T_r, can be rewritten as the product of t_r and n_r, the reconfiguration cycle time and the number of cycles needed to reconfigure the design. By utilising partial reconfiguration we can reduce n_r [8], and hence reduce the total impact reconfiguration has on R. n_r may also be reduced through improvements in technology and architectures that support fast reconfiguration through caches or context switches [10].

5 Generation of Custom Instruction

Compared to direct hardware implementations, instruction processors have the added overhead of instruction fetch and decode [7]. VLIW and EPIC architectures are attempts to reduce the ratio of fetches to execution. Customising instructions is also a technique for reducing the fetch and execute ratio to increase the performance of the instruction processor. The idea of incorporating custom instructions in an instruction processor has been reported [6]. Custom instructions are typically hand-crafted and incorporated at the processor instancing stage. While hand-crafted custom instructions provides the best performance, they are difficult to create, and require a skilled engineer with good knowledge of the system.

Opcode chaining can be used to reduce the ratio of the time spent on the control path and the data path of a FIP. Directly connecting up the data path of the sequence of opcodes that make up a procedure reduces the time spent on fetching and decoding instructions. Further, by converting a procedure call to a single instruction, the overhead of calling a procedure can be avoided; such overheads include preamble and postamble housekeeping routines, like storing program counters and shared registers, and refilling prefetch buffers.

Custom instructions have their own dedicated data path, making them suitable to exploit parallelism that may exist in opcodes; such as in instruction folding, up to four Java opcodes can be processed concurrently [3].

When creating custom instructions, we allow the available resources to grow as is needed to exploit as much data-level parallelism as possible. The introduction of a new custom instruction could introduce new possibilities for instruction-level parallelism in the FIP.

Other optimisations include device-specific optimisations such as using look-up table implementations. This exploits the high on-chip RAM capacity found in devices like Xilinx Virtex-E chips. Generalised look-up table based custom instructions can also be created, for instance; the same instruction can be used for cosine, sine and tangent operations, by reconfiguring the block RAM.

Streaming style instructions can also be incorporated. For example, an IP core that encrypts or decrypts a stream of data can be added as a custom instruction. Before a streaming instruction can be executed, it has to be initialised with relevant data such as the start position, length of the data stream and the location to write back to. The IP core is then activated via control channels that can be controlled by executing the custom instruction associated with the IP core. The IP core may be on a different clock domain from the FIP, in which case the relevant handshake protocols are used to communicate. Once the streaming instruction is activated, the FIP can then proceed to process other instructions. Buffers can also be used to store intermediate data if the core is not fully pipelined. This will allow the memory resources to be multiplexed between the core and FIP.

There are also optimisations related to reducing the overheads of run-time reconfiguration by reducing the amount of configuration storage required to store multiple designs and the time taken to reconfigure between these designs [9]. The following section will exemplify the process of creating a custom instruction.

	Java opcodes	Chained opcodes in custom instruction
a	iload_1	paramreg=TOS();
b	iconst_1 ishl	tempreg1=paramreg≪1;
c	iload_1 sipush 0x80 iand	tempreg2=param & 0x80
d	ifeq 0x9	if (tempreg2==0) jump 3;
e	getstatic 0x4f	tempreg2=0x1b;
f	goto 0x4	jump 2;
g	iconst_0	tempreg2=0;
h	ixor	tempreg2=tempreg2 ^tempreg;
i	int2byte	int2byte
j	ireturn	ireturn

Table 1. Sequential implementation of *FFmulx* in Java opcodes and chained opcodes. The Java opcode version takes 26.5 clock cycles on average plus another 4 cycles for the procedure preamble and post amble. The chained opcode version takes 8.5 clock cycles on average.

6 AES Example

We illustrate our approach by the AES (Rijndael) algorithm which is an iterated block cipher with variable block and key length. We have implementations of the cipher in two forms, a straight implementation (i) where we write code for the different component transformations of the cipher and a more efficient implementation (ii) where the component transformations are optimised into look-up tables.

In the first approach, the most frequently executed function, *FFmulx*, is a Galois matrix multiplication. The second column of Table 1 shows the Java opcodes required to implement the function. Depending on the outcome of the conditional branch `ifeq` opcode, this implementation takes between 25 to 28 clock cycles to execute.

The rightmost column of Table 1 shows the result of both opcode chaining and instruction folding. Opcode chaining involves storing intermediate results in temporary registers. By removing the need to push and pop values from the stack, the sequential structure imposed by the stack is eliminated. Next, instruction folding is applied. This allows several opcodes to be combined or folded into one instruction. In other words, several stack-based instructions are converted into one register-based instruction. Furthermore, since *FFmulx* is replaced by a single instruction, there is no longer a need to perform the preamble and postamble routines necessary for procedural calls. These techniques reduce the number of clock cycles in each application execution from 30 to 8.5 cycles.

Table 1 can be further optimised by identifying instructions that can execute in parallel, instruction b and c for instance. By introducing predicate registers, instructions d,e,g and h can be executed in parallel. Using this implementation, the original software *FFmulx* function has been optimised from 30 to 6 cycles, producing a 5-fold speedup. Similarly, the FIP (i) implementation is augmented by a single custom instruction involving direct connection of the data paths for the individual component transformations. This achieves an encryption of 128 bits of data with a 128 bit key in 99 cycles. Another implementation, FIP (ii), utilises lookup tables and achieves an encryption of 128 bits of data with a 128-bit key in 32 cycles.

Implementations	Cycles/Block	Hardware resources	Mbps/MHz	Flexible
Software[1] (C/C++)	340		0.4	Yes
FIP (i)	99	1770 Slices 2 BRAMs	1.3	Yes
FIP (ii)	32	1393 Slices 10 BRAMs	4	Yes
Hardware[5] (Spartan II 100-6)	11	460 Slices 10 BRAMs	11.5	No
Hardware[4] (Virtex-E 812-8)	1	2679 Slices 82 BRAMs	129.6	No

Table 2. Various AES implementations. Blocks are 128 bits with 128 bit keys. The C/C++ implementation runs on a 933MHz Pentium III. FIP implementations are written in Java and run on a sequential JVM implemented on a Spartan II 300E-6. The Spartan design is latency optimised and runs at 0.52 Gbps (45MHz). The Virtex-E design runs at a data rate of 7 Gbps (54MHz).

Table 2 compares different implementations of the AES algorithm. The fastest reported C/C++ implementation, by Gladman [1], achieves an encryption speed of about 350Mbps on a 933MHz Pentium 3. Running at 40MHz, FIP(i) encrypts at 51.7Mbps and FIP(ii) at 160 Mbps. FIP(ii) performs ten times better than software, in a Mbps per MHz comparison. Hand-placed hardware implementations provide good performance, but cannot be used for general computations. This flexibility has been compromised to improve performance. However these hardware implementations can be incorporated into FIPs as custom instructions, as outlined in Section 5.

The FIP approach provides a convenient compromise of trading off speed, flexibility and area. It provides the flexibility afforded by instruction processors and can be augmented with custom hardware to improve performance. Our proposed design-time and run-time system provides a means of customising these processors. It also provides a mechanism for these processors to adapt to environmental conditions, depending on usage patterns.

7 Concluding Remarks

We have described our work on run-time adaptive Flexible Instruction Processors, and the associated design and run-time environment. Run-time adaptability allows our system to automatically evolve and automatically refine the implementation to suit run-time conditions.Current and future work includes refining run-time statistics collection and reconfiguration strategies. The quality of the statistics gathered should allow the system to produce more optimal refinements. However the complexity of the monitoring hardware could affect FIP performance. We intend to obtain a better understanding of this trade-off between the quality of statistics and performance. We also continue to investigate strategies for reconfiguration, and to improve scalability [2] of our approach.

Acknowledgement. Thanks to A. Derbyshire and S. McKeever for their comments. The support of Celoxica Limited and the UK Engineering and Physical Sciences Research Council (Grant number GR/N 66599) is gratefully acknowledged.

References

1. B. Gladman. *Implementations of AES (Rijndael) in C/C++ and Assembler.* http://fp.gladman.plus.com/cryptography_technology/rijndael/.
2. J. A. Fisher. Customized instruction sets for embedded processors. In *Proc. 36th Design Automation Conference*, 1999.
3. H. McGhan and M. O'Connor. PicoJava: a direct execution engine for Java bytecode. *IEEE Computer.* October 1998.
4. M. McLoone and J. McCanny. Single-chip FPGA implementation of the Advanced Encryption Standard algorithm. In *Proc. FPL*, LNCS 2147. Springer, 2001.
5. N. Weaver and J. Wawrzynek. *Very high performance, compact AES implementations in Xilinx FPGAs.* http://www.cs.berkeley.edu/~nweaver/sfra/rijndael.pdf.
6. R. Razdan and M. D. Smith. A high-performance microarchitecture with hardware-programmable functional units. In *Proc. MICRO-27.* 1994.
7. S. Seng, W. Luk and P. Cheung. Flexible instruction processors. In *Proc. CASES.* ACM, 2000.
8. N. Shirazi, W. Luk and P. Cheung. Run-time management of dynamically reconfigurable designs. In *Proc. FPL*, LNCS 1482. Springer, 1998.
9. N. Shirazi, W. Luk and P. Cheung. Framework and tools for run-time reconfigurable designs. *IEE Proc.-Comput. Digit. Tech.*, May 2000.
10. S. Trimberger, D. Carberry and A. Johnson. A time-multiplexed FPGA. In *Proc. FCCM.* IEEE Computer Society Press, 1997.

DARP – A Digital Audio Reconfigurable Processor

José T. de Sousa[1], Fernando M. Gonçalves[1], Nuno Barreiro[2], and João Moura[2]

[1] INESC-ID/IST, Technical University of Lisbon,
R. Alves Redol, 9, 1000 Lisboa, Portugal,
{jose.desousa|fernando.goncalves}@inesc.pt,
http://{sca|figaro}.inesc.pt/{~jts|~fmg}
[2] COREWORKS — Audio and Video Projects,
R. Pinheiro Chagas, 101, 5-D, 1050-176 Lisboa,Portugal
{nuno.barreiro|joao.moura}@coreworks.pt,
http://www.coreworks.pt

Abstract. This paper presents DARP, a novel digital audio signal reconfigurable processor based on the low cost Spartan II XC2S200 FPGA device. The system can handle several tens of digital audio signals in parallel, and can be programmed and controlled by a host computer. Its main advantages are: multi-functionality, high performance, low cost and low power. Several digital audio cores have been developed, which can be combined in different ways to implement a variety of complex digital audio algorithms in DARP. Several expensive commercial systems would be needed to achieve the processing power that is possible with DARP. A case study of an 8x8 stereo audio matrix and format converter is presented. Our area, frequency and latency results show that FPGAs can compete with ASIC, processor or DSP solutions for implementing complex, cost effective and flexible digital audio systems.

1 Introduction

Reconfigurable systems are becoming a viable alternative for implementing electronic systems in a number of domains, from communications and networking to computing, signal processing and control[1]. In digital video processing, very successful applications have been implemented as demonstrated in [2]. Although many companies already use FPGAs in digital audio processing to implement some specific functions, for example, RME Intelligent Audio Solutions [17], DARP is, to the best of our knowledge, the only existing proposal for a multi-functional digital audio processor implemented with reconfigurable hardware.

Digital audio introduced the possibility of transmitting audio signals without any loss of sound quality [3]. The signals are conveyed using several standard formats which tend more and more to co-exist: AES3 (aka AES/EBU - 2 audio channels); SPDIF (consumer version of AES3) [5,6,7]; ADAT (8 audio channels), a proprietary format from Alesis, Inc [8,9]; MADI (48 audio channels) [4], and others.

M. Glesner, P. Zipf, and M. Renovell (Eds.): FPL 2002, LNCS 2438, pp. 556–566, 2002.

Typical operations that need to be performed on digital audio signals are the following: conversion among formats with a varying number of channels to allow equipment compatibility; change of signal sample rate also for compatibility reasons; alteration of signal connections using routing matrices; addition of special effects such as echo, reverberation or distortion; storing and retrieving signals in networked storage media.

DARP can perform the tasks identified above or others required by the users. It has I/O interfaces to several formats of digital audio signals, to analog signals using A/D and D/A conversion and to a host computer using a parallel port. Its function can be programmed by loading the FPGA with a configuration file. In this way, configuration files for various purposes can be provided to the final user, implementing various functions with the same hardware. This is significantly less expensive than using a collection of different dedicated systems. The programs for DARP can be written in a high-level hardware description language such as VHDL or VERILOG or a system language like HandelC or SystemC, taking about the same time to develop as DSP or processor software. The following features of DARP are highlighted: flexibility and multi-functionality, ease on handling concurrency and synchronization issues, high bandwidth only limited by the number of signal inputs, low clock frequency and power consumption compared to ASIC or DSP solutions.

2 System Architecture

The architecture of the DARP system is shown in Figure 1. The system, shown within the limits of the dashed line, consists of a central reconfigurable processor implemented with a FPGA and multiple interfaces to audio signals. DARP can be programmed by the host computer shown on the left using a parallel port interface. The user interacts with the host to select an FPGA configuration for performing a desired processing task. With a collection of different configuration files, many different algorithms can be run on DARP.

In its current configuration DARP uses a XC2S200 FPGA of the Xilinx Spartan II family [14]. This device can implement designs using about 200K system gates. The types of digital audio input/output interfaces are the following: optical digital signals, balanced digital signals using XLR type connections, unbalanced digital signals using RCA type connections, equivalent balanced and unbalanced analog signals using the same type of connections, respectively.

A prototype of DARP is being implemented using the Digilab 2 FPGA platform by Digilent Inc.[11]. The 50 MHz oscillator present on the board is used as a reference clock to mesure the frequency of a supplied external *word clock*. The term word clock is normally used to designate a clock at the audio sample rate frequency. Common word clock frequencies are 32, 44.1, 48, 88.2, 96, and, more recently, 192 KHz. A digital audio channel is normally encoded using 24-bit samples. The Digilab 2 platform provides 6 expansion connectors of 40 pins each; we use 2 of them to attach a daughter board containing our additional components: a VCO, a PLL, various I/O interfaces and respective circuitry.

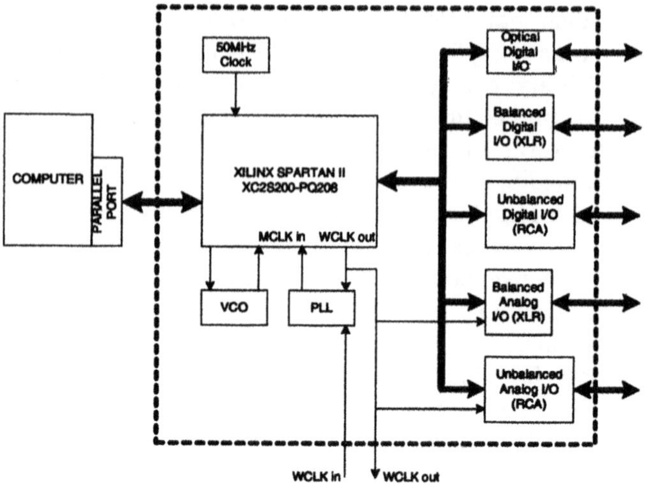

Fig. 1. The system architecture

In order to synchronize to one of the incoming audio signals, the VCO is controlled by a receiver unit implemented in the FPGA, which locks to the frequency of the input audio signal. In other words, the VCO recovers the *master clock* MCLK of the signal. MCLK is normally the bit clock (or a multiple of the bit clock) of the audio bitstream. MCLK is used as the clock for the synchronous sequential circuits that process the signal downstream the receiver unit.

Alternatively, the audio signals can be synchronous to an externally supplied word clock (*WCLK in*). In this case a PLL circuit is used to lock to the external word clock and multiply its frequency a certain number of times to obtain the master clock MCLK.

Professional balanced digital audio signals are usually conveyed by XLR cables, using the Audio Engineering Society/European Broadcasting Union AES3 (AES/EBU) standard interface format [5,6]. The use of low loss balanced cables enables audio signals to be transmitted over long distances, with high noise immunity and without causing ground loop problems. Terminations must contain a decoupling transformer and a matching impedance. These interfaces have been implemented and tested in the scope of the DARP project.

The unbalanced digital I/O interfaces using RCA type connections are used for consumer digital audio signals in the Sony/Philips Interface Format (SPDIF). This format is basically identical to the IEC-958 consumer standard[7], which, in turn, is similar to the AES3 standard discussed above. However, the use of unbalanced connections makes SPDIF less reliable for use in professional studios. No additional circuits are required for an SPDIF interface, which makes it less expensive.

For handling analog audio inputs and outputs, we have developed A/D and D/A converter circuits, which have been implemented and tested successfully. The A/D circuit employs a CS5333 A/D converter the D/A circuit uses a CS4396

D/A converter, both from Cirrus Logic [10]. The use of balanced or unbalanced cables are supported, with similar advantages and disadvantages as discussed for the digital signals.

Optical cables are popular for conveying audio signals, since they are free from nasty electrical effects like biasing, loss and noise, as well as for providing a wider bandwidth. DARP is prepared to receive and produce optical digital audio signals, since its I/O system contains Thermal Optical Switch (TOS) links to perform conversions between the optical and electrical domains. These interfaces have been implemented and tested.

Both the AES3 and the SPDIF digital audio formats carry 1 stereo audio channel or 2 mono channels of 24 bits per sample. These formats can be conveyed electrically or optically. Additionally, DARP supports a multichannel interface format: the Alesis Digital Audio Tape (ADAT), which is a patented and proprietary format of Alesis Corporation [9,8]. The ADAT format encodes 8 mono audio channels of 24 bits per sample, normally organized as 4 stereo channels. ADAT signals normally use optical connections.

3 FPGA Digital Audio Cores Developed

In the same way a computer needs programs to perform useful work, our DARP system needs FPGA configurations to process audio data. A number of FPGA IP cores have been developed to use in DARP: a multi-format digital audio receiver, two cores that convert from the ADAT format to the AES3/SPDIF formats and vice-versa, and a synchronous/asynchronous 8×8 stereo digital audio routing matrix. These cores have been developed using Xilinx's Webpack 4.1 freeware package and simulated using the Modelsim simulator from Modeltech Inc. [12]. All cores are written in VHDL. In the subsections that follow, these cores are described.

3.1 Digital Audio Receiver Unit

A high-level view of the multi-format digital audio receiver core is shown in Figure 2. It receives as input the signal *encoded audio in* and the master clock signal *MCLK*. It produces as outputs the following signals: *sync*, which indicates that the input bitstream is synchronized with MCLK; *WCLK*, the extracted word clock; *decoded audio out*, the decoded bitstream; *vco ctrl*, the signal that is used to adjust the VCO's frequency and phase to achieve synchronization. Note that it is the VCO that produces the MCLK signal, thus forming a closed feedback loop.

As in many other communication standards, audio bitstreams are encoded before transmission to facilitate clock recovery and eliminate the DC component. AES3/SPDIF utilizes biphase encoding, whereas ADAT utilizes non return to zero inverted (NRZI) encoding. Our decoder can be parameterized to handle either of these encodings.

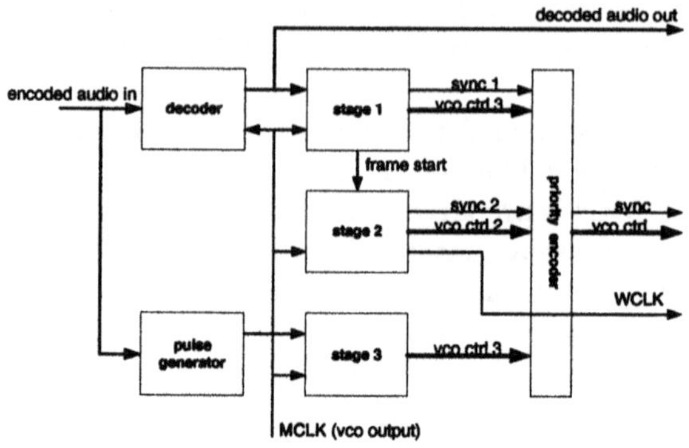

Fig. 2. Digital audio receiver implementation

Similarly to the receiver circuit recommended for the ADAT interface [8], ours consists of 3 synchronization stages: the first stage is in charge of recognizing the frame preamble; the second stage is responsible for making sure the number of MCLK cycles between preambles is within acceptable limits; the third stage performs phase locking. Note that digital audio signals are organized in frames separated by preambles, where each frame carries a certain number of time division multiplexed audio channels: 2 mono channels in the AES3/SPDIF formats and 8 mono channels in the ADAT format.

Stage 1 is a coarse frequency adjuster, stage 2 is a medium frequency adjuster and stage 3 does the fine tuning. The signals *sync 1* and *sync 2* indicate that stages 1 and 2 have achieved satisfactory synchronization. These 2 signals are used by the priority encoder to select which stage is driving the *vco ctrl* output, i.e., which stage is controlling the VCO to adjust the MCLK frequency. If *sync 1*=0 then stage 1 is in control of the VCO; else if *sync 2*=0 then stage 2 controls the VCO; if both *sync 1* and *sync 2* are asserted then it is stage 3 who is in charge of the VCO. Note that stage 1 sends a preamble start bit to stage 2 to restart its clock cycle count every time a frame preamble is detected.

3.2 Format Converters

Since we support ADAT and AES3/SPDIF formats, two converters have been developed: one from ADAT to AES3 and the other from AES3 to ADAT. In this paper we only have space to describe the external interfaces of these components, as illustrated in Figure 3. These converters have a latency of 1 sample.

For the AES3 to ADAT converter, the inputs on the left are the 4 AES3 stereo channels and their respective *sync* bits indicating that they are synchronized with MCLK and WCLK. Conversion is enabled only if the 4 *sync i in* bits are asserted. The outputs on the right are the ADAT signal *adat out*, formed with the 4 AES3 input channels, and the *sync out* signal indicating that the 4 inputs are synchronized, and thus the that the output ADAT signal is valid.

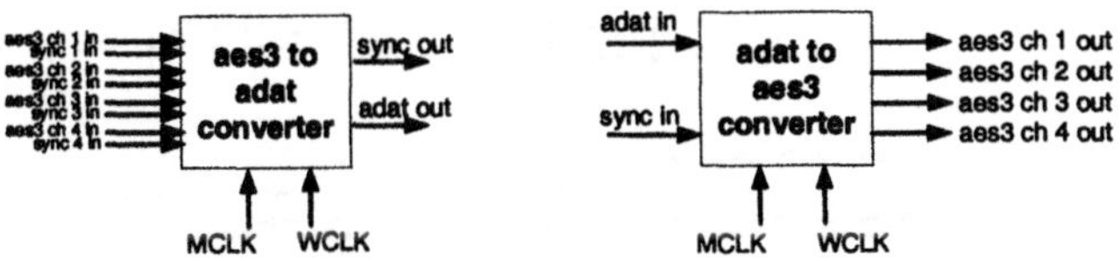

Fig. 3. ADAT to AES3 converter

For the ADAT to AES3 converter, the inputs on the left are the incoming ADAT signal *adat in* and the *sync in* bit indicating that the signal is synchronized with MCLK and WCLK. Only if the *sync in* bit is asserted will the conversion be enabled. The outputs on the right are the 4 AES3 channels *aes3 ch i out* that are extracted from the ADAT input signal.

3.3 Digital Audio Matrix

The need to frequently alter connections between various equipment justifies the use of digital audio routing matrices, which quickly became one of the most relevant productivity tools in the field. We have implemented the run-time configurable digital audio matrix illustrated in Figure 4. The matrix is aimed at routing individual stereo channels and supports the AES3 or SPDIF formats. The matrix inputs are on the left and its outputs are on the bottom. Each input channel is associated with a *sync i bit* indicating that the signal is synchronized with MCLK and WCLK. Each *sync i* signal is routed together with its channel to the outputs.

A signal may be routed in the biphase encoded or decoded forms, depending on the format present at the source and required at the destination. If a signal is routed in the decoded form, it may be biphase encoded at the outputs by the encoders shown. If a signal is routed in the encoded form then it leaves the matrix in the encoded form, without need to use the encoders. The *in select register* and the *out select register* control the choice of encoded/decoded inputs and outputs. Table 1 gives the values of these selection bits for all possible source and destination formats, so that latency is minimized.

Table 1. Selection of encoded/decoded inputs and outputs

Source	Destination	Encoded input	Encoded output
AES3/SPDIF	AES3/SPDIF	1	0
ADAT	AES3/SPDIF	0	1
—	ADAT	0	0

The desired routing can be set by programming the matrix crosspoints *Xpt (i,j)*, where i, j are the matrix horizontal and vertical coordinates, respectively. These are bit registers that, when asserted, determine if input i should be routed

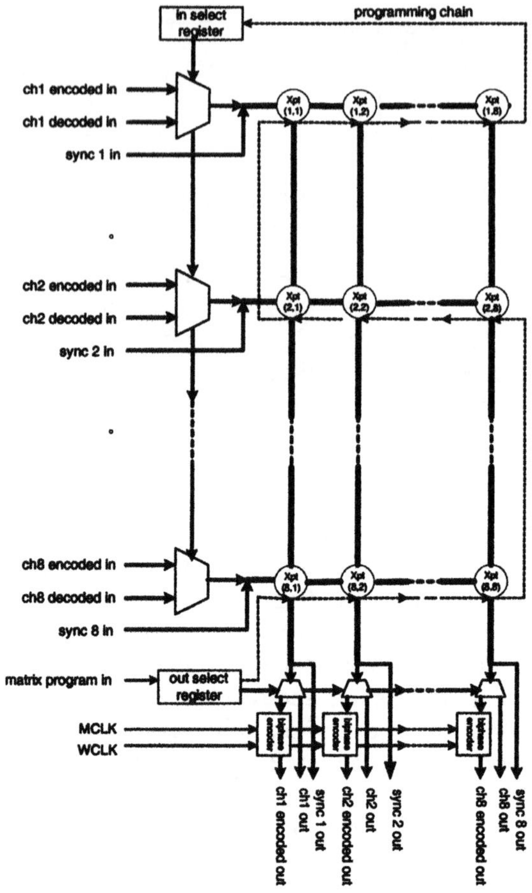

Fig. 4. Digital Audio Matrix

to output j. Many crosspoints can be asserted in a row, as it is possible to route a source to several destinations simultaneously. However, only one crosspoint can be asserted in a column, since an output can only be driven by a single input. The configuration software that runs on the host computer is in charge of checking for user errors or conflicts before generating the matrix programming data.

4 An Example: Routing Matrix with Format Conversion

A useful audio processing system is one that combines a routing matrix with format converters. Such a system provides for various digital audio signals to be interconnected, regardless of the way they are encoded. Until recently, the few existing systems of this type were high-end prohibitively expensive ma-

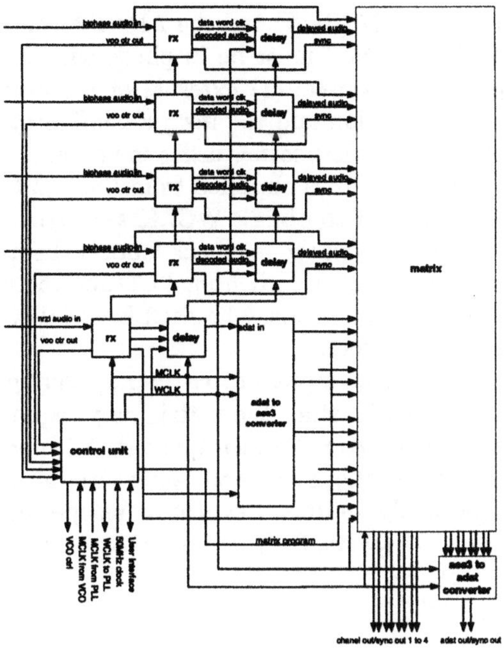

Fig. 5. An 8×8 stereo digital audio matrix with format conversion

chines [15,16]. Last year, RME [17] has released the first affordable format converter (ADI-8 DD), based on FPGAs. Since then some other manufacturers have released affordable audio matrices with format conversion [13]. However, the functionality of these systems cannot be changed, preventing them from taking full advantage of using reconfigurable hardware (FPGAs).

To demonstrate the capabilities of DARP, we will show how it can be configured to implement a routing matrix with format conversion, using the components described in the previous sections. The FPGA circuit can be viewed in Figure 5. It inputs 8 stereo digital audio channels, where 4 of them enter the system in the AES3/SPDIF format and the other 4 in the ADAT format. The system outputs 4 AES3/SPDIF signals and 1 ADAT signal. Each input can be routed to any output; if the input format is not the same as the one intended for the output, format conversion is activated. The desired routing and format conversions can be programmed by the user and changed while the system is running.

For each digital audio input on the left, we can see receiver units RX for synchronizing the signal with the system master clock MCLK. Each RX unit output is connected to an adjustable delay unit to align the samples with the system word clock WCLK. This is necessary only for the channels that will be combined into a single ADAT signal. The delay unit introduces a latency of at most 1 sample.

To support both the AES3/SPDIF and the ADAT formats, MCLK must be 256 times faster than WCLK and must be in phase with it. The user has two options to select the WCLK source: (1) external or (2) extracted from one of the input channels. This selection and the matrix configuration are sent to the control unit shown on the lower left corner using the parallel port user interface. If the user selects (1) then MCLK is obtained from the input *MCLK from PLL*. Its frequency is divided by 256 to obtain WCLK and fed back to the PLL as the *WCLK out* signal, thus closing the feedback loop. If the user selects (2) then MCLK is obtained from the input *MCLK from VCO* and the *vco ctrl i* of receiver *i* controls the FPGA output *VCO ctrl*. The MCLK and WCLK thus obtained are then used in the whole system.

It should be noted that some input/output audio signal pairs can work at a frequency different from WCLK, since the matrix only requires synchronization of the channels that form the ADAT output signal. All other routes can work asynchronously. In an asynchronous route the *sync i out* bit may be de-asserted and still the signal is perfectly audible. Asynchronous operation allows for routing of other devices like CD players, DAT or Mini-Disc recorders, without format conversion.

5 Summary

We have presented DARP, a FPGA-based reconfigurable processor for digital audio that can handle several tens of audio channels in parallel. The system can be programmed by a host computer using a parallel cable interface, after which it can work by itself. It has a SpartanII XC2S200 device for processing the signals, and several interfaces to audio signals: optical, digital and analog, balanced and unbalanced.

DARP can be reconfigured to execute various digital audio processing tasks, eliminating the need to use several expensive dedicated systems. It can be as easily programmed as a DSP or processor using a high-level language. Compared to those, DARP is more flexible in dealing with concurrency and synchronization issues, and its bandwidth can be easily scaled by just adding more I/Os. Note that DARP can synchronize simultaneously with different input channels or can even handle some channels asynchronously. This would be very difficult if not impossible to do with a processor or DSP system. DARP uses a 10 times lower clock frequency than a processor or DSP, which yields a much lower power consumption. Compared to an ASIC, the competitive price and flexibility of Xilinx Spartan FPGAs would require a very high production volume to make an ASIC a better option.

To demonstrate DARP's capabilities, we have configured it with an 8×8 run-time configurable stereo digital audio matrix with format conversion, supporting the AES3/SPDIF and ADAT formats. This system occupies about 35% of the XC2S200 device, and about 5% of the available RAM. We have obtained a master clock frequency of 75MHz, which indicates that signals sampled at a rate of 294KHz can be processed. Note that currently most systems work at

24bits@96KHz, and the forecoming standard is 24bits@192KHz. Some interesting features of our system are summarized in Table 2. In column 1 the features of interest are listed. In column 2 the obtained values for the implemented system are shown. In column 3 we estimate these values for a scaled up system that would occupy the whole of the FPGA (200K system gates). These estimations were made taking into account the fact that the matrix component is small compared to the format converters associated with the I/Os. Thus, we assumed that the size of the circuit is linear in the number of I/Os.

Table 2. Routing matrix with format converter features

Feature	Implemented system	Max. capacity system
No. of input mono channels	16	45
No. of output mono channels	16	45
Supported digital audio formats	AES3/SPDIF, ADAT	
Max. MCLK frequency	75 MHz	
Max. sample frequency	294 KHz	
Total I/O bandwidth	287.1 Mb/s	820.3 Mb/s
Total system gates	70,000	200,000
Total embedded RAM used	12 Kb	34.3 Kb
Worst case latency	3 samples	

As future work we plan to develop other digital audio FPGA cores such as MADI interfaces, sample rate converters and effects processors. We also envisage replacing the parallel port interface with a network card so that the system can be controlled remotely, including the possibility of sending digital audio channels over the network.

References

1. Special Issue on Configurable Computing, Scientific American, June (1997)
2. Haynes, S.D., Cheung, P.Y.K., Luk, W., Stone, J.: Video Image Processing with the SONIC Architecture, IEEE Computer, April 2000, 50—57
3. Pohlmann, Ken C.: Principles of Digital Audio. Fourth Edition. McGraw-Hill (2000)
4. AES10-1991: AES Recommended Practice for Digital Audio Engineering — Serial Multichannel Audio Digital Interface (MADI). JAES, vol. 39, no. 5, May (1991)
5. AES3-1992: AES Recommended Practice for Digital Audio Engineering — Serial Transmission Format for Two-Channel Linearly Represented Digital Audio Data. JAES, vol. 40, no. 3, March (1992)
6. EBU (European Broadcasting Union), Specification of the Digital Audio Interface. EBU Doc. Tech., 3250
7. International Standard IEC-598, digital audio Interface, First Edition, 1989-03
8. Barr, K., Zak, A., Ryle, M., Brown, D., Lafky, C.: Method and Apparatus for Providing a Digital Audio Interface Protocol. U.S. Patent 5,297,181, March 22 (1994)
9. Alesis Inc.: www.alesis.com

10. Cirrus Logic: www.crystal.com
11. Digilent, Inc.: www.digilentinc.com
12. Modeltech: www.model.com
13. Friend-chip: www.friend-chip.de
14. Xilinx, Inc.: www.xilinx.com
15. Kurzweil: www.kurzweilmusicsystems.com
16. Otari: www.otari.com
17. RME — Inteligent Audio Solutions: www.rme-audio.com

System-Level Modelling for Performance Estimation of Reconfigurable Coprocessors

Stephen Charlwood, Jonathan Mangnall, Steven Quigley

Digital Systems & Vision Processing Group
Electronic, Electrical and Computer Engineering
The University of Birmingham
Edgbaston, Birmingham, B15 2TT, UK

Abstract. The capabilities of general-purpose workstations are commonly enhanced by the addition of application-specific coprocessors located on the system expansion bus or a dedicated local bus. In order to determine the limits of applicability of such systems, performance estimation tools are required which are capable both of generating accurate predictions and supporting rapid evaluation of architectural alternatives. This paper describes a performance estimation method which meets these requirements. By combining data acquired using a variety of established techniques, and integrating these using a novel approach designed to capture far more of the intrinsic complexity of the system, extremely accurate estimates of performance can be generated. A detailed uncertainty analysis is provided, and the method is evaluated by comparing an application running on a coprocessor-enhanced workstation with model-based predictions, demonstrating estimation accuracy to be within ±5% of measured values.

1 Introduction

The trend in modern microprocessor architectures towards provision of SIMD instruction set extensions (such as Intel's MMX and SSE/SSE2) acknowledges the limitations of traditional superscalar microprocessor designs and highlights the increasing demand for parallel computation. However, the fixed width of the registers used by these extensions limits the parallelism which can be exploited. Research interest in computational surfaces capable of concurrent manipulation of much larger datasets, and their integration into general-purpose systems is therefore high.

A number of technologies may be used to provide such computational surfaces, including existing fine-grain reconfigurable devices (e.g. SRAM-based FPGAs), novel coarse-grain reconfigurable architectures, and alternative DRAM-based technologies such as active memories. This work is equally applicable to any of the above technologies, but focuses primarily on reconfigurable devices. By configuring FPGAs with application-specific circuits, and making full use of aggressive pipelining, parallel execution, custom memory hierarchies, wide datapaths and optimised operators, significant performance gains can be realised. Previous research has shown that for certain applications, the performance of general-purpose workstations can be

M. Glesner, P. Zipf, and M. Renovell (Eds.): FPL 2002, LNCS 2438, pp. 567-576, 2002.

substantially improved by the addition of a reconfigurable coprocessor [1][2][3]. Frequently, however, the relative performance gains of such enhanced systems are more modest, with reconfiguration overheads [4] and host-coprocessor communication bandwidth [5][6], being cited as the most significant limiting factors. As reconfigurable technologies mature, architectural innovations such as multiple configuration contexts will alleviate the problems associated with reconfiguration overheads. The use of more modern interconnect architectures will lead to improved communication bandwidths and thus higher performance. However, performance is still highly application-dependent, and for reconfigurable coprocessors to become a mainstream technology, it must be straightforward to i) identify which applications can benefit, ii) accurately quantify the probable benefits and iii) exploit the technology. It is therefore important to take a system-level view of performance, one which takes into account not only the physical characteristics of the various system components, but also the nature of target applications.

This paper presents a method for accurately quantifying the system-level performance of a general-purpose workstation enhanced with a reconfigurable coprocessor. The method integrates data acquired using existing commercial software tools and techniques, using a novel approach designed to achieve both high accuracy and rapid evaluation times. Previous work described how reliable performance estimates could be synthesised by combining direct measurements with model-based estimates, cycle-accurate simulation results and a model of application execution [7]. A number of enhancements to this work, including automatic generation of application execution models and performance estimates, support for analysis of reconfiguration overheads, and a detailed uncertainty analysis are presented here.

2 Modelling Performance

In this work, the target system represents a general-purpose uni-processor workstation enhanced with a reconfigurable coprocessor. Processing occurs in one of two *compute nodes*, the first represented by the host workstation itself, and the other by the reconfigurable coprocessor. The way in which the target system is modelled depends on whether or not both nodes are allowed to operate concurrently. The system can therefore be seen from two perspectives: the *heterogeneous parallel computer* view or the *host-coprocessor* view. The first of these treats the reconfigurable node as entirely independent and the second views it simply as extending the functionality of the general-purpose node. By assuming that processing of a given task occurs *only* in one node or the other, performance estimation is simplified considerably (an observation previously exploited by Chatha and Vemuri in their work on rapid prototyping [8]). Although this "enhanced workstation" model [7], could be viewed simply as a subset of a more generic model of computing, such as the Hybrid System Architecture (HySAM) model [9], it is considered an important subset and worth detailed analysis.

2.1 Alternative Approaches

The aim of modelling any system is to describe it in terms of its component parts, minimising the complexity of each whilst ensuring that the model still captures the characteristics of interest. Detailed models should be developed for those components which have the greatest effect on performance (in this case, those which affect reconfiguration and communication overheads). In general, the more detailed the model, the more accurately the model will reflect actual system behaviour. Models that represent a low level of abstraction typically provide highly accurate results, but require detailed workload information and result in long evaluation times [10]. Higher-level models require less information (and are hence less costly to develop), and may be evaluated more quickly, but at the expense of reduced accuracy.

Different methods of estimating performance exist. At one extreme, a simulator (or emulator) could be developed that has identical behaviour to that of the target system and thus could be used to produce cycle-accurate estimates of performance. This method is costly to develop, but offers support for architectural analysis and does not require the target system to be available. If the target system is available, and in-depth analysis is not a priority, then much faster profiling-based methods can be used. Profiling-based approaches obviate the need to model the target system and thus may be used where models are either too costly to develop, or where architectural details are proprietary and/or unavailable. They also have much shorter evaluation times than low-level simulation-based techniques.

In developing the method presented here, our design goals were high accuracy, flexibility, low cost of evaluation and low development cost. Support for analysis of alternative device, coprocessor and communication channel architectures was also a priority. By taking the *host-coprocessor* view of the system, which ensures processing in both compute nodes is mutually exclusive over time, entirely different methods of estimating performance could be applied to each node. For the reconfigurable node, a simulation-based approach was necessary in order to meet our goals. Development costs were reduced by the use of a commercial HDL simulation tool. For the general-purpose (software-executing) node, the choice of approach was more involved. The most flexible approaches to performance estimation of software are those based on analysis of source code, but they are also the least accurate - optimising compilers transform programs so aggressively that there is no longer any direct correspondence between high-level language constructs and executed code [11]. Even where analysis is based on object code, reasonable accuracy can only be achieved by taking into account pipeline effects and the complex memory hierarchies found in modern microprocessor-based systems. Any analysis of cache performance in general-purpose systems is fundamentally limited, however, by the effects of *intertask interference* [12] (assuming a pre-emptive multitasking operating system). This problem is caused by task pre-emption, which results in cache lines being displaced by newly-scheduled tasks. The displacement of cache lines results in memory access overheads becoming unpredictable. To avoid loss of accuracy, models of both the effects of concurrently-operating processes and the scheduling algorithms that manage them would be required. For these reasons, a profiling-based approach was selected for estimating the performance of the general-purpose compute node.

2.2 Analysis Goals

Once a system model has been constructed, model parameters may be varied in order to evaluate the effects of these changes on performance. Performance may be evaluated in a number of ways, but in general, performance analysis tools seek to provide information on one or more of the following design concerns:

- *Execution Time*: overall application run-time for a given set of application parameters, and for a particular system configuration.
- *Scalability*: an analysis of how execution time, resource usage and power consumption vary as application parameters or the system configuration changes.
- *Applicability*: the limits within which application parameters can be varied, given constraints on execution time, resource usage or power consumption.
- *Resource Usage*: a description of the resource requirements for a given set of application parameters.
- *Power Consumption*: an estimate of the power requirements of the system as a function of the parameters of the application.

This information can be used for a variety of purposes, including evaluation of alternative architectures and parallelism strategies, and the identification of performance-limiting factors. Of the design concerns listed above, applicability is our primary interest since FPGAs suffer from *catastrophic performance degradation* when capacity limits are exceeded (as FPGA resource requirements increase, step changes in performance are observed that can render the coprocessor redundant or no longer cost-effective).

3 Description of Method

Realistic parallel performance estimation (for a given application) depends critically on two key performance aspects: individual node performance and communication costs [13]. Our method models the two compute nodes separately and, unlike earlier work [8], explicitly characterises communication and control overheads in terms of the host interface, i.e. the coprocessor's API (application programming interface). Our approach differs from other performance modelling toolsets for reconfigurable computing, such as DRIVE [14] and ARC [15] in that the system model is more constrained and this is exploited to offer significantly improved accuracy. By directly measuring the performance of the general-purpose node (using our own *low-overhead* profiling techniques), much of the inherent complexity is automatically captured. This approach is fast, extremely accurate and allows existing compiler technologies to be used. A different approach is taken with the reconfigurable node, since greater understanding of this system component is required: simulation is used to generate cycle-accurate performance estimates. In our work, operations to be implemented on the coprocessor are described in VHDL, although other languages, such as JHDL or

Handel-C could be used, and characterisation is achieved using commercially-available HDL simulation and synthesis tools.

The model of host-coprocessor interaction is generated through extensive analysis of run-time characteristics. These measurements form a "micro-benchmark" of the coprocessor API in which the overheads associated with individual calls and sequences of frequently-used calls are measured, and their dependencies identified. The essential inputs of the analysis toolset are *profile data* concerning the application, a high-level *event trace* (the application execution model), multiple *basic block definitions* and the *API micro-benchmark.* The analysis toolset has been implemented in Perl and is currently command-line driven, although a Tk-based graphical interface is under development.

3.1 Model Construction

A simple method of generating an estimate of performance would be to describe the overall execution time of a program as the sum of the costs of its constituent *functions.* This approach cannot be used, however, since the cost of functions which have control dependencies is not necessarily constant. This problem can be avoided by identifying and then extracting a sequence $f_{n=1}, f_2, \dots f_N$ of *basic blocks* from within the program. A basic block is defined as a maximal-length sequence of instructions for which the only entry point is the first instruction and the only exit point is the last instruction [11]. It is then accurate to express execution time as the sum of the costs of its component basic blocks. Basic blocks are selected based on the proportion of the overall application execution time that can be attributed to them and the efficiency with which they can be implemented on a reconfigurable coprocessor. If suitable basic blocks cannot be extracted from the initial software implementation, it may be necessary to modify the software architecture in order to make this possible. By taking the *host-coprocessor* view of the system, a Equation (1) can be used to describe the total execution time of the application using a reconfigurable coprocessor, T_{RC}.

$$T_{RC} = T_{SW}^{mod} - \sum_{n=1}^{N} \left(T_{BB(n)}^{sw} - T_{BB(n)}^{rc} \right) \tag{1}$$

Equation (1) describes T_{RC} in terms of the cost of the *modified* software implementation and the cost of execution of the basic blocks in both the general-purpose node (i.e. in software) and on the reconfigurable coprocessor. Commercial software profilers were used to identify the most computationally-expensive elements of the original software implementation of the application. These elements were then assessed for suitability as basic blocks, taking into account Amdahl's Law.

3.2 Reconfiguration Overheads

Reconfiguration overheads represent one of the most significant factors limiting the overall performance of the system. Modelling these overheads, which are dependent both on the configuration subsystem of the target reconfigurable technology and the configuration management algorithms used, is very important. In a general-purpose system, frequent reconfiguration of the reconfigurable coprocessor is required. This necessitates ensuring reconfiguration overheads are small, in order that the benefits of using the coprocessor are not masked [16]. In our approach, overheads associated with configuration management are considered separately from the cost of physically altering the configuration data of a particular device. By incorporating management algorithms within the modified software implementation, their contribution to overall execution times can easily be determined. Physical costs are considered to be a function of the coprocessor API and are thus part of each basic block definition. Reconfiguration overheads are now supported by the analysis toolset, having enhanced the way in which basic block are defined. Whether or not a reconfiguration has taken place is determined from the high-level event trace (which is now automatically generated). The analysis toolset parses these traces and then selectively incorporates the relevant overheads associated with a particular basic block.

4 Uncertainty Analysis

In developing a performance model of any sort, it is necessary to generate a reliable estimate of the degree of uncertainty involved and hence determine some degree of confidence in the results produced using the model. Performance estimates for each of the system compute nodes are arrived at using different methods and therefore the associated uncertainty also varies. For the reconfigurable node, cycle-accurate simulations are performed to determine control overheads, latency and throughput. Determining the uncertainty associated with measuring the performance of the general-purpose node is more difficult. A wide range of factors contribute to the uncertainty, including the thread scheduling, memory allocation and virtual memory mechanisms of the host operating system, context switches, interrupts, cache misses, and operating system calls. Profiling encompasses the effects of all these components.

Characterising inter-node communications was achieved using a benchmarking program to measure the execution cost of each of the available API functions. The intrinsic variability of measurements taken on the target system represents a much more significant error in lower-cost API calls, hence the error associated with modelling communications in this way is highly variable. Sequences of API calls that would normally be found together in code were also tested in order to capture context-specific variations. The tests were run using a lightly-loaded system (defined in terms of context-switch activity), identical to that used for direct measurement of general-purpose node performance. A lightly-loaded system was used based on the assumption that if high performance for a given application is a priority, then the system will be a dedicated one.

4.1 Error Propagation

In order to be able to provide at least some analysis of the uncertainty, it is assumed that the error exhibited by direct measurements is normally distributed. In the case where the number of measurements taken is high then the Central Limit Theorem applies. The theorem states that when sampling *any* distribution, the distribution of the sample will approach the normal distribution as the number of samples tends to infinity. Having assumed normally-distributed errors, it is possible to determine how these errors propagate through a computation. If x is a function of two or more measured variables, $x = f(u, v, \ldots)$, and the errors in u and v are small, then the standard deviation of x can be approximated by the error propagation equation, given by Equation (2) [17].

$$\sigma_x^2 \cong \sigma_u^2\left(\frac{\partial x}{\partial u}\right)^2 + \sigma_v^2\left(\frac{\partial x}{\partial v}\right)^2 + \ldots + 2\sigma_{uv}^2\left(\frac{\partial x}{\partial u}\right)\left(\frac{\partial x}{\partial v}\right) + \ldots \tag{2}$$

From Equation (2), it can be shown that if the variations in the measured values u and v, are small and uncorrelated, then on average (and in the limit of a large random selection of observations), the third term in Equation (2), the covariance, should produce equal distributions of positive and negative values and hence vanish. Thus the standard deviation for $x = f(u, v)$ can be approximated by Equation (3).

$$\sigma_x^2 \cong \sigma_u^2\left(\frac{\partial x}{\partial u}\right)^2 + \sigma_v^2\left(\frac{\partial x}{\partial v}\right)^2 \tag{3}$$

From Equation (3), estimates of the standard deviation of x where the measured variables u, v, etc. are combined in some fashion can be derived. These results can then be extended for functions of more than two variables, i.e. $x = f(u, v, w, \ldots)$. The analysis toolset developed makes use of these results, and automatically generates estimates of uncertainty when computing predicted execution times.

5 Evaluation

Where a performance model reflects systems that can be built, the discrepancy between estimates generated by the model and measured results can be evaluated: for systems that cannot be realised, no such comparison can take place. However, where estimates for existing systems are shown to be accurate, this gives credibility to other estimates produced by the same method. Additional credibility is provided by quantifying the degree of uncertainty in the estimate, and then demonstrating that measured values fall within the computed distribution of the error. If model-based estimates are found to be very close to the measured results, then this suggests that the assumptions on which we have based our statistical analysis are reasonable. The aim of this analysis is not to try and eliminate all sources of uncertainty, but to ensure that the uncertainty is not so significant that it affects the conclusions that we wish to draw.

The greatest source of uncertainty in the model are the estimated quantities, or values based on them. In order to provide some assessment of the contribution of different components of the model to the overall uncertainty, profile data was acquired for a real system. The system consisted of a general-purpose workstation enhanced with an RC1000-PP reconfigurable coprocessor from Celoxica. The application used was a medical imaging problem whose computational expense is highly data-dependent [7]. Table 1 describes the modelling error associated with the estimation of T_{RC}, the execution cost of the application using the reconfigurable coprocessor. Tests were performed on six different images in order to assess the relationship between computational load and modelling error, and then repeated 50 times in order to be able to compute distributions. Table 2 provides examples of the errors in modelling basic block execution times. The data in Table 2 represents the measured and predicted costs associated with just a single basic block in each case, but the results are typical. Both tables describe modelling errors, which are defined here as the error in predicted values relative to measured values.

Table 1. Evaluation of modelling error in the estimation of T_{RC}

	T_{RC} Measured		T_{RC} Predicted		Error Bounds		Average Error	
	μ (ms)	σ (ms)	μ (ms)	σ (ms)	lower	upper	μ	σ
#1	307.2	0.6	312.3	7.5	-2.0%	-1.1%	1.7%	0.2%
#2	473.0	0.9	477.9	7.6	-1.3%	-0.6%	1.0%	0.2%
#3	730.5	0.8	731.5	7.6	-0.3%	+0.0%	0.1%	0.1%
#4	891.4	1.0	885.6	7.6	+0.4%	+1.1%	0.7%	0.1%
#5	1011.5	1.3	1004.0	7.0	+0.5%	+1.0%	0.7%	0.1%
#6	1383.6	4.3	1376.7	7.3	+0.2%	+1.6%	0.5%	0.3%

Table 2. Examples of modelling errors in the estimation of basic block execution times

	T_{RC} Measured		T_{RC} Predicted		Error Bounds		Average Error	
	μ (ms)	σ (ms)	μ (ms)	σ (ms)	lower	upper	μ	σ
#1	45.8	0.3	46.1	0.2	-1.2%	+2.2%	1.0%	0.2%
#2	48.1	0.5	48.5	0.2	-1.3%	+4.5%	1.2%	0.5%
#3	36.4	0.2	36.7	0.2	-1.2%	+2.6%	1.0%	0.3%
#4	48.2	0.5	48.7	0.2	-1.4%	+4.2%	1.3%	0.5%
#5	44.6	0.2	44.7	0.2	-0.7%	+1.7%	0.6%	0.2%
#6	48.5	0.2	49.0	0.2	-1.2%	+1.5%	1.1%	0.2%

Overall, the data indicates that the model produces slight overestimates of the cost of basic blocks, with the effect that speed-up is slightly *underestimated.* It is likely that as the number of basic blocks increases, the model will produce more accurate results. The reason for this is that statistical methods are often based on assumptions which are only reasonable when the sample size is large. The approach taken in characterising host-coprocessor communication thus becomes more appropriate when the number of API calls made increases. Failure to adequately characterise host-coprocessor communication overheads is considered to be the most significant shortcoming of earlier work. Also, although the results in Table 1 suggest an overall estimation accuracy of ±2.0% (compared with the ±8.1% previously reported [8]), the results in Table 2 indicate that errors in modelling basic blocks are closer to ±5%. Hence, in the limit where the entire execution time consists of basic blocks, the estimation error should approach ±5%. The asymmetry of the error bounds is due to the distribution of the profile data exhibiting positive skew. This skew is also the reason for the mean error being significantly smaller than the upper bound, and results in the modelling of inter-node communications contributing the most to the overall error.

This method uses a two-stage approach, the first involving data acquisition and the second involving combination the performance data with model-based estimates. The main limitation of this approach is the cost of acquiring performance data initially (i.e. hardware simulations and application profiling, which must be repeated for each set of application parameters of interest). Once performance data is available, model evaluation is very rapid (but dependent on the number of basic blocks extracted and thus theoretically unbounded). For the case study presented here, model evaluation required ~70ms on a 1.4GHz Pentium 4-based workstation.

6 Conclusions and Future Work

A method for modelling the performance of general-purpose workstations enhanced with a reconfigurable coprocessor has been presented. Initial results suggest that the method offers a greater degree of accuracy in estimating system-level performance than competing approaches. Accuracy is achieved through a combination of low-overhead profiling, cycle-accurate simulations and the use of an explicit profile-based model of inter-processor communication and control overheads. By combining the strengths of a commercial C/C++ compiler, profiler, HDL simulator and synthesis tool with a custom-designed analysis toolset, this method can be used to provide detailed information on execution times (along with an approximate uncertainty), scalability, applicability and resource usage. The toolset, which has been implemented in Perl, is currently being used to investigate the *limits of applicability* of reconfigurable coprocessors in general-purpose systems. The next stage of this work is to extend the model to support latency-toleration strategies, and then incorporate resource management algorithms for partially-reconfigurable and multi-context architectures.

Acknowledgements

The support of the UK Engineering & Physical Sciences Research Council (EPSRC) under grant GR/M16078 is gratefully acknowledged. The authors also wish to thank the anonymous referees for their constructive comments.

References

1. Y. Yamaguchi, A. Miyashita, T. Maruyama, T. Hoshino, "A Co-processor System with a Virtex FPGA for Evolutionary Computation", *Proc. 10th Intl. Workshop on Field Programmable Logic and Applications,* FPL'00, LNCS#1896, Springer-Verlag (2000)
2. K. Leung, K. Ma, W. Wong, P. Leong, "FPGA Implementation of a Microcoded Elliptic Curve Cryptographic Processor", *Proc. 8th Intl. Symposium on FPGAs for Custom Computing Machines,* FCCM'00, pp. 68-76, IEEE Computer Society (2000)
3. B. Carrión-Schäfer, S. Quigley, A. Chan, "Analysis and Implementation of the Discrete Element Method using a Dedicated Highly Parallel Architecture in Reconfigurable Computing", to appear in *Proc. 10th Intl. Symposium on FPGAs for Custom Computing Machines,* FCCM'02, IEEE Computer Society (2002)
4. S. Sudhir, N. Suman, S. Goldstein, "Configuration Caching and Swapping", *Proc. 11th Intl. Workshop on Field Programmable Logic and Applications*, FPL'01, LNCS#2147, pp. 192-202, Springer-Verlag (2001)
5. S. Singh, S. Slous, "Accelerating Adobe Photoshop with Reconfigurable Logic", *Proc. 6th Intl. Symposium on FPGAs for Custom Computing Machines,* FCCM'98, IEEE Computer Society (1998)
6. M. Dao, T. Cook, D. Silver, P. D'Urbano, "Acceleration of Template-Based Ray Casting for Volume Visualisation using FPGAs", *3rd Intl. Symposium on FPGAs for Custom Computing Machines*, FCCM'95, pp. 116-123, IEEE Computer Society (1995)
7. S. Charlwood, J. Mangnall, S. Quigley, "Model-Based Performance Analysis for Reconfigurable Coprocessors", in "Reconfigurable Technology: FPGAs and Reconfigurable Processors for Computing and Communications", Proc. of SPIE Vol. 4525, SPIE (2001)
8. K. Chatha, R. Vemuri, "Performance Evaluation Tool for Rapid Prototyping of Hardware-Software Codesigns", *Proc. 9th Intl. Workshop on Rapid System Prototyping*, RSP'98, IEEE Computer Society (1998)
9. K. Bondalapati, "Modeling and Mapping for Dynamically Reconfigurable Hybrid Architectures", PhD Thesis, University of Southern California (2001)
10. D. Kerbyson, E. Papeafstathiou, J. Harper, S. Perry, G. Nudd, "Is Predictive Tracing Too Late for HPC Users?", *High Performance Computing*, Plenum Press (1998)
11. Y. Li, S. Malik, "Performance Analysis of Embedded Software Using Implicit Path Enumeration", *Proc. 32nd ACM/IEEE Design Automation Conference*, DAC'95 (1995)
12. S.-S. Lim, Y. Bae, G., Jang, et al. "An Accurate Worst-Case Timing Analysis for RISC Processors", *IEEE Transactions on Software Engineering*, Vol. 21, No. 7, IEEE (1995)
13. T. Hey, A. Dunlop, E. Hernández, "Realistic Parallel Performance Estimation", *Parallel Computing*, Vol. 23, pp. 5-21 (1997)
14. K. Bondalapati, V. Prasanna, "DRIVE: An Interpretive Simulation and Visualization Environment for Dynamically Reconfigurable Systems", *Proc. 9th Intl. Workshop on Field Programmable Logic and Applications*, FPL'99, LNCS#1673, Springer-Verlag (1999)
15. J. Walrath, R. Vemuri, "A Performance Modeling and Analysis Environment for Reconfigurable Computers", *Proc. Reconfigurable Architectures Workshop,* RAW'98, LNCS#1388, Springer-Verlag (1998)
16. R. Hartenstein, M. Herz., T. Hoffman, U. Nageldinger, "On Reconfigurable Co-Processing Units", Proc. Reconfigurable Architectures Workshop, RAW'98, LNCS#1388, Springer-Verlag (1998)
17. P. Bevington, D. Robinson, "Data Reduction and Error Analysis for the Physical Sciences", 2nd Edition, McGraw-Hill (1994)

An FPGA Based SHA-256 Processor

Kurt K. Ting, Steve C.L. Yuen, K.H. Lee, and Philip H.W. Leong

Dept. of Computer Science and Engineering
The Chinese University of Hong Kong
New Territories, Hong Kong
{kting,clyuen,khlee,phwl}@cse.cuhk.edu.hk

Abstract. The design, implementation and system level performance of an efficient yet compact field programmable gate array (FPGA) based Secure Hash Algorithm 256 (SHA-256) processor is presented. On a Xilinx Virtex XCV300E-8 FPGA, the SHA-256 processor utilizes 1261 slices and has a throughput of 87 MB/s at 88 MHz. When measured on actual hardware operating at 66 MHz, it had a maximum measured system throughput of 53 MB/s.

1 Introduction

Field programmable gate array (FPGA) devices provide an excellent technology for the implementation of general purpose cryptographic devices. Compared with application specific integrated circuits (ASIC), FPGAs offer lower non-recurring engineering costs, shorter design time, greater flexibility and the ability to change the algorithm or design in the field. They have been used in a number of high performance cryptosystems including RSA [12], DES [13], Rijndael (AES) [6] and IDEA [10]. FPGA implementations of cryptographic algorithms have applications as coprocessors for microprocessor based systems or in high performance embedded applications.

The Secure Hash Signature Standard (SHS) was proposed by the US National Institute of Standards and Technology (NIST) in 2001 [9]. The standard describes four secure hash algorithms (SHA) and the version which outputs a 256-bit message digest is referred to as SHA-256. In this paper, only SHA-256 will be considered, although adapting the design to other digest sizes should be trivial.

Applications of the SHS include generating and verifying digital signatures, generating and verifying message authentication codes and also increasing the entropy in pseudo random number generators.

In this paper, a novel architecture for the implementation of the SHA-256 hash algorithm is presented. Making extensive use of shift registers, the design is compact yet achieves high performance. The system level performance of the SHA-256 core was tested on the Pilchard reconfigurable computing platform [11].

Although FPGA based processors for the MD5 hash algorithm have been proposed [4,5], we are not aware of any published designs for SHA-256 processors. A NIST validated commercial SHA-1 and MD5 core is available from Tality

M. Glesner, P. Zipf, and M. Renovell (Eds.): FPL 2002, LNCS 2438, pp. 577–585, 2002.

Corporation [1] which operates at 75MHz in $0.25\mu m$ technology and achieves 59 MB/s throughput.

SecuCore [2] is a commercial SHA-256 IPcore, featuring a maximum frequency of 166 MHz in a $0.18\mu m$ process with a throughput of 156 MB/s. Both the SecuCore processor and our FPGA-based SHA-256 processor use $0.18\mu m$ technology. The two designs require a similar number of clock cycles so the higher performance of the SecuCore implementation is due to the higher clock rate (166 MHz vs 88 MHz). One would expect an ASIC implementation to have a higher clock rate than an FPGA due its customized logic and routing.

The rest of the paper is organized as follows: in Section 2, the SHA-256 algorithm is described. Section 3 describes the architecture of the processor. Performance measurements are presented in Section 4, future work is described in Section 5, and conclusions are drawn in Section 6.

2 SHA-256 Algorithm

The SHA-256 algorithm takes a message of length less than 2^{64}-bits and produces as output, a message digest 256-bits in length. The digest serves as a concise representation of the message, and has the property that any change to the message is very likely to result in a change to the corresponding digest. The SHA-256 algorithm has a security of 128-bits, meaning that a birthday attack [7] can produce a collision in $O(2^{128})$ time.

In the SHA-256 algorithm, six logical functions which operate on 32-bit values are used:

$$\begin{aligned} Ch(x,y,z) &= (x \wedge y) \oplus (\sim x \wedge z) \\ Maj(x,y,z) &= (x \wedge y) \oplus (x \wedge z) \oplus (y \wedge z) \\ \Sigma_0(x) &= \mathrm{ROTR}^2(x) \oplus \mathrm{ROTR}^{13}(x) \oplus \mathrm{ROTR}^{22}(x) \\ \Sigma_1(x) &= \mathrm{ROTR}^6(x) \oplus \mathrm{ROTR}^{11}(x) \oplus \mathrm{ROTR}^{25}(x) \\ \sigma_0(x) &= \mathrm{ROTR}^7(x) \oplus \mathrm{ROTR}^{18}(x) \oplus \mathrm{SHR}^3(x) \\ \sigma_1(x) &= \mathrm{ROTR}^{17}(x) \oplus \mathrm{ROTR}^{19}(x) \oplus \mathrm{SHR}^{10}(x) \end{aligned}$$

where $\wedge$, $\sim$ and $\oplus$ are the bitwise AND, NOT and XOR operations; and ROTR and SHR are the rotate right and shift right functions respectively.

In order to hash a message M of l bits, a preprocessing step is first performed:

1. A "one" bit is appended to the end of the message, followed by k "zero" bits where k is the smallest non-negative solution to the equation $l + 1 + k \equiv 448 \bmod 512$. The binary representation of l as a 64-bit number is then appended so the length of the padded message is a multiple of 512-bits.
2. The padded message is then divided into N 512-bit blocks $M^{(1)}, M^{(2)}, \ldots M^{(N)}$.
3. The initial values of eight 32-bit words $H_j^{(0)}$ $(j = 0, 1, \ldots 7)$ are initialized to the first thirty-two bits of the fractional parts of the square roots of the first eight prime numbers.

The message blocks are then processed as follows for i = 1 to N:

1. The message schedule W_t ($t = 0 \ldots 63$) is prepared according to the equation

$$W_t = \begin{cases} M_t^{(i)} & 0 \le t \le 15 \\ \sigma_1(W_{t-2}) + W_{t-7} + \sigma_0(W_{t-15}) + W_{t-16} & 16 \le t \le 63 \end{cases} \quad (1)$$

2. Eight 32-bit working variables a, b, c, d, e, f, g, h are initialized to $H_0^{(i-1)}$, $H_1^{(i-1)}$, $H_2^{(i-1)}$, $H_3^{(i-1)}$, $H_4^{(i-1)}$, $H_5^{(i-1)}$, $H_6^{(i-1)}$, $H_7^{(i-1)}$ respectively.
3. The compression function is performed for t = 0 to 63:

$$T_1 = h + \Sigma_1(e) + Ch(e,f,g) + K_t + W_t; T_2 = \Sigma_0(a) + Maj(a,b,c)$$
$$h = g; g = f; f = e; e = d + T_1; d = c; c = b; b = a; a = T_1 + T_2$$

4. The intermediate hash $H^{(i)}$ is computed:

$$H_0^{(i)} = a + H_0^{(i-1)}; H_1^{(i)} = b + H_1^{(i-1)}; H_2^{(i)} = c + H_2^{(i-1)}; H_3^{(i)} = d + H_3^{(i-1)};$$
$$H_4^{(i)} = e + H_4^{(i-1)}; H_5^{(i)} = f + H_5^{(i-1)}; H_6^{(i)} = g + H_6^{(i-1)}; H_7^{(i)} = h + H_7^{(i-1)}$$

The final digest is formed by concatenating the final hash values

$$H_0^{(N)}, H_1^{(N)}, H_2^{(N)}, H_3^{(N)}, H_4^{(N)}, H_5^{(N)}, H_6^{(N)}, H_7^{(N)}$$

3 System Architecture

A shift register based approach was used to implement the SHA-256 algorithm which results in a fast and compact design. This architecture was inspired by NIST's descriptions of secure hash algorithms [8]. By inspecting the algorithm description in Section 2, it can be seen that the message schedule and compression function map naturally to a shift register structure.

The core contains three main components which implement the message scheduler, compression function and intermediate hash. These are controlled by a finite state machine which schedules the three blocks.

3.1 Message Scheduler

The message scheduler is implemented as a chain of sixteen 32-bit shift registers which store the intermediate message schedules W_t. Figure 1 shows the hardware architecture used to implement equation 1. It uses 16 cycles to load sixteen initial 32-bit words, ${M_t}^{(i)}$ for $t = 0$ to 15. During the 64 iterations of $t = 0$ to 63, it provides the message schedule W_t for the compression function by shifting the values in the chain from left to right. In the hardware implementation, W_t is added to the constant K_t to form W_K_t before being sent to the compression function. The rationale for moving the addition of K_t from the compression function to the message scheduler was to reduce the critical path of the compression function. This scheme results in a speedup of approximately 20%.

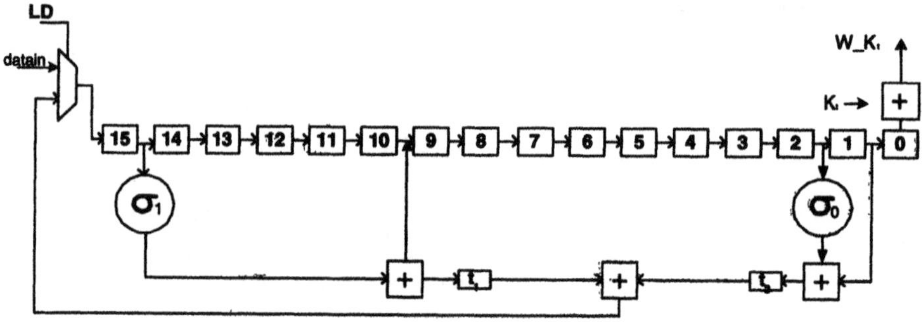

Fig. 1. Message scheduler block diagram.

3.2 Compression Function

The compression function module was implemented using shift registers, in a manner similar to the message scheduler. The 8 working variables $a, b, \ldots h$ are stored in eight 32-bit shift registers and connected according to Figure 2. The critical path in the design is the computation of $a = \sum_0 + Maj(a, b, c) + \sum_1 + Ch(e, f, g) + h + W + K_t$. The path was therefore pipelined by inserting a latch between $\sum_1 + Ch(e, f, g) + h + W\_K_t$ and $a = \sum_0 + Maj(a, b, c)$ (shown as "L" in Figure 2, with functions before "L" taking inputs earlier along the chain).

By-pass logic was also added between registers d and e to allow the outputs of the compression function, $a, b, \ldots h$ to be shifted out through h. The loading of values into the message scheduler is fully overlapped with the operations of the compression function, a new message block being loaded when the previous message block is in the 48th round of the compression function.

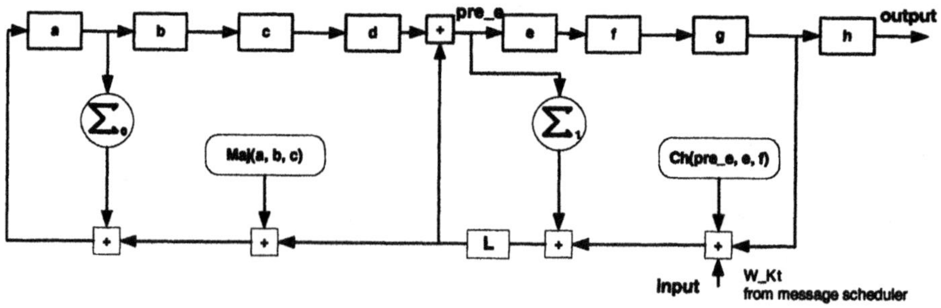

Fig. 2. Compression function block diagram.

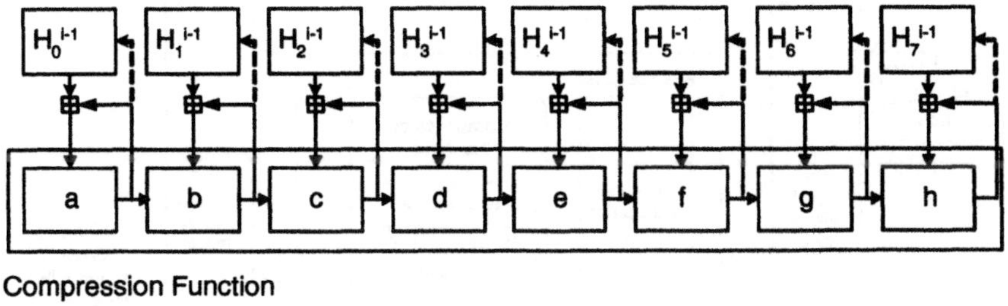

Fig. 3. Intermediate Hash from Compression Function.

3.3 Intermediate Hash

After 64 iterations of compression function, eight 32-bit intermediate values stored in the working variables $a, b, \ldots h$ are obtained. To compute the intermediate hash $H^{(i)}$, the working variables are added to the previous intermediate hash $H^{(i-1)}$ and written back to the registers. In the hardware implementation, $H^{(i-1)}$ is stored in another 256-bit latch and updated before the 64 iterations of the compression function begins. This is illustrated in Figure 3. The path in dashed lines is used for updating $H^{(i-1)}$ and the path in solid lines calculates the current intermediate hash $H^{(i)}$.

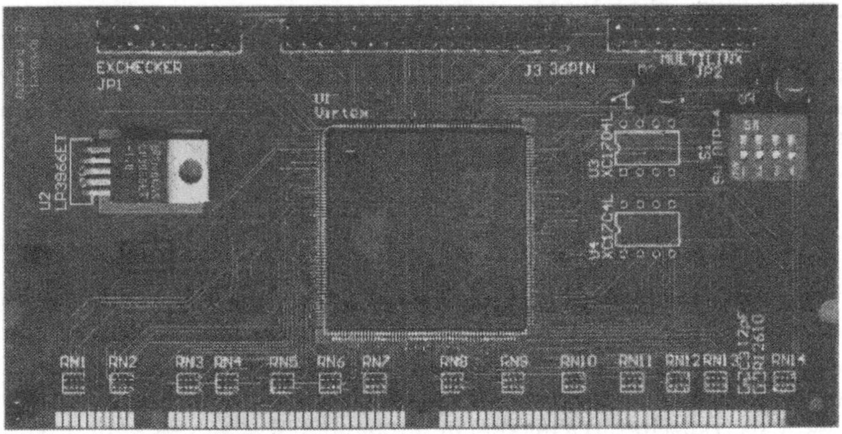

Fig. 4. Photograph of the Pilchard board.

3.4 PC Interface

The FPGA platform used was a Pilchard FPGA card (Figure 4) [11] populated with a Xilinx Virtex XCV300E-8 FPGA. Pilchard uses a SDRAM memory bus

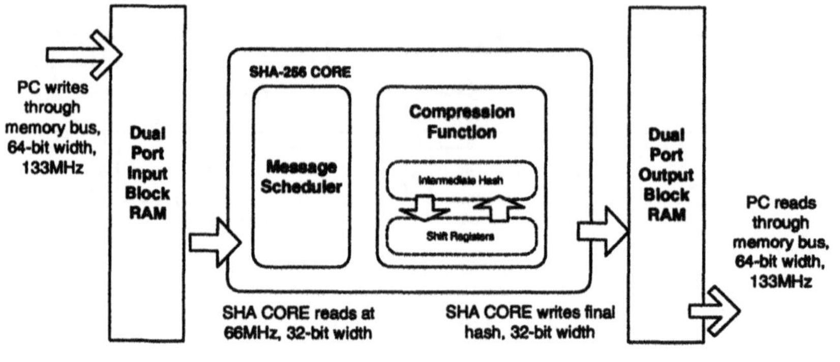

Fig. 5. PC interface block diagram.

interface instead of the conventional PCI bus and has much improved latency and bandwidth over the standard PCI bus.

The Pilchard platform provides a 64-bit wide memory mapped bus to the FPGA. In the current configuration, PC reads and writes operate at 133 MHz, which is the clock speed of the memory bus. The SHA core operates at a lower clock rate (66 MHz). In order to interface the two, on-chip dual port Block RAM was used. As shown in Figure 5, to compute a digest, the PC writes 64-bit data at 133 MHz to the input Block RAM. The SHA core reads 32-bit data at 66 MHz from the other port of the Block RAM and writes the resulting digest value to the 32-bit output Block RAM.

Polling was used to ensure reliable communications between the host PC and the SHA core. The PC signals the SHA core to start after it has filled the input buffer and polls the core until it signals that it has finished. It then fills the buffer again.

4 Results

The design was synthesized and implemented using the Xilinx ISE 4 tools and tested on the Pilchard platform. On a Xilinx Virtex XCV300E-8 FPGA, the SHA-256 core has a maximum frequency of 88 MHz (as reported by the Xilinx tools). Each 512-bit message block requires 8 cycles to load and 65 cycles to process. This translates to a maximum throughput of $\frac{512}{8\times65} \times 88 \times 10^6 = 87$ MB/s for an 88 MHz clock. In the actual implementation on Pilchard, the system clock was 133 MHz and the SHA-256 core was operated using a half rate 66 MHz clock. This configuration has a maximum throughput of 65 MB/s.

4.1 Resource Usage

A summary of the resource utilization of the SHA-256 implementation (including interface logic) in shown below. According to the Xilinx tools, the design

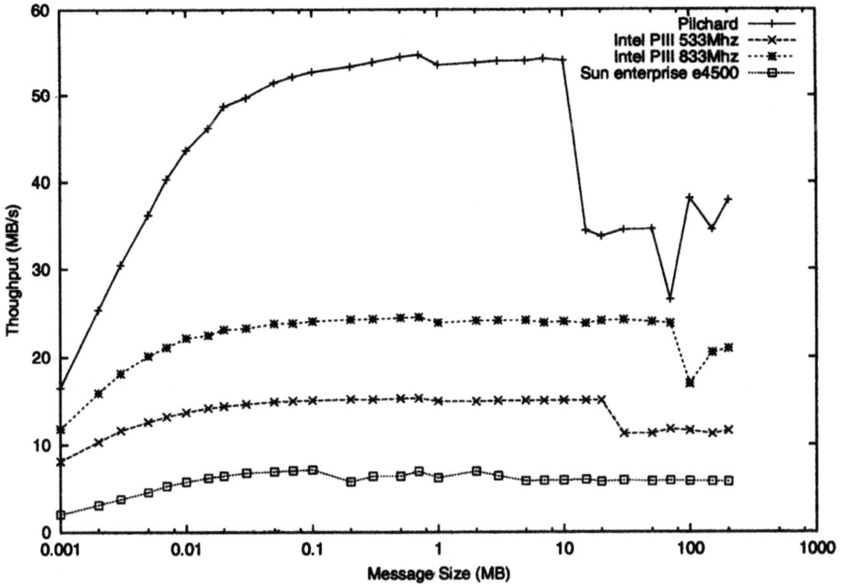

Fig. 6. Measured throughput of the Pilchard and software-only implementations as a function of the file size.

(including host interface) uses 1,261 Virtex slices and has an equivalent gate count of 167,190 gates.

The SHA-256 processor was tested on a Pilchard card hosted on a 533 MHz Intel Pentium III machine with 128MB RAM. Files containing randomly generated numbers with sizes between 1K and 200 MB were tested and the results verified with the mhash software library [3]. For each different input file size, the test was repeated 20 times and averaged.

The top trace of Figure 6 shows the measured system throughput in MB/s verses the input file size on a log scale. The results include all file I/O and operating system overheads as they are the times computed for computing a digest of an actual file. The throughput quickly saturates to a maximum value of 53 MB/s for file sizes greater than 200 KB. For the "uncacheable" memory type range register (MTRR) that was used, Pilchard is capable of a throughput of 132 MB/s, and the SHA-256 core 65 MB/s, thus the overall system throughput was limited by the handshaking overhead associated with the SHA-256 core.

For file sizes larger than 30 MB, throughput drops to approximately 30MB/s. A possible explanation for this strange phenomenon is that performance is greater for the smaller files due to the operating system caching the file reads.

The mhash optimized software implementation of SHA-256 [3] was also used for performance comparison purposes. Throughput measurements on Intel Pentium and Sun Enterprise machines are shown in the bottom traces of Figure 6. It is interesting to note a similar drop in throughput associated with large input file sizes in the software implementation. The hardware performance is more than double that of the 833 MHz Pentium III software implementation for file sizes up to 20 MB, and for larger file sizes, the FPGA version is about 50% faster.

The FPGA design has approximately a two times speed improvement over an 833 MHz Pentium III processor. However, this was achieved using a single chip compared with a workstation. FPGA based implementations have advantages in terms of cost, memory, energy and size over a software implementation, which may be important considerations in embedded applications.

5 Future Work

We are working on several improvements to the present design which could serve to improve the performance and flexibility of the SHA-256 system.

- Padding of the message is currently performed in software. In some applications it might be necessary to perform the message padding in hardware.
- Multiple SHA-256 processors could be instantiated in the FPGA as each only uses 40% of the resources. This would allow multiple files to be hashed simultaneously.
- With better floorplanning, routing delays could be significantly reduced and the performance of our design could be significantly improved.
- Larger buffers between the host and the SHA-256 core would serve to reduce the overheads associated with handshaking, increasing system throughput.
- It is possible to reduce the number of cycles, hence improving both latency and throughput via a parallel load facility so that several shift registers can be loaded in a single cycle.

6 Conclusion

In this paper, a shift register based architecture for implementing a SHA-256 processor was presented. This approach combines modest hardware requirements with high performance (87 MB/s). Detailed measurements of system level performance were reported, the system being about to compute SHA-256 digests with a throughput of 53 MB/s, the performance being limited by handshaking overheads. Suggestions for further improving the throughput of the system were given.

References

1. *www.tality.com.*
2. *http://www.secucore.com/products.htm.*
3. *http://mhash.sourceforge.net/.*
4. J. Arnold. Mapping the MD5 hash algorithm onto the NAPA architecture. In *Proceedings of the IEEE Symposium on Field-Programmable Custom Computing Machines (FCCM)*, pages 267–268, 1998.

5. J. Deepakumara, H.M. Heys, and R. Venkatesan. FPGA implementation of MD5 hash algorithm. In *Proceedings of the Canadian Conference on Electrical and Computer Engineering*, volume 2, pages 919–924, 2001.
6. M. McLoone and J. McCanny. High performance single-chip FPGA Rijndael algorithm implementations. In *Proceedings of the Cryptographic Hardware and Embedded Systems Workshop (CHES)*, pages 65–76. LNCS 2162, Springer, 2001.
7. A. Menezes, P. van Oorschoot, and S. Vanstone. *Handbook of Applied Cryptography*. CRC Press, 1997.
8. NIST. Descriptions of sha-256, sha-384, and sha-512. *available from http://csrc.nist.gov/encryption/shs/sha256-384-512.pdf*.
9. NIST. *Secure Hash Signature Standard (FIPS PUB 180-2)*. 2001.
10. O.Y.H. Cheung, K.H. Tsoi, K.H. Leung, P.H.W. Leong, and M.P. Leong. Tradeoffs in parallel and serial implementations of the international data encryption algorithm IDEA. In *Proceedings of the Cryptographic Hardware and Embedded Systems Workshop (CHES)*, pages 333–347. LNCS 2162, Springer, 2001.
11. P.H.W. Leong, M.P. Leong, O.Y.H. Cheung, T. Tung, C.M. Kwok, M.Y. Wong, and K.H. Lee. Pilchard – a reconfigurable computing platform with memory slot interface. In *Proceedings of the IEEE Symposium on Field-Programmable Custom Computing Machines (FCCM) – to appear*, 2001.
12. M. Shand and J. E. Vuillemin. Fast implementations of RSA cryptography. In E. E. Swartzlander, M. J. Irwin, and J. Jullien, editors, *Proceedings of the 11th IEEE Symposium on Computer Arithmetic*, pages 252–259. IEEE Computer Society Press, Los Alamitos, CA, 1993.
13. S. Trimberger, R. Pang, and A. Singh. A 12Gbps DES Encryptor/Decryptor core in an FPGA. In *Proceedings of the Cryptographic Hardware and Embedded Systems Workshop (CHES)*, pages 156–163. Springer, 2000.

Handling FPGA Faults and Configuration Sequencing Using a Hardware Extension

P. Zipf[1], M. Glesner[1], C. Bauer[2], and H. Wojtkowiak[2]

[1] Institute of Microelectronic Systems
Darmstadt University of Technology, Germany.
{zipf,glesner}@mes.tu-darmstadt.de
[2] Fachgruppe Technische Informatik
University of Siegen, Germany.
{bauer,wojtkowiak}@ti.et-inf.uni-siegen.de

Abstract. Run-time reconfiguration (RTR) applied to field-programmable logic allows for fast reconfiguration of parts of a user circuit in the presense of faults in the underlying programmable logic. The regular structure of field-programmable gate arrays (FPGAs) and the independence of the implemented system from the programmable hardware are the basis for a reasonable small implementation of a fault tolerance concept in hardware. In this paper we describe a hardware structure called *reconfiguration control unit* (RCU) which realizes a reconfiguration controller. Exchanging configurations is a frequent task in RTR applications, usually left to a host computer system. Applying the RCU to such tasks, a host system becomes obsolete and the time needed for reconfiguration can be minimized.

1 Introduction

Because of their regular structure, field programmable gate arrays (FPGAs) offer the possibility to detect occuring faults in their cells and react on them. When mapping arbitrary functions into groups of cells redundancy can be generated by leaving a fraction of the cells unused. These spare cells can serve as a replacement for faulty cells in their neighborhood by applying a different mapping of the logic functionality into the local cell group. The partial run-time reconfiguration capability can be used to reprogram an area containing the defect cell and thus exclude this cell from further use. There are several techniques to do this reported in [11] and [1].

Fault tolerance approaches for field programmable logic rely on an efficient way to react on a detected fault and to handle all necessary reconfiguration tasks. This is usually left to an attached host system performing the reconfiguration by executing specific software. Using software on an external system is a very inefficient way to reconfigure. A local handling mechanism for both performing the necessary steps for detecting a fault and doing the reconfiguration is needed. Ideally, such a mechanism would not need to access any external components but includes everything needed. Our *reconfiguration control unit* (RCU) proposed in

M. Glesner, P. Zipf, and M. Renovell (Eds.): FPL 2002, LNCS 2438, pp. 586–595, 2002.

[17] fulfils these requirements. After a fault is detected either by a configurated test circuit or by special hardware inside the FPGA logic cells, an algorithm implemented as hardware looks up a valid alternative configuration for the affected area and starts a reconfiguration cycle also directly implemented as hardware.

Because a reconfiguration after a fault is not different from a reconfiguration for sequencing successive user circuits on the programmable logic, the RCU can also be used for configuration sequencing. Like this, it can support (partial) run-time reconfiguration as used in many different areas of field programmable logic, ranging from simple task sequencing in [16] to virtual hardware in [4, 5].

Other research on the topic of fault handling that is considered here is about architectures for BIST/BISR, fault-detection by configurated circuits, fault bypassing by reconfiguration, and redundancy organization.

The built-in selftest and built-in self-repair approaches are both capable of detecting faults and making this information accessible. Durand and Piguet have proposed an FPGA architecture with cells suitable to detect run-time faults [6]. The single cells are extended by multiplexers and registers, allowing a sequential usage of different paths for the same operation, thus revealing different path results due to a fault. A complete row containing a faulty cell is bypassed and replaced by a spare row. In [14] and [1] the usage of a test structure configured into the FPGA is introduced. For this method of fault-detection, existing FPGAs can be used with only minor or no extensions. In [14] a reserved cell column holds a test control configuration while a second column is used as a cache for the cells in the column under test and takes over its functionality. The interchangeability of cells for testing purposes is accomplished by extra hardware inside the cells. Faults are signaled by an additional connection network. Row and column scanning test circuits called roving STARs are configured and moved over the FPGA in [1] to detect and locate faults. This aproach does not need special FPGA hardware and can be applied to any FPGA currently available. It is claimed that the fault scanning allows for cell testing without suspending the current operation. The method can also detect faults in the local interconnect. A method to bypass faulty cells in a cell group by providing alternative configurations for that group is proposed in [11]. For every possible fault position in a group, a configuration is provided that leaves exactly the cell containing the fault position unused. The alternative configurations must be generated in advance. It is assumed that faults are detected by other means. Finally, in [2] a first simulation model of our own FPGA prototype is descibed. It implements a fault detecting cell group organization where each group of 3 cells is complemented by one special cell used to detect faults in the group. The fault detection can be switched off leaving a fully functional group of 4 equivalent cells.

Based on the described methods it is possible to find and insert an appropriate replacement configuration after a fault is detected that does not use the defect cell anymore. We assume configuration data sets leaving one unused cell per block like the tiles in [11]. Reservation schemes for unused local resources can be found in [12, 13].

The basic concept and the structure of the RCU are presented in section 2. The application of the RCU as a reconfiguration controller is given in section 3. Finally, section 4 discusses first experimental results, and section 5 gives a summary and outlines our future plans.

2 The Reconfiguration Control Unit

The related work discussed provides solutions for different problems faced in implementing fault tolerant systems on FPGAs. There is no solution given of how to efficiently perform the reconfiguration. So far, a host system is assumed to do this. For embedded systems however, an external host system or even extensive software usage is unavailable or too costly.

We propose the *reconfiguration control unit* (RCU) to locally perform the tasks of recieving detected faults, mapping of fault positions on configuration blocks, and reconfiguration of the affected block, avoiding any external host system. The RCU is a hardware module which has access to the internal FPGA structures using the run-time reconfiguration port and special fault lines connecting it to the internal fault detection mechanism of the cells. Unlike other hardware-based approaches for reconfiguration, the RCU is not application specific and suitable for many FPGA-like reconfigurable cell arrays. It is integrated into the configuration port of the FPGA, avoiding an extra chip in the system. Figure 1 shows the structure of the RCU and its interaction with the FPGA and the configuration set memory.

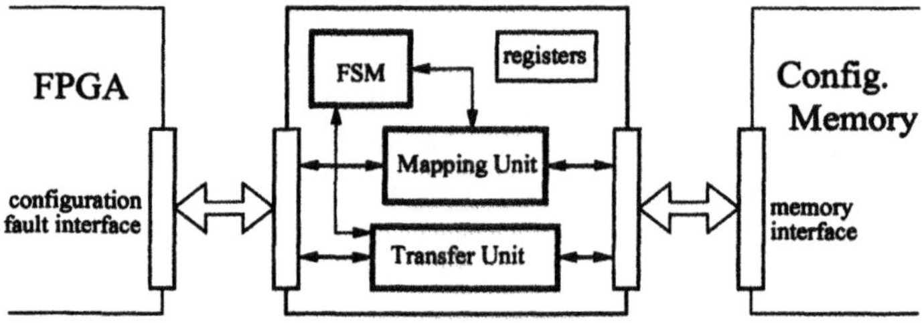

Fig. 1. *Structure of the RCU*

Prerequisite for an application of the RCU is an automatic fault detection inside the FPGA like in [6, 2]. Fault scanning algorithms based on configured test circuitry [14, 1] usually cause a high detection latency and seem to be not well suited to detect transient faults like single-event-upsets. Nevertheless, moving test configurations across the cell array being a typical reconfiguration task can be performed by an extended RCU. In our experimental FPGA model [2] we use a single-stuck-at and a single-event-upset (SEU) fault model for the cell data paths only. At the level of the implemented system however we can assume a more abstract model, distinguishing only between permanent and transient faults in the logic cells. Interconnect faults must be handled separately.

Recieving a Detected Fault After a fault is detected the corresponding fault lines are set to signal the fault position [2]. As pictured in figure 2, every cell is connected to an adjacent column and row line.

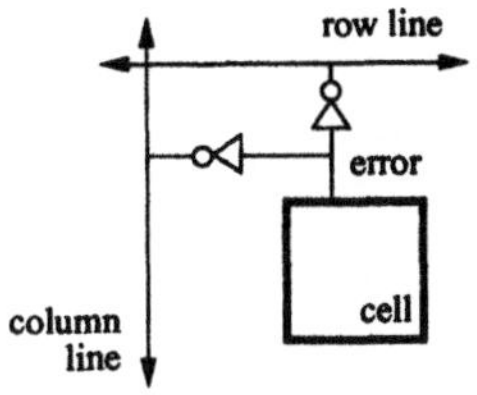

Fig. 2. *Fault lines*

In a subsequent encoder the row and column numbers are generated as bit vectors. The detected cell must now be removed from the cell set used by the configured user circuit.

It is always assumed that the fault disables the whole cell and is permanent. This reduces the test phase dramatically, because neither the FPGA's configuration RAM integrity nor the exact type of cell malfunction need to be checked. Permanent faults always lead to a reconfiguration of the block containing the faulty cell. The alternative configuration used defines the faulty cell's location as a spare [11].

Mapping of Fault Positions To bypass a faulty cell, another functional mapping, and thus a different configuration data set must be applied. For cell blocks with reserved spare cells, the minimal block size must be 2 cells, one active cell and one spare [13]. A more realistic block size would be 4 or 16 cells, including the one spare cell. The row and column fault position vectors are split into the block position and the position inside that block and both combined with their conterpart as shown in figure 3. At this point, a mapping table is used to de-

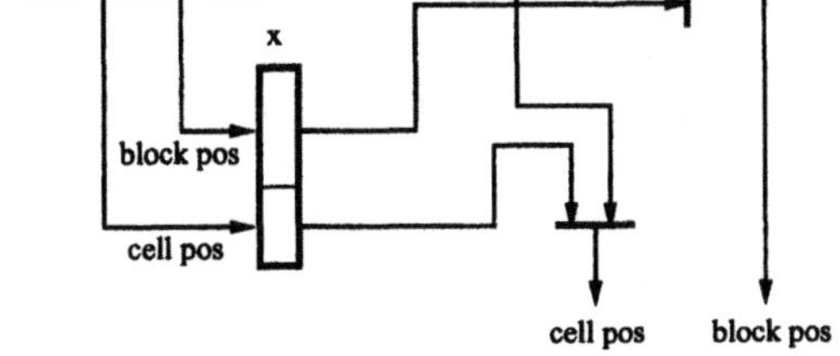

Fig. 3. *Cell position decoding*

termine a configuration set start address in memory from the cell position. The block position is used as an index into a lookup table associating a configuration set with its start address in memory. The cell position components inside the block then give the offset inside the sets as shown in figure 4. Adding this offset

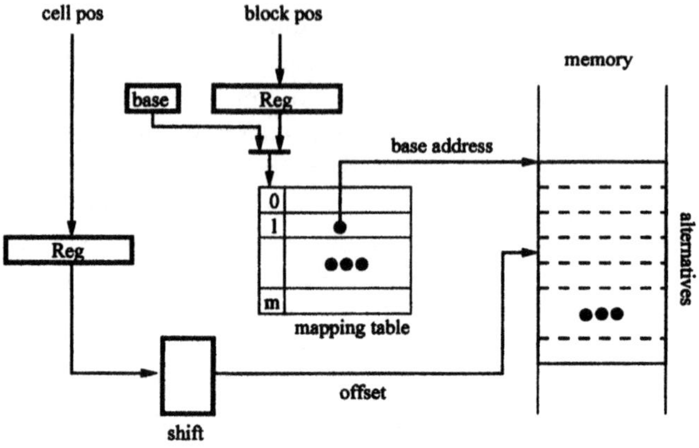

Fig. 4. *Configuration selection table*

to the configuration start address leads to an alternative set leaving the indexing cell as a spare. The lookup table for the block start addresses is located in the external configuration memory.

Reconfiguration To reconfigure the affected block, the RCU loads the transfer size for the block into an internal register and starts a data transfer from memory into the configuration RAM of the cell array.

To support this, the configuration data sets are structured in an address word/data word style. Currently, we are using an Xilinx 6200 series-like FPGA addressing scheme. Every data word has its corresponding address word. The address word gives the RAM position inside the cell array and the data word can be directly written to that location. The first word of the set is the number of words to transfer. Figure 5 shows the structure of a data set. Alternatively, if the RAM address is not provided for every single data word, an address generator scheme can be used because of the regular structure of the FPGA cell configuration memory.

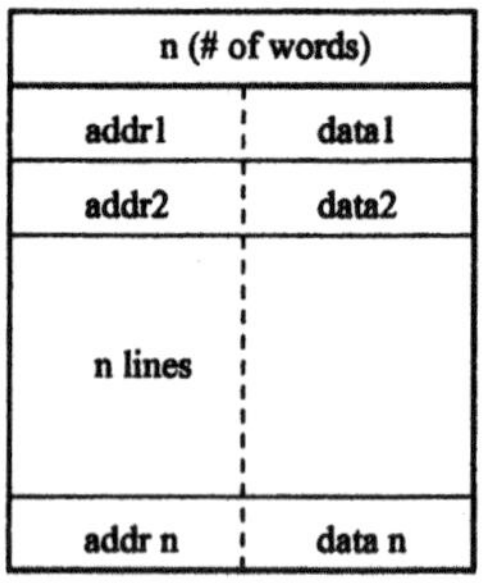

Fig. 5. *Configuration data set*

Fault positions are logged in a status register that is accessible from the application. It is possible to also generate an interrupt to notify the application.

As a reaction on the interrupt at a higher system level, error recovery measures can be taken. If the application supports checkpointing, a rollback operation could be initiated.

The described RCU tasks build up a complete fault reaction chain enabling the FPGA to regain a fault-free state within a minimum number of cycles.

3 Reconfiguration Tasks

The task of exchanging partial configurations of an FPGA is widely used in other applications of reconfigurable logic like the DISC processor [16], the RACE system [15], temporal partitioning [8], virtualized reconfigurable computing resources [4, 5], or the increase of FPGA functional density [7]. Often, an appropriate hardware extension could help to replace the external host system in its task to reconfigure the FPGA memory. Here we discuss a way to extend the data structures for reconfiguration data sets and the RCU functionality to allow for sequencing reconfigurations. There are basically three different situations that can occur.

(1) If there is an external host or processor controlling the task sequencing, it is enough to just write the data set start address into the transfer address register of the RCU and to start the reconfiguration. The more interesting situations are those where the RCU must manage the sequencing by itself without an external unit to intervene, discussed now.

(2) A fixed order of successive tasks implemented on the FPGA which implicates a fixed order of configuration data sets to be loaded as shown in [10] occurs whenever more than one algorithm has to be applied to several data sets. To implement this behaviour, every configuration data set must be extended by a pointer to the following data set. The new data set structure is shown in figure 6. An additional internal RCU register can be used to store this start address when

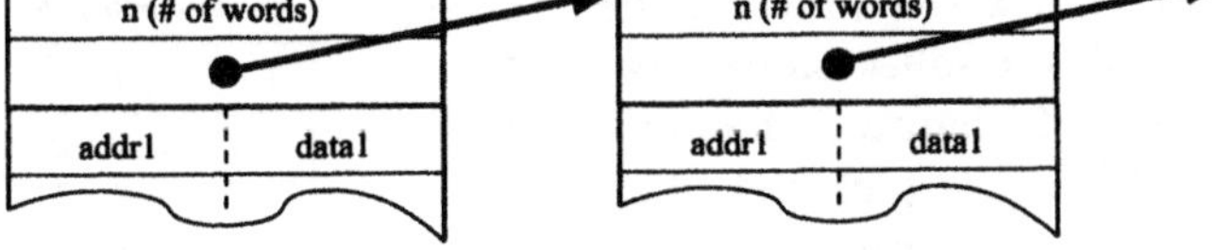

Fig. 6. *Linked data set list*

reading the current configuration set. After reconfiguration, the RCU stops operation and the user circuit is executed. To apply the next configuration, which is indicated by setting a line from within the user circuit, the pointer register is copied to the transfer address register and the normal reconfiguration sequence is started. Only minor changes to the state machine are needed to implement this behaviour.

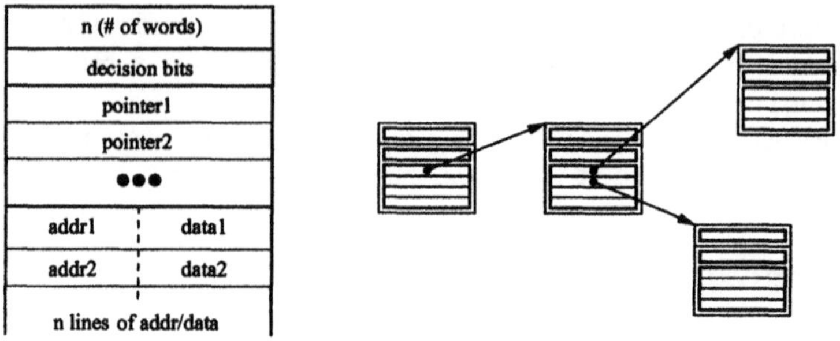

Fig. 7. *Headers of the multiple linked data set elements*

(3) For data dependent sequencing, the order of successive tasks cannot be predicted at design time. To implement this behaviour, a branch mechanism must be implemented depending on the results of previous operations or external events. The data structure must include a set of decision bits that are evaluated before a new configuration is loaded. Also, the different successor address pointers must be added. Figure 7 shows the new data structure.

As the number of possible successor data sets might differ for every reconfiguration, the according start addresses cannot be stored in advance like in the fixed successor case. Instead, the decision bits are stored in a new register and the start address of the current configuration data set must be saved in the pointer register. On a request for a new reconfiguration, the decision bits are used to calculate the branch index. Then the branch addresses stored in the old data set must be read and the one indexed is taken as the link to the next set. This implies an extension of the state machine. In figure 8 the structure of the extended FSM is pictured. This extended RCU can be a simple way to avoid an external host system or even a dedicated processor in an embedded system for many reconfiguration applications.

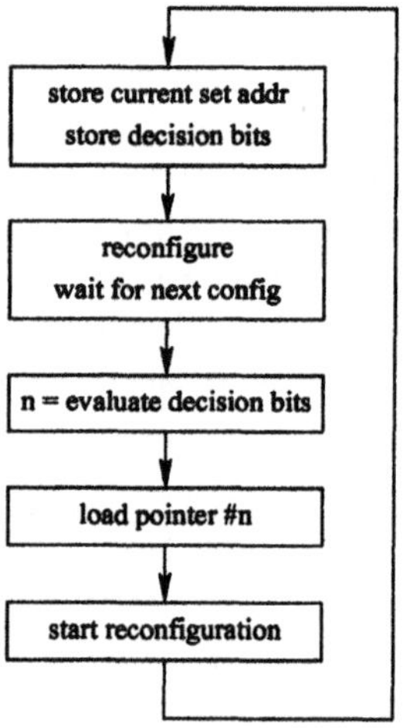

Fig. 8. *Structure of the FSM extension*

4 First Experimental Results

Our experimental system contains one or more FPGAs, a DLX-like RISC processor, RAM, and interface circuitry to its environment. At present, all parts of the system are available as simulation models only. First experiments with a simulation model of the RCU have shown an advantage compared to a software-based solution on the RISC processor. Figure 9 shows the software needed to transfer configuration data from memory to the FPGA cells, which are addressed by the word loaded to register r3, while the data for the specific location is loaded to register r4. The code needs $2 + 6 * n$ instructions corresponding to

```
      lw   r1, 0 (r0); transfer size
      lw   r2, 4 (r0); start address
loop: lw   r3, 0 (r2); load address
      lw   r4, 4 (r2); load data
      sw   0 (r3), r4; write data
      addi r2, r2, 8 ; incr. address
      subi r1, r1, 1 ; decr. size
      bnez r1, loop  ; while size
```

Fig. 9. *Assembler code of a RISC processor (DLX) for copying configuration data*

$7 + 6 * n$ cycles, depending on the number n of words to be transfered. The 5 additional cycles are needed to start the pipeline. As our processor does currently not support a pipeline, the calculation in our real simulation model takes $5 * 2 + 5 * 6 * n = 10 + 30 * n$ cycles. The number of cycles needed by the RCU is the number of steps its FSM needs to transfer the data. Starting with the error signal from the array, this are $6 + 8 * n$ cycles. Table 1 gives an overview of the number of cycles for a reconfiguration needed by the processor in compare to the RCU solution for two typical situations: a block reconfiguration of our FPGA and a region reconfiguration consisting of several blocks (of 4×4 cells). The table shows that the RCU is slightly slower than the pipelined version of

		clock cycles			memory accesses		
blocks	**# bytes**	**pipeline**	**no pipeline**	**RCU**	**processor**	**RCU**	**ratio**
1	16	103	300	134	144	50	2.88
16	256	1543	7690	2053	2308	770	~3

Table 1. *Clock cycles and memory accesses for configuration*

the processor. The reason for this is that the memory accesses the processor performs are based on a harvard architecture, thus hiding the real costs in a small system. To show the difference, the right side of the table compares the number of memory accesses needed by the processor and by the RCU. The RCU can obtain a saving in memory accesses of a factor up to three in compare to a processor. This saving directly depends on the fact that the RCU does not need to load code to perform its tasks.

These results are only reflecting the cycles needed for the reconfiguration. If a processor is present in the system, it will have other software to execute, so there will also be the costs for a context switch when the fault is detected. In many cases, when there is no processor needed in the system for its normal function, the advantage of not needing any additional hardware besides the FPGA with its integrated RCU and its external configuration data memory might be a more important argument. Finally, a lower memory bandwidth and less switching activity reduces the power consumption of the whole application.

First area estimations for a VLSI implementation of the RCU and the cells and 2×2 blocks of the FPGA from [2] for a $0.13\mu m$ AMS process give an area of $3{,}240\mu m^2$ for a cell (without configuration RAM), $136{,}591\mu m^2$ for a block (including all block RAM), and $126{,}399\mu m^2$ for the RCU.

5 Conclusions and Future Work

We have presented a hardware extension that enables FPGA based systems to react on faults and to form fault tolerance properties. These properties can be integrated in systems implemented on the extended FPGA hardware. A reconfiguration control unit implemented as hardware is able to perform all necessary steps to reobtain a fault-free system after a fault is detected. Proposals in different areas of reconfigurable logic can profit from the RCU by using it to perform their reconfiguration tasks. New fault tolerant applications can be implemented controlling faults on a near-netlist level gaining a low overhead fault tolerance appearance.

Detected errors are likely to have already changed computed values in an application, even if detected in the same clock cycle that they appear in. Because the hardware offers features like fast error detection and automatic self-repair, an application can exploit these properties by supporting appropriate mechanisms like fine grained checkpointing and rollback or delayed reexecution of computations with RCU status checks and result comparison. We integrated a checkpoint and rollback mechanism for programmable logic based on the FPGA prototype introduced in [2].

Another point of interest is the fault tolerance behaviour of the RCU itself. Currently, no measures are taken to guarantee its fault-free function. There are several possibilities to implement a fault tolerant version of the RCU. One is to build it as a tripple-modular-redundant system (TMR). Another, more resource saving approach would be to use a technique introduced in [9]. The state machine can be implemented as a bypass-pipeline described there. The datapath part of the RCU can be implemented using error correcting coding schemes for the registers.

Our future plans are to integrate the whole scheme into an automated design flow based on a codesign system [3], and to implement the FPGA with an integrated RCU as a VLSI chip.

References

[1] M. Abramovici, C. Stroud, C. Hamilton, S. Wijesuriya, and V. Verma. Using Roving STARs for On-Line Testing and Diagnosis of FPGAs in Fault-Tolerant Applications. In *Intl. Test Conference*, Atlantic City, NJ, Sept. 1999.

[2] T. Bartzick, M. Henze, J. Kickler, and K. Woska. Design of a Fault Tolerant FPGA. In *10th International Workshop on Field Programmable Logic and Applications*, pages 151–156, Villach, Austria, 2000.

[3] C. Bauer, P. Zipf, and H. Wojtkowiak. Integration von Fehlertoleranz im Codesign. In *Third ITG/GI/GMM-Wokshop*, 2000.

[4] G. Brebner. The Swappable Logic Unit: a Paradigm for Virtual Hardware. In *Proceedings of the IEEE Workshop on FPGAs for Custom Computing Machines*, Apr. 1997.

[5] E. Caspi, M. Chu, R. Huang, J. Yeh, J. Wawrzynek, and A. DeHon. Stream Computations Organized for Reconfigurable Execution (SCORE). In *10th International Workshop on Field Programmable Logic and Applications*, Villach, Austria, 2000.

[6] S. Durand and C. Piguet. FPGA with Selfrepair Capabilities. In *ACM International Workshop on Field-Programmable Gate Arrays*, Berkeley, CA, Feb. 1994.

[7] J. G. Eldredge and B. L. Hutchings. Run-Time Reconfiguration: A Method for Enhancing the Functional Density of SRAM-Based FPGAs. *Journal of VLSI Signal Processing*, 12:67–86, 1996.

[8] K. M. GajjalaPurna and D. Bhatia. Temporal Partitioning and Scheduling for Reconfigurable Computing. In *Proceedings of the IEEE Workshop on FPGAs for Custom Computing Machines*, Apr. 1998.

[9] A. Hertwig. *Synthesis of Fast Controllers Subject to Power Consumption, Testability and Fault Tolerance.* Ph.d. thesis, University of Siegen, Fachbereich Elektrotechnik und Informatik, 1999.

[10] B. L. Hutchings and M. J. Wirthlin. Implementation Approaches for Reconfigurable Logic Applications. In *5th International Workshop on Field Programmable Logic and Applications*, pages 419–428, Oxford, England, Aug. 1995.

[11] J. Lach, W. H. Mangione-Smith, and M. Potkonjak. Efficiently Supporting Fault-Tolerance in FPGAs. In *International Symposium on Field Programmable Gate Arrays*, 1998.

[12] L. E. LaForge. Configuration for Fault Tolerance. *4th Reconfigurable Architectures Workshop (RAW'97)*, Apr. 1997.

[13] L. E. LaForge. Configuration of locally spared arrays in the presence of multiple fault types. *IEEE Transactions on Computers*, 48(4), Apr. 1999.

[14] N. R. Shnidman, W. H. Mangione-Smith, and M. Potkonjak. On-line Fault Detection for Programmable Logic. In *17'th Conference on Advanced Research in VLSI*, Ann Arbor, Sept. 1997.

[15] D. Smith and D. Bhatia. RACE: Reconfigurable and Adaptive Computing Environment. *Lecture Notes in Computer Science*, 1142:87–95, 1996.

[16] M. Wirthlin and B. L. Hutchings. DISC: The dynamic instruction set computer. In J. Schewel, editor, *Field Programmable Gate Arrays (FPGAs) for Fast Board Development and Reconfigurable Computing*, pages 92–103, 1995.

[17] P. Zipf, C. Bauer, and H. Wojtkowiak. A Hardware Extensin to Improve Fault Handling in FPGA-Based Systems. In *Design and Diagnostics of Electronic Circuits ans Systems Workshop (DDECS)*, pages 233–236, Smolenice Castle, Slovakia, Apr. 2000.

On the Set of Target Path Delay Faults in Sequential Subcircuits of LUT-based FPGAs

Andrzej Krasniewski

Institute of Telecommunications, Warsaw University of Technology
Nowowiejska 15/19, 00-665 Warsaw, Poland
andrzej@tele.pw.edu.pl

Abstract. We show that the selection of the set of target path delay faults for a sequential subcircuit of a LUT-based FPGA is much more difficult, both conceptually and computationally, than it appears. An essential part of this problem is the identification of the set of irredundant logical paths, i.e. paths whose faults may affect the performance of the FPGA. We develop a classification of logical paths in a sequential subcircuit of a LUT-based FPGA that shows the relationship between irredundant logical paths and other types of logical paths. Based on this classification, we propose several ideas on how to define the set of target path delay faults, so that to allow the test designer to trade-off accuracy and computational complexity when evaluating the circuit testability or the quality of a particular test procedure.

1 Introduction

Most techniques for testing in-system reconfigurable FPGAs are intended to check, as exhaustively as possible, all possible operation modes of FPGA components – programmable logic blocks and parts of the interconnection structure (see, for example, [1]-[6]). It should, however, be noted that such a test strategy makes it possible to exercise only a small fraction of interconnection patterns that can be set by programming the device. In other words, only a small fraction of complete paths that exist in a particular user-defined circuit can be checked for possible delay faults.

To deal with FPGA delay faults more effectively, the concept of application-dependent testing (also referred to as a user test [2] or configuration-dependent testing [7]) has been proposed. The idea is to thoroughly exercise only that specific configuration of the FPGA which corresponds to the user-defined function. For LUT-based in-circuit reconfigurable FPGAs, application-dependent testing can rely on externally provided test patterns or on the BIST techniques. The BIST-based test procedure can be extended to account specifically for the detection of delay faults [8].

One of the major problems associated with testing delay faults is the evaluation of the test quality. Testability of delay faults in combinational circuits composed of simple gates (NOT, AND, NAND, OR, NOR) has been a subject of many studies (see, for example, [9]-[11]). It has been shown, however, that the methods and results obtained for such circuits are not applicable to FPGAs [12]. To evaluate the quality of testing for delay faults in FPGAs, new methods are, therefore, needed. In this paper, we focus on one key aspect of this problem – the selection of the set of target faults.

M. Glesner, P. Zipf, and M. Renovell (Eds.): FPL 2002, LNCS 2438, pp. 596-606, 2002.

2 Delay Faults in a Sequential Subcircuit of an FPGA

We consider a sequential subcircuit of the user-programmed LUT-based FPGAs (Fig. 1). The combinational part of such a subcircuit is represented as a network of interconnected single-output LUTs. For the purpose of our analysis, other logic components included in the combinational logic block, such as multiplexers, gates, etc., can be viewed as part of LUTs or part of the interconnection structure.

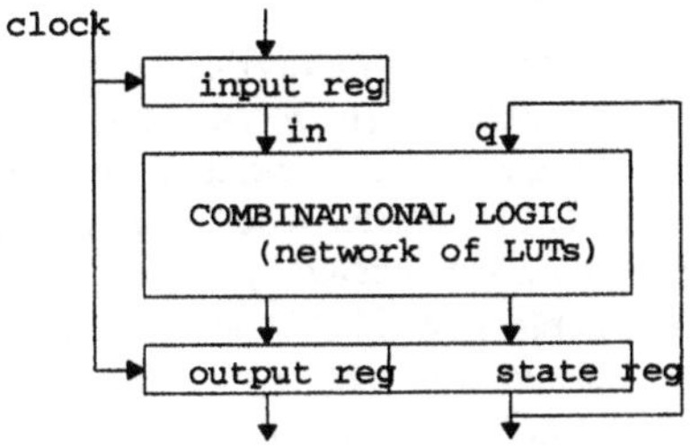

Fig. 1. Sequential subcircuit of an FPGA

As FPGA delay faults are mainly associated with interconnections, the path delay fault model is an obvious choice. We assume that all delays that contribute to the propagation delay of a path may depend on the polarity of "local" transitions that occur at the input of the path and at the outputs of LUTs along the path [5]. Thus, the propagation delay of a path can only be defined for a given *path transition pattern*, PTP, which specifies, for each connection along the path, whether a rising transition or a falling transition occurs at that connection. If a path transition pattern, PTP, defines for some connection a rising (falling) transition, we say that initial value 0 and final value 1 (initial value 1 and final value 0) are *consistent with PTP*.

We introduce the concept of a logical path as an extension of the same notion in a network of simple gates [9], [11]. A *logical path* π(PTP) is defined by a path π and some path transition pattern PTP associated with π. We say that a logical path π(PTP) *has a delay fault* if the propagation delay of path π corresponding to the path transition pattern PTP exceeds a given time T.

A logical path is *irredundant* if there exists a delay assignment, i.e. an assignment of propagation delays to all logic components and connections in the subcircuit, such that the propagation delay of that path determines the propagation delay of the circuit. This definition implies that only those delay faults that are associated with such paths can affect the performance of the circuit.

3 Attributes of Logical Paths

To formulate requirements that are satisfied by irredundant logical paths, we introduce a number of attributes of logical paths, namely their compliance with the LUT functions, their feasibility and their sensitizability.

3.1 Compliance with the LUT Functions

A single-output Boolean function F is *positive unate* (*negative unate*) in variable x_i if changing x_i from 0 to 1 does not affect the value of F or causes its change from 0 to 1 (from 1 to 0); function F is *binate* in x_i if it is neither positive nor negative unate in x_i.

A logical path π(PTP) *complies with the LUT functions* if for each LUT along path π, a transition at the on-path input of the LUT and a transition at the output of the LUT, determined by PTP, are of the same polarity (opposite polarity) if the function of the LUT is positive unate (negative unate) in its on-path input.

Example 1. Consider the sequential subcircuit of a LUT-based FPGA shown in Fig. 2. It has 4 input variables (a, b, c, d) and 3 state variables (u, w, y); variables u^+, w^+, y^+ are the next state variables. The functions implemented by the LUTs and their characteristics are given in Fig. 2 (LUTs and their functions are denoted by capital letters; output variables of LUTs and flip-flops and the corresponding connections are denoted by lower-case letters).

Consider the path $\pi = d\text{-}h\text{-}w^+$. As function H is binate in d and function W is positive unate in h, the set of logical paths associated with path π that comply with the LUT functions is $\{d{\uparrow}h{\uparrow}w^+{\uparrow},\ d{\uparrow}h{\downarrow}w^+{\downarrow},\ d{\downarrow}h{\downarrow}w^+{\downarrow},\ d{\downarrow}h{\uparrow}w^+{\uparrow}\}$ (symbol ↑ or ↓ that follows the symbol of a connection denotes a rising and falling transition at that connection, respectively).

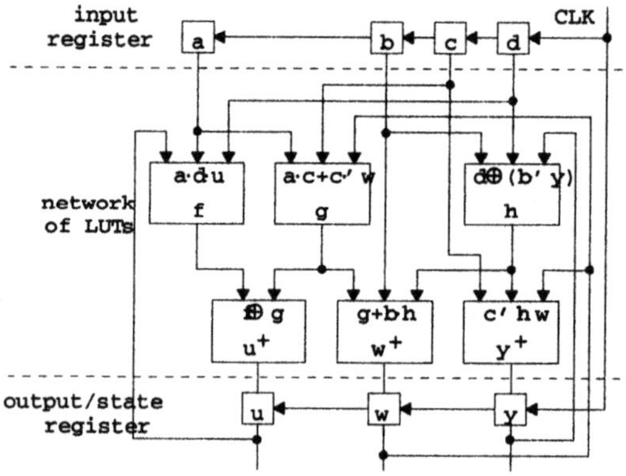

F: positive unate in a, d, u
G: positive unate in a, w
binate in c
H: binate in b, d, y
U: binate in f, g
W: positive unate in b, g, h
Y: positive unate in h, w
negative unate in c

Fig. 2. Sequential subcircuit of a LUT-based FPGA – an example

3.2 Feasibility

Let $in_{comb} = (in,q)$ denote a vector applied to the network of LUTs, where *in* is the content of the input register, and *q* is the content of the state register (Fig. 1). Let $<in_{comb}(1), in_{comb}(2)>$ be a pair of vectors produced in two consecutive clock cycles at the input of the network of LUTs.

We start with the concept of combinational feasibility of a logical path which is based on an assumption that all inputs to the combinational logic block of the sequential subcircuit of Fig. 1 are fully controllable, i.e. any possible vector in_{comb} can be applied to the network of LUTs during the first and the second clock cycle.

A logical path π(PTP) is *combinationally feasible* if there exists a pair of input vectors to the network of LUTs, <$in_{comb}(1)$, $in_{comb}(2)$>, which produces PTP. π(PTP) uniquely determines PTP(1) and PTP(2) – the sets of initial and final logic values associated with the connections along path π. Thus, $in_{comb}(1)$ and $in_{comb}(2)$ must produce PTP(1) and PTP(2), respectively.

Example 1 (cont.). Consider the path c-g-u^+. There are 8 logical paths comply with the LUT functions. Not all of these logical paths are, however, combinationally feasible. Consider the logical path c↑g↓u^+↑. PTP(2) is defined by c = 1, g = 0 and u^+ = 1. With c = 1, to produce g = 0, we must have a = 0. However, a = 0 implies f = 0, and this, in turn, with g = 0, implies u^+ = 0, which is inconsistent with PTP(2). Thus, c↑g↓u^+↑ is not combinationally feasible.

A logical path π(PTP) is *sequentially feasible* or, simply, *feasible* if there exists a triple <q(1), in(1), in(2)>, such that

a) state q(1) is reachable, i.e. for any initial state of the subcircuit, there exists a sequence of input vectors that produces state q(1);
b) the pair of vectors <$in_{comb}(1)$, $in_{comb}(2)$>, such that $in_{comb}(1)$ = (in(1),q(1)) and $in_{comb}(2) = (in(2),Q^+(in_{comb}(1)))$, produces PTP.

Clearly, a combinationally feasible logical path may not be sequentially feasible, as demonstrated by the following example.

Example 1 (cont.). Consider the logical path c↓g↑w^+↑ which can be shown to be combinationally feasible. To produce c = 0 and g = 1, as required by PTP(2), we must have w = 1. However, PTP implies $w^+(1)$ = 0, which, because of the sequential nature of the circuit, implies, in turn, w(2) = 0. This is inconsistent with PTP(2). Hence, c↓g↑w^+↑ is not sequentially feasible.

3.3 Sensitizability

For a LUT located on a logical path π(PTP) and represented by function F of N input variables, let $x \in \{0,1\}^N$ be an input vector, and $x^* \in \{0,1,*\}^N$ be an incompletely specified input vector. Let x_{op} be the on-path input and z be the output of the LUT. Let x*(-op) denote an input vector for which x_{op} = * and all the remaining bit positions (input variables) are specified.

A LUT input vector x*(-i) is a *sensitization vector consistent with PTP* for x_{op} if $F(x^*(-op)) = x_{op}$ ($F(x^*(-op)) = x_{op}'$) in the case when PTP defines the same polarity (different polarities) of transitions at x_{op} and at z.

Like in the case of feasibility, we start with the concept of combinational sensitizability which is based on an assumption that all inputs to the network of LUTs are fully controllable.

A logical path π(PTP) is *combinationally sensitizable* if there exists a pair of input vectors to the network of LUTs, <$in_{comb}(1)$, $in_{comb}(2)$>, which *sensitizes* π(PTP), i.e. such that

a) <$in_{comb}(1)$, $in_{comb}(2)$> produces PTP,
b) for each LUT along path π, $in_{comb}(2)$ produces, for the on-path input of that LUT, a sensitization vector consistent with PTP,

c) vector $in_{comb}^*(2)$, obtained from $in_{comb}(2)$ by complementing the bit that corresponds to the input of path π, produces PTP(1).

Conditions (a) and (b) in this definition correspond to the notion of a (static) sensitizable path, defined in the context of testing delay faults in networks of simple gates [11]. Condition (c) is specific to circuits whose basic logic components can implement arbitrary logic functions. It guarantees that, in the case when a transition that propagates along the path arrives at some logic component significantly late, the output of that component remains at its initial logic value and "waits" for an effect of the late transition to occur [12]. The concept of a combinationally sensitizable logical path is illustrated with the following Example.

Example 1 (cont.). Consider the logical path $d\uparrow h\uparrow w^+\uparrow$ and two input vectors to the network of LUTs: $in_{comb}(1)$, for which a = 0, b = 1, c = 1 and d = 0, and $in_{comb}(2)$ for which a = 0, b = 1, c = 1 and d = 1; $in_{comb}(1)$ produces PTP(1), whereas $in_{comb}(2)$ produces PTP(2). It can be seen that $in_{comb}(2)$ produces a sensitization vector consistent with PTP for input d of LUT H (because b = 1) and for input h of LUT W (because b = 1 and g = 0 is implied by a = 0 and c = 1). Consider now an input vector $in_{comb}^*(2)$ for which a = 0, b = 1, c = 1 and d = 0. This vector produces PTP(1) (d = 0, h = 0 and $w^+ = 0$). Thus, $<in_{comb}(1), in_{comb}(2)>$ satisfies conditions (a)-(c) in the above definition which means that $d\uparrow h\uparrow w^+\uparrow$ is combinationally sensitizable.

Under the assumed controllability of all the inputs to the LUT network, the combinational sensitizability of a logical path is a sufficient condition for the corresponding fault to affect the performance of the circuit (under some specific assignment of delays to the subcircuit components). However, it is not a necessary condition. The necessary condition corresponds to the concept of combinational functional sensitizability (combinational f-sensitizability) which is defined below.

An incompletely specified LUT input vector $x1 \in \{0,1,*\}^N$ is *covered by* another incompletely specified LUT input vector $x2 \in \{0,1,*\}^N$, which is denoted as $x1 \subset x2$, if for each bit position i, i = 1,..., N, $x1_i = x2_i$ or $x2_i = *$.

Given x(1) and x(2) – input vectors for the LUT produced by $in_{comb}(1)$ and $in_{comb}(2)$ – the *transition vector*, x(1,2), is defined as follows: for each position j, j = 1, ..., N:

$$x_j(1,2) = x_j(1), \text{ if } x_j(1) = x_j(2)$$
$$x_j(1,2) = *, \text{ otherwise.}$$

A logical path π(PTP) is *combinationally f-sensitizable* if there exists a pair of input vectors to the network of LUTs, $<in_{comb}(1), in_{comb}(2)>$, which *f-sensitizes* π(PTP), i.e. such that

a) $<in_{comb}(1), in_{comb}(2)>$ produces path transition pattern PTP,

b) for each LUT along path π and its on-path input x_{op}, $<in_{comb}(1), in_{comb}(2)>$ produces at the input of the LUT a transition vector x(1,2), such that there exists a vector $x^*(\text{-op}) \subset x(1,2)$ which is a sensitization vector consistent with PTP for x_{op}.

The concept of an f-sensitizable logical path was introduced in the context of testing delay faults in combinational networks of simple gates. Its idea is to account for the situation when a transition to the controlling value at the on-path input of a gate determines the delay of the path if it occurs earlier than similar transitions at other inputs of the gate [11]. Likewise, for a network of LUTs, this concept accounts for the situation when a transition arriving at the on-path input of a LUT forces the LUT output to a stable logic value (that cannot be changed by later transitions at the off-path inputs), thereby determining the propagation delay of the path. The notion of a combinationally f-sensitizable logical path is illustrated with the following Example.

Example 1 (cont.). Consider the logical path $y\uparrow h\downarrow w^{+}\downarrow$. A sensitization vector consistent with PTP for input y of LUT H requires b = 0 and d = 1. A sensitization vector consistent with PTP for input h of LUT W requires b = 1 and g = 0. The contradictory requirements on the value of b indicate that $y\uparrow h\downarrow w^{+}\downarrow$ is not combinationally sensitizable.

Consider now two input vectors to the network of LUTs: $in_{comb}(1)$, for which b = 1, c = 0, d = 1, w = 0, y = 0, and $in_{comb}(2)$, for which a = 0, b = 0, c = 1, d = 1, y = 1; $in_{comb}(1)$ produces PTP(1), whereas $in_{comb}(2)$ produces PTP(2). The input pair $<in_{comb}(1), in_{comb}(2)>$ produces at the input of LUT H, transition vector $x_H(b,d,y)$ = *1*, and at the input of LUT W, transition vector $x_W(b,g,h)$ = *0*. It can be seen that $01* \subset x_H(b,d,y)$ is a sensitization vector consistent with PTP for input y of LUT H, whereas $10* \subset x_W(b,g,h)$ is a sensitization vector consistent with PTP for input h of LUT W. Thus, $<in_{comb}(1), in_{comb}(2)>$ satisfies conditions (a)-(b) in the above definition which means that $y\uparrow h\downarrow w^{+}\downarrow$ is combinationally f-sensitizable.

We now take into account the sequential nature of the subcircuit.

A logical path π(PTP) is *sequentially sensitizable* (*sequentially f-sensitizable*) or, simply, *sensitizable* (*f-sensitizable*) if there exists a triple $<q(1), in(1), in(2)>$ such that

a) state q(1) is reachable,

b) the pair of vectors $<in_{comb}(1), in_{comb}(2)>$, such that $in_{comb}(1) = (in(1),q(1))$ and $in_{comb}(2) = (in(2),Q^{+}(in_{comb}(1)))$, sensitizes (f-sensitizes) π(PTP).

As alluded to earlier, the concept of f-sensitizability is very important from the practical point of view. This is because a logical path in a sequential subcircuit of a LUT-based FPGA is irredundant if and only if it is f-sensitizable [13]. This means that *the performance of a sequential subcircuit of a LUT-based FPGA can only be affected by delay faults associated with f-sensitizable logical paths.*

4 Classification of Logical Paths

The classification of logical paths in a sequential subcircuit of a LUT-based FPGA is shown in Fig. 3. For the circuit of Fig. 2, this classification is illustrated in Table 1, where for each physical path, the total number of logical paths and the number of logical paths corresponding to different areas in Fig. 3, denoted as A1-A11, is given (in Fig. 3, the name of a class, e.g. "seq. feasible", refers to the entire area of the corresponding oval, whereas symbol Ai refers to the area between external and internal oval(s)). The shaded areas in Fig. 3 and in Table 1 correspond to irredundant logical paths.

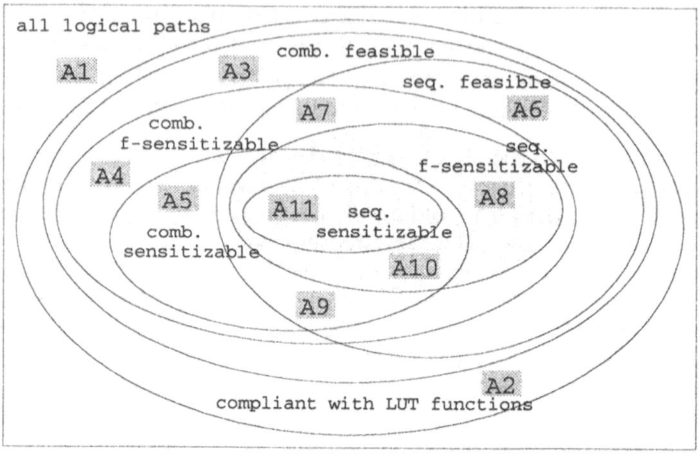

Fig. 3. Classification of logical paths associated with a physical path

Table 1. Logical paths for the circuit of Fig. 2

physical path	logical paths	A1	A2	A3	A4	A5	A6	A7	A8	A9	A10	A11
a-f-u$^+$	8	4				1					1	2
a-g-u$^+$	8	4	2									2
a-g-w$^+$	8	6										2
b-w$^+$	4	2										2
b-h-w$^+$	8	4					1		1		1	1
b-h-y$^+$	8	4								1	1	2
c-y$^+$	4	2										2
c-g-u$^+$	8	0	2			2						4
c-g-w$^+$	8	4				2						2
d-f-u$^+$	8	4				1					1	2
d-h-w$^+$	8	4		1			1					2
d-h-y$^+$	8	4				1						3
u-f-u$^+$	8	4				2						2
w-y$^+$	4	2				1						1
w-g-u$^+$	8	4				2						2
w-g-w$^+$	8	6				2						
y-h-w$^+$	8	4		1					3			
y-h-y$^+$	8	4				2						2
all paths	132	66	4	2	0	16	2	0	4	1	4	33

For a combinational subcircuit which can be thought of a special case of a sequential subcircuit, the class of (combinationally) feasible logical paths is – as a result of the sensitizability analysis – partitioned into three classes: unsensitizable logical paths, f-sensitizable logical paths, and sensitizable logical paths. In Fig. 3 (Table 1), these three classes would correspond to areas (columns) obtained by merging areas (columns) A3+A6, A4+A7+A8, and A5+A9+A10+A11, respectively.

5 How to Define the Set of Target Path Delay Faults?

The presented classification of logical paths is related to several practical problems associated with the evaluation of circuit testability or quality of a test sequence for delay faults in a sequential subcircuit of a LUT-based FPGA.

The circuit testability with regard to a specific class of faults, referred to as *fault testability*, is measured by the percentage of faults that are detectable, i.e. for which a test exists. In the case of path delay faults, the fault testability depends on the assumed type of tests (e.g. weak non-robust, strong non-robust, robust [14]). The quality of a test sequence produced by a given test procedure is usually measured by the *fault coverage* – the percentage of faults that are detected by that test sequence. Like in the case of testability, the coverage of path delay faults depends on the type of testability.

The calculation of path delay fault testability and path delay fault coverage requires that the set of *target faults* be defined. As stated in the Section 3, the performance of a sequential subcircuit of a LUT-based FPGA can only be affected by delay faults associated with f-sensitizable logical paths. Therefore, it appears that the set of target path delay faults should be defined as the set of faults associated with f-sensitizable logical paths.

Before we show difficulties associated with such a choice, we examine how the selection of the set of target faults affects the testability and coverage of path delay faults. For that purpose, we calculate these measures for the circuit of Fig. 2 for three different sets of target faults: the set of faults associated with f-sensitizable logical paths and two "extreme" sets: the set of faults associated with all logical paths and with all non-RD logical paths. (The concept of non-RD logical paths, not discussed so far in this paper, is related to the fact that not all f-sensitizable logical paths must be examined to guarantee that the circuit delay does not exceed a given threshold – so-called robust dependent (RD) paths may not be exercised [10], [11].)

In Table 2 and Table 3, we give the values of the testability and coverage of path delay faults for the circuit of Fig. 2, for the various types of testability. The entries in Table 3 correspond to an example pseudorandom test sequence.

Table 2. Testability of path delay faults for the circuit of Fig. 2

set of target faults	weak non-robust	strong non-robust	robust
all logical paths	42.4 %	25.0 %	24.2 %
f-sensitizable logical paths	100.0 %	80.5 %	78.0 %
non-RD logical paths	100.0 %	100.0 %	100.0 %

Table 3. Path delay fault coverage for an example test sequence applied to the circuit of Fig. 2

set of target faults	weak non-robust	strong non-robust	robust
all logical paths	40.1 %	18.2 %	15.2 %
f-sensitizable logical paths	85.4 %	58.5 %	48.8 %
non-RD logical paths	87.5 %	68.8 %	62.5 %

The data in Table 2 and Table 3, showing a significant impact of the selection of the set of target faults on the values of the testability and coverage of path delay faults, seems to support the claim that the evaluation of circuit testability and test quality should be based on the set of faults associated with f-sensitizable logical paths. Such a selection poses, however, the problem of computational complexity. It can be attributed not only to a large number of physical paths (which is typical for many types of circuits), but also to specific features of LUT-based networks, such as:

- a large number of logical paths associated with a particular physical path; the number of logical paths associated with a given physical path grows significantly, in the worst case exponentially, with the number of LUTs along the path,
- complexity of conditions that must be examined to decide whether or not a given logical path is f-sensitizable.

Because of the possibly unacceptable computational complexity associated with the identification of the set of f-sensitizable logical paths, alternative selections of the set of target faults can be considered, including:

- set of faults associated with a subset of all physical paths (set of critical paths), identified using a static timing analyzer or some other method,
- set of faults associated with a set of logical paths that is much easier to compute than the set of f-sensitizable logical paths, such as the set of logical paths that comply with the LUT functions or the set of combinationally or sequentially feasible logical paths.

For the circuit of Fig. 2 and the pseudorandom test sequence used to produce Table 3, the latter approach would yield the results shown in Table 4.

Table 4. Path delay fault coverage for an example test sequence applied to the circuit of Fig. 2

set of target faults	weak non-robust	strong non-robust	robust
log. paths compliant with LUT functions	81.8 %	36.4 %	15.2 %
combinationally feasible logical paths	83.9 %	38.7 %	32.3 %
sequentially feasible logical paths	81.8 %	52.3 %	45.5 %

It can be seen that the numbers in Table 4 give a reasonable approximation of the values corresponding to the set of irredundant logical paths (row "f-sensitizable logical paths" in Table 3) – much better than the numbers corresponding to the set of all logical paths. For some type of analyses, like a comparison of alternative methods for the modification of LUT functions, aimed at an enhancement of the efficiency of delay fault testing [15], such an approximation would usually be sufficient.

The selection of the set of target faults poses, however, another problem or dilemma, of a more fundamental character. It can be formulated as follows. Assume that there is a physical path with a relatively large (compared to other physical paths in the circuit) number of logical paths having a certain property (f-sensitizable, combinationally feasible, etc.). The question is: "should all these logical paths be taken into account when calculating the fault coverage?" The intuitive answer, consistent with the earlier analysis, would be "yes", but then, the calculated measure would be strongly biased by the coverage of faults associated with such a single physical path. To deal with this problem, the following ideas can be considered:

- introduction of a weighting factor that decreases the impact of faults associated with a physical path having a large number of logical paths,
- imposition of a limitation on the number of logical paths associated with a given physical path that are considered when estimating the fault coverage and introduction of some rules for the selection of a subset of such logical paths.

A more thorough analysis of this problem is, however, needed.

6 Conclusion

We develop a classification of logical paths in a sequential subcircuit of a LUT-based FPGA. This classification proves useful when dealing with practical problems, such as the evaluation of testability and coverage of path delay faults. It shows, in particular, the relationship between f-sensitizable logical paths, i.e. paths whose faults may affect the performance of the FPGA, and other classes of logical paths.

The experimental results show that the testability and coverage of path delay faults significantly depend on the selection of the set of target faults. It appears, therefore, that faults associated with f-sensitizable logical paths should be target faults. The identification of all f-sensitizable logical paths is, however, computationally so complex, that it may likely be intractable for most practical designs. Thus, based on the presented classification of logical paths and the results of a simple experimental study, alternative selections of the set of target faults are proposed.

Another problem with the selection of the set of target faults is caused by large differences in the number of faults (logical paths) associated with individual physical paths in LUT networks. Some ideas on how to deal with this difficulty are proposed.

The presented options regarding the selection of the set of target faults provide the test designer with a means to trade-off computational complexity with accuracy in the process of the development of a procedure for testing delay faults in a user-programmed FPGA.

In conclusion, it can, however, be stated that the problem of defining the set of target path delay faults for a sequential subcircuit of a LUT-based FPGA, not discussed so far in the literature, is much more difficult, both conceptually and computationally, than it appears. When discussing this problem, we have provided answers to some questions, but a large number of new questions have been posed.

References

1. Stroud, C., Konala, S., Chen, P., Abramovici, M.: Built-In Self-Test of Logic Blocks in FPGAs (Finally, a Free Lunch: BIST Without Overhead!). In: Proc. 14th VLSI Test Symp. (1996), 387-392
2. Renovell, M., Figueras, J., Zorian, Y.: Test of RAM-based FPGA: Methodology and Application to the Interconnect. In: Proc. 15th VLSI Test Symp. (1997) 230-237
3. Huang, W.K., Meyer, F.J., Chen, X.-T., Lombardi, F.: Testing Configurable LUT-Based FPGA's. IEEE Trans. on VLSI Systems, **6** (1998) 276-283

4. Renovell, M., Zorian, Y.: Different Experiments in Test Generation for XILINX FPGAs. In: Proc. IEEE Int. Test Conf. (2000) 854-862
5. Harris, I.G., Menon, P.R., Tessier, R.: BIST-Based Delay Path Testing in FPGA Architectures. In: Proc. IEEE Int. Test Conf. (2001) 932-938
6. Abramovici, M., Stroud, C.: BIST-Based Delay-Fault Testing in FPGAs. In: Proc. IEEE Int. On-Line Testing Workshop (2002)
7. Quddus, W., Jas, A., Touba, N.A.: Configuration Self-Test in FPGA-Based Reconfigurable Systems. In: Proc. ISCAS'99 (1999) 97-100
8. Krasniewski, A.: Application-Dependent Testing of FPGA Delay Faults. In: Proc. 25th EUROMICRO Conf., vol. 1 (1999) 260-267
9. Lam, W., Saldanha, A., Brayton, R., Sangiovanni-Vincentelli, A.: Delay Fault Coverage, Test Set Size and Performance Trade-Offs. In: IEEE Trans. on CAD, 1 (1995) 32-44
10. Sparmann, U., Luxenburger, D., Chang, K.-T., Reddy, S.M.: Fast Identification of Robust Dependent Path Delay Faults. In: Proc. 32nd ACM/IEEE Design Automation Conf. (1995) 119-125
11. Cheng, K.-T., Chen, H.-C.: Classification and Identification of Nonrobust Untestable Path Delay Faults. IEEE Trans. on CAD, 8 (1996) 845-853
12. Krasniewski, A.: Testing FPGA Delay Faults: It Is Much More Complicated Than It Appears. In: Proc. IFAC Workshop on Programmable Devices and Systems – PDS2001 (2001) 291-296
13. Krasniewski, A.: On Irredundant Path Delay Faults in LUT-Based FPGAs, Tech. Report, Inst. of Telecommunications, Warsaw Univ. of Technology (2002)
14. Underwood, B., Law, W.-O., Kang, S., Konuk, H.: Fastpath: A Path-Delay Test Generator for Standard Scan Designs. In: Proc. IEEE Int'l Test Conf. (1994) 154-163
15. Krasniewski, A.: Exploiting Reconfigurability for Effective Detection of Delay Faults in LUT-Based FPGAs. In: Hartenstein, R.W., Grunbacher H. (eds.), Proc. FPL 2000, LNCS, vol. 1896, Springer Verlag (2000) 675-684

Simulation-Based Analysis of SEU Effects on SRAM-based FPGAs*

M. Rebaudengo, M. Sonza Reorda, M. Violante

Politecnico di Torino - Dipartimento di Automatica e Informatica
Torino, Italy
http://www.cad.polito.it

Abstract. Commercial-Off-The-Shelf SRAM-based FPGA devices are becoming of interests for applications where high dependability and low cost are mandatory constraints. This paper proposes a new fault injection environment, which offers an alternative to radiation testing for evaluating the effects of charged particles on the configuration memory of SRAM-based FPGA devices. This paper describes the fault injection environment and reports preliminary results gathered on some benchmark circuits.

1. Introduction

Developers of fault tolerant systems must face new constraints that mandate new design approaches. On the one hand, there is a need for providing fault detection and possibly correction to applications where cost is a major issue. As an example, for many applications in the automotive or biomedical field the adoption of Commercial-Off-The-Shelf (COTS) hardware components is mandatory to reduce the design cost; moreover, classical solutions to guarantee fault tolerance such as triple modular redundancy are simply too expensive to be affordable. On the other hand, cost issues are becoming of interest also for domains where cost was normally a minor issue. For example, in the space domain there is a growing need for solutions able to combine reduced costs with faster and cheaper prototyping, and for solutions able to provide reconfigurations capabilities.

SRAM-based FPGA devices are able to match some of the aforementioned issues, since they combine low cost with high integration levels and in-the-field programming capability. Thanks to their high production volume, SRAM-based FPGA devices are much cheaper than ASIC devices and therefore costs can be drastically reduced. Furthermore, SRAM-based FPGA devices are now available that provide million of gates and advanced features such as large memory blocks, DSPs and CPUs, thus allowing to build an entire system on a single device. Finally, devices such as the Xilinx VIRTEX family offer partial reconfiguration features, making thus possible to reprogram the device even when it is already deployed in the field.

* This work has been partially supported by Center of Excellence on Multimedia Radio communications (CERCOM) of Politecnico di Torino and by Agenzia Spaziale Italiana.

M. Glesner, P. Zipf, and M. Renovell (Eds.): FPL 2002, LNCS 2438, pp. 607-615, 2002.

Despite the benefits SRAM-based devices offer, dependability issues limit their widespread adoption in safety- or mission-critical applications. If we consider for example the Xilinx Virtex family, we have that it is fabricated on thin-epitaxial silicon wafers exploiting a 0.22μm CMOS technology with 5 metal layers. Such a kind of technology is relatively sensible to Single Event Upsets (SEUs) [1] that may be originated by charged particles hitting the silicon substrate, and that interact with the memory elements by changing their logic state. Since the behavior of an SRAM-based FPGA is determined by the bitstream loaded and stored in it, the effects of SEUs may drastically alter the correct operations of FPGAs [2].

Although radiation hardened FPGA devices are available, they are much more expensive than COTS devices, and thus when cost is a major issue they are not affordable. In order to cope with dependability issues, FPGA vendors have developed design solutions able to harden Commercial-Off-The-Shelf SRAM-based FPGAs against SEU effects. These solutions usually come under the form of suggested design practices able to guarantee a certain level of immunity against SEUs [3].

Following the implementation of the adopted hardening solution, the obtained design should undergo an intense validation process whose aim is twofold. On the one hand, there is the need for validating the correctness of the implementation of the design hardening solutions. The design hardening process is indeed error prone, since it relies on designers for its implementation. To the best of our knowledge, automatic tools for design hardening are not yet available and thus the correctness of the design can not be guaranteed. On the other hand, there is a need for obtaining statistical evidence of the effectiveness of the adopted hardening solutions. This implies to measure figures that characterize the dependability of the hardened design (e.g., mean time between failures).

When addressing the validation of a design exploiting SRAM-based devices, two complementary aspects should be considered:

- SEUs may alter the memory elements the design embeds. For example, a SEU may alter the content of a register in the data-path, or the content of the state register of a control-unit.
- SEUs may alter the content of the memory storing the device configuration information. For example, a SEU may alter the content of a Look-Up Table (LUT) inside a Configurable Logic Block (CLB) or the routing of a signal in a CLB or between two CLBs.

The former aspect can be analyzed by resorting to well-known fault injection techniques [4] [5] [6] [7]. Once the model of the design is available, its memory elements (i.e., data-path/control-unit registers) can be easily altered, thus simulating the effect of SEUs, and the behavior of the system in presence of faults can be studied. In this context, the fault model that is normally adopted for mimicking the effects of SEUs is the transient single bit-flip, which corresponds to the inversion of the logic state of a memory bit.

Conversely, the latter aspect demands much more complex analysis capabilities. The simple bit-flip fault model can not be fruitfully exploited: the effects of SEUs in the device configuration memory are indeed not limited to modifications in the design memory elements, but may produce modifications in the interconnections inside a CLB and among different CLBs.

The usual solution for understating the effects of SEUs on both the memory elements the design embeds and the configuration memory is radiation testing [2]. A prototype of the system under analysis is exposed to a flux of charged particles, originated either by radioactive sources or by particle accelerators, which interacts with both the design memory elements and the configuration memory. Although this method allows detailed analysis of the SEU effects, it has two major drawbacks. First, it can be exploited only when a prototype of the system is available, and thus the validation phase can start at the end of the manufacturing process, only. Moreover, radiation testing experiments are very expensive: prototypes can be damaged by highly energized particles, and radiation facilities are expensive.

In this paper, we propose a new fault injection technique that is able to analyze the effects of charged particles in the FPGA configuration memory. The approach targets devices of the Xilinx Virtex family and exploits the reconfiguration feature they offer [8] to emulate the effects of SEUs. We resort to JBits [9] for reading back the content of all the memory elements of a FPGA, to alter its content according to the effects of SEUs, and to re-load the modified bit-stream in the device. Thanks to JBits we are able to emulate the effects of charged particles on a FPGA device without the need of expensive and time-consuming radiation experiments. A prototypical implementation of the proposed fault injection techniques allowed us to gather preliminary results that prove its feasibility and effectiveness.

A similar approach has been presented in [10] where an ad-hoc software and a prototypical board are used for performing fault injection experiments. The main novelties of our paper with respect to [10] are the adoption of JBits for analyzing the bitstream to avoid injecting faults in unused bits of the configuration memory and the use of a device simulator to analyze the FPGA behavior in presence of faults.

Please note that other authors have already proposed the use of JBits for performing fault injection experiments [11], but their focus was not on the analysis of SEUs inside the device configuration memory.

The paper is organized as follows. Section 2 describes the architecture of a typical fault injection environment and then it describes the environment we developed. Section 3 reports some preliminary experimental results showing the type of analysis our environment allows. Finally, section 4 draws some conclusions.

2. The Fault Injection System

This section first provides the reader with background information about the architecture of a typical fault injection system, and then it details the fault injection environment we developed in order to analyze the effects of SEUs on SRAM-based FPGA devices.

2.1. Background

For the purpose of this paper we assume that the analyzed system is a circuit to be implemented on an SRAM-based FPGA device.

The goal of a fault injection system [4] is to provide information about the behavior of the circuit when a fault is injected while a given set of stimuli are applied to the circuit.

The fault model we refer to is the *single transient bit-flip* in the memory elements storing the FPGA configuration bits. The bit-flip fault model (that matches the characteristics of SEUs [1]) corresponds to the flipping (from 0 to 1, or vice versa) of a memory bit. The bit-flip is random in time (it may occur whenever during the lifetime of a device), and in space (all the memory bits have the same probability of being affected).

We also assume that the input stimuli to be used during the analysis process are already available, and we do not deal with their generation or evaluation.

The fault injection process usually consists of three steps. The behavior of the fault-free circuit when the given input stimuli are applied is initially computed and stored. During the second step, for every fault to be considered, the given input stimuli are applied again to the circuit inputs, the fault is inoculated in the circuit, and the circuit behavior is observed. During the third step of the analysis process, the faulty circuit behavior is compared with the reference one (fault-free circuit) gathered during the first step, and the fault effects are classified according to the following categories:

- *Effect-less*: the output behavior of the faulty circuit corresponds to that of the fault-free one. A further characterization of the faults belonging to this category is possible by analyzing the value on the circuit flip-flops. In the case the contents of the flip-flops for the faulty circuit differ from those of the fault-free circuit, the fault is classified as *Latent*.
- *Wrong answer*: the output behavior of the faulty circuit does not match that of the fault-free one.

A typical fault injection environment is composed of three modules:

- *Fault List Manager*: it is in charge of analyzing the system and generating the list of faults to be injected.
- *Fault Injection Manager*: it is in charge of orchestrating the selection of a new fault, its injection in the system, and the observation of the resulting behavior.
- *Result Analyzer*: it analyzes the data produced by the previous module, categorizes faults according to their effects, and produces statistical information.

2.2. Fault Locations

Charged particles hitting SRAM-based FPGA devices are likely to alter the contents of devices configuration memory [2]. We can categorize the effects of the change introduced by the SEU in two broad categories.

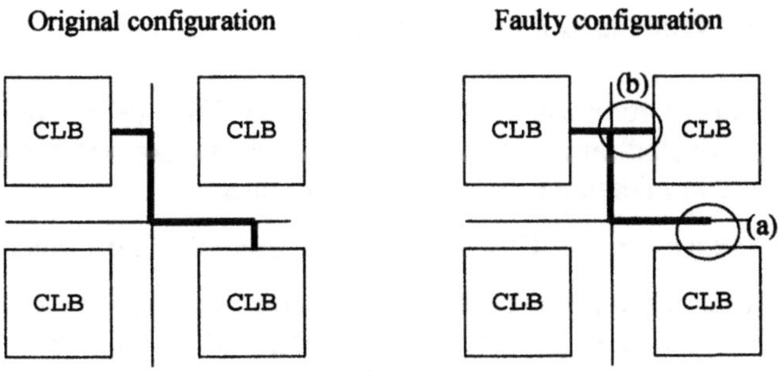

Figure 1: Example of inter-CLB effects

1. *Inter-CLB resources*: a SEU modifies the routing of signals between two CLBs; as a result, two CLBs that were connected before fault manifestation are no longer connected after the SEU reached the device (connection (a) in figure 1). Similarly, a connection between two CLBs may originate as a result of SEU occurrence (connection (b) in figure 1).
2. *Intra-CLB resources*: a SEU modifies the configuration of resources inside a single CLB of the device. When considering the architecture of a CLB, which is schematically reported in figure 2, we can classify the resources that can be altered in two types:
   a. *Routing*: the SEU modifies one of the configuration bits of the multiplexer the CLB embeds (resources A to C in figure 2).
   b. *Look-up tables*: the SEU modifies one bit in the look-up table the CLB embeds (resources LUT in figure 2).

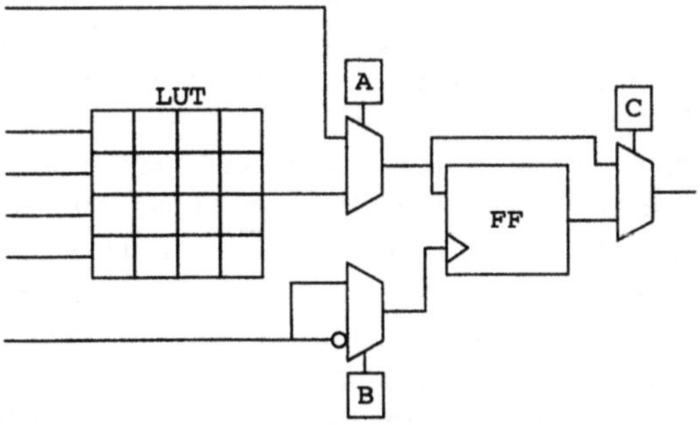

Figure 2: Intra-CLB resources.

Our fault injection environment supports the injection of bit-flips in both inter-CLB and intra-CLB resources. Thanks to the adoption of JBits, we are able to access and modify all the bits controlling the configuration of the mentioned resources. We are thus able to accurately model the effects of actual particles hitting the device.

2.3. JBits-Based Fault Injection Environment

The fault injection environment we developed exploits JBits [9] for generating the list of faults to be evaluated during the fault injection campaign and for inoculating the bit-flip during a fault injection experiment. In particular:

1. *Fault List Manager*: it is a JBits-based Java program that performs two tasks:
    a. It reads the bitstream the place and route tool produces and it identifies the FPGA resources that are actually used. This operation is motivated by the observation that injecting SEUs in un-used resources is useless, since they can not affect the circuit outputs.

    b. It generates the fault list. A fault is generated by randomly selecting as fault location one resource among the previously identified ones (i.e., FPGA resources that implement the considered circuit as described in the previous section). The time of the fault occurrence is randomly selected among the clock cycles that compose the set of input stimuli.
2. *Fault Injection Manager*: it is a JBits-based Java program that performs the following tasks:
    a. For every input vector in the set of input stimuli, it applies the vector to the circuit inputs, triggers the clock and observes the outputs the circuit produces.

    b. If the fault occurrence time is reached, a read-back operation is performed for loading the configuration memory from the FPGA. Then, the fault is injected by flipping the bit corresponding to the selected FPGA resource. Finally, the modified bitstream is re-loaded in the FPGA.

    c. The program also acts as Result Analyzer: it compares the outputs of the faulty device with those of the fault-free one which have been previously computed and stored, and it categorizes the fault effects according to the rules introduced in sub-section 2.1.

In the current implementation of our fault injection environment, the device under analysis is simulated through the VirtexDS program [9]. This solution offers a very simple way of analyzing fault effects on circuits and protects us against any damage of the FPGA device that may occur as side effects of the injected faults. As a major drawback, the adopted solution is rather time-consuming, since the VirtexDS is not optimized for speed and the simulation of large designs may require a long amount of time. In order to overcome this limitation, and by exploiting the features JBits offers, it is possible to replace the VirtexDS simulator with a board equipped with a real FPGA device.

2.4. The Fault Injection Process

The fault injection process consists in evaluating the effects of all the faults in the fault list on the analyzed circuits.

```
inject( fault list FL, input stimuli VL)
{  for each fault f ∈ FL do {
     reset FPGA board;
     download bitstream;
     time = 0;
     for every vector v ∈ VL do {
       if time == InjectionTime(f) then {
         read back bitstream;
         modify FaultyResource(f);
         write back bitstream; }
       apply v on the input;
       read output o;
       time++; }
     classify fault effect; }
}
```

Figure 3: the fault injection process

The sequence of operations that are performed during the fault injection process are described in figure 3.

3. Experimental Results

To evaluate the results our approach provides, we considered some circuits coming from the ITC'99 benchmark suite [12], we mapped them on FPGA devices and then we performed some fault injection experiments by injecting faults in the device configuration memory. We synthesized the benchmarks starting from their VHDL description resorting to the Synopsys FPGA Compiler II tool. Then, we performed the place and route operations exploiting the Alliance tool. The targeted device was a Virtex XCV300 and the adopted package was the PQ240.

The circuits characteristics are reported in table 1, where for each of them we report the number of VHDL lines, the FPGA resource occupation and the maximum clock frequency.

Circuit	VHDL lines	Used SLICEs out of 3072	Used IOBs out of 166	Clock frequency [MHz]
b01	110	10	5	107
b02	70	2	3	186
b03	141	20	9	121
b04	102	120	20	55
b08	89	26	14	88

Table 1: Circuit characteristics

During the injection experiments, we used as input stimuli some functional vectors provided by an automatic test pattern generator tool (`testgen` from Synopsys). Moreover, the fault list was randomly generated as described in section 2.3; for the purpose of this paper, and to limit the CPU time for each experiment, the fault list size was limited to 100 faults. The results we gathered are reported in table 2, where the circuit name, the number of faults and the length of the input stimuli are shown. Fault effects are classified in table 2 according to the categories introduced in section 2.1.

Circuit	Number of faults	Input stimuli length	Wrong answer	Effect-less	CPU time [s]
b01	100	129	65	35	1,036
b02	100	60	41	59	453
b03	100	174	34	66	1,929
b04	100	411	37	63	11,831
b08	100	411	54	46	7,502

Table 2: Fault injection results

Finally, the CPU times required for performing the injection experiments when the VirtexDS is used are reported. All the experiments have been performed on a personal computer based on a Pentium III processor running at 700 MHz and equipped with 640Mbytes of RAM memory.

These experiments confirm that faults originated in the device configuration memory may significantly affect the dependability of systems mapped on SRAM-based FPGA devices: the percentage of faults leading the circuits to produce wrong answers is indeed ranging from 34% to 65%. Moreover, a preliminary analysis of simulation traces suggests that faults modifying the signal routing cannot be neglected, thus tools able to support such a kind of faulty behavior are essential.

The major drawback of the current implementation of our fault injection environment is the high CPU time required by VirtexDS. A possible solution is to replace the simulator with a prototyping board equipped with a real FPGA device and by adopting a high-speed communication channel.

4. Conclusions

The paper presented a new fault injection environment that addresses the problem of assessing the effects of SEUs in the configuration memory of SRAM-based FPGA devices.

The approach exploits JBits for analyzing the bitstream loaded in the device to identify which are the most sensible portions of the FPGA. Then, a Java program based on the VirtexDS tool is used to perform fault injection experiments. The described environment has been used for analyzing the effects of charged particles on some benchmark circuits mapped on a Xilinx Virtex XCV300 device.

We are currently working on setting up a prototypical board suitable for radiation testing, whose purpose is to validate the results we gathered through simulation.

5. Acknowledgments

We would like to acknowledge Marco Palestro for implementing the described fault injection environments. We are also grateful to Mr. Brandon Blodget for his support in adapting JBits to our needs.

6. References

[1] M. Nikoladis, "Time Redundancy Based Soft-Error Tolerance to Rescue Nanometer Technologies", IEEE 17th VLSI Test Symposium, April 1999, pp. 86-94

[2] E. Fuller, M. Caffrey, A. Salazar, C. Carmichael, J. Fabula, "Radiation Characterization and SEU Mitigation of the Virtex FPGA for Space-Based Reconfigurable Computing", NSREC 2000

[3] C. Carmichael, "Correcting Single Event Upsets Through Virtex Partial Reconfiguration", Xilinx application note 216, XAPP216, 2000

[4] R. K. Iyer and D. Tang, "Experimental Analysis of Computer System Dependability", Chapter 5 of Fault-Tolerant Computer System Design, D. K. Pradhan (ed.), Prentice Hall, 1996

[5] E. Jenn, J. Arlat, M. Rimen, J. Ohlsson, J. Karlsson, "Fault Injection into VHDL Models: the MEFISTO Tool", Proc. FTCS-24, 1994, pp. 66-75

[6] G.A. Kanawati, N.A. Kanawati, J.A. Abraham, "FERRARI: A Flexible Software-Based Fault and Error Injection System", IEEE Trans. on Computers, Vol 44, N. 2, February 1995, pp. 248-260

[7] J. Arlat, M. Aguera, L. Amat, Y. Crouzet, J.C. Fabre, J.-C. Laprie, E. Martins, D. Powell, "Fault Injection for Dependability Validation: A Methodology and some Applications", IEEE Transactions on Software Engineering, Vol. 16, No. 2, February 1990

[8] "Virtex FPGA Series Configuration and Readback", Xilinx application note 138, XAPP138, 2001

[9] http://www.xilinx.com/products/jbits/

[10] F. Lima, C. Carmichael, J. Fabula, R. Padovani, R. Reis, "A Fault Injection Analysis of Virtex FPGA TMR Design Methodology", RADECS'2001

[11] L. Antoni, R. Leveugle, B. Fehér, "Using Run-time Reconfiguration for Fault Injection in Hardware Prototypes", IEEE International Symposium on Defect and Fault Tolerance in VLSI Systems, 2000, pp. 405-413

[12] F. Corno, M. Sonza Reorda, G. Squillero, "RT-Level ITC 99 Benchmarks and First ATPG Results", IEEE Design & Test of Computers, July-August 2000, pp. 44-53

Exploiting Reconfigurability for Effective Testing of Delay Faults in Sequential Subcircuits of LUT-based FPGAs

Andrzej Krasniewski

Institute of Telecommunications, Warsaw University of Technology
Nowowiejska 15/19, 00-665 Warsaw, Poland
andrzej@tele.pw.edu.pl

Abstract. We show how to extend the BIST-based test procedure for sequential subcircuits of LUT-based FPGAs, so that to increase the efficiency of delay fault detection. The proposed solution is based on the decomposition of the set of paths and the corresponding delay faults into two subsets, each exercised in a separate test phase. The detectability of path delay faults is enhanced through an appropriate modification of user-defined functions of the LUTs. An experimental study shows that the proposed extension reduces the length of test required to provide a specified detection probability for selected faults on average by a factor of more than 10, with the largest improvement for faults that are most difficult to detect by the original procedure.

1 Introduction

One of the key problems in testing FPGAs is the detection of timing-related (delay) faults. As timing-related faults are mostly associated with interconnection delays (this is especially true with the recent changes in the FPGA architectures, characterized by increasing popularity of cluster-based FPGAs [1]), testing for FPGA delay faults should focus on the interconnection structure.

Most techniques for testing in-circuit reconfigurable FPGAs exercise, as exhaustively as possible, all possible operation modes of FPGA programmable components (see, for example, [2]-[6]). With such a test strategy, however, it is possible to examine only a small fraction of interconnection patterns that can be set by programming the device. In other words, it is impossible to examine most complete paths (and the associated delay faults) existing in a particular user-defined circuit, even if the test technique itself is aimed at the detection of delay faults associated with interconnections, as is the BIST technique proposed in [7].

To deal with FPGA delay faults more effectively, application-dependent testing is advised. With this method, only one specific configuration of the FPGA – corresponding to the user-defined function – is thoroughly exercised [3], [8], [9].

In [8], a BIST-based procedure for application-dependent testing of in-circuit reconfigurable FPGAs is presented. During each of several test sessions, a selected part of an FPGA (configured to implement a user-defined function) is examined using the remaining portions of the FPGA, temporarily reconfigured into test pattern generators and test response compactors, in a similar way as for the conventional

M. Glesner, P. Zipf, and M. Renovell (Eds.): FPL 2002, LNCS 2438, pp. 616-626, 2002.

FPGA self-test techniques [2]. The development of the test procedure starts with the decomposition of the user-defined logic into a number of simple combinational and sequential subcircuits. For a sequential subcircuit, a two-phase test procedure, illustrated in Fig. 1, is applied.

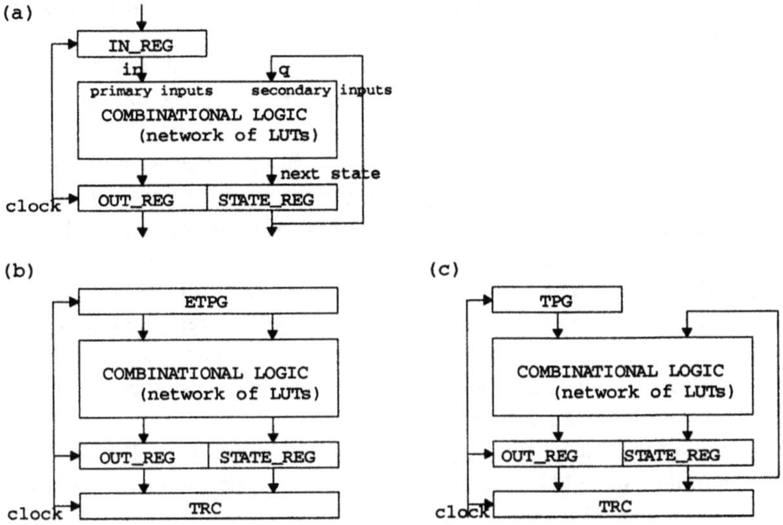

Fig. 1. Sequential subcircuit of an FPGA (a) and its reconfiguration for two-phase test procedure: test phase 1 (b) and test phase 2 (c)

The objective of test phase 1 is to exhaustively exercise the combinational logic. The feedback lines are broken and an exhaustive test pattern generator (ETPG) is placed on all the inputs of the combinational logic block. A test response compactor (TRC) collects responses of the subcircuit. During test phase 2, which is primarily intended to check the feedback lines, a test pattern generator (TPG) is placed only on the primary inputs of the subcircuit. The test responses are collected as for test phase 1.

During the test procedure shown in Fig. 1, test patterns are applied at-speed. The procedure is, therefore, quite suitable for the detection of timing-related problems. In this paper, we propose its extension which is oriented specifically towards delay faults. It involves the modification of user-defined functions of LUTs in the combinational logic block under test. Such a modification relies on an assumption that the propagation delay of a LUT does not depend on the implemented function.

In the earlier studies, the concept of the modification of user-defined LUT functions was exploited to enhance the testability of delay faults in combinational subcircuits of FPGAs through:

- the design of a BIST scheme that guarantees the coverage of all delay faults associated with physical paths from a selected set of critical paths, identified using a static timing analyzer or some other method [1];
- enhancement of the susceptibility of path delay faults to random testing [8].

The contribution presented in this paper is – to the best of our knowledge – the first attempt to exploit the idea of the modification of LUT functions in order to improve the detectability of delay faults in sequential subcircuits of FPGAs.

2 Testing Delay Faults in LUT-based FPGAs – Basic Concepts

We consider a sequential subcircuit of a user-programmed LUT-based FPGAs (Fig. 1(a)). The combinational part of such a subcircuit is represented as a network of interconnected single-output LUTs. For the purpose of our analysis, other logic components included in the combinational logic block, such as multiplexers, gates, etc., can be viewed as part of LUTs or part of the interconnection structure.

As FPGA delay faults are mainly associated with interconnections, the path delay fault model is an obvious choice. We assume that all delays that contribute to the propagation delay of a path may depend on the polarity of "local" transitions that occur at the input of the path and at the outputs of LUTs along the path [1]. Thus, the propagation delay of a path can only be defined for a given *path transition pattern*, PTP, which specifies, for each connection along the path, whether a rising transition or a falling transition occurs at that connection.

We introduce the concept of a logical path as an extension of the same notion in a network of simple gates [11]. A *logical path* π(PTP) is defined by a path π and some path transition pattern PTP associated with π. We say that a logical path π(PTP) *has a delay fault* if the propagation delay of path π corresponding to the path transition pattern PTP exceeds a given time T.

It has been shown that the methods and results of analysis of delay fault testability in circuits composed of simple logic gates (NOT, AND, NAND, OR, NOR) are not applicable to networks of LUTs [12]. This implies, in particular, that the concept of a test for a path delay fault must be redefined when moving from conventional circuits to FPGAs. In our earlier study, several types of tests for path delay faults in networks of LUTs, such as weak non-robust, strong non-robust and robust tests, are defined [12]. Here, we do not recall these definitions, but indirectly rely on them when defining tests for path delay faults in sequential subcircuits of FPGAs. In what follows, for the sake of brevity, we say "test for a logical path" instead of "test for the delay fault associated with a logical path".

For a sequential subcircuit, such as shown in Fig. 1(c), let in_{comb} = (in,q) denote a vector applied to the network of LUTs, where *in* is the content of TPG, and *q* is the content of STATE_REG. Consider a pair of vectors <$in_{comb}(1)$, $in_{comb}(2)$> produced in two consecutive clock cycles at the input of the network of LUTs. Let Q^+ be the next state function of the considered subcircuit. We say that state q is *reachable* if for any other state q', there exists a sequence of vectors applied to input *in* that moves the subcircuit from state q to state q'.

A *test* of type T (weak non-robust, etc.) for a logical path π(PTP) in a sequential subcircuit of an FPGA is a triple <q(1), in(1), in(2)>, such that state q(1) is reachable and a pair of vectors <$in_{comb}(1)$, $in_{comb}(2)$>, where $in_{comb}(1)$ = (in(1),q(1)) and $in_{comb}(2)$ = (in(2),Q^+($in_{comb}(1)$)), is a test of type T for π(PTP), as defined for the combinational part of the subcircuit (network of LUTs).

For a given type of testability T, the *detectability* (detection probability) of the delay fault associated with a logical path π(PTP) is the probability of producing, in two consecutive clock cycles, a triple of vectors <q(1), in(1), in(2)> which is a test of type T for π(PTP). The following assumptions are made regarding the test scheme of Fig. 1(c) when calculating the detectability of delay faults:

- a random sequence of vectors is produced by TPG, i.e. consecutive vectors are independent and the probability of a 0 (or 1) at each position of TPG is 0.5,
- the probability of a 1 at each position of STATE_REG is determined by the function of the LUT network, assuming a random sequence produced by TPG.

3 Proposed Extension of the Test Procedure

The proposed extension of the self-test procedure of Fig. 1 is based on splitting of test phase 2 into two test phases and modification of user-defined LUT functions for each of these new phases.

3.1 Splitting of Test Phase 2

To maximize the dependability of delay fault testing, the reconfiguration of a portion of the FPGA into BIST resources should not affect timing characteristics of that part of the FPGA which is exercised during a particular test session. This requirement can only be satisfied for test phase 2 of the self-test procedure of Fig. 1, and not for test phase 1 [8]. Therefore, the proposed extension, oriented toward delay faults, relies on the modification of test phase 2.

The set of paths in the subcircuit of Fig. 1 is "decomposed" into two subsets: paths that originate at the input register and paths that originate at the state register. Each of these two subsets is exercised in a separate phase of the test procedure. This means that the proposed extended procedure consists of three test phases:

phase 1: oriented toward the detection of static faults in the network of LUTs (as described in Section 1),
phase 2A: oriented toward the detection of delay faults associated with paths that originate at the input register,
phase 2B: oriented toward the detection of delay faults associated with paths that originate at the state register.

For phase 2A or 2B, the terms *active paths*, *active inputs* and *active variables* are used to denote target paths, inputs to the LUT network at which these paths originate, and variables associated with outputs of LUTs along these paths, respectively.

3.2 Modification of User-Defined LUT Functions

The splitting of the original test phase 2 into two phases (2A and 2B) allows for appropriate modification of user-defined LUT functions that makes active paths easier to test. The improvement in detectability of path delay faults is obtained through:

- deleting inactive variables from the functional input set of the LUTs,
- enhancement of the LUT testability characteristics for a given LUT functional input set.

The *functional input set* of a LUT is the set of LUT inputs that affect the LUT output (the functional input set may differ from the structural input set that includes all LUT inputs which are physically connected to the outputs of flip-flops or other LUTs). For a LUT located on an active path, making its output independent on inactive variables – as a result of a modification of the LUT function – makes it easier to satisfy the "local testability requirements" associated with that LUT. In other words, when deriving a test, fewer variables associated with that LUT must be assigned specific values.

The "local testability requirements" for a LUT can be made easier to satisfy without changing the functional input set of a LUT (or after reducing the functional input set of a LUT). A "library" of functions with optimal testability characteristics that can replace original LUT functions has been developed as part of our earlier studies on the enhancement of delay fault testability in LUT-based FPGAs [10].

A procedure for the modification of user-defined LUT functions must take into account the below discussed constraints.

The modification of user-defined LUT functions may affect path transition patterns associated with active paths. Therefore, the set of path delay faults that can occur in the normal operation of the modified subcircuit may differ from that of the original subcircuit. It is, therefore, essential to formulate requirements to be satisfied by the LUT modification procedure with regard to such changes. This complex problem is discussed in more detail in [13]. Below, only the main conclusion, formulated using the notion of the input-output transition pattern of a LUT, is presented.

The *input-output transition pattern* of a LUT determines how the LUT output changes in response to changes at its inputs, i.e., it specifies for each input whether the LUT function is positive unate, negative unate or binate in that input (a single-output Boolean function F is *positive/negative unate* in input variable x_i if changing x_i from 0 to 1 does not affect the value of F or causes its change from 0 to 1/from 1 to 0; function F is *binate* in x_i if it is neither positive nor negative unate in x_i).

The practical minimum requirement to be satisfied by the LUT modification procedure is to request no change in the input-output transition pattern for active variables of each LUT. This is referred to as the *LUT input-output transition pattern preservation* requirement.

The problem with the preservation of this requirement lies in that for some input-output transition patterns corresponding to LUT active variables, no functions that preserve these patterns exist if the set of their arguments is limited to the set of active variables [13]. The most trivial example would be a LUT that has just one active input variable and whose user-defined function is binate in that variable. As no single-input function exists that is binate in its only input variable, at least one inactive variable must remain in the functional input set of the considered LUT. Therefore, a straightforward idea to eliminate all inactive variables from the functional input set of each LUT is not always applicable.

Another reason for retaining inactive variables in functional input sets of the LUTs is to provide adequate controllability of state variables. The issue is relevant for test phase 2B. For this test phase, the complete elimination of inactive variables from functional input sets of the LUTs would make all the next state variables independent of the primary inputs of the circuit. Thus, the considered sequential subcircuit would become essentially non-controllable, with a disastrous impact on its testability. Therefore, for test phase 2B, some inactive variables must remain in the functional input sets of selected LUTs. When deciding which inactive variables are to be retained, we apply the following heuristic rules to maximize the "randomization" of the state of the circuit:

a) each next state variable must depend on at least one primary input variable;
b) the primary inputs should supply LUTs located close to the state register (ideally, LUTs that produce next state variables);
c) transitive functional input sets of individual next state variables (sets of primary and secondary input variables upon which next state variables depend) should be maximally disjoint with regard to inactive input variables.

All these constraints have an impact on the BIST scheme. The BIST scheme of Fig. 1(c) is "natural" for test phase 2A. For test phase 2B, variables associated with the primary inputs are inactive, but – as shown above – some of them must remain in the functional input sets of the LUTs. Therefore, we assume that, for both test phase 2A and test phase 2B, the BIST configuration is similar to that of Fig. 1(c). The only difference is that, to preserve the timing characteristics of the subcircuit under test, the input register (IN_REG in Fig. 1(a)) is not reconfigured into a test pattern generator – an extra test pattern generator is used to feed this register [8].

4 Experimental Study

In this section, we demonstrate the feasibility and effectiveness of our approach. For an example circuit, we compare the detectability of selected path delay faults for the phase 2 of the original test procedure (Fig. 1(c)) and for phase 2A and phase 2B of its proposed extension.

Consider the sequential subcircuit of a LUT-based FPGA shown in Fig. 2. It has 6 input variables (a, b, c, d, e, f) and 3 state variables (u, w, y). Variables u^+, w^+, y^+ are the next state variables. The functions implemented by the LUTs and their input-output transition patterns are shown in Fig. 2 (LUT functions are denoted by capital letters; output variables of LUTs and flip-flops are denoted by lower-case letters).

For test phase 2A, the set of active inputs is {a, b, c, d, e, f}, the set of active paths includes all the paths that originate at these inputs, and the set of active variables is {a, b, c, d, e, f, g, h, i, j, k, u^+, w^+, y^+}.

For each LUT, there exists at least one function whose functional input set includes only active variables and which preserves the input-output transition pattern of the original LUT function for these active variables.

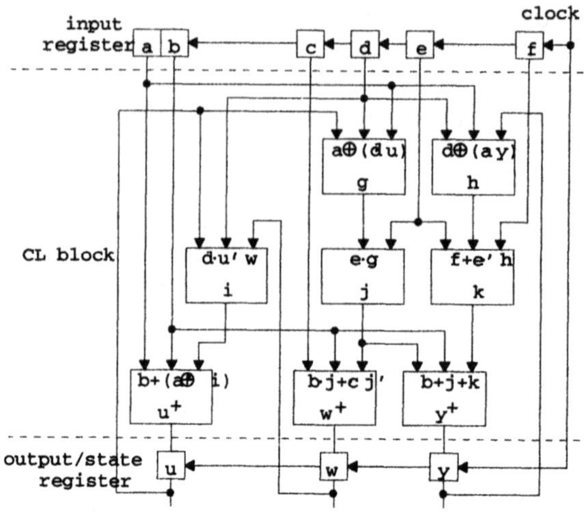

G: binate in a, d, u
H: binate in a, d, y
I: positive unate in d, w
negative unate in u
J: positive unate in e, g
K: positive unate in f, h
negative unate in e
U: positive unate in b
binate in a, i
W: positive unate in b, c
binate in j
Y: positive unate in b, j, k

Fig. 2. Sequential subcircuit of a LUT-based FPGA – an example

In Fig. 3(a), we show the subcircuit with LUT functions modified for test phase 2A. LUT inputs that are not included in the functional input sets of the LUTs are not connected. The LUT functions for which the functional input set is reduced (G, H, I) are obviously different from their original counterparts. Among functions whose original functional input sets include only variables that are active during test phase 2A, functions K and Y are modified, whereas functions J, U and W are not modified.

For test phase 2B, the set of active inputs is {u, w, y}, the set of active paths includes the paths that originate at these inputs, and the set of active variables is {u, w, y, g, h, i, j, k, u^+, w^+, y^+}.

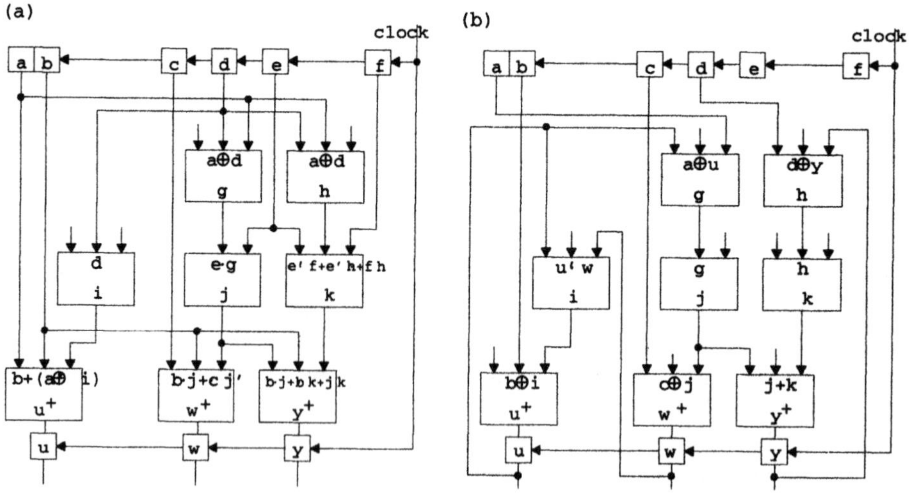

Fig. 3. Subcircuit modified for testing: test phase 2A (a) and test phase 2B (b)

It can be seen that each of the LUTs that implement functions G, H, U and W has only one active input variable and its original function is binate in that variable (e.g. function G shown in Fig. 2 is binate in its only active variable u). As was noted in Section 3, there exists no single-argument function that is binate in its only variable. This means that the functional input sets of functions G, H, U and W modified for test phase 2B must each include at least one inactive variable. This can be observed in Fig. 3(b) which shows the subcircuit with LUT functions modified for test phase 2B.

The characteristics of the original subcircuit and the subcircuit modified for phase 2A and phase 2B of the extended test procedure are given in Table 1. The controllability of the three next state variables, u^{+}, w^{+}, y^{+}, (next to the last row) is measured by their expected values (probabilities of the logic 1) – its optimal value is thus 0.5. In the last row, the values of a measure that characterizes the suitability of LUT functions for path delay fault testing, referred to as LUT sensitizability [13], are given.

Table 1. Characteristics of the original and modified subcircuit

subcircuit characteristic	original subcircuit	subcircuit modified for phase 2A	subcircuit modified for phase 2B
no. of active paths	21	16	5
no. of active inputs to the LUT network	9	6	3
no. of inactive inputs to the LUT network	0	3	6
no. of functional inputs (primary + secondary)	9 (6+3)	6 (6+0)	7 (4+3)
no. of active inputs to LUTs – for the subcircuit	23	19	10
no. of active inputs to LUTs – average for a LUT	2.56	2.38	1.25
no. of functional inputs to LUTs – for the subcircuit	23	19	14
no. of functional inputs to LUTs – average for a LUT	2.56	2.38	1.75
average no. of LUT off-path inputs for an active path	4.00	3.25 (3.75)*	2.00 (4.80)*
no. of transitive funct. inputs of next state variables	5, 6, 7	3, 5, 5	3, 3, 4
controllability of next state variables	0.75,0.45,0.8[illegible]	**	0.5, 0.5, 0.75
average LUT sensitizability	0.33	0.52	0.63

* the number in parentheses gives the related value for the original subcircuit (calculated for those paths in the original subcircuit that are active during a particular test phase)

** irrelevant because the functional input sets of the LUTs do not contain any state variables

The values of the detectability (detection probability) for two selected path delay faults in the original and modified subcircuits, calculated for three different types of testability under assumptions formulated in Section 2, are given in Table 2. For the modified subcircuits, the values for the logical path $d{\uparrow}g{\uparrow}j{\uparrow}y^{+}{\uparrow}$ are for test phase 2A, and the values for $y{\downarrow}h{\uparrow}k{\uparrow}y^{+}{\uparrow}$ are for test phase 2B. Besides detectability, in Table 2 we also show the size of transitive functional input sets for the considered paths (the transitive functional input set for a path is equal to the transitive functional input set of a variable at which that path terminates), the total number of functional off-path inputs for all the LUTs on the considered paths, and the average LUT sensitizability.

Table 2. Detectability of selected path delay faults for the original and modified subcircuit

fault	circuit	no. of transitive functional inputs	functional off-path inputs		average LUT sensitizability	detectability		
			active	inactive		weak non-robust	strong non-robust	robust
d↑g↑j↑y⁺↑	original	6	5	0	0.35	$1.17 \cdot 10^{-2}$	$1.95 \cdot 10^{-3}$	$9.77 \cdot 10^{-4}$
d↑g↑j↑y⁺↑	modified	5	4	0	0.50	$3.13 \cdot 10^{-2}$	$1.37 \cdot 10^{-2}$	$5.86 \cdot 10^{-3}$
y↓h↑k↑y⁺↑	original	7	6	0	0.30	$3.42 \cdot 10^{-3}$	$3.20 \cdot 10^{-3}$	$8.55 \cdot 10^{-4}$
y↓h↑k↑y⁺↑	modified	4	1	1	0.67	$4.69 \cdot 10^{-2}$	$4.69 \cdot 10^{-2}$	$2.34 \cdot 10^{-2}$

As expected, as a result of the modification of LUT functions, the detectability of the considered faults has substantially increased. It is seen even better if we compare the length of test required to detect the faults.

For a fault whose detectability is P, the expected length of test (number of randomly generated tests), L, required to detect that fault with a specified probability δ is [14]

$$L = \lceil \log(1-\delta)/\log(1-P) \rceil .$$

In Table 3, we show how the expected length of test required to detect the considered faults with probability $\delta = 0.99$ has decreased as a result of the LUT modifications (the value 27.6 in Table 3 means that the test for the subcircuit modified for test phase 2B is 27.6 times shorter than for the original subcircuit).

Table 3. Decrease in the expected length of test required to detect selected path delay faults with probability $\delta = 0.99$

fault	weak non-robust	strong non-robust	robust
d↑g↑j↑y⁺↑	2.7	7.0	6.0
y↓h↑k↑y⁺↑	14.0	14.9	27.6

The observed improvement in the detectability of delay faults can be attributed to the following changes in the characteristics of the subcircuit (cf. Table 1 and Table 2):

- reduction of the size of functional input sets for individual LUTs,
- reduction of the size of transitive functional input sets for individual paths,
- better testability characteristics of individual LUTs,
- reduction in the number (in the considered subcircuit – complete elimination) of state variables affecting the next state variables for test phase 2A,
- better controllability of next state variables for test phase 2B.

It can be seen (cf. Table 1 and Table 2) that those of the above characteristics which are relevant for both test phases of the extended procedure are more favorable for test phase 2B that accounts for paths which originate at the state register. This is reflected in Table 3: an improvement of detectability for fault y↓h↑k↑y⁺↑ is larger than for fault d↑g↑j↑y⁺↑. This property of the test development procedure, typical for sequential subcircuits in which the number of flip-flops is lower than the number of inputs, is beneficial because faults associated with paths that originate at the state register are generally more difficult to test.

5 Conclusion

We present an extension of the BIST-based application-dependent test procedure for sequential subcircuits of LUT-based FPGAs. A comparison of the efficiency of fault detection for the original 2-phase test procedure and for its proposed extension – the 3-phase test procedure – shows that a substantial improvement in the detectability of path delay faults can be observed for the extended procedure. In particular:

- for the examined subcircuit, the length of test required to provide a specified level of detectability is reduced on average by a factor of more than 10; for larger subcircuits, this reduction is expected to be even more significant;
- the improvement of detectability is more significant for faults associated with paths that originate at the state register, i.e. faults that are most difficult to detect by the original procedure.

Possible extensions of this work can go in two directions:

- Adding an optional step in the development of the test plan, intended to reduce the set of target paths. The reduced set would include only critical paths, identified using a static timing analyzer or some other method. Such an approach would increase the detectability of critical faults at the expense of neglecting faults associated with non-critical paths.
- Decomposition of set of paths into more than two subsets, each corresponding to a separate test phase. This would allow for a reduction of the number of variables in functional input sets of LUTs for each test phase and thereby would make active paths easier to test.

An implementation of these ideas would introduce additional trade-offs in the application-dependent testing of LUT-based FPGAs

References

1. Harris, I.G., Menon, P.R., Tessier, R.: BIST-Based Delay Path Testing in FPGA Architectures. In: Proc. IEEE Int. Test Conf. (2001) 932-938
2. Stroud, C., Konala, S., Chen, P., Abramovici, M.: Built-In Self-Test of Logic Blocks in FPGAs (Finally, a Free Lunch: BIST Without Overhead!). In: Proc. 14th VLSI Test Symp. (1996), 387-392
3. Renovell, M., Figueras, J., Zorian, Y.: Test of RAM-based FPGA: Methodology and Application to the Interconnect. In: Proc. 15th VLSI Test Symp. (1997) 230-237
4. Huang, W.K., Meyer, F.J., Chen, X.-T., Lombardi, F.: Testing Configurable LUT-Based FPGA's. IEEE Trans. on VLSI Systems, **6** (1998) 276-283
5. Metra, C., Mojoli, G., Pastore, S., Salvi, D., Sechi, G.: Novel Technique for Testing FPGAs. In: Proc. IEEE Design, Automation and Test in Europe Conf. (1998) 89-94

6. Renovell, M.: A Specific Test Methodology for Symmetric SRAM-Based FPGAs. In: Hartenstein, R.W., Grunbacher H. (eds.), Proc. FPL 2000, LNCS, vol. 1896, Springer Verlag (2000) 300-311
7. Abramovici, M., Stroud, C.: BIST-Based Delay-Fault Testing in FPGAs. In: Proc. IEEE Int. On-Line Testing Workshop (2002)
8. Krasniewski, A.: Application-Dependent Testing of FPGA Delay Faults. In: Proc. 25th EUROMICRO Conf., vol. 1 (1999) 260-267
9. Quddus, W., Jas, A., Touba, N.A.: Configuration Self-Test in FPGA-Based Reconfigurable Systems. In: Proc. ISCAS'99 (1999) 97-100
10. Krasniewski, A.: Exploiting Reconfigurability for Effective Detection of Delay Faults in LUT-Based FPGAs. In: Hartenstein, R.W., Grunbacher H. (eds.), Proc. FPL 2000, LNCS, vol. 1896, Springer Verlag (2000) 675-684
11. Cheng, K.-T., Chen, H.-C.: Classification and Identification of Nonrobust Untestable Path Delay Faults. IEEE Trans. on CAD, **8** (1996) 845-853
12. Krasniewski, A.: Testing FPGA Delay Faults: It Is Much More Complicated Than It Appears. In: Proc. IFAC Workshop on Programmable Devices and Systems – PDS2001 (2001) 291-296
13. Krasniewski, A.: Exploiting Reconfigurability for Effective Testing of Sequential Subcircuits in LUT-Based FPGAs, Tech. Report, Inst. of Telecommunications, Warsaw Univ. of Technology (2002)
14. David, R.: Random Testing of Digital Circuits: Theory and Applications, chapter 6, Marcel Dekker, Inc. (1998)

Logarithmic Number System and Floating-Point Arithmetics on FPGA

Rudolf Matoušek[1], Milan Tichý[1], Zdeněk Pohl[1], Jiří Kadlec[1], Chris Softley[2], and Nick Coleman[2]

[1] Institute for Information Theory and Automation,
Department of Signal Processing,
Pod vodárenskou věží 4,
182 08 Praha, Czech Republic
{matousek,tichy,xpohl,kadlec}@utia.cas.cz
http://www.utia.cas.cz/ZS
[2] Department of Electrical & Electronic Engineering,
Merz Court, University of Newcastle upon Tyne, UK
{c.i.softley, j.n.coleman}@ncl.ac.uk
http://napier.ncl.ac.uk/HSLA

Abstract. An introduction to a logarithmic number system (LNS) is presented. Range and precision of this arithmetic is briefly discussed. We show that the LNS arithmetic is suitable for a FPGA implementation. A case study will compare parameters of our LNS arithmetic library to a conventional floating-point arithmetic.

1 Introduction

In recent years we have investigated the use of a logarithmic number representation as an alternative to floating point. Efficient techniques have been developed to facilitate arithmetic comparable to single-precision floating-point in the logarithmic domain. One of goals of our project[1] is the development of IP cores for FPGA implementation, providing comprehensive and efficient real number processing capabilities.

1.1 LNS Number Representation

In LNS, a value x is represented as the fixed-point quantity $i = log|x|$, with an extra bit to indicate the sign of x and a special arrangement to accommodate zero and other exceptional values. Base-2 logarithms are used throughout our work, though in principle any base could be used. For two LNS values $i = log_2|x|$ and $j = log_2|y|$, LNS arithmetic involves the following computations:

[1] This work was supported by the ESPRIT Long-Term Research program: project "High Speed Logarithmic Arithmetic Unit", grant no. 33544.

M. Glesner, P. Zipf, and M. Renovell (Eds.): FPL 2002, LNCS 2438, pp. 627–636, 2002.

$$\log_2(x+y) = i + \log_2\left(1+2^{j-i}\right) \ , \tag{1}$$

$$\log_2(x-y) = i + \log_2\left(1-2^{j-i}\right) \ , \tag{2}$$

$$\log_2(x \cdot y) = i + j \ , \tag{3}$$

$$\log_2\left(\frac{x}{y}\right) = i - j \ , \tag{4}$$

$$\log_2\left(\sqrt{x}\right) = \frac{i}{2} \ , \tag{5}$$

where for (1) and (2), without loss of generality, we choose $j \leq i$. In all of the above the sign bits are handled separately by a simple logic.

The equations (3), (4) and (5) can be implemented as simple as fixed-point addition, subtraction and shift operations. Unfortunately the equations (1) and (2) require evaluation of a nonlinear function

$$F(r = j - i) = \log_2\left(1 \pm 2^r\right) \ , \tag{6}$$

which can be seen of figure 1. The solution of this problem is discussed in the next section.

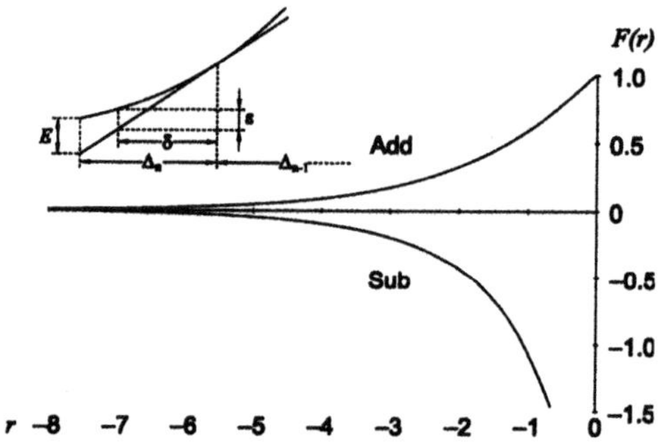

Fig. 1. LNS sum and difference functions. The inset shows an interpolation detail.

2 Arithmetic Algorithms

Historically ([1]), a look-up table was used to cover all possible values of equations (1) and (2). It is apparent that as the word length increases, the table sizes increase exponentially, which limits the practical utility of this approach.

A new approach [2] considered the implementation of the look-up table throughout r only at intervals of Δ, where $r = -n\Delta - \delta$. Intervening values were obtained by interpolation using the Taylor series

$$F(r) = F(-n\Delta) + \frac{D(-n\Delta)\,\delta}{1!} + \frac{D'(-n\Delta)\,\delta^2}{2!} + \cdots \ . \tag{7}$$

The scheme exposed a further problem intrinsic to LNS arithmetic: the difficulty of interpolating $F(r)$ in the region $-1 < r < 0$.

Our approach employs the first-order Taylor series approximation. The look-up tables are kept reasonable small by introducing an innovative error correction mechanism ([3]) and a range-shift algorithm ([4],[5]) for values in the range $-0.5 < r < 0$.

2.1 Conventional Addition and Subtraction

An interpolation detail of the function $F(r)$ is shown in figure 1. To minimise storage needs, Δ is progressively increased as the function becomes more linear with decreasing r. An intervening value of r lying in the n-th interval is thus correctly expressed as

$$r = \begin{cases} -\delta & \text{for } n = 0 \\ \sum_{i=0}^{n-1} (-\Delta_i) - \delta & \text{for } n > 0 \ . \end{cases} \tag{8}$$

For clarity of explanation, however, the following text will omit further reference to the variation in Δ and abbreviate the expression (8) to

$$r = -n\Delta - \delta \ . \tag{9}$$

As mentioned above, the Taylor series approximation was chosen. For the first-order case, the intervening value of r can be then obtained by formula

$$F(r) \approx F(-n\Delta) - \delta D(-n\Delta) \ . \tag{10}$$

Both $F(-n\Delta)$ and $D(-n\Delta)$ are stored in a look-up table.

The interpolation yields an error, as shown also on figure 1. The error corresponding to an intervening value r can be obtained by formula

$$\varepsilon(n, \delta) = F(-n\Delta) - \delta D(-n\Delta) - F(r) \ . \tag{11}$$

For each n, ε increases with δ to a maximum

$$E(n) \approx F(-n\Delta) - \Delta_n D(-n\Delta) - F(r) \ . \tag{12}$$

2.2 Error Correction Algorithm

For bigger word lengths, reasonable small look-up tables F and D yields too big error in the interpolation. An correction mechanism must be employed to meet our criteria.

Our mechanism is based on the observation that, for a given δ, the ratio

$$P(n, \delta) = \frac{\varepsilon(n, \delta)}{E(n)} \tag{13}$$

is roughly constant for all n. It is therefore possible to store, for one n, a table P of the error at successive points throughout each Δ, expressed as a proportion of the maximum error E attained in that interval. It is also necessary to store, together with F and D for each interval, its value of E. The error ε is then obtained for any (n, δ) as

$$\varepsilon(n, \delta) \approx E(n)P(c, \delta) \tag{14}$$

where c is a constant. This is accumulated into the result of the interpolation, thereby correcting the error.

This scheme has the major practical advantage that the lookups of $E(n)$ and $P(c, \delta)$ can be performed at the same time as those of $F(n)$ and $D(n)$ and their product can be evaluated simultaneously with the multiplication in the interpolation.

2.3 Subtractor Range Shifter

The range shifter simplifies the subtraction operation by obviating the interpolation in the region $-0.5 < r < 0$. The shifter simply replaces the subtraction $2^j - 2^i$ with two successive subtractions

$$2^j - 2^i = \left(2^i - 2^{j+k1}\right) - 2^{j+k2} \tag{15}$$

where

$$k2 = log_2 \left(1 - 2^{k1}\right) \ . \tag{16}$$

If we apply second-base logarithm to equation (15), we obtain a new subtraction formula in the form

$$log_2 \left(2^j - 2^i\right) = i_2 + F\left(r_2\right) \tag{17}$$

where

$$i_2 = i + F(r + k1) \tag{18}$$

$$r_2 = r + k2 - F(r + k1) \ . \tag{19}$$

For it to be possible to use existing hardware to evaluate (17), we require a means to evaluate i_2 and r_2. We therefore require a simple way to evaluate $F(r + k1)$. This is achieved by tabulating F in a table referred to as $F1$ throughout the range R over which the range-shift is required at intervals of Δ and choosing $k1$ such that the $F(r + k1)$ is a tabulated point. In practice, the address for the table $F1$ is obtained easily by a formula

$$I_1 = r \left\langle log_2 (R) - 1 + f \cdots log_2 (\Delta) + f \right\rangle \tag{20}$$

where operator $\langle\ \rangle$[2] denotes bitwise extraction and of course f makes a correction according to the fraction length. The $k1$ must be therefore chosen as

$$k1 = r \left\langle log_2 (\Delta) - 1 + f \cdots 0 \right\rangle \ . \tag{21}$$

[2] It is something like $r(10 \text{ downto } 0)$ in VHDL or $r[10:0]$ in VERILOG.

The $k2$ can be evaluated by tabulating all values of the right side of the equation (16) in the range given by $k1$, i.e. $-\Delta < r < 0$. The address can be again easily obtained by a formula

$$I_2 = r \langle log_2(\Delta) - 1 + f \cdots 0 \rangle \ . \tag{22}$$

Now, substituting back into (18) and (19):

$$i_2 = i + F1[I_1] \tag{23}$$

$$r_2 = r + F2[I_2] - F1[I_1] \tag{24}$$

where operator [ ][3] denotes table look-up. These new values are passed to the existing interpolator to evaluate the equation (17).

3 LNS Library Implementation

In the previous sections was shown, that the LNS arithmetic can perform multiplication, division, square and square-root operations simple and fast. On the other hand, the addition and subtraction algorithm is rather complex.

We will show here how to implement LNS arithmetic comparable to a single-precision IEEE floating-point standard. A low precision solution is also discussed.

3.1 Data Format, Range, and Precision

IEEE single-precision floating-point (FLP) representation uses a sign, 8-bit biased exponent and 23-bit mantissa. This format holds signed values in the range $1.2\text{E}-38$ to $3.4\text{E}+38$.

In the equivalent LNS representation, the integer and fractional parts are kept as a coherent two's complement fixed-point value in the range -128 to $\approx +128$. The real numbers represented are signed and in the range $\approx 2.9\text{E}-39$ to $3.4\text{E}+38$. One special value is used to represent the real number zero.

The 20-bit LNS format maintains the same range as the 32-bit, but has precision reduced to 11 fractional bits. It is comparable to the 16-bit FLP formats used on commercial DSP devices.

3.2 Design Structure

Adder and subtractor unit uses the theory from the section 2. Its structure is shown on the figure 2 and in [3]. Two operands are passed directly to magnitude comparator and zero, sign and control unit (ctrl unit). The magnitude comparator returns i, j, and r. It also detects equality. It passes its results regarding the relative magnitude of the two operands to the ctrl unit.

According to the comparator, addition/subtraction operations are completed in two specialised blocks of circuitry. Additions are passed directly to the add/sub

[3] Like in C/C++ for example.

unit, which interpolates the result using the Taylor expansion with the correction algorithm described above. In the case of subtraction, the data will follow one of two paths. If $-0.5 > r > 0$, the operands will be processed by the range shifter. After modification, or if $r \leq -0.5$ initially, the operands are forwarded to the add/sub where the operation is completed.

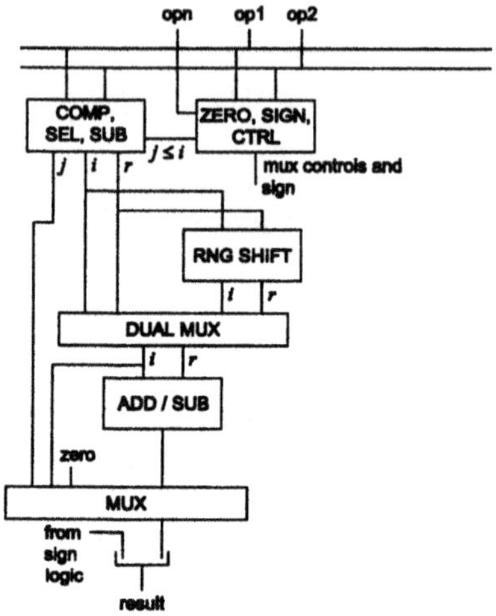

Fig. 2. Schematic of the LNS adder/subtractor.

The ctrl unit can detect zero operand values, and is supplied with information about the relative magnitude of the operands by the magnitude comparator. In cases involving one or more zero operands, or in cases where the two operands are equal, the result may either follow one of the operands, or be zero itself. Meanwhile the sign logic determines the sign of the result in accordance with the normal procedures for sign and magnitude comparator, and the sign bit is appended.

The multiplication and division cores are implemented using a common two's complement fixed-point adder resp. subtractor. Left and right shift operations are employed for the square and square-root macros. A simple logic is needed to handle special values, overflow and underflow.

3.3 Size and Speed

Our LNS core library implements all arithmetic cores in both 32-bit and 20-bit precision. All macros are optimised for Xilinx Virtex devices running at least at 50MHz.

The adder/subtractor is a 8-stage pipelined macro so a new calculation starts on each clock cycle. The arithmetic core of the algorithm consumes about 1300 slices (as known from Xilinx Virtex devices) for the 32-bit word length and about

720 slices for the low-precision solution. The lookup table memory consumes 96 BlockRAM cells (again Xilinx Virtex cell) in the 32-bit case and just 4 BlockRam cells in the 20-bit case.

The other macros in the library consumes each about 200 slices in the 32-bit case and about 160 slices in the 20-bit case. All these macros completes its operation exactly in one clock cycle.

4 Floating-Point Library

In the section 5 is provided a small comparison of our LNS library with a conventional floating-point library, and therefore, we outline some important library data here.

Information about three different floating-point libraries were available to us. We selected the most optimised pipelined solution. The important markers of this library, such as core size, clock rate and pipeline latency, are shown in table 1.

Table 1. Floating-point IP cores sizes and performance data. Slices are of Xilinx Virtex type, clock rate is in MHz. Latency describes the depth of the pipeline.

	20-bit			32-bit		
Operation	Slices	Frequency	Latency	Slices	Frequency	Latency
add/sub	208	153	11	420	130	12
mul	171	125	6	326	122	6
div	348	166	19	711	142	27
sqrt	620	173	19	780	146	27

5 Case Study

This section addresses the question of whether the performance of our LNS cores is comparable to the traditional floating-point solution. The best comparison is on an application, which is natural for that particular kind of arithmetic. Both floating-point and our LNS core libraries are to be used mostly in the DSP area, so we decided to make the comparison on a part of a RLS QRD algorithm. For a detailed information, please see [6].

5.1 QRD Algorithm

It can be shown, that the QRD algorithm can be easily mapped to a systolic array (see [6]). In fact, the array is a triangle composed of two types arithmetic elements: diagonal elements and the other elements. The diagonal elements are more complex, so the comparison will be based on them.

Our arithmetic element has to perform the following operations each time when a new data arrives:

$$d' = \sqrt{(\beta d)^2 + x^2} \tag{25}$$

$$c = \beta \frac{d}{d'} \tag{26}$$

$$s = \frac{x}{d'} \tag{27}$$

$$\delta_{out} = c\delta_{in} \tag{28}$$

where d, c and s must be stored internally. d' is the value of d for the next data cycle. β is a constant, x and δ_{in} are inputs and finally, δ_{out}, c and s are outputs of our element. For better understanding, our arithmetic cell is shown on figure 3.

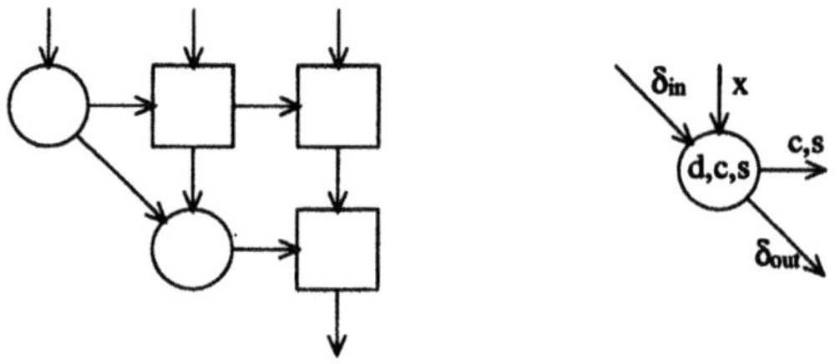

Fig. 3. The left sub-figure shows a schematic of a systolic array implementation of the QRD algorithm. A detail of one diagonal cell is shown on the right sub-figure.

5.2 LNS Solution

The LNS solution is straightforward and follows directly the algorithm critical path (see figure 4). One multiplier, one squarer (shared for both squares), one add/sub unit and one square-root macro are needed to evaluate the equation (25). It takes 11 clock cycles. Next, we can evaluate equations (26) and (27) in parallel. The product βd is already available as a part of equation (25), so only two divisions are needed to obtain results. The equation (28) depends on equation (26), and therefore just one divider can be employed without any additional delay to our algorithm critical path. Finally, the equation (28) can be evaluated by employing one multiplier. Evaluation of equations (26), (27), and (28) takes two clock cycles. Note, that just one pipeline stage of the adder cell is used, so the unit can be shared among up to 8 arithmetic cells.

In summary, we require 13 clock cycles to process a new data. We have utilised exactly one adder, multiplier, divider, squarer, and square-root unit. For 32-bit case, it will consume about 3000 slices of Xilinx Virtex device. A proper optimisation can keep the arithmetic cell running at 50MHz. Our QRD diagonal element can therefore process data at frequency $\approx$ 3.8MHz.

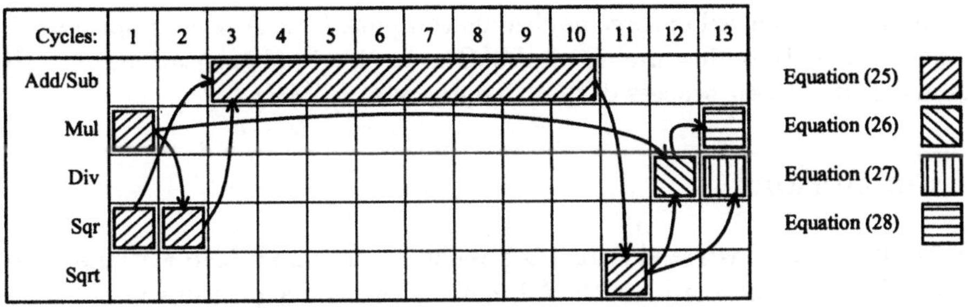

Fig. 4. A QRD diagonal cell implementation using the LNS library.

5.3 Floating-Point Solution

The floating-point solution is a little bit more complicated. As we know from table 1, all cells in library are pipelined. The latencies through the design will make the resource sharing more complicated. A sharing among other diagonal elements is probably simpler and more effective than a sharing inside of our single element.

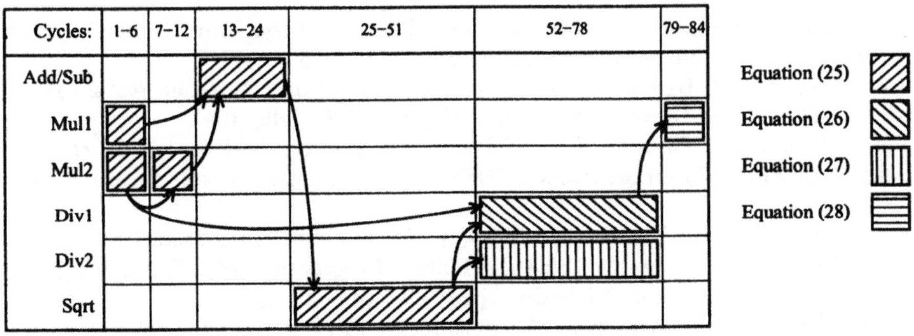

Fig. 5. A QRD diagonal cell implementation using the floating-point library.

To evaluate equation (25), two multipliers, one adder and one square root is needed (see figure 5). Total latency is 51 clock cycles. Next, we can evaluate (26) and (27) in parallel by employing two dividers with latency 27 clock cycles. Finally the equation (28) adds to design the delay of one multiplier, i.e. 6 clock cycles.

In summary, we require 84 clock cycles to process a new data. We have utilised one adder, two multipliers, two dividers and one square-root unit. For 32-bit case, it will consume about 3500 slices. Notice, that pipelining allows us to share all our cells among up to 6 diagonal cells. Adder, divider, and square-root unit can be even shared in some additional computations. A proper optimisation can keep the arithmetic running at 122MHz. In this implementation, our QRD diagonal element can process data at frequency ≈ 1.5MHz.

6 Conclusions

This work has demonstrated that it is possible to design an LNS arithmetic core library of a practical word length. All main arithmetic algorithms were shown.

A small case study at the end of this paper has shown that for some applications provides the LNS solution substantially better performance while consuming a comparable area. The strengths of the LNS lies in fast multiplications, divisions, squares and square-roots. It allows us to implement algorithms that are not suitable for pipelining. On the other hand, the size and BlockRAM utilisation of add/sub unit is the major weakness. The clock rate is also limited by the speed of table lookups.

Larger case study would bring out applications, which are suitable or unsuitable for this arithmetic library. However, such study overreaches the pages of this paper.

References

1. E.E. Swartzlander, and A.G. Alexopoulos: "The Sign/Logarithm Number System", IEEE Trans. Computers, vol. 24, pp. 1,238-1,242, 1975
2. L.K. Yu, and D.M. Lewis: "A 30-b Integrated Logarithmic Number System Processor", IEEE J. Solid-State Circuits, vol. 26, pp. 1,433-1,440, 1991
3. J.N. Coleman, E.I. Chester, C.I. Softley, and J. Kadlec: "Arithmetic on the European Logarithmic Microprocessor", IEEE Trans. Computers, vol. 49, pp. 702-715, 2000
4. J.N.Coleman and E.I.Chester: "A 32b Logarithmic Number System Processor and Its Performance Compared to Floating Point", Proceedings 14th IEEE Symposium on Computer Arithmetic, Adelaide, April 1999, pp. 142-152.
5. J.N.Coleman: "Simplification of Table Structure in Logarithmic Arithmetic", Electronics Letters, Oct. 1995, vol. 31, pp. 1905-6; and erratum Oct. 1996, vol. 32, p. 2103.
6. J. Kadlec, and J.P. Schier: "Numerical Analysis of a Normalised QR Filter Using Probability Description of Propagated Data", Research Report No. 1923, UTIA AV CR, 1998
7. M.G.Arnold, T.A. Bailey, J.R. Cowles, and M.D. Winkel, "Applying Features of IEEE 754 to Sign/Logarithm Arithmetic", IEEE Trans. Computers, vol. 41, pp. 1,040-1,050, 1992

Novel Optimizations for Hardware Floating-Point Units in a Modern FPGA Architecture*

Eric Roesler and Brent Nelson

Department of Electrical and Computer Engineering
Brigham Young University
Provo, UT 84602, USA
{eroesler,nelson}@ee.byu.edu

Abstract. As FPGA densities have increased, the feasibility of using floating-point computations on FPGAs has improved. Moreover, recent innovations in FPGA architecture have changed the design tradeoff space by providing new fixed circuit functions which may be employed in floating-point computations. These include high density multiplier blocks and shift registers. This paper evaluates the use of such blocks for the design of a family of floating-point units including add/sub, multiplier, and divider. Portions of the units that would receive the greatest benefit from the use of multipliers and shift registers are identified. It is shown that the use of these results in significant area savings compared to similar floating-point units based solely on conventional LUT/FF logic. Finally, a complete floating-point application circuit that solves a classic heat transfer problem is presented.

1 Introduction

Over the past few years the use of FPGAs in compute-intensive applications has been growing as evidenced by the number of papers on compute applications published yearly at conferences such as FPL and FCCM. The vast majority of such applications have employed fixed-point arithmetic due to its smaller size. The key advantage of floating-point over fixed-point is its ability to automatically scale to accommodate a wide range of values using its exponent. Floating-point is thus preferred by programmers for non-integer computations when it is available on CPUs due to its ease of use. However, this scaling behavior comes at the cost of reduced accuracy. A 32-bit fixed-point representation can have more accuracy (but less range) than a 32-bit floating-point representation.

Multiple authors have investigated the use of floating-point arithmetic in FPGAs and quantified its cost, anticipating the time when FPGAs have sufficient density to support it. In [1] the authors outline a pair of reduced width floating-point formats based on the IEEE format. Key features of the described representations include a biased exponent

* Effort sponsored by the Defense Advanced Research Projects Agency (DARPA) and Rome Laboratory, Air Force Materiel Command, USAF, under agreement number F30602-97-1-0222. The U.S. Government is authorized to reproduce and distribute reprints for Governmental purposes notwithstanding any copyright annotation thereon.

M. Glesner, P. Zipf, and M. Renovell (Eds.): FPL 2002, LNCS 2438, pp. 637–646, 2002.

representation and an implied leading '1' digit in the significand as in the IEEE standard. They also present basic designs for addition, multiplication, and division. In their paper, division is accomplished by computing the reciprocal of the mantissa (via table lookup) followed by a multiplication to complete the division. In addition, they present VHDL code samples for efficient coding of the shifters required for addition. The authors in [2] present a small unsigned floating-point representation specifically for use in HDTV applications. In it, they extend the above division algorithm by using a table lookup to compute a floating-point representation for the reciprocal of the mantissa. Finally, the authors in [3] outline a variety of approaches for doing 32-bit IEEE floating addition and multiplication in FPGAs. For example, their multiplier designs include versions based on bit- and digit-serial arithmetic and Booth recoding.

Not surprisingly, as time progresses and FPGA devices grow in capacity, floating-point becomes more feasible. However, recent innovations in FPGA architecture have changed the tradeoff space by providing new fixed circuit functions which may be employed in floating-point computations. These include high density multiplier blocks and shift registers, on-chip RAM, and special-purpose gates in the basic logic cell. The use of these innovations presents an interesting array of choices for the designer as well as a new series of tradeoffs. Since they are already committed to the silicon die at manufacture time, there is no added cost (in circuit area) if a designer chooses to use them. It may thus be advantageous at times to use them in what may seem to be inefficient or non-optimal ways. The decision may be driven more by *whether the design has any other use for them* rather than how area-efficiently they implement the computation. The purpose of this paper is to explore the impact these new features have on floating-point unit design in FPGAs and quantify the resulting area/performance characteristics.

When considering the design of arithmetic units a wide range of optimization goals present themselves including minimum area, minimum latency, or maximum throughput. When throughput is the key consideration (such as in the DSP applications outlined in [4] and [5]), the preferred design will be a feed-forward, pipelined design which will be optimized for a high clock rate and to produce one result every clock cycle. It is this style of design which is the focus of our work.

The outline of this paper is as follows. We first review floating point computations for add/sub, multiply, and divide. We then discuss optimizations that can be made using the special FPGA functional blocks mentioned above and compare the resulting circuits with generic LUT/FF circuits. Finally, a 2D heat transfer application using an array of floating-point units is provided as an example of the use of the resulting circuit modules.

2 Floating-Point Format and Basic Arithmetic

The ANSI/IEEE Std 754-1985 standard for floating-point specifies that the implementation of a floating-point number consists of three bit fields. The first, a single bit, represents the sign. The next field holds the value of the exponent. The exponent value is a biased representation, specifically excess-127 for 32-bit floating-point (float). The last field is the significand which must be normalized within the range $[1, 2)$. Since the MSB will always be a one, it is "implicit" in the field, i.e. the one is not actually present in the bit field but is assumed. The standard also specifies special combinations of exponent and significand values to represent zero, infinity, and NaN (not a number). The reader is referred to one of many books on computer arithmetic for more detail on the format.

The standard specifies formats for 32-bit and 64-bit representations. In this work, as in [1], an IEEE-like floating-point format is adopted for word sizes other than 32 and 64 bits. In every case the MSB is a sign bit with the remaining bits divided between exponent and significand according to the needs of the algorithm. As with IEEE, the exponent will always be biased but the bias will be based on the number of bits it occupies. Also, the implied leading '1' in the significand will be as in the IEEE standard.

2.1 Basic Floating-Point Arithmetic

The floating-point multiplier unit is the simplest of the arithmetic operations — the significands of the two operands are multiplied using a fixed-point multiplier and the exponents are summed (the extra bias must be removed in the process). After multiplication the possibility of a one-bit overflow exists. Handling this and doing the desired rounding are then completed. In all our designs the rounding mode implemented is *round to nearest even*, which is the default for the IEEE standard. The sign bit of the result is the XOR of the operand sign bits. Note that in this and all other operations described below, the implied '1' of each significand is prepended at the outset of the computation and then removed after its completion before the result is packed into the result word. Figure 1(a) shows a notional layout of a floating-point multiplier. It is drawn to reflect the relative sizes of its sub-parts — that the majority of the area is consumed by the fixed-point significand multiplier when built from LUTs and flip flops.

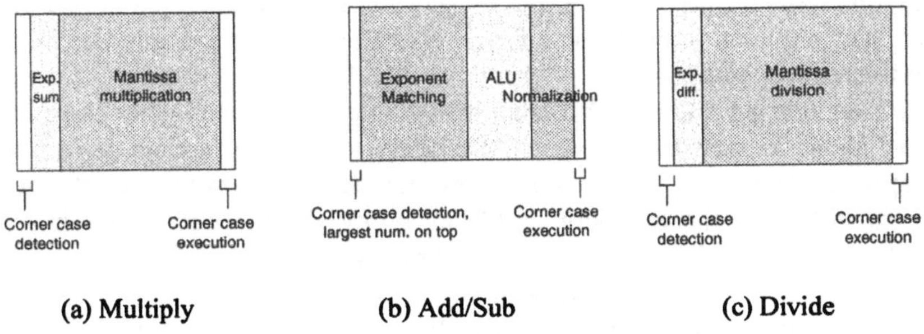

Fig. 1. Floating-Point Unit Floorplans

Floating-point addition is much more complicated than multiplication. The first step is to compare the two operands' exponents to determine which is larger. The significand of the operand with the smaller exponent is then shifted right dictated by the difference in exponents. The two matched significands are then added or subtracted, depending on the operands' sign bits. The result significand is then normalized to fall within the range $[1, 2)$ by shifting and the exponent adjusted. Finally, rounding is done and the result packed into the output word. Figure 1(b), shows a notional layout for a floating-point adder. Note that the exponent matching and normalization hardware dominate the area resources of the unit. Since the above adder requires an adder/subtractor as its core, subtraction of floating-point numbers is readily incorporated into the above design at the cost of a few gates' logic to determine when to add and when to subtract the significands.

A number of methods may be used for floating-point division in FPGAs. Division by reciprocal multiplication is discussed in both [1] and [2]. To accomplish this, the reciprocal of the denominator is computed via table lookup and then multiplied by the numerator. An n-bit significand requires a table with 2^n entries. This is problematic for anything other than small word sizes. A second approach based on multiplication is described later in this paper. It uses repeated multiplications to converge to the reciprocal of the denominator. In addition, for comparison purposes we present a restoring array divider design. The core of this array divider is the significand divider which consists of a series of stages, one per significand bit. Each stage consists of a subtractor and a multiplexor and two registers. As shown Figure 1(c) the array divider consumes the majority of the circuit area.

3 Floating-Point Module Generator Library

The design of floating-point datapaths is greatly simplified when a parameterizable library of floating-point module generators is available. The modules should be simple enough to be easily connected together, flexible, and optimized. Using parametric module generators the designer can quickly create an optimized minimum width data path for the specific problem at hand. A full-featured floating-point module generator library should minimally include modules that support all of the basic arithmetic operations including add, subtract, multiply, and divide, as well as conversion modules to facilitate use of the basic operations.

We have created a library that contains module generators for the basic functions outlined above as well as a square root module. All of the module generators were developed in JHDL [6]. The floating-point modules in our library are parametric in exponent width, significand width, and level of pipelining. All of the modules adhere to the IEEE 754 standard with three exceptions: (a) they support non-standard word sizes, (b) only one rounding mode is supported — round to nearest even, and (c) they do not support denormalized numbers. Our library also contains a set of utility module generators to perform conversion between any width fixed and floating point formats. A module for detection of floating-point special values such as NaN, infinity, and zero is also provided.

4 Candidates for Optimization

To understand the effect that special-purpose functional elements have on the design of floating-point modules in FPGAs, we have created two sets of module generators: one that is not targeted to any specific FPGA architecture (uses only LUTs and FFs) and one that is optimized to take advantage of the special functional elements in the Xilinx Virtex-II architecture.

The Virtex-II architecture has two special functional elements embedded into its fabric which we consider: SRL16's, and multipliers. The SRL16 design primitive allows a LUT to act instead as a 1-bit wide shift register with a depth of 1-16. Probably the most significant new feature of the Virtex-II architecture is its 18x18-bit signed embedded multipliers. In the larger Virtex-II chips, great numbers (>100) of these multipliers are available. To create a multiplier wider than 18x18, more than one of these multipliers can be combined with adders in a divide-and-conquer approach [7]. Finally, these multipliers can also be used to perform other tasks. As an example, a shift can be implemented using a decoder and a multiplier.

Please see [8] or [9] for detailed information about the Virtex-II architecture.

4.1 Using SRL16 Cells for Delay Lines

The JHDL floating-point modules are deeply pipelined to increase throughput and clock rates. This requires many delay lines, which quickly increases area for larger bit widths. Often the flip flops are free (logic cells exist which use only the LUT portion) but when long delays are needed, extra flip flops must be utilized. A single SRL16 (occupying a single LUT) can implement up to a sixteen stage delay line and thus can be used to replace up to sixteen flip flops.

4.2 Exponent Matching and Normalization

A floating-point adder or subtractor requires a shifter in two different places. The embedded multipliers can be used for this purpose. Prior to adding/subtracting the significands, the exponents must be matched. To match exponents, the significand of the smaller of the two values is shifted right. Shifters in FPGAs are typically implemented as a series of 2:1 muxes with an area that grows as $O(n \log(n))$ where n is the significand width. It is straightforward to pipeline such a shifter to increase throughput.

To use an unsigned multiplier as a left shifter, one only needs multiply by 2^k, where k is the number of bit positions to shift. It would be ridiculous to use a multiplier implemented in the normal FPGA fabric as a variable shifter. However, the embedded multipliers available in Virtex-II can be leveraged to implement such a shifter if they are not being used for other purposes. Since a right shift is desired, the wires of the significand are wired to the multiplier in reverse order and the multiplier used to do a left shift. In addition to the multiplier, a decoder (implemented as a ROM) is needed to generate the 2^k input to the embedded multiplier.

The second place where a shifter is needed is for postshifting after adding or subtracting the significands. Depending on the signs of the operands and the operation (add or sub), the resulting significand may be less than 1. To normalize this, the significand is shifted left until there is a one in the most significant bit. To use a multiplier to perform normalization, we must discover how far the first occurrence of the leading one is from the most significant bit. A priority encoder can be used to find this distance. The most efficient way to do this in an FPGA is to use a propagate-kill chain, to find the leading one and kill all occurrences of one after that. This is facilitated in FPGAs which have flexible fast carry logic which can be configured to perform the propagate-kill logic (Virtex-II is an example of this). The basic circuit is shown in Figure 2(a) and the details for one cell in the chain are shown in Figure 2(b). With an input of 00100101 this circuit will output 00100000. Reversing the bits leads to 00000100 which is the proper input to the multiplier to accomplish the required left shift.

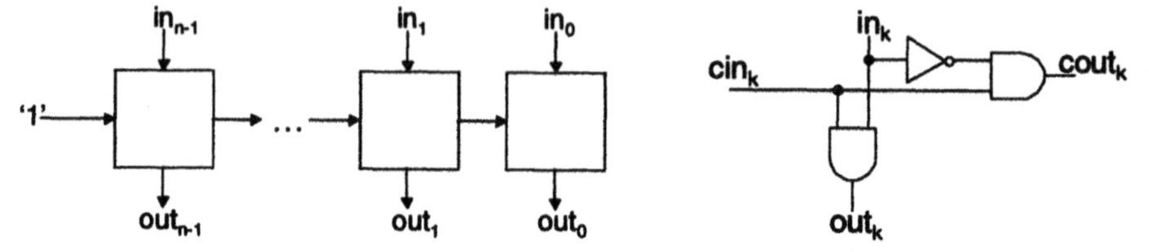

(a) Propagate-Kill Chain (b) Single Bit of Chain

Fig. 2. Propagate-Kill Chain for Normalization Priority Encoder

4.3 Significand Multiplication

The obvious candidate for replacement with embedded multipliers is the significand multiplier. In the non-optimized floating-point multiplier it consumes 76% of the area and is the limiting factor to cycle time. Table 2 shows that for a fully pipelined floating-point multiply unit, using the embedded multipliers results in a 77% area savings (this also includes the benefit obtained by using delay lines as well).

4.4 Significand Divider

Dividing via repeated multiplication is not novel [7] [10] , though using multipliers to implement a floating-point divider in FPGAs, to our knowledge, has never been published. One method of performing a divide function using multipliers is to generate the inverse of the denominator and then to multiply that inverse by the numerator. Previous authors [1] [2] have discussed the use of a lookup table to compute the inverse but this is only feasible for small word sizes. For arbitrary word sizes the Newton-Raphson method can be used to compute the inverse [7]. The Newton-Raphson method successively approximates the root of an equation as: $x^{i+1} = x^i - \frac{f(x^i)}{f'(x^i)}$. In our case, $f(x) = 1/x - d$ where d is the denominator in the original division. The above reduces to the following recurrence: $x^{(i+1)} = x^{(i)}(2 - x^{(i)}d)$, and the root is $\frac{1}{d}$.

It has been proven [7] that this requires $\log_2 k$ iterations of the recurrence to converge. The total number of multiplications required is then $2\log_2 k + 1$ (2 per iteration plus the last one to do $numerator \times 1/denominator$. This can be implemented as an iterative circuit or unrolled and pipelined (we choose the unrolled/pipelined version).

The number of iterations (or stages) may be reduced by using a lookup table to compute the result of the first few iterations [7]. An n-bit lookup table will reduce the number of iterations by $\log_2 n$. An important feature of this technique is that the number of multipliers required can be traded off against the size of the lookup table. In all our example designs, an 8-bit lookup table is used. Thus, for a 16-bit significand division only 1 stage is required instead of 4. For a 32-bit significand 2 stages are required. The number of multipliers required in each case is $(2 \times numStages) + 1$. Figure 3 shows an overall block diagram of a fixed-point divider based on multipliers.

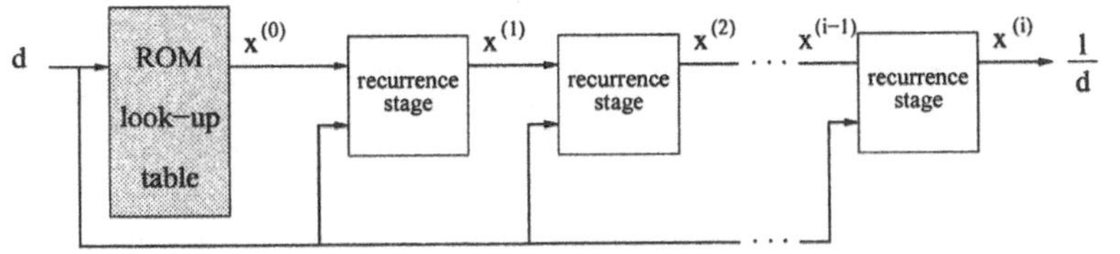

Fig. 3. Block Diagram For Divide Unit Based On Multipliers

5 Results/Comparisons

A series of designs were completed using our module generator library and run through the Xilinx 4.1 tools for a XC2V1000-6 part to obtain area and timing results. The generic and Virtex-II optimized designs were similar for the add/sub and multiplier units, with the optimized designs simply using shift registers and the 18x18 built-in multipliers. The divider units were fundamentally different from one another. The significand divider for the generic unit was a restoring array divider, while the optimized design used the 18x18 built-in multipliers as described in the previous sections. The word sizes tested which show the best performance for the optimizations presented include 16-bits (9-bit significand), 23-bits (16-bit significand), and 41-bits (32-bit significand). This is due to there being a good match between the significand size and the width of the available multiplier blocks in Virtex-II. In addition, a standard IEEE 32-bit format was run (23-bit significand) which shows less benefit due to not as good a match between significand size and multiplier block. In a configurable computing environment there may be no special significance to using the standard IEEE word sizes other than they match what is used on CPUs, simplifying validation. In many cases, however, non-standard word sizes may be profitably employed. Nevertheless, the results show that *sweet spots* exist in the design space.

Tables 1 through 3 show the area and performance characteristics of the modules tested. The areas reported are in slices (the multipliers don't contribute to the area measurements). Three different versions of each module are represented — the generic module, an optimized module which uses both built-in multipliers and shift register, and an optimized module which uses only built-in multipliers. Area improvements range from about 30% for the add/sub unit, about 80% for the multiplier, and about 50% for the divider. Of those area savings, the table shows that for the multiplier and divider the majority of the area savings was due to the use of the multipliers. The table also shows that SRL16's can make a significant difference in the area of add/sub units and a modest difference in the area of the dividers. Also note that the improvement due to SRL16's increases with word width. Finally, the table shows only modest changes in clock rate result from the Virtex-II optimizations.

Table 1. Comparison of a Add/Sub module with and without Virtex-II optimizations

Word Format (sign,exp, signf.)	Area (Generic) (slices)	Area (mult+ SRL16) (slices)	Change Area (mult+ SRL16)	Area (mult only) (slices)	Change (mult only)	Speed (Generic) (MHz)	Speed (mult+ SRL16) (MHz)	Change Speed (mult+ SRL16)	Latency (Gen.) (cycles)	Latency (V2 opt.) (cycles)	18x18 Mults used
16 (1,4,11)	392	254	-35%	280	-29%	235	225	-4%	20	14	2
23 (1,6,16)	584	371	-36%	421	-28%	197	204	4%	23	15	2
23 (1,5,17)	577	412	-29%	475	-18%	213	214	0%	23	16	7
24 (1,7,16)	601	381	-37%	431	-28%	197	210	7%	23	15	2
32 (1,8,23)	773	571	-26%	673	-13%	212	203	-4%	23	17	7
41 (1,8,32)	1010	807	-20%	936	-7%	173	174	1%	24	17	7

Table 2. Comparison of a Multiplier module with and without Virtex-II optimizations

Word Format (sign,exp, signf.)	Area (Generic) (slices)	Area (mult+ SRL16) (slices)	Change Area (mult+ SRL16)	Area (mult only) (slices)	Change (mult only)	Speed (Generic) (MHz)	Speed (mult+ SRL16) (MHz)	Change Speed (mult+ SRL16)	Latency (Gen.) (cycles)	Latency (V2 opt.) (cycles)	18x18 Mults used
16 (1,4,11)	339	81	-76%	66	-81%	213	248	16%	6	6	1
23 (1,6,16)	631	117	-81%	91	-86%	191	174	-9%	9	6	1
23 (1,5,17)	671	183	-73%	159	-76%	191	188	-2%	9	8	4
24 (1,7,16)	632	119	-81%	92	-85%	179	177	-1%	9	6	1
32 (1,8,23)	1156	248	-79%	221	-81%	166	170	2%	12	8	4
41 (1,8,32)	2024	308	-85%	270	-87%	175	173	-1%	17	8	4

6 Application - A Heat-Transfer Matrix Solver

To demonstrate the use of the above units, we provide a demonstration application where we compare two implementations: an implementation using generic floating-point modules, and an implementation using Virtex-II optimized modules.

This application is a classic heat transfer problem. Using relaxation, it computes a matrix representing temperatures at discrete points on a 2D surface where heat sources

Table 3. Comparison of a Divider module with and without Virtex-II optimizations

Word Format (sign,exp, signf.)	Area (Generic) (slices)	Area (mult+ SRL16) (slices)	Change Area (mult+ SRL16)	Area (mult only) (slices)	Change (mult only)	Speed (Generic) (MHz)	Speed (mult+ SRL16) (MHz)	Change Speed (mult+ SRL16)	Latency (Gen.) (cycles)	Latency (V2 opt.) (cycles)	18x18 Mults used
16 (1,4,11)	442	185	-58%	171	-61%	158	154	-3%	17	13	4
23 (1,6,16)	785	369	-53%	398	-49%	157	149	-5%	22	17	10
23 (1,5,17)	851	468	-45%	482	-43%	147	149	1%	23	21	16
24 (1,7,16)	806	385	-52%	411	-49%	158	147	-7%	22	17	10
32 (1,8,23)	1401	958	-32%	1182	-16%	147	140	-5%	29	29	24
41 (1,8,32)	2439	1192	-51%	1516	-38%	146	140	-4%	38	29	24

are applied at the edges. The temperatures at the surface edges (matrix boundaries) are known *a priori* - they are the inputs to the system. The matrix is computed by averaging each matrix element with its neighbors repeatedly until the matrix values converge to a set of stable values.

The FPGA implementation consists of a collection of concurrently operating PEs. Each PE contains three floating-point add/sub units and one floating-point multiplier for arithmetic, six BlockRam memories, and control logic. The PE loads a block of data from an external SRAM into five BlockRams which serve as its read cache. The PE then computes the new elements and writes them into another BlockRam which serves as a write cache. The write cache is emptied back to the external SRAM overlapped with the computation of new matrix elements. The PE design is heavily pipelined and represents a design optimized for high-throughput as described in [4] and [5]. The floating-point word size used throughout the design is 36 bits wide (1,8,27).

One PE based on our generic floating-point modules occupies 3, 603 slices and runs at 159 MHz, obtained by generating a PE design and running it through the Xilinx 4.1 tool chain. Note that nothing in the original design was placed — higher performance might result if hand placement were done. Taking into account our estimates for the circuitry required to coordinate their activities, a total of 9 such PE's fit onto an XC2V6000 part. This represents 27 floating-point add/sub units and 9 floating-point multipliers and uses 54 of the XC2V6000's BlockRAMs (it has 144 of them). The same PE design based on our modules optimized for Virtex-II occupies 2, 461 slices, runs at 171 MHz, and uses 130 embedded multipliers. A total of 13 such PE's will fit onto the same XC2V6000.

For this application, 25% of the clock cycles are spent doing real computation due to the need to read and write the matrix elements from the external SRAM. For this application, then, an XC2V6000 delivers a sustained floating-point performance of 2.2 GFlops. (13 PE's running at 171 MHz, each doing 4 floating-point operations per fourth cycle on average). For comparison, the sustained number is 1.4 GFlops for the version based on the generic floating-point modules.

7 Conclusions and Future Work

The purpose of this paper has been to quantify the effects of new FPGA features such as multipliers on the creation of floating-point modules for various word widths. The introduction of these FPGA features changes the tradeoff space and, at times, may result in using multipliers in unconventional ways or in ways which would not be warranted if the circuit were being built from LUTs and flip-flops. In addition, we have quantified the effect that shift register LUTs have on floating-point module design. A simple application was presented to give an idea of the levels of floating-point performance achievable with today's FPGA technology.

Much remains that could be done. A range of applications could be investigated and careful comparisons made with equivalent CPU-based implementations. That was not the focus of this work. Also, alternative floating-point modules for division could be developed. Examples might include modules based on SRT or other high-radix algorithms commonly found in VLSI implementations. Similarly, square root designs could be investigated. Another issue is that the range of rounding modes specified by the IEEE standard could be implemented as options to the module generator calls. In addition, we have ignored denormalized number representations as specified in the IEEE standard. Finally, interesting work would be a study which would propose new FPGA features which could be added specifically to enable more efficient floating-point computations.

References

1. N. Shirazi, A. Walters, and P. Athanas, "Quantitative analysis of floating point arithmetic on FPGA-based custom computing machines," in *Proceedings of IEEE Workshop on FPGAs for Custom Computing Machines*, D. A. Buell and K. L. Pocek, Eds., Napa, CA, Apr. 1995, pp. 155–163.
2. J. Dido, N. Geraudie, L. Loiseau, O. Payeur, Y. Savaria, and D. Poirier, "A flexible floating-point format for optimizing data-paths and operators in FPGA based DSPs," in *ACM/SIGDA International Symposium on Field Programmable Gate Arrays*, Monterey, CA, February 2002, ACM SIGDA, pp. 50–55, ACM Press.
3. W. Ligon, S. McMillan, G. Monn, K. Schoonover, F. Stivers, and K. Underwood, "A re-evaluation of the practicality of floating-point operations on FPGAs," in *Proceedings of the IEEE Symposium on FPGAs for Custom Computing Machines (FCCM '98)*, Kenneth L. Pocek and Jeffrey M. Arnold, Eds. IEEE Computer Society, April 1998, pp. 206–215, IEEE Computer Society Press.
4. B. Hutchings and B. Nelson, "Giga op DSP on FPGA," in *Proceedings of ICASSP 2001*, May 2001.
5. B. Nelson, "Configurable computing and sonar processing - architectures and implementations," in *ASILOMAR 2001*, November 2001.
6. B. Hutchings, P. Bellows, J. Hawkins, S. Hemmert, B. Nelson, and M. Rytting, "A CAD suite for high-performance FPGA design," in *Proceedings of the IEEE Workshop on FPGAs for Custom Computing Machines*, K. L. Pocek and J. M. Arnold, Eds., Napa, CA, April 1999, IEEE Computer Society, pp. 12–24, IEEE.
7. Behrooz Parhami, *Computer Arithmetic*, Oxford Press, 2000.
8. Xilinx, San Jose, CA, *The Virtex-II Logic Data Book*, 2000.
9. "Virtex-II handbook," *http://www.xilinx.com/products/virtex/handbook/index.htm*.
10. Joseph J. F. Cavanagh, *Digital Computer Arithmetic*, McGraw-Hill, 1984.

Morphable Multipliers

Silviu Chiricescu[1], Michael Schuette[1], Robin Glinton[2], and Herman Schmit[2]

[1] Digital DNA Labs, Motorola
Schaumburg, IL 60196 USA
{silviu,schuette}@ddna.labs.mot.com
[2] Dept. of Electrical and Computer Engineering, Carnegie Mellon University,
Pittsburgh, PA, 15213 USA
{rglinton,herman}@ece.cmu.edu

1 Introduction

This paper examines design techniques for reconfigurable functional units for embedded processors and DSPs. These reconfigurable functional units can be used to improve processor performance for certain applications by providing the operations that match the computational requirements of a particular application.

There are two approaches one can take to provide diverse functional unit resources in a processor. The first approach is to provide a general, FPGA-like, computational fabric that can be programmed into the required functional unit or units. This approach has been explored by PRISC [1], Chimeara [2], GARP [3]. The benefit of this approach is that the generality allows very application specific customization of the functional unit. This generality comes at the cost of performance and area. FPGA fabric will be slower and significantly larger on common operations such as multiplication and addition than on fixed implementation of those operators. Functional unit speed and efficiency is critically important in embedded processors and DSPs, therefore these fine-grained reconfigurable techniques will probably only be used for peripheral functions.

Another way to provide diverse functional unit resources is to specify a concise set of operations desired in a functional unit, and to design such a multi-mode functional unit for very high speed. We call such a functional unit a morphable functional unit, or MFU. The simple way to do this is to construct an individual implementation of each mode in the functional unit, and use a multiplexor to select the output based on the mode, as illustrated in Figure 1. Latches can be used to reduce power consumption of unused components in this MFU. The delay overhead for this level of reconfiguration consists of the multiplexor and latch delay, as well as the interconnect delay to move primary inputs and outputs to and from the different operators within the MFU.

Embedded processors and DSPs require a high level of performance on arithmetic operations. Because the delay of an MFU is not significantly greater than that of a single mode functional unit, its deployment in an embedded processor or DSP is feasible. In addition, an MFU conserves other important resources such as register file ports. Adding ports to a register file can significantly increase its delay and power consumption.

M. Glesner, P. Zipf, and M. Renovell (Eds.): FPL 2002, LNCS 2438, pp. 647–656, 2002.

Commercial microprocessors have used MFUs to support SIMD instructions like MMX [4]. These MFUs support a single type of operation, like addition, and vary the number and width of the operations. Our goal is to support sets of different operators. In this paper, we focus on the morphing between a set of multiplication and addition operations of various sizes.

A naive implementation of an MFU that can morph between addition and multiplication is presented in Figure 1. The MFU illustrated in Figure 1 is not very area efficient. Since the operators in the MFU are mutually exclusive, it is possible to share hardware between operators, as long as that does not significantly impact the critical path delay of the MFU. Hardware sharing in an MFU reduces area.

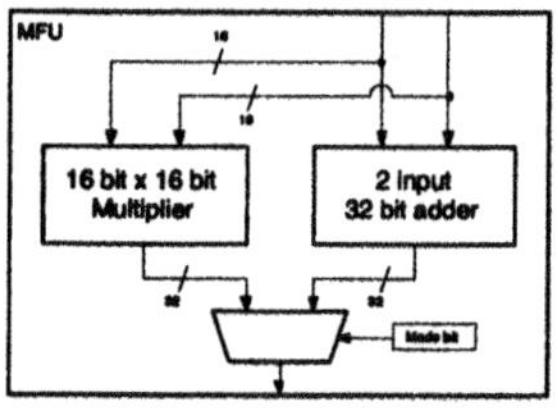

Fig. 1. Naive Implementation of two mode MFU.

Commercial synthesis tools are not capable of fully exploiting the mutual exclusivity of the different modes to reduce hardware area. Table 1 shows the area results of synthesizing an MFU identical to the one presented in Figure 1. The synthesis results shown are for a 0.18 micron standard cell library and are the best areas obtained using a variety of synthesis strategies and efforts. Because the area of the combined MFU is slightly larger than the total area of the components, we conclude that there is no hardware sharing occuring between the operators[1]. This result holds for a range of widths.

Table 1. Synthesis Results for MFU components separately and combined.

Unit	Area (sq. micron)
16x16 bit multiplier	114,720
32-bit adder	21,500
32-bit multiplexor	5,120
Component Sum	141,340
Combined MFU	142,280

[1] The combined MFU is larger than the sum of its components because the components used the same overall timing constraint, which meant that they had a little more timing slack than the MFU. As a result, the MFU was a little larger.

1.1 Related Work

As we have mentioned, a number of other architectures have explored fine-grained reconfigurable functional units [1, 2, 3]. Haynes and Cheung [5, 6] explored reconfigurable fabrics that are optimized for multiplication. These approaches take a much more general, programmable approach to design of morphable functional units. The area and performance overhead of these functional units are significant.

Custom functional unit designs have been constructed to support different modes of operation while exploiting some of the mutual exclusion of different modes. For example, [7] describes a floating point multiplier that supports both IEEE single-precision and double precision.

2 Morphable Multiplier Design

Multipliers in DSPs and embedded processors have high performance requirements. Therefore we use tree multipliers as the basis of our design evaluation. In a tree multiplier, the partial products can be generated using an array of AND gates, or more generally, radix-k Booth's multiple generators. The partial product reduction tree (PPRT) adds the partial products and produces a sum result in a redundant form. The redundant form is converted into a binary form by a carry propagate adder.

The PPRT design technique that will be used in this paper is based on the approach proposed in [8] which finds a globally optimal way of interconnecting low-level compressor stages. The method in [8] exploits the fact that the inputs and outputs of a compressor do not equally contribute to the delay of the multiplier.

2.1 Timing Slack to Morphability

The critical path through a tree multiplier will almost certainly run through compressors in the PPRT. Not all the compressors in the PPRT are on the critical path, however. Compressors that are not on the critical path have timing slack. The timing slack for each non-critical compressor is equal to the minimum delay that can be added to it in order to make that compressor critical. Using a compressor in more than one operation (e.g. add and multiply) requires some number of multiplexors to modify the connections of this compressor. A compressor with sufficient slack to allow the incorporation of multiplexors on its inputs is called a reusable compressor.

We have developed two methods of identifying the compressors that can be reused: a strict method and a relaxed method. We first present the strict method using an example. Figure 2 is one possible PPRT of a 6×6 bit multiplier. The optimal delay of this PPRT is equal to four equivalent XOR-gate delays[2].

[2] Throughout the remaining of this section, all delays will be expressed in equivalent XOR-gate delays. An equivalent XOR-gate delay is the delay through an XOR gate.

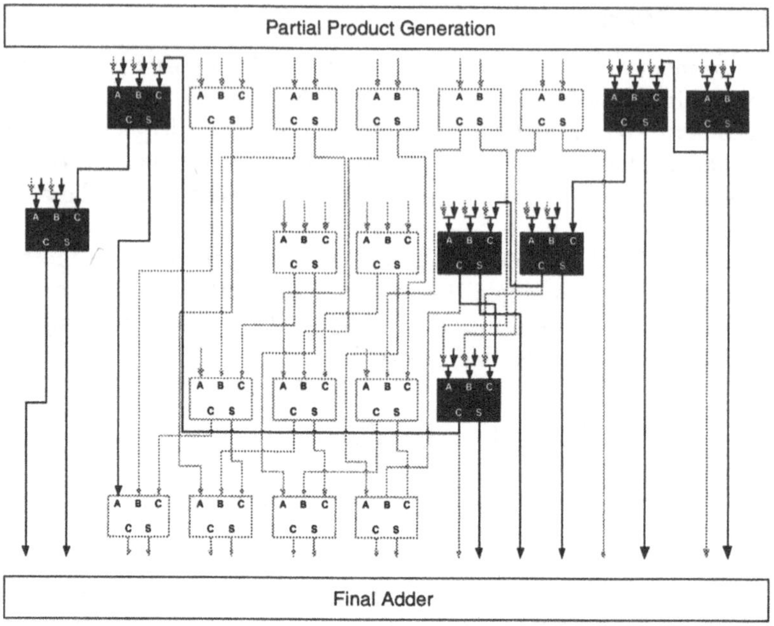

Fig. 2. A Morphable $6-bit \times 6-bit$ Multiplier using re-used adder cells. Gray wires show the PPRT in multiplier mode. The black adders are re-used in a 7-bit ripple carry adder.

Considering the PPRT alone, as if we had inserted a pipeline stage between the PPRT and the final adder, our goal is to identify the compressors that can be reused in a second mode subject to maintaining the delay through the PPRT equal to four.

Given a compressor that has timing slack, in the strict method, multiplexers are inserted at all its inputs. As a result of this insertion, the output delays of the compressor are recalculated and these changes are propagated through the fanout-tree of that compressor. If the recalculated delays of the PPRT outputs are less than or equal to a maximum tolerable delay, then the given compressor can be re-used when the MFU is used in another mode. For example, determining whether the compressor in vertical slice two (see Figure 2) is reusable or not involves the following steps:

1. Add multiplexors at all the inputs of the compressor.
2. Assuming that a multiplexor introduces a delay of 0.5, the sum and carry output delays of this compressor become 2.5 and 1.5 respectively.
3. As a result of the previously updated delay values, the delays of the last compressors from slices three and four are recalculated. Since the sum delays of slices three and four are less than 4, it is concluded that the compressor in slice two can be reused.

The algorithm detects all compressors that are individually reusable, and then selects a single compressor to "commit". Timing is recalculated for the PPRT including the input multiplexors of any committed compressor. The process of detecting and committing compressors is repeated until no more compressors are reusable. The sequence of committing reusable compressors will have an impact on the final set of reusable compressors. The heuristic employed currently commits compressors that are most significant and closest to the final adder first.

In Figure 2, the compressors that can be reused are shown in black. The black lines illustrate the connections that could be made to construct a seven-bit ripple carry adder.

The second method for identifying the reusable compressors exploits the existence, in the PPRT, of a path from the C_{out} of a compressor to the C_{in} of another compressor. For such paths, multiplexers have to be inserted only at inputs A and B of a FA. Hence, the reusable compressors found with the relaxed method are already chained in a ripple carry fashion. The reusable compressor chains are then wired up according to the techniques presented in the next section in order to build larger structures.

The relaxed method relies upon the existence of carry propagate chains inside a PPRT. In order to maximize the lengths of these paths, the algorithm for building a PPRT has to be slightly modified. In the algorithm presented in [8], the element of the input vector that is chosen to be wired to the C_{in} of a compressor is determined only by the value of the delay associated with the respective element. If a tie exists, the source of the signal that is chosen to be wired to the C_{in} input of a compressor is irrelevant. However, in our case, a tie-breaking rule is introduced. The tie breaking rule states that the signal that has as source the C_{out} output of another compressor is declared the winner.

2.2 Quantification of Timing Slack in PPRTs

Figure 3 illustrates the relationship between reuseable adder cells in a PPRT and the delay constraint for the PPRT. The four delay points on the x-axis are shown as a percentage of the critical path delay. The y-axis illustrates the percentage of adders that are found to be re-useable using the relaxed algorithm described above. Even at the critical path delay, a significant number of adders are reuseable. The ratio of reuseable adders quickly grows with small amounts of timing slack. At 130% of critical path delay all compressors in the PPRTs of both multiplier are reuseable.

3 Morphable Multiplier Evaluation

In the last section, we presented techniques to determine the number of compressors that can be extracted from the PPRT as a function of delay. In this section, we present techniques to use these compressors in functions other than multiplication and we present preliminary results for implementations of MFUs.

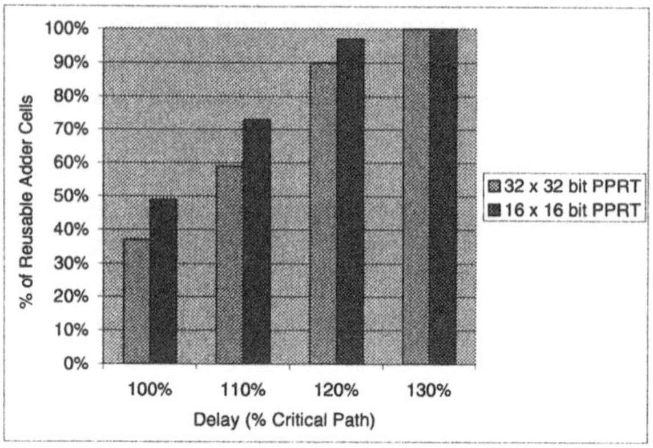

Fig. 3. Quantification of Re-useable adder cells in Two Different Partial Product Reduction Trees.

Our assumptions are that the delay specification for the MFU applies to all operations performed by the MFU. We will further assume that, among the operations performed by the MFU, the one that has the longest delay is a multiplication. We will investigate ways of reusing the compressors within the multiplier to reduce the hardware cost of a number of addition operations performed by the MFU.

3.1 Designing Hardware Efficient MFUs

Our problem definition is as follows: The MFU has two modes. This technique can be extended to more modes. Modes can contain multiplication or addition operations. Each multiplication operation in an MFU is specified by its input bitwidths and the architecture of the carry-propagate adder. All adders use a generalized block carry-lookahead structure. The user can specify the length of each adder block in the adder, and the maximum number of inputs in a CLA unit. This specification is sufficiently broad to allow specification of a ripple carry adder and a Brent-Kung adder in the extremes.

The architecture of each addition operation in either mode of the MFU is also specified. Finally, a delay constraint is specified. This delay constraint must be equal to or greater than the critical path delay of all operations in both modes of the MFU.

Our algorithm for designing efficient MFUs from this specification is illustrated in Figure 4. The basic idea is to analyze all operations in both modes to determine those chains of full adders in which the operations have adequate timing slack for insertion of multiplexors. This is performed by the multiplier and adder analysis blocks. The output of that stage is a set of adder chains for each mode. The second stage of the algorithm finds a maximum cover of adders that can be used to satisfy the adder chain requirements for the two modes. This stage of the algorithm outputs the set of adders that will be reconfigured between modes (labelled common), and the set of adders that will remain dedicated to each mode. In Figure 4, Mode 0 generates fewer adder chains, and all of its adder chains are reconfigured between modes. Mode 1 requires some adder chains that are not shared between modes.

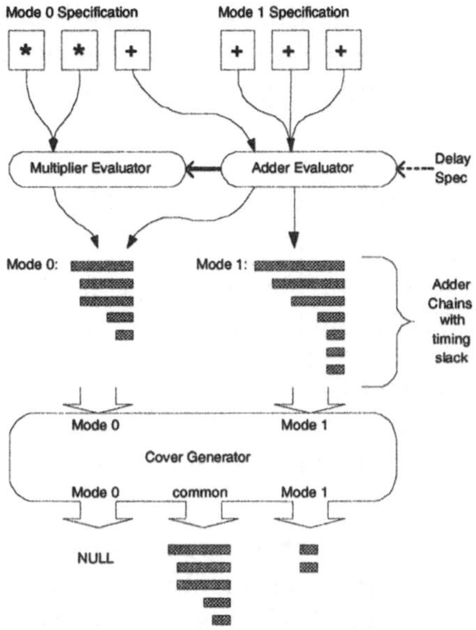

Fig. 4. MFU design algorithm.

The second stage of the algorithm is performed by formulating it as an instance of the maximum weighted graph matching problem. A bipartite graph is formed, whereby one set of nodes corresponds to the re-useable adders from one MFU mode. The other set corresponds to the re-useable adders in the other MFU mode. The resulting graph is a complete bipartite graph. Each arc has a weight that is equal to the minimum of the lengths of the adders connected by the arc.

The selection of an arc in this bipartite graph represents the sharing between two adder chains. Finding a maximal matching on this bipartite graph is equivalent to finding the best sharing between adder chains in the two MFU modes. Fortunately, maximal weighted matching can be solved in polynomial time. We use the Gabow algorithm [9], which does maximal matching on general graphs (not just bipartite graphs). This makes it easy to extend this algorithm to deal with more than two MFU modes.

Despite the fact that the sharing is optimal, this approach does not factor in secondary objectives to adder sharing. For example, two adders or multipliers in different modes might have common connections with other adders or carry logic blocks. This algorithm will ignore such secondary objectives.

3.2 Design Examples

In order to evaluate re-use, we will investigate the five two-mode MFUs described in Table 2. In Mode 1, all these MFUs implement a pipelined multiplier. The pipeline register is assumed to be between the PPRT and the final adder in these multipliers. All adders, including the final adder in the multiplier, use a BCLA structure with four-bit ripple carry adders at the leaves of the tree, and lookahead units that take four (P,G) pairs. We evaluate these designs using the critical path of the MFU, which always turns out to be the length of the critical path of the PPRT.

Table 2. Five MFU Specifications and Transistor Counts

Name	Mode 1 (all 2 stage)	Mode 2	Transistors (No Re-use)	Transistors (with Re-use)	Area Savings	Extra Area for Mode 2
MFU16-1	16 x 16 mult	1 32-bit add	8,648	7,260	16.0%	1.5%
MFU16-2	16 x 16 mult	2 32-bit add	10,144	7860	21.5%	11.4%
MFU32-1	32 x 32 mult	4 64-bit add	40,720	33,608	16.4%	19.1%
MFU32-2	32 x 32 mult	8 32-bit add	40,560	34,304	14.9%	20.7%
MFU64	64 x 64 mult	8 64-bit add	135,664	123,112	8.9%	10.9%

For this evaluation, we assume that the baseline functional unit is built from full adder cells consisting of 28 transistors. Using a pass transistor logic, we can add a 2:1 multiplexor on the A and B inputs of every cell with an additional of six transistors. Using this design, a re-useable adder chain with N adders requires only $6N + 7$ additional transistors. The additional seven transistor invert the select signals and multiplex the carry in signal. This amounts to 24% extra transistors for a 4-bit adder chain. An advantage to this approach is that the additional delay required by this implementation is only due to a single pass transistor delay.

The results for these MFUs are shown in Table 2. The fourth column shows the transistor counts for the implementation of MFUs without our reuse technique. The fifth column of the table shows the transistor count when our reuse technique is employed. The reduction in transistors is between 8.9% and 21.5%. In all cases, the morphable multiplier with re-use is as fast as the multiplier without re-use.

In most of these MFUs, the multiplier is significantly larger than the adders, which places a limit on the savings that can be obtained by our technique. Another way to think about these results is to consider the extra area required to add Mode 2 (the addition operations) to a multiplier. This extra area is shown as a proportion of the multiplier area. For example, in MFU16-1, it is possible to implement the 32-bit adder with an additional area of 1.5%. This overhead is so small because most of the carry-lookahead logic and full adders for Mode 2 are extracted from the multiplier's final adder. If Mode 2 has two adders, as in MFU16-2, the hardware for Mode 2 is contributed by both the final adder and the PPRT. In this case, Mode 2 requires extra carry lookahead logic, which pushes the extra area up significantly. In all cases, the addition of a large number of adder functions to our multiplier requires at most 21% extra area.

4 Applications

We have evaluated performance of a set of kernels on two hardware platforms. Platform1 is an embedded vector processor that contains two 16 × 16-bit multipliers, one 32-bit adder, one 32-bit shift unit and one 32-bit logic unit. All functional units have a delay of one clock cycle except for the multipliers, which are two cycle pipelined functional units. Platform2 is identical to Platform1 except for the multipliers, which are replaced by MFUs. The MFU in this case is identical to the MFU16-1. Our compiler technology does not currently support MFUs. In order to present a fair comparison between the two platforms, we have manually scheduled the kernels onto both platforms.

Table 3 presents the benchmark kernels along with a brief description of each of them. These kernels are being used in a broad range of DSP and image processing applications.

Table 3. Benchmark kernels.

Name		Mults	Adds	Description	Platform1 (cycles)	Platform2 (cycles)	Speedup (%)
quant		2	1	Quantization	2	2	0
dequant		2	1	Dequantization	2	2	0
8 × 8 dct	vdcth	5	29	Horizontal Processing	29	18	43.23
	vdctv	5	29	Vertical Processing	29	18	
	vdctc	1	0	Scaling	2	2	
fft		4	6	FFT (dec. in time)	6	5	20
pgp		4	6	Mult. prec. mult.	18	18	0
color-int		0	8	color interpolation	8	6	33.33
filter		8	10	3 × 3 filter	10	8	25

The results of manually scheduling the benchmark kernels on the two hardware platforms are presented in the fifth and sixth columns of Table 3. These columns show the number of cycles required to run a given kernel in the steady state. Column seven shows the speed-up obtained by using the MFU. The **dct** kernel is made up of multiple sub-kernels, and therefore the speed-up in column seven is computed by taking into account the "weight" of every sub-kernel. The **vdch** and **vdctv** sub-kernels are executed 8 times, while the **vdctc** sub-kernel is executed 64 times.

The execution time of the kernels that require a large number of additions is decreased if executed on Platform2 when compared to their execution time on Platform1. This behavior is expected since the MFUs, when working in *adder* mode, simply increase the number of resource instances onto which the additions can be mapped. However, due to output port contention, the adders that are available when the MFUs are configured in *adder* mode cannot be used until one cycle after the MFUs have been used in *multiplier* mode. This is the reason that **fft** and **dct** do not achieve higher performance.

A number of kernels do not obtain speedup on the Platform2, for a number of different reasons. The **quant** and **dequant** benchmarks do not contain enough additions. The **pgp** kernel does not achieve any speedup because its parallelism is limited by a loop-carried dependency.

5 Summary

The design of MFUs relies on the identification, selection, and sharing of adder chains. The identification phase uses timing slacks to identify re-usable adder cells. In a 16×16-bit tree multiplier, the percentage of reusable adder cells in the PPRT ranges from 45% with no speed penalty to 100% for a 30% speed penalty. The selection phase extracts a maximum cover of adder chains that are present in both modes of the MFU. The implementation phase adds multiplexers at the inputs of the required adder cells. Using these techniques, five different morphable multiplier designs were evaluated. The reduction in transistors, when all MFUs run at the maximum speed, is between 8.9% and 21.5%.

We evaluated the performance impact of MFUs in the context of an embedded processor. Nine kernels were scheduled on two platforms that were identical except that one had MFUs and one did not. The schedule for the kernels on the platform with MFUs was up to 43.3% faster than the platform without MFUs.

References

[1] R. Razdan and M. D. Smith, "A high-performance microarchitecture with hardware-programmable functional units," in *Proceedings of the 27th Annual International Symposium on Microarchitecture*, pp. 172–80, IEEE/ACM, Nov. 1994.

[2] S. Hauck, T. Fry, M. Hosler, and J. P. Kao, "The Chimaera reconfigurable functional unit," in *IEEE Symposium on FPGAs for Custom Computing Machines*, pp. 87–96, April 1997.

[3] J. Hauser and J. Wawrzynek, "Garp: A MIPS processor with a reconfigurable coprocessor," in *IEEE Symposium on FPGAs for Custom Computing Machines*, pp. 24–33, April 1997.

[4] A. Peleg, S. Wilkie, and U. Weiser, "Intel mmx for multimedia pcs," *Communications of the ACM*, vol. 40, no. 1, pp. 24–38, 1997.

[5] S. D. Haynes and P. Y. K. Cheung, "Configurable multiplier blocks for embedding in FPGAs," *IEE Electronic Letters*, vol. 34, pp. 638–639, Apr. 1998.

[6] S. D. Haynes, A. B. Ferrari, and P. Y. K. Cheung, "Flexible Reconfigurable Multiplier Blocks Suitable for Enhancing the Architecture of FPGAs," in *IEEE 1999 Custom Integrated Circuits Conference*, pp. 191–194, Apr. 1999.

[7] G. Even, S. M. Mueller, and P.-M. Seidel, "A Dual Mode IEEE Multiplier," in *Proceedings IEEE International Conference on Innovative Systems in Silicon*, pp. 282–289, 1997.

[8] P. Stelling, C. Martel, V. G. Oklobdzija, and P. Ravi, "Optimal Circuits for Parallel Multipliers," *IEEE Transactions on Computers*, vol. 47, pp. 273–285, Mar. 1998.

[9] Z. Galil, S. Micali, and H. Gabow, "Maximal Weighted Matching on General Graphs," in *Proceedings of 23rd Annual IEEE Symposium on Foundations of Computer Science*, pp. 255–261, 1982.

A Library of Parameterized Floating-Point Modules and Their Use

Pavle Belanović and Miriam Leeser

Department of Electrical and Computer Engineering
Northeastern University
Boston, MA, 02115, USA
{pbelanov,mel}@ece.neu.edu

Abstract. We present a parameterized floating-point library for use with reconfigurable hardware. Our format is both general and flexible. All IEEE formats are a subset of our format, as are all previously published floating-point formats for reconfigurable hardware. We have developed a library of fully parameterized hardware modules for format control, arithmetic operations and conversion to and from any fixed-point format. The format converters allow for hybrid implementations that combine both fixed and floating-point calculations. This permits the designer to choose between the increased range of floating-point and the increased precision of fixed-point within the same application. We illustrate the use of this library with a hybrid implementation of the K-means clustering algorithm applied to multispectral satellite images.

1 Introduction

Many image and signal processing applications benefit from acceleration with reconfigurable hardware. This acceleration results from the exploitation of fine-grained parallelism available in reconfigurable hardware. These applications are typically implemented initially in software using Matlab or C code, and variables and operations are assumed to be floating-point implemented using the IEEE standard 754. Reconfigurable implementations that exhibit speedup are possible if fixed-point or a more flexible floating-point representation than full IEEE precision is used, thus allowing for greater parallelism. We present a parameterized floating-point format and library of arithmetic operators to support it. This library supports a broad range of floating-point formats, including the IEEE standard formats as a subset.

1.1 Fixed-Point and Floating-Point Arithmetic

Representation of every numeric value, in any number system, is composed of an integer and a fractional part. The boundary that delimits them is called the radix point. The fixed-point format for representing numeric values derives its name from the fact that in this format, the radix point is fixed in a certain position. For integers this position is immediately to the right of the least significant digit.

M. Glesner, P. Zipf, and M. Renovell (Eds.): FPL 2002, LNCS 2438, pp. 657–666, 2002.

In scientific computation, it is frequently necessary to represent very large and very small values. This is difficult to achieve using the fixed-point format because the bitwidth required to maintain both the desired precision and the desired range grows large. In such situations, floating-point formats are used to represent real numbers. Floating-point formats resemble scientific notation, such as -3.2004×10^{17}. Every floating-point number can be divided into three fields: sign s, exponent e, and fraction f. Using the binary number system, it is possible to represent any floating-point number as:

$$(-1)^s \times 1.f \times 2^{e-BIAS} \tag{1}$$

Note that the exponent is *biased*, meaning that the stored value is shifted from 0 by a given value that depends on the bitwidth of the exponent field in the particular format. Also, the *fraction* represents the portion of the mantissa to the right of the radix point, while the term *mantissa* refers to the fractional and integer part.

A natural tradeoff exists between smaller bitwidths requiring fewer hardware resources and higher bitwidths providing better precision. Also, within a given total bitwidth, it is possible to assign various combinations of bitwidths to the exponent and fraction fields, where wider exponents result in higher range and wider fractions result in better precision.

The most widely used format for floating-point arithmetic is the IEEE standard 754 [1]. This standard details four floating-point formats - basic and extended, each in single and double precision bitwidths. The IEEE single precision format is the same as shown in Equation 1 with BIAS = 127, 8 bits for the exponent and 23 bits for the fraction, or a total of 32 bits. In IEEE format, numbers are normalized and only the fractional part is stored.

Optimal implementations of algorithms frequently do not require the bitwidths specified by the IEEE standard. Often, much smaller bitwidths than those specified in the 754 standard are sufficient to provide the desired precision. Reduced bitwidth implementations require fewer resources and thus allow for more parallel implementations than using the full IEEE standard format. In custom hardware designs, it is possible, and indeed desirable, to have full control and flexibility over the exact floating-point format implemented. Our library provides this flexibility.

1.2 Related Work

Investigation of using FPGAs to implement floating-point arithmetic by Fagin et al [4] showed that implementing IEEE single precision operators was possible, but also impractical on FPGA technology in 1994. Area was the critical constraint, with the authors reporting that no device in existence could contain a single multiplier circuit. Nevertheless, the authors suggest that custom, smaller, formats present a viable solution for FPGA architectures.

This line of thought was expanded on by the significant work of Shirazi et al [8], who provide two custom floating-point formats (16 bits and 18 bits total) as well as addition, subtraction, multiplication and division operators in those formats. A series of works [6, 5, 9, 7] ensued, all considering only IEEE single precision formats, usually with no rounding capabilities except in [5], where the authors implement rounding to nearest. Work on floating-point arithmetic was mostly centered on creating operator modules and optimizing them for area in order to utilize the expanding capabilities of new FPGAs.

Recent work by Dido et al[2] discusses optimization of datapaths, especially in image and video processing applications, by providing flexible floating-point formats. Their work presents a non-general floating-point format that is primarily used to represent the application specific range of scaled integer values through a format that resembles floating-point. Their format is unsigned and unnormalized, and cannot represent the IEEE single precision formats.

The floating-point formats presented here are a superset of all the previously published floating-point formats. They are both general and flexible. All the IEEE formats can be represented, as can all other instances of exponent and mantissa bitwidths.

2 Hardware Modules

We provide a library of parameterized components that are fully pipelined and cascadable to form pipelines of floating-point operations. Each component is parameterized by exponent and mantissa bitwidths. Each component has a ready and a done signal to allow them to be easily assembled into larger designs. Some error handling is supported, and errors detected are propagated to the end of the pipelined design.

The hardware modules presented fall into three categories. Format control modules support denormalizing, round and normalizing operations. The arithmetic operators include addition, subtraction and multiplication. The format conversion modules convert between fixed-point and floating-point representations. The names, functions and latencies (in clock cycles) of all modules presented are shown in Table 1. In order to operate on any custom floating-point

Table 1. Hardware modules

Module	Function	Latency
`denorm`	Introduction of implied integer digit	0
`rnd_norm`	Normalizing and rounding	2
`fp_add`	Addition	4
`fp_sub`	Subtraction	4
`fp_mul`	Multiplication	3
`fix2float`	Unsigned fixed-point to floating-point conversion	4
	Signed fixed-point to floating-point conversion	5
`float2fix`	Floating-point to unsigned fixed-point conversion	4
	Floating-point to signed fixed-point conversion	5

format, all the hardware modules have been parameterized. Every module's VHDL description accepts two parameters: *exp_bits* and *man_bits*, representing exponent and mantissa bitwidth respectively. These two values are sufficient to describe any floating-point format, since the third field, *s*, always has bitwidth of 1. The total bitwidth of the format is $1 + exp\_bits + man\_bits$. These parameters allow for the creation of a wide range of different modules through a single VHDL description. Values of the parameters help resolve the description at compile time and ensure synthesis of the correct amount of logic needed to perform the function of the module for the given format.

2.1 Denormalizing

The *normalized* format of a floating-point value is defined as the format in which exactly one non-zero digit forms the integer part of the mantissa. In binary, the integer part of every normalized floating-point number is '1'. Since this is redundant information, only the fractional part of the number is stored; the integer part is referred to as the *implied '1'*. While this provides efficient storage, the implied '1' is necessary to carry out arithmetic operation on the number and must be explicitly represented before any operations involving the number.

The `denorm` module inserts the implied '1' into the representation, unless the value being processed is zero. In the latter case, it will insert a '0', since floating-point formats represent the value zero by all zero exponent and mantissa. This module is purely combinational and is not pipelined.

2.2 Rounding and Normalizing

After arithmetic operations have been performed on the floating-point value, it is necessary to renormalize. During processing, mantissa bitwidth may increase, due to the introduction of guard digits during addition, for example. To normalize a floating-point value, we must remove the implied '1' which was introduced by the `denorm` module and reduce the fractional bitwidth to that specified by the particular floating-point format. Reduction of bitwidth introduces the need for rounding. The IEEE standard specifies four rounding modes: (1) round to zero, (2) round to nearest, (3) round to positive infinity ($+\infty$), and (4) round to negative infinity ($-\infty$).

We support the first two modes of rounding in the `round_norm` module, which handles rounding and normalizing of floating-point values. The input to this module is any floating-point value with the implied '1' explicitly represented and the mantissa bitwidth equal to or larger than that specified by the floating-point format in use. The output of the module is the normalized form of the input value, rounded to nearest (default) or to zero.

2.3 Addition and Subtraction

Addition is one of the most computationally complex operations in floating-point arithmetic. The algorithm of the addition operation for floating-point numbers is composed of four steps:

1. ensure the operand with larger magnitude is on input 1 (**swap**),
2. align the mantissas (**shift_adjust**),
3. add or subtract the mantissas (**add_sub**),
4. shift the result mantissa right by one bit and increment the exponent if addition overflow occurred (**correction**).

Each of the four steps of the algorithm is implemented in a dedicated module. The four sub-modules are assembled into the overall **fp_add** module as shown in Figure 1. The subtraction operation is similar to the addition operation, as $A - B = A + (-B)$. Thus, we use a slightly modified addition module to perform subtraction. The sign bit of B simply needs to be inverted.

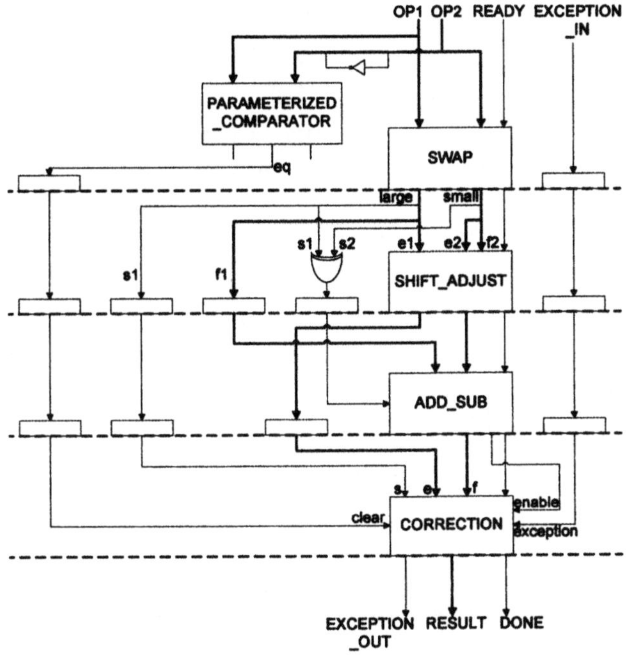

Fig. 1. Floating-point addition

2.4 Multiplication

Unlike in fixed-point, in floating-point arithmetic multiplication is a relatively straight-forward operation compared to addition. This is due to the sign-exponent-magnitude nature of the floating-point format. The sign of the product is the exclusive OR (XOR) of the operand signs. The exponent of the product is the sum of the operand exponents. The mantissa is the product of the operand mantissas. Note that the operations on all three fields of the floating-point format are independent and can be implemented in parallel. The structure of the floating-point multiplier is shown in Figure 2.

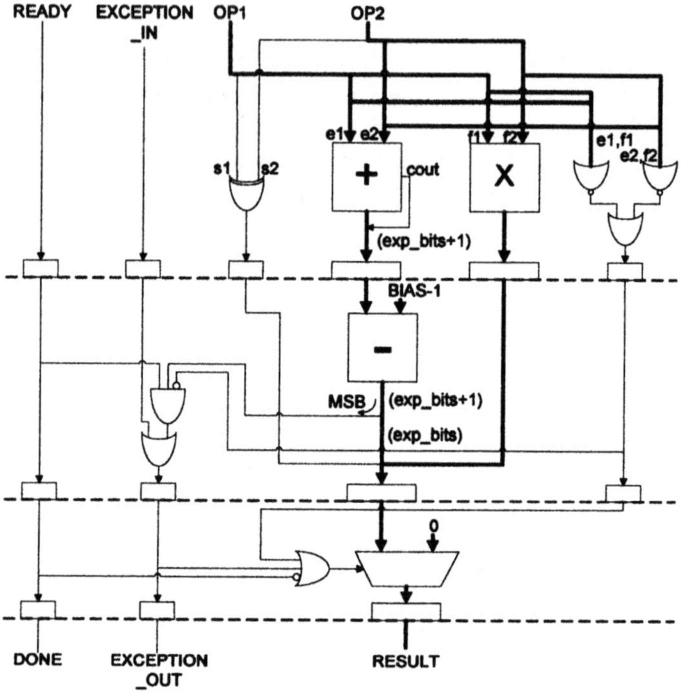

Fig. 2. Floating-point multiplication

2.5 Fixed-to-Float and Float-to-Fixed Conversion

Custom hardware designs, which are most likely to profit from parameterization of floating-point arithmetic, may derive extra efficiency from performing some parts of the algorithm in fixed-point and others in floating-point arithmetic. Hardware modules for converting between the two representations are thus required to implement hybrid designs.

The module `fix2float` converts from the fixed-point representation of a value to its floating-point representation, again rounding to nearest (default) or 0. This module has an additional parameter, *fix_bits*, to specify the bitwidth of the fixed-point value at the input. The output of the module is the floating-point representation of the value, and its format is again specified by *exp_bits* and *man_bits*. Two versions of the `fix2float` module have been developed: one for converting from signed and the other from unsigned fixed-point representations. The signed version is more complex due to handling of the two's complement representations of the input and this version hence has the longer latency of 5 clock cycles, as opposed to 4 clock cycles for the unsigned version (see Table 1).

The module `float2fix` implements the inverse function to that of the `fix2float` module: conversion from the floating-point representation of a value to its fixed-point representation. Similarly, rounding to nearest (default) and 0 are supported and the additional parameter *fix_bits* is in use to specify the width of the fixed-point output. As before, two versions of the `float2fix` module exist: one for converting to signed and the other to unsigned fixed point representation.

2.6 Results

All these modules are specified in VHDL and implemented on the Wildstar reconfigurable computing engine from Annapolis Microsystems, using a Xilinx XCV1000 FPGA. Synthesis results for parameterized arithmetic operator modules are presented in Table 2, for a set of floating-point formats labeled A0 through E2. The quantities for the area of each instance are expressed in slices

Table 2. Operator synthesis results

Format	Total bits	Exponent	Fraction	Area	
				fp_add	fp_mul
A0	8	2	5	39	46
A1	8	3	4	39	51
A2	8	4	3	32	36
B0	12	3	8	84	127
B1	12	4	7	80	140
B2	12	5	6	81	108
C0	16	4	11	121	208
C1	16	5	10	141	178
C2	16	6	9	113	150
D0	24	6	17	221	421
D1	24	8	15	216	431
D2	24	10	13	217	275
E0	32	5	26	328	766
E1	32	8	23	291	674
E2	32	11	20	284	536

of the Xilinx XCV1000 FPGA. Results for the `fp_add` module in Table 2 also represent the `fp_sub` module, which has the same amount of logic. The results in Table 2 show growth in area with increasing total bitwidth, for both modules. This growth is represented graphically in Figure 3.

To implement a single precision IEEE adder, the designer would use three parameterized modules: `denorm`, `fp_add` and `round_norm`. The floating-point format is 1 sign bit, *exp_bits* = 8 and *man_bits* = 23. Design E1 in Table 2 corre-

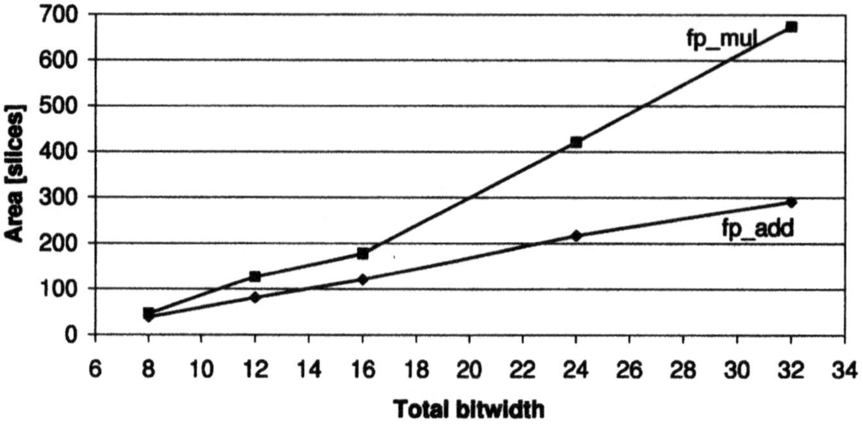

Fig. 3. Growth of area with increasing bitwidth

sponds to the adder. The total design mapped to a Xilinx Virtex 1000 takes up 305 slices, or just under 2.5% of the chip.

3 Application

We have used the parameterized hardware modules to implement a floating point-implementation of K-means clustering on multispectral satellite images. The K-means clustering algorithm consists of assigning each pixel in the image to one of K clusters, as well as accumulating the values of all pixels assigned to each cluster. These arithmetic operations can be implemented in fixed-point format, floating-point format, or a combination of the two, with format converters in suitable positions. A fixed-point implementation of K-means clustering on reconfigurable hardware [3] exhibits significant speedup over a software implementation.

The K-means algorithm processes images one pixel at a time, calculating the distance between the pixel and each of the K cluster centers. All K distances are then compared and the pixel is assigned to the closest cluster center. An accumulator and a counter are associated with each cluster. Once a pixel is assigned to a certain cluster, the value of the pixel is added to the cluster's accumulator and the cluster's counter is incremented.

The distance calculation is performed in 1-norm (Manhattan norm). The operations performed are: (1) subtract each pixel from each cluster center, each channel (dimension) processed separately, (2) take the absolute value of each difference, and (3) sum all the absolute values (dimensions). The distance of the pixel to the cluster center in the 1-norm is the resulting sum. The remaining operations are comparison of distances and accumulation.

The algorithm has been partitioned so the distance calculation is performed in floating-point arithmetic with 5 exponent and 6 fraction bits (1-5-6 format), while the comparison and accumulation operations are performed in 12-bit unsigned fixed-point format. Input data is in 12-bit unsigned fixed-point format, so it needs to be converted to the 1-5-6 floating-point representation. Similarly, the distance signal in 1-5-6 floating-point format needs to be converted into 16-bit unsigned fixed-point representation to be used by the comparison and accumulation circuits.

3.1 Results

The hybrid design of the K-means clustering algorithm resulted in a successful implementation using our library of parameterized modules. The design occupied 10,883 slices, or 88% of one of the three processing elements on the Wildstar board. This hybrid fixed and floating-point implementation was tested against an existing, purely fixed-point implementation and yielded satisfactory results, shown in Figure 4.

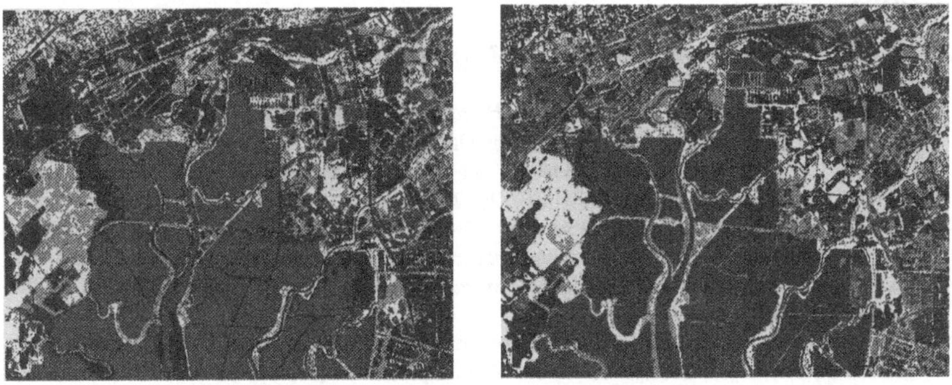

Fig. 4. Clustered image: pure fixed point (left) and hybrid (right)

The floating-point K-means distance calculation is significantly larger than the equivalent fixed-point implementation. In the fixed-point implementation, Manhattan distance was used to save space. In the floating-point version, 2-norm (Euclidean) distance will not take up significantly more space than the 1-norm calculation. The advantage of using the 2-norm distance is that the results match more closely with those achieved in software.

The hardware modules described in Section 2 lend themselves to the creation of finely customized datapaths. First, they give the hardware designer full freedom to implement various sections of the algorithm in the most suitable arithmetic form, be it in fixed or floating-point representation. Thus, the input data format does not influence the way the data is processed. Similarly, the results of processing can be returned in any format.

Also, all bitwidths in the datapath, whether in fixed or floating-point representation, can be optimized to the precision required for that signal. Hence, designing with our library of parameterized modules avoids expensive inefficiencies that are inherent in designs that operate only in the IEEE standard formats. In fact, such inefficiencies occur in any design that is restricted to using a small set of particular formats, even if these are custom. Using our library of parameterized modules provides the finest-grain control possible over datapath bitwidths. Finally, when using floating-point arithmetic, the designer has full control to trade off between range and precision. Because our modules are fully parameterized, the boundary between the exponent and the fraction for the same total bitwidth is flexible. Thus, with a wider exponent field, the designer has larger range for a value while sacrificing precision. Similarly, to increase the precision of a signal at the cost of reduced range, the designer chooses a narrower exponent and wider fraction field.

This research was funded in part by a grant from Los Alamos National Laboratory.

References

[1] IEEE Standards Board and ANSI. IEEE Standard for Binary Floating-Point Arithmetic, 1985. IEEE Std 754-1985.

[2] J. Dido, N. Geraudie, L. Loiseau, O. Payeur, Y. Savaria, and D. Poirier. A Flexible Floating-Point Format for Optimizing Data-Paths and Operators in FPGA Based DSPs. In *International Symposium on Field-Programmable Gate Arrays*, pages 50–55. ACM, ACM Press, February 2002.

[3] M. Estlick, M. Leeser, J. Theiler, and J. Szymanski. Algorithmic transformations in the implementation of k-means clustering on reconfigurable hardware. In *International Symposium on Field-Programmable Gate Arrays*, pages 103–110. ACM, February 2001.

[4] B. Fagin and C. Renard. Field Programmable Gate Arrays and Floating Point Arithmetic. *IEEE Transactions on VLSI Systems*, 2(3), September 1994.

[5] W. B. Ligon III, S. McMillan, G. Monn, K. Schoonover, F. Stivers, and K. D. Underwood. A Re-evaluation of the Practicality of Floating-Point Operations on FPGAs. In *Proceedings of the IEEE Symposium on FPGAs for Custom Computing Machines*, April 1998.

[6] L. Louca, T. A. Cook, and W. H. Johnson. Implementation of IEEE Single Precision Floating Point Addition and Multiplication on FPGAs. In K. L. Pocek and J. Arnold, editors, *Proceedings of the IEEE Symposium on FPGAs for Custom Computing Machines*, pages 107–116, April 1996.

[7] I. Sahin, C. S. Gloster, and C. Doss. Feasibility of Floating-Point Arithmetic in Reconfigurable Computing Systems. In *2000 MAPLD International Conference*, 2000.

[8] N. Shirazi, A. Walters, and P. Athanas. Quantitative Analysis of Floating Point Arithmetic on FPGA Based Custom Computing Machines. In *Proceedings of the IEEE Symposium on FPGAs for Custom Computing Machines*, April 1995.

[9] I. Stamoulis, M. White, and P. F. Lister. Pipelined Floating-Point Arithmetic Optimized for FPGA Architectures. In *9th International Workshop on Field Programmable Logic and Applications*, volume 1673 of *LNCS*, pages 365–370, August-September 1999.

Wordlength as an Architectural Parameter for Reconfigurable Computing Devices

Tony Stansfield

Elixent Limited, Castlemead, Lower Castle Street, Bristol BS1 3AG, United Kingdom
Tony.Stansfield@elixent.com

For a Reconfigurable Computing device the wordlength – the size of the basic unit of data transported by the routing network and operated on by the processing elements – is a key parameter. This paper shows that wordlengths around 4 or 5 represent a "sweet spot" that optimizes the fraction of the silicon area that is used for processing rather than routing.

Introduction

Traditionally, computing was performed by computers – von Neumann machines with a small number of complex processing elements and limited connectivity between those elements. Reconfigurable Computing – the use of large numbers of simple processing elements and a flexible routing fabric to create application-specific datapaths – provides an alternative. To date most work on reconfigurable computing is based on FPGAs, but other architectures have been proposed[1][3], which treat it as a "Computing" rather than a "Programmable logic" issue. A key feature of these architectures is a word-based (rather than bit-based) approach to data.

Architectural Parameters

This paper estimates how the size of a reconfigurable computing device varies with wordlength, using the following key architectural and implementation parameters.

Number of Inputs to a Processing Element and Wordlength

Previous studies [2] have considered the effect of changing the number of inputs to the lookup tables (LUTs) commonly used in FPGAs. Here we consider the effect of changing the bit width (or wordlength) of the inputs, and use the following symbols:

- n – the number of word-wide inputs to a processing element, and
- m – the number of bits in a word.

Silicon Area

Computing devices are ultimately constructed from logic gates (e.g. AND, NAND), memory (SRAMs and registers) and wires to link these elements together. Therefore the following parameters are used to estimate the size of a reconfigurable device:

M. Glesner, P. Zipf, and M. Renovell (Eds.): FPL 2002, LNCS 2438, pp. 667-676, 2002.

- A_{RAM} – The area of an SRAM memory cell
- A_{Gate} – The area of a 2-input simple logic gate (e.g. a CMOS NAND or NOR gate)
- W – The linear separation between wires (often referred to as the wire pitch)
- p – The fractional additional area required to add an extra port to a RAM cell

The following other components have sizes estimated from the RAM and gate areas:

- Registers. Based on a master-slave register design we can approximate
  $A_{Reg} = 2\ A_{RAM} + A_{Gate}$
- Multiplexers
  $A_{mux} = 2\ A_{Gate}$

All dimensions are normalized so that the area of a RAM cell, A_{RAM}, is 1, since it is the overall trend that is of interest rather than the size of a particular implementation. Values used for the area parameters are given at the end of this paper.

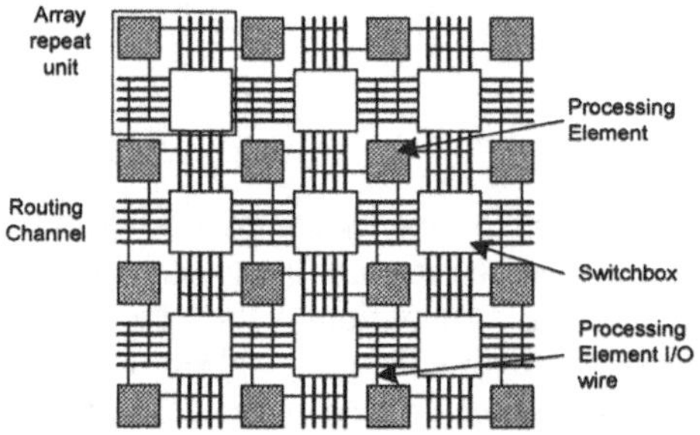

Fig. 1. Floorplan for a typical reconfigurable device

Why Is Wordlength Important?

Consider the effect of changing wordlength on the FPGA-style floorplan shown in Figure 1. If all 1-bit resources are replaced by *m*-bit equivalents then:

- The area of the logic increases by a factor of *m*,
- The number of wires in a routing channel, also increases by a factor of *m*, and so
- The area of the routing switchboxes increases by a factor of m^2

Logic and routing scale differently, so wordlength provides a useful tool to examine the relationship between logic and routing. The next two sections discuss the effect of wordlength in more detail, firstly for routing and then for the processing elements.

Routing Architecture

There are two factors to consider in the routing, summarized in these two questions:

- How big is a routing switch, and consequently a switchbox?
- How many wires (or buses) should there be in the routing network?

How Big Is a Switch?

A switch consists of 2 parts – a memory element (a register) to store the switch state and a logic element (a pass transistor) for the data routing. The total area is:

$$A_{SWreg} = A_{reg} + \tfrac{1}{2} m A_{Gate} = \tfrac{1}{2} A_{Gate}(k+m) \tag{1}$$

where $k = 2A_{reg}/A_{gate}$, and is typically between 4 and 5.

Alternatively, switch area can be estimated by counting the number of wires that cross it. This is not simply the *m* routing wires, there is an overhead to program the memory elements, which requires Vdd, ground, clocks and possibly a reset. With two extra wires in both the horizontal and vertical directions the area of a switch becomes:

$$A_{SWwire} = (2+m)^2 W^2 \tag{2}$$

The actual area associated with a switch is given by the larger of equations 1 and 2:

$$A_{SW} = Max(A_{SWwire}, A_{SWreg}) = Max((2+m)^2 W^2, A_{Reg} + \tfrac{1}{2} m A_{Gate}) \tag{3}$$

Using the parameter values at the end of this paper, for small wordlengths the logic area, with linear dependence on wordlength, is the limiting factor, while for larger wordlengths it is the quadratic dependence of the wiring area. The changeover comes at a wordlength of 4 or 5.

There are two possible ways of translating the area of a switch into the area of a switchbox, based on the answer to an architectural decision, either:

1. Choose a number of wires per channel, space them at a predefined pitch, and then see how many switches fit into the available area in the switchbox, or
2. Choose the number of wires per channel and the number of switches required to connect them, see how big the switchbox is and space the wires accordingly.

These two approaches are summarized below as "partially populated" and "fully-populated" switchboxes.

Partially-Populated Switchbox

With a partially populated switchbox the number and spacing of wires is fixed, and the number of switches derived from them. The number of switches per switchbox is equal to the switchbox area (defined by the wiring) divided by the area of the individual switch. With *B* buses per routing channel this gives:

$$\text{Number of switches} = \frac{(B(2+m)W)^2}{A_{SW}} = B^2 \frac{A_{SWwire}}{A_{SW}} \tag{4}$$

For a wiring-limited switch this reduces to B^2 - a fully populated switchbox, but for a logic-limited switch the area ratio is, by definition, less than 1. It is therefore not possible to have a switch at every crossing point of the horizontal and vertical buses, and the actual number of switches depends on how far from wire limited the switch is.

Fully-Populated Switchbox
A fully-populated switchbox has a switch at the crossover of every horizontal and vertical bus – this provides a representative example of the "predefined switch pattern" case described above.

With B buses per routing channel, the area of a fully-populated switchbox is:

$$\begin{aligned} \text{Area} &= B^2 A_{SW} \\ &= \tfrac{1}{2} B^2 A_{Gate}(k+m) \quad \text{(logic limited)} \\ &= (BW(2+m))^2 \quad \text{(wire limited)} \end{aligned} \tag{5}$$

The linear dimension of a switchbox, and consequently of a routing channel, therefore varies as $\sqrt{(k+m)}$ in the logic-limited case, which is much slower than the linear dependence assumed in the simple model used previously.

How Many Buses in the Routing Network – Rents Rule

Rents rule is the empirical observation that when a logic design is partitioned the number of terminals of a partition, T, seems to be proportional to the number of gates within a partition, G, raised to the power r, the Rent exponent:

$$T = sG^r \tag{6}$$

A change in the wordlength of a reconfigurable device can be regarded as a change in the size of the clusters that the processing logic is divided into, leading to a change in the number of cluster terminals to be connected via the wiring network. Using Rents rule, the number of terminals as a function of wordlength becomes:

$$T_m = s(mG)^r = sG^r m^r = T_1 m^r \tag{7}$$

And the number of buses required to contain this number of connections is:

$$\text{Number of buses, } B_m = T_m / m = B_1 m^{r-1} \tag{8}$$

With measured values of r typically in the range 0.5 to 0.7, this implies that the average number of routing buses per logic element (and therefore the number of buses required in the routing channels) *decreases* as the wordlength increases, varying approximately as $m^{-0.3}$ or $m^{-0.5}$

It is now possible to make more accurate estimates of the scaling of the routing network for the array of figure 1.

Partially-Populated Switchbox
Substituting equation 8 for the number of buses required into equation 4 gives:

$$\begin{aligned} \text{Number of switches} &= (B_1 m^{r-1})^2 \frac{((2+m)W)^2}{\tfrac{1}{2} A_{gate}(k+m)} \quad \text{(logic limited)} \\ &= (B_1 m^{r-1})^2 \quad \text{(wire limited)} \end{aligned} \tag{9}$$

And the number of switches per bus in the switchbox is:

$$\text{switches per bus} = B_1 m^{r-1} \frac{((2+m)W)^2}{\frac{1}{2}A_{gate}(k+m)} \quad \text{(logic limited)} \tag{10}$$
$$= B_1 m^{r-1} \quad \text{(wire limited)}$$

In the logic-limited case the number of switches per bus increases even though the number of buses is decreasing, and therefore the switchboxes provide better connectivity. The wire-limited case is simply a fully populated switchbox. Figure 2 is a plot of equation 10, the peak of the curves indicating the change from logic-limited to wire-limited switches. (The graph uses B_1 = 1, so the Y axis is expressed as a fraction of the switches required in the fully populated, wordlength = 1 case)

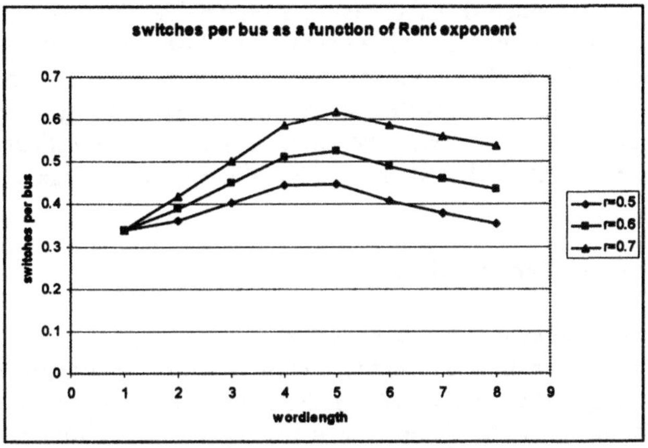

Fig. 2. Variation of number of switches per bus with wordlength and Rent exponent

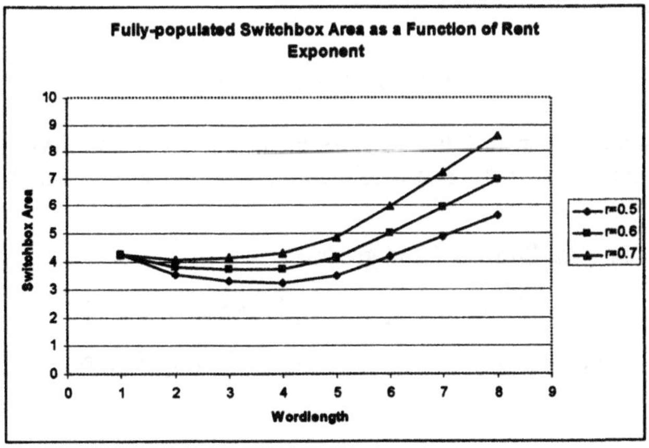

Fig. 3. Variation of fully-populated switchbox area with wordlength and Rent exponent

Fully-Populated Switchbox

For the fully populated switchbox, the area is obtained from equations 8 and 5:

$$\begin{aligned} \text{Area} &= \left(B_1 m^{r-1}\right)^2 \cdot \tfrac{1}{2} A_{Gate}(k+m) \quad \text{(logic limited)} \\ &= \left(B_1 m^{r-1} W(2+m)\right)^2 \qquad \text{(wire limited)} \end{aligned} \tag{11}$$

Figure 3 is a plot of equation 11 for a range of possible values of the Rent exponent, and shows that total switchbox area can decrease in the logic-limited region

Scaling Rules for Processing Elements

Previously it was assumed that the area of a processing element was proportional to the wordlength, since multiple 1-bit elements could be stacked side-by-side to create an m-bit element. This section contains more detailed estimates of processing element area. A major reason for considering word-based processing elements is for the efficient implementation of arithmetic circuits, and so we consider both traditional FPGA-like LUTs and ALU-based circuits, all with registered outputs.

FPGA-like Lookup Tables (LUTs)

A LUT can be constructed in two basic ways:

- A set of registers for the LUT contents, with a multiplexer tree to select the output
- A memory array with row and column decode to select the output.

There are also two ways to change the wordlength – either replicate everything, or have a shared memory section and replicate the decoding. Area estimates for the 4 combinations of LUT type and wordlength extension follow.

Multiplexer Tree

$$Area = 2^n m\left(A_{reg} + A_{mux}\right) + mA_{reg} \tag{12}$$

2^n registers to store the truth table, and the same number of multiplexers to select the output, plus an output register. The whole unit is then repeated m times.

Multiplexer Tree with Shared Configuration

$$Area = 2^n\left(A_{reg} + mA_{mux}\right) + mA_{reg} \tag{13}$$

A modified version of the above, with only one set of registers for configuration data.

Multiple SRAMs

$$Area = 2^n mA_{RAM}(1+p) + 2^{\frac{n}{2}} nmA_{gate} + 2^{\frac{n}{2}} m\left(A_{mux} + A_{gate}\right) + mA_{reg} \tag{14}$$

The RAM consists of the following components:

- An array of RAM cells, (with separate read and write ports for safe operation)
- Row decode – a set of gates decoding half of the address bits.
- Column decode – a multiplexer tree controlled by the other half of the address bits.
- A column equalize circuit, (modeled as a gate)

Multiport SRAM

$$Area = 2^n A_{RAM}(1 + mp) + 2^{\frac{n}{2}} m((n+1)A_{gate} + A_{mux}) + mA_{reg} \quad (15)$$

A modified version of the above, with a single (but multiported) memory array.

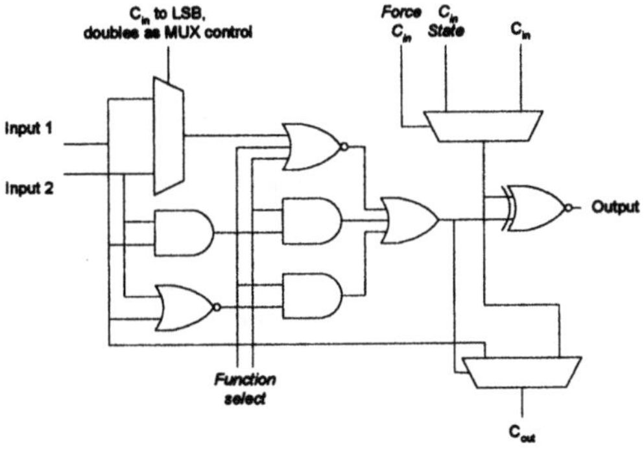

Fig. 4. Logic diagram of a simple bitslice

Arithmetic and Logic Units (ALUs)

This section considers ALUs that can perform simple operations such as add, subtract, bitwise AND, OR, XOR, and multiplexer operation. This covers the majority of the primitive operations provided by most programming languages (the main exceptions being multiplication and division). Figure 4 shows a bitslice for such an ALU. This bitslice can be implemented in the area of 6 2-input gates and 3 multiplexers per bit, plus 2 gates and 4 configuration bits (2 Function Select, Force C_{in} and C_{in} State) per 2-input ALU to set its function. An *n*-input ALU can be constructed as a tree of 2-input ALUs, so the size of an ALU is therefore:

$$Area = (n-1)(4A_{reg} + m(6A_{gate} + 3A_{mux})) + mA_{reg} \quad (16)$$

Relative Sizes of the Different Processing Elements

Figures 5 and 6 illustrate the area trends for 2 cases – fixed wordlength with variable number of inputs, and fixed number of inputs with variable wordlength. Areas are expressed as a percentage of the equivalent independent LUT circuit, so that the relative rather than absolute sizes of the different styles are emphasized.

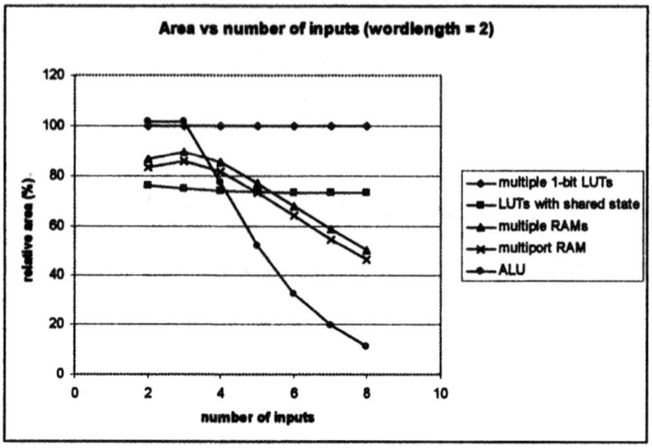

Fig. 5. Variation of area with number of inputs for the different processing elements

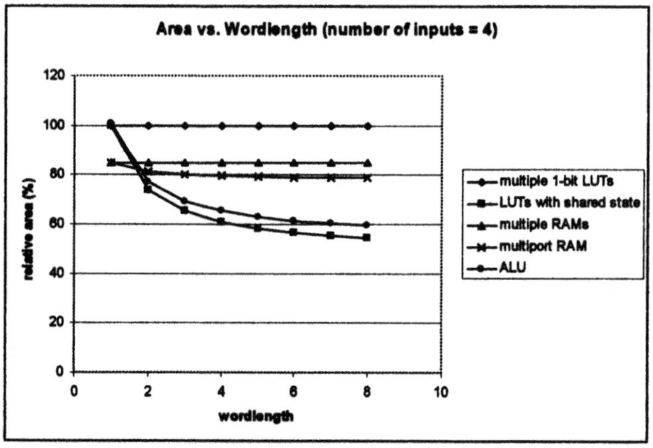

Fig. 6. Variation of area with wordlength for the different processing elements

Variation with Number of Inputs

The trends in figure 5 can be considered in 3 groups: LUTs, RAMs, and ALUs.

- Both types of LUT appear as essentially horizontal lines – in one case by definition, for the shared configuration state because the multiplexer tree rapidly becomes the dominant area factor.
- Both RAM types (with either shared or separate configuration memories) show an initial increase followed by a gradual decline in relative area as the number of

inputs increases. This reflects the changing relative size of the SRAM decode logic.
- ALUs show a rapid relative fall in area, due to their linear scaling with number of inputs, rather than the exponential one of both LUTs and RAMs.

Variation with Wordlength

The curves in figure 6 can be divided into 2 groups:
- Both RAMs, plus the LUT with independent configuration state, and
- ALUs, and the LUT with shared configuration state.

It may seem odd that LUTs with shared state have more in common with ALUs than with the independent LUTs. A consideration of the structure of the ALU and the shared LUT shows why this is the case – they both have a group of configuration bits whose outputs are control inputs to multiple copies of a block of logic, one copy for each bit of the input word. The scaling of the number of configuration bits is different (2^n vs $4n$), but for $n \leq 5$ the values of these two expressions are within a factor of 2. The main difference between ALU and shared state LUT is the form of the "bitslice".

Logic Area Vs Routing Area

Referring back to figure 1, the linear dimension of the repeat unit of the array is approximately equal to the sum of the linear dimensions of the switchbox and the processing element. From equations 11 and 17, the width (or height) of the repeat unit of an array with ALU-based processing elements can be expressed as:

$$\text{width} = B_1 m^{r-1}\sqrt{A_{SW}} + \sqrt{X + mY} \tag{17}$$

$$\text{where } X = 4(n-1)A_{reg} \text{ and } Y = (n-1)(6A_{gate} + 3A_{mux}) + A_{reg}$$

The fraction of the area devoted to the processing elements (the logic density) is:

$$\text{fraction of area for processing} = \left(1 + B_1 m^{r-1}\sqrt{\frac{A_{SW}}{X + mY}}\right)^{-2} \tag{18}$$

X and Y are the areas of the ALU periphery and bitslice, and are approximately equal. These equations contain an arbitrary parameter, B_1, the number of buses in a routing channel. Setting a value of this parameter is beyond the scope of this paper, however the following general comments can be made:
- For logic-limited switches the switch area (equation 3) varies as $k + m$. Equation 19 therefore contains two "small constant plus m" terms, which approximately cancel. The remaining Rent exponent term means that the logic density increases with m. (The actual values of the two constants provide a further 30% decrease in the square root term as m increases from 1 to 6, which reinforces this trend)
- For wiring-limited switches the switch area varies as $(2+m)^2$. In this case the square root term increases with m, and can be approximated as $\sqrt{m}$. Given the range of values of r, the result is a decrease in logic density with m.

These two comments together imply that logic density is maximized by a wordlength close to the changeover from logic-limited to wire-limited routing switches.

Conclusions

It has been shown that wordlength has a significant effect on logic density for reconfigurable computing devices. Of particular impact is the change from logic-limited to wiring-limited switchboxes, which occurs at a wordlength of 4 or 5.

Increased wordlength also makes it possible to reduce the number of buses in the routing network. Modeling this effect with Rents rule shows that the area of a logic-limited switchbox falls as wordlength increases, and the routing area is minimized at the wordlength corresponding to the change from logic- to wire-limited switches.

The variation of processing element size with wordlength has also been considered. For wordlengths around 4 the most compact processing elements are either ALU-based, or LUT-based with shared configuration state. These two designs have the same basic structure – a shared control and configuration area, and a repeated bitslice.

Sensitivity of the Conclusions to the Area Parameters

The most sensitive parameter is W, the wire pitch in the routing network. This appears in the calculation of wiring-limited switch area as W^2. Minimum wire pitch can vary by 50% or more between processes with the same nominal gate length, which implies a more than 100% variation in W^2. However, the appropriate wire pitch for reconfigurable wiring shows much less variation – such wires are commonly spaced at more than minimum pitch to avoid the extreme track-to-track capacitance seen with very closely spaced wires. The value of W=0.4 used here is derived from layout data for a standard CMOS process, and takes into account these effects.

Sensitivity to the other parameters is much less. Varying the gate area between 1.2 and 2.0 moves the wordlength at which the switch becomes wire limited by only 1 bit.

Values of Area Parameters

Parameter	Min	Typical	Max
A_{RAM}		1	
A_{gate}	1.2	1.5	2
W		0.4	
P		0.5	

References

1. Marshall, Stansfield, Kostarnov, Vuillemin & Hutchings "A Reconfigurable Arithmetic Array for Multimedia Applications" in FPGA 99 proceedings
2. Rose, Francis, Lewis & Chow "Architecture of Field-Programmable Gate Arrays: The effect of Logic Block Functionality on Area Efficiency" JSSC Oct. 1990 pp. 1217-1225
3. A DeHon, "Reconfigurable Architectures for General-Purpose Computing", MIT, Artificial Intelligence Laboratory, AI Technical Report No. 1586, 1996.

An Enhanced POLIS Framework for Fast Exploration and Implementation of I/O Subsystems on CSoC Platforms

Massimo Baleani[1], Massimo Conti[2], Alberto Ferrari[1], Valerio Frascolla[2], and Alberto Sangiovanni-Vincentelli[3]

[1] PARADES EEIG, Via San Pantaleo 66, 00186 Rome, Italy
{mbaleani,aferrari}@parades.rm.cnr.it
[2] Department of EA, University of Ancona, 60131 Ancona, Italy
{max,v.frascolla}@ea.unian.it
[3] Department of EECS, University of California, Berkeley CA 94709, USA
alberto@eecs.berkeley.edu

Abstract. The increasing complexity of embedded systems and demands for quicker turn-around times require reuse of hardware and software components. Reconfigurable hardware technology opens a new implementation space where software and hardware design cycles might be very close in time and where a broader range of applications can be mapped on. The exploitation of reconfigurable platforms is often hampered by the lack of a unified software/(reconfigurable) hardware design flow. In this paper, we presented an enhancement of the POLIS framework for fast exploration and implementation of input-output subsystems on configurable systems-on-chip (CSoCs). The designer, given the functionality of the system described in POLIS, explores different solutions at the co-design level. Those solutions that, based on the estimation of performances, violate the timing requirements are pruned without the need of any FPGA synthesis and validation steps. The explored solutions satisfying the constraints are then implemented. The automatic generation of the hardware description and the hardware-software interface make the implementation step extremely fast leading to very short system design cycles.

1 Introduction

Configurable system-on-a-chip architectures (CSoCs) that combine μprocessors and reconfigurable logic on the same chip are emerging as a promising alternative to both ASIC and standard micro-controller platforms, as witnessed by the number of currently available commercial platforms [1]. ASICs suffer from long design cycles, sky-rocketing NRE costs (SEMATECH estimates a cost of $1M for a 0.15$\mu$ mask set) and poor flexibility, while traditional micro-controllers do not meet performance requirements for demanding applications. The embedding of reconfigurable hardware (eFPGA) expands the range of problems for which post-fabrication solutions are viable. This eliminates the time and money spent in

M. Glesner, P. Zipf, and M. Renovell (Eds.): FPL 2002, LNCS 2438, pp. 677–686, 2002.

silicon design, fabrication and manufacturing verification. Reconfigurable hardware gives back designers their ability to add value and differentiate systems by post-fabrication selection and integration of components. This was typically done on-board and jeopardized by the advent of system-on-silicon technology.

In the last decade, FPGA-based systems have achieved significant speedups for a range of applications including data encryption, DNA sequence matching, automatic target recognition, genetic algorithms, image filtering and network processors (a good survey can be found in [2]). In these data-dominated applications the reconfigurable logic is employed as a hardware accelerator for computing and reconfigured for different computations during run-time.

With the advancement in process technology and increasing system requirements, embedded control applications, such as automotive control, avionics, robotics and industrial plant control processes, are also experiencing performance bottlenecks on traditional μcontroller platforms. The real-time constraints pose strong demands on both computational resources and I/O subsystems [3]. The CSoC architecture is particularly appealing since the programmable logic can be used to customize the integrated circuit, the CPU core and/or the I/O subsystem for particular applications, while retaining a certain degree of flexibility. It allows moving quickly part of the I/O subsystem from software to hardware and vice-versa without requiring expensive hardware redesign to explore different partitions.

A limiting factor in exploiting the power of reconfigurable platforms is the lack of a unified design flow that could easily move functionalities from software to the eFPGAs and back. For fully exploiting this flexibility in short time and with high degree of reliability, appropriate methodologies and tools for system specification, architecture selection, IP integration and automatic synthesis are essential. At this time, moving software, typically written in C, to hardware, typically written in some hardware description language (HDL), and vice versa is a long and tedious process hampered by the lack of a common abstraction. In this work we propose a novel approach to the exploration and implementation of flexible I/O subsystems on CSoC architectures. It is based on the design methodology and principles put forward in [4] and supported by an integrated hardware-software co-design framework built upon POLIS [5].

2 Related Work

A number of research efforts have studied development strategies and CAD tools for reconfigurable platforms. In most cases, they have come out with a unified hardware-software development environment, based upon a single language (C being the most popular) that can be effectively mapped to either hardware or software (*co-compilation*). PRISM [6] is likely the earliest work. PRISM analyzed C code to identify C functions that could be implemented with combinational logic. Other co-compilation approaches (e.g. [7, 8]) have been proposed where any grouping of instructions or rather computation intensive loop kernels are implemented exploiting the reconfigurable logic. One promising area of research relies on existing compilation techniques targeting VLIW architectures to study the benefits of various functional units and interconnect structures, as in [9].

Our approach starts from a higher level of abstraction where a common model of computation (CFSM) rather than a unique language represents the common ground for hardware and software components. Any textual (e.g. ESTEREL [10]) or graphical (e.g. State Transition Diagrams) language with underlying CFSM semantics can be employed. The system is captured as a network of CFSMs communicating asynchronously. While a C program has an underlying sequential semantics, this representation allows us to express the intrinsic parallelism among different components and the different pace at which they are evolving as they are mapped onto hardware and software resources.

As far as hw/sw partitioning is concerned, the methods proposed in the aforecited works, based on computation intensive kernels, do not apply to our case for which a more general approach to hw/sw partitioning is required. Due to the nature of the application domain we are focusing on, the main objective is not so much to speed up the execution of data intensive computations as to guarantee system "reactiveness" to external stimuli. Moreover, this generally involves heterogeneous decomposition of components (what we call *functional restructuring*) and the tecniques presented in the literature are ill-suited for this task. Since the decomposition is done to map parts of the function of the component into different implementation domains, the communication mechanism among the sub-components may be heterogeneous with respect to the communication mechanism at the component level. This is indeed what happens moving back and forth from hardware to software trying to achieve flexibility, cost, efficiency and to meet real-time constraints.

3 Design Methodology

In the POLIS co-design environment, a homogeneous behavioral representation is used to model hardware and software components. This common representation is based on the Co-design Finite State Machine (CFSM) model of computation [5] and several languages with underlying CFSM semantics, such as ESTEREL [10] or State Transition Diagrams, can be used to capture the behavior. System level functional simulation, performed in the PTOLEMY simulation environment [11], allows the designer to validate the functionality of the system without accounting for any implementation detail (e.g. hardware-software partition).

At this stage of the design flow, designers can explore the design space mapping behavioral functions onto architectural resources. Hardware-software partitioning (including *functional restructuring*), scheduling policy selection and communication refinement all take place at this point. All these steps and design decisions are manual in the proposed framework but are no more a result of designers' experience or intuition: performance evaluation can be carried out by simulating system behavior with an abstract timing model of the target architecture and it drives the designer to take the correct decisions. CFSMs mapped to hardware (hw-CFSMs) are supposed to execute in a single clock cycle (this as-

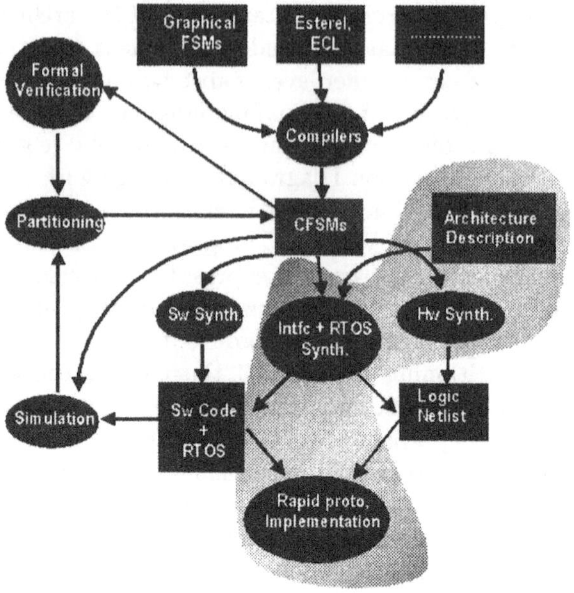

Fig. 1. The enhanced POLIS hw/sw co-design framework for configurable system-on-chip. The shadowed part represents our modification to the original framework

sumption has to be verified with a later timing analysis). Performance estimates of CFSMs mapped to software (sw-CFSMs) are derived using the technique presented in [12].

The automatic synthesis of hardware and of interfaces between the hardware and software partitions and their implementation onto the CSoC represent our original contribution to the co-design framework. POLIS automatically generates C code for each sw-CFSM and C code for a real-time OS, which is responsible for task scheduling and provides primitives for software-software, software-hardware and hardware-software communications. Several paths already exist for the synthesis of hw-CFSMs and automatic interface synthesis is also provided, to implement correctly the event-based asynchronous communication mechanism across implementation domains. However, we cannot leverage the entire synthesis flow "as is" as we are targeting CSoCs.

3.1 VHDL Synthesis

POLIS does already provide several paths for the synthesis of hardware CFSMs (i.e. CFSMs mapped onto the hardware partition). VHDL can be automatically generated from the intermediate CFSM format. It can be used for co-simulation, as shown in [13], but since it is a behavioral description it is not synthesizable at all, while it serves the purpose of verifying the behavior of the system via a VHDL simulator. Other VHDL synthesis flows exist, generating either behavioral, or gate level VHDL via the Berkeley Logic Intermediate Format (BLIF). However, the code turns out to be either a non-synthesizable description or not suitable for our design flow, e.g. the interface of BLIF-based VHDL makes it awkward to use the built-in CSoC hardware-software interfaces.

By-passing the generation of HDL code mapping directly onto the BLIF or Xilinx XNF descriptions is also possible. Unfortunately, not all the tools used to map onto CSoCs offered on the market support these formats, but all take a VHDL input. We aim at providing a general framework where not only different hardware-software partition can be evaluated and finally synthesized, but also different CSoC architectures (and thus generally supported by a different toolset) can be explored.

We have extended POLIS hardware synthesis capabilities to generate from the internal data representation (i.e. the memory image of the CFSM network and their individual behavior) a VHDL description of the hardware partition that can be efficiently synthesized onto the eFPGA using any available FPGA compiler. This mimics the software synthesis approach where a technology independent synthesis phase is kept separate from the compilation into the actual instruction set architecture. Further, since we are targeting fine-grain "standard" FPGAs, rather than customized coarse-grain reconfigurable fabrics often requiring assembly level programming [2], we can leverage a wealth of FPGA CAD synthesis tools.

The generated VHDL code is an RTL description of the hardware partition. Hardware CFSM execute in one clock cycle and are described each by a sequential process, representing the state of the machine, a reactive combinational process, computing the transition relation, and the associated data-path, consisting of relational, arithmetic and boolean operators, or even user-defined functions. Hardware synthesis can generate both an asynchronous Mealy implementation or a synchronous one. In the former case, CFSM outputs do not have a register, in the latter case they do. Note that the asynchronous option may cause combinational cycles between hardware CFSMs. Synchronous Mealy machines require a greater number of registers and introduce a unit delay (higher latency). This unit delay is compatible with the CFSM model, and ensures safe composability.

3.2 Interface Synthesis

In a synthesis-based flow, the interfaces among the different components of the design should also be automatically (and efficiently) generated. Homogeneous interfaces do not pose a problem. Software-to-software interfaces are implemented by the synthesized RTOS and so they are completely transparent. Hardware to hardware and hardware to environment interfaces use a wire to carry the event presence information, and a set of wires to carry the event value. The event presence bit is held high for exactly one clock cycle to signal the presence of an event. No latching or other overhead is required, since hardware CFSMs are executing one transition per clock cycle, and all their outputs are (possibly) latched for one cycle by the hardware synthesis procedure described above.

On the other hand, hardware-to-software and vice versa, environment-to-software and vice versa, and finally environment-to-hardware interfaces are more difficult to handle. To be compliant with the "one cycle per event" hardware protocol, we need to provide the appropriate interface logic between heterogeneous domains (see [5]).

Environment to software and hardware to software interfaces use a request-acknowledge protocol to make sure that the event is received by the RTOS, similar to the classical polling or interrupt acknowledge mechanism. Software to environment, software to hardware, and (optionally) environment to hardware interfaces use an edge detector to generate a one-clock-cycle event. Further, we need to provide the registers to hold the value (possibly) associated with each event.

On CSoC devices, the hardware side of the interfaces can be implemented on-chip employing the eFPGA block and/or using dedicated hardware-software communication resources available on the specific platform. Different choices result in different cost and logic complexity. For example, the Triscend E5/A7 family devices provide a native interface (i.e. multiplexing and decoding logic) between the reprogrammable fabric and the system bus. The use of these dedicated communication resources result in a more efficient and less costly interface than synthesizing the required logic onto the eFPGA. The capability to handle such communication resources represents a major enhancement over POLIS interface synthesis scheme.

POLIS interface synthesis only handles memory-mapped and port-based I/O for hardware-software communication. Memory-mapped I/O assumes that the memory address bus of the processor is accessible, uses a library of processor-dependent interface modules to adapt the protocol, and involves the synthesis of address decoders and the necessary glue-logic both for software to hardware and hardware to software interfaces. While this scheme is applicable to system-on-board integration, it does not scale to system-on-chip devices.

In POLIS, the available memory-mapped or port-based communication resources are specified by means of a text file (generally named *config.txt*) and the generation of the required interfaces is "hard-coded" into POLIS sources so that it is impossible to adapt interface generation to the specific CSoC platform. We have completely redefined the syntax and semantics of the configuration file in order to provide a completely new, flexible mechanism for specifying the available on-chip and off-chip communication resources, and supporting automatic synthesis and/or configuration of the specific hardware and software interfaces. A possible configuration file for the Triscend TE520S40 device is shown below.

```
.system
# part-I: address spaces
.addr_space XDATA start 0x9FFF stop 0x0000
#other space addresses ...
# part-II: resdef templates
.resdef CSL_Sel_hw2sw
unsign spaceaddr XDATA, integer wordnum 128, string bitmask "I"
```

```
    include triscend_TE520.inc
    code_sw "XDATA_CHAR(%name, %addr)"
    code_sw "#define %name &%name"
.resdefend
.resdef Port_one
    unsign startaddr 0x1FFF, integer wordnum 1, integer wordsize 16,
    string bitmask "I"
    include triscend_TE520.inc
    code_sw "CHAR_XDATA(%name, %addr);"
    code_sw "#define %name &%name"
.resdefend
# other resdefs ...
# part-III: resinst, i.e. implemented resdef's instances
.resinst CSL_Sel_hw2sw sel1
    wordnum 3
.resinstend
.resinst Port1 PortIN
.resinstend
.resinst Port1 PortOUT
    startaddr 0x001F, wordsize 8, bitmask "O"
.resinstend
# other resinsts ...
.end
```

The configuration file may be logically devided into three main sections. In the first section different *address spaces* may be defined. They can be used to implement memory-mapped communications.

The second section consists of a set of *res*ource *def*initions, each representing a sort of template for the communication resources available on the selected platform and specifying the maximum utilizable number of that specific resource. The meaning of the main fields is explained below. The interested reader is referred to [14] for a complete description of syntax and semantics of the configuration file.

spaceaddr: specifies one of the (optionally) predefined address spaces as the pool of addresses to be used for the specific resource;
startaddr: specifies a fixed address to start allocating from;
polisaddr: to specify restrictions on address allocation (none in this case);
bitmask: specifies the direction of the specific communication resource (i.e input, output or don't care);
wordsize: specifies the communication resource's width (if not given the default value of 8 bits is assumed).

Each resource definition may include also a user-specified, compiler-specific code needed to access the communication resource. The C code can be included from a text file, as given by the *include* directive, or can be specified via the reserved keyword *code_sw*. In the latter case, the C code can be parameterized (parameters are identified by the prefix '%') and will be automatically customized and embedded into the POLIS-synthesized real time operating system after resource allocation. For example, the following code lines (file *triscend_TE520.inc*) are included into the RTOS to use the Keil *u*Vision compiler for the Triscend E5 device:

```
#define CHAR_XDATA(name, location)
volatile unsigned char xdata name _at_ location;
```

The RTOS C code lines generated via the *code_sw* directive are instead reported below.

```
/* Resource CSL_Sel_hw2sw */
CHAR_XDATA(CSL_Sel_hw2sw__sel1_9fff, 0x9fff)
#define CSL_Sel_hw2sw__sel1_9fff &CSL_Sel_hw2sw__sel1_9fff
CHAR_XDATA(CSL_Sel_hw2sw__sel1_9ffe, 0x9ffe)
#define CSL_Sel_hw2sw__sel1_9ffe &CSL_Sel_hw2sw__sel1_9ffe
CHAR_XDATA(CSL_Sel_hw2sw__sel1_9ffd, 0x9ffd)
#define CSL_Sel_hw2sw__sel1_9ffd &CSL_Sel_hw2sw__sel1_9ffd
/* Resource Port_one */
CHAR_XDATA(Port_one__portIN, 0x1FFF)
#define Port_one__portIN &Port_one__portIN
CHAR_XDATA(Port_one__portOUT, 0x001F)
#define Port_one__portOUT &Port_one__portOUT
```

To ease debugging and/or improve comprehension of the allocation process variable names follow the following convention:

resdef-name__resinst-name_phisical-address

where *address* is automatically assigned according to the resource template.

The third section consists of *res*ource *inst*ances specifying how many resources are actually available in the target platform for each of resource type (i.e. resource definition). Each resinst must refer to a corresponding *resdef*, from which it inherits all the characteristics. For example, in the configuration file above, *sel1* consists of 3 of the 128 selectors totally available and subsequent *resinsts* referring to the same *resdef* will have three available addresses less. It is also possible to override the properties defined in the *resdef* template. For example the instance *PortOUT* redefines the fixed address, reduces the word length and specifies a different bitmask.

The resource assignment algorithm scans the list of required I/O events and values for the software partition, and assigns each of them to the first available resource with the required number of adjacent available bits. The allocation may be prioritized, priorities being assigned by the designer to reflect the relative cost and/or efficiency (e.g. in terms of power and/or latency) of each interface. The port assignment can be also customized by hand in order to keep the assignment of some or all resources the same, or to manually alter it.

Upon completion of the allocation stage, software procedures specified via the `sw_code` directive and needed to get access to communication resources are synthesized as part of the real-time OS. The RTOS is also responsible for task (i.e. software CFSMs) scheduling and software to software communications. The scheduler and the procedures implementing inter-task communications are synthesized using the POLIS standard synthesis flow.

At the same time, hardware interfaces are instantiated. For each type of resource used, this may implies the synthesis of interface logic onto the reconfigurable fabric and/or the configuration of built-in logic. Built-in logic configuration usually requires an interface to a proprietary CSoC development software. According to which kind of interface specification is provided, text or graphics, this process may or may not be completely automatized. POLIS (also in our enhanced version) can generate a report on the result of the resource allocation process [5]. When a textual interface is available, the information may be used by a set of target-dependent scripts to provide a completely automatic path to interface synthesis. Nevertheless, even in the latter case the information provided eases the (manual) configuration task.

4 Results and Concluding Remarks

One of the most difficult tasks in the implementation of embedded systems is the definition of the content of the input-output sub-system, i.e. the functionality mapped to the hardware that allows the system to communicate with the environment. While the use of CSoC allows the definition of this content even in the application field, the problem of the content selection is still up to the designer. In this paper, we presented an enhancement of the POLIS framework for fast exploration and implementation of input-output sub-systems on CSoCs. The designer, given the functionality of the system described in POLIS, explores different solutions at the co-design level. Those solutions that, based on the estimation of performances, violate the timing requirements are pruned without the need of any FPGA synthesis and validation steps [15]. The explored solutions satisfying the constraints are then implemented. The automatic generation of the VHDL describing the input-output sub-system and the hardware-software interface makes the implementation step extremely fast. Given the desired content of the input-output subsystem, the presented design flow reduces the design time to the eFPGA synthesis time, which might take hours for complex subsystems. In fact, POLIS generates the software partition as well as the hardware one. Moreover, the presented POLIS enhancement allows the use of dedicated resources for hardware-software (and vice-versa) communication that are typically provided by the target CSoC. This results in a more efficient use of the eFPGA area.

In [15] we presented the experience in applying the presented design methodology to the implementation of an automotive industrial case study onto a CSoC. POLIS confirmed to be an efficient basis for the fast exploration of hardware-software trade-offs. In fact, our approach allowed to evaluate a number of partitions in a few hours yielding what we believe to be an effective implementation of the functionality of the automotive subsystem.

We used less than an hour to move from a solution to another during architectural exploration, dropping all those alternatives which did not comply with our functional/performance requirements. The implementation design step, whose time is completely dominated by hardware synthesis, took no more than 8 hours to move from a first candidate solution to a second one.

Acnowledgments We wish to acknowledge the contributions of Giampiero Spugni for the extension of the POLIS synthesis flow and Luciano Lavagno from Cadence Berkeley Labs for his suggestions and original contribution to POLIS.

References

[1] Schaumont, P., Verbauwhede, I., Keutzer, K., Sarrafzadeh, M.: A quick safari in the reconfiguration jungle. In: Proceedings of the Design Automation Conference. (2001)

[2] Hartenstein, R.: A decade of reconfigurable computing: A visionary perspective. In: Proceedings of the European Design, Automation and Test Conference (DATE). (2000)

[3] Ferrari, A., Garue, S., Peri, M., Pezzini, S., Valsecchi, L., Andretta, F., Nesci, W.: Design and implementation of a dual processor platform for power-train systens. In: Proceedings of Convergence Conference. (2000)

[4] Keutzer, K., Malik, S., Newton, A.R., Rabaey, J.M., Sangiovanni-Vincentelli, A.: System-Level Design: Orthogonalization of Concerns and Platform-Based Design. IEEE Transactions on Computer-Aided Design **19** (2000) 1523–1543

[5] Balarin, F., Sentovich, E., Chiodo, M., Giusto, P., Hsieh, H., Tabbara, B., Jurecska, A., Lavagno, L., Passerone, C., Suzuki, K., Sangiovanni-Vincentelli, A.: Hardware-Software Co-design of Embedded Systems – The POLIS Approach. Kluwer Academic Publishers (1997)

[6] Athanas, P.M., Silverman, H.F.: Processor reconfiguration through instruction-set metamorphosis. IEEE Computer **26** (1993) 11–18

[7] Razdan, R., Brace, K., Smith, M.D.: PRISC software acceleration techniques. In: Proceedings of the International Conference on Computer Design. (1994) 145–149

[8] Li, Y., Callahan, T., Darnell, E., Harr, R., Kurkure, U., Stockwood, J.: Hardware-software co-design of embedded reconfigurable architectures. In: Proceedings of the Design Automation Conference. (2000) 507–512

[9] Proceler: Soft instruction set architectures for embedded computing (2002) [On-line] http://www.proceler.com.

[10] ESTEREL Team: The ESTEREL web (2002) [On-line] http://www.esterel.org.

[11] Buck, J., Ha, S., Lee, E., Masserschmitt, D.: Ptolemy: a framework for simulating and prototyping heterogeneous systems. International Journal of Computer Simulation **Special Issue on Simulation Software Development** (1990)

[12] Suzuki, K., Sangiovanni-Vincentelli, A.: Efficient software performance estimation methods for hardware/software codesign. In: Proceedings of the Design Automation Conference. (1996)

[13] Filippi, E., Lavagno, L., Licciardi, L., Montanaro, A., Paolini, M., Passerone, R., Sgroi, M., Sangiovanni-Vincentelli, A.: Intellectual property re-use in embedded system co-design: An industrial case study. In: Proceedings of International Symposium on System Synthesis. (1998)

[14] Frascolla, V.: Generazione automatica di interfacce hw/sw per metodologie di co-progettazione di sistemi dedicati nel settore automobilistico. Master's thesis, University of Ancona (2001)

[15] Baleani, M., Conti, M., Ferrari, A., Sangiovanni-Vincentelli, A.: HW/SW co-design of a multiple injection driver automotive subsystem using a configurable system-on-chip. In: Proceedings of the European Design, Automation and Test Conference (DATE). (2002)

Introducing ReConfigME: An Operating System for Reconfigurable Computing

Grant B. Wigley, David A. Kearney, and David Warren

Reconfigurable Computing Laboratory (RCL)
Advanced Computing Research Centre
University of South Australia
Mawson Lakes SA 5095
{Grant.Wigley, David.Kearney, David.Warren}@unisa.edu.au

Abstract. ReConfigME is a complete package to manage the dynamic reconfiguration of applications running on field programmable gate arrays. ReConfigME can also be viewed as an operating system for reconfigurable computing that handles the loading of IP cores on the FPGA platform and the dynamic arrangement and rearrangement of cores on the surface of the FPGA as the execution needs of multiple applications and multiple uses sharing the same platform evolve. ReConfigME can integrate with compilers for hardware software co-designed applications. We describe all the major components that make up the operating system and give preliminary results from the first prototype. These indicate that ReConfigME is a feasible basis for software like development of reconfigurable applications.

1 Introduction

Reconfigurable computing is becoming a mainstream technology, competing with general purpose processors in a growing marketplace for high performance and low power solutions for mobile and embedded systems. Yet if this scenario is to be realized reconfigurable computing must emerge from its roots as an alternative to application specific integrated circuits (ASICs) and move into a realm dominated by software. Even more ironical is that the engineer developing and debugging field programmable gate array (FPGA) applications is still typically using an ASIC hardware orientated methodology. In this paper we present a new approach to reconfigurable computing tools. We assume that the future application developers will consider themselves software engineers, that the design problem will no longer dominated by hardware resource constraints and that the development and debugging methodology will be orientated to a cost structure where bugs are just a nuisance to be worked around. For this new world we propose an operating system (OS) which facilitates multiple applications running on the same FPGA sharing the computing task with cooperating software only methods all written in a common language.

This paper is organized as follows. First we look at existing research. We then describe from the top down how applications will be written and run on our particular operating system. Then give a description of the major components of ReConfigME. Finally detail preliminary results from our first tests of the core components.

M. Glesner, P. Zipf, and M. Renovell (Eds.): FPL 2002, LNCS 2438, pp. 687-697, 2002.

2 Other Work

Operating systems traditionally provide run time support for applications. Surprisingly in view of the number of reconfigurable computer (RC) platforms and architectures proposed and built, very few of these projects have included a detailed investigation into run time support. Everybody who ever built a platform has seen the need for a single user loader, often in the guise of interface software between the RC platform and the host system. Some researchers have seen the need for a run time environment.

Brebner coined the term virtual hardware operating system [1]. He explored some of the fundamental issues that might influence the construction of any operating system for FPGA's with dynamic reconfiguration. He proposed that applications be designed into relocatable cores known as swappable logic units (SLU). He identified the main responsibilities of an operating system to be placement of SLU's and providing for "bus addressable" registers for communication between SLU's. The whole system described by him was not implemented on a real FPGA but simulated in C, including a simulation of the FPGA.

Shiraz [2] proposed a reconfiguration manager which comprises a monitor which seems to receive interrupt like requests from applications already running, notifying the loader to locate a new configuration at a particular place on the FPGA. This paper does not discuss how this new place is to be found (either in the initial load of the FPGA or subsequently). We assumed that this monitor is really just a mechanism for swapping between different cores in the same location. Thus there is no *allocation* in this proposal. The other elements of this proposal are a traditional loader and a configuration store.

Caspi [3] presents a Stream Computations Organized for Reconfigurable Execution, or SCORE. He presents a scalable, multi-threaded computation model and an associated architectural abstraction. Although SCORE introduces the idea of a run-time environment, it does not address the problems of dynamic logic resource allocation and real-time task graph partitioning. This is because SCORE has a fixed architecture and uses paging to swap tasks on and off the surface. It also has a fixed communication structure for inter-page communication. ReConfigME allows dynamic page sizes and as such requires online area allocation and potential online partitioning. Since ReConfigME does not have a fixed architecture a memory arbitrator had to be used.

In summary as far as we are aware, no-one has actually built an operating system for reconfigurable computing; if the definition of operating system is to extend to allocation of area resources and not just to be a loader of applications. We also note that the issue of resource sharing has been little touched in the reconfigurable OS related research although this is often thought to be a key issue in more traditional OS literature.

3 Compiler

In this section we provide a top down description of the OS application development environment. The first part of this, a compiler, is not a part of the OS proper. We describe it here to show the feasibility of generating the object modules we assume for the OS at a high level of abstraction.

ReConfigME is not restricted to any one language for implementing reconfigurable hardware. However to demonstrate the relationship between it and a compiler, we describe a proposed port of a Java compiler. The compiler actually compiles a superset of the Java language called Join Java; which has improved localized synchronization constructs that greatly simplify the specification of hardware like behavior in Java. In this section we give a short introduction to the syntax and semantics of Join Java. Readers who are interested in more information about Join Java are referred to [4]. Then we show how a simple hardware orientated application can be expressed in both Java and Join Java illustrating the advantages of Join Java in expressing hardware orientated behavior. We then show how Join Java can be used as a basis for the specification of task graphs; which are the fundamental structures used in defining applications for our operating system.

3.1 Introduction to Join Java

Join Java primarily adds a new type of method to Java called the *join pattern method* that gives the guarded process semantics of the Join calculus to Java. The body of a Join pattern method is not be executed until all the methods (*join fragments*) in the header are called. In the example in figure 1 the join fragments a(),b() and clock must all be called before the body will be executed. If Join patterns are defined with pure Java return types such as **void** and **int** they have blocking semantics. If the return type of the leading fragment is the new type *signal* the method is asynchronous and a new thread is created to execute the method. As shown in the example, parameters may be passed via the join fragments and although not shown in the example the join pattern method may return an object to the first calling fragment.

```
Hardware Class task1 {
  Asyn a(p1)&b(p2)&clock {
    p3=Add(p1,p2);
    c(p3);
  }
```

```
  Asyn c(p3)&d(p4)&clock {
    P5=Mult(p3,p4);
    e(p5);
  }
}
```

Figure 1. The body of a Join pattern method

3.2 Example Application in Join Java

In this section we give a small example that defines some of operations used in the image recognition phase of the geometric hashing algorithm [5]. In this example we present part of a reconfigurable hardware design for the transformation step in the geometric hashing algorithm to illustrate the advantages of join java over pure java in describing reconfigurable hardware applications. The presentation here is very short. For a more comprehensive treatment of possible hardware implementations of geometric hashing see [6]. A block diagram of the hardware is shown in figure 2.

Figure 4 is a multithreaded behavioral description of the pipeline in pure Java. The InputData class is a thread that initially performs an unconditional wait() for the clock. Every time the clock calls notify on the InputData object the InputData run method transfers data from RAM (simulated by an array) into the public variable *nextCoord.* Careful readers will notice that this code is not strictly correct since the Transformation stage must not start till the InputData is complete. Thus we need a guard before Transformation commences (unless both blocks complete exactly in the same number of clock cycles). In a native implementation, with two successive waits it is not possible to differentiate which wait will be notified by a particular object. So although Transform must wait for the Clock and InputData; it might be notified by two successive Clocks instead. A further problem is that the global clock must notify each functional unit at every clock tick using a reference to each functional unit passed back to it.

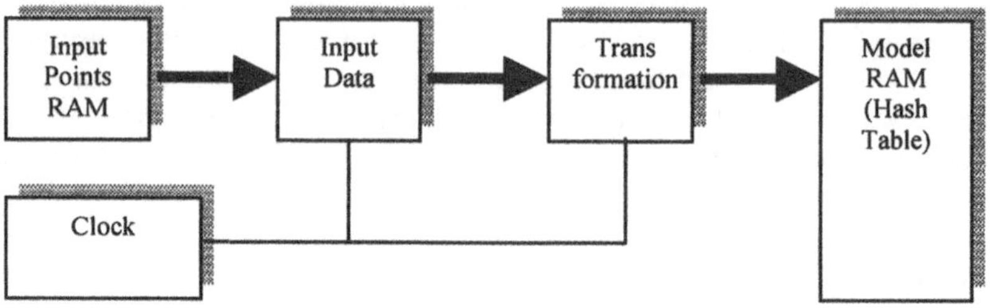

Figure 2. A block diagram of first two stages of geometric hashing

```
class Transformation extends Thread {
  InputData id;  static int
MAX_COORD=32;
    int outAddr;

    Transformation(InputData id) {
        this.id=id;
    }
    public synchronized void run() {
          while(true) {
            basis = new int[4];
            for(coordCount=0,
coordCount<4, coordCount++)
            {
                wait();

basis[coordCount]=id.nextCoord;
            }
            while(coordCount<MAX_COORD)
{
                wait();
                pointX=id.nextCoord;
                wait();
                pointY=id.nextCoord;
            }
        }
    }
```

Figure 3. Transformation

```
class InputData extends Thread {
      int[] ram =
public synchronized void run() {
     for (int i=0; i<32; i++) {
       wait()
       nextCoord=ram[i];
      }
     }
}
class Clock extends Thread {
   MasterClock(InputData                    id,
                 Transformation tr) {
       this.id=id;
       this.tr=tr;
   }
   public void run() {
       while(true) {
           synchronized (id) {
               id.notify();
           }
           synchronized (bs) {
               tr.notify();
           }
           this.sleep(clockPeriod);
       }
   }
}
```

Figure 4. Input Data Class

Figure 5 shows part of the same application in Join Java. In Join, the synchronization with the clock is written in the local definitions of the functional units as a join pattern guarding their execution.

```
Async ram(p1)&clock {
    p2=p1;
    inputData(p2);
}
```

```
Async  inputData(p3)&clock {
    p4=trHash(p3);
    Transform(p4);
}
```

Figure 5. Join Java Application

The Join version elegantly expresses the data flow nature of the pipeline and as we will show in the next section this makes for an easy translation of it to a task graph which is the object file format used on the operating system.

3.3 Task Graph and Join Java Hardware Class

The task graph defines the structure of reconfigurable hardware applications that run under the operating system. The task graph is a data flow graph where the nodes are pre-placed hardware cores and the arcs represent dependencies between the cores and their dataflow channels. The task graph can be generated directly from a Join Java *hardware class*. The body of join methods in a hardware class are currently assumed to be either defined as structural Java (such as JBits [7]) cores or as separate hardware native methods; which may have been synthesized from an RTL description. For performance reasons it is not currently permitted to have a software join method inside a hardware class.

There is a straight forward mapping from the join pattern methods to the task graph. The methods of the hardware class may have the special asynchronous method clock associated with them. If clock declarations are included then the graph can be explicitly pipelined; otherwise a clocked register is assumed at the start and the end of the task graph. Other compilers could be used in place of the Join Java if data flow graphs (task graphs) can be produced from the source code.

4 ReConfigME Components

In this section we describe the minimum set of components required in the ReConfigME operating system. To illustrate the role of each of the components we will describe the various phases that a task graph goes through during execution. Figure 6 shows a flow chart of a typical execution sequence. The solid lines refer to a successful completion of the task whereas the dotted lines refer to a failure of the task.

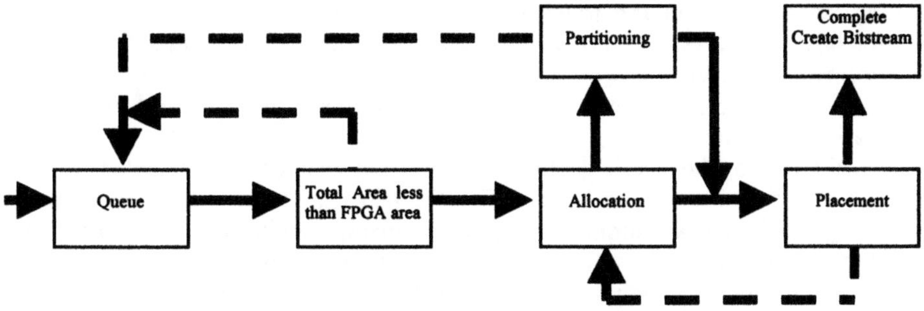

Figure 6. Flow Diagram of OS

Applications arrive as task graphs in the OS and form a ready queue. The graph at the front of the queue is compared with the maximum *space slice*, which is the maximum contiguous area a task graph may occupy on the FPGA. Fixing a maximum size for the space slice prevents large task graphs blocking small task graphs if they were to occupy all the remaining free space on the FPGA. If a task graph is smaller than the current space slice, the allocator will be asked to locate available logic area on the FPGA for it. If the allocator finds an available space, the placer will pre-pack the task graph into the rectangular space allocated. If the placer is successful the task graph will begin execution. If the task graph does not fit into the space slice it must be partitioned. If the placer fails to fit the task graph into the space slice then the partitioner must be called to reduce the number of nodes in the task graph segment. The partitioner itself may fail to find a feasible partition. If this is the case the task graph may have to rejoin the ready queue or the space slice may have to be increased. Further refinements relating to policy issues to allocating space of the FPGA can be accommodated in this flow chart by dynamically adjusting the space slice.

4.1 Packing

Unlike the traditional design method for field programmable gate arrays, where the designer would determine where to put the application on the FPGA and the design software would perform automatic placement at design time, ReConfigME is required it to make placement decisions at run-time. A combination of algorithms determine where to put the application onto the FPGA (allocation) and how to arrange the cores in a task according to a set of constraints (placement). We call this 2-stage process *Packing*. Figure 7 introduces the terms that we use in describing these steps.

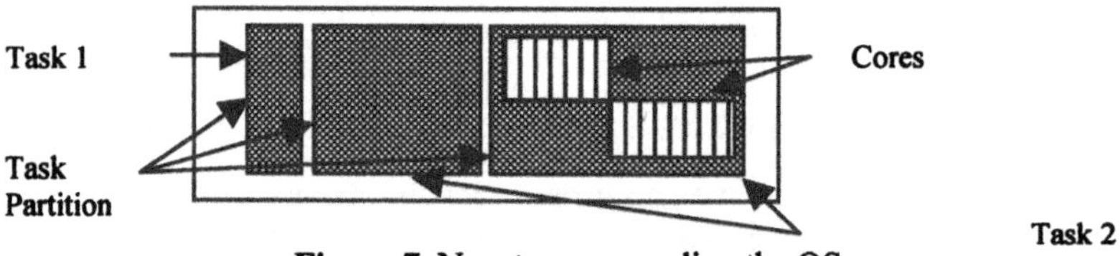

Figure 7. New terms regarding the OS

Allocation. Once ReConfigME has accepted the application, it has to determine on which part of the FPGA surface the task can go, without interfering with other executing tasks. We define this to be *Allocation.* The general geometrical problem of allocation has been investigated by many researchers. Several different solutions have been put forward [8]. Very few of these algorithms have been adapted for FPGA area allocation. We have implemented two algorithms and have proposed a third to solve the allocation problem.

In algorithm one, the available FPGA area is represented as a free list of area, analogous to a free list of disk blocks. The OS takes the next task from the ready queue and given its known minimum area requirement, searches the list of free space for contiguous area that will satisfy the area requirement, favoring area with square dimensions. The initial dimensions of the task graph are pre-calculated at compile time. This pre-compiled estimate of the space requirement is called a *virtual rectangle* because its aspect ratio is not yet determined. The OS initially places the virtual rectangle over the first free CLB position on the FPGA. If the virtual rectangle overlaps another task, the virtual rectangle is progressively and deterministically moved over the FPGA area and the process is repeated until a feasible position is found. The OS then marks the area as taken and the task partition has reserved area for itself. This algorithm has a time complexity of k, where k is the number of free CLBs on the FPGA. This complexity is likely to be a problem for larger FPGAs, and thus algorithm two was developed.

Algorithm two is based on a placement algorithm described in [9]. The algorithm consists of two parts: an empty space partitioning manager for insertion and deletion of task partitions, which is similar to algorithm one; and a set of rules for dividing up the free space. The algorithm differs from algorithm one in the way that is manages the free space. This algorithm stores the free space as a group of rectangles; each rectangle may have multiple CLBs. The complexity of searching for free space is thus linear in the number of rectangles, which is always less than the number of CLBs. When a task partition requests area, the algorithm searches the linked list of available rectangles looking for space with dimensions that are equal or larger than the incoming task partition. The allocation algorithm will place the virtual rectangle in the left-hand corner of the free space. The space left after this placement is then subdivided into two further rectangles. Although not mentioned in the original paper, this algorithm has more potential to fragment the FPGA surface because of the subdivisions it performs. We are currently working on a third algorithm, which has time complexity in between algorithms one and two but leads to less fragmentation than algorithm two.

Placement. The method of determining where to place the cores within the rectangles is defined as *placement*. Placement must be carried out under constraints that include placing communicating cores next to (or close to) each other to increase the chance of gaining a successful route and to reduce timing delays. Other placement constraints might include requiring a specific part of FPGA surface to be used, or to specify a placement that aligns with I/O pins.

The first placement algorithm implemented in ReConfigME is based on the placement algorithm developed by Gehring, a constructive placement algorithm for the Trianus System [10]. It attempts to place the communicating application cores next to each other. One application core is placed to the right of the communicating core, while the other is placed directly above the connecting core. A single input core only requires one connection and is placed immediately to the right of the connecting module. This process is repeated until the entire task graph partition has been placed. The placement results of this algorithm yield a good chance of a quick successful route and are repeatable. The algorithm avoids iterative techniques commonly employed by commercial tools, which significantly extend the run time. We are working on a more complex placement algorithm which while having a longer run-time, is better able to take care of constraints.

4.2 Partitioning

The process of selecting a hyper graph from a task graph that will fit into a particular contiguous area is our definition of partitioning. Although there has been a wide range of algorithms published that address the partitioning problem for FPGAs, most of these algorithms have an objective function of dividing the task graph into task partitions such that the inter-task communication is minimized or the task execution delay is minimized. In selecting a partitioning algorithm for use in the operating system, the objective function is to have a small, deterministic and bounded algorithm run time. It must be small because the run time is a direct overhead. A deterministic and bounded run-time is important to avoid unpredictable response times that would reduce the user ability of the operating system. These requirements exclude most partitioning algorithms based on combinatorial optimization heuristics. In this operating system we have modified an algorithm that was originally proposed for temporal parititioning [11]. Temporal partitioning aims to break a directed task graph into segments that might be dynamically reconfigured by a process analogous to time slicing. It was chosen over other partitioning algorithms as it had a near linear time complexity and it partitioned under area constraints.

We have modified the Purna temporal partition algorithm so that it can be called iteratively to find the closest fit to the target virtual rectangle area. The algorithm is now able to handle dynamically varying target rectangles and we have introduced a control variable (target fragmentation level) that allows the selection of the level of interaction between the partitioner and the packing algorithms. At one extreme of the control variable the partitioner will find a fitting partition with a single iteration or at the other extreme it will iterate to find the closest partition to the target. Clearly if the interaction is reduced there may be a considerable inefficiently in the use of area in the FPGA but there would be a reduction in the overheads in the run time of the partitioner.

4.3 JBits

JBits is a set of Java classes which provide an Application Program Interface (API) into the encrypted Xilinx FPGA bitstream. This interface operates on either bitstreams generated by Xilinx design tools, or on bitstreams read back from actual hardware, or on bitstreams created by JBits cores. JBits is used in ReConfigME to perform the last stages of the bitstream manipulation after the location of the application has been determined. As ReConfigME performs this at run-time, the traditional Xilinx design tools are unable to be used. Therefore, ReConfigME uses JRoute (JBits built in router) to complete the inter-core routes, and JBits to customize the application for the position it is loaded onto.

ReConfigME also strongly supports the use of JBits cores. The user can specify their task graph application as a combination of JBits cores. These cores are stored by ReConfigME in a library and are specified in the task graph at design time. ReConfigME will then allocate, partition (if necessary) and place these cores at run-time and then use the JBits API to create the corresponding bitstream. The user can also create new cores with JBits and upload these to ReConfigME's library.

Note that ReConfigME is not restricted to cores created with JBits. Cores may be created with any tool that can generate a partial bitstream. For example the JPG tool [12] allows VHDL synthesized cores to be included as nodes in a task graph.

4.4 Hardware Abstraction Layer

We assume that reconfigurable platform manufacturers provide a device driver for each of the supported software OS. On top of this is layer, is the Hardware abstraction layer (HAL) of ReConfigME. The distinctive feature of the HAL is that it comprises native methods when the language implementing the device driver (typically C) is different to the language used to implement ReConfigME (Java in the case in our prototype). The typical services provided by the HAL are starting and stopping the FPGA clock, configuring and (partially) reconfiguring the FPGA, loading and reading data from the on board RAM and loading and reading data from the FPGA registers. In our first prototype we are using the rc1000 java class provided in the JBits distribution as our HAL. The rc1000 class is compliant with the Xilinx Hardware XHWIF API definition and we have adopted this API definition for our HAL API.

4.5 Executable File Format and API

The OS has an API class that includes methods to execute task graphs. These methods assume that task graphs are store in a serialized pre-generated file. So for example **exec(tge, mem, pin, pout)** executes the task graph executable tge with input data taken from object pin and data output to pout object. The input and output data are stored temporality in the RAM attached directly to the FPGA at location specified by the object mem. The file tge will thus include the object defining the task graph, objects defining pre-placed cores (bitstreams) for each node in the graph and an object defining the memory locations of the input and output data in the RAM local to the FPGA. If the application consists of hardware only the data must come from an environment defined by the OS. If on the other hand the application includes both hardware and software elements the data for the hardware would be passed from the software language environment as parameters of the methods a hardware class which are stored temporarily in the local RAM of the FPGA. The most general example could have java software, java specified hardware and externally generated cores (from VHDL via a synthesis tool).

4.6 Thread Structure of the Operating System

ReConfigME and all concurrent hardware/software tasks executing on it are managed as separate threads running under a common Java Virtual Machine (JVM). This structure has been chosen for efficiency reasons. It is possible to have the OS and each hardware/software task running under a different JVM but this would incur overheads in inter-task communication at the software level; which we wanted to minimize. The drawback of using threads to manage tasks on the FPGA is that there is less protection between the software parts of these tasks than would be the case if they were managed from separate JVMs.

Each executing task graph is an instance of a base task thread class. When the base class is started it executes a method taken from the task graph executable (.tge) file. The structure of the .tge file is defined as the base class of the task thread. The object instances of this class are serializable and hence can be loaded from the .tge file at initialization. These include the bitstream objects (or classes that generate bitstreams on the fly) that make up the nodes of the task graph. The ReConfigMe thread is the first to run after the initialization of the JVM and it will itself have a tge file which may contain bitstreams to be loaded permanently onto the FPGA. The major difference between ReConfigME and other .tge applications is that it may have nodes (such as the major components described above) which are not associated with a task graph. This illustrates the flexibility needed in the definition of the .tge structure which must be able to accommodate applications which may range from just a single hardware only core to cases which are software only.

5 Prototype Performance

Fragmentation is usually associated in a traditional software OS environment with a loss of contiguous locations to store a particular application program. In the two dimensional environment of a RC there is a need to generalize this concept. We introduced two types of fragmentation in [13]. Internal fragmentation results from the inability of the placement algorithm to fully fill target rectangle size. External fragmentation arises from the inability of the allocation algorithm to make complete use of the free area on the FPGA. Clearly, the less fragmented the surface of the FPGA is the better the OS has performed in using expensive area resources. Figure 8 illustrates the performance of the current version of the prototype. It shows snapshots (from left to right and then down the page) of the FPGA surface as task graphs are added and removed from the FPGA. The shaded areas indicate occupied space and the dotted lines indicate where the allocation algorithm has divided the space.

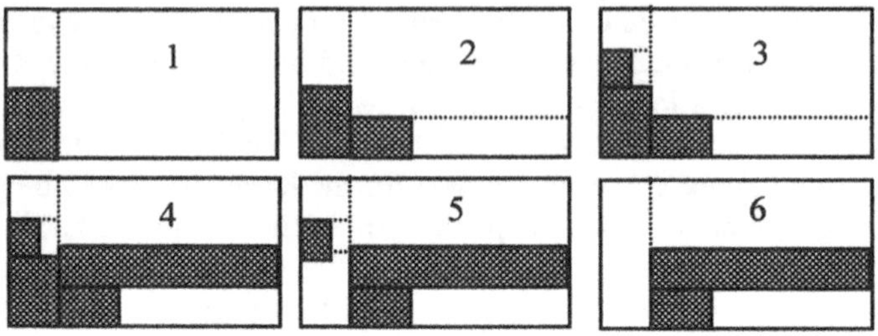

Figure 8. Snapshots of the OS

Figure 9 shows the operating system overheads for the current prototype as measured in elapsed time for a Celeron 800Mhz. The allocation time reported is for algorithm 2. These results do not include the time for routing between cores. We are currently working on a range of more elaborate benchmarks.

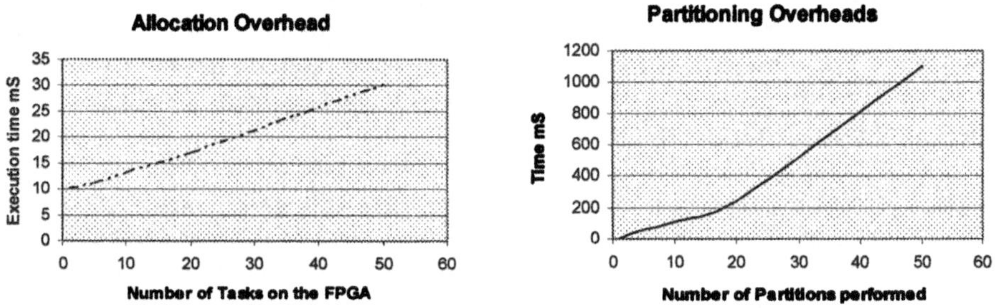

Figure 9. Allocation and Placement Overheads. Partitioning Overheads

6 Conclusion

In this paper we have described ReConfigME, an operating system implementation for FPGA-based applications. We have shown that existing research has proposed some of the key concepts of RC operating systems up till now no one has successfully implemented an OS for RC which combines all the necessary components. We have presented a compiler technology that is capable of generating executable files for ReConfigME. We have described in detail the algorithms used in each component of the OS, in some cases giving several possible algorithms, which have various trade offs between execution time and area fragmentation performance. Finally we have reported initial measurements of performance. The development of the operating system and associated compiler is a work in progress and we intend to enhance the implementation in several ways including better handing of inter-core communication, and improved placement under more realistic constraints. We also intend to better benchmark the OS by evaluating tradeoffs between OS performance and application performance. In order to do such research we are developing a number of applications for use with ReConfigME, including the well-known triple DES encryption, image fusion, where a infra-red and colored camera image are fused together, and an implementation of target recognition using geometric hashing are all under development.

7 References

[1] G. Brebner, "A Virtual Hardware Operating System for the Xilinx XC6200," 6th International Workshop on Field-Programmable Logic and Applications (FPL'96), Darmstadt, Germany, 1996.

[2] N. Shirazi, W. Luk, and P. Cheung, "Automating Production of Run-time Reconfigurable Designs," IEEE Symposium on FPGAs for Custom Computing Machines (FCCM'98), Napa Valley, CA, USA, 1998.

[3] E. Caspi, A. DeHon, and J. Wawrzynek, "A Streaming Multi-Threaded Model," Third Workshop on Media and Stream Processors, Austin, Texas, 2001.

[4] G. Itzstein and D. Kearney, "Applications of Join Java," Seventh Asia-Pacific Computer Systems Architecture Conference (ACSAC02), Melbourne, Australia, 2002.

[5] Y. Lamdan and H. Wolfson, "Geometric Hashing: A General and Efficient Model-Based Recognition Scheme," 2nd International Conference on Computer Vision, 1988.

[6] D. Warren, "Possible Hardware Implementations of Gemetric Hashing," University of South Australia, Adelaide 2002 2002.

[7] S. Guccione, D. Levi, and P. Sundararajan, "JBits: A Java-based Interface for Reconfigurable Computing," 2nd Annual Military and Aerospace Applications of Programmable Devices and Technologies Conference (MAPLD).

[8] P. Healy and M. Creavin, "An Optimal Algorithm for Rectangle Placement," University of Limerick, Limerick UL-CSIS-97-1, 1997 1997.

[9] K. Bazargan, R. Kastner, and M. Sarrafzadeh, "Fast Template Placement for Reconfigurable Computing Systems," in *IEEE Design & Test of Computers*, vol. 17, 2000, pp. 68-83.

[10] S. Gehring and S. Ludwig, "The Trianus System and its Application to Custom Computing," 6th International Workshop on Field-Programmable Logic and Applications (FPL'96), Darmstadt, Germany, 1996.

[11] K. Purna and D. Bhatia, "Temporal Partitioning and Scheduling Data Flow Graphs for Reconfigurable Computers," *IEEE Transactions on Computers*, vol. 48, pp. 579-590, 1999.

[12] A. Raghavan and P. Sutton, "JPG - A Partial Bitstream Generation Tool to Support Partial Reconfiguration in Virtex FPGAs," To appear in Reconfigurable Architecture Workshop (RAW02), 2002.

[13] G. Wigley and D. Kearney, "The Management of Applications for Reconfigurable Computing using an Operating System," Seventh Asia-Pacific Computer Systems Architecture Conference, Melbourne, Australia, 2002

Efficient Metacomputation Using Self-Reconfiguration*

Reetinder Sidhu and Viktor K. Prasanna

Department of EE-Systems, University of Southern California, Los Angeles, USA
sidhu@halcyon.usc.edu, prasanna@ganges.usc.edu

Abstract. Self-reconfiguration is a technique using which configured logic can quickly modify itself at runtime to suit application requirements. Although performance improvements using self-reconfiguration have been demonstrated, the technique itself has been only informally described. Based on an abstract reconfigurable device model, a precise definition of self-reconfiguration is presented in this paper. Various practical issues in efficiently implementing self-reconfiguration are also discussed.
A competing approach to self-reconfiguration is the use of a von Neumann processor on the same chip as the reconfigurable logic. Both alternatives can provide on-chip configuration modification. The performance of both alternatives is evaluated for a frequently used configuration modification operation. The approaches used for both alternatives are described and the performance of both approaches is evaluated. Self-reconfiguration is found to require significantly lesser area as well as significantly lesser time compared to the attached processor approach.

1 Introduction

Applications mapped using self-reconfiguration have been shown to improve performance over existing approaches [10][9][8]. A reconfigurable device architecture that supports efficient self-reconfiguration has also been developed [11]. However, the concept of self-reconfiguration has only been informally described so far. In the first part of this paper, a precise description of self-reconfiguration is presented (Section 2). An abstract reconfigurable device model is developed (Section 2.1) which is used to define and describe self-reconfiguration (Section 2.2). Practical considerations for efficient self-reconfiguration are also discussed (Section 2.3) and the work done to meet the requirements is summarized (Section 2.4).

A competing approach to self-reconfiguration is the use of a von Neumann processor on the same chip as the reconfigurable logic [3][2]. Both approaches can provide on-chip configuration modification, the former using reconfigurable logic and the latter using an attached processor. In the second part of the paper, the performance of both alternatives is evaluated for a frequently used configuration modification operation (Section 3). The approaches used for both alternatives are described (Sections 3.1 and 3.2) and the performance of both approaches is evaluated (Section 3.3). Finally, the contributions of the paper are summarized (Section 4).

* This work was supported by DARPA contract no. DABT63-99-1-0004 and by NSF grant no. CCR-9900613.

M. Glesner, P. Zipf, and M. Renovell (Eds.): FPL 2002, LNCS 2438, pp. 698–709, 2002.

2 Self-Reconfiguration

2.1 Reconfigurable Computing Machines

A reconfigurable computing machine is implemented as a digital integrated circuit[1]. So we begin with the fundamental model for digital circuits, the Mealy machine, which is shown in Figure 1(a). The input and output data are binary digits (bits). The combinational logic is a network of logic elements each of which performs a boolean function. The memory is composed of storage elements each of which can store a bit. The stored bits form the state of the machine. The above model is suitable for a device that performs a specific computation, such as an ASIC.

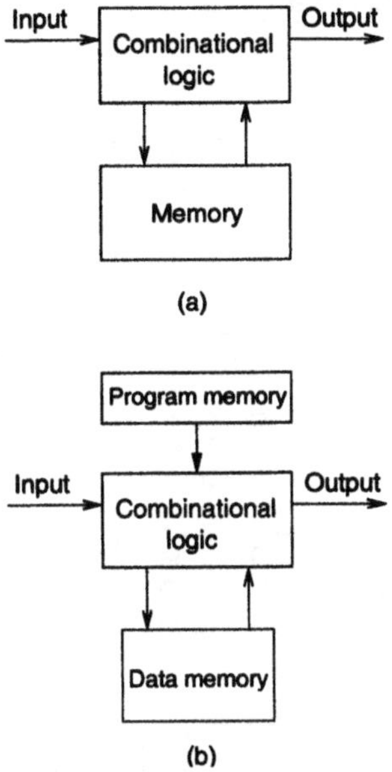

Fig. 1. (a) The Mealy machine model for digital circuits, (b) Programmable Mealy machine.

But a reconfigurable device is a general purpose machine. It can be programmed to perform a specific computation[2]. The program is the description of a logic circuit and so can be viewed as the description of a Mealy machine. The task of writing the program bits into memory is called *configuration* and the program bits are called *configuration bits*. The part of the memory that stores the configuration bits is called *configuration memory* and the part that stores data bits is called *data memory*. The Mealy machine described by the configuration bits is called *configured logic*. Once configured, a reconfigurable device functions as the configured logic would. The device reads input data, performs the same actions on it as the configured logic would have, and produces output data. The above task is called *execution* . By separating the program memory and data memory, we obtain the model shown in Figure 1(b). The solid arrow represents the connection used to configure the logic described by the configuration bits. The remaining arrows represent connections used by the configured logic, like a Mealy machine, for input, output and data memory access.

2.2 Self-Reconfiguration Definition and Description

Self-reconfiguration is informally defined as the modification of configured logic, during execution, by a part of the configured logic which remains unmodified throughout execution, the former part producing the output of the reconfigurable device and the latter part producing the configuration bits that modify the former part.

---

[1] Henceforth, reconfigurable device will be used as a synonym for reconfigurable computing machine.

[2] Assuming the reconfigurable device is large enough, it can perform any computation that can be performed by a universal Turing machine.

Using self-reconfiguration can improve computation efficiency because the configured logic can be quickly adapted to computation requirements during execution. Separation of the configured logic into the part modifies and the part that gets modified, makes it significantly simpler to design and debug the configured logic. Modification of configured logic means the modification of configuration bits that describe it. Therefore, to support self-reconfiguration, a reconfigurable device must enable the configured logic to read and write the configuration memory. Figure 2 shows the augmented device model. A precise definition of self-reconfiguration, based on the above model, is given below.

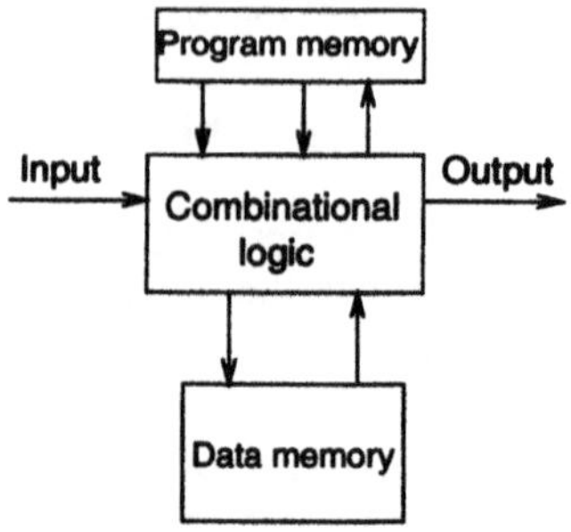

Fig. 2. Self-reconfigurable device model.

Self-reconfiguration requires that the logic be composed of two distinct but interacting Mealy machines. The Mealy machines, which we call C and M, perform different tasks. As shown in Figure 3(a), the input and output of C are respectively the input and output of the reconfigurable device and the state of C is stored in a part of the data memory. Therefore C performs all the actions required to produce the output data from the input data. The task performed by C is thus called *computation*. As shown in Figure 3(b), M has three possible inputs[3]: the input of the reconfigurable device, the state of C and the description of C. The output of M is configuration bits that modify the description of C. The state of M is stored in a part of the data memory[4]. M therefore performs all the actions required to modify C which in turn performs computation. The task performed by M is therefore called *metacomputation*.

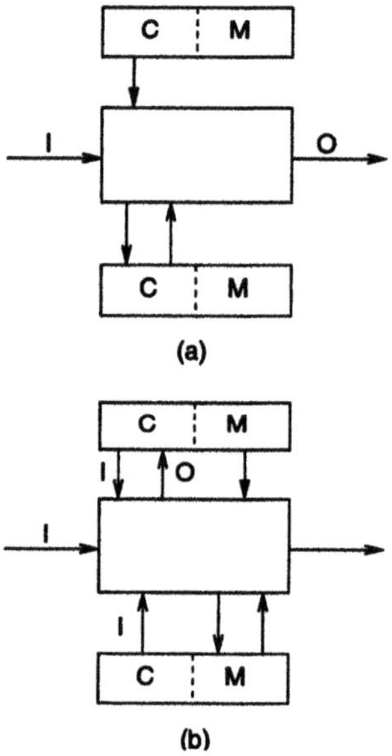

Fig. 3. (a) Computation, (b) Metacomputation.

The aim of self-reconfiguration is to improve the efficiency of computation or in other words, reduce the costs of computation. Using self-reconfiguration, computation logic can be adapted to the computation requirements during execution which is not possible if self-reconfiguration is not used. Therefore, the computation logic can be made more efficient using self-reconfiguration. On the other hand, self-reconfiguration requires metacomputation logic which is not required if self-reconfiguration is not used. Therefore, self-reconfiguration improves efficiency only if the decrease in computation costs due to C is greater than the computation costs due to M.

---

[3] M need not have all three inputs in all cases, but only those on which its output depends.

[4] States of C and M are stored in disjoint areas of the data memory.

The key strength of self-reconfiguration lies in computation logic modification based on input data available only after execution begins. It is only using the above type of self-reconfiguration, called *data-dependent* self-reconfiguration that optimizations can be made to the computation logic that are impossible to make during compilation. Data dependent self-reconfiguration requires that either the input data, or the state of C , or both should be inputs to M . Self-reconfiguration can also be used for computation logic modification which does not depend on input data. The above type of self-reconfiguration, called *data-independent* self-reconfiguration appears useful only for compressing the configuration bits that describe the configuration logic in order to reduce the are occupied by it. Data-independent self-reconfiguration cannot reduce the time required for the execution of the computation logic. Data independent self-reconfiguration requires that either M has the configuration bits that describe C as its only input, or M has no input.

The requirement of self-reconfiguration that configured logic modification can be performed only by part of the configured logic and that part cannot modify itself, significantly simplifies the tasks of designing, understanding and debugging configured logic that modifies itself. The above advantages would be lost if no restriction was placed on how the configured logic modifies itself.

2.3 Requirements for Efficient Self-Reconfiguration

Self-Reconfigurable Device Requirements In principle, a reconfigurable device, in order to support self-reconfiguration, need only provide some mechanism for the configured logic to read and write the configuration memory. But in practice, self-reconfiguration needs to be performed as quickly as possible and to do so, a reconfigurable device must provide the following features.

1. The configured logic must be able to read and write any location of configuration memory as quickly as possible. In other words, the reconfigurable device must provide configured logic fast, random access to the configuration memory.
2. Typically the metacomputation logic requires more than one clock cycle to compute the configuration bit values for the configuration memory cells whose contents need to be modified. If the bits are written into the configuration memory cells as soon as they are computed, then in any clock cycle when the modification is in progress, some of the cells would store new configuration bit values while others would retain old values. Therefore in any of the above clock cycles, the output of the computation logic being modified may not be correct. Therefore the reconfigurable device must provide either a mechanism to temporarily disconnect the logic being modified from its outputs[5], or a mechanism to store the configuration bits as they are being computed and to write all of them into the configuration memory cells in a single clock cycle.

[5] Reconfigurable device mechanism is not strictly necessary because extra logic to perform the disconnection can be added to the computation logic at design time. But doing so would make the computation logic larger and slower.

3. In typical applications the computation logic and the metacomputation logic do not compute at the same time. Therefore it would be a significant waste of area if logic for both parts remains configured at all times. In order to utilize area efficiently, therefore, the reconfigurable device must provide a mechanism to replace currently configured logic with some other logic. And to utilize time efficiently, the replacement must be as fast as possible. Note that the replacement involves saving not only the configuration bits for the logic being replaced, but also its state which is stored in a part of the data memory, and similarly for the replacing logic, restoring its configuration bits as well as its state which is restored to a a part of the data memory.

2.4 Self-Reconfigurable Logic Requirements

1. The configured logic needs to be designed to take advantage of self-reconfiguration. The computation logic must be made more efficient by exploiting the fact that it can be modified and the metacomputation logic must be designed such that it can make any of the computation logic modifications required.
2. Configured logic for performing basic metacomputation tasks such as configuring a LUT or creating a connection between logic cells must be designed. Doing so simplifies the task of designing metacomputation logic for a specific application.

2.5 Summary of Work Done on Self-Reconfiguration

The concept of self-reconfiguration was earliest presented in [5], where a small amount of static logic is added to a reconfigurable device based on an FPGA in order to build a self-reconfiguring processor. Being an architecture oriented work, no application of this concept is shown. The Xilinx XC6200 was also a self-reconfiguring device, and this ability has been used in [4] to define an abstract model of virtual circuitry, the Flexible URISC. This model still has a self-configuring capability, even though it is not used by the simple example presented in [4].

In order to satisfy the device requirements enumerated above, the Self-Reconfigurable Gate Array (SRGA) was developed [11]. The SRGA, a multicontext device, enable single clock cycle random access to its configuration memory and single clock cycle context switching. The former feature enables enables fast modification of the computation logic. By storing the metacomputation logic on a separate context, the latter feature enables the metacomputation logic to be configured only when required. The latter feature also prevents the computation logic from being active when it is being modified.

Using self-reconfiguration, significant speedups have been demonstrated for applications of simple string matching [10], genetic programming [9], regular expression matching [8] when compared with processor based implementations. Also, efficient configured logic to perform basic metacomputation tasks such as connecting two logic cells has been developed for the SRGA [11].

3 Metacomputation Performance Evaluation

Self-reconfiguration uses reconfigurable logic for metacomputation as well as computation. An alternate approach to modifying configuration bits would be to use a von Neumann processor for metacomputation, while retaining reconfigurable logic for computation. The above approach, commonly called runtime reconfiguration, has been used for several applications such as shortest path [1]. No commercial device like the SRGA exists that supports efficient self-reconfiguration. However, recent commercial devices combine a von Neumann processor with reconfigurable logic on the same chip [3][2]. Assuming that such as device provides the attached processor fast random access to the configuration memory, the metacomputation could be performed on the processor. It is therefore natural to ask the question how does metacomputation using a von Neumann processor compare with metacomputation using reconfigurable logic.

In order to answer the question, we compare the time and area required by both above approaches for the basic metacomputation task of connecting together two logic cells in the same row (or column) using non-local interconnections. The above task was chosen because for the above mentioned applications mapped using self-reconfiguration it was very frequently used and the most resource intensive.

The problem is to connect the output of a logic cell to the input of another in the same row, using only non-local[6] row tree wires and switches available in each row[7]. As

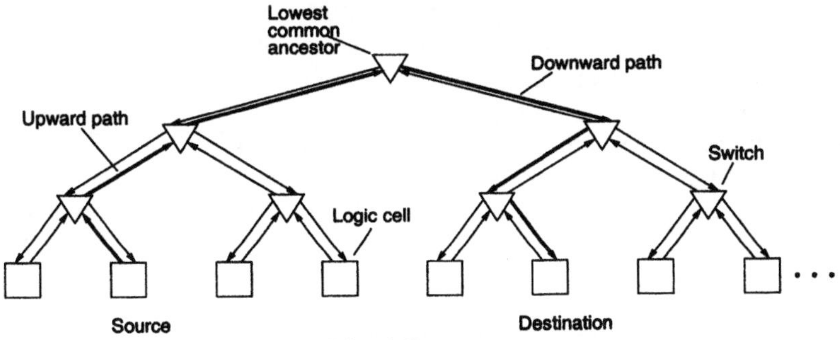

Fig. 4. Row tree.

shown in Figure 4, a row of the SRGA is structured as a complete binary tree with the logic cells forming the leaf nodes, the switches forming the non-leaf nodes, and a pair of wires carrying signals in opposite directions forming each edge. The switch structure is shown in Figure 5. A single configuration bit is required for each of its outputs. The configuration memory locations that store the above bits are organized as 3 rows of $N-1$ columns.

The inputs to the routing operation are the column numbers (s and d) of the source and destination logic cells[8]. The output of the routing operation is configuration bits that

[6] Connecting using only local, nearest neighbour wires is a much simpler problem. Also the routing delay would be linear compared to logarithmic in case of tree switches.

[7] Only non-local wires and switches are considered in the following discussion.

[8] The context number and the row number are required as well but they affect only where the configuration bits computed by the routing operation are written.

configure the switches to create the required connection. As can be seen from Figure 4, connections need to be created up the tree starting from the source logic cell, and then down the tree till the destination logic cell is reached. The highest node through which the connection passes is the *least common ancestor* of the source and destination logic cells. The switches used in the upward path are all ancestors of s, one at each level of the tree, and similarly the switches used in the downward path are all ancestors of d.

Since each of the above switches needs to connect one of its inputs to one of its outputs, only one mux needs to be configured in each switch. The problem therefore is to determine which switches need to be configured, which mux in each switch needs to be configured, and with what bit value is the mux to be configured. The above items determine respectively the configuration memory column numbers, the row address for each column number, and the configuration bit written at above row address and column number.

The row addresses of the locations are base_addr, base_addr+1 and base_addr+2 which store respectively configuration bits for the parent, left child and right child muxes. The column addresses vary from 0 to $N-2$ and each column stores the configuration bits of a switch. The order in which the switches are assigned to the columns is one in which they are encountered during an inorder traversal of the binary tree formed by the switches. For example, to connect the left input to the right output of the root switch ($N = 8$), a 0 needs to be written in row 2, column 3.

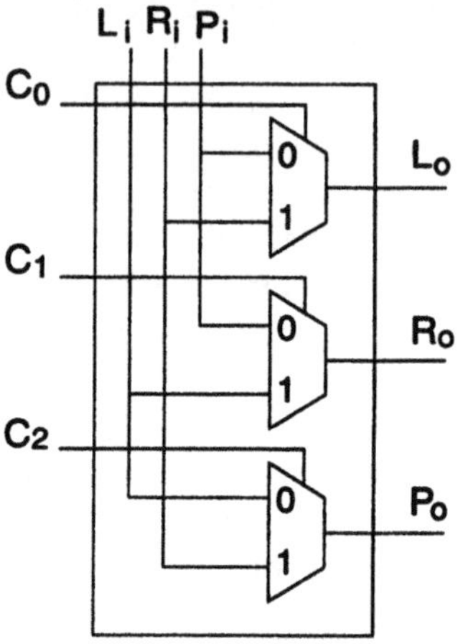

Fig. 5. Each switch receives an input from and sends an output to its left child (L_i, L_o), right child (R_i, R_o), and parent (P_i, P_o). The 3 configuration bits C_0, C_1 and C_2 control the connections between the inputs and outputs of the switch.

3.1 Row Routing Using Attached Processor

In this case, the row routing operation is performed by a program running on the von Neumann processor connected to the SRGA . The leaf nodes (logic cells) of the binary tree are assigned numbers $(0 \ldots N-1)$ from left to right. The levels of the tree are numbered $(0 \ldots \log_2 N)$ from bottom to top.

The configuration memory column number corresponding to every switch on the upward path can be obtained from the binary representation of s. The column number for the switch at level i is obtained by replacing the i least significant bits by 0 followed by $i-1$ 1s. For each switch on the upward path (except the least common ancestor) the mux to be configured is the one whose output connects to the parent switch. For the switch at level i on the upward path, whether the mux to be configured selects its left input or right input is determined by bit i of s.

The configuration memory column number corresponding to every switch on the downward path can be obtained from the binary representation of d. The column number for the switch at level i is obtained by replacing the i least significant bits by 0 followed by $i-1$ 1s. For each switch on the downward path (except the least common ancestor) the input selected by the mux to be configured is from the parent switch. For the switch at level i on the downward path, whether the mux to be configured is the one connecting to the left switch or the right switch is determined by bit i of d.

A row routing program, designed based on the above observations, is shown in Figure 6. In iteration i, the program configures two switches at level i, one on the upward path, and the other on the downward path. The last iteration is the one in which the switch encountered on the upward path is the same as the switch encountered on the downward path. The above switch is the lowest common ancestor. The program configures it and terminates.

Note that although the program has been written using C language syntax to simplify understanding, it is actually an assembly language level program. Each statement represents a machine instruction[9] each variable represents a machine register.

3.2 Row Routing Using Self-Reconfiguration

```
row_route(src, dest, base_addr)
{
  i = 0;
  z_mask = 0xfffe;
  p_mask = 0;

 loop: lr_bit = bit(src, i);
  src = src && z_mask;
  src = src || p_mask;

  lr_mux = bit(dest, i);
  dest = dest && z_mask;
  dest = dest || p_mask;

  if(src == dest)
    goto finish;

  write_bit(base_addr, src, lr_bit);
  write_bit(base_addr + lr_mux, dest, 1);

  z_mask = z_mask << 1;
  p_mask = (p_mask << 1)||1;
  ++i;
  goto loop;

 finish: write_bit(base_addr + lr_mux,
                   src, lr_bit);
}
```

Fig. 6. Row routing program.

We compute 4 bits for each switch—Bits L, P, R specify respectively whether the mux driving the left child, right child or parent outputs is to be configured, and bit C specifies with what value.

The logic used to compute the bits required consists of $N-1$ identical logic modules, one module corresponding to each row switch. Each module generates the 4 bits (L, R, P and C) for its corresponding switch. Figure 7 shows the structure of the logic module. Each module requires 5 logic cells. Just as the switches to be configured are arranged as complete binary tree, so also we configure the $N-1$ logic modules as a complete binary tree—each module and the switch it represents are in the same position in their respective trees. The edges of the logic module tree consist of

[9] To enable fast configuration modification, the processor is assumed to support the `write_bit(x, y, z)` instruction which writes the bit z in row x, column y of the configuration memory.

2 unidirectional links from each child node to its parent. The lowest level modules are connected to flip-flops—a pair of flip-flops represents each logic cell.

Computation starts by setting the flip-flops corresponding to the source and destination logic cells to contain 01 and 10 respectively. Each logic module receives 2 bits from each child node. If it receives 01 from one child and 00 from the other, it is on the upward path (see Figure 4). Thus it needs to configure the parent mux and hence writes a 1 into it. Based on whether the 01 was received from the left or right child, 0 or 1 is written to the C flip-flop (see Figure 5). The logic module passes the received 01 to its parent. If a node receives a 10 input from one child and 00 from the other, then it is on the downward path. The left or right mux needs to be configured and a 1 is written to the L or R flip-flop depending upon which child node the 10 was received from. In both cases, input from parent needs to be selected and hence 0 is written to the C flip-flop. The module passes 10 to its parent. Finally, if a module receives a 01 from one child and 10 from the other, it represents the switch which is the least common ancestor of the source and destination logic cells. A 1 is written to the L or R flip-flop depending upon whether the 10 was received from the left or right child. Also, a 1 is written to the C flip-flop since the left input needs to be connected to the right mux or vice versa. The logic module passes neither 01 or 10 to its parent.

The module logic shown in Figure 7 performs the above functions. Since only combinational logic is required to compute configuration bits, the signals travel up the tree and bits in all logic module are computed in a single clock cycle[10]. The subsequent task of writing configuration bits into the memory becomes very simple if the computed bits for a switch are located in the same column in which they are to be written. Therefore we map logic modules to $(N-1) \times 5$ logic cells, each module located in the column in which are to be written the 3 bits that configure the switch it represents.

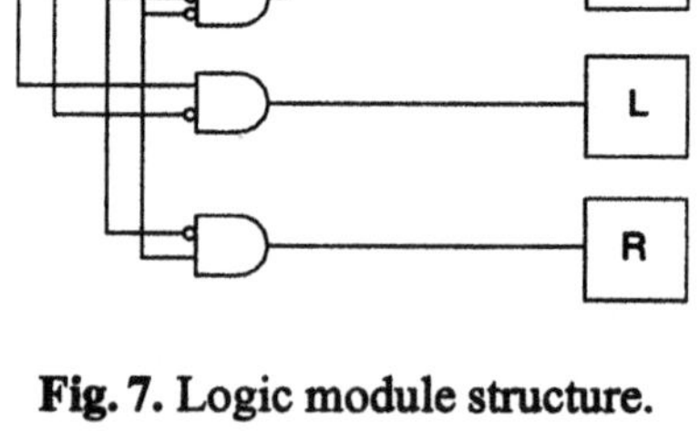

Fig. 7. Logic module structure.

Routing of the modules thus placed to connect them in a complete binary tree can be efficiently performed. Figure 8 shows how an $N-1$ ($N = 8$) node tree, with 2 logic cells per node can be configured with a single upward link from each child node to its parent. Since the required logic modules have 5 logic cells (and hence the tree requires 5 rows), they can be connected as a tree with 2 upward links from each child node to its parent.

Finally, the computed bits (L, R, P and C bits in all modules) are used to configure the switches. As discussed above, there are 3 $(N-1)$ bit memory locations, 1 each for the control bits of the muxes driving the left, right and parent outputs. Each clock cycle, the one of L, R or P bits in all the $N-1$ logic modules are inverted and written to the row mask register and the C bits of all $N-1$ logic modules are written to the location addressed by configuration memory address registers as described in [11].

[10] The clock period increases logarithmically with tree size.

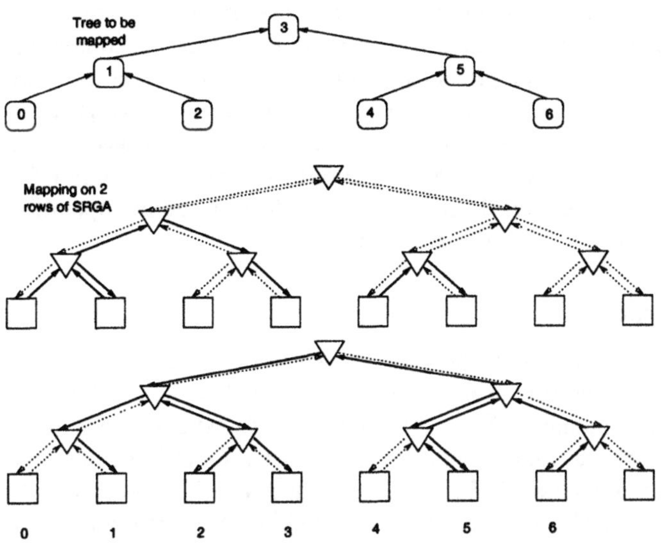

Fig. 8. Mapping of a complete $N-1$ node binary tree (with a unidirectional link from each child to parent) onto 2 rows of N logic cells. Each node consists of 2 logic cells.

In this manner, in only 3 clock cycles, the configuration bits to perform the routing operations are written. Thus, a connection between 2 logic cells in the same row (or column) can be created in a constant number of clock cycles—it does not depend upon the size of the row. The length of the clock cycle would depend upon the row length but it would grow only logarithmically with row length (since signals only need to propagate up the tree of logic modules). A related observation is that several such connections can be created in a row (or column) in parallel time if they occur in separate subtrees.

An alternate implementation would be to split the module logic into a 2 submodules and to store the logic for each submodule of all modules in a separate configuration context[11]. Compared to the implementation discussed above, the alternate implementation would require more time due to context switching and computation by logic on 2 contexts. But its key advantage is that only 2 rows of logic cells are required instead of 5 rows.

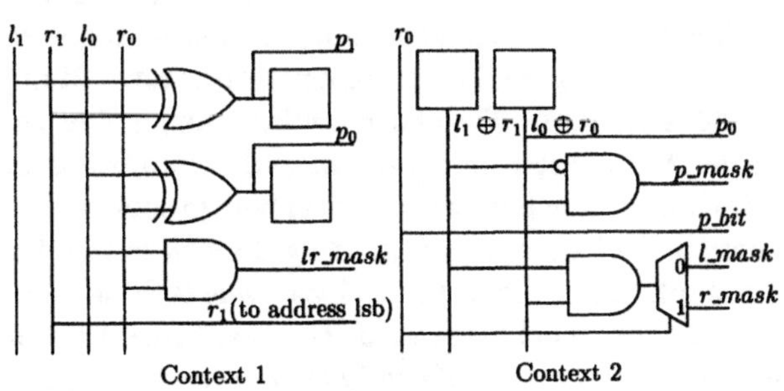

Fig. 9. Submodule structure. Each submodule fits into 2 logic cells.

The row routing operation can be done using trees of 2 submodule types which are shown in Figure 9. Initially, 01 and 11 are applied to the inputs corresponding to the source and destination logic cells respectively. 00 is applied to to all other inputs. In context 1, $l_1 \oplus r_1$ and $l_0 \oplus r_0$ are computed and stored in flip-flops to be used by logic on context 2. Also, $l_0 \cdot r_0$, the

[11] As explained in [11], each logic cell is associated with a memory block which can store upto 8 configuration contexts.

mask for the lowest common ancestor is computed. Whether the left or right mux needs to be configured is determined by r_1. For the lowest common ancestor, the content bit is 1 for all submodules. In context 2, the previously computed $l_1 \oplus r_1$ and $l_0 \oplus r_0$ are used to compute the mask and content bits for the parent mux which will configure the upward path. The previously computed bits are also used to compute the mask bits for the left and right muxes which will be used to configure the downward path. For the downward path the content bit is always 0. In this manner, the row routing operation can be accomplished using only a 2 rows of logic cells.

3.3 Performance Evaluation

Assuming each machine instruction of the program shown in Figure 6 executes in 1 clock cycle, the program would require at most $14 \times \log_2 32 + 4 = 74$ clock cycles to perform routing in a row containing $N = 32$ logic cells. To estimate how much time the attached processor would require and how much area it would occupy, we look at the recently introduced Altera ARM based Excalibur device [2] that combines reconfigurable logic with an ARM processor on the same chip. The ARM core 922T is used which operates at a clock speed of 200 MHz and occupies an area of 8.1 mm^2 [7][12]. Assuming negligible area for program and data storage, we can estimate that row routing for $N = 32$ using an ARM 922T requires 370 ns time and 8.1mm^2 area.

The recently announced Xilinx Virtex II Pro device utilizes the PowerPC 405 embedded processor. The 0.18 μm implementation of the processor occupies an area of 1.4 mm^2 and can operate at a clock speed of upto 390 MHz [6]. Assuming negligible area for program and data storage, we can estimate that row routing for $N = 32$ using a PowerPC 405 requires 190 ns time and 1.4mm^2 area.

To estimate performance using self-reconfiguration, we use an SRGA design using a 0.18μm standard cell library. The time required to compute the C, P, L and R bits for $N = 32$, using simulation to determine logic cell delays, is estimated to be 30 ns. Since three configuration memory rows need to be written, each requiring 10 ns[11], the total time required for row routing ($N = 32$) using self-reconfiguration on the SRGA is 60 ns. The total area occupied by a logic cell and its associated memory block is 15,425 μm^2[13]. As described in Section 3.2, 5×32 logic cells (and memory blocks) are required and therefore the total area occupied by reconfigurable logic that performs row routing using self-reconfiguration for $N = 64$ is 2.5 mm^2. The above implementation thus requires significantly lesser area than the ARM processor but significantly more area than the PowerPC processor. However, it requires much lesser time than both processors.

Using the alternate implementation, 9 clock cycles (including 2 clock cycles for context switching) are required. Thus total time with a 10 ns clock cycle is 90 ns. Approximately 64 logic cells (and their memory blocks) are used. Thus total area is about 1.0 mm^2. The above implementation thus requires significantly lesser time and significantly lesser area than both the ARM as well as the PowerPC processors.

[12] According to [2], the ARM core performance is comparable to a 0.18 μm ASIC implementation. Therefore it can be compared to with the SRGA implementation because the SRGA logic cells are implemented using a 0.18 μm process standard cell library.

[13] The area is significantly smaller than the area reported in [11] due to an improved memory block implementation.

4 Conclusion

In the first half of the paper, the notion of self-reconfiguration was precisely described using an abstract reconfigurable device model derived from the Mealy machine model. Practical requirements for self-reconfiguration and the work done to meet them were enumerated. In the second half of the paper, self-reconfiguration performance was compared with that of the competing approach of runtime reconfiguration. The results showed that self-reconfiguration required significantly lesser area and significantly lesser time when compared to the area and time requirements of an attached processor. This paper therefore presents a systematic development of the concept of self-reconfiguration, clearly separating the tasks of computation and metacomputation. Further, the performance evaluation results, although preliminary, suggest that reconfigurable logic may be superior to von Neumann processors for metacomputation as well.

References

[1] J. W. Babb, M. I. Frank, and A. Agarwal. Solving graph problems with dynamic computation structures. In John Schewel, editor, *High-Speed Computing, Digital Signal Processing, and Filtering Using reconfigurable Logic, Proc. SPIE 2914*, pages 225–236, Bellingham, WA, 1996. SPIE – The International Society for Optical Engineering.

[2] Altera Corp. Arm-based embedded processor device overview data sheet. http://www.altera.com/literature/ds/ds_arm.pdf.

[3] Atmel Corp. At94k series fpslic. http://www.atlmel.com/atmel/acrobat/doc1138.pdf.

[4] A. Donlin. Self modifying circuitry - a platform for tractable virtual circuitry. In *Eighth International Workshop on Field Programmable Logic and Applications*, 1998.

[5] P. C. French and R. W. Taylor. A self-reconfiguring processor. In D. A. Buell and K. L. Pocek, editors, *Proceedings of IEEE Workshop on FPGAs for Custom Computing Machines*, pages 50–59, Napa, CA, April 1993.

[6] Powerpc 405 embedded cores. www-3.ibm.com/chips/techlib/techlib.nsf/products- /PowerPC_405_Embedded_Cores.

[7] ARM Ltd. Arm920t and arm 922t. http://www.arm.com/armtech/ARM922T?Op- enDocument.

[8] R. Sidhu and V. K. Prasanna. Fast regular expression matching using fpgas. In *FCCM 20001. IEEE Symposium on Field-Programming Custom Computing Machines*, Apr. 2001.

[9] R. P. S. Sidhu, A. Mei, and V. K. Prasanna. Genetic programming using self-reconfigurable FPGAs. In *Field Programmable Logic and Applications - 9th International Workshop, FPL'99*, volume 1673 of *Lecture Notes in Computer Science*. Springer Verlag, 1999.

[10] R. P. S. Sidhu, A. Mei, and V. K. Prasanna. String matching on multicontext FPGAs using self-reconfiguration. In *FPGA '99. Proceedings of the 1999 ACM/SIGDA Seventh International Symposium on Field Programmable Gate Arrays*, pages 217–226, Feb. 1999.

[11] R. P. S. Sidhu, A. Mei, S. Wadhwa, and V. K. Prasanna. A self-reconfigurable gate array architecture. In *Field Programmable Logic and Applications - 10th International Workshop, FPL 2000*, Aug. 2000.

An FPGA Co-processor for Real-Time Visual Tracking

Miguel Arias-Estrada and Eduardo Rodríguez-Palacios

National Institute for Astrophysics, Optics and Electronics
Computer Science Department
A. Postal 51 y 216, Puebla, Pue. 72000, México
ariasm@inaoep.mx
http://cseg.inaoep.mx/~ariasm

Abstract. This paper presents the design overview and the post-synthesis simulation results of a digital co-processor for real-time visual tracking implemented in a Virtex-E field programmable gate array. The hardware description of the system was made in VHDL and the simulations show that the system performs up to 79 frames per second in a half-resolution VGA image format (320 x 240 pixels). The co-processor calculates edge/corner detection, stationary background and noise filtering, and the distance transform algorithm; these optimized operations implemented in the FPGA and the Hausdorff distance algorithm programmed in a general purpose processor implement a real-time visual tracking system.

1 Introduction

Image processing algorithms are expensive computing tasks, a simple algorithm as the edge detection of a VGA gray scale intensity image requires million of operations. Most of the image processing implementations are performed in software, limited to non-real-time processing, non-compact systems, non-low-power systems, etc. To solve this problems, a hardware version of the software algorithm could be wired; the system created is named a custom computing machine (CCM).

Custom computing machines are implemented using individual logic devices, ASICs or programmable hardware devices. The first solution is not used today because of the power dissipation, space, maintenance and other constraints. The second solution requires a lot of time, money and specialized people to design. The third solution is the most suitable to implement a CCM: programmable hardware devices offer a quick, safe and cheap design flow. The FPGA is one of the most used programmable hardware devices today, due to its capacity, speed and flexibility.

This work presents the design overview and the simulation results of a digital FPGA co-processor for real-time visual tracking. The co-processor is interfaced to a general purpose microprocessor, a memory bank and other input/output devices, implementing a tracking system using the Hausdorff distance. The architecture was designed using a top-down scheme coded with VHDL. Furthermore, the design use spatial and temporal parallelism concepts to meet real-time processing.

M. Glesner, P. Zipf, and M. Renovell (Eds.): FPL 2002, LNCS 2438, pp. 710-719, 2002.

Section 2 describes the tracking algorithm and its simulated performance in MatLab. Next, section 3 presents the design overview and the different modules inside the co-processor. The implementation and results of the architecture are presented in section 4, and finally some conclusions are given.

2 Tracking Algorithm and Performance

The chosen tracking algorithm is based on the Hausdorff distance [1][2] to track objets between consecutive frames of a video. The algorithm was chosen due to its hardware implementation feasibility and the following advantages: tracking non-rigid objects, tracking in cluttered scenes, tracking in scenes with more than one moving object, tracking with poor lighting conditions, tracking with moving camera, and tracking with large displacements of the objects in the image.

Figure 1 shows the flow chart of the tracking algorithm. The object to be tracked is represented by a model (i.e., a set of edge/corner binary features), the initial model is supplied by the user or is found by a special pre-processing step before the tracking. For simplicity lets consider that the initial object model and the features of the first frame are available. If M_t represents the initial model and I_t the feature image at time t, the algorithm to find the new tracked model M_{t+1} in the image I_{t+1} is as follows:

1. Compute the feature image[1] I_{t+1} from the gray scale intensity image in time $t+1$ using an edge/corner detection algorithm. The feature image can be obtained using the SUSAN algorithm [8].
2. Filter the stationary background between I_t and I_{t+1} and the noise that remains. The stationary background is filtered because it is unnecessary to track something that does not move.
3. Compute the distance transform [6] of the image found in the previous process. The distance transform (DT) is used to perform the Hausdorff distance in the next step.
4. Use the Hausdorff distance to obtain the best displacement of the model M_t in the image I_{t+1}. This process uses the distance transform of I_{t+1} and an iterative search based in a quad-tree partition scheme.
5. Update the model M_t that is part of I_t to the model M_{t+1} that is a subset of I_{t+1}.

The model M_{t+1} and the image I_{t+1} are used to find the model M_{t+2} in the image I_{t+2} and so on, the algorithm repeats until the last frame is processed. The result is a set of tracked models and its corresponding translations. Each translation specify the horizontal and vertical displacement of the model in the actual image. Huttenlocher et al. [1] implements this algorithm on a SPARCstation-2 and requires 6 seconds per frame for a half-resolution VGA video image.

---

[1] Some tracking systems use feature images instead of gray scale intensity images [3] [4]. Computing time of the image processing algorithms could be decreased or optimized using feature images, since them contain the most important information about the images and avoid operations over non-significant data.

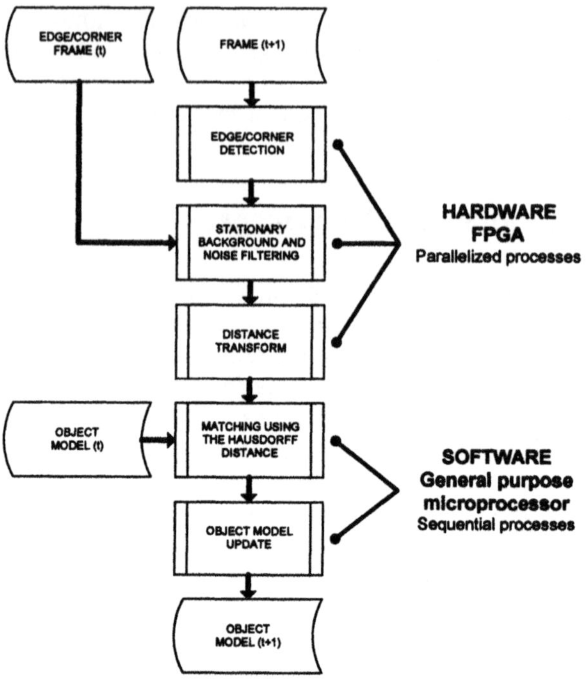

Fig. 1. Flow chart of the tracking algorithm using the Hausdorff distance

The algorithm was implemented to determine which processes of the figure 1 are candidates to implement in hardware using an FPGA or in software using a general purpose microprocessor. The algorithm was programmed in MatLab Version 5.3 using some functions of the Image Processing Toolbox and other specific functions. The test images are a 8 bit gray scale intensity sequence with 256 x 256 pixels. Each tracked frame requires 34.57 seconds. The edge/corner detection requires 55% of the total computing time, the stationary background and noise filtering the 2%, the distance transform the 37%, and the matching using the Hausdorff distance and the model update the 6%. The first three processes uses 94% of the total time and could be implemented in a custom computing machine using spatial and temporal parallelism to reduce the computing time. The last two processes could be implemented in a general purpose microprocessor since they are mainly sequential processes.

3 The Tracking Architecture

The proposed visual tracking system is performed by a video camera, an input/output module, a memory bank, an FPGA, a general purpose micro-processor, and an output device. The video camera supplies the frames to the internal memory bank via the input/output module; the input/output module coordinate the transmission of the frames between the camera and the memory bank and the transmission of the tracking results between the memory bank and an output device (i.e., a monitor or a post-processing personal computer). The memory bank includes two 512K x 16 bits single port RAM that stores the frames sent by the camera, the temporal tracking results and the final tracking models and translations. The general purpose microprocessor is programmed to performs the high sequential operations of the tracking algorithm (i.e., the addressing of the distance transform to obtain the Hausdorff distance, the quad-tree partition scheme, and the new model generation). The FPGA co-processor computes the edge/corner detection, stationary background and noise filtering, and the distance transform algorithm using high parallelism and pipeline.

The design and simulation of the tracking co-processor was coded using VHDL, synthesized and implemented in Xilinx Foundation 3.1i and simulated in Aldec Active-VHDL 4.1. Figure 2 shows the internal co-processor architecture; the main idea is that the memory address generator supplies the read and write necessary addresses for the other four modules. The edge/corner detection, filtering and DT algorithms are computed in the SUSAN, FILTER, FORWARD DT and BACKWARD DT modules (processing modules). Note that the distance transform algorithm is computed by two modules instead of one, this is because the algorithm is separable allowing to reduce hardware. The four processing modules receive and send data from and to the memory bank, only one of the four processing modules is active at a time.

3.1 The Memory Address Generator

A zoom of the memory address generator (MAG) is shown in figure 3. The MAG must meet two conditions: first, the read and write addresses should be generated simultaneous to enhance the speed processing of the four processing modules; second, the generator should be programmable to increment the flexibility to implement different read-write patterns. The four level pipeline superscalar datapath shown in figure 3 is the solution, the datapath is based in a RISC architecture [7].

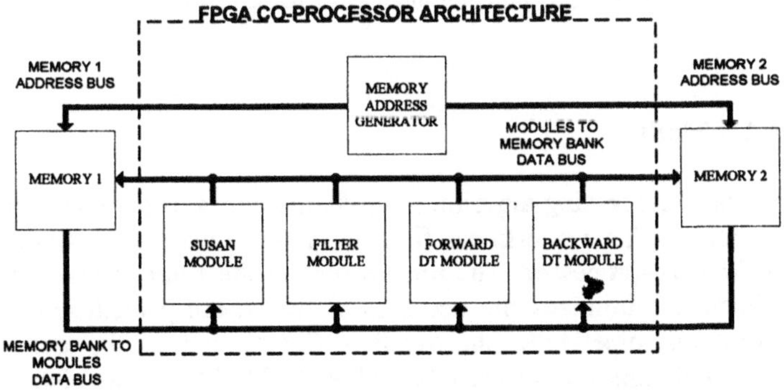

Fig. 2. Internal tracking co-processor architecture

The datapath performs 16 basic arithmetic and logic operations using only three array formats for simplicity. The first level in the datapath is the instruction fetch level, its principal action is the instruction read from the ROM program memory. The second level is the instruction decode, this level decodes the instruction to execute in the datapath and read the necessary registers from the register file. The register file contains the zero register, one input register, four output registers, and ten general purpose registers. Also, this level have the control and forwarding unit of the datapath, the last unit searches for possible data hazards in the decoded instructions and solve the problem before it happens. The third level correspond to the instruction execute, the instructions fetched and decoded are executed here using two arithmetic-logic units of 24 bits width each one. The fourth level is the write back level. In this level the branch logic decides if the branch instructions are taken or not, and the results are written in the register file. The synchronization of the MAG module and the active processing module is achieved by the input register and four flag output signals. The processing modules are independent so, there is no necessary synchronization between them.

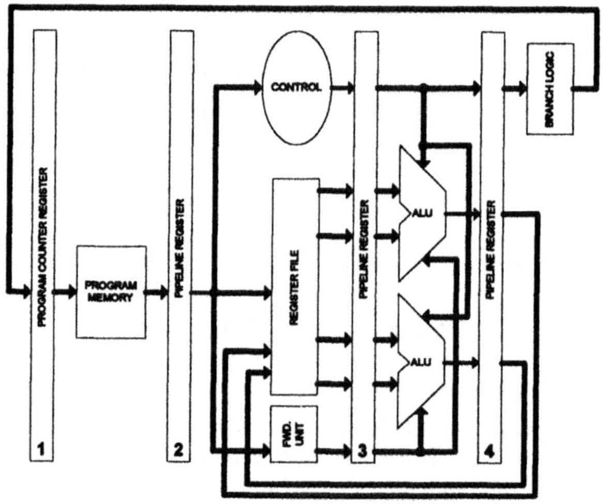

Fig. 3. MAG pipeline superscalar RISC architecture

3.2 The SUSAN Module

The SUSAN image processing algorithm detects the edges or corners in the intensity images to be tracked. This non-linear filter is implemented in the SUSAN module inside the tracking co-processor. The architecture of the filter follows the design in [8], the architecture minimizes the accesses to the memory bank and has parallel modules with internal pipeline to improve its performance (i.e., the architecture uses concurrency in 7 columns and 3 rows to speed up the USAN [5] calculation).

Figure 4 illustrates the architecture of the SUSAN module. The gray scale intensity image codified in 8 bits per pixel arrives to the SUSAN module in 16 bit blocks from the memory bank, the pixels are stored in 1 of the 22 NUCLEUS registers using the DECODER to select the destination. The stored pixels are passed to the systolic array that contains 21 USAN basic processors; each USAN processor has a 1 bit output signal. In order to write 16-bit blocks in the memory bank, the MUX-SUSAN-REGISTER post-processing is necessary: the individual USAN results are multiplexed to the SUSAN logic and the edges/corners binary pixels are stored in the REGISTER in a serial to parallel form. When a 16-bit block is filled, the block is written in the memory bank; the multiplexor MMUX selects the block corresponding to the first, second or third processing row. The thresholds G and T values are stored in configuration registers and all the control signals are generated by the CONTROL unit.

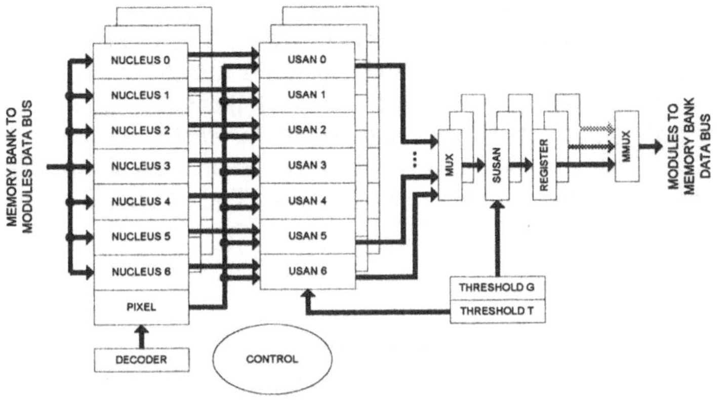

Fig. 4. SUSAN module architecture

3.3 The FILTER Module

The FILTER module performs the stationary background and noise filtering operations. A detailed view of the module is shown in figure 5, the architecture follows the Arias-Estrada and Torres-Huitzil [8] architecture, but the module includes a pre-processing section.

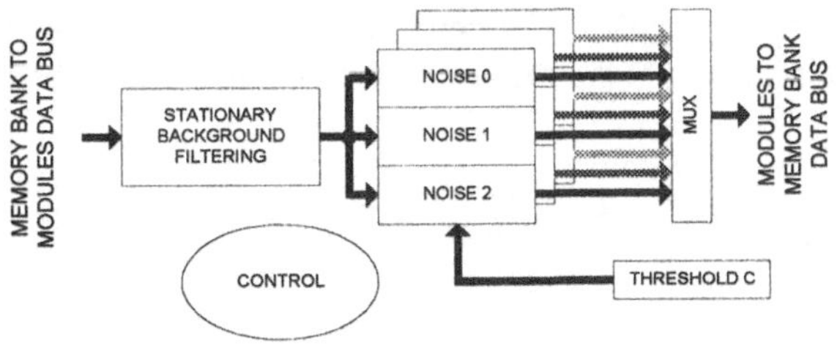

Fig. 5. FILTER module architecture

Two 16-bit blocks arrive to the stationary background filter (i.e., the pre-processing section) from the memory bank, each data block contains 16 edge/corner binary pixels. The output of the pre-processing section is passed to the systolic array that contains 9 NOISE basic processors, each NOISE processor has a 16-bit output signal. When a 16-bit block is filled by some of the NOISE processors, the block is multiplexed to the memory bank data bus and written in the specified address. The threshold C is stored in a configuration register and all the control signals are generated by the CONTROL unit.

3.4 The FORWARD and BACKWARD DT Modules

The distance transform algorithm is implemented in a separable form by two similar pipeline recursive architectures, the FORWARD DT and the BACKWARD DT modules. The difference between the architectures is that the FORWARD DT module works with 16-bit blocks where each block contains 16 edge/corner stationary background and noise filtered pixels, and the BACKWARD DT works with the same 16-bit blocks but each block contains 2 forward distance transform pixels. Also, the BACKWARD DT module compute the separable DT in reverse direction.

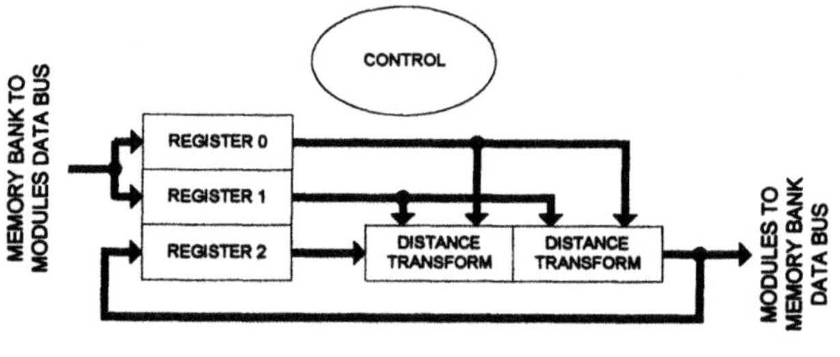

Fig. 6. FORWARD or BACKWARD DT architecture

Figure 6 presents a view of the DT architecture, either the forward or backward version. REGISTER 1 and 0 stores the nucleus and the neighbor pixels of the distance transform mask respectively. REGISTER 2 implements the delay to perform the architecture recursively. The two DISTANCE TRANSFORM cells after the registers are a simple systolic array that uses concurrency to enhance performance. The output of the right cell is written in the memory bank via the memory bank data bus.

4 Implementation and Results

The co-processor architecture was described with VHDL using a top-down design scheme, synthesized and implemented for a XCV1000EFG1156-8 Virtex-E Xilinx FPGA. The synthesis process was optimized for speed and the implementation was set to the default constraints (i.e., a better frequency system operation could be obtained using a pre-defined time and map constraints).

The design entry, synthesis and implementation operations were done with Xilinx Foundation software and the system was simulated with Aldec Active-VHDL. The test images were introduced to the simulation via text files into a RAM memory emulation described in VHDL. The FPGA tracking co-processor was tested simulating the following image operations and comparing the results with the MatLab algorithm implementation.

1. Edge/corner detection of two gray scale intensity images of 64 x 64 pixels using the SUSAN and the MAG modules.
2. Stationary background and noise filtering of the two edge/corner binary images obtained in the previous step using the FILTER and the MAG modules.
3. Forward distance transform of the stationary and noise filtered image obtained in the previous step using the FORWARD DT and the MAG modules.
4. Backward distance transform of the image obtained in the previous step using the BACKWARD DT and the MAG modules.

The co-processor synthetized frequency was 50.444 MHz. and simulations were carried out at 50 MHz. Table 1 shows the number and percentage of slices for the 5 modules after the implementation. Note that the systolic arrays SUSAN and FILTER use more than 70% of the design space.

Table 1. Number and percentage of slices for the co-processor modules

Module	Number of slices	% of design	% of FPGA
MAG	783	20.96	6.37
SUSAN	1,495	40.02	12.17
FILTER	1,288	34.48	10.48
FORWARD DT	82	2.19	0.67
BACKWARD DT	88	2.36	0.72
Total design	3,736	100.00	30.40

Table 2. Architecture performance at 50 and 66 MHz operating frequency

	50 MHz.				66 MHz.			
IMAGE SIZE	SUSAN	FILTER	DT	ALL	SUSAN	FILTER	DT	ALL
64x64	3,410	26,882	2,871	**1,473**	4,501	35,484	3,789	**1,945**
128x128	852	6,720	718	**368**	1,125	8,871	947	**486**
256x256	213	1,680	179	**92**	281	2,218	237	**122**
320x240	182	1,434	153	**79**	240	1,892	202	**104**
640x480	45	358	38	**20**	60	473	51	**26**

Table 2 contains the number of images per second processed when the FPGA tracking co-processor operates at the implemented operation frequency of 50 MHz and the estimated frequency 66 MHz. The DT column includes de forward and backward algorithms, the column ALL includes the number of images per second processed by all the modules of the co-processor. Finally, the simulated images are illustrated in figure 7. The results of the MatLab and Active-VHDL simulations are similar, so the co-processor architecture works correctly; the small differences between the images are consequence of the mask positions over the limits of the images in the software or hardware implementation of the algorithms.

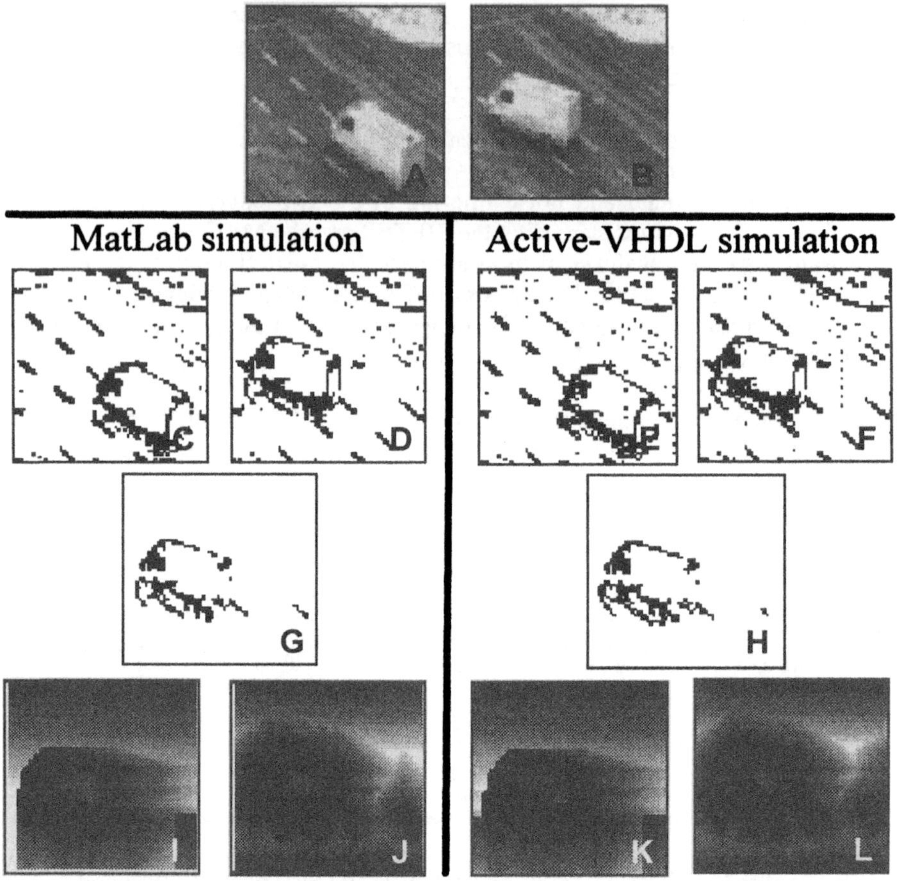

Fig. 7. Software and hardware simulated images. A and B are gray scale intensity 64 x 64 pixel images. C, D, E and F are edge/corner images; G and H are stationary background and noise filtered images; I and K are forward distance transform processed images; J and L are backward distance transform processed images

5 Conclusions

An FPGA tracking co-processor was developed. The co-processor computes the edge/corner detection algorithm, the stationary background and noise filtering algorithm, the forward distance transform algorithm and the backward distance transform algorithm using five modules. A four level pipeline superscalar RISC architecture datapath was designed for addressing the memory bank and to save the partial and final results of the processing. The datapath offers flexibility to program different addressing schemes or other procedures. Two systolic arrays using spatial and temporal parallelism were designed to implement the SUSAN, background and noise filtering in real-time. Two recursive filters were developed to implement the DT algorithm efficiently.

The co-processor architecture operates at 50 MHz and it can process up to 79 images per second in a half-resolution VGA image format. To achieve larger processing rates, the memory data bus could be increased or the design could be targeted to a faster FPGA device. Other possibility to enhance performance is to increment the concurrency in the systolic arrays, for example, the SUSAN module could process 7 columns and 7 rows simultaneously. Furthermore, the largest delay modules, such as the MAG execution block, could implement more pipeline steps to increase performance.

The modules of the FPGA co-processor could be used in other image processing applications where a real-time processing rate is needed. The FPGA is an ideal device to implement custom computing machines or hardware-software partition schemes systems.

Acknowledgements

This project is supported by the Consejo Nacional de Ciencia y Tecnología of Mexico (CONACyT), under project #143769.

References

[1] Daniel P. Huttenlocher, Jae J. Noh and William J. Rucklidge. Tracking Non-Rigid Objects in Complex Scenes. Technical report TR92-1320. (1992).

[2] Daniel P. Huttenlocher and William J. Rucklidge. A Multi-Resolution Technique for Comparing Images Using the Hausdorff Distance. Technical report TR92-1321. (1992).

[3] Christophe Deutsch. Suivi et localisation d'une cible complexe connue par vision monoculaire. Rapport pré-doctoral RT-LVSN-97-04. Université Laval. 1997.

[4] S.M. Smith. ASSET-2: Real-time Motion Segmentation and Object Tracking. Technical report TR95SMS2b. 1995.

[5] S.M. Smith and J.M. Brady. SUSAN- A New Approach to Low Level Image Processing. Technical report TR95SMS1c. (1995).

[6] Gunilla Borgefors. Distance Transformations in Digital Images. Computer Vision, Graphics and Image Processing. No. 34, 344-371. (1986).

[7] John L. Hennessy and David A. Patterson. Computer Organization and Design, the Hardware/Software Interface. Morgan Kaufmann Publishers. (1998).

[8] M. Arias-Estrada and C. Torres Huitzil. Real-time field programmable gate array architecture for computer vision. Journal of Electronic Imaging. Vol. 10, 289-296. (2001).

Implementation of 3-D Adaptive LUM Smoother in Reconfigurable Hardware

Viktor Fischer[1], Miloš Drutarovský[2], and Rastislav Lukac[2]

[1] Laboratoire Traitement du Signal et Instrumentation,
Unité Mixte de Recherche CNRS 5516, Université Jean Monnet, Saint-Etienne, France
fischer@univ-st-etienne.fr
[2] Department of Electronics and Multimedia Communications,
Technical University of Košice, Park Komenského 13, 041 20 Košice, Slovakia
{Milos.Drutarovsky, lukacr}@tuke.sk

Abstract. We present an implementation of a simplified scalable architecture for the efficient realization of 3-D adaptive LUM smoother in the Field Programmable Logic Devices (FPLDs). The proposed filter architecture takes advantages of a combination of recently provided Boolean LUM smoothers with bit-serial realization of stack filters. In order to decrease hardware requirements, we implemented a highly reduced filter structure that is completely modular, scalable and optimized for hardware implementation in FPLD. Introduced simplifications significantly decrease a circuit complexity, however they still provide excellent smoothing capability and provide real-time performance for processing of 3-D signals with sampling frequencies up to 65 Msamples/second.

1 Introduction

In general, nonlinear characteristics and performance of order-statistic filters results in their wide use in image/video applications. Especially, a class of a Lower-Upper-Middle (LUM) filters [6] have found many applications in digital image processing [3] such as edge sharpening, impulse noise smoothing and outliers rejection. When the LUM filter is designed as a smoother, it is characterized by the robustness against non-Gaussian or long-tailed noise distributions with the simultaneous signal-detail preservation.

Since the LUM smoother requires data sorting, it leads to an ineffective FPLD implementation. In order to avoid this disadvantage, it is possible to utilize the framework of stack filters, their design through Positive Boolean Functions (PBFs) [2] and implementation trough a bit-serial structure [1], [4] that results in a small chip area. In this paper, we focus on the FPLD implementation of 3-D modified adaptive LUM smoother having a reduced set of smoothing levels. Proposed approach is based on the well-known bit-serial realization of stack filters and recently developed Boolean expression of LUM smoothers [7],[8] allowing efficient implementation in current FPLDs. Our fully-pipelined, scalable VHDL implementation of the proposed 3-D

M. Glesner, P. Zipf, and M. Renovell (Eds.): FPL 2002, LNCS 2438, pp. 720-729, 2002.

filter with a window size $N = 27$ and 8-bit word length fits into a medium size Altera FPLD and provides sample frequency up to 65 Msamples/second. The reason for the choice of a cube window, i.e. $N = 27$, is that the above-mentioned window shape is the most frequently used filter window in the image sequence filtering [3],[6]. In addition, the proposed adaptive LUM smoothers with the cube filter window was successfully tested in smoothing applications [6],[9].

The rest of the paper is organized as follows. In the next Section, we describe structure, algorithm and properties of adaptive LUM smoothers based on a full set and a reduced set of thresholds. Section 3 focuses on implementation approach of the above-mentioned method for mapping into FPLD. The method uses efficiently fully pipelined bit-serial implementation and recently proposed simplification of LUM smoothers expressed through PBFs. In Section 4, we present results of algorithm mapping into selected Altera FPLDs. They are analyzed in terms of type of FPLD families employed, maximum usable clock frequency and necessary hardware resources expressed through Logic Cell (LC) count. Finally, the main ideas, achieved results and future plans are summarized.

2 Adaptive LUM Smoother Based on the Set of Thresholds

Let N be an odd window size and $x_1, x_2, ..., x_N$ an input set determined by a filter window. Let us consider the central sample x^* and the ordered input set $x_{(1)}, x_{(2)}, ..., x_{(N)}$, so that

$$x_{(1)} \leq x_{(2)} \leq ... \leq x_{(N)} \quad (1)$$

Then the output of standard LUM smoother is defined by

$$y_k = med\left\{x_{(k)}, x^*, x_{(N-k+1)}\right\} \quad (2)$$

where med is a median operator and $k = 1, 2, ..., (N+1)/2$ is a smoothing parameter. Clearly, the filter output is determined by comparison of lower $x_{(k)}$ and upper $x_{(N-k+1)}$ order statistic with the central sample x^* from a filter window. If x^* lies in a range formed by these order statistics, it is not modified. If x^* lies outside this range, it is replaced by a sample that lies closer to the median.

Let $y_1, y_2, ..., y_{(N+1)/2}$ be a set of all possible outputs of standard LUM smoothers and $Tol_1, Tol_2, ..., Tol_{(N+1)/2}$ a set of threshold values. Namely, in the case of spatiotemporal cube window with the window size $N = 27$, we achieve 14 outputs. For each smoothing level k, let us apply the following rule defined as

$$| y_k - x^* | \geq Tol_k \quad \text{for } k = 1, 2, ..., (N+1)/2 \quad (3)$$

where the optimal set of threshold values { Tol_k, $k = 1, 2, ..., 14$ } was found [6] as

$$Tol_{opt} = \{Tol_1, Tol_2, ..., Tol_{14}\} = \{0,4,5,7,9,12,15,16,22,23,38,43,48,52\} \quad (4)$$

Note that the LUM smoother with the smoothing parameter $k = 1$ is equivalent to an identity filter, where filter output is given by the central sample x^*. Thus, the necessary condition for a regular filter behavior is that the associated threshold value Tol_1 is forced to be equal to 0.

Since absolute differences between the central sample x^* and the standard LUM smoother output y_k are monotonous increasing, so that

$$|y_1 - x^*| \leq |y_2 - x^*| \leq \ldots \leq |y_{(N+1)/2} - x^*| \tag{5}$$

and the same restrictions are put on the optimal set of threshold values (see eq. (4)), i.e.

$$Tol_1 \leq Tol_2 \leq \ldots \leq Tol_{(N+1)/2} \tag{6}$$

it can be seen that the output of adaptive LUM smoother is equivalent to the standard LUM smoother with the largest k satisfying $|y_k - x^*| \geq Tol_k$ from (3). Mathematically, the output of adaptive LUM smoother is described as

$$y = y_k \quad \text{for the largest } k \text{ satisfying eq. (3)} \tag{7}$$

In order to decrease filter complexity related to the cube window, work [9] deals with the linear reduction of smoothing levels, where filter performance was analyzed for a wide range of reduction from 0 (full set of smoothing levels) to 12 (no smoothing levels). Experimental results showed that the presented method with a highly reduced filter structure (from an original set of 14 levels to a final set of 3 considered smoothing levels) had comparable performance with an original filter structure. The reduced set of considered smoothing levels is described as

$$y_{red} = \{y_1, y_7, y_{14}\} \tag{8}$$

and the corresponding set of optimal threshold values $Tol_{red} \subset Tol_{opt}$ is described as

$$Tol_{red} = \{Tol_1, Tol_7, Tol_{14}\} = \{0, 15, 52\} \tag{9}$$

Now, the filter output is provided by the LUM smoother (2) with the largest $k \in \{1, 7, 14\}$ satisfying $|y_k - x^*| \geq Tol_k$.

Note that the full version of adaptive LUM smoother is characterized by excellent performance, robustness against the impulse noise and independence on the intensity range [6]. The reduced adaptive LUM smoothers take the same properties. The architecture of the proposed filter is depicted in Figure 1. Nine B-bit samples of the 3-D window are input into two LUM filters (k=14 and k=7). Outputs of these filters are subtracted from the window central sample x^*. Absolute values of the subtraction results are compared to threshold values Tol_7 and Tol_{14}. Finally, the filter output is selected from the set of two LUM filters outputs and the central sample according to Eq.(7)-(9).

3 Proposed Realization

The most complicated block of the proposed algorithm is a LUM smoother. A bit-serial and word parallel realization first proposed by Chen [4] combined with new LUM smoother PBF expression [8] was chosen as the basis of an efficient FPLD implementation. This scheme is very suitable for hardware implementation, it provides the lowest complexity among all stack filters implementations and can be easily pipelined to increase data throughput.

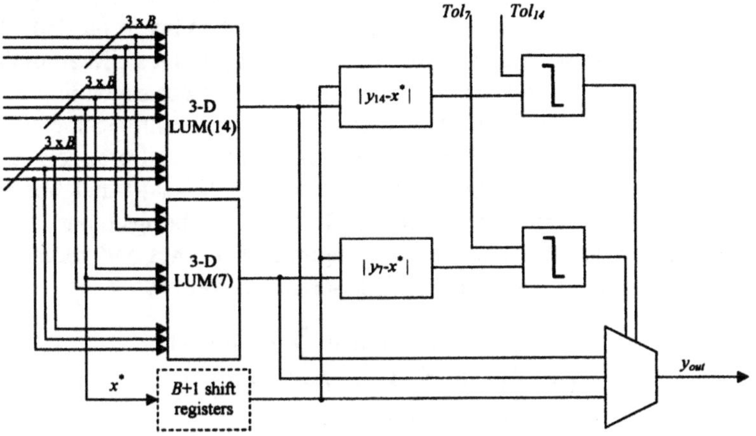

Fig. 1. Architecture of modified adaptive LUM smoother

3.1 Bit-Serial Realization

Let $f_{k,N}(.)$ be a PBF corresponding to the LUM smoother defined by smoothing parameter k and window size N. The algorithm for pipelined bit-serial word parallel realization of PBF-based LUM smoother with window size N and word-length B can be written by modification of Chen's algorithm [4] as

For $i = 1,\dots,N$ do in parallel
    set $p_{i0} = 1$
For $j = 1,\dots,B$ do in serial
  For $i = 1,\dots,N$ do in parallel
    Begin
    If $p_{ij-1} = 1$ then $d_{ij} = x_{ij}$
      else $d_{ij} = d_{ij-1}$
    $h_j = f_{k,N}(d_{1j}, d_{2j} \dots, d_{Nj})$
    If $p_{ij-1} = 1$ and $h_j \oplus x_{ij} = 1$ then set $p_{ij} = 0$
      else $p_{ij} = p_{ij-1}$
    End

where B-bit word values are represented in binary form as $\mathbf{x}_i = (x_{i1}, x_{i2}, \ldots x_{iB})$, $\mathbf{d}_i = (d_{i1}, d_{i2}, \ldots d_{iB})$ and h_j is the binary filter output determined by PBF $f_{k,N}(.)$. The algorithm introduces a propagation flags p_{ij} for each binary input channel i. When the flag p_{ij-1} is high, d_{ij} is equal to the input x_{ij}. Once $x_{ij} \neq h_j$ at step j, the flag p_{ij} for the input channel i and the next step is set to low.

3.2 Simplified Boolean Expression of LUM Smoothers

The fact that LUM smoothers are subclass of stack filters based on PBFs leads to the possibility of their Boolean expression. In order to express a LUM smoother with the smoothing parameter k and the window size N by its corresponding minimal PBF $f_{k,N}(.)$, a new conversion algorithm [7] was developed recently. Shortly, the minimal PBF is obtained by a logical summing (disjunction) of logical products of k samples including central sample x^* and logical products of $N-k+1$ neighboring samples (i.e. without central sample x^*). Concerning this fact, [8] brings binary analysis of the LUM smoothers in the dependence on configuration of ones and zeros inside binary input sets. The proposed simplification is described as follows

$$f_{k,N}(.) = \begin{cases} 1 & \text{if } x^* = 1 \text{ and } \sum W^* \geq k-1 \\ 1 & \text{if } \sum W^* \geq N-k+1 \\ 0 & \text{otherwise} \end{cases} \quad (10)$$

where the output value of $f_{k,N}(.)$ depends on binary value of the central sample x^* and the number of ones in the set W^* of $N-1$ neighboring binary samples. According to a representation of the logical summing and the logical product through MAX and MIN operators, each separately, to achieve $f_{k,N}(.) = 1$, at least the one logical product of $f_{k,N}(.)$ must result in 1. If the binary central sample is $x^* = 1$, the necessary and sufficient condition for $f_{k,N}(.) = 1$ lies in the need that at least $k-1$ neighboring samples will be equal to 1. If the binary central sample is $x^* = 0$, then the $f_{k,N}(.)$ depends on the neighboring samples and the output of $f_{k,N}(.)$ is equal to 1 if and only if at least $N-k+1$ neighboring samples are equal to 1. Another configurations of ones and zeros inside the filter window result in $f_{k,N}(.) = 0$.

Function $f_{k,N}(.)$ is very appropriate and highly simplified expression of PBF corresponding to LUM smoothers. We will show in the next chapters that LUM smoothers based on this function can be very efficiently implemented in FPLDs.

3.3 Algorithm Implementation

The algorithm starts by processing the most significant bits (MSB) of the N ($N = 27$ in our 3-D cube window) words $\mathbf{x}_1, \mathbf{x}_2 \ldots \mathbf{x}_N$ in the current window and by using $f_{k,N}(.)$ determines MSB of the desired LUM smoother output h_1. This output is then compared with the other MSBs of the window elements. The words whose MSB is not equal to the filter output h_1 replace their less significant bits at step 2. This process is continued up to processing the least significant bit at stage B.

Our hardware implementation of the LUM algorithm consists of two main blocks:

- LUM propagation cell (based on [5])
- Positive Boolean function $f_{k,N}(.)$ defined by (10)

In the propagation cell (see Figure 2) the output of $h_j = f_{k,N}(.)$ is compared with the data bit d_{ij-1} using a XNOR gate. The result of this operation is then multiplied (AND operation) with the propagation flag p_{ij-1} from the upper block. The propagation flag provides the information whether the data bit taken from previous level is a propagated one or the original.

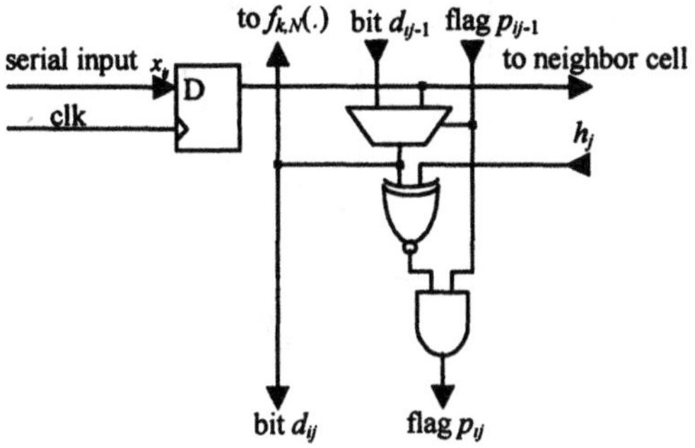

Fig. 2. Propagation cell of LUM smoother

If data bit is a propagating one, then the flag value p_{ij} will be 0, indicating that this data bit will continue propagating unchanged through lower levels. Otherwise, the flag will only depend on the result of the comparison of the filter-slice output with current data bit. One complete bit level of the LUM smoother is shown in Figure 3.

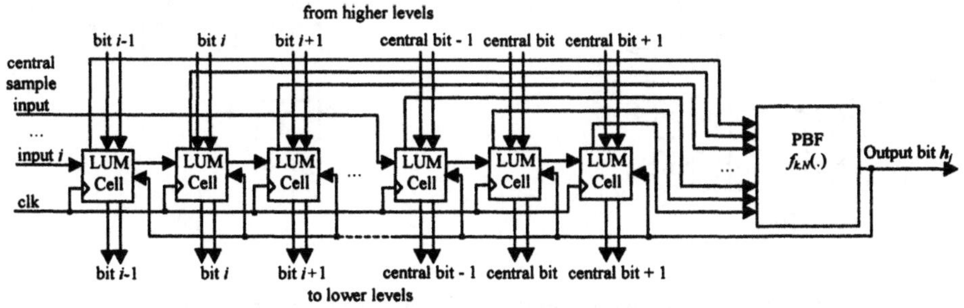

Fig. 3. One bit level of LUM smoother

3.4 Pipelined Architecture

Bit-serial nature of the algorithm enables to use very simple pipelined data path architecture. Identical 1-bit filter slices can be used in sequence (cascade configuration) in order to process input vectors in parallel. Thus, the bit-level pipelining can increase the filter throughput. Modified pipelined version of LUM filter propagation cell is depicted in Figure 4.

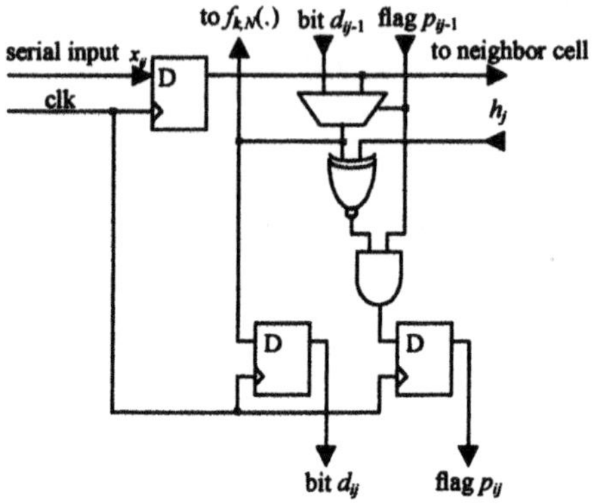

Fig. 4. Pipelined version of LUM filter propagation cell

However, in pipelined architecture shift registers have to be added (see Figure 5a and 5b) to delay input and output bit levels. Also, the central sample has to be delayed in B+1 clock periods (dashed block in Figure 1). The complete B-level LUM filter so computes B levels of B different samples in the same time. Since 3-D LUM filter needs nine input samples in parallel, nine input shift register triangles are needed, but only one output shift register triangle is necessary.

Fig. 5. Input (a) and output (b) shift registers in pipelined version

4 Implementation Results

Filter overall structure and all its blocks have been described in VHDL as parameterized modules. Principal parameters are word-length B and smoothing parameter k. 3-D window larger than $3\times3\times3$ samples seems to be impractical, therefore 3-D window size has fixed value $N = 27$. The filter has been synthesized using Altera Quartus II v. 1.1 and Leonardo Spectrum Level 3 v. 2001_1d VHDL compilers to be mapped to Altera ACEX [10], APEX [11] and APEXII [12] FPLD families. Placement and routing has always been realized using Quartus II v. 1.1 fitter. Timing analysis results presented in next tables have been obtained using Quartus tool, too. VHDL output generated by the fitter was used as timing simulation input for ModelSim v. 5.5 VHDL simulator. Output values have been compared with Matlab-generated test values in automatic testbench procedure.

While implementation of LUM propagation cell (both simple and pipelined version) is quite straightforward, expression $f_{k,N}(.)$ represents relatively complex N-input logical function. We have tested the influence of the smoothing parameter k on the overall complexity and the speed of the PBF function. While effect of k on the complexity/speed performance is insignificant (about 51 ± 2 logic cells for Leonardo Specturm compiler), synthesis result differences of Quartus and Leonardo Spectrum compilers were considerable. Number of logic cells (LCs) and input/output point-to-point delay (t_{pd}) for LUM PBF implementation in ACEX EP1K100-1, APEX EP20K100E-1 and APEXII EP2A15-7 for 27-input PBF are presented in Table 1.

Table 1. Results of $f_{k,N}(.)$ mapping into Altera ACEX, APEX and APEXII FPLD families

	ACEX 1K100-1		APEX 20K100E-1		APEXII 2A15-7	
Compiler	LCs	t_{pd} (ns)	LCs	t_{pd} (ns)	LCs	t_{pd} (ns)
Quartus II	127	64.1	121	42.3	121	24.9
Leonardo Spectrum	49	14.6	52	13.8	52	8.8

It can be seen that Leonardo Spectrum offers about three times better results in both speed and area parameters. Low number of logic cells and small point-to-point delay demonstrate excellent simplification of PBF expression (10) that allows implementing the LUM smoother function for relatively large window sizes. Achieved speed determines significantly the clock frequency of the final filter structure, since combinatorial function $f_{k,N}(.)$ is a part of the critical data path.

Implementation results for standard and pipelined LUM smoother with $N=27$, $B=8$ and $k=14$ are presented in Table 2 and 3, respectively.

Comparing parallel and pipelined version of standard LUM smoother we can see that at the expense of less than 50% area increase, the final filter speed in pipelined version is almost eight times higher. Critical data path in parallel version goes from bit level 7 (in 8-level filter structure) through all PBFs to the bit level 0. Input/output shift registers are not needed. Critical data path in pipelined version goes from bit registers in LUM cells through bit-level PBF and LUM cell multiplexer to propagation flag and bit output registers in the same level. Higher count of logic cells in pipelined version is caused by the use of input/output shift registers (nine input and one output shift register fields of 36 flip-flops). LUM cells matrix area stays practically unchanged (for 8 bit-levels and 27 input elements it is $27 \times 8 \times 3 = 648$ logic cells) for both filter versions. Since eight PBFs occupy about 400 LCs, total area estimation (1408) is very close to values obtained for three pipelined versions.

Table 2. Results of mapping of parallel LUM smoother into three Altera FPLD families

	ACEX 1K100-1		APEX 20K100E-1		APEXII 2A15-7	
Compiler	LCs	f (MHz)	LCs	f (MHz)	LCs	f (MHz)
Leonardo Spectrum	1011	8.68	1010	8.64	1010	12.49

Table 3. Results of mapping of pipelined LUM smoother into three Altera FPLD families

	ACEX 1K100-1		APEX 20K100E-1		APEXII 2A15-7	
Compiler	LCs	f (MHz)	LCs	f (MHz)	LCs	f (MHz)
Leonardo Spectrum	1510	59.52	1420	58.19	1420	79.74

Table 4. Results of mapping of pipelined adaptive LUM smoother into three Altera families

	ACEX 1K100-1		APEX 20K100E-1		APEXII 2A15-7	
Compiler	LCs	f (MHz)	LCs	f (MHz)	LCs	f (MHz)
Leonardo Spectrum	2628	55.25	2707	57.74	2725	65.24

Results of mapping of complete pipelined adaptive LUM filter from Figure 1 into three Altera FPLDs are presented in Table 4. Overall LC count is slightly lower than for two pipelined LUM filters, because two filters can share nine input shift register fields. Absolute value and comparison blocks from Figure 1 have been realized using standard Library of Parameterized Modules (functions lpm_abs and lpm_compare). Since outputs of these modules are registered, they do not influence the final filter speed. We can conclude that filter area is surprisingly small, so that it occupies only 52% of such a small device as ACEX 1K100.

5 Conclusions

In this paper, we have proposed Altera FPLD realization of novel adaptive 3-D LUM smoother based on reduced set of smoothing levels. The motivation for implementation of this method lies in its attractive properties such as excellent performance, robustness against the impulse noise, independence on the intensity range and last but not least relatively simple overall structure.

It was shown that our fully pipelined implementation can use sampling frequencies up to 65 Msamples/second and still requires relatively small amount of FPLD resources. These features allow using of proposed parameterized smoother block as a part of more complex System on Programmable Chip (SoPC) video systems.

In our future work we plan to integrate 3-D frame memory control logic with proposed adaptive LUM smoother and to create complete color video processing system based on Altera DSP Professional evaluation board with APEX 20K1500E [13].

References

1. Astola, J., Akopian, D., Vainio, O., Agaian, S.: New Digit-Serial Implementations of Stack Filters. Signal Processing 61 (1997) 181-197
2. Astola, J., Kuosmanen, P.: Fundamentals of Nonlinear Digital Filtering. CRC Press, (1997)
3. Bovik, A.: Handbook of Image & Video Processing. Academic Press (2000)
4. Chen, K.: Bit-Serial Realizations of a Class of Nonlinear Filters Based on Positive Boolean Functions. IEEE Transactions on Circuits and Systems 36 (1989) 785-794
5. Hatirnaz, I., Gurkaynak, F.K., and Leblebici, Y.: A modular and Scalable Architecture for the Realization of High-Speed Programmable Rank Order Filters. Proc. IEEE International Symposium on Circuits and Systems, Orlando FL, USA (1999)
6. Lukac, R., Marchevský, S.: LUM Smoother with Smooth Control for Noisy Image Sequences. EURASIP J. on Applied Signal Processing 2001 (2001) 110-120
7. Lukac, R., Marchevský, S.: Boolean Expression of LUM Smoothers. IEEE Signal Processing Letters 8 (2001) 292-294
8. Lukac, R.: Simplified Boolean LUM Smoothers. Proc. 4th EURASIP-IEEE Region 8 VIPromCom-2002 in Zadar, Croatia (2002) 159-162
9. Lukac, R., Fischer, V., Drutarovský, M.: 3-D Adaptive LUM Smoother Based On Reduced Set of Smoothing Levels. Proc. 9th IEEE International Conference on Electronics, Circuits and Systems in Dubrovnik, Croatia, (2002), accepted
10. ACEX 1K Programmable Logic Data Family, Data sheet, September 2001, ver.3.3, http://www.altera.com
11. APEX 20K Programmable Logic Data Family, Data sheet, February 2002, ver.4.3, http://www.altera.com
12. APEX II Programmable Logic Device Family, Data sheet, December 2001, ver.1.3, http://www.altera.com
13. APEX DSP Development Board (Professional version), Data sheet, March 2002, ver.1.2, http://www.altera.com

Custom Coprocessor Based Matrix Algorithms for Image and Signal Processing

A. Amira, A. Bouridane, P. Milligan, and F. Bensaali

School of Computer Science, The Queen's University of Belfast
Belfast BT7 1NN, Northern Ireland
a.amira@qub.ac.uk

Abstract. Matrix algorithms are important in many types of applications including image and signal processing. A close examination of the algorithms used in these, and related, applications reveals that many of the fundamental actions involve matrix algorithms such as matrix multiplication. This paper presents an investigation into the design and implementation of different matrix algorithms such as matrix operations, matrix transforms and matrix decompositions using a novel custom coprocessor system for MATrix algorithms based on Reconfigurable Computing (RCMAT). The proposed RCMAT architectures are scalable, modular and require less area and time complexity with reduced latency when compared with existing structures.

1 Introduction

In today's rapidly changing world, designers and researchers continuously demand significant increases in computer performance. Areas such as signal processing and imaging require enormous computing power. A close examination of the algorithms used in these, and other real world applications such as digital control, filtering, beamforming, etc. reveals that many of the fundamental actions involve matrix algorithms such as matrix operations, matrix transforms and matrix decompositions. For example, Discrete Orthogonal Transforms (DOTs) such as Discrete Cosine Transform (DCT), Discrete Fourier Transform (DFT)...etc. All use such matrix manipulations [1], [2].

There exist a number of systems, which have been developed to perform matrix algorithms using different approaches and platforms: MATRISC [3], MATCH [4] and PAMBlox [5]. An examination of the work mentioned above enables a number of limitations to be identified:

- A limited range of matrix algorithms can be performed using MATRISC, PAMBlox or MATCH systems;
- A system based on a static arrangement of multiple processors (as in the MATRISC system) will not be optimal for a range of algorithms which require different Processor Element (PE) arrangements;
- Many of the existing FPGA based matrix processing systems are built on older FPGA technologies rather than the Virtex FPGA series. This results in added complexity (e.g. multiple FPGAs being required) which could now be reduced or eliminated;
- Application developers in existing FPGA based systems require considerable FPGA knowledge to implement the different matrix algorithms; and

M. Glesner, P. Zipf, and M. Renovell (Eds.): FPL 2002, LNCS 2438, pp. 730-739, 2002.

- Existing environments do not support convenient experimentation and investigation into the best area/speed trade-offs. This process is an important part of the design cycle when using FPGAs.

The research work presented in here is aimed at addressing these limitations with the specific objectives:

- Using FPGAs as low cost accelerator for matrix algorithms applications;
- Developing novel, efficient and scalable architectures for matrix multiplication operations and matrix transforms, where both the area and the speed can be estimated for any matrix algorithm with any specific design parameters;
- Enabling application users to concentrate on experimenting conveniently with different algorithms and techniques to investigate the best area/speed trade-offs, rather than concentrating on the low level (and complex) structure of FPGAs; and
- Exploiting the potential of more recent FPGA devices (e.g. Virtex-E) [1].

The composition of the rest of the paper is as follows. The description of the RCMAT system architecture is given in section 2. Section 3 is concerned with the methodologies taken the performances achieved. Finally, concluding remarks are given in section 4.

2 RCMAT System Architecture

The RCMAT system consists of:

- A GUI for supporting experimentation with different parameters to enable the user to explore e.g. speed/area trade-offs;
- A library of architectures for matrix operations, matrix transforms and matrix decompositions. The application has the ability to choose and download existing files from the Standard Template Library (STL), to generate new files and to save those files either to the STL or to another application directory.
- A generator, which automatically produces VHDL code given the user, selected parameters and settings;
- A mechanism for making use of the standard (Xilinx) synthesis tools; and
- A coprocessor based on the Xilinx XCV1000E of the Virtex-E family [1].

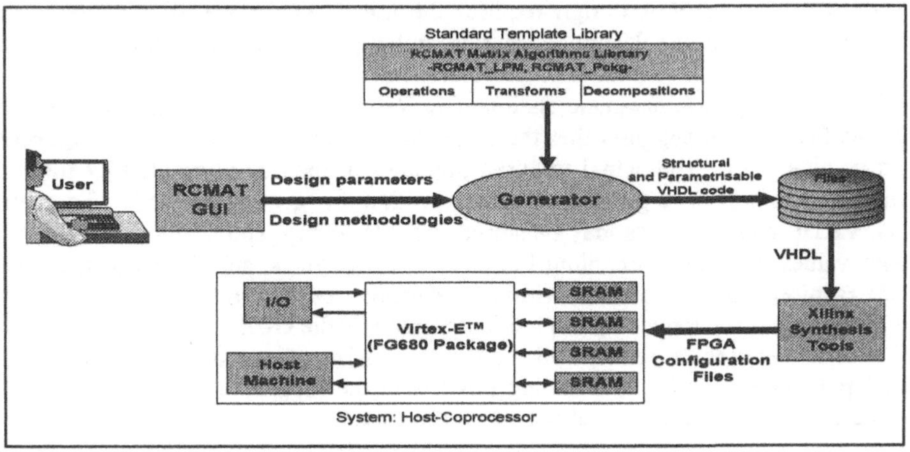

Figure 1. RCMAT System Architecture

2.1 RCMAT Graphic User Interface

As part of the system requirements the initial screen on the GUI presents the user with the following options:

- A choice of matrix algorithm from one of three categories (Operations, Transforms or Decompositions);
- A choice of design philosophy (Systolic Architecture (SA) or Distributed Arithmetic (DA)); and
- A choice of an arithmetic technique (Bit serial/parallel, digit serial, serial/parallel distributed arithmetic);

After setting these options, further panels allow the user to specify the design parameters such as the matrix size, transform length, digit size… etc.

The GUI is relatively simple and progress through the system is aided through consistent navigation facilities. The pathway followed in the creation of a template object for module generation requires only three steps:

- Select the options;
- Specify the design parameters; and
- Generate and download the module.

2.2 RCMAT Library

The RCMAT library contains three sub-libraries for matrix operations, matrix transforms and matrix decompositions using an arithmetic library containing our own parameterised arithmetic components such as adders, multipliers, subtracters, shift registers, etc

In the initial implementation, a number of common matrix operations have been chosen for development such as matrix multiplication and inversion. In the case of matrix algorithms based transforms, DCT, Fast Hadamard Transform (FHT) and Discrete Hartley Transform (DHT) have been chosen for development. In the case of matrix decomposition based applications, the following algorithms can be performed using the RCMAT system: SVD, LU decomposition and QR factorisation [1].

2.3 The Generator and Xilinx Synthesis Tools

Using VHDL for FPGA design requires the use of FPGA specific synthesis tools (Xilinx) to translate the design description, initially into a netlist, and eventually into gates.

VHDL code supports parameterisation. The VHDL module generator heavily relies on this factor, as it suggests that the code can be generalized for certain algorithms and architectures. The actual required module can then be controlled by the input parameters that exist as generic parameters within this generalized code. To achieve this, VHDL code modules may be stored in a file library, and a link to the specified input values provided. Enabling these input values to be substituted in the library code requires that the variables within are declared, but not initialized. Initialization of the variables is supplied by the input generated by the GUI.

The method chosen to perform this operation consists of creating a file that contains the input (a header file), and adding this file to the module file from the library to create a single “generated” module.

2.4 RCMAT Coprocessor

The RCMAT coprocessor is based on the Xilinx XCV1000E of the Virtex-E family, which has the following important features [6]:

- Fast, and high-density Field-Programmable Gate Array;
- Flexible architecture that balances speed and density; and
- Built-in clock- management circuitry.

3 Implementation Strategies of Some RCMAT Cores

This section describes the methodology used in the design, the mapping and the parametrisation of three typical examples. Basically, these are:

i) Orthogonal transforms based on matrix-matrix multiplication such us SVD and transforms based on matrix-vector multiplication such us DCT and DHT using a bit serial SA as deign methodology;

ii) FHT using bit serial DA principles; and

iii) Matrix multiplication based on Booth-Encoder algorithm [7] and using a bit parallel SA as design methodology.

3.1 Orthogonal Transforms

This section presents a novel architecture for DOTs which can be formulated as matrix vector multiplication. The approach taken uses the Baugh-Wooley multiplication algorithm [1] for a systolic architecture implementation.

3.1.1 Mathematical Model

Let the input data and the transformed data be represented by the two vectors X and Y of size N, respectively. Then Y can be written as follows:

$$Y_i = \sum_{k=0}^{N-1} H_{ik} X_k \tag{1}$$

If the elements of the matrix transform and the input vector are represented using the 2's complement number representation and using the Baugh-Wooley algorithm then:

$$Y_i = \sum_{k=0}^{N-1} \left[\begin{array}{l} \sum_{l=0}^{n-2} \sum_{m=0}^{n-2} 2^{l+m} h_{ik,l} x_{k,m} + 2^{2n-2} h_{ik,n-1} x_{k,n-1} + \\ \left(\sum_{l=0}^{n-2} -2^l h_{ik,l} x_{k,n-1} + \sum_{m=0}^{n-2} -2^m x_{k,m} h_{ik,n-1} \right) 2^{n-1} \end{array} \right] \tag{2}$$

where $h_{ik,l}$ and $x_{k,m}$ are the lth bit of H_{ik} and mth bit of X_k, (which are zero or one) and $h_{ik,n-1}$ and $x_{k,n-1}$ are the sign bits, where n is the word length.

3.1.2 Architecture Developed

Equation (2) can be mapped into the proposed architecture. Figure 2 shows the architecture obtained for N=4 and n=4. It consists of eight identical processing elements (PEs). Each PE comprises a serial-parallel Baugh-Wooley Multiplier (BWM) [8], a Flip Flop (FF) for saving the carry bit and a full adder that adds the result of the partial product and the result generated from the previous PE. The matrix elements H_{ij} are fed from the north in a parallel/serial fashion bit by bit Least Significant Bit First (LSBF) while the vector elements X_j are fed in a parallel fashion and remain fixed in their corresponding PE cell during the entire computation of the operation. Each bit of the final product of the PE is fed to the full adder of the preceding PE so that the corresponding output bit of each PE is added to complete the result bit using LSBF method. The architecture is symmetric. However, the odd and the even results can be obtained separately through the two processing stages and by selecting the input samples using the selector which depends on the index *i* values for the input coefficients. In addition, this architecture is regular, modular and can be generalised for any transform length and input word length.

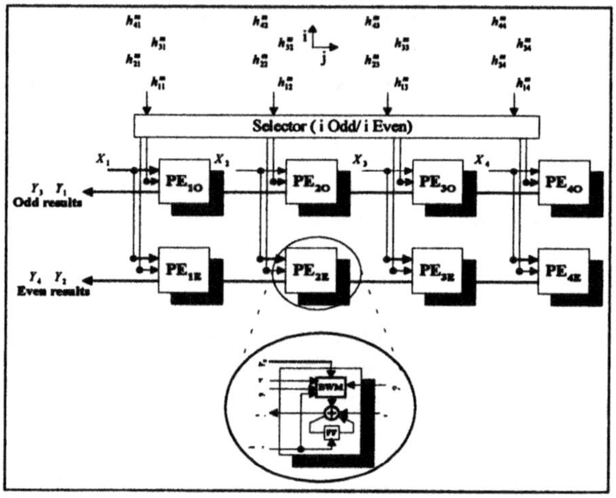

Figure 2. Proposed systolic architecture for transforms (N=4)

3.1.3 Algorithm Performance

The time complexity and the area of the structure are $n\,(N+1)T$ and $2N$, respectively. (where T is the clock cycle fixed by the total gate delay of the BWM multiplier).-See table1-.

Table 1. Comparison of proposed structure with the existing structures ([9],[8]) for computation of the transforms

Features	Proposed Structure	Structure of [9]	Structure of [8]
Computation time	$(n(N+1))T$	$(2n)T$	$(2nN)T$
Area Complexity	$O(2N)$	$O(N^2)$	$O(N)$

3.1.4 VHDL Design Library

As for multiplication, the VHDL codes for transforms are parametrisable with the generic parameters:

- The transform length N;
- The word width of the coefficients n; and
- The word width of the result n_{out}

3.1.5 RCMAT Implementation

The design is modular, regular and can be implemented for larger transform and input data word lengths. Table 2 illustrates the performance obtained for the proposed architecture in the case of N= 8 and n=8.

Table 2. Implementation report

Design Parameters	Slices	Speed (MHz)
Proposed architecture	188	31

3.2 Fast Hadammard Transform (FHT)

The Walsh-Hadamard transforms are important in many signal processing applications including speech compression, filtering and coding. This section presents a novel architecture for the Fast Hadamard Transforms using distributed arithmetic technique. The approach is based on both distributed arithmetic ROM and accumulator structure, and a sparse matrix factorisation technique.

3.2.1 Mathematical Model

Typically, a Hadamard matrix is defined iteratively as:

$$H_2 = \begin{bmatrix} 1 & 1 \\ 1 & -1 \end{bmatrix} \text{ and } H_{2N} = \begin{bmatrix} H_N & H_N \\ H_N & -H_N \end{bmatrix}.$$

where H_N is a Hadamard matrix of size NxN. Furthermore, if the transform length N is a power of two (i.e., $N = 2^p$), then a (FHT) algorithm (similar to Fast Fourier Transform (FFT)) can be used for its fast computation.

Let the input data and the transformed data be represented by the two vectors X and Y of size N, respectively. Then Y can be written as follows:

$$Y_i = \sum_{k=0}^{N-1} H_{ik} X_k \tag{3}$$

Applying the distributed arithmetic principles, equation 3 can be reformulated as follows:

$$Y_i = \sum_{m=0}^{n-1} Z_{n-1-m} 2^{-m} \tag{4}$$

where

$$Z_{n-1-m} = \sum_{k=0}^{N-1} H_{ik} x_{k,n-1-m} \quad (m \neq 0) \tag{5}$$

and

$$Z_{n-1} = -\sum_{k=0}^{N-1} H_{ik} x_{k,n-1} \quad (m = 0) \tag{6}$$

Since the term Z_m depends on the $x_{k,m}$ values it has only 2^N possible values, it is possible to precompute and store these values in a ROM. An input set of N bits $(x_{1,m}, x_{2,m}, ...x_{N,m})$ is used as an address to retrieve the corresponding Z_m values.

3.2.2 Architecture Developed

The architecture for the 1-D FHT is shown in figure 3. The n=8 bit inputs to the circuit are fed in a bit-serial fashion from a converter. The 4 separate RAC blocks calculate the 8 transforms as follows: a butterfly structure of bit-serial adders and subtracters is used to generate the elements of a new input matrix using sparse matrix factorization.

During the first 8 cycles eight bit-parallel outputs for each odd result are produced, and during the second 8 cycles eight bit-parallel outputs for each even results are produced. This implies a bit-parallel data organization with the maximum value in the ROM represented by 4 bits including the sign extension. Every n clock cycles the signal INVERT is used to compute the two's complement of the ROM's content by inverting the value and inserting a C_{in} (carry in of the adder) of value one while signal SELECT is used to select the odd and even input samples. The selector is basically a multiplexer (8→4), and the computation process runs from $m=0$ to $m = 2\times(n-1)$.

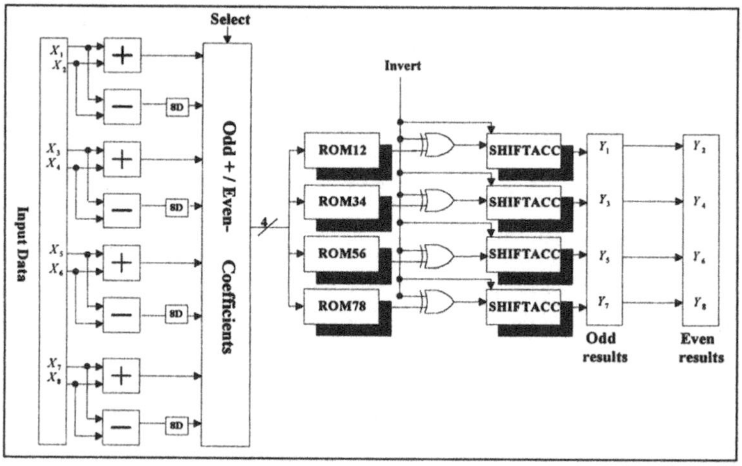

Figure 3. Proposed architecture for 1-D FHT (N=8)

3.2.3 Algorithm Performance

The algorithm performances are shown in Table 3.

Table 3. Comparison of proposed structure with the existing structures ([10],[11]) for computation of 1-D FHT

Feature	Proposed Structure	Structure of [11]	Structure of [10]
Computation time	$2n$	$(2N-1)(n+\log_2 N)$	$2N-1$

3.2.4 VHDL Design Library

As before the codes are parametrisable. The generic parameters being:

- The transform length N;
- The word width of the data n;
- The word width of the coefficients which depends on the type of the transform; and
- The word width of the result n_{out}

3.3.5 RCMAT Implementation

The design is modular, regular and can be implemented for larger transform and input data word lengths. Table 4 illustrates the performance obtained for the proposed architecture and [8] in the case of N= 8 and n=8.

Table 4. Implementation report for 1D FHT, (N=8,n=8)

Design Parameters	Slices	Speed (MHz)	(Area/Speed) Ratio
Proposed architecture	124	90	1.37
Structure [8]	136	45	3.02

3.3 Matrix Multiplication

This section investigates how some of the features of the Xilinx Virtex FPGA may be used to support efficient and optimised implementation of matrix product based on multiply and accumulate MAC. The approach used for matrix multiplication algorithm employs the idea used in the Modified Booth encoder Wallace trees Multiplication (MBWM).

3.3.1 Mathematical Model

Matrix multiplication can be formulated as follows:

$$C_{ij} = \sum_{k=0}^{N-1} A_{ik} B_{kj} \tag{7}$$

Applying the Modified Booth Encoder (MBE) algorithms, equation 7 can be rewritten as follows:

$$C_{ij} = \sum_{k=0}^{N-1} \sum_{m=0}^{(n/2)-1} (PP_{ik,m})\, 4^{m} \tag{8}$$

where $PP_{ik,m}$ are the MBE partial products [7], [12].

3.3.2 Architecture Developed

Equation (8) can be performed using the proposed MAC (figure 4). The proposed system exploits some of the Viretx FPGA features such as Block Select RAM and the fully digital DLL. The BlockRAM (*RAMB4_n_n*) available on the FPGA chips as an internal memory can be used to download the coefficients of the two matrices A and B using the dual port option available on this type of memories, where n is word-length of the data. The multiplication of two N x N matrices can be performed using N BlockRAMs to store the matrix coefficients. Clock skew and clock delay impact on device performance and the task of managing clock skew and clock delay with conventional clock trees becomes more difficult in large devices [6]. The Virtex series of devices resolve this potential problem by providing up to eight fully digital dedicated on-chip DLL circuits.
The heart of this algorithm is the multiply-accumulate component. This part takes two values (one row value from the A matrix and one column value from the B matrix), multiplies them and adds the result to the running total. Once N multiplications and additions have been completed, one value of the C matrix is obtained. The MAC has been used in this algorithm is basically based on the MBWM as shown in figure 4.

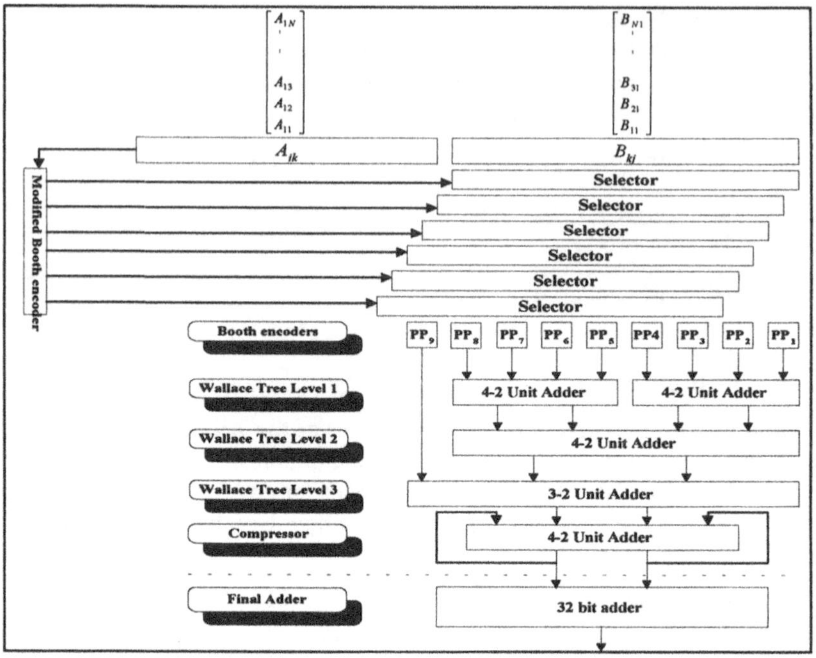

Figure 4. Proposed MAC architecture based on MBWM.

3.3.3 VHDL Design Library

The VHDL codes stored in the matrix algorithms library for matrix multiplication, using a bit parallel systolic architecture, are parameterisable and can be generated using the RCMAT GUI, to implement the design on the coprocessor. The generic parameters for each VHDL code are respectively:

- The matrix size N;
- The word width of the coefficients n; and
- The word width of the result n_{out}

3.3.4 RCMAT Implementation

The design is modular, regular and can be implemented for larger matrix product and input data word lengths. Table 5 illustrates the performance obtained for the proposed architecture for the case of N= 4 and n=8.

Table 5. Design parameters for the design implementation, (N=4, n=8)

Design parameters	CLBs	Speed (MHz)	(Area/Speed) Ratio
Proposed architecture	296	60	4.93
MAC (Multiplier + Adder)	270	46	5.87
***PAM-Blox* matrix multiplier [5]**	954/2=477	33	14.45

In comparison with *PAM-Blox* matrix multiplier [5], the design shows significant improvements when implemented on a single FPGA structure, requiring a single global clock, less area/speed ratio and reduced numbers of hardware slices for the logic operations used.

4 Conclusion

This paper describes the development of FPGA based environment for matrix-based computations. The system includes a GUI to help the user experimenting with different algorithms using different computer arithmetic techniques (bit serial, digit serial and bit parallel). The methodology adapted for the mapping of these techniques has been also described. The results so far obtained show that the proposed RCMAT environment provides substantial advantages when compared with similar systems such the RISC architectures. Furthermore the methodology used is modular and as such the system can easily be extended to include more matrix like algorithms. The proposed RCMAT architectures are scalable, modular and require less area and time complexity with reduced latency when compared with existing structures.

References

[1] A. Amira "A Custom Coprocessor for Matrix Algorithms." PhD thesis, Queen's University of Belfast, August 2001.
[2] J.P. Heron, "Design and Implementation of Reconfigurable DSP Circuit Architectures on FPGA." Ph.D thesis 1998, The Queen's University of Belfast.
[3] W. Marwood, "An Integrated Multiprocessor for Matrix Algorithms." Ph.D thesis 1995, University of Adelaide, Australia.
[4] S.P. Periyacheri, et *al* "A MATLAB compiler For Distributed, Heterogeneous, Reconfigurable Computing Systems." PDCS'99, November 3-5, 1999, Cambridge, MA - USA.
[5] O. Mencer, M. Morf and M.J. Flynn, *"PAM-Blox*: High Performance FPGA Design for Adaptive Computing." IEEE Symposium on FPGAs for Custom Computing Machines (FCCM), 1998 Napa Valley.
[6] URL: www.xilinx.com.
[7] J. Fadavi-Ardekani, "M x N Booth Encoded Multiplier Generator Using Optimised Wallace Trees." IEEE Transaction on VLSI Systems, VOL.1, NO. 2, pp 120-125, June 1993.
[8] A. Amira, A. Bouridane, P. Milligan and P. Sage "A High Throughput FPGA Implementation of A Bit-Level Matrix Product." Proceedings of the IEEE Workshop on Signal Processing Systems Design and Implementation (SIPS), pp 356-364, October 2000, Lousiana, USA.
[9] S.S. Nayak and P.K. Meher, "High throughput VLSI implementation of discrete orthogonal transforms using bit-level vector-matrix multiplier." IEEE Trans.on Circ.& Syst. II, Analog and Digital Sig. Proc., Vol.46, No.5, pp.655-658. 1999.
[10] S.Y.Kung,"VLSI Array Processors." Prentice Hall, USA, 1988.
[11] L.Chang and M.Chang Wu, "A bit level systolic array for Walsh-Hadamard transforms." Signal Processing Vol 31, pp 341-347, 1993.
[12] A. Amira, A. Bouridane and P. Milligan "Accelerating Matrix Product on Reconfigurable Hardware for Signal Processing." Proceedings of the International Conference on Field Programmable Logic (FPL), Lecture Notes in Computer Science, published by Springer Verlag, pp101-111, August 2001, Belfast.

Parallel FPGA Implementation of the Split and Merge Discrete Wavelet Transform

Nazeeh Aranki[1], Alex Moopenn[2], and Raoul Tawel[2]

[1] Department of Electrical Engineering-Systems
University of Southern California, Los Angeles, CA, 90089 USA
aranki@usc.edu
[2] Mosaix Technologies
176 Melrose Ave., Monrovia, CA 91016 USA
{amoopenn, rtawel}@mosaixtech.com

Abstract. The discrete wavelet transform has become a highly effective tool in many signal processing and data compression applications. In fact, it is widely accepted that JPEG2000, with its wavelet based image-coding technology will become the universally accepted format for digital images - whether on the web, over wireless systems, in digital cameras, printers, faxes or remote sensors. Various hardware implementations of the DWT were proposed by researchers to reduce its complexity and enhance its performance. In this paper we present an efficient hardware implementation of the discrete wavelet transform suitable for deployment on a reconfigurable FPGA based platform. Our implementation is a novel architecture based on the lifting factorization of the wavelet filter banks that uses the *Overlap-State* algorithm. It minimizes, memory usage, computational complexity, and communication overhead associated with parallel implementations.

1. Introduction

As a result of extensive research in recent years, transform coding techniques have come to virtually dominate every single image and video-coding scheme proposed to-date. Consequently, efficient software and hardware based transform coding system designs and implementations are a high priority objective at both academic and commercial research centers. While the wavelet transform offers a wide variety of useful features, it is computation intensive. Many VLSI architectural solutions for the DWT transform [1] have been proposed in order to meet the real time requirements of scientific and consumer applications. However, most of these solutions are special purpose parallel processors developed for specific wavelet filters and/or wavelet decomposition tree that implement high level abstraction of the pyramid algorithm. Vishwanath [2] proposed a systolic-parallel architecture for the 2-D DWT based on the recursive pyramid algorithm, but due to the approximations involved, these architectures cannot be used for exact reconstruction of the original data.

There is a clear need for a fast hardware DWT that allows flexibility in customizing the wavelet transform with regard to the filters being used and the structure of the wavelet decomposition. In many image processing applications, it is critical to compute the 2-D wavelet transform in real-time. In addition, JPEG2000

M. Glesner, P. Zipf, and M. Renovell (Eds.): FPL 2002, LNCS 2438, pp. 740-749, 2002.

provides capabilities for using different DWT filters, thereby requiring user programmable implementations. Field programmable gate arrays (FPGAs) offer a suitable platform (cost effective and highly flexible) for such an implementation. Several DWT hardware architectures were proposed for FPGA implementation. Reza and Turney [3] proposed an implementation of the polyphase representation of the DWT. Kim *et al* [4] presented a parallel architecture that can compute low pass and high pass DWT coefficients in the same clock cycle. However, these architectures either address specific filterbanks, or do not support block-based transform. In this paper, we propose an FPGA block-based parallel implementation which utilizes the *Overlap-State* technique [5]. This technique is based on a filterbank factorization described by Daubechies and Sweldens as "lifting" [6]. Such factorizations have attractive properties including fast computation and in-place calculation.

2. Lifting Factorization and Overlap-State Technique

The DWT in general is computation intensive. The Mallat style [7] multilevel octave-band wavelet decomposition, otherwise known as the standard DWT can be implemented as a pyramidal recursive filtering operation using the corresponding filter banks as shown in Figure 1. This algorithm is constrained by large latency, a high computational cost and requires a large buffer size to store intermediate results, which makes it impractical for real time applications with memory constraints.

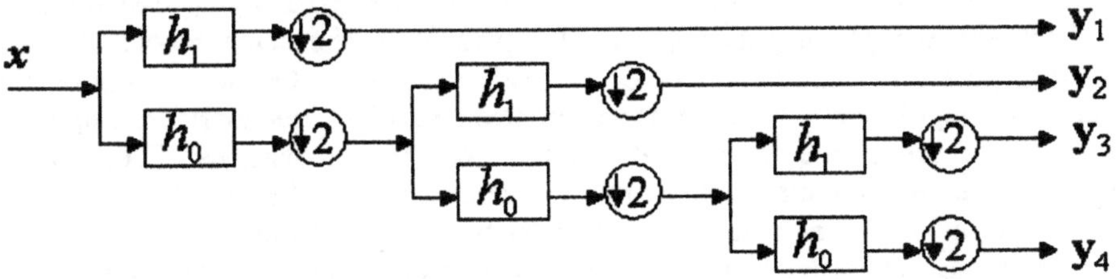

Fig. 1. Wavelet decomposition showing cascaded levels of filter banks.

The standard algorithm operates on the whole image in a sequential manner. An improved implementation would partition the image into several blocks and operate on each block independently and simultaneously in a parallel manner, and then merges the results to complete the DWT. A known disadvantage of such an approach is that it requires data exchanges between neighboring blocks at each decomposition level of the DWT and hence additional overhead due to inter-block communications.

2.1 Parallel Implementation of the 2-D Lifting DWT Algorithm

The key concept behind the lifting algorithm is to model the DWT as a Finite State Machine (FSM), which updates (or transforms) each raw input sample (initial state) progressively via intermediate states into a wavelet coefficient (final state). Any FIR wavelet filters pair can be represented as a polyphase matrix which can be factored into a cascaded set of elementary matrices (upper triangular and lower triangular ones). It has been shown that such a lifting-factorization based DWT algorithm can be twice as fast as the standard algorithm [6]. From a computational point of view, each of these matrices essentially updates the input data samples using linear convolutions [8]. The operation can be seen as a Finite State Machine where each elementary matrix $e^i(z)$ updates the FSM state $X^i(z)$ to the next higher level $X^{i+1}(z)$.

$$Y(z) = P(z)X(z) = e^{2m}(z)\cdots e^{1}(z)\underbrace{e^{0}(z)X^{0}(z)}_{X^1(z)} \tag{1}$$

$$\underbrace{e^{1}(z)e^{0}(z)X^{0}(z)}_{X^2(z)}, \qquad \underbrace{e^{2m}(z)\cdots e^{1}(z)e^{0}(z)X^{0}(z)}_{Y(z)=X^{2m}(z)}$$

DWT computations based on such lifting factorizations have some attractive properties, such as fast computation, and in-place computation that allows us to introduce the FSM model and motivated our hardware implementation. In this approach, boundary data is saved and exchanged between blocks at each decomposition level to complete DWT for block boundaries. This algorithm will be referred to as the overlap-save algorithm.

2.2 Overlap-State Algorithm

The overlap-state algorithm is a block-based parallel implementation that uses the same lifting model described in the previous section. While the DWT is still modeled as a Finite State Machine (FSM), raw input samples are updated progressively as long as there are enough neighboring samples present in the same block. Using this technique, the DWT can be computed correctly while the inter-block communication overhead is significantly reduced. Data samples near block boundaries are updated to intermediate states due to lack of enough neighboring samples. These partially updated boundary samples, called state information, are collected at each level and exchanged at the conclusion of the independent transform for each block. A postprocessing operation is initiated then to complete the transform for boundary samples. This technique was introduced by Jiang and Ortega [5][9] as the *Overlap-State* of the *Split-and-Merge* architecture, as shown in Figure 2.

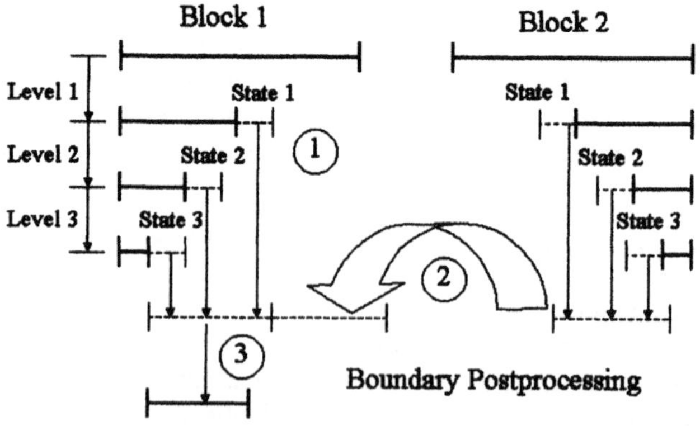

Fig. 2. Data flow chart of a three-level DWT decomposition using the Overlap-State technique

The three algorithms presented in this section were coded for the popular floating point Daubechies (9,7) DWT. While all these parallel architectures can be generalized to any wavelet filters pair, we selected the (9,7) filter pair for our initial evaluation due to its computational complexity and its insertion into the JPEG2000 standard.

The lifting factorization of the (9,7) DWT yields the following equations for the detail and smooth components[10]:

$$\begin{aligned} d_1[n] &= d_o[n] - \alpha_0 (s_0[n+1] + s_0[n]) \\ s_1[n] &= s_o[n] - \alpha_1 (d_1[n] + d_1[n-1]) \\ d_2[n] &= d_1[n] + \alpha_2 (s_1[n+1] + s_1[n]) \\ s_2[n] &= s_1[n] + \alpha_3 (d_2[n] + d_2[n-1]) \\ s[n] &= \beta_0 s_2[n] \end{aligned} \tag{2}$$

where

$$\begin{aligned} &\alpha_0 \approx 1.586134, \alpha_1 \approx 0.052980, \alpha_2 \approx 0.882911, \\ &\alpha_3 \approx 0.443506, \beta_0 \approx 0.812893, \beta_1 \approx 1/\beta_0. \end{aligned} \tag{3}$$

A strip-partitioning scheme was used to allocate input data sequence uniformly onto different processing units. Since this method has no segmentation is done in the row direction, data to be exchanged and state information obviously will only appear along up and down boundaries in each block.

3. Software Simulations

The parallel state-overlap algorithm partitions the raw image into ***n*** uniform stripes that get allocated to ***n*** processor units. Each unit computes its own allocated data up to the required DWT level, this is the *Split* stage. During each decomposition level, row and column transformations are completed first for all lines in a data stripe and stored back in their relative memory locations. The state information for all the stripes, other than the top stripe, is stored in the allocated state data locations to be communicated during the merge operation. The output from the *Split* stage consists of two parts: completely transformed coefficients, and the state information (partially updated boundary samples). During the next stage, *Merge*, a one-way communication is initiated and the state information is transferred from each processing unit to its top neighbor. For each stripe, the state information from the neighboring stripe is then combined together with its own corresponding state information to complete the whole DWT transform at each level.

Our software simulations were evaluated with the *Vegas* image (512x512 pixels) from the Signal and Image Processing archives of the University of Southern California. Our results for a 3-level DWT decomposition as it appears in memory and the corresponding reconstructed DWT image are shown in Figures 4 and 5. Results can be readily extended to color images. We evaluated the performance for the three parallel implementations in terms of memory usage and the total number computations. Our results showed that the *Overlap-State* has far less memory requirements (due to the in-place lifting computations) and significantly less computational overhead (due to the minimized inter-block communication). Scalability was verified by simulating the DWT with partions of 2, 4, 8 and 16 blocks for our *Vegas* test image [11].

In conclusion, our simulations demonstrated that the *Slit-and-Merge* technique has significantly less memory requirements, better performance, minimizes the inter-block communications and hence memory I/O operations, and is fully scalable.

Fig.3. "Vegas" – Original

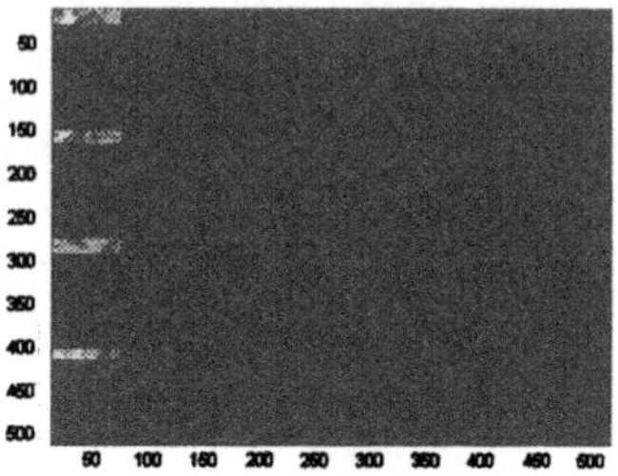

Fig.4. Memory map of DWT image

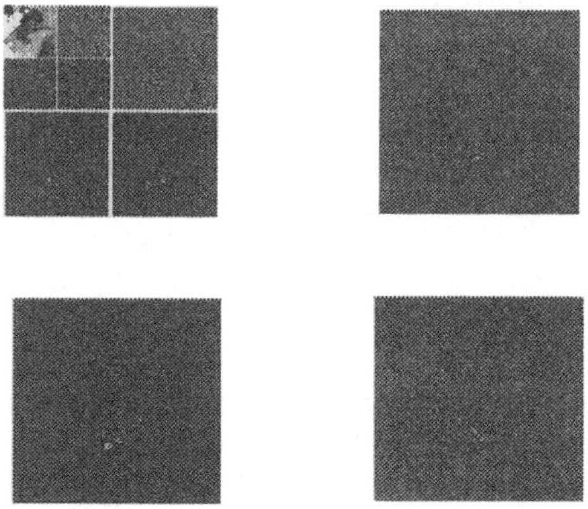

Fig.5. Reconstructed bands for DWT transformed "Vegas" image

4. Hardware Architecture

In this section we describe the architecture of a split-and-merge 2D-DWT system optimized for low-power, and real-time image encoding. Based on a highly parallel, SIMD-like architecture, our system incorporates multiple processors operating in parallel to achieve high processing throughput. The architecture exploits the unique properties of split-and-merge algorithm, enabling a very memory efficient and scalable design, and is particularly well suited for FPGA implementation. Our design supports dynamic and *in-situ* system reconfiguration for optimal performance under various operating parameters and hardware resources. In addition, variants of the parallel algorithms discussed earlier are also supported in our design.

4.1 System Architecture

The split-and-merge 2D-DWT system comprises a master processor and an array of slave coprocessors operating in a SIMD-like configuration, as shown in Figure 10. The central processor is referred to as the split-and-merge processor (SMP) and the coprocessors as DWT line processors (DLP's). The number of coprocessors can be scaled depending on system performance requirements and available hardware resources. The SMP is primarily responsible for implementing the top-level control and logic sequencing functions. The SMP also provides a host bus interface to an external host processor and I/O devices attached to the host bus. The SMP initiates and supervises all DLP's processing activities. The DLP's are special-function processing units optimized to perform high-speed computation of the 1D-DWT. The DLP's can perform their processing in parallel and independently. The system can operate in either a synchronous or non-synchronous mode. In the synchronous mode, the SMP instructs the DLP's to perform identical processing tasks in locked steps. In the non-synchronous mode, the DLP's processing is staggered. The non-synchronous mode provides a higher level of concurrency, but requires more complex scheduling and control logic.

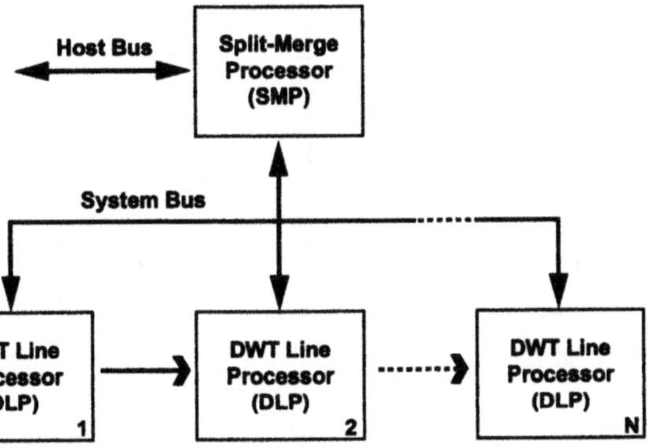

Fig. 6. Scalable multi-processor based system for the split-and-merge 2D DWT transform

The SMP communicates with DLP's via a high-speed system bus and initiates all system bus activities. The system bus consists of a bi-directional data bus, an address bus, and a set of control signals. A global address space is also defined to globally address the DLP's. Commands or write data addressed to a location in the global address space are written into all corresponding locations of the DLP's

4.2 Split-and-Merge Processor

The split-and-merge processor (SMP) is a global controller that manages the overall operation of the 2D-DWT system. The SMP's primary tasks include executing the top-level control and processing functions, as well as scheduling, supervising, monitoring the processing activities of the DLP coprocessors and managing internal data transfer between the DLP's and external data transfer between the 2D-DWT system and an external host. The SMP also performs various top-level processing tasks of the split-and-merge algorithm, including: a) system/global data initialization,

b) image boundary handling, c) boundary data initialization control, d) row and column transform control, e) boundary data transfer control, and f) decomposition level control. The SMP issues commands to the DLP's to perform various low-level DWT processing tasks including data line extension, and row/column 1D-DWT.

The SMP's basic processing flow is as follows: The SMP partitions the input data stream from external I/O into data blocks, performing partial buffering of the input data if necessary. In the non-synchronous mode, once a complete block has been downloaded to a DLP's local memory, the SMP instructs the DLP to perform the 2D-DWT on interior block data. In the synchronous mode, the SMP holds off DLP processing until data blocks are downloaded to all DLP's. When the 2D-DWT on the interior block data is completed, the SMP instructs the DLP's to merge the boundary data to complete the 2D-DWT of the entire data blocks. Finally, the SMP reads and outputs the transformed data from a DLP local block memory to the host processor.

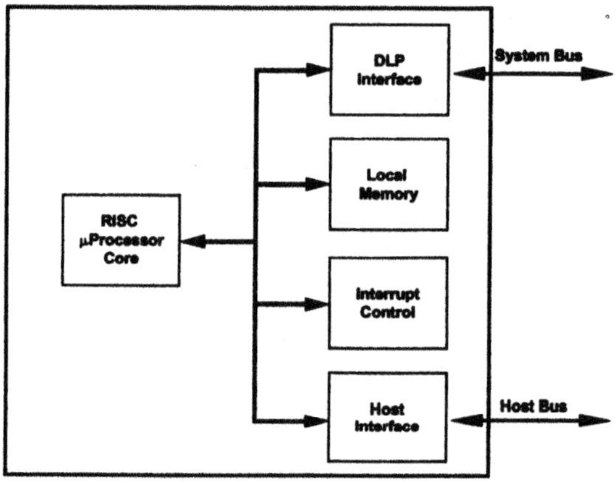

Fig. 7. Split-and-merge processor with system and host communication busses

The SMP communicates with a host processor via the host interface, which supports high-speed I/O data transfer to a host processor through the host processor bus. It also supports DMA data transfer to external I/O devices attached to the host bus. The SMP communicates with the DLP's via the DLP interface unit. The local memory stores the control and sequencing firmware, system parameters, user application configuration data, and provides partial buffering of external I/O data. The SMP issues commands to DLP's to initiate DLP processing (including 1-D DWT, reset and internal memory I/O) by writing to the DLP command registers.

4.3 DWT Line Processor

The DWT line processor (DLP) is a special-function coprocessor optimized for high-speed computation of the 2D-DWT. The DLP performs 2D-DWT on a data block as a sequence of row and column 1D-DWT's. The DLP comprises a controller, a set of local registers, a local memory, a memory control/interface unit, a pipelined arithmetic unit (PAU), and an SMP interface. The DLP controller performs various control and sequencing operations. Based on a multiple state-machine design, the controller is optimized for high processing concurrency and low latency. It decodes

SMP commands from the SMP interface and generates the required sequence of control signals to perform the various DWT processing functions. The DLP's local registers include control, status, and data registers. The local memory mainly stores the input data block. After a 1D-DWT is performed, the input data block is replaced with the output processed data. The memory also provides a line buffer for the 1D-DWT processing. The memory control/interface unit facilitates the transfer of data with the SMP and with neighboring DLP's during boundary data merge operation. The memory I/F unit provides separate input and output data ports for two neighboring DLP's. The ports contain internal buffers to allow parallel data transfer between DLP's. The DLPs communicate with the SMP over the system bus via the SMP interface unit and appear as "memory-mapped" devices on the bus. The SMP interface latches and buffers the address, data, and control signals on system bus during an active bus cycle. The address is decoded to determine if the current bus cycle is a local memory or register access. The SMP interface generates all the required handshake signaling as well as requests to perform the boundary merge when operating in the pipelined mode.

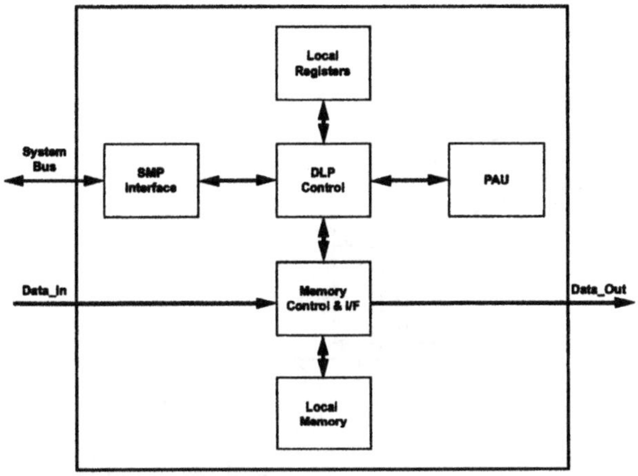

Fig. 8. DWT line processor with inter processor communication bus

The PAU is a fixed-point arithmetic accelerator designed to perform the numeric intensive 1D-DWT filtering operation using the in-place lifting technique. The PAU is based on a pipeline design and incorporates a set of multiplier-accumulator units (MACs) and data shift registers. The PAU pipeline cycle consists of loading two input data samples and reading out two output samples. The PAU operation starts by shifting in two input samples into the input registers of the first MAC unit in two clock cycles. Data in the input registers of the remaining MACs are shifted in the first clock cycle while additional clock cycles are used to perform the MAC operation. Two samples from the last MAC unit are then read out to complete the pipeline cycle.

The length of the DWT filter determines the number of MAC units and consequently the PAU pipeline latency. Internal data registers are provided in the PAU for storing the DWT filter coefficients. The shift register unit provides one- and two-clock cycle delayed data to the next pipelined stage in the PAU. The MAC, optimized for high speed and low latency, consists of an array multiplier and an accumulator with fast carry-chain logic for high-speed performance.

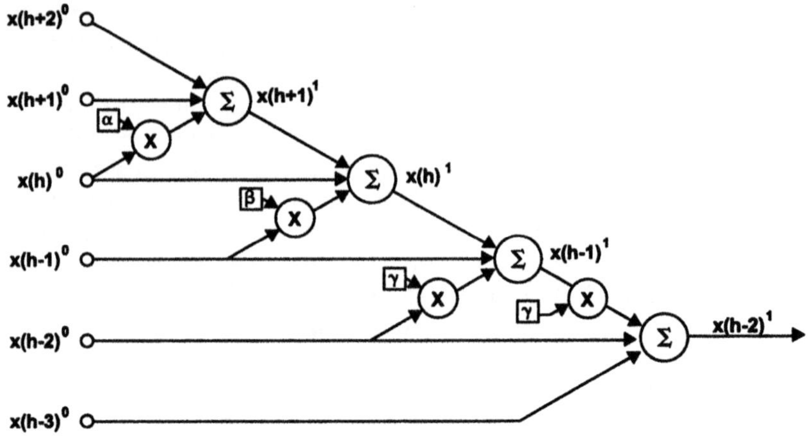

Fig. 9. DWT filtering with lifting flow graph.

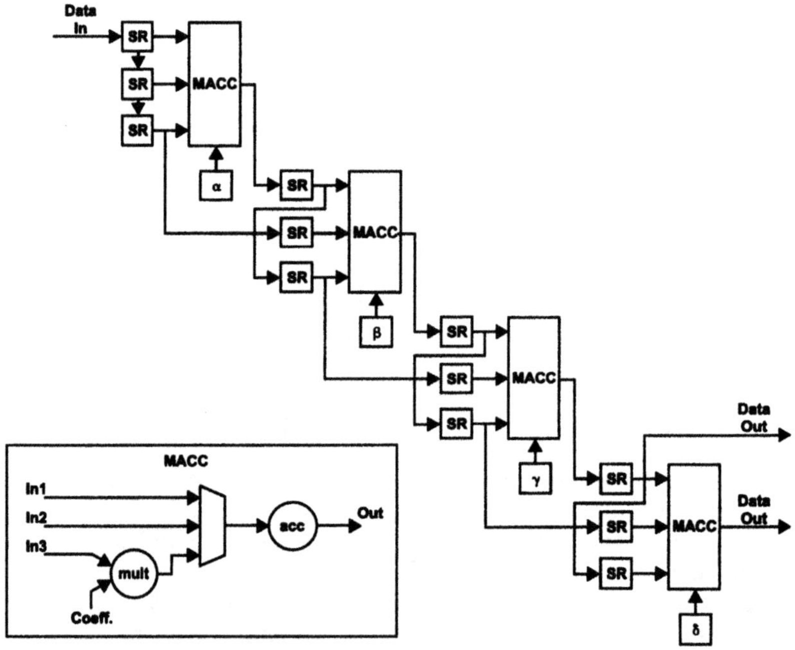

Fig. 10. Pipelined Arithmetic Unit (PAU).

Our DWT architecture was coded in VHDL and simulated. The design was then synthesized and ported to a Xilinx Virtex II FPGA platform. A Detailed description of our implementation and its deployment on the Virtex platform has been submitted for publication in a forthcoming issue of IEEE Transactions on Circuits and Systems.

5. Conclusion

We presented in this paper a compact hardware architecture for a novel image compression/signal decomposition algorithm based on the discrete wavelet transform (DWT). This is a fully parallel, low-power, scalable, multi-resolution implementation that is ideally suited FPGA deployment. Based on a highly efficient implementation of the wavelet transform, our approach makes use of the novel *overlap-state* wavelet decomposition algorithm that minimizes 1) memory usage (by allowing in-place transformation), 2) number of multiply-accumulate (MAC) arithmetic operations (by using lifting factorization), and 3) inter-processor communication overhead associated with parallel implementations (by using the overlap-state DWT implementation). With the proper lifting filtering factorization, this implementation can be extended to any desired customized DWT decomposition tree.

6. Acknowledgements

The authors would like to thank Antonio Ortega and Wenqing Jiang for sharing with us the overlap-state algorithm and for their support and helpful discussions. The research described in this paper was performed by Mosaix Technologies, Inc. and was sponsored by the National Science Foundation under Grant Number DMI-0109649

References

1. A. Grzeszczak, Mandal, M.K., S. Panchanathan, S. and T. Yeap, "VLSI implementation of discrete wavelet transform", IEEE Transs on VLSI Systems, V4, Dec. 1996, pp 421 –433
2. M. Vishwanath, "Discrete wavelet transform in VLSI", in Proc. IEEE Int. Conf. Appl. Specfic Array Processors, 1992, pp. 218-229.
3. A.M. Reza, R.D. Turney, "FPGA implementation of 2d wavelet transform", Signals, Systems, and Computers, Conf. Record of the 33rd Asilomar, 1999 Vol. 1, pp 584 –588
4. Y. Kim; K. Jun; K. Rhee, "FPGA implementation of subband image encoder using discrete wavelet transform", in Proc. of the IEEE Region 10 Conference, V2, 1999, pp 1335 -1338
5. W. Jiang and A. Ortega, "Parallel Architecture for the DWT Transform based on the Lifting Factorization" in Proc. of SPIE - Parallel and Distributed Methods for Image Proc. III, 1999
6. I. Daubechies and W. Sweldens, "Factoring wavelet transforms into lifting steps", J. Fourier Anal. Appl. 4 (3), 1998, pp. 247-269
7. S. Mallat, "A theory for multiresolution signal decomposition: The wavelet representation", IEEE Trans. on Patt. Anal. and Mach. Intell. 11 (7), 1989., pp. 674-693
8. W. Sweldens, "The lifting scheme:A new philosophy in biorthogonal wavelet constructions" in Wavelet Apps. in Signal and Image Processing III, Proc. SPIE 2569, 1995, pp. 68-79
9. W. Jiang, "Contribution to Transform Coding System Implementation", Ph.D. Thesis, USC, May 2000.
10. M. Adams and R. Ward, "Wavelet Transforms in the JPEG-2000 Standard", in Proc. of IEEE Pacific Rim Conference on Communications, Computers and Signal Processing, Victoria, BC, Canada, Aug. 2001, vol. 1, pp. 160-163.
11. A. Moopenn, "Final Report on Parallel Hardware Implementation of the Split and Merge DWT Transform for Wireless Comm.", SBIR Phase I, NSF Contract DMI-0109649, 2002

Fully Parameterizable Elliptic Curve Cryptography Processor over GF(2^m)

Tim Kerins[1], Emanuel Popovici[1], William Marnane[1], and Patrick Fitzpatrick[2]

[1] Dept of Electrical and Electronic Engineering,
University College Cork, College Rd., Cork City, Ireland.
{timk,emanuel,liam}@rennes.ucc.ie
[2] Dept of Mathematics,
University College Cork, College Rd., Cork City, Ireland.
p.fitzpatrick@ucc.ie

Abstract. In this paper we present an Elliptic Curve Point Multiplication processor over base fields GF(2^m), suitable for use in a wide range of commercial cryptography applications. Our design operates in a polynomial basis is fully parameterizable in the irreducible polynomial and the chosen Elliptic Curve over any base Galois Field up to a given size. High performance is achieved by use of a dedicated Galois Field arithmetic co-processor implemented on FPGA. The underlying FPGA architecture is used to increase calculation performance, taking advantage of the properties of this kind of programmable logic device to perform the large number of logical operations required. We discuss the performance of our processor for different Elliptic Curves and compare the results with recent implementations in terms of speed and security.

1 Introduction

In recent years a number of forces have elevated the importance of encryption. The expansive growth of the Internet has greatly increased the degree to which electronic systems connect and communicate. Public Key Cryptography is the basis of secure communication between unfamiliar hosts and is vital for secure E-commerce transactions. All standard mechanisms of network security such as Secure IP, Secure Sockets Layer (SSL) and Wireless Encryption Protocol (WEP) involve some form of public key cryptography. With bandwidth at a premium on E-commerce servers is it vital to have as much security per key bit as possible. Public key Elliptic Curve Cryptosystems (ECC) were introduced independently by Miller [1] and Koblitz [2]. The main strength of ECC is that the underlying mathematical problem is orders of magnitude more difficult than conventional public key algorithms so as a result the underlying key size can be made much smaller while retaining an equivalent level of security. For example a keysize of 200 bits in an ECC offers equavalent security to 1400 bit RSA [3]. Although elliptic curve systems offer greater security and utilize less bandwidth than conventional public key protocols the underlying arithmetic cannot be calculated as

M. Glesner, P. Zipf, and M. Renovell (Eds.): FPL 2002, LNCS 2438, pp. 750–759, 2002.

efficiently leading to slower communication. In contrast to RSA no single standard has been set for ECC and a large number of curves are currently in use, thus an ECC processor must be able to handle different curves and underlying fields.

The speed of ECC is dependent on the speed at which the underlying arithmetic can be calculated. A recent approach has been to use dedicated hardware to speed up these operations [4]. Many hardware implementations of processors have concentrated on curves over a particular field or particular class of fields and involve a large amount of precomputation and reconfiguration. This approach is impractical in the case of electronic transactions where it may be necessary to quickly vary the encryption strength/speed ratio where the parameters of the system change frequently. As an example consider a SSL server used for electronic transaction. Perhaps some communication is required at 151 bit encryption but needs to be performed at a very high speed. At a later time 239 bit encryption is required where speed is less critical. Our approach is to implement a dedicated arithmetic coprocessor on FPGA as part of a fully parameterizable ECC system. In contrast to other recent implementations it can operate on any required key size, up to a maximum size, without reconfiguration. This addresses the problem of non standardization as the ECC can be adjusted to easily operate on any elliptic curve on a per application basis. It is envisioned that this design could be used as part of a larger library of FPGA cryptography ciphers as suggested in [5]. FPGAs are very suitable for this type of application as they allow for rapid changes in protocol without any changes in underlying hardware and are well suited for applications relating to internet security [6].

2 Related Work

A number of implementations have been documented for the computation of point scalar multiplication, which is the basic operation used by ECC. Processors based on composite fields GF($(2^m)^n$) are reported in [7] and although they are efficient, questions have been raised about the mathematical security of this type of approach [8]. High performance FPGA and software implementations of ECC systems are reported in [9]. A significant stand alone elliptic curve processor is documented in [10]. In this case parameterization is achieved by reconfiguration of the FPGA. This adds an extra level of complexity to the design as reconfiguration time must be taken into account when switching field size. Our work is similar to [11] except that we achieve rapid parameterization of an ECC without reconfiguration. We believe our processor is an improvement over its predecessors due to its simplicity of design and efficient use of underlying hardware to achieve full parameterization. Our Galois Field processor design is based on that presented in [12].

3 Elliptic Curve Cryptography

To encrypt data in ECC, it is represented as a point on an elliptic curve over a finite field. In common with other public key schemes it relies on the existence of a "trapdoor function", ie one which is easy to perform but very difficult to reverse. In this case, when a point is added to itself a number of times, it is computationally intractable to recover the original point without knowing the exact number of additions. This is where the security of ECC resides. In some sense the number of point additions represents the secret key while a point on the curve represents the data to be encrypted. In this section we give a brief overview of the mathematical basis of elliptic curve cryptography. Additional information on elliptic curves and their applications is given in [3].

3.1 Elliptic Curve Arithmetic

The fundamental operation for ECC is point scalar multiplication, i.e. a point is added to itself k times.

$$\begin{aligned} Q &= kP \\ &= \underbrace{P \oplus P \oplus \ldots \oplus P}_{k\ times} \end{aligned} \tag{1}$$

Point addition is defined geometrically by the "chord-tangent" law of composition $\oplus$.

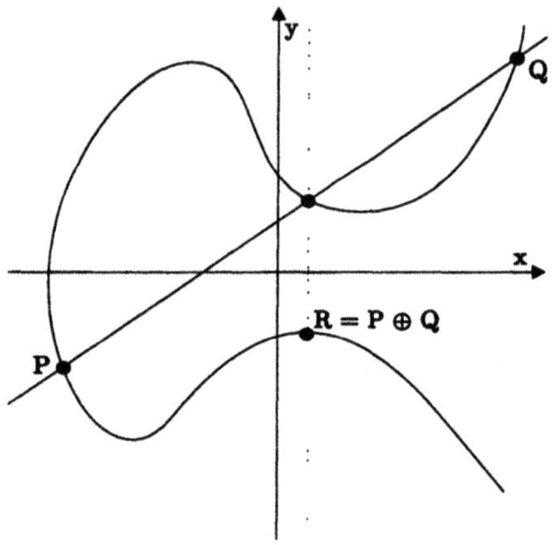

Fig. 1. Adding two points on an Elliptic Curve

To add two distinct points P and Q on an elliptic curve a chord is drawn between then and the third point of intersection of this line with the curve is reflected through the x axis. The reflection $R = P \oplus Q$. Adding a point P to itself (doubling P) is performed in a similar manner. In this case the tangent to the curve at P is taken. This line intersects the curve at exactly one other point which is then reflected through the x axis. This reflection is $2P = P \oplus P$. Point scalar multiplication is performed by successive doublings and addings of the base point P.

3.2 Elliptic Curves over Binary Finite Fields

For our implementation we choose elliptic curves over the field GF(2^m). The advantage of such a representation is that field elements are represented in hardware as m bit registers and addition of elements is a bitwise XOR. Field elements are represented in the canonical (polynomial) basis and multiplications and divisions are performed modulo a suitable irreducible polynomial p. A representation of an elliptic curve E, in affine coordinates, suitable for cryptography is defined to be the set of solutions $(x, y) \in GF(2^m) \times GF(2^m)$ to the equation

$$E : y^2 + xy = x^3 + ax^2 + b \tag{2}$$

where $a, b \in GF(2^m), b \neq 0$. Explicit rational formulas for the addition rule involve several operations in the underlying finite field. Given that $P = (x_1, y_1)$ and $Q = (x_2, y_2)$ are points on the elliptic curve then $R = (x_3, y_3) = P \oplus Q$ is defined when $P \neq Q$ (point addition) as

$$\lambda = \frac{y_1 + y_2}{x_1 + x_2} \tag{3}$$

$$x_3 = \lambda^2 + \lambda + x_1 + x_2 + a \tag{4}$$

$$y_3 = (x_1 + x_3)\lambda + x_3 + y_1 \tag{5}$$

and when $P = Q$ (point doubling) as

$$\lambda = x_1 + \frac{y_1}{x_1} \tag{6}$$

$$x_3 = \lambda^2 + \lambda + a \tag{7}$$

$$y_3 = (x_1 + x_3)\lambda + x_3 + y_1 \tag{8}$$

In either case the operation involves 1 division, 1 multiplication and 1 squaring in the underlying finite field. Traditionally inversion over a Galois Field is an expensive operation in terms of clock cycles and hardware. The speed at which it can be performed typically limits the speed at which an ECC over a polynomial basis in affine coordinates can operate.

3.3 Elliptic Curve Cryptosystems

Elliptic curve cryptography is based on the discrete logarithm problem applied to elliptic curves over a finite field. In particular for an elliptic curve E it relies on the fact that it is relatively easy to compute equation 1 while there is currently no known subexponential time algorithm to compute k given P and Q. In practice P is chosen so it is a generator of a finite cyclic subgroup of points on the curve and k is less than the order of this group. In implementing an elliptic curve cryptosystem a number of choices have to be made each of which will affect security and performance

- Size of underlying finite field $GF(2^m)$.
- Irreducible polynomial for finite field arithmetic $p(x)$.
- Suitable elliptic Curve E.
- Suitable base point P.

In a modern commercial communication environment an ECC processor needs to be parameterizable in each of the above so that the speed and strength of the cipher can be easily varied. There are elliptic curve analogs of most popular public key protocols such as elliptic curve Diffie-Hellman (ECDH) and elliptic curve ElGamal [3]. They are also used for secure hash function generation and digital signatures [3]. For example in ECDH a random base point P is chosen, this represents the public key, while k represents the private key. The shared secret key S between two parties A and B is easily calculated by

$$S = k_A(k_B P) = k_B(k_A P) \tag{9}$$

4 An Elliptic Curve Processor

Our processor uses FPGA technology to perform the most time critical operations, namely the Galois Field arithmetic, and its design is well suited to this type of application. It has a highly efficient inversion routine and ability to perform three field operations in parallel. The processor involves a dedicated Galois Field arithmetic coprocessor on FPGA, realized on the Celoxica PC-1000 bus "plug-in" card [13], containing a VirtexE2000 device [14]. The underlying Galois Field operations involved in the point addition (equations 3,4,5) and point doubling (eqations 6,7,8) are performed on FPGA, in communication with a host PC (Dell pentium 4 1.8 Ghz processor), which performs the scalar multiplication by successive point doublings and addings.

4.1 The ABC Galois Field Coprocessor

Our Galois Field processor design was first proposed in [12]. It performs the calculation

$$u = \frac{ab}{c} \; mod \; p \tag{10}$$

in $2m$ clock cycles, where $u, a, b, c \in GF(2^m)$ and p is the irreducible polynomial. An outline of the algorithm is displayed in figure 2. The (u_i, v_i) i=1,2,3 pairs are pairs of polynomials of maximum order m (m bit registers) and the discrepancies d_1 and d_2 are the x^ith coefficients (i^{th} bit in register) in

$$\begin{matrix} u_1 c + v_1 p \\ u_2 c + v_2 p \end{matrix} \tag{11}$$

respectively. The discrepancy d_3 is given by the x^ith coefficient in

$$u_3 c + v_3 p + ab \tag{12}$$

These operations are performed in the function ComputeDiscrepancies in figure 2 and are explained in detail in the next subsection. The pair (u_1, v_1) is defined to be smaller than (u_2, v_2) if the degree of u_1 is less than or equal to the degree of $u_2 + 1$. Let $k1$ denotes the index of (u_1, u_2) and $k2$ denotes the index of (u_2, v_2).

```
ABCprocessor(a,b,c,p){                // computes u=(ab/c)mod p
  var
    d1=0, d2=1, d3=0;                 // initialize discrepancies
    u1=1, v1=0;                       // initialize (u1,v1) registers
    u2=0, v2=1;                       // initialize (u2,v2) registers
    u3=0, v3=0;                       // initialize (u3,v3) registers
    k1=0, k2=1;                       // order of (u1,u2), (v1,v2)
    i;                                // iteration counter
  begin
    for(i=0; i<2*m; i++){
      ComputeDiscrepancies(a,b,c,p,d1,d2,d3);
        if((k1<=k2 && d1=1 && d2=1) || (d2=0 && d1=1)){
          u2=u2 XOR (u1 AND d2);      // XORs u2,u1 registers if d2=1
          v2=v2 XOR (v1 AND d2);      // XORs v2,v1 registers if d2=1
          u3=u3 XOR (u1 AND d3);      // XORs u3,u1 registers if d3=1
          v3=v3 XOR (v1 AND d3);      // XORs v3,v1 registers if d3=1
          u1=u1<<1;                   // left shift u1 : multiply by x
          v1=v1<<1;                   // left shift v1 : multiply by x
          k1=k1+1;}                   // increment order (u1,v1)
        else{
          u1=u2 XOR (u1 AND d1);      // XORs u2,u1 if d1=1
          v1=v2 XOR (v1 AND d1);      // XORs v2,v1 if d1=1
          u3=u3 XOR (u2 AND d3);      // XORs u3,u2 if d3=1
          v3=v3 XOR (u3 AND d3);      // XORs v3,u3 if d3=1
          u2=u2<<1;                   // left shift u2 : multiply by x
          v2=v2<<1;                   // left shift v2 : multiply by x
          k2=k2+1;}                   // increment order (u2,v2)
    return(u3);}                      // return result
```

Fig. 2. Pseudocode for the ABC Coprocessor

To perform arithmetic on a smaller field, the irreducible p' that generates the smaller Galois Field is loaded to the SRAMS from the PC and the same hardware is used for calculation of equation 10 for these smaller field elements, with faster calculation time depending on the degree of p'.

4.2 ABC Coprocessor Architecture on FPGA

Our processor used thirteen, 256 bit registers to calculate equation 10. Three holding registers are used for the initial loading of data, and the other ten are used for calculation as illustrated in figure 3. Initially the holding registers and register b are filled. During calculation the registers a, c and p are loaded bit serially from the holding registers and the (u_i,v_i) registers shifted or XORed as illustrated in figure 2. The calculation of the discrepancies (d_1,d_2 and d_3) is achieved by XORing the results of the Sum Blocks (Σ) as illustrated in equation 11 and equation 12. The Sum Blocks are the most hardware intensive part of the calculation and are well suited to implementation on FPGA as they can exploit the underlying technology. The architecture of a Sum Block for two 8 bit registers X and Y is illustrated in figure 4.

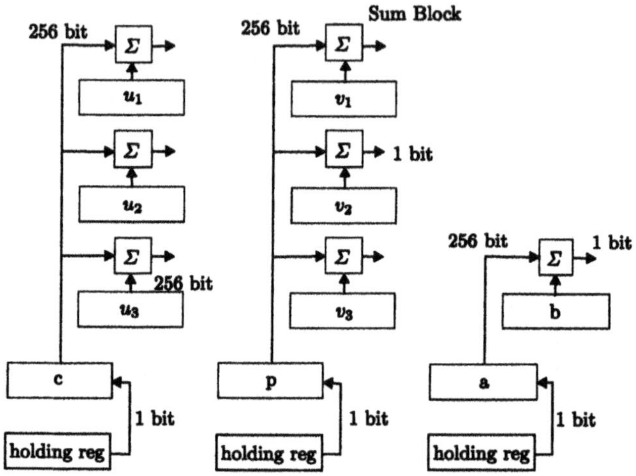

Fig. 3. The ABC coprocessor architecture

In our case with 256 bit registers each Sum Block has 8 levels of logic and represents the longest path delay in the ABC design. Our design contains 7 Sum Blocks.During synthesis one 256 bit Sum Bock is mapped to 68 CLBs. By mapping the logic to both the 4 bit LUTs and the carry XOR gates a sum block is reduced in complexity to only 3 levels of logic and optimizes CLB usage on the device as well as increasing overall performance.

4.3 Eliptic Curve Cryptosystem Using ABC Coprocessor

A schematic of our ECC processor is illustrated in figure 5. The ABC processor was developed in a VHDL environment using the Synopsys FPGA compiler tool and Xilinx Design Manager. The point scalar multiplication operation along with the maping of data to the SRAMS were coded in the C programming language, with the underlying Galois Field arithmetic being performed on the FPGA. Control, and the order of the field are communicated directly to the FPGA. Data is read from the PC in 32 bit blocks into the RC-1000 SRAMS by direct memory mapping. The FPGA then has control of the SRAMS and reads each of p, a, b, c in 128 bit blocks. After calculation the result $u3$ is written back to

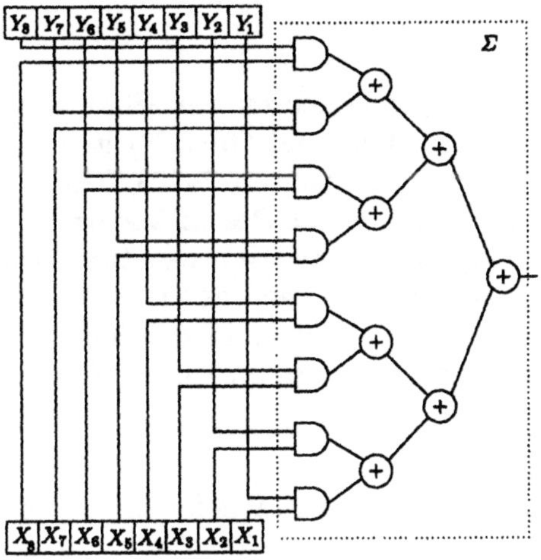

Fig. 4. The Σ Sum Block for 8 bit registers X and Y

the SRAMS, overwriting data c. The PC then has control of the SRAMS and accesses the result.

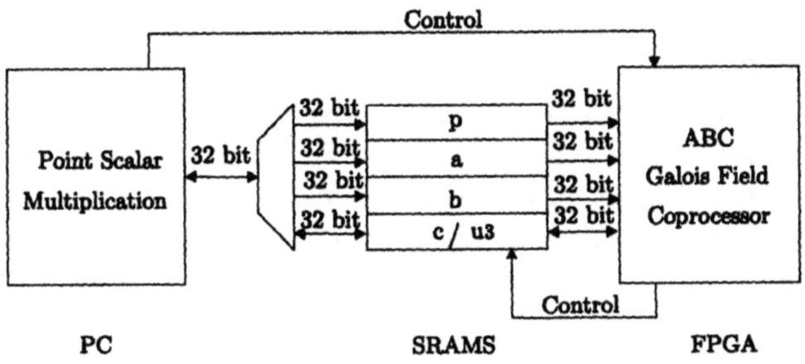

Fig. 5. Elliptic Curve Cryptography Processor

The required Galois Field arithmetic is performed by inputting data from equation 3 - 8 to the processor. For example to perform equation 6, $a := y_1$, $c := x_1$, $b := i$ (where i is the identity element 00...001), and the XOR operation is performed at the PC. In each point addition/doubling the ABC coprocessor is used 3 times. Using equation 1 the number of point doubling operations is approximately m (where m is the order of the field extension) and the number of point additions is approximately $m/2$ (given that the hamming weight of the binary expansion of k is $0.5m$). Thus to perform an elliptic curve point scalar multiplication the ABC processor is accessed approximately $4.5m$ times.

5 Results

The ABC processor was implemented on the Xilinx chip VX2000Bg560-6. For a 256 bit register size (maximum field GF(2^{255}) it was found to occupy 4048 slices, giving an equivalent gate count of 74103. This occupies approximately 20% of the total device. Using Xilinx Design Manager a clock frequency of 40 MHz was achieved for this design. As the access time between the SRAMS and PC is neglible at our data rates [13] and as the PC and FPGA can operate in parallel, an elliptic curve point scalar multiplication is calculated in $9m^2$ clock cycles. Execution times and data rates for various fields are illustrated in table 1.

Table 1. Execution Times and Data Rates for elliptic curve point scalar multiplication

Field Size (bits)	Time (ms)	Data Rate (Kbits/sec)
151	5.1	29.6
176	6.9	25.5
191	8.2	23.3
239	12.8	18.6

Our design performs well in comparison with [11], reporting a similar or decreased calculation time for point scalar multiplication, along with the added advantage that full parameterization is achieved without reconfiguration, for curves over any field up to GF(2^{255}). Reconfiguration time for Virtex Devices is known to be of the order of milliseconds unless dynamic reconfiguration is used [15]. The Galois Field coprocessor circuitry does not depend on the operation it is performing so it should be fully resistant to power analysis attacks. This in conjunction with a suitable method of securing FPGA to PC communications against side channel attacks increases the overall security of the system. By reconfiguration of the FPGA our processor can be expanded to GF(2^{1023}) with a degradation in performance.

6 Conclusions and Further Work

We have presented an implementation of an ECC processor fully parameterizable in the order of the underlying binary field m, the irreducible polynomial used to generate the field $p(x)$ and the elliptic curve used E. FPGA technology was used to perform the most time critical operations and performance compares well with recent implementations. It is well suited to applications where rapid parameterization is required (e.g. SSL servers) and can be included in a larger FPGA cipher library. As operations are carried out in the polynomial basis, basis conversions are not required when interfacing with other systems. We are currently investigating the effects of custom mapping the design to FPGA and moving more of the control logic to hardware. It is expected that these modifications will lead to large improvements in performance.

7 Acknowledgement

This work was carried out as part of an Enterprise Ireland Research Innovation Fund Project.

References

1. V. S. Miller: Use of Elliptic Curves in Cryptography. Advances in Cryptology Crypto'85, Lecture Notes in Computer Science No. 218, Springer-Verlag Berlin, (1985) 417-426.
2. N. Koblitz: Elliptic Curve Cryptosystems. Math Comp Vol. 48, (1987) 203-209.
3. I. Blake, G. Seroussi, N. Smart: Elliptic Curves in Cryptography, London Mathematical Society Lecture Note Series 265, Cambridge University Press (2000).
4. G. B. Agnew, R. C. Mullin, S. A. Vanstone: An implementation of elliptic curve cryptosystems over $F_{2^{155}}$, IEEE Transactions on Selected Areas in Communications. Vol. 11, (1993) 804-813.
5. T. Kerins, E. Popovici, A. Daly, W. Marnane: Hardware Encryption Engines for E-Commerce, Proceesings of Irish Signals and Systems Conference (2002) 89-94.
6. A. Dandalis, V. K. Prasanna: FPGA based cryptography for Internet Security, Online Syposium for Electronic Engineers, Nov 2000.
7. M. Rosner: Elliptic Curve Cryptosystems on Reconfigurable Hardware, Masters Thesis, ECE Dept., Worchester Polytechnic Institute, Worchester USA (1998).
8. P. Gaudry, F. Hess, N. P. Smart: Constructive and Destructive Facets of Weil Descent on Elliptic Curves, Journal of Cryptology, Vol. 15, No.1 (2002) 19-46.
9. D. Hankerson J. L. Hernadez A. Menezes: Software Implementation of Elliptic Curve Cryptography Over Binary fields, Proceeeding of CHES 2000, Lecture Notes in Computer Science, 1965 Springer-Verlag, (2000) 1-24.
10. G. Orlando, C. Paar: A High-Performance Reconfigurable Elliptic Curve Processor for GF(2^m), Proceedings of CHES 2000, Lecture Notes in Computer Science 1965, Springer-Verlag (2000). 41-56
11. K. H. Leung, K. W. Ma K. W. Wong P. H. W. Leong: FPGA implementation of a Microcoded Elliptic Curve Cryptographic Processor: Proceedings of Field Field-Programmable Custom Computing Machines (2000). 68-76
12. E. M. Popovici, P. Fitzpatrick: Algorithm and Architecture for a Galois Field Multiplicative Arithmetic Processor, submitted IEEE Trans on Information Theory Jan 2002.
13. http://www.celoxica.com.
14. http://www.xilinx.com.
15. A. G. Popovici: Reconfigurable Computing, Masters Thesis, National Microelectronics Research Centre, Cork Ireland. (2001).

6.78 Gigabits per Second Implementation of the IDEA Cryptographic Algorithm

Antti Hämäläinen, Matti Tommiska, and Jorma Skyttä

Signal Processing Laboratory
Helsinki University of Technology
Otakaari 5 A
FIN-02150, Finland
{Antti.Hamalainen, Matti.Tommiska, Jorma.Skytta}@hut.fi

Abstract. IDEA (International Data Encryption Algorithm) is one of the strongest secret-key block ciphers. The algorithm processes data in 16-bit subblocks and can be fully pipelined. The implementation of a fully pipelined IDEA algorithm achieves a clock rate of 105.9 MHz on Xilinx' XCV1000E-6BG560 FPGA of the Virtex-E device family. The implementation uses 18105 logic cells and achieves a throughput of 6.78 Gbps with a latency of 132 clock cycles.

1 Introduction

Cryptography is the science of keeping communication secure, so that eavesdroppers cannot decipher the transmitted messages. The transmission speeds of core networks require hardware-based cryptographic modules, since software-based cryptography cannot meet the required throughput requirements.

Field programmable gate arrays (FPGAs) are ideal components for fast cryptographic algorithms. The large capacities of FPGAs enable the fitting of fully pipelined algorithms on a single chip. The reprogrammability of FPGAs enables using the same hardware platform as a cryptographic engine for a multitude of communications protocols.

Cryptographic algorithms are divided into public-key and secret-key algorithms. In public-key algorithms both public and private keys are used, with the private key computed from the public key. Secret-key algorithms rely on secure distribution and management of the session key, which is used for encrypting and decrypting all messages. When it comes to both software- and hardware-based implementations, secret-key algorithms are 100 to 1000 times faster than public-key algorithms. For this reason, dual-key sessions use a secret-key algorithm for the bulk of communication, whereas the session specific secret keys are agreed on and distributed with a public key algorithm.

The International Data Encryption Algorithm (IDEA) was introduced by Lai and Massay in 1990 [1], and modified the following year [2]. IDEA has been patented in the U.S. and several European countries, but the non-commercial use of IDEA is free everywhere. The patent holder was originally Ascom AG,

M. Glesner, P. Zipf, and M. Renovell (Eds.): FPL 2002, LNCS 2438, pp. 760–769, 2002.

but in 1999 the intellectual property rights were transferred to Mediacrypt AG. Part of the fame of IDEA is due to its usage in Pretty Good Privacy (PGP).

IDEA is considered highly secure, and it has resisted all forms of attack tried by the academic community. No published attack (with the exception of attacks on weak keys) is better than exhaustive search on the 128-bit key space, which is computationally infeasible. The security of IDEA appears bounded only by the weaknesses arising from the relatively small (compared to its keylength) blocklength of 64 bits. [3]

Unlike many other cryptographic algorithms, IDEA can easily be implemented on 16-bit microcontrollers, since the algorithm operates on 16-bit subblocks. In 1999, a software-based implementation of four parallel IDEA algorithms (4-way IDEA) achieved a throughput of the order of 72 megabits per second (Mbps) on a 166 MHz MMX Pentium processor [4]. If this result is scaled to modern 2.533 GHz Pentium 4 processors, a software-based implementation of a 4-way IDEA achieves a throughput of 1.1 gigabits per second (1.1 Gbps). This sets a reference point for hardware-based implementations.

There have been several reported hardware implementations of IDEA in the published literature. Mediacrypt AG sells two hardware-based IDEA solutions, the IDEACrypt Coprocessor and the IDEACrypt Kernel. The IDEACrypt kernel is faster of these two and implements the IDEA algorithm with a three-stage pipeline. A 0.25 micron implementation has a throughput of 720 Mbps at a clock rate of 100 MHz. [5]

The Improved IDEA chip by Salomão et al. [6] achieved a throughput of 809 Mbps at a 100 MHz clock rate. If eight of these devices are connected in series, an estimated throughput of 6.5 Gbps can be achieved.

Cheung et al. [7] have investigated the tradeoffs in parallel and serial implementations of the IDEA algorithm. The parallel implementation achieved a throughput of 1.17 Gbps on a Xilinx Virtex XCV300-6 at a clock rate of 82 MHz, whereas the serial implementation achieved a throughput of 600 Mbps on the same device at a clock rate of 150 MHz. When two rounds of the IDEA algorithm were implemented, the parallel implementation required 79.56 per cent of the logic resources of an XCV300-6. The serial implementation of a single round required 93.68 per cent of the logic resources of the same device. It was estimated, that by utilizing linear scaling of the area requirements, a fully pipelined parallel implementation of the IDEA algorithm would fit into a XCV1000 Virtex device with a device utilization of 94.42 per cent. This would correspond to a throughput of 5.25 Gbps, if the clock rate remained unchanged.

2 Description of the IDEA Algorithm

IDEA encrypts 64-bit plaintext blocks into 64-bit ciphertext blocks using a 128-bit input key K. The algorithm consists of eight identical rounds followed by an output transformation. Each round uses six 16-bit subkeys $K_i^{(r)}$, $1 \leq i \leq 6$, to transform a 64-bit input X into an output of four 16-bit blocks, which are then input to the next round. All subkeys are derived from the 128-bit input key K. The subkey derivation process is different in decryption mode from the encryption mode, but otherwise encryption and decryption are performed with identical hardware.

IDEA uses only three operations on 16-bit sub-blocks a and b: bitwise XOR denoted by $\oplus$, unsigned addition mod (2^{16}) denoted by $\boxplus$ and modulo $(2^{16} + 1)$ multiplication, denoted by $\odot$. All these three operations are derived from different algebraic groups of 2^{16} elements, which is crucial to the algorithmic strength of IDEA. Of the three arithmetic operations, bitwise XOR and unsigned addition mod (2^{16}) are trivial to implement, whereas a both area-efficient and fast implementation of modulo $(2^{16} + 1)$ multiplication requires careful design and bit-level optimisation. The IDEA computation path is described in Fig. 1.

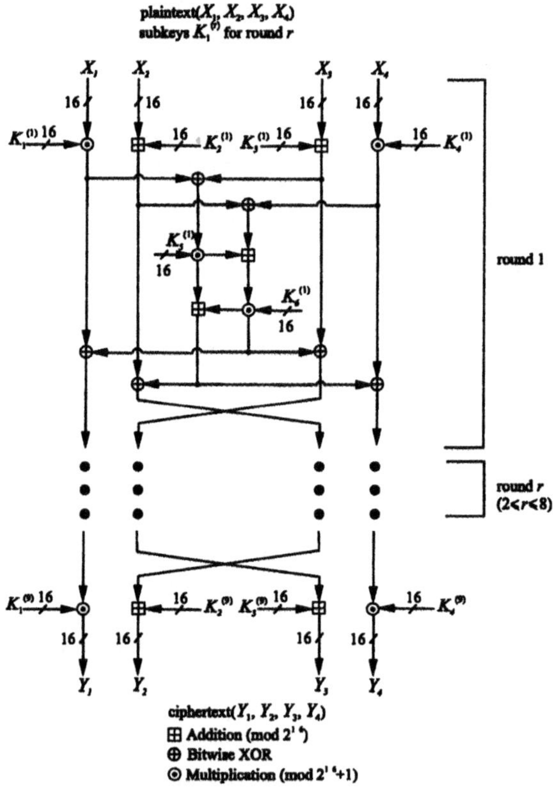

Fig. 1. The IDEA cryptographic algorithm

Except for key scheduling, the IDEA algorithm is defined as follows: [3]

INPUT: 64-bit plaintext $M = m_1...m_{64}$; 128-bit key $K = k_1...k_{128}$.
OUTPUT: 64-bit ciphertext block $Y = (Y_1, Y_2, Y_3, Y_4)$.

1. (Key schedule) Compute 16-bit subkeys $K_1^{(r)}, ..., K_6^{(r)}$ for rounds $1 \leq r \leq 8$, and $K_1^{(9)}, \ldots, K_4^{(9)}$ for the output transformation.

2. $(X_1, X_2, X_3, X_4) \leftarrow (m_1 \ldots m_{16}, m_{17} \ldots m_{32}, m_{33} \ldots m_{48}, m_{49} \ldots m_{64})$, where X_i is a 16-bit data store.
3. For round r from 1 to 8 do:
   (a) $X_1 \leftarrow X_1 \odot K_1^{(r)}$, $X_4 \leftarrow X_4 \odot K_4^{(r)}$, $X_2 \leftarrow X_2 \boxplus K_2^{(r)}$, $X_3 \leftarrow X_3 \boxplus K_3^{(r)}$.
   (b) $t_0 \leftarrow K_5^{(r)} \odot (X_1 \oplus X_3), t_1 \leftarrow K_6^{(r)} \odot (t_0 \boxplus (X_2 \oplus X_4)), t_2 \leftarrow t_0 \boxplus t_1$.
   (c) $X_1 \leftarrow X_1 \oplus t_1, X_4 \leftarrow X_4 \oplus t_2, a \leftarrow X_2 \oplus t_2, X_2 \leftarrow X_3 \oplus t_1, X_3 \leftarrow a$.
4. (Output transformation) $Y_1 \leftarrow X_1 \odot K_1^{(9)}, Y_4 \leftarrow X_4 \odot K_4^{(9)}, Y_2 \leftarrow X_3 \boxplus K_2^{(9)}, Y_3 \leftarrow X_2 \boxplus K_3^{(9)}$.

In IDEA, $a \odot b$ corresponds to modulo $(2^{16}+1)$ multiplication of two unsigned 16-bit integers a and b, where $0 \in \mathbb{Z}_{2^{16}}$ is associated with $2^{16} \in \mathbb{Z}_{2^{16}+1}$as follows: if $a = 0$ or $b = 0$, replace it by 2^{16} (which is $\equiv -1 \bmod (2^{16}+1)$) prior to modular multiplication; and if the result is 2^{16}, replace this by 0. Decryption is achieved with the ciphertext Y provided as input M. Key scheduling is described in standard textbooks on cryptography [3] [8], and its hardware requirements are negligible when compared to modulo $(2^{16}+1)$ multipliers.

2.1 Diminished-One Number Representation

The diminished-one number representation is often used in arithmetic modulo (2^n+1) [9]. In diminished-one number system the number A is represented by $A' = A - 1$ and the value 0 is represented by 2^n. In IDEA, $n = 16$, and consequentially, the value 0x0000 as a 16-bit unsigned integer is represented by 0x10000 in diminished-one representation.

The usage of diminished-one number system is advantageous in the implementation of modulo $(2^{16}+1)$ multipliers. There are also downsides in using the diminished-one number system: additional logic is required in adding up partial products and conversions are required to/from ordinary 16-bit unsigned integers. However, the advantages of using the diminished-one number system outweigh the disadvantages in the design described in this paper.

3 Design and Implementation

With the introduction of million-gate FPGAs, the implementation of fully unrolled secret-key cryptographic algorithms became feasible. If the entire algorithm with full inner and outer loop pipelining fits on a single FPGA, the limiting factor for throughput is the achieved clock rate as follows: [10]

$$\textit{Throughput} = \textit{block\_size} \times \textit{clock\_rate} \tag{1}$$

Since the block size of IDEA is fixed at 64 bits, a 100 MHz clock rate implies a throughput of 6.4 Gbps. Clock rates above 100 MHz can be achieved in modern FPGAs by carefully analysing the algorithm, partitioning the design into stages and pipelining the entire system. The disadvantage is increased latency measured in clock cycles, but this can usually be tolerated, since throughput is the dominant design factor in high-speed applications. The high-level block diagram of the fully pipelined IDEA implementation is described in Fig. 2

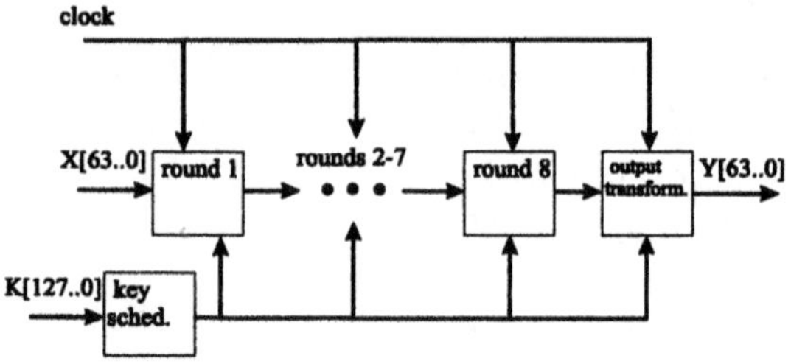

Fig. 2. Fully pipelined IDEA algorithm

A fully unrolled round of the IDEA algorithm is described in Fig. 3, which can be compared with Fig. 1. There are seven subrounds in one round, and the modulo $(2^{16}+1)$ multiplier is further divided into four sub-subrounds (See 3.2). A single round is calculated in 16 clock cycles, since three subrounds (1, 3, and 5) with modulo $(2^{16}+1)$ multipliers each require four clock cycles and four subrounds (2, 4, 6 and 7) are executed in a single clock cycle. After the 8th round, $8 \times 16 = 128$ clock cycles have been used. The final output transformation requires additional four clock cycles, since two modulo $(2^{16}+1)$ multiplication operations are executed in parallel. This adds up to a total latency of 132 clock cycles, which corresponds to 1.246 μs with the maximum clock rate of 105.9 MHz (See also Table 3).

3.1 Design Flows

The design was initially going to be implemented only in Handel-C [11], a high-level hardware description language with built-in directives for implementing parallelism in hardware. The design flow consisted of Celoxica's DK1 Design Suite v1.0 SP1, which produced a structural VHDL output file for logic synthesis with Synplicity's Synplify Pro 7.0 and subsequent place and route with Xilinx' ISE Foundation Series 4.1i.

A single round of the IDEA algorithm was coded in Handel-C, with the clock rate exceeding 80 MHz. However, as individual rounds were connected together, the performance of the overall design decelerated and the area requirements of the entire design increased in a non-linear manner for unknown reasons. Furthermore, compilation times exceeded ten hours, which made it impractical to improve the design within a single working day.

To achieve a clock rate of at least 100 MHz, it was decided to recode the entire design in synthesisable VHDL with Synplify Pro 7.0. Investigating the critical path revealed that the carry-save adder (CSA) structure (See 3.2) [12] was the most time-consuming part. The CSA structure was replaced with a simple three-stage adder tree, which both reduced area and increased the clock rate over the

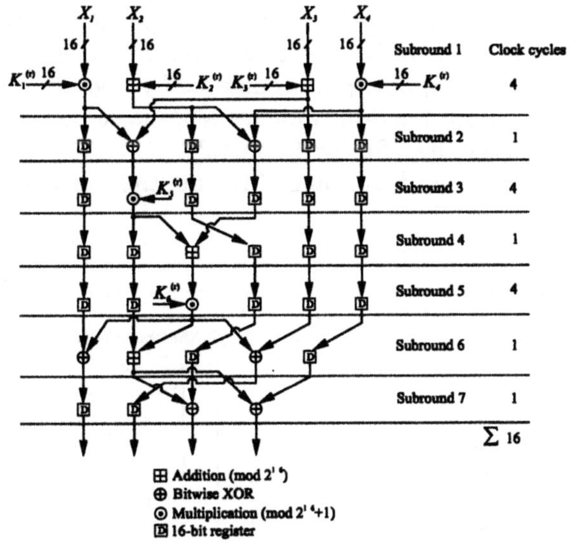

Fig. 3. A fully unrolled round of the IDEA algorithm

targeted 100 MHz. When the design was targeted for XCV1000E-6BG560, a clock rate of 105.9 MHz was achieved with 18105 logic cells (LCs).

The design flows are compared in Table 1 with further details in Table 3.

Table 1. A comparison of the two design flows. Note that the implementation of modulo $(2^{16}+1)$ multiplier was coded in different manner in Handel-C and VHDL.

Main Design Tool	Language	Other Tools	Performance of one round	Entire IDEA algorithm	Additional information
DK1 Design Suite	Handel-C	Synplify Pro 7.0 ISE 4.1i ModelSim	87.3 MHz 2902 LCs XCV1000E-6	13h compilation did not fit into an XCV2000E-6	CSA Array (See 3.2)
Synplify Pro 7.0	VHDL	ISE 4.1i ModelSim	105.9 MHz 2122 LCs XCV1000E-6	105.9 MHz 18105 LCs XCV1000E-6	Three-stage adder tree (See 3.2)

3.2 Modulo $(2^{16}+1)$ Multiplication

The critical part of an efficient hardware implementation of IDEA is the modulo $(2^{16}+1)$ multiplication operator. There has been a lot of academic activity in researching an optimum implementation of the modulo $(2^{16}+1)$ multiplier [12], [13], [14], but the research has been limited to full-custom design.

The partial product generation proposed by Ma [12] was used. The inputs to the partial product generation logic are 16-bit unsigned integers a and d in diminished-one representation. Since the second input d is always a subkey, it can be converted in advance in the key scheduling block. After simplifications, the eight partial products $p_0, \ldots, p_7$ are generated by a set of eight 8-to-1 multiplexers, whose control input is a 3-bit wide sequence from the subkey. Additional combinational logic is required for cyclic modulo left shifts, but the design fits into little over 200 logic cells. An outline of the multiplexer bank is presented in Fig. 4.

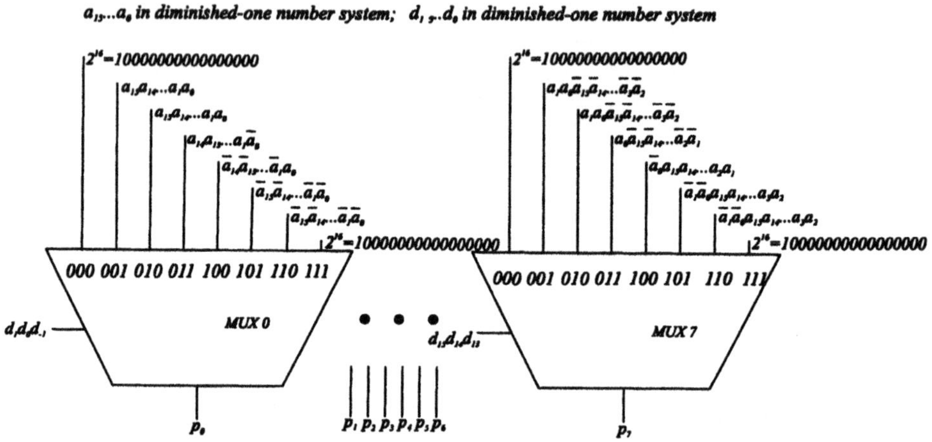

Fig. 4. An outline of the multiplexer bank. The outputs are eight partial products $p_0 \ldots p_7$ in diminished-one notation.

The produced partial products $p_0, \ldots, p_7$ are 17 bits wide, since zero is represented by 0x10000 in diminished-one number representation. To obtain the multiplication result, the partial products have to be summed together.

The CSA structure in [12] was coded in Handel-C, whereas a simpler three-stage adder tree was coded in synthesisable VHDL (See 3.1). It was noted, that the three-stage adder tree required fewer logic resources in the targeted devices of the Virtex-E family. CSA structures do not save area resources in FPGAs, but require more area resources than a straightforward implementation of the partial products summation. This is due to the efficient implementation of fast look-ahead carry logic chains in modern FPGAs, which leaves no practical room for optimisation of adder structures.

When adding two numbers a and b represented in diminished-one notation, attention must be given to the special case of zero. If zero is not used, addition in diminished-one number system looks as follows: [13]

$$(a+b+1) \bmod (2^n+1) = \begin{cases} (a+b) \bmod 2^n, & \text{if } a+b \geq 2^n \\ a+b+1, & \text{otherwise} \end{cases} \tag{2}$$

Modulo (2^n+1) addition can be realised by an end-around-carry adder, where the carry-out is inverted and fed back into the carry-in, i.e. $c_{in} = \overline{c_{out}}$.

This can be realized with two adders to prevent a combinational loop. The carry-out inversion logic does not work when both summands equal zero. Therefore an additional AND gate has to be added to produce the control input for a multiplexer, which selects the correct output $a + b = \text{0x10000}$, when $a = b = \text{0x10000}$. There are seven modulo $(2^n + 1)$ adders to sum up the eight partial products. This is described in detail in Fig. 5

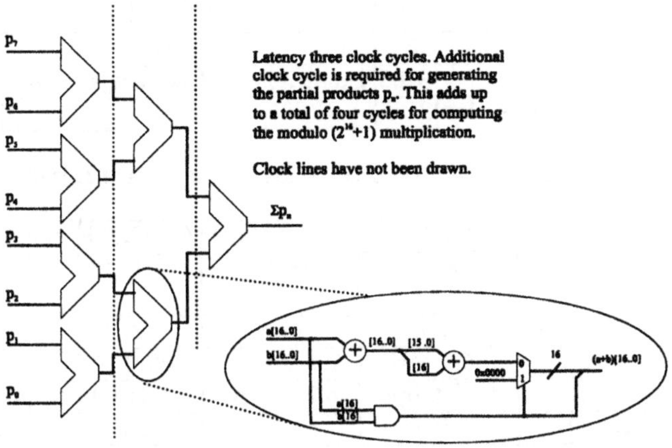

Fig. 5. The three-stage diminished-one adder tree used in IDEA implementation. The inner structure of a diminished-one adder includes extra control logic for the output multiplexer.

3.3 Results

The logic cell (LC) requirements of the seven subrounds (See Fig. 3) are summarized in Table 2. About 93 per cent of the area requirements of a single round are caused by modulo $(2^{16} + 1)$ multipliers implemented with a simple three-stage adder tree (See Fig. 5).

As mentioned, the two implementations of the modulo $(2^{16} + 1)$ multiplier differ in their area requirements, because a straightforward implementation of the three-level adder tree fits into a much smaller number of LCs than a more sophisticated CSA design (See also 3.2). A single modulo $(2^{16} + 1)$ multiplier implemented in Handel-C utilizing the CSA scheme [12] required 919 LCs compared to 463 LCs for the simpler VHDL-based multiplier.

To compare the results with those projected in [7], the VHDL-based design was targeted for an XCV1000E-6 device, and the area and timing characteristics are presented in Table 3. For comparison purposes, the design was compiled for certain Altera FPGAs, but these results must be viewed with caution, since no device-specific optimisations were made.

To verify the design in hardware, the IDEA algorithm was targeted for Xilinx' XCV2000E-6BG560 device on an RC1000 PCI card [15]. Logic synthesis with

Table 2. The area requirements of a single IDEA round in an XCV1000E-6.

Subround	LCs	Additional Information
1	969	2 multipliers, 2 adders
2	32	2 XORs
3	533	1 multiplier
4	16	1 adder
5	533	1 multiplier
6	48	2 XORs, 1 adder
7	32	2 XORs
Total	2163	4 multipliers, 4 adders, 6 XORs
After minimisation	2125	

Table 3. Timing and area characteristics of the entire IDEA algorithm.

	XCV1000E-6	XCV2000E-6	APEX20KC-8	EP2A40-8
LCs (Xilinx) ATOMs (Altera)	18105	18233	37289	37413
Device Utilisation	73 %	45 %	71 %	97%
Clock rate	105.9 MHz	105.9 MHz	32.0 MHz	66.2 MHz
Throughput	6.78 Gbps	6.78 Gbps	2.05 Gbps	4.24 Gbps
Latency (132 cycles)	1.25μs	1.25μs	4.13μs	1.99μs

Synplify Pro 7.0 and place and route with Xilinx' ISE Foundation Series 4.1i reported the same maximum clock rate of 105.9 MHz (See Table 3).

The RC1000 card has a programmable clock circuit with a maximum frequency of 100 MHz. The design fit into 45 per cent of the logic resources of an XCV2000E, and the functionality was verified with test vectors and with varying clock rates. Since the maximum clock frequency was 100 MHz, the functionality could not quite be tested at the reported maximum clock rate of 105.9 MHz.

4 Conclusions

The design and implementation of the IDEA algorithm at 6.78 Gbps on a single XCV1000E-6BG560 proves that entire unrolled and pipelined complex cryptographic functions can be implemented on a single FPGA. The limiting factors in achieving maximal throughput are the block size of the algorithm and the clock rate, which can be increased by carefully analysing the algorithm and partitioning the individual operations into subblocks executed in a single clock cycle.

An FPGA-based cryptographic module is a strong candidate, when high-performance cryptography is required. Applications include Virtual Private Networks (VPNs), satellite communications and hardware accelerators for encrypting huge files or entire disks.

An interesting research area is partial reprogrammability applied to cryptography. This is especially true for algorithms, which process data in small-sized blocks, whose other input is directly computed from the session key. IDEA is an example of this kind of an algorithm. Xilinx' Virtex FPGAs support partial run-time reconfiguration [16], and the area requirements of IDEA could be reduced by precalculating the optimum implementation for modulo $(2^{16}+1)$ multiplication for every 65536 subkeys. When a session key is changed, the device would be partially reconfigured with optimal modular multipliers.

References

1. X. Lai and J. L. Massey. "A proposal for a new block encryption standard", *Advances in Cryptology – EUROCRYPT 90*, volume 473 of *Lecture Notes in Computer Science*, Springer-Verlag, pp. 389–404.
2. X. Lai, J. L. Massey and S. Murphy "Markov ciphers and differential cryptanalysis", *Advances in Cryptology – EUROCRYPT 91*, pp. 17–38.
3. A.J. Menezes, PC. van Oorschot, S.A. Vanstone: *"Handbook of Applied Cryptography"*, CRC Press Ltd., 1997, pp. 263–266.
4. H Lipmaa. "IDEA: A Cipher for Multimedia Architectures?" *Selected Areas in Cryptography '98*, volume 1556 of *Lecture Notes in Computer Science*, Springer-Verlag, pp. 253–268.
5. IDEACrypt Kernel, http://www.mediacrypt.com/engl/Content/cryptkernel.htm
6. S.L.C. Salomão, J.M.S. Alcântara, V.C. Alves, F.M.G. Franca: "Improved IDEA", *Proceedings of the 13th Brazilian Symposium on Integrated Circuits and System Design - SBCCI 2000*, September 2000, Manaus, Brazil, pp. 47–52.
7. O.Y.H. Cheung, K.H. Tsoi, P.H.W. Leong, M.P. Leong, "Tradeoffs in Parallel and Serial Implementations of the International Data Encryption Algorithm IDEA", *Proceedings of the Third International Workshop on Cryptographic Hardware and Embedded Systems*, May 14–16, 2001, Paris, France, pp. 333–347.
8. B. Schneier: *"Applied Cryptography"*, John Wiley & Sons, 1996, pp. 319–324.
9. L.M. Leibowitz: "A Simplified Binary Arithmetic for the Fermat Number Transform", *IEEE Transactions on Acoustics, Speech and Signal Processing*, Vol. 24, No. 5, October 1976, pp. 356–359.
10. P. Chodowiec, P. Khuon, K. Gaj: "Fast Implementations of Secret-Key Block Ciphers Using Mixed Inner- and Outer-Round Pipelining", *Proceedings of the ACM/SIGDA Ninth International Symposium on Field Programmable Gate Arrays*, February 11-13, 2001, Monterey, California, USA, pp. 94–102.
11. *"Handel-C Language Reference Manual, Version 2.1"*, Celoxica Ltd., 2001
12. Y. Ma: "A Simplified Architecture for Modulo (2^n+1) Multiplication", *IEEE Transactions on Computers*, Vol. 47, No. 3, March 1998, pp. 333–337
13. R. Zimmermann: "Efficient VLSI Implementation of Modulo $(2^n \pm 1)$ Addition and Multiplication", *Proceedings of the 14th IEEE Symposium on Computer Arithmetic*, April 1999, Adelaide, Australia, pp. 158–167.
14. A. Curiger, H. Bonnenberg, H. Kaeslin: "Regular VLSI Architectures for Multiplication Modulo (2^n+1)", *IEEE Journal of Solid-state Circuits*, Vol. 26, No. 7, July 1991, pp. 990–994.
15. RC1000 Data Sheet, Celoxica RC1000, http://www.celoxica.com/products /technical_papers/datasheets/DATRHD002_0.pdf
16. Virtex Series Configuration Architecture User Guide, XAPP151 (v1.5), Xilinx Inc.

Rijndael Cryptographic Engine on the UltraSONIC Reconfigurable Platform

Emmanuel A. Moreira, Paul L. McAlpine, Simon D. Haynes

Sony Broadcast & Professional Research Labs, Basingstoke, Hampshire, UK
{emmanuel.moreira, paul.mcapline, simon.haynes}@adv.sonybpe.com

Abstract. This paper describes a high performance implementation of the Rijndael encryption algorithm using the UltraSONIC reconfigurable platform. We show how the UltraSONIC design methodology allowed us to develop a complete hardware/software solution in a matter of weeks. Reconfiguration is exploited to maximise the use of the available hardware resources. A modular implementation allows the trade off of encryption security against hardware resources. The flexibility of the UltraSONIC architecture allows a single implementation to process data from either the host computer or external real-time video sources. We are able to meet the requirements for processing high definition in real-time, achieving a throughput of 2.1 Gbit/sec. In software acceleration mode we are able to achieve more than 4 times speed up compared with a 1GHz Pentium III system.

1 Introduction

In the broadcast environment the creation, storage, and distribution of content is now almost entirely digital. With such high value content, some of the key benefits of digitally stored data –ease of distribution and loss-less copying– can become a major weakness. It is increasingly necessary to protect content in a highly secure manner.

There is a general trend of moving from custom hardware solutions towards more flexible computer based systems. Computers bring with them there own set of content piracy risks requiring the secure protection of data. Any solution should encrypt data stored on computers as easily as video data on more conventional storage media.

The Rijndael Algorithm, developed by Joan Daemen and Vincent Rijmen [1], has been chosen by the US National Security Agency (NSA) to become the Advanced Encryption Standard (AES), replacing the Data Encryption Standard (DES).

The Rijndael encryption scheme is expected to be robust against all known attacks but has also been designed to be fast and easy to implement in hardware [2]. It is not possible to implement it in software at anywhere approaching real-time rates for video, without reducing the key length, which severely compromises data security. An additional drawback to a software solution for encryption of data from external sources is the time taken to transfer the data to and from the computer.

UltraSONIC is a reconfigurable platform, developed at Sony Broadcast & Professional Research Labs. It is designed for rapid development and deployment of solutions to process real-time high and standard definition video. It is based on the

M. Glesner, P. Zipf, and M. Renovell (Eds.): FPL 2002, LNCS 2438, pp. 770-779, 2002.

earlier SONIC architecture [3]. It is a PCI plug-in card well suited to an environment where data is interchanged between computers and video hardware. The UltraSONIC architecture allows the design of the processing hardware to be independent of whether the data comes from external sources (such as VTRs) or from the host computer.

Other efficient FPGA based solutions have been suggested [4], but our aim is to demonstrate that it is possible to rapidly develop a solution based on generic reconfigurable hardware, without designing a custom platform.

2 The Rijndael Algorithm

The Rijndael algorithm takes plaintext (P) and transforms it into encrypted test (E) using a key (K). The algorithm operates by dividing the plain text into a number of blocks consisting of an array of bytes. The standard for the Rijndael algorithm specifies three possible lengths for the input blocks and the keys; 128,192 and 256 bits. This implementation encrypts 128 bit words using 128 bits keys.

The Rijndael algorithm can be decomposed into a number of rounds. Each round involves operations on these arrays of bytes such as substitutions, rows or columns manipulations and key (K) addition on this array. The rounds are not all exactly identical but they all have the general form shown in Fig. 1. Decryption rounds (Rd) are similar to encryption rounds (Re), but uses the inverse functions InvBS, InvSR and InvMC. For a detailed description of the Rijndael algorithm see [1].

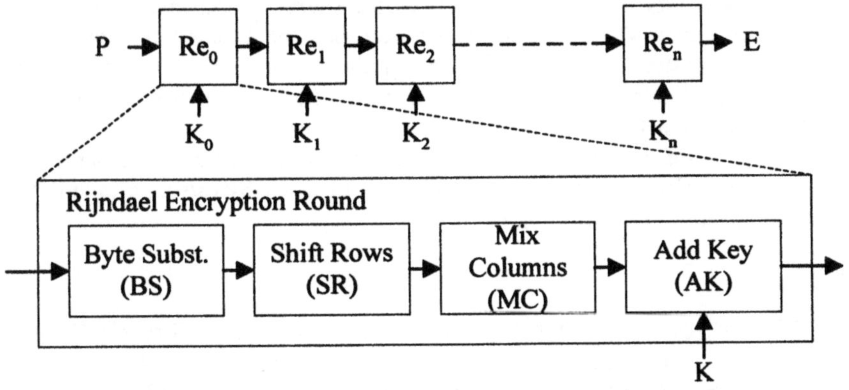

Fig. 1. The Rijndael encryption algorithm for n rounds. The Plaintext (P) is encrypted to produce the encrypted text (E). For each round a different key (K) is used.

One of the strong advantages of the Rijndael algorithm is that it can be implemented efficiently in hardware. Hardware resources can be traded off against performance by using an iterative or pipelined solution.

3 The UltraSONIC Platform

The UltraSONIC platform is shown in Fig. 2. It consists of up to 16 Plug-In Processing Elements (PIPEs) connected by PIPEflow buses and a PIPE bus. The PIPEs contain hardware for processing and/or interfacing to external hardware.

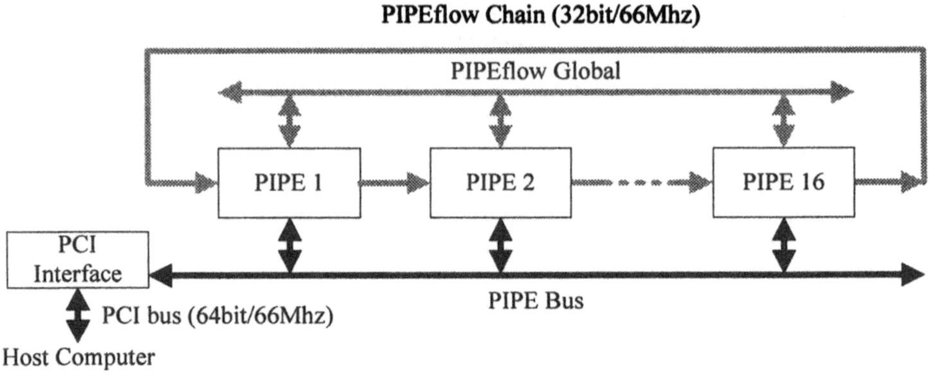

Fig. 2. The UltraSONIC Architecture; the PIPEflow buses are used for the transport of real-time video. The PIPEBus interfaces the PIPEs to the Host Computer using a 64bit/ 66Mhz PCI bus.

3.1 Bus Architecture

The UltraSONIC bus architecture consists of a shared global bus combined with a flexible pipeline bus. The PIPE bus is a global bus for transfer of data between the host computer and the PIPEs, matching the bandwidth of the PCI bus (528Mbyte/sec). The system uses this bus for fast transfer of video and control data (such as the keys for the Rijndael algorithm).

The PIPEflow buses are used for the synchronous transfer of video between PIPEs in a raster-scan fashion. They have a bandwidth of 264Mbytes/sec, allowing the real-time transfer of high-definition video.

3.2 PIPEs

The PIPEs are responsible for two main functions in the UltraSONIC platform: *Processing* and *I/O*. Processing PIPEs contain hardware used to implement the required algorithms (the Rijndael rounds in this case). For this application the type of processing PIPE used is called an *UltraPIPE*. I/O PIPEs allow the UltraSONIC platform to interface to external hardware.

UltraPIPEs
The architecture of the UltraPIPE processing PIPE is shown in Fig. 3. It consists of three conceptual elements: the PIPE engine, PIPE router, and PIPE memory.

The PIPE engine, implemented using a Xilinx Virtex 1000E, is responsible for implementing the required algorithm. The PIPE memory is used to store images and/or other data.

The PIPE router provides a number of fixed functions that allow the design of the PIPE engine to be abstracted from the low-level hardware details. The PIPE router can provide image data to the PIPE engine from any of the PIPEflow buses or from an image held in the PIPE memory; this enables an algorithm to operate in the same way regardless of whether the data comes from the computer (software acceleration) or from an I/O PIPE (real-time processing).

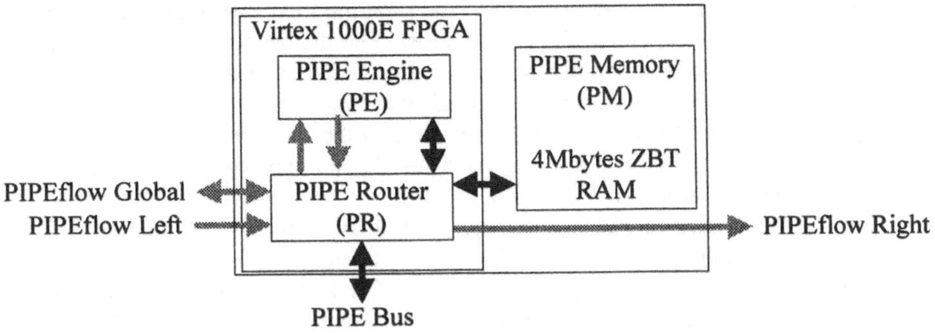

Fig. 3. Architecture of the UltraPIPE. The PIPE engine implements the algorithm, the PIPE Memory acts as an image store, and the PIPE router formats and moves the data.

SDI I/O PIPEs

Serial Digital Interface (SDI) is widely used in the professional broadcast industry for transporting video and audio data. SDI I/O PIPEs are similar to UltraPIPEs, but are used to interface video and audio data to or from external SDI equipment, such as VTRs or cameras. The architecture of the SDI PIPE is shown in Fig. 4.

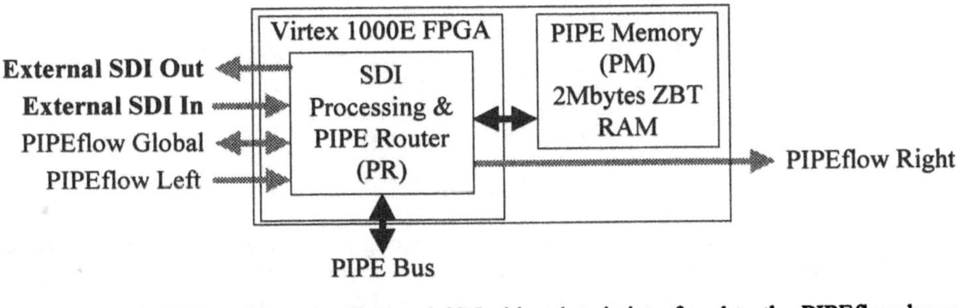

Fig. 4. SDI I/O PIPE architecture. External SDI video data is interfaced to the PIPEflow buses using the FPGA

3.3 UltraSONIC Application Program Interface (API)

The UltraSONIC platform has a powerful, yet easy to use, Application Program Interface (API). The API contains functions that allow a programmer to communicate with UltraSONIC. Functionality includes; performing data transfer between the PIPEs and the host computer, configuration of PIPEs, and reading and writing of data to and from PIPE registers.

4 Implementation of the Rijndael Algorithm

The UltraSONIC platform is well suited to the pipelined Rijndael algorithm shown in Fig. 1, because of the pipelined PIPEflow buses. The design strategy was to create a single PIPE engine design implementing as many rounds as possible. The PIPEflow buses were used to chain these designs together to increase the number of rounds: In this way, the number of PIPE modules used dictates the number of rounds that can be implemented. The Rijndael algorithm specifies the number of rounds and keys to apply depending of the size of P and (K_0, ... , K_n).

The PIPE bus is used to transfer the keys to the PIPE Engine from the host PC. The intended application determines how often the keys change.

There are two alternative designs for the PIPE Engine. The basic design can perform either encryption or decryption. An improved design takes advantage of reconfiguration to improve the performance by a factor of two.

Static Design
The static design, shown in Fig. 5, is a single design that can perform either encryption or decryption. In this case 6 PIPEs are required, each one capable of performing 2 rounds of Re or Rd. Each PIPE requires two keys. A register on the PIPE engine controls whether encryption or decryption is performed.

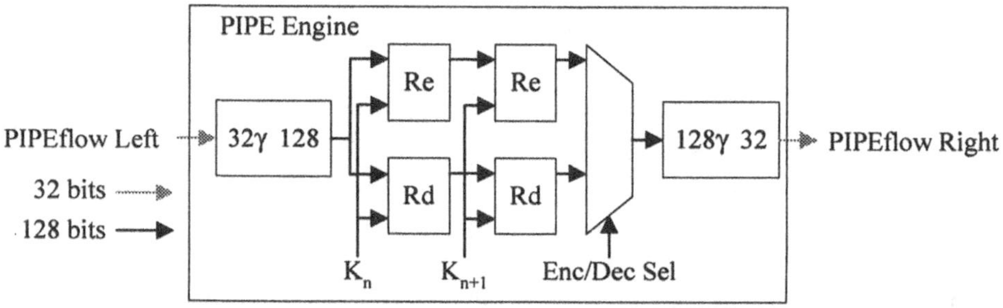

Fig. 5. The static design for a PIPE engine implementing the Rijndael algorithm. The design can either perform encryption (using the Re's) or decryption (using the Rd's). It is not necessary to reconfigure the PIPE between encryption and decryption.

Dynamic Design
The dynamic design requires *two* designs; one performing encryption, the other decryption. These are shown in Fig. 6. For dynamic configuration only 3 PIPEs are required, each one capable of performing 4 rounds of Re or Rd. The FPGA on the PIPE is reconfigured to switch between encryption and decryption.

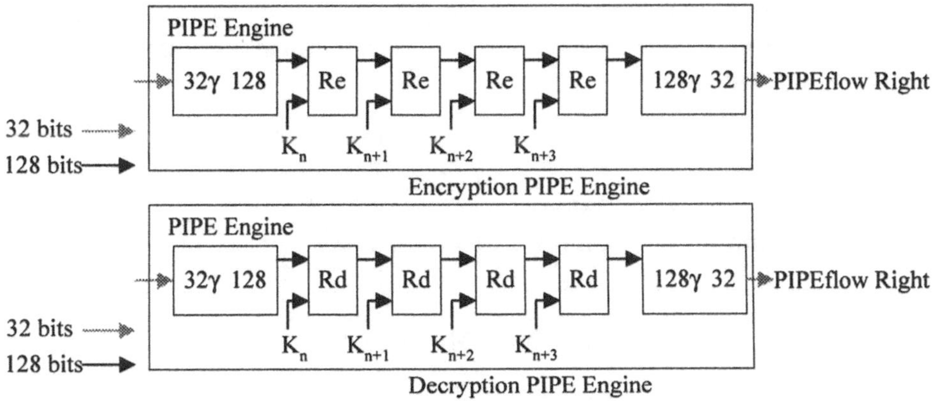

Fig. 6. The dynamic design for the PIPE engine. One design performs encryption, the other decryption. It is necessary to reconfigure the PIPE engine to switch between encryption and decryption.

5 Test Applications

Two modes were tested: a 'real-time' mode, and a 'software acceleration' mode. In the software acceleration mode both the source and target are host computer's disk storage: the data is taken from the hard drive, processed by the UltraSONIC, and then stored on the hard drive again. In the real-time mode the source stream is fed to UltraSONIC via SDI input PIPE (Fig. 7) Then, after it has been processed, the data is streamed out via SDI output PIPE. The same hardware design can be used for both these modes of operation because of the versatility of the UltraSONIC architecture.

5.1 Real-Time Video Encryption and Decryption

When the Rijndael cryptographic engine is used with real-time video, the data flow is entirely within UltraSONIC; no intervention from the host computer is required. The video data is transferred between PIPEs using UltraSONIC's PIPEflow buses. SDI PIPEs are used to interface the external video. The physical configuration of UltraSONIC is presented in Fig. 7. 5 PIPEs are used in total: 2 SDI PIPEs and 3 UltraPIPEs.

The system shown in Fig. 7 can be dynamically configured for either real-time Rijndael encryption or decryption by reprogramming the FPGAs on the UltraPIPEs. In the encryption mode, the 'Video In' signal contains non-encrypted video data. The input SDI PIPE (SDI PIPE 1) extracts the video payload, and transfers it to the first processing PIPE (UltraPIPE 1) using the appropriate PIPEflow bus. The PIPE router of UltraPIPE 1 routes the video data to the PIPE Engine where the first four rounds of encryption are applied. The data is then passed on to the PIPE engines of UltraPIPE 2 and 3 where a further eight rounds of encryption are applied. The resultant encrypted video is then transferred to the output SDI PIPE (SDI PIPE 2), where it is converted to an SDI signal and streamed out. It is worth noticing that although 'SDI PIPE 1' and

'SDI PIPE 2' perform two different functions, they are both the same type of PIPE but with different FPGA configurations. This, again, demonstrates the flexibility of UltraSONIC's architecture.

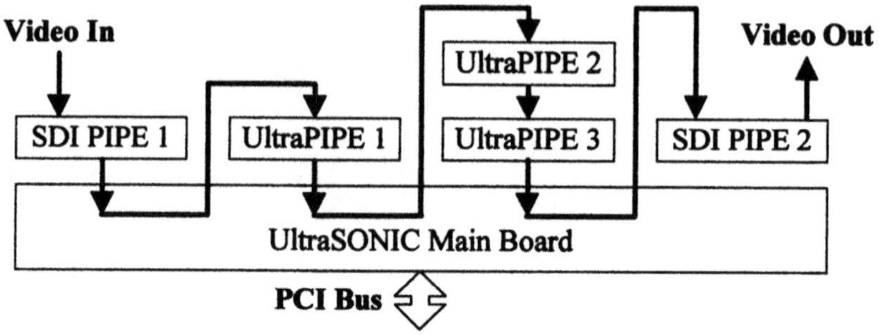

Fig. 7. Physical configuration of the UltraSONIC board for the encryption and decryption of real-time video.

The FPGAs on each UltraPIPE are capable of encrypting or decrypting of up to 4 Rijndael rounds each. The proposed system is therefore capable of up to 12-round encryption or decryption. Higher round count enables stronger encryption. Since it is possible to activate and deactivate each single round in the PIPE Engine design, it is possible to vary the strength of encryption using software in real time. What's more – the key for each round can also be altered in real time – which implies that encryption key can be changed on frame-by-frame basis, if necessary. This offers unparalleled flexibility for broadcasters.

In order to test the speed and effectiveness of the encryption and decryption process, the setup in Fig. 8 was used.

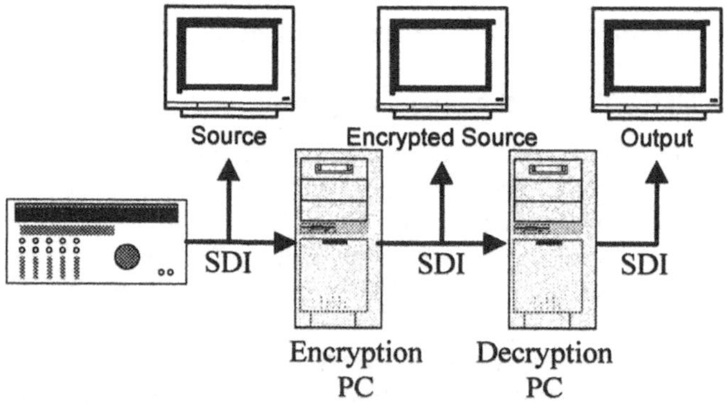

Fig. 8. Test setup for encryption and decryption of real-time video.

Two separate PCs were used. Both used the same UltraSONIC system configuration (as depicted in Fig. 7). The UltraPIPEs in the encryption PC were configured to perform encryption, while in the decryption PC they were configured to perform decryption – with the same strength and reversed keys. The source SDI signal produced by VTR was fed into UltraSONIC in the encryption PC. The encrypted SDI signal was then passed to the UltraSONIC in the decryption PC, where the video was decrypted to provide the original source. Three monitors were attached to observe the process.

5.2 Software Acceleration

The same UltraSONIC system configuration was used for software acceleration as for real-time mode; however the two SDI PIPEs were not used. Instead the data (a sequence of frames) was sourced from the hard drive, passed through the chain of UltraPIPEs, and then stored back again on the hard drive. Fig 8 shows the data flow in this case.

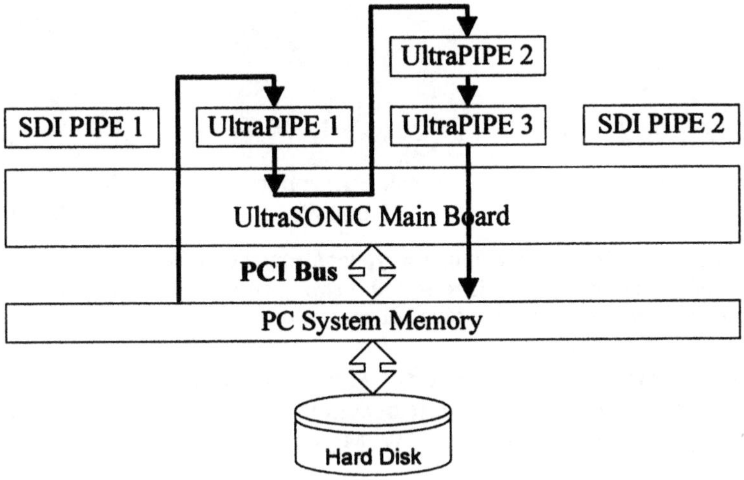

Fig. 9. Physical setup for the software acceleration mode of operation for the Rijndael engine on UltraSONIC.

The software acceleration mode was designed to measure the rate at which raw image data could be streamed out, encrypted/decrypted, and then stored back on the hard drive. Images were read from the disk to a contiguous buffer in the system memory. Then they were transferred to local memory of UltraPIPE 1 via the PCI bus, and streamed through to the local memory of UltraPIPE 3 – much in the same way as the real-time mode described earlier (i.e. using PIPEflow). It is worth noting that PIPE memory of 'UltraPIPE 1' and 'UltraPIPE 3' were used (unlike the real-time example). Although the source of data was different here (i.e. local PIPE memory, rather than input from SDI PIPE) – there was no need to reprogram the logic on FPGAs – due to versatility of the PIPE router.

6 Results

Tests both in real-time and software acceleration modes were carried out. In both cases a 1Ghz Pentium III system with 256Mbytes of RAM was used. In the real-time mode we were able to restore the original signal at the output. We were also able to monitor the strength of encryption on the encrypted source. The results of strong versus weak encryption can be seen in Fig. 10. The design was thoroughly tested using many different Rijndael keys. The throughput in real-time mode was a sustainable 2.1 Gbit/sec allowing real-time encryption and decryption of HD-quality raw video bitstream. Throughput is limited by the bandwidth of the PIPEflow buses, without this constraint 8.4 Gbit/sec is possible.

The sustainable throughput in software acceleration mode was 436Mbit/sec. The limiting factor in this mode was the bandwidth available to stream the data to and from the hard drive. Even so, this throughput corresponds to more than four times the rate at which the host computer could perform the same operation.

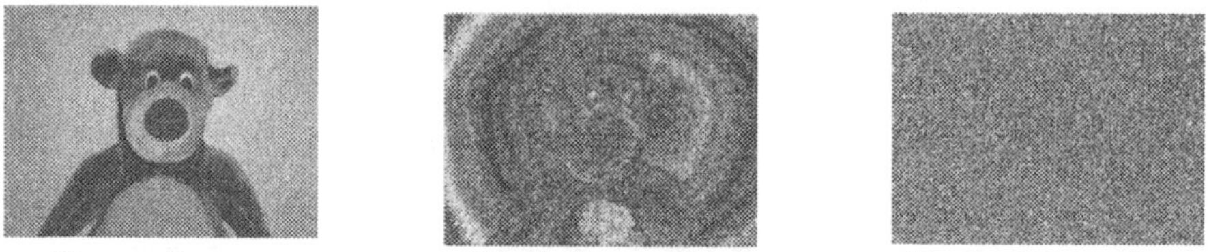

Source Image | Weak Encryption (1 round) | Strong Encryption (10 rounds)

Fig. 10. The results from the real-time encryption/decryption of video. It clearly illustrates the advantage of strong encryption: there is still a strong correlation between the encrypted data and the source image after only one round of encryption.

UltraSONIC performs well compared with other implementations of Rijndael on reconfigurable platforms. An implementation on the SLAAC-1V reconfigurable platform [5] obtained a throughput of 577Mbit/sec.

7 Conclusions

The UltraSONIC platform presents both hardware and software developers with an extremely powerful tool. It allows rapid prototyping, development and deployment of video processing solutions. Using UltraSONIC, we were able to quickly develop a complete software/hardware solution for Rijndael encryption and decryption in a matter of weeks. This development speed was possible due to several important factors: The UltraPIPE and SDI PIPE were used, so that no custom board design was required. The PIPE router allowed the hardware designer to concentrate on the implementation of the algorithm, without concerning themselves with details of I/O and data transfer. Finally, application software could be developed in parallel with the FPGA design, interfacing to the FPGA design using the powerful UltraSONIC Application Program Interface (API).

This implementation of the Rijndael algorithm is powerful enough to process high-definition video in real-time, with a throughput of 2.1Gbit/sec. We were also able to process data from the computer's hard drive at over four times the rate of the CPU; only the PC architecture itself prevented further speed-up. By exploiting the dynamic reconfiguration of the UltraSONIC platform, it has been possible to halve the amount of hardware required to implement a fixed number of rounds. Furthermore, taking advantage of the flexibility offered by the UltraSONIC platform, it has been possible to use the same hardware design for both real-time and off-line data processing.

In this paper we have presented only one application – real-time Rijndael encryption and decryption, but we believe that the UltraSONIC platform is well suited for a wide variety of applications.

References

1. Daemen, J., Rijmen, V.: AES Proposal: Rijndael, NIST AES Proposal, 1998.
2. Weeks, B., Bean, M., Rozylowicz, T., Ficke, C.: Hardware Performance Simulations of Round 2 (Advanced Encryption Standard) Algorithms, The Third {Advanced Encryption Standard} Candidate Conference, April 13--14, 2000, New York, NY, USA, 286-304
3. Haynes, S.D., Stone, J., Cheung, P.Y.K, Luk, W.: Video Image Processing with the Sonic Architecture. IEEE Computer, April 2000 50-57
4. McLoone, M., McCanny, J.V.: Single-Chip FPGA Implementation of the Advanced Encryption Standard (Rijndael), Proc. Of the Field-Programmable Logic and Applications 11th International Conference, FPL 2001, 162-171
5. Chodowiec, P., Gaj, K., Bellows, P., Schott, B.: Experimental Testing of the Gigabit IPSec – Compliant Implementations of the Rijndael and Triple DES Using SLAAC – 1V FPGA Accelerator board. Proc. Information Security Conference, 2001 220-234

GPSR Compliance

The European Union's (EU) General Product Safety Regulation (GPSR) is a set of rules that requires consumer products to be safe and our obligations to ensure this.

If you have any concerns about our products, you can contact us on ProductSafety@springernature.com

In case Publisher is established outside the EU, the EU authorized representative is:

Springer Nature Customer Service Center GmbH
Europaplatz 3
69115 Heidelberg, Germany

Batch number: 10682269

Printed by Printforce, the Netherlands